13

Robert Blatchford
and
El   ord

Contents

contents continued page 4 . . .

contents continued . . .

Once again it is our pleasure to welcome you to the latest issue of *The Family and Local History Handbook*. The thirteenth in the series. Since publishing number 12 we have been asked if we would publish the following issue with thirteen in its title. Obviously there is superstition about the number 13. We had many suggestions including missing out the 13 and calling it number 14. After some deliberation it was felt that this would be totally confusing for our readers! If not ourselves - and we are easily confused these days!

Thirteen is said to be an unlucky number but it is also lucky for some. Eizabeth's father was born on the 13th as was our youngest grandson. Those were both lucky occasions. If you are superstitious about the number please ignore it. This is in fact our fifteenth publication - *Herbert Chapman on Football (See Pages 15, 446 and www.herbectchapman.com for details)* and our Data Disk *The Family and Local History Handbook Omnibus* Volumes 1 - 10 *(See Pages 143, 447 and www.genealogical.co.uk for details)*. This latest edition offers a host of new articles and information.

Each issue of the Handbook stands alone and contains original and unpublished material commissioned by us. They are not reprints from other family history publications. We have tried, again, to provide a wide and interesting range of topics chosen from the several hundred articles submitted to us.

We hope *The Family and Local History Handbook 13* becomes an indispensable tool for your family and local history research. The listings in *The Genealogical Services Directory* section have been checked, updated and extended especially in relation to the Republic of Ireland and Northern Ireland.

This book is intended to be an essential companion to your research whether it is by using the extensive material in libraries, archives and museums or from the internet. However with regards to the internet, which serves us well, we must raise a cautionary note. There is a vast array of information on the internet and care should be taken when using unverified data found there as it can easily lead us astray. The fact that if it is on the internet *'it must be gospel'* leads many people to include erroneous information in their histories. Always remember when dealing with any information that nothing should be taken or granted and where possible original documention should e checked. It is important that our descendants are able rely upon the accuracy of our researches and by following advice given above you will create a family history which will come an heirloom.

The help from Elizabeth in producing this book eases with each issue and her input is invaluable. The design layout of the *Handbook* is my responsibility.

We are again grateful to all our authors for expertise and willingness to contribute to each issue.

We hope that you, our readers, enjoy th as much as our previous ones.

Robert and Eliza Blatchford

5

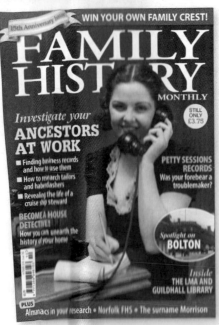

6

family & local history

In the beginning . . . .
A Beginner's Guide to Family History
Doreen Hopwood

This article will have you up and running with your own research and if you have already started then the advice here will help you get the most from your hobby . . .

If you're about to embark on a journey to your family's past – or if you've already made a start – these guidelines will help to keep you on track.

One of the great things about following the ancestral trail is that you don't know where it will take you – possibly not just across the United Kingdom, but much further afield. Wherever it leads you to, you'll pick up all kinds of interesting information *en route*.

When I started my journey (over 30 years ago), you had to go to London regularly in order to access any of the major resources. As I'm writing this – and certainly by the time that this handbook is published – more and more genealogical sources will become available at the click of your computer mouse. Obviously this is a great boon for researchers, but don't be tempted to try to carry out all of your research whilst seated at your computer desk. It's easy to assume that if a record can't be found on-line it doesn't exist, but in terms of genealogical resources, only a fraction is available electronically – although the numbers are always increasing. By not getting a copy of the original document, you'll not only miss the pleasure of seeing an ancestor's signature, but

the information on a database or other index may not provide all of the details from the original. The on-line version of a parish register entry will provide the facts, but some vicars couldn't resist writing margin notes in their registers – like the one at Rowley Regis in the late 19th century who attributed the death of a parishioner to the cold he caught in *'this cold, miserable parish church!'*

As you collect more information, you'll find yourself delving into the social history surrounding your ancestors' lives, such as finding what a puddler did for a living (an iron-worker) and whether or not the address of Court Heneage, Aston Manor was as grand as it sounded – it was actually a set of Birmingham back-to-back houses.

The *'Golden Rule of Genealogy'* is simply to ALWAYS work back from the known to the unknown – from yourself to your parents, then to your grandparents and so on. Even if you share your surname with a famous person from the past, don't try to come forwards to relate it to your family. Once you've worked back from yourself, you may find that there is a connection, but otherwise there's the danger that you'll end up an impressive family tree

which isn't YOUR family's.

Patience and perseverance are two *'musts,'* along with an open mind. Try to put yourself in the time period when your ancestors lived, rather than seeing (or judging) them with 21st century eyes. The death of an ancestor in a workhouse didn't necessarily mean that he/she was a pauper – until the advent of the welfare state, workhouse infirmaries may have been the only places where medical care was available.

Where to Start

Before going to visit record offices and libraries, gather together as much information as you can and write down what is known about each individual. You'll probably be surprised by the amount that you already know, and this will exercise will show the gaps you need to fill. Talk to members of your family and ask them for copies of any official documents, such as birth, marriage and death certificates, wills and grave papers, and anything else that might yield some biographical information. Photographs can be a great memory jogger, especially if talking to an older family member and can be a useful way of recording the 'who, when and where' details of each photo if this hasn't already been done. Whilst you'll need to verify any information with documentary evidence, don't discount the family myth – they're usually firmly based on the truth, but may have become distorted as they were passed down. Find out if anyone else in the family has already done some family history – or if is interested in joining in with you. This is an excellent way of sharing both the research work and the costs.

Get Organised

Contrary to popular belief, not everyone chooses to maintain their records on a computer, so don't feel compelled to rush out and buy software from the outset. You'll find reviews of programs etc in all of the family history magazines and there's plenty of information about computers for family history in the *Digital Genealogy* section of this

handbook. There are all kinds of printed record sheets available to buy, and your first investment should be a supply of A4 ring binders, loose-leaf pads, acid-free clear pockets and pencils. You could also use index cards, writing the basic details of each person on one and then filing them alphabetically in a storage box.

Major Sources
Birth Marriage and Death Certificates

Civil registration began on 1 July 1837 in England and Wales, and the General Register Office (GRO) indexes include all registrations from that date. Scotland, Ireland, the Channel Islands and the Isle of Man have separate registration systems which were established later.

Birth Certificates show:
• The names of the child and parents, including the mother's maiden name and father's occupation.
  • The date of birth and the address where the birth took place
  • The name and address of the person who registered the birth (usually a parent) and the date of registration (up to 42 days after the birth)

This information will then enable you to search for the marriage of the parents.

Marriage Certificates show:
  • The date and place of the marriage (could be a register office from 1837)
  • The names and ages of the bride and groom (although this may say 'full age' meaning they were over the age of majority – 21 until the late 20th century)
  • Their occupations and addresses at the time of the marriage
  • Their father's names and occupations
  • The names of witnesses (usually two) who

may be family members.

Death Certificates show:
• The name and age of the deceased and the date of place of death (possibly a hospital)
• The home address of the deceased and cause of death and whether there was an inquest
• The name and address of the informant (often a family member)
• From 1969 the date and place of birth of the deceased is shown and if a married woman, her maiden name is included. Death certificates do not show any burial/cremation details

Using The General Register Office Index:
• 1837-1983 each year is split into four quarters:
• March: events registered in January, February and March
• June: events registered in April, May and June
• September: events registered in July, August and September
• December: events registered in October, November and December
• From 1984 - there is one annual, cumulative index

Within each quarter/year, the indexes are arranged alphabetically by surname, then by forename(s), followed by the name of the registration district and the volume and page number: for example, a birth entry for the March Quarter of 1885 may read:

Knowles Walter S   Chorlton   8a 123

There are now numerous (subscription/pay-to-view) websites – such as www.ancestry.co.uk - www.findmypast.co.uk – the genealogist.co.uk – and increasingly you'll find that they have surname indexes which can save you time by not trawling through the quarterly indexes. However, be aware that surnames appear as they are spelt in the register where they are arranged in strict alphabetical order. This often means that they were written down as they were heard by the registrar, and if your ancestor couldn't read or write, he couldn't tell the registrar if the surname was mis-spelt. It's not unusual to find children of the same couple with different spellings of their surname on certificates, so try saying the surname out loud to find possible variations – for example, my family name of Knowles has appeared as Noles, Nowles and Knoles. Coverage currently ceases at around 2005 on these sites. There are also some free-to-view websites such as www.freebmd.rootsweb.com but coverage may not be as comprehensive

You'll find the indexes in microform (film or fiche) at many libraries and record offices, but also only up to 2005. Access to the more recent indexes (which include

civil partnerships) is at five centres in England and Wales and this system is likely to continue until the indexes have been fully digitised.

There is no public access to the civil registration registers – the only way of obtaining the information on them is by purchasing a copy of the certificate, and you can find out more about how to use the indexes and how to apply for certificates at www.direct.gov.uk There is a list of register offices in this handbook.

Census Returns

These can be seen as 'snapshots' of households at 10-yearly intervals throughout the Victorian period and although there is usually a period of 100 years before the information is made public, the 1911 census was released early and can be viewed at www.findmypast.co.uk (pay-to-view). The earlier census enumerators books (CEBs) are also available on many subscription websites, but there is also www.freecen.org.uk for the 1841-1901 returns. Censuses were taken from 1801, but those prior to 1841 were not required to be retained and many contained only statistical data. The 1841 census does not provide as much information as the later ones, which show:
• Address where the family was living – each household has a separate entry
• Name, age, marital status and sex of each individual in the household
• Relationship of each individual to the head of household – may include servants, lodgers, boarders, visitors etc
• Occupation of each individual – sometimes made a little grander than what it was!
• Place of birth of each individual – county and town/village/parish for those born in England and Wales, but often only the name of the country (ie Ireland) for those born elsewhere

You'll find a complete set of the CEBs for England and Wales at The National Archives -

www.nationalarchives.gov.uk - and most county and local record offices have them for their own area in microform. Addresses of these can be found in the directory in this handbook.

Church Records

The keeping of parish registers commenced in 1538 when Henry VIII broke away from the Catholic Church and declared himself as the head of the Church of England, and today they still record baptisms, marriages and burials, to complement the civil registration of births, marriages and deaths from 1837 in England and Wales. A few churches retain their own records, but in most cases, you'll find them deposited at the Diocesan Record Office (DRO), which may be at the same address as the County Record Office (CRO). Between 1754 and 1837 all marriages (except for Jews and Quakers) had to take place in the Church of England at a ceremony conducted by an Anglican vicar, and these register entries contain the following information:
• Date and place of the marriage
• Names of bride and groom, their marital status (bachelor/spinster or widow/widower)
• Where they were from (usually shows 'of this parish' – sometimes abbreviated to 'otp')
• Whether the marriage was by banns, licence or consent of parents (if either was under 21)
• The name of the officiating minister

• Signatures/marks of the bride and groom and (usually two) witnesses

Before 1813 baptism and burial registers usually provide only the minimum information – such the names and date of the event but after this, you'll find printed registers which also include the age and address of the deceased, and baptism records show the family address and occupation of the father. Some incumbents entered the date of birth of the person being baptised, but this wasn't a requirement. There is no central index to church registers, but some family histories societies have produced these for their area and you can find addresses and contact details in the directory in this handbook. The National Burial Index has just had its' third edition published, and more information about this can be found at www.fffhs.org.uk

The International Genealogical Index (IGI) is a world-wide resource on microfiche, produced by the Mormon Church and can also be accessed (free-to-view) at www.familysearch.org It includes entries taken from parish registers of baptism and marriage (but not burials) and also information submitted by individuals. It can be searched by name and by country/region, and generally (for England and Wales) covers Anglican churches for the period from the 1550s to around the 1850s – although this varies from county to county. It doesn't include every parish, so check to see if the one you want has been recorded on this resource. It's a really useful finding aid, but do always get a copy of the parish register entry, as it may include more information. You'll also find record at www.freereg.uk but again, this doesn't include all parishes.

Locating Records

The addresses and contact details of national, county and local record offices can be found in this handbook, as well as those of other repositories holding genealogical source materials, such as libraries, museums and specialist societies. Most have their own website, and before making a visit, check to see if you need to get a reader's ticket (you'll need to take some form of identity for this), book a place or order material in advance. Do as much background research as you can before going to a record office/library and set yourself realistic goals for your visit to make the most effective use of your time there.

Going Further
• Join your local family history society. You'll meet like-minded people and most societies hold regular meetings and arrange visits to

record offices etc. Once you find that your family was from a particular area, it's worthwhile joining the family history society for that area too.

• Enrol on a family history course. Local libraries will be able to advise you about any in your area, and there are on-line tutorials and distance learning courses available at all levels.

• Keep up to date with new developments by reading family history magazines and checking the websites of record offices. Some local authorities offer free access to subscription websites (such as ancestry) – usually in libraries/record offices.

Remember!

Success can also depend on the survival of records, if your family moved from place to place, their status in life, and even their surname. Having an unusual surname can be both a help and hindrance – especially if it can

be spelt in many ways, and although you may have to trawl through more records if your surname is a popular one – you're unlikely to find spelling variations for Jones.

As you progress with your research, you'll find many other sources which will help you to place your ancestors in their contemporary settings. Maps and photographs will give you a glimpse of where they lived, newspapers record local, national and international events, and help us to understand how these affected our families. You can investigate the stories told by an ancestor and find out if they really did happen – or if they became embellished as they were passed down the generations. Even if these don't help you to get further back with your research, they'll help you to understand your ancestor's lives and your own heritage.

Postcards: Windows on History
Jane Batchelor

Who has not enjoyed receiving a nice postcard from family or friends? But not all postcards are the same, their forms are many and as various as the ways in which they can be interpreted. Taken at a particular moment in time postcards may feature views and buildings that can no longer be seen, notable events, people going about their everyday lives but dressed in the clothes of the era they are living in and doing activities then routine, now of the past. Vanished houses; vanished shops: insight into a particularly local world.

In order to understand this it is useful to understand more about where postcards arose from and the different ways in which they can be read.

The Postcard Begins

The birth of photography in the United Kingdom around the 1840s coincided with the development of cheap and efficient railway travel which meant that travel was not just available to a privileged elite but to a much wider public, although still not to everyone.

In 1860 Francis Frith began travelling around the country in a

horse-drawn dark room recording popular images of places which people liked to see. Francis Frith's company has continued to flourish and the Francis Frith collection now provides, for a fee, an important source of postcard images both past and present.

Likewise Valentine's of Dundee specialised in photographs of Scottish views and later became an established picture postcard company. St Andrew's university library now holds the photographic archive for Valentine's; again a fee may be charged for the use of these pictures.

By 1870 plain postcards were in general use. By the 1890s the development of photographic techniques meant that picture postcards were readily available and many were now colour tinted. From 1894 it was possible to send picture postcards through the post. More information on the relationship between the postal system and postcards is available through the British Postal Museum and Archive and the Bath Postal Museum, which has an interesting collection of digitised

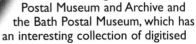

Miss Nellie Wills

postcards including some early Valentines' cards.

The Postcard Album

During the Edwardian era many people enthusiastically collected postcards in albums as they had previously collected images in scrapbooks, putting together collections of cards and often photographs which related to themselves and their lives. Such postcard albums have often been passed down from one family member to another, so it can be worth asking older relatives if they have such albums in their possession.

One such album which I have been lucky to see belonged to Miss Nellie Wills, who was born in 1910 and lived in Manchester. The postcard album includes an early picture of Manchester Road which is near the area where Nellie lived as a small child and a photograph of her at this age.

Also included in the album is a birthday card to Nellie dated 1914 when she would have been four years old. That the postcard is indeed sent to a young child is emphasised as it is addressed to "little Molly," Molly being a common term of affection for a young girl and by the sentimental picture on the front of a young boy giving flowers to a young girl. A short rhyme emphasises the love between the two figures and by inference the affection held for Nellie by the sender of the postcard. The card uses a small amount of colour tinting to great affect, highlighting the pretty hat of the girl and the flowers she is holding. Also noticeable is the address of the postcard which is the address of the Coppack family. The

Coppack family looked after Nellie after the death of her mother and the album originally belonged to them.

Wish you were here: postcards and the British seaside

The 1840s had seen the development of better travel and communications; but this acceleration really reached its height by the 1930s when cheaper travel and increased leisure time meant that many more ordinary people could travel to different places, of which the British seaside was one of the most popular. Paul Atterbury's entertaining *Branch line Britain* is structured as a journey across Britain and is illustrated by many photographs and postcards of high streets, scenic landscapes and seasides which could be accessed via branch lines and which continue to provide important documentary evidence of what different local places looked like and how people lived. Likewise, Gavin Weightman's book *The Seaside* uses photographs and postcards to capture the energy and excitement of British seaside visitors from 1920's - 1950's.

Energy and excitement; postcards from the sea were often not just scenic views but expressions of uninhibited fun, an opportunity for people to escape from everyday cares. The postcards of Donald McGill (1875-1962) represent a very popular type of British cheeky seaside humour and are discussed thoroughly in Elfreda Buckland detailed biography *The World of Donald McGill*, setting his work within the context of the postcard business. More recently there has been more appreciation of the skill such humour involves As I am writing this Tate Britain is holding an exhibition *Rude Britannia: British Comic Art (9th June 2010 – 5th September 2010)* which includes Donald Mc Gill's art and a **Donald McGill Museum** is being set up in the Isle of Wight (more information can be found on the website or by emailing info@donaldmgill.info)

United in Separation: War Postcards 1918-1945

Comic postcard or scenic view; postcards have always been very personal items. During the First World War beautifully woven silk postcards expressing the sentiments of loved ones, often, poignantly, soldiers separated from their families were very popular. Information given on such postcards can enable you to trace a soldier's address, family and military records. One such card featured in Nellie Wills's album is the

Wishes for your Birthday.
May your pleasures have no end
All your cares be few,
This the greeting that I send
Little one to you.

attractive postcard sent to C Mead during the First World War. It is a French card with the inscription *"Souvenir de la Grande Guerre"* (Souvenir of the Great war). The card features various flags and British crown in the centre of the card, suggesting that the card was designed for the British market.

The 1901 census records reveal C Mead to be Clarissa Mead, sister of Richard Mead who describes himself on the postcard as *"your loving brother."* The 1911 census shows that in 1911 Richard was employed as iron driller at a local gas works. The postcard also gives the details of where Richard was serving and from this it is possible to find his medal roll. A medal roll shows an individual's medal entitlement, rank and possibly where that person has served. Medal rolls can be seen at the National Archives at Kew.

The Second World War saw renewed popularity for postcards as a means of communicating with loved ones far away. Tonie and Valmai Holt's book *I'll be Seeing You* provides an interesting look at the variety of postcards sent during this period, with images showing a complex blend of the amusing, the heroic or intended propaganda.

In conclusion people have long wanted ways of sending short communications to others. Letters are long; postcards are short and even now in this age of fast communication there is still much pleasure to be had from receiving a colourful or interesting postcard. More than this, the postcards people write to each other can tell us all much about our history, our families and ourselves.

Select Bibliography

Paul Atterbury *Branch Line Britain*, David & Charles, Marlborough, Wiltshire 2006, first published 2004
Elfreda Buckland *The World of Donald McGill*, Blandford Press, Dorset, 1984
Tonie and Valmai Holt *I'll Be Seeing You: Picture Postcards of World War II*, Moorland Publishing, Ashbourne, Derbyshire, 1987
Robert Pols *Dating Old Photographs* (Countryside Books in association with The Federation of Family History Societies, 1993)
Pauline Saul *The Family Historians Enquire Within*, 5th edn, Federation of Family History Societies 1995
Gavin Weightman *Pictures from the Past: The Seaside*, Selecta Book Ltd, Devizes, Wiltshire 1995, first published Collins & Brown, 1991

Museums and Archives

British Postal Museum and Archive, Freeling House, Phoenix Place, London WC1X 0DL W: http://postalheritage.org.uk
Bath Postal Museum, 27 Northgate Street, Bath W: www.bathpostalmuseum.org
Donald McGill Museum, 15 Union Street, Ryde, Isle of Wight W: www.donaldmcgill.info The *Museum is not open at time of going to press but archive is available to interested users the website will state when museum is open*
Francis Frith Archive W: www.francisfrith.com/library
The National Archives, Kew, London W: www.nationalarchives.gov.uk
National Media Museum, Bradford, West Yorkshire BD1 1NQ W: www.nationalmediamuseum.org.uk *This museum has a special interest in photography and often has postcard exhibitions*
Tate Britain, Millbank London SW1P 4RG W: www.tate.org.uk
Valentines of Dundee Archive, University of St Andrews W: www.st-andrews.ac.uk/specialcollections/Photographiccollection

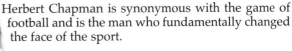

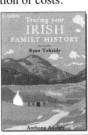

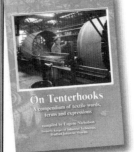

Doncaster and District Family History Society

Meetings
The last Wednesday of the month
(except December) at 7 pm for 7.30 pm
at Doncaster College for the Deaf,
Leger Way, Doncaster

Palgrave Research Centre
Adjacent to Doncaster Archives,
King Edward Road, Balby, Doncaster
Open: Mon, Tue, Weds and Fri 10 am to 4 pm
Sat 10 am to 2 pm **Bookings:** 01302 311390

Resources
Free Internet Access to Ancestry & FindMyPast
Extensive resources - on fiche, CDs, computers
and books - cover the whole of the Doncaster
Archdeaconry and much of the country

Annual Family History Day
Held at the end of October - with three speakers

Details from: Miss Kate Raistrick
8 Tenter Lane, Warmsworth, Doncaster,
South Yorkshire DN4 9PT
Tel: 01302 845809

Email: honsecretary@doncasterfhs.co.uk
www.doncasterfhs.co.uk

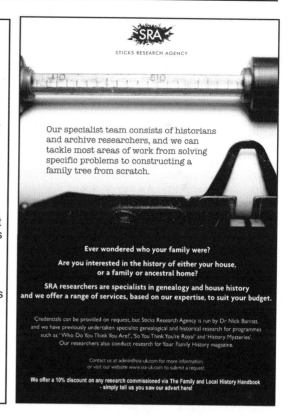

Our specialist team consists of historians and archive researchers, and we can tackle most areas of work from solving specific problems to constructing a family tree from scratch.

Ever wondered who your family were?

Are you interested in the history of either your house, or a family or ancestral home?

SRA researchers are specialists in genealogy and house history and we offer a range of services, based on our expertise, to suit your budget.

Credentials can be provided on request, but Sticks Research Agency is run by Dr Nick Barratt, and we have previously undertaken specialist genealogical and historical research for programmes such as 'Who Do You Think You Are?', 'So You Think You're Royal' and 'History Mysteries'. Our researchers also conduct research for Your Family History magazine.

Contact us at admin@sra-uk.com for more information, or visit our website www.sra-uk.com to submit a request.

We offer a 10% discount on any research commissioned via The Family and Local History Handbook - simply tell us you saw our advert here!

INSTITUTE OF HISTORICAL RESEARCH University of London School of Advanced Study

MA in Historical Research

- ❖ study at Britain's national centre for history
- ❖ 'cities and localities' module
- ❖ independent research project
- ❖ teaching undertaken in small groups
- ❖ full- and part-time study
- ❖ bursaries available

For further information visit:
www.history.ac.uk/students

or contact Dr Matthew Davies:
CMH, Institute of Historical Research,
Senate House, Malet Street, London WC1E 7HU
Tel: 020 7862 8698 Fax: 020 7862 8793
Email: matthew.davies@sas.ac.uk

FAMILY HISTORY RESEARCH
INCLUDING ALL PARISH RECORDS
CERTIFICATES, WILLS & CENSUS
IN
HERTFORDSHIRE AND LONDON
(BEDFORDSHIRE & BUCKINGHAMSHIRE
BY ARRANGEMENT)
ALL ENQUIRIES WELCOME

MRS CAROLYNN BOUCHER
(Cert Ed. Cert Genealogy Part II)
1 IVINGHOE CLOSE
CHILTERN PARK
ST. ALBANS
HERTS
AL4 9JR
Tel: 01727 833664

Email: carolynn.boucher@tesco.net

Who's the Daddy?

Finding the father of an illegitimate child

Joe O'Neill

Nothing is worse for a researcher, having located the correct document, than to find the relevant information has not been recorded. Few things are as disheartening as the silence of a parish register or a blank space on a registration certificate. And when this reticence conceals the paternity of a key ancestor it may leave you at a loss as to how to proceed.

Though commonplace in 21st century Britain the birth of a child outside wedlock was once regarded as a threat to an ordered society. As the terms used to refer to a child of an illicit union suggest people once frowned on illegitimacy. In our age when a third of all children are born outside wedlock it is hard to believe that illegitimacy once carried both a legal and social stigma. An Act of 1576 allowed Justices to imprison the parents of a bastard and one of 1610 provided for the imprisonment of the mother unless she provided securities as to her future good behaviour. In the 18th century unmarried mothers were often whipped through the streets.

Not surprisingly these sanctions and the dominance of Christian values of sexual morality combined to ensure that few children were born outside marriage. During the Tudor and Stuart periods illegitimacy was rare. In the years between 1600 and 1650 it was below 1% — about one in every one hundred and forty births — and never more than 3%. It began to rise mid-way through the 18th century with the onset of the industrial revolution, reaching one in every thirty-three births by 1750 and by the early 19th century had reached nearly 7%. Changes in social values and attitudes resulted in a steady decline up to the early 20th century when it was about 4%. The last census in 2001 showed one in three children born in England and Wales were born outside wedlock. The number continues to rise.

The reasons for these pre-20th century fluctuations are contentious. Some historians maintain the mid-18th century rise in illegitimacy was the result of the increasing shortage of accommodation and the accompanying difficulty of relocating outside the parish which put addition pressure on living conditions and led to overcrowding at a time when moral restrains were breaking down under the pressure of industrialisation.

Whatever the causes, the reaction of the authorities was always to try to legitimise children conceived outside marriage. Provided the couple married within eight months of the conception, the child was deemed legitimate. The mother's parish authorities were most keen to bring about a marriage, known as a knobstick wedding under such circumstances. This was because legitimate children took the father's settlement. Otherwise he became the responsibility of the parish in which he was born.

The Old Poor Law enshrined the principle that fathers should take responsibility for the maintenance of their children. The Overseer for the Poor and the churchwarden should require a mother likely to become a burden on the parish to identify the father. This questioning was known as an Examination.

The resultant bastardy examination records provide a fascinating insight into the lives of our ancestors and a glimpse of social history that remains largely unwritten. Among the 18th century Berkshire examination records are those relating to the Maidservant Elizabeth Grendall who explained that her unborn child was "begotten sometime last April on a couch in the hall of the dwelling house of Mr Sylvester [her employer] in Waltham St Lawrence, by his son Mr George Sylvester ... No other person than George Sylvester ever had carnal knowledge of her."

The next step, after the woman had identified the father, was for the officials to interview him with a view to getting him to enter into a bond to pay for the birth and maintenance expenses incurred by the child – a Bastardy Bond.

At this stage wealthy fathers often made a one-off payment in an effort to avoid scandal.

But this was unusual. In cases where the father was unable to pay birth and maintenance expenses, the parish frequently pressurised his family to take responsibility. In 1794 in Little Sampford, Essex, for instance, Mrs Willis paid £10 and Mr Woodham £20 for children fathered by their sons.

Fortunately for the family historian, many parishes recorded these transactions in Bastardy Books, which give the name of the father and details of payments. Where this is not the case check the Overseer's Account Books and Churchwardens' Accounts which give similar details.

Fathers often denied paternity. As unmarried expectant mothers were also reluctant to make their condition known the result was, in the view of poor law officials, that the public purse incurred an unacceptable burden. The problems of the Child Support Agency are clearly nothing new.

Consequently, the authorities gradually tightened the law. An Act of 1732 compelled any women pregnant with a bastard child to declare the fact and name the father under pain of imprisonment. It seems that this sanction was not often enforced, though some, like Sarah Mason of Bayford, found that the Overseer of her parish was a harsh man who in 1743 committed her to goal until such time as she named the father of her bastard child. During the 17th and 18th centuries some women were whipped.

The mother's word was sufficient to have a

man locked up until such time as he provided security to indemnify the parish. There is plenty of evidence to show that this sanction was actually imposed. Edward Woodhouse of Aldbury in Hertfordshire spent at least the whole of 1805 in custody for refusing to give sureties in relation to his illegitimate child.

However, this was exceptional. Until the mid-18th century, few legal sanctions were invoked against the parents of those born out of wedlock. Generally the parish officers dealt with mother and child in a sensible, compassionate manner with little fuss. Few were brought before the Quarter Sessions and often the only written record indicating that a child was a bastard is the baptismal record.

Parish registers provide the first clue to illegitimacy in the pre-registration period. Before 1813 – when printed forms were introduced – the priest was at liberty to elaborate on entries. At a time when most people lived in small towns and villages he was likely to know all his parishioners and have a good idea of what was going on in his parish. Consequently many recorded their belief as to the identity of the father.

Many mothers often left clues to the identity of the father. In certain parts of the country it was common for a couple to give their child a family surname as a middle name. If you find that an unmarried woman has given her child a surname in this way, investigate further as this could well be a clue to the child's paternity.

With the rise in illegitimacy a harsher approach became necessary. The New Poor Law of 1834 meant that illegitimate children might now become the responsibility not of the parish but of the Union and its Board of Guardians. In most cases the unmarried woman whose family could not support her had to go into the workhouse to give birth.

The alternative was to sue the father for maintenance in the Petty Sessions. If successful she was awarded a Bastardy Order, very similar in format to the old Bastardy Bond.

In practice, however, many mothers of illegitimate children often continued to receive outdoor relief. A great deal depended on the attitude of the Board of Guardians. Some such as that for Keighley in Yorkshire in 1843 seem to have been extremely open-handed. The minute book for that year shows that they continued to support Hannah Hodgson and her six illegitimate children. Other records tell a similar story.

After 1837 the key document indicating the illegitimacy of a child is the birth certificate. It usually shows a blank space

under 'name of the father' and 'occupation of the father.' The child is registered under the mother's name and her occupation – if she has one – is given. Until 1875 the mother was free to attribute the child's paternity to anyone and this was recorded. From that year, however, the father had to attend the registry office to have his name ascribed.

By the time registration was introduced in 1837 the number of illegitimate children born each year was significant. Statistics for England and Wales for 1880 to 1882 show that of approximately 850,000 births registered each year, about 43,000 were illegitimate. That works out at about 5%, or one in every twenty.

Many of these were abandoned. The more fortunate ended up with charitable foundations such as the Foundling Hospital, Barnado's, the Shaftesbury Homes, the Waifs and Strays Society or the Marine Society.

Poor law unions tried to identify the mothers of abandoned children. *The Poor Law Union Gazette,* for instance, contains advertisements for missing mothers which include interesting information not only about the mother but also perhaps about the father. An entry for 1859, for instance, includes an advertisement placed by the parish of St. James, Clerkenwell, seeking Harriet Matilda Purchase. It gives a description of the twenty-four year old mother and adds that she abandoned her child, Thomas Bullen Gill, at the surgery of a dentist, Mr Gill. It is not unreasonable to assume that Harriet believed the dentist was the child's father.

Those on the margins of society like Harriet were increasing likely to end up in the workhouse from the 1840s onward. Rejected by the father and often their own family, it was their only option. Consequently, a high percentage of illegitimate children were born in the workhouse. Once there, women were encouraged to have the Guardians seek an 'order of affiliation' (Bastardy Order) against the father, requiring him to accept financial responsibility for his child. Where these survive these records are usually found with other poor law records.

Quarter Sessions records also contain relevant material, such as orders for the maintenance of children. In 1839 responsibility for pursuing fathers became the task of the petty sessions and after 1844 clerks of the various divisions were required to make an annual return to the Secretary of State of all summons and orders relating to bastard children. These Bastardy Returns give the name of the mother, the date of the summons and the hearing, the result, the father's name, and the amount of maintenance awarded.

Occasionally, the address and occupation of the father also appears.

In summary there are eight different types of documents which should help to identify the father of an illegitimate child:

Bastardy Examination – in which the mother provides information about the identity of the father.

Bastardy Warrant – an order for the apprehension of the putative father.

Bastardy Recognizance – similar to a bail bond, requiring the father to appear at the next Quarter Sessions.

Bastardy Summons – instructs a Constable to bring a man to court.

Bastardy Order - gives details of who is to pay what.

Bastardy Certificate – this certifies that the father has paid up and releases him from the Bastardy Recognizance.

Bastardy Bond – a bondsmen promises to pay the parish any costs incurred by the father.

Notice of Application for Bastardy Order sent to the putative father ordering him to appear at the Quarter Sessions.

How many of these records survive varies greatly for parish to parish. Where they survive they give excellent information on the incidence of illegitimacy and how it was handled. Unfortunately, there are few areas for which comprehensive records have withstood the challenge of wartime paper shortage.

If a bastard child died, the overseers of the

parish in which it was legally settled would have paid for the burial, even in another parish. This should be noted in the Overseers' Accounts if they survive.

Bastardy payments ceased when the child was old enough to be apprenticed – usually no older than fourteen. Bastardy orders generally state for how long the money was to be paid. Payment was usually made to the parish supporting the child, but after 1834 some payments were made directly to the mother.

Like all sources in family history, bastardy records are most fruitful when combined with others. Apprenticeship indentures and settlement papers provide the ideal supplement as they indicate the subsequent course of the child's life.

Most of these documents are stored in the local CRO, many of which have produced name indexes to for the relevant material.

'It's a wise child who knows his own father,' Homer tells us. With guidance, perseverance and a little luck we can all attain to that wisdom.

Further Research & Reading:
Access to Archives (A2A) www.a2a.org.uk
Poor Law Union Records, Gibson, J. (FFHS)
Poor Relief in England and Wales, 1601 – 1834 Oxley G, David & Charles. 1974. (ISBN: 0715365673).
Annals of the Labouring Poor Snell K D M Cambridge University Press ISBN-10: 0521335582)
Copies of the *Poor Law Union Gazette* can be found at the British Library, Newspaper Library, Collingdale. www.n-e-n-a.co.uk/newsarchives.php
A number of counties have at least some of the relevant records online. Among these are Wiltshire: www.wiltshire.gov.uk/leisure-and-culture/access-to-records/wiltshire-and-swindon-record-office.htm
Devon: www.devon.gov.uk/record_office.htm
Berkshire: www.berkshirerecordoffice.org.uk/

The Odd Family
Fred Feather

The Essex Standard for the 5th August 1831
tells of THE ODD FAMILY

'In the reign of King William the Third there resided at Ipswich a family which, from the number of peculiarities belonging to it, was distinguished by the name of the odd family. Every event remarkably good or bad happened to this family on an odd day of the month and every member had something odd in his or her person, manner or behaviour; the very letters in their Christian names always happened to have an odd number. The husband's name was Peter, and his wife's Rabah; and they had seven children, all boys, viz., Solomon, Roger, James, Matthew, Jonas, David and Ezekiel. The husband had but one leg, his wife but one arm. Solomon was born blind of the left eye and Roger lost his sight by accident. James had his left ear bit off by a boy in a quarrel and Matthew was born with only three fingers on his right hand. Jonas had a stump foot and David was hump-backed. All these except David were remarkably short, whilst Ezekiel was six feet one inch high at the age of 19. The stump-footed Jonas and the humpbacked David got wives of fortune, but no girls in the borough would listen to the addresses of their brothers. The husband's hair was black as jet and the wife's remarkably white, yet every one of their children's hair was red. The husband was killed by accidentally falling in to a deep pit in the year 1701, and his wife, refusing all kinds of sustenance, died five days after him. In the year 1703 Ezekiel enlisted as a grenadier, and although he was afterwards wounded in 23 places, he recovered. Roger, James, Matthew, Jonas and David, it appears by the church registers, died in different places, and were buried on the same day, in the year 1713; and Solomon and Ezekiel were drowned together in crossing the Thames, in the year 1723.'

Which seems a little far fetched, unless an Ipswich parish register or some other clue puts them into someone's family tree.

Dating Family Photographs:
Researching Victorian and Edwardian Photographers and Studios
Jayne Shrimpton

Photographs of ancestors and more recent relatives are precious heirlooms and occupy an important place in the family archive. Wonderful to look at, old photographs offer a fascinating pictorial record of past generations, but, frustratingly, many have survived undated and may also be unidentified. In the interests of effective genealogical research, it is essential to try to establish an accurate, if approximate, date for inherited photographs, to assign them to their rightful place in history. It may never be possible to find out the exact year in which an unmarked photograph was taken, but a *date range* of a few years, or even around ten years, should help to identify an unknown subject, matching him or her to a name on the family tree. Equally, in cases where identity is already certain, a firm circa date will confirm at what stage of life the family member was portrayed. Various techniques can be used to determine the era of a photograph, including identifying the photographic format, recognising when the particular style of the card mount was fashionable, and estimating the date of the visual image from the studio setting and the styles of dress worn: these are all tried and tested approaches which provide a variety of clues and, when combined, they may result in a very useful date range. There is also another method, which researchers often wish to pursue and which may in some cases produce quite a close time span - investigating the operational dates for the photographer or studio that is named on the photograph. This article offers help with understanding the information provided by the photographer details, and practical tips for finding photographer names and addresses in primary sources, books and on the internet.

Photographer information

Any family picture collection which includes photographs from the Victorian and Edwardian eras prior to the First World War is certain to feature a large proportion of studio portraits – photographs taken by commercial photographers, as distinct from amateur snapshots. In many cases these professional photographs bear the name of and address of the photographer or studio and this provides significant historical evidence. Early photographs in the daguerrotype and ambrotype formats, cased or framed images on metal and glass plates respectively, may occasionally have the studio details embossed on the front of the case, or printed on a label stuck on the back, although these photographs, especially expensive daguerrotypes, are relatively rare survivals today. In 1861 the *carte de visite,* introduced into Britain from France in around 1858, overtook all other types of photograph - a photographic print pasted onto a small card measuring around 10 x 6.5 cms. In 1866 another card-mounted photograph arrived on the scene - the *cabinet print,* which typically measured 16.5 x 11.5cms, this larger format becoming

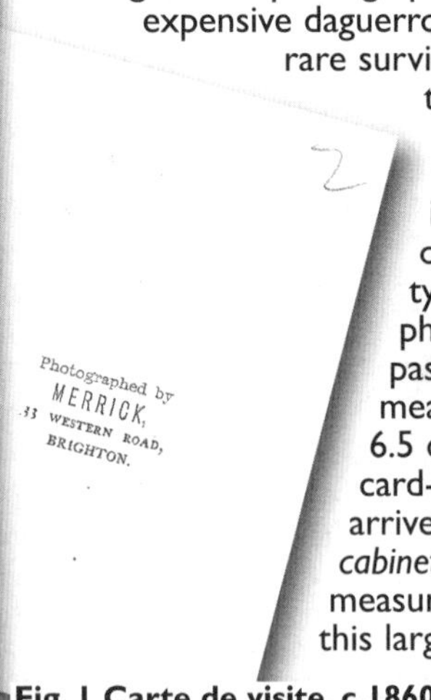

Photographed by
MERRICK
33 WESTERN ROAD,
BRIGHTON.

Fig. 1 Carte de visite, c.1860-65
Online research using the *Directory of Photographic Studios in Brighton & Hove, 1841-1910* shows that Merrick of 33 Western Road, Brighton operated from this address between 1859 and 1874 – a 15 year period which is helpful but does not offer a very close date range. In this case the visual clues, together with the neatly printed photographer details in the centre of the mount, suggest that this is an early carte de visite dating from c.1860-65.

popular by the 1880s. Further 19th century card formats appeared from time to time but none occur as frequently as the carte and cabinet photographs: these dominated portrait photography from the 1860s until the early-1900s, some still being produced in the early 1910s.

Card-mounted photographs provided commercial photographers with an ideal medium for identifying their work and advertising their business. Sometimes a name and studio address were printed in neat lettering on the front of the card, but the reverse offered a larger area and, excepting the few cases when the back was left blank, this was used to publicise the details of one or more studios and to elaborate on the services which the company offered. In around 1902 a postcard mount also began to be used by photography studios, the new photographic postcard being more common after 1906/7 and progressing to become the dominant format of the early 20th century, until the 1940s. Unfortunately many postcards did not mention the photographer, so vital trade evidence may be missing from these popular photographs, although sometimes a studio name (with or without an address) was printed on the back.

Geographical location

When studio details occur on a family photograph, whatever the format, they offer clear and precise information which, firstly, gives a helpful geographical setting and, secondly, offers researchers the potential for dating the picture. Photographers naturally specified the town or city in which they operated and this important fact at once suggests the place of residence for the ancestor(s) represented in the photograph, as customers usually visited a studio close to home - or their nearest town, if they lived in a rural area without a resident photographer. There may be occasional exceptions to this general rule: for instance an ancestor who moved around with their job may have visited a photographer's studio whilst studying or working away from home, or families may have had a photograph taken while enjoying a day trip or holiday at a seaside resort. Today's researchers may not, of course, be aware of every journey ever taken by family members in the past, but sometimes it is possible to form an idea of their usual movements. Ultimately, the geographical origin of a studio portrait always provides evidence that the ancestor or relative who posed for their photograph was, at some point, connected with that area, and this knowledge should help when considering possible candidates for an unidentified photograph.

Photographer operational dates

Photographer details may be very significant when it comes to dating a photograph, for establishing when a named photographer

mounts reprinted to include details of additional branches. When two or more studio addresses are specified on a photograph, as with Fig.7, it is necessary to find out when both or all were operating simultaneously; since some branches of a photography chain turned out to be fairly short lived, the period of multiple studios may have been relatively brief, so this can often help to narrow further the photograph's date range.

Researching photographers and studios

Discovering more about a 19th or early 20th century studio named on a photograph may take time, or can be surprisingly easy. Photographic history generates significant interest nowadays and a great deal of information has been compiled about past photographers and their operations. Institutions like the National Portrait Gallery, London (www.npg.org.uk) tend to focus on the work of eminent society photographers. Well-known portrait photographers, patronised by the social elite, may possibly have photographed prosperous and well-connected ancestors; if so researchers will find much written about them and their studios in books, gallery and exhibition catalogues and photography websites. However, most family historians will be concerned with investigating names from amongst the thousands of popular commercial photographers who operated high street studios across the country and catered for the mass market. Some transient photographers seem to have left little trace of their activities, but many others were recorded on census returns and may have advertised their businesses in local trade directories and newspapers, making it possible to trace their operations over a period of time as they expanded their business to include additional branches, joined up with new working partners or moved between different locations.

Sometimes it may be necessary to consult these original sources to find out when a photographer was recorded at a specific address. The British Library holds all UK daily, UK national daily and Sunday newspapers from 1801 to the present, as well as most UK and Irish regional and local newspapers. These can be viewed in the reading rooms at Colindale,

Fig.2 Carte de visite, 1866
Research into The London Mutual Photographic Association Ltd, using the online *Database of 19th Century Photographers and Allied Trades in London, 1841-1901* reveals that this company operated for just a few months during 1866. Too good to be true? Other evidence supports this data, for the busier style of the reverse and the mention of negatives indicates a date of at least mid-1860s, while the style of dress and hairstyle worn by this unidentified young woman are just right for that year.

operated at the address stated on the photograph will confirm the time period within which the picture must have been taken. If a photographer is only known to have run a particular studio for a few years, as in the case of Figs 2 and 3, then this suggests a close date-range for the image; however if he or she operated from the same studio for many years, as did the photographer named on Fig.1 then this can only offer a broad circa date for photographs taken at that address and a narrower time frame will still need to be ascertained using other dating methods, as mentioned above.

Photographers who expanded their business and took on extra studios generally lost little time in having their card

Fig.3 Carte de visite, c.1871-2
This photograph is also closely dated using information from the *Database of 19th Century Photographers and Allied Trades in London, 1841-1901*, which confirms that F J Meek was sole proprietor of the studio at 433, Strand during 1871 and 1872, having previously been in partnership with Hughes. The turquoise coloured card demonstrates the new 1870s vogue for coloured mounts, while the reverse is now quite detailed, the filigree scrollwork and ribbon banners both typical 1870s designs.

Fig.4 Carte de visite, c.1880-84

Research using the *Database of 19th Century Photographers and Allied Trades in London, 1841-1901* shows that A Eason & Co operated from 16 Dalston Lane, Kingsland for some years between 1875 and 1893. However the company also ran further studios between 1875 and 1879, which are not mentioned here, suggesting a closer date range for this photograph of c.1880-93. The elaborate style of the reverse, with slanting lettering and ornate capital letter, is characteristic of the late 1870s and 1880s, while the style of the young woman's dress suggests an early-1880s date.

North London, while selected titles are now available online: check the website to see if the geographical area of the photographer under investigation is covered – http://newspapers.bl.uk/blcs. Additionally the Irish Newspaper Archives is a project involving the complete digitisation of Ireland's national and many leading regional newspapers – www.irishnewsarchive.com. Trade directories – the historical equivalent of our Yellow Pages – were being produced regularly by the photographic era: the local library for the district in question should hold a good selection of local directories, while the Guildhall Library and Society of Genealogists in London both have impressive collections covering the entire United Kingdom. It is also possible to view some directories for free online at www.historicaldirectories.org or copies of directories on CD-Rom can be bought from various publishers. The census returns dating from 1851 onwards may be relevant when looking for photographers, especially the 1861 and later censuses. If using primary sources, do, though, bear in mind their limitations: census returns will only show a photographer's place of residence every 10 years and, while trade directories and newspaper notices are very useful, not all photographers advertised

5 Cabinet print, c.1893-4

...details were found online for T Wheeler & Son, and the company apparently didn't advertise at all, but the ...essional website *Photographers of Great Britain & Ireland, 1840-1940* supplied data confirming that a T ...eeler advertised at the Queen Street, Margate address 1895-1904. Wheeler must have worked with his ...efore these years, for the reverse design seen here, featuring bamboo, birds and fan, was common ...2-94, while this lady's sleeves are dateable to c.1893-4. The close date range deriving from combined ...nce has helped to identify these ancestors.

Fig.6 Cabinet print, c.1897
Another London photograph, studio dates of 1888-1900 were found for Edgar Prout of 76 St Paul's Road, Camden Square, using the *Database of 19th Century Photographers and Allied Trades in London, 1841-1901*. This 12-year date range confirmed the family's assumptions about the boys pictured here, their birth dates and knowledge of their careers suggesting that this was taken c.1897. The artistic reverse design, with classically-draped figures, is typical of the mid-1880s to late-1890s.

Fig.7 Cabinet print, c.1897-1902
There is no current online photographer index covering the Bucks and Herts area, but a Google search for 'Mr & Mrs S G Payne' led to a mention of this long-running photographic company on www.hertfordshire-genealogy.co.uk. Complete operational dates were not provided, but the entry confirmed that the Tring branch only ran between 1895 and 1907. This date range supports the young man's presumed identity, his appearance and the style of grey mount both suggesting a turn of century date.

Fig.8 Postcard, dated 1907
Studio details were only included on some of the postcard photographs which dominated the early 20th century. The USA Studios named here are not listed on any one photographer index but a general internet search led to various online references confirming that they operated from many branches in the late 19th and early 20th centuries. Fortunately the date is hand-written on the back and this seems to be reliable since the young woman, aged 14 here, was a relative born in 1893.

regularly in the press, so dates of individual advertisements found may not show the full picture. Local libraries and record offices may hold details of photographers who worked in their area and can be a good source of information. Some regional organisations have published guides to past photographers in their city or county and these are listed in the Published Regional Photographer Studies Section at the end of the article.

Internet resources
As with many aspects of genealogy, the internet is a valuable tool and may well provide an effective route to determining dates and addresses for a photographer or studio named on a photograph. A simple search should produce any online references to the individual or studio at the location named and, most helpfully, should reveal whether research into the photographer under investigation has already been carried out, and the results recorded for others to view online, perhaps on a specialised photographer website or database. At present there does not exist a complete searchable national online directory of 19th and early 20th century photographers; however several important photographer indexes and databases have been compiled by various national institutions, regional organisations, local and family historians and independent collectors and specialists. Most of these cover studios from a specific city or geographical area, giving A-Z photographer listings with dates of operation at each address, some entries also

including additional biographical details. Again, it is important to be aware of the limitations of the data, which usually derives from census returns, trade directories and newspaper advertisements. Some databases and indexes do not claim to supply complete operational data, but some cite details of the original sources of information used, and in these cases researchers can at least judge for themselves their scope and reliability. The principal searchable online indexes available at time of writing are listed in the Online Photographer Resources section below: in general, they offer a very useful short cut and if any cover the town or city of the photographer under investigation, they should provide some idea as to when he or she was in business. However data for some areas of the country has not yet been compiled, so if a photographer's dates cannot be found on an existing index, or anywhere else on the internet, and research in person using censuses and trade directories is not an option, researchers may wish to apply to a specialist professional offering photographer information for a small fee: such services are also listed below.

The images featured here represent the different photographic card formats to be found in family collections, their reverse views showing the photographer details. The styles of printed mount became increasingly elaborate between the 1860s and 1890s, slightly less ornate designs becoming fashionable around the turn of the century.

Online Photographer Resources
Database of 19th Century Photographers & Allied Trades in London, 1841-1901
www.photolondon.org.uk
History of Photography in Edinburgh   www.edinphoto.org.uk
Glasgow's Victorian Photographers   www.thelows.madasafish.com/main.htm
Victorian Professional Photographers in Wales, 1850-1925 www.genuki.org.uk/big/wal/VicPhoto1.html
Isle of Man Photographers www.isle-of-man.com/manxnotebook/tourism/pgrphrs
Photographers & Photographic Studios in Derbyshire
      www.genealogy.rootsweb.ancestry.com/~brett/photos/dbyphotos.html
Victorian Photography Studios in and around Birmingham and Warwickshire
      www.hunimex.com/warwick/photogs.html
Early Photographic Studios: A-Z directories of photographers in Norfolk, Suffolk and Cambridgeshire
      www.early-photographers.org.uk
Jersey Photographers and Studios   www.jerseyfamilyhistory.co.uk
Isle of Wight Photographers c.1840-1940   www.iowphotos.info/
Sussex Photo History   www.photohistory-sussex.co.uk/index.htm
Directory of Photographic Studios in Brighton & Hove 1841-1910
      www.spartacus.schoolnet.co.uk/Brighton-Photographers.htm
Photographers in Kent, 1855   www.kent-opc.org/photographers.html
Victorian and Edwardian Photographs – Roger Vaughan Personal Collection
      www.cartes.freeuk.com
Also links to list of **Bristol Photographers U.K. (1852-1972)** and **Photographic Studios for some parts of England and Wales in the year 1868.**
Index of UK Portrait & Studio Photographers c.1840-1950
      www.earlyphotographers.org.uk [May charge a fee]
Photographers of Great Britain and Ireland, 1840-1940
      www.cartedevisite.co.uk [Data provided for a small fee]
Published Regional Photographer Studies
London
A Directory of London Photographers 1841-1908, Michael Pritchard (PhotoResearch, 1994)
Birmingham
Professional photographers in Birmingham 1842-1914, C E John Aston et al (RPS Historical Group, 1987)
Leeds
Early Photography in Leeds, 1839-1870, Adrian Budge (Leeds Art Galleries, 1981)
Doncaster
Photographers in Victorian Doncaster 1842-1900, Keith I P Adamson (Doncaster Museum Service, 1998)
York
Photographs and Photographers of York: The early years 1844-1879, Hugh Murray (Yorkshire Architectural and York Archaeological Society, 1988)
Hampshire
Directory of Hampshire Photographers 1850-1969, Martin Norgate (Hampshire County Council Museums Service, 1995)
Wiltshire
Photographers in Wiltshire 1842-1939, Martin Norgate et al (Wiltshire Library & Museum Service, 1985)
Cornwall
Views and likenesses: early photographers and their work in Cornwall and the Isles of Scilly 1839-1870, Charles Thomas (Royal Institution of Cornwall, 1988)
Jersey
Jersey Through the Lens, Richard Mayne and Joan Stevens (Phillimore, 1975)
Ireland
Through the brass-lidded eye: photography in Ireland 1839-1900, E Chandler & P Walsh (Guinness Museum, 1989)
Scotland
Scottish Photography: A Bibliography 1839-1939, Sara Stevenson & A D Morrison-Low (Salvia Books & Scottish Society for the History of Photography, 1990)
Paisley Photographers 1850-1900, Don McCoo (Foulis Archive Press, Paisley, 1986)

To Stand Where They Stood

Anne Batchelor

'Family History research doesn't get better than this!'

I do worry about the future of Family History. So many modern families have a different structure to those of the past. We have artificial insemination by donor, surrogate mothers, or children born to a two-father partnership via a donated egg, and a loaned womb. How will it be possible to show those relationships on a family tree?

Then there are re-marriages or non-marriages. I once tried to show a class of school children how to draw a simple family tree, starting with their own name and the names of their mum and dad. "Please Miss," said a bewildered girl, *"Do you mean our dad, my real dad or mam's chap?"* 'Our dad,' was the man who fathered most of the family, 'my real dad' fathered her when her mother had a fling, and 'mum's chap' had recently moved in when 'our dad' went to prison. What a muddle!

With the coming of the computer age, I fear that thousands of family historians will spend their time sitting in the spare bedroom, pushing buttons, and miss out on the real magic of family research – that is real research at an archive with chance encounters with helpful fellow researchers. This is often the first step on the magical journey to the place where your family lived. There is nothing to beat the spine-tingling moment when you find yourself saying, *"They were here! Something of me stood here years and years ago!"*

Like many others of my generation, I was inspired by Alex Haley's story of his *"Roots."* His search for his ancestry led him to an African village where he was at last, after years of research, able to stand and say, *"This is my place, and these are my people."* We may not all be led to African roots but the journey to our places can be just as thrilling and satisfying.

When I started my research both my parents were still alive, and I well remember the moment when I took my elderly mother to the parish church at Crofton, where her parents were married. She stood in front of the altar, visibly moved, and then said, *"Just think, my lovely red-hared mother stood here on her wedding day. She must have been a lovely bride."* This was a very special moment for my mother, for she had only been four years old when her red-haired mother died, and all she could remember was her beautiful hair.

Later, I took her to Featherstone Parish Church, where she and all her siblings had been christened. The first child, little Hilda, had died at the age of two, of measles. The second child, George Henry, died at eleven months, of bronchitis; then came my mother Frances, a beautiful golden haired child with vivid blue eyes. As we stood at the font together, I found myself imagining their heart-felt prayer, *"Please God, let us keep this one."* In fact, it was the mother, Annie, who died young, at the age of twenty eight, while Frances – her child, lived to the grand age of eighty-nine.

Frances was brought up at the Godfrey Walker Home for Waifs and Strays in York from 1920 until she left school and went into service in 1931. It took me ages to locate the building, which I knew to be on Acomb Road, York, because many of the buildings had been renumbered. However, the Electoral Register for the area in the 1920's revealed the actual path taken by the person recording the inhabitants – *"to the top of Hobgate, then across Acomb Road"* – and there, opposite Hobgate, was the Home.

I was then able to confirm with the present owners that the house on the end of the terrace, once known as West Bank Terrace but now Acomb Road, was indeed a former children's home. On Mother's Day 1996, I took my mother on a visit. As we crossed the threshold together I saw, in my mind's eye, not that 82 year old lady but a nervous six year old with golden hear and vivid blue eyes being

Anne with her mother Frances at Middlethorpe Hall Hotel

handed over by Sister Tomlinson, of The Haven, Pontefract, into the keeping of two Anglican nuns in long black habits. These were Matron and Sister, who, along with the nineteen little girls who lived there, were to be her family for the next eleven years. It was so moving for me to stand where that little six year old had stood in January 1920.

Several times I have taken afternoon tea at Middlethorpe Hall, Bishopthorpe. This rather grand Country House Hotel, was once the home of the Paget family , where mum had her first job. She was a 'tweenie' (between stairs maid), the lowest ranking servant along with the scullery maid. As I sit in the drawing room, with my crustless smoked salmon sandwiches and tray of yummy cakes, I visualise my bonny little mother, on her knees, cleaning out the fireplace! It was in that same room, that, in 1998, we launched her book and I well remember her having a fit of the giggles when the waiter addressed her as *"Madam." "If only he knew!"* she whispered.

When I began to research my Batchelor roots I felt sure that it would be very easy, for were we not from York – only twenty miles from my present home? I knew that both my father and grandfather were born there. How was I to know at that point what a journey of discovery I would have to make, taking me into foreign parts south of Watford.

From their marriage certificate I knew that my grandparents, John Batchelor and Annie Gray, had been married at the church of All Saints, North Street, York on Christmas Day in 1897.

Annie had been born in one of the fifteenth century cottages alongside the church so she had only a short walk across the pavement to her wedding. I was allowed a peep inside the door of her home. It was such a tiny place in which to bring up seven children. Then I too crossed the pavement and went down the worn steps into the church.

There was a lovely stillness in the old building, and the bright sun sent coloured light through the famous stained glass windows and created amazing coloured patterns on the paved floor. I sat for a while and had the first of my *'just left'* feelings which I was to experience so many more times on my family journey – the vivid sensation that *'they were here only a few minutes ago. They've just left.'* Fanciful, I know, but that is how I feel. I believe that family history is not a list of cold facts studied by the head but also something felt in the heart.

When I came out into the daylight, I noticed at the end of the lane a little sweet shop, and remembered my old dad telling me how, as a child, he had bought his *'spice'* from Cissie Emmings in her family's corner shop. On impulse I went in and found an extremely old lady, Cissie, herself, behind the counter. I mentioned the Batchelor boys from Rougier Street and was ushered into her tiny back room for a cup of tea. What memories she had! Sadly, the next time I called I discovered that young intruders, stealing a few cigarettes, had beaten her about the head and put her in hospital, where the frail old lady had died. As my dad would have said, *"Their hands should drop off!"*

My grandfather's birth certificate showed that he was born in Paver Lane, in Walmgate, which was one of the poorest areas of York. Paver Lane still exists, but gone are the dark, cramped houses. Only the original pavements remain and an older building for storing hay. Nevertheless, I was able to walk, quite slowly and reverently, along the lane, saying to myself *"They were here."*

When I later discovered that my grandfather's parents, George and Eliza Batchelor, came from a small village in Hertfordshire, I felt so sorry for them coming to live in a dark, crowded slum. It was some comfort to me to realise that behind Paver Lane was the churchyard of St Margaret's, so there would have been a green area with trees nearby and perhaps the singing of birds.

In pursuit of my Hertfordshire ancestors I decided to get on a train and visit Berkhamsted where they had been born, and nearby Northchurch where they were married. I still remember the strange feelings as my train pulled into Berkhamsted station and I saw its name pass my carriage window. Suddenly, this was not just a name in an archive, but a real place!

The villages of Berkhamsted and Northchurch are connected by a long street called Gossoms End, so the next morning I set off to walk to St Mary's Northchurch, where my great grandparents George Batchelor and Eliza Ann Foskett were married in 1861. Though the main London road passed through Northchurch, the church of St Mary is in a tranquil spot set back from the road. As I was at that time a very inexperienced time-traveller, I had not thought about telling anyone I was coming. When I reached the church, the door was locked!

The folk at the pub opposite took pity on me and directed me to the home of Jack Reynolds who was, among other duties, the Keeper of the Key. He very kindly let me in and then left me to savour the moment.

It was a lovely summer day. The church was cool and quiet, apart from the sound of sparrows chirping outside. I sat in a pew near the front, and looked at the altar, thinking to myself *"That is where they exchanged vows."* Little did they know that over a hundred years later, I would be sitting here with their blood in my veins, having journeyed from far away Yorkshire.

They had no idea that fourteen years after

Wellington Row, York 2010

Cissie Emming's Shop, Wellington Row, North Street, York

Funeral of SSM Batchelor, Hartoft Street, York in 1906

Hartoft Street, York today

that marriage service they would be moving north to spend the rest of their lives in York. As I sat and experienced again my *'just left'* sensation, my eyes wandered to the stone column next to my seat. It bore graffiti dated 1717. How strange that it doesn't offend us when it is so old. The name beside the date was J. ROLFE. I couldn't believe my eyes – Theophilus Batchelor, cousin of my great grandfather, was the first of my family to come to York. He had been born in Northchurch and his mother was Elizabeth Rolfe! Perhaps this eighteenth century vandal was on of my distant relations by marriage.

Over the next few years I tracked my Batchelor family back through the centuries, spending many hours in record offices and archives, poring over original registers and wills. That in itself is a magical experience. Then, to my great surprise, I stumbled over David Batchiler. That discover was a prime case of serendipity.

I was researching at the Hertfordshire record Office and casually took a large book off the shelf, wondering to myself, *"What does Calendar of Salisbury Papers mean?"* In it was my first sighting of the man whose story was to add colour to my family tree. Daniel Bachiler was a Groom of the Privy Chamber to Anne of Denmark, the wife of King James I. His indentures, signed in 1586, when he was barely fifteen, identified him as the middle son of my Richard Bachiler, a farmer of Aston Clinton. In later life he was recognised as the leading lutenist and composer of his day. Putting together his story was a wonderful experience and an amazing feat for a self-taught, absolute beginning of a family historian.

No-one seemed to have discovered how he came to London in the reign of Elizabeth I. Finding him through his family I uncovered the fact that Daniel's uncle, Thomas Cardell, was lutenist and dancing master to the Queen. He took Daniel from his home on the farm in

Funeral of SSM Batchelor, Hartoft Street, York in 1906 with Hartoft Street, York today.

Aston Clinton into the court of Gloriana herself! It was uncle Thomas who taught the young boy to play the lute. He proved to be an exceptional musician and his rise to fame was swift and colourful. He went from his uncle's house in Kinges Street, Westminster, to be in charge of the music in the home of the powerful Sir Francis Walsingham.

From there he went into the household of Robert Devereux, Earl of Essex, and after the death of Elizabeth he was brought to court by Robert Devereux's widow, the Lady Frances (nee Walsingham). There he was made a Groom of the Privy Chamber and produced music for Anne of Denmark.

All the music books I consulted said things like, "Very little know of this man," or "this man's life is a complete blank." Because I had the full story I was able to visit the church where he was baptised in 1571, the Great Halls at Hampton Court, and Penshurst Place where his music had been played, and the deserted old churchyard of St Margaret's Lee, where he was buried in 1619.

As I stood by the font in the parish church of Aston Clinton, I thought about Richard and Elizabeth standing there, probably surrounded by their wide-eyed children, handing over their latest son, Daniel for baptism. They little knew that this tiny son was to become famous for his music for the next 440 years! Another lovely moment for me.

When I visited Hampton Court and Penshurst Place, I found a quiet corner to close my eyes and shut out the twentieth century. "These very stones," I thought, "echoed to his music. He was here."

No-one seemed to know when he had died, but I found Daniel in the burial register of St Margaret, Lee, for 1619. I immediately went to find a flower shop in nearby Blackheath and bought a single red rose to take to the churchyard. "Is it for someone special?" asked the assistant. She seemed quite taken-aback when I explained it was for a young member of my family who died three hundred and seventy years ago!

As there was no sign of a stone marking his last resting place, I chose an ivy-covered eighteenth century tomb and placed my rose on that. Then, being a true eccentric, I went behind the old ruined tower and sat on the grass. I put a piece of Daniel's music in my cassette player and listened to my favourite melody, 'Monsieur's Almaine.' It was quite an eerie experience, listening to what went on in his head and knowing that somewhere, close by, his body had been laid to rest.

My other exceptional visit was to Chapel Farm, St Leonard's where my earliest known ancestor, Andrew Batchelor, died in 1527, in the reign of Henry VIII. Amazingly, the occupier – Mrs Allen, believed my tale of the ancestors when I turned up at her door unannounced, and showed her my family tree and a copy of Andrew's will. As I was invited to step inside I had my 'Alex Haley' moment. Something of me was here four hundred and sixty one years ago.

Family history research doesn't get better than this! It felt both creepy and exhilarating.

Mrs Allen invited me to return to 'my house,' whenever I wished and so a year later, I brought my parents to see it. I could see that my old dad was trying to take in the idea that something of him, someone with his flesh and blood, had been there so long ago. He kept saying "Who'd have thought it? Well, flip me!"

This has been just a brief account of my 'just left' moments when researching my own family. I have not started to tell you all the other adventures I've had chasing other individuals whose stories have obsessed me! I've stood in the schoolhouse at Great Gaddesdon where Emily was headteacher in the 1870's. I've bowed my head in the front parlour of a little back-to-back house in York on the spot where 'My Gallant Hussar' – George Batchelor lay in his coffin awaiting his funeral in 1906, and I grieved for his young widow, left with three fatherless children and another baby on the way.

I've visited the house in Barnet where they Jukes family lived at the beginning of the twentieth century. I've walked in Trevor's garden and slept in Kathleen's room. I've stood on a wooden staircase in a house in Wales where John Manley, a Major in Cromwell's army , and his wife, Margaret had walked when they went up to bed.

Researching the diary of Augustus Frederick Manley (bought at an antiques' fair) I've followed his foot steps as he indulged his passion for the villages and mountains around Lake Lucern.

All of these experiences were 'Just Gone!' moments for me, when the centuries seem to telescope down, and I feel only a fingertip away from history. The people of the past are no longer names and dates on a family tree, but real people. Standing where they stood somehow brings them back to life for a moment.

I can recommend it. There is no thrill like it!

THE FAVERSHAM SOCIETY
FOUNDED 1962
FLEUR DE LIS HERITAGE CENTRE
ESTABLISHED 1977

Faversham, near Canterbury, is an unspoilt historic town and port with nearly
500 listed buildings. The Society, covering the town and nearby villages,
is a registered charity run by 100% voluntary effort. Our Heritage Centre,
Museum, Tourist Information Centre, Kentish bookshop and second-hand
bookshop are in 15th century buildings in the town centre.
Readers will be welcome here, at the nearby
Chart Gunpowder Mills (oldest in the world)
and at the medieval Maison Dieu on the A2, which we also administer.
One mile West, the Oare Gunpowder Works also welcomes visitors.
Our popular annual Open House event (oldest in the UK) takes place on
the first three Saturdays in July: around 25 buildings of historic interest
(and sometimes an historic sailing barge) are open to ticket-holders.
Over 100 individual historical studies in our "Faversham Papers" series
are on sale at our Heritage Centre.

Among many books and CD-ROMs (*) available
from the Society are:

Early Town Books of Faversham c 1251-1581 (Harrington & Hyde) (2 large & heavy vols)	£109.00
Faversham Book Trade (alphabetical listings of booksellers. printers etc)(Goulden)	£4.95
Faversham Folk at War 1914-1918: Roll of Honour & Decorations (P Stevens)	£6.95
Faversham Gunpowder Personnel Register 1573-1840 (Godfrey & Percival)	£6.95
Faversham Explosives Personnel Register 1840-1934 (Breeze) 3 vols Each	£6.95
Faversham Hundred Rental Transcripts 1532-1815 (Harrington & Hyde) (800 pp)	£17.50
Faversham Oyster Fishery through 11 Centuries (Hyde & Harrington)	£33.50
Faversham Registration District: Surname Index to 1841 Census (Breeze)	£6.95
Faversham Registration District: Surname Index to 1871 Census (Breeze)	£8.95
Faversham Tudor & Stuart Muster Rolls (Hyde & Harrington)	£17.50
Faversham's Reluctant Exiles (Transportees) (J Stevens)	£5.50
Hearth Tax Returns for Faversham Hundred 1662-1674 (Hyde & Harrington)	£27.50
More Faversham Reluctant Exiles (Transportees) (J Stevens)	£6.50
Nash Families of Goodnestone-next-Wingham (Nash Mills)	£6.50
Selling Church & Churchyard Monumental Inscriptions (Neame)	£4.75
Taylor Papers, The (Fry)	£7.95

Prices are post-free to UK destinations: for others, please enquire
Payment with order, please

We may be able to help with local and family history enquiries.
In this event please write, letting us know all you know as well as what you want to know!
10-13 Preston Street, Faversham, Kent ME13 8NS
W:www.faversham.org/society **E:** ticfaversham@btconnect.com **T:** +44 (0) 1795 534542

FAVERSHAM
MARKET TOWN OF KINGS

Did Your Ancestor Work on The Railway?

Frank Hardy F.S.G

For the purposes of this article, I am going to assume that your ancestor was employed before 1923. I will attempt to give you some general guidance on tracing railway staff. My background is that I was a civil engineer working for British Railways, and later Railtrack and Network Rail, from 1959 to 2009 during which time I had professional dealing with many other departments. As far as family history is concerned, I have been researching my extended family since 1975. Since 1985, I have been helping others in their search for the elusive ancestor in their family.

Records for staff joining after 1923 are relatively few and far between, and for those of us who joined after 1948, there are virtually no surviving records unfortunately. Do not despair however, your relations will probably have most of the detail tucked away in a corner of their memory.

Your family story says that Uncle Joe worked on the railway. Well, the first thing to do is to establish whether the story is true or a fanciful myth. My background as a railway civil engineer AND as a family historian tells me that there are a number of facts that have to be proven before it is worth trying to find a trail through the railway records that survive at *The National Archives* and around the country in record offices.

Throughout, I have assumed that you will be searching for a man, as there were so few women employed, and then only in a very limited range of jobs.

I have given the histories of George and Henry Wainscott to illustrate what can be done to trace a railwayman. I have not cited detailed references, as the histories are provided to give you a taste of what information can be obtained by using a variety of sources.

A personal history of George Wainscott

George Wainscott was born in 1844 at Hereford, the son of James Wainscott, railway ticket collector on the Newport, Abergavenney and Hereford Railway at Hereford (from birth certificate). When George married in 1864, the marriage certificate described him as a railway servant. According to the records of the North Staffordshire Railway, he was appointed Yardman at Leek in Nov 1869. On the April 1871 Census, he was staying with his father in Hereford, but by the next month was living at Fenton, Stoke-on-Trent; this may have been a railway owned house. In 1878, he was a points man, living at Havelock Street, Shelton. In the following year, his son Henry was born at Leek. On the 1881 Census he was living at Leek. In January 1889, he was appointed Signalman at Leek at a weekly wage of 23s.0d; and 2s.0d was deducted weekly for rent of a railway house. He was cautioned in Jan 1902 for *'irregular signalling.'* He resigned 19 Apr 1903 and a retiring gratuity of £10 was allowed by the Directors of the company at their meeting on 21 Apr 1903. He died a few months later.

A personal history of Henry Wainscott from railway records and family papers

Born 5th Mar 1879 at Barnfields, Leek, son of George Wainscott, and baptised 20 Jul 1879 at St Luke, Leek. On 1 Aug 1898 Henry joined the Manchester, Sheffield and Lincolnshire Railway as a goods clerk at Broughton Lane Station, Sheffield at 20s.0d per week. On 1 July 1899 his pay was increased to 22s.6d per week. He resigned 7 Apr 1900, and on the following day was presented with a writing case, bible and prayer book by his colleagues at Broughton Lane Station, by then

Opening of Britannia Railway Bridge
© Robert Blatchford

ERECTED ANNO
ROBERT STEPHENSON

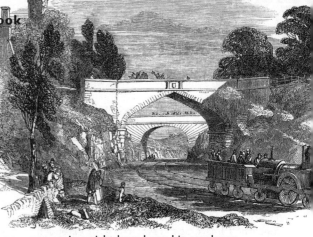

on the Great Central Railway, to mark his departure to the Boer War. He served as Private H Wainscott no 1120 in the 5th detachment (Sheffield) of the St John Ambulance Brigade as an ambulance man. He served as an Orderly at No 13 Stationary Hospital at Wynberg and Johannesburg. He returned from South Africa, and rejoined the Great Central Railway 18 Mar 1901 as Goods Clerk at Staveley at 22s 6d per week. His pay rose to 25s.0d on 1 Jul 1901 and to 27s 6d on 1 Jul 1902. On 12 Nov 1902 he was transferred to Leicester Station as Goods Clerk. In 1903, he was living at 19 Roman St., Narborough Road, Leicester. His pay was increased to 30s.9d on 1 Jan 1905. On 20 Mar 1905, he was transferred to be a Goods Clerk at Doncaster. Married 24 Mar 1905 at Leicester Register Office, and the witnesses were Ernest Alfred Wordsworth and Sophia Mary Wordsworth. At the time of his marriage Henry was a railway clerk living at 5 Shaftesbury Road, Leicester. By 1906 he had moved to a post at Wheatley, Yorkshire. Resigned from the Great Central Railway 25 Aug 1906 and emigrated to New Zealand and joined the New Zealand Railways in Dec 1906. Became a guard at Woodville, Wellington and Auckland (in 1914 was living at Alma St., Newmarket, Auckland); shift clerk at Pahiatua and Mangatimoka. Became a Station Master, and was stationed at Mauriceville (1921-1927), Lawrenceville, Cross Creek at the foot of the Rimutaka Incline, Masterton and Patea. In 1933-1941, was described as a clerk, living at 61 Lincoln Rd., Masterton. Died 3 Jan 1941 at Patea, whilst on relief duty and was buried at Masterton, New Zealand.

Now, how can you trace your ancestor?

The primary questions to be answered are 'Where', 'When', 'What'. Some are easy with the availability of the Census Return on the Internet. Birth marriage and death dates and places can only be answered with the actual certificates from the General Register Office.

Where, exactly, did he live?

The answer to this is crucial to enable you to start a search for his railway history. If the answer is, say, London, Birmingham, Glasgow or Manchester, please go away and get a street address as this may be a route to clarifying which railway company might have been his employer. From the Census Returns note the details of the house where he was living. In general, railway employees lived within walking distance of their workplace, and so knowledge of an address enables you to look at a detailed map such as the *Alan Godfrey* series of reproductions of Ordnance Survey maps to see which railway company might have been involved. There are also specialist maps of the railways that can help identify which

companies might have been his employer. When was he living there?

The railways were built over a period from 1825 to 1900, and if there was no railway close by at the time your ancestor was living at a particular address it will be extremely unlikely that he was employed by a railway company. It will be necessary to look into the history of the railways in the area to see when the lines were built.

By checking all census returns between 1851 and 1911 this may well reveal his movements, and help to locate him, possibly on more than one railway. Men moved around the railway industry to get promotion, if it was slow where they had started, or to fill posts on a new railway line.

As well as Census Returns, information can be gleaned from the birth certificates from his children, or from Marriage and Death certificates. A death certificate can be particularly revealing in the case of a fatality on the railway.

What was his occupation?

This can be found from the census returns, which may if you are lucky, show that he was an engine driver working for a particular railway. However, I should issue a word or two of caution. The description 'engine driver' on a census return or on a certificate issued by a registrar does not mean that the person worked on the railway. He might well have been the driver of a stationary engine providing power for a works or cotton mill.

The term 'fireman' can be even more misleading: just look at this selection of jobs which were called a fireman:

Did he ride on a red Fire Engine ringing a bell? – if so it is unlikely that he worked for the railway unless it was at one of the large workshop complexes, such as the works at Swindon, Crewe or Doncaster.

Was he a firemen stoking a stationary steam boiler in a factory? Again he would only have been employed by the railway if this was a big workshop.

Was he a fireman (stoker) on a ship? He will only appear on railway records if he had been on one of the ferry services across the Channel, North Sea, Irish Sea or on the Clyde

Did he work for a main-line railway, or was he employed in some sort of factory working on a small locomotive to move wagons around a factory complex? Many large companies had their own private railways (e.g. the breweries around Burton on Trent)

Of course the situation gets even complex when the occupation is simply given as labourer. This term can refer to a labourer in many departments of a railway, but there are also many thousands of labourers employed in industry and on farms all over the country.

Another pitfall is that the railway industry employed people of virtually every trade, some in large numbers, but others, such as nurses, in small numbers at a very few locations. The only occupation that I am certain had no one employed by any railway company was undertaker.

What was his date of birth?

Almost all railway staff records use the Date of Birth to identify the person until the introduction in the middle of the 20th Century of National Insurance numbers. Likewise with manual records on cards or in ledgers, the railway staff clerks used the date of birth (DoB), and sometimes as an additional check, the Date Entered Service (DeS).

How many railwaymen and women were there?

This is a very difficult question to answer. I have seen a suggestion by Christian Wolmar in his book *'Fire and Steam'* that in 1901 there were 650,000 people employed by the railway companies. I think this must have been somewhere near the maximum number employed at any one time. My reasoning is that in Victorian times the number of lines was growing and services were expanding. By the start of the 20th Century a reduction in the numbers employed started as faster trains resulted in better productivity.

Gradually after 1900, the working day was reduced from 12 or more hours down to 8 hours

and this did slow down the drop in numbers. Then there was a further decline arising from the introduction of electrification which eliminated the need for locomotive firemen.

One also has to take into account that many employees worked for the railway industry for up to 50 years, when trying to make an assessment of the number of individuals who were employed between 1830 and 1948. On this basis, my estimate is that there must be somewhere between 2 and 3 million individuals, employed at one time or another from 1830 up to 1948.

Women in the railways

There is a tendency to think that the employment of women is relatively recent, but some women were employed by the railways from the 1840's, although they were in occupations where women were necessary such as Ladies Waiting Room Attendants. Gradually the refreshment rooms employed women as waitresses.

The first widespread use of women really dates from the First World War in 1914-18, when the railways were forced to replace the men called up for military service. With the Armistice, the men returned to their civilian employment and most of the women were dismissed, having been employed on short-term agreements. A few women were employed between the wars, frequently in office positions, such as clerks, typists, telephone switchboard operators as well as the Waiting Room Attendants and Waitresses.

With the Second World War, the railways found themselves in the same state as before for staff, and recruited women into many roles formerly considered the preserve of men. There were platform staff, booking clerks, train guards, shunters, some track repair gangs, locomotive cleaners and women signalmen and level crossing keepers as well as the clerical and office roles.

After the end of the war in 1945, as previously, a lot of the women were displaced by men returning from military service. Within a few years, a lot of clerical duties were carried out by women, and in the 1960's a number of women were employed in the various drawing offices within the engineering departments. Gradually more and more women moved into management roles in all departments of the railway; at retirement in 2009, my immediate line manager was a woman. As I write this on a train, both the driver and train manager are women, and this is, in the 21st century, commonplace.

1923 and 1948

What is the significance of these two dates? Simply, these were the dates of major reorganisations affecting the

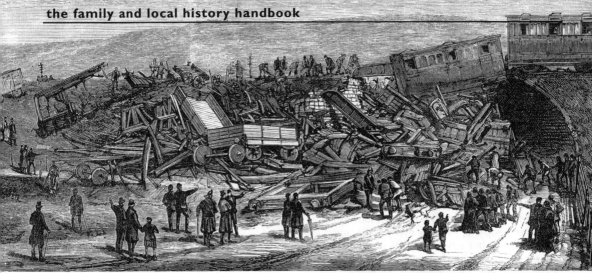

whole railway industry.

On 1st January 1923, the Railways Act of 1921 came into effect and created the Big Four railway companies, by enforced amalgamation. A simplified description of the areas covered by each company follows:

London, Midland & Scottish Railway – covering lines out of London (Euston and St Pancras) to Birmingham, North Wales, the North West of England Sheffield and parts of Scotland to Perth, Inverness and Wick, and the Tilbury line to Southend. The principal companies in the group from the pre 1923 era were:
London, Tilbury & Southend; Midland; London & North Western, Lancashire & Yorkshire, Furness, Glasgow & South Western, Maryport & Carlisle, Caledonian and Highland Railways.

London and North Eastern Railway – covering East Anglia, London (Marylebone) to Sheffield and Manchester, Kings Cross to Edinburgh, Leeds and Scarborough and South East and East of Scotland. The principal companies in the group from the pre 1923 era were: Great Northern, Great Eastern, Great Central, North Eastern and North British Railways.

Great Western Railway – covering London (Paddington) to Penzance, South and Mid Wales, Birmingham and Birkenhead. The principal companies in the group from the pre 1923 era were: Great Western, Barry, Taff Vale, Rhymney, Brecon & Merthyr Railways.

Southern Railway – South of the River Thames to Ramsgate and the whole south coast round to Weymouth and the Isle of Wight and London – Salisbury – Exeter and North Devon. The principal companies in the group from the pre 1923 era were: South Eastern, London Chatham & Dover, London Brighton & South Coast, London & South Western, Isle of Wight, Isle of Wight Central and Freshwater Yarmouth & Newport Railways. There were also some jointly operated lines: Cheshire Lines Committee, Somerset and Dorset Railway, Midland and Great Northern Railway

Many minor railways were not included in the 1923 amalgamation including: Festiniog, Talyllyn, Southwold, Kent & East Sussex, East Kent Railways and the Hundred of Manhood & Selsey Tramway.

On the 1st January 1948, the railways of England, Scotland and Wales were nationalised under the authority of the Railways Act of 1947 with an umbrella organisation entitled 'The Railway Executive of the British Transport Commission.' Day to day running of the railways were delegated to six regions, Scottish, North Eastern, London Midland, Eastern, Western and Southern. Very few staff records survive from post 1948, so I do not propose to go into any detail of the organisation which changed from the pre-1948 period.

What staff records can you find?

Thanks to the government enforced reorganisations in 1923 and 1948, records of staff are not plentiful. Every reorganisation causes files to be lost in transit or destroyed under the principle 'That is of no interest to anyone!' If I were to say that for the period 1923 to 1948 there are less than two pages listed in 'Was your Grandfather a Railwayman?' and more than 30 pages for the period before 1923 you will get some idea of the amount available. Except for a few records in local and personal archives, virtually no paper records survive for after 1948. There are no records available to the public held by the Train Operating Companies, infrastructure companies or Network Rail. When I retired, my staff history was on computer in an incomplete form; basically only the last 6 or so years of my career had survived, without any details of my qualifications.

The one company that had the least number of reorganisations, the Great Western Railway, has the best kept and largest collection of staff records, although it would seem that some dates and places are absent.

The surviving staff records are mainly located at The National Archives, and a full list of the National Archives and other record office holdings is given in Was your Grandfather a Railwayman (ISBN: 978-1860061615 FFHS).

The records that survive are not complete; my perusal of the listing of surviving material shows many gaps. Complete departments are often missing, or for other companies, only a selection of the stations or depots are available

The records that were retained after an amalgamation were those that related to staff still employed. Volumes relating to retired and deceased staff were generally consigned to the bottom of a dusty cupboard only to be destroyed at the next reorganisation or office move. Having moved offices during my career, I have experienced this at first hand with old records of civil engineering work, which had been overtaken by events, and either not carried out, or demolished and a new structure built.

Scottish railway records are generally held in Edinburgh.

As an aside, I found it fascinating to read some of the records from the 1880's. The terminology used by the clerks then, was exactly the same as that used in the 1960's and 70's by the British Railways staff clerks – 'given advice for his future actions' means he was given a verbal warning that had been formally recorded on his record!

What other records mention staff

The minutes of the various committees of Directors can sometime give some personal details of a member of staff. For Managers, their appointment may be recorded, and on retirement the Directors may have decided to grant the man a pension. Staff below the level of managers would normally only come to notice for doing something meritorious or, alternatively, exceptionally blameworthy. A good job was the expected state of affairs for all grades.

As many of these Minute books appear to be un-indexed, it could be a long slog to find information about a particular person. The starting point must be the date of an appointment of promotion or a retirement; a search through minute books back from the date might give some details of an individual.

If you have the date of an accident to an individual, resulting in premature retirement or death, there may be a mention of the Directors awarding a gratuity or pension to the man or his widow.

Railway Clearing House

With the complex railway system that had developed even as early as 1840, it became necessary to apportion passenger fares and good charges equitably between the railways involved. A passenger travelling over the East Coast Route from Kings Cross to Edinburgh would be travelling over the Great Northern, North Eastern and North British Railways, each of which wanted their share.

To carry out the apportionment, the Railway Clearing House was established in 1842 near Euston Station, and it was sent details of the number of tickets sold for each route and pair of stations. For the Goods traffic, it employed number-takers at junctions who recorded the wagon numbers passing from one company to another.

Some records of the staff employed by the Railway Clearing House exist at The National Archives at Kew.

People who were not Railway staff

The railways were constructed by Contractors, often called navvies (or Navigators – a term derived from the construction of canals). These men were employed by men like Thomas Brassey or Samuel Morton Peto. I doubt if any reliable record of the individuals employed on the construction survives, if it ever existed. In my experience in the 20th Century, companies carrying out construction work often have little information about their employees who are hired and fired as the work needs a particular skill.

Many of the Locomotives, Carriage and Wagons used were constructed by outside firms to the drawings and requirements of the railway companies. These contractors were frequently used when the Railway Company's own workshops were working to capacity.

Accidents

In general, reports of accidents do not give any personal details of the individuals, other than length of service. To make the best use of the Railway Accident Reports produced by the Inspecting Officers for the Board of Trade, it would be necessary to know the exact date and place to track down any details in the reports. The reports give names of witnesses and other people involved in the major train accidents where passengers have been killed.

The first passenger and goods railway was the Liverpool and Manchester Railway opened in 1830 and, on its opening day, achieved notoriety by having the first case of a person being struck by a train and killed on the railway. William Huskisson M.P. has his place in history!

Staff fatalities were not generally the subject of a report by an inspecting officer, and would generally feature in statistical tables in the Annual Reports of the Inspecting Officers.

However, I understand that some accidents to staff and others working on the railway were tabulated in some detail in British Parliamentary Papers annually by Railway Company as a Return of Accidents. Some Central Libraries may hold these volumes as well as copies being in the Parliamentary

Records. I must point out that you would need the date and railway company concerned to be able to trace the accident.

A good source for reports of accidents of all kinds and any associated Coroner's Inquest would be local newspapers of the day, but once again, a precise date will be needed unless you want to plough through a mass of paper.

Newspaper and Magazine Reports

Newspapers are a good source for information about the construction of a railway, frequently featuring regular reports on the construction of the earthworks and bridges. These would be followed by an account of the festivities associated with the opening of the railway through the town.

As far as individuals are concerned, accidents might be mentioned in greater or lesser detail. With a fatality, there might be an account of the Coroner's Inquest. Promotions, particularly of station masters, might get a mention where the individual had been prominent in local affairs. Similarly there might be a report of the festivities when a long-serving member of staff retired.

From 1897, the Railway Magazine has been published monthly and for the first 50 years of its existence gave potted biographies, and sometimes a photograph, of long serving inspectors and those managers who had recently retired. Many libraries have a run of the Railway Magazine as well as copies being at the National; Railway Museum.

I was doing some research for a cousin who had an ancestor living in Sheffield around 1900 working on the Great Central Railway. I found that he was in the St John Ambulance Brigade, and

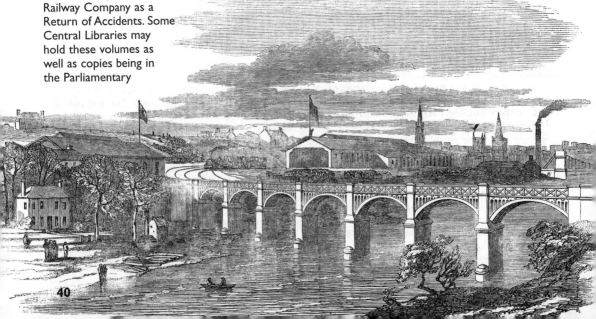

temporarily left the railway to go to South Africa. I managed to track down, in the local archives, a photograph of the St John group taken before they left Sheffield along with a local report of their departure.

Staff Magazines

Runs of the staff magazines that were published by some companies from about 1880 onwards are to be found in the Search Engine area of the National Railway Museum and at The National Archives. These volumes are good for tracking down individuals who have been promoted or retired, whatever their grade, but I have not discovered any with truly comprehensive indexes of names.

Trade Unions

Most railway workers from the 1880 onwards belonged to a trade union. There are three principal trade unions, formed between 1870 and 1900 with a series of mergers and amalgamations nearly as complex as those of the railway companies.

The unions are the National Union of Railwaymen (for station staff, signalmen and guards); Associated Society of Locomotive Engineers and Firemen (for drivers and firemen) and the Transport Salaried Staff Association (for clerical staff). Men in the railway workshops like Swindon, Crewe and Doncaster were often recruited into 'outside' trade unions such as those for engineering trades.

Membership records for the railway trade unions are mainly to be found at the Modern Records Centre of the University of Warwick. Some local branch records may have been deposited at a county Record Office or other local Archive, so it can also be worth looking into local holdings.

Seven Ways to Find Your Railway Ancestor
1. Know his date of birth and obtain birth certificate.
2. Know where he was living at a given date. Use marriage certificates and birth certificates of any children to get accurate addresses and occupations.
3. Using maps find which railway companies he could have worked for. Use the 'Pre-Grouping Atlas and Gazetteer' or 'The Railways of Great Britain – A Historical Atlas' (see Further Reading below) or use the appropriate 25 inch Ordnance Survey maps or the reproductions by Alan Godfrey Maps.
4. Do some research in railway histories to check date of opening of lines. (See the 'Regional History of the Railways of Great Britain' and the 'Bibliography of Railway History'
5. Check whether staff records survive for the company/companies. Use 'Was your Grandfather a Railwayman?' or 'Railway Ancestors' to check. (see Further Reading)
6. Check that departmental and depot records for your ancestor have survived as there is no point in looking for a Station Master in the Locomotive department or in a workshop. Likewise a fitter would not normally be found in the Traffic department
7. Visit Record Office/National Archives where staff records are held and search records.

Having done all that, where next?

My suggestion is that you search the internet for any references to the name, and then see if anyone else is interested in the family.

Join your local Family History Society, where there are usually people who are willing to help you in your research; attending the meetings can give you ideas to follow up in your further research. Searching for railway ancestors is no different to searching for an ancestor in any other occupation, and you need the stimulus of other peoples ideas.

Local reference libraries may have some of the books mentioned in the 'Further Reading' section below.

Has anyone else written up details of the family?

If the history of the family has been printed, then it is possible that a copy has been deposited at the Library of the Society of Genealogists – see their catalogue on their website at www.sog.org.uk and go to the Library Catalogue tab and search for the surname under 'Subject.' A substantial collection of unpublished and un-indexed material is held in the manuscript collections of the Society, but lists of surnames contained in the three manuscript collections is available on the Library pages of the website.

Further Reading
Was Your Grandfather a Railwayman? by Tom Richards (Author and Federation of Family History Societies 4th Edition 2002). The definitive listing of all known railway staff records and includes some overseas railway companies, mainly in the Commonwealth. (New Edition expected in 2011)
My Ancestor was a Railway Worker by Frank Hardy (Society of Genealogists 2009). A short guide to railway ancestry, with a glossary of terms and lists of workshops and private companies building railway locomotives and trains.
A Bibliography of Railway History by George Ottley (Volume 1 George Allen & Unwin 1965, 2nd edition HMSO 1983; Volume 2, Supplement 7951-12956 HMSO 1988 plus Second Supplement 12957-19605 National Railway Museum with Railway & Canal Historical Society)
Railway Ancestors: A Guide to the Staff Records of the Railway Companies of England and Wales 1822-1947 (ISBN: 978-0750950589 The History Press £20.00) by David Hawkings contains a listing of The National Archives holdings and has a useful list of the railway companies that served a particular county.
Railway Records: a Guide to Sources by Cliff Edwards (Public Record Office 2001)
The Railway Navvies by Terry Coleman (Hutchinson 1965, reprinted Pimlico 2000).
A Regional History of the Railways of Great Britain in

14 volumes by various authors (David & Charles 1960 - 1975)

Fire & Steam by Christian Wolmar (Atlantic Books 2008) - a wide ranging railway history looking at how the coming of the railways transformed Britain.

For the Kings Service – Railway Ships at War by A J Mullay (Pendragon Press 2008

Pre-Grouping Atlas and Gazetteer (Ian Allan Ltd) – Shows the railway system at 1922, with lines and stations marked with the owning/operating company.

The Railways of Great Britain – A Historical Atlas – Col M H Cobb (2 volumes, Ian Allan 2004).

Railways of Britain – Colin & David McCarthy (Ian Allan Ltd 2006 onwards) – a series of atlas books each covering one or two counties showing all railways known to have been constructed.

Tracing Your Railway Ancestors – Di Drummond (Pen & Sword Books, 2010).

Railwaywomen: Exploitation, betrayal and triumph in the workplace Helena Wojtczak ISBN: 978-1904109044 Hastings Press (2005) £30.00

The Fair Sex – Women and the Great Western Railway Rosa Matheson ISBN 978-0752444192 The History Press Ltd (2007) £12.99

Anchoring Your Ancestors

Karen Foy's guide to Canal Ancestors

It usually happens quite by chance. One day, someone drops into the conversation that Great Uncle Jack helped build the Caledonian Canal, that your Great, Great Grandfather transported coal on his narrow boat on the Trent and Mersey Canal or a distant relative on your father's side was a Toll Keeper somewhere in the Fens.

It only takes the seed of curiosity to be sown and you're hooked – suddenly your family history stretches out before you with a dozen questions you want answered.

As one of the world's fastest growing pastimes, 'genealogy' or researching your family history can become an addictive hobby. Once you start to dig deeper it won't be long before what started as a passing interest becomes a labour of love as your quest for knowledge grows.

So now that the bug has bitten, just how do you go about tracing your ancestors who have connections to Britain's rich and vibrant waterways heritage? There's a massive amount of information out there if you just know the right places to look.

As with any new project it's best to start with the basics. Gather as much information as you can from living relatives – you may even be lucky enough to discover a will containing details of your boating ancestor's life or an obituary detailing their waterways employment. Research back through your own parents, grandparents and great grandparents until you reach the relative you want to investigate in greater detail. As always, the golden rule is to begin with 'proved' information and the latest document, then work backwards.

Hatches, Matches and Dispatches . . .

The first stage is to confirm your facts using birth, marriage and death certificates (BMD'S). These certificates can be located using indexes. The indexes help to pinpoint what year and quarter of the year your ancestor was born, married or died and can be found at your local Records Office, Church of the Latter Day Saints (Mormons) or on the websites such as www.ancestry.co.uk and www.findmypast.co.uk

Consider where your ancestor worked at a particular time. Although some may have lived on canal boats, they would still need to get married, have their children christened and arrange a burial of their loved ones – use your investigative skills to work out the parishes and churches where these events may have taken place.

There is nothing quite like seeing a copy of their birth, marriage or death (BMD) certificate. These documents confirm so many facts from dates and addresses to parents, spouses, next of kin and even the cause of death ensuring you're not off on a wild goose chase researching the wrong person.

Searching the Census . . .

Census Returns are taken every ten years and are most effective from 1841 onwards. Each decade on census night the enumerators visited all houses, vessels and institutions and recorded the people who lived at these addresses. The evidence gathered included the names of the inhabitants, whether they were married, single, male or female, their ages, place of birth and a description of their occupation – ideal for finding out more about their specific role. Recorded vessels and institutions can supply a whole host of facts especially if your ancestor was amongst them. From this you can trace any siblings that your ancestor had and follow their lives and

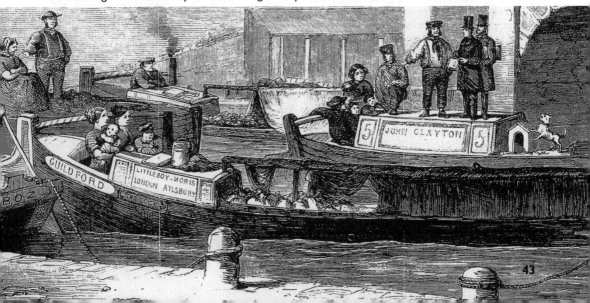

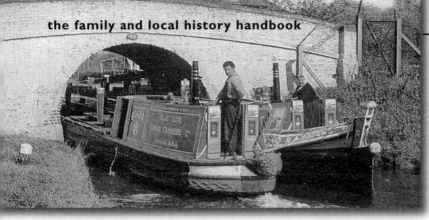

who navigated a large, flat bottomed boat in shallow waters.

In Depth Investigations . . .

Armed with your latest findings and confirmed facts you can now try to dig a little deeper. For example, if there is documented evidence that your ancestor worked in Cheshire – this is your starting point. Specific records relate to certain areas of the trade and your first *port of call* should be to contact the local archives or records office in the area where your chosen ancestor lived or worked, enquire what documents they hold and arrange a visit.

The following resources may be available to you:

Trade Directories break each area down into its towns, villages and districts, listing the names of merchants, traders and inhabitants and the services they provided. Each book is dated with the year of compilation and lists the traders around the dock areas from canal agents to boat builders as well as canal companies, carriers, customs officials, toll keepers and pilots. These directories – *Pigot's*, *Kelly's* and *White's* - are indispensable in creating a 'picture' of the area in which your ancestor lived and can also be searched online at www.historicaldirectories.org

From 1795, every vessel was required to be registered with the Clerk of the Peace. You may be lucky enough to discover some of these Registers of Vessels at your local archive although it is down to each individual facility as to what has survived. Cheshire, for example, holds an earlier Register of Vessels used on the inland waterways including canal barges, from between 1795 and 1812 and covers mainly Northwich vessels. Each register usually gives the name of the owner, sometimes a list of the crewmen on board, the master of the vessel and who built it. Crew lists were compiled to document the men on each voyage – Gloucester holds a vast number of these lists so if your ancestor worked in this area it is well worth a look.

This line of enquiry could, in turn, lead you deeper into research on boat builders where Gauging Tables were used to note the boat builder and the year of construction, its owner as well as the length of the vessel and where it traded.

If you're interest lies in tracing a particular vessel then locating a boat's Log Book can provide a whole host of valuable information. Survival rates of these documents are limited and can be

careers with each decade's new census.

So what did your ancestor do for a living?

With any luck the census will have helped you to shed some light on to your ancestor's employment on the canal and where they were located in the country at the start of a particular decade. Below is a glossary of just some of the job titles he could have taken.

Wharfinger – he was the owner or keeper of a wharf and was responsible for its day to day running and the goods which were delivered there. Working from his office on the wharf he would ensure that the tide tables were correct, that the slipways were maintained and that any disputes with employees or boatmen were dealt with.

Boatman – he would work on, repair, operate or hire out boats.

Waterman – this is another term for a boatman and describes someone who either works or lives on the water. He is skilful at boat operation and makes his money hiring his boat on the inland waterways or harbour areas.

Bargeman – this man would operate, work upon or master the crew of a barge.

Lock / Toll Keeper – Living in a house beside the lock, the lock keeper would keep a register of each passing vessel and the cargo it carried and then calculate the appropriate toll. This money was then paid to the Canal Office.

Boat builder – these were skilled craftsmen of flat bottomed canal boats and other vessels.

Bridgeman – this term describes the man who would open a bridge for anyone passing along the canal – his duties can also involve managing the loading and unloading of cargoes at a landing dock. He would be the public face of the Canal Company - not only to those using the canal but also to those crossing the bridges on foot.

Docker – this man would be employed to load and unload cargoes at the dockside or harbour – manually or with the aid of machinery.

Pilot – this person would be qualified to conduct vessels in and out or certain bodies of water or a port.

Flatman – a term used to describe someone

difficult to find but they can offer details of the Captain or owner and what kind of cargo was being carried. One particular Winsford Log Book records the Salt Cargo carried from Winsford but does not detail the vessel's return cargos which would give an idea of what was being bought back into this area dominated by the Salt Industry.

Cargo records give a real insight into the social history of the time from the transportation of staple ingredients such as butter, sugar and wine to bales of cloth, timber, clay and coal. One list dating from late 1770's details the measurements used during this era - one *Pipe* of Wine, two *barrels* of Porter and three *Balks* of timber – marvellous snippets from the history of trade.

The Canal Boat Act of 1877 – 1884 was used to improve the standard of living aboard the boats and documents relating to this *can* be found but for other related occupations why not track down the Waterways Index, compiled in the late 1970's by a lady in search of her own ancestor. Today, John Roberts of Sutton Coldfield in the West Midlands continues to add information contributed by other genealogists and extracted from various sources so that the record now has details on over 10,000 men who were once employed on our waterways. This is an active source and information is still sought from other genealogists who can contribute information from their own family records. Details of the index can be found via links on Cyndi's List alongside a whole host of other links to the history and resources surrounding Britain's canal network. www.cyndislist.com/canals.htm

Click for Clues ...

Perhaps you want to find out more about the construction and development of our inland waterways, then why not contact the Railway and Canal Historical Society. - www.rchs.org.uk/trial/gwpf.php?wpage=Home

Within the organisation they also have individual research groups – one being on Waterways History – which may be able to help you with your quest and inspire further investigation.

Examples of the records held at the National Archives include documents detailing the Canal Transport System inherited from Canal Companies pre- nationalisation (1948) or when they had been taken over by other companies such as the Railways. These 'take over' papers date mainly from 1850's onwards. By 1919, the Ministry of Transport had been created and they took on much of this paperwork which is also searchable here. The Historical Record section deals with documents related to particular companies, maps, plans and photographs, and early records for the funding of specific projects such as building the Caledonian Canal from 1807 – 1825. If you know where your ancestor may have been working, a trip to the National Archives could well prove fruitful. The National Archives (TNA), Ruskin Avenue, Kew, Richmond, Surrey. TW9 4DU T: 020 8876 3444 W: www.nationalarchives.gov.uk/ N.B. Always do your homework before you visit a Records Office so that you don't loose valuable research time. By all means use the wonderful resources on the internet but where possible always confirm your facts by seeing the original documented evidence. There is nothing like seeing an original log book with your ancestors name written in copperplate writing. Be prepared and take pencils (pens are not usually allowed), paper, your notes, money for photocopying and your digital camera.

Completing the picture ...

Learning more about what your ancestors did in their everyday lives is half the fun. Although you may not have photographs of individual relatives, you can still build up photographic evidence of similar workers, their costumes and living and working conditions by visiting canal museums in person - or even online. Gradually, you will get a feel for a certain period in history by creating an overall representation of what tools they used, the clothes they wore and the food they ate, helping to breathe life into what was once just a name on your family tree.

An essential online resource is the Virtual Waterways Archive Catalogue – searchable free at www.virtualwaterways.co.uk/home.html

For more information on the Lock Keepers of

Gloucester see www.gloucesterdocks.me.uk/people/dockco/lockkeepers.htm

By collecting and preserving a whole host of photographs, documents, plans and memorabilia related to this area of Britain's history *and* making it publicly available, this is one of the most comprehensive 'windows into the world of the waterways.' From the 17th century to the present day you can search the catalogue and be

directed to one of fifteen repositories to arrange viewing. At present, you are unable to view the documents online but with the rapid development of uploading records to the World Wide Web, I'm sure it won't be long before this area of the service has been enhanced.

Don't be surprised that now you've started you want to find out more. What began as a journey to find out what happened to Great Uncle Ivor, has now led you on a mission to research his career as a river pilot or that your Grandfather's teenage years in Norfolk has now got you hooked on finding the Toll Keeper's cottage in which he and his parents once lived. Its all part of the fantastic world of genealogy and what's even better is that its part of *your* life too!

Some of the best UK Canal Museums include:
The London Canal Museum, 12-13 New Wharf Road, London N1 9RT
T: 020 7713 0836 W: www.canalmuseum.org.uk
The National Waterways Museum, Ellesmere Port, South Pier Road, Ellesmere Port, Cheshire CH65 4FW T: 0151 355 5017
W: www.thewaterwaystrust.org.uk/museums/ellesmere.shtml
The National Waterways Museum in Gloucester T: 01452 318200
W: www.nwm.org.uk
The Union Canal Museum, Linlithgow Canal Centre, Manse Road Basin, Linlithgow, West Lothian, Scotland EH49 6AJ Tel: 01506 671215
W: www.lucs.org.uk
The Foxton Canal Museum, Foxton Inclined Plane Trust, Foxton Canal Museum, Middle Lock, Gumley Road, Foxton, Leicestershire, LE16 7RA T: 0116 2792 657
W: www.fipt.org.uk

The National Waterways Museum
Karen Foy

reports on the wealth of information available to help your research.

If you've got canal related connections in your family tree, then visiting a canal themed museum will really help you to both visualise and perhaps experience – in a small way - what life was like for your ancestors.

I'd visited Ellesmere Port Boat Museum several years ago and after a much publicised refit and development scheme as well as its renaming to The National Waterways Museum Ellesmere Port, I decided to go along and see the improvements for myself and was not disappointed. As with everything these days, the cost of entry to many places is going up but I thought the admission fee of £6.00 for adults was well worth the money.

Situated in a 200-year old historic dock complex on the south bank of the River Mersey, the museum has undergone a £2 million makeover and enabled the historic port buildings to be successfully merged with and complemented by the new exhibitions and their 21st century technology.

The facilities are excellent from the bright, open café which looks out onto part of the canal and outbuildings to the onsite shop which sells all the usual memorabilia alongside a vast array of publications on the canal industry and local history books on the surrounding Wirral area. There is also a section set aside for the Boat Museum Society with details of how to join and purchase copies of their Waterways Journal.

A large car park means arrival by car, minibus or coach party proves no problem and there are toilet facilities dotted throughout the museum.

Explore and Investigate . . .

There isn't a set format to the way you walk around the grounds and are free to wander at your leisure moving from outdoor canal-side areas of interest to indoor displays. Wherever you are there are information boards detailing what you are looking at or explaining how a piece of machinery was used. Side buildings hold independent exhibitions and the first one I came across concentrated on the changing face of Ellesmere Port. Large boards explained the history of the town's canal trade mainly during the 19th century and what I found interesting were the enlarged photographs of what life was like during this period. Men, women and children feature in scenes showing their living and working conditions, clothing of the period, road transport and the bustling area around the canal which was the hub of their lives. Newspaper cuttings, theatre advertisements, commercial correspondence and receipts all help to provide a bigger picture.

Moving outside once again allows you to see the locks which dominate this part of the canal. Ellesmere Port's first locks were built here in 1795 to help link them to the River Mersey which were wide enough to enable river barges to use them. Narrow locks were built in 1843 to alleviate the busy traffic of narrow boats using the docks here. Dotted along this section are numerous tugs, barges and narrow boats for you to view complimented with full explanations about each vessel, their construction and the cargoes they once carried.

Complex Construction . . .

For me, one of the most fascinating areas was the replica boat builder's yard and exhibition inside the Island Warehouse Galleries. A great deal of effort has gone into creating this showcase to provide as much detail as possible which not only focuses on the boat making itself but also travel and trade upon the canals– ideal if you have a boat building ancestor in your family.

Between 1721 and 1971, 2000 vessels were built in the Northwich and Winsford areas of Cheshire which at the time had a thriving ship building industry. The displays chart the history of the craft and explain how iron and steel gradually replaced wood for construction. The size of individual boat yards varied, some were family run concerns situated alongside the canal with perhaps a father and son in-charge and a couple of employees whilst others were much larger in scale with building and repair yards employing up to 300 people in roles from blacksmiths, riveters and foundry men to patternmakers, painters and shipwrights. Many employed boys as young as 14 to work as apprentices and learn the trade over seven or eight years – in the early 1900s they would earn three shillings per week rising to ten shillings by the end of their apprenticeship.

During the late 18th and 19th centuries, as the number of canals increased so did the amount of traffic and, in turn, the number of

LEEDS & LIVERPOOL CANAL COMPANY
CAUTION
CYCLING AND TRESPASSING
ON THE TOWING PATH

NOTICE IS HEREBY GIVEN THAT PROCEEDINGS WILL BE TAKEN UNDER THE COMPANYS BYELAWS AGAINST ALL PERSONS CYCLING OR OTHERWISE TRESPASSING ON THE TOWING PATH. CANAL OFFICE LIVERPOOL JULY 1911 BY ORDER

boat yards. Some were launching a new boat every few week. One of the exhibits explains that eight men could build a horse drawn narrow boat in six weeks whereas repairs, improvements and painting could be done in less than seven days. Even their equipment used is on display with descriptions of how augers were used for boring holes, planes for smoothing the edges of the timber planks and bevel gauges for measuring angles.

Equally fascinating is the recreated shed - built of scrap timber – belonging to the boatyard painter. Here, he would store his materials of linseed, turpentine, bags of paint pigments and putty to paint everything from masts and stands to tillers and slides. Alongside these practical and essential items he would also use his artistic skills to decorate lamps, stools, water cans and tunnel lamps – not only for the boats built in the yard but also as private commissions.

His work would include painting the all important name of the boat in traditional yet elaborate style along the side of the vessel. These names were usually chosen by the owners or boat companies who looked to towns, cities, birds, animals, fish, flowers, royalty and mythical beasts as just some of the subjects for inspiration.

I liked the fact that there was seating in most exhibition areas and interactive displays for the children from making your own signs to understanding how things work. Computer terminals are dotted throughout with specialised programs to help you find out more. Each display includes a good mix of textual explanation, photographs or imagery and actual items which you can physically touch and experience.

A Step Back in Time ...

For a real insight into what life was like on and around the waterways, why not wander to the area known as *Porters Row* - a row of cottages originally built in 1833 for the employees of the Ellesmere and Chester Canal Company at a cost of £780 – which, once restored was opened to the public in 1986. Initially, twelve were built but today only four remain, gaining the name 'Porters Row' as they were occupied mainly by the porters (and their families) who moved the cargoes between the boats and the warehouses on the canal docks. By the 1850s there were also blacksmiths, shipwrights and watermen living here. Each cottage has been cleverly reconstructed and decorated to portray a particular era over their 180 year history.

For those who chose to take to the water and live aboard a narrow boat, the museum even allows you to experience the complexities of raising a family and carrying out your day to day activities of eating and sleeping in a confined space.

An authentically equipped canal boat shows

where a whole family would have lived in cramped conditions, kept warm around and cooked upon a black leaded stove and slept in a makeshift compartment or any available space they could find. Lit by oil lamps, a bull's-eye lamp would have been set into the roof to allow light to flood the centre of the cabin. The walls and shelves would be adorned with horse brasses, and the needlework skills of the womenfolk in the form of handmade lace would sit comfortably alongside the vibrantly coloured barge wear painted with a traditional 'Roses and Castles' design enabling the family to decorate their little homes and brighten up their surroundings.

A Working Life ...

Between 1760 and 1840, a network of canals spread across the countryside joining city to city and creating a transport system which had the potential to ship heavy goods around Britain and ultimately, to the world beyond. This generated employment for thousands from those who financed and supervised these projects to the men who dug these new river channels or 'cuts'.

Life may have been good for the engineers and surveyors who were responsible for the overall construction of the canals but for the navvies who moved from job to job, conditions were far from comfortable.

A display in the Island Warehouse Galleries shows a navvy living in a temporary wooden hut - built of timber and canvas - shared with one or two co-workers. With only the bare essentials and no furniture or running water, their evening meal may have been a poached rabbit, cooked on a makeshift fire outside his hut. Although comradeship must have reinforced many friendships it is likely that the men regularly wished they were home with their families.

Certain areas of the country required or produced specific raw materials which then became the cargo of the boatmen. Cheshire was famous for its salt mining, the steel industry required iron ore, limestone and coal from the Peak District and Wales whilst the potteries in Stoke on Trent could not function without china clay from Cornwall. In turn, the finished products would then also need transporting to their new

destinations making the canals a vital commercial highway.

The boatmen employed to do this work expected to work long and gruelling hours to make ends meet – often from 4.a.m. or 5.a.m. in the morning and finish 12 or 15 hours later. They were paid per ton of cargo delivered and expected to load and unload each shipment. Only the captain would be paid and would then disperse these earnings between his crew – which in the majority of cases would be his wife and children.

Although in the 1830s, working was forbidden on a Sunday, many boatmen would still try to continue travelling with their loads in order to make their trips in the fastest times possible. Gradually, education was provided for the children of the families alongside the edge of the canal as well as Sunday School and religious studies which were taught by Missions and Friendly Societies. The Grand Union Canal Company later provided a school room at their Bulls Bridge Depot where all the children could learn together but it wasn't until the Boat Children's Education Act of 1920 that brought about a reform and stated that the children must attend school for at least 200 days a year.

Machine Mastery ...

A visit to Ellesmere Port is not complete without a look behind the scenes at the machines which made canal work and operation possible. The Blacksmith's Forge was where all of the Canal Company's ironwork was made and is still in operation today. The Pump House is home to the steam driven pumping engines which supplied the power for the hydraulic cranes and capstans around the dock which loaded the cargo from the boast and barges whilst the Power Hall houses a variety of engines that supplied the power for many of the boats and other canal related activities.

More to Explore ...

Ellesmere Port, Gloucester Docks and Stoke Bruerne comprise the three museums which are home to Britain's Inland Waterways Collection. Between them they house over 80 historic boats, 5000 canal related items and 40,000 records. Together these pieces allow us to chart the history of the waterways from the late 18th century well into the mid 19th century and beyond.

Due to the size of the collection not all of the exhibits are on display at any one time but you can always expect to see a wide range of examples on show from painted canal wares and traditional dress to larger working machines such as crane, engines and barges.

Ellesmere Port's archive has a large assembly of primary material relating to the history of Britain's canals and inland waterways with a document collection of working records and boat building plans, and photographic collections of work by Michael Ware, Robert Aickman and Eric de Mare.

Those attracted to the local history of the area may be interested to know that their archives also consist of collections relating to the Weaver Navigation Trust, the Manchester Ship Canal and Middlewich Wharf. The museum is happy to grant free access to the archives but a prior booking must be made.

A research service is also available for those unable to visit in person. You can find out more by contacting Linda Barley T: 0151 373 4378 Email: linda.barley@thewaterwaystrust.org.uk

The UK can boast over 2000 miles of waterways. Over their history they have provided work for people from all walks of life. It's not surprising then that many genealogists and local historians find this area of our heritage completely fascinating. Trying to discover our own ancestors who have links to what was once the backbone of Britain's transport system can prove to be both an intriguing and challenging task so why not arrange a trip to Ellesmere Port and get a feel for what life was really like – I can guarantee you won't be disappointed.
National Waterways Museum
Ellesmere Port, South Pier Road, Ellesmere Port, Cheshire CH65 4FW T: 0151 355 5017
E: ellesmereport@thewaterwaystrust.org.uk
W: www.nwm.org.uk/ellesmere/

Karen Foy has been a keen family historian for just over ten years. As a freelance writer her articles appear regularly in family history magazines such as Family History Monthly.

ABM Publishing Ltd, 61 Great Whyte, Ramsey, Huntingdon PE26 1HJ.

Henry Jenkins
– That Surprising and Wonderful Man
Alan Plowright

Are you beginning to feel your age? Do you consider that the allotted three score years and ten is a good innings? If either of these is the case, take heart and visit the village of Bolton on Swale. There, in the churchyard of St Mary's Parish Church, you will find a monument to the memory of Henry Jenkins, reputedly Yorkshire's oldest man, who made the normal life expectancy of seventy years seem a very short span.

He was born in the neighbouring tiny village of Ellerton on Swale in 1500. History relates that he spent all his life in the locality and finally expired at the ripe old age of 169 years. Ellerton and Bolton lie at the edge of the pastoral Vale of Conyers and Mowbray, that is sandwiched between the Yorkshire Dales and the North York Moors. Walkers may be familiar with Bolton on Swale, for it lies on Wainwright's popular Coast to Coast Walk.

Henry was born into an age of discovery, when horizons were broadening and hitherto unknown continents were being unearthed. Columbus was in the midst of his global voyages, having recently discovered Trinidad and the mainland of South America. Other great seafaring explorers were also very active. Vasco da Gama became the first European to open up the sea route to India during an expedition from his native Portugal. A little earlier, he had sighted Natal on the South African coast and also discovered Mozambique. The Venetian, Cabot, sailed on a voyage of exploration to Newfoundland and Nova Scotia, believing them to be part of Asia. His countryman, Sebastian Cabot, subsequently journeyed in search of the

North West Passage and entered Hudson Bay.

It was also a time of progress in science and the arts, particularly music. The violin family of instruments made their appearance during the year of his birth, together with the earliest form of harpsichord known as the virginals. The Dutch were developing pumping machinery to help drain and reclaim some of their land and the coiled spring for operating clocks was invented in Nuremburg. British activity included the establishment of the Press in Fleet Street.

The modern age is considered to be the most rapidly changing one, but Henry must have observed many remarkable developments during his extensive life-span. One of his earliest remembered activities was taking a horse, loaded with arrows, to Northallerton for supply to the English army, which marched to Flodden Field in 1513. Henry recalled the incident with pride many years later, for the Scots were defeated at the battle, mainly through the efforts of the formidable English bowmen.

He lived to see a total of nine monarchs on the English throne. His birth occurred during the reign of Henry VII and he survived until that of Charles II. In the interim period Henry VIII, Edward VI, Jane, Mary, Elizabeth I, James I and Charles I all came and went. Despite Henry VIII's philandering and monetary meddling, he was, in Henry's opinion, the most memorable. This is a remarkable tribute considering that this is the king who caused rampant inflation by his dispersal of his predecessor's fortune and his debasement of the coinage.

During the reigns of this imposing list of monarchs, Henry would have recollections of many great events, such as Drake's world voyages and his battle with the Spanish Armada. Another memory would be of the Pilgrim Fathers setting sail from Plymouth in 1620 for the New World. He lived through the Civil War, which began in 1642, when fellow-countrymen fought each other and the monarchy was temporarily destroyed. Towards the end of his life there occurred, in relatively quick succession, the Great Plague and the Great Fire of London in the mid-1660's. At that time, Sir Isaac Newton was conducting his experiments on gravitation and evolving his revolutionary mathematical theories.

Also at that time, land was in great demand. It provided the major source of employment to a population that was gradually increasing following the ravages of the Black Death, when a third, or possibly one half, of the inhabitants of the kingdom died of the plague in less than two years.

Henry's earliest memory relates to accompanying his father to market with his horse and cart to sell vegetables. At the age of eleven or twelve he left home to escape his father's temper and beatings.

After jobbing for two years he was taken into the service of a local gentleman called Mills. He rose to become footman and eventually butler and stayed for a period of roughly twelve years. Henry then obtained the situation of butler to Lord John Conyers of Hornby, Constable of Richmond, who had led the local contingent at the Battle of Flodden. During that period he had frequent contact with the monks of Fountains Abbey through the carrying of messages for his master. He became friendly with them and they gave him roast beef and strong ale. Unfortunately, these times lasted for only a few years as the monasteries were soon to be dissolved and the last Abbot, whom Henry came to know well, had to sign the Deed of Surrender.

After the death of Lord Conyers in 1557, Henry earned a living by fishing in the River Swale and he continued to do this for over 100 years until 1661. He often swam in the rivers and it is recorded that he crossed the Swale in spate when well past his century and swam in it for many more years.

Henry was finally persuaded to retire at the age of 161 by the local gentry who considered him too old to work and somewhat of a celebrity. They kindly supported him during his remaining years by the provision of food and a small dole.

When he was 163 he was persuaded to dictate his life history to Mrs. Ann Saville who had moved to Bolton on Swale and heard of Henry's great age. Sceptical of the tales that she had been told, she decided to obtain the true facts from the man himself. She wrote an account of them and they were published as a short volume and many years later a copy was found by accident amongst some old books purchased at an auction in York. It was already very old, for it was printed in Old English and had become badly faded and worm eaten. The purchaser could, however, make out that it bore the signature of Mrs. Saville and he set about transcribing it into a legible form. From

THE
ONLY GENUINE AND AUTHENTIC EDITION
OF THE

Life and Memoirs
OF THAT
SURPRISING AND WONDERFUL MAN

Henry Jenkins
COMMONLY CALLED

OLD JENKINS,
Of Ellerton - upon - Swale in Yorkshire,

WHO LIVED TO THE ASTONISHING AGE
OF
169 YEARS AND UPWARDS
WHICH IS
SEVENTEEN YEARS LONGER THAN OLD PARR
AND THE
Oldest Man to be met with in the Annals of England

Written from his own dictation at the Age of One Hundred and
Sixty-three Years.

BY MRS ANN SAVILLE
Of Bolton, in Yorkshire,

Where a Monument is erected to his Memory by Public Subscription.
an Abstract of which was published in the 3d vol. of the
Philosophical Transactions, and is likewise
under his Print, by Worlodge.

PRINTED FOR THE EDITOR
BY J.A. GILMOUR, MARKET PLACE, SALISBURY.

Title Page of book by Ann Saville

his enquiries he found that it had long been out of print and he decided to re-publish it under the title, *The Life and Memoirs of That Surprising and Wonderful Man, Henry Jenkins*. A claim appears on the title page stating that it is the only genuine and authentic account of the man commonly called 'Old Jenkins,' a nickname that had been widely used during his latter years by the people of the district. Another statement describes Henry as *'The Oldest Man to be met within the Annals of England.'*

A copy of this revealing book is held in the Local Studies section of Bradford Central Library. It tells how, initially, his grandmother and then his mother became self-styled village 'doctresses.' This came about through his great uncle, who had been a ship's surgeon, giving his drugs, medical apparatus and treatment book to his sister when he had no further use for them. Expert medical attention was, at that time, the province of only the rich, and people from the surrounding area consequently flocked to his grandmother when anything ailed them and likewise to his mother after her death. Henry gave the treatment book entitled *A Collection of 604 Valuable Receipts* to Mrs Saville as he had no use for it, being unable to read or write. The collection of remedies is quite an eye-opener and it gives a good indication of how treatments have changed over the years.

St Mary's Parish Church, Bolton on Swale

The monument to Henry Jenkins in the graveyard of
St Mary's Parish Church

constituted a slow poisoning of the system and led to premature death. The best water to drink, he advised, was rainwater, caught in an earthen pan. After settling it could be drawn off clean into another vessel and kept sweet for a long time. *'Early to bed and early to rise,'* was another of his maxims, which he adhered to all his life and a half-hour walk after supper was always taken to assist the digestion before retiring to bed.

Whether or not these habits were truly beneficial can only be judged by their results. Because all the family enjoyed good health and retained full use of their faculties throughout their long lives, they were not without merit. Mrs. Saville recorded that Henry, although a great age at the time of his dictation to her, displayed clear thought and a good memory.

No-one can be absolutely certain that Henry survived to such a great age, but, according to Mrs. Saville, an intelligent authoress, who was converted from her scepticism, Henry could clearly remember facts from his early life, which add weight to his claim. Other facts, quoted by Henry during his interview, helped to convince Mrs. Saville that he was telling the truth. Henry always gave his age as approximate, whereas an impostor would have been more definite. He maintained that his mother told him that he was born in 1500, but, due to the absence of parish records at that time, he could not definitely authenticate this fact.

Henry's recollection of the Battle of Flodden and the fact that he knew King Henry was away fighting in France at the time and that the leader of the British troops was the Earl of Surrey indicate that he was born before 1513. He could not have read about such events because, as stated previously, he had never learnt to read. Another fact that aids Henry's claim is that when Lord Conyers, whom he served for some years, died in 1557, Henry's name was listed amongst his servants, which confirms that he must have lived for at least 120 years. Henry's local knowledge, especially concerning land ownership before the anarchy and confiscations of the Civil War, was used at court hearings, which he was often summoned to attend. There were records in the King's Remembrancer's Office, in the Exchequer, of his appearance as a court witness, such as in 1655 at Kettering, in Yorkshire. He was also frequently at York Assizes, to which he travelled a distance of fifty miles, on foot. Here, in 1655, he testified, on oath, that he remembered a

He did, however, have a good knowledge of cures for various ailments and swore by certain precautions and remedies, to which he attributed his longevity. The wearing of flannel next to the skin was one such precaution, to be followed both in summer and winter. If this was done when young it would ward off old age and prevent the limbs from taking cold. The custom had been passed down through generations of his family and may have been the reason why none of them ever suffered from gout or rheumatism and all lived to a great age. His sister, for example, who was two years older than Henry, died when he was 113 years old.

His diet consisted of plain food, such as bread and cheese, or cold meat with onions. Raw onions, he maintained, were very beneficial in many respects, including promoting sleep and warming the system. Henry only ate when hungry and drank when thirsty, seldom drinking anything but water or small beer. Occasionally, after a hard day's work, he would drink a pint of strong beer, but, in his opinion, the regular consumption of strong and spirituous liquors

right of way to be in existence in 1540 and Henry's age and evidence were never questioned during cases concerning tithes at Catterick in 1667.

Henry swore in Chancery and other courts to possessing above 140 years memory, in fact it is recorded that he once proved that a father was 140 years old and that his son was 100. Several other elderly witnesses at court hearings testified that they knew Henry Jenkins and that he was already very old when they first knew him.

If you get the chance, do visit his monument in Bolton on Swale churchyard. This imposing edifice, erected through public subscription in 1743, towers proudly above the surrounding gravestones. His still-discernable name is carved on its base. Inside the charming fourteenth-century church you will find a large tablet of black marble on the south wall, near to the chancel arch. This was installed in 1748 to commemorate Henry's long life.

Should you thirst for more evidence of his existence, you can visit the Henry Jenkins Inn at Kirkby Malzeard. Henry is depicted, complete with flowing white beard, on the sign outside this hostelry, which stands in the main street of the village. According to local parish records, it has been there for at least 150 years and it replaced the original inn that was situated in Bolton on Swale. Unfortunately, I cannot explain the reason for its transfer to Kirkby Malzeard. Inside the present inn hangs a copy of a genuine portrait of Henry painted by Robert Walker, who was painter to Cromwell. Alongside the portrait are photographs of the monument, church and tablet at Bolton on Swale.

An inexpensive leaflet is available from the inn, which outlines Henry's life and contains the following anecdote regarding the visit to his home by a lawyer searching for evidence in a legal case. As the advocate approached the cottage he saw a feeble, white-haired figure sitting in the front garden. When questioned, this ancient-looking individual said that he knew nothing about the matter and suggested that the visitor entered the cottage and asked his father. The lawyer, mystified, followed his suggestion and inside he found an even older looking man nodding by the fire. Once again the lawyer was frustrated because this man claimed that his memory was failing, but, his father, who was in the back garden chopping sticks, could tell him all that he needed to know. To his astonishment, the lawyer found Henry in the garden, looking remarkably fit at the age of 166 and far more vigorous than his son and grandson. He was conveniently able to provide the necessary information, which enabled the lawyer to win his case.

If, after reading this account of Henry's remarkable life, you have been galvanised into improving the quality and length of your life and those of your family, the following extracts from A Collection of 604 Valuable Receipts may be of assistance. They contain, not only remedies for ailments, but hints on dieting and child care. One word of caution, I cannot vouch for their potency!

A Cold in the Head - Pare very thin the yellow rind of an orange, roll it up inside out and thrust a roll into each nostril.

Bleeding at the Nose - To prevent - Drink much whey every morning and eat a great many raisins.

Gout in the Foot, or Hand - Apply a raw, lean beef-steak, change it every twelve hours till cured.

Indigestion - The best remedy is to eat as much very old Cheshire cheese as you can.

Blisters on the Feet, occasioned by walking - Are cured by drawing a needlefull of worsted through them and leave it till the skin peels off.

Windy Cholic - The best remedy is to eat plentifully of parched peas and also of raw onions.

General Ailments - Cold baths will cure Ague, Apoplexy, Leprosy, Lunacy, The Plague and the bite of a mad dog.

Drowned Persons - Rub the trunk of the body all over with salt. It will recover those that seem dead.

In Extreme Fat - (Dieting) - Use a total vegetable diet, that is, dine on turnips, carrots, or other roots, drinking only water. Breakfast and sup on milk and water with bread only, for a year.

Children - To Prevent Rickets, Tenderness and Weakness - Dip them in cold water every morning till they are eight or nine months old.

It is best to wean a child when seven months old. It should lie in a cradle at least a year. Their drink should be water only. Tea they should never taste till ten or twelve years old. Milk, porrage and water gruel are the proper breakfasts for children.

Extracted from *A Glimpse of Yorkshire* by Alan Plowright - Moorfield Press ISBN: 0 95301192 5

Masonic Ancestors in England and Wales?
A guide to some of the methods and pitfalls
Peter Lambert

When looking for information about ancestors who you know were or may have been Freemasons there are several ways where additional information may be discovered which may assist in filling in some gaps in their history.

Before I go further in to how more information may be obtained I would first like to give you a bit of background on Freemasonry which will hopefully assist you in understanding some of the terms you may come across in your researches.

Freemasonry in England and Wales as it exists today can trace it origins back to at least 1717, when the first or 'Premier' Grand Lodge was formed, but it is known that Freemasons were made many years before that date.

Scotland and Ireland have their own constitutions with their own history, rules and regulations so I will concentrate on Freemasons under the United Grand Lodge of England (which includes Wales) and the Grand Lodges that made this up. Women also have their own version of Freemasonry but this is completely separate organisation.

Every Freemason when they are brought in joins a Lodge. This Lodge is made up of a number of individuals usually between 10 and 100 in number (about 30 is a common number). This Lodge is a private entity run by and for its members under certain rules established by a Provincial, District or Metropolitan Grand Lodge and by the United Grand Lodge of England itself.

Each Lodge has a number and a name which is unique to it within the English constitution and this number and name can assist in getting you more detailed information about your ancestor.

If you have any old paperwork belonging to the ancestor in question you may find this Lodge name and number or sometimes just the number on this but care needs to be exercised here as it is common for Freemasons to visit other Lodges than their own and therefore unless your ancestor's name is actually on the document it cannot be assumed that he was a member of that Lodge. Photographs are also useful if the ancestor in question is in Masonic regalia as a lot can be gleaned from by an experienced eye.

Like every branch of ancestral research the more information you have the more information you can obtain.

Once you have established all that you can then the first point of call could be to contact the United Grand Lodge of England themselves where the Library and Museum offers a service for a small fee to members of the public and can search their records even when the Lodge name or number is not known.

Please remember that if enquiries refer to or concern individuals who are still alive the Library and Museum may not be able to assist

as they must abide by the data protection act. The United Grand Lodge of England is a membership organisation and therefore has to abide by this act where a date of death cannot be supplied or reasonably assumed.

Information about individual members held at the Library and Museum is based on Annual Returns of members compiled by individual lodges and sent to Grand Lodge. The earliest such Returns date from about 1768. These were used to create registers of members grouped by their membership of a lodge.

There is no complete alphabetical index of members. Membership Registers cannot be made available to individuals to conduct their own researches due to the conservation needs of the records although Membership Registers from 1768 to 1886 are available in digital format for public use at the Library and Museum.

There are some lists of members for periods from 1723 to 1740 found in the minute books of Grand Lodge. These are transcribed and indexed in Volume X of *Quatuor Coronatorum Antigrapha* (Class Mark: A31 QUA fol) a copy of which is held at the Library and Museum.

The type of information normally recorded in the membership registers are age, address and occupation and date of joining the lodge. The records do not contain any personal details regarding date of birth or marriage, details of family members or change of address. The records of the United Grand Lodge of England cover England and Wales and certain overseas areas now forming part of the Commonwealth. As I said there are separate Grand Lodges for Scotland, Ireland, France and other European countries. In the USA there are separate Grand Lodges for each state. The Library and Museum can advise of contact details for other countries. Alternatively most of these addresses can be found via the website of the United Grand Lodge of England at www.ugle.org.uk in the section Information for Freemasons.

Requests for family history and genealogical information are available upon application to the Library and Museum either in writing to The Library and Museum of Freemasonry, Freemasons' Hall, 60 Great Queen Street, WC2B 5AZ or on line at www.freemasonry.london.museum/family-history.php

On this web-site they provide a form to be completed with all of the information you know about your ancestor which will enable them to get as much information back to you as possible.

If you can get to London it is worth visiting the Library and Museum of Freemasonry which is open free of charge to the public every week Monday to Friday 10am to 5pm (except bank holidays). The Library and Museum of

F. Kapp & Co CALCUTTA & DARJEELING.

Freemasonry also arranges tours of Freemasons' Hall in which it is based which has been the centre of English Freemasonry for over 230 years.

Once an ancestor's Lodge name and number are established it may be possible to get more information about them from the Lodge history which may be in the Library and Museum (but not all Lodges have histories).

My thanks go to Diane Clements and the staff of the Library and Museum of Freemasonry for all of the assistance they have given me in putting together this article.

Masonic Portrait of The Duke of Sussex 1843

The Jews' Free School
Doreen Berger

On Tuesday, the 18th of January in the year 1876 an illustrious visitor was a guest at the establishment known as the Jews' Free School. He examined the children for three hours and was so pleased with their proficiency that, to the delight of the children, he requested their renowned headmaster, Mr. Moses Angel, to grant them a holiday. As the Government examination was near at hand, the children were told they would have to wait for their treat.

He then partook of a French luncheon at the school and, before leaving, wrote in the Visitors' Book: "I have been exceedingly pleased with all that I have seen at this school, and delighted with the singing and the knowledge of Hebrew", signing the book, L.L. Bonaparte.

This school was the pride and joy of the community, the pet charity of the Rothschild family, and the only opportunity for any education at all for the thousands of poor, often ragamuffin children who made their way through its ranks. Its origins were, of course, not in the leafy suburbs, where now it lies, but in the poverty stricken Jewish quarter of the East End of London.

In 1732 a religious school, called the Talmud Torah, was established in connection with the Great Synagogue in the City of London. Funded entirely by private donations from the wealthy segment of the German and Polish Jewish congregation, the school was, of course, only open to boys. The Spanish and Portuguese congregation had established their own school, called the Gates of Hope, as long ago as 1664, just eight years after the date that is recognised as the official re-establishment of the Jewish community in England, but the German and Polish congregation were comparative newcomers. The new school at first met in the houses of the teachers until a lease was taken for a large room in Cutler Street, and then in Gun Square.

It was not easy to be admitted to the school, although priority was given to orphan boys, but a ballot would take place whenever the school was oversubscribed. Successful applicants had to be aged between six and nine years, of legitimate birth and able to read the Hebrew language. In addition, the parents of successful pupils had to be residents of London for a minimum of three years and to be of unblemished character. Obviously, these requirements meant that many of the children of the poor were not eligible for free schooling.

Once accepted as a pupil, the boys were not allowed to absent themselves without written permission from either the President of the school or a member of the committee. They had to attend morning and evening prayers at the Great Synagogue and funerals, and one of their number would be nominated to recite the memorial prayer following the death of a synagogue member.

There were considerable advantages in being a pupil. The school clothed them, allowed the boys the left over candle ends after services and an occasional goblet of wine after a circumcision had taken place. On reaching the age of thirteen, the traditional age of manhood, each boy was given a suit of clothes, a new hat, a shirt and a pair of shoes and stockings. Apprenticeships were available for them to masters of good character, particularly in the trades of tailoring, pencil-making, watch-making and glass-cutting.

In 1788 it was agreed to broaden the range of lessons and the boys now spent less time in studying religious subjects. From nine until noon they had tuition in Hebrew, but in the afternoon there were lessons in English and arithmetic.

It was, however, becoming increasingly obvious that all was not well amongst the steadily increasing Jewish poor. Most of them lived by their wits, while their children ran around the streets, dirty and ignorant, but well versed in the art

Napoleon III & Prince Louis Napoleon

of selling what ever wares they could to help their parents feed their large families. There was no law in force for parents to send their children to school, but in the early years of the nineteenth century missionary schools were established in the Jewish quarter, which managed to attract some of these itinerant children. Something had to be done, and in 1815 a lease was taken on a plot of land known as Petticoat Lane, a building was erected and an entrance made through Ebenezer Square.

The new building opened on April the 13th, 1817 when one hundred and two boys were enrolled. With the aid of its new, talented, head master, Henry Solomon, its reputation slowly grew, and in the January, of 1822 the school moved to nearby Bell Lane, changing the name to the Jews' Free School. Four hundred and forty seven new boys were admitted, and this time a number of girls were included amongst the pupils.

It had now been realised that female children had been sadly neglected and that they, too, would benefit from receiving an education. The attendance of the girls was not as regular as that of the boys, as it was recognised that they were sometimes needed at home. In acknowledgment that the girls' role in life was different, emphasis was placed on domestic subjects, amongst which needlework, dressmaking, laundry and the cleaning of the classrooms was part of their school day.

One of the most famous headmasters of his day, Moses Angel, made the greatest difference at the school. He was, however, not all he seemed. His real name was, in fact, Angel Moses and some of his past is still shrouded in mystery. What we do know about his family background is that both his sister and his father, a publican who was known to have nefarious dealings in stolen goods, stood trial at the Old Bailey for their part in a daring robbery. His sister, Alice, was considered to have been under the influence of her father and treated more sympathetically, with four months' hard labour, but "Money Moses" was sentenced to transportation to Australia for fourteen long years. He did not survive this humiliation, and his son was not the first man to turn his back on unfortunate events in his past and to make a success of his future.

Under the leadership of Moses Angel the school thrived and government inspection was encouraged. He was a stern disciplinarian and an autocrat, but many a small boy, perhaps with foreign-born parents, certainly from a poverty-stricken background, knew Mr. Angel was not to be trifled with and owed his later career to this headmaster. Moses Angel stayed at the helm until the end of 1897, his career at the Free School spanning fiftyfive years.

The school was described in 1869 in a volume of sketches by Dinah Maria Mulock Craik, the authoress of John Halifax. *'The building at Bell Lane, Spitalfields was approached,'* she said, *'through a wilderness of narrow, insanitary streets. When the unkempt children saw a carriage approaching the school, they would break into a grinning welcome, for they knew that no carriages were likely to pass in that foul area unless they were from the charitable family that they knew and loved.'* 'These women,' Miss Mulock Craik wrote, *'provided schooling to the poor of their nation, carrying on a system of unobtrusive, personal benevolence, and going about the dark haunts of Houndsditch and Spitalfields as familiarly as City missionaries.'*

She was referring to the ladies of the wealthy banking family of Rothschild, to whom this school held a special place in their hearts. Hannah Rothschild clothed the children herself for many years before the name of their anonymous benefactor became known to the public. Her son, Anthony was elected its President in 1847, when there were over four hundred boys and nearly three hundred girls as pupils, and continued in this position until his death in 1876. If

Anthony was known as the father of the school, his sister-in-law, Charlotte, was its mother. She visited the school each week, taking a special interest particularly in the girls, even teaching them herself and writing serious, thought-provoking books for them. Anthony's wife, Louisa, took a special interest in the Free School, writing religious books for the pupils, and the Rothschild ladies encouraged their daughters to do the same. Others amongst the Anglo-Jewish elite were willing patrons, but the Rothschild family stood in loco parentis to the school and took their responsibilities seriously. In many ways, the Jews' Free School was the favourite charity of the Jewish establishment.

So successful was the school that it is worth describing the annual visit made by Her Majesty's Inspector of Schools, Mathew Arnold, accompanied by the Inspector-General of Paris schools, at the beginning of July, 1862. The two gentlemen were received by Louisa de Rothschild, her daughters and members of the school committee. Mr. Arnold went through every class in both the boys' and the girls' schools, examining pupils at random, and testing the classes in arithmetic, dictation, grammar, geography and history. At the end of his visit, he pronounced that the institution was in all respects quite extraordinary, that it might vie with any similar establishment in the country, while he found it superior to many in cleanliness and arrangements connected with the health of the pupils. Before leaving, Mr. Arnold examined five young female pupil-teachers, who were preparing for their matriculation at the University of London, in Greek. The school had come a long way, indeed, since its stumbling beginnings.

When the influx of immigrants fleeing, often for their lives, from Eastern Europe at the end of the nineteenth and beginning of the twentieth centuries, the Free School was ready to take these foreign children and attempt to turn them into little English gentlemen, or ladies, in the case of the girls. Many of the children only spoke Yiddish, and much work would have to be done before they could be successfully integrated into British society, but most of them had the will to succeed, and, on the whole, their parents believed in their offspring receiving an education. The children were encouraged to show patriotism and to speak English at home, and in this way the parents were helped to learn. This all may have been an experiment, but it was a very successful experiment.

The school survived a number of crises. The first of these was the Education Act of 1870, when rate maintained Board schools were introduced, but the school, largely still dependent on voluntary contributions, managed to survive. Then the London County Council seriously considered its closure during the nineteen twenties, but the school stayed open. The last of these was crises when the school was bombed in 1941, but it managed to re-open and, realising that the Jewish population was shifting from the East of London, moved itself to Camden Town.

Today the school is a large comprehensive school in the north west London suburbs, educating pupils between the ages of eleven to eighteen years, and the largest Jewish school in Europe. It has a very successful sixth form and there is a strong partnership between the parents and the school. The school has been named as the top mixed comprehensive school in official league tables and placed in the top one per cent for value-added achievements. In 2007 its excellent academic record saw fifty three per cent of their results for GCSE exams receiving grades of A* or A. In spite of all its many problems since its inception in 1732, and recent controversies regarding faith schools, which are still unresolved, it looks to the future with well deserved confidence.

Surviving admittance and discharge registers from 1869 until 1939 can be seen at the London Metropolitan Archives under reference LMA/4297, and some partial lists of pupils in minute books. A comprehensive book, J.F.S., The History of the Jews' Free School, London since 1732, by Dr. Gerry Black, was published by Tymsder Publishing in 1998.

For those with Jewish ancestry, The Jewish Victorian reference books are available from Robert Boyd Publications, 260 Colwell Drive, Witney, Oxfordshire OX8 7LW.

These books contain the published vital records of the community, including genealogies and anecdotal stories. To find out more about your heritage, please contact The Jewish Genealogical Society.

The Day the Magistrates Paid Up

A story from the Quarter Sessions
Stephen Wade

In 1892, the landlord of the British Queen beer house in Croydon was in court. He was sentenced to three years' penal servitude. This gentleman, John Henry Hook, had applied for the renewal of his licence. He had been in charge of the pub for just two months. Unsurprisingly, because of his prison sentence, the application for renewal was refused. This was not an uncommon occurrence, but what was unusual in this case was that the great barrister, Marshall Hall, applied on behalf of the owners of the pub for the renewal. He was opposed by Mr Forman, representing the Church of England Temperance Society. There was even talk of the state running all the pubs, but as one writer put it, *'The beer and spirit-drinking public of free Englishmen would object to having their drinks served out by a man in uniform, and would still more object to a huge state monopoly as would be necessitated by the adoption of this system . . .'*

These court appearances were happening all over the land, and it was difficult to fight the magistrates for licence renewal; landlords across the land were receiving scrutiny and severe criticism, but in rural Lincolnshire at that time, there was a notable triumph for the publicans.

In 1893 Mrs Ann Robinson, a widow, kept a public house in Market Rasen, Lincolnshire. At that time in England, there was no shortage of inns, pubs and beer shops. In fact, the small market town where she ran her business had an excess of them. But she began to have some problems, and the police took action. Her pub, the White Lion Inn, had a tap room which attracted the worst

sort of men, notably tramps and apprentices out for a good time.

Running a country inn at that time was one of the most demanding occupations for anyone, let alone a widow. A series of drawings published in 1879 depict scenes from the life of a public house: one picture shows a group of around twenty people –men, women and children – waiting for a public house to open; another shows *'men, women and children drinking gin'* in a pub and the last shows a drunkard causing havoc. The Illustrations in Punch for the later Victorian years often show violent drunks and pubs in upheaval as the gin and beer have done their work. Only seven years before Ann had her license withdrawn, a landlady of a pub in Barton on Humber had to stand by while a brawl broke out in her bar: pots were smashed and when a constable came to sort it out, he was beaten up.

In June 1892, Ann was convicted of permitting drunkenness on her premises and fined £3 with costs. Again, she was later convicted of serving liquor to drunks. The law clearly stated that *'The holder of a justice's licence shall not permit drunkenness or any violent, quarrelsome or riotous conduct to take place on his premises, nor sell intoxicating liquor to a drunken person.'* The trade had always been a tough one for the landlord or landlady: in 1861 a new beer house had opened in the village of Navenby, for instance, and on the first night, the unfortunate landlord had a fight on his premises involving three brothers, and had to call the police. He started with a big black mark in the minds of the local constabulary. The local police took against Ann Robinson and three officers stated at the Great Grimsby quarter sessions that there were several reasons why her licence should be removed. They listed these charges:

There was no stabling at the inn.
Within ten yards of her premises there were two other fully licensed pubs, and only twelve yards away there was a beer shop.
There had been the two convictions against her. Police officers had stated that the place was badly conducted.

Sergeant John Parker stated that he had noted that the taproom was *'the resort of apprentice boys'* and Constable James Cooke said that he had never seen the landlady in the tap room. He complained: *'It has been left to the care of a young servant girl.'*

The magistrates wrote to give notice that Ann Robinson's licence was to be withdrawn. That was enough for Ann: she was going to fight the decision. She went to her solicitor and a campaign began to clear her name and have her licence retained. It was a time when the licensing of pubs and beer shops was in the news. Up and down the land, in special quarter sessions called *'Brewster Sessions'* licensing had been in the news. In August that year in Blackburn, the Chief Constable had objected to licence renewal of 17 out of 40 places of refreshment; he won his case, and in addition, another nine businesses, including an off-licence and five more beer houses were refused licences.

A month later in Liverpool, a grocer called Franklyn applied for a licence to sell beer. His solicitor gathered references of good character for the man , and the ground landlords, together with the Lord Mayor of the city, gave support to the waiving of restrictions in the so-called *'restricted area'* where the grocer traded. Even with all that support, Franklyn was given a wine and spirits licence but was refused permission to sell beer.

The late Victorian years and the Edwardian period saw a rapid increase in beer shops. Workers often had a drink in the early morning on the way to work, and then stopped off again for beer on the way home.

Ann Robinson was trading at that time, with hot competition down the road, and as a widow, she would have been alone in her fight. But she

had very good and talented solicitors. She was sure that the magistrates were being most unfair and she took them to court. In the Market Rasen petty sessions for October 1893, she appealed, on the basis that there was insufficient proof given or tendered to the bench, and that the White Lion inn was not at all badly conducted. Ann was feeling victimised. Amazingly, she was successful, and the justices were ordered to pay £29.14s and 10p *'for the reasonable charges and costs of the said appellant by them sustained and incurred.'*

What Ann had done was enlist the help of the brewery in Lincoln with whom she worked. Their man, and the local solicitor, had chased up every charge and reference, even sending a man to check on the stated offences. But there was also an issue on a larger scale. Questions had been asked in parliament in July that year: the Home Secretary was asked if a temperance advocate was allowed to sit as a magistrate, and he had answered in the affirmative. Obviously, there were likely to be Temperance men on the benches up and down the land. The Temperance Movement was gaining strength as the beer shops increased, and marches through the towns, in which Temperance banners were held high, were common sights. Taking the pledge was fashionable, although in many cases it was a matter of show rather than resolve.

In 1904 the Licensing Act tackled the question of the proliferation of licensed premises and reduced their number to a considerable extent. There had been statutory licensing of alehouses by justices in England since 1552, and the annual Brewster sessions had become an institution, dealing with a motley assemblage of licensing cases. The beer shops had arrived after 1830, when the Beer Act was passed; but Ann's place was an inn. What had affected her was the 1872 act which dealt more directly with drunkenness- hence her conviction for selling to a drunkard. We can appreciate the scale of the problem of social drinking when we note that in 1869, according to Paul Jennings, there were 118,500 licences given for premises to sell alcoholic drinks. There was a gradual decline after the 1872 act, and by 1901 there were *'a little under 103,000 licences'* Jennings notes.

That national picture places Ann Robinson's fight to remain in business in context: she stood against the tide of repression and reform because she felt that she was the victim of an injustice. The statement resulting from her appeal reads that 'the refusal to renew such licence was contrary to law and inequitable' and so the Rev. William Waldo Cooper, Louis Charles Tennyson d'Eyncourt, Cook Holdershaw and Gerard Young esquires would have had to reach into their considerable pockets and pay up. The member of the Tennyson family, Louis Charles, had been a

Metropolitan Police magistrate also; he died in 1896. As for Ann, she returned to her work with, undoubtedly, a wonderful feeling of triumph, although we can be sure that she spent some time in the tap room and was more severe with the noisy drunks. But she had been one unusual instance in a national debate. The Bishop of Chester spoke out on the 'Drink question' and caused a stir. One correspondent wrote to *The Times* to insist that the much-maligned landlords were actually worthy of a second look, writing that 'The reports presented by the police to the licensing magistrates at the Brewster Sessions now being held furnish pretty conclusive evidence that

publicans are by no means what their enemies imagine them to be, but are essentially a law-abiding section of the community.'

Sources

Paul Jennings 'Liquor Licensing and the Local Historian: The Licensing Act 1904 and its Administration The Local Historian Vol.39 no. 1 Feb. 2009 p. 48-61
For sources regarding the Robinson case, thanks are due to Lincolnshire Archives Ref. 4/BM/19/8/4/1 - material from the Quarter Sessions, Petty Sessional division.
The Times 3 September, 1893 letter from 'W H W'

Quarter Sessions - *What They Could Do For You*
Audrey Buxton

Some of you who have been fortunate enough to collect and keep *The Family and Local History Handbook* series may remember that I made a brief mention in Issues 9 and 10 (with more detail: see *Clothing the Bones*) of Rutland's Quarter Sessions which run, with some missing years, from 1743-1972. These are held at the Leicestershire, Leicester and Rutland County Record Office in Wigston.

Since writing about these records I have been given four printed volumes of the *Calendar to the Sessions Records* of Middlesex, 1612-1618 following the death of my cousin Margaret Halstead in Enfield, plus a later book of reports for other years to 1751 by the same editor, who had already spent 26 years on his monumental task and was hoping for more money to complete the series which had already reached 21 volumes. It

struck me as an interesting exercise to devote an entire article to them, and compare and contrast the contents and sentences handed out for similar offences in the different centuries between the two, and to see how many of the people brought before the courts came from other counties. In the end this proved nearly impossible, as the "Reports" only mentions the most interesting eighteenth-century cases and dwells more on the appearance of well-known people, national events and topography of London. These topics are equally of interest to the local historian; e.g. the introduction of street lighting in 1745 and licensing to build, including the fact that no house could be divided without permission.

However, I was grateful to find that all four of the Middlesex calendar books have separate indices by name, occupation, offence, punishment and places, and contain Gaol Delivery Registers as well as a list of Justices, Juries and Constables, making it very easy to find a specific person. Alas, such is not the case with the early hand-written Rutland Sessions, but unless you are in a tearing hurry it is no hardship, as the contents are a fascinating snapshot of the age.

Then, how could I tie the two counties together? Serendipity is a wonderful thing! The change of venue from *"The Castle"* tavern in St. John Street Clerkenwell, at the beginning of December 1612, involves Rutland; for the court sessions of 13-14 January 1612/13 notes that a new Sessions House (also in St. John Street) had been erected and paid for and gifted by the youngest son of a wealthy mercer of London; Sir Baptist Hicks, whose descendants were to play a large part in the history of Rutland. Created Baron Hicks of Ilmington and Viscount Campden in 1628 according to Gerard Noel's book *Sir Gerard Noel MP and the Noels of Chipping Campden and Exton*, q.v. the year before he died

nowe in Nugate for hurtinge one Leonard Lorie one the Noss with a Spitt, and whoe is lately dead" having lingered for a week after the end of a spit was pushed up his right nostril. Ugh!

In contrast, John Attwood, a King's constable in St. Martin's-in-the- Fields in 1613, found himself on the wrong side of his own law by allowing fifteen vagrants to go free. This was the second time he had appeared in two days, the sentence being removal from office, although he had a third chance the following September. Alas, he was absent for the swearing-in and was fined forty shillings: not surprisingly, he does not appear thereafter.

Several people were tried for practising 'evil and diabolic arts called witchcraft, enchantments, charms and sorceries' around this time. The sale of meat during Lent was indictable offence, as was lewd behaviour (particularly on a Sunday) and failure to attend church. Two men were hauled up for refusing to 'watch' and it was an offence not to pay one's share in keeping the streets paved properly. Back in Rutland the following century, the parishes were answerable rather than individuals, but today it is interesting to note that those living in private roads are each responsible for its maintenance along their frontages, and the same applies to riparian owners regarding streams and rivers.

The law in 1614 appears to have dealt very harshly with bastardy. John Owen of Islington, baker, was ordered to be whipped at a cart's tail through his borough for "begetting Mary Waford with child; and she to be whipped when she is recovered of her sickness", he to pay eighteen pence a week for its upkeep when the child was born; roughly about £10 in today's money. Not all couples met the same fate, however, and sentences vary according to status and willingness to contribute more money towards the upbringing of the child. Equally harsh was the branding with an 'R' on his left shoulder of the seven year old Julius Laney of Westminster, labourer, for being "an incorrigible rogue and a dangerous beggar, wandering about to the great danger of the inferior sort of people at the same, and for fighting in face of the Court" in 1613. No Social Services then . . .

(N.B. the preface to Middlesex's volume I states 1625) he sired no sons; but the wording of the grant ensured that any title would pass to the husband of the elder of his two daughters, Juliana, who had married Edward, Sir Andrew Noel's son.

On his father-in-law's death Edward, created Baron Noel of Ridlington in 1617, keeper of the king's deer park there and visited by King James I at Brooke in 1612 (when he was already Keeper of Game in Leighfield Forest), became the second Viscount Campden. Edward and Juliana made Baptist's magnificent house at Chipping Campden in Oxfordshire their main residence, having added to the family's holdings in Rutland by the purchase of the manor of Exton in 1614. Thus, 'money' enhanced 'position' to the satisfaction of all concerned, not least the ordinary folk who benefited from Sir Baptist's generosity and largesse which continues to this day.

Apparently the new court was not to everybody's taste (possibly because there was no means of purchasing ale!) and although the record does not specify the name of his inn in St. John's Street, it makes one wonder if James Ewer - indicted for not carrying away his dung from his door at Hicks Hall gate and making insulting speeches, for which he was bailed at the same Sessions - happened to be landlord of "The Castle."

There are so very many interesting cases in Middlesex at that time that it is hard to pick out even a handful without regretting the lack of room for more. There are the usual breaches of the peace, removals, lewd behaviour, drunkenness (the stocks), petty theft (whipping), robberies including highway robberies, burglaries - even King James's Whitehall mansion was relieved in 1613 of soft furnishings worth £166 10s. by one 'Humming' or 'Bacon' Tom, who was sent to Tyburn. More serious were the assaults, cases of grievous bodily harm, manslaughter and murder. One of these sounds particularly horrid, in that the murderer was a woman, Susan Fisher, who "is

One case in particular in the Sessions Register of 1615 (and Gaol Delivery 1-3 August) amused me, showing a young draper of Edgware cocking a snook at the law, abusing the constable of Little Stanmore and telling him that "he would not come to the Musters, and diswadinge others askinge them if they woulde goe see a footeball playe;" probably not much different a response from yesterday's teenagers, forced to join the National Service only they would not have got away with it!

Book IV shows no-one from Rutland transgressing in Middlesex, but several interesting cases including two of the Watch in Hackney; Henry Wells and Henry Meakins, both blacksmiths, for absenting themselves on the night of 7 August 1617 *"continuyng tiplinge and takinge tobacco most parte of ye night."* In this case we are told they were found not guilty, but were 'respited' for sureties for good behaviour in the future.

Towards the end of the period the clerks have been more forthcoming. One of the accounts in Volume III is truly gruesome. The crime took place, it is said, because of a series of misfortunes causing the perpetrator, who had been a wealthy man, to lose two ships in storms and £1000 worth of goods in them, although it was to his credit that the entire crew of twenty in the second ship had been saved. However, on 3 September 1616 Thomas Sampson of St Margaret's Westminster had counterfeited a writing in the name of the king, purporting to be a licence for Francis Baildon of London to beg in various places in England, presumably to cover his losses. But the forgery of the Great Seal of England cannot have been good enough because he was sentenced on 12 April 1616 to be drawn and hanged, his body to be cut into four parts and his head to be cut off and his entrails burnt in the fire. This terrible fate befell one other person during the period, (for an equally treasonable offence, i.e. clipping gold). Again, although Thomas did the deed presumably for money, there does not appear to be any retribution for Francis Baildon.

Lists of sentences are recorded in the indexes of all four books under the heading *"Punishments."* I expected to find more transportations over the six years covered but there were only 190, the first being a quite unexpected venue. On 4 April 1614 Thomas Batle of Paul's Wharf, a waterman, was called to give evidence against Barnaby Littgold for burglary. He was sent to prison for sureties, *or to be sent to Greenland by order of the Lord Mayor*. Discovered by Frobisher in 1576, it appears that nobody knew quite where this island was for a considerable time. Whether he actually went is debatable; if he did it wasn't for long, for in Book II the name Barnaby Littgold appears again - this time he has stolen a cloak and is to be transported to "Barmowdes" [sic]. Perhaps the climate in Greenland was not considered to be very suitable for colonisation, but Bermuda doesn't sound much of a punishment to me

Although plenty of people were moving up and down the country, and there were many from counties around the periphery of London, only two Rutlanders appear to have got themselves into trouble with the law during this period. There was no-one in the first book. Volume II has, on 6 January 1614/15 one Ralph Treswell of Hosier Lane, St. Sepulchre's, gentleman, to give evidence against Andrew Caldecott or Caldycott of Ketton for robbing Ralph Treswell of St. Sepulchre's, the items not stated. Two men stood surety for him to appear at the next sessions, but the letters 'G.D.R.', which stand for Gaol Delivery Roll, appear after the entry. Since the rolls had been undone and some replaced in the wrong order, the whole being wrapped in the G.D.R., this may mean that Andrew went to jail before the hearing rather than afterwards and we do not know the outcome. Unfortunately, in the main the Sessions Rolls have to be consulted to find out what happened in most of these cases, but the next one was considered to be so serious that it got a special mention in the preface to Book III.

In the sessions held on 29 November and 1 December 1615, Anthony Bevis or Bevys and John Garraway of Tottenham Court stood surety for William James of the same, a locksmith. He and John Baker, his master, were accused of making a key which opened a chest in the Earl of Lincoln's house in Cannon Row, out of which was stolen £1000 in gold. Sir Henry Fines or Fynes [Fiennes] of Westminster, knight, for Francis Needham his servant and Richard Browne of Ketton, gentleman, both bound over in the sum of £1000: the Earl of Lincoln had complained that the chest had been opened with a false key. But again, maddeningly, it does not say whether the men were proved guilty or not.

although, to be fair, the sentence involved slavery. It is not until 1749 that a woman was transported to *"some of his Majesty's Colonys and Plantations"* in America for seven years.

On 20 June (the same dates as the above case concerning Thomas Batle) Henry Bourne is to be hanged, not for stealing twenty sheep, but for a felony committed in London city; his co-defendant William Clarke who had taken sixteen sheep, guilty as charged, *"seeks the book but does not have it because he had it before, therefore to be hanged."* Respited for the Bermudas.

AT THE SESSIONS.

Counsel "DO YOU KNOW THE NATURE OF AN OATH, MY GOOD WOMAN?"
Witness (with a black eye). "I DID OUGHT TO, SIR! MY 'USBAN' 'S A COVIN' GARDEN PORTER, SIR!"

Evidently this new venue was becoming popular, for Joan (or Jane) Sansome was lucky to be found not guilty on 14 July, otherwise this was to be her destination too. Two days later Thomas Burrows and Robert Everett both of Edgware were convicted of assault and robbery including highway robbery, both to be hanged but sentence commuted to.. Yes, the Bermudas, and the same result was recorded on 27 July: Richard Storie for stealing a mare.

The phrase *'seeks'* or *'was shown'* the book is one of the curiosities found which was new to me. Robin Jenkins, Keeper (Collections) at Wigston tells me that this stems from the mediaeval idea of seeking *'benefit of clergy.'* He believes it arose from the dispute between crown and church over jurisdiction in secular courts over the clergy: the ecclesiastical courts were granted the right of jurisdiction of clergymen, and the traditional test was to get the accused to read a passage from the Bible. Mr. Jenkins believes that it was retained as a means of mitigating the severity of the penal system whereby thousands more would have been hanged for offences we would regard as fairly trivial today, but this excuse could be used only once, as can be seen above.

The ability to read was much prized, and if the person in the dock could read the sentence was lessened, particularly if the alternative would have been hanging (except in the case of William Clarke, who had not learned his lesson). Book learning earned a felon the privilege of holding on

to his lands if he had any but not his chattels, and to be branded rather than hanged if the amount involved did not merit being sent overseas. But if you were a rogue, vagabond or sturdy beggar, you could be sent to be a slave in the new colonies anyway.

The worst thing to do was to say nothing when asked to plead. Unlike today, when all prisoners have a right to remain silent, in the seventeenth century this brought an automatic punishment of *'peine fort et dure.'* This was a death sentence of unimaginable brutality. The unfortunate was either taken to a shallow pit and a board placed upon him; or - in Middlesex - to a dark room, naked, and laid face down upon the floor, being fed upon three morsels of sour bread on alternate days and 'the worst water in between'. In both cases, stones were placed upon the body by degrees, more and more, until death occurred. Remarkably, no less than seven people opted for this terrible death rather than give evidence and be hanged.

In contrast, the Rutland Quarter Sessions are very clear, with the list of cases heard at Uppingham on 14 July 1743 starting with Tyc[h]o Wing appointed as *Coroner. (see The Family & Local History Handbook 10)* Ten Constables looked after the five Hundreds together with five Bailiffs. Next came eighteen Jurors chosen from nine of Rutland's villages. The list of those bailed to appear comes next together with the names and villages of those standing surety for them and the amounts.

The names and sentences of those found guilty at a previous session show a woman from Exton being whipped for disturbing the peace in Barrowden. In addition, for stealing striped jersey and linen and a brass pan she is to be kept in jail until the three sets of fees, each 19s. 2d., are paid. Another, from St. Bride's in London is fined for disturbing the peace. Since she was not from Rutland she was to be kept in Oakham gaol until the next sessions, as no doubt happened similarly to non-Londers in Middlesex; only I fancy the conditions in Oakham prison were very much more salubrious. At least, I did not find anyone dying from gaol fever in Rutland.

The third case is from an apprentice girl whose master has not provided her with clothes according to his covenant, for which she was awarded one guinea, followed by an Uppingham man convicted of setting two wire snares. Since he had no money he could not pay the £5 fine for this first offence, and was sent to the House of Correction in Oakham for three months.

One James Le Pla of Oakham is appointed Justice of the Peace, and William Cheselden of Ridlington is to be Gamekeeper for Leigh Forest as of 27 March 1743/43. John Billington of Uppingham, having attained 70 years of age, is excused jury duties as happens today. Two Settlement cases follow, and close the proceedings. How different this is from the hurly-burly of London, a seething pot of vice, where within one fourteen-month period 1614-16, of 421 persons tried, three stood mute, 100 were hanged, 59 were branded, 73 whipped, nine either pilloried or put in the stocks, 14 transported, eight outlawed, 34 sent to gaol, eight given hard labour, two evicted and one woman ducked.

The Michaelmas Sessions were also heard in rotation at Uppingham and followed a similar easy form and pace. There seems not to have been a court held in March, as the next page (all of which are numbered) has the Quarter Sessions sitting in Oakham with the big case being the dreadful offence of Thomas Bird of Stamford driving a loaded wagon pulled by six horses over a hayfield, for which he was fined 2s. 6d.! And the Overseers of the Poor, surveyors, and collectors of house-duty for Leighfield were each fined five shillings for not appearing at a special Sessions.

The court then moved to Glaston for Michaelmas 1744, where William Larratt of Liddington appears to have had a set-to with one of the Chief Constables and did him "great damage" for which he was fined £20. This entry is followed by the laconic remark: "Verdict - All things are well." The main item on the following page, dated 6 June at Glaston, is a call to arms on behalf of King George II for "the speedy and effectual recruiting of his Majesty's Regiments of ffoot Service in Flanders, Minorca, Gibraltar and the Plantations and the Regiments of Marines."which were to take place on Thursday 30 June in the house of one William Buning of Uppingham, with a second opportunity to enlist on 27 June. Sessions then revert to Oakham, when in July 1746 William Larratt is again in trouble, this time for fighting with Edward Vines. Fined six shillings. The Larratt family seem to have been in the thick of it fairly regularly as Daniel and James, of North Luffenham, are, this time, at the wrong end and being assaulted by Robert Ratcliff, who was fined two guineas. (Robert must have calmed down in later years, as he is appointed one of the jurors for the Uppingham Sessions in April 1761.)

In amongst the disorder and crime is the granting of a licence to hold Presbyterian worship in a house in Manton, and a licence for a higler to sell poultry, eggs, butter, fish, etc. in Oakham Market.

After this the orderly progress of Rutland's courts seems to have had a hiccup, as between 1748 and 1756 there are only two terse comments, both from the Clerke, the newly appointed Robert Ridlington of Glaston; firstly, that the Rolls between July 1748 and Epiphany 1756 appear to be missing; and secondly that indeed at that Epiphany, no session was held as there were none of the Justices of the Peace assigned!

Thereafter the wheels run smoothly, except in the case of the many vagrants passing through Rutland and the high cost of transporting them. At the following meeting the treasurer, Henry Sheild, proposes that the transportation of these persons is outsourced and contracted to

Epiphany 1756 no session was held as there were no Justices of the Peace assigned!

Thomas Wyles at so much per head according to the number of people being carried, i.e. three pence (3d) each per mile for 1 to 3 miles. Then it was two pence (2d) per mile for 4 to 10 miles and three halfpence per mile for 10 to 20 miles. All those beyond this figure a guinea a mile - to which the court agrees.

I wonder what would happen today if, as in July 1756, and January and April 1757 there were no J.P.s to sit on the Bench, or as in March 1772 the weather was too inclement? From what is written there were no sessions from April 1757 to January 1758, except that following the appointment of Charles Ayre as a gamekeeper on 8 Sep 1758 the Enclosure Articles for Tinwell are given in full detail; a wonderful tool for anyone interested in the apportionment of these lands. A little further on, out of sequence and dated 1755, is the account of the enclosure of Tinwell's fields, then Edith Weston, and Ketton in 1768 with the signature of Vincent Wing. Later are others including Uppingham; all these accounts contain priceless information for local historians, especially if the corresponding maps have survived.

I had hoped to compare and contrast the doings in Rutland with those of Middlesex, but so far they could well have been in different countries, rather than counties. Rutland seems to have decided that whipping people, including 'rogues and vagabonds' or fining them, was the best way of completing the matter (and certainly they didn't take up many days in the cells). Their Justices seemed a little lax about attendance, and one of their Coroners, William Gilson, was considered negligent by not having examined Thos. Sheild ("who did violence to him self by Cutting his throat") when asked to carry out an inquest in July 1762. The Sheilds were an important family and could have expected more assiduous attention.

What Rutland's Quarter Sessions do extremely well is to document the life of the common people in the county, their petty doings, their quarrels and their licences, the removals, settlements and bastardy orders of poor people and those of no fixed abode; the apprentices' grievances, the minor officials who kept order in this small and lovely former county, now an impoverished Unitary Authority. Their helplessness against the enclosure acts resonates with what is happening in our country today. What did London know or care about these country people's affairs, and do those in power at Westminster today behave any differently? I've often said there is acoustic double-glazing five miles high around the House of Commons; but don't get me started ...

We are so fortunate that so many of these records have survived of these old county Quarter Sessions; for a list of holdings I recommend *Quarter Sessions Records for Family Historians*, by Jeremy Gibson. Sadly, not all counties have early records, but Northamptonshire CRO holds a printed record for 1630 (in Latin) 1657 and 1657/58. Lastly, remember to search any relevant newspapers where cases would have been reported and where you may find a great deal more information; e.g. the *Stamford Mercury* for Rutland, Lincolnshire and perhaps further afield.

Sources:
Rutland Quarter Sessions Minute Book Ref. RQ3. 2/16
Middlesex Sessions Records pub. By Sir Ernest Hart MBE, Clerk of the Peace, The Guildhall, Westminster, 1928
Sir Gerard Noel MP, author Gerard Noel, ISBN 0-9511434-9-2
My thanks to Robin Jenkins of the Leicestershire, Leicester & Rutland County Record Office, Long Street, Wigston, Leicestershire.

How We Shopped, How We Worked:
The Marks & Spencer Company Archive
Matthew Tattony

Marks and Spencer ltd - Portsmouth

When, in February 2010, the Marks & Spencer Company Archive exhibited at the *Who Do You Think You Are? Live* event at London's Olympia, we were delighted with the reception we got from the public. Many visitors, however, were initially surprised to see us there: what was Marks & Spencer, a multi-national retailer, doing at a family and local history event?

In fact, as one of the UK's oldest and best-established brands, Marks & Spencer has long been devoted to preserving its history. The Marks & Spencer Company Archive, formally established in 1984, holds around 60,000 records that illustrate in great detail the Company's development from a market stall in 1884, to penny bazaars, to the well-loved chain of stores all over the UK and abroad.

Within the archive there are thousands of company documents, including reports, letters, contracts, magazines and other business records, alongside journals and photograph albums kept by employees over the years. Extensive store photograph albums give a dynamic picture of changing high streets. A large collection of merchandise (clothing, toys, books, homeware, etc) as well as food packaging and other promotional materials show what people were buying in decades gone by.

On a day-to-day basis the Marks & Spencer Company Archive primarily serves as a business resource for Marks & Spencer. It provides stimulus for new product designs, advice on the Company's past, and

information for use in legal matters. In 2009 the archive played a central role in Marks & Spencer's 125th anniversary celebrations, supplying research and materials for use in special commemorative events, media, packaging and product lines. Outside the business, the archive has served as a valuable research resource for academics and historians, assisting with a number of books on retail history.

The archive, however, can tell you about much, much more than just one business. As a record of one of the UK's biggest retailers – and employers – it has considerable applications for social history. From a customer's point of view, items such as magazines, fashion supplements, checking lists and the products themselves can show what your predecessors were wearing, how much they paid for it, and how it was advertised as the fashion of the day. The same can be said for food: packaging, advertisements, articles and even own-brand cookery books shed light on changing tastes and prices.

If someone in your family ever worked for Marks & Spencer, then there is a great deal of behind-the-scenes information to be learned about their working lives as well. Uniforms, training materials, and all manner of employee documents dating from before the term "Human Resources" even existed will show how your relative would have worked, the standards of appearance and service to which they adhered, and how they carried out their

Marks and Spencer Ltd - Chatham

Song Sheets sold at a
Marks and Spencer Penny Bazaar

jobs. Employee magazines from the 1930s onward can tell you about the foreign holidays, theatre productions, sporting contests and other social events that were regularly organised by store employees after hours. There is also a considerable amount of material, both official and personal, from the Second World War, such as biographical accounts, ARP training manuals, and the "Forces Bulletin" sent out from Head Office to Marks & Spencer employees on active service and in POW camps. These show how those Marks & Spencer staff who were serving in the armed forces kept in touch and rejoined the company after demobilisation, and those who remained at home continued with their work under drastically different circumstances while the nation made arrangements for war.

The archive is currently closed to the public as it undertakes an ambitious relocation project (see below for more details). Until it opens there is, however, a fantastic exhibition which you can visit all year round. Admission is free and if you would like to a guided tour for your group we would be more than happy to arrange one for you as long as you email in advance. To book a guided tour, please email: exhibitionbookings@marks-and-spencer.com

The Marks in Time exhibition, located in the Parkinson Building at the University of Leeds, opened in 2009 as a core feature of Marks & Spencer's 125th anniversary celebrations.

Key items from the archive's collections are woven into an audio-visual narrative that explores the inter-relationship between Marks & Spencer and British social and economic history.

A visitor to Marks in Time can find out how Britain's culinary habits changed over the decades as freezers and microwaves appeared in our kitchens and Chinese and Indian food seduced the nation; you can find out how fashions moved with the times by viewing articles that your family would have been wearing from the 1920s to the present day; you can see how innovations in employee welfare, corporate governance, and retail practices changed the way we worked. And you'll be able to see how Marks & Spencer led the way in all these areas, becoming an intrinsic part of the fabric of British society in the process.

If you can't make it to Leeds, we also have an interactive website which illustrates the key themes and objects from the exhibition, and provides educational downloads for Key Stages 2 and 3. Please visit us at *http://marksintime.marksandspencer.com/Main/* for more information.

The Marks in Time exhibition is the first phase of Marks & Spencer's new partnership with the University of Leeds. The second phase is the relocation of the Marks & Spencer Company Archive to a brand new facility on the University's campus, which will make its collections open to academics, researchers and the general public for the first time. The catalogue will be taken online and core areas of the collection, such as clothing and food packaging, will be digitised to allow even greater access. This is an enormous undertaking, which has necessitated the closure of the archive to the public for the time being, but we are aiming to have the project completed and opened to the public in the autumn of 2011.

While we are currently unable to undertake new research, we are very happy to answer enquiries based on a wealth of existing research and already-catalogued material. You are welcome to contact us with enquiries (for example: when your local Marks & Spencer opened, what your grandmother's uniform looked like, and so on) and we will do our best to answer them. Additionally, we are always happy to receive donations of material of all kinds relating to Marks & Spencer's history. If you would

like to follow the progress of our relocation project, you are invited to join our Friends of the Marks & Spencer Company Archive scheme. For information on all of the above, please email us at company.archive@marks-and-spencer.com.

When it opens in the autumn of next year, the new Marks & Spencer Company Archive facility will provide a first-class resource for family and local history researchers, and until then the Marks in Time exhibition is an excellent way to see the highlights from the collections in the wider context of how daily life, working and shopping in the UK have changed since the 1880s. There is ample scope to learn more about the past from the collections of a company that has

Marks and Spencer Ltd - Marble Arch
Christmas Shopping 1945

been a fixture on local high streets for 126 years, has employed hundreds of thousands of people over successive generations, and whose products have been purchased by millions.

A Police Murder In Hertfordshire
Death of the Parish Constable of Shenley - James Grainge
Fred Feather

The initial report is to be found in the **Chelmsford Chronicle** for 2nd January 1824, entitled '*Another murder in Hertfordshire*.' This incident had occurred on the previous Wednesday 31st December 1823, at Rabley House, near South Mimms and about a mile from Shenley Hill, in the parish of Ridge. Rabley House was owned by Captain Nestor and occupied by a Mrs Brown and Patrick Connolly, an Irishman (another source said he was born in England in 1784) and former surgeon to the City of Dublin Militia.

Mr Stephens, an attorney from London, accompanied by a Sheriff's Officer and his assistant, tried to gain entry to the house to serve process and Connolly wounded Thomas Watson with a pitchfork. A false rumour went round the village that there had been a murder. Stephens went to the local Magistrate and obtained a warrant for assault, which local constables Thomas Lock and James Grainge had to serve. Connolly had, in the meantime, borrowed a gun and some powder. Grainge was shot in the arm and died during the following afternoon Thursday 1st January 1824, after amputation of the limb. He left a wife and

four infant children. Connolly and his servant Hugh Moran were arrested and kept overnight in the cage at Barnet without heating or bedding whilst three other occupants of the house were secured at an inn.

Connolly had previously been in a successful practice at Brighton. He left the district after an officer named Andrews had sued him for defamation and secured substantial damages. Connolly was married to a '*West India*' lady of considerable fortune who resided at Portsea, one brother James was a chemist and druggist in Regent Street another brother was also a surgeon. It was considered likely that the attorney was acting for Andrews, who was trying to legally obtain his damages and that Connolly had no intention of paying him.

The '*Chronicle*' for 9th January 1824 reported upon the inquest, which was held by Hertfordshire's Coroner Rooke on Saturday 3rd January 1824 in the White Horse Public House. Mr George Neville Ridley a St.Albans surgeon, and Mr Lloyd Morgan told of attempts to treat Grainge, then they heard of the action taken by St.Albans surgeon Mr Webster.

Edward Tinsley spoke of a second shot,

aimed at a man named William Walston, after Grainge had been wounded. Lousia Howard, a single woman under 20, told the court that she lived at Mr Bartholomew's Rabley Farm nearby and had, knowing Mrs Brown the occupier of Rabley House, loaned Moran the gun and ammunition. Thomas Bush was in no doubt that he had seen Connolly shoot Grainge. He then said that Connolly shot at him 5 or 10 minutes later. He was present when the Reverend Newcombe promised Doctor Connolly safe passage, after which he surrendered.

Some £40 was then collected for the widow and orphans, including £3 from the magistrates and £5 from Captain Nestor. The jury returned a verdict of Murder in the First Degree against Connolly and in the Second degree against the four other occupants of the house.

On page 86 in the edition of the weekly newspaper *'John Bull'* for Sunday 7th March 1824, there is a report from the Hertfordshire Assizes of the trial which took place on the previous Friday 5th March 1824 and there is another in the *'Chelmsford Chronicle'* for Friday 12th March 1824.

Pat Connolly, Hugh Moran, Edw. Travers, Elizabeth Brown and Amelia Morgan appeared, indicted by a Coroner's Inquisition, *'for the wilful murder of James Grainge on 31st December 1823 at Ridge in the County of Hertford.'* They all pleaded *'Not Guilty'*. Mr Justice Best called the attention of the Grand Jury to the charges and further charges of Manslaughter against Connolly and Moran. There could be no accessory to that crime and both were charged similarly. Defence Counsel, Mr Dowling, pointed out that there were only 11 signatories to the Coroner's Inquisition when there should have been 12. Mr Justice Best decided that the inquest had thus been 'informal.' Travers, Brown and Morgan were acquitted and retired from the dock.

Connolly and Moran were also indicted for Manslaughter on a bill of the Grand Jury. The Prosecutor, Mr Serjeant Taddy, outlined the case and called William Cannon, clerk to Mr Stephen, who told the court of an attempt to execute process on Connolly, who then threatened him and the officers with death. They had then obtained a Magistrate's Warrant and gave it to James Grainge, Constable of Shenley, to execute. Connolly was alleged to have said *'If you attempt to take me, by Heaven I will shoot you.'* Grainge said *' If you will not open I must break the door down'*. The reply *'By Heaven, if you do, I will shoot you dead.'* Cannon then told Grainge to break down the door. whereupon an axe was given to the Constable and he began to batter the door. A shot was then fired and Grainge reeled off the steps exclaiming *'You have shot my arm off.'*

Thos. Watson, Thos. Hesketh, Thomas Walsall, Wm. Scares were then called as prosecution witnesses. Everyone commented on the reasonable tone that Grainge had adopted in dealing with the defendants, but to no avail. Mr G. F. Ridley, Surgeon, said that the arm was amputated by a naval surgeon, but Grainge had lost too much blood and as a result died. It was admitted that Grainge had drunk some spirits, perhaps too much before or during the operation. Mr Dowling then blamed the incident on the outrageous conduct of the witnesses and inferred that Connolly was justified in defending his home. Moran pleaded that he only acted in obedience to the commands of his master, Connolly.

Mr Justice Best summed up and gave his opinion, that the offence of manslaughter was the one to be proved and that the offence could equally be proved against Moran. The Jury later pronounced both *'Guilty.'* The judge said that Connolly's conduct must have brought him to an ignominious death on Monday next (15th March) but for an irregularity in procedure. (This apparently referred to the fact that the coroner's inquisition was signed by 11 jurors and the Coroner, when there should have been one more juror). He contended that the constable was the least at fault of any of the participants and that Connolly should not plead using the excuse of his wife and family as he had not only shown no remorse but had compounded the offence by his attitude to the deceased. He was instead transported for life. Moran was imprisoned for 6 months in the House of Correction, with *'Hard labour.'* Connolly bowed deeply and respectfully after the sentence. Within a few weeks he had appealed to the King, on the grounds that transportation was too severe a sentence for

Manslaughter. This was rejected as at least two others had received a similar sentence.

Dr Connolly was transported to Van Diemen's Land on 29th March 1824 on the 'Phoenix 11' under Captain Robert White. it may be that, as a surgeon he was of some assistance to the ship's medical officer Charles Quaide. They arrived in what is now Tasmania on 21st July 1824. He died there 30 years later on 16th July 1854 at the age of 70.

James Grainge was buried in St. Botolph's Church at Shenley on 8th January 1824, his abode given as Shenley Hill, his age 44 and his occupation Constable –

John Rice in Melbourne, Australia then consulted their records for me. He found:

Patrick Connnolly: Born 1784 England, Died 16/7/1854 in

Tasmania Australia, Age 70. No marriage, children, or siblings located in Tasmania. Tried Herts Assizes (Lent Session) 4/3/1824 sentenced to transportation for Life to Australia. Crime: Manslaughter (charged Murder), 1) Stabbing the Sheriff's Officer Thomas WATSON with intent to murder and the Murder of James Grainge with a gun. Departed England 29/3/1824 on board 'Phoenix II' arrived Van Diemens Land (Now Tasmania) 21/7/1824. The captain of the ship was Robert White, the Medical Officer Charles Queade.

Copies of shipping records showing Patrick and some information on his physical appearance etc. may be available here.

Sources:

Convicts to VDL, *'Transported Beyond the Seas'* (Hertfordshire FHS), Archives Office of Tasmania. *Hertfordshire People* (Burial index)

South African Research – *Frequently Asked Questions*
Rosemary Dixon Smith

If you're an experienced family historian accustomed to using British records, you'll find that a mind shift is required when you begin tracing South African ancestors. The following FAQ highlight the differences between UK and SA procedures and clarify the avenues open to you in South African research.

Q: How do I obtain SA BMD certificates?

A: In the UK, acquiring relevant certificates is standard practice. In the South African context, this isn't the recommended first line of attack. BMD registers and indexes are held by the Department of Home Affairs. The only way to obtain an official certificate is through the Department or, if you live overseas, through the South African embassy or consulate.

The Department of Home Affairs won't consider applications for certificates unless you provide full details i.e. names, precise date and location of the event. Generally these are what the family historian is trying to find out. If you know all the facts, is it really worth going through the frustrating ordering process? It could take six months to acquire a certificate; there's no guarantee of a result. If the only information you have is a vague idea that the ancestor was born or married 'in the Cape', don't waste time applying for a certificate.

If your forebear was born prior to the start of civil registration, a birth certificate will not be available.

Cape Town, South Africa

Durban, South Africa 1860

Compulsory official registration of BMD commenced in SA as below:

Cape: marriages 1700; births and deaths 1895
Natal: marriages 1845; births 1868; deaths 1888
Transvaal: marriages 1870; births and deaths 1901
Orange Free State: marriages 1848; births and deaths 1903

Marriage certificates are uninformative: no parents' names appear on the document. If the happy couple later divorced, a copy of the marriage certificate is likely to be among the documents generated by the court proceedings; this is one good reason to access a divorce file. In early civil marriages, where the bride was under age, her parents' signatures would appear on the entry, indicating their consent to the marriage.

There are other possible avenues for finding SA birth and marriage records but the discussion here relates to obtaining *official certificates* for such events.

If you have the full details of an ancestor's death you could apply for a death certificate, but do you really need the piece of paper? A more sensible approach may be to find your ancestor's death notice.

Q: What's the difference between a death certificate and a death notice?

A: The South African death certificate is a civil document usually completed by a doctor. The death notice is a legal document usually, though not invariably, completed by the next-of-kin; it forms part of the deceased estate.

More informative than the death certificate, ideally the death notice should supply the full name of the deceased, birthplace, parents'

names, deceased's age at death, occupation, place of residence, marital status, place of last marriage, names of surviving and pre-deceased spouses, deceased's date and place of death and names of children. Assets in the estate are indicated and whether they exceed a certain

value; it's also mentioned if the deceased left a will. The document is signed by the informant, stating if they were present at the death. Note that the accuracy of the information given in a death notice is in direct proportion to the knowledge of the informant. Sometimes parents' names are not given and reference to birthplace may be vague e.g. England, rather than a town or county. In most cases, though, the death notice will be a rewarding source.

The only fact stated in a death certificate which doesn't appear in a death notice is the cause of death.

Q: Where's the best place to start my search?

A: Go to www.national.archives.gov.za/ and explore NAAIRS (National Automated Archival Information Retrieval System), the portal to SA public records. NAAIRS is an online index enabling you to identify and locate records held in SA government archival repositories. If you haven't used this index before, read the site's introductory pages explaining information categories, abbreviations, source codes and search tips. It's surprising how many family historians do not make use of these helpful facilities – and then complain that they 'can't navigate NAAIRS'.

To begin searching, if you're uncertain as to location, try the 'RSA' database (all South Africa) entering your ancestor's forenames and surname as well as a 'beginning' and 'ending' date parameter. If you believe he died in Natal you could limit your search to the 'NAB' database (Pietermaritzburg Archives Repository) or to the database for another relevant province, and see if a deceased estate file reference emerges.

There are numerous other file types which can prove useful to the family historian. Explore the index to find out what is on offer.

Q: Why can't I find a reference to my ancestor on NAAIRS?

A: Should no reference emerge it doesn't necessarily mean that your ancestor did not spend some time in SA. It could be that his activities weren't a matter for public record, or that his sojourn was brief.

A deceased estate file was not opened for *everyone* who died in SA. Reasons for this vary e.g. minimal assets at date of death would imply literally no 'estate'. If the ancestor died comparatively recently (say within the past 20-30 years) his deceased estate file, presuming there is one, would not be referenced on NAAIRS. In such an instance, the records would be held by the Master of the Supreme Court in the area where the death took place.

Your ancestor might not have died in SA but moved on elsewhere, to another colony perhaps, or even returned to his place of origin. The name you believe was his may not be correct – it wasn't unknown for an emigrant to change his name when starting afresh in the colonies.

If you don't immediately find a reference to your ancestor on the index, don't give up. Information is being added continually so keep checking.

Q: What about census records?

A: This resource, a favourite of those researching UK ancestors, is not an option in SA, where census records are destroyed after statistics are taken. The UK census can be useful in conjunction with SA sources: pinpointing the year an ancestor was last recorded as residing in UK could help establish an approximate time-frame for his emigration.

Q: Are church records available?

A: The short answer is yes, but you need some basic facts: a reasonable date parameter, place of event and the religious denomination. Church records are not all centrally held; many are still kept in the parishes and some registers may not have survived the ravages of time. There are numerous denominations in SA. It's advisable to make some headway on NAAIRS before going the diffuse church records route.

Q: When did my ancestor arrive in SA and on which ship?

A: Passenger lists are not a good starting point. Organized emigration schemes are well-documented but if your ancestor paid his own passage as an independent traveller his arrival may remain invisible. Registers which have survived are not all-inclusive and are rarely indexed; steerage passengers are seldom named. It's impossible to speak in terms of a national database of SA passenger arrivals or departures: no such source exists. Very few passenger lists are available online: someone has had to transcribe these from original registers held in archival repositories or from newspaper shipping columns.

Rather than pinning your hopes on finding your forebear on a passenger list, focus on whether he eventually died in SA. If you fail to find a relevant deceased estate file, look for any other likely reference on the index: a divorce, an application for employment or even a mortgage bond. Be imaginative in your search terms.

Finally, don't neglect the Family History Library Catalogue at www.familysearch.org Numerous SA records are available on film.

European Immigration Index and Registers in Natal, South Africa
Rosemary Dixon-Smith

Natal was proclaimed a British Colony in 1845. Attempts to encourage immigration to this new outpost of the Empire followed, with varying degrees of success. Competing with destinations such as America and Canada, where the influx of immigrants was enormous, Natal was 'the Cinderella Colony' for much of the 19th century. Nevertheless, Joseph Byrne's and other private as well as government-aided immigration schemes brought many British settlers to Natal.

Family historians seeking British ancestors who emigrated to Natal are fortunate: a large proportion of original incoming passenger registers have been preserved.

If you believe your ancestor arrived at Durban (earlier called Port Natal) by sea during the middle to late 19th century you have a good chance of finding him or her on a passenger list. This is due to a useful resource, the European Immigration (EI) Index, and original passenger registers from which this Index was compiled. The Index and registers are held at Pietermaritzburg Archives Repository.

The handwritten registers are arranged chronologically by date of arrival. They are not all-inclusive. Some are lists compiled by the Port Captain and among these are valuable records of steerage passengers on certain voyages. Registers exist from the mid-1840s and continue through to about 1911, and the Index reflects the same date parameter.

In terms of British history the 1840s seem very recent, but remember that the first group of Europeans to form a small trading settlement at Port Natal arrived in 1824. It took another two decades for the area to be stable enough to be declared a Colony and before immigration from Britain and elsewhere became feasible. From that point incoming passenger arrivals would be officially recorded. Transcripts of arrivals during the 1840s (as well as those of later decades) can be seen at www.genealogyworld.net/rose/natal.html

Not every vessel entering the bay of Natal was an immigrant ship: there were coasters like the schooner Rosebud operating between Table Bay and Natal, calling at smaller ports en route, cargo ships from Bourbon (Mauritius) and private chartered vessels from Britain and other countries.

Immigration began in earnest with the arrival in Natal of the first group of settlers under the Byrne scheme in 1849. Almost 5 000 immigrants would sail from Britain to Natal during the next three years. This era is well-documented in published sources and some passenger lists are available online.

In the EI registers, reasonable coverage of arrivals continues to about 1890. With the approach of the 20th century, factors such as a dramatic increase in the volume of shipping at Durban, inconsistent record-keeping and gaps where registers haven't survived could hamper the search for individual arrivals.

This dovetails well with the data now available through the ancestorsonboard passenger search facility powered by findmypast.com covering departures from Britain to South Africa (and other destinations) after 1890. If your ancestor sailed to Natal before 1890, the EI Index could be helpful. Utilising both these options, if he sailed after 1890 you may be able to find his departure from Britain as well as his arrival in Natal.

The EI Index is a finding aid for arrivals entered in the handwritten registers. A no-frills card index, it is filed alphabetically by surname. EI Index data is not included in NAAIRS, the online index of the South African National Archives and Records Service. The EI Index is not online at all, which may be

Emigrant Ship - 1850

Durban. South Africa 1890s

employer or a relative if the surname is the same as that of the immigrant, though confusion can arise if the previously-settled colonist is a brother-in-law or a friend of the new settler. If a brother-in-law this might provide a clue as to the maiden name of the new settler's wife.

disappointing for those who prefer information to appear magically at the click of the mouse. Alternative means of access are discussed below.

Also included in the index are selected references from shipping columns of The Natal Witness; these entries can be followed up using the date of the edition given.

Minor errors in the EI Index do occur. In the case of two immigrant families of the same name arriving on the same ship, the second family had been included on the index but the first had not. Looking at the original register, the two families were separated by one individual entry of a different surname: this person turned out to be the mother-in-law of the head of the family. Above her entry were the missing couple, presumably overlooked by the compiler of the Index. Such omissions are not the norm.

Usually surnames only are given on the Index, though initials may be included and very occasionally the full first name. What isn't clear from the Index is which person of that surname is the head of the family. Recourse to the original register is necessary to establish family groups and the ages of individuals.

Even in the original register, the first name appearing in a family group may not necessarily be the male head of the family. Frequently in the Natal settler context it's his spouse, travelling with their children. The husband's name could appear in a separate column under 'applicant', indicating that he'd arrived in the Colony earlier on an LSD trip (Look, See and Decide) in preparation for his family to come out on a later ship.

The name given in the applicant column is often that of the prospective employer of the male immigrant, but could also be the name of a family member who had arrived in Natal earlier and then offered to stand surety for a relative wishing to join him in the Colony. It may be easy to tell whether the applicant is an

A commonly-found surname such as Smith will bring up several references. If a close date parameter for the arrival is known, which happens rarely, it might be possible to identify the correct contender, but this is difficult if no initials are given. It would be necessary to access the appropriate register for that time-frame for further clues.

If you're unable to make a personal visit to Pietermaritzburg Archives Repository one option is to delegate to a local professional researcher who would check the EI Index and, if a likely arrival is found, access the relevant register for further detail, taking digital copies of the entry.

Contact details for private researchers are on the Main Page menu at www.national.archives.gov.za/

For those who prefer the hands-on approach, numerous original records held in the European Immigration Department at Pietermaritzburg Archives Repository have been filmed by the Church of Latter-Day Saints. Explore the Library Catalogue on the Family Search website www.familysearch.org

To access a list of available films, click on Place Search, then enter Natal, South Africa. Next, click on 'South Africa, Natal, Emigration and Immigration'. Select 'Immigrant Records 1845-1911'. There's a wealth of material, from passenger lists to applications for assisted immigration and deeds of naturalisation: order films from a Family History Centre near you.

Passenger lists online:
www.genealogyworld.net
http://sa-passenger-list.za.net/
[Like most records, passenger registers were not generated for the benefit of future family historians. It's up to us to interpret the information.

Philip's Fall from Grace
Linda Ingle

Finding a criminal ancestor whilst researching family history generates a variety of emotions such as shock, interest, excitement and speculation as to what motivated the person to commit a crime. Life could be exceptionally hard for some people in the 19th century and poverty was extreme, an individual could sometimes be forced into a life of crime in order to live. Harsh sentences were imposed for what today would be considered very trivial offences such as spitting in the street, swearing, being drunk and disorderly, as well as the more serious crimes such as rape, burglary and grievous bodily harm. A person could be transported to Australia for stealing as little as a loaf of bread. Later in the century prisoners were only transported for committing murder and the last transportation took place in 1866.

Victorians felt that prisons should be as unpleasant as possible to deter people from committing crimes. Once inside the prisoner had to be made to face up to their faults by keeping them in silence and making them do hard, boring and often pointless work. There were two sorts of prisons, local and convict. Local prisons were used for prisoners serving shorter sentences and acted as a deterrent therefore standards of accommodation and sanitation were lower and the hard labour more severe. Convict prisons attempted to reform their inmates and standards were generally better. For many of the poorer convicts, the conditions and food were often better than they had at home consequently they would re-offend just to have some warmth and food.

It was therefore with a great deal of interest that I discovered my paternal great grandfather Philip Gilleard languishing in Wakefield Gaol on the 1861 census. Philip was born in 1816 in Goole, the eldest child of Cornelius Gilleard and Mary Wheater. According to the records he appears to have been well educated as he could read and write well and his occupations bore this out, his occupations have been listed variously as Shipping Agent's Clerk, Bookkeeper, Accountant and Commission Agent. Although he lived predominantly in Hull, he had also lived and worked in Huddersfield, which, at that time, was growing from a small market town to a thriving industrial town with many new mills being built.

Philip's crime was forging a bill of exchange. According to the online Glossary of Financial Terms a bill of exchange is:

An old fashioned term relating to a non-interest-bearing order in writing by one person to another to pay a specified sum to a specified person or bearer on a particular date. They provide a method for the provision of credit, i.e. a loan. The bill is negotiable during its life and it can be passed by one person to another a s a medium of exchange, effectively serving the purpose of money. It is used primarily for international trade and must be signed and dated.

At the time of his arrest, Philip was working as a Commission Agent in Hull. The definition of a Commission Agent is that they acted as agents for other parties. It is obvious from the records that Philip came from a loving and caring family and committing this crime appeared to be out of character for him. The records do not state why he committed this crime but Hull like Huddersfield, had endured a population explosion in the mid 19th century, but work in Hull was scarce therefore crime had escalated. It is possible that Philip's job was insecure, he had two young children aged 5 and 3 and another on the way, it could have been panic that drove him or chance that he would

York Prison & Assize Court

not be found out. Whatever the reason, he was arrested in Hull on Thursday 21st March 1860 and taken to Hull Prison. The shock to his wife must have been so great that she gave birth to their third daughter the next day on 22nd March. Emily's birth certificate stated her father's occupation as Shipping Agent's Clerk. Philip was kept in Hull Prison until the Magistrates Court hearing on Saturday 31st March 1860 whereby he stated his name, date of birth and address. Present at the hearing was Mr Wells for the Prosecution; Mr Lannerets for the Defence, also present were Thomas H Turner and B. Blyth. As the crime was very serious he was immediately transferred to York Castle to await trial at York Assizes four months later.

The trial was heard on 9th July 1860 where he pleaded guilty; sentencing took place on 23rd August 1860. The Assize records state that he was 44 years of age, had seven children (four from a previous marriage who were at that time grown up and earning their own living), could read and write well. It was his first offence and he was sentenced to three years in gaol, the first part in Wakefield then transferred to Portland Gaol, Dorset on 8th May 1861. *The Yorkshire Gazette* dated 25th August 1860 states that Philip, along with fifteen other prisoners was transported on Wednesday last from York Castle to Wakefield

to commence their sentences.

Whilst on remand in the local prison in Hull and in York Philip was kept separate from other convicted prisoners until his case came up for hearing. He was treated as a Class 3 prisoner which meant that he was allowed certain privileges such as better standard of food, could wear his own clothes, could work for profit and have visits from his wife and family. Once convicted, he had to work his way through from Class 1 to Class 4. Prisons had a class system for hard labour; Class 1 was the most severe, with Classes 2 and 3 less severe. Prisoners who were not fit enough for hard labour were generally employed within the prison on tasks such as tailoring, joinery and gardening.

Wakefield, along with Leicester and Millbank acted as *"holding"* gaols for male convicts at the start of their sentences. Philip was a Class 1 prisoner, which meant he had to serve nine months in separate confinement and perform hard labour. The purpose of separate confinement dictated that he was only allowed to speak to warders and the chaplain and no contact was allowed with the other prisoners. The idea was to hold prisoners in solitude to protect them from the negative influence of other convicts. Being left in complete silence with only their own thoughts and the Bible was supposed to bring about a spiritual

The Prison Gates Portland **Weymouth.**

Prisoners returning from Work, Portland

cleanliness. The medical officer gave a cursory examination to determine if he was fit for hard labour, taking note of his height, weight and physical description. Unfortunately, these records do not survive and had he been convicted ten years later there would have been a photograph. A long list of the prison rules would be read out to him and the punishments given for breaking the rules included being placed in leg irons, confined to the cell, bread and water for a short period, lose any remission and whipping. His clothes and belongings were taken from him and a uniform given.

renewal of the offender who would see the error of his ways. They were kept in solitary confinement in order to think about their life and crime and face up to themselves. The chaplain usually encouraged them to turn to religion. Even when taking exercise or in chapel, the prisoners were not allowed to make eye contact or talk to each other. It was felt that a strict diet of work and military discipline would help them to turn away from crime. It also worked to enhance the discipline for the prison staff due to the low ratio of warders to prisoners. However, prisoners needed to be monitored on the effects of separate confinement on their mental and physical health as it had been noted in previous years that long periods of separate confinement caused mental deterioration. It was therefore advocated that prisoners had two hours of brisk exercise each day.

The records do not state what form of hard labour Philip had to endure but it was quite likely that it would have been oakum picking as this could be done on his own in his cell. Oakum picking was a favourite "hard labour" task popular in both prisons and the workhouse. It consisted of a piece of tarred rope to be unpicked to its individual fibres so they could be used again – hence the saying *"money for old rope."* Unpicking the rope caused the hands and fingers to bleed and was very painful. It was not uncommon for the prisoner to have to unpick up to 4lbs per day and if this were not done he would be punished. Vast quantities were used by the Royal Navy to make the ships watertight.

Upon arrival in prison Philip was searched for any dangerous items, which could facilitate injury or escape, all personal items taken from him, he was not even allowed a photograph of his wife and family. He was given a number by which he would be known until his release. A tepid bath was given to him and his hair cut very short for the purposes of health and

The purpose of wearing a uniform was that it identified the inmates thereby making it more difficult to escape undetected. It also allowed a better standard of hygiene in the gaol. This mainly referred to some prisoners who were vagrants or so poor they had filthy clothes. The uniform was standard across the country and consisted of prison dress, coat, waistcoat, knickerbocker trousers, shirt, shoes and stockings.

Wakefield Gaol cells were small measuring approximately 7ft x 13ft, it would have had a small glazed window at one end and a black painted door at the other. Once the door was shut it would be very dark. Philip had to sleep on wooden planks for the first month then a straw mattress was given as well as sheets and blankets. No pillow was allowed. He would also have been given eating and drinking utensils, a sweeping brush and a slop bucket with lid, which could be used for sitting on and a copy of the prison regulations. By comparison the Portland cells were much more basic due to the fact that most of the prisoners spent a lot of their time outdoors. They have been described as "no more than a small corrugated iron kennel with a stone or slate floor".

Portland Gaol, Dorset was built in 1845 and held 1500 convicts serving the second stage of their sentence on public works, the first part having been in solitary or separate confinement. Portland itself is situated at the end of a peninsula joined to the mainland by a narrow treacherous shingle causeway. The gaol was renowned for its cruel treatment of prisoners; it was also very cold especially in winter when even the warders doing their nightly rounds, wore blankets around their shoulders and heads, so the conditions for the prisoners must have been even worse. The hard labour in Portland required the prisoners to work the stone quarries, it was such hard work

PORTLAND PRISON.
CONVICTS BEING SEARCHED ON RETURN FROM WORK

that an average of one life per week was lost. Other labour was building the breakwater in Portland Harbour. The breakwater forms one of the largest harbours in the world and work started in 1849 when Prince Albert laid the foundation stone. The work was completed in 1872. It cost the lives of twenty-two men.

Convict prisons used a stage system for enforcing discipline and to reward good behaviour. Marks could be earned for good behaviour that would entitle the prisoner to privileges, one of which was to have one pint of tea per day instead of gruel. It could also mean an early remission of the sentence, but marks could also be taken away for misbehaving. Philip's Portland records are very comprehensive but unfortunately it does not state what form of labour he had to undergo. It does state however, that the second stage was due 9th March 1862 and the third stage 9th January 1863.

Throughout Philip's time in Hull, York, Wakefield and Portland his records state that his conduct was good and very good. He seemed to progress through the stages fairly quickly and earned gratuities, this indicated he had earned money, which would have gone towards his expenses for returning home at the end of his sentence. His religion was given as Protestant, state of health good and progress at school very good.

Education was considered important and an important element in reform. At least half an hour each evening was devoted to schooling

and the Visiting Justices directed that reading and writing be taught. Most prisons had libraries where books could be borrowed. Religion was also considered important and each prisoner was given a Bible and Prayer Book and had to attend chapel each Sunday, which broke the monotony of daily prison life.

Prison diets were varied according to the labour the prisoner had to perform, but it generally consisted of bread, gruel, potatoes, meat, soup and cocoa. A prisoner would not necessarily have had all of those but generally had bread and gruel for breakfast and supper. On alternate days he would have meat with potatoes and soup the other day. The soup had to contain per pint, 3oz cooked meat without bone, 3oz potato, 1oz barley, rice or oatmeal and 1oz onion or leeks with salt and pepper.

Philip was only allowed to see his family twice a year as the authorities believed that convicts should be kept away from the influence of their families. Letters could be sent and received every quarter. Prisoners were not allowed to write about the conditions in the gaol only let their families know they were alright. It would have been very difficult for Philip's wife to visit Portland not just due to the distance, but she was running a boarding house in Hull, in addition to bringing up a young family. Philip's records show his wife Elizabeth as his next of kin but his father Cornelius of Goole was also named so it is more than likely that Cornelius would have visited his son instead.

Due to his excellent behaviour, Philip, along with many other convicts from various gaols, spent the last six months of his sentence helping to build Broadmoor Hospital. He had earned early remission and was discharged on licence on 9th January 1863 but would have to report every week to the police in Hull until August 1863 when his sentence would have expired.

There is no doubt that Philip ruined his life by committing his crime. The shame and stigma of his crime and subsequent gaol sentence must have had a devastating effect on his entire family and it is fortunate that Elizabeth had a source of income from the boarding house though it is likely her father in law helped to support her and the children. Philip and Elizabeth had another baby born nine months after his release in October 1863, soon after the birth they moved to Huddersfield where no one would have known him, although his son from his first marriage lived there. They had two more children, and the last three birth certificates give Philip's occupation as Bookkeeper but in actual fact he never worked again. His youngest son's copy birth certificate was for unemployment insurance and the 1871 census states he was an unemployed Commission Agent. It is doubtful that the children from this marriage would have known about their father's crime as they would have been too young and there are no family stories relating to this event.

Not only did Philip ruin his life, he also ruined his health. He died thirteen years later of TB aged 61 in 1876. The death certificate does not state how long he had had this disease, but it is likely that he picked up the source of the infection whilst in gaol as the ventilation and sanitary conditions were appalling, in addition to which, the cold and cruel regime in Portland, plus working outside in all weathers would contribute to this condition. There was also an inherent weakness of the respiratory system in the family as his parents and siblings all died of lung conditions.

Cornelius in his will in 1874, left money to be shared between his children and grandchildren all of whom he named, but the children of the second family were not mentioned and this suggests that they had had their share whilst Philip was in gaol.

Unfortunately, it will never be known exactly why Philip committed his crime but he paid dearly for a moment of weakness for the rest of his life. My initial feelings of elation to find a criminal ancestor changed to sadness during the research at the grim reality of Victorian gaols and the harsh and cruel regime inflicted on Philip who must have suffered untold trauma as well as the shame he brought upon his family. Due to the nature of his previous occupation he would have found it almost impossible to obtain a position of trust again.

Sources
Birth, Marriage and Death Certificates
Berkshire Archive Office: Broadmoor Records
Hull Archive Office: Magistrates Court Records,
Yorkshire Gazette Newspaper
Internet: www.finance-glossary.com/define/bill-of-exchange/154 :Victorian Crime & Punishment April 2010
The National Archives: Censuses 1841-1871
Will of Cornelius Gilleard
York Archives:York Assize Records
Further Reading:
Higgs M. **Prison Life in Victorian England** Published by: The History Press Ltd ISBN: 978-0752442556 2007

Georgian Blacksmiths
Prudence Bebb

Was one of your ancestors a blacksmith? If not, I'm surprised. Many people in this country are descended from a blacksmith and no wonder! He was a village necessity. Not only did he shoe the horses, he did so much else as well. If you made a hole in your kettle or iron candlestick, you went straight to the forge where the smith could mend it. In our village the doors in the Georgian houses all have the same hinges made of iron in the shape of an 'H', the work of either Lupton or Illingworth, the blacksmiths in George III's time. Visiting the forge was fun. Everyone gathered there and the air was filled with gossip. In hot weather it was exchanged under the spreading chestnut tree, which had been planted there to provide shade for horses that were waiting to be shod.

The blacksmith wore a leather apron which was split at the front so that he could pull the horse's foot between his legs. He gripped it there whilst he worked on it. He had to pare and clean the natural hoof before fitting the new shoe, so he really gave the equine customer a pedicure. Then he fitted a shoe which was suitable for the individual horse's needs. It might be a riding horse, requiring a lighter weight of shoe, or it might be a draught animal pulling heavy loads along muddy and rutted roads. Such a working horse would need a heavier shoe and consequently more nails to secure it.

The job was a very skilled one. Some

blacksmiths had been trained by their fathers at the family forge. Others became apprenticed to a blacksmith who would teach them the trade and for whom the apprentice would work whilst learning. He would promise to serve in honesty and not to frequent any alehouses: "At Cards, Dice, Tables or any other unlawful games he shall not play". So there was no chance of a flutter for fun during the seven years of his apprenticeship, as can be noted from this indenture of 1757. Here Joseph Smith, the suitably named blacksmith, takes as apprentice Richard Harris, son of William Harris in Warwickshire. Richard was illiterate and had to sign the document with a cross. Obedience and honesty were more important than a facility with the written word.

Even if he could not read his indenture, the apprentice probably longed to visit an alehouse so that he could get away from the smoke-filled forge. Parts of it were very dark because the smith wanted to test the colour of the iron without sunlight giving him a false impression.

The workplace could be noisy as well. The blacksmith hammered the horseshoes into shape on his anvil. The composer, Verdi, had evidently listened to that sound ringing out before he wrote the impressive Anvil Chorus. The hammering of iron on iron would be a common sound near any blacksmith's shop.

The apprentice would learn how to use the great bellows to fan a small fire into a hotter one. It was not unusual for the smith to work a twelve-hour stretch for he was in constant demand. A gardener, who already had a strong wooden pole, wanted a metal shoe to fasten on it and turn it into a spade. A cottager, who made her own rushlights, wanted an iron taperstick to hold them safely when alight. A farmer needed his cob shoeing. And, of course, everyone required their things at once.

Some people, living far from a dentist, even went to the

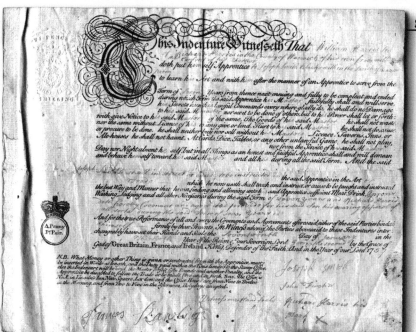

the smithy with a riding horse or even two. He wanted them shod in the best way for travelling on Spanish tracks, even over the Pyrenees, and the smith, who had never left England, had to work out what type of horseshoe would be best in the Iberian Peninsula.

Cartwheels, made of wood by the local wheelwright, would be brought to the blacksmith before use. It was his task to make a metal rim to fix round the outer part of the wheel to lengthen its life as it rumbled over the rough tracks and cobbled streets of the area. To facilitate this job, the smith had a template which usually lay on the ground nearby; he used to stretch the new rim round it to be sure it would fit the cartwheel. Over the country there must be numerous iron templates which have sunk in to the soft ground outside an old forge. We have one in our village which has been seen in living memory but is now hidden under grass and wildflowers, lying embedded in the earth. The old forge was demolished some years ago but the iron wheel still lies undisturbed near the place where the blacksmith's cottage used to be.

Besides making tools for other people the smith had a big collection of his own, including many sizes of hammers, from a great sledgehammer downwards. He had iron shears, numerous bolts, nails and screws of his own making, and tongs with which he moved pieces of red-hot iron. He could cool it rapidly by immersing it in the trough of water kept near the fire. Banging and clanging, sizzling and raking, all such sounds told the village that the blacksmith was at work. Many of the tools used on nearby farmland had been made by him. People came to him with very specific requirements and his years of experience (and those of his father before him) enabled him to work out how to make what was wanted. He knew exactly what colour the iron should be when he started to shape the required object, for the colour told him how hot the metal was.

Many people depended for their livelihood on the blacksmith's work. For example, the

blacksmith to have a tooth extracted. This was not always a good idea. A newspaper recorded in 1811: "Mr Cradock of Langtoft, Lincolnshire, contrary to the advice of a surgeon, had a double tooth extracted by a blacksmith with a pair of pincers, which occasioned a broken jaw, and ultimately his death."

The blacksmith's forge was not the safest place in which to linger. In 1812 a Staffordshire farmer went there carrying a bag of gunpowder, which he had just bought. He probably kept away from the fire but he seems to have forgotten that striking iron can produce sparks. He opened the top of his gunpowder sack whilst the smith was hammering on his anvil. A spark flew to the sack and an explosion resulted, blowing up the smith's house and the next door house. The blacksmith, his apprentice and three children had to be dug out of the ruins. Miraculously, there were no serious injuries although the farmer suffered the pain of a broken arm. The vibration shook the whole of Loynton where the smithy was.

A blacksmith might invent variations of horseshoe to suit the foot of a particular equine. Some horses walked in a manner which caused the back foot to strike the front leg, causing injury. A cleverly-designed shoe could overcome this problem.

Of course, an individual owner might give the blacksmith specific instructions about the kind of footwear he required for his horse. During the French Wars (1793 – 1815) a scarlet-coated officer, due to leave England shortly to fight against the French in Spain, might enter

thatcher required the correct tools to enable him to mend roofs or thatch ricks. Most kitchens in the village contained the smith's handiwork in brackets, nails, hooks and lanterns. At some time everyone would have been in his shop, smelling the familiar odour of burning hoof and probably coughing in the smoke. On a winter's day the forge was a wonderful refuge, the fire contrasting with the ground frost outside. There was a hood over the smithy fire to direct the smoke into the chilly air.

Not every blacksmith worked in a village forge. The reign of George III was a time of industrial experiment and some smiths made parts for machinery, working near a watermill or a textile mill. Those living in coastal areas might get a job helping with shipbuilding. Whilst fighting Napoleon, the Royal Navy needed extra ships which required thousands of nails and people to find new ways of doing old jobs. The ships were made largely of wood but they contained much ironwork too. A village blacksmith with a large family to support might consider going to Whitby or Scarborough, where there was a thriving shipbuilding industry.

Some places, such as Beverley, Doncaster and Epsom, needed good blacksmiths for the racehorses which were brought there for race meetings. There were no horse-boxes to bring the animals to the racecourse; they made the journey on the hoof and probably needed the blacksmith when they arrived. Many a blacksmith was also a farrier.

If you entered the village smithy, you needed to be careful not to fall over or tread on some tool; for tools were everywhere. The smith mended other people's and made his own. If he needed a special tool for a particular job, he simply made it. There were knives of every imaginable size so he could remove a stone of any dimension from a hoof before shoeing it. His many hammers hung from homemade hooks near the anvil.

No matter what the weather was, the blacksmith was unlikely to be cold. He used a lot of energy and his fire burned steadily under its hood.

Your ancestors may have decorated brackets and made household objects with fancy scroll ends. He probably enjoyed the opportunity of making something attractive after spending days creating farm tools of a very functional nature, such as tines for a rake or links of chain to attach a draught animal to a plough. Some of his work has probably survived. He worked steel as well as iron, making strong blades for scythes and sickles. He knew how hot the steel should be before he doused it in water to cool

it; the repetition of this action strengthened the blade.

Not every blacksmith owned his forge; some were employed to work on another man's premises. In April 1811 an advertisement was printed in the York Herald which said: "Wanted. Two Hinds and a Blacksmith. They must be married men. For particulars apply to Mr Charles Willis, Black Horse, Pavement." It is easy to see that an innkeeper would find a blacksmith a very useful member of the establishment.

Although blacksmiths were widely needed, they did not always make a good living. Sometimes they combined the job with something else to improve their prospects. That didn't always succeed; in 1819 William Dodsworth, a ship's carpenter, went bankrupt despite being able to do the work of a blacksmith as well. When his effects were sold to pay off his debts, they included: "1 pair blacksmith's bellows, 1 anvil, 1 pair vice, all new and sundry tools, iron, and etc."

The blacksmith, in the village next to ours, had his forge beside the river bank and augmented his income by operating the ferry which took people across to the other side where there was a towpath enabling them to walk to York.

A blacksmith who was also a farrier would be sure of customers who wanted him, not only to shoe their horses, but to diagnose their illnesses and mix suitable medicines for them. Such a smith probably had recourse to a ten and sixpenny book called *Every Man His Own Farrier or the Whole Art of Farriery Laid Open.* The author claimed that the book contained 'an accurate view of the Causes, Symptoms, and most approved methods of Care for every disease to which a Horse is liable.' This sweeping claim was backed up by an appendix to the book containing recipes for medicaments suitable for equine complaints.

Perhaps your ancestor was a creative smith who could make wrought-iron. If so, he would have heated the metal until it was white-hot; then it would be clamped in a vice and the smith would take up his tongs and use them to twist it.

When he became a journeyman, which meant a day-labourer, no longer an apprentice but fully trained and eligible to a wage for a day's work, he could earn from three to five shillings per day. He worked very hard for that, from sunrise to sunset, but he was a free man no longer bound to the smith by an indenture. He could even go to the alehouse and play with cards and dice!

The Parish Vestry
Ray Whitehand

What was a parish vestry?

The term vestry can be used in two very differing forms. The *church (or chapel) vestry* is a room either in or attached to the church where vestments were stored. This is where, invariably the genealogist's favourite piece of furniture *the parish chest,* with its horde of poor law documents and other ecclesiastical material of the 16th to 19th century can be found. It was also the place where the *parish vestry* would convene to administer the day to day events of the local community. The *parish vestry* was a committee of parishioners responsible for the administration of just about anything and everything in the local community.

It is difficult to pin down when the *parish vestry* first became an entity. It was definitely in operation by the end of the 14th century, running side by side with the manorial courts. Basically *a parish* could best be defined as a township or group of townships possessing its own church and parson, to whom it paid its tithes and other ecclesiastical dues, whereas *a manor was* better described as an 'estate' held by the (land)lord, who was himself a tenant of the crown. So basically you have the one administration system owned by the church,

the other owned by the crown. In medieval England the two systems had run along side each other, but totally separate. Boundaries were not the same, hence a parish might contain more than one manor though equally a manor might cover more than one parish. Physically there was no comparison.

With the decline of the manorial concept in the early part of the 16th century the emphasis moved more towards the parochial system of administration. Parliament orchestrated a series of statutes in the 15th and 16th centuries which actively encouraged the transformation of the parish into a self governing authority promoting the parish vestry as the new form of local government.

There were two types of parish vestry, the *open vestry* and the *select vestry*. An *open vestry* was a general meeting where male rate payers (and on occasion females) could attend and vote on the civic functions of a parish, with some authority in the expenditure of the church rate. There were exceptions to this where ancient customs relating to the manorial customs remained and were in conflict with parochial ones.

However this open system was not necessarily the best administrative solution in populous areas. Some vestries decided to convert - by act of parliament - from open into select vestries, whereby the membership was acquired either by nomination in the original act or subsequently by co-option when a vacancy occurred – the rate payers had no electoral right in the matter.

Where these *select vestries* were formed, more often than not, they consisted of the wealthier members and land-owners of the parish. As the act

allowed any vacancies to be filled without consultation with the parishioners, this could easily, and was often mismanaged and open to abuse. This frequently lead to an imbalance of the representation of the committee which often caused much resentment especially in areas where

ROTATION OF CROPS

Rural Dean. "TUT-T-T! OH, I DON'T LIKE THIS! THIS IS VERY — TELL MR. TWISTER"
"THAT I STRONGLY OBJECT TO HIS PUTTING THE CHURCHYARD TO THIS USE. I'M REALLY SURPRISED!"
Rural Churchwarden. "'ZACTLY WHAT I SAID, SIR! I'VE SPOOKE TO 'M OOVER AN' OOVER AGAIN! 'LOR' BLESS ME,' I SAYS,
'YOU KEEP A WHEATIN' ON 'T AN' A WHEATIN' ON 'T! WHY DON'T YOU 'TATER IT?' I SAYS!!"

there had been a strong *open vestry*. A *select vestry* could be established with anything between twelve and twenty four members. These committees were often known by their size, hence *'the twelve', 'fifteen', 'sixteen', 'company of four and twenty.'*

Both methods of selection had their merits. The *open vestry* was more democratic, while one of the attractions of the *select vestry* rested on its ability to manage the affairs of a populous area better than an open meeting which could become quite raucous. Also, the act establishing the *select vestry* could override the manorial powers that were, by custom, empowered on the *open vestries*.

While two acts known as *Sturges Bourne Vestries acts of 1818, and 1819* played with the voting rules the *Hobhouse vestry act 1831*, permitted the establishment of a *select vestry* elected by rate payers, with out the necessity of an act of parliament which opened the way for all parishioners who paid rates for one year to be part of the voting system. On the request of five rate payers a secret ballot could be held. In the main a vestryman had to be assessed at £10 or more per annum. One third of the elected representatives retired each year.

Many of the roles of the *vestry* – for the reasons shown above – tended to overlap those of the manor courts. One of these *'overlaps'* was the election of the various officers. Constables, Waywards and Overseers were all positions held in manorial times, but by

the 16th centuries vestries were regularly electing these posts, sometime running parallel to and sometimes in conflict with those elected by the lord of the manor.

The most common method of selection of officers was by way of what became known as the *House-row*. This was a system whereby parish officers were chosen by rotation according to the position of a selected rate payer's house. This method was also used in determining which house should be next to take on a parish apprentice. It was simply a method by which the ratepayer was chosen in the order in which the house stood in the locality. Listings of house row in minute books can be used to identify parishioners.

Vestry meetings were normally held annually around Easter week. The officers would present their accounts to the vestry for auditing. As the manorial system deteriorated so the role of the vestry increased and strengthened. As auditors of poor law accounts the officers felt they should have a say in setting the laws which governed the local poor rates. As this involvement gained momentum so the vestry's responsibility for making many of the local laws grew, often to the dismay of the rate payers, especially with regard to the self governing select vestries, where there was no recourse to the rate payers.

The Officers and their duties:

The Churchwardens: alternative names include: churchman, churchmaster, church reeve and kirkmaster

As the name suggests, this was an ecclesiastical position with responsibility for the maintenance of the church and representing the people in parochial matters. It was an ancient but temporary post with two churchwardens usually appointed each easter tuesday. The vestry would normally choose one, the bishop selected the other. Their duties would include:
- the management of parish property and income;
- representing the views of the parishioners in parochial and collective matters;
- the upkeep of the church fabric, the provision of faculties for worship and the allocation of pews
- to attend the archdeacon's court
- to supervise the education and relief of the poor in collaboration with the overseers of the poor
- to control and extermination of vermin

In the case of large parishes up to four churchwardens might be appointed to represent the various townships or villages.

The Sexton:

The jack of all trades, with responsibilities which included grave digging, bell ringing and general maintenance of the church structure including paths, gates and fences etc.

Collector of the Poor:

This role was short lived. It operated from the first Poor Law Act of 1563 until the creation of the Overseer of the Poor. The 1563 act enabled two or more able persons to be appointed gatherers and collectors of the charitable alms of all residues of the people inhabiting a parish. A fine of twenty

shillings was imposed on any parishioner who refused to act in this post. The collectors accounted for monies each quarter.

Overseer of the Poor: *subject to the approval of the Justice of the Peace,*

This office was established by the Poor Law Act of 1597/8 then made compulsory by the Poor Relief Act of 1601. It superseded the less formal office of collector of the poor. Normally at least two persons were appointed annually by the vestry, subject to the approval of the justice of the peace, to levy a poor rate and supervise its distribution. They were unpaid and selected from among the parishioners. Most of their duties were transferred to the guardians of the poor in 1834, leaving the overseer with the duty of assessing and collecting the rate, although legislation enabled the parish to appoint paid collectors under the control of the overseers. The office was finally abolished by the Rating and Valuation Act 1925.

The Surveyors of the Highway: *alternative names include boonmaster, overseer of the highways, stonemen, stone wardens waymaker, waywarden and wayman*

Created by the highways act of 1555, the surveyor was selected by the vestry. In 1691 the law was altered so that the vestry gave the justices of the peace a list of land owners eligible for selection and the justices chose, usually by rotation. The officer's duty was to survey the highways three times a year and organise the workforce which was provided by land holders to repair the roads, or else collect the monetary commutations.

The Parish Constables: *subject to the approval of the justice of the peace, with alternative names including headborough, petty constable, thirdborough.*

An officer appointed by the vestry with a wide range of duties which varied over the centuries. They included:
- the upkeep of the village stocks, lock ups, or any other means of punishment and imprisonment .
- the apprenticing of poor children and the collection of child maintenance from absent fathers.
- the supervision and removal of itinerant strangers and beggars
- collaboration with other officials in the relief of the poor.
- the collection of the county rate and of any specially levied national taxes
- the maintenance of the parish arms and the training of the local militia
- the care of the parish bull.
- assistance at shipwrecks in the locality

- the apprehension and detention of suspected criminals and the arrest of escaped prisoners
- the compilation of jurors lists

Originally a manorial appointment, as vestries became more powerful the constable's responsibilities fell on them, but for a period of time it was not unusual for both manor and vestry to appoint constables within the same parish. The vestries finally assumed full responsibilities for the position, subject to the approval of the Justices in 1842.

Meresman:

A parish officer appointed to maintain the boundaries of the parish, but often also involved in the upkeep of roads, bridges and waterways.

Parish Clerk:

The post was a temporary one although he would often be appointed by the incumbent in earlier times, and he would usually be in holy orders himself. A parish clerk arranged baptisms, and communions. Acted a sexton, rang the church bells, for service and even led the responses at services and was therefore sometimes called an amen man.

Some Vestry Minute Examples

The work of the parish vestry is best illustrated in surviving vestry minutes. These records highlight the many responsibilities of the officers. The annual election of officials, and their accounts get good representation. In the 16th and 17th centuries the parish was responsible for administering its own poor relief. The enormous amount of physical and paperwork this generated fell on the vestry and its officers. The results of which can be found recorded in the aforementioned minute books including settlement examinations, and certificates, removal orders and bastard papers. By the 19th century these minute books become formidable in size as the vestries become responsible for public hygiene, roads, weights and measures, early building controls and street cleaning.

The vestry minutes for Barking illustrate how the vestry accountancy system worked. Each of the officers would keep accurate accounts of their annual income and expenditure. These would then be taken along to the annual vestry meeting. once the accounts were audited any gain by the officer would be handed over to the treasurer, while any shortfall would be made up to the officer.

What is interesting in the Barking minutes is that this vestry was responsible for overseeing the proceedings of the three neighbouring hamlets of Barking, Needham and Darmsden, even though they each had their own church and overseer. The first pages give details of the

election of the churchwardens and overseers for each of the hamlets authorised by the signatures of the eight members of the vestry at the base of each parish.

Emphasising the fact that most of the officer's work was unpaid, an entry in the minutes of the public parish meeting held at Barking church on 30th April 1723 details an instance where remuneration was given. Following the setting of the poor rate of 1½d in the £ for the coming year, there was a motion put forward and carried that the churchwardens shall be paid *'only for 2 ringing days viz 29th May and the 5th November except it shall be upon a particular occasion'*. Frustratingly there is no reason given for the ringing of nor for the other 'particular occasions'.

A page from the vestry book for Combs vestry for the period 1718-1837 details the account of J W Dennington for the year from Easter 1836

Southgate for sparrows £2 13. 7d (1)
Woolby 3/-
Bird (carpenter) £1.16.2d
Frewer (Stow Constable) 15/- (2)
Gladwell (clean path & Usper bill) 17.7d
Churchwardens bill £2.17.10d
Gross Bill hund cuff etc 19/- (3)
Cooper (Glazier) 19.11d
Fisk £2.15.2d
Green (Constable) £5.2d

Green (Constable) serving warrant 7/-
Southgate (Constable) serving warrant 7/-
Revd Mr Nunn a years registers 10/-
(sub total) £29-0-1^{1}/2d
balance from other side due to the churchwardens last easter
£2-3-10d
Total £31-3-11 ^{1}/2d
less rate receipts £29-5-9^{3}/4d (4)
balance due to churchwardens £1-18-2 (5)
(poor) rate set 4 April 1836 at 4d in the pound

(1). the sparrows would have been eating the freshly
sown seed crops. Rates for this were in the region of 3d
per dozen, showing the large numbers of birds caught.
This was normally a job for the young lads, snaring or
catapulting were the most common form of capture. The
birds would be given to the poor for food. Some
accounts show entries of eggs collected to prevent the
young being hatched, more food for the poor.
(2). It is interesting to note the payment made to the
Stow constable, this may have been for removing a
pauper back to Combs.
(3). surely not another constable
(4). poor rate receipts
(5). this is the short fall accumulated in the
churchwardens accounts over the year

Previously in the same book:

*on 25th November 1717 it was this day agreed between the
officers of ye town of combs & ye inhabitants whose names are
here under written & John Welham of Combs, that ye said
Welham shall take a male bastard child Caled Matthew Cole
from ye day of the date hereof for the sum of ten pounds to be
now paid until ye sd Matthew Cole shall attain a proper age to
be put out apprenticed, and if it shall happen that the said child
shall die before he be put apprenticed ye said John Welham will
oblige himself to repay ye said ten pounds except one shilling
and six pence per week for so long as he hath kept the sd child
and necessary cloathing and farther doth agree to take ye sd*

*child apprentice for the sum of seven pounds more to be paid
by the town of combs when ye sd Matthew Cole shall be bound
apprentice THE MARK OF JOHN WELSUM*

This was a regular method of dealing with
orphaned, abandoned or illegitimate children.
Parishioners would agree to care for these
children in rotation, paid for at least in part
from the parish overseers accounts. The child
would be taken on for various periods of time,
until they were of an age where they could be
apprenticed.

Another contemporary entry can be found in
the minutes of the public meeting on 11th
January 1724 when it was agreed and ordered
that Mr Prior & Simon Parker churchwardens
of parish should build up - at the cost and
charge of the said parish - a shed at the lower
end of the churchyard which may contain ten
or twelve horses for the common use and
convenience of the parishioners coming to
church. No doubt the car park of the 18th
century before the advent of the combustible
engine.

As already mentioned as we move into the
19th century so the role of the vestry increased
dramatically. The Wickham Market vestry book
shows the range of items under discussion.
These include the voting of applicants for
Bishop Wood's charity - lighting the streets
with gas following the result of a poll - repairs
to Dallinghoo road and a proposal to
appropriate £85.0.0d of parish money to buy
lands for the cemetery. On 6th March 1857 a
list of men residing within the parish suitably
qualified and liable to serve as constables was
recorded, then on 17th July 1868 a rate was set
of 4^{1}/2d in the pound for occupiers of property
and 1^{1}/2d for all occupiers of land in the town

The role of the *vestry men* was wide and
varied. One duty was that of *walking the bounds*
or *beating the bounds*. In the days before road
maps it was necessary to watch, maintain and
police the boundaries of the parish. This was
normally carried out on Rogation tide – the
three days before Ascension Day. The
incumbent, parish officers, prominent
vestrymen and a good many school children
would do this. The job was to check the
location of the boundary stones, and to ensure
that no buildings encroached on parish
territory without the knowledge and
authorisation of the parish. Often seen as a
social occasion the tradition continued well
into the second half of the nineteenth century,
long after maps made the occasion somewhat
irrelevant.

An incidental role of the vestry came about
as a result of the 1834 new poor law act. The

former parish workhouse buildings were now obsolete and the vestry became responsible for the eventuality of these now idle places of residence and employment. While some vestries found alternative uses for them –schools, almshouses etc, others saw the cash incentive of selling them off. On 3rd August 1837 the Parham vestry meeting of the rate-paying guardians of the poor agreed to apply to the Poor Law Commission (P.L.C.) for authorisation to sell their workhouse. The application described the premises as 'a freehold brick and tile messuage divided into four tenements with appurtenances in three quarters an acre of land'. Either permission was not granted or they could not find a buyer, for at a subsequent vestry meeting on 15th January 1838 it was agreed by a majority of the rate payers to let the poor house at the following rents: Mrs Smith £3-10-00; George Last £3, Jasper Smith £3, and David Nicholson £3-10-00.

Sources

Main sources all at Ipswich Record Office
Parham Vestry Minutes 1834-1854, FC110/A1/1
Barking Vestry books 1723-1740; FB15/A1/1
Framlingham Constables Account 1619, FC101/11/1
Wickham Market vestry book EG62/A1/1
Combs Vestry book 1718-1837 FBA211/A1/1
The Local Historian's Encyclopaedia by J Richardson

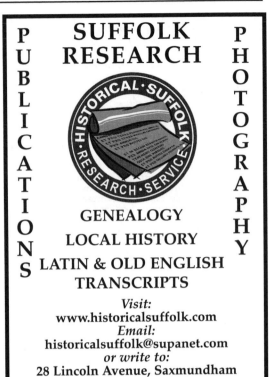

We'll All End Up In The Workhouse!

Anne Batchelor

It was in the early 1950's and my mum needed a new winter coat. I remember, vividly, as a young girl, going into town with her and trailing around the shops. Then she spotted it – in the window of a rather posh shop selling real fur coats. In her childhood she had been brought up in a Waifs and Strays home, and then gone into service as a housemaid/cook/nanny, so she never had expensive clothes.

Now, she had saved up for *'a good coat,'* and this was it! She tried it on and looked like a film-star in the quite modest coat with real squirrel collar. So she bought it to wear *'for best'* – this was at weddings, funerals, church on Sundays and *'up in the Gods'* at the theatre (in the days when theatre going was a dressed-up occasion; not the jeans and tee shirt events we see today).

As we came out of the shop she turned to me and said, *"Whatever you do don't tell your dad how much I paid. If he knew he would say, 'We'll all end up in the workhouse!'"* Her posh coat cost a massive £9.10 shillings (£9.50p).

Such a saying would be meaningless to young people of today, but to my parents' generation the workhouse was considered to be a shameful destination and a fate worse than death. Older residents of Leeds still remember when the famous Jimmy's (St James Hospital) was the local workhouse and many were distressed beyond measure when sent for treatment in the geriatric wards which were based in the original workhouse building.

Now, thankfully, that part of the hospital has become the famous *Thackray Medical Museum.*

There is a striking photograph displayed there showing some early workhouse residents – poor, sad, lost-looking souls in faded, shapeless uniforms. My eye is always drawn to one face which stands out as being out of place. She is a young, pleasant-faces, bright looking girl – probably sent to the workhouse because she had a baby out of wedlock. Such a wicked girl!

In the eighteenth and early nineteenth centuries the workhouse had been the responsibility of each parish. They paid for its upkeep and paid the wages of the Master of the Workhouse, who was answerable to them for its efficient running. He had to be at least twenty-one years old, able to keep accounts, and 'a person of sufficient education, strength of will and firmness of purpose, and yet considerate and gentle in his bearing, without servility, or disrespect to the Guardians – and without intolerance or laxity to the inmates.' He was to exhibit self-control over his temper and not use profane language. It was helpful if he had a wife to share his duties. It was his responsibility to see that all his charges were fed and clothes, given work to do and provided with medical care when necessary. He was expected to give regular reports to the Guardians of the workhouse and keep regular accounts.

Most workhouses had a very strict regime. At Aylesbury in 1831 the list of rules includes :-

'Every person in health shall rise by six o'clock and by seven in winter, and commence their work by six o'clock in the morning and work till six o'clock at night, allowing half an hour for breakfast, one hour for dinner, and half an hour for supper. Anyone refusing to work shall, for the first offence, go without their next meal and for the second offence, be reported that they may otherwise be punished. Any of the poor, guilty of stealing, selling their provisions, or clothing, or of drunkenness, swearing, quarrelling, fighting or in any other way disturbing the peace of the house, or of being in anyway saucy or abusive to the Master or Mistress, shall be punished with the utmost severity of the law.'

Should anyone think that going into the workhouse was going to be an easy way of avoiding working for their

living, the reverend H. H. Milman, writing in 1832, makes it clear that they are mistaken. *"The workhouse,"* he says, *"should be a place of hardship, of coarse fare, of degredation and humility; it should be administered with strictness, with severity; it should be as repulsive as is consistent with humanity."* I think that is what we would call, *'as cold as charity.'*

So the discovery of William Borrow, a compassionate and caring workhouse master at Knaresborough (Yorkshire) in 1791/2 was a real eye-opener for me. I had taken my family history beginners' class for a visit to Claremont – the Leeds Library of the Yorkshire Family History Society, and had asked the archivist to make available to us some original documents from the archives. As part of the display he had put out for us *'The Daybook of the Master of Knaresborough Workhouse – 1791/2'* I opened it up somewhere in the middle and read:

"Old Susana Atkinson, gentlemen, to tell you truly she is a muckey hanfull" (sic)

Further on, I read his account of a violent incident involving *'Nutty'* – a volatile young woman, who on August 15th 1792, refused to get out of bed.

'I said, is not it time to get up near eight of clock if thou wilt not get up I will help thee up. I at her with the birch wand. She up with chamberpot and spild sum of it onto flower (floor) she swore by her maker she would drownd me and – we had sum very high words Thou bitch and whore I said though shall to the house of correction she greved me so ill – but realy I was afraid of that durt coming upon me.'

Sitting down, I began to read this Daybook from the beginning. It was like a window into the past. It was in two parts, the first by an unnamed master. His entries were mundane and boring -

'Jm. Owthwate at work
Wm.Brown at work
Danial Leevak at work
The rest as useall'

On just a few occasions, he got carried away and wrote something more interesting ;-

'Robert Jefferey at Patley with his mother
The childer a haladay half day
Robert Jefferey Drinking All Day'

However, with the arrival of the new Master

and Mistress, the contents of the Daybook soon changed. On July 6th 1791, William Borrow and his wife come and within a month, the entries became more interesting ;-

'Mary Thorp rocking credle and looking to childer.
Elizh Clemshay senr walking to and fro with her child.
Elizh Clemshay senr talking dutch'

(What we could call *'double-dutch'* or rubbish)

Before long, a picture of life in the house is revealed along with indications of William Borrow's attitude to his charges. There are forty-six people living in the house – the old and destitute, single mothers and little children. In many other workhouses children under seven were moved out to live elsewhere but at Knaresborough, children of all ages, from birth, lived with their quarrelsome elders. They were taught (after a fashion) by old William Brown, but were often naughty and disrespectful, running rings round the poor old chap.

Even the children were expected to work. The Master coaxes and encourages them:

'I told them they are brave barns and I will give you every one an apple or a bit of spice'

He also gives them a holiday so that they can attend Knaresborough Fair –

'Being the fair now my dear barns I have given you all fairings and likewise Mr Forth hath given you sixpence.'

Evidence of William's kindness can be seen in the way he treats sick members of what he calls his 'family.'

October 8th 1791

'Mary Iles was sick and great pain in her head and went to bed. I went to her and said pal whats the matter with thee thinks thou. She said I am sick and pain in my head. I said I will get thee anything aples pears ginbread wine or anything thou desires.'

October 31st 1791

'Ann Palferman is badly for sure but I said nany cheir up you must not fall badly now and just going to married. We will send for this true love of yours and will see what he can do for you. We will send for Joseph Smith his tears will drop onto your face and that will be better then docktor.'

I became so interested in life in William Borrow's workhouse that I began to get a feel of the man himself and longed to know more about him. In her account of the workhouse, Ruth Strong, writes of him as 'hard pressed, a kindly soul doing his best to steer a middle course between extracting the maximum amount of work from his charges and caring for them with sympathy and understanding.'

As well as maintaining control by use of his birch 'wand,' William would threaten wrong-doers, with the dungeon where they could be sent to cool off. To me, he seemed a caring man who carried out his duties with amazing patience and good humour, just giving way at times to exasperation.

I was surprised to discover than another researcher had spent a considerable amount of time studying my William. She was Maria F. Garcia-Bermejo Giner of the University of Salamanca, Spain. She became interested in William's Daybook as part of her study of Yorkshire dialect in the eighteenth century.

The Yorkshire Dialect Society were able to provide me with a copy of her transcript and notes. Like me, she found William Borrow a shadowy and elusive figure who seems to be unrecorded anywhere but in the Daybook. The I.G.I. (International Genealogical Index) gives over two hundred William Borrows around this time, but there seems no way of knowing which, if any, is our man. A William Barrow married Hannah Thomas, widow, on July 29th 1794, but our William was already married, when, in 1791, he took the job as Master of the Workhouse. Perhaps Hannah was his second wife?

In the Bishop's Transcripts for Knaresborough parish church, there is recorded a burial of a William Burrow of Bond End, Knaresborough, on August 3rd 1802. This might well be my William – but who knows? So all that I know about him for certain comes from his own writings in the Daybook.

Come and wander with me for a while through the twelve months between August 1791 and September 1792. To help I have inserted punctuation where necessary as William just rattles on without a full stop in sight!

'Gentlemen their hath been a Sore bout betwixt Old Eliz Clemshay and me. She said she wod not spin. I said then you shall have nothing to eat. She fell sulky and said nothing but she fell on and I got her work done. I proved Conquor of an ill wild beast.'

Sept 7th 1791

'Their comes this man about Eliz Crabtree and he would marryer hir derectly. She told me it was him that begot her child. They teasd me very much and they go a shilling of me.'

Sept 16th 1791

'Eliz Clemshay and Mary Thorp, I promist them if they would get their work done they should all go to Harragate races and I would go with them and buy them every one sum ginsbead.'

On **October 4th 1791**, William and his wife receive one of the perks of the job:

'Gentlemen, I humbly thank you for the favour of you all for a little backah (tobacco) for my wife and me." He assures them that he deserves it, too - "My good Honourable Gentlemen you seem to take to me and my wife and that we ought to be very trusty. I will be as good as ever I can to do that at is wright to the Town and to the Poor likewise. We have two or three that would gladly do rong but ill (tempered) wild beast hath often short horns.'

October 19th 1791

'The childer they bide sum driving and is dilatery but when fair words doth not do I is forst to use my rod. Old Elizh Clemshay cryed out pitifully to be for a peticoat. Saith I if you will but spin hard I will speak to Mr Couper. Come on I have told you ofton that you wear dilatery, you and your daughter both only spins three hands a day. If you will but spin four I will speak to Mr Couper. She said I am poorly both sick and lame but I will do my best. Pray seek for me for a petticoat.'

October 22nd 1791

'Sarah Lemin wer cros for she wanted butter to her pudin but I told her a good stomok wod do without so much soas. She said I wanted more soas and more pudin. I said you had as much as others had. Good people have you not all had plenty of pudin. They all about said, they had enough.'

There always seems to be trouble when Nutty is around!

October 29th 1791

'Nutty and my wife is a throng as three in a bed for Nutty grows very heavy now when she comes near note (the time of calving).' Old Susana Atkinson said 'Nutty, thou hath been an ill husey. Nutty

93

I rather suspect that Nutty enjoyed her battles with various other women. It brought some excitement into a rather dull existence.

William records very little trouble with the men of his family. Most of them were out at work during the day rather than being shut up in the claustrophobic workhouse. He does mention one incident involving William Steel and William Otes who were –
'Drunk all day till nine o'clock night. Willm Steel behaved very ill. He cared not for the Oversears nor the worst they could do and for all the Masters and Mistris that ever they had, they was all gon to the divil, and for the present Master the divil was a stride of his neck, but dam them all for I car not a dam for them all. They may do their worst.'

The Master records this wonderful drunken rant but explains his caution at dealing with it, thus – *"I never came at him. I wod not come near that drunken ass. He is a very stuped man."* A very sensible decision in my opinion!

Illness in the house caused William a great deal of worry. In January 1792, there was an outbreak of *'kingkof'* among the children – perhaps whooping cough? Much of the illness William had to cope with was the result of old age and frailty. It is here we see him at his most compassionate.

January 19th 1792
'Old Jane Whelas (Wheelhouse) every day poorly but she eats well. She saith pray Master get me a gill of ale. I said Giny will that cure you aught. She said it will comfort my hart. Giny, as long as you can eat and drink well you will not die but do not ask me tomorrow again and I will get you a gill of ale. She saith I is now going to die. No, no, I said, you will live to see many bright eye dim before you die.'

Sadly, we watch old Jane's deterioration – at the end of January William describes her as *'like pinwire,'* that is very thin. By February, he reports *"She eats a little but lies in bed and that makes me think she will not be long, but I get her a little gin every day or what she desires to have. She is worn like a little child and nothing but skin and bone."*

Old Susana Atkinson, too, is now on her last legs, spending all her time in bed and constantly

said you little better than I. Susana said thou dirty husey, I will drop thee. They had both ill word till they came at blows. They cald out for my wife. She said, As they begun, let them end, but there was no blood shed. I said whats hear to do with you. I will put you and Nutt into black hole. Quoth she, I do not care a fart for you or the wors you can do.'

Poor William had his patience tested to breaking point with 'all guns blazing ' Nutty. After her child was born Nutty was found to have sold some of its baby clothes in the town for money to buy drink. When William reprimanded her, she threatened to leave the newborn child with him and go out on the town to get another! In his opinion, to keep the young woman on the straight and narrow –
'I said it was the best way to have sum parts of them disfigard and then the men wod not be so kien of coming about them.'

Meanwhile Nutty continues stirring up trouble – this time with Mary Steele -
'Mary Steel wanted a sop of milk for her lad. Well saith my wife I will get you some. I will go down into saller, saith Nutt, she wans it for herself, for her own guts. Thou bitch, saith Steel's wife, and whore. High words were betwixt them soon and come to blows presently.'

having to be cleaned up. She was, according to William, *"a mucky handful,"* when she came into the workhouse and old age and infirmity have not improved matters.

November 29th 1791

'Old Susana makes durty work but she saith she eateth nothing, but there is a deal comes from her. I said their must be sum ingate or else their wodnot be such an outgate!'

The younger women continue to grumble about their food. William treats them with sarcasm.

December 3rd 1791

'Sarah Lemin could not eat beef. It was not good, Sarah I said, what would you have? Sumthing at is good, she said, for a woman that gives suck (ie a nursing mother). Now Sarah I know your meaning. We will get you a brase of parteriges espeshely for a lady of pleasure but I will tell you ye shall fair no better than the rest.'

When he had other problems with the same young woman, he threatened to send her to the dreaded House of Correction -

'For you are always creating strife with sumbody, but you shall be no master over me, for I will not allow hens to crow, for it is a sign of sum ill luck, they eather lay wind eggs or sumthing, but I wod put their heads under their wings and so ly them to sleep.'

In other words – *'I shall be Master in my own house!'*

There were not many occasions for laughter in Knaresborough, but I guess the incident on the 10th February, raised some giggles. Sarah Ousman had gone to the outside loo (the little house) probably with her child's potty, not noticing a small toy had fallen in. Let William tell the story – *'Sarah Ousman was at Little House door and had thrown sum little baby lacon (lakin – a toy) into the durt and she goes to fetch it out, slips in over head. Nanny Palferman happens to be near, runs in and clicks her by hair of her head and drags her out, or else she had been in great danger of her life.'* What an awful way to 'go' that would have been.

So the year 1792 passed, with the usual squabbles and complaints, and yet with all his problems William – forever the optimist, writes on March 20th –

"Now we all quiat, and I hope we can keep our family in order."

Poor, dear man, how I feel for him with his troublesome family! He does venture to give advice to the overseers -

'Gentlemen, at your meeting my advise is not to take a poor family in that hath six or seven poor naked childer in, that wants cleathing for that is expensive. Rather, give them a few shillings to bide whear they are, for the least expence. Gentlemen, I think they come from all parts of the world to Knaresborough, for I think they know whear they get much made on. Pox take them all, for as one goes off another comes on. So, gentlemen, I think you are always in trouble and expence.'

Now, William Borrow has slipped away into the mists of time, leaving behind his Daybook as his only footprint. I do hope that the rest of his life was happy. He certainly deserved it. His workhouse provided a safety net for those broken individuals whose life without it would have been unbearable. Their argumentative, peevish, violent behaviour was evidence of their will to survive, and at the end of their days, when old, weak and frail, William and his wife were there, to do the best they could for them.

As a personal footnote, my family owes a great deal to the existence of workhouses. When researching my own family history, I discovered that, when my great grandparents moved from their home in Berkhamstead (Herts), northwards to settle in York, George Batchelor's old mother stayed behind. Probably saying, *'I don't want to end my days in a strange town, among strangers, I am not moving anywhere!'* She stayed put. It was a moving moment when I discovered that she died in the Berkhamstead Union Workhouse.

My late mother told me that her father, dying of cancer in his forties, was nursed in the Pontefract Infirmary. When I tried to find some record of his admission, there was no sign of him. Then a helpful archivist suggested that perhaps he had been in the Workhouse Hospital. That would make sense. His young wife had died twenty years before, his only son was serving in the army and his only daughter, (my mum) was *'in service'* living in the house where she worked.

There would have been no family member able to nurse him, so the Pontefract Workhouse Hospital would have been his salvation. Knowing her feelings about *'the Workhouse,'* I never did tell mum that he died there!

Caribbean Family History Research
- from 17th century to Present Day
Sharon Tomlin

Researching my Jamaican family roots has involved the well-known process of patience and perseverance. The journey has been enjoyable and continues to be so as I have been able to connect with family members that have been previously been disconnected for one reason or another. In order to research Jamaican family roots one of the key aspects to emerge is the need to obtain understanding of the local and social history from which the Jamaican ancestor originates. I will attempt to explain the strategies involved as well as shed light on genealogical data gathering relevant to researching your Jamaican family roots as well as give an overview of both the local and social history of the island.

Caribbean family

Typically today for many Caribbean families particularly of African ancestry in most instances from the line of ancestry of the great-grandparents usually have no knowledge of their names or able to recall the names. Why is this so? According to researchers factors such as the construction of the Caribbean family was borne out of factors such as African - Caribbean desire to retain the cultural and social structure brought over from Africa during the period of enforced enslavement were able to maintain despite the effects of the oppressive regimes during this period. In addition during the period of colonisation of Jamaica the social construct of the family introduced by European system initially by the Spanish and Portuguese then English of administration of African people in the Caribbean resulted in the early creation of colour system used to identify skin complexion of people of predominantly African features that has resulted in enforced adaption to conditions to slavery and the aftermath.

Today's Caribbean family is ethnically diverse with the majority of the population of African ancestry and mixed African heritage with Chinese, Indian, Lebanese, Jewish and European backgrounds making up the minority of the population. Families of African – Caribbean ancestry still tend to be traditionally matrifocal with grandmother playing the dominant role of nurturing and caretaker of her grandchildren, particularly so when parents frequently migrate to countries such as United States of America and Europe. Caribbean family members can be found participating in all aspect of society today. The motto of the island is *'out of many one people,'* indicative of the embracing and acceptance of diverse ethnic make-up of the Caribbean people.

RESTING AFTER A DAY'S WORK ON BANANA FIELD.

Earliest arrivals to Caribbean

The Africans and Europeans were not the earliest settlers to Jamaica – the earliest settlers were Caribs and Taino Indians. Between 2000BC and 300BC, Tainos and Caribs nomads are believed to have travelled from Venezuela, Guyana and Yucatan Peninsula in sailing vessels fashioned in the shape of canoes to explore coastal waters and nearby Caribbean archipelago (Sherlock and Bennett 1998). Caribs chose to settle in the southern islands of the archipelago while the Tainos inhabited the larger islands Hispaniola, Puerto Rico, Cuba, Jamaica and Bahama Islands. Caribs were more warlike than the Tainos. Tainos were also known as Arawaks. Jamaica was inhabited by Tainos between AD 600 and 900, considered Jamaica's first freedom fighters. When Spanish conquered the island and began to enslave them they resisted to the death. Some committed suicide rather than lose their freedom; they made refuge in Blue Mountain in Jamaica that later provided refuge to runaway African slaves. Some escaped to the other interior mountainous region and established hide outs in the densely forested interior that was later utilised by African rebelling against oppression. Gradually the numbers were reduced by disease as a result of being less resistance to European illnesses and were gradually absorbed by numerous African resisters. African people were brought over to the Caribbean islands involuntarily basis primarily to fill the loss of labour owing to reduction in size of the population of Tainos and Caribs – the beginnings of Transatlantic Slave Trade.

1625 saw the overtaking of Barbados by the English conquest and 1655 saw the overtaking of Jamaica by the English conquests. Prior to 1625 Caribbean countries were ruled mainly by the Spanish of which by then present were around 1500 Africans then residing in Jamaica (Sherlock & Bennett 1998,).

Early Caribbean families: during the period of slavery

Transatlantic Slave trade – trading of African people from Africa through Europe then to the Americas - was established in the Caribbean during 15th century commencing with Portuguese and Spanish.

English involvement of trading in the Transatlantic Slave trade route earliest known was early 17th century. After establishing a network of colonies in Virginia in 1607 they initially then conquered Barbados in 1625. Jamaica was conquered in 1655.

During this period described are some of the instances that occurred in Jamaica that affected the population.

- The classification of scales of skin complexion of enslaved people was established to regulate registration and administration of slaves.
- The emergence of the planter class in Jamaica resulting in establishment of wealth, privilege and mercantile trading of huge profits, governance of the island and the establishment of correspondence between Great Britain and Jamaica.
- The setting up of governance of Caribbean English ruled countries such as Jamaica. For instance, the establishment of the Jamaica Assembly and role of Church of England in registration of vital events such as baptisms, marriages and burials as well as parochial administration.
- Creation of new laws to regulate restriction of freedom for slaves to be educated and to participate in religious practices brought over from Africa.
- To regulation of the many insurgencies and insurrections that arose from attempts to liberate enslaved people of Jamaica. As a result committees were set up by the assemblies to enact laws against rebellion. Fight for freedom and emancipation from slavery that involved individuals such as Thomas Clarkson, William Wilberforce, William Knibb and Maroons as well as enslaved population. During the period of slavery, the ethnicity and social conditions of Jamaican family would generally comprise:
- People of African ancestry that were enslaved, had no political, social, civil nor economic freedom. Some were manumitted
- Freed people of Colour: individuals of mixed African and European heritage as a result of involuntary relationships between white men and black

nity
edral,
idad.

women of which the product of such relationships produced children that were usually manumitted or born free from being identified as a slave.
• European families: comprise predominantly Jewish, English, Irish, Scottish and Welsh families. To lesser extent Swiss, German, Italian and Eastern European families.

• Indentured Jewish, Irish, English and Scottish individuals

1808 saw the ending of The Atlantic Slave trade to Jamaica and the abolishment of the institution of slavery in 1838 with a four year interim of apprenticeship system.

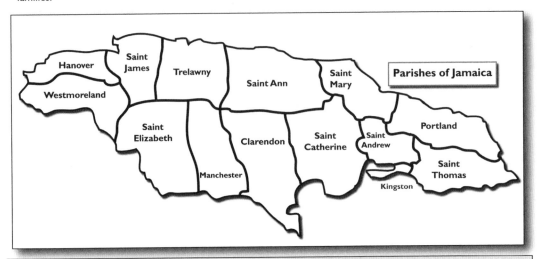

Parishes of Jamaica

Map show parishes of Jamaica fixed since 1865 to present
Today, Jamaica has fourteen administrative parishes as illustrated below

Jamaican Parishes

Parish	Capital	Notes
Kingston		Part of Port Royal which was an original parish. Eliminated by 1866 absorbed by Kingston and St Andrew
St Andrew	Kingston	Original parish Part of Port Royal which was an original parish. Eliminated by 1866 absorbed by Kingston and St Andrew
St Thomas	Port Morant	Original parish
Portland	Port Antonio	Created from St. George parish and St. Thomas in the East parish, 1723 St.George, original parish, absorbed by Portland in 1866 St. David - original parish, absorbed by St. Thomas in the East, 1866 St.Thomas in the East - original parish, portion absorbed by Portland 1866
St Catherine	Spanish Town	Original parish St John parish was part of St Catherine as an original parish, absorbed by St Catherine in 1866 St. Dorothy, original parish - Separated from Clarendon, 1675; absorbed by St. Catherine, 1866
St Mary	Port Maria	Original parish Metcalfe parish created from St.George and St. Mary in 1841; absorbed by St. Mary, 1866
St Ann	St Anns Bay	Original parish
Clarendon	May Pen	Original parish Separated from original parish of Vere in 1673, reabsorbed 1866 St. Dorothy, original parish - Separated from Clarendon, 1675; absorbed by St. Catherine, 1866
Manchester	Mandeville	Created from Clarendon, Vere and St Elizabeth in 1814
St Elizabeth		Original parish
Westmoreland	Savanna - La- Mar	Separated from St Elizabeth in 1703
Hanover	Lucea	Separated from Westmoreland in 1723
St James	Montego Bay	Original parish
Trelawny	Falmouth	Trelawny - separated from St. James, 1770

The parishes are subdivided further into distinct regions called counties namely:
Cornwall: Westmoreland, Hanover, St James, St Elizabeth
Middlesex: Clarendon, Manchester, Trelawny, St Ann
Surrey: St Mary, Portland, St Thomas, Kingston, St Andrew
Counties were created in 1758 as a result of imposition of the English system of government. Today names remain fixed, however they are of no administrative consequence.

Jamaica
Place names

Before arriving in Jamaica in 1494, Columbus heard the name *Yamaye* or *Xamaye* – name given to Jamaica by the Taino people. The suffix *ca* of Jamaica is typical of Amerindian language and Jamai (or Yamaye) identified as the place or where people lived (Higman and Hudson 2009). As early as 1512 the name Jamaica was identified. (Higman and Hudson 2009).

Early place names in Jamaica and the Caribbean derived from influence of colonial government and the population. By eighteenth century there was the complete settlement of landowners and continued landownership system that gave names to districts that reflected the dominance of the British planter class settlers and the imposition of essentially an English system of administration. Place names in Jamaica became accepted and naturalised as part of the culture of Jamaican creole that marked the identity of the people. The names ceased to sound foreign as the names became part of the natural language of the place, Jamaican (Higman and Hudson 2009).

Presently the majority of place names in Jamaica derived from the British Isles. Over 60% from England, over 20% from Scotland, around 8% from Ireland and 3% from Wales.

Around 1880 cadastral maps shows around 157 names were transferred from Continental Europe, North America, Africa, Asia, Central and South America (Higman and Hudson 2009).

Jamaican Registration Records

The Church of England was the main governance for Jamaica. The earliest records commenced soon after the Church of England took over the administration of records post 1655 in Jamaica. Records date back from earliest recorded entries being 1663 for Clarendon and St Andrew 1668 for baptisms

Early non-conformist records held included: Roman Catholic, Moravian, Baptist, Wesleyan, Methodist, Jewish and Quakers. Each denomination held own records within each Caribbean island.

Registration Records in Jamaica 17th to 1824

Diocese of the Church of England recorded baptisms, marriages and burials for each parish. The Rector for each parish was responsible for the administration of vital events as well as undertook parochial administration. Practice was in line with early English system of church administration. In 1824, the Diocese of Jamaica was established and the register of office was established in 1825.

Pre - 1825 records

Pre - 1825 records were called Copy Registers that featured entries for baptisms, marriages and burials. Entries tended to record 'one line' of information. For example for baptisms, details recorded included:
• Name of individual baptised
• Date of birth (not always and sometimes absent)
• Date of baptism (some parishes recorded witnesses present)
• Name of parents

For marriages recorded would be the names of individuals getting married, the condition whether spinster, bachelor, widow or widower, name of marriage officer and parish of marriage.

Registration Records in Jamaica from 1825 - 1870

Created were Parish Registers and New Series registers reflecting the new administration of the Diocese of Jamaica. Records are that of Bishop`s Transcript as records were transcribed by the Rector or curate, once transcribed records were sent to the Diocesan Office where the clerks transcribed them into books. Information recorded tended to include further details, in addition to entries stated for records pre-1825, for baptisms details would include:
• Occupation of the father
• Place individual was born
• Place father and mother resided at time of baptism
• Complexion of the individual (entries were inconsistent for each parish, recorded during one decade)

Parish Registers and New Series: the Diocese of

Jamaica was established in 1824, new system of recording set up. Events recorded between 1825 – 1869.

Dissenter records: Records of non-Anglican members recorded between 1844 – 1854, records of births and deaths, marriages 1818-1880.

Registration Records in Jamaica from 1870 - 1880

Creation of the Law 6 series arose out of further change in administration of records following discussions on creating new constitution to be framed and regulations to be made to manage the organisation of the Church of England to that of a voluntary principle. In 1870 a law to enact the disendowment of the Church of England in Jamaica. Law 6 series recorded vital events of baptisms, marriages and burials of individuals within the Church of England churches of Jamaica.

Brief History of Civil Registration in Jamaica

Civil Registration Records began in 1844. The period lasted for about seven years. The law was revoked due to few persons registering the event as required by law.

Civil registration was instituted in earnest in 1878. Compulsory registration of births and deaths commenced on 1st April 1878, followed by marriage in 1st January 1880. The implementation was a result of *"Law for the Registration of Births and Deaths in Jamaica"* (Law 19 of 1877). One feature of the new marriage law required that only a duly appointed Marriage Officer should solemnise the marriage in the presence of two witnesses.

Civil Registers post 1878

To research entries post 1878 an index is available for each parish of which contains details such as:
• Births: name of parent(s) registering child, year of birth (heading), name of child and reference number which is the alphanumeric code (see below)
• Marriages: names of individuals married, year of marriage (heading) reference number in the form of a number of the certificate. Entries are listed by parish which are in turn listed according the letter assigned to each parish, listings are in alphabetical order.
• Deaths: name of individual, year of death (heading), reference number which is the alphanumeric code (see below)

Information gathered from the index will then refer to seek further details on the individual obtained from the certificate

Events of births, marriages or deaths were recorded on single registered certificate. Codes were assigned for each parish and district from 1878. The event is assigned an alphanumeric code.

Jamaica: Codes Assigned to Each Parish Since 1878

A: Kingston	B: St Andrew
C: St Thomas	D: Portland
E: St Catherine	F: St Mary
G: St Ann	H: Clarendon
I: Manchester	K: St Elizabeth
L: Westmoreland	M: Hanover
N: St James	O: Trelawny
P: Cayman Islands	

ON THE RIO COBRE RIVER, JAMAICA

Barbados Registration Records

Each parish was assigned a letter to identify individual parishes.
Parishes created were:

Parish	Births	Marriages		Deaths
Christ Church	X	1637	1643	1643
St.Philip P	1648	1672/3		1673 (all imperfect before 1757)
St.Michael	M	1648/9	1648/9	1648/9
St.James S	1693	1693		1693
St.Joseph	O	1718	1717/8	1717/8
St.Thomas	T	1728	1723	1723
St.Lucy	L	1714	1749	1748
St.Peter E	1779	1779		1779 (lacking baptisms 1825-1834)
St.George	G	1801	1801	1801
St.John	J	1805	1657	1657 (baptisms imperfect before 1825)
St.Andrew	A	1825	1825	1825

Source: Barbados: www.rootsweb.ancestry.com/~atgwgw/resources/bsource.html

Barbados

Barbados Registration Records

Since early 16th century Spanish and Portuguese were present in Barbados by the early 17th century the English settlers arrived. During 17th and 18th century period Barbados was divided into eleven parishes of which each had administrative responsibilities.

Early settlers included English, Irish prisoners of war, Scottish prisoners of war, voluntary indentured labour from England, Ireland and Scotland. Like Jamaica, earliest settlers in Barbados were Caribs and Arawaks.

Leeward Islands – St Kitts, Nevis, and Anguilla

Leeward islands are situated north of Lesser Antilles are so called due to the prevailing wind that blows easterly. Comprise islands that are predominantly of volcanic geological formation (Macpherson 1970). In 1806 Leeward Island Caribees Government was split into two groups of which St Christopher (St Kitts), Nevis and Anguilla along with British Virgin islands were in one group. Group remained until 1816 when they split. Anguilla continued to be administered with St Christopher and Nevis.

Anguilla

Lies 60 miles north of St Kitts, administered as part of the Leeward Islands until 1825, incorporated in St Christopher (St Kitts) and Nevis. Anguilla succeeded in becoming a separate dependency of Great Britain in 1969.

St Kitts & Nevis

St Kitts and Nevis are both volcanic islands with unpredictable geological history and lush vegetation. Originally inhabited by the Caribs knew the island as *Liamuiga or 'fertile land.'* Christopher Columbus arrived 1493 by then were long established settled communities of Caribs and Arawaks Indian population.

St Kitts was formerly known as St Christopher

Colonization began in St Kitts in 1623 by the English and French who sought refuge after losing fight with Spanish galleon. Carib Indians were massacred by the groups of which by 17th century European diseases wiped out Carib Indian population in Nevis additionally were victims of Spanish attacks. From St Kitts the English colonized Nevis, Antigua, Barbuda, Tortuga and Montserrat, while the French claimed Martinique.

Registration Records for Anguilla, St Kitts and Nevis

Early registration of vital events records incorporated the islands Anguilla, St Christopher and Nevis. For St Kitts no surviving Roman Catholic records available before 1865.

Register indexes consist of records for individual islands of St Christopher (St Kitts), Nevis and Anguilla.

Migration from Caribbean to England and Wales, Canada and United States of America (USA)

Migration of Caribbean people from Caribbean to England, Wales, Canada and USA has been a longstanding tradition dating back to the 17th century since.
Types of Caribbean migrants included:
• Servants
• Primitive preachers
• Labourers
• Ship workers
• Trade
• Seek or further education, Scholars
• Seek work
• Continued work with employer – in service
• Farm working opportunities – commenced in Caribbean during the 1940s
• Continued professional development

Sources for Research
Newspapers

Barbados: newspapers published since 1731. Few single issues were published 1733, 1742, 1745-1747, 1753, 1761, 1766, 1775, 1781, 1783 and 1803 and for most years since 1805
Jamaica: earliest known published in early 1700s, printing began with Weekly Jamaica Courant in 1718. The Gleaner created 1830s. National Library of Jamaica holds collection dating back 1718.

Gleaner available online, web address:
http://gleaner.newspaperarchive.com

Wills and Probate

Wills in existence for all Caribbean islands from 17th century. Located in repository for the island of origin. Wills are also located in The National Archives in Kew, Richmond UK. Generally written when individual resided in England who had property in the Caribbean or died on route during return to England.

Jamaica: Register General Office; V L Oliver`s Caribbeana published printed index of wills 1663 -1750 also lists wills probated in Prerogative Court of Canterbury

Barbados: Wills held at Barbados Department of Archives, Barbados 1743 – 1959. V L Oliver's Caribbeana published printed index of wills

Selection of Internet sources

www.movinghere.org.uk - Database of passenger lists, images, documents and life stories.

www.rootsweb.ancestry.com/~caribgw

Jamaican Family Search: http://jamaicanfamilysearch.com - Subscription based online library. Free samples available

Society of Genealogists: www.sog.org.uk/index.shtml selection of materials relating to the West Indies

Family Search: www.familysearch.org - International collection of genealogical records available to view on microfiche, microfilm and online.

London Family History Centre: www.londonfhc.org

Barbados: www.rootsweb.ancestry.com/~brbwgw/index.htm Rootsweb resource on 1680 census, repositories

Candoo: www.candoo.com/genresources Free online surname study database covers the Caribbean and other resources.

British West Indian Colonies in 1815

List of British West Indian colonies in 1815, with dates when they became British colonies and the name of the former colonial power. The British government included British Honduras (now Belize), British Guiana (now Guyana) and the Bermudas as part of the West Indies.

Anguilla (1650)	
Antigua and Barbuda (1632)	
Bahamas (from 1629)	
Barbados (1625)	
Bermudas (1612)	
British Guiana (1814)	Dutch
British Honduras (1638)	
British Virgin Islands (from 1666)	Dutch
Cayman Islands (1670)	Spanish

Dominica (1763)	French
Grenada (1763)	French
Jamaica (1655)	Spanish
Montserrat (1632)	
Nevis (1628)	
St Christopher (1623)	joint French and British
St Lucia (1814)	French
St Vincent & the Grenadines (1763)	French
Tobago (1814)	Courlanders/Dutch/French
Trinidad (1797)	Spanish
Turks and Caicos Islands (1678)	

Useful addresses and websites

Public Record Office, Kew, Surrey, TW9 4DU Tel: 020 8392 5200, Internet: www.pro.gov.uk

British Library, Newspaper Library, Colindale, London NW9 5HE, Internet: prodigi.bl.uk/nlcat/

Church of Jesus Christ of Latter-Day Saints British Isles Family History Service, 185 Penns Lanes, Sutton Coldfield, Birmingham B76 1JU, Internet: www.familysearch.com

Historical Manuscripts Commission Quality House, Quality Court, London WC1A IHPW: www.hmc.gov.uk

Caribbean Genealogical Web Project: www.rootsweb.com/~caribgw/

Cyndi Howell's Online Gateway to resources for Hispanic, South American and Caribbean family history: www.cyndislist.com/hispanic.htm

Antigua and Barbuda

Antigua National Archives, Rappaport Centre, Victoria Park, St John's, Antigua
Registrar General, High Street, St John's, Antigua

Bahamas

Public Records Office, Department of Archives, PO Box SS-6341, Nassau, Bahamas
Registrar General's Office, PO Box N532, Nassau, Bahamas

Barbados

Department of Archives, Lazaretto Building, Black Rock, St Michael, Barbados
Registration Department, Supreme Court of Barbados, Law Courts, Colleridge St, Bridgetown, Barbados

Belize

Belize Archives Department, 26/28 Unity Boulevard, Belmopan, Belize

Bermuda

Bermuda National Archives, Government Administration Building, 30 Parliament St, Hamilton HM 12, Bermuda

British Virgin Islands

Library Services Department, Flemming St, Road Town, Tortola, British Virgin Islands

Cayman Islands

Cayman Islands National Archive, Government Administration Building, George Town, Grand Cayman
Registrar General, Tower Building, George Town,

Grand Cayman
Dominica
National Documentation Centre, Government
Headquarters, Roseau, Commonwealth of
Dominica
General Registrar, Bay Front, Roseau,
Commonwealth of Dominica
Grenada
National Museum, Young St, St George's, Grenada
Registrar General, Church St, St George's,
Grenada
Guyana
National Archives of Guyana, River Police Building,
Stabroek Square, Georgetown, Guyana
General Register Office, GPO Building, Robb St,
Georgetown, Guyana
Jamaica
Jamaica Archives, Spanish Town, Jamaica
The Registrar General, Vital Records Information,
Twickenham Park, Spanish Town, Jamaica
Montserrat
Montserrat Public Library, Government
Headquarters, Plymouth, Montserrat
Registrar General, PO Box 22, Plymouth,
Montserrat

St Christopher and Nevis
National Archives, Government Headquarters,
Church St, Box 186, Basseterre, St Kitts
Registrar General, PO Box 236, Basseterre, St
Kitts
St Lucia
St Lucia National Archives, PO Box 3060, Clarke
St, Vigie, Castries, St Lucia
St Vincent and the Grenadines
Archives Department, Cotton Ginnery
Compound, Frenches, Kingstown, St Vincent
Registrar General, Kingstown, St Vincent
Trinidad and Tobago
National Archives, PO Box 763, 105 St Vincent St,
Port-of-Spain, Trinidad
Registrar General's Office, Registration House,
South Quay, Port-of-Spain, Trinidad.

Sharon Tomlin is a researcher of family
history and genealogist. She has over fifteen
years experience working with records. At
present she runs workshops on *How To
Research Caribbean Roots* with emphasis on
Jamaican records.

The Wages of Sin
Sue Hoddinott

Family businesses come in many guises but
one of the more unusual is Brothel keeping. Of
course prostitution is the oldest profession in
the world so they say but even in these liberal
times it's not an element of the customer
service industry one is keen to brag about. Yet
within the family history fraternity scandal
involving our ancestors in any salacious activity
or crime is often viewed as winning the family
history jackpot.

Of course few people are handed down
family stories of how Great Aunt Sally was a
prize prostitute, or Great Uncle Alfred owned
a chain of houses of ill repute. The divining of
the truth is somewhat more subtle and we are
left to find the clues within the census records
as a starting point.

So it was with my Mannerings family from
Chatham Kent. Originally as Ag Labs in
common with 90% of the United Kingdom in
the early 19th century my Great Great Great
Great Grand Grandfather Benjamin Mannerings
managed to become a beer shop owner and
later tenant landlord at various sawdust and
spit pubs in the town. His retirement at the age
of 55 years to a smart new area of Chatham
left me with a niggling worry of how he
managed to finance this but one I easily set
aside for a while.

Benjamin had a number of children who also
followed into the licensed trade and the
defining moment came in the form of the 1871
census for one of his sons Thomas Abraham
Mannerings who ran a pub called the Coach
and Horses in High Street Chatham. It struck
me that listed on this census at his hostelry
were quite a few unmarried 'ladies' who were
described as 'visitors.' This could have been
quite innocent but nonetheless appreciating the
basic nature of the pub in question and this
being Naval and Army Garrison town I became
curious as to whether Thomas had an
additional and illegal source of revenue.

I did not have to search far. In the same
census year Thomas' son George, who the
licensee of the notorious inn called the
'Trumpet' and my hunch was realised. George
aged a mere 22 years married with two young
daughters had no fewer than six 'ladies' under
his roof all unmarried and variously described
as lodgers – some with occupations such as
stay maker or weaver some with none at all!
There were also listed a few single men one
whose name was not known and described as
'Stranger.' This time the evidence was
compelling that the 'Trumpet' Inn was indeed a
'den of iniquity.' It is hard to believe George was
so naïve or stupid to admit to not knowing the

George Mannerings with the over riding conclusion that they were perhaps not the brightest of brothel keepers given the size and relevant success of this industry. Brian Joyce writes *'Mannerings was unlucky – many publicans were able to flout the Licensing Act.'* The way this was achieved was *'for many publicans to let cottages to prostitutes. This way they could claim that the girls were not resident in the pub, and so the pub itself was not a brothel. The publicans had the advantage of still taking a cut of the women's immoral earnings but at far less risk to themselves and their licences.'*

identities of people who were staying under his roof.

For the area of Chatham and neighbouring towns and villages an excellent resource exists on the internet called *'Cityark'* which is run by Medway Archives http://cityark.medway.gov.uk. This website gives access to many records including some of the licensing records for this period. Scrolling through these records it did not take long to realise that not only had the Mannerings family tenanted numerous pubs, inns and beer shops in and around Chatham exceeding over twenty in number but the brothel keeping industry also extended to other sons of Thomas Abraham Mannerings. On 31 July 1876 William, the second son of Thomas was now tenant of the Coach and Horses where he was convicted of *'permitting his premises to be a brothel'* according to the petty session records and was duly fined £10 with 12 shillings costs and licence revoked. During this period his brother George was similarly convicted. Both brothers were able to pay the fines of £10 and avoid a month of hard labour.

I soon learnt that such was the problem of binge drinking, prostitution and brothel keeping in Chatham that the situation had lead to Government intervention. In the book *'The Chatham Scandal'* the author Brian Joyce thoroughly charts the evolution of Prostitution in Chatham and its environs as well as some of the characters involved. From this book I learnt that the Mannerings clan were indeed harbouring and operating some of the town's most notorious prostitutes.

On pages 194 and 195 of *'The Chatham Scandal'* Joyce gives an in-depth account of the apprehension by the Police of both William and

This was exactly the method Alfred Mannerings, the third son of Thomas Abraham adopted. In September 1881 Alfred was convicted of running a brothel at the *'Oxford'* Pub in Chatham where he was tenant Landlord. At the same time his sister in law Charlotte the now widow of his brother William was convicted as tenant Landlady of the Cross Keys for the same offences.

Alfred was a strange solitary character. In the 1870's he had joined his eldest brother Thomas in living in Junction City Kansas USA but sometime around 1876 he had returned to Chatham. Alfred never married but lived in humble reduced circumstances as a lodger until his death in 1924. However what his brothers may have lacked in business sense Alfred made up for as he invested in a number of *'cottages'* and humble dwellings where the sources of his income were installed to carry on their work unhindered by the law.

The activity of outsourcing the 'working ladies' seems commonplace in Victorian Britain and may obscure many ancestors who were once engaged in such an activity. A couple of ladies living at a given address described as 'Dressmaker' or *'Seamstress'* on a census would not usually arouse suspicions in regard to their lifestyle and income.

It seems from these immoral earnings Alfred then invested in legitimate enterprises as well as schools, Gas and water companies and other institutions. Meanwhile he lived a life of near poverty- the local Chatham Newspaper reporting after his death

'Mr Mannerings lived a very secluded life, hardly allowing himself the necessaries of existence. His life was practically that of a Miser and the news that he was wealthy man has

Indenture for Thomas Cape
1721. 2nd series, no.1
Reproduced by permission of Exeter City Council

offices. Pauper indentures are likely to give the names of parish overseers rather than the names of parents. Many of them relate to bastards.

Three imperatives governed the attitude of the authorities towards pauper children: fear, cost, and charity. The fear of beggars amongst the ruling classes verged on paranoia. Beggars had to be controlled, otherwise, the result would be anarchy. Apprenticeship offered one useful means of control. Apprentices were meant to be under the strict supervision of their masters, who were supposed to be established tradesmen and householders.

Apprenticeship also offered a means of reducing expenditure on the poor rates: once a small premium had been paid to the master, the maintenance of the apprentice became his responsibility, and no further expenditure would be incurred by the parish.

Charity was the third imperative behind the system, but it was a poor third. Charity was thought to mean that the poor should be enabled to earn their own living at the earliest possible moment.

Pauper apprenticeship was wide open to abuse. Once children were apprenticed, which could be as early as age 7, many parish overseers felt themselves relieved of any responsibility for them. Supervision of masters was spasmodic, and many apprentices suffered from over-work, poor nutrition, physical violence, and worse. Boys were frequently apprenticed to husbandry, girls to 'housewifery.' In the late eighteenth and early nineteenth centuries, many were sent to northern factories, where conditions were sometimes harsh. Pauper apprentices were regarded by employers as a ready supply of cheap labour. Children were frequently apprenticed to occupations which required nimble fingers but no great skill. Little attention was paid to their long-term prospects.

The potential for abuse of pauper apprentices was recognised by Parliament. From 1766, London parishes had to keep registers of apprentices bound by their overseers. This requirement was extended to the whole country in 1802, and lasted until 1844, when responsibility for pauper apprentices was transferred to Poor Law

The information in apprenticeship registers is taken from the indentures. Both registers and indentures are likely to give an apprentice's name, the date of binding, the name(s) of parents or guardians, the names of masters (and perhaps their wives), the names of other parties, such as sponsoring charities, the trade that was to be taught, the premium (if any), the term which the apprentice was to serve, and the provision that was to be made for the apprentice at the end of the term. It should be signed by both master and apprentice (or his sponsor), and by witnesses. Sometimes the master only signed the apprentice's copy of the indenture, and the apprentice only signed his master's copy. It is worth noting the names of witnesses, since these may be relatives.

The indentures signed by overseers do not differ greatly from private indentures, although sometimes they are printed. They can be found with other parish records in local record

Unions (some of whom continued to keep registers).

These registers frequently survive. They are frequently written in printed books of forms. Sometimes, they give more information than apprenticeship indentures (particularly parents' names). The details given include the names, ages, sex, and parents of apprentices. Registers also name masters, their trades, and their residences, stating the premium paid, and the term of the apprenticeship. Many Devon registers have been published by Devon Family History Society www.devonfhs.org.uk/publications.htm#Joint. For Somerset and Dorset, they are available in the 'Specialist Records' collection at www.findmypast.co.uk. 'Staffordshire Apprenticeship Records' are at www.staffsnameindexes.org.uk

Apprenticeship indentures entered into by charities follow much the same format as those of private apprentices. They are likely to name the charity concerned, and to give the names of its officers. The master and wardens of Exeter's Guild of Weavers, Fullers, and Shearmen, for example, administered a charity established by the will of a Mr. Crispin. In 1710, they paid £5 to apprentice Tobias Carter, whose father had died. His master was to be William Jenkins, cordwainer. The master and wardens signed the indentures. Carter was to serve for eight years. At the end of this term, he was to be made free of the Incorporation of Cordwainers and Curriers, and of the City of Exeter. Children apprenticed by trade guilds were not necessarily apprenticed to the guild's own trade.

In one respect, the apprenticeship indentures of charities, and, indeed, of parochial overseers, did diverge from those of private indentures. They were not liable to the tax on apprenticeship indentures imposed by the Stamp Duty Act of 1709. This act levied a duty of 6d in the pound on all apprenticeship premiums of £50 or less, and one shilling in the pound on all premiums in excess of that amount. The duty was abolished in 1804, but the last payments were not made until 1811.

Registers of the duty paid were kept. These are now held in the National Archives, class IR 1. A detailed guide to 'Apprenticeship Records as Sources for Genealogy' is available at www.nationalarchives.gov.uk/catalogue/RdLeaflet.asp?sLeafletID=295. The registers summarise the information on apprentices and masters given in the indentures, and give details of the duty paid. The amount of information provided tails off after 1760.

Abstracts of some stamp duty registers are available at the Society of Genealogists, and

Apprentices at their Looms
© Robert Blatchford Collection

have been digitised for an online database, 'Apprentices of Great Britain 1710-1774' www.originsnetwork.com/help/aboutbo-appgb.aspx. This is a pay per view database containing some 350,000 entries. There is also an online database covering Cambridgeshire Masters and their Apprentices 1763-1811 www.cfhs.org.uk/Apprentices/index.html

Indentures should have been stamped to show that duty had been paid. However, there was a great deal of evasion, and much legislation was passed which attempted to deal with it. London masters in particular frequently avoided payment. Consequently, failure to find an apprentice in these registers does not indicate that no apprenticeship was served.

Indentures, apprenticeship registers, and stamp duty registers, record details of apprentices when their indentures were drawn up. The careers of apprentices can also be followed when they completed their terms of service. Indentures frequently obligated masters to ensure that their apprentices were granted the freedom of their guilds, and the freedom of their cities, once they had served their terms. The 'freedom' gave them the protection of their guilds, the right to trade within their borough, and frequently the right to vote in local and Parliamentary elections. Freedom could be acquired by serving an apprenticeship, by patrimony, and by purchase[5].

Grants of the freedom were frequently recorded in registers. These registers of freemen can frequently be found amongst city archives in local record offices. They usually record the name of the tradesman and his master, his trade, the nature of his entitlement, and the date freedom was granted. It is important, however, to bear in mind that there was frequently a gap - sometimes a substantial gap - between the date on which an apprentice completed his servitude, and the date on which he applied for grant of the freedom. The importance of the freedom for trading

Tuckers Hall, Exeter, headquarters of
The Guild of Weavers Fullers and Shearmen

contain much useful information.

Other information can be found in newspapers, many of which are now available online at 'British Newspapers 1800-1900' http://newspapers.bl.uk/blcs. A search on this pay per view database using the term 'apprentice' gives over 126,000 entries. Many of these relate to advertisements. Masters advertised for apprentices; parents advertised for masters. Masters also sometimes advertised for runaway apprentices. When Cornelius Brinkley absconded in 1780, his master advertised that he was thought to be *'lurking in the neighbourhood of Exeter or Collumpton. No reward will be given for apprehending him, but his master will be obliged to any press gang that will lay hold of him.'*

purposes declined during the eighteenth century, but that did not apply to Parliamentary elections. Elections were frequently marked by large numbers of applications for admittance to the freedom from ex-apprentices who had not previously bothered to exercise their rights.

Many registers of freemen have been published, for example, those from Chester[6], Leicester[7] and Newcastle upon Tyne[8]. The Exeter register[9] records the names of most of the apprentices whose indentures are held in the City Archives (in Devon Record Office). It also records many names of apprentices whose indentures have been lost. It is particularly noticeable that many freemen were granted the freedom just before the Parliamentary election of 1722.

Apprentices can also be traced in a variety of other records. The records of the poor law contain much useful information. Overseers accounts are likely to record the payment of premiums paid for apprenticing children, together with other expenses. Settlement examinations, conducted by Justices of the Peace, give mini-biographies of the poor, and are likely to record whether examinees served an apprenticeship.

Justices of the Peace were also authorised to adjudicate on complaints made by both masters and apprentices. Sometimes, they kept their own notebooks, where they recorded the decisions that they had made personally[10]. Such notebooks frequently record apprenticeship matters. Many decisions were also made at Quarter Sessions and Assizes, whose records

Notes:
[1]. HOLLIS, D., et al., eds. *Calendar of the Bristol apprentice book, 1532-1565.* 3 vols. Bristol Record Society, 14, 33 & 43. 1948-80.
[2]. BARLOW, JILL, ed. *A calendar of the registers of the apprentices of the City of Gloucester, 1595-1700.* Gloucestershire Record series 14. Bristol & Gloucestershire Archaeological Society, 2001.
[3]. WILLIS, ARTHUR JOHN, & MERSON, ALLAN LESLIE, eds. *A Calendar of Southampton apprenticeship registers, 1609-1740.* Southampton records series 12. 1968.
[4].RISING, WINIFRED M., & MILLICAN, PERCY, eds. *An index of indentures of Norwich apprentices enrolled with the Norwich Assembly, Henry VII-George II.* Norfolk Record Society 29. 1959.
[5]. For a detailed account of the freedom in London, consult ALDOUS, VIVIENNE E. *My ancestors were freemen of the City of London.* Society of Genealogists, 1999.
[6]. BENNETT, J.H.E., ed. *The rolls of the freemen of the City of Chester.* 2 pts. Lancashire & Cheshire Record Society, 51 & 55. 1906-08.
[7]. HARTOPP, HENRY, ed. *Register of the freemen of Leicester.* 2 pts. Records of the Borough of Leicester, new series 1-2. 1927-33
[8]. DODDS, MADELAINE HOPE, ed. *The Register of Freemen of Newcastle upon Tyne, from the Corporation, guild and admission books chiefly of the seventeenth century.* Newcastle upon Tyne Records Committee publication 63. 1923.
[9]. ROWE, MARGERY MARY, & JACKSON, ANDREW MACPHERSON, eds. *Exeter freemen 1266-1967.* Devon & Cornwall Record Society Extra Series 1. 1973.
[10]. See, for eample, MORGAN, GWENDA, & RUSHTON, PETER, eds. *The justicing notebook (1750-64) of Edmund Tew, rector of Boldon.* Surtees Society 205. 2000.
[11]. I have modernised the spelling in this extract.

Stuart Raymond is the author of numerous handbooks and guides for family historians. He is the author of *My ancestor Was An Apprentice* which is published by the Society of Genealogists.

FAMILY HISTORY
BOOKSHOP

Our Family History Bookshop has over **1,000 items** to choose from including books, family history software, large printed charts, magazine and certificate binders, jigsaw puzzles, accessories and maps, as well as subscriptions and back issues.

Whether it's a general guide to family history or a specific booklet you need, the Family History Bookshop has a wide range, with new releases and established titles.

www.familyhistorybookshop.co.uk

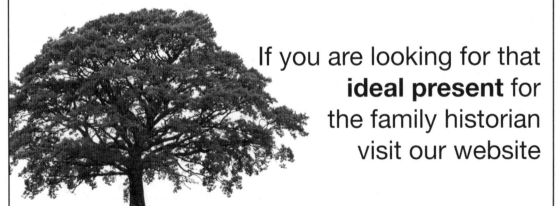

If you are looking for that **ideal present** for the family historian visit our website

ABM Publishing Ltd, 61 Great Whyte, Ramsey, Huntingdon PE26 1HJ.

Using The National Archives
Mark Pearsall
Principal Records Specialist The Family History Team

The National Archives (TNA) now has a dedicated family history team led by Mark Pearsall, which is part of the larger Military, Maritime, Transport and Family team headed by Roger Kershaw. Our aim is to provide advice and guidance to members of the public online and onsite about the genealogical records held in The National Archives and records held elsewhere. The onus is very much on opening up access to the records and facilitating research, not doing the research for people, which is just not practical given the many commitments that The National Archives has as the archives for England, Wales and the United Kingdom. The family history team consists of Principal Records Specialist Mark Pearsall, Records Specialist Audrey Collins, and Reader Advisers Richard Elvin, Tamara Brown-Milberg, Gerry Toop, and Reading Room Assistant Pad Kumlertsakul. The team came together following departmental reorganization in late 2009. Audrey, Gerry, Richard and Pad had previously been members of TNA staff at the Family Records Centre in Islington until they relocated to Kew in 2008.

Talks and Events

The family history team runs The National Archives talks programme with talks held every Thursday at 2pm in the Talks Room. Admission is by ticket, free of charge, and tickets can be

collected on the day of the event only, from the Information point in the Start Here Zone (or at the door if people arrive after 1:50pm). We do this to keep track of attendance, and although the tickets are not bookable in advance, we have never had to turn anyone away! We have a mixture of in-house and external speakers, and we also aim to strike a balance between family history and general historical and records-based topics catering for all interests.

TNA is represented at Who Do You Think You Are Live every year, in 2010 we provided speakers on all three days of the event. We usually attend two other fairs each year; in 2010 we attended the Yorkshire Family History Fair at York in June and the National Family History Fair at Newcastle in September. We can provide outside speakers to give talks about The National Archives and how its resources can complement family and local history research. We can also give talks on specific aspects of the records and record series held by TNA and other archives. We charge a fee and travelling expenses, but we are only limited by the travelling distance from London, unless the cost of overnight accommodation can be provided.

Online Resources and Research Sign Posts

The National Archives Catalogue and Documents Online, Access to Archives and the National Register of Archives allow people to identify information held in TNA, county record offices, local archives and other institutions. A visit to TNA is of most benefit to researchers who need to consult original records about specific aspects of their ancestors' lives. There is no need to come to The National Archives to begin your family history research. The basic sources are widely available online. All public libraries have computers for members of the public to use and many have subscriptions to commercial genealogical services online. Please check what is available in your local area before making a long journey to Kew. Visitors to The National Archives should be able and willing to do their own research themselves. Staff will of course be happy to advise and assist, but we are unable to do research for you. Our most popular records are increasingly available online. The system for ordering up original documents at Kew is also computer-based and in order to get the most out of a visit to TNA, people should have a basic level of IT skills.

Researchers will get the most benefit from a visit to TNA if they do some preparation in advance. Basic and detailed guidance on a wide range of topics is available on our website and our catalogue can be searched online. There are quick animated guides (20 minute tutorials) on preparing for research, how to use indexes, how the records are arranged, etc so you will know what to expect and how to get the most out of your visit. Researchers at TNA only need a reader's ticket to order up original documents. You do not need a reader's ticket to use online or microform resources, or to make photocopies and printouts of surrogate records. If you are likely to need a reader's ticket you should bring with you two forms of ID: one providing proof of identity and one providing proof of current address. A reader's ticket is currently valid for three years and is applied for onsite. Part of the application process involves an online preservation tutorial so applying for a reader's ticket can take up to twenty minutes. The National Archives website www.nationalarchives.gov.uk is now more intuitive and user friendly. As well as the research guides, which provide in-depth subject information, we now have a series of research sign posts for those who are looking for a person, place, or subject. The research signposts can help you uncover a person's history. Each one tells you where you can find relevant records and how they can be accessed. The signposts also point to records in other archives and organizations and tell you which records are available online. The looking for a place signposts help you investigate the history of places, including towns and villages, prisons, workhouses and foreign countries. The subject signposts allow you to research political and military history and society, industry and the arts.

Projects

There are a number of projects that are of benefit to family historians. The MH 12 project has opened up some of the original correspondence in series MH 12 of the poor law boards and their officials with the Poor Law Commission, Poor Law Board and Local Government Board. The project covered only a small selection of Poor Law Unions, but digital selections of these records can be accessed on TNA's Documents Online pages, and as the project was undertaken with the aid of volunteers in different parts of the country, the records are available to download for free. The volunteers worked on particular Poor Law Unions which are listed on the Documents Online page www.nationalarchvies.gov.uk/documentsonline/workhouse.asp The records cover correspondence

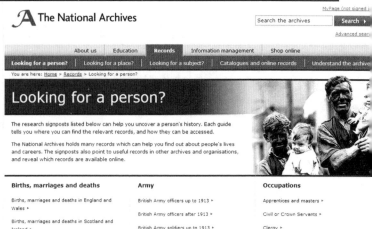

from the 1830s, 1840s and 1850s, and in the case of two unions correspondence to 1871. You can search by first and last name of a person, place name, occupation and subject. The records include letters, memoranda, reports, accounts and other returns. These can include details of individual paupers, cases of neglect and cruelty, appointments of officials, conditions in the workhouse, financial matters and public health.

Another recently completed cataloguing project is the Medical Journals of the Royal Navy in Admiralty series ADM 101. These records are a selection of the journals kept by surgeons of HM ships, naval hospitals, naval brigades and shore parties. They also include some convict and emigrant ships where a naval surgeon was provided. You can search volumes 1 to 293 covering dates between 1793 and 1880, by name of individual, subject and ship. The records have not been digitized, but it is now much easier to identify material from the catalogue www.nationalarchvies.gov.uk/catalogues/search.asp . The project has improved access to the records for, among others, medical historians and family historians. There are a number of other on-going cataloging projects aiming to make searching the catalogue and identifying material easier. These include expanding the descriptions of the First World War officers' service files in WO 339 and Airmen's records in AIR 79 by including full name of the individual in the descriptions. Other records being worked on are Greenwich Hospital school admission papers in ADM 73, Royal Navy allotment registers in ADM 27 and Royal Marines attestation forms in ADM 157.

Members of the family history team have also worked on the descriptions of the Land Tax assessments of 1798 in series IR 23, which at present are only listed by county. These records show all owners (proprietors) and occupiers (tenants) of land arranged by parish or township in England and Wales. When completed, you will be able to search for a parish or township and order copies of the return for that particular place. These records are especially useful for finding out who the landowners and the main tenants were in a particular place when seeking to trace estate, manorial and farm records. Other Land Tax assessments from 1780 to 1832 can be found locally in county record offices. What we have discovered while working on this project is that some counties made returns for 1799 as well, and occasionally a parish or township supplied a return for 1799 and 1800, which found their way to the board of Taxes office in London.

Our Collections

Our most popular records are the census returns from 1841 to 1911. These records are now all available online and can be accessed at home and in many libraries and archives. The 1841 to 1891 censuses are available at www.Ancestry.co.uk. The 1901 returns at www.1901censusonline.com and the 1911 census through www.Findmypast.com at www.1911census.co.uk

The returns cover England and Wales, the Channel Islands and the Isle of Man. From 1861 British ships on the high seas are enumerated, and in 1911 British army units overseas are recorded for the first time.

Military and naval records are, after the census returns, the next most popular records, particularly military service records. Findmypast have now made available online the Soldiers' Documents from 1760 to 1913 (TNA series WO 97). First World War service records in series WO 363 and 364 are available on Ancestry. From September 2011 the Militia service records in series WO 96 will also be available online. Many other army records are available in original format such as muster rolls (WO 10-13 and 16) and operational records for campaigns from dispatches in the 17th century to war diaries in the 20th century.

Naval service records for ratings of the Royal Navy can be searched on our Document Online web pages from 1853 to 1928. Officers' service records, including Royal Marine officers (series ADM 196), are searchable on Documents Online covering men serving from 1756 to 1917, although not all returns survive, particularly in the late 18th and early 19th centuries. Warrant officers can also be found in this series and also their certificates of service can be found by searching the catalogue for series ADM 29. Royal Marines records of service (ADM 159) can also be searched on Documents Online. Ships' musters and pay books (TNA series ADM 31-39, ADM 115, 117 and 119) can be searched for on the catalogue and are original documents.

Records of merchant seamen and the merchant service can be found among the records of the Board of Trade. Registers of seamen's service cover the period from 1835 to 1857 and from 1917 to 1972. You can search the catalogue by name to see if a seaman's pouch (registration documents) covering the period 1941 to 1972 survives in series BT 372 or 391. First and Second World War medals can be searched on Documents Online. A 10% sample of Agreements and Crew lists survives from 1861 in series BT 99. Indexes to the crew lists can be searched on Findmypast.

Legal records are some of the most fruitful sources of social and biographical material for family history. The Home Office Criminal Registers (HO 26 and 27) cover Middlesex from 1791 and England and Wales from 1805 to 1892, showing all those who were tried for indictable offences. These registers show where trials were held, whether at borough and quarter sessions or at the assizes. Assize records are held in TNA and include Crown minute and gaol books, indictments and depositions. There is a research guide and key to criminal trials arranged by county. In addition to the Assize records there are the records of the central law courts; King's Bench, Common Pleas, Exchequer and Chancery to 1875, and the divisions of the High Court and Supreme Court of Judicature from 1876. All these legal records are original documents, but searching the online catalogue can identify relevant material and often individuals.

The research sign posts and in-depth research guides will give you more information on what is available, what you need to know, what records are available online and which you need to visit The National Archives to access as original material.

The Reading Rooms

The 'Start Here' zone is for all first time users of The National Archives, not just family historians. Here staff will assess your requirements and either show you to a computer where you can familiarize yourself with our online resources, or if you have done some research on our website beforehand, direct you to the relevant part of the Open Reading Room, depending on whether your research relates to military, maritime, transport or family history, or to modern social, political, colonial or diplomatic history. On the second floor is the Map and Large Document Reading Room. Here you can consult maps and plans and medieval and early modern records. The 'Start Here' zone will allow people to familiarize themselves with our catalogue, research guides and sign-posts and other online resources. There will also be short film animations played on the plasma screens in the zone to familiarize you with our procedures. Staff will provide help and guidance, but we are unable to do research for you. If you have never used a computer before then you should bring a family member or friend who has computer skills to assist you. The desks in the 'Start Here' zone are designed for two people to sit together for that reason. Once people are comfortable using the catalogue and online resources they can move on to the other areas to work. Records Specialists, Reader Advisers and Reading Room Assistants will be on duty at the desks in the Open Reading Room to answer record enquiries. In the future we aim to continue to improve our services and online resources, and also open up to you some of the many records that are not accessible online, and are in some cases not easily identifiable from the online catalogue. Through our licensed internet associations a number of popular record series have been, and are being, made available on commercial websites. We are also making more series of records available on our Documents Online web pages through digitization. Some of these will not be directly searchable as they will not have been indexed, but you will be able to browse the images as though

you were looking at the original document. Sign up to our free online enewsletter, which you will receive monthly, giving you updates on recently released government files, newly digitized records and new online resources www.nationalarchives.gov.uk/news/enewsletter.htm

You can also access The National Archives Facebook page for news and information or follow #UkNatArchives on Twitter. A little time beforehand spent using the website and the resources available will reward you in time saved when you come and undertake research at Kew.

Getting Better All the Time
Joe O'Neill

Did Florence Maybrick avenge the victims of Jack the Ripper? What was Thomas De Quincey's state of mind when his marriage bond was issued? Could the servant writing to his master in 1605 of the capture of Guy Fawkes have guessed that four centuries later, in the wake of the MPs' expenses scandal, a writer to the *Times* would describe the miscreant as the only man ever to enter Parliament with honourable intentions?

Just some of the thoughts prompted by three documents among the millions which the Lancashire Record Office houses in its bright and pleasant purpose built home. They chart the county's history from the 12th century to the present day and are the focus of those who pore over them in the Search Room. But the Office does a great deal more than merely make these archives available to the wide range of visitors it attracts. As Kathryn Newman, Public Service Archivist, explains, the Office offers the expertise and enthusiasm of a team of facilitators. "Every member of staff is fascinated with our archives and keen to get

the most out of them. We may not know the answer to a query, but we'll do everything possible to find out."

The life of both the historic and the modern county of Lancashire is documented in LRO's eight miles of shelving. There are many sources relating to local government administration at all levels and a vast array of maps and plans. The sources of particular interest to the family historian include Poor Law and Quarter Session records; probate records of the Archdeaconries of Chester and Richmond; records of Anglican, Roman Catholic and nonconformist churches, including registers of baptisms, marriages and burials; taxation records, including those for land tax; prison and hospital records; electoral registers; school records, including log books and admissions registers; trade directories; private records, including manorial and estate records, family papers, and the records of businesses and societies; the records of private charities, many linked to churches, and copies of some national sources, including census returns for the whole

County Palatine.

The present-day boundaries of the administrative county do not fully incorporate the ancient County Palatine of Lancashire. They exclude the areas of Merseyside, Greater Manchester and South Lakeland. Whilst those areas have their own record offices, many records relating to them are stored at LRO. If what you want is not at the LRO, staff will point you in the right direction.

Making the most of your visit

It is always helpful to contact the Record Office before making a visit. You should also check that the Office has the documents you need. Consult its online catalogue via www.lancashire.gov.uk/education/record_office/about/overview.asp You can also view some of the Office catalogue via the Access to Archives website: www.nationalarchives.gov.uk/A2A/default.aspx

The Office does not operate a booking system but in order to access original documents you will need a reader's ticket, which requires proof of identity.

Kathryn Newman of LRO advises readers to set themselves a specific question and to allow plenty of time for their first visit. Trawling documents is engrossing and time passes very quickly.

Any first-time visitor will be pleasantly surprised. There's a buzz of productive activity as enthusiasts of all ages use the excellent facilities. Nor will you be left to your own devices simply to get on with it. A member of staff will help you get the most out of your visit by explaining how to use the indexes and catalogues and showing you relevant leaflets and instruction notices. You'll discover how to order records. Staff are very welcoming and as many have charted their own ancestry, they appreciate what is involved.

Whether seeking information when planning a visit or using the enquiry service, the LRO prefers to deal with queries by letter, fax or email. Staff are fully occupied helping researchers and the required documents are not always readily to hand which makes it difficult to answer telephone queries.

The enquiry service enables you to obtain for a fee a report on research into records where access is sometimes restricted, such as school records, police service records, closed hospital records, rate books and vehicle licensing records. The Office has a designated staff member who does this on your behalf.

Even experienced researchers, however, enjoy and benefit from Office courses. Among these is a free research consultation, when you

---

LANCASHIRE
RECORD OFFICE

Lancashire
County
Council

Times of Opening:

Monday   09.00 - 17.00 Tuesday 09.00 - 19.30 Wednesday 09.00 - 17.00
Thursday 10.00 - 17.00   Friday 09.00 - 17.00

Also open on the second Saturday of each month from 10.00 - 16.00

- Main family and local history sources for Lancashire
- No need to book to see original material or microform copies
- County Archive Research Network (CARN) reader's ticket required for access to original material
  please bring official ID with your name, address and signature
- Full colour document imaging service available and photography permitted
- Close to Preston Railway station and free visitor only car parking
- Hot drink vending machine and eating area available

During spring and summer 2011 there will be major work carried out at Lancashire Record Office and some closures may be necessary.
If you are intending to visit and think your visit may be affected, please contact us for advice and up to date information.

Lancashire Record Office, Bow Lane, Preston PR1 2RE
Website: www.archives.lancashire.gov.uk Phone: 01772 533039 Email: record.office@lancashire.gov.uk

discuss your research needs with an archivist so as to identify likely sources. There is also a monthly newsletter with information on recent deposits, cataloguing developments and other items of interest to researchers.

Of particular interest to family history societies - but also widely used by schools – are the group tours. This is an opportunity to learn at firsthand how the office works and to see behind the scenes. The visit is adapted to the group's special interests and typically includes an introductory talk, a tour of part of the office and an exhibition of original documents, possibly including local material, by arrangement with the member of staff hosting the visit.

Kathryn Newman leads 'Getting to Know' sessions on the first Thursday of every month. These are particularly popular with family history groups and may include a visit to the strong room.

The Friends of Lancashire Archives are valuable ancillaries to the work of the Office. They promote, support, assist and improve the Office in its crucial work of protecting and conserving the archival heritage of the county, and making it available to the public. They provide a forum through which the Office can explain, publicise and promote its work and policies whilst users can put forward ideas and suggestions for improvement and comment upon proposals. The FLA has also helped fund several projects, most recently the purchase of deeds relating to the Forton area of Lancashire, which otherwise would have gone out of the county. They meet socially and enjoy visits to other Record Offices and to places of historical and archival interest, including those not normally accessible to the general public.

The Friends – the largest archival support groups in the country - also host a range of workshops, with guest speakers on a wide variety of subjects. They have worked on valuable indexing projects designed to help the family historian, such as the creation of an index to Amounderness disputed wills and are currently working on apprenticeship records. You can find out more about the Friends by writing to the Secretary, Mrs E Hedley 5 Birchfield, Much Hoole, Preston, Lancashire PR4 4HD.

With so much to offer, it's hardly surprising that the LRO is one of the best-used in the country, attracting researchers with a huge variety of interests from all over the world. Its continued appeal is assured as its collection grows, necessitating the addition of a second new storage tower in the near future.

It's not only the archives that are growing. As Kathryn explains, staff work with visitors in constantly questioning the sources. *"We learn something new every day. Hopefully, we're getting better and better at helping people trace ancestors who otherwise would have no voice."*

Note: During 2011 major work will be carried out at Lancashire Record Office and some closures may be necessary. If you are intending to visit and think your visit may be affected please contact the Record Office by telephone – 01772 533 039 or email record.office@lancashire.gov.uk for advice and up to date information

Reference DP 189/13
The South Prospect of Preston engraved 1728 by S & N Buck
Reproduced with permission of the County Archivist, Lancashire Record Office

Was My Ancestor a Wife Murderer, Arsonist or Just Unlucky?

Theresa Mcloughin

Plumpton Hall

John Heskett was born 21st November 1753[1] in Plumpton Hall Cumberland to James Heskett and Isabel Ebdale. Plumpton Hall was a working farm and had been in the family since 1675. His father like many of his ancestors were Yeoman farmers

His Uncle William Heskett was Rector of Denton in Cumberland and John decided to follow in his footsteps and go into the church to train as a minister. On the 4th August 1776 a notice was posted in the Parish church of Heskett in the Forest Cumberland giving notice of his forthcoming entry into the church as a curate.[2] The Testimonial dated 9th August included J Cowper the Vicar of Penrith, William Cowper the Vicar of Dacre and William Heskett (his uncle) Rector of Denton recommending him as a candidate for the Holy Orders of Deacon.[3]

On the 15th August 1776 Edward Wilson Rector of Washington appointed him curate for the sum of £30 a year.[4] He appears to have led a quiet life here as no further information can be found.

John moved from Washington to Kirknewton from about 1778. He married his first wife Jane Pringle from Doddington on the 27 July 1780 at Kirknewton. Jane died in April 1781 without bearing any children.. A testimonial to the Bishop of Durham from J Hogarth Vicar of Kirknewton on the 18th August[5] recommended him to be admitted to the Holy Orders of priests. He was accepted as a curate on the 1st September 1781 for the yearly sum of £30. John seems to have become frustrated during this time as his requests of confirmation of his age from his home parish of Hesket in the Forest was delayed or lost. J Hogath wrote to the Bishop of Durham on the 12th September 1881[6] to explain the reason for the delay and his disappointment over the last year at not being ordained a priest.

On the 14th March 1783 married Dorothy Morton daughter of

Ralph Morton of Wooler. They had three children. John born 1784, Charles James born 1785 and George born 1786. It would appear that Charles James must have died soon after his birth as no further records can be found. His wife Dorothy died 3rd November 1787 in Kirknewton. During his short time as a minister in Kirknewton the church unfortunately had a fire in 1785[7] and the parish records were destroyed. John was now left with two sons to bring up on his own.

John now appears to have moved to Whitburn a small fishing village close to Monkwearmouth. I would think this would be about 1789. Baronet Hedworth Williamson owned Whitburn and Monkwearmouth and was also a member of the Freemasons.

The fire in St Peters Monkwearmouth broke out on the 12th April 1790. It is thought to have been due to a candle knocked over by Revd. Jonathan Ivison and it destroyed Monkwearmouth Hall and all the parish registers. It is rather strange that another fire occurred while he was in the vicinity and he was so keen to become a priest. Did he have some input with the fire to cause stress and worry to the now aging Iveson in order to gain his position? The records recreated[8] after the fire show Baptism entries for his sons John and George in St Peters even though they were baptised at Kirknewton. Is it a coincidence that he was obviously around to recreate these records?

During his time at Kirknewton I feel that he may have visited Sunderland to visit Tipping

Phoenix Masonic Lodge

Brown who was a physician and Master of the Masonic lodge No 207 in the latter part of 1781 which was in Vine Street. It is possible that the two met while they were both studying in Durham or while he was curate at Washington. On the 19th November 1783[9] the Masonic Hall in Vine Street, somehow took fire and was entirely destroyed, another incident of his connections and another fire.

A new lodge was built in Queen St Sunderland and dedicated on the 5th April 1785. The lodge was to be named the Phoenix Lodge.

St Peter's Monkwearmouth

On the 17th January 1793 John was nominated by Tipping Brown to be a mason. On the 7th February 1793 at the lodge meeting he was made a mason. His first request at that meeting was to ask for money for the Free School in Cumberland; his request was rejected he did not waste any time in asking for favours did he?

On the 3rd March 1793[10] at the Masonic Lodge meeting a Committee was appointed to arrange and set the future entertainment for the Lodge. John was elected as one of the Committee members. Was his entertainment to be a bonfire I wonder!!!!

The minutes of the Masonic meeting on the 3rd April 1793[11] show that he is now the Chaplain of the lodge with Tipping Brown still the Master.

On the 12th June 1793[12] he married by Licence Elizabeth Wild widow of John Wild a wine importer at St Michaels Bishopwearmouth. At this time he was clerk at Whitburn Parish Church. Tipping Brown stood guarantor for his bond for the sum of £200.

On 24th September 1793 a service was held in Holy Trinity Church by John Heskett as chaplain, attended by all the local magistrates and dignitaries prior to the laying of the foundation stone for the new Iron Bridge across the River Wear by Rowland Burdon. In *Garbutts The History of Sunderland*[13] that John Heskett gave a rousing sermon.

John was still chaplain of the Phoenix lodge in 1796 when the Wearmouth Bridge was opened and took part in all the ceremonies connected to this day.

He does not appear in any records of the Phoenix lodge after 1797 so it is not known whether he may have moved lodges to possibly Monkwearmouth. It is rather strange that his friend Tipping Brown also disappears from the lodge records.

A testimonial[14] dated 26th July 1898 recommends that he become curate of St Peters in Sunderland. The testimonial is signed by Henry Black Rector of Boldon Church and George Stephenson curate of Bishopwearmouth

His wife Elizabeth died on Feb 13th 1806 in Monkwearmouth. On August 28th 1808 he married his 4th wife Jane Strahan in Monkwearmouth. On October 10th 1810 John died in Monkwearmouth. A year later on 6th October his son George who was a mariner died. Only his son John survived and all the Heskett's in Sunderland are descended from him.

During his life he came into contact with many of the memorable people from the town of Sunderland. Baronet Hedworth Williamson Tipping Brown (1759 – 1811) Vice president of the Humane Society, James Field Stanfield (1749-1824), a sailor, actor and wine merchant who was involved in the campaign for the abolition of the slave trade. Michael Scarth (1766 – 1805), who was a partner with Messrs Grimshaw, Webster and Mills in a Patent Ropery which was established in 1793 on the banks of the River Wear and many more through his connections with the freemasons.

The above are facts that I have unearthed during my research. I do not have any proof of his influencing the early deaths of his wives or his directly setting fire to these buildings but it does seem strange that he had four wives and was always in the area at the time of the fires.

A footnote to the story of John Heskett. His descendant who my cousin Ralph Heskett will was ordained Bishop of Gibraltar on July 10th 2010. So it looks like I have Good Minister and Bad Minister in my family tree!

References
1. Letter confirming birth from Parish Records
2. Personal papers from Durham University Library
3. Personal papers from Durham University Library
4. Personal papers testimonial from Edward Wilson from Durham University Library
5. Personal Papers from Durham University Library
6. Personal Papers from Durham University
7. Extract from "A Short History of Kirknewton Church"
8. Parish Records of St Peters Monkwearmouth
9. Minutes of the Freemason Registers
10. Minutes of the Freemason Registers
11. Minutes of the Freemason Registers
12. Marriage Licence from Durham University Library and Parish Records
13. Garbutts the History of Sunderland
14. Personal papers from Durham University Library

A Helping Hand: Charities

Doreen Hopwood

Charities today can be multi-national organisations distributing tonnes of aid where it's needed, but until the founding of the welfare state in the United Kingdom, many of ancestors would have relied on some form of charity in times of need.

Charities often originate from religious houses and hospitals, such as that of St Oswald in Worcester, founded in about 990 AD, and many evolved into almshouses, which still exist as charitable institutions. At first they provided shelter and alms (usually bread and ale) to travellers, as well as to the sick and infirm, and this is reflected in the alternative title of 'Spital' or 'Spittle House,' derived from 'hospital.'

Following the dissolution of the monasteries, many of the almshouses which had been run by religious orders disappeared, and responsibility for the sick and poor fell to the parish. Today, it doesn't matter if you don't know the name of the parish where you live, but until the introduction of the New Poor Law in 1834, this knowledge was crucial, especially if you needed help. The parish officers were responsible for the moral and physical welfare of their parishioners and were, in effect, your chancellors of the exchequer who collected and distributed the parish funds. As such they went to great lengths to ensure that only those who had a

right to help received it. By looking at the accounts of the overseers of the poor and the churchwarden, you'll see which families or individuals were the most needy and how their needs were catered for. Sometimes financial help was given, but most commonly support took the form of goods or services, such as clothing or the provision of a nurse. In some parishes, the poor were employed to wash the church linen or to look after the parish crops rather than being given charity, and these payments also appear in the accounts. You'll find these records (known as 'the parish chest') deposited with the parish registers at the relevant Diocesan record office, but survival rates vary.

Charities were commonly established through bequests made in the wills of the wealthy, and became known by the name of their benefactor, such as the George Fentham Trust, whose will of 1690 provided for 'the buying and paying for ten as good coats as for the sum of ten pounds might be had without fraud.' The clergy encouraged these bequests, as it was good for the soul to remember the poor. The Trust or Deed by which the charity was set up often included a clause under which beneficiaries were required to pray for the benefactors on a regular basis (sometimes several times a day) or maintain his tomb or memorial. You'll find a copy of

the benefactor's will within the documents of the charity, and this can provide a real insight into the relative values of the time. In 1558, Eleanor Palmer bequeathed two acres of meadow land and its income 'for the benefit of the poor of Kentish Town and Chipping Barnet forever' which could still be valuable today, unlike the bequest from George Fentham mentioned above.

The Charity Commission was founded in the 1850s and is now responsible for the registration and regulation of charities in the United Kingdom. The Central Register of Charities is open to public inspection and copies of the accounts of registered charities can be obtained from the Commission. However, only charities with a gross income or expenditure of over £10,000 in any financial year are required to submit their accounts to the Charity Commission, so you may need to contact the charity itself. You can search the Central Register of Charities at www.charity-commission.gov.uk/registeredcharities by present or former name of the charity or

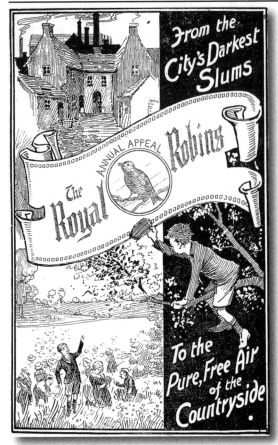

by keyword. This then provides the contact details and further information.

You'll find lists of charities in the relevant Victoria County History, and copies of these are available in main reference libraries/record offices with some also on-line at www.british-history.ac.uk. Brief histories of an area's main charities may also be included in Kelly's or Post Office directories, and these can also be searched on-line at www.historicaldirectories.org.uk

After the introduction of the New Poor Law, some parishes continued to operate existing charities and some introduced new ones. *The Bread Charity Distribution Book of Samuel Wheeley*, of Edgbaston in the 1840s, suggests that details of the recipients would be given, and whilst this is the case for a short period, later records simply show the number of loaves distributed on certain dates. Churches were keen to help parishioners in need, but as in earlier times, applicants were carefully vetted. In the later Victorian period, relief normally took the form of coal, food and dispensary notes, and one Birmingham relief register shows numerous Co-op vouchers, each worth 1/6d, and medical tickets being given out. However, when Florence Timmins who had an unemployed husband and a weekly rent of 4/9d to find, applied for help she was

given a one-off hand-out of a pint of milk and a bottle of Bovril.

Cathedral, market and guild towns have a large number of ancient charities, but the growth of industrial towns in the nineteenth century, was highlighting the plight of the poor in these urban environments. They became the focus of the Victorian *'social conscience'* which was linked to the belief that the rich could genuinely help the poor by philanthropic action. This, in turn was part of the increasing interest in evangelicalism and the urge to do useful work. These charities depended upon donations and subscriptions to fund their activities, and, whilst their methods of fund raising varied, they all had one thing in common - they differentiated between the *'deserving poor'* and those who were considered to be scroungers.

Most charities operated a ticket system by which subscribers were issued with a number of tickets, dependent on the amount of their subscription. They then gave them to *'deserving'* persons who presented the ticket to the charity office where they were interviewed before their case was considered. *The Edgbaston Mendicity Society* was formed in 1870 and was very clear about whom it would and whom it wouldn't help. Applicants were divided into two classes - *'that which trades upon public charity [mendicants] and that which has been thrown upon it by circumstances [deserving poor].'* The Society was keen to ensure that it wasn't taken advantage of and published some of the ploys used by people to get money from them. Nevertheless, in 1872 over two and a half thousand applications were granted and over three and a half tons of food were distributed. The poor soon got to know of any offices where relief tickets were about to be issued and long queues formed outside. The social consciences of the better off were stirred by images of the deserving poor which were published in magazines such as the *Illustrated London News* and as they were also the subject of paintings by famous artists such as Sir Luke Fildes these images adorned art galleries too.

Access to medical care was generally by a ticket system and subscribers to medical missions and hospitals were able to nominate patients. In the 1870s, an outpatient's ticket for the *Birmingham Lying-in Hospital* cost five shillings and one for an inpatient cost fifteen shillings. Help was normally restricted to married women, but the hospital admitted all destitute midwifery cases which were recommended by the clergy, and hospitals with 'Free' in their title treated any person in need of medical help.

Educational charities, such as the Blue Coat Schools, used a system by which subscribers and benefactors were able to nominate children to be accepted as pupils. Lists of nominees and their sponsors can be found within the minutes or annual reports which can then lead to a search of the school's registers. Each had some criteria for acceptance, such as the child having already been baptised and that he/she wasn't illegitimate. Following the introduction of compulsory education, some charity schools were taken over by the relevant council and their records may still be with the Local Education Authority, at the school itself, or deposited at the county/local record office, whilst others have become independent or endowed schools, retaining their records.

The Charity Organisation Society (COS) was founded in order to co-ordinate the work of voluntary and charitable organisations in London and soon had branches in major cities. However, it became known for its strict vetting procedures and its initials (COS) were interpreted as 'Cringe Or Starve' by some. The annual reports of these organisations include a complete list of all local charities, institutions and philanthropic societies in the area, together with details of the type of help they offered – and the qualifications people needed to access that help.

Not all charities were specifically for the benefit of the poor or for local people. The Manchester Society for Relieving Really Distressed Foreigners was a small organisation, and in 1880 The German Seamen's Mission was founded in South Shields to look after sailors visiting the Tyne. Long before the founding of the RSPCA, Thomas Ingram bequeathed money to pay for sermons to be read advocating merciful treatment of animals, especially horses. In 1825 twelve such sermons were made.

Paupers were expected to be suitably grateful for any charity they received, but in many cases the donors had little idea of what it was like to be needy. Always quick to comment on social issues, Punch Magazine regularly published articles about the rich and the poor. The first line of 'The Pauper's Song' of 1845 infers that criminals were better treated than those who had fallen on hard times:

> 'Houseless, famish'd, desperate man: a ragged wretch am I! And how and where and when I can, I feed and lodge and lie. And I must to the workhouse go, if better may no be: Aye, if indeed! The Workhouse! No! – The gaol, the gaol for me!'

Philanthropic societies depended on subscriptions and donations to enable them to function, and you may find an ancestor listed as a subscriber rather than as a recipient. Their names and addresses and the amount of their subscription were published in annual reports, together with details of the officers and trustees. Philanthropy was one of the few activities deemed suitable for middle class women, and by 1900, some 500,000 were regularly carrying out charitable work. The names of the wives and spinster daughters of the local gentry or manufacturers often appear as lady visitors, and many worked for more than one charity.

Local newspapers reported on charitable events and you may be fortunate enough to find a photograph of an ancestor participating in a fund-raising activity. Many also had their own charities, such as the Birmingham Mail Christmas Tree Fund, and some organised public appeals to purchase clothing. However, these items were not always gratefully received - boots provided by the Daily Mail made recipients instantly recognisable because they had the letters D and M pierced on the toecaps so that they couldn't be pawned.

The majority of almshouses catered for elderly woman, who usually had to be of sound mind, physically able to care for themselves, be over 50 years of age – and 'of good character.' Surviving records are usually at county record offices, and minute books, admission registers, correspondence with the Charity Commissioners and matron's reports can help build up a picture of everyday life in these institutions. In 1873, Martha Rhodes provided for the building of 15 almshouses and a matron's house at Handsworth, and in between references to the sweeping of chimneys and deliveries of coal, there are snippets of biographical information about new arrivals and the demise of older residents. There were obviously some rooms that were more desirable than others, as residents applied to move into these once they became vacant. The matron's reports also give an idea of the dynamics of the almshouses - the sad case of Miss Dowler occupied the attention of the matron and Trustees for some time in 1855 after she locked herself in her room and threw the keys out of the window. Numerous meetings with relatives ensued, and the other residents requested that she should be removed 'for the safety of the buildings and the peace and happiness of all.' She was eventually taken away by relatives.

Residential charitable institutions often provided their residents with a uniform which in some cases had to be worn at all times. For the majority, however, it was required only on certain days, but always when the person went outside of the institution. The ex-servicemen at the Coningsby Hospital in Hereford were supplied with a ginger suit, a hat with a red and white border, a military jerkin and cape and a sword for when they ventured 'abroad.' Probably the most famous of these uniforms is that worn by Chelsea Pensioners who are ex-soldiers living at the Royal Hospital Chelsea.

You'll find that many large charities, such as the Red Cross and Salvation Army, have their own archives and contact details are given on their websites.

Most of us have ancestors who fell on hard times and it's easy to assume that they ended up in the workhouse, but the safety net provided by many of the local charitable institutions may have enabled them to retain their independence and remain in the local community.

Where There's a Will – There's an Argument
Depositions and Allegations: The gold dust of probate documents
Jill Groves

In this article I will discuss the documents called Depositions and Allegations and the insights they can give into family and local life in the seventeenth and eighteenth centuries. The twenty-seven sets of documents I have used to research this article come from one or two parishes in North-east Cheshire. (This is because I have been (and still am) studying and transcribing Wills and other probate documents in the parishes of Bowdon and Ashton-on-Mersey for a number of years.)

What Are Depositions and Allegations?

These documents were created when wills were disputed or there was a dispute over who should administer the deceased person's estate. The person or people disputing the will or administrator (the plaintiff) took their complaint to the diocesan consistory court. Every diocese had a consistory court. These church courts had very wide powers to try cases (or causes as they were called) on morality, tithe payment disputes, matrimonial cases, and to licence schoolmasters, midwives, physicians and surgeons. In addition, the consistory court was where wills for testators with estates over £5 were proved, hence disputes over wills and a deceased's estate came before this court.

Allegations were documents (accusations) created from the complaint of the plaintiff if the person or people complained of (the defendant) denied them. If the defendant didn't deny them the plaintiff's complaint was called a libel.

Depositions were the replies of witnesses for either side to the allegations. By this time lawyers were involved, who should have been advocates (the church court equivalent of barristers), but were often wrongly proctors (the church court equivalent of solicitors). It was they who presented the documents to the judge of the consistory court. And in this sort of case the court sat on paper. It was not often that in these probate cases witnesses, plaintiffs and defendants appeared in person before the court.

This is a very simple description of how consistory courts worked on probate cases. For a better and more detailed description of the workings of church courts see *Sin, Sex and Probate: Ecclesiastical Courts, Officials and Records*[4]

In many consistory courts the cases were bound into sequential or annual volumes. However, in the diocese of Chester most of the probate case documents were collated together with the Will, probate inventory and other probate documents. John Addy complained in 1987 that the court books for Chester diocese

were not foliated and all subsequent hearings were added on the date on which the cause began.[1] Now, much of the Consistory Court Act Books for this diocese have been indexed, calendared and put on the Access to Archives website, available via The National Archives website. But most of the cases listed are morality, matrimonial cases or tithe disputes.

How Common are Depositions and Allegations?

Considering the incidence of Depositions and Allegations in the parishes of Bowdon and Ashton-on-Mersey, in the seven townships looked at – Altrincham, Bowdon, Dunham Massey, Hale, Timperley, Ashton-on-Mersey and Sale – out of 572 probate documents between 1600 and 1760, there were twenty-seven with Depositions and Allegations. That is one set of depositions and allegations per twenty-one probate documents. Of the just over 23,000 Cheshire Wills dating between 1590 and 1760, 2119 had codicils which might contain Depositions and Allegations – one codicil per eleven probate documents. So, although these types of probate document are not common, they are not that rare. And thank goodness for that because the stories they can tell are fascinating.

What Sort of Cases Came to Court?

When I first started looking at Depositions and Allegations for this article, I thought most disputes would arise from Nuncupative Wills and cases of intestacy (disputes over administrators of the estates of people dying without making a will). However, only seven of the twenty-seven were over Nuncupative Wills and only five over the administration of an intestate's estate. More than half the disputes, fifteen, were over written Wills.

Nuncupative Wills were declared verbally before witnesses and then written down after the death of the testator. The potential for fraud was high. Parliament recognised this and passed the 1678 Statute of Frauds. This required the Nuncupative Will to be made in the testator's own home, during his/her last illness, and to be witnessed by at least three people, who were to arrange to have the words written down within six days, and confirmed within fourteen days at a consistory court. After the 1837 Wills Act a verbal will was only valid if made by a soldier on active service or a seaman or mariner at sea.[2]

Information Contained in Depositions and Allegations

If one of your ancestors was a witness in a probate dispute you will usually discover their age and the parish in which they lived. If you are a little more lucky you will find out what they did for a living. And what they were doing when the deceased made their will or died. For example, in April 1638 Jane Devis and her husband William were walking the fields with a neighbour, Edward Ogden, in early Spring, checking the crops, when Mr Ogden suddenly fell ill and collapsed, and declared his nuncupative will. And the difference in the ages given between Jane and her husband – Jane was sixteen years younger than her husband – makes it very possible that she was a second wife.

Of course, most of all probate disputes give evidence of family feuds and arguments. In 1607, after the death of his brother John, young Hugh Williamson marched into the widow's house and found his brother's boots ready to give to someone. John's widow, Joanna, said he came to her house and

'fyndeinge the same ready and haveing occasion to use the same as she beleeveth did without any leave of this Respondent take awaie the same with him sythence [since] when she never had the same restored againe or satiffacccon for the same.'[3]

His thoughtless actions caused a rift between himself, his other older brothers and the widow, especially over the value of items given to each, and whether they should have been given before an inventory of John Williamson's goods had been made.

Through the Depositions and Allegations to the third will of Maudie Tipping of Dunham Massey in 1613, the Consistory Court at Chester was interested to learn – from many witnesses – that both Robert Massey, a servant in Maudie Tipping's household, and George Moores, kinsman and neighbour to Maudie, had illegitimate children. However, Robert Massey was married and no one named his adulterous girlfriend. But, again, many people could name George Moores' *'love,'* his young maidservant, Mathilda Artenstall, who had screamed out his name to three local midwives as she laboured to give birth to his child. George Moores was a fifty-four year old widower, so two years later he married young Mathilda.

Depositions and Allegations are very good at showing how wills were actually created and how sometimes, probably through ignorance, occasionally through too much haste mistakes were made. For example, Maudie Tipping's will should have been read over to her before she signed it. Which was not done. Why it wasn't done is a matter of conjecture, but it possibly smelt as fishy to the Consistory Court as it does to anyone reading the documents today. And as Maudie commented herself on the matter to her son-in-law William Rowcroft a few days later, *'I cannot tell what they have made'* – *'They'* being her eldest son Robert, his kinsman George Moores and the writer of the will, George Vawdrey the Parish clerk for Bowdon.

Until the late seventeenth century in the greater Altrincham and Sale area of Cheshire, when a sick person wished to write a will a member of the household (servant or young child) was sent running to the nearest neighbour known to be literate. Occasionally the parish clerk was sent for, as in the case of Maudie Tipping. Ralph Wright alias Vergus of Hale had someone dash out for a literate neighbour, Hugh Janney, in 1602.

Someone in the household of Ralph Chorlton of Altrincham in 1634 had the very unofficial 'township clerk' of Hale, John Goulden, sent for.[4] John Goulden was a puritan thorn in the side of Bishop Bridgeman of Chester, so the Consistory Court was more interested that he should have been the one chosen to write Ralph Chorlton's will, especially since Altrincham was out of his area, than in what interested the objectors to the will, namely Ralph Chorlton's state of mind at the time which the objectors implied might have been impaired because of his three-month long illness.

The change in will writing that came at the end of the seventeenth century with the entry of attorneys/lawyers into the business is well-documented in the Depositions and Allegations.

Amongst these attorneys was George Clayton. A descendant of a husbandman family from nearby Sinderland, he seems to have instituted a system whereby a client lodged a proforma will with him. This proforma was produced when the client decided to make a will proper. It was taken to the client's house by one of George Clayton's many young apprentices and amended to take account of the client's new wishes, if any. Then it was taken back to the 'office' and rewritten neatly by another apprentice before being returned to the client for signing/marking and witnessing. This is what happened with the will of William Higginson of Altrincham, butcher, in 1725.

Another attorney, who may have also been one of George Clayton's apprentices at one time, Isaac Worthington, had a different approach. He went in person to the client and discussed the will and the client's wishes with the client. He did not use proforma wills. When John Coppock, a wealthy old tanner of Timperley, wanted to have a new will written, Isaac Worthington jumped onto his horse and out rode out to him. As the lawyer entered the house he was presented with minutes written by the client. He looked these over, and took other notes as the old tanner made clear what he wanted. Worthington then took the minutes and the notes into another room and wrote the will. He took it back into John Coppock's bedchamber and read it over to him. The old tanner wasn't quite satisfied and asked that the words *'over and besides her wages'* referring to a young servant be added. Then John Coppock signed the will in the presence of three witnesses, including the lawyer.

Occasionally Depositions and Allegations provide information on marriage and separation in the early modern period. The Depositions and Allegations to the Will of George Jackson of Sale, yeoman, 1738 illustrate this. The main problem was not the will itself, but how to pay a legacy to a kinswoman, Mary Taylor, without her estranged and separated husband John getting his hands on the money. John and Mary Taylor had been separated for years and he had not paid her maintenance in all that time. If the money, £30, was paid to the skinflint husband (as the law might demand when they were still married, although officially separated) there was a very good chance that Mary wouldn't see a penny of it! The executor, Jeremy Hardy, said he wanted to pay the money to Mary directly, but that there was a problem – the estranged husband demanding the money be paid to him. Whether Mary Taylor got her money in the end isn't known.

As has been previously mentioned, what Depositions and Allegations mostly show is family relationships, and conflict in families. The Depositions and Allegations to Maudie Tipping's third will in 1613 show jealousy between Robert Tipping and his brother John, and their much younger brother-in-law William Rowcroft. Both Robert Tipping and Rowcroft worked for the same master, Sir George Booth of Dunham Massey, Robert as the steward. But William

Rowcroft had just landed a very valuable tenancy, a dairy worth £100 a year on land Sir George had bought at Wilmslow. Robert Tipping wasn't jealous for himself, but for his youngest brother John who thought he was due something too and hadn't got it. Robert must have been very fond of his brother or very jealous of his young brother-in-law to do what he did. To make his elderly, sick mother believe that her only and very loving daughter Alice, who had been her main carer for some years even after her marriage, was dead, when she wasn't. And to tell that lie, straight-faced to most of the village too. The aim was to reduce what Maudie gave to her daughter, by making sure she gave it to her granddaughter Isabella Rowcroft instead. The effect was probably to estrange poor Alice and her family from her brothers.

This particular case also shows the caring love of Alice Rowcroft for her mother, who only went home to Wilmslow when she was exhausted. And the social interactions in the house of an old lady in the seventeenth century. Most of the village seemed to have tramped through Maudie's

bedroom, paying their respects, helping Alice – and probably hoping for a little something in Maudie's will.

When Mary Massey of Sale, eldest daughter of Richard Massey of Sale Hall, esquire, married the man of her dreams, the Reverend Hugh Hobson, curate of Ashton-on-Mersey in 1663, it caused a rift between herself and her father. Not only that, but the whole tale came out in the Consistory Court records because Mary's mother Barbara felt very angry that her great efforts on behalf of her wayward daughter to get her husband to relent and give his eldest daughter any legacy at all were not only unrecognised by Mary herself, but deemed to be not enough.

The story of the marriage at Chester between Mary and Hugh, as told by Mary, was all sweetness and light. Her father approved it and even sent a couple of servants with Mary to the church in Chester, and welcomed the happy couple on their return. (Why, if Richard Massey approved, did Mary and Hugh think it necessary to get a licence and get married thirty miles away from home?)

The story told by Mary's mother and her

maternal uncle, John Gleave of Pulford near Chester, was radically different. They said Richard Massey was 'highly incensed and displeased' that Hugh Hobson was courting Mary. Several times Mary declared that if she didn't marry Hugh 'she would drown or make herself away.' It was a bit melodramatic (like a teenager in a flounce) and said, before witnesses, to her father in order to force him to consent to the marriage. Instead, Richard sent her away to stay with her uncle John Gleave at Pulford near Chester to cure her of this infatuation for the curate.

On her return a few weeks later, Mary seemed cured at first, but then she met Hugh again. Shortly afterwards the pair ran off to Chester to get married, without Richard Massey's consent.

The Consistory Court gave sentence in favour Barbara Massey and John Gleave.

Mary went on to have at least ten years of happy marriage with the Reverend Hobson. Her mother, however, only forgave her after the death of Hugh Hobson, and her will only gave Mary £10. Bequests to other siblings were higher.

When she heard her father's will in 1725, Esther Higginson, daughter of William Higginson of Altrincham, butcher, asked her mother Elizabeth if she 'had been born a bastard; that she came to be omitted out of her father's will.' William Higginson was originally not keen on leaving Esther a legacy, she had argued with him and he considered her an undutiful daughter, and was not speaking to her. Esther was said to be *'at Coventry.'* But his wife persuaded him he should leave Esther a legacy. The will had been amended on the spot by young John Stafford, who scratched out *'three daughters'* and wrote in *'four daughters,'* but not very legibly.

The will was sloppily drafted and the omission of Esther was not the only problem. Mr Higginson had left his clothes to his grandson William, without giving the boy a surname. So two other daughters, Elizabeth Davenport and Jane Broom, joined in objecting to the will. All because a thoughtless eighteen year old apprentice lawyer who knew it all, probably in too much of a hurry to get back to a hectic social life rather than deal properly with the will of a cantankerous old man, couldn't be bothered. We can only hope that Master Stafford learnt a lesson from this.

The case of John Coppock of Timperley, tanner, in 1753 shows a father exasperated with the behaviour of his only surviving adult son William and the paranoia of that son.

John Coppock had written two wills in two years, between 1751 and 1753. He had lost another son, Bryan, curate at Bowdon, in 1748, and he, poor man, was trying to be even handed between his only remaining son, William, and his daughter Jane and her husband James Lowe. There was a change of only £20 extra being given to James Lowe. This was because the responsibility for paying for John Coppock's funeral was now put on his son-in-law. The change was because Mr Coppock didn't trust his son to do things properly.

However, William didn't see it this way. He saw a conspiracy by Jane and James Lowe to get more of his father's large estate into their hands. Why else had he been sent to the local pub on the day his father made his will?

When William brought his case in the Consistory Court, many witnesses gave damning evidence on William's character, his deteriorating relations with his father and what he really did on the day the will was written. William was well-known throughout the parish of Bowdon for the scandal of his *'idle, drunken and disorderly course of life.'* John Coppock, in despair at his son's attitude, had often been heard to threaten to disinherit William. But he didn't. In fact, William's inheritance was very handsome for the time – all his father's land and the tannery. William was only objecting to having to raise £100 as a mortgage on that land to pay his sister and brother-in-law.

As for being sent to the pub on the day the will was made, his father would have preferred him to remain at home. Nevertheless, William took himself off to the pub. He later returned home drunk.

William also tried to claim that his father was suffering from what we now might called dementia, and was incompetent to make a will. Everyone else found the old tanner to be *of 'sound mind and good remembrance.'* The Consistory Court let the will stand and James Lowe execute it.

The case can't have enhanced William Coppock's reputation locally.

I have two sets Depositions and Allegations which give evidence on how credit was obtained. In one case, the will of Robert Newton of Hale, 1734. The will as security against a loan. Robert Newton, then living with his daughter

Alice, wife of George Ashley of Hale, made the will in 1724, but, just before he died in 1728, one of the executors and his son-in-law died. This meant that most of Robert Newton's estate came to his young grandson Robert Ashley. Meanwhile, Robert Newton's daughter Alice remarried William Gandy.

Then young Robert Ashley died and it wasn't clear who should get what from Robert Newton's will. However, Alice and William Gandy thought they should have control over the will and the estate.

But, along came a complication, the result of which was a long paperchase through the offices of various local attorneys in 1734 for the will. The will was seized as collateral by people chasing Alice Gandy's second husband for the debts of her first. At the end of this long case, the Consistory Court decided William Gandy wasn't liable for the debts of George Ashley.

To add to *'where's the will,'* William Gandy, once his wife got the will back the first time, used it, with other papers, as surety for a loan of £40 from Thomas Gandy, his brother. Two lawyers were asked for their opinion of the will as surety. One at least thought it was good security against £40, since it mentioned a lease on a property in Mobberley.

The Consistory Court decided that the main creditor of George Ashley, Robert Frith of Altrincham, could be the executor/administrator of Robert Newton's will (finally found in the hands of Thomas Gandy), not least because two of the remaining executors, sensing trouble, had renounced their executorships. However, the

Consistory Court evened things up by making Mr Frith pay the court costs.

And finally, a tale of unsavoury methods of lending from the end of the seventeenth century. John Jackson of Rostherne makes Shylock look like Mother Theresa of Calcutta.

On a day in early May 1697 John Jackson was accompanying George Aldcroft of Altrincham back to his house. The two had been in Rostherne where fifty-nine year old George Aldcroft had been Jackson's witness in a commission held at the Rams Head, Rostherne (courts, particularly petty sessions courts often met in pubs in the seventeenth and eighteenth century). George Aldcroft was a literate man. He would have called himself an attorney, but really he was little more than a scrivener.

George Aldcroft was one of two witnesses to what was done and said that fateful May afternoon.

John Jackson asked George Aldcroft to ride with him to the pub in Bowdon run by Thomas Jones on the main road from Chester to Altrincham to drink a glass of ale. When Jackson and Aldcroft were sat down in one of the pub's rooms, each with a glass of ale in his hand, a man came in, Thomas Warburton of Bowdon, wheelwright. He had buried his wife Mary less than a fortnight before and was still in a very distressed state – not all of it grief. He saw John Jackson and approached him.

Warburton had just discovered his late wife owed money for malt to two Altrincham men, John Parker and Henry Smith. They threatened him. The wheelwright told Jackson Warburton had borrowed money from Jackson before. Now he needed £17. The Rostherne man havered slightly, claiming he didn't have the money. Then he relented and agreed to lend the wheelwright £29 17s 10d.

John Jackson took Thomas Warburton off to Altrincham to get the bond drawn up and signed. George Aldcroft left the party at this point. The next witness, Francis Newton of Altrincham, schoolmaster, appeared once the couple were ensconced in John Clayton's inn in Altrincham. John Jackson had sent for the schoolmaster to write and witness the document. Jackson admitted to Mr Newton that Warburton really only owed him about £6, but he wanted the wheelwright to put his mark on a warrant of attorney for £50, £50 which he, John Jackson, owed to others.

Jackson plied Thomas Warburton with drink and assurances. Warburton put his mark at the warrant.

Jackson tucked the warrant inside his coat, took up his glass of ale and raised it to Mr Newton. 'Now I have tricked him and done my business,' Jackson whispered to Newton. The wheelwright overheard. 'I hope you will not take further

advantage of me, Master Jackson,' he asked. 'What you have done should not anywise prejudice you,' answered Master Jackson. 'If you would tomorrow or at any time after pay me the £5, with lawful interest, I would accept it. And there is no more due to me,' Jackson lied. Thomas Warburton accepted Jackson's words and went home, satisfied. The wheelwright fell ill and he died eleven days later on 18 May 1696.

John Jackson then took over Thomas Warburton's estate. To give the man his due, he did arrange for a coffin and a wake, because Warburton's son Aldcroft was too ill to bury his father. He began selling up the wheelwright's estate to pay himself and other debts such as for the nursing of Thomas Warburton and his wife, and the horse doctor's bill for the grey mare. And he did pay for the upkeep of Aldcroft and his two sisters.

However, Aldcroft Warburton began to question what Jackson was doing and he asked for the accounts to be audited. There were many discrepancies between the amounts paid for items and the amounts entered in the accounts. But by the time the case came to court two years later John Jackson was dead.

John Jackson's actions were questionable at the time, but since he was dead the court could do no more than apply the law as it was then. And the wheelwright's children lost out.

Conclusion

As you can see from this article, most of human life can be found in the Depositions and Allegations. They are worth wading through the bad handwriting – and even worse Latin in the seventeenth century ones. They show how people in a community interacted with each other. They throw up all kinds of details of life. And, just occasionally, they record what people actually said to each other.

There are many more stories I have not been able to tell, such as the double-dealing curate, who managed to raise two lots of mortgages on one property.

So take a look at the Depositions and Allegations for the area where your ancestors lived, and see what details of local life they can tell you.

Notes

[1]. John Addy in the introduction to the *Diary of Henry Prescott, Deputy Registrar of the Diocese of Chester*, Vol.1, Record Society of Lancashire and Cheshire.
[2]. *Sin, Sex and Probate: Ecclesiastical Courts, Officials and Records* by Colin R. Chapman ISBN 978-1873686157
[3]. Depositions and Allegations to the Letters of Administration of John Williamson of Bowdon, 1607.
[4]. I have called him and his uncle, another John Goulden, the *'unofficial'* township clerks of Hale, because a) they were not approved of by the diocese of Chester because of their very puritan views, b) they wrote nearly all the wills for the people of Hale between 1610 and 1660, when John Goulden junior died.

The Pentrich Uprising
Ann Bogue

When my mum died, in 2001, she left my brother John and me some of her family's birth certificates, including hers, her parents and her siblings. There was also some interesting information about her grandparents and an old family bible, which I remembered seeing at her parents' house when I was a child. These items, from the Wheeler and Clayton sides of my family ancestry took second place to the general turmoil, disruption and necessary grieving process that dominated family life for a while. Bible, other family icons and paperwork were carefully wrapped, boxed and stored away in the under drawer.

It would be 4 or more years before they were to see the light of day again. A short break for a cuppa, during springcleaning, was to turn into a need to trace my roots as I browsed through the paperwork from the rediscovered cardboard box. Sipping coffee and nibbling a biscuit, I read and I wondered; who, what, when, where, why . . . oh, and how?

I immediately began tracing my mother's forebears, the Wheeler and Clayton sides of my family, until my curiosity had been partially satisfied. I did not appreciate at the time, how addicted I would eventually become with my family history. It would be a further 4 years before, during a conversation with my cousin Rich (from my father's side of the family); I mentioned that I was considering investigating our grandma's genealogy. We already knew that grandad was at least fifth generation farrier and blacksmith, and local. He informed me that his father, my uncle Fred, had kept many of the certificates relating to our fathers' family. These were Booth and Fletcher (grandma's maiden name). As soon as I saw them, I was at it again.

Our grandma, Mary Alice Fletcher, was born, according to her birth certificate, on the 30th of December 1879, and her father was deceased. She married Joseph Booth in December 1904, and died on Good Friday 1958.

I contacted our cousin Brenda, in Australia, who had been researching our ancestry for about 10 years, her information was the same as mine. Great grandfather William had died, according to family lore, in a mining accident just prior to grandma's birth. The 1881 census shows her living with her mother and 4 siblings, and confirmed that William had died. The 1891 census however, informed me that her mother had remarried, and that she had 3 more siblings

We found a record of William's marriage (10th of July 1870), in Wombwell, near Barnsley. He was a bachelor and miner, aged 25, and his father was

Vincent Fletcher. That name should have made things relatively easy, shouldn't it? William was born around 1845, if the certificate was to be believed. The 1851 census showed him living with father Vincent, mother Eliza and siblings Alice, Joseph and Thomas. It did not help though, as he had been recorded as Vencent Hitchin. By 1861, William was boarding with the family of James and Tryphena Street, and he was a miner. We could find no record of his birth anywhere, so we sent for a copy of his death certificate. He had died on the 24th of November 1879, aged 34, from Tubercular Peritonitis, his brother Joseph, a pit deputy, present.... No mining accident then!

Brenda and I then decided to send for a birth certificate for his brother Joseph, who was a couple of years younger than William. The certificate informed us that their father was Vincent, but his mother was Mary Turner. No wonder that William's birth was hard to find. We were aware, from the 1851 census, that he was in the Alfreton area of Derbyshire, and after a few intensive hours in the Matlock archive I eventually found him in the Parish records.

Vincent Fletcher had married Mary Turner on the 12th of January 1845. Coincidentally, William Fletcher had been baptized on the very same day in Alfreton.

Next stop was Mary's death, sadly, she had died, aged 25 on the 18th of August 1849 in Swanwick, Derbyshire, but we knew from her marriage certificate, that her father was Thomas Turner, a labourer. We also discovered that Vincent had died aged 33 on the 5th of February 1852 in Swanwick. Poor William! He had no mother or father, and at the age of 16 he was lodging with a family by the name of Street.

We were stuck again, until Cousin Brenda experienced a 'light bulb' moment and decided to investigate the Street family, where she found a marriage between James Street and Tryphena Turner in North Wingfield on the 26th of August 1849. Tryphena's birthplace was recorded as South Wingfield. This information led us to Thomas and Martha Turner. They had 6 daughters, including Mary and Tryphena, and an illegitimate son by the name of William Taylor. William Turner led us to Thomas Turner's marriage, on the 14th of March 1820, to Martha Taylor.

A sortie into *Genes Reunited* led me to a lady by the name of Frances Bedford. At last Lady Luck was with me, I contacted Frances to see if we had relatives in common, and she allowed me access to her family tree, which included deaths in Derby Gaol and transportation to Australia. Frances, in turn, encouraged me to contact a lady by the name of Sylvia Mason, who was also very helpful by telling me about The Pentrich Riots of 1817.

Once again I was in Matlock, double checking the information that I had been given, and we found Thomas Turner's father, Samuel, born in 1757 and his grandfather, William, born 1720. This William Turner had been married twice, having 3 children including John, Alice and Samuel with his first wife and then 6 more children with his second wife, William, Robert, Betty, Salathiel, Joseph and George.

Samuel's brother John had 10 children, including William who was born in 1771, John who was born in 1783 and Edward born 1785.

John (1783) had a son Joseph, who was born in Manchester in 1798, hence the name Joseph 'Manchester' Turner. Joseph had marched as one of the peaceful protesters who became known as the Manchester Blanketeers, in March 1817. A later open air meeting of Manchester people in 1819, at St Peters Fields, ended in bloodshed when they were charged by the yeomanry and hussars. This incident became known as the Peterloo massacre, with 500 injured and 11 dead.

Martha Turner's parents were Benjamin Massey Taylor and Mally Ludlam. Mally Ludlam was one of 10 children that included a brother Isaac who was born in 1765.

The Turners and the Ludlams were destined to play a significant part in the Pentrich Riots of 1817. The riots were so called because the men of the Derbyshire village of Pentrich formed themselves into an armed force and marched towards Nottingham. They expected to be part of a national uprising aimed at overthrowing the government. The reason for this unrest was anger and despair with the lack of work and food after the Napoleonic War together with the enactment of the Corn Laws in 1815.

Along with Jeremiah Brandreth (aka Jeremiah Coke), some members of each family were fated to be found guilty of High Treason for their involvement, by a government intent on quelling the unrest throughout the country.

Cousin Rich visited Huddersfield Library to see Mr Simon Craddock in the reference section, and returned with a memory stick that contained a complete transcript of the trial. The publication, The trials of Jeremiah Brandreth, William Turner, Isaac Ludlam, George Weightman and others, for High Treason.

As Brandreth, a late substitute for a man by the name of Wain, who was considered to be too ill to participate in the uprising, was in the dock, Thomas Turner, giving evidence, stated that he was present at his father's house on the evening of the 9th of June 1817. At a little before nine in the evening; He, Samuel Ludlam and John Walker went to opposite the meeting house, very near to Colonel Halton's gates. (It would appear that he was a willing participant then, not one of the marchers who had been forced to join). It was while standing there that he first saw a stranger who was referred to as the Nottingham captain, it was Brandreth. He was standing with George Weightman and William Turner. They all had guns.

The group of men assembled there, were formed into ranks and set off to march to Nottingham, commanded by William Turner and Brandreth. Thomas carried a bag of bullets, which he said he preferred, rather than carrying a pike as some others did. It was while a group of them were at Hunts Barn that a servant of Widow Hepworth was shot and killed by Jeremiah Brandreth, for refusing to open the door.

Thomas said 'You shouldn't have shot a poor innocent man.' Brandreth replied 'It was my duty, and if you say anything more about it, I will blow your brains out.'

When asked if William Turner was present at the time of the shooting, Thomas replied 'I do not believe that he was there at the time.'

The men marched through the night, in very bad weather, trying to enlist support on the way. They had been promised meals, ale, and a substantial sum of money. On the way they stopped frequently, taking alcohol and promising to pay after the government had been overthrown. They unsuccessfully tried to get support, cannon and ammunition from the

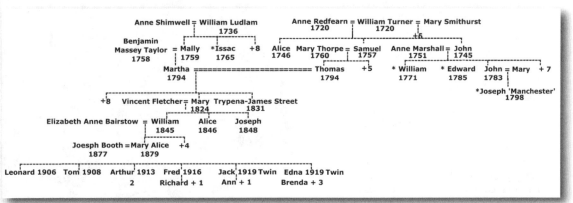

Butterley Ironworks.

Brandreth had assured the several hundred men assembled at Pentrich & Ripley that they would find mass support as they marched the 14 miles to Nottingham. Support would be coming from Birmingham 150,000 men, from Derby, Nottingham and Leicester 30,000, Leeds 10,000, Sheffield 10,000and Barnsley 5,000.

At one point, George Weightman rode off on a pony, borrowed from a Mr Booth (ironic eh?), towards Nottingham to check on the progress of the other supporters of the uprising. It is suggested that he did not actually go all the way there, but that he had probably been intercepted by a government agent, who misled him into believing that all was going to plan, and that the army would stay in their barracks.

As we now know there was no extra support, and in the heavy rain they were easily dispersed by the hussars between 2.00 and 3.00 am on the morning of June 10th.

Thomas later states in his evidence that he was carrying a pike as the group arrived at a point around two or three miles beyond Eastwood (they had travelled 10 miles as the crow flies, by my reckoning), where he discarded his weapon and made his escape, noting many pikes that had been discarded by others who had managed to leave the group before him.

Of the 170 or so men who marched on that fateful night, 3 were hanged and beheaded, 12 were transported to Australia for life, 3 transported for 14 years, 6 jailed for between 6 months and 2 years, 23 charged but not tried, 23 apprehended and released, the rest were not apprehended.

On the 24th of October, William Turner petitioned for leniency to HRH Frederick, Duke of York, on the strength of his exemplary service after enlisting into the Derby Militia in 1797, and later volunteering into the 20th Regiment of Foot. He had served in Holland and then in Egypt from 1799 until the termination of hostilities. He also claimed that he supported his aged father & mother. The sentences on him, Brandreth, Ludlam and Weightman were subsequently reduced from Hanging, Drawing and Quartering, to Hanging and Beheading.

Edward Turner and 'Manchester' Turner had their death sentences commuted to Transportation to Australia for life. Those who were transported travelled aboard the ships Isabella, which took around 5 months and 2 weeks, and Tottenham, 10 months, due to bad weather and storm damage. Their Tickets of Leave give us an image of height and colouring, 'Manchester' having a pearl in one eye. Their entry papers, pardons and the Australian musters, copies of which were obtained by

our cousin Brenda, tell us that both Turners did very well in their new life, and ended up with property and new families.

On Edward's Australian marriage entry (he already had a wife and children in England), his marital status is shown as 'Not Stated.'

6th November 1817 – Execution Day
(according to the Pentrich Historical Society)

10.30 Prisoners went to chapel, Brandreth had slept well and seemed totally unaffected by what was to happen, Turner and Ludlam had spent the night praying and singing psalms. They looked like *'walking spectres.'*

11.30 All other prisoners left the chapel.

12.00 Mr Simpson. The Under Sheriff and some javelin men and special constables appeared. Brandreth and George Weightman had their irons removed, Turner and Ludlam were still praying. Their chains were removed shortly afterwards.

12.15 The 'Hurdle' was drawn up at the door, turned flat side down and the horse attached. Brandreth tumbled himself onto it. At this point Weightman was informed that his penalty had been respited for one week. It was eventually commuted to 25 years transportation. Brandreth passed from the hurdle into the passage of the prison, soon to be joined by Turner, whom he took by the hand; they kissed each other as Ludlam was being drawn on the hurdle.

Mr Pickering, the Chaplain of Derby County Jail,

and Brandreth passed up the ladder, preceded by the executioner and his assistant. The noose was too high for Brandreth and had to be adjusted, and then secured round his neck.

Turner ascended the ladder, faltered before calling out *'This is all Oliver and the Government, the Lord have mercy on my soul,'* then the rope was placed over his neck.

Ludlam ascended the ladder and spoke, *'Oh Lord forgive my sins, and receive my soul . . .'*

Executioners put the caps on their heads and pulled them over their faces.

12.45 The drop.

1.15 The bodies were cut down.

Brandreth was laid on the block and beheaded, followed by Turner, then Ludlam.

Their bodies were later interred in St Werburgh's Churchyard, Derby.

During the aftermath, properties belonging to those found guilty were destroyed, the families dispersed and their land redistributed.

William Turner's denouncement on the gallows of *'Oliver'* and the Government was instrumental in causing a change of attitude by the government, probably brought about by a huge public reaction to the punishments meted out. *'Oliver'* was William Oliver who had been recruited as a Home Office spy whilst in the *Fleet Prison* for debt. It was because of his actions that the Pentrich men were arrested by the army.

These were the last people sentenced to Hanging, Drawing and Quartering in England.

An item in the Derbyshire Courier dated 27th April 1839 records a Coroner's Inquest verdict on the body of Thomas Turner, our great great great grandfather. The deceased was at work in a limestone quarry, when a quantity of earth fell upon him and so severely crushed him as to cause death. The verdict was returned as Accidental death.

Footnote

1817 was not the best time to be one of the less well off in England; they had few friends in Parliament. There were no representatives for places such as Leeds or Manchester, whereas Cornwall had 44. At this time some MP's represented what would later be referred to as Rotten Boroughs (there weren't any houses in Old Sarum, Wiltshire , and much of Old Dulwich in Suffolk was in the North Sea), or Pocket Boroughs (these were owned by wealthy landowners who could evict tenants if they did not vote in line with their landlord's wishes). An attempt by Sir Francis Burdett to reform the commons had already been defeated by 265 votes to 77.

'The Great Reform Act of 1832' introduced by the Whigs, after around 47 years of practically successive Tory governments (the only break being Lord Grenville's Whigs 1806-07), would eventually change the situation. Landowners would no longer have the right to nominate, or suggest MP's, and almost ½ million new voters were enfranchised, townspeople occupying property worth at least £10 a year.

The Industrial Revolution was gathering momentum, and the urban population was growing. Meetings of over 50 people had been banned by the government. People were also being held without trial, Habeas Corpus having been suspended. Spies were being sent out all over the country to infiltrate the population, and William J Richards (masquerading as Oliver, plus various other aliases), was obviously one of these. He was later to be exposed as an *'Agent Provocateur'* because of his participation in the uprising, rather than merely observing and reporting what was happening.

Robert Banks Jenkinson 2nd Earl Liverpool, the Tory PM 1812-1827, had been in Paris at the age of 19 and had witnessed the storming of the Bastille on the 14th of July 1789. Obviously he and his advisors had worked on a strategy to ensure that nothing similar would be allowed to happen in England. His tactics would appear to be entrapment by Oliver and subsequent trials for High Treason.

The years of the later 18th and early 19th Century were not a happy time for the planet in general. There was much volcanic activity; a large eruption in Iceland, followed later by a massive one in Indonesia, Mount Tambora in 1816 (4 times more destructive than the well known Krakatoa), global weather patterns were disrupted by the ash that was projected into the atmosphere and millions of people around the world died of starvation. In England 1816 was known as the year without a summer. Crops either didn't grow or ripen and many were ploughed back into the soil.

Getting to Know the Constables
A survey of some sources for police ancestors
Stephen Wade

Searching for police records in the hope of finding details of the life and career of an ancestor can be a frustrating business: records can be fragmentary and many have been lose forever. But the records are more diverse than might be thought. In this article, I am reporting on an investigation into some fascinating sources with regard to the Hull City Police, Lincolnshire Constabulary, and other smaller forces at the end of the nineteenth century.

Superannuation Records

These two records exemplify the range of materials open to the family historian looking for a police ancestor: minute books are minimal, giving names and short lists of payments made by various councils, vestries and other organisations, whereas superannuation records may often be voluminous. But with minute books there may be surprises, as other writers on this subject have commented, there tend to be packs of miscellaneous papers attached to minute book records.

In Quarter Session minute books, for instance, there may often be accounts of events by Chief Constables who wrote quarterly reports. There may be pay sheets also. But often the bare record gives a name and a reason for payments given, such as extra duties or special duties.

On the other hand, superannuation records are usually substantial, and they provide the researcher with the opportunity to locate quite detailed information about a constable, including of course length of service, also a career summary, and in the cases of early retirement due to ill health, even more information on the person in question. Basic details, as in this extract, from the Hull Police of superannuation based on medical grounds, provides a basis for further work:

Hull Policemen Receiving Superannuation on Medical Grounds 1851-1866

Policeman	Date pension Given	Employment status
Supt. McManus	May 1851	Died in post Apr. 1866
PC Cox	Nov. 1851	Retired on medical grounds

Much more may be gleaned when the medical records and statements or requests for payments are studied. County archives will in most cases have these. Here are some examples from the East Riding Archives based on papers from the East Riding Constabulary superannuation records.

First, a general one-off payment:
Aug. 17 1859 'As required by 19 and 20 Vic. I certify that Police Sergeant William Ford burst a Blood vessel in the execution of his duty on the night of 5 June past. I recommend him for a gratuity of 6 months pay from the superannuation funds.'
This is a request giving career length of service:
'Superintendent Joseph Young is totally unfit for duty. Vide medical certificate C and D.

'Superintendent J D Wright has served 37 years. 3 years in Newcastle, 13 as a rural policeman and 21 years as superintendent with the present organisation.

Similarly, George Cordukes's career was:

'39 years as a P.C. – 10 years in the Leeds Borough Police; 6 years as a superintendent with the West Riding Constabulary and

He has been a P.C. for 20 and 4/12 years, has served 10 years as a superintendent in this Riding and 14and 9/12 have been in the present organisation.'

Note: this item has one of those extra details which add character profiles, as the surgeon has added to the medical certificate: '*I may add that he has been under me since 12 July and it was in direct opposition to my wishes that he attended the Assize at York.*'

Then, some accounts give information regarding the areas covered by individuals within a specific constabulary, as in this medical certificate:

At the general quarter session of the peace, 19th day of October, 1873, before the chairman and justices:

Motion: *That there is a recommendation to the Chief Constable that*

A pension be granted to Superintendent Wilkinson who is incapable from infirmity of body to perform the duties of his office.

And that a Sergeant or Inspector be appointed to the new lock-up at St. John's Wood and also that an additional constable be appointed to the police station at Dairycotes....

By the court,

GEO. LEEMAN *Clerk of the Peace.*

Finally, some superannuation requests contain a more exact career summary of an officer, such as this:

20 years with the present organisation.'

It may be seen from this that pension and superannuation payments, from ex gratia to proportional retirement pay, provide considerable biographical depth of material.

Personnel and Discipline Books

In county archives, personnel books will be in the form of such items as 'Record book of appointments' or '*officer's journal.*' At times these could be itemised as such things as 'abstracts of pay (with dates) for particular areas or divisions. These are merely lists of names, of course, but again, they provide a starting-point for more research.

But sometimes, as in the case of the Croydon Police records. (see **Box below**)

Far more informative are discipline books. A typical example is this extract from a discipline book of the Borough of Liverpool Police for 1838, relating to severe criticism expressed by a Commission reporting in line with the 1835 Municipal Reform Act. Between 1 January and 31 December, 1838, there were 185 officers on charges of being drunk on duty and 694 for being absent from beats.

Here are some extracts from the Watch Committee records for June, 1838:

Extract from '*Service Given to Croydon Police 1829-1840*' from research by Doris Hobbs (see bibliography):

Name	Enrolled	Resigned	Reason		Other information
Richard Coleman	24.10.29	24.10.38		persistent drunkenness	Sergeant, Formerly Bow Street Patrol
John White		12.9.29	11.4.31	neglect of duty	None
William Rochford	11.3.35	6.1.36		Not offered place on permanent strength	Formerly Met.
William Wood	4.1.37	11.1.37		Employed one week during Lewis's suspension	labourer.

2/6/1838
Resolved:

> That John Edwards, No.65, be fined one shilling for being drunk coming out of a public house when off duty at 12 o'clock on Friday night.

4/6/1838
Ditto

> That John Harper, No. 338, be fined one shilling for appearing for Duty without his greatcoat.

4/6/1838
Ditto

> That William Byrne, No 217, be fined one shilling for being asleep in a stable at 20 minutes past 2 o'clock on Sunday evening

Similarly, but with more wide-ranging material, the Police Orders, instituted from the beginning in the Metropolitan Police, have listings of such things as dismissals, as in these from 1862:

Dismissals.

P C Turner;

drunk on duty, losing his truncheon and three keys belonging to premises; and complained of by two civilians for assaulting them with his rattle; pay to 16th.

Reduction

P C 404, Hammett;

making use of an improper remark as the relief was marching for duty; pay as first class to 17th.

Fines

P C 315 Burnham;

admonished for not reporting his having the purse at once. The money returned by the P C proves to be the whole amount lost.

Occurrence Books

These were sometimes referred to as incident books or even station diaries. These books were always placed in the stations and were used to record all happenings of any note, from trivial to very important. Routine duties were also included. From an anonymous writer who served in the 1850's:

> 'The ordinary police duty at this time was performed as follows: the night duty was from 10 p.m. to 6 a.m.; the second from 9 a.m. to 3 p.m. at which time the first relief came in again until 10 ... Frequently in the London season the relief which came off at 9 a.m. had to turn out to attend on her Majesty and Prince Albert when these royal personages arrived or departed from a railway station.'

This kind of explanation of the normal work and the special duties covers the spectrum of events recorded. These listings in the occurrence books note arrivals, charged or not, and officers who are involved, they give names and ranks, and also help to compile a fuller profile of individual constables.

A similar document was a day book, and there is a perfect example of this from 1845-1846, written by P C Jones of the Denbighshire Constabulary, researched by Dr F. Clements (see bibliography). Jones includes the kind of thing normally in routine occurrence books, such as,

December 1845

I left at 7 a.m. for Burras, 12 p.m.
On duty at residence 6 a.m. and went round the public houses, 12 p.m.

He then includes fuller details when there is an actual event, such as:

> 'On duty at Burras and Wrexham fair ... put a man in bridewell June 17th
> Got the man remanded till the next day. He was remanded till the next day.
> He was discharged, no proof against him for stealing a dog ...'

Order Books

Order Books can provide a wealth of detail about an officer and are indeed a particularly exciting prospect when they provide details of a career and also personal qualities. For instance, the record in this respect for the Lincolnshire Constabulary provides a profile of Sergeant John

Dawson. In the section for appointments, promotions and reductions, we learn that Dawson was appointed in January, 1857 as a constable; in 1864 he was promoted to sergeant and in April 1866 he was sergeant *'extra class.'* There is a description of him, noting that he was a native of the village of Welton; he was five feet six and a half feet tall, eyes grey, body 'stout' and complexion 'fresh' In religion he was a 'churchman' and was married with five children. Dawson had previously been in the army, serving in the 60th Rifles and the Royal 9th Lincs Militia. Sergeant Dawson was discharged in December, 1873 with a pension of £36 8.0 per annum and he died on May 16, 1884.

Charge Books

Interestingly, calendars of prisoners add a little narrative to the charge book. If a line in a calendar says, *'John Clay Oct 13. for stealing one cotton shirt, the property of Matthew Sharman'* we have the next stage from the charge book, which records the constable's name, the alleged offence and the potential offender. A charge book basically records the details at the station of these basic facts, and how the prisoner was disposed of.

A typical charge book will be a huge and heavy folio volume with these headings across two pages:

Date/ name/ occupation/ charge/ arresting officer/ custody record/ magistrate/ sentence and other notes. So in these records we have simply the name of the officer involved, as in this detail from 1861:

William Wass, shoemaker, was arrested by P C 47, Henry Booth, for an assault on a constable in the execution of his duty.

And in 1862 William Wilkinson stole a heifer and was arrested by Superintendent Horsley. He was given six months in Louth gaol.

The charge books give an enlightening account of the range and nature of all levels of crime, and they also testify to the high number of assaults on police. Occasionally an officer is involved in more serious crime as in the case of Emma Taylor in 1861 who was charged with feloniously killing Ann Gray in the parish of Nickenby. She was arrested by a superintendent (no name) but was discharged at the Assizes.

Though it may be piecemeal, assembling these various records, offers the possibility of building a fuller picture of a police officer to the researcher. As with all historical study, the secret is a workable mix of patience and persistence.

Bibliography:
Thanks to Ian Mason, archivist at the East Yorkshire Archives, Beverley.
See these monographs also:
Dr F Clements *'Policing in Denbighshire 1800-1850'* Journal of the Police History Society no. 22 (2007 pp. 21-24
Doris Hobbs *'The Croyden Police 1829-1840'* Journal of the Police History Society (1987) pp. 66-79

Wipe the Slate Clean
Kath Jones

More than 500 million years ago the slate deposits around Britain were formed by volcanic action and environmental disturbances. The mountains that were created formed the mountainous terrain which provided the country with the mineral wealth which helped build the modern nation of the country, it has also played a large part in the social structure of our society adding to the physical appearance that the country has inherited today. Our slate mining ancestors did a fantastic job, working in such a dangerous occupation, distributing their products around the world making some investors very wealthy whilst at the same time making others penniless.

History of the Slate Industry . . .

Slate has been an important product in Wales from as far back as the Roman times. The industry developed slowly during the early part of the 18th century but grew rapidly until the late 19th century. It was at the beginning of the Industrial Revolution that demands for the product increased when the usefulness of this natural building material was realised.

Wales was one of the largest and most significant slate producing areas. The two largest slate quarries were Penrhyn and Dinorwig and the largest slate mine was the Oakeley mine at Blaenau Ffestiniog. Most slate was used for roofing but thicker slabs are cut to be used as flooring, worktops and headstones.

Roofing slates from local Welsh quarries not only became popular all over Britain but also in countries throughout Europe and North America. Villages throughout Wales were transformed into busy industrial towns and tiny harbours became bustling ports as the slate industry flourished and the products were shipped abroad. This rapid growth brought work for thousands of men in and around the local communities and by the latter quarter of the 19th century, the Dinorwig Quarry in North Wales was the largest in the world.

The Daily Working Conditions . . .

The working conditions of the quarrymen across Wales were unforgiving. Before the introduction of regular transport the men would face a long journey on foot carrying their food rations for the week. This was due to the fact they had to travel so far to the mines and meant they could only return home to their families on a Saturday afternoon until Monday morning. Some would walk at least ten miles or more and then would *still* have to catch the quarry train to their place of employment.

Many miners lived and worked like this for up to fifty years of their lives and the daily toil of hard work showed on their faces.

Each worker had to complete a five year apprenticeship before he could class himself as a qualified quarryman and even though the work was skilled, it was undoubtedly an unhealthy, dirty and dangerous job. Even in the Dressing Shed where slate was shaped they couldn't get away from the hazards of slate dust.

At the tender age of ten, many of the worker's sons would serve a premature apprenticeship where they would deliver blunt tools by cart from the quarry to the blacksmith's shop for sharpening. They would then improve their skills by learning how to split and chip the slate and later move on to become journeymen or a *jermon* by chipping the slates of a regular quarryman. Although this initial apprenticeship was compulsory, no written qualification was received.

Quarrying . . .

Slate was blasted from the rock face by using *gunpowder* as an explosive. Dynamite or gelignite would have been too intense and would shatter the slate, so they were only used to remove the surrounding rock and rubble to expose the slate vein. A special Powder House was used to store the gunpowder and strict rules were put in place so that if anyone should enter this store they had to wear copper soled clogs to reduce the danger of creating a spark which would ignite the explosive. Once the worker had obtained the correct amount of gunpowder and put it in a cloth or rubber powder bag, it was carried to the quarry ready to create the blast – yet another day to day hazard of their work.

Some of the jobs were equally as tough and especially for the rock men who had the added danger of working with the explosive - gunpowder - during quarry blasting. Their role involved being suspended from ropes over the side of the rock face where they would use hammers and chisels to chip away at each terrace of slate. They were expected to work in all conditions from the summer when the sun reflected back at them from the surface of the rock to the winter months

when rainfall made the slate slippery to stand on.

The slate was first extracted in large blocks then needed to be reduced in size using a mallet and chisel to cut *across* the grain – this part of the process was later replaced by sawing. Each worker would then have a manageable portion to work with and by splitting the slate *down* the grain, an experienced worker - using an anvil and a knife known as a whittle - could obtain four roof slates from a piece approximately one inch thick. At the end of the day these were carried outside and piled in the Stacking Plot, counted in threes and graded by size and thickness.

The Chief Engineer was responsible for all aspects of engineering work which took place within the quarry and was ultimately accountable for supervising all the staff and much of the work's correspondence.

Quarry Workshops . . .

All the machinery in the quarry had to be maintained to a high standard so the Foundry played an important role in the whole operation. The slate sawing equipment, wagons, trucks, steam engines and the vast amount of railway lines – usually made of cast iron - all had to have new components due to the heavy duty workload they endured so it was essential that the quarry made their own substitutes in the foundry.

A Huge Success . . .

The quarry owners invested their money in ensuring that there were enough roads and railways to connect their quarries to the ports for export. At first, the slate would have been carried in panniers on horseback and in wagons but transporting the slate began to get more expensive to transfer than it did to produce it. At Dinorwig in particular, the Padarn Steam Railway was built which would convey the slate to the port where it was loaded onto sailing ships and transported around the world.

As Time Evolved . . .

As slate quarrying became a thriving industry it was necessary to improve techniques to speed up slate production. Steam power was introduced in 1807 at Hafodlas Quarry to keep the works free of water but it took a number of years before this method was fully accepted. Water wheels were the main source of power in many areas although it was not unusual to sometimes see a windmill used to provide the energy to drive the

equipment. Quite often a network of dams were built to supply the water wheels with the water, sometimes this was carried for long distances in wooden or slate lined leats. At the quarry there were sometimes two or more wheels in tandem - the water from the first going on to power the second etc.

It was during the 1850's at the Llechwedd Slate Caverns in Blaenau Ffestiniog, John W. Greaves designed his own sawing table using waterpower to help split the slate into manageable pieces and also a slate dressing machine which enabled the workers to trim the slate for use as roof tiles. His improved equipment considerably aided the output of the quarries.

Candles were the main source of lighting during this time but it was Llechwedd who first installed electricity in 1890 at the insistence of quarry manager, Warren Roberts. The dynamoes were driven using waterpower and the effect was so significant that other quarries saw the benefits and followed in their footsteps improving conditions no end.

It is difficult to imagine the lives and hardships that these men endured on a daily basis. Many jobs were completed by hand without the aid of machinery, in a severe environment, often risking their lives to help add to the coffers of the already wealthy quarry owners. Their skills literally helped to shape the face of Wales, making their mark on the countryside as they chiselled out the slate which would ultimately roof the houses of properties around the world.

Today, we can remember these craftsmen and labourers at institutions like the National Slate Museum and Llechwedd which, with the aid of exhibitions, displays and demonstrations help us to get a feel for what life as a Welsh quarryman was like.

The owners of the quarries made vast amounts of money from their slate quarrying interests, none more so than the owners of Penrhyn Quarry at Bethesda in North Wales – the Pennants. Their wealth combined with profits made from Jamaican sugar enabled them to build the impressive family home of Penrhyn Castle, a far cry from the living conditions of their poorly paid workers.

Living Conditions ...

Accommodation was provided by the quarry owner in the form of barracks which were usually situated on the hillside. Many of the barracks were damp, cold and miserable places to spend their week but often the quarry was too remote to make daily travel realistic possibility. The living quarters didn't have the comfort of their own homes but *included* a living room and bedroom. They were sparsely equipped with furniture made by the men's own hands – sacking ripped up to act as rugs, beds separated by slate slabs, dense brown paper was used to blackout the windows and old newspapers were used as tablecloths.

No electricity was installed in the barracks so their only means of light would be a paraffin lamp or candle. There was no running water only the use of a nearby freshwater brook or a standpipe which would be used for cooking and washing.

Each barrack could house four people – two adults and two youngsters – often these were members of the same family. Every one would have their own responsibilities – fetching water, bucketing coal or cooking.

The quarrymen's work attire

was corduroy trousers, a flannel shirt and hob nailed boots topped off with a flat cap. Their dress was about as distinctive as their food which would be cooked on the open fire and all the pans and kettles were left blackened with thick soot and smoke.

Their diet consisted mainly of stew, together with bread and butter washed down by strong tea drunk out of tin mugs or jam jars – not what most workers today would expect from the life of a quarryman. These workers stayed sane by amusing themselves with card games, ludo, domino's, draught's, newspapers or magazines. The barracks did however turn into great social institutions helping to develop the men's social skills and where they would have debates about politics and religion. Each barrack housed a Bible and some evenings the men would visit one of the local churches. However, some slate miners lived a more comfortable life in quarry cottages which were very basic but at least had the comfort of a lounge, kitchen, and a bedroom and where some were lucky enough to have their families living with them too.

Sombre Salary ...

The average wage of a quarryman in 1845 was the equivalent of 75p per week now. Out of this they were expected to pay rent, feed and cloth their families and themselves, buy household goods and candles and purchase their own equipment for work such as ropes, fuses and gunpowder. Some quarries but not all provided corn free of charge for their workers and it was not surprising that the number of ships leaving Welsh ports for America increased during this time as people left in search of better lives.

Twenty five years later, the demand for slate had risen considerably and thankfully, for the quarrymen, so did their wages reaching the equivalent of 27p per day helping to make their lives slightly more bearable.

For many of those living in Wales during the late 19th Century, working at Llechwedd not only provided a wage, but it created a vibrant society full of political debate, poetry, song and a stronghold for the Welsh language.

A Specialist Service . . .

Some quarries had their own hospitals and a fine example of a quarry hospital still exists at the Dinorwig Quarry, erected to deal with the inevitable casualties who could be injured in such dangerous surroundings. The most common accidents would be due to a sudden rock fall injuring the workers or their own ropes becoming over used and breaking.

At Dinorwig, the hospital was run by volunteer quarrymen who were St John's Ambulance trained. They received no extra pay for the service they provided. One of the site medics was a Dr Mills Roberts who – with the help of the workshop smithy - is reported to have helped create two metal arms for a quarryman who lost both of his arms in an accident.

Medical advice was administered in an attempt to prolong the workers lives from the threat of silicosis and tuberculosis. Hazards in the quarry together with overcrowded housing and poor diet provided the men and their families with inferior health. Their families suffered from tuberculosis and the workers from silicosis – the result of the slate dust.

Each worker knew the value of having a hospital on site, for minor ailments as well as those dreaded accidents or diseases. The local community would often hold concerts and events to raise money for the upkeep of the hospital or for those who had suffered an accident at work. In an attempt to cover themselves against such an eventuality a 'hospital shilling' was deducted from the men's pay to allow them to be treated in the hospital for free.

Fascinating Facts . . .

The stone dais on which Prince Charles sat for his Investiture as Caernarfon Castle was supplied by the Dinorwig Slate Quarry.

Slate can be used for blackboards, billiard tables, floor covering, headstones and fireplaces.

Slate will not distort with heat and will withstand acid.

Being able to mark slate and then rub it off again has enabled us to have one of our most popular sayings - *Wiping the slate clean* - meaning *to start again or forget our problems.*

Places to Visit . . .
National Slate Museum, Llanberis, Gwynedd LL55 4TY T: 01286 870630
W: www.museumwales.ac.uk/en/slate/ Open Daily. Free Entry.
The Museum was opened in May 1972 and provides a wealth of information on the lives of the men at the Dinorwig Quarry. It is located in some of the old quarry workshops. The displays include a row of recreated Victorian slate-workers' cottages that once stood at Tanygrisiau near Blaenau Ffestiniog known as 'Fron Haul'. There are many exhibits, it has a multi-media display showing the lives and work of the men who quarried slate here. The museum has the largest working water wheel in the United Kingdom. A restored incline formerly used to carry slate waggons uphill and downhill is also erected in the museums grounds. You are also able to visit the Chief Engineers House. At the same time call at the fascinating Quarry Hospital where you can see how the men were treated during their illnesses. There is a small entrance fee to the hospital but it is well worth a visit. It is the ideal place to get a feel for what your ancestor's life was really like.
Llechwedd Slate Caverns, Blaenau Ffestiniog, Gwynedd LL41 3NB T: 01766 830 306
W: www.llechwedd-slate-caverns.co.uk/ E: info@llechwedd-slate-caverns.co.uk
Llechwedd Slate Caverns of Blaenau Ffestiniog is still part of a living, working slate mine which has been working since 1836. There are two impressive underground tours to explore the underground world of the Victorian Slate Miner.
The Deep Mine Tour – will take you deep underground where you can discover the world of the Welsh Slate Miner during the late nineteenth Century. The Deep Mine, opened in 1979 and is accessed by Britain's steepest passenger railway.
The Tramway Tour - will take you for a guided tour on the Miners' Tramway to the 'Cathedral Chambers,' where you can discover the world of the Welsh Slate Miner, during the reign of Queen Victoria, as you travel underground for a third of a mile at surface level. You will hear stories of the 'Caban' and experience what it was like to see those great man-made caverns - by candlelight. The train will return to the Slate Mill (1852) where most of the slate blocks were split by hand and prepared for shipping - to the rest of the world. This mine is both interesting and educating and well worth a visit. So why not visit as an individual, a family or a school group.
Gwynedd Archives Service, Gwynedd Council, Council Offices, Caernarfon, Gwynedd. LL55 1SH.T: 01286 672255
Slatesite - www.llechicymru.info/index.english.htm This is a fascinating website which has information on everything you want to know on the slate industry.

Willie's candles did not drip! or when snuffing ruled! Aspects of traditional candle making

Brian Elliott

It wasn't that long ago that itinerant chandlers travelled from home to home and village to village making candles in situ from saved kitchen fats or sold them ready-made from small workshops. Every town and parish had one or more working tallow chandlers. But, because of their raw materials, some of the larger businesses were also involved in soap manufacture, mixed aromas wafting through the country air. According to *A Book of English Trades*, originally published in 1804, London tallow chandlers operated in restricted space, from cellars, reached by stairs, extremely smelly places of work. Little appears to have been wasted, however, by-products fed to dogs and market-bound ducks.

Candles were an integral part of our ancestors' lives and of course their sacred as well as decorative usage continues to the present day. Until the 1830s methods of manufacture had changed little since medieval times. They were hand-made via dipping or moulded (and occasionally rolled, using wax). Two raw materials were used, tallow and beeswax. The best was beeswax, usually obtained from collections or ranges of straw hives known as skeps, sometimes housed in purpose-built recesses in walls of gardens, orchards and houses; and generally known as bee boles. Relatively light in weight, sweet smelling and with a long lasting and bright flame, beeswax candles were elite luxury products, limited to the wealthy and the religious houses.

Hives and beeswax are occasionally mentioned in early wills. The Elizabethan will of John Storey of Burton Grange, near the site of Monk Bretton Priory, part of the ancient Yorkshire parish of Royston (near Barnsley) included a very special bequest of '*one bee hyve to the church of Roiston and the commoditie thereof to find way to make one candall to burne at the hie masse before the Sacrement ...*' Storey's widow, Alice, left '*three of my best chandles and one great candlestyke*' to a nephew. An earlier Yorkshire example, dated 1442, concerns the will of John Sunderland of Tickhill (near Doncaster) who was active in buying land and property in nearby Stainton parish, including a field called Candleland, for which a wax candle had to be kept burning in Stainton church before the statue of St John the Baptist during Sundays and at church festivals.

Tallow, the hard fatty substance obtained by rendering the suet of sheep or cattle, was the main constituent of everyday candles. They were not very efficient or pleasant to use. The seventeeeth-century diarist John Evelyn petitioned parliament against chandlers and butchers '*because of those horrid stinks and unwholesome smells.*' When lit, tallow candles also tended to dribble, had a short burning time and needed frequent '*snuffing.*' The latter did not mean

A tallow chandler at work in a London cellar. Fat would have been obtained from local butchers and rendered by the chandler to produce the tallow. London ducks were fed the waste products.
From *A Book of English Trades*, 1804

extinguishing the flame but trimming the wicks (the charred part was the snuff) with '*snuffer scissors.*' In large households this was the regular and tedious job of a servant, often the footman in country houses, and was an essential task for theatre staff. Without snuffing the light was dismal one. Variations of the word '*snuff*' continued in common usage, Thomas Hardy, for example, saying that his study had '*just been stuffed so the room was brightly illuminated.*' Here are a few others:

'*She was going out like the snuff of a candle.*' (Trollope)
'*You don't care the snuff of a candle.*' (WS Gilbert)
'*They got up in a snuffe to bed ... without taking leave of them.*' (Pepys)

And of course a context that has continued into modern parlance: '*If the old codger were to snuff it ...*'

Even the Houses of Parliament were subject to dismal lighting. On 4 February 1836, King William IV struggled to read the royal speech, not helped by his poor sight. After great efforts the librarian came to his rescue, bringing along two beeswax candles,

Dipped and mould-made candles making
© Brian Elliott collection

links with beekeeping organisations and sponsors the National Honey Show - www.waxchandlers.org.uk

High quality wax candles continue to made today, usually on a craft basis by a small number of family concerns. An exceptionally good example is

whereupon the king, now in a perfectly distinct voice said, 'I have hitherto not been able, from want of light, to read this speech in the way its importance deserves, but as lights are now brought to me, I will read it again from the commencement . . .'

From medieval times candle making came under the control of two London livery companies. The Worshipful Company of Wax Chandlers (coat of arms motto: Truth and Light) is the most ancient, its charter granted by Richard III in 1484 (the only one granted by this monarch), though it had been functioning as a guild from at least a century earlier. After the Reformation it lost control over manufacture and by the end of the eighteenth century, in the wake of cheaper materials, the making of beeswax candles became a rarity. Its Hall, rebuilt several times, is situated in Gresham Street. In addition to its charitable role the Company has

the White Rose Candle Workshop (www.whiterosecandles.co.uk), established in 1971 by Mick and Jenny White, idyllically located in an old water mill near Wensley in the Yorkshire Dales. Here visitors can see traditional dipping techniques and casting methods. Although very much a working site, a wonderful array of candles and candle products can be viewed and purchased either direct or via mail order.

The Worshipful Company of Tallow Chandlers, located on Dowgate Hill, London, was granted full livery status in 1462 but had been operational from at least 1300 (www. tallowchandlers.org). In 1404, every London home was supposed to display a lantern, lit by a tallow candle when nights were dark, the precursor of street lighting. The Company also dealt with an array of other products, including soap, vinegar, salt, sauces, oils, even herrings. Its Hall

---

Huddersfield & District Family History Society

Registered Charity No. 702199

The Huddersfield & District Family History Society caters for those researching and with interests in the Kirklees Metropolitan area which covers about 160 square miles. Within our boundaries lie the ancient parishes of Almondbury, Batley, Birstall, Dewsbury, Emley, Hartshead, Huddersfield, Kirkburton, Kirkheaton, Mirfield and Thornhill.

We have a research room and library in Meltham, at which all our databases of transcribed Parish Records and the 1841/1851 census are available for searching, together fiche/film/CD parish records for all churches and most non-conformist chapels in Kirklees. Access to Ancestry and FindMyPast is available through our computer room, we also have an extensive collection of reference books.

The Society has over 500 publications for sale, all can be purchased in person or by mail at our research room or on-line through the Society's website. The Society also has a research service which can be accessed by email, letter or on-line.

For further details please contact:-
The Secretary - (Email: secretary@hdfhs.org.uk)
33a Green's End Road, Meltham, Holmfirth, Huddersfield, West Yorkshire HD9 5NW
or visit
our website at www.hdfhs.org.uk

was destroyed in the Great Fire of London and rebuilt in 1670. By the early eighteenth century the traditional role of the *Tallow Chandlers' Company* had declined and by c.1850 rendered tallow was little used for candle making. One Yorkshire exception was in the Wensleydale hamlet of Burtersett, where a man, just about within living memory, made candles from the fat of dead sheep and the pith of rushes for the wick, apparently locally in demand because *'Willie's candles did not drip!'*

Richard Richardson of Brierley (a small West Riding settlement between Barnsley and Wakefield) made his will in the winter of 1728, calling himself a *'soap boyler.'* His soap-making interests were quite considerable, supplying shops in Doncaster and Barnsley. Richardson's probate inventory provides us with a detailed insight into the scale and extent of his trade. Candles were sold by weight so that *'a dozen candles'* probably meant twelve pounds of candles. He had a large and small pair of weigh scales in his candle warehouse, along with a variety of tubs and moulds. His stock of candles included eleven and a half dozen valued at five shillings a dozen. If a single candle weighed about half an ounce there were about 30 candles to the pound. Richardson therefore had somewhere in the region of 4,000 candles in his warehouse. He also had stocks of tallow, a furnace valued at £30 (about £2,600 today) and a sale book from his customers amounting to about £150 (about £13,000 today). He could have had a turnover involving the manufacture of at least 100,000 candles

a year, a staggering production figure even by modern standards. A search at the Registry of Deeds at Wakefield showed that he was an enterprising fellow, involved in a variety of private and commercial property deals in Barnsley; and his Brierley Park home and workshops must have been well known, albeit strategically sited away from the village. Interestingly, by 1721, he was described more specifically as *'candler'* in deeds and his eldest son worked as a chandler in Wakefield. So some chandlers could be wealthy businessmen before new materials and new technology made their activities obsolete.

The demand for candles before c.1850 was huge. They were in widespread use not only in our ancestors' homes but in a variety of commercial, industrial and public settings, in shops, workshops, factories and mines, in schools, theatres, inns and alehouses, carriages, for illuminating show caves, magic lantern shows and so on. As well as for lighting candles were also used as clocks and for time measurement.

In 2007, I interviewed a retired coal miner who recalled attaching a candle to the tub of coal that he was pushing or *'tramming'* in a Yorkshire drift mine during the 1930s, evocative of their highly dangerous potential during the nineteenth century. Some mining companies had their candles dyed with a distinctive colour (such as green) in order to reduce pilfering.

As late as the twentieth century candles were used as night tapers in country villages and for emergency lighting on fire engines and ships.

For most families *'Price'* was the household name in candle manufacture. The founders were in fact William Wilson and Benjamin Lancaster who used a fictitious name for their enterprise. Founded in London in 1830 as *Edward Price and Company*, Price's had become the world leader of candle manufacture by the end of the century, introducing innovative processes and producing inexpensive stearine candles (as against ordinary tallow) which were not that far below the quality of beeswax. With factories in London and Liverpool, the company employed 2,300 workers by 1855, many of them boys. Child labour was cheap and allowed some intricate tasks to be done well but Wilson, deeply religious, was an enlightened employer. His philanthropic approach was reflected in schools for his young workers, free breakfasts and suppers, baths and leisure facilities. A model village was developed on a greenfield site in Liverpool, copied by both *Lever's Port Sunlight* and *Cadbury's Bournville*. By the 1860s, Price's were producing 32 million night lights a year and as late as 1939 45,000 tons of candles were still being made, about three dozen candles

Mick White of White Rose Candles hand-making wax candles via his home-made heated dustbin in the White Rose Workshop.
© Brian Elliott

per head of population.

At the 1861 census there were 381 persons aged from 5 to 84 employed in Yorkshire in the tallow chandling trade. Almost two-thirds of which worked in the industrial West Riding. Sheffield had 18 chandlers, Rotherham 7, Barnsley 5 and Doncaster 4. A small candle factory functioned at Kilnhurst, near Rotherham until about 1970. In more rural West Yorkshire, at Netherton, traditional methods were used with a small workforce at *JW Turner and Son*, each person hand-dipping about 200 candles, and each batch taking 20-25 minutes depending on the temperature. They also made candles in sets of moulds. *Turners* had to buy their paraffin wax from the Far East though more expensive but better quality American wax was preferred.

Tapered candles were through strands of wick being passed from a drum via a frame and wound on to another drum some distance away. The strands were then dipped in a vat of boiling wax, wound slowly to give a good coating in time to harden before starting the process again. The strand, gradually acquiring the necessary thickness for tapers, was passed through a machine which cut them into twelve-inch lengths. After bundling, the wicks were dipped into boiling water to make the wick for lighting.

Technical innovation and the use of new materials had a massive impact on traditional candle manufacture. The developing whale industry in the late eighteenth century revolutionised the trade when oil from the sperm whale was crystallised into a form of wax. *Spermaceti* did not have the bad smell of tallow when burned, was harder than both tallow and beeswax so did not soften or bend in the summer months. Oils from imported plants also began to be used, some producing smokeless flames; and the French chemists Chevreul and Gay-Lussac had patented steain in 1811. In 1834, Joseph Morgan devised a machine that moulded candles by the use of a cylinder with a moveable piston to eject candles if they solidified, allowing continuous mechanised production. After 1850, paraffin was increasingly used in candle manufacture following James Young's experiments with coal distillation and by the end of the century the addition of *stearic acid* improved candle quality even further. The use of oil, gas and electricity reduced and eliminated the usage of candles as the main lighting source during the twentieth century but our long history of candle making should not be forgotten.

N.B. *Price's Patent Candles Limited* are now owned by an Italian Company, but continue to be proud of their Royal Warrant. Traditional beeswax candles are also still made by a small independent producer, Moorlands Dipped Candles, based at Alston, in Cumbria (www.moorlands-candles.co.uk).

Acknowledgements
Borthwick Institute for Historical Research (York), Leeds Local Studies Library, Prices Patent Candles Ltd, Wakefield Registry of Deeds, White Rose Candles (of Wensley), Worshipful Company of Tallow Chandlers, Worshipful Company of Wax Chandlers

The Great Plague of London
Brian Parnaby

Following the havoc wrought by the Black Death* in the Fourteenth century, which depleted England's population - according to varying figures, by up to half? (questionable, but certainly reducing it drastically) - the country had been troubled only by occasional outbreaks of Plague, usually of the bubonic type, highly virulent but a little less deadly than .the other varieties – septicemic and pneumonic. These spasmodic occurrences had, fortunately, not embraced vast swathes of the countryside but, instead, had been confined to the larger, urban populations, especially London, the commercial hub of the country; many of the citizens of these larger conurbations living in conditions of the utmost squalor. The open sewers and lack of even the most elementary hygiene precautions – even amongst the wealthy, educated hierarchy, were appalling by present-day standards. Conditions therefore were ideal for an outbreak of pestilence.

This plague was also of the septicemic and pneumonic type, but bubonic plague was the most common manifestation of the disease, caused by a bacillus in fleas that lived on black rats.)

The origin of this new threat to the inhabitants of England has been traced to the Netherlands, the carriers identified, probably correctly, as being those merchant vessels carrying cotton to England, for the burgeoning English manufacturing industry. Apparently, this trade endured despite the occasional bouts of warfare between the two great sea-going nations of the Netherlands and Britain. An epidemic of bubonic plague had struck Amsterdam in 1663-1664, although there had been intermittent outbreaks during the previous century.

The disease claimed its first victims in England in early 1665 (probably in April), in the London Dock area of St. Giles-in-the-Field, amongst the shacks or 'stews' where the poorest of the poor existed, these people being largely employed as dock workers. Thus, they quickly came into contact both with the infected cargoes

The Bubonic form of the Plague was generally known as the 'Black Death' and had been identified as such since the first recorded Plague struck England in 1348.

and with the Dutch seamen from the merchant ships. Although records were not fully maintained and certainly were not always accurate, especially in the case of the poverty-stricken (probably judged worthless by their 'betters') – there was a great chronicler of events on the London stage – Samuel Pepys (1633 - 1703).

Pepys was a great diarist – later to become a household name - which he commenced writing in 1660; it was written in cipher which was only decoded in the mid-Nineteenth century.) At the time of the outbreak of the Great Plague in 1665 he was involved in the administration of the Navy as 'Clerk of the Acts' and was later to become Secretary to the Admiralty.

On the 7th June 1665, recorded as an oppressively hot day, whilst walking in Drury Lane, Pepys noticed several houses with Red Crosses marked on the doors – a sign that Plague was present. His diary quaintly records that 'it put me into an ill conception of myself and my smell, so that I was forced to buy some roll-tobacco to smell and to chew, which took away the apprehension.'

During the month of June the plague increased rapidly, to such an extent that the redoubtable Pepys wrote that, shortly after his stroll along Drury Lane, the coachman conveying him home from his office, was forced to abandon the carriage, claiming that he had been struck down by the plague. Yet Pepys remained in London, at his post, whilst many of his colleagues fled the city.

By the third week of June, the streets of London were crowded with wagons, coaches, and throngs of foot-travellers, deserting the city for the countryside. A 'London Bill of Mortality' published for that week showed that a total of 267 people had died during that week only. The mortality rate increased week on week and, by the second week of July, it had reached one thousand a week. One even more disheartening aspect of the exodus from the city was that many medical practitioners also departed, along with large numbers of clergymen. The result was that there was a decreasing number of doctors to tend the victims. 'Plague Doctors,' qualified and unqualified, roamed the streets of the city, offering succour to any victims, highly laudable in view of the fact that is was highly likely that they themselves could fall victim to the disease, as indeed many did. The Monarch King Charles II

Pest House during The Great Plague

The Broad Stone, East Retford, Nottinghamshire, – on which money, previously immersed in Vinegar, was placed in exchange for goods during the Great Plague

not necessarily by any means escaping the disease - they were taken by relatives and friends to special 'pest-houses,' for confinement, the sick along with the well, until they either died or recovered! In most cases these people had no option. The authorities often sealed the doors of houses where the occupants were known or suspected of having the disease, with a large Red Cross painted on the door, together with the words 'Lord have mercy on us.' Guards were placed outside the doors to ensure that the occupants did not escape and some people wore grotesque home-made masks to repel the feared 'miasma' (a highly unpleasant or unhealthy smell, generally associated with carrying of the bad 'humours' on the air; the fanciful notion being that these 'humours' were the cause of the disease.

The incubation period was 4-6 days, when usual signs of bubonic plague appeared on the victim's body – formation of 'buboes' which were swollen glands in the groin or armpit, and a blackening of parts of the sufferer's body. Headaches and vomiting were common throughout the progress of the disease, and death could occur with a week or so.

To compound the distress of the country at the effects of the plague, the Dutch Government boasted that their enemy (England) had been dealt a mortal blow, which was grossly untrue.

The authorities – those who resolutely remained at their posts, that is – adopted a range of tactics and procedures to ward off the pestilence, most of them totally ineffectual. Some of these were quite ludicrous, including the distribution of various herbal-type substances such as hops, incense and pepper being burned in the forlorn hope that their aromas would ward off the infection. Adult citizens remaining in the city were even urged to smoke tobacco. Inns and lodging-houses were closed and markets cancelled – all wise moves, even though done by accident. Thousands of dogs and cats were slaughtered – what about the black rats? This did not help matters at all, rather the reverse, as there were now no natural predators to catch the rats, who had, and were, spreading, the disease.

The weekly death toll continued to rise inexorably for several months, increasing from the July figure of 1,000, to 7,000 in September; truly astonishing and alarming figures, September being the peak month for deaths. On the advent of the cooler weather, the numbers of dead began to decrease as the rampaging of the plague lessened. By the end of the year (1665) the death toll was low and, in February 1666, it was deemed safe for the Royal party to return to London. Eventually, only isolated cases occurred and the Great Plague was adjudged to be over.

Although the Plague was centred on London and the South-East, it spread to various parts of the

and his family left the city in July, firstly for Salisbury, later removing to Oxfordshire, though London's Aldermen elected to remain at their posts. Those people wealthy enough to afford to leave the city also fled. Astonishingly, the Mayor, Sir John Lawrence, although also remaining in London, quarantined himself in a specially constructed glass case, sealed off from the 'ill-humours' (bad moisture in the air!) to enable him to carry out his duties. The efficacy of this precaution is hard to confirm, although Sir John survived the epidemic.

During August the death toll approached three thousand a week and the 'Bills of Mortality' continued to rise inexorably.

Scenes of almost unimaginable horror now became commonplace throughout the city. Corpses were carried openly through the streets; 'Plague pits' were dug to dump the rotting corpses; afflicted people walked about displaying open sores or sat in the doorways of their homes (hovels usually) wrapped and muffled, awaiting death, as recovery was, in many cases, highly unlikely. Plague helpers drew carts around the city, calling out 'Bring out your Dead,' for conveyance to the burial pits. In London, two of these pits were located at Aldgate and Finsbury Fields. Mourning bells tolled constantly announcing new deaths. The authorities employed temporary 'plague examiners,' whose duty was to find and report plague victims. They also hired 'scavengers' to clean the streets and some women were employed to enter the houses of the sick to check on the dead or dying, prior to their removal to 'plague pits.' when the inevitable occurred. It was reported that up to 10,000 Londoners hired boats and sat in the River Thames, hoping to avoid the plague's effects – dodging the invisible 'miasma' or the 'humours.'

In some cases, where people did not confine themselves to their own homes with their families –

country, even as far as the North Midlands; York was also severely affected and the dead were buried outside the walls of the city. The cause of this was probably the contamination of previously uninfected people coming into contact with Londoners, perhaps, unwittingly or otherwise being contaminated who had fled to the Provinces. Possibly also, or even probably in some cases, goods sent from London may have been infected and the infection passed to the recipient of the goods. This is probably true of Eyam, a little village in Derbyshire, where a parcel of clothing, believed to be have been laundry, was brought by a traveller. Eighty per cent of the village's population perished and, but for the courage of one of the villagers, William Mompesson, who persuaded the villagers not to abandon their homes, the disease could have spread throughout Derbyshire had they fled.

Happily, with the coming of winter, the scourge of the plague began to disappear, almost concurrently with the virtual destruction of the city caused by the Great Fire of London in September 1666. At the time, to many people, this horrendous conflagration was responsible for the demise of the Plague but this has since been refuted. It is possible though that, by

the destruction of many of the vermin-ridden, insanitary dwellings of the poor and down-trodden, it may have had some minor effect on the spread of the remnants of the disease, already on the wane at the time of the Fire. At the very least the Great Fire would have killed many of the disease-ridden black rats and fleas that infested these human rabbit-warrens.

The total estimated death toll in London attributed directly to the Great Plague was set at a minimum of 70,000. A more realistic figure would be one approaching 100,000, in view of the lack of adequate records held, especially in respect of the poor of the metropolis. Blame for the large number of deaths was attributed to the poor living conditions and this is a reasonable conclusion. It became noticeable that deaths in the more affluent areas of the city were proportionately lower than in the congested 'stews' of the city.

The next such 'Plague' to strike England would be the 'Spanish Flu' Pandemic of 1918. By then, despite huge advances in medical knowledge through research, medicines and hygiene practices the death toll world wide was enormous.

London before The Great Fire

The Great Fire of London
Brian Parnaby

Rapidly following the end of the Great Plague, another disaster was to strike the great city of London. It seemed to some Londoners that a curse had fallen on the city; to many others however the conflagration which would envelop the city was a blessing in disguise. The destruction by fire of the sordid rabbit-warrens of 'stews.'[1] would clear the city of a festering malaise which had disfigured and shamed the leading city of the known world.

The noted diarist Samuel Pepys was an astute chronicler of the Fire which broke out in the early hours of Sunday 2nd September 1666, following a prolonged drought in the south-east of the country. Some of his observations will follow.

The Fire began in Pudding Lane, appropriately enough in a baker's shop owned by one Thomas Farynor (or Farriner), a baker to the Sovereign, King Charles II. Initially, the blaze was confined to Farynor's house, but it being made principally of

wood, the presence of a strong wind and dry atmosphere because of the drought, helped the fire to spread quickly. It was later ascertained that one of Farynor's employees, a maid, had failed to extinguish the bakery ovens on the Saturday evening. The continuing and resultant excess of heat from the ovens caused sparks to ignite parts of the premises. In her panic to escape, after warning her employer the maid, unfortunately, was consumed by the flames and perished.

Many of the houses and business premises adjoining Farynor's bakery were built mainly of wood and pitch, so a combination of carelessness, weather conditions favouring the spread of the fire and highly flammable materials, conspired to spread to neighbouring properties, with predictable and disastrous consequences. When Pepys was awoken by one of his servants at about 3am., he was informed that a fire had started in the city, in the vicinity of Mark Lane. He judged it to be of little consequence and once more retired to bed. When he arose at 7.a.m. the fire appeared to have diminished but his maid informed him that she had received reports from other servants that the fire had increased in strength, had already destroyed over three hundred dwellings and was 'raging' along Fish Street.

In view of Pepys's important position in public life (he was Clerk to the Acts of the Navy) and intrepid and inveterate diarist that he was, he decided to investigate the cause and effects of the fire. In his diary he later recorded that he walked up to the Tower (of London) and, a half-mile to the West lay London Bridge with the *'the Northern side houses all in flames and a great fire blazing between Thames Street and the River Thames.'* He described that area as being *'a huddled infinity of timber-built, pitch-coated little houses and warehouses full of oil, tallow and spirits, providing enough fuel to light all of London.'* Pepys then took a boat and travelled along the river, noting that the riverside houses of many of his friends were ablaze. The inhabitants of all the burning - or soon to be consumed – houses, mainly wealthy merchants (the poor had scant possessions), were frantically removing their goods and flinging them into boats (lighters) along the river bank, even into the river itself. Acute observer that he was, Pepys noted that, whilst people were frantically trying to save their personal goods, no-one seemed to be making any efforts to stem the blaze. Pepys then ordered his boatman to row him to Whitehall, where he had an immediate audience with the King and the Duke of York (later King James II), advising him to give instructions to the Lord Mayor,[2] to destroy buildings in the path of the fire, so as to save as much of the city as possible. The instructions being duly given, Pepys proceeded to see the Lord Mayor, finding him virtually helpless, having already overseen the demolition of houses, to no avail, as the fire was out of control. Having done what he could and fearful that his own home could fall victim to the fire, Pepys

then returned there and set about packing and evacuating his possessions, which he, his wife and the servants worked all night in doing, transferring everything by cart to safety in the Bethnal Green area. Pepys was fortunate; his house was not destroyed by the Fire and he was able to return home with all of his possessions intact. He also took the precaution of having a deep pit dug in the garden of the Navy Office (his place of work) wherein he proposed to bury his personal stock of wine, parmesan cheese and personal papers! Being a Civil Servant and mindful of his responsibilities, he sent for Dockyard hands from Woolwich and Deptford, recruiting them to fight the fire. He was also thoughtful enough to write to the appropriate authority (Sir William Coventry, Secretary to the Duke of York), for permission to pull down houses in the path of the Fire; there being an ancient rule in the City that whoever destroyed his neighbour's dwelling should pay for its rebuilding. Meanwhile the Duke of York and his soldiers were busily engaged in blowing up houses on Ludgate Hill, a fruitless task as it turned out.

Meanwhile, to return to the broader picture. Despite the fire hazards, the King and the rest of the Royal family remained in London. During the havoc caused by the still recent Great Plague, they had quickly decamped to Salisbury and then to Oxford which had rather sullied their reputations. This time they responded admirably to their responsibilities. Indeed, Charles made great efforts to take charge of the situation and was responsible for ordering the creation of fire-breaks – the demolition of many perfectly good buildings, thus denying the fire the timber it needed to feed on. This was a standard procedure at the time in cases of outbreaks of fire. He also ordered navy rations to be given to the homeless who had fled the city.

The Old St. Paul's Cathedral was badly damaged, reports at the time stating that the lead roof had completely melted and lead was flowing down the streets. The virtual destruction of this medieval

The Great Fire of London

Newgate Prison burning

conflagration. Without belittling the tragic loss of these lives, it is important to highlight the enormous destruction of property in the city. About 430 acres of property, representing almost 80% of the buildings in the city was destroyed. One must remember that the area encompassed by the city of London of four centuries was much smaller than the huge conurbation that it is today. Even so, to Londoners of the day, it presented an almost unimaginable scene of destruction. Thirteen thousand houses, more than eighty Churches and fifty-two Guildhalls were destroyed. Thousands of Londoners were financially ruined and lost their homes.

Cathedral in the Great Fire of London later provided the opportunity for Sir Christopher Wren to design and build (1675-1710) the present magnificent baroque Cathedral on Ludgate Hill. This new St. Paul's fortunately defied the efforts of the Luftwaffe to destroy it in the Blitz, being guarded by volunteer fire-watchers who doused most of the incendiary bombs dropped on the Cathedral; only relatively slight damage was caused and St. Paul's became a symbol of Londoners' resistance to Nazi aggression.

To return to the indefatigable Pepys: he arranged for Trained Bands[3] to be called in, to demolish buildings in the path of the fire, by using gunpowder. Their actions were in vain however as the necessity to clear rubble before blasting permitted a clear path for the flames to spread.

The Fire continued virtually unchecked for several days, rampaging throughout the areas shown on the map before it abated at a point near the Temple Church. Before people could breathe a collective sigh of relief it suddenly came to life again and continued towards Westminster.

At least there was one consoling feature of the Fire in that it was confined to the North side of the River Thames, when, feasibly, it could have crossed the River, via the Bridges or by sparks from the inferno. (There were buildings, stalls, huts etc. situated along the bridges in those days.) Fate in the form of the vagaries of the wind intervened; its direction changed and drove the fire in a northerly direction, that is, back upon itself. Having thus done so, finding nothing remaining to burn, after four nightmare days, the fire gradually died out.

Most surprisingly, perhaps because of the rapid action taken under the direction of Samuel Pepys and other notables, with the possible exception of the, at first unconcerned, and then panic-stricken, Lord Mayor, the death toll was insignificant. Only an estimated sixteen people perished in the

On the credit side as regards the future of London it must be recorded that the Fire destroyed those rat-infested areas of the city into which it came in contact. The 'Fleet' – a tributary flowing into the River Thames, had been a running cess-pit for countless years, through the deposit of rubbish and human waste and had been a source of various diseases, as the poorest of the poor used it for drinking water. The heat from the inferno destroyed all the waste which had accumulated and cleansed the water.

The last word comes from the diary of Samuel Pepys:

Personally he had been very fortunate in that his house and possessions had been spared. He remarked: *'St. Paul's is burned, and all Cheapside.' 'The Lord of Heaven make me thankful and continue me therein!'*

[1] *'Stews'*: a term used at that time to denote what today would be called a slum. Middle English, probably derived from the Old French word *'estui,'* from *'estoier'* - meaning 'confine,' because of the cramped living conditions.)(infinitely worse than later 19th and 20th century slums)

[2] It was later reported that the Lord Mayor, had shown such disregard for the severity of the fire, despite the visual evidence to the contrary, that he had caustically remarked that *'a woman could piss it out.'*

[3] Trained Bands: these were civilian 'soldiers,' raised to assist the Government in times of civilian emergencies – somewhat similar to Special Constables or Territorial Army soldiers, but used only to maintain civil order.

Another fire, in 1676, destroyed over 600 houses South of the River Thames.

The 1918 Flu Pandemic
Brian Parnaby

The world has had its share of disasters, both man-made and natural; but even the barbaric killings by the evil Russian dictator Joseph Stalin and his Chinese counterpart Mao Tse Tung, pale into insignificance against the slaughter of tens of millions of people within a short space of time, immediately following the Great War of 1914-1918. This was the feared Influenza pandemic of 1918, which caused the deaths of tens of millions of people within the space of two years.

The now notorious 'Spanish Flu' (or 'La Grippe') has been recorded as the most devastating pandemic in world history. It was a global disaster on an epic scale, severely restricting all aspects of life - social, trade and commerce and travel especially.

Firstly let us examine the origin of the influenza virus which tends to occur in epidemics and pandemics. As most of us will know, influenza is an acute respiratory illness, with symptoms of headache, fever and muscular pain. The mortality rate amongst the elderly and infirm is high because of their reduced resistance to the disease; as also it is with young children. Although the British Government (and others) now provide vaccination against 'flu,' as it is commonly termed, this is not always successful in warding off the illness as the virus mutates into different strains, each with different *antigenic* properties. (The Dictionary definition of an *antigen* is: a toxin or other foreign substance which induces an immune response in the body, especially in the production of antibodies.)

The name *'influenza'* is derived from the Latin *influential coeli*, a medieval name for the disease, which was thought to be due to the influence of the sky! How this conclusion was arrived at, heaven only knows!

The disease acquired its name *'Spanish Flu'* in the following way: the First World War was in its final stages when the virus first began to spread, apparently from Asia throughout the Continental United States and Europe. Strict censorship was still imposed during the War Years but Spain was a neutral country; it was in the interests of all the combating nations to preserve this censorship when the virus first manifested itself. However, Spain being neutral, had no censorship regulations and, consequently, issued public statements when the virus arrived in Spain – one of the last countries in Europe to be affected. In that country it was called *'La Grippe,'* simply *'influenza.'*

As already mentioned, the influenza epidemic (later to become a pandemic - that is, it assumed global proportions) first became recognised in the United States, (in Kansas) in the Spring of 1918 but only became a source of concern to American doctors in the early autumn of 1918 when the virus began to proliferate rapidly. Throughout the world during the two year ravages by the virus, a fifth of the world's population was infected.

Strangely, this particular strain of 'flu,' did not follow the usual pattern of attacking the very young, the old and the weak, but proved deadly to the younger adult members of society - in the 20 to 40 year-old range.

To use the large population of the United States as an example of the havoc caused by the disease, it has been estimated that the average life-span in that country was lowered for a decade. The normal mortality rate for an influenza epidemic was less than 0.1%; but, during the pandemic, the death rate rose to 2.5%. Young adults in the 15-34 year range were especially severely affected, deaths from influenza and resulting pneumonia being twenty times above normal.

A particular and unpleasant aspect of this strain of virus was the speed in which it struck, with fatal consequences. People could suddenly become infected and die within hours, from a particularly virulent form of pneumonia which blocked the airways and suffocated them. Bleeding from the ears, hæmorrhage from mucous membranes – especially from the nose and stomach – were common symptoms. In many cases misdiagnoses were made, symptoms identified as cholera or typhoid, with fatal results, not unusual in view of the fact that no antidote had been found.

There were numerous reports of people retiring for the night, apparently quite well, and being dead by morning; or going to work as usual and dying shortly thereafter. The number of reports of these types of occurrence were legion throughout the world. A macabre little song was sung by children:

'I had a little bird,
Its name was Enza.
I opened the window,
And in-flu-enza.'

The virus circled the globe and spread its contamination by the usual means: through shipping lanes; the movement of troops from the United States to Europe, in those closing months of the Great War; the return of troops from mainland Europe to their home countries (usually America), either repatriated as wounded or, following the cessation of hostilities, their discharge from the Forces; and the general intermingling of the population of all countries, going about their everyday business. In short, the virus had ready access to virtually all the world's population.

A rumour spread that the disease had originated in Europe, being heralded by enemies of Germany as a biological weapon, either following on from the use of mustard gas and chlorine (used by both sets of combatants); or as an indirect result of the use of these gases percolating into the atmosphere. These allegations were patently false.

Despite the urgent investigation by the world's scientists into the cause and effects of the virus, no vaccine became available to combat and stop its rapid spread. It continued its remorseless journey, spreading death wherever it struck. Scientists theorised, with reasonable accuracy, that the origin of the virus had been in China where it had struck with unparalleled ferocity. Frankly, when the virus first appeared, there had been only slight concern as it was thought to be one of the *'run-of the mill'* influenza epidemics which appeared, at irregular occasions throughout the world. Only when its symptoms clearly manifested themselves was it identified as a new and most unusual virus. By then, it had a grip on the world's population. Although this lack of action was later criticised, by then the

damage had been done. Even today, scientists have not been able to isolate and identify the virus and claim a cure is available. The latest *'swine-fever'* scare of Spring 2009 is a case in point; fortunately, this virus, although serious, is in no way comparable to the *Spanish Flu'* pandemic.

Several serious side effects of the pandemic duly manifested themselves. Firstly, the announcement of the Armistice in November 1918, resulted in huge numbers of people congregating at central points in major towns and cities throughout the world. This resulted in simply assisting the progress and spread of the disease. Secondly, the demands on the medical services increased tremendously. Medical staff, including General Practitioners and Nurses – already in short supply in civilian hospitals because of the demands for treatment of the wounded in battle - were hopelessly overworked in dealing with the influenza outbreaks. Medical Students at Universities had their studies curtailed as they were drafted in to help in ministering to the sick, in support of qualified staff. Despite their invaluable help, uncountable numbers of affected members of the public were not attended to and, tragically, usually died unaided.

The disease continued its rampage for over two years, all the while scientists attempting to restrict its progress. Eventually, it died out, having by then killed an estimated 50 million people - although some estimates have been as high as 100 million – the greatest mass slaughter in recorded history.

Among the many famous, often household, names recorded as victims of the pandemic were:
Louis Botha - First Prime Minister of the Union of South Africa;
Gustav Klimt - Famous symbolist Painter;
William Leefe-Robinson VC - The first Airman to shoot down a German Zeppelin over England;
Harold Lockwood - American Silent Film Star;
Yukov Sverdlov - Bolshevik Party Leader;
Frederick Trump - Grandfather of American businessman Donald Trump;
Famous Survivors:
Walt Disney - Cartoonist;
David Lloyd George - British Prime Minister during the Great War;
Edward Munch - Norwegian Painter;
Mary Pickford - American Silent Film Star;
Franklin D. Roosevelt - U.S. President;
Haile Selassie - Emperor of Ethiopia;
Wilhelm II - German Emperor during the Great War
The epidemic was not selective in its attacks on the population and being rich and famous did not exclude one from infection by the virus.

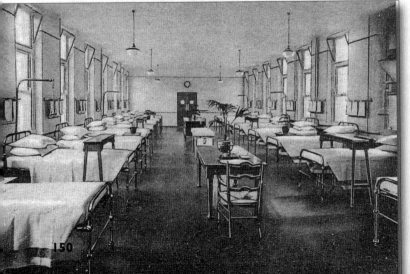

Wash Away the Blues

The days when taking in washing was a common line of work are now long gone. Automatic washing machines have replaced the old fashioned washing utensils of yesteryear which made washing such a hard task. Dolly tubs, mangles, washboards and flat irons are all a thing of the past but have become the collector's items of today. Nowadays, children are only familiar with the automatic washing machine which washes, spins and even dries our clothes and don't consider the extensive hours of labour that our forebears endured so we would benefit in future years. **Kath Jones** *finds out more.*

A Hard Job to Follow ...

In the days of our ancestors washing took place down by the river or stream. The washerwomen would congregate at the waters edge, immerse their washing in the water and rub the clothes with their hands or slap them against a large flat rock and using sand as an abrasive to rid the garments of dirt until the stream carried the grime away. Sand was later replaced by home-made soap and eventually by soap powder.

Finally, the ladies would wring out the clothes with their hands but large items such as sheets and blankets needed two women, one at each end twisting in opposite directions - ridding the garments of excess water - before hanging them out to dry. In the country, the wet clothes were often laid on hedgerows to dry whereas in the towns it was a common sight to see back alleys criss-crossed with washing lines, sheets billowing in the wind.

Some people didn't live by a stream so had to do their washing in water-tight vats. The vats stood in their back yard and were filled with hot water that had been boiled on the fire. Once the washing was submerged, the women stood in the tub and agitated the garments with their feet or simply rubbed them by hand which often made their hands sore. It was natural for groups of women to gather together in the street and carry out a communal wash. For many, it was their only opportunity of getting social time in what was otherwise a life of constant drudgery. Children joined in or played alongside whilst their mothers worked.

Working from Home ...

Many washerwomen worked from home, collecting the laundry from a number of homes and working long hours sometimes seven days a week to supplement their husband's earnings. Having large families meant the man's wage was insufficient to provide for them all. Women, young or old, widowed or single found it crucial to earn a living and took in washing from neighbours or even advertised by standing in the street.

Knowing that washing was a full day's job, the washerwomen would get up at five or six in the morning to do her own housework, make breakfast, and do the shopping before starting a day's hard toil.

Before indoor plumbing, water often needed to be carried quite a distance before work could begin and to make life easier, every effort was made to collect rain water in water butts for later use. The boiler was filled from the water butt and then lit; when hot, it was poured into a metal dolly tub. A wooden dolly or maid was then used to agitate the clothes or they were rubbed with soap on a metal or glass rippled washboard. They were often washed in sequence from the whites to coloureds due to the fact that the coloureds would loose their dye and precious water would have to be changed more often. After a final rinse they were lifted out of the dolly tub with a pair of wooden tongs and fed through the mangle to remove the excess water and finally hung out to dry. The clothes were very heavy and took a lot of strength to lift - adding to the gruelling work load.

Unlike the grander properties where a purpose built laundry was constructed, often washing was done in an outside shed, communal wash-house – if she was lucky enough to have one - or out in the

Profile of a Washerwoman – Florence Margaret Baxter (1923-1984)

Florence was born in a small village in Derbyshire in 1923. The youngest of seven children, she grew up helping her mother do the washing. Her father and brothers were miners and so washing wasn't an easy job. Working for a living was bred into her from an early age.

As time passed, Florence had two children and moved to Folkestone in Kent. She worked in Domestic Service in a boarding house where she gained even more experience in washing laundry. Life was hard and money was scarce and whilst there, Florence had another two children. The owners thought highly of her and whilst she worked they looked after her youngest child.

Moving back to a Derbyshire mining village, she re-married and had four more children. Money was tighter than ever with eight mouths to feed so she used her experience to take in washing at home.

Through word of mouth and satisfied customers washing for miners became her trade. She would starch and press the garments and return the finished items to their owners at which point she would be paid.

Using a gas boiler with a mangle attached she boiled away the whites – her result showed when pit towels fifteen years old were still as white as snow. She used this method until 1969 when she bought a twin tub, followed a few years later by an automatic washing machine. Referring to the automatic she would often say, *"You can't beat a bit of elbow grease! The machine doesn't get them clean!"*

back yard.

If the weather wasn't good enough to dry the clothes outside they were hung over a clothes horse - making the house damp - or on a pulley which was suspended from the ceiling over the fire.

More Jobs than One ...

Not only did a washerwoman wash the clothes but she was a multi tasker too. Mending and ironing was an important part of her service. Socks, sweaters cardigans and gloves were darned using wool and a wooden mushroom - pushed inside the sock to hold it taut. Sheets were patched using old ones or cut up to make the better ones last longer. Collars that needed starching were dipped into hot starch made up in a bucket then the excess starch was scraped off and the collars hung up to dry. Flat irons heated up on the fire were used to iron the clothes - whilst others were warming on the grate. The pain and physical toil would take its toll and many of these hard working women looked older than their years.

It is believed that during the Victorian era, many of the women who worked in what was known as 'sweated trades' such as the washerwomen, escaped the Census investigators when it was feared that penalties might have to paid if their full income was declared. In 1851, out of a female population of just over 10 million, 145, 000 washerwomen and 55, 000 charwomen declared their occupation on the census so it is always worth checking to see if your ancestor was listed. To search online visit www.ancestry.co.uk

Workhouse for Washerwomen ...

For the poorer working class society, there was always the threat that if they did not earn enough money their family would be put in the workhouse. Many penniless, homeless families were forced to live in such conditions. For those trying to avoid the workhouse, the job of the washerwomen or laundress was passed on to their daughters and the girls were brought up expecting to help. Boys were also involved by fetching the washing or sorting it

into heaps on the floor.

To learn more about the life of a washerwoman's daughter and her life in the Victorian era, visit http://victorianweb.org/gender/sullivan.html

Catherine Cookson the famous author worked in a South Shield's Workhouse laundry and by the age of 23 - in 1930 - was a manageress at a workhouse laundry in Essex, where she earned £3. 6s a week . Records can be found at www.institutions.org.uk/workhouses/england/dur/ south_shields_workhouse.htm

The Life of Domestic Servants ...

In 1851, just over one million people were employed in domestic service but by 1871, this figure had risen to over one and a quarter million. Alongside butlers and ladies maid's, laundry maids would be an essential resource to every wealthy home.

For many young women finding a position as a domestic servant in a large wealthy house or on a country estate meant leaving home to live-in with their employers. For most of them, this would have been their first time away from home. Laundry maids would have been an essential asset in these large houses and equally as important as the butlers and kitchen maids. They only earned £16 per year plus their keep which would include all meals, uniform and a small room in the attic. The experience of living away from home and the strict household standards, taught them what would be expected in the future.

Laundry maids would rise early and before breakfast collect the water, which would be heated up on the fire which they had already lit. The washing was sorted into piles, the dirtiest items put in to soak to remove any stains. The washing took the maids all day. On average three maids and the Head Laundry Maid were expected to do the washing for the sizeable household of up to fifty people including guests and other servants.

The maids were chosen to do specific laundry jobs and only those more experienced were allowed to wash the family's clothes, whilst the others dealt with household linen and bedding. The housekeeper kept a record of all linen and clothing; she would also discipline the maids if they failed to fulfil their duties sufficiently. A seperate day was allotted to ironing, starching and folding the garments before returning them to their rightful places within the house. By the time the girls went to bed they were exhausted, backs aching and their hands chapped from being immersed in water most of the day. They would only get a half day off each week however, they always hoped that if they worked hard enough they would move up the ladder to Head Laundry Maid or even Housekeeper.

To experience the life of a domestic laundry maid, why not visit one of the many museums or country houses where the laundry has been recreated complete with copper boilers, dolly tubs and homemade soap. Shugborough Hall or Erddig in North Wales are good examples of the way laundry maids lived and worked and where staff dress in period costume and perform the duties of their Victorian equivalents.

The laundry shows all the implements used for washing, drying and ironing the clothes. Erddig had its own laundry business taking in from areas surrounding the large estate. Visit www.erddig.co.uk and www.shugborough.org.uk

Tools for the Task ...

Monday, was the most common day chosen by women to do their washing and Tuesday allotted for the task of ironing. As the Industrial Revolution swept across Britain, the progression of labour saving devices and appliances were being developed to speed up the washing process. Devices and patents were filed all over the world expanding the laundry industry and therefore giving women greater freedom as we moved into the 20th century.

A Collector's Piece ...

Many of these old washing utensils have become collectors' items. The following objects are just a few that have become popular:

Mangles ...

Although much of the wringing out of laundry would be done by hand, with large quantities this became impossible and the use of a wringer or mangle would be crucial. By regulating the rollers through which the laundry would pass and turning a handle on the side of the device, you could squeeze out more and more water each time enabling the washing to dry quicker. To appeal to the housewife, one mangle sold under the trade name of the 'Little Nipper'. Mangles can be bought from car boots, antique centres or old house clearances from as little as £50 and as much as £200.

Washboards ...

Washboards, an important part of laundry equipment, were used in conjunction with the mangle. Usually made of corrugated glass or metal and wood, they allowed the user to rub the soiled clothes up and down the board helping to remove the dirt. It was essential that the boards were checked for any damage before use in case rough or jagged edges should tear the clothes or hands. These washboards can be purchased today between £10 and £20 depending on condition.

Washing machines ...

In the early 1900's, the previous two appliances were combined into what was basically a tub on legs with a hand operated mangle attached. As popularity for this product grew, an electrically powered agitator was added to improve the process. This was the forerunner to every washerwoman's dream. John Fisher, an American engineer, invented the first electric washing machine in 1908 manufactured by the Hurley Machine Company of Chicago. Power driven dollies which agitated the clothes and special wringers were added later. Well known brand names for these early washers were Napier Kimber, Savage and GEC. Hotpoint and Hoover also developed their own versions and in 1957, Hoover added a spin dryer and produced its first twin tub.

Although washing

Baby BURCO

machines were in use in the latter part of the 19th century, they were expensive to buy and use. Now vintage machines can still be picked up for as little as £10 or as much as £1,000.

Tongs ...

Vintage wooden washing tongs hinged with a metal strip can be bought for as little as £5.00 whereas small copper and wooden dolly possers used to agitate the clothes in the tub can command between £10 and £15 with larger examples fetching even more.

Irons ...

Ironing was tedious task and often required great skill to achieve a good finish to the garments. Various irons and tongs would achieve different results from scissor shaped crimping tongs for frills and children's clothes to an Italian iron used to provide less pressure on materials such as velvet. Most common was the Flat iron.

From as early as the 1st Century BC, the Chinese used metal pans filled with charcoal to smooth out their laundry but it wasn't until the 17th century when cast iron gadgets were made specifically for this purpose. These heavy implements were heated in the fire on a trivet or had a compartment into which hot coals could be placed to retain the heat. A drawback to this was that the handle got very hot so a pot holder or cloth had to be used to protect the hands until a simple wooden handle was developed to solve the problem. Throughout the years, various types of fuel have been used to power the iron including whale oil, natural gas and even gasoline.

The first electric iron appeared in France in 1880 heated by an electric arc of two carbon electrodes. Originally cordless, it had to be placed on a stand and then plugged in to 100 volt supplies to heat it up. By 1912, Universal irons were available for travelling which could be operated on 100 or 200 volts and by 1930; a basic heat regulator was added to allow different temperatures to be chosen for different materials. Steam irons were not introduced into Britain until 1953, although early varieties had been in use in the US since 1926.

Laundry irons tend to be the most collectable of washday items with prices starting from as little as £5 to £20 for an early 20th century smoothing iron. This still represents reasonable value for money. Prices of cylindrical barrel Goffering Irons which were heated internally by inserting a red hot poker, depends on age, size, and the number of barrels featured. The simplest are usually found at around £40 with the Georgian polished brass examples, which have large and small barrels on tripod feet, rarely priced at less than £300. Irons make great paper weights or doorstops and are ideal as "small" collectables in the modern world.

Sinks

As with any laundry duties, a sink was always essential and next to the cooker it was at the hub of the kitchen. Large ceramic sinks are often found at Architectural Reclamation sites and look great installed in today's kitchens to give a real period feel. Belfast (Butler) and Chisel sinks can be bought for as little as £45.00. Butler sinks is a term used to describe traditional sinks which are at least 3 – 4 cm thick. A Belfast sink is one with an overflow whereas a London sink is very similar but with no overflow designed to prevent water wastage.

Tracing ancestors ...

If you want to trace your ancestors to find out if you have a washerwomen in your family tree, early evidence of washerwomen can be found by visiting the following sites

http://www.rootsweb.com/~ialee/data/census/1860blk-mul.htm

http://www.nathanielturner.com/washerwomeninbrooklyn1923.htm

http://www.wirksworth.org.uk/C61-occ.htm
http://www.1901censusonline.com/

Checkout these websites for further information:-

Image sources ...

For an 18th century image of a laundry maid by artist Henry Robert Morland
www.tate.org.uk/servlet/ViewWork?workid=10302
For a picture of The Washerwomen by Pierre-Auguste Renoir (1841-1919) visit
www.abcgallery.com/R/renoir/renoirlist.html
For a great image of Welsh washer women doing their washing in a stream at the public washing place From Costume of Great Britain by William Henry Pyne London 1808 Aquatintat
www.alamy.com/image-details-popup.asp?srch=&imageid=%7B5F358D24-FE29-4656-80CD-A1A80BCF6212%7Dvisit
Picture of Washer women from the army
www.cottonbalers.lynchburg.net/Laundresses.JPG

Port Sunlight ...

In 1887, William Lever made the decision to move his successful soap works from Warrington to a new location on the Wirral. His aim was to build a village for his workers but with access to road and rail links to transport his wares. When a new site close to the River Mersey became available, he set his new plans in motion.

Named *Port Sunlight* after his most popular brand of household soap, the factory opened in June 1889. Within six years they were producing 1600 tonnes of soap a week rising to 2400 tonnes, two years later.

Containing copra and pine kernel oil and packaged in his trade mark wrappers, *Sunlight Soap* created a lather much easier than rival varieties made from animal fats and by 1899, *Sunlight Flakes* had been developed to make the life of the housewife and laundry maid that little bit easier.

A visit to the Port Sunlight Museum and Lady Lever Art Gallery on the Wirral is a must. A fantastic array of items on show and entrance is free. Email: archives@unilver.com or visit Unilever plc, Unilever Archives & Records Management. PO Box 69, Port Sunlight, Wirral CH62 4ZD, Tel: (0151) 641 4551 to find out more.

The Life and Adventures of William Pilbeam
Malcolm Pilbeam

1873 - 1888 William's Early Life

This is the life story of my grandfather, William Pilbeam, who was born in Burwash, Sussex. It is a life full of adventure and intrigue - from his impoverished childhood, through service to his country where he experienced physical hardships and injuries, to becoming a loyal and trusted attendant to one of the world's richest people, culminating in an adventure which made the front pages of the national newspapers.

William was born on 21st February 1873 in Ham Lane, Burwash, Sussex, one of 9 children. He was born into a family that had resided in Burwash for many years. Both his father and grandfather had been blacksmiths in the village.

William's father and grandfather had a reputation for both drinking and violence and were fined a number of times. His grandmother not only had to bring up a large family but had to cope with her husband's violent episodes which unfortunately sometimes were directed against her.

On 14th December 1886, when William was 13, his grandfather wandered away from his son's house and nothing further was heard of him until 21st January 1887 when his body was discovered in a large pond. The local newspaper reported his body was not very decomposed because it had been covered in ice for some weeks. He may have been drunk and fallen into the pond.

1888 - 1896 Army Service

On 13th November 1888 William enlisted at

Hastings as a regular soldier. He lied about his age because his army records state he was 18 when in fact he was only 15. In his records he is described as being 5 feet 5 inches tall, of fresh complexion with brown hair and grey eyes, having a mole on his left shoulder and a scar on his right calf.

He was initially posted to Winchester with the Rifle Brigade for training. During his early days in the army he found it difficult to accept discipline facing charges on three occasions. However, his behaviour was not all bad because he was granted his first Good Conduct badge, although in March 1890 he was charged with being absent from the base and was confined to barracks for four days.

If he joined the army to see the world then his wish was granted. On his 18th birthday, he was posted to India with the 1st Battalion Rifle Brigade. The first posting was to a place called Ranikhet, where he arrived with 122 fellow riflemen on 11th April 1891. His transport to India was on HMS Malabar, a voyage of about 17 days. The Battalion stayed here until the end of October when they moved down to Bareilly for the cold weather! Here camp life was relatively quiet, with the various Companies in camp competing in both football and cricket tournaments. Later in William's life there is evidence that he was both a good footballer and cricketer so it is likely he participated in these tournaments.

On 9th November 1892 the Battalion started its march for Lower Bengal reaching Allahabad on the 20th November. By 26th December, having marched 480 miles they boarded trains at Asansol and arrived at Calcutta the following morning. On 13th November 1894 William was awarded his second Good Conduct Badge.

The next stage of William's army life took him to Hong Kong. Early on the morning of 30th November 1894 the Battalion embarked on the Warren Hastings at the Kiddespur docks and set sail around 9.00.a.m. steaming slowly down the River Hughti. After stopping off briefly at Singapore for the ship to take on coal, they ran into a monsoon for a couple of days which did cause a considerable amount of sea-sickness, but at 4.00. p.m. on 15th December they dropped anchor in Hong Kong.

The summer was hot and the Rifle Brigade were fitted with new khaki suits similar to what they had brought with them from India. However, water-bottles, which should have been provided upon the Battalion's arrival in Hong Kong, were not received until 8 months later! There were some cases of the plague in the spring and several men were sent to various houses to ensure that it did not spread.

Towards the end of 1895 William's time in the Rifle Brigade was nearing an end and on Christmas Eve he set sail for the UK on the hired freightship Teucer. He arrived home on 6th February 1896 and on 9th February was formally transferred to the Army Reserve.

1896 - 1899 Back to Civilian Life

Presumably William travelled back to Hastings where his parents then lived to seek employment and on 12 April he commenced duties at the West Cliffe branch of Ticehurst House mental institution.

Little did he know where this employment was to lead in the later years of his life. Although initially employed at West Cliffe at some stage during the following three years he was transferred to Ticehurst House itself which is located just outside the village of Ticehurst, Sussex. During this time in Ticehurst he became captain of Ticehurst Football Club.

1899 - 1901 The Boer War in South Africa

War was declared by the Boer Republics on 11th October 1899. At this time William was still in the Army Reserve and on 11th November 1899 he was recalled to army service under Special Order. He left his job on 14th November and was back at the Rifle Depot on 21st November.

Transfer to South Africa was quick and William sailed from Liverpool on Wednesday 13th December 1899 on HMS Majestic with just over 2000 other troops and one passenger, the Spanish Military Attache arriving in Cape Town on Friday 29th December, but William together with the majority of troops on board, sailed on to Natal.

Reservists from the 2nd Rifle Brigade initially formed part of the Composite Rifle Battalion commanded by Major Montagu-Stuart-Wortly of the Kings Royal Rifles. After landing at Durban, the most likely first stop for William would have been the camp at Frere. From Frere the Battalion moved on to Chievely guarding the line and rail-head.

The Battalion was then put into the 11th (Lancashire) Brigade under Major General Wynne. They were the first troops to enter Colenso on 20th February and the next day crossed the Tugela river in hot and tiring conditions. On 22nd February there was heavy fighting, including that at a flat topped hill just outside Colenso called Groblers Kloof and it was here that William was shot and wounded in the knee.

The battles around the Tugela Heights were aimed at relieving the siege at Ladysmith which had begun in November 1899. Within the town were over 21,000 civilian and military personnel who suffered disease and starvation on an unprecedented scale. After much fighting en route the first small contingent of relief troops finally entered Ladysmith on 28th February. It is not known if William's injury prevented him from participating in the march into Ladysmith.

1901 - Serious Injury and Discharge Home

On 12th January 1901 an accident occurred which resulted in an injury to his left eye which ultimately would lead to the loss of that eye. In a statement made by William on 2nd February 1901 at a Court of Enquiry at Pretoria he said. 'On the

afternoon of 12th January at Daspoort Camp, Pretoria I was helping the Armourer with some rifles. One of the rifles had a cartridge jammed in the breach. I tried to get it out with the extractor, but it did not succeed so I took a small file, and using the pointed end, I tried to get it over the rim of the cartridge. Suddenly I accidentally struck the cap of the cartridge with the file, and the cartridge exploded, a piece of metal was blown into my left eye; my eye has since been taken out. I first walked to the 11th Field Hospital and there I was attended to.'

The Medical Officer's report to the enquiry said: 'No 9774 Pte Pilbeam W 2nd Rifle Brigade was admitted into No 2 General Hospital Pretoria on 14.1.1901 suffering from wound to left eye said to have been caused by the explosion of a cartridge accidentally. The injury is likely to interfere with his efficiency as a soldier in the future.'

On 28th January the eye was extracted at the No 2 General Hospital Pretoria. By the 25 February William had been transferred to Wynberg No 1 General Hospital near Cape Town. He departed from Cape Town on the hospital ship SS Catalonia leaving on Monday 11th March and arrived back in Southampton on 11th April.

Arriving back in the UK William was transferred to the Herbert Hospital, Woolwich, London. His medical records state that the socket of his injured (left) eye was healthy and fit for an artificial eye which was recommended and subsequently fitted. He was put on a diet of varied roast and allowed stout as an extra! Following a period of recuperation William returned home to resume his job as an attendant at Ticehurst .

To conclude the story of his military life he was awarded the Queen's South Africa Medal under Army Order No 223 issued on 1st October 1902

with clasps for Tugela Heights, Relief of Ladysmith, Laings Nek and Belfast (Bergendal). Clearly a medal thoroughly earned.

1901 – Events that shape the rest of his life

Upon his return to employment at Ticehurst House William became attendant to a Prince Ahmed Seif-ed-Din who had been transferred the previous year from a prison in Cairo, Egypt after attempting to kill Prince Fuad, who later was to become king of Egypt. Prince Fuad was married to Seif-ed-Din's sister, Princess Chievekar. It was an unhappy marriage and the Princess had run away but Prince Fuad hauled her back. There was talk of divorce and Cairo was awash with rumour and scandal.

Prince Seif-ed-Din was unhappy with the way his sister was being treated so much so that on 7th May 1898 at the exclusive Khedivial Club he forced his way in and shot Prince Fuad three times including in his throat. Amazingly Prince Fuad survived the shooting. Prince Seif-ed-Din was arrested and was sentenced to five years penal servitude and he was sent to Gizeh prison. It was rumoured that the Prince was mad and formal papers show that in 1899 he made a homicidal attack against an official with a penknife he had somehow obtained, barricading himself in his cell and exhibiting all the symptoms of extreme terror. He had uttered murderous threats against the Prime Minister and was adamant that the English had made a plot to assassinate all the Khedivial family. (The Khedives were Turkish viceroys who governed Egypt between 1867 and 1914). He was formally declared insane in December 1899.

There was no suitable mental institution in which to hold him in Egypt and after consultation with Lord Cromer, the British Consul General, it was decided to send him to Dr. Newington's home for wealthy unbalanced people, Ticehurst House. A medical examination of the Prince took place at Claridges Hotel in London where it was found he was suffering from Delusional Insanity with ideas of persecution and was admitted to Ticehurst House on 27th July 1900.

Another examination took place on 29th August 1900 where it was noted in the records 'He has libidinous desires in regards to youths and boys' At a further examination on 29th January 1901 the Prince denied it was he who shot Prince Fuad, saying it was an assassin who escaped from prison in Baghdad!

Although the Prince was one of the wealthiest people in the world, because of his declared insanity the Egyptian authorities would not allow him access to his wealth. However he was given a substantial monthly allowance.

Over the course of the next 24 years William became a very trusted attendant to the Prince which ultimately would lead to the adventure of a lifetime in 1925. On 5th October 1901 William married Bessie Pearson at the parish

church in Westerham, Kent. Whether this was a quick romance or he had known Bessie prior to going off to South Africa I do not know. Bessie was born in Salehurst, Sussex in 1873 and both the 1891 and 1901 census returns show her as a servant at Rusthall Lodge near Tunbridge Wells.

1902 - 1924 – The Settled years

For a time William seemed reasonably settled. He and Bessie had five children and he had a steady job at Ticehurst House as attendant to the Prince.

The Prince had moved into what is known as the Highlands at Ticehurst House, a separate detached building, paying an extra £600 per annum, on top of the standard fees of £800, for the privilege and enjoying a life of relative luxury and, to a certain extent as the years went by, freedom. Although he had been declared insane his behaviour by some was said to be more eccentric than mad, although an episode is recorded in the Ticehurst House records in July 1904 which states he 'jumped out of his carriage and rushed to his Italian organ men and asked them to kill that William his attendant. Afterwards told his attendant he could not help it.'

By the time of the 1911 Census the family had moved to The Platts in Ticehurst. Meanwhile, back at Ticehurst House, as time went by the Prince was allowed out but William had to accompany him at all times. Records at Ticehurst House show that William was signed out for up to 15 hours some days, presumably when out with the Prince.

It was not an unusual sight for the Prince, with William and a driver, to be seen passing through the village where he was well known and would wave to the locals.

Such trips often involved a visit to St Leonard's near Hastings where the other branch of Ticehurst House, known as Westcliffe was located. These trips to St Leonard's would often involve a visit to the local cinema (Cinema de Luxe on the seafront) where the Prince would book a box, take tea at the Queen's hotel and walk along the promenade listening to the band playing. At all times, however, William would be at his side. Although the Prince obviously thought a lot of William his 'insanity' must at times caused some concern. In 1912, for example, they were at Sheerness (in north of Kent) and seeing the battleships off shore the Prince said to William he had surrounded this island with them and

intended to kill everybody but promised him (William) he would be left till last. William also took the Prince to visit his brother Harry who was a policeman at Hayward's Heath police station.

By 1922 William and Bessie had moved to 28 Sunnyside and at one point he was interested in buying some land to start a chicken farm. The seemingly settled life of the Pilbeam family was, however, about to come to an abrupt end in August 1925 when William shot to national fame for his part in helping Prince Seif-ed-Din escape from Ticehurst House and flee the country.

The escape plot must have taken considerable planning. William must have been sworn to secrecy and continued his normal routine right up to the last minute including playing cricket. So secret was it, that not even Bessie was aware.

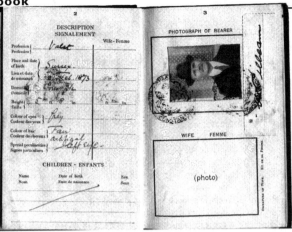

1925 – The Escape of The Prince

Although officially declared insane by the Egyptian authorities his mother, Princess Nougan, never doubted her son's sanity and over the years she employed the best lawyers to try to obtain his release. She even visited England and gained the interest of Ramsay MacDonald, a senior politician, who became Prime Minister in 1924. He also made efforts to secure the release of the Prince. Then all of a sudden at the beginning of September the national newspapers reported the disappearances of the Prince and William.

In the immediate period prior to the escape there were rumours of renewed efforts to secure his release and Ticehurst House even admitted they had put extra security on the Prince for fear of kidnap.

One theory was that an American was instrumental in planning the escape. On one visit to England Princess Nougan met an American attorney frequently and after she left the country the Attorney met William and John Bastone, his friend who worked at St Leonard's. Some years later Bastone said William introduced him to a New York attorney whilst walking along Hastings seafront and told him of the escape plot.

On July 7th 1925 two Turkish visitors, Princess Nougan and Ibrahim Faridun Pasha, a high official in the Turkish government and husband of the Princess(and step father to the Prince), took rooms at the Royal Victoria Hotel in St Leonard's. Hotel staff said they met a well dressed man at the hotel and made enquiries in Deal about hiring a fast boat for a trip to France. During August Bank Holiday William took a day trip to Boulogne, missed the boat back and sent a telegram to his wife to say he had to stay overnight and would return the next day.

On 30th August the Prince was driven in his own luxurious car from Ticehurst to Hastings accompanied by William and another attendant, Hyland. Upon arrival in Hastings the Prince, with William and Hyland went to the promenade on

Hastings Pier and listened to the band for a short while. At around 11.30.a.m. the Prince asked for a newspaper and William, being the senior attendant, sent Hyland to Hastings railway station to buy one.

As soon as Hyland left for the station they tried to buy tickets for Boulogne. Their first attempt was unsuccessful. It is not clear why and one story was that they were only selling tickets to Eastbourne at the time and the other was that the ticket seller saw the Prince not to be English or French so declined to sell a ticket to him. At this delay they went for a beer at the refreshment buffet and shortly afterwards managed to purchase tickets to Boulogne. They then boarded the *PS Devonia* for the trip across the channel.

By the time they had boarded the *Devonia* they had been joined by Bastone the attendant from Westcliffe. On the trip to Boulogne William shaved off the Prince's beard. They also drank whisky and the Prince smoked almost continuously. The Prince suffered from sea-sickness.

In 1937 a book about the life of the Prince Ibrahim Faridun Pasha recounted details of the escape at the end of September 1925.

Upon arrival in Boulogne they were met by the Prince's mother and step father and boarded a plane which flew them to Paris. (*Some years later when Bastone returned to England he stated that they went to Paris by fast car*) In Paris, however, an unexpected delay arose over their passports which prevented their onward journey. In the meantime fifteen detectives had been sent from England to try to trace the Prince, whose photos were in all the French newspapers. To avoid detection they moved from one hotel to another.

At one hotel they were nearly caught. At 4 00.a.m. one of the detectives traced their whereabouts but a faithful friend managed to tip them off and they fled the hotel minutes before the detectives arrived.

After several days in Paris their passports arrived and they motored to Marseilles on the Mediterranean coast where they embarked on the *SS Phrygle* which was bound for eastern ports.

They travelled as second class passengers assuming they would be less likely to be recognized,

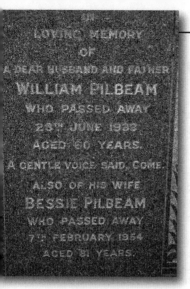

In
LOVING MEMORY
OF
A DEAR HUSBAND AND FATHER
WILLIAM PILBEAM
WHO PASSED AWAY
28TH JUNE 1933
AGED 60 YEARS
A GENTLE VOICE SAID, COME
ALSO OF HIS WIFE
BESSIE PILBEAM
WHO PASSED AWAY
7TH FEBRUARY 1954
AGED 81 YEARS.

an assumption that proved incorrect. In fact a Frenchman both recognized and spoke to them. Fortunately he proved friendly not only in keeping the secret but helping them in the rough and ready ways of actually being second class passengers.

1925 - 1932 Life in Constantinople (Turkey) and return to England

William and Bastone did not find life easy at first in Constantinople. The Prince, relishing his new found freedom, was not an easy master. It appears William and Bastone lived in a hotel and travelled each day to attend to the Prince. They were forever on the move and found it extremely tiring. Bastone especially was finding it difficult to cope with; he found things dull and complained bitterly about the lack of company. They also found the hot climate difficult to deal with. William coped much better than Bastone. He was genuinely attached to the Prince and, to quote the 1937 book *'made Seif-ed-Din fortunes his own and took the rough luck with philosophy.'*

In the spring of 1928 Bastone had had enough and left. When he arrived back in England he was arrested, taken to Hastings and charged with *'aiding and abetting Pilbeam, a mental attendant at Dr Newington's Home* (i.e. Ticehurst House) *to assist a patient to escape from the Home on 31st August 1925.'* He pleaded *'Guilty'* and was fined the maximum penalty of £20.

I have been told by family members that my father, Frank and his first wife Olive (and probably other members of the family) met William in Boulogne a couple of years after the escape. Looking at William's passport visa stamps it shows he visited France in the summer of 1927 and again in 1931. Bessie obtained a passport in June 1927 and probably went with my father to meet her husband in Boulogne. The passport shows she visited Turkey in 1929.

In 1930 William became very ill and told the Prince he wished to return home to England. It is not clear when this illness started but there is a photo of William with a Dr Essa(?) Pacha taken in 1929

The Prince could not bear the thought of William leaving and implored him to stay. William agreed but only on the condition that Bessie could join him in Turkey. From Bessie's passport it appears she spent a few weeks with William in 1929 because her visa was only valid for two months. She returned to

England then went back to Turkey permanently in the summer of 1931. For this journey it appears William returned to France to meet her and accompany her back to Turkey.

In order to help William the Prince called in the best doctors available. However, they could do nothing for him and knowing he was going to die he decided to return to England for good with Bessie towards the end of 1932. In December of that year he said a final farewell to the Prince.

Knowing he was a *'wanted'* man he wrote to his brother Harry, an ex police sergeant. Harry then arranged for a detective to accompany him to Dover to meet William off the boat from France. As soon as he set foot on English soil William was arrested. When in court William pleaded *'Guilty'* and was fined the maximum penalty of £20. This was of little consequence to him as the Prince had been financially generous.

After his court appearance William and Bessie went to live with their daughter Dorothy in Etchingham, East Sussex, where he spent the last few months of his life. He lived long enough, however, to learn that the Prince had married Princess Ulviya whose father was a pre-war Governor of Constantinople.

1933 William's Death

William died on 28th June 1933 at the Tunbridge Wells General Hospital. Although relatively young at the age of 60 his life had undoubtedly been an adventurous, and at times, a painful one. William was buried at St Mary's church in Ticehurst.

The general impression to most people was that William did not return from Turkey a wealthy man. However, in a note written many years ago by Harry's daughter she states *'Aunt Bessie declared to the world at large that they were penniless but she showed us the money belts around her body with a fortune of money and jewels.'* Certainly after William's death Bessie move back to Ticehurst and was able to live in relative luxury until her death on 7th February 1954.

Malcolm Pilbeam

Malcolm started his family history research some 20 years ago but gave it up after a short time. After taking early retirement he decided research his grandfather. He continues to expand the rest of the family tree. Malcolm has been married to Shirley for 38 years in June and they have two children and two grandchildren. Malcolm and his children are West Ham United Football Club season ticket holders. Malcolm has written a book about his grandfather and can be contacted by email at malcolm_pilbeam@yahoo.com

The Wreck of the Royal Charter
Karen Foy

Gold bullion, the Australian Colonies and one of the fastest clipper ships of the 1850's provides a fascinating tale combining tragedy, heroism and a fight for survival. Culminating in disaster off the coast of North Wales, Karen Foy finds out more.

When Stephen Roose Hughes married Jane Ann Moulsdale in 1843, he was no doubt happy with his ordinary life and looking forward to a long career with the church, but sixteen years later his faith would be tested with a tragedy that shocked the world.

A Step Back in Time . . .

The year was 1855 and at *Sandycroft Ironworks* on the banks of the River Dee, a new type of ship had just been built. The steam clipper's new design meant that in the absence of wind, the ship could run on its auxiliary steam engines. Weighing 2719 tons and stretching to 102.4 metres long, she was built by *George Cramm* and completed by engineer *William Patterson*, an expert in his field who had overseen the construction of two of *Brunel's* ships – the *Great Britain* and the *Great Western*.

Launched as the *Royal Charter* in front of a crowd of spectators and *'christened'* by a Mrs S. Bright , the majestic ship was built for the *Australian Screw Steamship Company – Gibbs, Bright and Co* – which would later become the *Liverpool and Australian Navigation Company*. For three years she was recognised as a top class passenger ship making regular journeys to Australia transporting up to 600 travellers in first class luxury accommodation with room for additional cargo if needed. Such was the speed of this powerful ship she could complete the passage in 60 days.

On the Brink of Disaster . . .

In late August 1859, the *Royal Charter* set sail from Melbourne laden with over 500 passengers and crew and an estimated £320,000 worth of gold bullion as cargo. Many on board were wealthy gold miners who had struck it rich in Australia's gold fields eager to return home with their rewards on one of the fastest ships of the day.

After 58 days at sea, the *Royal Charter* docked in Ireland and dropped off seventeen of its passengers before making the final leg of the journey to Liverpool but it was on the following night that disaster struck. The onboard barometer was dropping rapidly and a storm was brewing in the Irish Sea that soon developed to gale force winds which continued to rise to force 12 - or hurricane force - on the Beaufort Scale.

Making the decision *not* to head to Holyhead harbour to sit out the storm, Captain Thomas Taylor continued on to Liverpool. In the early hours of the 26th of October 1859, the *Royal Charter* was in serious trouble. Attempts to slow

Panton Arms, Pentraeth

rescued. These amounted to 18 of 376 passengers, 5 of 11 riggers working their passage and 18 of more than 100 crew members – none of them officers. Over 400 others perished needlessly beneath the waves.

In Search of the Truth . . .

When news of the tragedy hit the headlines, it was claimed that more could have been done for the victims and that the villagers were only interested in the gold which was being washed ashore. It was at this time that Charles Dickens - the essayist and novelist who also provided reports for periodic journals - came to Anglesey to find out the *true* story.

Staying at the Panton Arms in the nearby village of Pentraeth, Dickens discovered a completely different version of events to those sensationalised by the Victorian press.

Instrumental in tending to the bodies of the victims was Reverend Stephen Roose Hughes, rector of the local parish church of St Gallgo. Dickens witnessed the tenderness and care which Reverend Hughes showed to the victims who lay in a makeshift morgue within the church. Going to meticulous lengths to record any distinguishing features about the bodies, the contents of their pockets, even cutting buttons from their clothes as identification, Hughes went on to write 1075 letters to the relatives, answering queries and trying to provide comfort and consolation.

With his brother, Reverend Hugh Robert Hughes, they buried 140 victims, some unidentified, in the churchyard at St Gallgo. Those washed ashore further along the coast were buried by the brothers at Llaneugrad, Penrhosllugwy, Amlwch, Llanddona, Llanbedrgoch and Llanddyfnan.

Dickens felt that the villagers and their compassionate Reverend had been wrongly accused. Claims for valuables and personal property were settled by the government and the cargo was dealt with by the owners and insurance brokers. The fishing community of Moelfre was deeply affected by the events of the shipwreck as bodies continued to be washed up on land or tragically caught in their nets so they were by no means having the easy time of it that was being portrayed in the press.

her movement by chopping off sails, rigging and masts were to no avail; her anchor chains snapped and at Point Lynus near Moelfre, Anglesey, the vessel - pushed towards the rocks by the ferocious winds - began to break up.

Despite repeated distress signals in the form of lights, flares and cannon, in winds of over 100 mph it was impossible to launch the Moelfre Lifeboat and local men, Thomas Hughes and Mesech Williams watched helplessly from the shore as the scene unfolded before them. Desperate to assist the stricken vessel they looked on as Joseph Rogers, an anglicised Maltese member of the *Royal Charter* crew, managed to swim with a rope - despite being driven back three times - to the nearby rocks enabling a rescue attempt to begin. Forming a human chain and using the *'boson's chair'* method of winching the victims ashore, twenty eight local men worked in dangerous conditions, tirelessly trying to save as many survivors as possible. That night 41 people were

A Lasting Memorial . . .

Dickens was so strongly influenced by what he'd observed that along with his report, he wrote an account of the catastrophe in his book *'The Uncommercial Traveller'* giving such vivid descriptions gleaned from his conversations with the Reverend Hughes, clarifying the power of the storm and its aftermath.

'So tremendous had the force of the sea been when it broke the ship, that it had beaten one

St Gallgo's Church

THIS MONUMENT
has been erected by
PUBLIC SUBSCRIPTION.
TO THE MEMORY OF
those who perished in the wreck
of the ROYAL CHARTER,
off MOELFRE
on the coast of ANGLESEY
on her passage from
AUSTRALIA to ENGLAND,
WEDNESDAY, THE 26TH DAY OF OCTOBER
A. D. 1859.

In the months that followed the strain of the experience began to take its toll on the kind hearted Reverend Hughes. Although immortalised in Dickens book, Rev Stephen Roose Hughes died three years later on 4th February 1862, aged 47. Oak panelling inside the church is dedicated to his memory and his gravestone, alongside that of so many others that he'd buried, bears a fitting inscription by his widow, Jane:

His noble and disinterested exertions on the memorable occasion of the terrible Wreck of the Royal Charter are well known throughout the World. The subsequent effects of those exertions proved too much for his constitution and suddenly bought him to an early Grave.

Every year on the date of his death, Reverend Stephen's life is celebrated at St Gallgo's Church with a commemorative service.

Today, as you walk through the tranquil village of Moelfre and along this rugged piece of coastline it's hard to imagine the terrible disaster which affected so many lives. Up on the headland Coastal Path, overlooking the site of the *Royal Charter's* final hours, stands a permanent reminder of those who perished in one of the worst shipwrecks to occur on Britain's shores in the form of a stone memorial. The dangers faced by seamen in this area can also be noted in that exactly one hundred years after the *Royal Charter* disaster, the ship, the *Hindlea* also struck these same rocks in another gale but thankfully, this time, all the crew were saved by the Moelfre Lifeboat under the command of Coxswain, Richard Evans.

great ingot of gold, deep into a strong and heavy piece of her solid iron-work: in which also several loose sovereigns that the ingot had swept in before it, had been found, as firmly embedded as though the iron had been liquid when they were forced there.'

He also helped to acquire donations to build a memorial to the victims in the form of an obelisk. At one stage this stood inside the church above the mass grave of many of the unidentified victims but during the 20th century it was moved to a peaceful location within the churchyard.

Local Heroes ...

The St Gallgo Church website at www.royalcharterchurch.org.uk/wreck.html records the names of the 28 local men whose names are sadly not to be found on any monument to commemorate their bravery and courage. There is a fitting quote from Ecclesiasticus 43 verses 8 and 9: '*Some there by who have left behind them a name to be commemorated in story. Others are unremembered; they are perished as though they had never existed.*'

THE MOELFRE TWENTY EIGHT

Thomas Roberts	Owen Roberts	Owen Roberts jr.	David Williams
Mesech Williams	Robert Lewis	Thomas Hughes	John Hughes
William Owen	Richard Hughes	Evan Williams	John Parry
John Owens	Thomas Parry	John Lewis	Joseph Williams
Thomas Owen	William Williams	Richard Mathew	Israel Mathew
William Pritchard	Owen Hughes	Richard Evans	David Owen
John Lewis Jr	William Owen	Lewis Francis	John Francis

Facts and Figures

The Illustrated London News of October 1859 reported that in the '*Board of Trade Wreck Register of 1859*' there were 133 wrecks and 90 casualties resulting in 798 lives lost during the heavy storms of October 25th and 26th 1859.

Although much of the gold was recovered by salvage divers in the months following the disaster many artefacts have been recovered in recent years including spectacles, pistols, sovereigns and other personal items.

Folklore suggests that some of the large old houses in Moelfre were funded on gold washed ashore from the wreck with some of the island families becoming rich overnight.

Joseph Rogers (birth name Giuseppi (Guze) Ruggier) was awarded a gold medal and five pounds for his bravery as well as a citation by the *Royal National Lifeboat Institution* which reads:

"That the Gold medal and £5 be presented to Joseph Rogers in testimony of his heroic conduct in swimming ashore with a line from the Steam Ship Royal Charter, whereby many lives were saved, on the occasion of the unfortunate wreck of that vessel, during a very heavy gale of wind on the Anglesey Coast on the night of the 25th October 1859."

In 2009, in commemoration of the 150th Anniversary of the disaster a pair of bronze sculptures by Sam Holland was unveiled at the Moelfre Seawatch Centre on Anglesey. One depicts Joseph Rogers climbing a rock face whilst the other shows the wrecked *Royal Charter*. The

inscription reads *'Joseph Rodgers* (notice spelling) *A hero of the Royal Charter.'* Underneath is an eight pointed Maltese Cross in recognition of his nationality. For more fascinating information on Rogers and his life after the disaster why not visit a dedicated website at www.agius.com/maltese/ruggier.htm

Henry Nelson O'Neil, historical genre painter and friend of Charles Dickens was inspired to create an oil painting entitled *'A Volunteer'* after the incident which depicts Joseph Rogers just before his leap of faith into the stormy sea in an attempt to rescue some of the Charter's passengers. In later years, the piece is believed to have formed part of the art collection of rock star Rod Stewart who sold the painting at Sotheby's in 2001.

As a result of the tragedy, the Meteorological Office, overseen by Captain Robert Fitzroy, brought in the first gale warning service to help prevent similar tragedies in the future. Fitzroy had achieved lasting fame as the Captain of the HMS Beagle on Charles Darwin's famous voyage and is also credited with making accurate weather forecasting a reality as a direct result of the work he carried out, inspired by the *Royal Charter* disaster.

Today, the remains of the wreck lie in less than 5 metres of water as a series of iron bulkheads and ribs which become covered and uncovered by the sands each year.

Further Reading –

The Golden Wreck by Alexander McKee gives a detailed account of the doomed ship, the *Royal Charter* and the lives of those affected by the tragedy. Avid Publications April 2000. ISBN-10: 1902964020

Details and snippets about the vessel and its fate as recorded in the Mersey Times can be found online at www.old-merseytimes.co.uk/ROYALCHARTER.html with more information at the Liverpool Records Office.

**Charles Dickens
1843**

Karen Foy has been a keen family historian for just over ten years . As a freelance writer her articles appear regularly in family history magazines such as Family History Monthly.

A Maritime Memorial . . .

Far from the island shores of Anglesey, on the opposite side of Great Britain is the fishing town of Whitby. It is here that another connection with the Royal Charter lies.

On 5th October 1789, in the village of Cropton, North Yorkshire, William Scoresby was born to a master mariner and arctic whaler, William Scoresby. In the years that followed, he too became a distinguished sailor accompanying his father on numerous voyages and later became an Arctic explorer in his own right. At the age of 21, he was given his first command and initially brought back the produce of thirty whales to Whitby but his accomplishments did not stop there.

On voyages between 1815 and 1822, he reported his maritime observations and made improvements to the magnetic compass culminating in his version of the compass needle being showcased at an exhibition of the British Association for the Advancement of Science in 1836. As a result, the Admiralty acknowledged the improvements made and the design was officially produced and put into use. His many discoveries and explorations charting the arctic oceans and laying the foundations for future polar expeditions led to the East Greenlandic town of Scoresbysund and the suburb of Scoresby in Melbourne, Australia being named after him.

A slight deviation or possibly an addition to this maritime career took place in 1826 when William Scoresby was ordained and after a time as Curate in Bessingby, as Chaplain at the Mariner's Church in Liverpool and incumbent in Exeter, he came to preach at St Mary's Church in Whitby at a memorial service in commemoration of two of the town's whaling ships which had been lost in the Greenland seas. By 1856, he took a commission to test the effect of iron ships on his compass and to adjust it to suit this new type of vessel. He spent the voyage on the Royal Charter – a sailing clipper with a small 200 hp steam engine and an iron hull – built in the period between wooden sailing ships and steamers.

When the Royal Charter was wrecked on a subsequent voyage the Scoresby Chair was later made from its timbers in honour of the work and achievements of William Scoresby. Ornately carved and embellished with anchors, ropes, a compass and the Scoresby crest, the chair was presented in 1922 to St Mary's Church in Whitby by Dr Scoresby Jackson, where it remains on display to this day.

St Mary's Church, Whitby
home of
The Scoresby Chair

The Scoresby Chair

Definitely not a Gentleman
- One Master Mariner in the Age of Sail
Len Barnett

Over the years I have studied numerous sets of mercantile crew agreements, crew lists and ships' official logs where discipline had broken down and this has been reflected occasionally in my commercial writing: such as in the 7th edition of *The Family and Local History Handbook*. Time and again these logs show the same negative tendencies of crew members, but because they were written exclusively from the command's perspective it can be difficult coming to objective conclusions as to what actually occurred: especially as records giving others' perspectives are exceedingly rare and masters have automatically been regarded as beyond reproach.

The following is overwhelmingly based on the crew lists and ship's official log of one such voyage. However, reference to other records; such as the vessel's certificate of registration; *Lloyd's Register of British and Foreign Shipping*; *Lloyd's List*; Board of Trade registers of certificates; and newspaper reports has also been made.

By the 1850s while it is not that unusual to see clauses in agreements stating that voyages could last anything up to five years, before viewing these particular records I have never seen a trading voyage that lasted longer than three. Transcribing this log (actually four bound together) covering almost five years, some of the entries showed aspects not normally recorded. Investigating further, it has become possible not only to *prove* less than respectable behaviour of the master mariner, but also to shed light on other aspects that might be of interest to genealogists.

For reasons that should become apparent, it is worth pointing out that I might have been the first person ever to have read this log. Although shipping masters, or other officials, were supposed to view these documents periodically, it is highly likely that no one bothered in this case. This is because both the crew lists and log are in a complete mess. (There are no agreements surviving.) For a start, the handwriting is absolutely foul. *Many* of the dates and places of signing on and discharge in the crew lists are provably incorrect, with numerous mariners that cannot be identified both through poor record keeping and probably also through giving false information. There also seems to be at least one sheet missing. As for the log, among complexities, the master had his own way of compiling entries, whereby individuals were given '*blocks*' of pages, added to over time. As and when space was running short, blank spaces would be filled in. Additionally, some pages have been ripped out,

the remains of a few still evident.

Constructed in 1856 the *Dennis Hill* was a Newcastle-built barque of 349 tons, with an A1 rating from *Lloyd's Register*. Bound for Shanghai, on 22nd December 1857 she sailed from London, under the command of Robert Atkin. Born in Warkworth, Northumberland, he was then 43. Holding a master's certificate of service, although an experienced master, prior to gaining this berth on her building his only previous command had been of a *far* smaller vessel for ten years. He was also a minority shareholder of the *Dennis Hill*, with eight of the sixty-four, the rest held by a Hill family from England's north east.

Clearing the Downs on 26th December, via the Sunda Strait her first landfalls were Woosung and Shanghai in the Celestial Empire in June 1858. By mid September she had transited the Chinese coast to Swatow, where she probably remained to late October. Until March 1859 she was effectively either at Swatow, or Shanghai. In April she was at Amoy, before returning to Shanghai. It was not until July that she again sailed, this time for Nagasaki and Kanagawa, in Japan. She was still at the latter place in November, possibly at Shanghai in December and Whampoa in January, before definitely arriving in Hong Kong in late January 1860. Later in February she sailed for Bangkok, Thailand, but was back at Hong Kong in May. Until late November she was at Hong Kong, Shanghai

Dennis Hill

or Foo-Chow-Foo. Her next leg was a departure from the recent past, in being bound for Melbourne, Australia. Shortly before Christmas she was in the vicinity of the volcanic island of Krakatoa and arrived at Melbourne in early February 1861. Via Newcastle, N.S.W. in April, her next calling place was Wellington, New Zealand as of mid May. She was still at Wellington late in July and her next definite landfall was again Kanagawa in mid September. Most of October was spent back at Shanghai, shifting to Foo-Chow-Foo late in the month. Chartered for New York from there, she was at Hong Kong for four days later in November. She passed through the Sunda Straits early in December and with a short stay at Saint Helena in late January, arrived at New York in March 1862. Possibly via Baton Rouge in mid May, her next destination was Kingston, Jamaica: arriving sometime in early June. Off again in August, northwards she was at Saint John's, Newfoundland for eight days in September. Finally, with an unplanned short stay at Stromness, in the Orkneys, the *Dennis Hill* arrived in London on 25th October 1862.

As might be expected the original crew was disposed of variously and substitutes were signed on as and when necessary. Immediately striking was in the sheer number of seamen officers employed.

Of the eleven, or possibly twelve, in mates' berths; seven were discharged; one was discharged to hospital; but also one is said to have gone insane; and two deserted. Even of those discharged, only one seems to have lasted over six months and one other over a year. The average for all the others was three months onboard.

As for second mates, the position was even more unusual. Of the probable eight in total, three were known to have been discharged. Beforehand two of these had been disrated. Another was probably discharged, having been temporarily disrated. Three others had deserted and two were gaoled. One of the latter had deserted and been gaoled, the other having been disrated and gaoled. Only two appear to have remained more than a year and again the average time onboard for the others discharged was three months.

It should also be mentioned that at least on one seaborne leg Robert Atkin was the only seaman officer onboard. Presumably he took personal charge of one watch, with someone unknown the other.

The mate on sailing from London was Willoughby Arthur Granger, 29 years old and from Gosport, Hampshire. In late February 1858 the master logged his first criticism, stating that he had been *'conducting himself in a most unofficer like manner.'* By late March *serious* problems had arisen with his professionalism. According to the official log the mate became increasingly argumentative and strange. On 17th April 1858 he was relieved of his watch and confined to his cabin: although allowed exercise on deck under strict conditions that he did not live up to. Due to difficulties in discharging cargo and in accounting for stores, it is known that Willoughby Granger had been returned to duty on arrival at Shanghai. However, the day after a scuffle with the master he was taken before the British Consul. On 14th July 1858 Willoughby Arthur Granger forfeited two months' wages and was ordered to be discharged.

What subsequently happened to this chap is far from clear. He might have been dead by 1861 when his certificate was returned to London and there are no further ink entries in the Board of Trade registers. Also, it is relatively safe to conclude that Robert Atkin's loggings on him were accurate, as prior to signing on to the *Dennis Hill* there had been numerous detrimental reports in the register.

Another mate whose career seems to have ended on leaving this vessel was Daniel Crerar: 28 years old from Nova Scotia, with a master's certificate of competency. As the dates in the crew lists cannot be reconciled with loggings, in all likelihood he signed onto her around mid August 1858 at Shanghai, lasted at least until late November and possibly late December, when he was discharged to hospital.

Patterns can be detected from the seamen officers that deserted though. George Lawrence Leask was mate for only a number of days. An Aberdonian of 22, at that time he only held a second mate's ticket for competency, but this was unimportant in the *'Far Flung'* at that time. He

probably signed on at Shanghai on 6th August 1858, was certainly onboard on the 7th and 8th and had gone by the 11th, but possibly earlier. With a slightly chequered career, by 1865 he had a (first) mate's ticket and continued at sea until 1873.

William Cowen was a 22 year-old Liverpudlian that was said to have signed on at Hong Kong, on 15th October 1860, as mate. The following day John Stafford, a Dubliner of the same age, joined as second mate. On 9th December both came into conflict with the master, mostly over their failure to wash down the deck during the morning watch. The master accused Cowen of being 'mutinous' ten days later. Further criticism of the mate followed in January. Prior to 13th March 1861, while in Hobsons Bay, Melbourne, both mates quietly slipped away. Nothing can be determined as to William Cowen's subsequent life, as he had no certificate. Had he remained in this region he would not have really needed one until the implementation of the Merchant Shipping (Colonial) Act of 1869. John Stafford, on the other hand, at the time had an only mate's certificate; eventually an ordinary master's of competency; and seems to have had a respectable career through to 1890.

Little is recorded of Thomas Brown, the second mate after John Stafford. According to the crew lists he was a 33 year-old Londoner and signed on in Melbourne on 11th March 1861. Apart from being absent from the vessel for twelve hours a few days later, the only other logging is when he quietly deserted between 25th and 26th May 1861. (At the time of writing, I have found out nothing further on him.)

John Tucker's case is fascinating. About 27 years old from Devonport, although he too held an ordinary master's ticket of competency, probably signed on as second mate at Shanghai on 23rd March 1859. He witnessed a logging on 20th June, when David Scotland, the sailmaker, had lost a scraper over the side. A week later the second

mate was threatened and abused by the carpenter, James Smith, returning off shore drunk. The master, Robert Atkin, intervened and inflamed the situation, resulting in the carpenter being gaoled for a month. On 1st July Tucker attempted and failed to transfer to another vessel and then get discharged from his present one. Immediately withdrawing his labour, he then went shore without leave as he pleased and tried to see the Consul: deserting on 8th July. Four days later at one bell (0.30 a.m.) there was a curious incident onboard. Two European sailors in a small Chinese boat were detected stealing two 'swivell' guns, with another still lying on the deck. David Scotland was one of the witnesses to a claimed conversation days before in which essentially John Tucker planned to rob the Lazarette in lieu of his wages. On supplying this information to the local Superintendent of Police John Tucker was tried and convicted on 15th July. He received '3 months imprisonment with hard labour in H.M. Consular Jail' for the theft and another three months for desertion, with his pay 'to go as far as possible towards pay for the guns.'

After this he found his way back to the United Kingdom and continued his career. Mostly in mates' billets, he had one command, but as second mate of the Niagara was drowned in 1876. Possibly due to the shambles of the paper work, there was no mention of his time on the Dennis Hill, or his conviction in his entry in the relevant Board of Trade register.

David Scotland has already been mentioned. Originally he signed on in London as second mate. A Scot from Kincardine, he was 42 years old but had only had a mate's ticket of service for three years. Other than one minor case of leave breaking before sailing, there is no indication that he did not acquit himself well in the worrying period when Willoughby Granger had gone insane. Nevertheless, he was not reappointed as mate. Instead, an able seaman, Thomas Normandale, was put in charge of the mate's

watch. By mid November at Shanghai David Scotland was obviously disenchanted, as he hadgone on shore without leave twice. On the second occasion he had tried to make complaints to the Consul but was told to return on board. On the 19th his complaint was heard but dismissed and it appears that the Consul wanted him to be discharged. Instead, Robert Atkin disrated him to able seaman and sailmaker. Seemingly it was not until two days later that David Scotland learned of his loss of status and wanted to go to see the Consul once again. While he remained onboard as sailmaker until discharged in Hong Kong in October 1860 without apparent further trouble, the scraper logging seems more than slightly petty. Also, while impossible to prove one way or the other, I certainly wonder if some revenge was exacted on John Tucker in the theft of the swivel guns. Anyway, after another billet as a second mate, in 1863 he then shipped as sailmaker of the *General Windham* from London for Otago: dying at sea in 1864.

Thomas King's time as second mate can only be guessed at. Someone apparently signed on in this berth in July 1859 and was stated as being discharged at Kanagawa that September. However, there is no sign of any second mate in the log until August 1860 when Thomas King was disrated for being asleep on watch. (Falling asleep on watch was all too common, for perfectly understandable reasons and was still evident in my time at sea.) Having then withdrawn his labour through claiming illness, it is not clear whether he was also incarcerated until being 'returned to duty' five days later. In September when seemingly in harbour he witnessed a logging as 'second mate,' although confusingly Robert Atkin had a tendency

to refer to the disrated in the log in their previous positions. Anyway, it would appear that the second mate was got rid of in early October at Shanghai.

The last second mate that was disrated was James Lumsden. A 25 year-old Scot probably from Fraserburgh (as applications for mates' certificates that should have identified him appear to have been falsified to hide his time on the *Dennis Hill*), he was said to have signed on at Shanghai on 14th October 1861 as boatswain. He is first recorded in the log on the 20th as second mate, but on 29th November he too was disrated for being asleep on watch. The carpenter, David Carmichael, was detailed to take charge of his watch. Nevertheless, on 10th December Lumsden was re-appointed as second mate: the carpenter being too busy with his own work. James Lumsden was discharged at New York.

The last second mate, William Hunter, was not formally disrated, but ended up in a worse situation. A 24 year-old islander from Stromness with an only mate's ticket, he signed on at New York in April 1862. Found asleep on watch more than once on the way to Jamaica, he lost his watch to the boatswain, Jacob Mercer, on 1st June. Unusually, Robert Atkin tried to have him paid off twelve days later, but Hunter refused. The master then had him imprisoned onboard. On the 21st this defaulter refused to be ejected to the forecastle and demanded to see a magistrate. There are no further entries in the log, but on the crew list William Hunter was discharged and 'left in Jail' on 15th July.

In voyages where discipline disintegrated it was not unusual for the petty officers (also known as 'idlers') and seamen to be disrated. This too occurred on the *Dennis Hill*, although the level was not spectacularly high. From loggings, the first cook, an American named John Williams, seems to have been a homicidal maniac! He was disrated on 14th March 1858, presumably with the steward, George Ramsden, also acting as cook. In mid September, Ramsden, in turn was disrated, generally for being 'slovenly,' although also because he fought back on being assaulted by the master: with an ordinary seaman, William Drury, being detailed off for stewarding. Ramsden's complaints not having been taken seriously either by naval officers or the Consul at Swatow, eventually he managed to escape legally. In December, while at Shanghai, George Ramsden signed onto a man-o-war: *Nimrod*. The first sailmaker and carpenter, Thomas Robertson, had caused violent drunken trouble in August and November 1858 while at Shanghai and it may well have been that he was an alcoholic. Interestingly, when the carpenter took his complaints to the Consul, the mate was fined one dollar, although the complainant was also severely reprimanded. On 30th December the

reasons entered into ships' official logs for withdrawal of labour and the stock answer in most published masters' memoirs has been that 'the people' have been 'the scum of the earth:' determined to cause mayhem and desert. Undoubtedly, there were some pretty hard characters that were seafarers, but this simply does not wear. Whatever the reasons and there could have been many to choose (from inedible food, poor pay, foul living conditions, unseaworthy vessels and brutal mates), often situations became extremely violent, with defaulters imprisoned in irons on bread and water.

master criticised Thomas Robertson professionally, who took this badly and the end result was that the carpenter was disrated. While in port Robertson continued to do precisely what he liked and eventually deserted at Shanghai in March 1859. As well as at least one threat to another carpenter, David Carmichael, three seamen were disrated from able to ordinary seamen.

By the standards of the era, the numbers desertions of seamen, or those joining men-o-war were not all that noticeable. Even so, there are aspects that are. Having been at anchor for months and repeatedly making representations to Consuls without success, seamen often ran at the point of sailing: probably to lessen the chances of being apprehended and returned. Also, there must have been a sorry state of affairs aboard this vessel if even the master's apprentice son, Robert Foreman Atkin, deserted. Perhaps unfortunately for this lad, he was deposited back onboard some days later!

The day-to-day offences and punishment on this merchantman are identical to many others where the logs have survived. Commonly, men have objected to orders given by mates, whereby bad language, blows or wounds were exchanged. Not infrequently these have been at times of great stress during adverse weather at sea and commands have made much of these occurrences as 'mutinous.' But, in my experience it is precisely at such times when those that see themselves abused do crack. Then there are the routine loggings where the people throughout time became disinterested, argumentative and violent. Not infrequently they point blank refused to turn to (work). Decades before mariners began to organise themselves in trade unions, this withdrawal of labour must have been regarded as a legitimate action by those with grievances: even if not recognised by the Board of Trade. Other than for medical problems, hardly ever were

As on many other merchantmen, while in port the disaffected continually attempted to have their complaints heard by naval authorities and Consuls: whether given leave and permission or not. With the 'system' obviously weighted against them, it is comparatively rare to see complainants getting what they regarded as justice from these State officials. In many respects, the best that they could hope to get was paid off 'by mutual consent.' This can be seen frequently in other logs, but is clear that Robert Atkin did not approve of this at all and so, the unsatisfied acted as they saw fit: legally, or illegally. There were times on this vessel when almost the entire ship's company was in serious dispute with the command.

The description of treatment of one particular able seaman is invaluable, as it gives *real* insights into this master. William Broom, a 22 year-old Londoner signed on at Melbourne in March 1861. While at Wellington in June he repeatedly refused duty due to a 'sore throat.' As per normal with medical cases, Robert Atkin reckoned that this AB was merely 'skulking:' with various clashes. Considering that William Broom was made out to be such a desperado later on, when the master ordered him to shift into the cabin he refused and this *may* indicate that he thought it safer in the forecastle. Refusing to ask the master 'in a proper manner' to go ashore to complain about him on July 5th, William Broom was turned over to the police and 'sentenced to two hours imprisonment and to forfeit two days pay' for his pains. It was not until the next day that he got to see a doctor ashore, who basically said that he was on the mend. According to the ship's log, on this same day while ashore William Broom then assaulted Robert Atkin. This time he was 'sentenced to

to fear this able seaman and both he and the mate *'watched the working of Broom's countenance up through the Skylight.'* Atkin confided in Collier that William Broom was *'either going mad or pretending.'* This AB might well have been *'mad,'* but not necessarily in the psychiatric sense.

All the way through at sea it had been usual for one or two to be locked up and in irons. Only identified as *'W Bender,'* earlier in the month had claimed to been ill, but had refused to see the master *'for medicine,'* when at Saint Helena in late January 1862 there was another mutiny. Bender was *'off duty pretending to be Sick'* when the mate, William Collier entered the forecastle. There were two different versions of events logged: multiple loggings being another trait in this document. Whether the seaman really tried to assault the mate with a *'slung shot'* cannot be determined, but seemingly the two mates dragged Bender back aft. His messmates, including Broom attempted to physically stop this. Nevertheless, Bender was sent ashore to a doctor, which is what he had wanted in the first place. In all likelihood not wanting him landed, the medic opined that the seaman's *'liver was a little sluggish but that he was able to work'* and given a prescription. Similarly, to William Broom earlier the seaman Bender refused to shift his sleeping berth out of the forecastle. Early in February AB Broom had complained to the master that they were only receiving *'4 ounces of Beef to the pound'* among shortages and of course, neither of the mates had any idea that this had been going on!

Although it might well be that William Broom had generally only been attempting to defend the seamen's rights, by 5th February 1862 Robert Atkin was convinced otherwise. He regarded this AB as such a danger that he conspired with William Collier to have Broom put in irons. Far from being the mutinous mob that the command maintained, the crew appear to have been cowed and they allowed a search of the forecastle. Not finding the firearms that they expected, the two seamen officers uncovered two journals: written by seamen Broom and Bender. Reading these only seems to have increased Robert Atkin's paranoia about Broom and the rest of the crew. Also, by then the second mate, James Lumsden, was regarded by the command as being with the mutineers. This was something that not only he,

fourteen days imprisonment with hard labour.' If there was a sensible time to discharge this man *'by mutual consent,'* it was then.

Instead, although nowhere near ready to sail, Able Seaman Broom was brought back onboard at Robert Atkin's request on 10th July. Apparently while under police escort the prisoner assaulted the constable, William Harries and the former was 'secured' in the cabin in irons. Nothing more is mentioned until on 20th October at Shanghai, William Broom had *'evidently'* been one of the ringleaders in an incident that prevented the vessel being unmoored. This was on a Sunday and essentially, was a mutiny even if as the men saw it, they were only defending their *'rights.'* Eleven days later, the *'crew'* was ordered to pump ship. This task was backbreaking and in order to keep time, shanties were sung as a matter of course. William Broom began singing and was ordered to stop by the then mate, William Collier. A 25 year old from Chatham, he was inexperienced in merchant service. Prior to gaining his second mate's ticket in 1858 he had only been in the Royal Navy. The able seaman let the mate know that he was not impressed. There were further probably minor clashes with the mate. Next, on 16th January 1862 while on the wheel, Robert Atkin is said to have had cause to pick up William Broom. It would appear by this time that the master was beginning

but also the *'idlers'* went on record to deny.

19th March 1862 must have been a busy day onboard. Reaching New York Light Ship, dozens of loggings were read out to defaulters. The directions to masters within logs were not entirely consistent. On one hand, loggings were to be made as soon as possible after events, but these needed only to be read out to defaulters before making landfall (if at sea). While late readings might be allowable under these directions, defaulters on this particular vessel frequently objected to this and to an unusually high degree, also commented that these were false. Another practice cannot have been legitimate though. More than one mate witnessed entries for incidents when they had not even been on the vessel's articles!

William Broom was still incarcerated onboard and the master wanted the British Consul ashore to try him. Said not to have this power, he was advised just to pay Broom off. Refusing, Robert Atkin was referred to the local magistrates or city prison authorities. By the time that Atkin finally managed to get this process started, Broom had broken out and departed ashore: only to be picked up by a marshal. The U.S. authorities arranged for a lawyer to act for the suspect: found through a sailors' boarding house keeper. With their help, Broom took out a counter suit against Atkin and Collier and they had to pay a small fortune to remain on bail. Robert Atkin complained that the British consular officials refused to aid him in any way. The next log entry details a naval court held *'for the purpose of ascertaining the amount of wages due to William Broom . . . and also investigating the grounds on which the master, Robert Atkin claims to make certain deductions from the Wages.'* While some deductions were accepted, essentially the court was scathing towards Robert Atkin: of the *'opinion that the master used unnecessary violence in placing Broom in Irons.'*

Intriguingly, a published account by another master mentions the legal situation in New York twenty years later. Another hard-fighting man, he was of the opinion that the British Consul was weak and the American authorities corrupt.

Up to this point there are unmentioned elements and that is for a reason: further evidence relating to this voyage and Robert Atkin. There is an unusual *'black book'* entry for him. While no action was taken by the Board of Trade to suspend, or cancel his certificate, this referred to a gaol sentence that Robert Atkin served *'for writing a threatening letter'* in 1865. When investigated, it turned out that he had held up a broker in London (previously dealt with in New York) with a pistol that he had reckoned had led to his bankruptcy. For a long time I had wondered whether, prior to the world-wide development of

the telegraph system, master mariners had got into financial difficulty in securing return cargoes abroad. This proves that at least one did.

Robert Atkin's use of a pistol in this affair confirms further what was within the log, but under completely different circumstances. The use of fists, firearms and other weapons against rebellious crews is not infrequently gloried in within published masters' memoirs, but normally there is precious little evidence in original records. Atkin mentioned at least some in his log though: partially in passing. Apart from thrashings and canings, on at least one occasion he was armed with a sword and on two others made threats with a pistol. As previously mentioned, there had also been swivel guns onboard (probably for anti-piracy defence), but these disappeared over time. In all likelihood Robert Atkin was anxious that these would be turned on him, but as no sign of these were found, were probably sold, or dumped over the side by crewmembers wishing to get rid of this potential threat to them!

In winding this up, a few other points might be made. Although everything that went wrong seems to have been attributed to others, as loggings are full of criticisms, he appears to have been a competent enough seaman. Of the *'piling on sail'* school, studding sails characterise seagoing entries and it can be seen from positions noted that the *Dennis Hill* was capable of making considerable speed.

The rate of death and injury onboard was also astoundingly low: Able Seaman Normandale dying of chronic diarrhoea and there were less than a handful of hospital cases. Whether this was down to sheer luck, or not, cannot be determined from the surviving documents.

In business Robert Atkins was clearly out of his depth though. Prior to this he had only been in command coastwise and on short-sea voyages. Therefore, it is highly likely that he will have had no business contacts in the Far East. Trade with China always had been exceedingly problematical and potentially hazardous; and Japan had only very recently been *'opened up'* to western trade.

Although not losing his ticket through his London gaoling, he only had one further seagoing command for one voyage. However, in his younger days he had signed on as a carpenter: highly unusual for professional seamen. Also, at the time of the London hold-up, he was said to have been a farmer in Walthamstow. So, obviously he could turn his hand to other things. He also seems to have had a way with women. Not only was he married twice, while threatening the broker he had an unidentified female in tow!

Readers might be interested in reading a transcript of this saga. This is within my online guide at www.barnettmaritime.co.uk.

General Register Office - Certificate Services
Melanie Lee - GRO Communications

From 1st April 2008 The General Register Office (GRO) became part of the Identity and Passport Service, an Executive Agency of the Home Office. GRO Scotland and GRO Northern Ireland remain the responsibility of the devolved administrations.

The primary role of the GRO is to carry out the statutory functions of the Registrar General, and to oversee and support local authorities and registrars in delivering the local registration service. GRO maintains the national record of all events (birth, marriage, death etc) which have taken place in England and Wales from July 1837. Since this date, each entry made in a register of births, marriages or deaths has been copied to the centrally held national record maintained by GRO. By law, the General Register Office for England and Wales can only provide information in the form of a certificate on payment of a statutory fee.

Many customers who apply to GRO require a certificate for legal or administrative purposes, such as applying for a passport or pension; but by far the largest proportion of applications are from family historians and professional genealogists. GRO produces a useful guide for family historians and this is available online via the Directgov website. The booklet is called *"Discover Your Family History"* and copies can be downloaded via www.directgov.uk/gro

Certificate Services at Smedley Hydro

All certificate applications are processed by Certificate Services at Smedley Hydro, Southport, Merseyside. Many people have asked about the unusual name of the office where their certificates are produced. Smedley Hydro was built in early Victorian times and known as the Birkdale College for the education of young gentlemen. It then became a Hydropathic Hotel, whose electro-chemical baths were extremely popular *'in restoring the work-weary, the enfeebled and those of a naturally delicate organisation'*. With the outbreak of the Second World War, the building was requisitioned by His Majesty's government for the purpose of National Registration.

Applying for certificates online:

The quickest and easiest way to order a certificate is by using the GRO's online ordering service. Certificates can be ordered online for birth, death, marriage, civil partnership and adoption events registered in England and Wales, and for certain British Nationals who were born, married or died overseas.

The GRO website provides an efficient and secure method of placing an order. For further information, visit: www.direct.gov.uk/gro

If you are using the online ordering facility for the first time, you will need to complete an online registration process. You will only need to register your details the first time you use the service.

Applying for certificates by Telephone:

The Contact Centre telephone number is + 44 (0) 845 603 7788. You will hear a menu selection before being transferred to an operator, who can take your order details and arrange for your certificate(s) to be posted out to you. Payment can be made by Visa credit card, debit card or Visa Electon, MasterCard, Solo and Maestro. Telephone the Contact Centre, Monday to Friday 8am to 8pm and Saturday 9am to 4pm.

Applying for certificates by post:

If you are applying by post you will be asked to complete a GRO application form.

To request a birth, marriage or death application form, you can:
• Email GRO at certificate.services@ips.gsi.gov.uk
• Please insert GQ in the subject line of your email to ensure a personal response, stating which type of application form you require, how many copies and also your name and address.
• Telephone the Contact Centre +44 (0) 845 603 7788.

Application forms should be completed in full and returned to GRO, together with the correct payment either by cheque, postal order or credit card. Cheques should be made payable to 'IPS' (Identity and Passport Service). It should be noted that these

Smedley Hydro, Southport
Reproduced with the permission of Martin Perry, Southport Civic Society

applications should not be faxed or photocopied. The original form should be returned by post to: *General Register Office, PO Box 2, Southport, Merseyside PR8 2JD*

Fees

The fee is the same if you apply online, by telephone or by post. For the latest information on fees visit www.direct.gov.uk/gro or contact GRO and ask for a copy of the booklet *'How to order and pay for certificates.'* Some commercial companies also offer a service to get certificates for you, but these organisations apply to the GRO or the local registration service on your behalf so it's cheaper and quicker to order direct.

Application to a local Register Office:

If you know exactly where the birth, marriage or death that you are looking for took place, you may also apply to the local Register Office covering that area. The Superintendent Registrar will be able to provide you with a certificate from their records for a statutory fee.

If you do not know the exact details of the event, you should provide an approximate date and location; the Superintendent Registrar will make a limited search of the indexes on your behalf. Local Register Offices store religious marriage records for all buildings in which weddings have taken place. Registration districts may contain a large number of religious buildings; over 100 in some cases. The registrar will be unable to search all the records on your behalf, so in the case of religious marriages you must specify exactly where the marriage took place. There is also a facility for you to make a general search of the indexes, usually by appointment, with the Superintendent Registrar. There is a statutory charge for making a general search. Some local authorities have made their indexes available on the Internet, see www.ukbmd.org.uk for details.

THE GRO INDEX

The GRO indexes are arranged by year, and then alphabetically by surname. Before 1983, the indexes were also split into quarter of the year in which the event was registered e.g. events registered in January, February or March are indexed in the March quarter for the relevant year.

You may wish to look for the GRO reference number at one of the many centres around the country which hold copies of the national GRO index on microfiche. There are over 100 such locations including libraries, County Records Offices and Family History Centres within the UK and overseas. To find out the nearest one to you, visit www.direct.gov.uk/gro or telephone the Contact Centre +44 (0) 845 603 7788.

The full range of GRO Indexes, including births, deaths, marriages, civil partnerships, adoptions and overseas events are held at:

Birmingham Central Library
Local Studies and History Service, Chamberlain Square, Birmingham B3 3HQ Tel: 0121 303 4511
Bridgend Reference & Information Library,
Coed Parc, Park Street, Bridgend CF31 4BA Tel: 01656 767451
City of Westminster Archives Centre
10 St Ann's Street, London SW1P 2DE, Tel: 0207 641 5180
London Metropolitan Archives
40 Northampton Road, London, EC1R 0HB, Tel: 0207 332 3820
Manchester City Library
Elliot House, 151 Deansgate, Manchester, M3 3WD, Tel: 0161 234 1979 or 1980
Plymouth Central Library
Local and Naval Studies Department, Drake Circus, Plymouth PL4 8AL Tel: 01752 305909
The British Library
96 Euston Road, London, NW1 2DB Tel: 0870 444 1500
Alternatively, you may wish to view the indexes online and there are several third party websites where you can do this.

Please note that it is not possible for members of the public to search the indexes in person at the Southport office.

If you are unable to decipher part of a GRO index reference, GRO offers a microfiche index checking service. Contact GRO for clarification by:
• Email : unclearfiche@ips.gsi.gov.uk
• Telephone the Contact Centre +44 (0) 845 603 7788
• Post : Unclear fiche, GRO, PO Box 2, Southport, Merseyside, PR8 2JD.

This service clarifies the reference number for you but will not confirm that it is the entry you are looking for.

Unable to find a birth, marriage or death in the Index?

Prior to 1875, there was no legal obligation to register an event and therefore some were missed. In addition, some events may have taken place outside of England and Wales. An important factor to remember when searching is that there could be some variations in the spelling of names, as many people could not read or write and the registrar would have to interpret the spelling of them.

Births

• the child may have been registered under a forename/surname other than that by which he/she was known in later life.
• the child could have been registered before the parents had chosen a forename, in which case the entry in our indexes would be at the alphabetical end of the listing under female/male.
• the child could have been born in a period other than that searched. Ages on census records and marriage certificates should be treated with caution. No proof of age was required and often people did not actually know their own age.

Marriages

• marriages sometimes took place after the birth of the first child; so widen the timescale searched.
• the bride may have been married more than once; so check under the name of the groom instead.
• couples often lived together as man and wife as divorce was rare and expensive. Often, couples never married, or did not remarry after their spouse died.

Deaths

• widen the timescale that you believe the death occurred as it could have been registered some time after the event i.e. if an inquest took place.
• widen the search for the place of death; the person may have died in a different location to where they actually lived.
• in a minority of cases, deaths would be registered without a name i.e. if there was nobody to identify a body. These are listed as 'unknown' in the indexes and appear at the end of each quarter.

What if you do not know the GRO reference number of the entry you want?

If you do not wish to conduct your own search of the indexes, GRO are happy to do this for you. The GRO will undertake a search of the indexes for the year in which you believe the event occurred, and if necessary, a year either side. Due to the additional searches involved, this service takes a little longer. Once the application is received, the certificate is posted out within 15 working days. Should GRO be unable to find the entry, a full refund will be returned to you with an email or letter of explanation.

To assist GRO in the search, you will need to provide as much information as possible about the person on the certificate you are trying to obtain. For a birth, full name, date of birth, place of birth and if known, the parent's names including the mother's maiden name. For a marriage, you will need to supply the names of both the bride and groom, date of marriage, place of marriage and if known, the father's name for both bride and groom. For a death you will need to supply a full name, date of death, place of death and if a female, her marital status. The occupation of the deceased is also helpful.

Other certificates available from GRO:

1. Overseas Records

The General Register Office holds records of births, marriages, civil partnerships and deaths of British nationals and members of the British Armed Forces, where the event has taken place abroad and is registered with the British authorities concerned e.g. British Consuls, High Commissions, HM Forces, the Civil Aviation Authority and the Register of Shipping and Seamen. However, it should be noted that the majority of the registrations held are non-compulsory; therefore, it is possible that the record you are looking for may not be held at the General Register Office.

Furthermore, you should be aware that there are certain countries where there is no provision for the registration of births, marriages or deaths by the British Consul or High Commission for example: Australia; Canada; Falkland Islands; New Zealand; South Africa; Zimbabwe. In these circumstances, you may have to apply to the relevant authority in the country concerned to try to obtain a locally issued certificate.

Overseas records held at GRO do not cover every event which takes place involving a British national. The oldest records held by the GRO are the British Army 'Regimental Records' which date back to 1761. GRO also hold the death records of those who fell during both World Wars and the Boer War. The types of registrations held and relevant dates are:

• Regimental births/baptisms 1761-1924
• Regimental marriages 1786-1924 (the regiment is needed for any search to be undertaken).
• Ionian Islands births/baptisms, marriages and some burial records relating to the British civil and military population on the Islands of Corfu 1818-1864.
• Marine births and deaths since 1837.
• Consul births, marriages and deaths since 1849.

War Deaths:
• Boer War 1899-1902
• First World War 1914-1921
• Second World War 1939-1948

Entries held at GRO do not show place of burial or next of kin. Certificates only record Unit/Regiment, service number, name, age at death, country of birth, place (theatre of war) and cause of death (e.g. 'killed in action' or 'died of wounds').

• Army births, marriages and deaths from 1880-1956.
• High Commission births, marriages and deaths from date of Independence (e.g. India 1949).
• Air births and deaths (events on British aircraft) since 1947.
• Deposited foreign marriage certificates since 1947.
• Armed Forces births, marriages and deaths since 1957.
• Hovercraft births and deaths (on British hovercraft) since 1972.
• Offshore Installation deaths (on British gas and oilrigs) since 1972.

The indexes to overseas events are available at some libraries, family history societies and can also be viewed online.

Application for certificates of overseas events can be made in the following ways:

• Online at www.direct.gov.uk/gro.
• Telephone the Contact Centre +44 (0) 845 603 7788.
• Post using a GRO application form to: The General Register Office, PO Box 2, Southport, Merseyside, PR8 2JD.

Overseas birth, marriage and death application forms may be requested by:

• Email to: certificate.services@ips.gsi.gov.uk, inserting GQ in the subject line of your email to ensure a personal response to your request. Please state which type of application form you require, how many copies and also your name and address.
• Telephone the Contact Centre: +44 (0) 845 603 7788.

2. Commemorative Marriage Certificates

Special commemoratives certificates for Silver (25th), Ruby (40th), Golden (50th), and Diamond (60th) wedding anniversaries make a thoughtful gift and treasured keepsake. Printed on specially designed certificates, they feature the original marriage details and are mounted within a presentation box; making an unusual and attractive gift.

Order online

Please ensure you place your order at least 10

days before you need the certificate. For further information visit www.direct.gov.uk/gro or telephone the Contact Centre: +44 (0) 0845 603 7788.

3. Stillbirth certificates.

The GRO holds records of all stillbirths registered in England and Wales since 1 July 1927. Certified copies of these records can only be obtained with the Registrar General's consent. The following conditions apply:

- A certificate will only be issued to the mother or father of a stillborn child.
- Siblings may apply if their mother and father are no longer alive. They need to provide details of their parents' dates of death with the application.

If you would like more information, including an application form, please contact GRO by: T: +44 (0) 845 603 7788.

Post: General Register Office, PO Box 2, Southport, Merseyside, PR8 2JD.

How to contact GRO

Email: The email address is certificate.services@ips.gsi.gov.uk. Please insert GQ in the subject box to ensure a personal response. A reply to your email will be provided within 5 working days.

Telephone: The Contact Centre telephone number is + 44 (0) 845 603 7788. You will hear a menu selection before being transferred to an operator, who can take your order details and arrange for your certificate(s) to be posted out to you. Payment can be made by Visa, MasterCard, Maestro or Visa Electron. Telephone the Contact Centre, Monday to Friday 8am to 8pm and Saturday 9am to 4pm.

The Contact Centre is 'Typetalk' enabled. This means that customers with hearing difficulties can communicate with the office via the National Telephone Relay Service, who set up a link with the GRO and act as an intermediary on their behalf. Text: 18001 (followed by) + 44 (0)845 603 7788 Please note that some calls may be recorded for training and monitoring purposes.

Post: Write to GRO at: The General Register Office, PO Box 2, Southport, Merseyside, PR8 2JD.

Certificate Services welcomes feedback:

The GRO welcomes feedback and customer input on the level and quality of service being provided. If you have any comments about the service, please contact GRO by:

Email: certificate.services@ips.gsi.gov.uk. Please insert GQ in the subject box to ensure a personal response. Telephone: +44 (0) 845 603 7788 Monday to Friday 8am to 8pm and Saturday 9am to 4pm. Write: GRO, PO Box 2, Southport, Merseyside, PR8 2JD.

General Register Office - Adoptions
Melanie Lee - GRO Communications

Adoptions policy in England and Wales is governed by the Looked After Children's Branch of the Department for Children, Schools and Families. The General Register Office (GRO) administers four statutory functions which have come into being since 1926 and are governed by the Adoption and Children Act 2002.

The Adopted Children Register is a record of all adoptions granted by courts in England and Wales since 1927. When an adoption has been granted, the court issues an order, which is the authority for an entry to be made in the Adopted Children Register. The entire process, which includes instructing the registrar who holds the original birth entry, may take up to six weeks. Once this process is complete the adoptive parent(s) will receive a free short adoption certificate.

An adoption certificate is a replacement birth certificate but in an adopted person's new name. It is expected to be used by an adopted person for all legal and administrative purposes in place of the original birth certificate. Replacement certificates can be purchased on-line at www.direct.gov.uk/gro or by telephone on +44 (0) 0845 603 7788. Lines are open (excluding bank holidays) Monday - Friday 8.a.m. - 8.p.m. and Saturday 9.a.m. - 4.p.m.

The Adopted Children Register also contains some registrations of overseas adoptions. Adoptions which have taken place overseas may be registered at GRO when the adoptive parents were habitually resident in England or Wales at the time of the adoption; or the child was born in England or Wales. The country in which the adoption occurred is recognised from list of designated and convention countries approved by the Department for Children, Schools and Families. A Registrable Foreign Adoption application may be made by, the adoptive parents(s), any other person who has appropriate parental responsibility for the adopted child or the adopted person when aged 18 or over.

Information on access to birth details for an adopted person

If you were adopted through a court in England or Wales and are aged 18 years or over the law allows you to gain access to your birth details. These details will enable you to purchase a certified copy of your original birth entry:

If you were adopted before 12th November 1975 you are required to attend an informal meeting to receive information from an approved adoption advisor. This can be an advisor at either your local Social Services, at GRO in Southport, a registered Intermediary Agency or, under certain circumstances, at the agency that handled your adoption. The adoption advisor will be able to able to offer practical advice and guidance as well as discussing any concerns or issues important to you.

If you were adopted on or after 12th November 1975 you have the choice whether you would like to see an approved adoption advisor or have the information sent to you direct. You may find it helpful to see an adoption advisor as they will be able to offer practical advice and guidance as well as discussing any concerns or issues important to you.

If you were adopted in England or Wales and now live outside the UK you can also apply to access your birth records. If you are required to attend an informal meeting to receive your information from an adoption advisor; it may be possible for this to take place in the country where you are currently residing, as long as a suitable body or organisation is available. The GRO maintains a list of approved overseas Adoption organisations that may be able to provide this service.

If you were adopted after 30th December 2005, once you have reached aged 18 years or over you can gain access to your birth details through the agency or social services that dealt with your adoption. If the name of the agency or social services is not known, the adopted person may contact GRO for this information.

Information on access to adoption records for birth relatives

From 30th December 2005, a birth relative wishing to make contact with an adopted person can apply to a registered Intermediary Agency, whose role is to help facilitate contact between birth relatives and adopted people. The Intermediary Agency can apply to GRO for the name of the organisation involved in the adoption or if that is not available the name of the court granting the adoption. They can also apply for post-adoptive information which will enable an application to be made for an adoption certificate and information from the Adoption Contact Register.

Intermediary Agencies

Registered Intermediary Agencies may accept approaches from adopted people and birth relatives, aged 18 years or over, to help convey their wishes for communication and contact. A list of registered intermediary agencies can be found at Commission for Social Care Inspection (CSCI) now part of the Childrens Social Care Functions of Ofsted which covers England and Care Standard Inspectorate for Wales (CSIW). When visiting the CSIW website please note that your search results will appear at

the bottom of the Services and Inspection reports page. Alternatively you can contact GRO, please telephone 0151 471 4830.

Adoption Contact Register

The Adoption Contact Register was created in 1991 to put adopted people and their birth relatives in touch with each other if that is what they both wish. The Contact Register cannot help an adopted person to learn of the whereabouts of a birth relative or to know their birth relatives wishes unless the relative has also entered their details on the Contact Register.

The Contact Register is in two parts and to be eligible for registration applicants need to be 18 years or over. Part 1 allows for an adopted person to register their details for a fee of £15 and record their wishes for contact, non contact or specific contact with any birth relative(s). Part 2 allows for a birth relative to register their details for a fee of £30 and record their wishes for contact or non contact only.

If a wish for contact is registered and a link is made both parties will be notified, but only the adopted person will be provided with the current name and address of the party wishing to make contact.

Adoption services

For further information about adoption services, visit www.direct.gov.uk/gro or Tel: 0151 471 4830.

Applying for Adoption Certificates

Applying for adoption certificates online:

The GRO website provides an efficient and secure method of placing an order. For further information, visit: www.direct.gov.uk/gro.

Applying for certificates by telephone:

The Contact Centre telephone number is + 44 (0) 845 603 7788. You will hear a menu selection before being transferred to an operator, who can take your order details and arrange for your certificate(s) to be posted out to you. Payment can be made by Visa, MasterCard, Maestro or Visa Electron. Telephone the Contact Centre, Monday to Friday 8 a.m. to 8 p.m. and Saturday 9 a.m. to 4 p.m.

Applying for certificates by post:

If you are applying by post you will be asked to complete a GRO applications form.

To request an adoption application form, you can contact GRO by:

Email: certificate.services@ips.gsi.gov.uk. Please insert GQ in the subject line of your email to ensure a personal response, stating which type of application form you require, how many copies and also your name and address.

Telephone: +44 (0) 845 603 7788.

Application forms should be completed in full and returned to GRO, together with the correct payment either by cheque, postal order or credit card. Cheques should be made payable to 'IPS' (Identity and Passport Service). It should be noted that these applications should not be faxed or photocopied. The original should be returned by post to: **General Register Office, PO Box 2, Southport, Merseyside PR8 2JD.**

Researching Family History in a Social Context
Linda Ingle

Great Grandfather Henry Firth Hollingworth was born into poverty in 1846 and rose to become a manufacturer and employer. This study looks at his life, together with the conditions and changes that took place within the Huddersfield and district woollen industry during the latter part of the 19th century, which in turn, enabled him to achieve this. It also looks at the growth and prosperity of the textile industry and how it affected the wider community.

West Yorkshire has produced wool since Roman times; it began as a cottage industry. The clothiers would buy the raw wool; the amount bought would depend upon the prosperity of the clothier. The wool would then be picked over by hand to remove bits of vegetation and dirt before being brought home to the women to spin and weave. *(Teasdale Page 15 - 2006)* The clothier would then take the rolls of cloth to market to sell. If the clothier was poor, he would carry the cloth on his shoulders and walk to the nearest market, the wealthy ones would have a packhorse.

Conditions in the Huddersfield and Holmfirth area were ideal for this occupation due to the soft water needed for washing the wool, and in later years, for driving the machinery, which would spin and weave the cloth. The Holmfirth of the 18th and 19th century was very inhospitable consisting of moorland which was not suitable for arable farming, and steep hills dropping down to a narrow valley. These conditions were ideal for sheep who were able to graze easily on weeds. Small hamlets were scattered on the hillsides and it was in one of these that Henry Hollingworth was born in August 1846.

Henry was the youngest child of George Hollingworth and Nancy Wood. Both parents were weavers and were

poor. It is assumed that George died young as he no longer appears after the 1851 census, but his wife worked as a weaver until she was well into her seventies. George and Nancy were not typical of families of that time as they only had two children, but this could have been due to the possible early death of George, and Nancy did not remarry. She lived close to George's relatives who may have helped in the care of the children.

Past generations of Hollingworths had been Clothiers but Henry's grandfather John Hollingworth, together with his sons, ran a farm, they did everything from rearing and shearing the sheep, washing and combing the wool, whilst the women did the spinning and weaving. John would then take the finished product to market to sell. John was married twice and had five children to his first wife, the eldest of whom was George, Henry's father, and nine children to his second. The farm consisted of twenty two acres, was self sufficient, and was situated in an isolated position high up on the moors above Holmfirth, and according to a descendant of the second family, life was very hard and it was difficult to eke out a living. The younger sons of the family christened the farm *'Bare Arse Farm.'* This was indicative of the extreme poverty the family had to endure, the inference being torn breeches or threadbare clothes. (Oral interview with Mrs L Harrison, great granddaughter of John Hollingworth. 2008) There were none of the modern comforts taken for granted today, for example, no electricity, no running water, no supermarkets or shops nearby; the nearest church would be several miles away. In addition, there would be little leisure time. The 1851 census shows fourteen people living at the farm,

Great Grandfather Henry Firth Hollingworth

it, dried and put on the loom. (Teasdale, 2006. Page 11)

After his wife's death in 1877 Henry then moved to Lockwood, now a suburb of Huddersfield, but then a very desirable place to live boasting a spa and a Town Hall. He became a Power Loom Weaver and on his second marriage in 1880 to Hannah Hodgkinson, was a Mill Manager. Hannah born in 1854 was the youngest of eight children, four of whom died as teenagers of poverty related illnesses; it is therefore very unlikely that Hannah would have brought any money to the marriage.

Henry and Hannah had four children, James 1882, Percy 1884, Minnie 1890 and Harry 1899. He had also had a son with Sarah Ann Battye who was born in 1868 but died of TB aged twenty-three in 1891.

By 1881 Henry was a Designer. This meant he had to be part artist and part engineer; it was a very important job, the hub of the whole process. A designer took the first instruction from the manufacturer who would tell him what weight of cloth he needed, for example a twelve ounce piece may be needed or for overcoats twenty to twenty five ounces of cloth. This meant a lot of complicated working out with a slide rule as to how many ends (threads) per pitch, which fabrics to use, i.e. wool and linen blend and work out how many ounces of wool per yard was needed. In addition, he had to work out the intricate designs of the cloth and work out which colours were needed and in which order they went on to the loom. (Oral interview with Mr K Hanselman 2010).

In the latter part of the 19th century there had been a new innovation in the production of cloth and this was known as worsted coatings. It was woven from wool yarns that have been combed to make the fibres parallel and tends to have a smoother surface. Yorkshire began to produce mixed worsted cloth (cloth of cotton warp and worsted weft), which had a much wider market and was cheaper. From the 1880s fashion began to change and manufacturers were quick to follow. Another local manufacture was of fancy woollens that had very intricate designs and weaves but, as today, fashion changed rapidly and the larger manufacturers found it too risky because they could have been left with large stocks that were unusable. This then left a niche for the smaller manufacturer. The high demand in 1881 for fashion novelties such as dog hair, feathers and rabbit fur required new ideas and designs almost annually so the manufacturers experimented with different fibres. The Huddersfield district was in advance of other manufacturers in nearby towns. (Jenkins, Page 253. 1992)

By 1884 Henry was trading as Henry Hollingworth & Co. Ltd and leasing part of Albert Mills, Lockwood. (Huddersfield Archive Library) The

therefore twenty two acres of grassland could not support such a large family so as the sons grew up and married they left home. George had already left when he married in 1841 where he found work in one of the local mills.

During the 19th century the textile industry was gradually being mechanised much to the consternation of the home based weavers as some of these machines could do the work of two or more men and there was a great deal of strife and lockouts. Consequently during the earlier part of the century the industry did not develop as quickly as it could have done. (Leeds & Yorkshire Woollen Industry - Internet - 2009) However, mechanisation was there to stay and new mills were being built along the bottom of the valley from Holmfirth right down to Huddersfield alongside the River Holme. This was so that the water could be used for washing the wool and for powering the machines. Eventually by the middle of the century the mills employed the majority of the people. Also from that time, people began to move nearer to the mills and small villages began to appear alongside the river. Over time, these spread as far as Huddersfield. The 1851 census revealed that in England for the first time, more people were living in urban areas due to industrialisation, than rural ones, and this trend has continued ever since.

The 1861 census shows Henry aged fourteen, living with his mother and sister in Holmfirth. His occupation is given as a Piecer; this meant that he was employed in a spinning mill to piece together any threads that broke. Although women and children usually did this job it does suggest that this was his first employment, as he would have left school at the age of thirteen.

Henry married Sarah Ann Battye in 1867 and they moved further down the valley where he was employed for eleven years as a Woollen Warper. Warp were threads running along the length of woven cloth and a warper would wind yarn onto a warp mill to lay out threads in the correct length, width and colours for the loom. The yarn was then sized with glue to strengthen

1891 census states he was a Commission Weaver, Manufacturer and Employer. A Commission Weaver, worked on commission, had to have his own looms and helped the larger manufacturer to fulfil his orders. By 1894 he had taken on a partner and six shareholders and changed the name of the company to Hollingworth Wood & Co. Ltd. The company manufactured fancy worsted and woollens, as well as suitings and overcoats, serges and vicuna fabrics. (Teasdale. Page 105. 2006) The company exported all over the world. Vicuna is very expensive wool that is lighter, softer and warmer.

Henry retired in 1905 at the age of sixty-five and on his son's marriage certificate in 1907 his occupation was given as 'Gentleman.' The 1911 census states he was a retired Woollen Manufacturer. He died suddenly at home in 1918.

All Henry's sons followed him into the textile industry becoming dyers and finishers. James, a Master Dyer, became a director of Longwood Finishing Company, his son Frank followed in his footsteps becoming a dyer also at Longwood Finishing Company and later at L B Hollidays. This meant that six successive generations of Hollingworths had been involved in the woollen industry in one form or another.

Most of Henry's relatives and neighbours were weavers working from home, but by the middle of the 19th century most were employed in the mills that were springing up in the valley. Even when Henry moved to the more prosperous area of Lockwood, his neighbours were involved in the production of cloth in some way. The mechanisation of the woollen industry, which in turn spawned other industries such as dyeing and

finishing, making and maintenance of the machines, building mills and homes for the workers to live in, inevitably affected the wider community and brought more prosperity to them.

Research into the life of Henry Hollingworth and his family has provided a picture of how many people lived in the small corner of Yorkshire in the mid 19th century, and how they coped with the many difficulties that came their way. The dire poverty experienced by Henry's grandfather led Henry and others like him to seize opportunities to better himself and rise up the social scale to die as a 'Gentleman.' As to how he achieved this was due to a combination of factors, the most significant of which appears to be his change in fortune after his second marriage in 1880. It may have been that his wife was the driving force behind his success, as per the saying 'behind every successful man is a good woman!' This then, combined with the changes in the textile industry and the swift changes in fashion, enabled Henry to take advantage of the need for a smaller manufacturer to fulfil the required shorter runs of cloth. He would have been very well prepared having worked through many of the processes of manufacture due to his many jobs within the industry. In order to be a designer he would have had to be creative and this was quite possibly inherited as production of cloth in its various forms had been done by generations of Hollingworths before him. It is also reasonable to assume he had a good degree of intelligence that enabled him to assimilate and carry out such complicated design work. He was clearly prepared to take a risk and would have been considered an entrepreneur of his time, in common with many others of that era. It was at this time that the woollen industry was thriving and was famous throughout the world and it appears that Henry was in the right place at the right time.

Bibliography

Jenkins, D. T. (1992) *Textiles and Other Industries 1851-1914.* Haigh E.A. Ed.
Kirklees Cultural Services, Huddersfield
    Huddersfield A Most Handsome Town.
Teasdale, V. (2006) *Huddersfield Mills, A Textile Heritage.* Wharncliffe Books
Leeds and Yorkshire Woollen Industry: Internet November 2009

Sources

Birth, Death and Marriage Certificates
1851-1911 censuses. The National Archives
Huddersfield Archive Library (Ledger of Hollingworth Wood & Co. Ltd.)
Huddersfield Family History Society
Oral Interview with Mrs L Harrison,
    John Hollingworth's great granddaughter 2008
Oral Interview with Mr K Hanselman 2010
Parish Registers
Information, such as how the machines worked and what they did, has been given to me by people who worked in the textile industry.

The Roots of Spinal Tap
Anthony Adolph

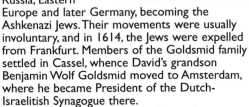

Because his father Peter worked for the United Nations and was posted to New York, Christopher Haden-Guest was born and bred an American. Born in New York on 5th February 1948, he was educated at the city's High School for Music and Arts. Inspired by Peter Sellers' characterisation of Inspector Clouseau in the Pink Panther films, he became an actor, debuting on Broadway in 1970 in *Room Service*. He worked extensively for *National Lampoon* and, in 1983, wrote the satirical film *Spinal Tap*, in which he also starred as guitarist Nigel Tufnel. His many acting and directorial jobs include an appearance in *St Elsewhere* and direction of *Attack of the 50 Ft. Woman*. He is married to actress Jamie Lee Curtis, and has two adopted children.

From a first glance at his family tree, it seems surprising Christopher inherited his family title, when two living persons, his cousin Hadley and half-brother Anthony, are older than him. However, as Charles Mosely, editor of *Burke's Peerage* sagely points out, Hadley is in fact a girl whilst Anthony was born two years *before* his parents married, thus barring him from succeeding to the family title which Christopher now enjoys.

Ostensibly, Christopher and Jamie's backgrounds seem very different. She is the daughter of actor Tony Curtis, originally called Bernard Schwartz, who was born in New York in 1925 to immigrant parents Emanuel and Helen Schwartz. But when we started digging into Christopher's origins, we found that, before his immediate English aristocratic forebears, he too has European immigrant ancestry. Through his grandmother Muriel Goldsmid, a line stretches right back to David Goldsmid of Frankfurt-on-Maine, Germany in the early 17th century.

Christopher's blue blood stems from his Oldham-born grandfather Leslie Haden Guest (1877-1960). Educated in Manchester, Leslie served in the Boer and 1st World Wars and then became a Labour M.P., founding the Anglo-French Commission of the Red Cross Society and sitting on the Parliamentary Committee on Evacuation of Civil populations in 1938- an emotive period for anyone with European Jewish connections. After the War he was Lord-in-Waiting to George VI.

The Goldsmid's story is monumental, stretching from Biblical times to the ghettos of Europe and thence to the heady days of Jewish emancipation in Britain. The family claimed descent from the princely Hasmonean family of Judea and the Maccabee hero-sons of Matthias the priest, whilst they derived their *kinnui* of Goldsmid - the name by which they were known to the Gentile world - from an even earlier forebear, Bazalel ben Uri, the goldsmith employed to decorate the Tabernacle, as described in Exodus xxxi, 4. After the fall of Jerusalem in the 1st century AD, the Jewish Diaspora began. Some settled in the western Mediterranean and were the ancestors of Sephardic Jews, whilst others made their homes in Russia, Eastern Europe and later Germany, becoming the Ashkenazi Jews. Their movements were usually involuntary, and in 1614, the Jews were expelled from Frankfurt. Members of the Goldsmid family settled in Cassel, whence David's grandson Benjamin Wolf Goldsmid moved to Amsterdam, where he became President of the Dutch-Israelitish Synagogue there.

Benjamin's grandson Aaron- from whom Christopher is descended through two different lines- arrived in London in 1763. He rapidly established himself as a merchant and one of the most prominent members of the Ashkenazi Jewish community. After his death his sons formed a partnership with the Mocattas to create a formidable firm of gold bullion merchants. The youngest two sons, **Abraham** and **Benjamin Goldsmid** (Benjamin was Christopher's direct ancestor) became bill brokers who broke the monopoly which a clique of (Gentile) bankers held over Government loans. The Government got a better deal, and Goldsmids became fabulously wealthy, becoming the leading members of the Stock Exchange. Although posthumously slated in a vitriolic attack by the anti-Semitic William Cobbett, Abraham and Benjamin were generous philanthropists, contributing to many causes, Jewish and Gentile, founding the *Mashebat Nephesh*, the Jewish Bread, Meat and Coal Society and what became the Royal Naval Assylum. When Abraham died, it is said that £100,000 worth of I.O.U.s were found in his office, each carefully torn up to render them void.

Horatio, later Lord, Nelson was such a close friend of Benjamin's that he spent his last night in England at the financier's house in Roehampton. After his death at Trafalgar, Nelson's grief-stricken and cash-strapped lover Lady Hamilton was generously bailed out by the Goldsmids. On an even more exalted level, they were amongst the first Jews to move in royal circles. Abraham once had George III to an informal lunch at his country house at Morden and escorted the three royal dukes to a service at the Great Synagogue in 1809. The friendship between the Hanovers and Goldsmiths did much to break down anti-Semitic prejudice in English society.

But wealth did not bring the brothers

happiness: subject to occasional bouts of melancholy, Benjamin committed suicide in 1808. In 1810, Abraham and Sir Francis Baring raised the Government a £14 million loan to help finance the last stage of the war with Napoleon. But faced with resulting financial difficulties, Abraham killed himself. News of his death caused a massive overnight drop of 2³/4 in consols (irredeemable British government securities). 'We question', commented the *Morning Post, 'whether peace or war . . . ever created such a bustle as the death of Mr Goldsmid.'*

Most of the next generation converted to Anglicanism and became fully assimilated into British society. Indeed Christopher's great grandfather **Col. Albert Edward Goldsmid** had no idea of his Jewish ancestry until he was an adult. Born in the heart of British India, he was brought up as Englishman, with a private tutor who had brought up the Tsar of Russia and Queen of Prussia. He joined the Royal Munster Fusiliers in 1866, becoming chief of staff in the 6th Division British in the Boer War, and survived having his horse shot from under him at the Battle of Paardeberg. He became Commandant in the Orange River Colony and Inspector-General of the lines: he remained in the army until 1903, and was awarded the Victorian Order.

Albert's discovery of his Jewish roots had a profound effect on him, and as such his story was the basis for George Eliot's *Daniel Deronda*. In 1892 he went to Argentina to organise the colonies established there by Baron de Hirsch for Jewish refugees from Tsarist Russia. Back in London, he helped found the Jewish Lads Brigade and was a prominent leader of the *Choveve Zion*, the organisation which promoted the settlement of Jews in Palestine, to the extent that, had Israel been established in his life-time, it is believed he would have held high office there. He died in Paris on 27th March 1904 and was buried at the Jewish Cemetery at Willesden.

The most prominent of all Goldsmids was a prominent nephew of Abraham and Benjamin, and Christopher's 2nd cousin 4 x removed, **Isaac Lyon Goldsmid**. An earlier promoter of railways (he helped finance the Croydon, Merstham & Godstone Railway), he also supported the creation of the London docks, helped found the non-sectarian University College, London (as a means for Jews to obtain degrees away from the repressive atmosphere of Oxford and Cambridge) and University College Hospital and is widely regarded as the creator of modern Hove. He was a passionate promoter of Jewish emancipation and a supporter of Wilberforce's anti-slavery campaigns, and of Elizabeth Fry's attempts to reform prisons and abolish the death penalty for offences other than homicide, and spent many long nights in prison with men and women about to be executed for more trivial offences. And his efforts did not go unrewarded by the Establishment: he was the first member of the Jewish community to be made an English baronet and Baron de Palmeira in Portugal.

Hull, Hell and Halifax
Pam Bielby

Edward Frederick Lindley Wood (Lord Halifax) was born on 16th April 1881 at Powderham Castle, Devon, this being the home of his maternal grandfather William R Courtenay, the Earl of Devon. Edward was the fourth son and youngest child of Charles Lindley Wood and Agnes Elizabeth Courtenay.

Edward was born into what has been described as a somewhat sickly family; his three elder brothers died young leaving him as heir to the family estates and the Lord Halifax title. He was himself born with a withered left arm and no hand, this didn't seem to impede him too much, as he became skilled in riding, shooting and hunting. His two sisters Alexandra Mary Elizabeth born 1871 and Mary Agnes Emily born 1877, both lived into old age.

His father Charles Lindley Wood has been described as one of the most prominent names in the history of the Catholic revival within the Church of England. The young Edward grew up with his father's unquestioning faith in God, and developed his own deep commitment to the Anglo-Catholic religion. Edward's unquestionable faith, wily quick-wittedness and love of fox hunting led Winston Churchill to bestow upon him the nickname of 'The Holy Fox.'

Like Lord Halifax, Herbert Stanley Hawkins (my maternal grandfather) was also born at the home of his maternal grandfather Richard Major Allison and his wife Hannah Garratt. However in sharp contrast to the palatial Powderham Castle, 6 South Parade, Hilderthorpe Road, Bridlington was little more than a large middle terraced house, now used as a hairdressers. In the mid 1880's Hilderthorpe Road would have been in the heart of the bustling community, surrounding the Harbour. The house backed onto the Gipsy Race, now little more than a ditch, but back in Victorian times this would have been a busy river. The then relatively new railway ran just yards away from the Allison's home taking grain, fish, goods and people from the quayside to the rest of the country.

Herbert was born on 5th February 1884, the second child and only son of John Stocks Hawkins

(Junior) and Ada Allison. They also had three daughters, all born in Bridlington, Ada Florence 1882, Hilda Hannah 1885 and Dora 1887. At Herbert's birth the occupation of John Stocks Hawkins (Junior) was given as Naval Engineer, however as he had resigned from the Navy some years before this is a puzzle. It may have been that he was working as a civilian engineer with the Navy, or he had re-joined.

Dora died in 1918 at the age of 31 years; possibly from Influenza although this has not been confirmed. Hilda Hannah died at the age of 53 years and Ada Florence emigrated to Canada; they all married Swedish seamen.

Whereas Edward had a strong affiliation to the Catholic Church, Herbert and his sisters were ardent supporters of the Salvation Army. Herbert loved music and had a passion for playing the piano, something which he encouraged his own children to continue.

Unlike Edward, Herbert was not born with any disability; however he battled most of his adult life with crippling bronchitis.

Edward's father, Charles Lindley Wood was born in 1839; his family came from a long line of lawyers, clergymen, Naval Officers and Political

John Stocks Hawkins (junior) in Naval Uniform circa 1878

figures. Charles was an accomplished writer, and wrote numerous ghost stories. After attending Eton School, Berkshire, Charles held the title of Groom of the Bedchamber to HRH the Prince of Wales, later King Edward VII. Only resigning this position when he was elected to the newly formed England Church Union, he had met the Prince, and future King, when they were both children. They remained close friends until the death of the King in 1910. Charles Lindley Wood succeeded to the titles of 2nd Viscount Halifax of Monk Bretton and 4th Baronet of Barnsley in 1885, and held the office of Deputy Lieutenant of the West Riding of Yorkshire.

Edward Wood's great great grandfather Captain Sir Charles Wood died from his wounds on active service aboard HMS Worcester, off Madras in 1782. More distant ancestry can be traced to William Wode, the last Prior of Bridlington, who was executed at Tyburn, Knavesmire, York for his part in the Pilgrimage of Grace, during the reign of Henry VIII in 1536.

Herbert's father John Stocks Hawkins (Junior) was born at Dunnington Manor, East Yorkshire on 11th January 1858. His father John Stocks Hawkins (Senior) later moved his wife and young family to Moor Grange a moated Manor house dating back to 1293 and once farmed as part of the Meaux Abbey estate. The house had been owned by John Stocks, uncle of John Stocks Hawkins (senior), until his death in 1872. Johns Stocks Hawkins (Senior) had married Bessey Hought in April 1858; she came from a prominent farming family of North Frodingham. Bessey Hought's elderly unmarried uncles Leonard and Richard Hought also lived with the family.

Leonard Hought would later buy The Tiger, Public House, at Beeford, East Yorkshire (still in existence today). At the age of just nine years of age Fanny Gertrude Hawkins daughter of John Stocks Hawkins (Senior) and Bessey Hought inherited this Inn from her Uncle. The reasons why Leonard chose to do this are unknown. Fanny was just 19 years old and unmarried when 'The Tiger' was sold to John Smith's Brewery. The beneficiary of the sale proceeds has not been identified.

Ada Allison's father Richard Major Allison worked as a Tin Smith, he came from a family of Master Cooper's. His family had once owned numerous workshops and retail properties in and around the Bridlington area. Richard's cousin and uncle married the sister and niece of one John Barker of Kent. In the 1800's John Barker opened 'Barker's' the famous Kensington drapery store which traded for over 135 years, and was later bought out by the House of Fraser.

John Stocks Hawkins (Junior) bought himself out of the Royal Navy for the price of £12 in February 1880, after serving just 18 months of a

10 year commitment. The Naval Records show that he had served mainly on HMS Asia a prison ship, moored off Portsmouth. It is difficult to ascertain why he had wished to leave the Navy after such a short period of service, but it was to become a fateful decision.

Tragedy struck the family on the 8th February 1889, when John Stocks Hawkins (Junior) was lost in the North Sea onboard the steam ship Adventure (H1500). The Hull registered trawler is said to have been the first steam trawler to be lost from the port of Hull. The Lost Hull Fisherman register lists him as J Hawkins (30) Chief Engineer, of Dunnington, misspelt as Donnington.

After this tragedy Ada appeared to try to hide her children, stating that she was 'scared' that the family would take them away. Hilda Hannah and Ada Florence recalled being followed around by 'men in black hats'. The Hawkins children all reported spending some time in orphanages.

The only evidence of this is the 1891 census when Ada Florence is shown to be at the Sailors Orphanage in Hull. At the same time the widow Ada Hawkins is recorded as living in Hull, with daughters Hilda Hannah and Dora. Herbert Stanley is listed both with his grandfather in Bridlington and his mother in Hull so it is difficult to ascertain his whereabouts.

In March 1893 Ada Hawkins re-married in St Stephens Church, Hull. Her new husband was George Frost a blacksmith from Skidby, East Yorkshire. Soon afterwards the Hawkins children took the on the surname of their new step-father.

A few years' later Ada and George adopted a son also born in Bridlington; on the 1901 census he was listed as T Banks aged 4. Reportedly dying in the Far East and last seen on the 1911 census, as Bertie Frost, firewood dealer, there are no further identifiable details.

Edward Wood and Lady Dorothy Evelyn Augusta Onslow, daughter of the 4th Earl of Onslow married in 1909. They had five children two daughters and three sons, one girl died in infancy and their middle son was killed on active service in Egypt during World War II. Their surviving sons took up Political office and their remaining daughter married the 3rd Earl of Feversham of Ryedale.

Another wedding took place in 1909 that of Herbert Stanley Hawkins and Mary Elizabeth Moran, daughter of a Hull fisherman; the couple had six children five daughters and a son, although one girl died in infancy. Their surviving children married and lived the rest of their lives in Hull.

With a growing family Herbert found work as a Fish Bobber on St. Andrew's fish dock, Hull. Fish Bobbers were employed to land the fish brought in daily by the large fishing fleet of the day. The work of Fish Bobbers would have been arduous, wet, cold and odourous. In Hull it is said that Fish Bobbers earned a 'bob a week' hence the name 'Bobber.'

Whilst life was unfolding within the Hawkins family, Edward Wood was making a name for himself in the Political field. He became the Member of Parliament for Ripon and saw some active service in World War I, although this was mainly behind the lines. He was elevated to the Peerage in 1925; then just prior to World War II he became perhaps the most famous Foreign Secretary of all time. He accompanied Neville Chamberlain to Munich for talks with Adolf Hitler. It was during this visit that he is understood to have assumed Hitler was a doorman, much to the Fuehrer's consternation.

In the Political field there were those who thought Edward Wood was the best candidate for Prime Minister. But it is said that he had neither the charisma nor inclination for the post and was happy to leave it to Winston Churchill.

In contrast to Edward Wood's Second World War experience, Herbert Hawkins and his family remained in the city of Hull, reputedly one of the most bombed areas of the country. By then almost disabled from poor health and recurrent chest complaints Herbert worked as an Air Raid Warden, frequently risking his own life to ensure others were safe. Living in close proximity to the dock area of the city, Herbert and his family witnessed many bombs falling and the resulting devastation.

Herbert Stanley Hawkins (far left) at work on St Andrew's Dock, Hull as a Fish Bobber circa 1930

Ill health was eventually to catch up with Herbert Stanley Hawkins and he died at the age of 67years on 15th February 1951, at the Western General Hospital, Hull.

Edward Frederick Lindley Wood survived Herbert by a few more years dying at the family estate of Hickleton, West

Yorkshire on 23rd December 1959 at the age of 78 years.

Like the Wood family, the Hawkins were also descended from a long line of lawyers, clergymen, Naval Officers and Political figures, in fact they were descended from the same family. But whereas Edward Wood could trace his family directly back through the male side, the Hawkins ancestry travelled along the female side. A well known and respected family, the Woods owned estates and property in Yorkshire and London. Beeford Grange in East Yorkshire was the seat of Sir George Wood, Knight; he was the brother of Elizabeth Wood and cousin of Charles Lindley Wood.

So what did happen within the Hawkins family to take them so far away from the privileged world of Lord Halifax to the fishing community of Hull?

On 9th January 1816 Elizabeth Stocks (daughter of Elizabeth Wood and John Stocks (gentleman farmer of Moor Grange) eloped to marry Philip Hawkins, in Skeffling-cum-Burstwick, East Yorkshire. She was barely 16 years of age, the occupation of Philip was given as a 'Farm Bailiff.' Elizabeth and

Edward Frederick Lindley Wood (Lord Halifax)

Philip would have 11 children in all, six of whom would be born at the family estate in Royston, West Yorkshire. John Stocks Hawkins (Senior) father of John Stocks Hawkins (Junior) was one of the children born in there, in 1832. Philip Hawkins was to die in 1860 at the age of 67, however he had been committed to a mental institution in 1842, it is not known what condition he was suffering from.

The Hawkins returned to Beeford around 1835, on the death of Elizabeth's mother, Elizabeth Wood, who had farmed at Beeford Grange. Dunnington Manor came into the possession of John Stocks Hawkins (Senior) and his wife following the accidental death of William de France Stocks nephew of John Stocks. William's sudden demise had left a void which the newlywed John Stocks Hawkins was the obvious family successor to take over. He and his family remained at Dunnington Manor for approximately 13 years, until they moved into Moor Grange on the death of John Stocks in December 1872.

Six of the ten children of John Stocks Hawkins and Bessey Hought were born at Dunnington

Manor, their eldest child being John Stocks Hawkins (Junior) born 11th January 1858, their youngest child Bessey Mosey Hawkins was born in 1877 in Hilderthorpe, Bridlington. The Hawkins family continued to live and farm at Moor Grange, until 1876, when John Stocks Hawkins (Senior) was declared bankrupt at Hull County Court. There is documented evidence of failed property deals and mounting gambling debts, throughout most of his marriage to Bessey Hought.

In August 1874 John Stocks Hawkins (Senior) purchased a property at Southcliffe Terrace, Bridlington, and moved his family in following the bankruptcy declaration. Evidence then begins to emerge that the marriage of John Stocks Hawkins (Senior) and Bessey Hought was collapsing and they started to live apart. Bessey was then named as the sole owner of the Bridlington property.

Running the property as a Bed and Breakfast business, by 1878 Bessey was forced to re-mortgage in order to cater for the ever increasing numbers of summer boarders. However with so many young children to care for times must have been tough for the family.

Sadly the youngest Hawkins children Clara and Bessey Mosey were just 4 and 2 years of age when on 12th November 1879, their 40 year old mother Bessey died of Pneumonia in the Southcliffe property.

Present at Bessey's death was one Anne Hopper; it is difficult to say exactly who Anne Hopper was as information regarding her ancestry changes frequently. But whoever she was on 16th April 1881 she married John Stocks Hawkins (Senior) and took over the running of the Southcliffe Terrace property.

Just prior to this marriage John Stocks Hawkins (Junior) had desperately tried to raise a second mortgage on the family home. Having failed to raise money and with increasingly mounting debts Southcliffe Terrace was sold and the family moved into a smaller property on Railway Crescent, Bridlington. Despite the house being smaller the family continued in the Bed and Breakfast trade. The railways at the time would have been bringing holidaymakers, by the score, from the industrial

**Herbert Stanley Hawkins
as young man**

Mansfield   245, ANLABY ROAD
HULL.

towns of West Yorkshire, and trade should have been good.

In 1881 the Bridlington Free Press listed that, including the Hawkins family, a total of 24 persons were living or staying at the Railway Crescent address. Shortly after this the Hawkins children are seen to depart the family home with increasing regularity. Both John Stocks Hawkins (Junior) and William Hought Hawkins married in 1881, their sister Charlotte Stocks Hawkins married William Ralph Skelton Tigar. The grandfather of William Tigar was Pennock Tigar, Alderman and Lord Mayor of Beverley and proprietor of the Tigar Manure Works, from which the family had amassed their capital. Of the other Hawkins children George Wood Hawkins eloped and later left for Canada, Elizabeth Jane would marry John the supposed son of Annie Hopper. Margaret Louisa died young, Clara would die in childbirth leaving two children, Mary never married, Bessey would marry twice and Fanny Gertrude would later marry and move to Hartlepool.

On 17th May 1887 John Stocks Hawkins (Senior) died aged 56years at the house in Railway Crescent. The cause of death was listed as a tumour of the neck. He is buried in an unmarked grave in Bridlington cemetery. After his death, even though he was an un-discharged bankrupt, legal documents show that John Stocks

Hawkins (Senior) continued to have considerable influence over various properties held in trust funds.

Following her husband's death Anne Hopper moved out of Railway Crescent and into a newly built property in St Georges Avenue, Bridlington, with her brother Robert Hopper and Anne Sullivan. Anne Sullivan appears to have been yet another illegitimate child of Anne's.

The two youngest Hawkins children, Clara and Bessey Mosey were also taken along and employed as servants in the new lodging business. It is unknown as to how this business venture was financed, but it continued for some time.

By 1901 the lease of the property was in the possession of Anne Sullivan, both Clara and Bessey Hawkins continued to live there until they married. Anne Hopper herself re-located to Leeds were she died on 2nd November 1920. Anne Hopper and Anne Sullivan are buried in the same unmarked grave of John Stocks Hawkins in Bridlington.

There is well documented evidence of how events shaped both the Wood and Hawkins families, but as usual with genealogy there are frequently more questions than answers. What is evident though is that the downturn in the fortunes and status of the Hawkins family had much to do with marriage, debts and fate.

Life may have been very different if Elizabeth Stocks had followed her head and not her heart. Similarly is the decision of John Stocks Hawkins (Junior) to leave the Navy. Would he have actually lived any longer, or would he have succumbed to illness or disease, had he stayed put.

What sort of Prime Minister would Edward have made?

And what of the concerns of Ada Allison, were people really after her children and if so who? It is difficult to imagine any of the Hawkins family being interested so what was she so scared about?

Then there is Anne Hopper what was her true identity? Was she a gold digger or someone genuinely in love, no one will never know.

For the inquisitive visitor to Bridlington there is a house on West Street, once owned by George Wood Hawkins. Ironically he named it Stockswood, after Sir George Wood and John Stocks, a timely reminder of an intriguing family once described as almost 'legendary' in the Bridlington area.

Sources
Lord Halifax
www.spartacus.schoolnet.co.uk/2WWhalifaxL.htm
Lord Halifax tried to negotiate peace with the Nazis
www.telegraph.co.uk/news/uknews/2650832/Lord-Halifax-tried-to-negotiate-peace-with-the-Nazis.html
Queen Mother wanted peace with Hitler
www.fpp.co.uk/bookchapters/WSC/Monckton.html
Lord Halifax Biography

www.basicfamouspeople.com/index.php?aid=694
Census www.ancestry.co.uk/
Searching for Clara Peter Bolton (Unknown) (a personal search to find his mother's identity)
History of Beeford and Moor Grange, Stocks family information
www.british-history.ac.uk/place.aspx?region=6- and www.genuki.org.uk/big/eng/YKS/ERY/Beeford/index.html
Birth, marriages and deaths in England and Wales 1837-2005 www.bmdindex.co.uk/
Hawkins Family Papers and Documents, which include birth, marriage and death certificates, the Will of Elizabeth Hawkins and auction documents relating to Beeford Grange.
The story of John Barker & Co Ltd, Kensington, London www.gla.ac.uk/media/media_91174_en.pdf
Lost Trawlermen of the Port of Hull, Hull City Archives, www.hullcc.gov.uk
Navy discharge papers of John Stocks Hawkins (Junior) www.nationalarchives.gov.uk/ -
Lundy Darryl www.thepeerage.com/ - The Wood family
'The Holy Fox' The Life of Lord Halifax, A Roberts 1991 Phoenix Press
www.stortfordhistory.co.uk/guide7/grange_paddocks.html
Tigar and Champney Family Papers and documents, East Riding of Yorkshire Archives and Local Studies Service, Beverley, archives.service@eastriding.gov.uk
The will of George Wood www.hullcc.gov.uk
St Andrews Dock, Hull (1962)
www.yfaonline.com/yfapublic/assetDetails.cfm?film=2249&keyword
Lost Trawlers of Hull 1835-1987 Alec Gill Pub: Hutton Press

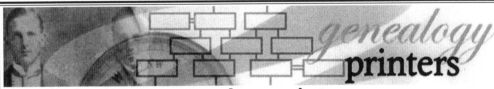

From Milling to Movie Making
Martin Limon

One of the most potent symbols in the history of movie making is of a large muscular man in shorts and with an oiled torso swinging a huge hammer to strike a gong. This familiar image was the trademark of J Arthur Rank (1888-1972), one of Hull's most famous citizens, a member of a prosperous mill-owning family in the city and who rose to become the dominant force in the British film industry during the 1930s and 1940s.

Truth is often stranger than fiction and the story of J Arthur Rank the miller turned movie-mogul is a case in point. Often seen as a rather dull bumbling figure, ordinary in appearance, shy and slow in speech much of Arthur Rank's early life was lived in the shadow of a successful father. Joseph Rank was a Methodist business tycoon who established the family's fortunes through a dynamic and lucrative flour-milling business that began in Hull.

The towers of windmills were once a familiar sight in towns and villages across Yorkshire for the power of the wind was once used to grind corn into flour. One such windmill (now restored as part of a public house) can still be seen on Hull's Holderness Road and it was here that the story of a great northern business family began. Joseph Rank was a formidable figure in Victorian and Edwardian Hull and had begun work at the age of fourteen at the Holderness Road mill and from these modest beginnings built up a huge flour-milling business at ports throughout Britain at a time when imported wheat was fast becoming the trend.

Publicity photograph of J Arthur Rank from the 1940s

Arthur Rank was the sixth of Joseph's eight children and he had a strict Victorian upbringing. Joseph Rank was a ruthless domineering figure whose strict Methodist values insisted on family attendance at church three times on Sundays and an outright ban on drinking alcohol, theatre-going and dancing in public. Like many self-made men of those times he could also be hard on his own children. Arthur was sent away to a Methodist boarding school (1901-1906) but he was obviously no great scholar for his father told him that he was *"a dunce at school and that the only way he would succeed was through the family business."* This prophecy seemed to come true for when Arthur tried his hand at running his own firm after the First World War (Peterkin's Self Raising Flour) this was a failure and he had to return to his father's milling business where he had served his initial 'apprenticeship.'

So how was this rather dull, slow-witted man able to make the transition in middle age from an unsuccessful self-employed businessman to a successful moviemaker? The main factors seem to have been Arthur Rank's deep religious faith and his access to money. In 1920 he received an early inheritance of one million pounds from his father (who wished to avoid death duties) and this gave him the means to pursue his own ambitions. It was also from his father that Arthur inherited an enthusiasm for Wesleyan Methodism; in 1919 he became a Sunday school teacher and in 1925 bought the newspaper 'The Methodist Times' to spread his Christian message. Inspired by what he considered to be a 'divine calling' the making of films with a strong moral message was the next logical step and would help to counteract the negative influence of Hollywood on British society.

In 1933 he started the Religious Films Society and collaborated with a Methodist minister to make a movie called 'Mastership' costing £2,700. This gave him a taste of what could be achieved and meant that he could combine his enthusiasm for risk-taking in business with evangelical Christianity. A fellow enthusiast, Lady Yule, soon joined him; she had been left nine million pounds by her late husband and saw movie making as a way to combat her boredom! Together they set up a new production company called British National (1934) and made another movie with strong religious themes, *'Turn of the Tide',* about the rivalry between two Yorkshire fishing families. Unfortunately the reluctance of the distributors meant that the film was never widely shown

187

The newly restored windmill on Hull's Holderness Road. It was here that Joseph Rank (1854-1943) was born. He later established the milling firm of Joseph Rank Limited.

declare that "I am in films because of the Holy Spirit" and he seems to have believed, genuinely, that films could be a force for good. However although he was a committed Christian he was enough of a businessman to realise that 'religious films' had only a limited appeal and as a result the flavour of his movies became more 'mainstream.' He did this in order to compete with the Americans who provided about 80% of the films seen on British cinema screens up to the Second World War.

By the time war broke out in 1939 Arthur Rank was well on the way to becoming the closest thing to a movie mogul that Britain has ever seen with his Rank Organisation having a controlling interest in the movie studios at Pinewood, Ealing and Elstree and moving into every area of film from newsreels, to comedies, to Shakespeare adaptations and to costume melodramas. Although reviled by some as stuffy and prudish

and Rank quickly realised that he would need to control the distribution of films if he was to be a producer who could rival the big Hollywood studios. With this aim in mind he bought out General Film Distributors who were the UK distributors for Universal Pictures (1936). Two years later to strengthen his hold on the exhibition of films he bought the Odeon cinema chain too and with further acquisitions the Rank Organisation controlled over six hundred cinemas by 1942.

Rank's investment in film production was also continuing at breakneck speed. In collaboration with Lady Yule and the Sheffield building tycoon Sir Charles Boot, Heatherden Hall in Buckinghamshire was bought and turned into 'Pinewood Studios' at a cost of over one million pounds. As the name suggests it was designed to rival the best that Hollywood had to offer. The continuing religious motivation of Rank's work was revealed at the opening of the new studios with the production facilities there being 'blessed' by the Reverend Benjamin Gregory (the editor of the 'Methodist Times' and honorary secretary of the Religious Films Society). Rank was to

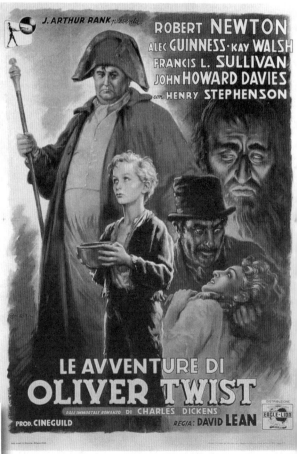

J. ARTHUR RANK presenta
ROBERT NEWTON
ALEC GUINNESS · KAY WALSH
FRANCIS L. SULLIVAN
JOHN HOWARD DAVIES
con HENRY STEPHENSON

LE AVVENTURE DI
OLIVER TWIST
DALL'IMMORTALE ROMANZO DI CHARLES DICKENS
PROD. CINEGUILD   REGIA: DAVID LEAN
EAGLE-LION

Publicity poster for J Arthur Rank's film of 'Oliver Twist' (1948). Directed by David Lean The film was popular with foreign audiences as well as British ones

and by others as dangerous monopolist in reality his 'light touch' in the day-to-day business of producing movies made the 1940s a 'golden age' of British film making. Arthur Rank was the first to admit that he knew little about the artistic side of film production but had the good sense and the money to hire the best brains to handle this for him. Affectionately known to his staff as 'Uncle Arthur' he provided the finance to make movies that no one else would have made and provided the enthusiasm and organising ability of a visionary who wanted the British film industry to succeed in a market dominated by the Americans.

Under his leadership a group called 'Independent Producers Limited' were given free rein to produce the kind of films they wanted to make without the kind of intrusive interference that was so much a feature of Hollywood. By doing this, he reasoned, the quality work they produced would enable him to break into the all-important American market. Three of the talented directors who worked for him were David Lean, Michael Powell and Emeric Pressburger and all were in the enviable position of being able to count on Rank's generosity in the funding of their films. David Lean was to say of Rank's benevolent approach: *"We can make any subject we wish with as much money as we think that subject should have spent on it."*

The result of Rank's 'hands-off' style of management was a series of classic British movies like *'Brief Encounter'* (1945) *'Great Expectations'* (1946) *'The Red Shoes'* (1948), *Oliver Twist* (1948), and *Genevieve* (1953). To all outward appearances the Rank Organisation was a success with, in 1946, a staff of 31,000 and a turnover of £45 million. However the downside to this picture was that as the organisation grew it became less efficient with much overspending on film budgets and expenditure on doubtful projects such as the 'Rank Charm School' where young starlets were trained in the finer points of their craft. In addition Arthur Rank's missionary zeal in trying to break into the American market with his films was met with frustration and disappointment, partly caused by the actions of the new Labour Government after 1945 in adopting protectionist policies.

After 1952 the death of his only remaining brother forced Arthur Rank to concentrate on the family's milling business with the result that the day-to-day operation of the film studios were left to his vice-chairman, the accountant John Davis. Unlike Rank he was less inclined towards taking risks so that quality suffered. Safer low-budget comedies like Norman Wisdom films, the *'Doctor'* series of movies and *'Carry On'* films were now the order of the day. Furthermore the organisation he had created was badly hit by the growth of television from the mid-1950s after which cinema audiences went into decline.

By the time of Arthur Rank's death in 1972 the organisation that bore his name had moved on to more lucrative areas of business like Rank Xerox copying machines and bingo halls and no longer made films. Looking back at his importance to the British film industry in the 1930s and 1940s (for which he was raised to the peerage) and to the movie empire that he built, it seems incredible that it vanished so quickly. Today this Hull-born pioneer is best remembered for a string of superbly crafted British films that made the Rank Organisation the envy of the world and for his charitable work through the Rank Foundation. This was established by Arthur Rank in 1953 and continues to support worthy causes among, for example, the young and the old to this day.

Rank studios had a number of successes with 'Carry On' films. This is a publicity photo for 'Carry On-Don't Lose your Head' starring Sid James and Kenneth Williams. (Courtesy of the Rank Organisation)

Chancel Repair Liability
- A Contemporary Problem

Stephen Rickitt

Local historians may have come across references to Chancel Repair Liability in post reformation land transactions and, occasionally, in the most detailed legal textbooks. Until relatively recently, most lawyers were completely unaware of its existence. The writer used it as an interview question to sort out the wafflers from the honest even as late as the mid 2000s.

This article will briefly examine the origins of the liability and explain why in the next few years local historians with a detailed knowledge of an area with a pre-Reformation church and /or subsequent Enclosure Awards can anticipate detailed questions both on land ownership during Henry VIII's reign and the detail of the enclosure process.

It will then close by indicating where to find further information on this involved, anachronistic and yet potentially economically significant issue

Origins

My understanding is that uniquely within medieval Western Christendom, the rector of the parish church in England and Wales was responsible for the maintenance of the CHANCEL of the church, the parishioners being responsible for the remainder. The chancel is the eastern end of the church, containing the altar and usually the choir. In other parts of Western Europe, the parish

priest had responsibility for maintaining the entire church building.

The liability has its origins in the mists of Common Law before the accession of Richard I in 1189, a time deemed to be the start of English and Welsh legal memory. Later in this article, I shall indicate a possible modern day difference between Wales and England as a result of the disestablishment of the Church of Wales in 1920.

Usually the lord of the manor gave land for the erection of the parish church, but did not wish to retain a liability for the church's maintenance. That responsibility fell to the rector, who in turn needed some method of providing for his living expenses and those of repairing the church chancel. Land was therefore allocated to the rector and this became known as GLEBE or GLEBE LAND. The rector got both the income from the Glebe and the tithes from the parishioners. Originally tithes were one-tenth of parishioners' produce but over the centuries became monetary payments.

Changes over the next centuries

The picture then changes with alterations in society.

The first major change was the Reformation under Henry VIII. Before then many rectorships had been the property of the monasteries. A vicar would be appointed, and paid, to act as the priest based in the parish dealing with spiritual needs but he

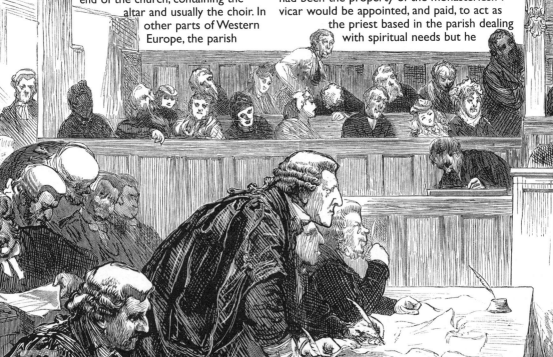

would not have the rights to the glebe nor the tithes. On the dissolution of the religious houses, specific legislation was passed enabling the glebe land to become the property of laymen, but accompanied with the obligation to repair the chancel.

The next set of changes came with the Enclosure Acts and Awards, especially in the 18th and 19th Centuries. In many cases, specific provision was made for the rector to receive an allotment of land in exchange for surrendering his tithe rights. It is the opinion of the leading legal experts that the obligation to repair the chancel will now be a burden on that area of land.

There were also further changes with the reform and eventual abolition of tithes during the late 19th and 20th Centuries.

Until the late 1980s, there were very occasions when chancel repair liability permeated the legal consciousness, let alone that of the public. There was a flurry of interest following the imprisonment of a landowner for failure to comply with an ecclesiastical court ruling resulting in the passage of the *Chancel Repair Act 1932*. That Act did not deal with the liability, merely in which court enforcement proceedings should be taken. There were a few judicial decisions in the 1930s and one in 1955 (where the Air Ministry unsuccessfully tried to avoid liability).

The Law Commission were asked to look at the issues in 1983, and their working paper is generally regarded as the authoritive statement of the law as it was, and to a great extent, still is.

This was followed by a report in 1985 recommending abolition being phased over a ten year period. The principle of abolition had been accepted by both the English and Welsh Anglican Churches, although they would have preferred the phasing to be twenty years. Government took no action on the recommendation.

The Aston Cantlow Case

In January 1995 the court proceedings began which have now changed the legal landscape. The Parochial Church Council for the Parish Church of St John the Baptist in Aston Cantlow began a claim against a local landowner for the cost of repairing the chancel.

[The village of Aston Cantlow lies about three miles to the north west of Stratford-upon-Avon. It has a long history. The parish church, St John the Baptist, stands on an ancient Saxon site. Two images of its exterior can be seen on the website Pictorial Images of Warwickshire, www.genuki.org.uk/big/eng/WAR/images. It is the church where Shakespeare's mother, Mary Arden, who lived at Wilmcote within the parish, married John Shakespeare. The earliest part of the present structure is the chancel which has been there since the late 13th century. It was built in the decorated style and contains a fine example of the use of flowing tracery: Pevsner and Wedgewood, *The Buildings of England: Warwickshire*, (1965) pp 19, 75.].

The proceeding went from the Chancery Division, to the Court of Appeal, and finally in 2003 to the House of Lords (sitting in its then judicial capacity). To the surprise of many, it was decided that chancel repair liability was alive & kicking and the landowners were ordered to pay for the costs of repairs.

The greatest problem faced by property lawyers is there is no central place where a search can be made to see if there is any chancel repair liability affecting a particular piece of land. I recall being told by a colleague in a leading City of London firm that they had carried out an experiment and it took a highly educated lawyer two days to trace records through the National Archives at Kew, and even then they were unable to give a clear yes/no answer.

At the same time as the House of Lords gave its ruling, the Land Registry were introducing their new scheme for registering land and had assumed chancel repair liability would not survive the challenge in the courts. They then had to rapidly introduce legislation to cater for the newly revived liability and try to make some provision to enable land transactions to take place without a risk of suddenly finding an onerous obligation to repair part of the local church. It was also apparent that the scope of the potentially affected land within England and Wales extended to a significant percentage of the land with the two countries. The best estimates are that chancel repair liability affects about 5200 parish churches (no one is quite sure and the Churches and The Law Commission say it's between 4000 and 6000), about one-third of all parishes in Wales and England.

With the costs of repairing what are inevitably ancient structures rising all the time, the 1995 estimate for the repairs to St John the Baptist was over £95 thousand, the esoteric legal question suddenly became highly significant in land transactions.

The Land Registry's solution was to provide a ten year period until October 2013 for chancel repair obligations to be registered as a caution at the Land Registry. As the cut-off date approaches, it is possible that local historians will be approached by either the Parochial Church Council, or the affected landowners seeking evidence to support or rebut claims for chancel repair liability. Unregistered liability will still exist in certain circumstances beyond October 2013, and perhaps pressure will grow for a solution to be imposed by Parliament.

There have been suggestions that the legislation which removed the responsibility for church repairs from the priest to the Parochial Church Council MAY mean that some Anglican rectors in Wales may still have the common law duty of repairing their chancels. The argument concerns the wording of the legislation which led to Welsh disestablishment in 1920. As far as I am aware, no one though has seriously pursued this avenue (as yet).

It must also be stressed that the liability only affects Anglican churches.

Where to start research

The Law Commission and others seem to think it will be almost impossible to trace the pre-Reformation Glebe Land. I am not so sure, with the increasing numbers of sales and break-up of the larger estates in the past decades, I consider it is not unreasonable for research to uncover Glebe Land.

Keen historians, ramblers, riders and others are already well versed in tracing highways created by Enclosure Awards. It will be as easy to trace land given to rectors in exchange for tithes.

Some of the other ways in which the liability attaches to land will be more complex and I can only refer the truly dedicated to the papers below for a starting point.

The National Archives have good research guides on Chancel Repairs and Tithes, to which I would refer the initial researcher.

The Church of England's Legal Advisory Commission have also published an Opinion giving details on the process of registration but also setting out a case for not enforcing or registering chancel repair liability where, for example it might adversely affect the Church's pastoral mission in a community.

Further Information

1: There is an excellent lecture given by Derek Wellman, Registrar of the Diocese of Lincoln, to members of the Ecclesiastical Law Association on 8 April 2000, available via the Peterborough Diocesan website at
www.peterboroughdiocesanregistry.co.uk/wellman.pdf
2: The most authorative survey of the legal position up to the mid 1980s is contained in a 1983 Working Paper titled *Transfer of Land – Liability for Chancel Repairs* produced by The Law Commission and available online at
www.bailii.org/ew/other/EWLC/1983/c86.pdf
3: The subsequent report by The Law Commission in 1985 is available at
www.bailii.org/ew/other/EWLC/1985/152.pdf
4: The judgment of the House of Lords in the Aston Cantlow case is at
www.bailii.org/uk/cases/UKHL/2003/37.html

5: The National Archives Legal Records Information Leaflet 33 (Chancel Repair) is at
www.nationalarchives.gov.uk/catalogue/RdLeaflet.asp?sLe afletID=223&j=1
6: The National Archives Domestic Information Research Guide 41 (Tithes) is at
www.nationalarchives.gov.uk/catalogue/RdLeaflet.asp?sLe afletID=100
7: The Church of England's Legal Advisory Commission's Opinion is available via
www.cofe.anglican.org/about/churchlawlegis/guidance/

Stephen Rickitt is a solicitor with Northumberland County Council in the lucky position of combining his interests in history with his work in the area of highways and property. The views in this article are his own. He is grateful to his colleagues for their forbearance over the years when he raises CHANCEL REPAIR LIABILITY yet again!

The History of Portrait Miniatures

Sandra Hargreaves

Quite recently I made contact with a distant cousin descended from a couple who were also my great, great grandparents. We exchanged emails to confirm that we belonged to the same tree, and then within the space of a few minutes a scanned copy of an old photograph of the couple was appearing on my computer screen. I had never seen their likeness before and it was definitely one of the highlights of the years spent researching my ancestors. Within the space of twenty four hours, a photograph was in my possession here in Australia which had been sent from Canada. Truly amazing and I began to wonder what John and Elizabeth Hargreaves would have thought about the technology which enabled their photograph, taken in about 1870, to wing its way almost instantaneously around the world in 2009. The photograph had almost certainly been taken to Canada when one of their sons had left England's shores for a new life. Today we take photography for granted, but what of the days before photographic images were possible?

Sometime ago I had received a copy of the will of Thomas Hargreaves who died in Wakefield, Yorkshire on the 3rd October 1845. He was described as a painter. Although he seemed to have no apparent connection to my own Hargreaves family line, I followed this up by sending for a copy of the will of his son George Hargreaves, also a painter, who died on the 26th of January 1864. It contained the following paragraph, " and the oil paintings painted by myself and my half share in the oil paintings painted by or formerly belonging to my late father." Although I wrote to various art galleries, I was unable to locate any of the paintings mentioned in George's will. Several months later I was browsing through an index to the *Dictionary of National Biography*, when I noticed the name of Thomas Hargreaves (1774-1846) listed as an artist. However, artist Thomas was shown as living in Liverpool and further research into Thomas of Wakefield had shown him to be a coach painter and gilder by trade, not an artist. I was sufficiently intrigued, however, to search for the entry in the Dictionary of National Biography.

Thomas Hargreaves of Liverpool was the son of Henry Hargreaves, a woollen draper of Castle Street, and had been baptised on the 7th of April 1774 at the church of St Nicholas in Liverpool. As a child he had shown great artistic talent and when the eminent artist Sir Thomas Lawrence saw his work Thomas was encouraged to go to London as Lawrence's apprentice. He was to serve a two year apprenticeship at 50 guineas a year, before returning to Liverpool where he set himself up as a miniature artist. He exhibited at the Royal Academy in 1798, 1808 and 1809 and in 1811 Thomas became a member of the Liverpool Academy. He was a prolific painter and was a founder member of the Society of British Artists in Suffolk Street in 1824. It is known that amongst his sitters were the family of W.E. Gladstone, the politician. There are a considerable number of surviving portrait miniatures done by Thomas and I have come across quite a few online which have been for sale. They have a considerable value today.

On a more personal note Thomas Hargreaves of Liverpool was married to Sophia Shaw. Their son George was baptised at St Peters in Liverpool on the 14th of January in 1797. One of their sons was perhaps significantly named Lawrence. Their other known children were Charles, Emma, William and Augustus. Thomas trained talented young artists in the skills of creating portrait miniatures. One of his students was Anne Langton, who became a competent miniature artist. She painted portraits of her family members and friends, which show the delicate skill she possessed. She and most of her family emigrated to Canada after a decline in the family fortunes, during the 1830's. In the census of 1841 Thomas Hargreaves was living in Bold Street Liverpool where, according to trade directories, he had lived since at least 1827. He was sixty seven years old and still working as an artist. His son George, also a miniature portrait artist of some note was living there too. Son Charles had followed his grandfather Henry's trade and was a tailor and draper. On the 23rd of December 1846, Thomas the artist died in Liverpool.

His son George died in 1870. There seems to be no family connection between the two men called Thomas Hargreaves although both had a similar lifespan, both had a

A Painting by George Hargreaves

son called George and both had a love of painting. In spite of this, the beautiful miniatures I had seen online encouraged me to find out more about the art of painting miniatures.

The Liverpool Mercury of Friday January 8th 1847 contained the following obituary for Thomas Hargreaves:

Death of Thomas Hargreaves Esq.

We lament to state that our esteemed fellow townsman, Thomas Hargreaves Esq. of Hope Place, Hope Street, breathed his last on Tuesday. As an artist of great merit and considerable standing and influence, his name will be long remembered and fondly cherished. In the profession of a miniature portrait painter, he had very few equals. His likenesses were remarkably striking, and he was probably more celebrated for the faithful and yet strictly natural manner in which he depicted female beauty and loveliness than for any of his other miniature representations. He had the singular good fortune of enjoying friendship and intimate acquaintanceship with two great patrons of art, whose names will be handed down to posterity with honour and renown - we mean the late Sir Thomas Lawrence and Mr Roscoe. He was several years under Sir Thomas, in London, studying as an oil and portrait painter; but the smell of the oil having disagreed with his health, he was compelled to abandon that department of the profession, and to dedicate his talents to miniature painting, which he followed during the remainder of his life. The keen discernment and highly cultivated taste of Roscoe were not slow in discovering genius of a very high order in the works of our deceased friend, and once that he was patronised by Roscoe his house and studio became the resort of those numerous admirers of art which Liverpool then and now justly boasted. In public life Mr Hargreaves was highly and very justly respected; and in private he was remarkable for that extreme mildness of disposition and gentleness of manners, which are the certain accompaniments of genuine talent as well as for the most gentlemanly deportment. One particular trait in his character will be remembered by many. He became the friend and patron of every rising artist and wherever he discovered a young man struggling for fame, he was ever ready to afford him the benefit of his advice and experience and to usher him into those societies in which he would be most likely to succeed. Though his health had been suffering for many years from a nervous affection he lived to the advanced age of seventy three, and retained the friendship and esteem of his numerous friends and acquaintances to the last.

We have all admired magnificent portraits hanging on the walls of stately homes, recording a line of illustrious or occasionally notorious ancestors. There were many reasons why people would have commissioned portraits, but the kind seen in stately homes usually did not prove to be very mobile. They could not be transported easily and could have been easily damaged if taken down from the safety of the wall. However, miniature portraits were far more practical and by the late seventeenth century and early eighteenth century they were extremely popular. Way back in the sixteenth century, when wealthy families arranged marriages for their children into suitable families great distances away, a miniature portrait could be

sent with an envoy. The portrait could be used to infer a beauty which perhaps did not exist and there must have been many a disappointment when the betrothed couple met for the first time. At first it was the nobility who created images this way but gradually the practice became more popular and a sailor or soldier might have a portrait with him, of someone dear to him at home. Merchants who travelled and were in foreign countries for long periods of time might exchange small portraits with loved ones left behind. This all led to an increase in the numbers of portrait painters in Britain, who initially used watercolour paints on a stretched vellum surface. In Europe, this miniature painting did not achieve quite the popularity it enjoyed in England. However, on the continent portrait miniatures were more likely to be of enamel. That is using the technique of painting with metallic oxide paints onto a metal surface. Usually copper, it was prepared by covering it with white enamel paste. Each colour was painted onto the surface and fired in a kiln after each separate colour had been applied.

The earliest miniature portrait painters were the illuminators of beautiful hand written books. Their delicate skills, acquired during their painstaking work, were ideal for portrait painting. As the invention of printing created less demand for illustrators of books an increasing demand for their portrait painting skills continued. Early in the sixteenth century, portrait miniatures were commissioned by the English and French courts and the techniques were learned by Hans Holbein, King Henry VIII's portrait painter. Portrait miniatures were often small enough to be worn as jewellery or carried incorporated into items such as tiny boxes. From this time until the beginning of the eighteenth century, the portraits were painted on to vellum which was stuck onto a card made from several layers of paper glued together. The surface was then prepared by burnishing with a dog's tooth set into a wooden handle. Squirrel hair brushes, set into a quill, were used to apply the paint made by the artist using a range of pigments. These were made from plants, insects, mineral powders with gold and silver leaf.

The beginning of the eighteenth century saw vellum replaced by thin sheets of ivory obtained from elephants' tusks. This surface presented its

St George's Square, Liverpool

own problems and to make the paint adhere to the surface more readily, the ivory was slightly roughened. The paints too had to be prepared differently and gum arabic was used to make the paint stickier. Liquid from the gall bladder of a cow or bull was also used as it was said to make the paint easier to apply. The sheets of ivory became thinner as the cutter's skills improved and this added to the translucency of the painting. As with all things, the desire for these portraits spread to the wealthier classes beyond the royal courts and by the late eighteenth century, many such portraits were exchanged. They were tokens of affection and sometimes memorials of the dear departed. Often the paintings were oval or round and were set into beautiful frames. The frame might incorporate a lock of hair as a love or memorial token. Some framed paintings were presented in velvet lined boxes to protect them when taken on journeys. Most were of the head and shoulders of the sitter and often the background was of soft clouds in a pale blue sky. Most of those I have seen do not have smiling faces. It would have been much more difficult to maintain such a pose for the length of time required at a sitting. Many are of children but all are a fascinating image of a member of someone's family from the past. Unfortunately, many that have survived are of unknown people painted by unknown artists.

The demand for portrait miniatures continued unabated, until the art of the photographer reached the high streets of towns during the mid nineteenth century. The camera does not lie it is said, but for me the portrait miniatures represent an age when life was not rushed and there was an atmosphere of calm surrounding the creating of a portrait. I can accept their 'enhancements' for they were perhaps the equivalent of air brushing

techniques of today. Not only do portrait miniatures possess a hypnotic appeal of an individual from so long ago, they show us the popular hairstyles and fashions from a by-gone age. If you are really lucky, you may one day find the serene face of an ancestor gazing back at you from a small gilded frame.

Sources and Bibliography
Census 1841 HO 107 -0560, Folio 6/7, Page 7, Entry 25
Dictionary of National Biography
http://www.archive.org
Archives of Ontario: References to Anne Langton
Don Shelton's: Artists and Ancestors - Miniature Portrait Art Collection http://portrait-miniature.blogspot.com
Gores 1827 Directory of Liverpool
Pigots 1828/9 Liverpool Directory
Universal Directories of Liverpool 1791 and 1796
Liverpool Mercury: Friday January 8th 1847

Further Reading
Coombs, Katherine (1998) The Portrait Miniature in England Victoria and Albert Museum, London
Foskett, Daphne (1987) Miniatures: Dictionary and Guide Antique Collectors' Club, London

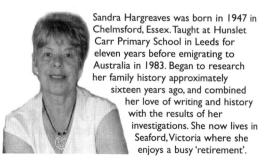

Sandra Hargreaves was born in 1947 in Chelmsford, Essex. Taught at Hunslet Carr Primary School in Leeds for eleven years before emigrating to Australia in 1983. Began to research her family history approximately sixteen years ago, and combined her love of writing and history with the results of her investigations. She now lives in Seaford, Victoria where she enjoys a busy 'retirement'.

THE
City of York & District
Family History Society

The City of York & District Family History Society, Founded 1975,
covers the modern Archdeaconry of York, a large area of Yorkshire,
which stretches from Coxwold, Hovingham and Sherburn in Harfordlythe in the North
to Ledsham, Birkin, Selby and Drax in the South,
and from Bramham, Bilton and Sherburn in Elmet in the West
to Huggate and Bubwith in the East

check our website for full details:

www.yorkfamilyhistory.org.uk

**Wherever you are, if you have ancestors from our area, or even
if you live locally and are researching elsewhere, come and join us!**

We meet on the **first Wednesday of each month**, excluding August, at:

The Folk Hall, New Earswick, York
at 7pm for 7.30pm

The Society's **Research Room** *is located
at The Study Centre
The Raylor Centre, James Street, York YO10 3DW*

Phone: 01904 412204

email: yorkfamilyhistory@btopenworld.com

Our own
YORK FAMILY HISTORY FAIR
Held every year on a Saturday in March

For details of this and other Society activities
please see our web-site: www.yorkfamilyhistory.org.uk
or contact the Secretary, enclosing s.a.e.
Mrs Anne Weir, 26 Nursery Road, Nether Poppleton, York YO26 6NN
email: secretary@yorkfamilyhistory.org.uk

Registered Charity No. 1085228

Adultery, Murder and Petty Treason

Fred Feather

I was working in the fine County Record Office at Wigston on newspapers for the year 1825. My Leicestershire remit was to search for the trial and execution of Hannah Read in Leicester. This proved to be no problem, for both the *Leicester Chronicle* and *Leicester Journal* reported the events of the torrid spring and summer of 1825. *James Read* was a 39 year old labourer and army pensioner of Shearsby, whose military service would have taken him back to Waterloo or the previous Napoleonic battles. He was baptised at Lubenham on 16th July 1786. In 1824 he had gone missing from his picturesque village, nestling between the county town and Market Harborough, it was said over a debt he had incurred after buying a calf.

His 36 year old wife *Hannah* (daughter of *William Packwood* and his wife - nee Binley, who was baptised at Foxton on 7th June 1790) was living at Sheepshead. She had gone there in 1824 to nurse 19 year old *John Waterfield's* wife, the latter having given birth. Hannah herself had five children, two of them were *'illicit,'* they were Ann aged 16 and William aged 11, both born before her 1816 wedding to Read in St.Margarets, Leicester. To *Read* she had borne Elizabeth in 1816, Uriah in 1820 and Emmanuel in 1823. Both the *Waterfield* patients, mother and baby died, and it was suggested that damp linen had been the cause. Hannah stayed on, living as man and wife with the widowed *John Waterfield* and it must be conjectured that he was an early example of a toy-boy. Hannah bore him a child in February 1825. When *Waterfield* suggested that she should

return to her husband, she threatened both suicide and fatal consequences to James Read. At 4am on 21st April Read went with a Constable to the home of Jane Wright where he knew them to be living together. Hannah threw a stocking maker's bobbin at him through the window and threatened him.

On 25th April 1825, after her co-villagers had threatened to douse her with water if she did not return to James, a reconciliation was mooted and she sent a child to invite him to meet her near her own village of Foxton. Foxton Locks are the spectacular series of canal locks which were the apogee of Georgian water engineering. That evening she returned to Foxton carrying Read's hat and stick. She told Thomas, her husband's brother and employer, that *'Jem'* had run off, after going mad and eating grass. Thomas Read's search of the canal bank soon located the body of James Read under a bridge on the route to Gumley. James was buried at Shearsby on 29th April 1825. The village constable (pre-police) then took her into custody and the inquest resulted in her being sent for trial charged with murder at the Leicester Summer Assize. To murder a husband at that time was considered as a crime against the state and thus *'Petty Treason.'*

Her trial took place on Wednesday 3rd August 1825, in front of Mr Justice Park. She was described as decently dressed, but had the appearance of a morose, violently tempered woman, with black hair, sallow complexion and small dark eyes. After her plea of *'Not Guilty'* the jury heard evidence from witnesses Thomas Read, Parish Constable John Abney, Mary Gamble, Elizabeth Whitmore, Ann Elliott, Ann Robinson, Jonathan Beaumont Collins and the boatman who found the body Robert Johnson. The jury deliberated for about 15 minutes then pronounced her *'Guilty.'* Her screams and interruptions were of no avail and she was sentenced to die. Forty years previously she would have been sentenced to be burned at the stake (which actually happened to Catherine Hayes in 1782) for Petty Treason (or a wife murdering her husband) was considered a more serious crime than mere murder. Thomas Denton and John Jones were executed for Petty Treason in 1789, in their case, for coining.

The wretched Hannah was not only to be hanged but had first to be dragged on a sledge to her execution, as the law then was. At dawn on the morning of Friday 5th

August 1825 she was tied to the horse-drawn sledge, on which bedding had been placed so that she would not be too uncomfortable, and removed from the Bridewell to the place of execution. After prayers and comforting by the gaoler's wife, Mrs Musson, she was thence dragged to the scaffold and executed at 11am.

The paper reported that during her last grief-stricken days she had thrown down the bible given her by the Reverend R.Burnaby. The Shearsby carter, Mr Johnson, had brought her four young children to see her but they did not realise the significance, that it was to be their last meeting, and just played in the cell. Waterfield's baby was with her and this had finally been forcibly taken from her after assurances that it would be looked after. On the evening of the 4th August she had made a confession to two visiting acquaintances. She told them that she had met 'Jem' by the 'navigation' and he was playing with Waterfield's baby. She had told him how silly his

smock looked and he was adjusting it whilst she held his hat and stick. As he drew it over his head she pushed him into the canal. Three times he came up and she poked him down with his stick. She never quite got to admitting it, but the inference taken by the newspapers was that the death of Waterfield's wife (buried Shearsby March 1824) would have stood further examination. John Waterfield had been no support during her ordeal and she enjoined her daughter Ann (who was unable to visit her as she was suffering from smallpox) to shun him. Not long since he had been taken by a military recruiting party. The besotted woman had gone into Leicester to pledge her wedding ring and earrings to raise enough money to get him out of the army's clutches. That year of 1825 pre-empted Victorian moralising and was a more robust time. This tale of forbidden love is, as I write, lodged in Canada and will clarify one family legend.

Anglian Curiosities
Fred Feather

Some of you family detectives might enjoy a challenge. Here are mainly Anglian characters, about whom you may be able to enhance the information, explain, identify or even fix their actual family. Anything bizarre enough from elsewhere has not been eschewed.

A piece of cake Holmes!

The Ipswich Journal reports upon the Tiptree Fair of 1831; 'On Wednesday week there was a pugalistic set-to between Jacob Harrington and Charles Kendle, which lasted one hour and thirty-five minutes. Harrington was taken off the ground, and died four hours later. Kendle has been committed to Chelmsford Gaol under the Coroner's warrant'. The fate of the winner is being investigated.

Little and Large

The Essex Standard had more to tell, for it then reported a heartrending case concerning giants and a dwarf thus; 'A 'Scotch Giantess' six feet six inches high, who has lately been exhibited in a van in an open space of ground between the Westminster road and the new Bethlem, attempted to poison herself on Monday, with Arsenic, in consequence of her husband, who is only half her size, having suspected that she intrigued with a man called the 'Spanish Giant.' When the husband returned home to the van he discovered the Giantess apparently in the agonies of death, in consequence of having taken poison. Finding a portion of it in a cup he swallowed it, and was immediately seized with violent sickness. They were removed to Guy's hospital.'

I suppose what we would need to know first is;

Where is the above location? Then does Guy's Hospital have archive material. Or, does anyone have a Scottish Giantess up their family tree.

A bit heavy

At the Central Criminal Court (Old Bailey) on 10th December 1841 (not long after the inauguration of the Penny Post) William Henry Mence, a G.P.O. messenger was convicted of stealing one penny and was 'Transported for Life.' (Chelmsford Chronicle).

Did she fall or was she pushed?

The Ipswich Journal for the 23rd March 1762 was concerned with Hertfordshire matters; 'At the Assize held at Hertford on Thursday and Friday last 11 Prisoners were tried, only one received Sentence of Death, viz., Joseph Trant for a Footpad Robbery. The Rev. Mr John Dolben, of St Albans, surrendered, and was tried for the wilful Murder of Mrs Margaret Cook, his aunt, by giving her a mortal Bruise on her Head. The principal Evidence was Joseph Furkins, a Lad, his Servant, whose Testimony was contradicted by the next Evidence (the Maid-Servant) who was by when the old Lady fell; but upon Dr Cotton, a Physician, and Mr. Knowlton, a Surgeon and Apothecary, (who were instantly sent for by Mr Dolben) deposing they attended her till she died, and that she died of an Apoplectic Fit, and had neither Wound nor Bruise upon her, the Counsel for the Prosecution gave it up, and he was acquitted without going thro the rest of his Evidence'. Did she leave a will and I wonder who was the beneficiary?

The Sailor's Grave.

Now, for those who like to visit graveyards or antique shops, a search for the Sailor's Grave at Thursley in Surrey will be of interest. W.H. Goss Ltd, makers of the finest crested china sold models of the gravestone, which are rare;

In Memory of
a generous but unfortunate Sailor
Who was barbarously murdered on Hindhead
On Sept. 24th 1786
By three Villains,
After he had liberally treated them
and promised them his farther Assistance
On the Road to Portsmouth

When pitying Eyes to see my Grave shall come
And with a generous Tear bedew my Tomb
Here shall they read my melancholy Fate
With Murder and Barbarity complete
In perfect Health and in the Flower of Age
Hell a Viel to three Ruffians Rage
On bended Knee I mercy strove t' obtain
Their Th(reat ?)of Blood made all Entreat (vain ?)
No dear Relation or still dearer Friend,
Weeps my hard Lot, or miserable End;
Yet o'er my sad Remains (my Name unknown)
A generous Public have inscrib'd this Stone.

(brackets indicate that the text cannot be deciphered on the postcard)

According to Arthur Mee in *The King's England* (Surrey volume) – '*The gibbet on which they were hanged stood on a site marked by a stone at Hindhead.*' The last four lines come from the entry for Thursley in David Saunders' '*Britain's Maritime Memorials and Mementoes.*'

Just checking?

The Essex Constabulary was formed in February 1840, at which time the Essex Quarter Sessions had some interesting happenings. In August 1840 a man called Charles Calcraft was taken before the magistrates, charged with robbery. The facts were that Mrs Charles Lamb, wife of the licensee of the Bull Public House at Great Baddow, had allowed Calcraft to sleep on the premises. On going upstairs to waken him that same evening she had found him in a state of undress in her bedroom, clutching seven shillings, the same amount of money that was missing from her purse. He was committed for trial, the *Essex Standard* gleefully reporting that he was the brother of '*that eminent Newgate functionary, Jack Ketch*' by which they meant William Calcraft (1800-1879) the famous hangman. He had been born at Baddow and his family lived at nearby Hatfield Peverel. In the October issue Charles Calcraft was found guilty at the Colchester Quarter Sessions and given 3 months imprisonment with Hard Labour. This was a real find as to my knowledge Charles Calcraft joined the Essex Constabulary for about 3 months in 1842 and was sacked for '*leaving his guard (an old name for a beat) with a prostitute.*' Were there any vetting procedures at the time and how effective were they?

Whatever happened to Mehuman Newman

At the northern end of the county, in the same month that Charles Calcraft was jailed, Constable 38 Josiah Hawkins Radley (24) tried to arrest the inhumanly named Mehuman Newman of High Street Green, Sible Hedingham. He acted on the suspicion that Mehuman had stolen a sheep and, for his pains, was beaten unconscious by Newman and his father James (72). The rules of engagement in those days appeared to be rather simpler, thus Superintendent Thomas Redin (25) of nearby Castle Hedingham shortly arrived. Levelling a pistol at father and son, he then offered to '*blow their brains out*' at which the newspaper's only comment was that '*the prisoners - intimidated, were secured.*' For the very serious assault on Radley they were each given one month's hard labour. Note again what Calcraft got for stealing 7 shillings. However, on a second charge of stealing a sheep, Mehuman was transported for 15 years. I have often pondered if he ever returned from the Antipodes and what name he was using at the time. Being called Mehuman whilst existing with a bunch of presumably hardened convicts brings to mind the thinking behind Johnny Cash's infamous prison song 'A boy called Sue.'

Unlucky in love.

John Turner, leader of a gang of robbers at Runwell was executed at Chelmsford on 21st December 1827. His widow later married James Passfield, but romance was short-lived, as her new husband was also hanged at Springfield Jail in Chelmsford in 1835 for arson at Toppesfield. Unlucky - period!

According to another newspaper, the *Essex Chronicle* for 1874, Thomas Goodeve a Halstead horse stealer was '*turned off*' one evening in 1767. His Majesty's '*respite*' arrived 12 hours afterwards.

So much for 2nd class post.

An eclectic concatenation

The following concatenation (look it up) from the *Chelmsford Chronicle* indicates that this publication could always be relied on for a bit of fun. The issue for 10th September 1841 reported under the headline 'Bodkin versus sword' the heavy wagering upon a race of 150 yards along New London Road, Chelmsford. In this McLean, 'the flying tailor,' beat Windebank, (a Recruiting Sergeant based in the town), by half a yard.

Jolly Boating Weather

Not wishing to leave you in gloom and despair I present a little something from the same newspaper's edition of Thursday 10th July 1766;

'The *perfon* that went *acrofs* the Thames on Saturday night *laft* in a butcher's tray, which he performed with *eafe* in eight minutes, and on which no *lefs* than 1800 l. (£) was depending in the neighbourhood of Claremarket, has engaged, for a very considerable wager, to cross again tomorrow evening, standing on his head in the *fame* tray; which undertaking is looked upon as the *moft* extraordinary attempt within the memory of man. One Gentleman has laid no less than 650 l. that the person will do it within twenty minutes.'

I regret that I cannot name the '*perfon*'(person), but he would grace any family's tree.

My Old Rat and Mouse in the Smoke

Joe O'Neill

The Cockney, as instantly recognisable as Colonel Blimp and the bluff Northerner, is one of the standard English stereotypes. Londoners have been regarded as a distinct type since the beginning of the 19th century. In more recent times the East Ender – born within the sound of the bells of St Mary le Bow — came to be seen as the archetypal Londoner, the Cockney. Chirpy, witty and flash he is streetwise and cynical, working class with a strong materialistic bent redeemed by an irrepressible optimism which sustains him through every hardship.

This image owes much to Arthur Morrison who recorded and popularised the Cockney persona. In *Tales of the Mean Streets* and *A Child of the Jago* he enshrined the characteristics of the Cockney. By the 1930 the image was inextricably associated with street markets and rhyming slang.

Yet the home of the Cockney, London, was in a constant state of change. It was a city of strangers, for most of its history existing in a state of flux. In the 19th century the population soared. During a single decade, 1841 to 1851, 330,000 people flooded into London. From Ireland alone 46,000 came, increasing the capital's Irish community to 130,000. As early as 1841, 40% of Londoners were born elsewhere. The number of these provincials increased throughout the 19th century – during the sixty years to the end of the 19th century, between 30,000 and 50,000 newcomers arrived each year.

In order to accommodate the soaring population the city was constantly expanding. Between 1890 and 1945 Greater London grew from 5.6 to 8.7 million. The difference was that whereas growth had been urban until around 1850 it now became suburban.

Though it was the lore of wealth that drew millions to the capital, the reality is that throughout the 19th century London was dominated by a low wage economy. Most Londoners had some experience of poverty, a large minority drifted in and out of poverty and many lived their whole lives in poverty.

Newcomers generally settled on the periphery of London and left the old central areas to the Cockneys. However, it is impossible to make a clear distinction between new Londoners and Cockneys. Intermarriage was common – in particular country women seem to have been very attractive to Cockney men. Many a Cockney memoir of this period mentions a common practice which can create a difficulty for the family historian. Frequently these new Londoners – including those of Irish origin – adopted Anglicised forms of their surname. They did this to deflect prejudice against foreigners.

Both new arrivals and the Cockneys lived with

Fulham Church 1843

constant change. The great rebuilding of the central districts between 1851 and 1881 drove 150,000 people from their homes. Amid all this movement areas of the city were in a state of perpetual change: once respectable areas were being dragged down by newcomers and rebuilding was raising the status of areas that were once slums. Those who were driven from the inner cities often relocated to what some writers describe as 'suburban slums.' The threadbare Langford Road area of Fulham became home to those whose homes in Drury Lane were demolished in the 1890s. Former residents of Somers Town – evicted to make way for the railway – ended up in the Junction Road, Archway. Those whose homes were buried under Marylebone Station found shelter in Kensal New Town. In London, nothing and no one stood still.

What's more many established Cockneys left their homes for long periods. Among these were those who wintered in the capital and spent the summer months elsewhere, as farm labourers, navvying on canals, roads or railways, travelling the country with circuses and shows or simply tramping about in search of casual labour. When the days shortened and the temperatures fell, they made their way back to London's more temperate clime, with its workhouses, an abundance of cheap lodging houses and free shelter provided by religious charities.

Census returns during the nineteenth century show that the areas where the London-born were concentrated were in the centre of the city. Bethnal Green, for instance, boasted 82% of its population London born in 1851 and that figure had increased to 85% by 1881. In this case this was due to the importance of the silk-weaving industry in the area, which meant that craftsmen clustered there. Other areas with similar figures were Mile End, Shoreditch, Stepney, Poplar,

Limehouse, Clerkenwell and parts of Finsbury, Lambeth, Bankside, Walworth, Bermondsey and Rotherhithe.

Throughout this period the Cockney areas of the city were distinctive in a number of ways. They were marked by high fertility, early marriage and poverty. Social investigators reported that the incidence of poverty in these areas was between 45% and 50% compared to 30% throughout the capital as a whole. The natives of these areas spoke a language of their own – a source of endless fascination to outsiders. The transportation of the letters v and w meant the Cockney spoke of his 'vife' instead of his 'wife,' dropped his aitches, used double negatives and double superlatives and a rich array of slang of both the rhyming and the back variety. At its most pure it was found among costermongers, thieves and flower sellers – the archetypal Cockney characters.

It was not only the costermongers and the flower sellers who lived a hand-to-mouth existence during the 19th century. As the centre of a great trading empire London employed 500,000 men in the docks and in import-related occupations alone in 1900. The Empire guaranteed enormous employment opportunities in both the City and Whitehall which in turn created an insatiable demand for labour in the food, retail, transport, domestic service industries, building, catering, clothing and retail industries. This is why even in the worst days of the 1930s depression, London, with its wide spread of employment opportunities, was relatively unscathed by the blight of unemployment. In the 1930s slump over one thousand London factories closed – but 1,573 opened, almost half the national total. Two out of every three new jobs created in Britain in the inter-war period were in Greater London. All the British industries that prospered during this period were London-based – wireless, electronics, telephones, vacuum cleaners and processed foods, such as Horlicks and Heinz. At the same time many of the traditional inner-city industrial jobs and those in traditional trades began to decline though there was still a demand for casual and workshop labour.

The new industries of aircrafts, engineering and cars were among those which relocated to London's outer suburbs. Elstree Croydon, Surbiton, Pinewood, Cricklewood and Ealing were host to the film industry. The capital's greatest acquisition,

however, was the Ford motor works at Dagenham.

Many Cockneys went on what was known as their annual *'hopping holiday'* – a week spent in the fields of Kent harvesting hops. The irony of this holiday was that for others the toil entailed was more rigorous than anything they did during their working lives. Yet for many it was the highlight of the year. It was customary for people from each part of London to go to the same village every year. Battersea people, for instance, went to Headcorn.

Industrial disputes featured large in the lives of Cockneys. These became increasingly frequent during the second half of the 19th century up to the outbreak of war in 1914 and again during the 1920s. The famous *'Match Girls' Strike'* of 1888 when 1,400 women working at the Bryant & May match factory went on strike over conditions and pay, and the Dock Strike of 1889, notable successes for unskilled labour, became part of Cockney lore. Yet most cockneys lived a precarious existence when healthy and inevitably fell into poverty when ill.

During the Victorian period, most of the able-bodied applicants for relief were sick. In areas such as Shoreditch and Camberwell, more than a third of workhouse paupers went into the infirmary.

London was generally unhealthy. Apart from cholera epidemics, the death rate was generally higher than the norm – and in some areas appalling. In the 1830s, one in every three children born in *St. Giles in the Fields*, died in their first year. A major contributory factor was inadequate housing. The 1841 census showed the extent of overcrowding in the Tottenham Court Road, for instance, where 27 houses were home to no fewer than 485 people. For all the building and improvement during the 19th century accommodation remained an intractable problem. As late as 1901 more than a third of the families in many of London's inner boroughs lived in one or two rooms. Philanthropic efforts to improve housing, such as Peabody Buildings, which housed 20,000 by 1900, did nothing for those at the bottom of the economic pile. These were the occasional labourers, street sellers, loafers, semi-criminals, inmates of common lodging houses and the homeless who find shelter night by night.

Just above these were the casual labourers, who Rowntree classified as the very poor. In East London the largest group consisted of dockers, who averaged less than three days' work a week. This class of casual labourers made up about ten per cent of the city's population. In other forms of dockside employment long periods of poverty were due to other factors. Many of the sawyers working in the timber yards that dotted the banks of the Thames were paid three-monthly. The weeks immediately before payday were often hungry.

The capital's street population was about 40,000 in the 1850s. Many of these were based in the East End, the focus of most concern, with the worst slums and the highest death rate. Events such as the Ripper murders of 1888 served to crystallize public fears. The area was the centre of recent immigration – in the 1880s there were 40,000 Jews there and by 1901 42,000 Russians and Poles in Stepney – a figure exceeded by only five towns in Poland itself.

Stepney and Shoreditch became the worst slums of the 1930s. Virtually no housing was built for the poor in central London during the Victorian period. It was the LCC that made the biggest improvement after 1900 when it began to rehouse workers in tenements in greenbelt sites beyond its boundaries – Totterdown Fields, Tooting, Newbury, White Hart Lane, Tottenham and Old Oak in West London.

The major development came after research in the early 1920s showed that almost 200,000 people in the LCC were living in 'unhealthy' districts and over half a million were in 'unsatisfactory' conditions. Though the enormous council estates of Roehampton, Bellingham and Becontree – the latter

Damage caused by German Zeppelins 1915

became the world's largest council estate – had few facilities, they were a great improvement for the families who lived there. Most of the households were those of skilled workers or people in regular employment – the poorest could afford neither the rent nor the fares to travel to work. By the 1930s the emphasis had changed from the great peripheral estates to the tenement blocks, mainly in Southwark, Lewisham, Wandsworth, Lambeth, Bermondsey, Finsbury, Fulham and Woolwich.

The advent of the electric trams – which first appeared in 1901—made possible the growth of suburban areas of private houses. Gradually the electric railway – ideal for the stop-start of commuter trains – appeared in the years before the Great War. Further improvements in the 1920s and 1930s meant that by 1945 cheap, new housing in Thundersley, Billericay and Rayleigh was a possibility for working class families.

The war fuelled competition for housing in Cockney London to crisis level. The city had many significant ethnic communities – Italians in Finsbury, Germans in Fitzrovia, Camden Town and Kentish Town, areas in which many Greek Cypriots settled in the 1960s. In the 1960s, the New Commonwealth immigrants arrived in large numbers – West Indians, Indians and Pakistanis. Most of these settled initially in Brixton, Notting Hill, Camden Town and Southall. For decades there was plenty of work and most enjoyed the prosperity they had come in search of. But by the last decade of the century things were very different. There developed significant pockets of unemployment – by 1990 Hackney, Harringey and King's Cross were only some of the areas with high levels of unemployment. By 1992, more than one in ten Londoners was on income support.

But the vulnerability of Cockney London, however, was evident long before that. The Great War had a profound impact. Many men were keen to join up. Leaving aside patriotism, it was a time of high unemployment and for many the war gave them a purpose. For many it meant that they had their photograph taken. Countless photographs of men in their military uniforms date from this period.

It brought about other changes. Before the war there was a great deal of kudos attached to receiving a letter or a postcard. The arrival of the postman was an event and every proud recipient of a written communication was sure to drop it into conversation with his neighbours. Now people dreaded the approach of the postman as he so often brought news of a son or father's death at the front.

On 31st May 1915 the German Zeppelins dropped incendiaries from Stoke Newington to Hackney and Stepney, killing six and injuring 35. A warning system was introduced – the police fired rockets when a Zeppelin was spotted and then took to their bicycles, displaying 'Take Cover' signs. Boy scouts bugled the all-clear.

The inter-war years saw many East Enders leave in search of work. Some simply went 'on the tramp' hoping to get casual employment. Those who remained in employment – at a time of falling prices and the increased availability of consumer goods – enjoyed a period of relative prosperity. Further, there was a general improvement from the mid-1930s, as the car, gas, electricity and consumer durable industries all boomed in the capital.

There was also some slum clearance during this period and the building of council accommodation – usually in the form of flats which contained all modern amenities in areas such as Merton, Mitcham and Wallington.

The Blitz came to London on 7th September 1940. The Germans dropped 1,400 incendiaries from Woolwich Arsenal to the Surrey Commercial Docks. It drove 150,000 to sleep in the Tube and in December 1940 the bombing burnt out the commercial centre of the city. In total there were 50,000 casualties in the London County Council area. But the most terrifying period began in June 1944 with the arrival of the V1 flying bomb, closely followed by the even more terrifying V2 rocket. The first V2 announced its deadly arrival on 25th November

London Slums 1930s

1944 when it scored a direct hit on the New Cross *Woolworth's* which was packed with Saturday afternoon shoppers and killed 160. In total flying bombs damaged almost half of the capital's housing stock, destroying much of Stepney, Poplar and Bermondsey. Stepney's population fell by half as a direct result of the War.

The War, more than any other single factor, destroyed traditional Cockney communities. Many residents of Bow, Bermondsey and Bethnal Green decamped to the suburbs. The War made at least 1.5 million Londoners homeless. Many left when their homes were damaged and never returned.

In post-war London, dominated by shortages, queues and austerity, rebuilding was slow and

In 1976 the Environment Secretary expressed his concern at the 'unbalanced migration' from the centre of London, which was leaving the city with a disproportionate residue of unskilled and semi-skilled workers, the unemployed, single parent families, immigrant communities and overcrowded and inadequate housing.

The gradual decline of Commonwealth trade bled the Docks of its vitality – and the new towns that sprang up beyond the Green Belt, such as Stevenage and Crawley sucked out hundreds of thousands of those who'd lived in the city. Within the city the shortage of housing remained a constant. The council's response was often to build extremely unpopular blocks of high-rise flats. In the decade after 1964 almost four hundred tower blocks were built. Those who had the means moved out. The disasters of 'sixties housing led to a reduction in government expenditure on housing and a spectacular rise in house prices – which in turn drove more people out of the city.

But it has also sparked yet another change in the East End. Former working class terraced houses have now become eminently desirable. Many have been bought and modernised by the aspiring middle class. As always, Cockney London is in a state of flux.

Street Party, London 1935

disjointed. But at least there was full employment – in particular, electrical industries, vehicle building and engineering prospered and Dagenham's car industry, which by 1960 provided 30,000 jobs, was a major boon. BOAC, BEA and Heathrow were all major employers and there was plenty of employment in East London. But there were other less benign developments.

Foreign competition was undermining the capital's manufacturing base. Fifty per cent of manufacturing jobs disappeared during the 1970s, a development signalled by the collapse of Hounslow and Ealing's engineering and electrical industries and the demise of the iconic *Pears* factory. This was also reflected in commerce's gradual relocation away from the city to avoid all its attendant problems — congestion, high rents and high wages. Unemployment, unknown since the 1930s, began to reappear in the capital in the 1970s.

Further Reading:

There are numerous readable social histories of London. Among the most accessible are *London in the 19th Century* (Vintage) and *London in the 20th Century* (Vintage) both by Jerry White, *Victorian London* (Weidenfeld & Nicolson) by Liza Picard, *London: A Social History* (Penguin Books Ltd) by Roy Porter, *London: the Biography* (Vintage) by Peter Ackroyd, *The Times History of London* (Times Books) Hugh Clout and *Thames: Sacred River* (Vintage) by Peter Ackroyd. Gilda O'Neill's books are wonderfully evocative of all aspects of Cockney life. Among the best of these are *Our Street: East End Life in the Second World War, Lost Voices: Memories of a Vanished Way of Life, My East End: Memories of Life in Cockney London*, and *The Good Old Days: Poverty, Crime and Terror in Victorian London*, all by Penguin. The recent DVD, *East End through the Ages* (Green Umbrella DVDs) contains some excellent archive footage. Two fascinating websites are The History of the East End of London at www.eastlondonhistory.com/ and the East London History Society at www.mernick.org.uk/elhs/ELHS.htm

Bridport Daggers and The Devil's Arse!

Making ropes, discovering one of our most important craft industries

Brian Elliott

Our ancestors made use of rope and nets in a variety of settings: in the home and garden, on farms and in workshops, factories and mines; and the maritime context was considerable: from small sailing and fishing boats to the new and fast developing ocean liners such as the SS *Great Britain*. Cordage was constantly, especially in wartime, always in demand by the Navy. Specialist rope was also needed for a variety of civil engineering, leisure and sporting activities.

There was also the macabre use as gallows ropes for the hangman. In this context, Bridport's pre-eminence as a rope making centre included the grim retort, '*You'll live to be stabbed with a Bridport dagger!*' which may have misled the Tudor antiquary John Leland who referred to the town as a place where '*good daggers*' were made!

This article is concerned with traditional rope making using natural materials. Rope making is one of our most ancient crafts. The range of products was huge, and the scale considerable, from candle wicks to massive anchor ropes.

After *hackling* (cleaning and sorting of hemp fibres), often by women the spinning of the yarn took place in a *rope walk*. This was a long narrow shed which could be up to a quarter of a mile or more in length. It was open to the elements in places and could be freezing cold in winter and red hot in summer. The rope yarn was attached to hooks (called *crooks*) on a twisting machine (or *jack*) usually hand operated by a boy towards a single hook on the distant *sledge*. The distance between the two determined the rope length. Making the rope meant walking miles backwards and forwards every day and operators had to be very fit and dexterous.

Rope was such a vital commodity that manufacturing was once a widespread industry throughout the the United Kingdom. Individual users and businesses were never far from a rope maker's distinctive workplace or a seller of ropes. This was particularly true in the market towns of Britain, where the rural economy depended so much on rope and twine. At the national census of 1861 there were almost 1200 people employed as rope and cordmakers in Yorkshire, at over 50 locations. The industrial West Riding had by far the greatest concentration (69%), particularly at Wakefield (110 workers), Bradford (47), Leeds (43), Hunslet (40), Halifax (35) and Thorne (26). York also had 29 rope workers and the other concentrations were at coastal ports - Scarborough (20), Whitby (23), Hull (31) and Scunthorpe (55). An analysis of workers' ages

shows that there were 204 workers aged up to fourteen of which 46 were aged nine or younger. Almost one in twenty workers were children, perhaps reflecting the family context of the trade as much as dexterity or cheap labour. Only 63 females were recorded, primarily working in the West Riding of Yorkshire. Another closely related occupation concerns persons employed in hemp and fibrous materials and the census shows that over 80% of over 2,000 workers in Yorkshire were female and were probably involved in the *hackling* process.

Some areas of course became centres of excellence for the trade. Family firms were near to each other and competed for business with fishermen and nautical users of rope.

After the hackling or cleaning of natural fibres such as hemp the next stage of ropemaking involved a man drawing out or spinning a loosened batch carried around his waist. The fibres are attached to hooks on a wheel turned by a handle, usually by a boy after which the man slowly walks backwards drawing out more fibre.
From A Book of English Trades, c.1804

The main stage of ropemaking involved the spinning, stretching and twisting into various thickness and lengths in rope walks which, with their associated sheds, formed highly distinctive features in town locations, as can be seen in this example, c. 1900.
The yarn can be seen supported via wooden frames spaced at regular intervals along the walks.
© Brian Elliott

combined in the face of opportunities at home and abroad from the new industries. Doncaster based *British Ropes* (now *Bridon International Ltd*) was able to market and service Yorkshire and other coalfield regions, becoming a world leader in wire, steel and synthetic rope materials. Other companies gradually diversified away but remained loyal and proud of their roots.

Mudfords of Sheffield was founded in 1832, making hand-spun ropes, but seven generations later their 'The Ropeman' logo continues but across a range of industrial textiles: covers, sheets, tarpaulins, slings, janitorial products and protective clothing; as well as natural and synthetic rope.

The natural raw materials for traditional rope making include flax, sisal, jute, and hemp and in summer, most of them can be seen growing at the *Eden Centre* in Cornwall amid a spectacular rope man sculpture. Fields surrounding Bridport once flourished with hemp and the attractive blue-flowered flax, grown in enormous quantities.

Old Bridport, with its wide main thoroughfares of South, East and West Street and long narrow alleys stretching backwards, once occupied by family owned rope walks, owes its layout to the trade. For centuries, rope and net making was largely a cottage industry here, very much a family affair, women and young

The most notable was at Bridport in West Dorset, internationally famous for its net making and a major supplier of cordage for the Navy from the thirteenth century. Cordage workers worked day and night on rigging for the King John's navy. By the reign of Henry VIII Bridport ropes were of such high quality that the King gave the town a short-lived monopoly of supply. From 1618 Chatham in Kent, with its naval dockyard, began producing the great ropes for anchors and hawsers as well as meeting the incessant need for miles and miles of rigging. Similar facilities emerged at Portsmouth, Devonport, Plymouth and Woolwich. In fact, wherever there was shipbuilding, rope works flourished, be it in Newcastle-upon-Tyne, on the banks of the Clyde or in Northern Ireland at Belfast.

Inland industrial regions also demanded easily obtainable rope products and a variety of family and company concerns helped to serve this need. In the twentieth century some small family firms

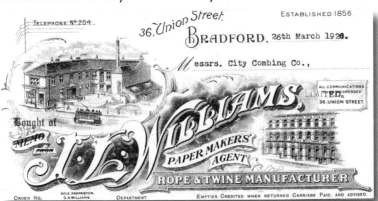

TELEPHONE No 204.
ESTABLISHED 1856

36, Union Street.
BRADFORD, 26th March 1929.

Messrs. City Combing Co.,

ALL COMMUNICATIONS ADDRESSED TO 36, UNION STREET.

LIMITED

Bought of J.L.WILLIAMS,

MEMO FROM

PAPER MAKERS' AGENT

ROPE & TWINE MANUFACTURER

ORDER No.   SOLE PROPRIETOR. S.A.WILLIAMS.   DEPARTMENT   EMPTIES CREDITED WHEN RETURNED CARRIAGE PAID, AND ADVISED.

The impressive letter-head of J.L. Williams of Bradford, paper agents and rope manufacturers.
© Brian Elliott collection

A typical advertisement of a ropemaker's wares,
Mallinsons of Barnsley, 1914
© Brian Elliott Collection

manufacturers that are world leaders in their fields: *Amsafe* (textile products for aviation) and *Edward Sports* (nets and equipment for sports).

If your ancestor was a rope maker there are several places well worth a visit in order to appreciate aspects of the trade. Three excellent ones are:

The Victorian Ropery at The Historic Dockyard - www.thedockyard.co.uk - still has its long double workhouse, said to be the only traditional ropewalk from the Age of Sail to survive anywhere in the world. Here costumed guides provide works tours.

Outhwaites Ltd - www.ropemakers.com - of Hawes in the Yorkshire Dales. Established in 1905, the business was extended and enhanced from the mid-1970s by Peter and Ruth Annison and has now become an important tourist and educational centre. Apart from a shop Traditional rope making can be seen.

Peak Cavern, Castleton, Debyshire - www.peakcavern.co.uk

Traditional rope making can be seen in this most extraordinary location, in the great entrance area, affectionately known as *The Devil's Arse*. These days only demonstrations are given to visitors. However, from the seventeenth century until about 1915 a small subterranean community lived and worked here, making ropes for sale to the local lead miners. Some of the ropers doubled as guides, taking curious visitors into the inner cave. The last of the commercial rope men was Bert Marrison who retired at the age of 89 in 1974.

children involved in the craft, neighbours helping out during busy periods to supplement land or sea associated work. Nearby villages had *braiders* who specialised in particular mesh sizes and patterns, an outworking tradition that continued until recent years. One exceptional Bridport pioneer was Samuel Gundry whose seventeenth century family business expanded to become the largest net works (*Bridport - Gundry plc*) in Europe. Today, Bridport's rope making tradition survives in the hands of two designers and

Although traditional rope making has almost disappeared there are an abundance of place names to remind us of their former importance. The street name *Rope Walk* can be found in places such as Birmingham, Bristol, Edinburgh, Ipswich, London (several occurrences), Nottingham, Nuneaton, Reading, Skipton, Ross-on-Wye and St Ives (and you may know of others). Occasionally, as at Barton-upon-Humber, part of an old rope maker's building has been adapted for art and heritage usage.

Acknowledgements

Peter and Ruth Annison (Outhwaites Ltd), Bridport Museum Service, Dorset Libraries and Arts, John Harrison (Peak Cavern), Leeds Central Library, Richard Mudford (Mudfords of Sheffield)

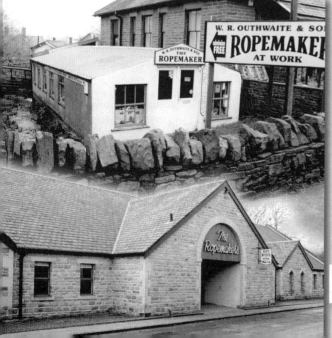

The fronts of the old and new ropeworks at Outhwaites, Hawes in the Yorkshire Dales.
© Brian Elliott

On The Right Track

Kath Jones

Trams were part of our public transport through most of the 19th century and at least a third of the 20th century. Many children will not remember the trams of our past but may well have travelled on the famous Blackpool trams of today bringing back the nostalgia of yesteryear. Some cities and seaside towns are renovating some of the old trams or purchasing new ones and bringing them back to our streets either for commercial business or simply for enjoyment.

A touch of History ...

Trams were first known in Britain as tramcars but in America called streetcars, trolleys or trollycars, they were designed to run on fixed rails - known as tramways. The tramways were usually developed out of industrial haulage routes or the tracks of omnibuses which first ran on our streets back in the 1820's. They shared road space with pedestrians and other traffic and were used as a form of urban passenger transport carrying people to and from places of work or purely for pleasure. Occasionally, they also served their purpose for industry transportation. Trams differed from our conventional trains in the way they were usually shorter and lighter.

The first horse-drawn tramways were introduced in the early 19th century and were a large improvement from the omnibus. The advantages of these trams to previous forms of transport was the low rolling resistance of the metal wheels on steel rails - which were grooved from 1852 - allowing the horses to pull greater loads even in severe weather conditions. Some problems which arose from using animals were that horses could only work a few hours per day, each horse usually covering a distance of around twelve miles which took around four to five hours to complete, therefore many systems needed a minimum of a ten horse team for each horsecar tram. These animals had to be housed and cared for, groomed and fed costing the streetcar company a large sum of money, even the enormous amount of manure they produced had to be disposed of by the company which also added to expenses.

The first tram introduced to Britain's streets was on the Swansea and Mumbles Railway in South Wales: it was horse-drawn and later was converted to steam and finally electric power. The first passenger railway started operating in 1807 after the Mumbles Railway Act was passed by the British Parliament in 1804.

A horse-drawn tram still operates as a tourist attraction on a tramway along the sea front at Douglas in the Isle of Man.

Horse-power to Man-power ...

As time evolved, horse-power was replaced by steam driven trams, operated by a small boiler engine fitted at the front of a leading tram which was followed by one or two carriages – known as the tram engine – similar to today's small train. Another style of steam tram had the engine inserted in the body again known as the tram engine or steam dummy. Paris was the most notable city for this type of tram.

Cable trams followed the steam; they were pulled along by an overhead cable which moved continuously at a constant speed whilst the individual trams gripped and released the cable to stop and start. Some of these cable trams operated on Highgate Hill in North London and from Kennington to Brixton Hill in South London. Cable tram no 72/73 is the sole survivor of the fleet in Upper Douglas in the Isle-of-Man.

Although these more advanced trams were being transformed to electric with new technology some of the old horse-drawn trams were returned to service temporarily throughout World War Two to conserve fuel. Many electric trams were introduced to Britain throughout the late 19th century; but Blackpool was the first location to have the electric street tramway. The Blackpool Tramway was opened on the 29th September 1885, running along the promenade to nearby Fleetwood using conduit current collection which was later replaced by overhead power supply. Since the closure of the Glasgow Corporation Tramways 1962, this has been the only first-generation operational tramway in the UK which still remains in operation today and is one of the countries most famous tourist attractions - loved by both young and old alike.

A Toast Rack near Rhos Depot

The most extensive tramway systems were to be found in many of the large cities in Britain including Manchester, London, Birmingham and Glasgow.

Tramway systems started to disappear during the mid 20th century, when most of the lines were torn out of our cities by bus manufacturing or oil marketing companies for the specific reason of replacing the trams with buses because their ever improving technical features meant that buses became more reliable and had a less costly infrastructure.

Funicular Fun ...

The basic principal operation of a funicular - known as a funicular railway or cliff railway - is a pair of tram-like vehicles which are permanently attached to one another by a cable which runs through a pully at the top of an incline. This moves the ascending and descending vehicles on rails up and down a steep incline, counterbalancing each other. The rails were laid with enough space between them to let the cars pass at mid point. Funiculars have changed drastically over the years and now mainly run by the introduction of electricity.

The seaside town of Scarborough in North Yorkshire is situated on the east coast of Britain. It is home to one of the first cliff railways and at one time had five working funicular railways but only three remain in use today. The North Bay in Scarborough had two cliff railways, whilst the South Bay had three. The three existing lifts on the South Bay remain in service and run from May to October each year.

The Scarborough South Cliff Tramway Limited was created in 1873 so that they could link the South Cliff esplanade with the South sands. A Mr Lucas designed the lift which was built by Crossley Brothers of Manchester. The fourteen passenger cars were constructed by the Metropolitan Carriage Company of Birmingham. The lift was first using sea water as a counterweight. In 1879, two Crossley gas engines were replaced by a steam pump which pumped the sea water up a pipe - which lay between the two parallel tracks - to fill the upper car and the bathing pool. The Spa lift on the South Cliff opened and started operating on the 6th July 1875 then costing the huge amount of £8,000.

The success of the South Cliff Lift was the promotion of a similar line on the North Bay. The Scarborough Queen's Parade Tramway Company Limited was created on March 4th 1878 to link the Queen's Parade, on the top of the North Cliff, to the sands and more precisely to the Promenade Pier. Unfortunately on opening day a cabin broke loose and serious damage was caused to the lower station. The lift was closed for the rest of the year. This lift should have taken the number thirteen because it was really unlucky, with an accident every year involving pump engine, water supply failures and landslips. A further landslip in 1887 stopped the use of the lift all together.

St Nicholas Cliff was built by the Medway Safety Lift Company Ltd and opened on 5th August 1929 to help the great number of passengers on the Central Tramway Cliff Lift which is located just behind the Grand Hotel. The control equipment was incorporated in the upper station and no station was provided at the bottom of the lift, where passengers stepped directly out on the pavement.

The North Cliff Lift was built by the Medway Safety Lift Company Ltd in 1930. The lift was part of a large Corporation development at Peasholm Gap. It closed in September 1996. It has been dismantled and will now be re-assembled in Launceston, Cornwall.

Another seaside resort which boasts a cliff lift is Saltburn-by-the-Sea which is also in North Yorkshire further up the coast from Scarborough. This distinguished Victorian resort developed around the former smuggling village of Old Saltburn, when Middlesbrough's manufacturers wanted to escape the dirt and dust for a holiday which could be achieved travelling by railway.

Although this resort became particularly popular in the 1870's the only drawback was that it was perched on a cliff top and people found it difficult to access the beach and its newly constructed pier. With the beach being 120ft below the town, engineer John Anderson's expertise

SOUTH CLIFF, SCARBOROUGH
H.9229

was called for and his solution was to construct a wooden lift which was approached by a narrow walkway. The rickety structure had a cage which carried up to twenty people at one time; it descended from the town to the beach below. The cage was raised or lowered by pouring water into, or out of, a tank which counterbalanced the enclosure and its passengers. Although, the lift proved to be a huge success and carried passengers for thirteen years, Saltburn's tramway - as it is known - replaced the old vertical lift, which was closed on safety grounds in 1883. The cliff tramway opened a year later and provided transport between the pier and the town just as the old lift had done.

This funicular is a real classic as it still operates by 'water balance', i.e. a tank on the top car is filled with water, when the car reaches the bottom the water is discharged into the sea. But, since 1924 the water pump has been electrically operated. The first major maintenance was carried out in 1998, when the main winding wheel was replaced and a new braking system installed. The cliff funicular is one of the world's oldest water-powered cliff lifts, (the oldest being the Bom Jesus funicular in Braga, Portugal).

These are a few more of the UK's funicular railways:

Aberystwyth Cliff Railway, Babbacombe Cliff Railway, Bridgnorth Cliff Railway, Cairngorm Mountain Railway, Clifton Rocks Railway, East Cliff Railway, East Hill Cliff Railway, Fisherman's Walk Cliff Railway, Great Orme Tramway, Lynton and Lynmouth Cliff Railway, National Railway Museum Inclinator, Scarborough funiculars, Shipley Glen Tramway , Southend Cliff Railway, West Cliff Railway West Hill Cliff Railway, Worsley Navigable Levels.

Llandudno and Colwyn Bay Electric Tramway. A Brief History ...

Llandudno's most distinctive feature is the Great Orme. The Summit Complex hosts the site

Saltburn Cliff Lift

of the Great Orme Tramway terminus as well as some magnificent views over the Conwy estuary of the Welsh mountains and as far as the Isle of Man, Blackpool and the Lake District. There is an exhibition of the history of this funicular tramway at the half-way station. The Great Orme Tramway opened to the public in July 1902 after local people realised how much money could be made from funicular railways after the first cliff railway had opened in Scarborough in 1875 and by 1893 at least thirteen had been built in the UK.

Llandudno's tramway is still working each summer season and runs on a daily basis from late March to late October

Cliff Tramway, Saltburn-by-Sea

The Great Orme Tramway

The Opening of the Line ...

The Tramway started to take shape and finally the line opened on Thursday 17th October 1907. The first passenger trip was a private affair, directors and other dignitaries joined the journey as well as the company and guests. The line was opened to the public two days later on the 19th October with a fleet of fourteen single-decker cars.

On the first day of public use over 4,300 trips were made and £45 in fares was taken. Even after this short period it seemed that the tramway was going to be a phenomenal success.

Lucky Number Seven

Tram number 7 seems to fit the bill with the year of the launch of the Electric Tramway – 1907 and also the Centenary in 2007. A full sized renovated replica of the tram is being restored and will be on public display in numerous locations within Llandudno, Rhos on Sea and Colwyn Bay.

Tram car number 6 used on the Llandudno and Colwyn Bay Electric Railway was built in 1914 for the Bournemouth Corporation System. Of all the trams used in that period this was the only car to survive when the line closed in 1956. It was bought, conserved and displayed by the British Transport Commission in London's Clapham Museum throughout the 1960's.

When the museum ceased the collection from the Electric Railway was split between two museums – The National Railway Museum in York and the London Transport Museum in Covent Garden.

Tram number 6 wasn't required in either of the collections and so became the property of the Science Museum. Both a Llandudno and Bournemouth group of supporters put forward two bids to restore the tram, the Llandudno group lost and Bournemouth restored the tram to its original colours and its original number 85 was displayed. It now takes pride of place in the Southern Electric Museum in Christchurch, Dorset. Knowing they didn't have a purpose to carry on the group from Llandudno split up.

In 1980, Roger Best – a tramway enthusiast – purchased the body of number 126 from Bournemouth and together with other like minded followers started to recreate the tram and renamed it tram number 7 which seemed appropriate for the centenary. The tram is sited at Glanwydden and is being reinstated as a towable replica. Some of the original fixtures and fittings were found in the Orme areas of Llandudno and Colwyn Bay and will be used for this project.

taking visitors to the summit of The Great Orme, climbing a mile of track to the summit complex at a height of 679 ft (207)m.

The Great Orme Tramway is the only cable hauled tramway still operating on British public roads. It runs from Church Walks in Llandudno.

With the Orme tramway doing so well another proposition was put to the citizens of Llandudno and Colwyn Bay to build an Electric Tramway. Initially, this was to run four and a half miles between Llandudno and Rhos-on-Sea and would be constructed using a 3' 6" gauge tramway with a cost of £28,000. Interested local parties applied for a Light Railway Order which was lead by George Griffiths but was rejected at a hearing in Colwyn Bay on the 23rd February 1897 on the grounds of the interest of landowners and Llandudno Urban District Council.

A second Order was applied for, this time for the same gauge but for eight miles in length running between Llandudno and Old Colwyn. The cost was estimated at £65,000 for the considerably longer line. Once again the order was declined on account of Llandudno Urban District Council who had made an application for a Board of Trade Provisional Tramway Order to construct two miles of the line themselves. The Council discarded the scheme and the order was eventually granted in 1898 and the promoters were given three years to purchase the land and finish the line.

This wasn't going to be easy. Many more obstacles were to stand in their way - the lack of time and money together with legal costs mounted, making it difficult to get started so they applied for an extension to the time granted to finish the line. In 1899, with lots of persuasion approval was given to the company for another four years and six months with the stipulation that if it wasn't finished within this time the order would close.

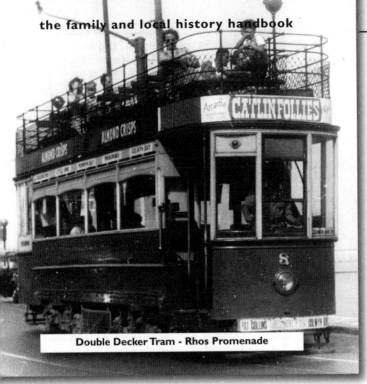

Double Decker Tram - Rhos Promenade

from West Shore, Llandudno to Old Colwyn passing through Craig Y Don, Penrhynside, Penrhyn Bay, Rhos on Sea and Colwyn Bay, several times throughout the season.

Moving on . . .

Modern trams or light railways are quite different from the first Victorian and early 20th century trams, which carried passengers around our towns and cities - from the smallest to the largest. Light rail which have now replaced some of our tramways generally have a lesser capacity and lower speed than the heavy rail systems but a faster and higher capacity than that of our old tram systems. Light rail is the term used to describe the new streetcar transformations which have taken over from the old tramways.

At the moment there are eight new tramway/light rail systems running in the UK, these include Croydon, London's docklands, Birmingham, Manchester, Sheffield, Newcastle, Nottingham and Blackpool. Other new light rail schemes are being planned for South–Central London and Edinburgh. At the same time systems are proposed for Leeds and Liverpool, although funding has been refused by the government, making them unlikely to proceed; for the same reason plans for schemes in Bristol and Portsmouth have been discarded.

Some historic town tramway systems in the United Kingdom

England

Alford and Sutton; Barnsley and District; Birmingham

Another Bournemouth tram, number 86, has been acquired by the Society and is currently at Long Whatton, near East Midlands Airport, awaiting reconstruction by master craftsmen to become a running replica of number six. When the tram is fully restored to its former glory it is hoped it will run on a half mile demonstration track at a venue yet to be sited, possibly in Llandudno.

Yesteryear lives on . . .

They recreated this nostalgic era in the summer of 2007 when they hauled the towable replica tram number 7 along the original track route

Museums to visit . . .

Why not take time out and visit one of the numerous fascinating tram museums around the country.

Crich Tramway Village in Derbyshire is home to **The National Tramway Museum** which is situated in the heart of Derbyshire overlooking the Derwent Valley. This period village has been affectionately restored to include the Tramway museum and its world famous archives. For further information contact Crich Tramway Village near Matlock, Derbyshire, DE4 5DP T: 01773 854321 W: www.tramway.co.uk/ E: via website

Birkenhead on the Wirral is home to the **Birkenhead Tramway and Wirral Transport Museum**. It was here that Europe's first tramway was built, the idea of an American flamboyant entrepreneur by the name of George Francis Train. The first trams to run on the line were horse-drawn but by 1907 they had all been converted to electric operation. These trams ran for quite some years but with the speed of evolution in public and private transport the tramway was forced to close down on the 17th July 1937.

Today part of this line has re-opened and you can take a ride on one of the historic trams from Woodside visitors' centre to the terminus at Taylor's Street. Most of the trams you can ride on today are replicas of a 1948 design and which worked our streets through the forties and fifties. Even though they may sound old when they are clanging on the rails they are fairly new!! They were built in Japan and painted to the Birkenhead specification of Cream and Maroon and included British engines. P & O containers shipped them to the Wirral.

A fine example of one of the electric double-decker trams - first launched on the tramway in 1901- can be seen on display in the Transport Museum, together with the Birkenhead 20, Wallasey 78 – 1920, Liverpool 762-1931 and many other momentous trams which had been sold for scrap. These trams were rescued and lovingly restored by members of the Merseyside Tramway preservation Society. The Museum is well worth a visit.

There are several other museums for you to explore. To find out the locations or times of opening of the museums search the internet or visit your local information centre.

Corporation; Blackpool; Brill; Bristol; Chatham & District; Chesterfield; City of Birmingham; Dearne District; Derby; Doncaster; Dover; Grimsby & Immingham; Grimsby District; Heaton Park; Hull; Ilkeston; Kingsway (London); Leeds; Leicester; Liverpool; London County Council; London United; Lowestoft; Maidstone Corporation; Manchester Corporation; Mansfield & District; Matlock; Mexborough & Swinton; Nottingham Corporation; Nottingham & District; Nottinghamshire and Derbyshire; Portsdown and Horndean; Portsmouth; Rotherham; Scarborough funiculars; Seaton; Sheffield; Southampton · Warrington; Wisbech and Upwell; Wolverton and Stony; Stratford

Wales
Great Orme; Swansea and Mumbles Railway; Pwllheli and Llanbedrog

Scotland
Aberdeen; Dundee; Edinburgh; Glasgow; Scottish Tramway & Transport Society
Northern Ireland
Belfast Giant's Causeway Tramway
Isle of Man
Douglas Bay Horse Tramway; Douglas Southern Electric Tramway; Manx Electric Railway; Snaefell Mountain Railway; Upper Douglas Cable Tramway
Industry: Maley & Taunton

Why not research your family history on www.ancestry.co.uk or another family history website to find out if any of your ancestors worked on the trams, either as a driver, conductor or even a maintenance man.

Lunatic Asylums and Mental Hospitals
Institutionalisation or care in the community?
Doreen Hopwood

'Care in the Community' has come full circle over the last six hundred years or so, and its return was heralded by Enoch Powell's stirring speech of 1961 when he was the Minister of Health. It brought about the demise of the purpose-built 'isolated, majestic and impressive' edifices which had appeared on the outskirts of towns and cities during the Victorian period, based on architectural designs recommended by the Commissioners of Lunacy. They were typically surrounded by land - Holloway, which opened in 1885, was set in 22 acres of parkland – and this provided outdoor employment and a place of exercise for the patients. The location also fulfilled another purpose in that it protected the mentally ill from society, and protected society from them.

The term 'bedlam' originates from the Priory of St Mary of Bethlehem, founded in London in 1247 and which became one of the world's first hospitals for the treatment of mental illnesses, but following its move to a new building at Moorfields, as the Royal Bethlem Hospital, it became notorious for allowing visitors to pay to watch the antics of the inmates in its galleries, a practice which stopped in 1770. 'Bedlam' was the only public asylum in the country until the early 19th Century when an act of 1808 encouraged counties to establish their own. However, public subscriptions had to be raised in order to build asylums, so between 1807 and 1841 only about 20 had been erected, despite the fact that it was estimated that the number of people being classed as mentally ill had risen six-fold. It's difficult to understand the reason for this dramatic rise, but suggestions include rapid urbanisation, displacement and a growing desire to seclude mentally ill relatives in institutions rather than keeping them at home.

Until their dissolution by Henry VIII,

monasteries were often the places where the mentally ill found refuge, but following this and the extension of the poor laws, pauper lunatics were increasingly being confined in madhouses. Despite being known as private asylums, these licensed houses were not designed for the wealthy as they had generally been looked after within their own homes. They were primarily run for profit and their income came from the Overseers of the patient's parish who paid a weekly sum for each patient placed there. Details of these payments should be amongst the Overseer of the Poor's accounts within the parish chest, and these will probably be at the relevant Diocesan Record Office. The experience of inmates of these institutions varied. The poet, William Cowper, spent 18 months in a private asylum in St Albans in the 1750s, and said of his attendant 'He maintained such an affectionate watchfulness over me during my whole illness.' On the other hand, inmates at an asylum in Middlesex in 1827 were obliged to remain in bed for the whole of Sunday so that their keepers could visit friends. If there was more than one inmate, the asylum had to be licensed, so there should be an entry in the Quarter Sessions records, which can usually be found at the relevant county record office. Adverts for private asylums often appeared in local and national newspapers from the late 18th century, and you'll probably find some in county and town directories from the mid 19th century. The Middle Class Idiot Asylum in Warwickshire in the 1870s produced a booklet , illustrated with testimonials of the good effects their training and care had on patients, and whilst surviving records may be at the local/county record office, The National Archives holds one register of admissions to private asylums outside London for the period 1798 to 1812. This

Hogarth's Vision of an Asylum

asylums, but special institutions, such as Broadmoor in Berkshire were later built for them.

The Crown held custody of the lands of persons certified by the Masters of Lunacy as being of unsound mind to prevent misappropriation of his/her estate. These individuals were known as 'Chancery Lunatics' and records can be found at The National Archives. The Act of 1845 was also intended to prevent the placing of wealthy relatives in asylums and regulations concerning certification were tightened. You can download a very useful leaflet (*Lunacy and the State: Domestic Records Information 105*) from the National Archives at www.nationalarchives.gov.uk.

contains almost 1800 names and is indexed by the surnames of both inmates and keepers. The classification of mental illness was very woolly at this time, and when a list giving reasons for the admission of patients to the Bethlem was compiled in 1810, it included *'troubles, religion, disappointment and love.'* As counties were slow to respond to the 1808 *'invitation'* to erect mental asylums, the *Metropolitan Commissioners in Lunacy* carried out a *'census of the insane'* and this showed that only half of these individuals were in asylums or hospitals whilst the rest were in workhouses, gaols or in receipt of outdoor relief. This resulted in the **Lunacy Act 1845**, which was effectively the birth of the asylum system. Under this, authorities had to receive patients at a weekly cost of not more than 14 shillings (70p) per person. This meant that pauper lunatics who should have been placed in the Duddeston Asylum, near Birmingham (at a cost of eleven shillings (55p) per week) were sent to the Northampton Asylum where the weekly charge was nine shillings (45p). This could account for you not finding an ancestor in his/her own parish when the census was taken and once discharged, the person may have remained in the area.

The purpose-built Birmingham Borough Lunatic Asylum opened in 1850 and its 1862 report shows that it was 'home' to patients from Hastings, Leicester, London, Lincoln and Bridgnorth as well as those from adjacent counties at a weekly net cost of 7/9d (39p). Whilst the population consisted mainly of pauper lunatics, asylums also took in private patients for whom the cost was borne by friends or relatives. Criminal lunatics were either confined in gaols or

Although we tend to think that Victorian asylums were places where people were incarcerated and then forgotten, by the mid 19th century there was a more humane approach to mental illness, with an emphasis on treatment rather than just confinement and an understanding that it could be caused by social problems, such as poverty or grief, and physical conditions, such as head injury and venereal diseases. This belief that most mental illnesses were curable resulted in some radical treatments in order to restore the patients' sanity. These included cooling the brain by pouring water over the patient's head and other water treatments, and patients were spun round and round in the hope of re-positioning the components of the brain into the right order.

Over time, the terms used to describe mental illness and those affected by it have changed dramatically, and the terminology used here is as it appeared in contemporary records. Today, we consider many of the words as being derogatory, but when they were being used they were seen as a genuine attempt to describe particular conditions. When the census asked householders to identify any 'imbecile, idiot or lunatic' resident in the household, answers were not always given. Either families were reluctant to admit that any of them had a mental disability or they could have been unaware of any problem, especially in respect of children. When *'idiot'* was substituted by *'feeble-minded'* in 1901 there was a marked increase in the number of individuals listed,

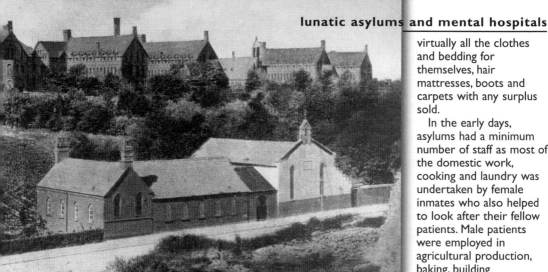

Rubery Asylum

virtually all the clothes and bedding for themselves, hair mattresses, boots and carpets with any surplus sold.

In the early days, asylums had a minimum number of staff as most of the domestic work, cooking and laundry was undertaken by female inmates who also helped to look after their fellow patients. Male patients were employed in agricultural production, baking, building maintenance and supervision. The Medical Superintendent/Officer

possibly because this term didn't have the same stigma, and it could include elderly persons with senile dementia.

On admission to an asylum, an attempt was made to diagnose the type of mental illness of each patient and 'mania' appears as a generic term to cover symptoms such as hysteria, obsessive behaviour and excitability. This may have been further defined as religious mania, and patients showing signs of depression were diagnosed as melancholic. The Victorians devised a new term – *monomania* – which seemed to apply to both conditions.

The demarcation line between *'idiot'* and *'lunatic'* had always been problematic and the former was defined as *'One who hath no understanding from his nativity and therefore, is by law assumed never likely to attain any.'* This would probably equate to *'learning difficulties'* today. The definition of *'lunatic'* was *'One who hath had understanding, but by reason of disease, grief or other accident hath lost the use of his reason'* and would now relate to mental disorder or psychiatric illness. When, in 1930, asylums became mental hospitals, pauper lunatics were re-defined as *'rate-aided persons of unsound mind.'*

Conditions in asylums varied across time and place and legislation tried to standardise the experience of inmates. The active employment of patients was a key element in their daily lives, and this served a double purpose by keeping them occupied and ensuring that the asylum remained self-sufficient - if it made a profit, so much the better. At Colney Hatch Asylum in Middlesex over a hundred trades and occupations were represented by patients admitted in 1852 and they were assigned to work which was familiar to them. Patients at the Birmingham Borough Asylum were kept busy by making and repairing articles of clothing and furnishings which, in 1862 included

had overall responsibility for the inmates, assisted by a matron and her deputy and several attendants of both sexes, many of whom 'lived in.' The Medical Superintendent at Littlemore Asylum received £450 per annum in the 1860s whilst matrons received £100 and the annual pay for a male attendant ranged between £20 and £25, with that of female attendants varying from £14 to £18.

The survival rate of archives varies, sometimes due to the fact that when a mental hospital closed, the records may have remained in the building for several years in less than ideal conditions. You may be lucky enough to find a complete range of sources relating to an ancestor, but there are often gaps in coverage. The sheer number of forms and paperwork generated by the system means that you should find something amongst the following:

The Patient Index is a good starting point as there is usually a name index covering a span of years, showing the dates of admission and discharge.

Medical Superintendent's Reports rarely provide information about individual patients, but give an insight into the daily running of the asylum.

Visiting Books include regular reports by the Visiting Committee and the Commissioners of the Board of Control who monitored the paupers their parish was charged with supporting.

Registers of Admission include personal information about the individual, including details of any transfers from other institutions and usually give the patient's number which can lead to other records, such as case books.

Medical Registers similar information to admission registers, but there are separate ones

Male Casebook

surrounding his/her admission and updated notes/observations for the period of time spent in the asylum.

Post-Mortem Books may be cross-referenced to the casebooks.

Reception Orders were signed by a Justice of the Peace and contain personal and medical history of the patient. As these were loose sheets, their survival rate varies.

Patients' Ledgers show costs to other Unions, or in the case of private patients, to family/friends, for maintaining the patient.

Civil Registers of Deaths of Patients contain similar information to that shown on a death certificate.

Access to hospital records is regulated by the **Public Records Acts**. Generally speaking, public records are closed for 30 years, so whilst material relating to the general running of the hospital can be accessed, records of individuals are closed for a period of a hundred years. This closure also applies to other sensitive material, but it may be possible to gain access to these records and the archivist at the office holding the records will advise you about this. Until the introduction of the National Health Service in 1946, public asylums and mental hospitals were administered locally and so you'll find the majority of records at local or county record offices rather than at The National Archives. Many have on-line catalogues or lists of the types of records

for male and female patients. Private and pauper patients are listed (sometimes separately) and entries for criminal patients are in red ink.

Medical Superintendent's Registers of Admission and Discharge include the information shown in the admissions registers, with the addition of the patient's religious persuasion and any risk of suicide.

Discharges and Deaths Registers vary in their content. At best, they include details from the medical certificate, personal, family and medical history whilst others may only show the dates of admission and discharge/death. They may show details of transfer to another mental hospital or institution.

Casebooks usually include a physical description of the patient, the circumstances

Map of Winsom Green, Birmingham

WYE HOUSE ASYLUM, BUXTON, DERBYSHIRE.

ESTABLISHMENT FOR THE CARE AND TREATMENT OF THE INSANE OF THE HIGHER AND MIDDLE CLASSES.

Resident Physician and Proprietor—F. K. DICKSON, F.R.C.P. and F.R.C.S. Edin.

ERECTED IN 1861 BY HIS GRACE THE DUKE OF DEVONSHIRE.

This Institution has been established for the reception of patients of **BOTH SEXES** of the Higher and Middle Classes, for whom it is admirably adapted by its position and appointments.

It is erected on an eminence surrounded with scenery of the most varied character, and the views from the House and Terrace extend over many miles of picturesque country.

The house is furnished throughout on the most liberal scale, and fitted up and arranged to resemble as much as possible an ordinary dwelling-house, with Bath-rooms and every necessary convenience.

The Proprietor lives in the House, and is assisted in his duties by a Resident House Surgeon and an experienced Lady Supt.

The House is heated throughout by means of hot-water apparatus, and is well and thoroughly ventilated.

Buxton is situated on the Mountain Limestone Formation, at an elevation of 1,000 feet above the level of the sea, and is accessible by Railway from Manchester and Liverpool by Stockport, or by the Great Northern and Midland Railways *via* Ambergate and Derby.

It is also connected by Telegraph with all parts of the kingdom.

Particulars of Terms and Forms of Admission can be obtained on application to the Resident Physician. [120]

years. Many mental hospitals published their own staff magazines and these generally include details of staff appointments, promotions and retirements. You'll probably find these in local studies departments of libraries rather than at record offices.

If there are no surviving archives, there may be yearbooks, reports or histories of the institution and it's possible that these are also deposited at the local reference library. Many local/family history societies have produced material relating to institutions and you may even find that some oral history recordings have been made by people who either worked or were resident in mental hospitals in the 20th century. Local Studies libraries will probably have copies of books written about institutions in their area and you may find that there are websites under the name of the asylum, some of which have bulletin boards or forums.

they hold and the Hospital Records Database at www.nationalarchives.gov.uk/hospitalrecords is the best place to search for the location of material for a specific asylum/mental hospital. You can search this by its name, keyword or location and this is particularly helpful as many of these changed their name when they became mental hospitals in the 1930s or were incorporated into general hospitals. The search results show contact details of the repository holding the records and a list of the material they have for that institution. Surviving staff personnel records prior to the introduction of the NHS should be at the relevant record office, but these are also closed for 100

In 1904 a Royal Commission examined the existing provision for the mentally ill and concluded that there were almost 150,000 mental defectives in England and Wales, of whom 76% were classed as feeble-minded. This group were considered suitable for specialised training to enable them to adapt to society and carry out useful employment, but this resulted in many individuals being placed in institutions (known as colonies) for the rest of their lives. From 1913 authorities were given wider powers to remove individuals from the community to asylums and many of these had their own residential schools catering for children aged between 7 and 16 years. Many of the imposing Gothic buildings survive today and have been put to other uses, whilst others have been entirely demolished, leaving no trace of their former architectural grandeur. Fortunately for family, local and social historians many of their records have been carefully conserved so that we can still gain an insight into what it was like to live and work in these institutions.

SOME KEY DATES CONCERNING MENTAL HEALTH LEGISLATION

1808 Asylum Act
Empowered counties to build asylums if they so wished.

1828 Madhouse Act
Regulated private asylums

1845 Lunacy Act
Compelled local authorities to build and maintain asylums

1874 Four Shillings Act
Subsidised the transfer of mentally ill to asylums from workhouses

1890 Lunacy Act
Regulated the arrest, certification and detention of the mentally ill. A medical certificate had to be signed by two medical doctors who had independently examined the patient

1904 Royal Commission Investigated provision for the mentally ill and introduced specialised institutions (colonies) where the feeble minded could be trained for employment.

1913 Mental Deficiency Act
Empowered authorities to remove individuals from the community and place them in special institutions, including residential schools for children over the age of seven who were certified as being mentally defective.

1930 Mental Treatment Act
Asylums became mental hospitals and could accept voluntary and temporary patients.

1946 NHS Act
Control of mental hospitals passed from local authorities to NHS

1960s - Emphasis on *'care in the community.'*

Sir George Cayley: *The Father of Flight*
Martin Limon

tells the inspiring story of Sir George Cayley from Brompton, near Scarborough whose pioneering aviation work in the nineteenth century was to be of vital importance in the development of powered flight.

For centuries mankind had dreamed of following the birds by taking to the skies but it was not until the 19th century that serious scientific research took place to find out how this could be achieved. Ask anyone the question: *'Who invented powered flight?'* and most people will instantly reply *'the Wright Brothers'* for as every schoolboy knows it was Orville and Wilbur Wright who succeeded in getting their *'flying machine'* off the ground at Kitty Hawk, USA for a brief twelve seconds in December 1903. However when Orville Wright was later asked about the inspiration for their pioneering achievement he singled-out the Yorkshire baronet Sir George Cayley (1773-1857) as a major factor by saying:

'Cayley was a remarkable man. He knew more of the principles of aeronautics and as much as anyone that followed him up to the end of the nineteenth century. His published work was a most important contribution to the science.'

Yet George Cayley's work was more than just theory and it is only in recent times that his importance in the story of flight has been widely recognised. In Yorkshire however Cayley has long been a hero and there are those who are determined to keep his achievements in the public eye. Anyone visiting his home village of Brompton-by-Sawdon between Scarborough and Pickering will see at the entrance to the village (on the A170 road) a sign saying *'birthplace of aviation'* as well as a public house and a road named in honour of their most famous son.

Sir George Cayley was born in Scarborough but after succeeding to his father's title in 1792 lived at Brompton Hall for the rest of his life. Privately educated Cayley showed a considerable talent for scientific investigation and in his school notebooks there are cartoons suggesting that even at an early age he was developing ideas and theories on how flight might be achieved. Another surviving piece of evidence is a silver disc (from 1799) on which Cayley had engraved the forces that governed flight and on the reverse side the design of an aircraft with a fixed wing, a fuselage and a tail. Experiments with varying

A nineteenth century portrait of Sir George Cayley.
In addition to his work on aeronautics Cayley was a considerable scientist and engineer and among his projects were self-righting lifeboats, caterpillar tractors and tension-spoke wheels.

wing sections in the stairwells at Brompton Hall led him to develop theories about the forces that would influence an aircraft: thrust, lift, drag and gravity. At an early stage Cayley recognised that the answer to the question of flight was "to make a surface support a given weight by the application of power to the resistance of the air." His observations of birds soaring great distances by simply twisting their arched wing surfaces led him to deduce that aircraft could fly if their wings were cambered to maximise lift.

Cayley was a meticulous researcher conducting experiments with models and keeping careful notes of his observations and he was the first investigator to apply the methods of science and engineering to the question of how to achieve flight. On these grounds alone Cayley can be regarded as the first aeronautical engineer in history and the *'father of aerodynamics.'* By 1808 he had advanced from experimenting with model gliders to building full-size craft with a wing area of 172 square feet and with the essential features of modern-day aircraft (inclined rigid wings to provide lift, a tail assembly for stability and a rudder steering control).

The outcome of his experimental work was a landmark three-part treatise called *'On Aerial Navigation'* published in Nicholson's Journal (November 1809 - March 1810) setting out the basic principles of aeroplane flight and later the inspiration of other pioneers including the Wright Brothers. Unfortunately in 1810 Cayley's revolutionary theories were well ahead of their time for to suggest that *'man could fly'* was to invite ridicule. As he said: *'to the public aerial navigation is a subject bordering on the ludicrous.'*

As a result his efforts to generate enthusiasm for aeronautics failed and his attempts to form aeronautical societies were unsuccessful. Therefore for many years he concentrated on other subjects of scientific or mechanical interest instead: things that seemed to offer more immediate results (like

of any other power source the kite shaped glider would have used the muscle power of estate workers pulling downhill on ropes to launch it across the valley on its short flight. According to Cayley's granddaughter the pilot was the Brompton Hall coachman, John Appleby. She later wrote:

'The coachman went in the machine and landed on the west side at about the same level. The coachman got himself clear and when the watchers got across he shouted: 'Please Sir George, I wish to give notice. I was hired to drive not to fly.'

This first flight by a man in a heavier-than-air fixed wing aircraft may have been nerve wracking for the pilot and short in duration but the plane that he flew had all the essential features needed for lift and for horizontal and vertical control even if it lacked an engine. The flight served to prove Cayley's assertion that air passing over a curved wing generated lift. This is why the achievements of Sir George Cayley have been celebrated in the one hundred and fifty years since his death and why a replica of the 1853 plane was flown in the 1970s and 1980s at Brompton Dale in recognition of his contribution to aeronautics. The year 2003 was also an opportunity to mark Cayley's work as part of the centenary celebrations of powered flight. Using a replica glider built by BAE Systems at Brough in East Yorkshire Sir Richard Branson took off and flew for about fifty yards at a height of about six feet to recreate that first flight before landing on the other side of Brompton Dale (July 2003)

When the celebration of powered flight moved to the Yorkshire Air Museum a day later it was therefore only fitting that the museum replica of the Cayley aircraft should stand proudly alongside a replica of the Wright Brother's Flyer. As Ian Dewar the museum's operations manager pointed out: 'Sir

---

A photograph of Sir George Cayley 1850s
(Image courtesy of the National Air and Space Museum, Washington)

---

railways, artificial limbs and caterpillar tractors).

In order to develop a successful aeroplane in the modern sense of the word Cayley had to find a way to provide thrust. Sustained flight needed a lightweight engine and Cayley recognised that the steam engines available in the early nineteenth century would never be suitable since they were too heavy. To provide an alternative he tried, and failed, to develop other power plants driven by hot air and gunpowder.

It was not until towards the end of his life that Cayley returned to his major passion of aeronautics, possibly encouraged and helped by his grandson George John Cayley (1826-1878). His crowning achievement was the construction of a large glider that Cayley described as a *'governable parachute.'* It was this machine that made a well-documented heavier than air flight at Brompton Dale around June 1853 (fifty years before the Wright Brothers). In the absence

A replica of George Cayley's glider at The Yorkshire Air Museum
(image courtesy of Nigel Coates)

was the originator of the airplane. He conceived the configuration that is now seen as conventional: a body or fuselage supporting one main wing, with horizontal and vertical tails positioned aft.'

George Cayley's achievements have long been understated in Britain. My generation was brought up to believe that the Wright brothers were the fathers of aviation but in fact they attributed their success to his achievements. After their first flight, they said they owed it all to George Cayley.'

In Britain Sir George Cayley was long seen as an eccentric aristocratic and an amateur enthusiast and his work was often ignored or neglected. However this was not the case abroad and many experts (especially in the United States) regard him as the hero of the aviation story. One organisation said of his achievements: 'Cayley

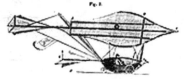

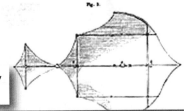

A glider by Sir George Cayley
Mechanics Magazine 1852

Victorian Trade Cards
Karen Foy

For sheer commercial creativity and artistic license, the world of Victorian Trade Cards makes a fascinating subject for any social historian or ephemera collector - especially where space is at a premium. Karen Foy takes a look at these 'mini marketing marvels' and finds out more about this interesting and affordable area of research.

Today, television, radio and newspaper mediums are just some of the methods we use to advertise products but in the Victorian era, one of the most successful means of marketing a seller's wares was in the form of 'trade cards'. Although used in the UK, these highly coloured and decorative works of art became increasingly popular in the United States. For those of us with ancestors who may have immigrated to America, this technique of promoting new products, gadgets and services would have been part of their everyday lives – the examples featured give us an insight into their 'shopping experiences' overseas.

Accessible Advertising ...

Throughout the 1800's, most merchants and shopkeepers had decorative cards produced which would be given away to promote either their business or particular products sold – the idea of which is thought to have originated from similar cards used by craftsmen in the 1700's to publicise their particular line of work. This trend gradually became extremely fashionable in America and whilst many European countries had

their own decorative versions, it was not quite so popular in Britain until a smaller type of card was later issued with cigarettes and brands of tea which became collectable in their own right. As a result, from an enthusiast's point of view, any early British examples are highly sought after and rightly take pride of place in any collection.

Unlike today's business cards which are often plain or limited in colour and usually bear only a name and company address, the Victorian alternative was much more elaborate. They varied in sized from tiny 3cm x 7cm versions to large A5 style creations often given out at Christmas or other significant times of the year and largely depended on the wealth of each individual business as to how much they could afford to spend on marketing.

The front of each card was decorated with an image – not always related to the product sold – some would feature a slogan to aid publicity whilst the reverse would be embellished with text giving full details of the products and services and possibly even a testimonial from a satisfied customer. Simpler versions had plain backs which were stamped with the name of the shop whilst some were die cut into specific shapes or useful bookmarks.

It's widely known that the Victorians were hoarders – their houses were crammed with ornaments and trinkets ensuring that a cluttered room adorned with ornate accessories met the strict fashion guidelines of the day. At the time, the pretty designs featured on the trade cards made the perfect collectable for the modern Victorian who would paste examples into scrapbooks and arrange them in subjects that were appealing and decorative ensuring that products were not forgotten as their collections grew. The craze for collecting increased as people sought out the more complex designs when colour lithography of the 1870's became more abundant. The 1876 Centennial World's Fair held in Philadelphia, Pennsylvania – ten years after the end of the Civil War - was a remarkable event celebrating original patents, inventions, printing methods and signalling a new era. The Trade Card provided the perfect medium to market these innovative ideas and display the testimonials of happy customers.

Each card falls mainly into two categories – 'Stock' cards which had an image on the front with a plain back on which the details of the advertiser or product could be printed. These were ideal for a small business as the cards could be made to apply to any item which needed promoting at the time.

CLARK'S
TRADE
O.N.T.
MARK
SPOOL COTTON

If the Lady who reads this card, when in want of Spool Cotton, will buy

CLARK'S O.N.T. SPOOL COTTON,

SHE WILL GET THE

BEST THREAD FOR HAND & MACHINE SEWING.

IT IS WOUND ON

WHITE SPOOLS.

The bottom label of every spool reads as below.

CLARK'S
TRADE
O.N.T.
MARK
SPOOL COTTON

'Custom' cards were specifically created at the request of the advertiser. The designs could be 'one offs' produced for a limited print run or special images of a company's products – the details of which would be printed on the reverse of the card.

The majority of American cards - produced on coated card stock - can be dated to the 1850s and 1860s (the first example of its kind was printed in 1852) well before trade card advertising reached its peak. Coated card stock refers to the process of applying a chemical substance to paper to give it a glossy finish. In the mid 1800s, this chemical could have been created from kaolin (often known as china clay), white lead (which was highly toxic) or even animal hide glue – to name but a few. This coating thickened the paper and allowed ink which was printed onto the card's surface to remain there rather than sink into the paper – giving sharp, shiny and vibrant text and images – in turn, attracting the customer's attention. Bear this in mind and you may discover some early examples to add to your collection.

Creative Commerce . . .
New inventions played a huge part in the subjects chosen for illustration. At the time, the introduction of a lawnmower which could be pushed by a man rather than pulled by an animal was a commercial success. The creation of a side-wheel machine developed in England which was lightweight and inexpensive caught on all over the world and gradually found its way onto trade cards that showed the ease of operation to its customers – even Kodak chose to use this method of advertising to showcase its latest

HOW TO KEEP HUSBANDS AT HOME, NIGHTS.

camera equipment.

Sewing, whether by hand or machine was an important part of a woman's daily life during the 19th century and the cotton thread or cotton spool was in great demand. Clark's Spool Cotton was one of the most popular brands and featured on a wide variety of trade cards with bobbins of thread incorporated into each picture. Baby images were used to show how white, soft or silky their threads were, adding captions like 'A Favourite with the Ladies' to imply that their female customers had excellent taste. Other companies such as Coats, Merrick and California Silk competed with images featuring elephants, whales and strong men to promote how strong and durable their brand of thread was.

Educational subjects, famous characters, occupations and nautical scenes provide fascinating topics in which to specialise allowing you to create a complete gallery of US Presidents, military figures or chart specific events in history. Clipper ships were used to advertise particular voyages by the maritime companies and distributed during the mid 1800's showing that these cards were essential in promoting services as well as products.

Mechanical banks made of cast iron were produced after the American Civil War allowing a coin to be placed in the mechanical arm of the object which could then be tipped inside and used as a form of savings or 'piggy' bank. These items were so popular that their images were reproduced on trade cards in limited numbers but their bright colours and high quality images of characters such as Punch and Judy, Uncle Sam or Humpty Dumpty mean that they now command high prices.

Various artists soon became known for their style of work and series were produced which could include between two and ten numbered cards that told a story in sequence. The subjects were covered imaginatively in a comic strip or informative format and publicised everything from cigars to soap. One particular series is from the Liebig meat extract company – their sets are very collectable, attractive to look at with a great amount of thought and detail given to the subjects covered. The reverse often held a recipe or product description and proved so popular that they were published in many countries in various languages. Each set is numbered and catalogues for collectors are available from specialist dealers.

Elegant ladies or fashion accessories of the day featured on cards given out by chemists and make colourful additions to an album whilst other entertaining designs to look out for are those printed by William B. Burford Lithographers of Indiana which advertised medicines sold by Dr Joseph Haas, a veterinary surgeon within the

Be sure to see the Celebrated

MEHLIN

PIANOS

The Mehlin Pianos are creating more favorable comment than any others. They are considered by expert judges to be the Finest Pianos now made. Your inspection is earnestly solicited by

T. C. HEFFNER,
5 North 8th Street, READING, PA.

county. The cards produced in the early 1880's are distinctive in that the images show animals taking on human characteristics and although difficult to track down, they can add a great comedy element to a collection.

But it was not only animals that benefited from the latest medical treatments. 'Dr Kilmer' was one of the best known American herbal remedies of the day with a wide array of cards foretelling the benefits of potions such as Indian Cough Cure or Parilla Liver Pills. Wistar's Balsam of Wild Cherry was advertised as 'a remedy for coughs, consumption and all lung diseases' optimistically claiming that *'Consumption can be cured by a timely resort to this standard remedy, as is proved by hundreds of testimonials it has received'*. The image used to promote this product depicted two healthy children, fit and well, perhaps cured of all ills, and even climbing trees!

Health care related cards can make not only an interesting read but also a fascinating area in which to specialise.

Rogue Traders . . .

Although most of the illustrations had some connection to the advertised product there were many occasions when there was no connection whatsoever. Set against a backdrop of an old mill and a gently flowing stream, a small trade card promotes Dr Morse's compound syrup of Yellow Dockroot – *to regulate the digestive organs and purify the blood* – on the reverse, this miracle cure promises to treat a list of ailments including dyspepsia, biliousness and headaches…not bad for $1.00 per quarter bottle!

Musical instruments were widely promoted but

opposite are two examples of the images used not quite depicting the product or service offered. First is a scene of a young farmhand sleeping next to a haystack which has been used on a card promoting a Violin Repairer in Boston, whilst another card claims that *'over 40000 families have been made happy owning a Kroeger Piano'*. Sadly, the retailer didn't think that having a picture of the product on his cards would increase sales and instead chose a portrait of a young girl to attract more customers.

The food and beverage industries featured some classic text and imagery mismatches. Newman's Pure Gold Baking Powder declared it was *sold by all the first class grocers in the country and used by 50,000 families in the United States, Canada and British Provinces.* A clear engraving of this essential commodity adorned the back of the trade cards but in our example a very elegant shoe festooned with a posy of flowers was the image chosen for the front. These designs could have been a clever attempt by the Ad men to appeal to the avid Victorian collectors who would spend hours poring over their scrapbooks arranging cards and swapping their duplicates whilst never forgetting an advertised product that was in their collection.

Changing Times . . .

The use of trade cards reached their peak in the 1890s. Advertising policies began to change so magazines and newspapers took advantage of this potential income by offering advertising space within their pages. This wider readership outshone the amount of coverage a business could receive compared to handing out trade cards to each customer; it was also more cost effective.

This particular period marked the beginning of the postcard age. Those who had previously collected trade cards now switched allegiance and sought out the latest themed postcards of locations they had visited. Inevitably, the purpose of the trade card from both an advertisers and collectors point of view gradually began to fade.

Providing additional resources for the family historian, even a small collection of Victorian trade cards can give a glimpse into life during this era. From medical supplies to musical instruments, washing powders to the latest perfumes, they allow us to understand the types of products and services our ancestors may have used and bring their world to life.

From the pretty to the preposterous, the religious to the risqué, there is something here to interest everyone. If you're lucky enough to have bought or inherited a partial collection, why not look at it with fresh eyes…dig deeper and bring an old pastime back to life. I can guarantee you

won't regret it!
Creating a Collection . . .

From coffee and cocoa to soaps and shoe polish, trade cards have covered a wide range of subjects but where can you find these historical gems?

Specialist auctions and trade fairs are held specifically for the buying and selling of these cards. Their artistic value alone can make them highly sought after as well as the way they reflect all that was new and innovative during the 19th century.

Check out auction sites such as www.ebay.com where they are readily available but also track down items at Antique and Ephemera Fairs. Sometimes examples can be found tucked into boxes underneath a stall or hidden in pristine condition within the tatty pages of an old scrapbook. Don't miss an opportunity to rummage for a long forgotten item concealed within a less than eye-catching display case – the shabby outside might be protecting some unseen treasures within.

A wide selection of cards can be bought from as little as £1 or £2 per item rising to as much as £50 - £100 for really collectable items in fine condition.

Successful Suggestions . . .

Check the backs of cards to ensure that the advertising details have not been ripped away if removed from an album.

Avoid any rips or creases and where possible always buy the best examples that your pocket will allow.

Care should be taken when attempting to soak off cards which have been glued to old scrapbook pages to avoid ruining nice examples – if in doubt seek advice from a dealer or experienced ephemera collector.

Display in divided pockets or scrapbooks which are acid and lignum free to prolong the life and colour intensity of the cards.

Store out of direct sunlight – avoid areas which are prone to damp or moisture

Eager to find out more?
Victorian Trade Cards: Historical Reference and Value Guide by Dave Cheadle (Paperback - 5 Jun 1996) ISBN-13: 978-0891457060
Collecting Cigarette and Trade Cards (Paperback) by Gordon Howesden. New Cavendish Books Jan 1999. ISBN-13: 978-1872727875

The Police
Fred Feather

I suppose it is the sign of advancing years that a simple phrase can work you into a paroxysm of bile. In my case such is the phrase which I have used for my title. Quote - '***The Police*** *did such and such.*' Quote - '*My ancestor was in* ***The Police***.' My reply is usually '*What exactly do you mean by* ***The Police***?' There have been a couple of hundred different organisations within that definition and there are still at least 43. Forty-one years service with the brutal and licentious constabulary have left me with an enduring impression that there is no such thing. To me the Service (politically correct term) has always had a kaleidoscope of facets which were a constant source of wonder. Often the question was posed '*How can I trace my ancestor? His marriage, census or death record described him as 'policeman''* (and increasingly in enquiries '*policewoman.*') Please forgive me if, in my reply, I occasionally become subjective and refer to the county of Essex, in which I was the first and founding curator of its Police Museum.

In one force (which is the 'f' word,' no longer used by those who yearn to achieve higher rank) we had a shift whose members included *Sage, Onions* and *Bacon*. Our jailer at Southend was a Fellow of the *Royal Microscopical Society* and I cannot count all those who left to became clergymen. *Lord Nelson* was, a few years since, a Detective Constable in Hertfordshire. From 1831 there were Special Constables raised for special occasions, the most famous being the future Emperor Napoleon III.

Louis-Napoleon walked the beat in Kensington ,at the time of the Chartist problem and his duty armband is currently in the care of the Chelmsford and Essex Museum at Chelmsford. I always delighted in 'canteen culture,' where the stories of life and derring-do made my occupation something called 'The Job', alas nowadays mostly described as 'a job.'

We will assume that you will set about your task in two ways, that is, with the aid of a computer, or the other way. First, with a computer. I will start by quoting Bill Wood, the list owner of a rootsweb list (POLICE-UK-D-request@rootsweb.com) for persons seeking police ancestors. He writes 'There is no such thing as a centralised record of policemen'

Nothing more true will ever be circulated. Alternatively: How to do it without a computer. Exactly the same truth prevails.

Prior to 1829 there were police forces, such as those in Glasgow and on the River Thames. The grave of the founder of the latter can be found in Paglesham churchyard, to the east of Southend and the west of Belgium. From London an organisation, pursuant to Bow Street Runners and known as the Horse and Foot Patrols, spread investigations out towards surrounding counties. Lists of officers are available, but they often became members of the Metropolitan Police when it was formed in 1829. The Public Record Office at Kew is strong on records of 'The Met' and the other large forces, such as the pre-1922 Royal Irish Constabulary. P.R.O. leaflets on police subjects can be downloaded from their website.

Forces with the title 'Police'.

From an Act of Parliament of 1835 small towns with a charter began to employ policemen. In Essex they were Colchester, Harwich, Maldon and Saffron Walden. The early beat book of Colchester from 1836 has survived and is the basis of an index of officers of that town, up to a 1947 amalgamation. Minutes of the Watch Committee, controlling body of a town force, have survived. In Colchester each new officer was introduced by name to that committee, their names minuted. Harwich and Saffron Walden officers are being traced from the 1841 and 1851 censuses and newspaper reports until their demise, when they and many other small forces ceased to exist in 1857, as policing of all areas became compulsory. Maldon, officers traced in a similar fashion, lasted until made obsolete by future legislation and amalgamated in 1889. Those large enough to survive independently used the title 'Police'. The largest town forces retained the title for another 130 years. The two big London services, the Metropolitan Police and City of London Police, always retained this title. My own force, Essex Police,

assumed it in 1974, when their former title, The Essex and Southend on Sea Joint Constabulary, became too unwieldy for administration and cap badges. Watch Committees disappeared nearly forty years ago.

Forces called 'Constabulary'

Under the provisions of an 1839 Act of Parliament, Rural Police emerged, Wiltshire late in that year. Essex and various others began a few weeks later in 1840. Where a larger county force amalgamated with a smaller Police or Constabulary, the title 'Constabulary' usually survived.

In Essex we believe that we have records of everyone serving since 1840 and, with the use of our Giggins Index, can nearly always produce a biography. There is also the index of everyone who served with the former Southend on Sea Constabulary (1914-1969). Constabulary records can be found in the papers of Quarter Sessions, their supervising authority, usually reported in newspapers or retained as originals in Record Offices. Later this body became the Standing Joint Committee, now Police Committee. Others, such as Hertfordshire Constabulary (1841-to date), destroyed their records many years since, and painful reconstructions from newspapers will be required. Kent Constabulary was not formed until 1857. Many of the 43 UK forces retain the word 'Constabulary', many others are still called it despite disposing of the name many years since.

Other policemen

All those referred to as policemen were not necessarily in a Town Police or a County Constabulary. Within my own county I recall security men at Southend Airport (Southend on Sea Constabulary Special Constables) and later at Stansted Airport (British Airports Constabulary). On the railways we had members of the London Transport Police, Eastern Counties Railway pre-1947, the London Midland & Scottish and London and North Eastern Railways, the London Tilbury and

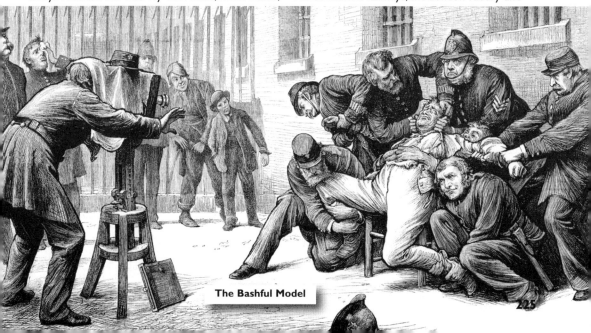

The Bashful Model

Southend Railway (who in Victorian times sponsored an Essex Constabulary officer). One enquiry I answered assured a lady that she was not going mad, in that successive censuses showed her target being promoted from Detective Constable to Station Master. The Metropolitan Police positioned Special Branch officers at immigration points such as the port of Harwich. Whilst working on the 1851 Devon census I discovered a pocket of Metropolitan Policemen stationed in Royal Docks, such as Portsmouth and Devonport. Royal residences also drew their men. Commercial Docks had policemen and that is what they were called, until a short time ago, when established forces such as the Royal Parks Constabulary, Docks Police, Ministry of Defence Police and British Rail Police became 'agencies.' In Essex we maintain a strays register, the Bayliss Index, of men and women of other forces who were temporarily in our county.

A miscellany of police museums.

Police Museums come and go, based on the whims of those who command. Bad news for the museum of the former Essex Constabulary (1840-1969), loaded onto the launch 'Vigilant' and ordered dumped somewhere off Southend Pier in the early 1970s. Someone wanted a computer suite in the room it occupied. Good news; some rebellious spirit rescued most of the goodies and put them in a room where normally only dogs practising sniffing for drugs would find them. Most are now in the reconstituted museum of 1991. Other collections have been mothballed, including, I believe, Cambridgeshire, Cheshire and Cumbria though some part of these collections may be in Record Offices. Many towns such as Huntingdon and Kings Lynn have excellent police museums. Others such as Kent have placed theirs within a tourist facility, Chatham Historic Dockyard. Many respected museums, such as that of Devon and Cornwall, have in the past come and gone or were on the back burner due to the loss of the services of the person with the knowledge to run them. And, these can return to the game at any time. There are also well-funded and independent museums such as that of Greater Manchester and the West Midlands services. Of the situation above the border I am ignorant but

informed that there also centres of excellence there. In London the City Police have a museum with an excellent curator. The Metropolitan Police museum, for many years a dream, now exists in West London. Do not confuse this project with the Science (formerly the Black) Museum at New Scotland Yard. That is not about policemen, it is the world's oldest crime-museum, mainly devoted to criminality and artefacts. At Weathersfield in Essex we also have the excellent museum of the Ministry of Defence Police (its forebears, the civilian police of Army, Navy and Air Force). Military organisations such as the Royal Military Police, the R.A.F. Police and the Navy (Chatham Dockyard) have police museums.

How to identify a policeman from a picture.

Senior officers were most photographed, but few in number. Wiltshire and Essex had not a dozen chief constables between them in over 320 years joint service. Victorian uniforms can be sumptuous but, a word of warning, there were many ex-military senior officers that uniforms can be confusing. We have no picture of the founding Chief Constable of Essex, John Bunch Bonnemaison McHardy, (served 1841-1881), perhaps because he was a full Admiral and could have as much braid as he required.

Ranks were mostly denoted by military insignia. Constables wore numbers, a prime source for police humour; One Training Officer numbered a good friend '40 Watts.' Said Brian: 'Are they suggesting I am not too bright?' At one time 'PC49' provoked laughter after a 1940's radio show. PC 1001 was described as 'Clean round the bend.' Essex did not for many years issue '666' or '999' as anyone with those numbers attending a pub brawl would be under extra pressure, neither, in deference to his family, has the number of a late lamented colleague, murdered on duty. How long will that tradition last? Our collection of photographs, with the helmet or collar showing a number, is a prime source for identification. Acting sergeants had stripes and numbers, full and station sergeants had crowned stripes. Inspectors wore Bath Stars, Superintendents and above, crowns, 'pips' and laurels. This of course varied between forces and eras. The Essex Constabulary in 1840 had only Superintendents and Constables, later Inspectors were added, but only in 1855 did the Sergeant appear. In different times there were Chief Inspectors and Chief Superintendents. In London the chiefs of both forces

IDENTITY.

Enthusiastic Amateur (at the National Gallery), "CAN YOU TELL ME WHERE I CAN FIND THE NEW 'CONSTABLE'?"

Hibernian Officer, "SHURE IT'S MESELF YE MUST MANE, SOR! I CAME ON JEWTEE HERE FOR THE FORST TOIME THIS WEEK, SOR!"

were Commissioners. Some smaller forces had High Constables

When first formed the police took a non-army profile, with reinforced civilian top hats, but from the 1870s the majority of working policemen wore helmets. There are three distinct shapes:

1. a **Roman style comb** from front to back, this was, and still is, worn by the City of London Police, but the Victorian Metropolitan Police also wore it for several decades. It is presently used by Essex, Kent, Thames Valley and many others. The comb has a small filigree front, in the majority of these forces featuring a Maltese Cross, whilst Essex has the cockle-shell in honour of Southend Constabulary.

2. a **military looking spike & ball** on the top, these include *Humberside, Devon & Cornwall* and *Royal Parks Constabulary.*

3. the commonest helmet has **a rose-top** and is used by the present Metropolitan Police and many others.

From 1970 red, blue and green insignia arrived, pioneered by *Greater Manchester, Metropolitan, Essex* and *Kent.* Kepis were the working headgear of senior officers but with the advent of the car the peaked cap became fashionable. In Scotland a cap with the black and white diced band replaced the helmet some 70 years ago, whilst in England caps were plain blue until about 1970, when diced bands were adopted (but not by Surrey for many years).

Heraldry identifies uniforms geographically, and the period can be identified by the crown used. Not all forces used a crown, some forces, including Norfolk, did not use helmet badges. There are three types of crown; A) Geulphic or Victorian - a distinct high sided shape worn until 1901. In Essex they sawed these off when the old Queen died and soldered on B) The Edward or King's crown, much heavier but with a lower profile. A good place to learn the difference is on old postage stamps. Kings wore the Edward crown until 1952, since then we have the familiar C) or Queen's crown.

Jackets - The wearing of the arm band indicated whether an officer was on duty and can be a good ageing or identifying mark. The City of London still wear theirs in red/white vertical stripes. The Metropolitan Police wore blue/white vertical stripes. In Colchester Police the armband was horizontal blue/white.

Medals are a good dating method, their configuration and shape identify a military and police career. Those issued by the sovereign are worn on the left breast, those by other authorities on the right breast. Victorian medals are for temperance, marksmanship and for bravery awarded by local authority, by the Royal Society for the Protection of Life from Fire, the Royal Humane Society and sundry other worthy groups. Registers for some of these awards are with parent organisations and the National Archives. Familiar Sovereign's ribbons are the blue/white/blue of the Long Service & Good Conduct Medal, issued from 1952 and the red/white/black of the Special Constabulary medal, issued since the Great War.

Decorated truncheons are a subject that follows many of the above rules but should be taken to an expert for analysis. They mostly pre-date Victoria or were issued within her reign, although special presentations continued until this day.

Memorials and Diversions.

In Lancashire, former Sergeant Anthony Rae of Preston has been charting the deaths of officers of all UK forces killed on duty with a National Role of Honour. Essex Police has a web-site as a memorial to about 150 officers who died violently on duty or in the service of their country. There are Rolls of Honour in Chelmsford, Belfast, Scotland Yard and many others with such details. Another unusual source could be Coventry Cathedral, where is housed the National Register and Memorial to all special constables killed on duty, poignantly dominated by Reserve Constables of the Royal Ulster Constabulary. The earliest page is devoted to Henry Trigg, Parish Constable of Berden in Essex, murdered in the course of a robbery in 1814. At our Chelmsford Museum we also have details of the investigators of that case, Bow Street Runners Vickery, Bishop and Stafford. I know because I arranged both entries.

Now to endeavour (was that not Inspector Morse's Christian name?) to get the Freemason canard out of the way. In Victorian times senior officers often had a prominent social position within a community, but were not allowed to openly support political parties, which meant that they could not join the Liberal or Conservative clubs or frequent certain pubs. Masons provided one means of socialising with peer groups which is nowadays provided by golf clubs. Masonics were then often very open and brothers named in all newspaper reports of funerals etc. Over the years many joined, some, it is suggested, in the hope of socialising with those who could promote them. I personally think those days are past and that there are now comparatively few police Masons but many more golfers. Read all about it in *'My Ancestor was a Freemason'* by Pat Lewis. If you suspect that police ancestor of mixing with clergy, schoolteachers, soldiers, sailors, marines, firemen, solicitors and other local worthies, you could try to trace the present whereabouts of their Lodge and write to them. You may be pleased with the response.

How to contact police sources.

Here are some things you might consider:

Contact the Record Office in the area in which you suspect your target was located. Ask about local police records and if the local service has a museum.

Post your enquiry on the internet police rootsweb. Metropolitan enquiries get responses from Scotland Yard archivists.

Log on to the Internet and search for force histories (www.police.uk). Some service sites, such as Lincolnshire, Merseyside and Bradford may give you a pleasant surprise. Written histories such as East Yorkshire and Sunderland are interesting. To mark the 150th anniversary of foundation many counties produced histories in 1989/1990. Look out for the Police Vehicle Enthusiasts Club.

Write to one of the 43 UK services, or perhaps the Garde Siocanna in Dublin, or the various agencies. Address it to the Chief Officer, enclosing a self addressed envelope. This puts pressure on the recipient. Ask what facilities they have, who is interested in their force history and if anyone answers historical enquiries. Enclose a clear copy of your photograph and they may point you in the right direction.

Please note that the Police History Society is an academic society devoted to research on police subjects and is not usually geared to accepting enquiries about individual officers. There is no central source.

Finally ...

Now, I have tried to show you that **The Police** is a touch too bland a title for such a varied organisation and be assured that generalisations can often be shot down in flames. My advice is **No quick e-mailed** 'do me a look-up.' The information is probably there, but you will have to work for it.

What The Dickens!
Chris Webber

Ian Wray always knew that his great, great, great uncle was one of Charles Dickens' best friends but little did he realise that other forebears changed the course of English history.

The surprising story of how Charles Dickens was inspired by trips to the quiet North Yorkshire market town of Malton are becoming well known.

The old solicitors' offices in the town's Chancery Lane, believed to have influenced the great writer's depictions of Scrooge's offices in *A Christmas Carol*, is to be turned into a museum and the whole story has been featured on the BBC.

But for Ian Wray, a former insurance worker, Dickens' friendship with great, great, great uncle Charles Smithson was, and will always remain, primarily a family story, told many times down the years, that took dedicated research to verify.

Mr Wray, who was always interested in his family history, explained that the family tales of Dickens were only the beginning of his research into his family history. Delving back deep into the Middle and even Dark ages, he has discovered remarkable ancestors that were part of some of Britain's most important moments.

One was a knight at the Battle of Bannockburn, another, John Wray, a mariner at the Battle of

Trafalgar. There's even a connection to Hugh Despenser who ended up being brutally executed by jealous barons for his influence over the weak 14th Century king Edward II.

And yet Mr Wray finds himself returning often to the story of how Charles Dickens, the author who told the world about the horrific social problems of early industrialised, urban society, was inspired by the picturesque rural town of Malton.

In retirement Mr Wray, who lives in Malton, went on to research the story from his mother's side of the family, and has produced a booklet for the town's Dickens Society outlining just how Dickens was influenced by his family and Malton. He was helped by the fact that his family had founded and run for generations the Malton Messenger, a well-regarded local newspaper now incorporated into the Ryedale Gazette and Herald. In other words a small newspaper owned by his ancestors detailing the weekly goings on of their relatively small world is available to Mr Wray – a gift to research that many family historians could only dream about.

He also took from compilation books copies of letters, now scattered in museums around the world, from Dickens himself referring to Charles Smithson, some that the great writer sent to his wife. Most of the letters are now held in museums around the world but, partly thanks to Mr Wray, copies are available to read in the friendly café in the street inside the old Palace Cinema, opposite the 'Scrooge offices' on Chancery Lane.

These kind of records offer some hard evidence of Dickens' friendship with Smithson and have attracted serious scholars to Mr Wray's door. However, Mr Wray readily admits, some of the most interesting details of how Dickens was inspired to create characters based on Smithson and other people in the Malton area, rely on his own family's stories.

"It's oral history, but I have no doubt it's true," he says. "A lot of the stories are backed up to some extent by the letters. For example Dickens sent Charles Smithson's widow a copy of A Christmas Carol soon after it was published and it's clear in the letter they've talked about it.

"A lot of the stories came, I believe, from Richard John Smithson, Charles Smithson's nephew, who was 15 when Charles (Smithson) died but who my grandmother would have known. It seems a long time ago, but in fact it's only a couple of generations from him that we get the stories. That said, we're scrupulous about separating what is verifiable by literature and what is oral, family history."

In his first extensive interview Mr Wray tells the story of how Dickens came to be so closely connected with his family and Malton.

He explained that the Smithson family had solicitors' offices in both Malton and London, in a shared practice.

Aged 19 Charles Smithson was being trained by his eldest brother in Malton but John Smithson died. Charles was forced to move to London to continue his training with his other brother, Henry. Three years later their father, Richard, died and Henry returned to Malton leaving Charles alone in London. Mr Wray's own great, great, great grandfather, Richard, had already died.

It was during the period that Charles Smithson was alone in London that Charles Dickens acted as surety for a friend to buy into the Smithson's London business. The pair became lifelong friends.

Smithson, along with a partner, was the London agent for Richard Barnes, the attorney at Barnard

Castle, who became the model for John Brodie in Nicholas Nickleby. Smithson himself is mentioned in the preface as the professional friend from whom Dickens obtained a letter of introduction to Barnes.

Charles Smithson's period in London came to an end when his older brother Henry then died and he was forced to return to Malton.

He lived at Easthorpe Hall – now destroyed - until the autumn of 1843 and then the Abbey House in Old Malton, behind St Mary's Priory Church . Charles Dickens – and his wife Catherine – are known to have stayed at Easthorpe for three weeks in the July of 1843 because of various letters Dickens wrote from there. He also wrote a poem there and part of Martin Chuzzlewit. The character of Sairey Gamp is reckoned to be a housekeeper employed by Smithson who was mentioned in several of Dickens' letters.

The long visit was also recorded by newspapers. For example The Yorkshire Gazette of July 8th 1843 reported that 'the admired and talented author of Pickwick,' had 'visited the Old Malton Abbey and other remarkable places in the vicinity.'

It was during this sojourn that Dickens got to know a couple called Mr and Mrs Jump who lived in a house on what is now Middlecave Road . It is believed Mrs Jump was the model for Mrs MacStinger in Domeby and Son.

Perhaps not surprisingly, the 'Scrooge' offices on Chancery Lane and the bells in A Christmas Carol are said to be those of St Leonard 's Church on Church Hill in the town catch the public imagination most vividly. Here Mr Wray relies mainly on oral family stories. And yet there is still the copy sent to Charles Smithson's widow and the lay-out of the offices themselves which closely match those described in A Christmas Carol.

It's been a long process, on-going without any Government funding, but slowly the offices are taking the shape of an office, thanks largely to the town's admirable Dickens Society.

After Charles Smithson died, aged on 39, Dickens apparently told the family he based the character of Mr Spenlow in David Copperfield on his old friend.

CHARLES DICKENS

229

Charles Smithson, despite being a solicitor, had failed to leave a will. *"Every place has been searched that could be thought of and nothing has been found,"* wrote Dickens. The Spenlow character did the same thing.

What is certain is that Charles Dickens attended the funeral of Charles Smithson. A letter Dickens wrote to his wife about the event testifies to his sorrow. We even know the details of Dickens, heading north to attend at short notice, leaving York by fast carriage at 7.a.m. on April 5th and arriving just in time for the funeral at 9.30.a.m, a journey that takes about half-an-hour by car today.

Mr Wray's research gave him a thirst for more family research. The Trafalgar connection, from his father's side of the family, is certain as the family had a Trafalgar ribbon.

The trace further and further back to the time of the Norman Conquest and beyond makes Mr Wray's family tree look like something akin to that of the Royal Family's.

With that inspiring thought Mr Wray gets down to the business in the process of processing the enormous family tree into comprehensible copies for his own descendants.

Chancery Lane, Malton North Yorkshire

Monarchs and Muscle

Robert Blatchford

In *The Family and Local History Handbook 12* Anne Batchelor wrote about Lillian Ellis – Volta in her article – *Can U Lifter*. In the article Anne described that not even the strongest men could lift her. It was a phenomenon which attracted fame and media attention.

However there was an earlier performer of these amazing feats. Our attention was brought to this by one of our readers – Jackson W Roberts of the Isle of Wight. (Jackson has told me that his first name has been used in his family since the 1840s.)

Apparently Jackson was an avid reader of The Strand magazine as a child and still has four bound volumes. The Strand magazine was the publication that serialised work by many famous authors – Arthur Conan Doyle with Sherlock Holmes and Rider Haggard with his adventure stories.

In the bound volume for 1893 there is an article by Miss Phyllis Bentley – Monarchs and Muscle. The introduction to the article says that

'Miss Phyllis Bentley is well know to the public by her clever exhibition of experiments in lifting and balancing. These experiments she has had the honour of performing before many Crowned Heads of Europe, and in ... [her] interesting article [she] relates her experience of these Royal personages.'

Miss Phyllis Bentley

The Czar attempting to lift Miss Bentley

The first court she had the privilege of visiting was the Danish Court during the Golden Wedding Celebrations of the King and Queen of Denmark. Amongst the guests were The Czar of Russia, Crown Princes from Denmark and Greece and the Duke of Cumberland. Apparently the Czar had enormous strength and Phyllis was apprehensive when the Czar would attempt to lift her He had a reputation for a lack of 'gentleness where his purpose was thwarted.' The Czar took Phyllis by her elbows with the purpose of lifting her. To him at first it seemed an easy task and he did not use all his strength. However Phyllis remained firmly on the ground and the Czar began to lift in earnest. In spite of his efforts the Czar was unable to lift Phyllis from the ground. Finding that his efforts were in vain the Czar questioned Phyllis on how she had defeated his efforts. Phyllis explained that the angle she stood contained the secret of the power of resistance. The Czar then transferred his efforts to the Princess of Wales who he easily lifted and the same happened with the Czarina. However the task of lifting the Crown Princess of Denmark, who was of almost masculine build (Phyllis' description), proved to be somewhat more difficult. In the end the lack of the Princess's experience and the Czar's strength prevailed and he was able to lift her. He could not however lift Phyllis.

It was not only this test of strength that Phyllis demonstrated. She would hold up a billiard cue in her open hands and attempts would be made to push it to the ground. In one demonstration Prince George of Greece in exerting himself was unable to push the cue to the ground and merely snapped it in two. Phyllis says he did not strain her arms although he used the utmost effort.

Perhaps we should let Phyllis explain herself:

'I remember reading in a French newspaper a few months back an extraordinary account of my alleged mesmeric power, in which it was minutely explained how on one occasion I had mesmerised the Czar. His Majesty, it went on to say, told me to stand, against a wall, but I refused, and defied him to push me there. He raised his arm for that purpose, but I looked him in the eye, made certain passes over him, and, lo and behold, he was hypnotized!

What really happened was this: I placed the tips of my fingers against a wall, and asked the Czar to put his hands upon my shoulders and push me against the wall. His Majesty tried and did not succeed, that was all. There was, of course, nothing mesmeric about the experiment, it being performed upon precisely the same basis as the other tests I did with His Majesty; but, the story, as I have told, was that on this occasion I had actually mesmerized the Czar, and several times since I have been asked to do "the mesmeric test you did with the Emperor of Russia." I have repeated the test, but not as an exhibition of mesmerism, about which subject I neither care nor know anything.

I wish it to be clearly understood that there is nothing of a supernatural character about my

The Czar trying to push Miss Bentley against the wall.

exhibitions. What I do is perfectly understandable, and although the experiments are apparently widely different from each other, they are really one and all, with the exception of the chair test, performed upon precisely the same basis - that of the diversion of physical force.

There is nothing of the character of a trick about my experiments; the secret lies in the position I assume and the angle at which the cues are held. In this way I can, without the slightest strain or physical effort, nullify the force displayed by the strongest men. It is curious that it should be so, but so it is.

Some people think I must be exceedingly strong; on the contrary, I am anything but strong or robustly built, whilst my weight does not exceed eight stone. I have a knowledge of dynamics and a certain quickness of perception blended with a sufficiency of nerve and self-possession.

In the chair test everything depends upon how the chair is packed. I do not care how heavy the four or five men who sit upon it at one time really are, as long as they are properly balanced. I do not grasp the sides of the chair with my hands, as I actually use no physical effort in the act of getting the chair with its living weight up; I merely, as I say, catch it on the swing, and up it goes.

It not infrequently happens that when the men packed on the chair lose their balance the whole of them fall to the ground, a confused mass of struggling bodies and moving arms and legs. Such a sight is much relished by an audience

At one Palace the poor chair, in spite of its solidity, ran a serious risk of being broken into matchwood. Some members of the Court thought they would sit on the chair on their own account, whilst another exalted

Miss Bentley lifting the Czar, The Crown Prince of Denmark, Prince George of Greece and The Duke of Cumberland

personage did the lifting. They took their places, but, before the exalted personage had got himself in position, they slipped, and over they went, taking the chair with them. They kicked and struggled, whilst, amidst a roar of laughter, another member of the Court made a hasty sketch of the scene. I would much have liked to have gained possession of that sketch, it was all so exceedingly comic.

I am afraid I am indirectly responsible for a great many damaged Royal chairs and broken billiard-cues, for, as I have intimated elsewhere, my visit to a Court has always been followed by a vigorous attempt to reproduce my experiments, with the result that chairs have become disjointed under the strain of an unexpected weight, and cues have snapped at the angle at which they have been held.'

As Jackson surmised perhaps Lillian Ellis was related to Phyllis Bentley or the more likely explanation is that Lillian knew Phyllis and received training from her or merely perfected the techniques that Phyllis used. We shall never really know.

**Lillian Ellis
CAN U LIFTER?**

Image © Llyfrgell Genedlaethol Cymru The National Library of Wale

Sources for Welsh Family History
at Llyfrgell Genedlaethol Cymru – The National Library of Wales
Beryl Evans
South Reading Room Manager & Family History Co-ordinator

By tracing your Welsh family history you will be partaking in an ancient Welsh tradition dating back to beyond the Laws of Hywel Dda when it was necessary to know one's relatives to the ninth remove. In order to pursue this tradition you will at some point visit The National Library of Wales, which is considered to be the main centre for Welsh family history. The Library holds an abundance of records pertaining to the whole of Wales. The majority of these records can be consulted within the South Reading Room.

However, before a visit to the Library or indeed to any archive office, some preparatory work needs to be done, so as not to waste your time or that of the staff during a visit. Gather together as much information as you know and ask relatives for further details, searching for evidence such as certificates, photographs, letter and diaries. Organise this information and decide which branch you intend to follow and make a list of sources to be checked during the visit.

It is advisable for you to make yourself familiar with the website www.llgc.org.uk and to register online for a reader's ticket in advance www.llgc.org.uk/readersticket. Remember to bring with you two forms of identification to finish processing the application, one showing your current address. The National Library of Wales can be a great day out for all, not only those wishing to use the facilities in the Reading Rooms. On Mondays and Wednesdays at 11.00am and 2.15pm respectively, behind the scenes tours of the Library are held. All day on Wednesdays Reader Surgeries are held on topics such as family and local history, maps and photographs and the online catalogue and e-resources. Also, there are numerous exhibitions, a

café and shop. Further details can be found on the website which is constantly being updated.

Access to the majority of family history resources can be made in the South Reading Room. The records of civil registration for England and Wales since 1 July 1837 are held centrally by the General Register Office (GRO) or by the Superintendent Registrars of the local districts. The National Library of Wales does not hold or issue certificates, these can be obtained from the GRO or local registry offices. However, the Library does hold microfiche indexes from 1837 to 1998 and free online access from 1837 to 2006 through Findmypast and Ancestry.

Census returns are also available free of charge through these websites, including the 1911 census. The Library also holds microform copies of the census returns from 1841 to 1901 for the whole of Wales and some bordering English parishes. Also held are many transcripts and indexes to returns compiled by individuals and family history societies.

Since 1538 it has been necessary to keep a record of every baptism, marriage and burial in every parish, however, the earliest surviving registers for most Welsh parishes do not commence until 1660, with starting dates varying from parish to parish. The National Library of Wales holds copies of registers for over five hundred parishes, along with transcripts and indexes for many more. For dates of surviving parish register see Cofrestri Plwyf Cymru/Parish Registers of Wales, ed. By C J Williams and J Watts-Williams (Aberystwyth, 2000).

A joint project between the GSU and the Library has seen the digitisation of all available parish registers throughout Wales. These will in due course be available to view at the Library and archive offices throughout Wales.

From 1598 to around 1860 the incumbent of each parish sent transcripts of each register to the Bishop of the diocese, these are commonly known as bishop's transcripts. Again not many transcripts from Welsh parishes survive prior to 1660. All surviving bishop's transcripts are held at The National Library of Wales. For dates of surviving bishop's transcripts see Cofrestri Plwyf Cymru/Parish Registers of Wales, ed. By C J Williams and J Watts-Williams (Aberystwyth, 2000). Transcripts cease at dates varying from parish to parish during the mid to late nineteenth century; transcripts of marriages tended to cease in 1837 with the introduction of civil registration. The transcripts for the diocese of Bangor and Llandaf can be viewed on microfiche, whilst the original transcripts for the diocese of St David's, St Asaph and Swansea and Brecon can be consulted.

At The National Library of Wales there are bonds and affidavits relating to approximately 90,000 marriages that took place in Wales between 1616 and 1837. These were marriages that took place by licence rather than after banns. Both types of marriages were recorded in the parish register. Prior to the introduction of civil registration in 1837, almost every marriage in Wales had to take place in the parish church, between 1754 and 1836 nobody except Jews and Quakers were permitted by law to marry elsewhere. From 1837 onwards it was permissible to marry in a register office, a nonconformist chapel or Roman Catholic Church. The covering dates for each diocese are as follows:-

Bangor: 1757-1931 with four documents 1691-96;

Llandaf: 1690-1941 with a few 1665-1708;

St Asaph: 1690-1938 with a few 1616-89;

St David's: 1661-1867 with two documents 1616-1621.

The indexes to the pre-1837 bonds and affidavits can be searched online at http://cat.llgc.org.uk/cgi-bin/gw/chameleon?lng=en&skin=fh

Before marrying in a parish church you had to make sure there was no impediment to the marriage. This was usually done by publishing banns, by making a public declaration of the intention to marriage on three consecutive Sundays prior to the marriage. If both parties were from different parishes, banns had to be published at both parish churches.

The better off were able to avoid such publicity and delay by obtaining a licence, therefore, no banns were published. In Wales a licence was issued in the name of the Bishop. To obtain a licence the bridegroom would appear before a person authorised to act on behalf of the Bishop's court and swear on oath that he knew of no impediment to the marriage.

If the marriage took place in Wales it is quite likely that the affidavit or bond if survived is among those held at the Library.

Wills, letters of administration and other probate records provide another invaluable genealogical source. It must be realised that for most people neither a will or administration ever existed, however, it is always worth investigating. The wills

Llyfrgell Genedlaethol Cymru
The National Library of Wales

can be a rich source of information specially for the period prior to civil registration, listing family members, acquaintances, land and property owned or rented, along with details of personal effects.

Wills and administrations, proved before the introduction of Civil Probate on 11 January 1858 were proved by the ecclesiastical courts, these have been deposited at the Library. These wills have been indexed and free access is now available to the digital images of these wills through the Library website www.llgc.org.uk/probate

Wills of persons owning property in more than one diocese would be proved in the Prerogative Court of Canterbury. The Library holds microfilm copies of these wills from 1701 to 1858, the originals being held at The National Archives, Kew (PROB 11/459-2263).

The Library does not hold original wills after 1858 but has custody of register copy wills from five registries covering the Welsh counties except Montgomeryshire. The annual index to the wills and administrations for England and Wales (Calendar of Grants) is also available from 1858 to 1972.

The records of the nonconformists in Wales may be less comprehensive than those of the Anglican Church in Wales, however, they should not be forgotten. Many registers of dissenting congregations were deposited with the Registrar-General after the Civil Registration Act of 1836 and are now held at The National Archives. Microfilm copies of these registers can be viewed at The National Library of Wales. The registers can also be searched online at www.bmdregisters.co.uk

Some pre-1837 registers were copied locally before being surrendered to the Registrar-General others did not make it to London at all. Some of these registers have now been deposited at the Library. For covering dates of surviving registers please consult *Cofrestri Anghydffurfiol Cymru/Nonconformist Registers of Wales* ed. Dafydd Ifans (Aberystwyth: NLW, 1994).

There are many other nonconformist records that are of genealogical value such as members lists, contribution books and annual reports. Details of records in addition to registers can be found on the CAPELI database that can be accessed within the South Reading Room at the Library.

Denominational magazines often contain a section for births, marriages and deaths. Although primarily of value for particulars of members of the denomination in question, notes on members of other denominations may often appear in the

Image © Llyfrgell Genedlaethol Cymru – The National Library of Wales

following publications:

Yr Eurgrawn Wesleyaidd (1809, Wesleyan Methodist)

Seren Gomer (1818, Baptist)

Y Drysorfa (1831, Calvinistic Methodist)

Yr Haul (1835, Anglican Church in Wales)

Y Diwygiwr (1935, Congregational)

Yr Ymofynydd (1847, Unitarian)

For more information relating to denominational magazines visit the website www.llgc.org.uk/index.php?id+516

The Court of Great Sessions was established by the Second Act of Union in 1542 and remained in existence until its abolition in 1830. These records often relate to legal actions before various courts of law, but even information about persons of unimpeachable character as well as wrongdoers themselves is often given. Transcations concerning land were also conducted before some of these courts.

As far as family historians are concerned they are a class worth considering as occasionally challenge pedigrees were filed in connection with certain actions. A challenge pedigree was drawn up by the plaintiff to prove that he (or his wife) was related in the fourth degree in consanguinity to the sheriff (or his wife); the sheriff being normally responsible for empanelling the jury. Such a pedigree would be drawn up in order to request the court to appoint the coroner instead of the sheriff to appoint a jury.

The only class of Great Sessions records to be individually indexed are the Gaol Files. These are criminal records, usually serious offences (felonies) that came before the court. The Crime and Punishment database can be searched on the Library's website www.llgc.org.uk/sesiwn_fawr/index_s.htm For further information relating to the whole collection of records refer to Glyn Parry's book *A Guide to the Records of the Great Sessions in Wales* (Aberystwyth: NLW, 1995).

The manorial records held by the Library are mainly to be found with the estate records and listed with them. They are most comprehensive for Montgomeryshire (mainly the Powis Castle and Wynnstay estate records) with substanstial holdings for Glamorgan and Monmouthsire also (mainly, Badminton, Bute and Tredegar estate records) it should be noted that in many parts of Wales the manorial system never really took root. In conjunction with HMC, the Library produced a manorial database for Wales, which is available to search at www.nationalarchives.gov.uk/mdr/ and a volume, entitled *Welsh Manors and Their Records* by Helen Watt, (Aberystwyth, 2000) has also been published by the Library.

Most of the estate records and personal papers held by the Library are detailed in typescript schedules which are now also available to search on the Library's website http://isys.llgc.org.uk The estate records contain title deeds, rentals, account books, correspondence etc. Rentals may prove particularly useful in indicating a death or change of residence when a name disappears from a series of rentals. Records drawn up in the administration of an estate may enable you to discover names of owners and occupiers over several centuries.

The Library also holds many manuscript pedigrees. These vary from descendents of nobility, compiled in the later Middle Ages and copied time and again with additions by later genealogists, to charts which are the work of amateurs of modern times who have given copies of their compilations to the Library. For searchers particularly interested in the pedigrees of gentry families there are several important printed works available. Further information and a list of some of these works can be seen on our website www.llgc.org.uk/index.php?id=492

The above is far from being a comprehensive list of sources held at The National Library of Wales of genealogical sources. For further information on source for family history research it is worth consulting the Library's website www.llgc.org.uk/index.php?id=247

Probate Records at The National Library of Wales
Beryl Evans
South Reading Room Manager & Family History Co-ordinator

Pre-1858 Records

Wills, letters of administration and other probate records provide an invaluable historical and genealogical source of information not only to the family historian but also for social and local historians alike. It must be realised, however, that for most people neither will nor administration ever existed. Today, someone may consider making a will in mid-life by consulting a solicitor, however, until the mid-nineteenth century making a will tended to be a last minute consideration to tidy affairs in the last few days or even hours of life.

The testator would name the executor of his/her will and it is the duty of this person to obtain legal permission to administer the estate, this being called 'probate.' If someone dies without making a will or the will is invalid for any reason, that person will have died 'intestate.' In this situation the next of kin can obtain 'letters of administration' to distribute the estate. Probate was usually granted within a few months and mostly within a year of death. However, there are a few instances were it was granted on a later death within the family.

Until 1858, the making of a will was considered to be a religious duty and the proving of wills and granting letters of administration in England and Wales was the responsibility of ecclesiastical courts each having its own area of jurisdiction. Which court had jurisdiction in any given case was determined largely by the place of death and the extent and location of the estate of the deceased. Wills were normally proved in the Episcopal consistory court (the diocesan or bishop's court). If the estate comprised goods in two or more dioceses within the same province, probate was granted in either of the two provincial courts of the Archbishop of York and the Archbishop of Canterbury. The Prerogative Court of the Archbishop of York (PCY) administered the northern province (the northern dioceses of England which included the southern detachment of Flint), while the Prerogative Court of the Archbishop of Canterbury (PCC) covered the southern province

Image © Llyfrgell Genedlaethol Cymru - The National Library of Wales

(the southern English dioceses and Wales). If the deceased had held goods in both provinces, probate was undertaken by PCC that had over-riding jurisdiction throughout England and Wales.

The right to grant probate was also held by certain church and secular courts called peculiars because they were 'of peculiar or exempt jurisdiction' i.e. outside the authority of the archdeacon or bishop. There was only one peculiar in Wales, that of Hawarden, co. Flint, which had jurisdiction in the parish of Hawarden only.

The pre-1858 probate records deposited at The National Library of Wales comprise those of the Episcopal consistory courts of **St. Asaph, Bangor, St. David's,** and **Llandaff,** the consistory court of the archdeaconry of **Brecon,** the peculiar of

The following is a brief summary of the position in Wales:

Probate Court	Jurisdiction (counties)
St. Asaph	Most of Denbigh and Flint; Parts of Caernarfon, Meirioneth, Montgomery and Salop
Bangor	Bangor, Anglesey; most of Caernarfon; parts of Denbigh, Meirioneth and Montgomery
St. Davids	Cardigan, Carmarthen and Pembroke; part of Glamorgan (deanery of Gower)
Llandaff	Most of Glamorgan and Monmouth
Brecon	Brecon; most of Radnor; parts of Monmouth, Montgomery and Hereford
Hawarden	Parish of Hawarden, co. Flint
Chester	Parts of Flint and Denbigh (one Parish – Holt)
Hereford	This group has been transferred to the Herefordshire Record Office. Parts of Monmouth, Montgomery, and Radnor. This court also had jurisdiction in those parishes which were partly in Shropshire and partly in Montgomery i.e. Alberbury, Mainstone and Worthen

Hawarden, and the Welsh wills proved at Episcopal consistory court of **Chester**. There were no ecclesiastical courts in Wales below the diocesan level. In probate matters, the consistory court of the archdeaconry of Brecon, one of the four archdeaconries of the diocese of St. David's, acted as the diocesan court in a local capacity.

In tracing a pre-1858 will/administration, the first step is to establish in which court the grant might have been made and where that court's records are held. Since probate jurisdictions did not always follow county boundaries, this can sometimes prove difficult, especially with regard to parishes bordering England and Wales.

Information concerning the probate courts having jurisdiction in Wales, the counties and parishes they covered, and the dates of surviving records is given below. Two indispensable guides to probate records in general are *Probate Jurisdictions: Where to look for wills* by Jeremy Gibson and Else Churchill (FFHS, 5th ed., 2002) and *Wills and other probate records* by Karen Grannum and Nigel Taylor (TNA, 2004). The series of county/parish maps published by the Institute of Heraldic and Genealogical Studies, Northgate, Canterbury, Kent, is very useful for showing the pre-1858 ecclesiastical jurisdictions. These maps, covering Wales, England and Scotland can be consulted in the South Reading Room of The National Library of Wales.

The pre-1858 records at the Library cover the whole of Wales except for fifteen border parishes which came within the jurisdiction of the Episcopal consistory court of Hereford, but they include seventeen English parishes which came under Welsh courts.

The main types of probate records are the will, the administration bond and the inventory. Inventories are not common after the 18th century. Associated documents which occasionally accompany the main records include executors' and administrators' accounts, and documents such as deposition and bond of tuition and curation.

The original wills and administration bonds generally survive from about 1600 except for Bangor, where very few have survived prior to 1635. There are, however, records in original or copy form dating back to the latter half of the 16th century, but survivals are few. The earliest surviving volumes of register copy wills are for St. Asaph (from 1565) and Brecon (from 1543) both pre-dating the surviving original records. During the Interregnum, the local courts ceased to function, with resultant gaps in the Bangor and St. Asaph records between 1648 and 1660 and in Brecon and Carmarthen (St. David's diocese) between 1653 and 1660. Despite this, some wills, mainly for Glamorgan, were proved during this period at Llandaf. The records of the court of civil commission which functioned during the Commonwealth are filed at The National Archives with those of PCC.

The following is a brief summary of the holdings for each court, giving covering dates only. Gaps in the series have not been noted. The complete index is now available to search online through the Library website.

The holdings of the Welsh Probate Courts in the Library

St. Asaph	Original wills etc, 1557-1858. Register copy wills 1521-1709. MS indexes, 1583-1857
Bangor	Original wills etc, 1576-1858. (There are very few wills before 1635). Register copy wills and administrations, 1790, 1851-8. Published index to pre-1700 records. MS indexes, 1700-1858
St. David's	Original wills etc, 1556-1858. Register copy wills, 1703-1858. MS indexes, 1600-1858 (archdeaconries of St David's (Pembrokeshire), Cardigan and Carmarthen). [The archdeaconries are roughly equivalent to the historic counties, but the archdeaconry of Cardigan included a good number of north Pembrokeshire and some Carmarthenshire parishes, and the archdeaconry of Carmarthen included 23 Glamorgan parishes – deanery of Gower]
Llandaff	Original wills etc, 1568-1857. Register copy wills, 1695-1844. MS indexes, 1575-1857
Brecon	Original wills etc, 1557-1857. Register copy wills, 1543-1858. Published index to pre-1660 records. MS indexes, 1660-1857
Hawarden	Original wills etc, 1554-1858. Printed index, 1554-1800 in Publications of Flintshire Historical Society, Vol IV. MS indexes, 1752-1857
Chester	Original wills etc, 1521-1858. Typescript indexes, 1521-1857. Printed indexes, 1545-1837 in Publications of Lancashire and Cheshire Record Society

Probate act books are available for all the courts (except Bangor and Brecon and for the Welsh wills proved at Chester), but surviving series are incomplete.

An *Index of the Probate Records of the Bangor Consistory Court, Vol I: Pre-1700* was published by the Library in 1980 and *Archdeaconry of Brecon Probate Records, Vol I: Pre-1660* in 1989. Abstracts and indexes, of most of the pre-1858 wills for the consistory courts of Bangor, St. Asaph, Llandaff and St. Davids, and the archdeaconry of Brecon are also available on microfiche prepared by the Genealogical Society of Utah and available through their website www.familysearch.org

The pre-1858 wills have been indexed and free access is now available to the digital images of these wills through The National Library of Wales website www.llgc.org.uk/probate

Post 1858 Records

In 1858, responsibility for probate was transferred from the complex system of church courts to a simpler system of civil probate registries. The search for a post-1858 will become a comparatively easier task. Since 12 January 1858, wills and administrations in England and Wales have been proved and granted in either the Principal Registry

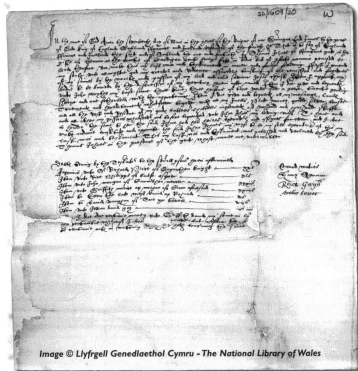

Image © Llyfrgell Genedlaethol Cymru - The National Library of Wales

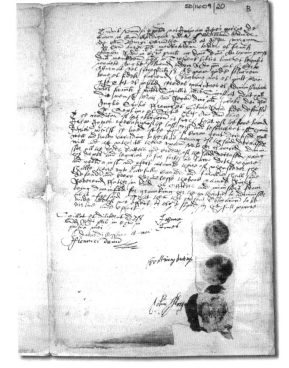

Image © Llyfrgell Genedlaethol Cymru - The National Library of Wales

of the Family Division, or the appropriate district registry. Until 1941, the district registries made a second copy of the will which was entered and bound into volumes of register copy wills. It is these volumes of copy wills from the district registries having jurisdiction in Wales which constitute the post-1858 probate records deposited in the Library.

The post-1858 records comprise those from the district registries at **St. Asaph, Bangor, Carmarthen, Llandaff** and **Hereford**. The exception is Shrewsbury which covered Montgomeryshire. The following details regarding jurisdictions and record holdings are based on information contained in the typescript schedule of probate records. It should be noted that the jurisdictions reflect the territorial position contemporary with the period of records i.e. 1858-1941, not the current situation. Territorial jurisdiction was abolished in 1926, and the registries at St. Asaph and Hereford were closed in 1928.

District Registry	Jurisdiction (counties)
St. Asaph	Denbigh, Flint and Merioneth
Bangor	Anglesey and Caernarfon
Carmarthen	Cardigan, Carmarthen, Pembroke, and part of Glamorgan (Gower)
Llandaff	Monmouth and Glamorgan (except Gower)
Hereford	Brecon, Radnor and Hereford

The post-1858 records consist of large bound volumes of copy wills spanning the years 1858 to 1941, when registries ceased to copy wills into registers. They cover all the historic counties of Wales (except for Montgomeryshire), and one

English county – Herefordshire. Post-1858 Montgomeryshire wills were proved at the Shrewsbury District Registry whose records are at the Shropshire Record Office.

Contemporary manuscript indexes together with modern card indexes cover most of the records. Deficiencies can be made up by using the printed *Calendar of Grants*, an annual index of all wills and administrations granted in England and Wales since 1858. This index is available at The Principal Registry, most District Probate Registries and some local record offices, and for the period 1858-1972 at The National Library of Wales.

A brief summary of the holdings for each registry is given below.

St. Asaph
Register copy wills, 1858-1928. There are no separate MS indexes, but indexes can be found in the volumes for 1860-1 and 1865-1923

Bangor
Register copy wills, 1858-1941. Card index, 1858-1941

Carmarthen
Register copy wills, 1858-1941. MS indexes, 1858-1923. Card index, 1924-1941

Llandaff
Register copy wills, 1858-1940. MS indexes, 1858-1905

Hereford
Register copy wills, 1858-1928. MS indexes, 1858-1928

In addition to the official probate records, some wills and inventories and other papers associated with probate can be found in the consistory court papers filed with the diocesan records of the Church in Wales. The index to these records can be accessed through The National Library of Wales online catalogue http://cat.llgc.org.uk Hundreds of wills occur in the Library's collections of family estate and personal papers; some of these may not survive in the official probate records or may never have been proved, or may have been proved outside of Wales, these can also be searched for using the online catalogue.

Of the 190,00 or so wills held at the Library, only some 1000 documents have been written in Welsh, with over three quarters of these in the Diocese of Bangor. To give some indication as to the variety of information that can be gleaned from a will here are a few examples. Amongst the collection are wills of the famous – Twm Sion Cati alias Thomas Johnes, Fountaine Gate, Caron (SD1609-20), the Welsh Robin Hood and that of Howell Harris, the famous Welsh religious reformer (BR1773-51). Details of a philanderer namely Oakley Leigh, Lampeter (SD1788-80) 'Agent to the tyrannical Squire, Sir Herbert Lloyd.' The parish register recorded his extramarital exploits and no less than eleven 'natural' children were named as beneficiaries in his will.

Miles Bassett of Cardiff (LL1680-10) gives details of a family disagreement! 'And [I could put] as little

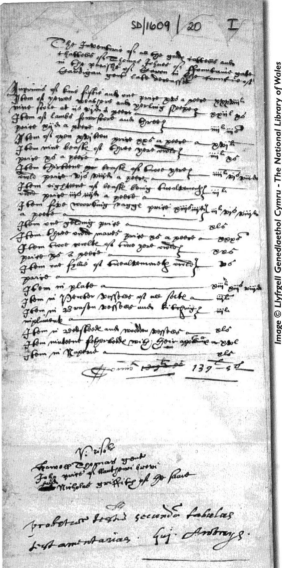

Image © Lyfrgell Genedlaethol Cymru - The National Library of Wales

confidence in my crabbed churlish unnaturall, heathenish and unhuman sonne inlaw Leyson Evans and Anne his wife; I never found noe love, shame nor honestie with them . . . but basenesse and falsehood, knaverie and deceipt in them all, ever unto me . . . they were my greatest Enemies, I had no comfort in anie of them, but trouble & sorrow ever, they sued me in Londone in the Exchequier and in the Comonplease, and in the Marches at Ludlowe, and in the great Sessions at Cardiff and thus they have vexed me ever of a long time.'

Therefore, a lot of interesting information can be found in many of the wills, giving an insight into the social conditions, family life and much more. Wills and inventories are an unvaluable source for family historians and should not be overlooked.

Genes, Dixons and Edinburgh
Glenys Shepherd

The most fascinating thing to me when I study my Family History is the way in which past generations constantly re-emerge in their descendants.

When a child is born it is only a matter of days or even hours before doting relatives begin to offer their opinions on *who the baby looks like.* Move on a few years when the child takes up activities, interests and develop abilities of their own, when the next query comes *I wonder who she/he takes after to be good at that?*

Just one unusual snippet of information is enough to send me on a trail, down a road which eventually leads to many different avenues. In my case, the trail of *The Dixon's* led me to Sudbury in Suffolk, to the Archives of the Grenadier Guards at Wellington Barracks in London, Scunthorpe, Liverpool, Bolton, Wigan, Scarborough and, most recently, to Fife, Dundee and Edinburgh, which is not where the trail ends as I had thought. More of that later.

Here a word of caution! If consecutive Census Returns place your family into two or three areas, don't jump to the conclusion that that is where they were during the ten year periods of census. They could quite easily have moved away, but then moved back to one of the areas.

Computers and web sites are of course great tools but it's much more interesting to spend time in the area you are researching. Also local sources and personalities in the area can be a valuable tool in your research.

My research into my *Dixon Family* began in the 1950's when I was ten years old (my mother, Florence, was one of six children born to George Edward Shawcross Dixon and Eliza Cant during the1890's to early, 1900's). I was the youngest of all

the grandchildren so granny was in her late 70's and my only remaining grandparent when she told me some family stories. Of course, over time, memories play tricks and some facts become distorted, so over the years I have realised that some of the stories were not completely accurate (after all, grandmas don't want to bare their souls to ten year olds!) and realised later on that granny had quite a dry sense of humour. Let me give you an example, granny told me that granddad (who died in 1914) had been the Leader of the Grenadier Guards' Orchestra and had been rewarded for his services to music. The truth was, granddad had been entered into the 2nd Battalion of the Grenadier Guards for a term of twelve years at the age of thirteen to *make a man of him'* (he was then small for his age) and on the Census of 1881 was listed as *'a drummer.'* As his father was a Professor of Music, he obviously thought it would be good career move for the young George, so he was entered as *'Drummer Boy.'* In fact, he strongly disliked his period of service. He did eventually achieve the post of Full Drummer with excellent standards of musical abilities in playing the drums, fife and probably piano.

A copy of granny and granddad's Marriage Certificate led me to the Archives of Wellington Barracks, where I was given a photocopy of his service history. When he left the Guards, he entered the music halls.

Tracing his story then became difficult, but I eventually pieced it together using dates on Birth Certificates and with occasional photographs lent to me by my cousins. It transpired that his children were mostly born in several towns in which he had worked - Scunthorpe; Stockport; Bolton and finally Wigan. He died aged 44 in 1914, leaving a family of eight children, and many of the girls went into service at the earliest opportunity (which they all hated!). One of the little snippets of information I obtained from granddad George's Army History was that during the period of time he was in the Guards, great granddad George had changed his next of kin address from Scarborough to Fife, but I didn't have an exact date; I only knew it was somewhere between 1883 - 1895 whilst granddad was in the Guards. So I now reached the conclusion, quite wrongly as it happened, that great granddad George had taken his family to Scotland, as I had photographs of 1906 taken in Edinburgh, one labelled *'Granddad George visiting his brothers at their grocers shop in Princes Street, Edinburgh.'* It later emerged that I had put two and two together and made not four, but five.

I decided to go to Edinburgh and also to visit Fife - I could not work out what he was doing there if the shop was in Edinburgh.

With two of my family for support, I went to

Great Grandad's Brothers in their Edinburgh shop waiting for George to visit

Edinburgh. The next full day we went to Kirkcaldy. The change of address on granddad's army record was difficult to decipher due partly to the quality of the handwriting but this was compounded by the fact that the address had been altered on the records. To me it looked like:

Next of Kin: George (Father) 6, Deckhand (or Decksland) Bridge Street *(Indecipherable word?)* Kirkcaldy.

We spent time at the Library and at the Kirkcaldy Museum but we could not find any address which corresponded to the address we had in spite of lengthy searches of Census etc. Then we did have a small breakthrough. The Librarian Researcher found a Trade Directory for the right time span showing a *'Dickson'* trading at Dicks Land and it was near to Bridge Street about a mile from the town centre, close to the coast. There was a stream, a Bridge Street and an old mill (now converted into other uses). The buildings around corresponded with an old street map - the only place *'Dicks Land'* could have been was a small piece of land between the mill and the stream, so for the time being that was it. It appeared to have been a fruitless search as we tried to find out what our Professor of Music great grandfather was doing in a little business premises in Kirkcaldy - we thought it had to be correct even if Dixon was spelled differently so, at that time, I filed the information for *'future perusal'* whilst being completely confused about why he would be there (more later!).

Now for query number two, the grocery photograph *'In Princes Street.'* A brief walk down the street was perfectly useless (never mind it was a dry day!). *'The truth about the shop.'* For a small fee, I spent a few hours at the Scottish Genealogical Society headquarters in Edinburgh. The members were incredibly efficient and knowledgeable. I went without an appointment but was shown around their little gem of beautifully catalogued resources. I was asked to show them the information I already had and tell them what I would like to research. Immediately they pointed out that grand though the premises were, they would definitely not be located on Princes Street.

A search through a few Trade Directories revealed *'Dixon Brothers - Provision and Tea Merchants.'* The address proved to be about a mile from Princes Street, very close to a rear entrance to Holyrood. Unfortunately the store had been demolished, so, once again, we only had a photograph of *'where the shop had been'* but we did happily think that because it was a very substantial business close to the Palace, *'Dixon Brothers'* might have supplied Royalty at some time! So, the Dixon family had moved from Scarborough to Edinburgh in the 1890's hadn't they? Well, actually - er - no. Wrong again.

I spent some time in the Edinburgh Room at Edinburgh Central Library. I wanted to find out

more about the Dixon family so I started with the Telephone and Trade Directories for 1940, then worked my way back through the last available one of 1880, checking each *'Dixon'* entry. From my notes I then made a flow chart of all the family members, entering their address and businesses. The last one was from 1880. Hold on a minute! They were not there then - they were in Scarborough on the 1881 Census!

Time ran out, we left Edinburgh with more questions than answers. Never mind, a good excuse to go back to Edinburgh. I do not work for the Edinburgh Tourist Board, but I have to say that it is a city of fantastic resources for Family Historians. A lot of assistance is available if you encounter difficulties with your research. The organisation at the Records Office and New Century House is excellent. I made an appointment with the assisted research service, sent advance copies of what I had, and an outline of what I wanted to know - from this they decided it should be possible to help me to achieve my aims, and confirmed an appointment. There is a fee payable per hour (in 2010 it was £20 per hour).

In one hour I discovered the answers to so many unanswered questions and also dispelled a lot of

myths and misconceptions.

One thing I had wanted to find out was where great granddad George was buried in Edinburgh. Surprise, surprise - he had not died anywhere in Scotland. From the dates on Births, Marriages and Death Certificates, it was possible to put his death into a time span of 1924 - 1940 but not in Scotland. But also, after the 1881 census, it transpired that great grandmother had died before 1891, the youngest child was very young, so the family rumour that he had married for a second time appeared to be correct - but it didn't occur in Scotland, so it appeared that after her death, he moved to Scotland but eventually moved back to England to re-marry.

So I checked in the 1891 census to see if the Dixon's were established by then in Edinburgh. Yes, there was a Dixon family in Edinburgh on the 1891 census but, although most of the children's names were almost identical to great granddad's children, they were a different family.

I checked again! - great granddad George and children (no wife, who had died by now) had actually moved to Dundee. From the census, I found the children's ages and jobs. 'Apprentice Grocer' etc. So the boys had qualified to 'Master Grocers' by the time they moved to Edinburgh. (Probably these moves were assisted by passenger boat from Scarborough - to Dundee).

So what of 'the other' Edinburgh Dixon family? They had moved from England to Edinburgh with their many children - only the last one had been born in Edinburgh. It appears that the father was most likely to have been a brother of great granddad George.

It became obvious that my granddad was only one of his generation to have followed a musical career, but his sisters were milliners, 'fashion modistes' and artists. Two of the sisters who were milliners and moved to Denton near Manchester, where their husbands ran 'Hat Manufacturers' businesses, for which Denton was renowned. One of the sisters - Marguerite - married an electrical engineer in 1902 in Dundee. I had been told her surname was Mackerslie (a name, I must admit, I had not heard of)

but from their wedding certificate it emerged that her husband John had changed his name from Muckersie when they married (it sounded better). They moved to Denton, but later on, on retirement, they moved to Angus. From an American Web Site, my sister found brief details of Arthur A. Dixon, Anna Dixon and Arthur Percy Dixon, all portrait painters and/or artists.

From a visit to the R.S.A. in Edinburgh (Research Room) I obtained a list of 'Dixon' Artists - names - dates of birth and death, list of addresses of where they were living when the listed paintings were produced - and yes they were relatives! Anna in particular was very prolific, as she lived to 1959 - she was 86 when she died. I would love to see some of their work, but I do not know if it will be possible. The other milliner sister, Edie, married John Broadbent and they had a son called Lees.

When great granddad George died, all his children, except the very youngest one, could play at least two instruments. Of their children, my cousins, there are professional musicians, artists and singers. And the present generation? One of the boys is a Director of Music, and, like my granddad George and great granddad George, is an excellent musician who has moved house a few times to further his career, and another is a flautist. And the next up and coming generation? We will have to wait and see, but flutes and keyboards are beginning to appear. So, a lot of queries answered. Many myths dispelled. Proof that abilities can and do descend through the genes. Also, a photograph of granddad George and one of my brothers - same face - 50 years between. Great Aunt Marguerite's photograph - identical to my mother. Great Aunt Edie - identical to one of my cousins. So, talents and appearances go on through the generations - how long will this continue!

Now then - I'd like to know more about . . . ! (Next time!)

Thank you to my brother Trevor and sister Pam for accompanying me on one of my trips to Edinburgh, and to Karen Roach at the Records Office, to the Library Staff at the Edinburgh Room and the members of the Scottish Genealogical Society.

Great Grandad's
Funeral Procession
Lower Ince, Wigan

243

Scottish Land and Property Records

Chris Paton

If there are two fundamental rules which apply when carrying out Scottish family history research, they are:
• Always work from the known to the unknown, and
• Scotland is not England!

Nowhere does this become more obvious then in the records of Scottish land and property ownership, which are completely unlike those of the rest of the United Kingdom.

Familiar sources

If carrying out research into a Scottish property, there are a lot of useful resources available which will be familiar to everyone. Basic occupancy of a property – essentially who was where and when – can often be revealed through the registration of vital records in a family, whilst various list records such as directories, electoral rolls and census entries can be found in local libraries and archives, or online at sites such as ScotlandsPeople - www.scotlandspeople.gov.uk and Ancestry - www.ancestry.co.uk

It is always worth understanding the nature of the records you are looking at, for example, early directories may be a year out of date prior to their publication, and sometimes simply lifted information from the previous edition without it being checked again. Census entries on the other hand can be much more useful than simply noting who was in the house, with additional columns such as that detailing how many rooms there were in the house with one or more windows.

Maps can also be very revealing, providing a fascinating insight into how your ancestors' environments have changed over the years, particularly when considered in chronological order. The best maps source to get started with is the fantastic National Library of Scotland collection at www.nls.uk/maps/index.html with holds over 20,000 digitised images. This includes town maps from 1580 onwards, Timothy Pont's maps from the late 16th Century and Ordnance Survey maps from the mid 19th to early 20th centuries. The Royal Commission on the Ancient and Historical Monuments of Scotland website at www.rcahms.gov.uk contains the equally useful Canmap service, which allows you to search for historic sites, and the Canmore database, which provides all sorts of information on properties, including some old photos and diagrams. Much of this information is now also accessible on the new ScotlandsPlaces website at www.scotlandsplaces.gov.uk which also provides free to view 18th century tax records for every county, and additional resources.

Such resources can sometimes throw up remarkable stories about a property. Whilst working for the BBC in 2002, I commissioned an archaeological dig in the grounds of Castle Menzies in Perthshire for the untransmitted pilot programme of what eventually became the BBC2 series 'Time Flyers.' The dig was commissioned on the basis of an aerial photograph discovered on Canmore which showed an unusual crop mark immediately to the castle's east. An old map by Pont, found on the NLS map site, seemed to imply this might have been a former garden. During the excavation we soon confirmed that this was indeed the case, and from documents discovered that it had been abandoned during the second Jacobite rebellion of 1745-46, when the Duke of Cumberland had ordered the garden's walls to be torn down.

Knowing who lived in a property or area, and gaining an understanding of that property or area are two sides of the triangle to pursue with land research – the third is ownership.

Feudalism

The big difference between Scotland and the rest of the United Kingdom concerning land ownership is that until 2004, Scottish land was held through the feudal

Excavation at Castle Menzies in 2001 confirming the former garden as depicted on a 16th century map by Timothy Pont
©Chris Paton

system, long abandoned in England and Wales in the Middle Ages.

Feudalism was introduced to Scotland in the 12th century. It basically concerned a series of relationships between dominant *'superiors'* and their subordinate *'vassals,'* with the monarch the highest superior in the land. To manage the Crown's estates, large tracts were carved up by the monarch into parcels of land known as *'feus'* and passed on to various high ranking nobles or institutions as *'feuars.'* In return, the feuars made an annual or twice yearly payment called a *'feu duty'* to the superior (originally through military service), after which they were said to be *'infeft.'* These feudal agreements were hereditary, and so the land could be passed on to a feuar's heir after death. For most of these great landholders, the agreements were secure, with rebellion the only real event that could possibly see them dispossessed (as happened to many after the Jacobite uprisings of the 18th century).

These vassals could in turn become superiors themselves by further dividing the land into smaller portions. This was known as *'subinfeudation'* and made the monarch's vassals into *'subject superiors,'* with their own vassals beneath them becoming feuars also. This process of subdivision carried on again and again down a sort of feudal pyramid, to the level of common merchants and lesser nobles with much smaller holdings. As long as the feu duties continued to trickle up to the Crown, everyone was happy.

Not all of Scotland was feudal, however. An exception was the system known as *'allodial'* *'odal'* or *'udal'* tenure, basically granting outright ownership. Church property was held in this way, and Odal Law still exists in the Orkney and Shetland islands to this day, particularly on the coastline, where land had anciently become the absolute freehold property of a family once it had remained in the family for four generations.

Charters

Scottish property transactions under the feudal system were recorded in charters or writs, which stipulated various agreed conditions between the vassal and the superior, including the amount of feu duty to be paid, and any penalty clauses.

Charters could exist in many forms. A

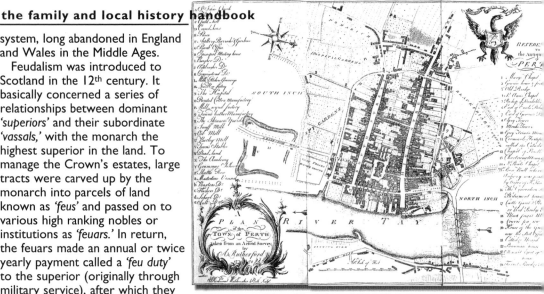

Map of Perth from 1774 ©Chris Paton

'Charter of Feu' was granted upon the original creation of a feu, and was usually reproduced almost word for word in subsequent charters dealing with the same property. If a feuar sold his property to another buyer, a *'Charter of Resignation'* was issued, temporarily returning the land on which it was built to the control of the superior, and a *'Charter of Confirmation'* then granted to the new owner to complete the purchase. A *'Charter of Novodamus'* could also be granted, where land was temporarily returned to a superior for a mistake to be corrected in the wording or a change made to the document, before being granted back to the vassal.

Charters are held in many locations. The National Archives of Scotland (NAS) holds a *Calendar of Charters* under RH6, which is indexed (containing details on charters recorded between 1142 and 1600), and also a series of legal writs under RH7 (for records from 1601 to 1830). Additional charters are also found within its Gifts and Deposits collections (GD), searchable online at www.nas.gov.uk/onlinecatalogue

The Scottish Archive Network (SCAN) at www.scan.org.uk describes charters held within local archives, whilst the National Register of Archives for Scotland (NRAS) is another possibility at www.nas.gov.uk/onlineRegister for privately held records. Some charter summaries for records in Dundonald (1219-1672) and Wigtown (1214-1681) can be found on Ancestry, whilst the *Records of the Parliament of Scotland to 1707* site at **www.rps.ac.uk** has some records for the pre-Union period with England, from 1235 to 1707.

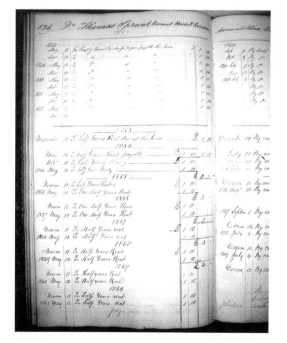

Charter showing the 'resignation' of lands of Blackfriars in Perth back into the control of its feudal superior *'ad remanentiem'* i.e. permanently ©Chris Paton

Sasines

Charters are often difficult to find, but sasines (pronounced 'sayzins') are a much handier alternative. At the end of any charter, a superior would give an instruction to bailies to draw up an *'Instrument of Sasine,'* a legal document to allow the transaction to be recorded in the *Register of Sasines,* with 'sasine' being the act of taking possession of the land.

Property transactions have been recorded in these registers from as early as 1599 in some counties, though mostly from 1617 onwards. Until 1868 they were recorded in *'Burgh Registers'* for the country's royal burghs (with most pre-1809 registers still held in local archives), in *'Particular Registers'* for individual counties across the country; or in a *'General Register'* based in Edinburgh, for transactions across most of Scotland (with the exception of the three Lothian counties), including property based across two or more counties.

Digitised abridgements for the particular and

Rental book from King James VI Hospital in Perth ©Chris Paton

general registers from 1781 to 1868 have been made available for view at the NAS. They can be searched by surname or place name, and will usually give enough information to let you know who granted a piece of land, the name of the recipient, and the arrangement by which it was transferred. However, the original sasine itself can also be ordered up, and can provide further information such as a description of the land in question – useful for noting the exact boundaries of a property, and some physical details of the house itself.

A list of printed indexes for registers prior to 1781 can be consulted online at www.nas.gov.uk/guides/sasines.asp. The pay-per-view Genhound website at www.genhound.com contains an index to many pre-1781 particular registers, whilst many sasine records can also be ordered up through the FamilySearch catalogue www.familysearch.org on microfilm and viewed at a Family History Centre,

In 1868 the General Register was reorganised into county based divisions, and the Particular Registers were abolished (though burgh registers continued for some time after). An index to entries within this new General Register, compiled by place name from 1872, can be consulted at the NAS.

From 1979, a newly created *'Land Register,'* maintained by Registers of Scotland www.ros.gov.uk has in turn been slowly replacing the General Register. In the old system, properties were identified within sasines by a physical description of which other properties bordered it in all sides. In the new Land Register, they are now pinpointed using Ordnance Survey data. From 1870, a series of search sheets was created for each property listed in the old General Registers, and those from 1875 to 1993 have been digitised and can be consulted at the Registers of Scotland offices in Glasgow or Edinburgh, for a small fee. They are invaluable, giving long lists of transactions for a property from the present day back to 1875.

Inheritance

Inheritance was another way through which land could be conveyed, but Scottish land and property could not be bequeathed in a will until 1868. Prior to this the inheritance rules of primogeniture applied. Before heirs could legally take possession of a property, they had to have the fact that they were heirs recognised by the superior to whom they were about to become the vassal. Many just moved in without sorting out the paperwork, only to realise years later that they needed the document when seeking to sell the property on, whilst others argued about who had the legal right to inherit in the first place! As such, don't always expect to find the relevant documents immediately after the previous owner's death.

There were two ways to be so recognised, dependent on where the superiority lay. If an heir was to take hold of property which had the Crown as its direct superior, he or she would have to go before a jury of local landowners to have the right to inherit confirmed. The jury would deliberate and then return or 'retour' its findings to the Royal Chancery in Edinburgh, with a copy issued to the heir. These recorded 'Services of Heirs' were mainly written in Latin until 1847. Records from 1530 to 1699 were indexed as the *Inquisitionum ad Capellam Regis Retornatarum Abbreviatio*, available at the NAS or on a CD from the Scottish Genealogy Society - www.scotsgenealogy.com

From 1700 you then need to consult the *Indexes to the Services of Heirs* at the NAS, but again, the index from 1700 to 1859 is available on a CD. The process continued until 1964, but at this point most land was being conveyed through wills, making the process virtually redundant. The records usually show genealogical relationships identifying from whom the property was inherited, and also contain terms such as 'Heir General' (a person succeeding by force of law), or 'Heirs-Portioners' (women who jointly inherited a property if there was no male successor), which can be equally revealing genealogically. It is important to note that some Services were never retoured from sheriff and burgh courts, but may still be recorded in their registers, whilst courts for areas known as 'regalities' were never required to send them to the Royal Chancery in the first place – so you may have to dig a little deeper!

If the land was controlled by a subject superior lower down the chain, rather than the Crown, an heir could instead make do with a document known as a 'Precept of Clare Constat,' which showed that the subject superior clearly recognised the heir's right to inherit. Even with this the heir could still go through the Services of Heirs procedure, to make the position absolutely crystal clear.

Occasionally you might come across mention of the words 'tailzie' within the records of wealthier families. It was actually possible for a landowner to dictate the course of his land's

The Registers of Scotland Office George Square, Glasgow
©Chris Paton

disposal long after his death by creating a deed called a tailzie, through which he could lay down a series of conditions that had to be adhered to. The breach of such conditions could actually force his successor to give up the land altogether. Tailzies can be extremely useful in identifying entire families, as they would list the name of the person to whom the land should go upon the death of the present incumbent, but also suggest alternative lines should that person die, and in the order that that succession should take place. Often within a tailzie, if the line of inheritance should fall onto a daughter or other female member of the family, a condition would be set whereby she could only inherit the land if she first married somebody with the same surname as the creator of the tailzie, or somebody who would be willing to take on that name. In addition, that husband would also have to assume the set of Arms inherited by his wife.

This would allow the identity of that family, and more importantly, the political weight of that family name, to remain undiminished in an area. The Register of Tailzies, kept from 1688, is located at the NAS (RT1, with an index catalogued under RT3/1-3). Land could be removed from a tailzie, or *'disentailed,'* from 1848 onwards, the details of which are also included in the register. From 1914, the register in fact only has details of such disentails.

Rents, valuations and estate papers

Feuars could lease out their properties to tenants. Locating such agreements through estate records, rental rolls, etc., can be done through the catalogues mentioned above, though such records can be patchy.

A useful set of records which can be of immense help is the Valuation Rolls from 1855 to 1989, which recorded annual rents worth more than £4 in value, along with the sitting tenants and their occupations, the owners, and any feu duties or payments due. The rolls are held both in local county archives and at the NAS, where a copy was legally required to be deposited, and which can now be consulted on microfilm. The Valuation Roll for Glasgow in 1913-14 can be viewed online at www.theglasgowstory.com

For Dumfriesshire, several rolls from 1896-97 have been digitised and made freely available at www.maxwellancestry.com/ancestry/resources.htm

At the time of writing, digitised records for Perthshire from 1857-1899 are being indexed by Ancestry, and many more records for the whole country are soon due to be placed onto the ScotlandsPeople website - www.scotlandspeople.gov.uk from 1855 to 1916.

Another useful online tool is found on the FamilyRelatives subscription based website www.familyrelatives.com being a *Return of Scottish Landowners* as printed by the House of Lords in 1874. This details the names and addresses of every landowner holding more than one acre in Scotland, and is arranged in counties. It details returns for all those living outside of a burgh containing more than 20,000 individuals, and separately for those living within such a burgh. The records also record how much land was owned, the annual value of the land and the heritage derived from it, with the definition of an owner including feuars, leaseholders of 99 years or more, and liferenters. The same records are also available at The Genealogist website - www.genealogysupplies.com

For earlier periods, estate papers are your likeliest source for finding evidence of rentals for poorer folk and the labouring classes. The first thing that you need to identify is the identity of the local feudal superior, i.e. the landowner. The easiest way to try to establish this is to consult the Old and New Statistical Accounts at the University of Edinburgh's EDINA website www.edina.ac.uk/stat-acc-scot - Google Books or Electric Scotland www.electricscotland.com - which in many cases will usually list the names of landowners in the 1790s and the 1840s. Once you know who owned the land, the next job is to then find if any estate records exist. These can be located absolutely anywhere in Scotland, so this may take a bit of digging to turn up.

Again, the NAS holds many records from estates amongst its Gifts and Deposits collection (GD), with particularly good examples including the Breadalbane Muniments (GD112) and the Grandtully Muniments (GD237) for Perthshire, and the Duke of Gordon's papers (GD44) for his Aberdeenshire lands. Other records of use can be found with the RH9 and RH11 series and the CR series (Commissioners of Crown Estates).

The following are examples of rental payments concerning a relative of mine who lived in Airntully, parish of Kinclaven, Perthshire:

Perth: Rental of the baronies of Strathbraan, Murthly and Airntully dated 1801 (Source: NAS CR4/23)
John Henderson crop 1801
Entry 1793
Endurance 19
Expiration 1812
Coals 4 bolls 4 hens
£26 13s 5d

This not only tells me about the rent that John had to pay annually, but also that he had a nineteen years lease. Rental records rarely list anybody other than the head of household, but the fact that they can show the presence of an ancestor in the parish at a particular time is still extremely useful.

Beyond the NAS, you may find estate papers held at county records offices, or still in private hands. To locate these you will need to use the SCAN catalogue or that of the National Register of Archives for Scotland. Some records may also be listed through the English equivalent at www.nationalarchives.gov.uk/nra

This article has been adapted from my book *'Researching Scottish Family History,'* ISBN: 978 1 9062802 2 2 available from the Family History Partnership, PO Box 502, Bury, Lancashire BL8 9EP W: www.familyhistorypartnership.com

General Register Office for Scotland

Registration of Births, Deaths and Marriages in Scotland

Registration of baptisms and proclamations of marriage was first enacted in Scotland by a Council of the Scottish clergy in 1551. The earliest surviving register is for a baptism of 27th December 1553 for Errol in Perthshire.

Following the Reformation, registration of births, deaths and marriages became the responsibility of the ministers and session clerks of the Church of Scotland. Standards of record-keeping varied greatly from parish to parish, however, and even from year to year. This together with evidence of the deterioration and loss of register volumes through neglect led to calls for the introduction of a compulsory and comprehensive civil registration system for Scotland. This came into being on 1st January 1855 with the establishment of the General Register Office for Scotland headed by the Registrar General and the setting up of 1027 registration districts. New Register House in Edinburgh was constructed to house the statutory records and was opened in 1861.

One point to note is the fact that birth registration took rather longer to bed down, which is evidenced by the first Registrar General for Scotland, William Pitt Dundas, stating in his first annual report, published in 1861, that: *'there is good reason for believing that very few births indeed now escape registration.'* Thus in a few instances there are births registered in Old Parish Registers but not the statutory records between 1855 to around 1861.

By 2006 registration districts numbered 156 and on the 1st January 2007 the number had reduced to 32 to mirror the number of Local Authorities and for the boundaries to be contiguous with the Local Authority boundaries.

Records in the custody of the Registrar General

The main series of vital events records of interest to genealogists are held by the Registrar General at New Register House in Edinburgh. They are as follows:

Old Parish Registers (1553-1854): the 3500 surviving register volumes (the OPRs) compiled by the Church of Scotland session clerks were transferred to the custody of the Registrar General after 1855. They record the births and baptisms; proclamations of banns and marriages; and deaths and burials in some 900 Scottish parishes. They are far from complete, however, and most entries contain relatively little information. Deaths and burials generally recorded the burial in the churchyard or the hiring of the parish mortcloth.

There are registrations for earlier events going back to 1539 but they are transcriptions and were not registered until sometime between 1570-1590. There are also a small number of OPRs beyond 1854, which were recorded whilst the system of civil registration, introduced in 1855, bedded in.

Register of Neglected Entries (1801-1854): Births, deaths and marriages proved to have occurred in Scotland between 1801 and 1854 but which had not been recorded in the OPRs. These events were registered after 1854 but can be found in the indexes for OPRs under the date of the event.

Statutory Registers of Births, Deaths, Marriages, Civil Partnerships and Dissolutions (from 1855): the statutory civil registers which district registrars have compiled since 1st January 1855.

Adopted Children Register (from 1930):

Persons Adopted under orders made by the Scottish Courts. The earliest entry is for a birth in October 1909 and the book opens with the first adoption dated 25rd November 1930. Where a court makes an adoption order, the Registrar General annotates the entry in the register of births as well as making a separate entry in the adoption register. The information necessary to link the two entries is kept confidential. Copies of the entries in the adopted children's register are only available on microfiche at the ScotlandsPeople Centre and only a maximum of three entries can be ordered any day.

Register of Divorces (from 1984): records the names of the parties, the date and place of marriage, the date and place of divorce and details of any order made by the court regarding financial provision or custody of children. Prior to May 1984 a divorce would be recorded in the RCE (formerly the Register of Corrected Entries, now the Register of Corrections Etc), and a cross-reference would be added to the marriage entry.

Births, Deaths and Marriages occurring outside Scotland (The Minor Records)
These relate to persons who are or were usually resident in Scotland.
Marine Register of Births and Deaths (from 1855)
Air Register (from 1948)
Service Records (from 1881)
War Registers - Boer War (1899-1902), two World Wars
Consular returns (from 1914)
High Commissioners' returns (from 1964)
Foreign Marriages (from 1947)
Register of births, deaths and marriages in foreign countries (1860-1965)
Census records (from 1841)

These are the enumerators' manuscript books of the decennial census of the population of Scotland. They record the name, age, marital state, occupation and birthplace of every member of a household present on census night. Census records are closed for 100 years and only the schedules for the 1841 to 1911 census are open to the public.

To discover more details about the history of these records please see www.scotlandspeoplehub.gov.uk and look under the 'Research' tab .

Searching at the ScotlandsPeople Centre
The ScotlandsPeople Centre is the largest family history centre in Scotland and is located at the east end of Princes Street in Edinburgh. The Centre has search rooms, a small reference library, access to websites of genealogical interest, a café, shop and seminar facilities across a campus and is open 09:00 to 16:30 weekdays except for some public holidays. The campus comprises General Register House, which was opened in 1788 as the first purpose built

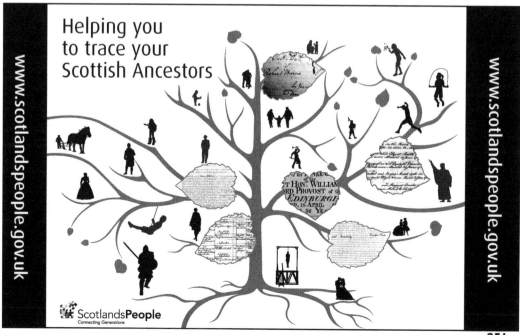

Helping you to trace your Scottish Ancestors

www.scotlandspeople.gov.uk

ScotlandsPeople
Connecting Generations

repository for public records and New Register House, which was opened in 1861 as a purpose-built repository for Scotland's civil registration records.

The Centre has over 160 search places. Day search tickets can be purchased either at the Centre or by ringing 0131 314 4300. Season tickets are also available for regular searchers. Further information about services is available at http://www.scotlandspeoplehub.gov.uk/ . Free introductory taster sessions for limited periods of time are also available but it is not possible to book these sessions.

It is recommended that you pre-pay if you plan to visit the Centre because it means that your seat and user name is allocated in advance so that you can go direct to your seat and start searching once you have inputted a unique password. A user name is established for every customer so that they have their own unique user account. Customers can put money on their account to allow them to print or make electronic saves.

The following records can be searched on the ScotlandsPeople Centre network:
Scottish Statutory Records – 1855 to modern day (dissolutions of civil partnerships will be available in the future)
Old Parish Registers – 1553 to 1854
Census Returns – 1841-1911
Wills and Testaments – 1513-1901.
(1902-1925 available by early 2012)
Coats of Arms – 1627 – last 100 years
There are plans to add valuation rolls and Catholic parish records over the next few years.

The main difference between the Centre and the internet website is the fact that you can view the indexes and images of the digitised records deemed to be modern day at the Centre. On the internet, only the indexes for the modern day records can be viewed.

You can obtain official extracts of any statutory record, Old Parish Record and census record. It is also possible to print unofficial copies of all records or make electronic saves with the exception of prints of the Coats of Arms, which must be ordered. Separate charges apply for prints, electronic saves and prints of Coats of Arms.

Local Family History Centres
The Family History Centre, Park Circus, Glasgow plans to relocate to the Mitchell Library during 2011. Once relocated, this facility will have access to many of the ScotlandsPeople records.
The Burns Monument Centre Kilmarnock provides access to the ScotlandsPeople internet website.
Scottish Local Authorities who satisfy specific standards required by GROS and NAS and who have local family history centres will be eventually be linked to the ScotlandsPeople network.
Local Authority Access to the New Register House Indexes. The all-Scotland computerised indexes and images can also be accessed from local registration offices which have links to the New Register House DIGROS system. Some offices provide search room facilities.

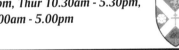

The Irish Family History Foundation
Karel Kiely M.A.

The Irish Family History Foundation, with its cross-border network of local centres, is the largest provider of family history research services in Ireland. The IFHF operates on an all-island and a not for profit basis. In the late 1980s the IFHF identified the various church records of baptisms, marriages and deaths as a priority for computerization. Other primary sources such as Griffith's Valuation, the Tithe Applotment Books, the 1901 and 1911 census and gravestone inscriptions were also included. A common computer system was user with custom designed software based on a unique Standard Surname function; this allows users to search across all variants of a surname.

The county genealogy centres are a valuable part of the heritage and tourism infrastructure in their communities throughout the island of Ireland. As the IFHF and its member centres are not for profit organizations the revenues generated are re-invested in the centres and in the provision of a local, community based approach to genealogy provision for the benefit of our people and the local communities where the records belong. The availability of the online search facility is the most significant development in genealogy to date in Ireland making it possible to find one's ancestors in a particular county. Because it has a network of locally based centres supporting the online database the IFHF can offer a service that no other provider can replicate.

The IFHF began the roll out of an online research service in mid 2007. The project has been achieved in two phases. The first phase culminated in a launch of the *Genealogical Online Research System* at the Navan Centre, Armagh, in November 30th 2007. It was officially launched by the Church leaders of the four main denominations in Ireland whose records form the core of the database, Cardinal Sean Brady, Most Rev. Alan Harper, Archbishop of Armagh & Primate of All Ireland, Most Rev. John Finlay, Moderator of the Presbyterian Church of Ireland and Most Rev. Cooper, President, Methodist Church.

In this initial phase there was a searchable online site provided for each individual centre hosting their birth, baptismal, marriage and death records for Counties Armagh, Cork North and East, Dublin North, Dublin South, Fermanagh, Galway West, Kildare, Leitrim, Roscommon, Tipperary North, Tipperary South, Tyrone. Cardinal Sean Brady welcomed the development and called for the task of completing the database to be supported, as it offers those who wish to trace their family history a real chance of locating their ancestor's origins, especially for those who do not know the county of origin of their ancestor.

The second phase of the project was the development and launch of a All Ireland Central Search System

in March 2008. Minister Seamus Brennan, Department of Arts, Sports and Tourism, and Deputy First Minister Martin McGuinness launched the service on the Jeanie Johnston famine ship replica at the Dublin Docks. This phase included over 17 million records from Counties Antrim, Armagh, Cavan, Cork North and East, Down, Dublin North, Dublin South, Fermanagh, Galway East, Galway West, Kildare, Kilkenny, Leitrim, Louth, Limerick, Mayo North, Mayo South, Roscommon, Tipperary North, Tipperary South, Tyrone, and Westmeath. Since the launch in March 2008 the IFHF has assisted Counties Sligo, Wicklow, Longford and Meath to make their data available online.

In 2009 Counties Derry and Donegal joined the online service and further records from the counties already participating were also added. In 2010 the online service expanded further with with the addition of data from Counties Laois and Offaly, while other participating centres added further data. The IFHF continues to support and assist its centres in computerizing the remaining church records sources.

It has developed an enhanced search facility and redesigned the website in its ongoing quest to make the site the premier Irish genealogical resource. As well as a access to a free basic search facility across millions of records there is an Advanced Search which adds a number of fields to the search criteria for birth or baptismal and marriage records.

Birth and Baptismal records

For birth or baptismal records, in addition to the search fields available using the Standard Search option, users can now search by Mother's First name and Surname. By combining this with the Father's First name and Surname users have the opportunity to find all siblings of a family.

Marriage Records

For marriage records, in addition to all the search fields in the Standard Search option, users can search using any or all of the following: Spouse's First Name, Spouse's Surname, Father's First Name (please note that the names of parents may not been recorded in the original record), Father's Surname, Mother's First Name (please note that the names of parents may not have been recorded in the original record), Mother's Surname.

Users can purchase the entire record set located at a reduced cost. By entering as much detail into the search form as possible users can narrow a search to produce as few matches as possible. The cost of buying records within the Advanced Search option is dependent on the number of records in the result set that is returned. The website contains a list of the SOURCES searchable online for any county, as well as advice and samples of records.

The county genealogy centres also continue to offer a commissioned research service for those who do not want to carry out their own research. The funds that are generated through our service have enabled the computerization of further records.

The IFHF is working to establish centres where there is currently no local genealogy service in operation. It will continue to improve the databases, support centres and promote the services it offers to a local and worldwide audience.

*Voted one of the 10 best websites for International Searches in 2009 by *Family Tree Magazine* along with some the world's most recognized genealogy websites.

Presbyterians in Ireland:
A Guide to Denominations and Documentary Records
William Roulston
Research Director - Ulster Historical Foundation

Through my participation at The National Family History Fair in Gateshead over the last four years, I have met many people looking for Irish ancestors who were Presbyterians. For some there is understandable confusion at the bewildering array of manifestations of Presbyterianism in Ireland – Seceder, Non-Subscribing, Reformed, Free, and Evangelical. The aim of this article is to help those with Irish Presbyterian ancestors find out more about their forebears. It considers the different strands of Presbyterianism in Ireland, distinguishing between each of the historic Presbyterian denominations, and explores the range of records generated by these churches.

The Presbyterian Church in Ireland

Presbyterianism emerged in Scotland in the late sixteenth century. It is characterised by worship services where reading the Bible and preaching have greatest importance and where there is a lack of emphasis on ritual and liturgy. The basic unit in the Presbyterian Church in Ireland is the congregation. In terms of church government it is democratic rather than hierarchical: every minister is considered equal, and to assist him each congregation will appoint a number of *'elders,'* collectively known as the session. Church buildings have historically been known as *'meeting*

houses' reflecting the belief that the significance of the edifice lies not in and of itself, but rather in the group of people who have gathered there.

In the early seventeenth century, with the influx of large numbers of Scottish settlers, a number of clergymen with Presbyterian convictions arrived in Ulster from Scotland. To begin with they were accommodated within the Church of Ireland and were allowed a certain amount of freedom to practise their beliefs. However, in the 1630s there were moves to bring the Church of Ireland more closely into line with the Church of England. This resulted in the expulsion of those ministers with Presbyterian beliefs.

In 1642 an army from Scotland landed at Carrickfergus to defend Scottish settlers from attacks from Irish insurgents. Accompanying this army were a number of Presbyterian ministers acting as chaplains, and here the first Irish presbytery was founded. In the 1650s, during the Cromwellian regime, there was considerable freedom of worship and many ministers in Ulster were Scottish Presbyterians. Following the Restoration of 1660, ministers who refused to conform to the teachings and government of the newly reinstated Church of Ireland were dismissed. Despite periods of persecution, Presbyterians began to form congregations and

Belfast's
First (Non-Subscribing) Presbyterian Church

build their own churches from the 1660s. In 1690 an overarching ruling body known as the General Synod or Synod of Ulster was established.

For many members of the establishment, Presbyterians were regarded as more of a threat than Catholics, especially because of their numerical superiority over Anglicans in much of Ulster. Certain restrictions were placed on Presbyterians as a result of the Penal Laws passed in the Irish parliament. For example, in 1704 a law was passed which required persons holding public office to produce a certificate stating that they had received communion in a Church of Ireland church. Twenty-four Presbyterian members of the Londonderry corporation resigned rather than submit to the 'Test Act.' Even after the passing of the Toleration Act in 1719, under which Presbyterians were granted freedom of worship, there was a strong sense of estrangement from the Anglican and landed establishment, and this was a contributory factor in the large-scale emigration of Presbyterians from Ulster to America in the eighteenth century.

The distinguished historian ATQ Stewart famously observed, 'The Presbyterian is happiest when he is being a radical.' Political radicalism was never more obvious than in the 1790s when Presbyterians were instrumental in the creation of the United Irishmen and were heavily involved in the revolutionary activities that led to the 1798 Rebellion. In the nineteenth century Presbyterians were active in the movement for land reform that resulted in the dismantling of the landed estate system. With the rise of Irish nationalism and the campaigns for Home Rule in the late nineteenth century, the great majority of Presbyterians became unionist in their political outlook.

Today the Presbyterian Church is the largest Protestant denomination in Northern Ireland with some 560 congregations, overwhelmingly in Northern Ireland, but with a significant number of congregations in other parts of the island, especially counties Donegal and Monaghan as well as the city of Dublin. The website of the Presbyterian Church in Ireland is www.presbyterianireland.org. This includes an extensive, though incomplete directory of congregations.

Published Works relating to the Presbyterian Church in Ireland
Histories

There is no shortage of published works on Irish Presbyterianism. In the nineteenth century several men, usually ministers in the Church, began to write detailed histories of Irish Presbyterians. Foremost among them was James Seaton Reid who wrote the magisterial History of the Presbyterian Church in Ireland, ed. W. D. Killen (3 vols, 2nd edition, Belfast, 1867). Others works include Thomas Witherow, Historical and literary

St Johnstown Presbyterian Church County Donegal

memorials of Presbyterianism in Ireland (2 vols, Belfast 1879-80) and W. D. Killen, History of the congregations of the Presbyterian Church in Ireland (Belfast, 1886). Some of these early volumes can now be read on Google Books or Archive.org.

Most of these books look at the Church from an institutional point of view, focussing on structures of government and prominent ministers. In the twentieth century academics began to research and study Presbyterianism from different viewpoints. An academic study that considers the mental worlds of Presbyterian is The Shaping of Ulster Presbyterian Belief and Practice, 1770-1840 by Andrew Holmes (Oxford, 2006). A recent handsomely-produced volume that provides a good overview of Irish Presbyterianism is Presbyterians in Ireland: An Illustrated History, Laurence Kirkpatrick (Holywood, 2006). This volume includes photographs of virtually every Presbyterian meeting house in Ireland. Presbyterianism in Dublin is expertly covered in Dictionary of Dublin Dissent – Dublin's Protestant Dissenting Meeting Houses 1660-1920 by Steven C. Smyrl (Dublin, 2009)

Information on Congregations

An indispensable guide to the Presbyterian Church in Ireland is the History of Congregations published by the Presbyterian Historical Society in 1982. It provides brief sketches of each of the congregations, mainly focusing on the succession of ministers. It is particularly useful in determining when a particular congregation came into being. A Supplement of Additions, Emendations and Corrections with an Index was published in association with the Ulster Historical Foundation in 1996. The text of both publications can now be read online on the website of the Presbyterian Historical Society (www.presbyterianhistoryireland.com).

In many of the larger towns and villages in Northern Ireland there are two or more Presbyterian congregations and the *History of Congregations* is particularly useful in working out their chronology and how they relate to one another. Newtownards, for example, has several Presbyterian congregations. First, Newtownards is the oldest and dates back to the seventeenth century. Second, Newtownards originally had Seceder connections, while Regent Street was established in 1834. The formation of the Greenwell Street congregation can be linked to the 1859 Revival. Strean Presbyterian Church outside the town came into existence following a disagreement in First Newtownards in 1865. It was named after its main instigator, Thomas Strean, who gave over £8,000 to build a meeting house.

Information on Presbyterian Ministers

Biographical information on Presbyterian ministers was published as *Fasti of the Irish Presbyterian Church, 1613–1840* compiled by James McConnell and revised by his son Samuel G. McConnell (Belfast: Presbyterian Historical Society, 1951). After 1840 biographical information was published as *Fasti of the General Assembly of the Presbyterian Church in Ireland, 1840-1910*, compiled by John M. Barkley, and issued in three parts by the Presbyterian Historical Society of Ireland (1986-7). The biographical sketches are fairly succinct, but can include the name of the father and possibly mother of the minister, his own family details, where he was educated and where he served. Publications, if any, may also be noted, and perhaps something exceptional about his career.

Congregational Histories

In his book, *The Shaping of Ulster Presbyterian Belief and Practice,* the historian Dr Andrew Holmes has observed that there is a *'seemingly unique obsession of Ulster Presbyterians with writing and reading congregational histories.'* To a large extent this is a reflection of the importance of the congregation within the Presbyterian system, and the way in which its identity is intertwined with its locality and the families who, often for generations, have been associated with it.

A great many congregations have their own published histories. Many of these will include appendices providing very useful information on past members of the congregation and surrounding district. For example, the appendices to John Rutherford's *Donagheady Presbyterian Churches and Parish* (1953) include the following lists of names – ratepayers in the electoral divisions of Dunalong, Ballyneaner, Dunamanagh, and Mountcastle in 1856; Donagheady wills pre-1858, the Donagheady poll book of c.1662, and hearth money rolls for Donagheady from the 1660s, as well as various other extracts from sources.

The best collection of congregational histories is in the Presbyterian Historical Society Library. There are also good collections of these histories at the Linen Hall Library and Central Library in Belfast, and in the library of the Public Record Office of Northern Ireland.

Seceders, Non-Subscribers, and Covenanters

The Secession Presbyterian Church

The Secession Church was a branch of Presbyterianism that emerged following a split in the Church of Scotland in 1712 over the issue of official patronage. Before long it had gained a foothold in Ulster and began to spread rapidly, especially in those areas where the Presbyterian Church had hitherto not been as strong. In the nineteenth century nearly all of the Secession churches were received into the Presbyterian Church in Ireland. Therefore, in the *Guide to Church Records* congregations that originated as

Limerick

Secession churches will be found listed as Presbyterian churches.

Essential reading for an understanding of the Secession Church in Ulster is David Stewart's *The Seceders in Ireland: With Annals of Their Congregations* (Belfast, 1950). Brief biographical sketches of Secession clergy appear in *Fasti of Seceder Ministers Ordained or Installed in Ireland 1746-1948*, arranged and edited by W.D. Bailie and L.S. Kirkpatrick, published by the Presbyterian Historical Society 2005.

The Non-Subscribing Presbyterian Church

The ethos of the Non-Subscribing Presbyterian Church is 'faith guided by reason and conscience'. The origins of this denomination go back to a dispute within the Presbyterian Church over the issue of subscription to the Westminster Confession of Faith, the statement of doctrine of the Presbyterian Church. Those who denied the necessity of subscribing to this work were known as 'New Light' Presbyterians or 'Non-Subscribers.' In 1725, in an attempt to deal with the situation, ministers and congregations of the 'New Light' persuasion were placed in the Presbytery of Antrim (this did not mean that all the congregations were in County Antrim).

About 100 years later the issue of subscription again became a source of contention within Presbyterianism, and in 1829 a small section of the Presbyterian Church withdrew and the following year formed what was known as the Remonstrant Synod. In 1910 the General Synod of the Non-Subscribing Presbyterian Church was created following a union of the Presbytery of Antrim and the Remonstrant Synod. In 1935 this body was joined by the Synod of Munster. Today there are around 34 congregations, mainly in counties Antrim and Down.

Some of the early Non-Subscribing Presbyterian Church records, created before the split, are in fact Presbyterian records. For example, the early records of Scarva Street Presbyterian Church in Banbridge are to be found in Banbridge Non-Subscribing Presbyterian Church records. In a number of instances a Non-Subscribing Presbyterian Church will be known as the First (Old) Presbyterian Church. Rosemary Street Non-Subscribing Presbyterian Church in Belfast, for example, is generally known as First Presbyterian Church. This can give rise to confusion if there is a Presbyterian Church in a town with the designation First.

For a brief background to this denomination see *A Short History of the Non-Subscribing Presbyterian Church of Ireland* by John Campbell (Belfast: 1914). The denomination's website (www.nspresbyterian.org) includes a map showing the location of all congregations.

The Reformed Presbyterian (Covenanter) Church

The Covenanter or Reformed Presbyterian Church was composed of those who adhered most strongly to the Covenants of 1638 and 1643 and who rejected the Revolution Settlement of 1691 in Scotland. The National Covenant of 1638 was a reaction against the attempts by Charles I to bring the Scottish Church into closer conformity with the episcopal Church of England and to introduce greater ritual and a prescribed liturgy to services. It firmly established the Presbyterian form of church government in Scotland, and bound the people to uphold the principles of the Reformation. The Solemn League and Covenant of 1643 was composed on similar lines and affected England and Ireland as well as Scotland. During the reigns of Charles II (1660–85) and James II (1685–8) there was considerable persecution of Covenanters, and many were executed or banished. This ended with the accession of William III. In 1691 Covenanters refused to accept the Revolution Settlement as it gave the government a role in the running of the Church of Scotland. Covenanters, therefore, stood apart from mainstream Presbyterianism in Scotland.

Of the early history of the Covenanters in Ireland very little is known, save that the denomination was small and scattered. It was not until the latter part of the eighteenth century that congregations began to be organised and ministers were ordained. Very few Reformed Presbyterian records have survived from the eighteenth century. This can be partly explained by the paucity of ministers at this time; many baptisms and marriages were performed by visiting ministers from Scotland and there is little evidence of proper records being kept of these events. Congregations were divided into societies, composed of several families living within a short distance of each other. From the middle of the eighteenth century Covenanters in Ireland became much more organised with the creation

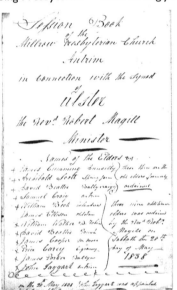

Antrim Session Book

of an Irish Reformed Presbytery in 1763. In 1811 a Synod of the Reformed Presbyterian Church was established. Today there are around 35 congregations.

For background information on this denomination see *The Covenanters in Ireland: A History of the Reformed Presbyterian Church of Ireland* by Adam Loughridge (Belfast, 1984). For information on ministers in the Reformed Presbyterian Church see *Fasti of the Reformed Presbyterian Church of Ireland* compiled and edited by Adam Loughridge (Belfast, 1970). An updated *fasti* with short historical sketches of each Reformed Presbyterian congregation is currently in preparation. A recent article on researching Covenanter ancestors is 'The Origins of the Reformed Presbyterian Church of Ireland with some comments on its records' by William Roulston, published in *Familia: Ulster Genealogical Review* (2008), pages 86-110. The website of this denomination is www.rpc.org. This includes a map showing the location of congregations.

Documentary Records

There is little difference in the types of record generated by the three historic Presbyterian denominations, though there may be occasional differences in emphasis. Therefore, the different categories of Presbyterian records can be considered together. One point I would make at this stage is that it is always worth looking at Church of Ireland registers for baptisms, marriages and burials involving Presbyterians. This is because until 1870 the Church of Ireland was the established or state church in Ireland and because of its status many people who ordinarily belonged to another denomination can turn up in the pages of its registers. Even Catholic records should not be discounted for there was much more intermarriage in Irish society than is often supposed.

Registers of Baptisms, Marriages and Burials

Baptismal Registers

Presbyterians practise infant baptism, and the registers of these baptisms form one of the most useful categories of record when looking for Irish ancestors, especially in the period prior to the introduction of civil registration of births in 1864. The basic information provided in a baptismal register is the name of the child, the name of the father and the date of baptism. The mother's name will usually be given as will a specific

location. The occupation of the father and the date of birth of the child may also be provided.

Although there are a number of very early Presbyterian registers of baptism, including Drumbo (1692), Killyleagh (1693), Lisburn (1692), and Portaferry (1699), in the majority of cases, baptismal records do not pre-date the nineteenth century. This may be for the very simple reason that the congregation was not established until the 1800s. Less systematic record keeping was also a factor.

Many Presbyterian baptismal registers begin in 1819 or shortly thereafter for at the Synod of 1819 the following instructions were issued:

> 'That every minister of and Baptism the Synod be enjoined to register, or cause to be registered, in a book to be kept for that purpose, the names of all children baptised by him; the dates of their birth and baptism; the names of their parents, and the places of residence. This book shall be carefully preserved, and considered as the property of the congregation – to remain with them on the death, resignation, or removal of the Minister, and to be handed to his Successor, for the purpose of continuing the registry.'

Even with the ruling of 1819 some Presbyterian

Page from Belfast Funeral Register

congregations do not have complete sets of nineteenth-century registers of baptisms. Some records were accidentally destroyed as the following extract from the baptismal register of West Church, Ballymena records:

> *'I preached at Churchtown on the 5th of November 1848 according to appointment by Presbytery and the list of children baptised on that day having been accidentally destroyed in my absence, I am necessitated to leave blank in the register at the same time noting its cause.'*

Due to the *'negligence and disobedience of a female servant'* the records of Bready Reformed Presbyterian Church were lost in a fire in the home of the clerk of session in September 1868. Other records were destroyed deliberately. One nineteenth-century Reformed Presbyterian minister became convinced that infant baptism was contrary to Scripture and left his congregation, but not before he had destroyed many of the baptismal registers. The baptismal records of Rosemary Street Presbyterian Church, 1868-1941, were destroyed as a result of the *'Belfast Blitz'* during the 2nd World War.

On other occasions record-keeping was simply lax. A visitation of 1st Donagheady Presbyterian Church in County Tyrone in 1865 found that there was no baptismal register, no communicants' roll, and no session or committee minute books. In 1876 it was noted that no minutes of any committee meeting had been kept since 1871. It was not until 1878 that a baptismal register was provided. Frequently registers disappeared around the time that a minister died or moved to a new congregation.

For the most part baptismal registers will follow a fairly routine format. Occasionally, however, an entry of some interest might appear. One such entry appears in the baptismal register of Crossgar Presbyterian Church in County Londonderry. Following a record of the baptism on 4 May 1888 of David Campbell at the age of 46 the entry continues:

> *This D. Campbell spent 21 years and 43 days in the Army (4 years in England, 1 in Scotland, 3 in Ireland, 12 years and 27 days in India) before his baptism. While in the Army be was an Episcopalian, having gone over from the Presbyterian Church like a great many others; when he got off he attended the Episcopal Church in Macosquin for some time, but he wrote on a letter asking me to baptise him which I did on sincere profession of his faith.*

Marriage Registers

One of the main grievances of Presbyterians in the early eighteenth century concerned the right of their ministers to conduct marriages. In 1737 an act of parliament was passed which, with certain caveats, permitted two Presbyterians to marry. At last in 1782 marriages performed by a Presbyterian minister were legally recognised as being *'as good in law'* as those performed by a minister of the Church of Ireland. However, it was not until the passing of another act of parliament in 1844 that Presbyterians ministers were permitted to marry a Presbyterian and a member of the Church of Ireland.

Prior to the standardisation of marriage registers from 1 April 1845, when all non-Catholic marriages were to be officially registered, these will give in their simplest form the date of the marriage and the names of the bride and groom. The residence and the name of the father of each party are occasionally provided. The names of the witnesses may also be given. At the same Synod of 1819 that exhorted ministers to keep registers of baptisms, similar directions were given for the keeping of marriage registers:

> *Overtured and unanimously agreed to – That every Minister of this Synod shall keep, or cause to be kept, a regular registry of all marriages celebrated by him; stating the date of each marriage, the names of the parties, the Congregations or Parishes in which they reside, and the names of at least two of the witnesses present at the celebration of the ceremony.*

It was also agreed that every minister would be required to submit annually to his respective presbytery an accurate list of the marriages he had conducted in the previous year. These marriages would then be copied by the clerk of presbytery into a separate volume. Relatively few of these presbytery marriage books seem to have survived, or at least are in the public domain. One that does relates to the Tyrone Presbytery and covers marriages in the following congregations:

> *Cookstown (possibly 1st), 1820-8, Loughgall, 1819-22, Tobermore, 1819-22, Vinecash, 1825-8, Carland, 1826-8, Magherafelt, 1819-28, Dungannon (possibly 1st), 1819-28, Benburb, 1827-8, Cloveneden, 1826-8, Richhill, 1826-8, Stewartstown (possibly 1st), 1820-7, Coagh, 1820-2 and Minterburn, 1819-22 (PRONI, MIC/1P/460).*

From 1st April 1845, with the introduction of civil registration of non-Catholic marriages, the information on the individuals getting married includes their name, age, status, and occupation. The names and occupations of their fathers are also given. The church, the officiating minister and the witnesses to the ceremony are named. In most cases the exact age of the parties is not given, and the entry will simply read *'full age'* (i.e. over 21) or *'minor'* (i.e. under 21). If the father of one of the parties was no longer living, this may be indicated in the marriage certificate by the word *'deceased'* or by leaving the space blank, but in many cases it is not.

Burial Registers

Few Presbyterian congregations have very old burial registers. Part of the reason for this, as will be discussed presently, is the fact that not every Presbyterian meeting house has an adjoining graveyard. Those burial registers that do exist were mainly started in the late nineteenth or even the early twentieth century. Burial registers can be fairly uninformative, with the name of the deceased, the date of burial and occasionally the occupation and age at death given.

One very interesting early eighteenth-century document relating to the burial of Presbyterians survives among the records of Rosemary Street Non-Subscribing Presbyterian Church in Belfast. It is a register of the hiring of funeral gear – palls, cloaks and hats – for about 2,000 funerals which took place in Belfast between 1712 and 1736. It has been published as *Funeral register of Rosemary Street Non-Subscribing Presbyterian Church (known as the First Presbyterian Church of Belfast), 1712-36*, edited by Jean Agnew (Belfast: Ulster Historical Foundation, 1995).

Other Congregational Records

A variety of other items may be found among the records kept by individual Presbyterian congregations. Some of these are discussed below.

Minutes of Session Meetings

The session was the ruling body in each congregation and was composed of the minister, designated the moderator at meetings of session, and elders in a particular congregation. One of the elders served as *'clerk of session'* and was responsible for recording the minutes of the meetings. Session records cover a range of matters, many of which relate to the internal discipline of members of the congregation for a variety of transgressions. Occasionally they may contain baptisms and marriages that are not recorded elsewhere.

Family Records and Congregational Censuses

A real boon to any researcher seeking information on the families that belonged to a particular congregation will be a congregational census. These can take different forms. At their simplest they may be a list of members of the congregation. More detailed census returns will provide the townland and will include the names of all members of the family. For example, the records of Rademon Non-Subscribing Presbyterian Church, County Down, include a census of families arranged by townland, 1836-7, with notes added at a later date indicating those

who died or got married, those who left the congregation and those who had emigrated. For Carrigallen Presbyterian Church in County Leitrim there is a visitation book with details of each family by townland and dates of baptisms of children, 1837-92.

A remarkable volume is Rev. Robert Magill's family record book for the congregation of 1st Antrim (Millrow). This includes detailed information on the families that belonged to the congregation in the early nineteenth century and includes baptisms, marriages and deaths. On a number of occasions Magill even went so far as to sketch out family trees, with figure drawings of the various family members. This volume is available for inspection at the Presbyterian Historical Society Library.

Lists of Communicants

These are similar to congregational census, but they only list the names of communicant members of a particular congregation. Sometimes there may be a separate list of the names of new communicants. Occasionally lists of communicants are annotated with additional information, such as when a communicant married, emigrated or died.

Transfer Certificates

Members of one congregation who wished to transfer their congregation to another would be issued with a certificate testifying to their good standing in the church. Frequently a transfer certificate would be issued to those who were emigrating. For example, the transfer certificate given to David Carson by the Rev. Hugh Hamill of 1st Donagheady in 1784 certified that Carson was *'born and bred of honest Protestant dissenting parents and brought up in that faith, and has lived a sober, regular life which we hope will recommend him to our brethren in America, whom he may chance to associate with.'* Carson took no chances and also sought and received a similar testimonial from a local Reformed Presbyterian Church. For a number of congregations there are lists of people who left the congregation to emigrate abroad.

Financial Records

The financial records of a congregation should not be overlooked when searching for a

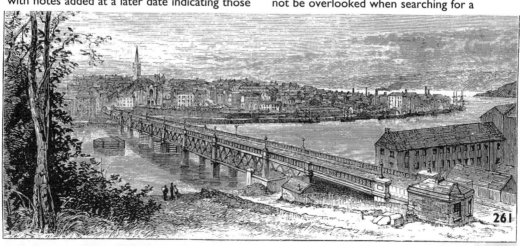

Presbyterian ancestor. Occasionally they will survive for a period for which registers of baptisms and marriages are absent. These records range from stipend lists (the stipend being the minister's salary), pew rent books, and account books. For 1st Lisburn Presbyterian Church there is a subscription list for the new meeting house from 1764-5.

Pew rent books can be particularly interesting documents. Formerly, the greater part of the minister's stipend was derived from pew rents, that is, from the letting of pews or seats within the meeting house for a fixed annual sum. In some congregations there were different classes of pew-sitters, reflecting a certain social stratification. For example, in Glendermott Presbyterian Church pew-sitters were divided into gentlemen, farmers, and artisans/cottiers. Some pew rent books survive from the early eighteenth century. For instance, for Rosemary Street Presbyterian Church in Belfast there are surviving pew rent books, 1726-73, 1788-96, 1816-56 and 1866-73.

Calls to Ministers

When a congregation had settled on their choice for a new minister a 'call' was issued to him, signed by the members. It was then up to the individual to whom the call was issued to decide whether or not he wished to accept that call. Some of these calls can incorporate fairly extensive lists of names of members of individual congregations. For example, the call issued to Thomas Clark by the Presbyterians of Ballyalbany, County Monaghan, in 1751 contains the names of over 160 individuals. It was published in S. Lyle Orr and Alex Haslett, *Historical Sketch of Ballyalbany Presbyterian Church* (1940), pages 10-12.

Education Records

Within Presbyterianism there was a strong emphasis on education, especially on literacy and the ability to read the Bible for oneself. Many ministers conducted classes in their home or in the session room of their meeting house. Providing a Classical education, these schools were often used to prepare young men for the ministry. Few records relating to these establishments survive.

Education records that do survive among congregational records relate principally to the Sunday schools that were established in their hundreds in the early nineteenth century. For

example, among the records of 2nd Portglenone Presbyterian Church, County Antrim, is a Sunday school roll book, 1821-67. The records for Antrim (Millrow) Presbyterian Church include a Sabbath School library loan book, 1870, and a Sabbath School receipt and expenditure book, 1835-62, incorporating a weekly roll of teachers and salaries, 1840-41.

Administrative Records: Minutes of Meetings of Presbytery and Synod

The Presbytery was the middle layer of government in the Presbyterian Church, above session and below Synod. It comprised the ministers and ruling elders of the congregations affiliated to the Presbytery. It dealt with matters that could not be settled at the level of session, either because there was a dispute of a nature that could not be resolved without recourse to a higher authority or because the issues related to more than one congregation. Presbytery meetings were held on a regular basis. Presbyteries were frequently reorganised. In addition, individual congregations could change presbytery if it meant that a dispute would be resolved.

The surviving minute book for the Presbytery of Strabane, covering the period 1717–40, reveals that the Presbytery dealt with a variety of matters relating to the members of the congregations within its bounds. For instance, in December 1718 John Alison came before Strabane presbytery desiring a certificate testifying to his credentials as a good Presbyterian as he was preparing to emigrate. Presbytery decided not to issue him with one until just before he was ready to leave, and then only conditional on his continued good behaviour.

The Synod of Ulster was the highest authority in the Presbyterian Church in Ulster. It met once a year, usually in June, and was composed of representatives from every congregation in each of the presbyteries. The records of the Synod of Ulster meetings for the period 1690–1820 were published in three volumes by the Presbyterian Church in 1891 (available to read online at www.archive.org). Much of the minutes deal with matters of a fairly routine nature. Occasionally, however, an item of real value will be recorded. From 1840, when the Synod of Ulster and the Secession Synod United,

Presbyterian College, Belfast

there are the printed minutes of the General Assembly, a set of which is in the library of the Presbyterian Historical Society.

Presbyterian Graveyards and Gravestone Inscriptions

Many, but by no means, all Presbyterian meeting houses have adjoining burial grounds. Few of the inscriptions in graveyards surrounding Presbyterian churches pre-date 1800 and in fact the practise of burying within the grounds of Presbyterian churches does not seem to have happened until the late eighteenth century. The burial ground attached to Castlereagh Presbyterian church is unusual in having several memorials dating from the late eighteenth century. An exception to this generalisation is the graveyard at Drumbo Presbyterian Church, which includes memorials from the late seventeenth century. However, in the case of Drumbo the meeting house is unique, so far as the present writer knows, in that it stands on the site of a medieval parish church.

If looking for the burial places of Presbyterian ancestors prior to the nineteenth century, the most obvious place to check will be the old parish graveyard, probably dating from the medieval period, and which may or may not have a functioning Church of Ireland church within its bounds. Even after burial grounds began to be laid out around Presbyterian meeting houses, the practise of interment in these older graveyards continued for some families.

It was not until the second half of the nineteenth century that Presbyterians were legally entitled to open a burial ground that did not adjoin one of their own meeting houses. The background to the opening of Balmoral Cemetery in 1855 was an incident in which a Church of Ireland minister obstructed a funeral being conducted by two Presbyterian ministers. One of the ministers involved, Rev. Joseph Mackenzie, secured the ground for the cemetery, and remained its owner, though it was managed by a board of trustees. Though the cemetery was never exclusively Presbyterian, it was predominantly so and was the only burial place of its kind in nineteenth-century Ulster.

The inscriptions from many Presbyterian churchyards have been published in one form or another. The Ulster Historical Foundation has published the inscriptions from more than 50 Presbyterian churchyards in County Down as well as several more in County Antrim. A number of local historical societies have also been involved in transcribing and publishing gravestone inscriptions. Many inscriptions have been made available on the internet.

Locating Records

Over the years the Public Record Office of Northern Ireland (PRONI) has done a tremendous job in acquiring originals or copies of records kept by individual Presbyterian congregations. Most of the Presbyterian records in its custody are on microfilm. The coverage is so extensive that there are relatively few congregations whose records have not been deposited in some form in PRONI (www.proni.gov.uk). The majority of these records are available on microfilm, though there are also some original documents, as well as photocopies.

The Presbyterian Historical Society, about which more will be said presently, has copies of most of the microfilms of Presbyterian registers held by PRONI and can be viewed on a microfilm reader at the Society's office in Church House, Belfast. A small number of Presbyterian records are only available at the Presbyterian Historical Society. These include some very early session books, including those of Dundonald and Aghadowey, as well as some registers of baptisms and marriages. A few pre-1900 Presbyterian registers are still in local custody.

With the advent of the internet, the indexing and digitisation of church records has gathered pace. Many of the centres affiliated to the Irish Family History Foundation have indexed Presbyterian registers for their respective counties and made these available online on a pay-per-view arrangement (www.rootsireland.ie), though coverage is far from complete. Local endeavour has also resulted in many registers being made available online for free.

The Presbyterian Historical Society

The Presbyterian Historical Society was

Queen's Bridge, Belfast

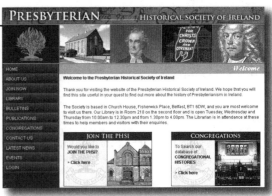

founded in 1906 to promote public awareness of the history of the various strands of Presbyterianism in Ireland. Once described as a *'Treasure House of Ulster's History,'* the Society's library possesses some 12,000 books and pamphlets. These are mainly concerned with ecclesiastical history and in particular Presbyterian history. The collection includes a large number of congregational histories. A set of *The Witness*, a Presbyterian newspaper, covering the period 1874-1941, is also available for consultation as are the printed minutes of the General Assembly beginning in 1840.

Manuscript material includes session minutes, baptisms and marriages from individual churches as well as some presbytery minutes. These include session accounts for Armagh Presbyterian Church for 1707-32, session minutes for Aghadowey Presbyterian Church for 1702-61 and baptisms from Cullybackey (Cunningham Memorial) Presbyterian Church covering the period 1726-1815. In addition the records of a number of now defunct congregations in the Republic of Ireland have been deposited for safekeeping in its Library. The Society also has a duplicate set of the microfilm copies of Presbyterian Church registers held by PRONI covering the vast majority of Presbyterian congregations in Ireland.

Of particular interest is the large amount of biographical data available on Presbyterian ministers. This material can be accessed through a card index, while there are also handwritten and printed *'fasti'* providing information on clergymen. A small collection of private papers of Presbyterian ministers is also available. These include some of the papers of the most distinguished Presbyterian minister in the nineteenth century, the Reverend Henry Cooke.

The Society's library has been built up gradually over many years through donations, bequests and purchases. The Society is funded through donations and fees, together with a valuable financial contribution each year from the Incidental Fund of the General Assembly of the Presbyterian Church in Ireland. Queries on membership are welcomed and should be addressed to the Society's Librarian, Valerie Adams.

The Society now has its own website (www.presbyterianhistoryireland.com) which contains information on upcoming events, membership, and other news. Members of the Society can access a digitised version of the History of Congregations, as well as past editions of the Society's annual publication, The Bulletin. A history of the Society has been published – Times Passing: The Story of the Presbyterian Historical Society of Ireland from 1907-2007 by Dr Joe Thompson.

At the time of writing, the Society is making preparations for a move to new premises at College Green beside Union Theological College in Belfast.

Conclusion

Researching Irish Presbyterian ancestors can be as fulfilling or frustrating as investigating forebears from any one of the many other denominations on this island. Among the chief frustrations is the fact that relatively few congregations have registers of baptisms and marriages prior to the 1800s. On the other hand, the large number of administrative and other records that were generated by individual congregations means that it can be possible to put real flesh on the bones of Presbyterian ancestors and so understand more about their social and religious worlds.

Irish Marriage and Death Certificates
The Parameters of the Next Generation
Joe O'Neill

The cynic and the poet will attach some significance to the fact that marriage and death are grouped together here. Their significance for the genealogist, however, is far more obvious. Together they usually mark the beginning of a period of stability in an ancestor's life and in Ireland – where illegitimacy was until recently extremely rare – the beginning and the end of the period in which the next generation was born. Together with birth certificates, marriage and death certificates constitute the trunk which supports the whole structure of your family tree. Full civil or state registration of all births, marriages and deaths began in Ireland on 1 January 1864. (Non-Catholic marriages had been registered since 1845.) This meant that from then all parents were required to inform the authorities of the birth of a child. Responsibility for registering a marriage rested with the officiating clergyman while deaths could be done by anyone but were usually done by a relative or a doctor.

The poor law structure of the day was used to carry out registration. In 1864 Ireland was already divided into 163 areas, known as poor law unions. Each was responsible for providing a workhouse for its poor, a place where they went when they could not support themselves. Within these unions, which were large areas, there were smaller divisions, known as Dispensary Districts, each of which had a medical officer responsible for caring for the poor. Most unions contained six or seven of these districts. When civil registration was introduced in 1864, recording births, marriages and deaths within each of these districts became the responsibility of a registrar. In fact, in many cases this new registrar was the medical officer.

All certificates state the county, Registration District and the Superintendent Registrar's District.

In addition to these registrars, the government appointed a superintendent registrar for each poor law union, with responsibility for overseeing the registration of births, marriages and deaths within that union. There was also a Registrar General, based in Dublin, with overall responsibility for registration throughout the country.

The information was sent up the chain of authority to Dublin, where it was recorded. The General Register Office was also responsible for creating an index to the records for the whole country. The original records were then returned to the Superintendent Registrars, where they remain to this day.

When a couple's marriage is registered the registrar issues a marriage certificate. It contains a host of invaluable information.

What the Marriage Certificate Tells Us

Marriage records give more information than other civil registration documents and are in fact the most useful of the three. As the certificate had to be completed within three days of the ceremony, the date recorded is generally correct.

The most important information about the couple contained in the marriage certificate is:

their names: ages: status – spinster, widow, bachelor, widower: occupation: residence at time of marriage: names and occupations of their fathers: the church: the name of the officiating minister: the names of the witnesses.

A Note of Caution

This all seems very straightforward. Unfortunately, the information recorded on the certificate is, like that on other civil registration documents, only as reliable as the informant.

Not every clergyman registered every marriage. Though fewer marriages than births went unregistered many genealogists feel that as many a ten per cent of marriages may have gone unregistered.

In many cases the exact age of the couple is not recorded. Instead you will often find 'full age' that is, 21 or over, or 'minor' that is less than 21. The significance of this is that those of full age were free to marry without parental consent. Consequently, where parental consent was not forthcoming, a person who was under full age might give a false age.

Sometimes people lied about their age for other reasons. It was generally assumed that a man would be older than his wife. In order to spare the bride's embarrassment in situations

Sackville Street, Dublin renamed O'Connell Street in 1924 in honour of Daniel O'Connell the early 19th century nationalist leader whose statue now stands facing O'Connell Bridge

where this was not the case, the couple might be flexible with the truth, adding a few years to his age, trimming a few from hers.

It is also important to appreciate that many people did not know their exact age. For most of the 19th and early 20th century people attached little significance to their precise date of birth. Before compulsory education, state pensions and the welfare state, when the celebration of birthdays was largely confined to the wealthy, it was of little significance.

The husband's occupation was recorded though until comparatively recently this was seldom done for the bride.

Sometimes, where the father of one of the couple was deceased, this is recorded. However, this is not always the case.

The residences of the both husband and wife at the time of the wedding were recorded and, from 1957, their intended place of residence after marriage, if within Eire.

Signatures of the witnesses can be interesting. Usually, witnesses were close relatives of the couple, often brothers or sisters.

What the Death certificate Tells us

The most important information about the deceased on the death certificate is:

date and place of death: full name: age: gender: status – married, spinster, widow, bachelor, widower occupation: cause of death: it is usually stated if the informant is a child of the deceased but otherwise the relationship is usually not mentioned

Trinity College Library - Dublin

A Word of Caution

Many of the considerations that apply to birth and marriage certificates also apply to death certificates, though of all three events deaths were the least likely to go unregistered. On the other hand, more than any other record, its accuracy depends on the reliability of the informant.

The age recorded may be only approximately correct, for the reasons mentioned above. The cause of death, unless specified by a doctor, may be vague or general.

Where to Find the Records
In the Republic

The **General Register Office (GRO), Dublin**, has responsibility for the records. For several years now there has been talk of the indexes becoming available on line, but this has not yet materialised. You can search the indexes at the GRO or pay to have someone there do it for you. All the information is on the website. Once you've located it you may order the certificate by post, telephone or email.

If you know the relevant registration district of the marriage or death you can search the records there. You will find the address in a telephone directory, under 'Health Service Executive'.

Most indexes – though not all – and the actual records are on microfilm which you can access at any Family History Centre, Dublin City Library and South Dublin City Library, Tallaght. It is also possible to search some of the records at the County Heritage Centre. Some, such as Clare, Derry, Mayo and South Tipperary have created a database of the local records.

In Northern Ireland

All Northern Ireland records from 1922 onwards are with the General Register Office in Belfast and are available on microfilms at Family History Centres. However, the original centralised records up to 1922 remain in Dublin.

You must arrange a time to visit to search the index and you may then order the certificate by post, telephone or email. The Office has computerized indexes for the North from 1845 and copies of death records from 1864. Marriage records from 1864 are with the district registrars, held by the local councils. You will find database copies with the County Heritage Centres.

To complete this stage of your research you must acquire a copy of the certificate from the appropriate GRO. But there are other sources of information.

The Church of the Latter-Day Saints (LDS or Mormons) has microfilm copies of some registers and indexes to the records held by the GROs. What's better is that some parts of the early of registration are accessible online through the LDS International Genealogical Index (IGI) which you can search at www.familysearch.org/

The beauty of this is that you can enjoy free access to this LDS material at any of their Family History Centres.

Going to Mass

GRONI holds the following additional records:
deaths at sea of all those born in Northern Ireland who died after 1 January 1922;
deaths and marriages of men serving in the army and their dependents registered on or after 1 January 1927 under the Births, Marriages and Deaths (Army) Act 1879;
deaths of Northern Ireland people registered by British consuls abroad on or after 1 January 1922;
marriages of Northern Ireland people registered by British consuls abroad on or after 1 January 1923;
deaths and marriages of Northern Ireland people registered by the British High Commissioner in Commonwealth countries on or after 1 January 1950;
copies of certificates, with translations, relating to the marriages of people from Northern Ireland in certain Commonwealth countries, according to the laws of these countries, without the presence of a British consular official;
deaths of Northern Ireland people who died on war service between 1939 and 1948.

Unusual Cases

All this is fine if your ancestor was registered in the normal way. But what about those cases that are slightly unusual?

What about ancestors who were normally resident in Ireland but married or died outside the country? (Remember, we are not talking here about Irish people who emigrated. Emigrants registered with their adopted country. We are here dealing with people who normally lived in Ireland but were temporarily away from home, intending to return almost immediately.)

The Registrar General in Dublin has a number of records relating to such people. Prior to 1922 Irish people abroad wishing to register a marriage or death did so with the GRO in London. You may search these records at both www.1837online.com and the Family History Centre in London.

The Dublin GRO maintains the following records covering a range of other unusual cases:

a register of all Irish-born people who died at sea between 1 January 1864 and 31 December 1921, and thereafter of Irish-born people other than those born in the North;
registers of deaths of Irish-born people certified by British Consuls abroad, between the above dates;
a register of the marriages celebrated in Dublin by Rev J.F.G. Schulze, Minister of the German Protestant Church, Poolbeg Street, Dublin, from 1806 to 1837;
registers under the Births, Deaths and Marriages (Army) Act, 1879;
a register of certain births and deaths outside the state and a register of certain Lourdes marriages.
There is also a searchable index for deaths since 1864 and one of marriages since 1845.

Contacts:

The General Register Office (Oifig An Ard-Chláraitheora), Government Offices,, Convent Road, Roscommon T: +353 (0) 90 663 2900 W: www.groireland.ie/ Email certificate application (must be sent with appropriate downloadable form) The General Register Office also maintains a family history research facility at 3rd Floor, Block 7, Irish Life Centre, Lower Abbey Street, Dublin 1

General Register Office (GRO) Oxford House, 49-55 Chichester Street, Belfast BT1 4HL. Tel.: 028 9025 2000 web.: www.groni.gov.uk

Details of all the LDS Family History Centres are available online at www.familysearch.org/

The British Library, Oriental and India Office Collections, 96, Euston Road, London NW1 2DB tel.:0207 412 7873 W: www.bl.uk/collections/orientalandindian.htm

General Register Office, London W: *www.direct.gov.uk/en/Governmentcitizensandrights/Registeringlifeevents/Familyhistoryandresearch/index.htm*
For copies of certificates contact Certificate Services Section, PO Box 2, Southport PR8 2JD T: 0845 603 7788 W: *www.gro.gov.uk/gro/content/certificates/* E: *certificate.service@gro.gsi.gov.uk*

take a closer look inside...

Search for your Irish roots online using a database of the largest collection of parish records and other sources on the island of Ireland. Or commission one of our county genealogy centres to research your Irish family history.

www.rootsireland.ie

The Public Record Office of Northern Ireland
The Future of our History
Ann McVeigh

Exciting times are ahead for the Public Record Office of Northern Ireland (PRONI). In April 2011 a new state-of-the-art national archive will open to the public in **Titanic Quarter, Belfast.**

The new accommodation will comprise an expansive search room (with integral microfilm area, internet access and laptop-enabled tables) and reading rooms providing greatly enhanced capacity and facilities for researchers, including access to the Electronic Catalogue and ordering system. The storage repositories will also be greatly expanded and improved with bespoke 'rolling rack' shelving systems, fully compliant with the British Standard for the preservation of archival documents. A spacious ground floor area equipped with Wi-Fi will house exhibitions and lectures, orientation points, public utilities, and a café with internet access, making it a great place to meet friends old and new and chat about the latest research successes.

To facilitate this move PRONI will be closed to the public for a period of up to eight months. However we are committed to continue to provide the best service we can to all our customers during this period. In line with that commitment, we will be working hard to ensure that while we are closed to the public (from close of business on Friday 3rd September, 2010) researchers will not be inconvenienced too much. Our website, recently improved and easy to navigate, will not only keep researchers abreast of the latest developments, but will have a number of very useful features added.

PRONI Website

The website is a great place to start your research as it contains information on the most useful archives to consult at PRONI, an updated set of PRONI's family and local history leaflets, and information on other sites that may be useful to your area of study. To assist researchers a list of *Alternative Sources for Archival Information* has been compiled to provide advice on what is available either on-line or through libraries and other institutions and organisations. The *'Frequently Asked Questions'* page covers a host of topics. One of the most useful and popular parts of the PRONI website is our extensive introductions to over 140 major private collections. These give users an excellent overview of each archive as well as detailed historical background information. Increasingly, however, we are putting more databases and guides on-line.

Records Available On-line

Several major databases are available on-line:

The Freeholders' Records

Relating to the six counties of Northern Ireland from the mid 18th to early 19th centuries, record the name and place of residence of those who were entitled to vote (or who actually voted) at elections. This on-line resource of over 5,000 high quality images of the registers is fully searchable and provides direct access to a unique resource for family and local history for a period that has a scarcity of documentary evidence.

The Ulster Covenant

This contains the names and addresses of those who opposed Home Rule in the early part of the twentieth century. Almost half a million people signed either the Covenant (men), or the Declaration (women). The database is searchable by surname and each surname is linked to an image of the actual document showing the handwritten signature.

The Wills Index

Wills and Letters of Administration 1858 - c.1920 and the index is now searchable on-line. Although

QUEEN'S BRIDGE, BELFAST.

the original wills were destroyed and it is simply copies of the wills that have survived, they are the earliest complete set proved by the Supreme Court of Judicature in Ireland, who assumed responsibility for granting probate and letters of administration in 1858. The index is based on the entries in the will calendars that summarise every will proved and all letters of administration granted, amounting to over 148,000 entries. Although many wills relate to the professional classes and the landed gentry, most walks of life are covered, from farmers, labourers and grocers, to blacksmiths, innkeepers, watchmakers, and even a few people who died in the workhouse! The last testaments of well-known personalities are also represented, for example, Thomas Andrews, the director of Harland & Wolff who was aboard the Titanic when it sank in 1912, and Charles Lanyon, civil engineer and architect, who designed many of the finest buildings in Belfast, including Queen's University, the Custom House, and the Crumlin Road Court House.

Street Directories

These volumes, previously on open access in the Search Room, were very heavily used and damage was becoming critical. Further handling would have endangered their long term preservation so it was decided to scan the directories to provide an on-line search. The directories on-line cover the years 1819 to 1900 but with some gaps in the series. PRONI does not hold copies of all street directories and even when the main run of the *Belfast and Ulster Street Directory* begins in 1852 there are gaps in the series up to 1900. The directories were published for trade and business purposes largely as a result of the growth in trade at home and with the wider world, hence the emphasis on the listing of manufacturers, traders and merchants. Some, for example, Matier's 1835-6 *Directory* and the 1831-2 *Directory* feature only Belfast, but will also generally include a list of the gentry in the neighbourhood. These 'village directories' include a list of the principal inhabitants living on the outskirts of Belfast, for example in Dunmurry, Jordanstown and Newtownbreda, as well as an alphabetical listing referred to as 'Country Residents'. Occasionally the directory is only for some provincial towns, for example the 1840 *New Commercial Directory of Armagh, Newry, Londonderry*, etc. While there are problems with their accuracy,

they are, nevertheless, an invaluable resource for family and local historians.

Names Index

The Name Search launched in 2009 currently includes the following sets of indexes:

Index to pre-1858 wills (these are copies of original wills and are to be found in various collections in PRONI) and a selection of diocesan will indexes [1]

Surviving fragments of the 1740 and the 1766 religious census returns

1775 dissenters petitions

Pre-1910 coroners' inquest papers

About the pre-1858 wills index

Although most originals were destroyed in the fire in the Public Record Office of Ireland (Dublin) in 1922, copies of testamentary records or extracts from them survive in a wide variety of PRONI sources. The pre-1858 wills index is an attempt to bring together pre-1858 wills and administrations found within the archives in PRONI. There are over 15,500 entries in this index.

About the 1740 and 1766 religious census

These returns are not only of value to the family and local historian but to those interested in Irish surnames and how they have been anglicised. The returns list the names of heads of households arranged largely by county, barony and parish and in at least half of the returns there is a breakdown by town. No further information is given about the individuals. The returns show religion as either Roman Catholic (referred to as 'Papists') or Protestant. Protestants were sometimes distinguished as either Church of Ireland, or Dissenters, with Dissenters being mainly Presbyterians. The returns also give an account of any Roman Catholic priests operating in the parish and their names. There is often more than one person of the same name listed in a townland/parish but we have no way of knowing whether this was in fact the case or if names were duplicated in transcription.

About the Dissenters' Petition

The petitions are lists of names of Dissenters arranged either by parish, by congregation, by town and neighbourhood or in one instance by barony. Occasionally, members of the Established Church also signed the petitions. The lists usually indicate whether the signatories were Dissenters or Established Church members, although there are occasions when no such information is recorded.

About the pre-1910 coroners' inquest papers

Coroners in Northern Ireland are either barristers or solicitors and are appointed by the Lord Chancellor. They inquire into deaths that are unexpected or unexplained, a result of violence, negligence or accident, or any other unusual circumstances. In total, 5,911 files and papers relating to Coroners' Inquests, 1872-1909 are now referenced on Name Search, containing details of the surname, forename, address, date of death and date of inquest.

On-line Guide to Church Records:

Church records are an invaluable source for the family historian, especially those that pre-date Civil Registration of births, deaths and marriages, which was introduced in Ireland in 1864. PRONI's Guide to Church Records is an easy way to identify what churches are in a parish, what records exist for each church, the covering dates for each series of records (for example, baptisms, marriages, vestry minutes etc.) and their PRONI reference number.

Denominations included are: Church of Ireland, Roman Catholic, Presbyterian, Non-Subscribing Presbyterian, Reformed Presbyterian, Methodist, Moravian, Congregational, Baptist and Religious Society of Friends ('Quakers'). Normally, there will be more than one denomination of church in each parish. The denomination of a church can be identified in the Guide by the preceding code (for example, C.I. = Church of Ireland; P. = Presbyterian Church and R.C. = Roman Catholic Church). The majority of parishes covered in the Guide are located within the six counties of Northern Ireland, however, PRONI holds some records from parishes in the Republic of Ireland, particularly the border counties of Donegal, Cavan, Monaghan, Leitrim and Louth. You will still have to visit PRONI to see the actual records but at least by checking this guide, you can be confident that your journey will not be wasted.

Electronic Catalogue

Perhaps the jewel in our website's crown, the Electronic Catalogue (E-Catalogue) enables researchers to browse the lists of practically all our collections from the comfort of their own computers. Providing web access to over one and a quarter million catalogue entries, the E-Catalogue contains approximately 70% of PRONI's total catalogue of which almost 92% is relevant to family history. The database can be searched by keyword, such as a name, townland or subject matter; by date; or by PRONI reference number. Some private documents have been transcribed, thus removing the need to see the original in a number of cases. This resource has made it so much easier to carry out research 24/7.

Coming Soon

Work is currently underway to digitise the **Re-Valuation Books** (VAL/12B) to make these records available on-line in the future. The First General (Griffith's) Valuation was completed by 1864. However, this could be considered simply a snapshot in time as changes to land ownership and property developments are not recorded, hence the introduction in 1864 of the re-valuation books which noted any changes in land use. Thereafter, properties were valued annually until the early 1930s, with each volume of the re-valuation books covering approximately a ten-year period. Each year, assessors recorded any change in the quality or dimensions of the properties, or in the names of occupiers or immediate lessors, and any differences in the acreage and value. The changes were recorded in different colours of ink, one colour for each year, and the alterations are usually dated. This can help to establish significant dates in family history, such as dates of death, sale or migration.

It is hoped that the information available on the PRONI website will help researchers to continue their work but unfortunately, not everything can be put on-line. For this reason, the microfilmed copies of our most popular records will be available at an alternative venue while we are in transit to the new building.

PRONI Self-Service Facility to move to Cregagh Library

PRONI has worked with Libraries NI – the new single library service for Northern Ireland – to make sure these family history resources will be available for research during this time. The Self-Service microfilm Facility will find a temporary home at Cregagh Library, 409-413 Cregagh Road, Belfast, from September until PRONI re-opens in April 2011. This popular family history resource, which includes church records, copy will books, and copies of the Registry of Deeds, will be available during their normal library opening hours.

During the transit period, PRONI staff will be working hard to ensure the smooth implementation of new processes and procedures. We are planning a number of outreach events such as lectures, presentations, conferences, and family history fairs. Keep checking our website for updates.

Public Records

Many people are under the impression that, due to the fire in the Public Record Office of Ireland in the Four Courts in Dublin, there are no surviving public records before in 1922. In fact, there are many series of records that go back to the early 19th and even into the 18th century. For example, the Grand Jury Presentment Books that give the names of those who received money for the construction and repair of roads, bridges, gaols, and other public works, date back to the 1760s.

Other early sources include:

Valuation records, dating from 1830s to the present day

Tithe Applotment books, 1823-37,

Copy wills, 1838-c.1900,

Original wills, 1900 to 2002;

Registers and inspectors' observation books of approximately 1,600 national/public elementary/primary schools, 1870s – c.1950s

Grant-aid applications of the Commissioners of National Education, 1832 to 1889;

Ordnance Survey maps (various scales) 1831 - present;

Minutes, indoor and outdoor relief registers, and other papers of the Boards of Guardians who administered the workhouse system from 1838 to 1948;

Records, including admission registers, of lunatic asylums, some dating back to the mid-19th century (but these are subject to extended closure for 100 years);

Title deeds, leases and wills in the Irish Land Commission and the Land Purchase Commission archive, some of which date back into the 18th century.

Guides to using the more popular collections, such as the tithe applotment books, the large scale Ordnance Survey town plans, education records and probate records, are available in the PRONI search room.

Private Archives

Privately deposited records are also available at PRONI and can often be very adequate substitutes for those public records destroyed in the Four Courts Fire. The most important of those are:

Records of solicitors' firms, which include copies of wills, leases and title deeds;

Great landed estates (many of which go back into the 17th and 18th centuries);

Railway companies, who bought up a considerable amount of land;

Churches, where generations were baptised and married.

Equally useful are family and personal papers, and the working notes of antiquarians and genealogists who worked in the Public Record Office of Ireland prior to the fire of 1922. These scholars took copious notes from the early records and their notebooks contain information on documents dating back to the mid 17th centuries.

Almost all the major estate archives for Northern Ireland are held in PRONI and you can find descriptions of many of them on the PRONI website. Among the more notable estate archives are: Downshire (Cos Down and Antrim); Antrim (Co. Antrim); Abercorn (Co. Tyrone); Belmore (Co. Fermanagh); Gosford, Brownlow and Caledon (Co. Armagh); and Drapers' Company (Co. Londonderry). Other estate papers are also available.

Opening Times

PRONI will continue to operate as normal until close of business on Friday, 3 September. This means we will be open to the public Mon - Wed and Fri 9.00 am – 4.45 pm; Thurs - 10.00 am – 8.45 pm. Latest time for ordering documents is 4.15 pm (Thursdays, 6.30 pm). There is no need to make an appointment unless you intend to bring a group. Group visits are very welcome but must be booked in advance.

Research is free for those pursuing personal and educational research, however, all visitors will need to obtain a Visitor Registration card at Reception which requires photographic proof of identity.

PRONI staff look forward to welcoming visitors old and new to our new home in Titanic Quarter in April 2011. In the meantime, please keep checking our website for updates and information.

•**Please note, the original bonds referred to in the indexes no longer exist. There is no further information available other than that recorded in the indexes and therefore copies of the actual administration bonds cannot be provided**

Digital Communication
The Metropolitan
Telegraph Gallery
1871

digital genealogy

273

My Ancestor Was On The Census - Well They Should Have Been!

John Hanson

We have all in our research asked the question above – if not then you have been extremely lucky so far and you are bound to get there sometime As a general rule I suspect that the majority of us can find about 80% of our ancestors easily – it is the remainder that are the problem and here I want to explore the reason why

There are many reasons as to why but they generally fall into one of the following which will be explored later in more detail:

- Not in the Country or not at home
- Missing or Damaged pages
- Failure to provide information
- Quality Matters
- Enumeration and Indexing errors

Before we go into the detail on these I need to point out that this article is based mainly on the censuses of England and Wales – see the end for details relating to Scotland and Ireland Also the information contained here is based on the situation when the article was written in August 2010

Also, before we get into the specifics we ought to clear up some initials points which may help

If you can't find them on one website search engine - try another – it could be just a simple case of mis-indexing (see below) or it could be that the company concerned has missed a complete or part piece number So if you normally use Ancestry - www ancestry co uk - try Find My Past - www findmypast co uk - but do bear in mind that not all of the companies may have indexes all of the censuses

The top four sites all offer a subscription service as well as pay-per-view options One needs to remember that the subscription options will normally allow unlimited access to all of the material that is available on the site, not just the census

Whilst these are the commercial companies it doesn't mean that they are the only options,

however they are the only ones to offer images to go with the transcriptions so that you can check the entries yourself It is worth exploring the internet for other indexes but first you may want to try one of the following websites:

www censusfinder com

Whilst predominantly American based there is a growing list of UK transcriptions that exist

www ukbmd org uk

Whilst this website is mainly concerned with birth, marriage and death it has a growing list of references to census indexes which can be found either on the county based pages or on the separate pages dedicated to the census

www freecen org uk

This site is a sister to the freebmd www freebmd org uk site but aims to provide a similar sort of service but for the census returns of 1841-1871 and 1891 Because it is an ongoing project you must remember that your area may not have been done yet – if this is the case, why not volunteer to index that part of the census, do your research at the same time and also help others

The Church of Jesus Christ of Latter Day Saints website **www familysearch org** has the 1881 census transcript for England and Wales (with the exception of The Genealogist this is the same index that both Ancestry and FindMyPast used to start with) It also has the 1881 for Canada and the 1880 for the United States (all free) If you look at new Record Pilot Search (found on the Search Records list) you will notice the 1841 and 1861 census transcripts – licensed from elsewhere – however the search options are not as comprehensive as the main commercial sites

Just because a search input screen has lots of boxes, you don't have to fill them all in The reason for this is simple Despite what you may think, computers are dumb and have to match all off the characters in all the fields that you have completed Therefore the more you enter

Census Year	1841	1851	1861	1871	1881	1891	1901	1911
www FindMyPast co uk	All	All	All	All	All	All	All	All
www Ancestry co uk	All	All	All	All	All	All	All	All
www TheGenealogist co uk	All	All	All	All	All	All	All	All
www originsnetwork com	All		All	All				
www 1901censusonline com							All	
www 1911census co uk								All

The following table should be a help to understand who has what:

the more the chance there is of not finding what you want

You can often get away with the minimum of information and in some cases just a name Take for example the 1901 census and my grandmother Zilpah Bird – there is only one yet there are 50 (using the Find My Past website) possible entries for her brother Stanley Add a birth year to Stanley (1897 +/- 1 year) and you get only 15 It doesn't take long then to look down that list for the possible entry I never work with exact year of birth with census returns as none of my ancestors were that accurate! You do also need to bear in mind possible age transcription errors and the fact that our ancestors, men and women alike, sometimes lied!

Most census websites with search facilities of their own allow you to use a *'wild card '* A *'wild card'* is a single character, normally an asterisk *, that can be used to represent one or more characters and therefore allows you to search for one or more versions of a name or place at the same time However all of the sites do not use the same rules Most sites will insist on two characters before you can use the wild card, but Ancestry insists on three whereas Find My Past enables you to use the wild card at the beginning of a word as well

Your ancestor may well have been in an institution Depending on the type of institution this can create its own set of problems

Workhouses and hospitals are not normally a problem – other than the ones who insisted on putting the names the wrong way round on the census returns and were indexed with the surname and first names reversed so you end up with Smith John – so if you can't find your John Smith try Smith John

The problem is more likely to lie with prisons and asylums where the person is more often than not listed simply by their initials If the place of birth is accurate then you should be able to find them

There is a useful trick with Ancestry that you might like to try Take any census year and go down below the search screen and select a country – lets try England Then select just the county of Lancashire and enter no other information When Ancestry displays a result from such a search without a name it displays the result in alphabetical order of forename within surname What you get at the beginning, as this result shows (see figure 2), is all those entries that are either hard to read or a real puzzle! Try it with the county of interest for your missing ancestor and you might be surprised

Not in the Country or not at home

We have to remember that our ancestors were a lot more mobile than we sometimes give them credit for My grandmother Zilpah Bird was born in West Suffolk in 1892 and married in Edmonton, Middlesex in 1923 In the 1901 census the family was living in Barking, Essex - somewhere that my mother had no idea that the family had ever lived So try to be broad with your searching and not assume where you think they are living

Quite often you will find that young men are missing from the census returns prior to 1911. The reason is that they are most likely to be in the Army The British Army overseas was not included

Punch 1851

FILLING UP THE CENSUS PAPER
Wife of his Bosom." Upon my word, Mr. Peewitt! Is this the Way you Fill up your Census? So you call Yourself the 'Head of the Family'-do you-and me a 'Female?'"

in the census returns for the first time till 1911 So if he is between 16 and 36 try looking in the new Chelsea Pensioners British Army Service Records (classes WO96 and WO97 at the National Archives, Kew) which have now been digitised, indexed and available on FindMyPast If his papers are not there then it is possible that they were extracted and merged with

THE CENSUS.

Head of the Family (filling up the paper). "WELL, MISS PRIMROSE, AS A VISITOR, I MUST PUT YOUR AGE IN ! WHAT SHALL WE SAY ?
Miss P. "OH, IT'S BEST TO BE STRAIGHTFORWARD. THE SAME AS DEAR FLORA. TWENTY LAST BIRTHDAY !"

PUNCH APRIL 20,

his papers for WW1 (TNA classes WO363 and WO364) which are available on Ancestry However with the WW1 papers remember that only about 40% of them exist With the Census Returns for the army included in 1911 there should be none missing You could also try reading one of the books on British Army ancestors such as the *'My Ancestor was   '* series for the Society of Genealogists

If the your ancestor was in the Royal Navy then he should be included in the returns as they have always been included no matter where in the world the ship was as a Royal Naval ship is classed as part of the 'mainland' If they were in the Merchant Navy then it is more a question of suck it and see If the ship was in port then it should be included in the returns but of course it might not be where you expect it to be as it could be in port anywhere in the country If the ship was going to be at sea then the master was given a return, asked to complete it and hand it in at the port of arrival (if in the UK) – how many did I wonder! There are again several books available of tracing both Royal and Merchant Navy ancestors

In the 1911 census the problem is with the women and not the men and relates to the suffragettes To quote from the 1911 census website help pages www 1911census co uk/content/default aspx?r=33&98

'**The suffragettes** As part of the protest against the government's continued refusal to grant women the vote, the suffragettes organised a mass

boycott of the census Exact numbers will never be known, but it is estimated that thousands of women may be missing from the 1911 census Many women made sure that they stayed away from the family home all night, and were not listed on the census at all In such cases, they will simply be untraceable via the census '

It is also possible that your ancestor went abroad, either permanently or just to work for a while The passenger lists for those leaving for far flung places exist from about 1890 onwards and are at TNA (class BT27 for outbound and BT26 for inbound) Both have been digitised, indexed and are online BT27 with FindMyPast and BT26 with Ancestry You could also try searching the census returns for the USA and Canada (available on www ancestry com) In both cases the place of birth is likely to be listed as just 'England ' Unfortunately the census returns for Australia were not kept until the year 2001 so no census returns there to help

Missing/Damaged pages

The main sites tend to list known complete missing piece numbers from any census and you will also find them listed in TNA catalogue with the term 'missing' or *'part missing '*

Occasionally pages will get damaged and the best example is the problems with the 1851 returns for Manchester which were water damaged With the help of Manchester and Lancashire Family History Society a lot of the material has been salvaged and you can read about it at www 1851-unfilmed org uk

The 1861 is known for the problem of missing front and end pages of many enumeration books, caused by too much handling I suspect If you had wanted to look at the 1861 census in the 1950's you would have been giving the original book – how often is that likely to happen these days!

Odd pages can become damaged – missing corners, pieces torn off were they have been caught somewhere, half pages or even single pages that have become detached and the information gives no idea as to where it is There are also pages where the enumerator or a checking clerk has spilt the ink pot over the page after it has been completed

Failure to provide information

There is often the question someone asks about those that really do seem to vanish Well there are at least a couple of examples that I can quote Look at John Travers in the 1841 census (HO107/723 Book 12 Folio 6 Page6 – fined £5 for his sins) or have a look at Piece RG10/544 Folio 117 Page 41 in the 1871 for a page of unknown sailors who seem to have enjoyed themselves in the process! (do you think that the enumerator was trying to say something about the status of the women?)

People in institutions, especially in an area away from their home, often have an unknown place or birth or at best just a county

Quality Matters

Quality here is about the quality of the image being scanned – was it black/white or greyscale? I have seen pages on Ancestry that are almost unreadable yet the image on Find My Past is perfectly readable – however I have seen it the other way round as well This is partly caused by the fact that every company had to create their own images from the films provided by TNA The 1911 is totally different of course having been scanned in full colour and should any other company want to create an index to the 1911 then they will license a copy of the images created by BrightSolid

Enumeration and Indexing errors

The biggest problem relates to those people that have been mis-transcribed – or have they been? With the exception of the 1911 census, what we actually look at is a transcription of the household schedules into enumeration books The schedules for the earlier censuses would have looked similar to those of the 1911 So the error may well have been created when the enumerator copied the entries or perhaps it is what he thought that he heard There is a problem as many of us will have seen with the check marks created by the clerks collating the statistics at the time of the census who always seem to have crossed through that vital word or number that we want to read If only they would go back and re-scan them in full colour as all the check marks (certainly for the 1891 census) are in different colours and make reading the text so much easier

The 1911 is more likely to generate errors than the earlier census returns simply because of the number of different sets of handwriting that exist – some 8 million as opposed to 30,000

Have a look at the entry for Snowbear Hatham in the 1881 census (Piece 4943 Folio 42 Page 21), you can just imagine the enumerator struggling with that one Also there is the family of fellow Census Detective Jeanne Bunting whose grandfather

Page 28

NAME and SURNAME or Initials of Inmates	(1) RELATION to Head of Family—or (2) Position in the Institution	CONDITION	AGE [last Birthday] of MALES / FEMALES	RANK, PROFESSION, or OCCUPATION	WHERE BORN	If Deaf-and-Dumb or Blind
1 5447 J. M.	Prisoner	U	55	Hawker	Scotland	●
2		Mard	52	Labr	Middx London	
3 5780 R. C.		Mard	54	Labr	Cumb Sandy Camp	
4 1 C. F.		Mard	24	Hairdresser	Ireland	
5 2 G. C.		Mard	32	Shoemaker	Hants Southampton	
6 3 B.		U	21	Labr	Lanc Liverpool	
7 1/2 J. J.		Mard	43	Tobacconist	Norfolk Melton	
8 7 J. J.		U	28	Collier	Staffordshy Sheffield	
9 9 R. K.		U	28	Boatman	Warwick Birmingham	
10 10 J. W.		U	32	Sailor	Ireland	
11 1 F. C.		Mard	25	Power Weaver	Lanc Colne	
12 2 J. P.		U	30	Hawker	Yorks Leeds	
13 3 A. R.		U	78	Agl Labr	Essex Nazeing	
14 8 G. H.		Marrd	78	Labr	Monmouth Churchill	
15 20 A. A.		U	40	Fileculler	Surry Reigningham	
16 2 C. J.		U	31	Frogman Man	Stafford Sheffield	
17 3 R. K.		Mard	69	Labr	Lanc Morley	

© Crown Copyright Images reproduced by courtesy of The National Archives, London, England.

Foulds Cronshaw appears to have been a habitual criminal as his criminal record shows – details can be found on www halstedresearch org uk/ui07 htm He was sentenced at Preston, Lancashire, on 23 May 1859 to serving 4 years Penal Servitude for 'Larceny before conviction of felony' and can be seen here in Dartmoor, Prison He is entry number 11

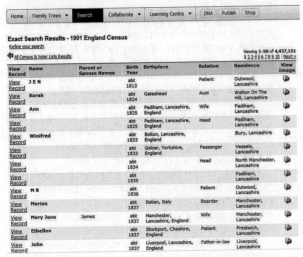

| | Home | Family Trees ▼ | Search | Collaborate ▼ | Learning Centre ▼ | DNA | Publish | Shop |

Exact Search Results - 1901 England Census

Refine your search

◄ All Census & Voter Lists Results

Viewing 1-50 of 4,437,151
1 2 3 4 5 6 7 8 9 10 | Next »

View Record	Name	Parent or Spouse Names	Birth Year	Birthplace	Relation	Residence	View Image
View Record	J E N		abt 1813		Patient	Outwood, Lancashire	🔍
View Record	Sarah		abt 1824	Gateshead	Aunt	Walton On The Hill, Lancashire	🔍
View Record	Ann		abt 1825	Padiham, Lancashire, England	Wife	Padiham, Lancashire	🔍
View Record			abt 1825	Padiham, Lancashire, England	Head	Padiham, Lancashire	🔍
View Record	Winifred		abt 1833	Bolton, Lancashire, England		Bury, Lancashire	🔍
View Record			abt 1833	Golcar, Yorkshire, England	Passenger	Vessels, Lancashire	🔍
View Record			abt 1834		Head	North Manchester, Lancashire	🔍
View Record			abt 1835			Padiham, Lancashire	🔍
View Record	M B		abt 1836		Patient	Outwood, Lancashire	🔍
View Record	Marian		abt 1837	Italian, Italy	Boarder	Manchester, Lancashire	🔍
View Record	Mary Jane	James	abt 1837	Manchester, Lancashire, England	Wife	Manchester, Lancashire	🔍
View Record	Ethellon		abt 1837	Stockport, Cheshire, England	Patient	Prestwich, Lancashire	🔍
View Record	John		abt 1837	Liverpool, Lancashire, England	Father-in-law	Liverpool, Lancashire	🔍

The result of searching for everyone living in Lancashire in the 1901 census showing the start of the 4,437,151 entries! The fourth entry down is one of many from the same page where there is little information yet the information is correctly indexed on Find My Past – the problem is caused by the poor image quality of the Ancestry image

Rueben Attersley is there as Robert, his wife Rosa as Rebecca and daughter Ruth as Rachel (RG13/1591 Folio 148 Page 17) Was it the enumerator or the head of the household that got it wrong? How can we be certain that they are one and the same? – the couple were married from that address, the daughter was born there as well and also the surname is fairly rare so that there are only 30 entries in the 1901 census and it is also Jeanne's one-name study

So how do you find those elusive ancestors?

Well, if you are still stumped after all of the above here are some more tips

Forget the surname – just searching on first name, age and place of birth will produce a list of possible people all you need to do is look down the list of surnames looking for the most likely contender

With Ancestry I prefer to go to the 'old style' search which means that I have total control over the search rather than let ancestry make its, at times vague, suggestions With the 'old style' search screen there is a box in the top left that lets you select 'exact match' only allowing you absolutely total control The other option that Ancestry suggest is 'soundex' – a means to linking similar surnames but the system is now outdated and I much prefer the system of variant names offered by FindMyPast – assuming that you tick the 'include variants' box

Place names can often be difficult to read and I tend to abbreviate them to just the first four letters followed by the wild card character So a place like Ripponden becomes Ripp* which will cover most of the mis-transcriptions of the name

As we said earlier 'less is best' – if you get too many results from your search criteria you can always go back and add more information to reduce the numbers which is easier that trying to take it away because you never know what you got wrong

Scotland

At present the only real place to consult Scottish census returns from 1841-1901 is on the pay-per-view website Scotland Online www scotlandonline gov uk as it is the only one with the images The 1911 for Scotland is covered by different laws from those in England and Wales and therefore will not be released until after 100 years – now whether that is 3rd April 2011 or the first working day in 2012 is still uncertain Ancestry co uk do have an index to the census to 1901 but have no images

Ireland

To all intents and purposes the census returns prior to 1901 were all destroyed in World War I or the uprising of 1922 The returns for 1901 and 1911 are available free via the National Archives of Ireland www census nationalarchives ie – I was surprised to find several people for the one-name study I work on there as servants

About the Author

John Hanson is a founder member of the Census Detectives www censusdetectives org uk who travel the country giving free advice He is also the author of **'Getting the Best from the 1911 census'** published by the Society of Genealogists www sog org uk He has been interested in family history for the past 25 years, in particular the use of computers and the Internet for research He is the Research Director for The Halsted Trust, maintains the research website www halstedresearch org uk and was made a Fellow of the Society of Genealogists in 2005 for 'services to genealogy '

It's Good to Talk
Joe O'Neill

Every single guide to family history advises the initiate genealogist to begin by interviewing members of your family This, we are always told, is the foundation of all subsequent research, the rooting soil from which the great edifice of your family tree will spring

Certainly, your most valuable source is the memories of your family Without it, you are like a man crossing the desert without a compass: you don't know where you are going or how to get there Your family will give you those all-important pointers, an outline of the family structure and vital clues about where to find the relevant documentation They will also save you countless hours of fruitless searching

However, though all this is accepted, few writers say much more about how to get the most from this invaluable resource It's almost as if they assume that interviewing members of the family is without pitfalls and that unlike scrutinizing court records or overseers' accounts it is without its hazard Unfortunately, this is not the case and in order to maximise the potential of your family you must prepare carefully and anticipate problems

But don't take too long to get started The longer you leave it the greater the possibility that those with invaluable information will no longer be available Obviously, this is particularly so with older relatives If, for instance, you are able to interview your grandmother, she will probably be able to give you some information about her grandparents Immediately you have information on four generations of ancestors without consulting a single written record

Before you speak to anyone, sketch out a family tree using all the information you already have Don't worry about gaps At this stage everything is provisional Later you can use it in discussion with your relatives to confirm or question the links you have made and to fill gaps It may also serve as a means of bringing your interview to a conclusion

Photographs are also helpful Have any family photographs to hand when you are interviewing Many people recall faces better than names and a wedding photograph is an excellent means of jogging memories

Both the family tree and the photographs provide a good way of rounding off an interview or of rescuing it if it seems to be floundering

Which family members do you talk to?

Ideally you should speak to all of them Lore suggests that women, who usually take responsibility for remembering birthdays and anniversaries, are a better source of information than their male counterparts Anecdotal evidence suggests that not only do they have a far better recollection for the details of family history, but also that they are often aware of nuances in relationships to which men are oblivious

Who to Interview

- Brothers / sisters
- Cousins
- Aunts / uncles
- Parents
- Grandparents
- Family friends

Don't think that going to such lengths is unnecessary Information about a family passes down the generations in an erratic and unpredictable manner There may be many aspects of a family's story which are familiar to the older siblings, but entirely unknown to the younger On the other hand, the youngest children often lived at home after the older ones had left They are therefore likely to have become the repository of a great many family documents in addition to knowing most about their parents' later lives Every relative you don't speak to is a potential source of information neglected

Let those you speak to know that you are undertaking a serious piece of research and would welcome help

Group or Individual Interview?

Should you convene a family gathering or speak to each person separately? Speaking in a group makes for an informal and open atmosphere, reduces the pressure on each individual and is likely to be productive as one person's recollections may well prompt others' memories But it may be difficult to arrange

Even if you opt for a group interview, you will almost invariably find when you review your records, that there are gaps in your information Perhaps the information you have gathered prompts new questions Either way you will almost certainly want to speak individually to at least some of those who formed the original group

The Interview

There is no need to reinvent the wheel Ask if any other member of the family is already researching your family history or has shown an interest in doing so You may discover that

• Explain that you are gathering information to write an accurate family history Make it clear from the outset that you do not want to discuss any issues which your respondent would rather avoid nor will you divulge anything told in confidence
• Keep a record by making notes, a sound recording or cam cording
• Several short sessions are better than one mammoth sitting
• Record everything and don't dismiss even the flimsiest recollection as insignificant

One of my great aunts, for instance, told me that her grandfather's house was called 'Mallow ' At the time this seemed unimportant Later, however, it proved invaluable as it allowed me to identify the town in County Cork where he was born

Remember that family myths and legends with caution are not always totally accurate narratives They usually contain at least a grain of truth and often the irritation of this grain may prompt you to pursue a productive line of research However, beware of those that seem to be too good to be true Almost every family has a story of a wealthy ancestor who left a large, unclaimed inheritance Every member of my family assured me that we were all directly descended from the high kings of Ireland To date I have found no evidence of royal lineage Unless there is some concrete evidence to suggest that you are descended from Lord Nelson, don't waste time trying to prove it

Certain subjects require sensitivity Some episodes of family history are so painful that people don't want to resurrect them It's also important to realise that many members of the older generation do not share current blasé attitudes to illegitimacy, homosexuality, certain illness – especially mental illness – and criminality They may not wish to broach such matters

Don't let this annoy you It is, of course, inconvenient and you may be tempted to press where you feel the interviewee is reticent This is never the right thing to do We have no right to make anyone feel uncomfortable
– apart from which it is

some of the preliminary work has already been done Failing that, you may have a fellow enthusiast, someone willing to share the expenditure of money and time and keep you on track A word of warning, however: a good historian always checks the findings of others, not because he is mistrustful but because even the most meticulous researcher can misinterpret a source

When interviewing, you are likely to get more information *if you begin by asking open, as opposed to closed, questions* 'When was your father born?' is a closed question and is likely to elicit no more than a date If however, you ask the open question, *'What do you know about your father's early life?'* you are likely to prompt a fuller, discursive response which may well turn up all sorts of information Once you have broached the wider topic of your father's early life, you may then clarify details by asking closed questions, such as *'So he wasn't born in Manchester?'*

How to Interview

• Don't make it seem like an interrogation Create a relaxed atmosphere conducive to reminisces and nostalgia

counterproductive People are most likely to share what they know with us when we are sensitive to their feelings

A face to face conversation is the best way to gather information If that is not possible, you will have to settle for speaking over the phone, by email or letter

During the course of the interview ask your relative if you may see anything they have that may be helpful

Ask to See

- Old family photographs
- A family Bible
- Birth, marriage and death certificates: these are the building blocks of any genealogy
- Certificates of qualification or membership
- Memorial cards – particularly popular among Catholics
- Personal documents – letters, address books
- Newspaper cuttings, such as announcements and obituaries or accounts of incidents which affected the family
- Military or other medals
- Mementoes of an ancestor – a father's watch, for instance

Structure your interview by asking about each of the following in this order:

- The person himself
- Their brothers and sisters
- Their parents and uncles and aunts
- Their grandparents and relations of the same generation
- Their own and their siblings descendents

When recording information, it's a good idea to allocate a fresh sheet of paper to each relative and to ensure that for each ancestor you discover as much as possible You will find a suggested list of questions, which, of course, you may modify as you think appropriate

Key Questions

- Full name and nickname
- Date and place of birth
- The names of other members of the family and their relationship
- The person's appearance and anything that was distinctive about it
- Education
- Occupations and training or apprenticeships Did any of these run in the family?
- Homes / residences, with dates
- Hobbies or membership of clubs, associations or societies
- Spouse and how the marriages ended e g death of spouse, divorce
- Children
- Did they serve in the armed forces? Details of time spent in the armed forces are invaluable in locating service records

- Holidays and outings – where they went and with whom Past generations often spent holidays visiting family members
- Did they emigrate?
- Religion and churches attended
- Where buried
- Anything else e g political views, attitudes to social issues, values, quirks or eccentricities

Keeping a Record

It's best to make a written record, by making notes as you talk This has the advantage of forcing you to concentrate on what you are being told and encouraging you to prompt for clarification and further explanation The disadvantage, however, is that some people find it very off-putting to have someone writing down what they are saying It certainly doesn't help to build up a rapport and can be very time-consuming

You may opt for a sound recorder, preferably unobtrusive

In recent times many use a camcorder Ideally, you could get the informant to tell part of his story where it took place and record that Apart from making any account clearer, revisiting a significant location may revive memories

You may choose to use a combination of all three But regardless of how you record information, you should always note the name of the person who provided it and the date of the interview This is invaluable when it comes to cross checking information And remember: everything you are told must eventually be corroborated by other sources

It is no more than basic courtesy to give those who have helped you periodic updates on your progress They will appreciate it and feel that you value their help Your findings may also prompt memories thought long forgotten and lead to further discussion

The information you've gathered is pure genealogical gold which can't be mined in any record office or unearthed in any library

Social Networking and Genealogy
Chris Paton

A few decades ago, a family history community was one which basically existed in the form of a local society or organisation, where people could meet on a regular basis to discuss their mutual interests and to share resources The rapid development of communications technology, however, has now radically transformed the way that we can interact, from the increasing use of mobile phones to the most sophisticated social networking facilities on the internet Increasingly, online communities are proving to be just as popular as their historical counterparts

Before discussing how online social networks can today help us with our genealogical research, it is first worth pointing out that the world has not ended, and we have not evolved beyond the need for mouths to communicate! You can still do your research, even in today's day and age, without the use of a computer or any other gadget, though it might take you considerably longer to achieve and cost you a bit more money Social networking sites on the internet have not replaced such traditional methods, but have merely added another tool to the genealogical kitbag

So what is a social networking website? It is essentially a web portal that allows you to communicate with others when doing your research and to make your own contributions; it may even carry original genealogical data sources in its own right Using the web we can collaborate in constructing family trees with relatives, create life based archive projects, and share information in a variety of different ways And in many cases it won't cost you a penny

As a way to pool our resources the social network has become so popular that there are even websites set up to specifically keep on top of what is out there, such as the excellent Genealogy Wise - **www genealogywise com** - which hosts many dedicated research groups for names, territories or interests, chat rooms and discussion forums, blogs, a video room and much more In this article, I'll take a look at some of the types of sites that are around at present and explain how they can help with your research

Discussion Forums

An effective way to participate in a topic based conversation with likeminded historians is to subscribe to a discussion forum The forerunner to the discussion forum was the message board, of which there are still many in existence, with one of the longest running being Ancestry com's excellent Rootsweb site at **www rootsweb ancestry com** These are basically discussion threads that are gathered by category, in Ancestry's case by surname or by geographic location, and can be searched by keyword

An online forum is just an updated version of this concept, which acts in a similar way Discussion threads can be gathered together within thematic sections e g "*census queries*" or "*Hertfordshire,*" and individual discussion threads then created within these to discuss specific topics You can answer other people's comments with your own observations, amend your own comments with an update, and with some you can even add photographic content or other images One of the best around is the Rootschat forum at **www rootschat com**, which serves all countries of the United Kingdom with dedicated areas, each of which contains county based threads Similar nationwide based sites include the British Genealogy forum at **www british-genealogy com** and Genealogy Forum UK - **www genealogyforum co uk**

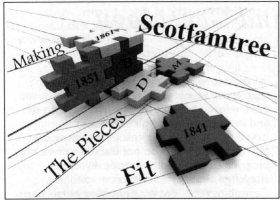

An interesting forum based community in Scotland is that of ScotFamTree - **http://scotfamtree 11 forumer com**

Structured around two main membership tiers, the first is free to enter and provides a general talking shop on all matters historically and genealogically Scottish The second, however, is a subscription based service (costing just £8 a year at time of writing), which unleashes a whole new raft of services, including dedicated forum areas for Scottish counties, occupations, vital records and census transcription copies, as well as various subject based look up areas, many of which contain digitised records You can also submit your family tree via a Gedcom file to the site's 'SFT Families' facility and have it hosted in a searchable format for those wishing to make connections with others What makes ScotFamTree stand out is its constant attempts to innovate – it even recently launched its own online television channel The ScotFamTree channel -**www livestream com/scotlandsfamilytreechannel** - carries streamed Scottish material that can be found on the web, along with specially shot interviews by the forum's moderators with key archivists and museum around the country, as well as videos of its members' meetings and gatherings In essence, it is the virtual 21st century progression of the family history society, which not only exists in an online environment but which also holds regular gatherings, attracting members from across the world

Forums also exist for specialist subject areas, for example, the truly essential Great War Forum at **http://1914-1918 invisionzone com/forums** has all you need to know about the First World War – if you can't find what you are looking for here, it is possible that you are looking at the wrong war! Many genealogy magazines also provide forums, such as *Your*

Family Tree (**http://forum yourfamilytreemag co uk**), ABM Publishing's *Practical Family History* and *Family Tree* magazines (**www familyhistoryforum co uk**), and *Who Do You Think You Are?* magazine (**www bbcwhodoyouthinkyouaremagazine com/forum**) which provides for a degree of interactivity between the readers, but also the editorial teams Make an interesting post on a forum and you may even be invited to write it up further for the magazine itself

Facebook

For most people, when you mention an instant messaging website, the first thing that comes to mind is the Facebook website at **www facebook com** It is estimated that there are currently more than 150 million people around the world who have a Facebook account, which allows them to share instant gossip, photographs, videos, news and more Increasingly genealogy companies are using the site to help spread the message of their product, but also to create communities of loyal subscribers who interact with company staff Subscribers can communicate with each other and with staff, share tips about research, ancestral stories, they can even complain when they feel the service has not been good enough Family history societies and archives are also increasingly turning to the site as a way to communicate with members in an almost real time environment around the world, a good example being that of Aberdeen and North East Scotland FHS at **www facebook com/anesfhs**, which regularly posts old photographic queries, genealogical curios, and regular news and events alerts

The site is free to join, though in the past has sometimes been plagued with negative press concerning its privacy settings, basically what you wish for people to know about you and what you don't You can be asked to join up to 'causes' and to sign up to applications which use the network you have built up of friends and family to propagate themselves and to make money However this can be easily controlled by monitoring your privacy settings Similar sites to Facebook include Bebo - **www bebo com** and MySpace - **www myspace com**

Blogging

If you can blag, blether or blunder your way through your family history experience, the chances are that you can 'blog' your way through it also! A blog is an online diary, short for 'web log', which allows you to make a daily, weekly, or completely infrequent post of your experiences or any news that you may wish to share Bloggers' posts can then be commented on by readers who can also bookmark or subscribe to the site to keep up to date

There are many types of blogs A couple of years ago a former client of mine, Chere Athey, made a once in a lifetime trip to Scotland with two of her cousins from the USA, in order that they could trace their family roots together To keep other members back in the States appraised of their progress, they created a daily blog of their discoveries, with information on new found relatives, historic buildings, and the occasional good old fashioned knees up, all of which is faithfully recorded online at **http://chereathey blogspot com** At the other extreme, a blog site can be extremely useful as a research tool The North Antrim Local Interest List at **http://nalil blogspot com** is an excellent example of a project created to share not just interesting historical facts about the area around the Giant's Causeway in Northern Ireland, but also the current news and updates of a community still very active today

On the news front there are several blogs of interest for genealogists Eastman's Online Genealogy Newsletter is an American based site located at **http://blog eogn com** that has been running for several years, providing information primarily on American developments, but also from the around the world, including the UK The site has two levels of subscription, the first being the basic newsletter which is free, and then the 'Plus' newsletter which you need to pay to subscribe to, with additional features by site founder Dick Eastman and others There are other news providers much closer to home, such as Alan Stewart's *Grow Your Own Family Tree* at **http://growyourownfamilytree wordpress com** and my own *Scottish GENES (GEnealogy News and EventS)* blog at **www**

scottishancestry blogspot com, whilst Canadian based ex-pat John Reid also keeps the useful *Anglo-Celtic Connections* blog at **www anglo-celtic-connections blogspot com**

Again, genealogy vendors are also getting in on the act, with blogs from Your Family Tree magazine - **www yourfamilytreemag com**, FindmyPast - **http://blog findmypast co uk** - and Ancestry - **http://blogs ancestry com/uk** - as good examples, with many others also continuing to promote their wares Useful blogging directory sites include Alltop - **http://genealogy alltop com** - and Geneabloggers - **www geneabloggers com**

There are many sites that offer the potential to set up a blog, but the two most popular are Google's Blogger service - **www blogger com** - and Wordpress- **http://wordpress org** Blogger allows you to construct sites using templates hosted online, though you'll need a free Google account, whilst Wordpress requires you to download software to get up and running Both platforms are free and easy to use

Twitter

A new form of communication growing ever more popular by the day is the Twitter website at **http://twitter com**, the most popular of what are known as *'microblogging services,'* which allows you to leave short status messages known as *'tweets'* to your followers on your home page The messages can only be 140 characters in length, which may seem very short, but which can be used to provide a quick status update, a link to an interesting website that you have found and more In 2010, some 65 million tweets were being registered per day around the world

You can look at other people's sites without subscribing, though simply clicking on *'Follow'* means that tweets from those you subscribe to will appear on your home page as they happen My Twitter account, for example, is **http://twitter com/chrismpaton**, which in my case I use to alert people to both Scottish and UK wide news developments People can *'follow'* me, but I can also *'block'* them if I think they are essentially 'spamming' (advertising indiscriminately) People can send messages to me by including **@chrismpaton** in their message, or I can make a post and put a *'tag'* in it, essentially a keyword which people may be searching for posts on, by putting a hash symbol (#) before a word So for example, a message to me by someone

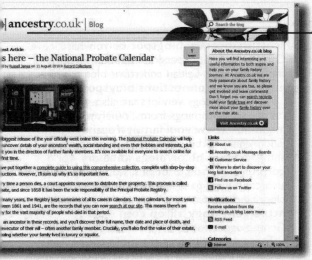

est Article

s here – the National Probate Calendar

by Russell James on 11 August 2010 in Record Collections

else might read

@chrismpaton Love the new #genealogy site at www example com! #scotland #ancestry

Increasingly, Twitter is being used for more creative purposes During the summer of 2010, military historian Paul Reed (**http://twitter com/sommecourt**) used the site to post an online tribute each day to members of the Few, the Battle of Britain pilots who were shot down during the aerial conflict of 1940, whilst the National Archives (**http://twitter com/UkNatArchives**) posted real time updates of the war as fought seventy years ago using cabinet minutes, a surprisingly effective way to understand the conflict's development from the top levels of the government

Family Trees

One of the key tools for the family historian is of course the family tree itself, the diagram of our ancestral lines and the information gathered from our research There are many software programmes that can be purchased which will allow us to collate and present all of our findings, but there are increasingly many appearing online that can let you do the same thing, and with a few added bells and whistles TreeView 2 is one example from the Genealogist website at **www thegenealogist co uk/tree**, which will allow you to record the details of your family history, and to make the information visually accessible in many ways The site was recently redesigned to incorporate two major social networking additions, searching and messaging, which have dramatically enhanced its potential as a research tool in its own right By setting your account on the site to 'Public' in the Privacy Options tab, you can allow others to search for individuals within your tree, allowing you to make connections with possible distant cousins and other relatives The site protects your

privacy by allowing only the surnames of those still alive to be displayed from your tree in such a search, and your own personal information cannot be accessed

There are of course other sites providing similar options Genes Reunited - **www genesreunited com**, recently taken over by FindmyPast's parent company Brightsolid Ltd, is possibly the best known of these The site offers an online tree building facility through a paid subscription, which also allows you to similarly search through other members' trees for possible connections, as well as provide access to certain records collections, such as English and Welsh censuses It also notifies you by e-mail of potential 'hot matches' that it thinks you may have yet to discover, a very handy facility when you have an unusual name in the tree, Unfortunately it can also offer decidedly luke warm matches also, particularly if you have names such as Smith, when it can throw up some truly creative errors!

The Israeli based MyHeritage site - **www myheritage com** - has a tree building and social networking facility through which you can upload photos which the site can recognise and organise possible relatives from other trees through facial tagging software, as well as classic searching It also allows you to download a copy of its *Family Tree Builder* software, another excellent free software package Similarly, Geni is another useful site at **www geni com**, though can be a bit aggressive in its emailing of notifications and updates, whilst Arcalife- **www arcalife com** - is a further social networking site which allows you not only to build a tree, but also an entire life based archive, preserving your story in a variety of ways from 'life cubes' to web based *'time capsules '* Through this site you can upload videos, photos, and other forms of *'digital estate'* – you can even send pre-written e-mails to people for up to ten years following your death! The basic subscription is free, and there are various other paid for subscription levels providing more storage and additional features

On a slightly different tack, the Lost Cousins - **www lostcousins com** - website foregoes the tree as a common platform and instead focuses on genealogical information as contained in particular UK censuses, allowing you to look for matches with potential distant cousins who may have input the same details The censuses it bases its network on include 1841 and 1881 for England and Wales, 1881 for Scotland and 1911 for Ireland

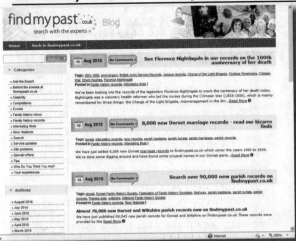

Geographically Based

Increasingly many new forms of social networking are being developed that use different criteria to form links with others One of the most innovative in recent times has involved the use of geography as a background to establish links, rather than names Ancestral Atlas - **www ancestralatlas com** - is a site that uses maps as a starting point, allowing you to tag a location with a note concerning a historic event that took place there, and to view the tags placed by others in the same area If a vital event of interest is noted on a tag on the same street where your ancestor lived, you can contact the person who placed it online through the site for further information In addition the site provides additional features such as historical maps for the area that you are looking at, to compare and contrast, and again has a basic free subscription level

An equally interesting approach comes form the History Pin website - **www historypin com** - established by social action movement We Are What We Do, essentially as an excuse for different generations to be able to get together around a computer and discuss what life was like in the past It does this through the clever integration of Google's Maps and Street View applications, and the addition of historic photos uploaded by users of the site It works by comparing images of a place both from a modern and historic perspective, using a modern Street View image compared to a historic photograph taken from the same spot A good example might be to show a modern shopping centre and to compare it with an image of the same area during the Blitz after a particularly

destructive raid However you don't have to just sit around a computer to tell the story – you can add stories from anywhere in the world and build up a community view of that place from many different perspectives When you take into consideration that Kodak estimates there to be some 12 billion non-digital photographs in existence in the world today, that's a lot of history to exploit!

Other geographically focussed sites include Curious Fox - **www curiousfox com** - which allows you to forge connections with other researchers by a shared village or town of interest You can search for a particular place and then look at various forum posts for that location which may contain information that ties into your research

Community based online archives are another emergent way to interact and share experiences, and to help build up a grass roots perspective of our local environments Sites such as StoryVault - **www storyvault com**, for example, host an archive of stories submitted by people from all over the world, in video or text format, with an online family tree capability

And finally, even death cannot escape the clutches of the social networking phenomenon Obituary sites such as Everlasting - **www everlasting uk com** - providing an opportunity to leave a final tribute to a loved one, or to construct an archive of tributes, which can remain hosted online in perpetuity Possibly more tasteful then emailing people ten years after your death!

Chris Paton is the author of Tracing Your Family History on the Internet (Pen and Sword, March 2011) and writes the monthly internet column for Family History Monthly

Chelsea Pensioners British Army Service Records: A Wealth of Information

Amy Sell

How well do you really know your ancestors? It's fairly easy to establish key facts about them: when they were born, when and whom they married and when they died A much trickier task is to discover what they were like as individuals and to begin piecing together what their day-to-day lives would have been like

In 2010 the online launch took place of the Chelsea Pensioners British Army Service Records, findmypast co uk's most exciting project since the 1911 census was made available in 2009 These records, categorised as WO97 at The National Archives, are one of the largest and most popular record collections in the reading rooms at Kew as family historians and genealogists have realised how valuable they are for taking their research one step further

The collection comprises the service records of over 1 5 million soldiers pensioned out of the British Army between 1760 and 1913 These army pensions were administered by The Royal Hospital Chelsea, hence these soldiers were referred to as Chelsea Pensioners regardless of whether they resided at The Royal Hospital or were among the much larger group of 'out-pensioners' who continued to live with their own families

Many of the soldiers recorded in the collection served in some of Britain's most significant wars, including the Battle of

Waterloo, the Crimean War and the Boer Wars Significantly, the records document the service of soldiers of 'other ranks'; many other military resources of this period often only provide information about the officer classes This means that the Chelsea Pensioners British Army Service Records actually provide historians with a different perspective on these wars and also make it much more likely that family historians will discover ancestors in the collection

Who were the Chelsea Pensioners?

Pensions were awarded to soldiers who had either completed their full service of 12 years or who had been discharged from the army due to wounds or illness Consequently, the men described as Chelsea Pensioners both here and on census forms after their army careers, often differ greatly from our modern-day understanding of a 'Pensioner' As you will see in the examples that follow, Chelsea Pensioners were often fairly young, having joined at the age of 17 or 18 and having been discharged due to illness perhaps halfway through the 12 years of service This meant that many soldiers became pensioners in their twenties, thirties and even some in their late teens

Of course, there are many other examples of soldiers who served well beyond the term of full service, being pensioned out of the army perhaps in their forties Indeed, the fact that it is impossible to specify an exact profile of a Chelsea Pensioner is a reflection of the records themselves No two soldiers' service records are the same, meaning the soldiers emerge as individuals

An unparalleled Level of Detail

What really sets the Chelsea Pensioners Service Records apart from other historical records is the sheer volume of information and level of detail that is provided about each soldier Previously, the richest information available online about an ancestor tended to come from a census record

287

Even the 1911 census, which is the most in-depth census currently available, only gives one line per individual. This, at the very most, can provide the family historian with 17 pieces of information about an ancestor

In contrast, each service record is a mine of information Each individual soldier's record consists of a bundle of a minimum of four pages and could in fact be up to 20 pages long The first example we shall delve into, the service record of Joseph Grandy who served in the British Army between 1870 and 1899, comprises 10 pages The information listed differs from soldier to soldier but tends to include a number of the following:

- Date and place of birth
- Age
- Height
- Chest size
- Complexion
- Hair colour
- Eye colour
- Distinguishing features
- Occupation before joining the army
- Name and address of next of kin
- Date the soldier signed up and date of discharge, including the reason for discharge
- Regiments served in and at what rank
- Countries where and dates when the soldier served
- Service history including promotions, campaigns fought in, plus any medals that were awarded
- Medical history
- Conduct and character observations
- Details of marriage during army service
- Names and dates of birth of children born during army service

Painting a picture of Joseph Grandy

The Chelsea Pensioners British Army Service Records are an invaluable tool for family historians as they list a number of details about a soldier's appearance Many of the records predate the age of photography, meaning they are one of the only ways to establish what an ancestor looked like Even when a photograph is available, as is the case with Joseph Grandy, the soldier's service record can provide some key additional information

Joseph Grandy's service record states that he joined the army on 28 January 1870 at the age of 19 years and three months The photograph that survives of him shows him some years later with a wife and young child The photograph provides an idea of Grandy's facial features and body shape; however, his service record contains a number of important details that can give the image an extra dimension

At the commencement of his army career, Grandy was recorded as being of fresh complexion with hazel eyes and dark brown hair (Figure 2) This information allows us to add colour to the black and white photograph that has survived Grandy himself is not recorded as having any distinctive marks; however, the vast majority of Chelsea Pensioners Service Records refer to tattoos, birth marks and/or scars on the soldier's person For instance, Benjamin Jones was listed as having the tattoo of a 'B J' and crossed flags on right forearm, anchor and figure of Welsh woman on the left' when he joined the army in 1886 (Figure 3)

The description also places Grandy's height at a rather specific 5ft 10 5/8 inches Clearly, while a photograph can give some idea of an ancestor's height, the service record supplies an unparalleled level of detail which can bring the family historian much closer to understanding what an ancestor was like It is much easier to relate to somebody if you are able to directly compare that person with yourself The service record also goes on to state that Joseph Grandy had a 35-inch chest – rather small in comparison with modern sizes

An important New Resource for Family Historians

In addition to the information provided about Grandy's appearance, the document also records two events that it would have been difficult to unearth details of elsewhere Firstly, we are informed that Joseph Grandy had been born in the British territory of Gibraltar This is demonstrative of a general trend in the

Joseph Grandy, wife and child Date unknown

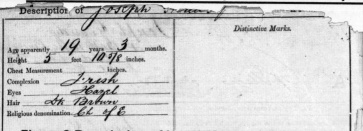

Description of Joseph Grandy

Distinctive Marks.

Age apparently	19 years 3	months.
Height	5 feet 10 7/8	inches.
Chest Measurement		inches.
Complexion	Irish	
Eyes	Hazel	
Hair	Dk Brown	
Religious denomination	Ch of E	

Figure 2 Description of Joseph Grandy on enlistment
Crown copyright WO97/2920/106 reproduced courtesy of
The National Archives and findmypast.co.uk

Description of Benjamin Jones. **on Enlistment.**

..re physically equivalent to	24 years	months.
..eight	5 feet 6	inches.
..eight	140	lbs.
..est Measurement	35 1/2	inches.
..mplexion	Dark	
..es	Hazel	
..ir		
..ligious denomination	Church of Eng.	

‡ *Distinctive Marks.*

"B.J. + cross flags a
R. Forearm, anchor
figure of welsh woman
on left"

Figure 3 Description of Benjamin Jones on enlistment
Crown copyright WO97/2920/106 reproduced courtesy of
The National Archives and findmypast.co.uk

Chelsea Pensioners British Army Service Records It is apparent that while the majority of soldiers had been born in England, Ireland, Scotland and Wales, a significant proportion came from other parts of the British Empire In particular, there are a number of soldiers recorded as having been born in India and the Caribbean

While not an unusual find in these records, discovering that an ancestor was born overseas can be a real boon for family historians who may have previously struggled to find a birth in the General Register Office's index of births in England and

GRANDFIELD ...	John	Canada	1836-37	736
GRANDY	John Joseph	Gibraltar	1847-49	117
—	Joseph Samuel	Gibraltar	1850-59	110
.. ..	Robert Henry	Gibraltar	1850-59	741
GRANE	Helen	Malta	1877-78	693
GRANET	Mary Anne	Mauritius	1844-46	667
GRANEY	James	Bombay	1830	236

Figure 4 Listing of Joseph Grandy's birth
Crown copyright WO97/2920/106 reproduced courtesy of
The National Archives and findmypast.co.uk

Wales With this fresh information, it is easy to spot Joseph Grandy in the index of British citizens born overseas which is available to search at findmypast co uk (Figure 4) The index confirms that Grandy was born in Gibraltar and also records his full name, Joseph Samuel

Grandy As with the birth index for England and Wales, it is possible to order a birth certificate from the General Register Office by using the references provided on the right Here we see that Grandy's birth record appears on page 110 of the births registered in Gibraltar between 1850 and 1859

The second event documented in Grandy's service record was his marriage to Catherine Louisa Taylor (Figure 5) The marriage took place in Dublin on 16th September 1873, three years and eight months into Grandy's 29 years of army service The service record goes on to inform us that Catherine lived with the battalion, accompanying her husband to India and Burma (Figure 6) Irish ancestry is renowned for being fairly difficult to trace, owing to the fact that many core records were destroyed when the Public Records Office of Ireland burnt down in 1922 Consequently, the Chelsea Pensioners British Army Service Records are a fantastic

	To whom	Catherine Louisa Taylor
Married		Spinster
	Place and date	Dublin - 16th September 1873

Figure 5 Record of Joseph Grandy's marriage
Crown copyright WO97/2920/106 reproduced courtesy of
The National Archives and findmypast.co.uk

new resource to add to the Irish family historian's toolbox

Life in the British Army

A key part of a soldier's service record is obviously the documentation of his military career, including a record of any promotions or medals he was awarded and a list of the campaigns he fought in This information allows a real insight into both what an ancestor's character and day-to-day life were like

Joseph Grandy's service record informs us that he joined the Fourth Battalion Rifle Brigade in 1870 as a Private, before being promoted to the rank of Corporal after one year and 110 days of service (Figure 7) As a Corporal, Grandy would have been in command of around 10 men within the battalion Clearly, promotions equated to increased responsibilities and were a sign of a soldier's proficiency and trustworthiness

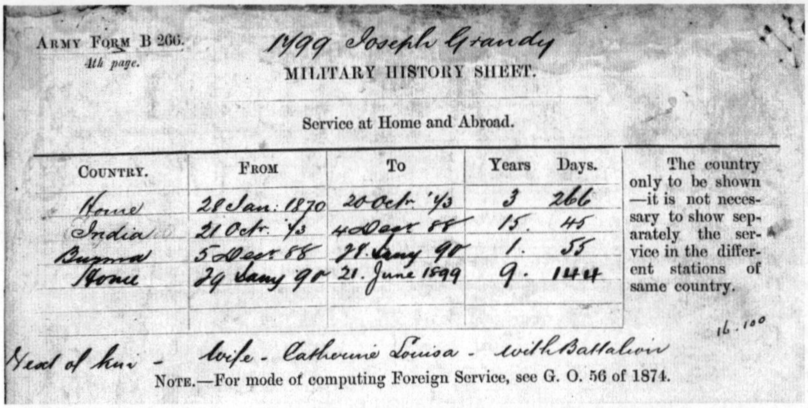

his army service

In addition to the Good Conduct medal, Grandy was also awarded a decoration for his service in the 'Ali Musjid' Afghan Campaign of 1878-79, the beginning of what is known as the Second Anglo-Afghan War In the nineteenth century, Afghanistan was seen as a key area which separated the Russian empire from

Figure 6 Joseph Grandy's service at home and abroad
Crown copyright WO97/2920/106 reproduced courtesy of
The National Archives and findmypast.co.uk

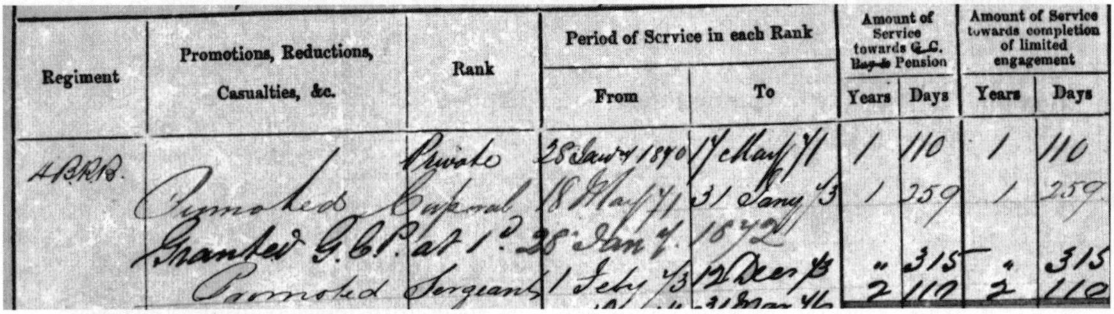

Figure 7 oseph Grandy's promotions
Image is Crown copyright WO97/2920/106
reproduced courtesy of The National Archives
and findmypast.co.uk

Grandy was evidently considered to be a very capable soldier as his service record states that he was promoted again to the rank of Sergeant after serving as a Corporal for one year and 259 days, placing him second-in-command of a platoon of up to about 40 soldiers

The portion of Grandy's service record shown in Figure 7 also states that he was awarded Good Conduct Pay on 28th January 1872 Grandy was actually awarded this on three other occasions during his army career and another section of his service record reveals that he was also awarded a Good Conduct medal (Figure 8) By taking these points into consideration, the service record can shed some light on Joseph Grandy's personality as it is evident that he was seen to be dependable and hard-working throughout

the British territory of India When the Amir of Afghanistan refused to receive a British diplomatic mission in 1878 despite a Russian mission having already entered the country's capital, the British Army (including the Fourth Battalion Rifle Brigade) invaded

Information about the campaigns in which a soldier fought is a fantastic starting point for family historians wishing to establish what army life was like for an ancestor Many accounts of the conditions that soldiers faced during particular wars and campaigns exist and can be unearthed as the next step of research Accounts of the Ali Musjid campaign that Joseph Grandy served in make much reference to the fatigue of the soldiers, owing to a lack of supplies For instance, one General stated that,

I asked Colonel Newdigate and Colonel Turton if their men could go on, and they said they were quite exhausted There was no water further on, and the whole of the baggage might have been carried off and the escort cut up if we had deserted it, and

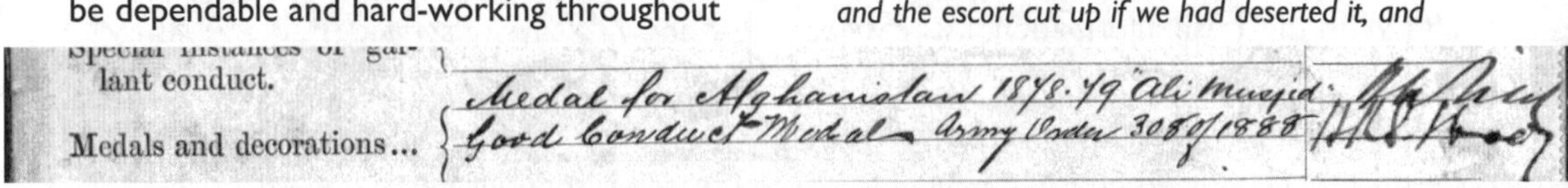

Figure 8 Joseph Grandy's medals and decorations
Image is Crown copyright WO97/2920/106 reproduced courtesy of
The National Archives and findmypast.co.uk

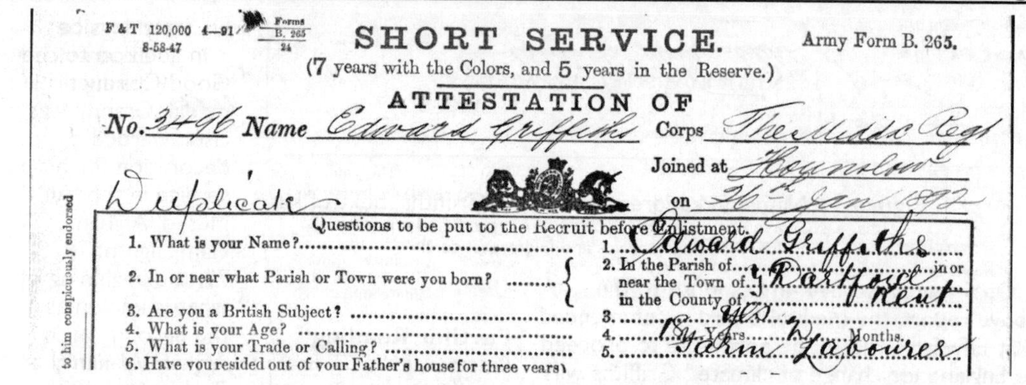

F & T 120,000 4—91 Forms B. 265 24
8-58-47

SHORT SERVICE. Army Form B. 265.

(7 years with the Colors, and 5 years in the Reserve.)

ATTESTATION OF

No. 3496 Name Edward Griffiths Corps The Middx Regt

Joined at Hounslow

Duplicate on 26th Jan 1892

Questions to be put to the Recruit before Enlistment.

1. What is your Name? .... 1. Edward Griffiths
2. In or near what Parish or Town were you born? .... 2. In the Parish of........in or near the Town of Dartford in the County of Kent
3. Are you a British Subject? .... 3. yes
4. What is your Age? .... 4. 18 Years 2 Months.
5. What is your Trade or Calling? .... 5. Farm Labourer
6. Have you resided out of your Father's house for three years

to him conspicuously endorsed

Figure 9 Edward Griffiths' attestation paper
Image is Crown copyright WO97/2936/057 reproduced courtesy of The National Archives and findmypast.co.uk

Tytler's baggage was all behind my Brigade (Journal of General MacPherson in Hanna, H B , *The Second Afghan War, its Causes, its Conduct and its Consequences*, Vol 2, 1904

Unexpected Information about Edward Griffiths

It is often worth searching the Chelsea Pensioners British Army Service Records for an ancestor even if he had no apparent connection to the British Army Soldiers often served for very short periods and their Pensioner status may not have been recorded in other documents The service record of Edward Griffiths, a Private in The Middlesex Regiment, is an astonishing example of this

Griffiths joined the army on 23rd January 1892 at the age of 18 years and two months (Figure 9) He was recorded as being a Farm Labourer at the time of enlistment which matches his occupation in the 1891 census, taken a year earlier Griffiths also appears in the next census, taken in 1901, as he completed just seven years of army service and was discharged as an invalid in 1899 In 1901 Griffiths was working as a General Labourer and was living at 206 Dartford Road in Dartford, Kent with his family (Figure 10) This corresponds with the name and address of Griffiths' next of kin that was listed in his service record Here, Griffiths had stated that his father Henry Griffiths lived at 206 Mile End Terrace, Dartford Road (Figure 11)

Of greater interest is the information about Edward Griffiths' army career that went unmentioned in his 1901 census listing It is evident that no reference was made to Griffiths having served in the British Army nor to the fact that he was in a receipt of an army pension Yet Griffiths' service record reveals even more about what his life was like, describing the reason he was discharged in 1899 in great detail

The six pages relating to Edward Griffiths' medical history reveal that by the end of his army career he was suffering severely from both rheumatism and syphilis On 31st December 1898, four months before he was discharged as an invalid, a Medical Officer described Griffiths' symptoms in the following terms,

He is much reduced in weight, is unable to walk about from chronic [swelling] of left knee joint; there has been much [excess fluid] in this joint and any attempt at walking causes a [return] of the inflammatory symptoms – in this and in the right knee joint His right deltoid muscle is somewhat [wasted], his right testicle is enlarged as also the lymphatic glands in both groins He has improved in condition under mercury and potassium iodide but is unfit for service

The Medical Officer stated that Griffiths had caught syphilis while serving in Gibraltar in June 1873, spending 159 days in hospital because of the disease that year Secondary syphilis, or orchitis, had appeared in 1896 while he was serving in India Griffiths had then developed rheumatism a year later and had spent 177 days in hospital because of it

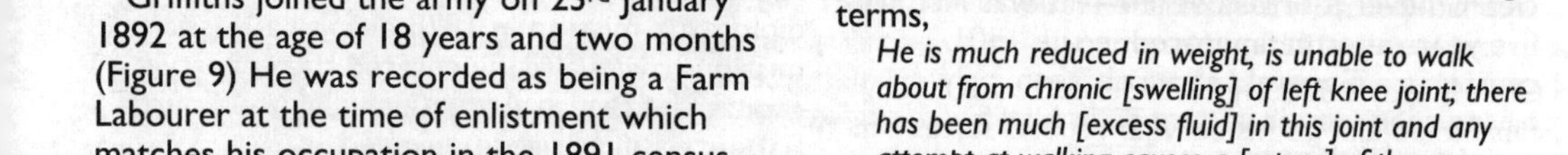

206	Do	1	Henry Griffiths	Head	M	51		General Labourer	Worker	Do Dartford
			Elizabeth Griffiths	Wife	M		50			Do Wilmington
			Edward Griffiths	Son	S	26		General Labourer	Worker	Do Dartford
			Reuben Griffiths	Son	S	22		Wharf Labourer	Worker	Do do
			Grace E. Griffiths	Daur	S		18	[illegible]	[illegible]	Do Crayford

Figure 10 Edward Griffiths in the 1901 census
Image is Crown copyright RG 13/703 reproduced courtesy of The National Archives and findmypast.co.uk

	refunded .. (2) On _(Credited to the public in the Accounts of____ to____)_ £ _million & Terrace_	things he
12. Name and Address of next of kin .. ..]	_Father, Henry Griffiths, 206 Dartford_ _Rd., Dartford, Kent,_ _nus_	experienced during his life

Figure 11 Name and address of Edward Griffiths' next of kin
Image is Crown copyright WO97/2936/057 reproduced courtesy of
The National Archives and findmypast.co.uk

On 9th January 1899, in response to the above report, the Medical Board recommended that Edward Griffiths 'be permitted to proceed to England for change of climate ' Griffiths was transferred from India to the Royal Victoria Hospital in Netley, Hampshire, arriving almost three months after the recommendation on 3rd March 1899 He spent a further 54 days in hospital before finally being discharged from the army as an invalid on 25th April 1899

This wealth of information allows an acute appreciation of what Edward Griffiths' life was like, something that is simply not possible through *'core'* birth, marriage, death and census records alone Indeed, if the Chelsea Pensioners British Army Service Records had not been speculatively searched, there would have been no way of knowing that Edward Griffiths had ever served in the army nor that he had suffered so badly with rheumatism and syphilis Edward Griffiths died in Dartford at the age of 32 having clearly never fully recovered This was just five years after he appeared in the 1901 census as a General Labourer, seemingly having seen very little change in his life since the 1891 census

The increasing popularity of family history as a hobby is not surprising when we consider the type of information that is now easily accessible from the comfort of our own homes In just seven years, online resources have expanded from purely factual birth, marriage and death indexes (the indexes for England and Wales were made available online for the first time in 2003 by findmypast co uk's former site, 1837online com) to records that hold the level of detail discussed here It is now not only possible to find out key facts about our ancestors' lives, but also to start piecing together what they were actually like as people By using the Chelsea Pensioners British Army Service Records, family historians can now really begin to establish what an ancestor looked like, get a sense of his personality and character traits and also gain an awareness of the

Further Reading

Brereton, J M , *The British Soldier, a Social History from 1661 to the Present Day*, Bodley Head, 1986
Ewing, G *The Second Anglo-Afghan War 1878-1880* www angloafghanwar info
Hanna, H B , *The Second Afghan War, its Causes, its Conduct and its Consequences*, Archibald Constable & Co , 3 volumes, 1899, 1904, 1910
Spencer, W , *Army Records, a Guide for Family Historians*, The National Archives, 2008
Watts, M and C Watts, *My Ancestor was in the British Army*, Society of Genealogists 2009

ScotlandsPeople
Connecting Generations

Davina Williams
Head of ScotlandsPeople Centre

ScotlandsPeople is a partnership between the General Register Office for Scotland (GROS), the National Archives of Scotland (NAS) and the Court of the Lord Lyon The ScotlandsPeople pay-per-view website at http://www scotlandspeople gov uk/ , which provides access to the records held by the partners, was launched in 2002 and is enabled by Brightsolid, a leading provider of web-based business solutions

ScotlandsPeople gives access to a uniquely comprehensive range of Scottish genealogical data This includes:

Statutory Registers held by the General Register Office for Scotland (GROS) For the births; indexes and digitised images are available for all records from 1855 to the last 100 years For the modern day records registered during the last 100 years only the indexes are available For these modern records sets 'Extracts' can be ordered either directly on line or through GROS

For the marriages; indexes and digitised images are available for all records from 1855 to the last 75 years and for the deaths; from 1855 to the last 50 years For the modern day records within the 75 and 50 year periods only the indexes are available For these records Extracts can be ordered either directly on line

or through GROS

Register of Corrected Entries (RCE) related to a specific birth, death or marriage held by GROS The words 'RCE' or 'Reg Cor Ent ' will be entered in the left hand column of the register if a RCE applies to that particular entry RCEs were written if after an entry in a register had been completed, an error was discovered or some other amendment was required as a result of new information A RCE was required because it was not possible to amend the original entry

The various cut-off dates detailed for records deemed to be modern have been applied to avoid raising concerns about browsing on the Internet among records relating to living people

At the beginning of each year, these records are updated to renew what is deemed to be outwith the 100, 75 and 50 year cut off dates for the various record sets listed above

Old Parish Registers [OPRs] of births and baptisms from 1553 to 1854 and banns and marriages and deaths and burials from 1538 to 1854 held byGROS There are also a small number of OPRs which were registered after 1854 These records are automatically displayed in the index list if the search period requested is up to 1854

Catholic Parish Registers

These records, which are held by the Scottish Catholic Archives, cover all Scottish parishes in existence by 1855, the records of the main Catholic cemeteries in Edinburgh and Glasgow and the records of the RC Bishopric of the Forces, which records all sacramental events for British Catholic service men and women serving in the armed forces worldwide

Indexes and digitised images are available for birth and baptismal records from 1703 to the last 100 years; banns and marriages from 1703 to the last 75 years, and deaths and burials from 1847 to the last 50 years There are also indexes and images for other events like communicants, sick calls, status animarum; convents, first confessions and seat rents Further information is available at www scottishcatholicarchives org uk/

Census Records for the census returns for Scotland for 1841, 1851, 1861, 1871,1881, 1891, 1901 and 1911 held by the General Register

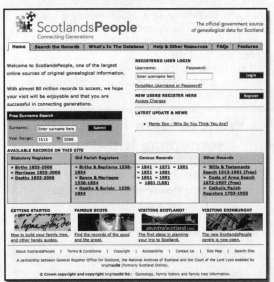

Office for Scotland (GROS) have been indexed and digitised For 1881 only, transcriptions can also be viewed, which are a cooperative product of GROS, the Scottish Association of Family History Societies and the Genealogical Society of Utah, now known as Familysearch These transcriptions are structured differently to the other censuses

Wills and testaments held by the National Archives of Scotland (NAS) Indexes and digitised images are available from 1513 to 1901 Searching of the indexes is free for this set of records Records sets from 1902 to 1925 are due during 2011 or early 2012

Coats of Arms from the Public Register of all Arms and Bearings in Scotland maintained by the Court of the Lord Lyon Indexes and digital images from 1672 to the last 100 years Searching of the indexes is free for this set of records

Valuation Rolls, which list properties across Scotland, their proprietors, tenants, occupiers and their valuation held by the National Archives of Scotland (NAS) will start to be released during 2011 All of the years half way between the open census since 1851 up to 1955 will be indexed and imaged

Features

The site includes a number of free features, including a free forename and surname search where the customer can see how many index entries there are relating to their particular forename or surnames, features on famous Scots, help with Scottish handwriting, occupations, and unusual words and news items Search results for most records can be viewed on a map of Scotland The site also offers a timeline feature to help customers keep track of the records they have found

Searching

The search facilities are straightforward and allow searches on a type of record including details of surname and/or forename and/or year range and/or geographical area Wildcards can be used for only one character on either a forename and/or surname Variations of name can be searched using fuzzy searching, name variants, metaphone options and wildcards In order to help reduce the

numberof results for a search, customers should search by name, forename, time period and/or geographical area Result pages are displayed in pages each containing a maximum of 25 records The index page will indicate if a digital image of each record is available - if so, it can be accessed at the click of a mouse and redemption of the appropriate number of credits

Registration

Customers need to register the first time they access the database Once registered, customers only need to use their username and password when they return to the site The site uses customer registration forms and order forms so that customers can request particular products, but does not handle credit or debit card details This information is entered once customers have been directed to a secure payment gateway system No credit card or debit card information, is retained by Brightsolid or GROS at any time

Credits or vouchers can be purchased to search and view all of the records held by GROS and the Scottish Catholic Archive and last for a period of 90 days (starting from the time a credit or debit card payment is authorised), however many times the customer logs on and off in that time Further credits can be purchased

No charge is made for accessing the index to Scottish wills and testaments and the Coats of Arms but access to the related colour digital images costs £5 for a will regardless of length Access to the images of the Coats of Arms costs £10 Customers can access any of the previous records they have downloaded outside the 90 day registration period

If a customer wishes to order an Extract of any GROS register entry found in the index, they can do this on-line, again making a credit card payment The system automatically transfers the request to GROS to fulfil the order and mail the extract

If customers encounter difficulties with the site, they can contact GROS or Brightsolid via the 'contact us' button

Courtesy of Apple

Census Returns

A Census has been taken every 10 years since 1801
except in 1941 during the Second World War
Most of the census returns for 1801, 1811, 1821, 1831 were not preserved
However there are some areas where returns for these years
have been found - (see *Pre -1841 Censuses* by *Colin Chapman*)
The first nationwide census returns useful to researchers are those for 1841

The Censuses took place on:

1841	7th June 1841	1851	30th March 1851	1861	7th April 1861
1871	2nd April 1871	1881	3rd April 1881	1891	5th April 1891
1901	31st March 1901	1911	2nd April 1911	1921	19th June 1921
1931	26th April 1931	1941	No Census	1951	8th April 1951
1961	23rd April 1961	1971	25th April 1971	1981	6th April 1981
1991	21st April 1991	2001	29th April 2001	2011	27th March 2011

• The future of the census is in doubt and the 2011 will be the last of its kind according to Francis Maud - Cabinet Minister in The Coalition Government He said that the present system was expensive (Estimated at £482 million in 2011), prone to error and abuse Mr Maude suggested that other sources of information could be used to provide a snapshot of the nation every five years The suggested sources that could be used include credit reference databases, Royal Mail and existing government databases

military history

Remembering the Fallen
Peter Francis
Head of External Communications
- Commonwealth War Graves Commission

On 19th July 2010, more than five and half thousand people gathered in the small French village of Fromelles, in northern France, to witness the reburial of an unknown First World War soldier, in one of the immaculately maintained war cemeteries that dot that part of northern Europe. Millions more were watching or listening at home in Australia and the United Kingdom as the event was transmitted live to both countries.

With the growth of interest in the two world wars, and remembrance generally, a casual viewer may not have initially thought such level of ceremony and interest was unusual, but there was nothing "*routine*" or "*ordinary*" about either the funeral or the cemetery.

For more than two years the *Commonwealth War Graves Commission,* on behalf of the Australian and British governments, managed a unique project to recover, rebury with dignity, and where possible identify, the remains of 250 Australian and British casualties of the Great War. To give these men the dignity in death they so richly deserved, the Commission, for the first time in more than fifty years, designed and built a new war cemetery – Fromelles (Pheasant Wood) Military Cemetery.

It is difficult for those of us who have grown up with remembrance, the 11th of November, the two minute silence and the red poppy, to appreciate that remembrance of the war dead as we know it is a relatively new phenomenon.

Historically, public opinion of the Army was low – Wellington famously referred to his troops as *'the scum of the earth'* – while ordinary soldiers were often buried in mass graves with little or no form of permanent memorial.

The First World War changed that. For the first time the ranks of Britain's army were swelled with volunteers from every walk of life, and as that army suffered terrible losses, so the public demanded they be remembered. At the same time, an incredible organisation grew out of the destruction – an organisation that for the first time memorialised that sacrifice in stone. An organisation whose very existence was to ensure *'Their Name Liveth For Evermore.'*

War cemeteries and memorials, like that at Fromelles, play a vital role in our remembrance of the dead. They are the very fabric upon which our remembrance is focussed and the Commonwealth War Graves Commission takes great pride in their construction, ongoing care, the comfort they bring to families, comrades and nations and the role they play in keeping alive the names of the fallen. But what is often less well know by those who visit such places, and perhaps take them for granted, is how they came to exist at all, the form they take, who built them and how are they looked after. Incredibly, one man is largely responsible for the existence of the Commission. His name was Fabian Ware.

Fabian Ware arrived in France in September 1914 to command a

King George V with Fabian Ware at Tyne Cot Cemetery

Reproduced with permission of The Commonwealth War Graves Commission - © The Commonwealth War Graves Commission

Sir Fabian Ware

scale of slaughter and noted there was no organisation in place to record the final resting places of casualties. Fabian became concerned that graves would be lost forever and so his unit took it upon themselves to register and care for all the graves they could find. By 1915 the unit was given official recognition by the War Office, becoming the Graves Registration Commission.

As the war progressed, Fabian, concerned about the fate of the graves once the war was over, became convinced of the need for an official organisation representing the Imperial nature of the war effort, the equality of treatment due to the dead and the permanence of graves or memorials. With the support of The Prince of Wales, Ware submitted a memorandum to the Imperial War Conference in 1917. It was unanimously approved and *The Imperial War Graves Commission* was established by Royal Charter on 21st May, 1917.

From the outset, the Commission sought perfection and permanence for the physical forms of commemoration and settled on three of the most eminent architects of the day to begin the work of design and construction of the cemeteries and memorials - Sir Edwin Lutyens, Sir Herbert Baker and Sir Reginald

British Red Cross Unit. He'd had a varied career and as journalist had reported on the Boer War and how the treatment of the dead in that conflict had caused many people great distress.

Upon his arrival he was shocked by the sheer

Fromelles - Excavation Site and Fromelles (Pheasant Wood) Military Cemetery

Fromelles - Archaeologists at work at the mass grave site

Blomfield. However, no one had ever attempted to commemorate the fallen on such a scale before and almost immediately, challenges arose over the type, size, and cost of the cemeteries and memorials the Commission was to build.

In desperation, Fabian turned to Sir Frederic Kenyon, Director of the British Museum, and gave him the task of bringing together the differing views. His report, presented to the Commission in November 1918, articulated principles still held by the Commission today.

• that each of the dead should be commemorated individually by name either on the headstone on the grave or by an inscription on a memorial;
• that the headstones and memorials should be permanent;

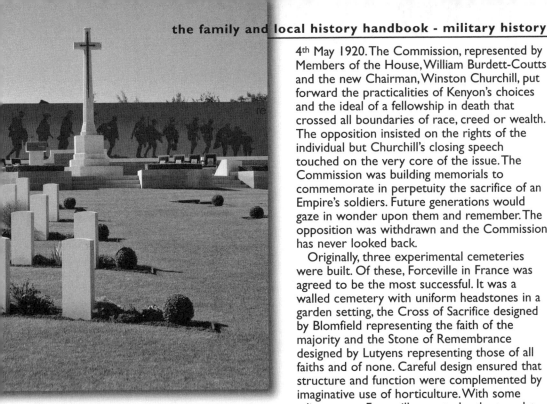

4th May 1920. The Commission, represented by Members of the House, William Burdett-Coutts and the new Chairman, Winston Churchill, put forward the practicalities of Kenyon's choices and the ideal of a fellowship in death that crossed all boundaries of race, creed or wealth. The opposition insisted on the rights of the individual but Churchill's closing speech touched on the very core of the issue. The Commission was building memorials to commemorate in perpetuity the sacrifice of an Empire's soldiers. Future generations would gaze in wonder upon them and remember. The opposition was withdrawn and the Commission has never looked back.

Originally, three experimental cemeteries were built. Of these, Forceville in France was agreed to be the most successful. It was a walled cemetery with uniform headstones in a garden setting, the Cross of Sacrifice designed by Blomfield representing the faith of the majority and the Stone of Remembrance designed by Lutyens representing those of all faiths and of none. Careful design ensured that structure and function were complemented by imaginative use of horticulture. With some adjustments, Forceville was to be the template for the building programme.

• that the headstones should be uniform;
• that there should be no distinction made on account of military or civil rank, race, or creed.

In particular, decisions on non-repatriation of remains and private memorials were designed to avoid class distinctions that would conflict with the feeling of 'brotherhood' which had developed between all ranks serving at the Front. These far sighted principles and the wider report settled disagreements within the Commission but a bigger storm was brewing. The restriction of personal choice with regard to repatriation and the form of grave markers, led to powerful and vocal opposition.

The debate on how to commemorate the fallen went to Parliament, reaching its climax on

Fromelles (Pheasant Wood) Military Cemetery has been designed and built in the tradition of these *'Great War'* cemeteries – albeit using modern construction techniques and equipment. It reflects the fact that the original burials date from 1916, but also has modifications to fulfil 21st-century access requirements for visitors with mobility impairments – something that was not a consideration in the 1920s and 30s.

The new cemetery uses traditional materials that would have been familiar to Lutyens and Blomfield. Its distinctive hexagonal shape has as its focus the Cross of Sacrifice, from which the

Fromelles Carriage Party 19th July 2010

HRH The Prince of Wales with the Cortege 19th July 2010

particular engagement of the Great War, highlights one of the saddest truths of that terrible conflict. With so many of the dead lost without trace the Commission was called upon to build numerous memorials to the missing between 1923 and 1938. The largest, the Thiepval Memorial in France stands at over 45 metres high and carries the names of over 72,000 casualties from the Battle of the Somme with no known grave. The memorials signify the Commission's commitment to commemorate individuals; as Rudyard Kipling put it, 'Their Glory Shall Not be Blotted Out.'

However, it was the provision of over 500,000 headstones that was perhaps the greatest single challenge facing the Commission after the First World War. Apart from finding enough high quality stone, engraving regimental badges and inscriptions was a time-consuming affair. In an early indication of the Commission's willingness to innovate, a Lancashire firm designed for the Commission a machine to trace details onto headstones; this considerably increased the speed of the engraving process.

Today, a computer controlled engraving machine called an *Incisograph*, programmed with the regimental badges and the Commission's unique fonts, runs at full capacity all year round. To the Commission, a broken or illegible headstone is a brave man or woman forgotten and that is unacceptable – and so a considerable amount of staff and financial resource is focussed on the constant cycle of

avenues and rows of headstones radiate outwards. From the Cross itself, on its elevated terrace, there are distant views of the Fromelles battlefield and V.C. Corner, the other cemetery most closely associated with the battle in which these men died.

Dedicated by HRH The Prince of Wales on 19th July 2010, it joins thousands of other cemeteries in France, Belgium and elsewhere as a place of dignified remembrance of the fallen, of comfort, pilgrimage and interest for generations to come.

The project at Fromelles, to recover, rebury and where possible identify the fallen from one

The Dedication Ceremony 19th July 2010

remembering|fromelles

Fromelles 19th July 2010

headstones were required. In Normandy alone, almost 25 kilometres of concrete beams were needed to hold headstones. However, by October 1956, 90% of graves were marked with a permanent headstone.

The *Dieppe Canadian War Cemetery*, completed in 1949, was the first of the Second World War cemeteries to be finished. However, a shortage of men, tools and machinery, coupled with post-war unrest in some regions and the fact that even in 1956 bodies were still being recovered from the route of the *'Death Railway'* in Burma, meant that construction work was not finished until the 1960's. In all, the Commission built 559 new cemeteries, and thirty-six new memorials to add to those cemeteries and memorials built after 1918.

With another 600,000 names to be added to records already in excess of 1,100,000, the Commission kept pace with the task of recording the names and details of Second World War casualties. In 1947 over 60% were accounted for and by 1959 over 400,000 names were recorded and over 100,000 registers had been produced for the public. Now these records are available to a much wider audience thanks to the Commission's website at www.cwgc.org Launched in 1998 the website still receives more than 300,000 visits a month – rising to more than a million during major anniversaries or the annual remembrance period.

The Commission also reorganised its structure to cope with the increased (in terms of numbers and geographical spread) task of commemoration. War Graves Agreements were extended or established with the countries where the Commission had to carry out the bulk of its work and international committees were formed. In 1956 a Commonwealth, German and French Joint Committee meeting was held in London. Through common suffering, the Commission was bridging the gap between old enemies. The Commission recognised that the name *'Imperial'* in its title was not in tune with the post war strengthening of national and regional feelings and in 1960 the name of the organisation was changed to the *'Commonwealth War Graves Commission.'*

Today, the Commission is responsible for the graves of and memorials to 1.7 million

headstone inspection, re-engraving and ultimately replacement. More than 6,500 new headstones are manufactured by the Commission at our offices in France every year, while a headstone renovation programme aims to re-engrave every First World War headstone in our care – something that will take 28 man years and some £5 million pounds to complete.

Started in 1919, the Great War building programme was not finished until 1938. Just one year later, war once more engulfed Europe and, although the Commission had gained from its previous experience, the task of burial and commemoration was to prove no less daunting. Learning the sad lessons of the First World War, the Services organised graves registration units from the start and early on land was earmarked for use as cemeteries.

The Commission also recognised the changing face of warfare. The increased use of air power meant that casualties were no longer restricted to military personnel. Ware urged the commemoration of all civilian deaths caused by enemy action and this took the form of a roll of honour, which on completion numbered over 66,000 names. In 1956 it was placed near St George's Chapel at Westminster Abbey, London. A new page is turned every day.

As the tide of war moved in the Allies' favour, the Commission was able to return to many of its 1914 - 1918 cemeteries and memorials; thankfully, most were undamaged structurally but in many cases horticultural work had to start again. Remarkably, within three years, the pre-war standards had almost been restored.

Once more, the Commission took on the challenge of construction work to commemorate the 600,000 Commonwealth dead of this latest conflict. Over 350,000

Commonwealth men and women who gave their lives in the world wars. The work takes place in over 23,000 locations in 150 countries throughout the world.

The task is never-ending – the Commission's dedicated workforce, some 1,200 strong, paying the debt we all owe to those who lost their lives in two world wars. In some ways, our task is one of horticultural and structural maintenance and without doubt, these roles take up much of our time.

Many readers may be keen gardeners? Well, the Commission 'gardens' on a mammoth scale. We measure our headstone borders in kilometres, not metres, and garden in almost every climate to be found on the globe. Tens of thousands of new plants are used each year to keep the horticultural standards in the cemeteries and memorials up to scratch, while the Commission is proud of the fact that nearly all of its horticultural waste is recycled.

The horticulture in our cemeteries is not a luxury but an essential part of our commemoration of the dead – as can be seen at the newest of our cemeteries at Fromelles, where it softens the new stonework and where the colour and life of the plants is symbolic of the life we enjoy thanks to the sacrifices made by so many brave individuals. The plants also create the right atmosphere in which to remember the fallen – there should be nothing

'gloomy' about a Commonwealth war cemetery.

Of course, gardening is a labour intensive activity and in areas where there are large concentrations of cemeteries, like France and Belgium, mobile horticultural teams are used to maintain the graves. In other countries, a small workforce, in some cases the third generation of a particular family to work for us, will lovingly care for a single Commission cemetery their entire Commission career.

Without exception, our staff are dedicated to the task in hand and in many cases, highly skilled and innovative – developing, adapting and trialling the latest machinery or developing drought tolerant plants that will better equip the Commission to cope with a changing climate. In some cases this work will filter down to the domestic gardener.

Gardening takes place all year round while regular inspection and maintenance keeps the now aging structures in good repair. But the Commission is so much more than just a maintenance organisation.

Engaging a new generation in our work and the importance of remembrance is a new but vital role for the organisation. For the first time, the Commission has engaged with teachers and students and developed education resources to meet their interest and needs. We see the importance of this work only increasing as we move further away from the two world wars. At the same time, the website and our online records will continue to be developed to meet the ever growing need and interest in the two world wars and, more generally in family history research.

The twentieth century's two great wars have done much to shape today's world and the debt we owe to those who fought cannot be overestimated. The veterans, their ranks thinning now, have had a chance to speak for themselves. They have told us how it was to fight, to be parted from family, to lose comrades. We know the lessons we should learn from their sacrifice. But the dead are silent. We have to look to what they left behind for their testimony, and must find it in the ranks of headstones and panels of names that remain. They have a message for the twenty-first century, and it is the Commission's duty to give them a voice.

More information about the Commonwealth War Graves Commission, including the casualty records, can be found at www.cwgc.org

For more information about Fromelles visit www.fromelles.org

Bletchley Park – Britain's Best Kept Secret
Claire Urwin

© Bletchley Park Ltd

A Visit to the Bletchley Park Museum

Entering through the Bletchley Park gates is stepping back into the 1940s. The wonderfully quirky and ostentatious Victorian mansion set against the beautiful gardens and lake is conspicuously at odds with the original utilitarian wooden code breaking huts, still standing after seventy years. Much of Bletchley Park remains completely unchanged from the days it was occupied by the most brilliant brains in Britain and you can almost feel the ghostly presence of vibrant, young individuals dashing about in Harris tweeds and college scarves; the weight of Britain's survival on their shoulders.

A whole day is easily absorbed by the wide variety of displays and exhibitions. From the Enigma and Lorenz machines to the rebuilds of Colossus and the Turing Bombe the whole code breaking process is explained from intercept through to decisive military action. In addition there are a number of privately owned collections ranging from classic cars to a toy museum and a large range of Churchill memorabilia. Bletchley Park also now houses The National Museum of Computing which traces the development of the computer from Colossus to the modern PCs of today, celebrating the Park's place as the spiritual home of the Information Age which underpins everything we do today.

A visit to Bletchley Park is a day of entertainment, education, thought-provoking admiration, nostalgia and a celebration of one of Britain's greatest success stories. To visit Bletchley Park is to experience a true 'sense of place' and to relive a completely remarkable episode in history and in the history of human achievement.

A Victorian Country Estate

Fifty miles (80km) north west of London lies Bletchley Park. In 1883, it became home to the Leon family, whose patriarch was a wealthy City of London financier. Herbert Samuel Leon bought over 300 acres of land beside the London and North-Western Railway line that passed through Bletchley, Buckinghamshire, developing sixty of those acres into his country estate. At the heart of the estate, he built a mansion in a curious mixture of architectural styles. One of Bletchley's greatest benefactors, he was much loved by the local people. He was awarded a baronetcy in 1911.

Following the deaths of Sir Herbert and Lady Fanny Leon, the Park fell into the hands of property developer Captain Hubert Faulkner, who intended to demolish the buildings and sell the land as a housing site.

Captain Ridley's Shooting Party

But the Government was about to intervene. It was 1938 and the threat of war loomed as Hitler invaded first Austria and then Czechoslovakia. The Government Code and Cypher School, then based in London, needed a safer home where its intelligence work could carry on unhindered by enemy air attacks. At a junction of major road, rail and teleprinter connections to all parts of the country and located conveniently between Oxford and Cambridge , Bletchley Park was eminently suitable.

Commanded by Alastair Denniston, the Park

> 'The work here at Bletchley Park was no optional extra; no engaging very British sideshow; it was utterly fundamental to the survival of Britain and to the triumph of the West and I'm not actually sure that I can think of very many other places where I could say something as unequivocal as that.
> **This is sacred ground. If this isn't worth preserving, what is?'**
> **Professor Richard Holmes, Military Historian**

was given the cover name Station X, being the tenth of a large number of sites acquired by MI6 for its wartime operations.

The Outbreak of War

After meticulous preparation and a series of trial runs, the codebreakers arrived in earnest in August 1939. They masqueraded as 'Captain Ridley's Shooting Party' to disguise their true identity. It was to be the first instalment in one of the most remarkable stories of the Second World War.

Enigma

The Enigma cypher was the backbone of German military and intelligence communications. Invented in 1918, it was initially designed to secure banking communications, but achieved little success in that sphere. The German military, however, were quick to see its potential.

They thought it to be unbreakable, and not without good reason. Enigma's complexity was bewildering. Typing in a letter of plain German into the machine sent electrical impulses through a series of rotating wheels, electrical contacts and wires to produce the encyphered letter, which lit up on a panel above the keyboard. By typing the resulting code into his own machine, the recipient saw the decyphered message light up letter by letter. The rotors and wires of the machine could be configured in many, many different ways. The odds against anyone who did not know the settings being able to break Enigma were a staggering 158, million, million, million to one.

The Poles had broken the original and simpler version of Enigma in 1932, when the encoding machine was undergoing trials with the German Army. They even managed to reconstruct a machine. At that time, the cypher altered only once every few months but with the advent of war, it changed at least once a day increasing the complexity of the challenge enormously, as, to deal with the task effectively, the codes needed to be broken much more quickly. The Poles were locked out and in July 1939, they had passed on their knowledge to the British and the French. This enabled the codebreakers to make critical progress in working out the order in which the keys were attached to the electrical circuits, a task that had been impossible without an Enigma machine in front of them.

Codebreaking Begins in Earnest

Armed with this knowledge, the codebreakers were then able to exploit a chink in Enigma's armour. A fundamental design flaw meant that no letter could ever be encrypted as itself; an A in the original message, for example, could never appear as an A in the code. This gave the codebreakers a toehold. Errors in messages sent by tired, stressed or lazy German operators also gave clues. In January 1940 came the first break into Enigma by the great Codebreaker Dilly Knox in Cottage 3 of the Park.

It was in Huts 3, 6, 4 and 8 that the highly effective Enigma decrypt teams worked. The huts operated in pairs and, for security reasons, were known only by their numbers. The codebreakers concentrating on the Army and Air Force cyphers were based in Hut 6, supported by a team in the neighbouring Hut 3 who turned the decyphered messages into intelligence reports. Hut 8 decoded messages from the German Navy, with Hut 4 the associated naval intelligence hut. Their raw material came from the 'Y' Stations: a web of wireless intercept stations dotted around Britain and in a number of countries overseas. These stations listened in to the enemy's radio messages and sent them to Bletchley Park to be decoded and analysed.

The Turing-Welchman Bombe

To speed up the codebreaking process, the brilliant mathematician Alan Turing developed an idea originally proposed by Polish cryptanalysts. The result was the Bombe: an electro-mechanical machine that greatly reduced the odds, and thereby the time required, to break the daily-changing Enigma keys.

Lorenz

The Lorenz was an even more complex cipher machine than Enigma. Made by the Lorenz company, it was used exclusively for the most important messages passed between the German Army Field marshals and their Central High Command in Berlin. Its size meant that it was not a portable device like Enigma. Bletchley Park code breakers called the machine 'Tunny' and the coded messages 'Fish'.

Lorenz used the 'International Teleprinter Code', in which each letter of the alphabet is represented by a series of five electrical impulses. Messages were enciphered by adding, character by character, a series of apparently randomly generated letters to the original text. Crucially, to decrypt the enciphered message, the receiving Lorenz simply added exactly the same obsuring letters back to the ciphertext. The obsuring letters were generated by Lorenz's 12 rotors, five of which followed a regular pattern, while another five followed a pattern dictated by two pin wheels. Cracking Fish again relied on determining the starting position of the Lorenz machine's rotors.

Tunny and Heath-Robinson

The great Cryptanalyst, John Tiltman broke the first Fish messages at Bletchley in 1941 using hand-methods that relied on statistical analysis, but by 1944 the Germans had introduced complications which made it virtually impossible to break Tunny by hand alone. Dr Max Newman and his team in the 'Newmanry' were assigned the task of building machines to break Tunny.

The first machine designed to break the Lorenz was built at the Post Office research department at Dollis Hill and called 'Heath Robinson' after the cartoonist designer of fantastic machines. Although Heath Robinson worked well enough to show that Max Newman's concepts were correct, it was slow and unreliable.

Flowers and Colossus

Max Newman called in the help of Tommy Flowers, a brilliant Post Office Electronics Engineer. Flowers went on to design and build 'Colossus', a much faster and more reliable machine that used 1,500 thermionic valves (vacuum tubes). The first Colossus machine arrived at Bletchley in December 1943. This was the world's first practical electronic digital information processing machine - a forerunner of today's computers.

Lorenz had to be cracked by carrying out complex statistical analyses on the intercepted messages. Colossus could read paper tape at 5,000 characters per second and the paper tape in its wheels travelled at 30 miles per hour. This meant that the huge amount of mathematical work that needed to be done could be carried out in hours, rather than weeks.

D-Day

Mark I Colossus was upgraded to a Mark II in June 1944, and was working in time for Eisenhower and Montgomery to be sure that Hitler had swallowed the deception campaigns prior to D-Day on June 6th 1944. There were eventually 10 working Colossus machines at Bletchley Park.

The End of War

With the declaration of peace, the frenzy of codebreaking activity ceased. Much of the 'incriminating' evidence was destroyed. As the Second World War gave way to the Cold War, it was vital that Britain's former ally, the USSR, should learn nothing of Bletchley Park's wartime achievements.

The Secret

The thousands who had worked there departed with no public recognition, and many with no knowledge, of the fact that they had contributed to a feat so colossal that at times the Allies were receiving enemy messages even before Hitler's own Generals. For decades, the codebreakers would remain silent about their achievements. Some continued to use their remarkable expertise to break other countries' cyphers, working under a new name: the Government Communications Headquarters (GCHQ). The site became home to a variety of training schools: for teachers, Post Office workers, air traffic control system engineers, and members of GCHQ. In 1987, after a fifty-year association with British Intelligence, Bletchley Park was finally decommissioned.

The Truth Emerges

It was not until the wartime information was declassified in the mid-1970s that the truth would begin to emerge. The impact of those achievements on the outcome of the war and subsequent developments in communications still has not been recognised fully. Historians agree that the work done in wartime Bletchley Park effectively shortened the war by up to two years, saving countless

lives. Not only is Bletchley Park accredited as being the birthplace of the Information Age with the world's first semi-programmable electronic computer in the form of Colossus, but it was also the catalyst in transforming national communications and intelligence from a one-room activity through to an industry from which our modern GCHQ has emerged, countering the threats posed by terrorists, drugs and serious crime.

Bletchley Park Today

Today, Bletchley Park Trust is a charity; its mission is to build on the World War Two codebreakers' legacy, drawing inspiration from the history and preserve the heritage site for future generations. Ultimately the Trust aims to transform Bletchley Park into the world-class heritage and education centre it deserves to be, reflecting the profound significance of its impact on WW2, the twentieth century and the way we all live today. It receives no ongoing public funding and relies heavily on its revenue stream from museum visitors as well as conferences, weddings and its Science and Innovation Centre, where Bletchley Park has returned to world-leading research after 60 years.

Recent Developments

Bletchley Park Trust, conscious of the debt we all owe to great and famous WW2 heroes, especially Churchill, but also to unsung intellectual warriors like Turing, Knox and Welchman, work tirelessly to develop the site. Over the last few years, in addition to the opening of the Science and Innovation Centre, the Bletchley Park Trust has restored the Mansion roof; Codebreaking Huts 4, 8 and 12; Blocks A, B and E; established an American Garden Trail; a number of impressive exhibitions, including fully-operational Bombe and Colossus Rebuilds, and developed unique mathematics learning resources for students and educators. The Park is open every day to the public and visitors from all over the world now share the Secrets of Bletchley Park.

Bletchley Park Ltd, The Mansion, Bletchley Park, Milton Keynes MK3 6EB T: +44 (0) 1908 640404 W: www.bletchleypark.org.uk

Opening Times

Open daily except Christmas Eve, Christmas Day, Boxing Day and New Year's Day
1st November to 31st March - 10.30am to 4.00pm
1st April to 31st October - 9.30am to 5.00pm
Weekends & Bank Holidays: 1st November to 31st March - 10.30 am to 4.00pm : 1st April to 31st October - 10.30am to 5.00pm
The gates will not be open before the times stated. Not ALL exhibitions are open every day. Please always check before travelling on 01908 640404 or visit www.bletchleypark.org.uk

Four Bombs in Two Minutes:
One Enemy Air Attack during the Blitz 1940

Len Barnett

To most, Crouch End, a pleasant suburb in North London might not be associated with the Second World War. Nevertheless, like many others away from the East End this area was subjected not only to enemy air attacks during the Blitz of 1940-41, but more during the *'tip and run'* phase through to 1944 and again by the infamous V-weapons in 1944 and 1945.

Already aware of this, at least in general terms, I had no particular reason to think that a piece of derelict land behind my home had any connection with such events: even if an apple tree lies at a crazy angle. With the intention of re-creating a garden, I encountered an inordinate amount of rubble. Scanning the brick-built mid-Victorian houses all around, at first sight none had the appearance of having had damage repaired. Looking closer though, I noted slight differences in one row of semi-detached houses: two being less ornate, having slightly cleaner brickwork and at the front, a gap in the plane trees along the road. Dawning on me that these were of post-war construction, I decided to investigate.

After an initial unsuccessful foray in the local newspaper, *The Hornsey Journal*, I reckoned that Air Raid Precaution Wardens' records would be a logical source and this proved the case.

Since councils were responsible for the A.R.P. at their level, any surviving documents should be found in local archives. For the then Borough of Hornsey, covering Crouch End, these are at Bruce Castle, Tottenham. From there, reports of raids in the local newspaper began to make sense. Identities of the dead were then learned, or confirmed through the Commonwealth War Graves Commission. The relevant official history named *Civil Defence*; a booklet published by Hornsey Historical Society entitled *Home Fires*; and also *Kelly's Directory* were helpful.

At approximately 8.20 p.m. on 8th October 1940 four high-explosive bombs fell within a quarter of a mile of each other. As the two types of A.R.P. written reports do not entirely tally, it is not possible to state with absolute certainty the order in which they fell. The incident log records five events over this night. It is not unlikely that this was compiled later, as all entries are in the same hand and kept *very* neatly. Even so, there are slight irregularities. The first incident of the day logged was numbered two and timed at '20.26.' Incident three was recorded as occurring at '20.20'; with four and five at '20.22.' A situation report the following afternoon tidied up the times to two each at '20.20' and '20.22.' Therefore, it may have been that the information for the incident log came from hastily written notes and a zero was inadvertently entered as six. (The last event occurred over a mile away to the south at a cinema near Finsbury Park later that evening.) If my assumption is correct, then the first two bombs landed at 8.20 p.m. One was at the rear of Dunn's bakery; and the

other on or near 56 Crouch Hall Road. While the former was literally a stone's throw from an A.R.P. report centre and wardens' post, at Hornsey Town Hall, the latter was in a road that leads off from the Broadway at the clock-tower. According to the official version reports of both detonations were received about five minutes later. Of the other two that apparently fell at 8.22 p.m.; the third landed behind what was then a Lyon's corner house and a café run by Sainsbury's on the corner of the Broadway and Coleridge Road; while the fourth struck a terraced row in Tivoli Road, parallel with Park Road, near the cricket fields. It was not until twenty and twenty-nine minutes later respectively that reports reached the A.R.P. authorities of the latter incidents.

It is likely that the first known incident had been the one behind Dunn's, as it was so close to the town hall. This had hit the bakery's stables, killing three horses and damaging the premises of the Hornsey Gas Company next door (the latter now Barclays Bank). While one person was injured *The Hornsey Journal* mentioned not only that debris had fallen in front of 'municipal offices,' but also that 'twin babies' nearby had 'remained sleeping' throughout. It would appear that the coal gas main was also ruptured.

Even with the danger of major fires near the Broadway, the situation in Crouch Hall Road was more immediately serious. Two houses (four semi-detached properties 56 to 60) had been demolished, others were seriously damaged, four people were said to have been killed, with a further five injured.

The corner of the Broadway and Coleridge Road is directly across the road from Dunn's bakery. Even then an area of

mixed usage, behind the Lyons' corner house (now a branch of Costa) and Sainsbury's Mecca Café (presently an unoccupied shop and Bank Santander) the initially unnoticed bomb that dropped there destroyed the mission hall of the Plymouth Brethren. One person was slightly injured and the gas main was damaged there as well.

Unfortunately, the fourth incident in Tivoli Road was the worst of the night locally. This had demolished three of the terraced houses (15 to 19), with others grievously affected and a fire caused by the coal gas main that had been extinguished by the following afternoon. At that latter time it was thought that eight people had been killed, with six injured: but that others were 'still believed under wreckage.'

By then the corpses had been removed to mortuaries and the injured to hospital. Rescue Parties were still searching for dead and injured at Crouch Hall Road and Tivoli Road; and Repair Gangs were making surrounding structures safe. Furniture was still being removed and stored. Not only had a section of Crouch Hall Road been closed to traffic, so too had one of main north-south roads bordering the southern end of the Broadway, due to shaky chimneystacks. Three repair parties had been at work in the vicinity of the town hall. This was seemingly more than for the two residential locations with fatalities, but as a large public air-raid shelter (capacity 186) nearby may well have been in use by then, this may be seen as defensible.

The minutes of Hornsey Council's monthly meetings (found in the local library) give the impression of efficiency, even if the detailed reports submitted have not been retained for posterity. Items in the local press gave other views: some not so positive. Prior to these attacks a few readers had been so angered at the officiousness of individual A.R.P. wardens that they wrote to the paper. Another citizen had publically asked why councillors were apparently being paid £5 per week as full-time wardens. This was because not only did these officials have other incomes, their duties meant that they could not be full-time wardens and that the other full-timers by then were only getting £3 5s. This spurred numerous letters from voluntary A.R.P. wardens, frustrated variously. For a start, the full-time cadre of paid wardens had been cut back from the September 1939 numbers to a point where they could not even get one day off per week without the goodwill of unpaid volunteers covering for them. (This decision had been taken at governmental level, as a cost-cutting measure.) Many of the volunteers had not even received boiler-suits and boots, entirely necessary for carrying out their duties, never mind additional clothing for coping with the increasingly cold nights. (Unbeknown to these wardens, the government had no intention of having these issued on a large scale.) Also, they were only beginning to receive nightly rations, such as 'dry biscuits' and 'mouldy cheese': that were considered as giving little sustenance. There were also significant complaints concerning public air raid shelters and trenches. More than one resident's letter opined that for such a high rate-paying borough the council served residents poorly and a petition had even been sent to Whitehall. Of course, the local authorities responded to these charges, either in sharp denials or defences (as in the better-paid councillor wardens), or alternatively, in upbeat explanatory editorials. All these add significantly to an understanding to what is liable to have happened that October night.

For civil defence purposes, at local level boroughs were first split by ward and from there into sectors, peppered with wardens' posts: presumably connected to reporting centres by telephone lines of some sort. At least some of these posts were *said* to be of a pillbox type construction and were manned by the full-time wardens. Supporting them were the part-time volunteers, both men and women

that maintained constant foot patrols as far as possible. Principally, it was the latter's responsibility to locate and report incidents to the posts. Although the patrolling wardens also aided people in other ways, if the Auxiliary Fire Service was not required, the A.R.P. Rescue Parties were next on the scene. These were made up of men over thirty in the building trades and each party should have had a foreman, bricklayer, carpenter and plumber, as well as labourers. Four of Hornsey's twenty Rescue Parties were of volunteer council workers. There were also Decontamination Parties, in the event of poison gas being used by the enemy. While all were said to be trained in first aid, there were also A.R.P. medical units: some with ambulances. The utility companies were informed by the A.R.P. authorities and it would seem logical that their workers also attended incidents: for assistance with damaged and therefore, highly dangerous gas, electric and water mains. Anyway, after locations had been secured through the efforts of the Rescue Parties, by demolition if necessary, it was the turn of the Salvage Parties to sort and re-cycle building materials. At the time of these attacks the Auxiliary Military Pioneer Corps were doing this, but soon after a Labour Reserve scheme was announced nationally. Unemployed men were requested to volunteer for this war work. Also, members of the clergy were ex officio members of the A.R.P. for the giving the *Last Rites*.

Returning to the A.R.P. reports of October 8th, in all likelihood patrolling wardens, or others ran from Crouch Hall Road to the town hall almost as soon as the bombs dropped, with the damaged nearby buildings also noticed shortly before. Presumably one Rescue Party will have been immediately despatched to Crouch Hall Road from the depots off Hornsey High Street and two ambulances as soon as it was established that there were people injured: possibly from the mobile A.R.P. unit then based at the town hall. Interestingly, there is no mention of a fire at this location, but I have dug up a number of pieces of charred timber within layers of brick and ironwork, broken crockery and other personal possessions. Perhaps neighbours with stirrup pumps put out fires there: as citizens were then being encouraged to set up their own 'fire services.'

It is far more difficult trying to make sense of events at Tivoli Road. Mid-way between two wardens' posts, both were approximately only 75 yards away from this bombing. Assuming that these were manned, not only should this

context. Although not subjected to the intense hammering of London's East End, like many other boroughs, even prior to the opening of the Blitz on September 7th there had been some bombings: but most were very light. The night of September 8th to 9th had been heavy though, with almost forty incidents logged in A.R.P. records. While there had been an increase of tempo towards the end of that month again this tailed off and for some days there had been no incidents. On the night of October 7th to 8th a handful of oil-bombs and one high-explosive bomb had been scattered across the borough, seemingly in three waves, but with little damage. On the night of 9th to 10th the area around Hornsey High Street (with a few apparent strays elsewhere) was subjected to at least fifty incendiaries. The next night it was the turn of the foot of Alexandra Palace and Muswell Hill. With the housing spaced out more, few lives were lost: although three people were killed in the Anderson shelter in their garden. Early on October 16th there was a serious incident, when there was a near miss to the public trench off Tottenham Lane, on Broad Lane. While well over fifty people escaped or were rescued, at least eleven and possibly more than seventeen were killed when it caved in. Finally, virtually across the road from the destroyed houses in Crouch Hall Road, behind what was then Wilson's department store (now *Budgens* to the discount book shop) a bomb dropped on the evening of October 21st. Either not detonating due to hitting soft tarmac or through having a time delayed fuse, not only was the large public air-raid shelter (capacity 145 persons) deemed unsafe for some days, all properties within a thirty-yard radius were evacuated.

Even without studying surviving *Luftwaffe* records at Freiburg, Germany much can be learned of their activities over Britain. Apart from numerous published histories on the perspectives of both sides' air forces, the Air Ministry's daily intelligence summaries (seen at the R.A.F. Museum Hendon) give an astonishing amount of detail. Further data, such as on the weather was located within Ultra decryptions of enemy signal traffic and British army anti-aircraft unit diaries at The National Archives, Kew.

Daylight operations on October 8th had been complex; primarily with long-range bomber reconnaissance ranging far and wide (as far north as Liverpool); and hundreds of small raids throughout England's South East and

detonation have been heard, in particular the flames should have become visible to the post at the foot of Wolseley Road on Park Road. It should not have taken any longer than four minutes to get to the site of devastation and back to the post. Whatever actually occurred, when reported only one Rescue Party was dispatched to this location.

The Plymouth Brethren meeting hall was probably well out of sight of the Broadway. Therefore, with the other three incidents and resources probably significantly stretched it is hardly surprising that this was not discovered for some time.

It is worth pointing out other difficulties. Apart from diversions through closed roads, driving for the emergency services cannot have been at all easy in the blackout, even in moonlight. Although there was a rising moon, it was overcast that night and probably raining at times. For the rescue and repair parties, especially at night and even without corpses, the work must have been both extremely dangerous and grim.

The situation report of October 9th maintained that the *'population'* was *'calm.'* Since little meaning can be taken from this phrase, it might be useful to put these events into

London by fighter-bombers (hastily converted Messerschmitt Bf. 109s).

Night operations began with a sweep and raid on a broad front between Portland and Portsmouth. London was a major target with a *'stream'* of aircraft from France and Holland following on. Nevertheless, it was noted that many of these aircraft passed on to attack aerodromes north of the metropolis. Essentially there was absolutely *no* pattern to the hits on London. The most serious were on the south side of the Thames near London Bridge; in Shoreditch, north east of the City; and Chiswick and Hammersmith in the west. There were also 50 major and 320 minor incidents. In the immediate vicinity of Crouch End, the other areas affected that night were Hampstead, Finsbury Park, Islington, Tottenham, Edmonton and Southgate.

Drawing on all this tactical information and after discussion with an air historian, tentative conclusions can be drawn on these specific attacks. Of the 190 enemy bombers involved (Heinkel IIIs, Dornier 17s and Junkers 88s), at least one passed over Crouch End. If the A.R.P. reports were in error and they were all dropped at the same time, this could have been due to one aircraft on an approximate course of 310 degrees (magnetic), dropping a rather badly spaced stick. Cloud cover at medium height had been increasing and reached 100 per cent by 9 p.m. So it may have been that Crouch End had been one unseen target for one bomber, navigating by radio beacons. An *Ultra* decrypt would seem to indicate that the British

had *not* been jamming these enemy beacons during that particular 24-hour period. Alternatively, there could have been two machines on slightly different courses. Even though the anti-aircraft defences to the south saw no enemy aircraft, with two of the detonations being *so* close to each other, perhaps they had descended to below cloud level. The bomb-aimer of the second machine, seeing fires from the first, may have also dropped two of his bombs close by two minutes later.

Regarding fatalities the A.R.P. reports state that at Crouch Hall Road there were four deaths. However, only three names are in *The Commonwealth War Graves Commission* records: a couple and their six-year old son. Also, at Tivoli Road the C.W.G.C. records give a final death toll of ten people: including another child. One of the adults was an A.R.P. stretcher leader, but as his wife was also killed, presumably he was a volunteer not then on duty. In attempting to resolve these matters, I contacted the local Coroner's office. As a class these documents are subject to a 75 year closure period and so, those from 1940 will not be open to the public until 2016. Being for a London borough they will be at the London Metropolitan Archives. In the interim, requests can be made to the Coroner for information. It should be pointed out that whether any is forthcoming, or not, is entirely down to these officials as *individuals*.

Although there were no relevant obituaries in the local newspaper, there were some useful snippets. At Crouch Hall Road a *'man had spoken through the debris to his rescuers, but was dead when they reached him.'* Also, four out of the five injured in this attack were named and said to have been treated at a first aid post (again probably on Park Road).

With air attacks on the British Isles from Aberdeen to the Scilly Isles that affected civilians in this war, there will have been a *vast* number of incidents worthy of research. Locations of records will vary according to local organisation and archiving, but hopefully this article will spur others to look into this area of local and family history.

⊙ ROYAL AIR FORCE museum

Paul Hudson M.A (Oxon) MCIM MInstSMM - *Head of Marketing*

The aim of the Royal Air Force Museum is to inform present and future generations about the history and traditions of the Royal Air Force; to educate individuals about Air Power and Defence; and to promote the Royal Air Force.

This is done through many different methods. Through the integrated use of the Museum's exhibitions and collections at both its London and Cosford sites; through the development of online resources which are free for the public to use; and through the expertise of the Museum's staff who are able to offer assistance to both the professional and amateur historian.

The History of the Museum

After the Battle of Britain and the subsequent victory for the Allies in World War II there was a substantial groundswell of opinion amongst British politicians and the general public for the creation of a museum dedicated solely to the history of RAF. Greater priorities after World War II, such as re-building the country's shattered infrastructure and economy, meant that the building of such a museum was put on hold until the nation's and the M.O.D's budgets could accommodate this project.

However, in anticipation of the existence of such a museum, various air-frames that were considered to be of historic importance were placed into storage, or reserve collections, at various RAF stations around the country.

In 1962 the Air Force Board formed a committee, under the chairmanship of Marshal of the Royal Air Force Sir Dermot Boyle, to advise the Board on historical and museum matters. Arising from the committee's deliberations was a recommendation that the time was now appropriate to establish a Royal Air Force Museum.

A Board of Trustees was formed to look after the Museum's interests, with Sir Dermot Boyle as its chairman and Dr. John Tanner, from the staff of the RAF College, Cranwell, as Director of the Museum.

The Museum's London site at RAF Hendon was chosen as the most suitable site for the Museum as it had a long aviation history, from

the earliest days of aviation (1909) and on 15 November 1972, Her Majesty the Queen officially opened the Royal Air Force Museum at RAF Hendon in London. On its opening; the museum's London hangars housed some 36 aircraft.

The London site today

Today the Museum's London site consists of 5 Galleries containing over 100 aircraft, enabling visitors to navigate their way through the history of aviation from the earliest balloon flights right up to the development of the *DA2 Eurofighter Typhoon.*

The *'Milestones of Flight'* Exhibition Hall was opened on the 17th December 2003, exactly 100 years to the day from the first powered flight by Orville Wright. It contains a dramatic display of suspended aircraft, split level views, touch screen plinths, timeline wall, cutting edge screen displays and a breathtaking 3-D film.

The Main Aircraft Hall, consisting of two First World War hangars, displays aircraft from the early days of aviation to the Tornado GR1 and the impressive Chinook Helicopter used in the Falklands conflict. Life in the past and present RAF is covered through both interactive and static displays located around the Hall.

Among the aircraft within the Bomber Command Hall are the Lancaster, Halifax, Wellington and Flying Fortress of the Second World War, the diminutive FE2b of earlier days

and the Vulcan of the Cold War era. A special exhibition chronicles the events of the heroic *'Dambusters'* Raid, making use of archive film footage and artefacts associated with the people involved.

The Grahame-White Factory harks back to the glory days of Hendon's aviation past. This Grade II listed building has been renovated and relocated closer to the main Museum site. It stands complete, with its five huge timber *'Belfast Trusses,'* spanning the full width of the building. Inside it are the Museum's collection of early aircraft and other associated exhibits. This enables the building to be re-used in a situation that is very similar to its original purpose.

The Battle of Britain Hall focuses on the epic struggle of 1940. Apart from the unique collection of British, German and Italian aircraft, visitors can sit and watch *'Our Finest Hour,'* a lively and stimulating interpretation of the Battle of Britain. This multi-media approach neither trivialises the events of the Battle nor endows them with false glamour, but it aims to attract and educate an audience for whom the Second World War is not recent history. Visitors can also see a V1 flying bomb and a V2 rocket, or walk through the mighty Sunderland flying boat; giving them a taste of what life would have been like for the Sunderland's crew on a two or three week mission.

315

ACH98/20/15

O/as Fighting School
Bedgford
Norfolk.

h. 3. 19.

dly dear Ira
To business first, thank you very much for making the garments for me, its awful decent of you — (making me decent). well there are one or 2 alterations that would improve them — first of all they bulge between the b... at the back ... remedy I sugg... make the band ... longer, so th... fit lower down, or round a higger f... the waist, or I suppose you could on... barn... the back is fitted with small... they will be O.K.

Now we are settled on the ... tell you all about them, there are 9.
A = Kitchen
B = Common Room, not yet complete.
C = Officers — divided into 3.

I May 1979 and was born out of a collection of historic ground instructional airframes on inventory at the Royal Air Force's base at Cosford. Other aircraft were added to the collection from the RAF's Reserve Collections of Historic Aircraft scattered about the Country. The Trustees of the Royal Air Force Museum took over the management of the collection, in 1979, under a Ministry of Defence Management Agreement, as a Museum independent of the RAF Museum at Hendon in London, and employed two staff.

The Museum continued to grow until 1995 when forward plans indicated that expenditure would overtake income by 1998 if public facilities were not improved and visitor numbers increased. Applications were made to the Heritage Lottery Fund, the European Regional Development Fund and an appeal was launched to build a Visitor Centre in which to accommodate first class public facilities and a conference centre.

In addition, an art gallery, a temporary exhibitions gallery and two other subject galleries (Missiles and the History of Cosford) were built and opened by His Royal Highness The Duke of Gloucester on 21st June 1998.

Centres of Excellence

On 13th May 2002, Marshal of the Royal Air Force Sir Michael Beetham opened a new Conservation Centre named after him. This Centre was the culmination of seven years of planning to move the RAF Museum's Reserve Collection to Stafford and the Conservation Centre to Cosford, from Cardington in Bedfordshire. Since its opening the Centre's work has won a plethora of awards and it is open twice a year, for a week at a time, enabling the public to view the latest projects undertaken by the Museum's Aircraft Conservation Team.

On 7th February 2007 the National Cold War Exhibition, a landmark building containing 18 aircraft, military transport, missiles, memorabilia, interactive kiosks and information hotspots was officially opened by HRH Princess Royal.

This unique exhibition tells the story of the Cold War period, from national, international, social/political as well as cultural perspectives, in an innovative way. A major feature of this unique exhibition is Britain's three post-war V-Bombers the Vulcan, Victor and Valiant. A Number of these aircraft are suspended in

Interwoven throughout the artefacts in each of these Hangars are displays both static and interactive that shed further light on the social aspects of the history they narrate. Whether it be *'Diversity in the Royal Air Force'* since the Service's early days (Historic Hangars) or the political and economic uncertainties that lead to the fall of the Weimar Republic, the rise of fascism across Europe and the Second World War (Battle of Britain Hall).

Throughout the year, the Museum hold historic pageants, enabling the public to interact with characters from a given period of aviation history and to empathise with those individuals' hopes and fears for the future; making their histories more real and immediate. The Museum's Handling Collection, which is used regularly throughout the year, for museum events and schools, affords visitors the opportunity to touch the actual equipment and try on the actual kit that their RAF ancestors would have used in their day to day duties.

Royal Air Force Museum Cosford

The Royal Air Force Museum Cosford, just outside Wolverhampton, houses like its sister museum in London, one of the largest aviation collections in the UK. 70 historic aircraft are displayed in three wartime hangars and within the site's latest gallery, the National Cold War Exhibition.

The Aerospace Museum at Cosford (as the Museum was previously know) was opened on

flying attitudes including a Dakota, Canberra, Meteor, Lightning and Javelin. Visitors are able to view them from an elevated viewing gallery. In addition to these aircraft, this gallery contains, seven mini-theatres or immersive hotspots which enable the public to explore interactively the social and economic tensions of this period.

Mascots and Boy Entrants – Social History at Cosford

As well as the 70 aircraft on display at Cosford the Museum is also home to a number of smaller unique exhibitions such as the site's Lucky Mascots exhibition. The aim of these exhibitions is to educate the public about the social history that is bound up with the Museum's collection.

With Lucky Mascots the public explore how charms and the emotional ties to them can take many forms. Some are traditional good luck items such as a rabbit's foot or medal of Saint Christopher (the patron saint of travellers). Others are mundane objects with a special meaning to the individual - a coin given by a relative, or a girlfriend's silk stocking.

Lucky charms were often used during wartime as the danger and stress of operational life tended to encourage belief in a favourite mascot. Such mascots helped to maintain morale and give aircrews the courage and confidence to face each operation. Even highly experienced aircrew had their own lucky mascots, showing that they knew skill alone was not enough to ensure their well being.

The display at RAF Museum Cosford features mascots from both the RAF's early history up to the modern day and include Lucky Gremlins, Percy the Parachuting Penguin, Wing Commander Roland Rat, Scotch Jock and Teddy Cooper.

Another unique exhibition at Cosford which examines social history within the RAF is the new permanent exhibition which honours Boy Entrants. This newly refurbished and extended exhibition dedicated to the RAF Boy Entrant Scheme has been produced in collaboration with the Boy Entrants Association, highlighting the role played in the RAF by young men aged between 15 and 17 1/2.

Beginning in 1934 with 150 boys the scheme ran until 1965, with a break from 1940-1947, during which time over 38,000 boys had been trained. Entrants underwent 18 months of trade training in a myriad of roles ranging from wireless operators and armourers to nursing attendants and stewards, as well as continuing their education and participating in unrivalled social and leisure time pursuits. Many of these boys went on to adult careers in the RAF; a significant number were commissioned and earned promotion to senior rank and an equally significant number were regularly included in the annual New Year's Honours List.

Boy Entrant training took place at various RAF stations including Hereford, St. Athan in South Wales, and Yatesbury in Wiltshire, and RAF Cosford itself was one of the principal centres, accommodating up to 1000 Boy Entrants at a time.

Assistance for Professional and Amateur Researchers

The Museum's Department of Research and Information Services (known as DoRIS) is based at the Royal Air Force Museum's London site and manages the Archive and Library collections. Although the service records of individuals are not held on site, the collections contain a range of material useful to family and local historians.

A wealth of information about service life can be gleaned from original documents such as letters, diaries, ephemera, photograph albums and log books. The majority of these are found amongst the numerous personal papers of men and women who have served with the British air services held by the Museum. The papers of individuals of the Allied air forces (especially those who served with the RAF from Occupied Europe during the Second World War) and the air forces of the Dominions and British Commonwealth are also kept at Hendon.

Depending on what is known already, or the focus of your research, specific sources can provide useful detail. The Archive holds documents relating to the early days of flight; the papers of aviation companies and of those instrumental in developing aviation in this country. The Royal Aero Club collection is also held at Hendon. This will be of interest if your relative was a civil aviator, although for much of the First World War military personnel had to qualify for a civil flying licence too. The Museum holds the card index for these licences which provide personal details including rank or profession; the qualification date, place and type of aircraft flown. The majority of these cards have a photograph associated with them too. Copies of these are available via the Ancestry website www.ancestry.co.uk

For tracing specific details about your relative the Army and Navy Lists will be of interest as well as the Royal Air Force Muster Roll of 1918. This was compiled when the Royal Air Force was formed and lists the NCOs and airmen serving at this point in time. It

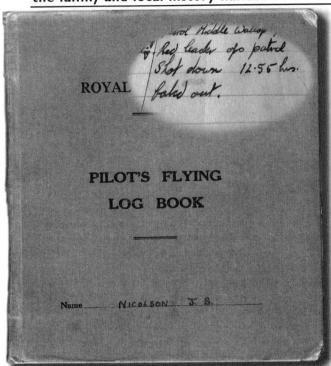

essential to know the date and the aircraft type.

The extensive Library collection also contains a vast array of detail for individuals including losses, awards, and biographical information. A broad range of books from published memoirs and historical studies to the more technical aspects of aviation is available for consultation. One of the largest collections is the series of manuals known as Air Publications issued by the Royal Air Force and its predecessors. They cover details of aircraft and engines used by the RAF, policy matters and training material. Complementing these are instructional posters known as Air Diagrams which cover a variety of topics. Of particular interest will be the periodicals and magazines produced by RAF stations and units which provide a fascinating insight into service life.

For those interested in a particular station or geographical area the Museum holds a large collection of site plans for airfields and non-flying stations in the UK and abroad. These show the lay-out of the stations and the type of buildings to be found on site. Many were constructed to standard designs and a collection of building drawings are held by the Museum. The Library also holds a significant collection of aeronautical maps including navigational charts and target maps.

The Department is unable to undertake detailed research but does offer an enquiry service with email and postal enquiries answered within 20 working days. Visitors can use the reading room at Hendon where material from the collections can be consulted. This facility is currently open Tuesday to Friday 10.00.a.m. to 5.00.p.m. by appointment. Curatorial staff can offer guidance to researchers during their visit and an interpretation service of documents and artefacts. If you would like to find out more, visit the Museum's web-site - www.rafmuseum.org.uk/research/ - or contact the department if you would like assistance at research@rafmuseum.org

The Royal Air Force Museum is open daily from 10am to 6pm except for Christmas Day, Boxing Day and New Year's Day. The museum closes, at both sites, for an annual Spring Clean in January. Please check the website for dates. Admission to the Museum is free of charge, with last admission being at 5.30 pm (London) and 5 pm (Cosford). www.rafmuseum.org.

provides details such as pay, rank and trade but is ordered by service number not alphabetically. The Air Force List was also issued from 1918 until quite recently. These volumes are indexed alphabetically and provide the service number as well as rank and date of seniority for officers. Those covering 1920-1938 also show where an officer was serving.

Information concerning casualties or those injured during active service is available. The Museum holds an extensive set of record cards relating to the deaths, injuries and illness suffered by Royal Flying Corps and Royal Air Force personnel from 1914-1928. These Casualty Cards, and Casualty Forms, can provide additional service history information and next of kin detail. Records covering the Second World War include a set of Bomber Command Loss Cards which can be consulted on microfiche and a collection of Effect Records for deceased personnel. These are available to next of kin only and are essentially final statements that close the financial accounts for the individual. The details provided include pay owing and any deductions required, for example mess bills. Accident Cards, or Form 1180, are also held on microfilm. These include reports on accidents involving RAF aircraft from 1930s to the 1970s although there are gaps. To trace a specific accident it is

In Which Regiment Did Your Ancestor Serve?

Bridget Hill

My interest in family history started at a very early age but progress was slow. I was eight years old and although the internet had been invented (just!) it had yet to impact on what was then largely a hobby for the retired ie. those with time to visit records offices and wander around cemeteries. My pocket money did not go far when all letters had to be accompanied by a stamped addressed envelope and there certainly wasn't much left for magazines or certificates.

My curiosity had been sparked by the unannounced arrival of my uncle at the family home. I had answered the door and been extremely confused when a gentleman asked for my father and said he was his brother. My father, very politely, asked the man to leave but invited him to return a couple of hours later. By the time he returned I had a found out that my father was not the eldest of two from Somerset but the youngest of eight from Birmingham, my aunt was no blood relation to me, neither was my grandfather but my grandmother was actually my first cousin, once removed and that I was not related to anyone

Private (later Acting Serjeant) Arthur Dommett
1st Battalion Honourable Artillery Company

with the same surname but for my parents and brother. Apparently this was all to do with a war and something to do with evacuation and adoption. It was a lot for an eight year old to take in but thus started my lifelong interest in family history and my subsequent interest in military history.

Despite being so radically affected by the Second World War my family is not a military one. During that war my grandfather worked in a factory making wings for Spitfires but was not medically fit to serve on the grounds of his poor eyesight. However, having spent many years researching my three lines I decided to look more carefully at the life of my other grandfather, my mother's father - Arthur Dommett, who had died just before I was two years old. I had been told that he was a local government officer, clerk to the rural district council and registrar of births, marriages and deaths but a photo of him in army uniform during the First World War was produced from the family archive. No one in the family could tell me what regiment he had served in but all had presumed that it would have probably been the local county regiment, the Somerset Light Infantry.

This wonderful studio photograph showed my grandfather, Arthur Dommett, bear-headed (so no cap with badge) and with no distinguishable design on the buttons on his uniform. However with magnifying glass in hand I managed to distinguish two metal letters on his shoulder – A and C. There appeared to be another letter in front of these but I could not make it out. I set off to the library and found a book which listed army regiments of the period together with their recognised abbreviations. After some trawling I found the Honourable Artillery Company – H.A.C. I wondered if it might be his regiment but after further research almost discounted it. Why would a young man working for the council in Somerset be in an officer training regiment in London?

All budding family historians know the first thing to do to get started is to talk to your living relatives. As an eight year old this had been relatively easy as older generations were quite happy to tell me their stories. I thought that all possible information had been gleaned some years before. However when I asked my mother whether her father had served with

Honourable Artillery Company Shoulder Title

the HAC she put the question again to her elder brother. He didn't know but almost as an aside mentioned that he had his medals, a pocket diary and a piece of shrapnel which had been removed from his neck during the war! Of course the medals were a vital source of information as they showed not only his regiment – the Honourable Artillery Company – but also his rank and service number. The first lesson to finding out which regiment your ancestor was in during the First World War is therefore to ask if anyone in the family has the medals. Unfortunately this doesn't assist in Second World War Research as medals were issued unnamed.

So, if you are not lucky enough to have an absent minded uncle with hidden treasures, how do you find out what regiment your ancestor served with? It is amazing how many people still assume that it had to be the county regiment of the place where he was born or was known to have lived. Whilst much has been made, and rightly so, of the sacrifice made by Pals Battalions and devastation caused to communities when lads from a small geographical area or social group joined up, served and died together the fact is that many men had no obvious link to the regiment they joined.

Certain regiments have traditionally recruited in surprising areas and recruitment officers regularly travelled to other areas to find men. Local newspapers frequently printed articles stating how many men of eligible age had joined up, and how many were yet to do so. If your ancestor was in the Coldstream Guards for example, would you assume he was a Londoner? He could have been from Devon - a traditional recruitment area for the Coldstream Guards. Similarly the Grenadier Guards have a long history of recruiting in the Manchester area. Soldiers on leave might be invited to speak to boys at their former school, so encouraging them to join a particular unit. I became aware a few years ago that many Second World War veterans of the Oxfordshire and Buckinghamshire Light Infantry settled in Exeter having become fond of the area (or a

young lady in it maybe) whilst training for the assault on Pegasus Bridge at a similar bridge in the area. That will be one for future generations of family historians to ponder!

Thousands of men served in corps with no geographical allegiance such as the Army Ordnance

Honourable Artillery Company Cap Badge

Corps, Royal Engineers, Army Cyclist Corps, Royal Artillery, Royal Flying Corps, Royal Army Medical Corps etc. Men joined these corps from all over the country. Sometimes they joined a corps because they had a specific skill eg. doctors in the RAMC, miners in the Royal Engineers etc. but it isn't safe to assume that just because your ancestor was in a particular corps he had a pre-war skill, trade or training relevant to it. The army frequently took what it could and made it into what it needed.

Not all recruiting serjeants (that's how they spelt it during the Great War) were happy to ignore the lies told by boys attempting to join the army under age. If the recruiting serjeant of the local regiment was known to the family boys would often go elsewhere to join up knowing that they had far less chance of being rejected as under age, or in some cases over age . Of course others simply walked around the block and presented themselves again only to be accepted.

Some men simply couldn't wait to get to the Front and so looked for regiments which they thought would get them there more quickly. The brother of Honourable Artillery Company VC winner Capt A O Pollard was posted as a deserter from the HAC. He had become so restless when they did not get to France as quickly as he wanted that he 'left' and joined the Grenadier Guards instead. Now I know they could both be thought of as London units - but he could so easily have gone to a county regiment or a corps unit.

Another reason for an ancestor appearing to have served with an illogical regiment was as a result of previous actions during the war. My great, great uncle started his army life in the Somerset Light Infantry, he was after all a Somerset man. However, when his battalion were so reduced in number after a battle that it could not continue as an effective force all those left fit to fight were transferred to the

The Author with her Grandad, Arthur Dommett in March 1968 five months before he died

unit next in the line. Thus when he made the ultimate sacrifice it was not under the badge of the Somerset Light Infantry but the Royal Inniskilling Fusiliers. To my knowledge he had never seen Ireland and I have not a drop of Irish blood in me.

One of the great sources of information about casualties of the Great War is a publication (now available online) called *Soldiers Died in the Great War 1914-19*. As I write I have in front of me Part 37 which relates to the Duke of Cornwall's Light Infantry, although it could be any volume. Reading the birth places of the casualties of the 1st Battalion illustrates this very topic; Staffordshire, London, Banffshire, Warwick, Devon . The 14th casualty on the list is the first to herald from Cornwall. In fact of the first 50 casualties listed for the battalion only 6 came from Cornwall.

Of course the easiest way to identify your ancestor's regiment is from a photo which includes a cap badge. All you have to know is which cap badge you are looking at – and there were literally hundreds during the First World War.

The Cardwell Reforms of 1881 had redesignated the regiments by name rather than number so making it necessary for regimental badges to be redesigned. A universal star helmet plate was created with a space in

the centre measuring one and seven eighths of an inch (how British is that!) to take a standardised badge. This consisted of a circle bearing the name of the new regiment and a device in the centre, often a collar badge.

Field service caps first became general wear in the 1890's. Helmet plates were too large for the new caps and were therefore temporarily replaced with a collar badge but by about 1898 most regiments of both cavalry and infantry had sealed patterns for cap badges. Exactly when a regiment, battalion or man started to use a particular cap badge cannot always be accurately determined. Battalions serving abroad when new badges were issued frequently had to wait until their return home. Some changes were delayed due to objections raised by Commanding Officers who managed a degree of autonomy in far distant regions of the Empire.

By the outbreak of the First World War in August 1914 cap badges were established as the symbol of a regiment or corps. Although not the only insignia worn during the period, the cap badge goes some way to defining the experience of that soldier, and so provides insight into the lives of our ancestors. Was your ancestor in the cavalry, the infantry, the Royal Artillery or Royal Engineers for example? In addition it is possible to access records of a particular regiment or battalion, such as the published regimental history or the war diaries at the National Archives, to find out its movements during the Great War. So, whilst an individual man probably won't be named in the war diaries, it is possible to make educated guesses as to his wartime experience based on his cap badge.

As for my grandfather, whilst trawling through some local newspapers I found a very small article which announced that Arthur Dommett and his friend, a colleague from the council, had gone to London to join the Honourable Artillery Company because his friend was a Londoner and had heard the reputation of the regiment! Although the regiment had been used as an officer training unit more than once during the war it also fought on the Western Front and in other theatres.

You can find more information about cap badges and details of our free cap badge recognition service on the Military Heritage website and blog at www.militaryheritage.co.uk.

Good luck with your research.

'Wee Are Not Greedy Of Jurisdiccon In Matters Of Blood'

Jill Groves

looks at Bristol City Council and its relationship with the Admiralty in the case of HMS Lizard and the Tyger merchantman

Introduction

This article is based mainly on a small collection of twelve documents in Bristol Record Office (BCC/J/Adm/5/1-12). I found these documents when researching a distant branch of my mother's family, the Mighells/Mitchels of Lowestoft. This branch of mum's family were connected with the Royal Navy – they were Royal Navy officers, ranging from midshipmen to full-blown admirals.

This collection of documents, a series of letters and memoranda between the Bristol authorities and Admiralty in London, concerned that most notorious of Royal Navy activities in times of war – the Press Gang. In this case it was a press gang that went wrong. I have written about this story of a Press-ganging that ended in two murders, several men in Bristol gaol and a blighted naval career. But what I wish to explore in this article is the light this incident throws on relations between a port authority like Bristol and the Admiralty.

The Bristol authorities were faced by a number of dilemmas in 1707. Ports like Bristol needed the Royal Navy to patrol the seas nearby and keep them safe, and to escort the ships of Bristol merchants to and from the Bristol Channel (then known as the River Severn or the Severn Sea or Saint George's Sea/Channel). In order to do that the Royal Navy needed to impress men into its service to crew it ships, since its 'volunteer' scheme was not yielding enough to compensate for the great losses the Royal Navy incurred that year. Ports like Bristol needed to attract lucrative commercial shipping trading with North America, Russia, Africa, the Caribbean, etc, which it could not do if it was known that the Royal Navy were close by, 'fishing' for sailors. Trade would go elsewhere, say to Liverpool. The Royal Navy, contrary to popular opinion, did not want to press-gang men with no knowledge of the sea or sailing. They preferred to press-gang merchant seamen, experienced sailors who knew one end of a rope from another and who knew how to set sail.

The Press-gang Incident

HMS *Lizard* had been patrolling between Exeter and Milford Haven since the late spring 1707, and also escorting merchant ships

between the ports of Exeter, Plymouth, Falmouth, Bristol, Newport and Milford Haven. For which the merchant ship-owners were very grateful. However, when the *Lizard* was ordered to turn fox against the chickens it was guarding, they were probably less so.

The *Lizard* was ordered by Admiralty to begin press-gaging merchant seamen as they arrived at the entrance to the River Avon. Commanding such a press-gang in a long boat or a larger sloop (often rated ships had smaller ones as tenders) was often the first command of a very young junior lieutenant or even a senior midshipman. In the *Lizard's* case it fell to its sailing master/mate, who was also a young man of sailing ability, but without the money and influence to be a midshipman first. It should have fallen to the *Lizard's* second lieutenant, if it had one, but didn't because the captain, Josiah Mighells, had been taken ill and died the day before the expedition.

The Royal Navy needed a lot of extra men in 1707, even before the catastrophic loss of life on the night of 20th / 21st October – 1,400 men and officers and a large number of ships lost in a great storm off the Scillies.

When the *Lizard's* press-gang in long boat and a pinnace went to impress the eighteen men on the long boat of the *Tyger* [1] there were no warning shots given, just firing of muskets into the body of the boat, killing one man and badly wounding two others, one of whom was at least able to give evidence to the Bristol authorities (the mayor and aldermen) two days later.

The Bristol authorities were horrified by the callous way the *Lizard's* crew went about the impressments and by shots being fired before giving a warning, thereby *'wounding killing and murthering.'* The crew of the *Tyger's* long boat *'were forced and brought by the Crew of the said Pinnace on board the ship Lizard.'* The mayor, George Stephens, and aldermen, then gave their five water bailiffs a warrant to arrest the men of the *Lizard* pinnace, especially the sailing master, Mr Parker Rowe, [2] and also to bring the *Tyger's* men to Bristol to give evidence. The warrant was accompanied by a letter addressed to *'the commanding officer of the Lizard,'* suggesting that the mayor and aldermen of Bristol already knew that Captain Josiah Mighells had died of disease four days before and had been buried at Pill, the nearest parish on the coast of Somerset.

Bristol City Authorities and the Admiralty

Although in the first report made by the mayor and aldermen, they seemed to deplore the impressments of the *Tyger's* crew, in the letter to the acting captain they assured him that if he sent the *Tyger's* crew ashore as witnesses they would be returned to the *Lizard*. But *'If soe be you suspect the retorne of the persons we send for you may send what guard you please along with them.'* But the mayor and aldermen knew they might have a riot on their hands if it became widely known throughout the city that one man had been *'murthered'* and two others badly wounded by a press-gang.

'the Resentm[en]t both by the neighbouring Countys and this City run very high for this way of killing', they

said in a later letter to the Secretary of the Admiralty, Josiah Burchett, 'yet it shalbe our Care . . . that Justice and Law shalbe kept in their bounds.'
[BCC/J/Adm/5/8]

But they also wanted the acting captain of the *Lizard* to co-operate. They had to be seen to be doing something by the merchants, and the populace, but not so heavy-handed that the Royal Navy withdrew protective escorts.

Acting Captain William Besille had probably already sent a report of the press gang by courier (or ship) to Admiralty in London (he would be a fool not to). This dawned on the mayor and aldermen a day after they learnt of the incident. A letter was sent off to Prince George, Prince Consort to Queen Anne and Lord Admiral, post haste, with a short resume of the facts. They also assured the Prince that although they intended to prosecute the perpetrators in Bristol, as they considered they had every right to do under Bristol's own court of admiralty, 'wee shall be very carefull not to Incroach on your Hignesses Jurydiction of Admirall, soe wee doubt not of yo[u]r Highnesses Countenance in the Prosecution of soe Barbarous an Action as this Appears to be.'
[BCC/J/Adm/5/4]

Meanwhile Acting Captain Besille had partially complied with the Bristol authorities' arrest warrant. He had allowed at least some of the crew of the *Tyger* to go ashore and give evidence, guarded by at least six men from the *Lizard*, including two who had already gone to Bristol to guard the two badly wounded men taken to Bristol for medical treatment. However, Lieutenant Besille had completely failed the warrant in one very important respect. 'Wee are told that the officers on board the Lizard have p[er]mitted the master of the shipp [Parker Rowe] who (as wee are informed) ordered the putting the armes into the Boate and to fire upon the men to escape.' Parker Rowe, the person the Bristol authorities blamed for the murder of the by now two men of the *Tyger* (a second man, Richard Kinaston having died six days after the incident), now could not be found.[2]

The mayor and aldermen were highly incensed by this cavalier attitude of the Royal Navy to their authority and warrant. Bristol took action. The six men from the *Lizard* were put in Bristol Gaol, pending enquiries and any court case in Bristol.

What happened to the men from the *Tyger* is unknown, but they were probably returned to the *Lizard* as promised, showing that even if the

Royal Navy couldn't act honourably Bristol's common council could.

Then a note came back from Prince George on 8 September 1707 at Windsor, via Josiah Burchett – in practice Josiah Burchett's advice to Prince George via Josiah Burchett. This note said that since the offence took place on water the case would be tried by Admiralty Court Martial under a law passed by Parliament in the reign of Charles II, some forty-five years before. [BCC/J/Adm/5/5]

The mayor and the common council of Bristol were rightly angry at this. Admiralty, in the person of Josiah Burchett, had trodden very heavily on the ancient rights of Bristol's own admiralty court. Rights which Bristol had had since the late thirteenth century, and reinforced in the fifteenth century, and confirmed as recently as the reign of Charles I some sixty to eighty years before, and they had never been questioned of superseded in more than 250 years until September 1707.

What was more, these rights had worked to the advantage of both Bristol and Admiralty in London.

'And this Jurisdicc[i]on has been very often serviceable to the state by taking Fugitives without waiting for any Admiralty warrant. And to our selves by arresting our debt[ors] without staying for an Admiralty process.' [BCC/J/Adm/5/8]

Bristol Admiralty Court in the person of the mayor replied to Josiah Burchett by pointing this out. He also said the Bristol court did not recognise the Act of Charles II as pertaining in this case. Bristol Admiralty Court pointed out that Admiralty in London did not have 'Jurisdicc[i]on of any murther, or killing but on board a shipp. And that a Court Martiall has power over such only who are in her Ma[jes]ties pay... And if a Court Martiall shall try Saylers in her Ma[jes]ties service, for killing he subjects that are not soe, Our Citizens must for beare going on the water while the Lizard is in the road [King Road, close to the mouth of the River Avon].' [BCC/J/Adm/5/8]

The Bristol authorities wanted their authority as an admiralty court since the fourteenth century – and reinforced in the fifteenth century and in the time of Charles II – acknowledged in this matter by Admiralty in London. The mayor and the aldermen kept George, Prince of Denmark, the Lord High Admiral and the Secretary of the Admiralty, Josiah Burchett, informed about the incident as a matter of courtesy. Admiralty thought it had jurisdiction as a matter of course because it had taken place a float in the Bristol Channel. Bristol said it had taken place in the mouth of the River Avon and therefore fell within the jurisdiction of the Bristol Court of Admiralty.

So if Josiah Burchett and the Admiralty wanted the case tried by court martial and so trample all over the ancient rights of the city and port of Bristol, Admiralty, the Royal Navy, and even the whole government in London, would lose all co-operation with the Bristol authorities over deserters and other fugitives from justice. The Bristol authorities would warn ships to stay away whilst HMS *Lizard*, or any other Royal Navy ship on a similar mission, was in the Severn Sea. Thus Bristol would be barred to the Royal Navy Impressment service. Bristol might lose money from port taxes and import duties, but so would the government. In the end Admiralty and the government would lose more than Bristol. And what if word of this incident got out? What if other port cities with similar rights did the same?

The Bristol authorities pointed out that they had tried a similar case three years before. In that case, Admiralty had not interfered. So why was it interfering now? Well, the case in 1704 involved only one man and that an ordinary sailor. The case in 1707 involved about twenty sailors, and potentially (if he could be found) a Royal Navy officer and possibly even a lieutenant of marines.[3] Admiralty did not like the thought of a local court like Bristol trying Navy men. They might not be acquitted. They might even be hanged for murder! [4]

Josiah Burchett stood by his decision that since the offence was committed afloat it should be tried by Court Martial in London – and thereby ensure that the principles were acquitted. He even got an opinion from Sir Charles Hedges, judge of the High Court of Admiralty on 25th September 1707 (who naturally would say he was entitled to judge it). The Bristol authorities also got opinions from their legal people in October 1707.

But by the end of October 1707 perhaps Admiralty had to be a little more conciliatory. They had at least 1400-2000 men and officers and several ships to replace after the disaster on 21st October 1707, when the renowned admiralty, Sir Cloudesley Shovell, and five ships

of his fleet foundered in a great storm off the Scillies. At the same time French privateers such as the Comte de Forbin were capturing Royal Navy and merchant ships in large numbers. Both the Bristol authorities and Admiralty needed each other.

Bridges needed to be repaired, normal relations resumed. It cannot be proved from the papers in Bristol Record Office, but possibly a lot of horse-trading went on. The Bristol authorities probably won to some extent. They were allowed to try the *Lizard*'s men they had in Bristol gaol. However, did they find any guilty of the murders of John Edwards and Richard Kinnaston? Have a guess.

Six of them were found not guilty, but not released from Bristol gaol until mid-November 1707, after a petition to Admiralty and Admiralty had written to the mayor of Bristol. Which means that four, including Parker Rowe (if he had been caught), were either in custody awaiting Court Martial in London or dead of gaol fever or acquitted and free. Of all the options, the two latter are more likely.

Ports like Bristol and its merchant families provided a lot of volunteers for the Royal Navy, mostly expert sailing masters and officers. In those days the career lines between merchant shipping owners and captains of merchant ships, and Royal Navy officers were very fluid, as between merchant seamen and Royal Navy sailors. Later in the eighteenth century, as Richard Woodman details in his *Britannia's Realm*, when the Royal Navy was larger, Admiralty had fewer such dilemmas and the press-gang seems to have been used more often, even illegally, and often much more violently than was the case here. Local courts, when they were involved, were very much more supine to the wishes of Admiralty. Even in cases of blatant murder by the press gang, these courts acquitted the perpetrators.[4]

Local Courts of Admiralty

So what were these local admiralty courts and what sort of cases did they handle? From the end of the thirteenth century and before 1887 the coast of England and Wales was divided into nineteen districts, for each of which there was a vice-admiral of the coast. Each vice-admiral of the coast had a local court of admiralty, such as the court at Bristol. There would have been a Judge Official and Commissary of the Court of Admiralty of wherever, who was probably also the vice-admiral of the local coast. Far from being Royal Navy or even people with merchant navy experience, the vice-admirals of the coast were normally local court judges. Even Sir Charles Hedges, judge of the High Court of Admiral in 1707, was a legal man, not a sailor.

These courts of admiralty acted mainly as receivers of wrecks. But they could also act in the case of local ships and maritime law. And they did so in Bristol with the help of the city authorities and aldermen, most of whom were magistrates anyway. (http://en.wikipedia.org/wiki/Admiralty_court)

In America in the 1760s, similar admiralty courts had much weaker evidence standards than criminal courts and the judges were paid a percentage of the fines levied. Was this also true of English local court admiralty courts in the eighteenth century? From the papers in the 1707 Bristol case possibly it was true that weaker evidence standards were used, which was why Josiah Burchett and the High Court of Admiralty were so keen to try the case in London and make it more favourable to the Navy.

As regards judges being paid a part of the fines, that might have been a later refinement in the 1760s, especially for the American colonies as a means of encouraging admiralty court judges and raising revenues for HM Government. American admiralty courts had no jury, only a judge.

Postscript – Bristol Merchants and Letters of Marque, 1707-1711

The *Tyger* merchant ship, with a slight bit of irony, became a privateer with Letters of Marque in 1708 and in 1710, with a change of owners. In other words, the *Tyger* became, briefly, a part of the Royal Navy. It was kitted out at the expense of its owners with 16 guns and a crew of forty in 1708, and with 20 guns in 1710.[5] Edward Malcome/Malcolm, captain of the *Tyger* in August 1707, wasn't her captain in 1708 and 1710. He had moved to on another smaller merchant ship with Letters of Marque, the *Severn Galley*, with twenty-six men and 10 guns.

Between 1708 and early 1711, nearly fifty Bristol-owned merchants ships were commissioned with 'Letters of Marque' and kitted out with arms. This was much larger than ports like Portsmouth and Plymouth – two and six respectively – although it came nowhere near the 200 granted to London merchants.

The Bristol privateers ranged in size from the 250 ton *Hannibal Frigate* with a crew of eighty and 22 guns (the size of a small sixth-rate frigate) to the *Wincanton Galley* with a crew of twenty-two and only 8 guns. (*Hannibal Frigate* was not the largest, but had the most crew and guns.)

Whilst the Mayor and Common Council of Bristol didn't directly own any of the Bristol

privateers, they had relatives who did. William Stevens, who was related to the Mayor, was lieutenant of the *Duckenfield Galley* in 1709. John Day, related to a member of the Common Council, part owned the *Scipio Frigate* and the *Mary Galley* in 1708; Francis Rogers, related to another member of the Common Council, was part owner of five privateers. (TNA, Records of the High Court of Admiralty and colonial Vice-Admiralty Courts, HCA 26/13-14.)

In years when Britain was at war and trade was not going well, then a lot of shipowners resorted to 'Letters of Marque' on the grounds that if the owners couldn't make money from trade they could at least make money from their ships taking enemy merchant shipping. That so many Bristol and London shipowners were granted 'Letters of Marque' trade must have been very bad for those ports between 1707 and 1711. (Plymouth and Portsmouth were mostly Royal Navy ports.) There was a lot of French naval and privateer activity between Land's End and Lisbon and between The Nore (Kent) and Archangel in 1707 (Lisbon and Archangel being two places where British merchants traded a great deal), especially by the Comte de Forbin and his friend René Duguay-Tronin. Both of them seemed to be everywhere in the autumn of 1707 and they captured a large number merchant ships in October.

Notes

1. The long boat that set out from the *Tyger* might have been a way of getting twenty seamen off the merchant ship and out of the clutches of a press-gang raid on the ship. In the 1780s, whalers about to enter the River Tyne would send a number of their crew ashore in long boats to escape the Royal Navy impressment service in the port of Newcastle, and then trust to press-gang protection papers for the rest of the

crew. The Royal Navy got wise to this and would send ships to raid whalers' long boats and then the whalers themselves once they got into port. *Britannia's Realm* by Richard Woodman, The History Press, details a number of such incidents.

A pinnace was a small sail boat used to ferry goods and people ship to ship or ship to port. They could also be slightly larger vessels, much favoured by the Dutch, merchants and others for smuggling and raiding in shallow waters.

2. By the time the water bailiffs arrived on board the *Lizard* Parker Rowe had, so the acting captain said, escaped. However, perhaps he was hidden on board. In 1786, a certain, later-renowned, captain on a Royal Navy ship in the Caribbean, one Horatio Nelson, hid his boatswain when the latter had been on a press-gang raid into the stews of a port and killed a man. In this case Admiralty took a dim view, though. (*Britannia's Realm* by Richard Woodman, The History Press.)

3. In June 1709, an *Edmund* Broadstreet petitioned Admiralty for confirmation of his commission as a lieutenant of Marines. (TNA, Privy Council Office, PC 1/2/183.) An *Edward* Broadstreet was listed as a member of the impressment gang. It would have been common to take marines as part of a press-gang. So perhaps *Edmund* and *Edward* Broadstreet are the same person and the lieutenant of Marines. However, this is speculation and could be very, very wrong.

4. By the 1780s, Admiralty could be quite secure in the thought that local courts would acquit the members of Royal Navy press-gangs, even when they had committed murders far worse than Mr Parker Rowe and the *Lizard* press-gang. (*Britannia's Realm* by Richard Woodman, The History Press.)

5. The National Archives (TNA), High Court of Admiralty and colonial Vice-Admiralty Courts, Prize Court: Registers of Declarations for Letters of Marque, HCA 26/13 and HCA 26/14.

Bibliography

Bristol Record Office, BCC/J/Adm/5/1-12, the Case of the *Lizard* and the *Tyger*
TNA, Records of the High Court of Admiralty and colonial Vice-Admiralty Courts, HCA 26/13 and HCA 26/14
Britannia's Realm by Richard Woodman, The History Press, published 2009.
TNA, Privy Council Office, PC 1/2/183
http://en.wikipedia.org/wiki/Admiralty_court, accessed 25 March 2010

The Story of a Badge
Research behind a schoolboy 'swop' from the 1960's
David Barnes

Class of 1967 David Barnes (left) Michael Applebee (right)

Class of 1968 David Barnes and Michael Applebee

Having been brought up in the 1960's I saw war films such as *The Dambusters*, *Reach for the Sky* on television and *633 Squadron* and *The Battle of Britain* at the cinema. To me there was always something fascinating about the Royal Air Force and its part in the Second World War.

My father had served in the Home Guard and the Royal Navy during the Second World War, but the father of one of my school friends from Primary School had served in the Royal Air Force and had been a Prisoner of War. One thing most of us did not do was ask those who served in the Forces about what their war was actually like. Maybe an early attempt to ask was brushed off, or we were told by others not to ask them about the war.

As schoolboys we played war games with toy soldiers or pretended to be soldiers fighting battles on local waste ground, spent hours with metal military vehicles and built Airfix plastic construction kits.

Another popular pastime of that era was 'swopping items', exchanging anything from themed collectors cards that were free with tea or with chewing gum, or toy soldiers, Matchbox, Dinky or Corgi cars etc.

One item I obtained from one such swop was the half-wing Brevet of a RAF Air Gunner from the son of the RAF Prisoner of War mentioned above.

Disappointingly the badge has been lost over the years, but I recently decided recently to do some research on this serviceman, who had sadly passed away.

There were three things that I knew, his name, the fact that he had been a prisoner of war and that he had been awarded a gallantry medal.

Being aware that the Ministry of Defence still held his WW2 service records and being located many miles from the National Archives,

I decided to use some secondary sources to piece together the story of the serviceman who had been awarded this badge.

During the Second World War there were periodic listings published by HMSO of all British and Allied Prisoners of War in Germany and German Occupied Territory, but these are difficult to locate. However reprints of the May 1945 listing, split into three Volumes were published by J B Hayward in 1990 as: *Prisoners of War, British Army 1939-1945*, *Prisoners of War, Naval and Air Forces of Great Britain and Empire 1939-1945* and *Prisoners of War, Armies and Other Land Forces of the British Empire 1939-1945*.

A full listing of Honours and Awards to the RAF and Dominion Air Forces during World War 2 appears in *Honour the Air Forces* Michael Manton, Token Publishing.

Awards were published in the London Gazette, as were all Officers' commissions and promotions. Using the Gazette online search facility I was able to follow his rise through the ranks.

In the process I discovered one squadron that he served with, and discovered that there had been a recently published history of that squadron. *Battle-Axe Blenheims – No.105 Squadron RAF at War 1940-41* by Stuart R Scott, - Alan Sutton Publishing Ltd 1996 and *The Bristol Blenheim – A Complete History* by Graham Warner, - Crecy Publishing 2002

The information I have discovered so far is as follows:

Eric W Applebee

Joined the ranks for the Royal Air Force and was allocated the Service Number 537379, which is from a batch of numbers 505001 – 549999 which was allocated to civilian enlistments into the ranks of the Royal Air Force from October 1925. It therefore appears likely that he joined the RAF in the early-mid

105 Squadron 1941   Prisoner of War 1945
44982 P/O (later F/O) Eric William Applebee DFM

1930's.

On enlistment he would have been given the rank of Aircraftman 2nd Class, and the usual period of engagement was six years. It was normal for semi-skilled men to undergo a training period of between eight to fourteen months. He trained as a Wireless Operator / Air Gunner

Promoted Corporal

16th May 1940 Flight Lieut. Simon N L Maude, with Sgt A J Hawkins and Corporal E W Applebee in Bristol Blenheim IV P6920 of 114 Squadron were ordered to return to England, but managed another sortie before evacuation from Crecy. Leaving at 8.00am the reconnaissance was to fly to the Montcornet-Rumigny-Dugigny areas to the north, then down to Rethel and the River Aisne in the south. They spotted three Henschel Hs.126 spotter aircraft circling Montcornet and attacked these with his single fixed machine gun, shooting down one and damaging another

Promoted Sergeant (Between May and October) 1940

All RAF Non-Commissioned Wireless Operator / Air Gunner were promoted to Temporary Sergeant from 27th April 1940, and later it became possible for Air Gunners to be commissioned as officers in the Royal Air Force.

Gazette Issue 34976 published on the 22nd October 1940

Air Ministry, 22nd October, 1940 ROYAL AIR FORCE. The KING has been graciously pleased to approve the under-mentioned award: -
Awarded the Distinguished Flying Medal. 537379 Sergeant Eric William APPLEBEE

(This gallantry award was for service with 114 Squadron, operating Bristol Blenheim aircraft as part of the Air Advanced Striking Force in France 1940). 114 Squadron sustained heavy losses in France during the German advances in 1940

London Gazette Issue 35019 published on the 20th December 1940

Air Ministry, 17th December, 1940. ROYAL AIR FORCE. GENERAL DUTIES BRANCH.
The under-mentioned is granted commission for the duration of hostilities as Pilot Officer on probation: Sergeant 2nd Dec. 1940 (Seniority 13th Nov. 1940) 537379 Eric William APPLEBEE (44982)

Whilst serving with 18 Squadron in Bristol Blenheim IV's he was personally invited by Wing Commander Hughie Idwal Edwards VC DFC, Commanding Officer of 105 Squadron to join the Malta Detachment in 1941. Pilot Officer E W Applebee had gained a reputation for developing a technique of shooting down enemy fighters flying at sea-level. At just the right range he would shout to the pilot, who would throw the engines into +9 boost and haul the aircraft skywards, effectively mimicking a shipping attack. As the aircraft rotated, forcing its nose upwards, the Wireless Operator / Air Gunner would get a clear field of fire over the tail. Pilot Officer E W Applebee DFM was reputed to have simultaneously shot down two German Bf 109 fighters over the North Sea with this tactic.

Joined 105 Squadron at Swanton Morley, Norfolk in July 1941

On 14th July 1941 105 Squadron was involved in a daylight raid on Rotterdam along with 18, 21, 139 and 226 Squadrons. Flight Lieut G E Goode DFC (Pilot), F A Harbord (Observer) and Pilot Officer E W Applebee (Wireless Operator / Air Gunner) in Bristol Blenheim IV Z7488, Coded F were engaged in circling smoke markers out in the North Sea, where they then shepherded a Hawker Hurricane escort from RAF Coltishall to cover the withdrawal of the Bristol Blenheims from the Rotterdam raid.

Left Swanton Morley, Norfolk on 25th July 1941 en route to Malta flying via Portreath, Cornwall and Gibraltar with Squadron Leader G E Goode DFC (Pilot) and Sgt F A Harbord (Observer).

On 28th July 1941 he arrived at Luqu airfield, Malta and took part in his first Mediterranean anti-shipping operation taking off at 18.40

hours on 31st July 1941 in Bristol Blenheim IV Z7503 Coded J as Wireless Operator / Air Gunner to Acting Squadron Leader George E Goode DFC (B Flight Commander), with Sgt Frank A Harbord (Observer). A convoy of four cargo ships was sighted, but it was escorted by a cruisers, six destroyers and half a dozen Italian fighters, giving aerial protection. At this time 105 Squadron had been instructed not to attack battleships, to the six British aircraft headed back to Malta.

At Dusk on 3rd August 1941 Squadron Leader led five aircraft to bomb shipping in the heavily defended port of Tripoli. Two ships were hit along with the Enemy Air HQ building by four of the attacking Blenheims

On 7th August 1941 this crew led an attack on an enemy convoy of merchant ships, escorted by five destroyers and a motor torpedo boat and several Italian Fiat CR.42 fighters.

On 8th August 1941, Squadron Leader G E Goode lead a flight of six aircraft to make an attack on shipping in the port of Catania in Sicily at dusk, however the attack was aborted after some 30 Italian CR.42 Falco fighters were seen over the target. The flight returned to Malta.

A lone unescorted merchant vessel was seen on 10th August 1941 70 miles south-west of Lampedusa, heading North. Squadron Leader G E Goode was leading three aircraft and the Vichy French vessel was attacked off the Tunisian coast and sunk.

11th August 1941 105 Squadron. Blenheim IV, serial number Z7503, coded J, took off from Luqa, Malta at 17.52 hrs, engaged on a bombing raid on a Chemical Works manufacturing nitrates at Crotone, in the Bay of Taranto, Southern Italy. After successfully hitting the target the aircraft was hit in the port engine by Flak (anti-aircraft fire) from Italian Corvettes anchored just offshore, whilst flying over the harbor on its second run-in. With burning oil smoking from the engine, the pilot searched for a suitable site to crash land whilst trying to release a 500 lb bomb the crew believed to be stuck in the aircraft. Crossing the bay the aircraft gained enough height to cross the cliffs at Capo delle Colonna and made a forced landing in a field. After destroying their documents they were attempting to set fire to their aircraft before being shot at by a group of 27 Italian soldiers. An Italian Naval Officer, Captail Val Dambrini arrived on the scene and took charge of the situation and took the three RAF Aircrew into his custody. 44982 Pilot Officer E W Applebee DFM, Wireless Operator / Air Gunner taken Prisoner of War 11th August 1941 in Italy, with 81675 Squadron Leader George E Goode DFC (Pilot) and 987185 Sgt N A Nicholl (Observer) were taken to a Naval Base at Crontone, Italy

After being interrogated at an airfield at Centocelle, South-East of Rome Squadron Leader G E Goode and Pilot Officer E W Applebee were taken north, to an Officers Jail, situated in an old monastry at Piacenza.

He was held in a Civilian Jail, situated on the top of a mountain overlooking the village of Gavi, some 20 miles from Genoa, Italy. This was inhabited by Prisoners of War considered troublemakers. He remained there until after capitulation of Italy on 8th September 1943 when he and his fellow Prisoners of War were moved, travelling through Austria to reach Germany.

Eric Applebee ended up in Stalag Luft III at Sagan, made famous by the film 'The Great Escape,' when seventy nine Allied officers escaped on the night of 24 - 25 Mach 1944. Whilst three reached Great Britain, (Sgt P Bergsland, RAF, Pilot Officer J E Muller, RAF and Flt Lieut B van der Stok, RAF), seventy six were recaptured and of these, fifty were shot in degrading circumstances on the

Eric William Applebee's Prisoner of War Card

Bristol Blenheim IV - 1941

he successfully reached England, via Sweden in November 1943

Whilst held as a Prisoner of War, two promotions were

personal orders of Adolf Hitler.

Although Eric Applebee did not participate in the *'Great Escape,'* he had been involved in the earlier 'Wooden Horse' episode during July - October 1943.

Three Officers, Flight Lieut. Eric E Williams, RAF, Lieut. R Michael C Codner, Royal Artillery and Flight Lieut. Oliver S L Philpot, RAF successfully escaped from Stalag Luft III using a wooden vaulting horse to cover the building of an escape tunnel. The operation began on 8th July 1943 and the three broke out of the tunnel on the evening 29th October 1943. Eric Williams and Mike Codner travelled to Stettin and reached England, via Sweden in December 1943. Oliver Philpot had headed to Danzig, and

gazetted:

London Gazette Issue 35483
Published on the 10th March 1942
Pilot Officer (probationary) confirmed in appointment and to be Flying Officer (war substantive): E. W. APPLEBEE, D.F.M. (44982). 2nd Dec. 1941 (Seniority. 13th Nov. 1941)

London Gazette Issue 35996
Published on the 27th April 1943
Air Ministry, 30th April, 1943 GENERAL DUTIES BRANCH. Flying Officer to be Flight Lieutenant (war substantive): E. W. APPLEBEE (44982) 2nd Dec. 1942 (Seniority 13th Nov. 1942)

In 1945 he was still held at Stalag Luft III, located Sagan, administered by Wehrkreis VIII - Breslau (Wroclaw). He was assigned German P.O.W. Number 228325. He was released after the German Surrender in 1945 and returned to England remaining in the Royal Air Force.

London Gazette Issue 37497
Published on the 8th March 1946
Transfer between branches. Flt. Lt. E. W. APPLEBEE (44982) from General Duties Branch to the Administrative and Special Duties Branch 21st Feb. 1946

London Gazette Issue 37952
Published on the 9th May 1947
Transfer between branches. Administrative and Special Duties Branch to the Secretarial Branch retaining their seniority: Flight Lieutenant E. W. APPLEBEE, D.F.M. (44982) to the Aircraft Control Branch as Flight Lieutenant (temp.). 31st Mar. 1947 (seniority 16th Nov. 1943)

London Gazette Issue 38194
Published on the 30th January 1948
AIRCRAFT CONTROL BRANCH The under-mentioned are granted the substantive rank of Flight Lieutenant, 1st Nov. 1947, with the seniority stated: E W APPLEBEE, D.F.M (44982). 1st Sept 1945

Hopefully this story is not the end of my research, and it will serve as a guide or reminder of those 'odd' items that can be found amongst family possessions, that could end up being useful in researching family history and also how useful secondary sources can be.

Bristol Blenheim

SPECIFICATIONS AND PERFORMANCE

BRISTOL BLENHEIM (MARK IVF)

DIMENSIONS:	Span, 56 ft., 4 in.; length, 39 ft., 9 in.; height, 9 ft., 10 in.; wing area, 469 sq. ft.
CREW:	Three: pilot, navigator-bombardier, and radio operator.
WEIGHT:	Empty, 8,250 lb.; loaded, 14,400 lb.
PERFORMANCE:	Maximum speed, 295 m.p.h. at 15,000 ft.; range, 1,900 miles at 220 m.p.h.; initial rate of climb, 1,500 ft. per minute; service ceiling, 27,000 ft.
POWER PLANT:	Two 920-h.p.(each) Bristol Mercury XV air-cooled motors.
ARMAMENT:	One fixed forward-firing, .30-caliber machine gun in port wing; a retracting, hydraulically operated top turret with two .30-caliber guns; and one rear-firing .30-caliber gun under nose.

Of Sea Service, Ships & Men
- Basic Definitions of Maritime Terms
Len Barnett

When compared, English as a language is free of many restrictive grammatical rules of others. Nevertheless, many words and phrases are technical, specific and not interchangeable. Contrary to popular usage, this is certainly the case with maritime terms. This article explores the fundamentals of these with the idea of aiding genealogists in their understanding of records of individuals in British service.

Sea Service

It is important to stress that those that earn their living from the sea overwhelmingly have done so for *others*, rather than for *themselves* and it has always been this way. Consequently, this has had an effect on how it has been described.

'Merchant' service has not only covered those in mercantile activities, in other words, in *all* the trades that there have been (including in human beings as slaves), but often for the want of proper definition also in other seagoing industries: as in whaling and fishing. Until the twentieth century the collective terms were the merchant or mercantile marine. Alternatively, individuals were *in* merchant or mercantile service. When those engaged in whaling and fishing *en masse* were mentioned they were said to be of the whaling or fishing

fleets. With one exception in the 1850s, it was not until the Great War 1914-19 that the designation *'merchant navy'* made an appearance. Even then this was only occasionally and as far as I can determine, only by naval officers with particular political aims of forcing merchant mariners under naval control. Post war the title *'Merchant Navy'* was bestowed on the mercantile marine by King George V. Arguably it was not until 1941 when the Merchant Navy Reserve Pool came into existence that this term had any veracity though. Even then, apparently *many* merchant mariners hated this title, as they regarded themselves as private individuals rather than as merely part of a *'navy.'*

Even time in the Royal Navy has not quite been as clear cut as might be expected. Nevertheless, this can be defined as being in service of the State, although until well into the nineteenth century often had far more to do with tribal loyalties of commanders and their followers. Additionally, from the late 1850s onwards the Royal Naval Reserve was developed: until 1958 (when reorganised) almost entirely from professionals in merchant and fishing service. In 1909 another reserve came into being: the Royal Naval Volunteer

Reserve. The *'wavy navy'* as it was called due to the pattern of rings for commissioned officers, was overwhelmingly made up of non-professional seafarers, or landsmen. Even so, there were rare occasions of merchant mariners within the R.N.V.R. and also, during the Second World War, this was the normal way into the navy for commissioned ranks (sometimes transferring into the RN proper in 1945). It should also be realised that there were also various colonial naval forces, with their own reserves.

Ships

Even the seemingly simple term *'ship'* is absolutely full of misunderstanding! For a start, it is not interchangeable with *'boat!'*

When a youngster in the Royal Navy I was told that essentially the difference in these was in their relative sizes: ships being large and boats small. Of course, there were exceptions, in that destroyers, submarines and small craft were referred to as *'boats.'* Decades on, I have learned that a small minority of merchant vessels have also been called *'boats'* by their crews. But, as far as I can make out, this refers to particular trades and corporate cultures. Also, with the exception of the massive modern processing vessels, fishing craft have always been known as boats. So, after thought, in the twentieth century and with exceptions I would define *'ships'* as vessels that can sustain 'normal' living (even if 'normality' in some types has been extremely squalid); whereas, *'boats'* are small craft for particular forms of work and the saving of life.

Going back to the age of sail, the term *'ship'* held different meanings though. For merchantmen, technically these vessels were *'full-rigged ships:'* although men of the sea almost always dropped the prefix full-rigged. In explanation, merchant vessels were rated by their rigging and ships had three or more masts that were square-rigged and a bowsprit. They tended to be the largest and being labour-intensive required the largest crews. To be *'square-rigged'* meant (and to a limited degree still means) when there were yards supporting the primary sails across the breadth of the vessel (within working tolerances). Barks, or barques, were similar, except that their aftermost mast was rigged *'fore and aft.'* Masts rigged fore and aft were simpler affairs, with booms holding the sails along the length of the vessel (again within working tolerances). There were also numerous other types of civilian sailing vessels, named after their rigs: for instance, brigs, snows, barquentines, brigantines, schooners, ketches and smacks. It might also be mentioned that vessels could be re-rigged, for instance ships becoming barques in cost-cutting exercises.

The gradual development of various technologies throughout the nineteenth century meant vast changes in how shipping was conducted. Incidentally, the term *'shipping'* does not have anything inherently to do with ships. Instead, it relates to the shifting of goods. Especially through the introduction of reliable triple-expansion steam engine as of the 1880s, services to timetable became realistic and aided

These all have specific meanings, even if sometimes they lose their original names and roles. Two examples of these may be of interest. Destroyers were developed to deal with ultra fast French torpedo-boats in the latter nineteenth century and were first known as torpedo-boat destroyers. And, the currently twenty-five year-old 'aircraft carriers' are actually through deck cruisers (as they cannot handle fixed-wing aircraft) and now give the limited air support for fleet and amphibious operations that H.M. Government apparently wants.

Men

Once again, all sorts of confusion has arisen over what to call men that earn their living from the sea. (I make no apology for using the term men. While there have been and indeed, still are women seafarers, the sea has overwhelmingly been a male environment.) One to begin with is that of the so-called 'able-bodied' seaman. No such creature has legitimately existed at sea: even if some mid nineteenth-century British legislation drawn up by landsmen civil servants mistakenly states this! The correct term has always been able seaman.

In merchant service, with exceptions, the seamen managers with overall responsibility for vessels have been masters and later, master mariners. (Not strictly accurate, for centuries they have also often been called captains and occasionally, as in the East India Companies, commanders.) Their direct assistants in ship-handling and navigation have been mates: sometimes dubbed officers. In support of these seamen managers have been petty officer specialists. More often known by their derogatory nickname of 'idlers' (by seamen, as they did not keep watches), on sailing ships they have been the cooks, stewards, carpenters, sailmakers and surgeons (the latter categories when carried). Below them were 'the people', who as seamen were supposed to be rated according to their skill. These could range from boatswains (foremen that may, or may not be classed as petty officers); quartermasters (such as in mail packet services); able seamen, efficient deck hands (in the twentieth century), ordinary seamen, boys and apprentices

the rise of the 'liner' companies greatly. In the public mind these have been remembered exclusively as floating hotels, but even the most glamorous passenger liners also shifted cargo: both general and bulk. For that matter, those unfairly denigrated as mere 'tramps' that in reality ensured that *many* trades operated smoothly and populations did not suffer shortages of goods and commodities, sometimes also carried passengers.

Prior to the development of iron and steam in warships, again during the nineteenth century, the term 'ship' had different meanings. Excluding custom-built vessels of war in the ancient world, ships first appeared as purpose-built battleships-of-the-line in the seventeenth century. This was when the first modern battlefleet tactics were also developed during the wars especially against the Dutch during the Commonwealth period. (There is an irony that the modern Royal Navy has its real roots in Parliament, as opposed to the monarchy.) These battleships were 'rated' by their size as gunnery platforms. So, first-class ships-of-the-line were the largest: by the end of the seventeenth century with approximately 100 guns. The smallest of these, fifth and sixth-class men-o-war (another name for warships), were also known as frigates. Warships smaller than frigates were unrated and could be known either by their rig; as in sloops and brigs; or by their role, as in bomb vessels.

With industrial processes changing warship and weapons design radically, from the mid nineteenth century onwards new types of men-o-war have been developed. Battleships-of-the-line became 'Dreadnoughts' and 'Super-Dreadnoughts' prior to the Great War 1914-19, before gradually disappearing far later in the twentieth century. Sometimes, older names were reused: as in cruisers, frigates, sloops and cutters. Entirely new roles brought about very different vessels: such as destroyers, submarines, aircraft carriers and assault ships.

(sometimes called cadets and midshipmen in companies that regarded themselves as prestigious). With the introduction of steam then motor vessels, other branches have evolved. For handling of the machinery, there have been engineers, firemen, (coal) trimmers and later others, such as greasers. While Donkeymen were also part of the engineering department, their duties were in operating auxiliary engines (known as donkeys) for aiding seamen in cargo shifting and other tasks. On passenger liners, a great many other ratings in the 'hotel' departments have evolved: including a bewildering variety of stewards and waiters.

Fishing craft, being tiny, have had far simpler structures. Essentially, commanding them have been skippers, with one mate per boat and a number of hands. Whaling ships used conventional mercantile ranks and rates for the ship-handling, with all sorts of specialists for the killing and processing of their prey.

Although there always have been similarities to those in civilian service, ranks and rates in armed service have been highly complicated for centuries. Taken directly from a military officers' rank the ship-handling managers in command have been known as captains. Their direct assistants were originally lieutenants, but additional ranks have been added, such as commander and two other grades of lieutenancy. All these sea officers held commissions. Below them were also the specialists: masters, gunners, boatswains, carpenters, pursers, surgeons and cooks.

(Masters were specialist navigators that had evolved out of the mercantile understanding of the term until the military men took over the roles of ship-handling and overall command.) These sea officers held warrants. Confusingly, there was also a second, lower grade of warrant officer, rated as petty officers. They included armourers, masters-at-arms and sailmakers. And, there were also other petty officers not holding warrants, including midshipmen and masters' mates. By the Revolutionary and Napoleonic Wars 1793-1815 were all sorts of rates below petty officer: yeomen, clerks, stewards, able seamen, ordinary seamen, landsmen and boys of various descriptions. Through the nineteenth century additional layers of responsibility were added, such as chief petty officers and leading seamen. Collectively, petty officers and men formed 'the people' on men-o-war.

When new branches were introduced into the Royal Navy, from the nineteenth century onwards new rank and rating systems have also been developed. Also the status of warrant officers changed: some for the better, others the worse. In detail, these have been *immensely* complex and might form the basis of a further article on its own.

Readers might be interested to know that many of the organisations and trades have been dealt with in more depth in past articles in *The Family and Local History Handbook*. Also, more information on the naval ranks and ratings can be found within my online guides at www.barnettmaritime.co.uk

Tracing Prisoners of War

Sarah Paterson

Family History Librarian - Department of Printed Books

The Imperial War Museum does not hold any official documentation or comprehensive listings of Prisoners of War, but it does have extensive material that will be helpful for providing information and understanding about their experience. This leaflet should be used in conjunction with the relevant leaflet for the individual's branch of service – Army, Royal Air Force, Royal Navy or Merchant Navy. The Collections Division welcomes visitors by appointment, and has different types of material, such as art, books, documents, three-dimensional objects, film, photographs and sound recordings.

Collections Enquiry Service, Imperial War Museum, Lambeth Road, London SE1 6HZ
T: (+44) 020 7416 5342 F: (+44) 020 7416 5246
E: collections@iwm.org.uk W: www.iwm.org.uk

Where to Find Prisoner of War Records

Records of prisoners of war (POWs) were compiled by each national branch of the Red Cross and are now held centrally by the **Archives Division and Research Service, International Committee of the Red Cross, 19 Avenue de la Paix, CH-1202 Geneva, Switzerland**. Because of their personal nature, these records are not accessible to the general public but paid searches can be conducted (currently 200 Swiss Francs for First World War enquiries) – please be patient as this may take several months. Second World War or later searches, carried out for former prisoners or their next of kin may be free of charge. You will need to know the **full name** and **nationality** of the individual you are researching. Additional details such as regiment, number, place and date of birth, date of capture and name of father are likely to aid your enquiry. More information is available on the website at www.icrc.org/eng (click on Info Resources, and then ICRC Archives information Sources – an electronic application form can be found under 'Requests for personnal [sic] data').

Some details about those who died in captivity during both World Wars will be held by the **Commonwealth War Graves Commission**. The computerised database *Debt of Honour* can be accessed on the website at www.cwgc.org The Commission can be contacted at **2 Marlow Road, Maidenhead, Berkshire SL6 7DX (Tel: 01628 507200)**.

Any official documentation relating to British POWs is held by **The National Archives, Ruskin Avenue, Kew, Richmond, Surrey TW9 4DU (Tel: 020 8876 3444; Website: www.nationalarchives.gov.uk** More information about these records can be found in the research guides *British Prisoners of War, c1760 – 1919* and *British Prisoners of War, 1939 – 1953* on the website. The interviews and reports provided by repatriated or escaped prisoners from the First World War in record class *WO 161* can now be viewed online at: www.nationalarchives.gov.uk/documentsonline/pow.asp Although more than 3,000 individuals are represented, this is only a very small percentage of those who were held captive. There is also a very slim possibility that you

he War Illustrated - Robert Blatchford Collection

QUEEN VICTORIA'S RIFLES : Officers taken prisoner after the defence of Calais, at the German camp, Oflag VII C., Laufen. The two on the left and the one on the right are unidentified ; the others, left to right, are Lieut. Courtenay, Capt. J. A. Brown, Lt.-Col. J. A. M. Ellison-Macartney, Capt. P. J. E. Monico, Capt. A. N. L. Munby, and Lieut. S. J. Saunders.

OFLAG IX A : British prisoners-of-war in cheerful mood, for they have received eagerly awaited parcels from home.

The War Illustrated - Robert Blatchford Collection

research.

First World War

The *List of British Officers Taken Prisoner in the Various Theatres of War Between August 1914 and November 1918*, compiled by the military agents Cox and Co in 1919 will prove helpful if you are seeking an individual who was commissioned. Another useful source is the monthly **Enquiry Lists** issued by the **Enquiry for the Wounded and Missing Department** of the **British Red Cross and Order of St John**. Our holdings of this are not complete (although we do have copies of all those known to exist), with better coverage for some periods than others.

The IWM's **Women's Work Collection** contains some information about soldiers and non-commissioned officers who were taken prisoner before Christmas 1914, and were therefore eligible to receive Princess Mary's Gift Box. These lists are arranged by regiment in sections BO 2 1/11 – BO 2 1/328. Already available commercially on microfilm, the collection is now available as a searchable web database (by paid subscription to Gale Digital Collections (**Women, War and Society, 1914-1918**) or free at point of access within the Museum). There is also a wealth of general material on this that will help you to understand more about the First World War prisoner experience, especially from the point of view of benevolent organisations in the UK sending aid to prisoners of war.

A map gazetteer compiled by Mrs Pope-Hennessey, showing the locations of the principal Central Powers prisoner of war camps in Germany and Austria was published by Nisbet and Co during the First World War and can be viewed in the Explore History Centre.

Second World War

Three useful volumes have been reprinted by John Hayward in conjunction with the Imperial War Museum. These are nominal rolls of POWs held in Germany and German Occupied Territories, corrected up to the end of March 1945. Volume one is entitled *Prisoners of War: British Army 1939-1945: Alphabetical Nominal Registers (Including Rank, POW Number, Regiment or Corps and Camp Location Details) Listing*

may find correspondence or reports on prisoners of war in *FO 383*.

The National Archives (TNA) has Japanese prisoner of war index cards in *WO 345*. TNA also holds liberated prisoner of war interrogation questionnaires in *WO 344*. These were the debriefing reports given by prisoners released from German or Japanese captivity at the end of the Second World War. The COFEPOW website is compiling a database of all Far East prisoners of war, containing basic information and a copy of the front page of the prisoner's liberation questionnaire, if one was completed: www.cofepowdb.org.uk

Sources at the Imperial War Museum (IWM) include personal papers and diaries, autobiographies, camp journals and recorded interviews, although inevitably some locations are better documented than others. Please contact us to find out more about the particular camps you are interested in, or visit www.iwmcollections.org.uk
http://www.iwmcollections.org.uk The following items may be helpful for starting your

British prisoners at Stalag XX Aat Thorn, in Poland.
Among these soldiers are C. W. Davis (front centre), K. J.Brydson,
A. Cross, H. K. Wright, M. Fox, N. C. Baker, A. Johnstone,
A. H. Berrisford, F. Nurse, A. L. Gosling

www.nzetc.org/tm/scholarly/tei-WH2Pris.html

Issues of *The Prisoner of War: the Official Organ of the Prisoners of War Department of the Red Cross and St John War Organisation*, contain interesting background information, particularly about activities in POW camps in Occupied Europe.

For those interested in prisoners in the Far East, *Prisoners of the Japanese in World War II: Statistical History, Personal Narratives, and Memorials Concerning POWs in Camps and Hellships, Civilian Internees, Asian Slave Laborers and Others Captured in the Pacific Theater* by Van Waterford (Jefferson, North Carolina: McFarland, 1994) provides helpful guidance, information about the camps and suggestions for further reading.

Over 107,000 British Army Prisoners of War of All Ranks Held in Germany and German Occupied Territories. Volume two covers *Armies and Other Land Forces of the British Empire* and volume three covers *Naval and Air Forces of Great Britain and the Empire*. This information can now be accessed via the subscription website www.ancestry.co.uk

Two recent publications covering RAF prisoners are *Footprints on the Sands of Time: RAF Bomber Command Prisoners-of-War in Germany 1939-1945* by Oliver Clutton-Brock (London: Grub Street, 2003) and *Unsung Heroes of the Royal Air Force: the Far East Prisoners of War 1941-1945* by Les and Pam Stubbs (Grantham, Lincolnshire: Barry Books, 2002).

Probably the best single volume work dealing with POWs generally is *Official History of New Zealand in the Second World War, 1939 – 1945: Prisoners of War* by W Wynne Mason (Wellington, New Zealand: War History Branch, Department of Internal Affairs, 1954). This can now

Korean War

Prisoners of War Korea, 1950 – 1953: the British Army compiled by Peter Gaston (London: London Stamp Exchange, 1976) lists men taken prisoner.

Useful Contacts

There are too many worthwhile organisations to list here and we would suggest that enquirers contact the Collections Enquiry Service for advice on addresses, including details of the various branches and regional Far East Prisoner of War associations. The following have websites that contain helpful links to other sites as well as useful information:

The National Ex-Prisoner of War Association: www.prisonerofwar.org.uk

Royal Air Forces Ex-POW Association: www.rafinfo.org.uk/rafexpow

COFEPOW (Children (and Families) of the Far East Prisoners of War): www.cofepow.org.uk

Family History Books from The Imperial War Museum

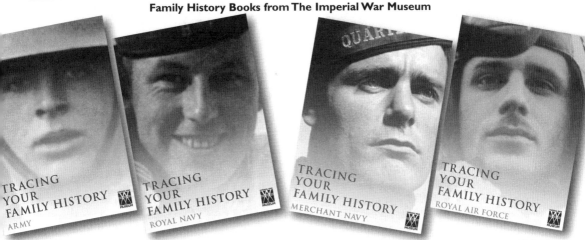

'A York Sailor Killed'

Janet Wilson

Based solely upon an Official Telegram, sent to a father of a submariner who had died at sea Janet Wilson shares with us her research and findings on the detailed press coverage which gives fascinating details regarding this tragic episode in the First World War.

The Official Announcement

Mr Charles Edward Wilson received the following telegram from the Admiralty:

> 'Deeply regret to inform you that Fred Wilson Stoker 1st Class, Official number K1405, reported killed in Submarine E13 on 19th August 1915 letter follows.'

The letter received shortly afterwards read:

> 'I regret to have to inform you that telegraphic information has reached this department that Fred Wilson, stoker first-class, official number K 1405, belonging to His Majesty's submarine E13 lost his life when that vessel grounded on the 19th inst. on the Danish island of Saltholm in the Sound'

During August 1915 the following headlines appeared in National and Local Newspapers

'A YORK SAILOR KILLED'
HOME-COMING OF DEAD
GREAT TRIBUTE TO HEROES OF E13
'HOW THE CREW OF THE E13 FACED DEATH'
'IMPRESSIVE INCIDENTS AT HULL'

The report in the *Yorkshire Evening Press* stated that on Monday 23rd August 1915, the British Submarine E13, whilst on passage to the Baltic ran aground in Danish territorial waters of the Island of Saltholm. What happened next according to the communiqué issued by the Admiralty on 21st August 1915 was:

> 'Lieut. Commander Layton reports that the submarine under his command grounded in the early morning of 19th and all efforts failed to re float her. At 5.00.a.m. a Danish torpedo boat appeared on the scene and communicated to E13 that she would be allowed 24 hours to try to get off. At the same time a German torpedo-boat destroyer arrived and remained close to the submarine until two more Danish torpedo-boats came up, when she withdrew.
> At 9.00.a.m. while three Danish torpedo boats were anchored close to the submarine, two German torpedo boat destroyers hoisted a commercial flag signal, but before the commanding officer of E13 had had time to read it, the German destroyer fired a torpedo at her from a distance of about 300 yards, which

exploded on hitting the bottom close to her. At the same moment the German destroyer fired with her guns and Lieut. Commander Layton, seeing that his submarine was on fire and unable to defend himself owing to being aground, gave orders for the crew to abandon her. While the men were in the water they were fired on by machine guns and with shrapnel.
> One of the Danish torpedo boats immediately lowered her boats and steamed between the submarine and German destroyers, who therefore had to cease fire and withdraw.'

In August 1915 the British Submarine E13 under the command of Lieutenant Commander Geoffrey Layton was ordered to join the Royal Navy Submarines operating with the Russian Navy in the Baltic. On 19th August 1915 as the E13 was entering the Baltic Sea there was a gyro failure and the submarine grounded on

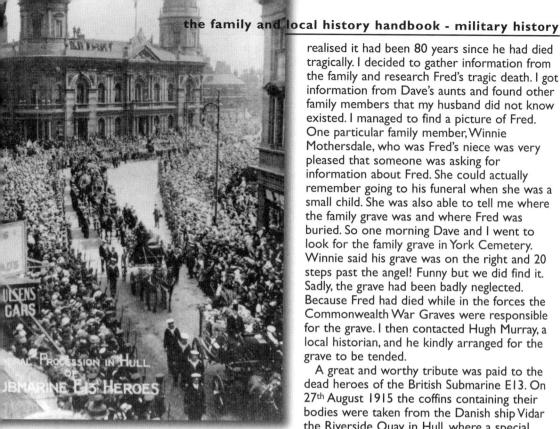

FUNERAL PROCESSION IN HULL OF SUBMARINE E13 HEROES

the Danish Island of Saltholm. During *World War I* Denmark was neutral and gave the submarine twenty four hours to free herself and leave Danish waters otherwise it would be interned for the duration of the War.

The First Lieutenant Paul Eddis was sent ashore to make arrangements for some assistance. Meanwhile the Captain and the rest of the crew tried to free the submarine under the observation of the Danish Navy who could not help to re-float E13. Warships of the Imperial German Navy arrived, saw what was happening, and without warning opened fire on E13 despite Danish ships being between E13 and the Germans. The submarine was very badly damaged. The crew attempted to escape by swimming to shore but fifteen were either killed on the Submarine or whilst swimming to the shore. The Submarine E13 was a total loss and after the war was sold for scrap.
The surviving Crew were interned in Denmark for the remainder of the War.
The remains of those killed were returned to England by the Danes and were buried at home. From a crew of thirty submariners fifteen sailors died including Fred Wilson.

Fred Wilson was my husband Dave's great Uncle, and his late father was named after him, I originally came across Fred Wilson in 1995. I

realised it had been 80 years since he had died tragically. I decided to gather information from the family and research Fred's tragic death. I got information from Dave's aunts and found other family members that my husband did not know existed. I managed to find a picture of Fred. One particular family member, Winnie Mothersdale, who was Fred's niece was very pleased that someone was asking for information about Fred. She could actually remember going to his funeral when she was a small child. She was also able to tell me where the family grave was and where Fred was buried. So one morning Dave and I went to look for the family grave in York Cemetery. Winnie said his grave was on the right and 20 steps past the angel! Funny but we did find it. Sadly, the grave had been badly neglected. Because Fred had died while in the forces the Commonwealth War Graves were responsible for the grave. I then contacted Hugh Murray, a local historian, and he kindly arranged for the grave to be tended.

A great and worthy tribute was paid to the dead heroes of the British Submarine E13. On 27th August 1915 the coffins containing their bodies were taken from the Danish ship Vidar the Riverside Quay in Hull, where a special gangway covered with black cloth and white centrepiece had been erected; palms and plants had also been arranged, and many dignities accompanied the procession. Fifteen exquisite wreaths of arum lilies sent by Queen Alexandra were placed in rows, each label bearing the signature of Her Majesty. Through densely crowded streets to Paragon Station, Hull the coffins were then transported home to their respective relatives.

The train from Hull arrived at York Station on Platform 4, the same day, and the cortège left at 3.40.p.m. Before long, a large crowd of people began to assemble in the vicinity along Queen Street; the city walls as far as Micklegate bar were lined with people and along the route where the body of the gallant sailor was being taken to York Cemetery. Hundreds of people gathered and several wreaths were placed on the coffin including those from Queen Alexandra, York Admiralty Recruiting Office and the Sergeants mess of the Scots Greys. As the cortège moved off, the band of the West Yorkshire Regiment played *'Beethoven's Funeral March.'* The deepest sympathy was shown by the crowds which lined the route to the Cemetery, which was via Queen Street, Nunnery Lane, Bishopthorpe and Fishergate. Heads were uncovered, many soldiers saluted and at the cemetery the band played *Chopin's Funeral March*.

Over the following years I have continued researching the E13 and have been in contact with the Portsmouth museum who were very interested in my findings and pictures, and together we have been able to share information. A family member kindly visited the museum and sent a photo to me of the E13's bell, which is on display at the RN Submarine Museum in Gosport, as is also a section of HP airline from the E13 pierced by German machine-gun bullets when she was stranded on Saltholm Island, this was presented to the museum by G Layton, her Commanding Officer, at the time. More recently I have had a communication from the Archivist, Mr George A Malcolmson, that Fred Wilson is listed in the *Submarine Book of Remembrance* which is kept in the *Submarine Memorial Chapel* in Gosport. The museum also contains a strong memorial theme and Fred is listed in their *Area of Remembrance*, this quiet area on the museum site containing a wall of names showing all British Submariners lost on active service. Through researching Fred and the E13 since 1995 much more information is available on the internet, there are a number of sites that you can download information including Naval Ratings Service Records from the National Archive at Kew www.nationalarchives.gov.uk and the Commonwealth War Graves Commission at www.cwgc.org.

Fred was born in October 1885 in Norton, near Malton in the North Riding of Yorkshire (now North Yorkshire) the fifth son of Mr and Mrs Charles Wilson. The family later moved to York and lived for some time at the Railway Crossing, Wigginton Road, York. He was well known in York as he was for some years

engaged in the central signal box at York Railway Station: he was very involved in signalling and spent many evenings on the top of York Minster signalling to Strensall Camp and other places in the district. At one time he served in the York Volunteers and held the rank of Corporal, and also the signaller's certificate. Fred joined the Navy in 1908 and served two years on HMS Philomel; he was shot in the shoulder while engaged in the Persian Gulf and was awarded the Russian Cross of St George Fourth Class.

Further Reading
A Naval History of World War I Paul Halpen ISBN: 978 1857284980 Publised by Routledge
Beneath the Waves A. S. Evans ISBN: 978 1848842922 Pen & Sword Books 2010
Baltic Assignment - British Submariners in Russia, 1914-19 Michael Wilson ISBN: 978 0436578014 Published Secker & Warburg 1985

Acknowledgement
I would like to thank the Royal Navy Submarine Museum in Gosport for all the help and support in obtaining and recording the events of the E13.

In Memory of
Stoker 1st Class F WILSON

K/1405, Submarine E.13., Royal Navy
who died age 30
on 19 August 1915

Cross of St. George, 4th Class (Russia). Son of Charles Edward and Annie Wilson, of 5, Filey Terr. York. Served in the Persian Gulf, 1909-1914. Born at Norton Malton, Yorks.
Remembered with honour
YORK CEMETERY, Yorkshire

Commemorated in perpetuity by
the Commonwealth War Graves Commission

**Fred Wilson's
Commonwealth War Graves Commission
Certificate of Remembrance.**

Alfred Wilson (Fred's brother) and Francis Grey's wedding on Easter Saturday April 11th 1914 at Benwell Parish Church Newcastle -upon-Tyne.

Fred Wilson is in uniform

The other man on the back row is Charles Wilson Fred's father.

The Captain, Officers and Crew of E13

The Fatalities in the attack on the E13 were:

Petty Officer William George Warren	Haslar Cemetery
Leading Seaman Henry Thomas Pedder	Haslar Cemetery
Able Seaman Harold Joiner	Haslar Cemetery
Able Seaman Alfred John Payne	Lewisham (Ladywell) Cemetery
Able Seaman Robert Thomas Smart	Haslar Cemetery
Ordinary Signalman Herbert Goulden	Loughborough (Leicester Road) Cemetery
Ordinary Telegraphist Ernest Stuart Charles Holt	Haslar Cemetery
Engine Room Artificer Herbert Staples	Grimsby (Scarthe Road) Cemetery
Chief Stoker Benjamin Pink	Haslar Cemetery
Leading Stoker William Hayes Thomas	Cosheston (St Michael) Churchyard
Stoker Thomas Charles Greenwood	Haslar Cemetery
Stoker Arthur Long	Wimborne Minster Cemetery in Dorset
Stoker Walter Thomas Wilcox	Woodlands (The Ascension) Churchyard, Dorset
Stoker Fred Wilson	**York Cemetery**
Stoker Walter Albert Yearsley	Haslar Cemetery

The Survivors were:

Lieutenant Commander Geoffrey Layton	Retired as an Admiral. Died: 1964.
Lieutenant Paul Leathley Eddis	Lost as Commanding Officer of L24 in January 1924
Lieutenant William Garriock, RNR	Retired as Lieutenant Commander, RNR. Died: 1953
Petty Officer Charles Bowden	Pensioned 1924.
Petty Officer Alfred Frederick French	Lost in K5 in January 1921
Leading Seaman Herbert Lincoln	Demobilised 1919
Able Seaman Walter Edwin Brewer	Died: 26th Mar 1920 – three weeks after
'Demobilisation.'	
Able Seaman Charles Frederick Rendolson Hunt	Pensioned 1929
Able Seaman Benjamin Nix Watson	'Demobilised' in May 1919
Engine Room Artificer Walter Augustus Varcoe	Released Early August 1923
Engine Room Artificer Albert Thomas Henry Abrams	Pensioned 1924
Engine Room Artificer Edgar Tennison Lukey	Free discharge April 1920, Enlisted again Oct 1921
Leading Stoker William Whatley	'Invalided' out 1920
Stoker Frederick George Stubbington	Pensioned 1925
Stoker F W Smith	No further information

The New Explore History Centre
at The Imperial War Museum

Sarah Paterson - *Family History Librarian Department of Printed Books*

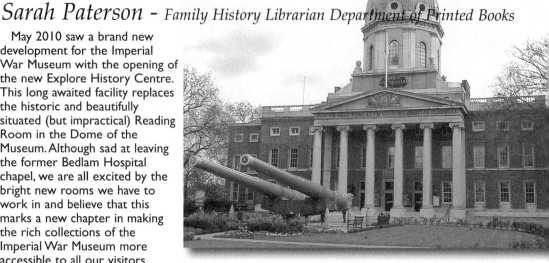

May 2010 saw a brand new development for the Imperial War Museum with the opening of the new Explore History Centre. This long awaited facility replaces the historic and beautifully situated (but impractical) Reading Room in the Dome of the Museum. Although sad at leaving the former Bedlam Hospital chapel, we are all excited by the bright new rooms we have to work in and believe that this marks a new chapter in making the rich collections of the Imperial War Museum more accessible to all our visitors.

The Explore History Centre is a drop-in room leading directly off the first floor galleries, so anyone can just wander in and take advantage of the interactive media displays, the online catalogue and staff expertise. The catalogue features objects from all of the Museum's Collections, and you can sit and view photographs, look at artworks, listen to sound recordings as well as check to see what books and personal papers we have. The family history pages provide basic advice to start you off on your quest, and also provide access to some relevant websites. The Searchlight feature allows you to look at a wide variety of different subjects through a curatorial overview highlighting different objects in the Museum's Collections.

You can also look at the Common Objects case featuring objects that will be familiar to many of you as they are the types of precious things that would have been treasured by family members, such as medals, ration books, cap badges, letters and cards, etc. You can sit in comfortable chairs and watch selected film footage. Interactive coverage of iconic images featured in the 1940 exhibition ensure that you gain new insight into these and can examine and understand their significance in great detail. There are also books on the shelves and tables that can be looked at (though it should be emphasised that this is not the library of the Museum – you can order titles from this through our online catalogue). Expert staff are also on hand to offer assistance. The Explore

History Centre is open between 10.00.a.m and 5.00.p.m, every day except for Sunday when it opens at 11.00am.

The Research Room next door is the more direct successor to the old Reading Room. Again, this is light and airy, but an appointment needs to be made before you can visit. If there is space, it may be possible to transfer from the Explore History Centre to the Research Room, but there are only 35 seats and it is proving to be a very popular facility. If you want to do research it is best to contact us in advance and make an appointment – we are very happy to talk you through the various options, and make helpful suggestions. You can look at our collections of books, and unpublished personal papers here, as well as listen to interviews with veterans. The Research Room is open 10.00am to 5.00pm, Monday to Friday.

The building work has resulted in quite a bit of disruption, and some books are still in storage. This means not everything that can be seen in the Research Room is currently accessible, so please check to see what the situation is when you make your appointment.

We look forward to welcoming you to the Explore History Centre – please do pop in and see us on your next visit to the Imperial War Museum.

Imperial War Museum, Collections Enquiry Service, Lambeth Road, London SE1 6HZ
T: 020 7416 5346 E: collections@iwm.org.uk W: www.iwm.org.uk

A Great Yorkshire Sea Battle
Martin Limon

Martin Limon tells the story of the epic encounter between American national hero John Paul Jones and the Royal Navy that took place off Flamborough Head in September 1779.

For those many Yorkshire folk who head to the coast each year Flamborough Head is a place they associate with spectacular scenery for this eight-mile long chalk promontory is a popular holiday destination in the summer months. More than two centuries ago however Flamborough Head became famous for a very different reason. On the evening of September 23rd 1779, local people were to hear gunfire out at sea and those who hastened to the cliffs at Flamborough were able to watch one of the most desperate naval battles in history taking place by moonlight!

The Battle of Flamborough Head was the zenith of the career of the controversial American naval commander John Paul Jones. He had been born in Scotland in 1747 and after an eventful career at sea had settled in Virginia in 1773 at a time when there were growing tensions between Britain and her American colonies. These were to lead to the American *Declaration of Independence* (4th July 1776) and so America's fledgling navy, in their struggles against the much superior Royal Navy, soon needed the seafaring abilities of John Paul Jones. Jones saw that America's tiny navy was not strong enough to protect its own coasts and said that it should attack the British where they least expected it and where they were most vulnerable. This strategy was to lead to him to Europe where Jones was able to launch a kind of guerrilla warfare against the British in their own home waters with the idea of forcing them to re-assign some of their naval squadrons away from the American coast.

The new strategy began in April 1778 and his success in carrying out hit-and-run attacks in the

Irish Sea made the name of John Paul Jones feared throughout Britain although at the time he was reviled as a *"freebooter"* or a *"blood-thirsty pirate."*

In alliance with France his victories off Britain's west coast meant that Jones was given command of a new flotilla of ships. One of these was the Duc de Duras, an old merchant vessel given to America by a French shipping magnate, which Jones transformed into a warship with 40 guns and re-named the Bonhomme Richard. In addition to this Commodore Jones had at his disposal the Alliance a frigate with 36 guns and commanded by a Frenchman, and the Pallas a French ship of 32 guns together with a smaller vessel. On the 14th August 1779 this flotilla of ships set sail on a mission that had the aim of destroying or capturing British ships involved in the Baltic trade.

On the 23rd September 1779 the American fleet of four ships encountered a Baltic convoy off the Yorkshire coast and prepared to intercept it. The forty one merchant ships were protected by two British warships: the Serapis with fifty guns and the Countess of Scarborough with twenty guns. On the face of it the Americans lacked the firepower to deal with such formidable British warships but such was the tenacity of Commodore Jones that he did not consider the possibility of giving up without a fight. Although the main interest in the battle off Flamborough Head centred on the duel between the Bonhomme Richard commanded by Jones himself and the Serapis commanded by Richard Pearson, there was a second battle between the Pallas and the Countess of Scarborough.

The battle commenced around 7.p.m. under moonlit skies and on a 'millpond' sea with the Bonhomme Richard and the Serapis firing broadsides at each other. Given the superiority in guns of the Serapis, Jones could not hope to win by firepower alone especially since during the Bonhomme Richard's second broadside two of his biggest guns exploded killing both officers and men. Jones was therefore forced by circumstances to opt for close-quarters fighting and by skilful seamanship he was able to bring the Bonhomme Richard alongside the Serapis by using grappling hooks and lines. There then began a desperate and bloody fight between the crews of the two vessels as a prelude to sending across boarding parties. Even with the two ships locked together the British gunners continued to fire, wreaking havoc

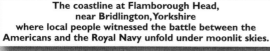

The coastline at Flamborough Head, near Bridlington, Yorkshire where local people witnessed the battle between the Americans and the Royal Navy unfold under moonlit skies.

Portrait of John Paul Jones c. 1890
by George Matthews based on an earlier picture
by Charles Peale (1741-1827)

with the hull and lower decks of the Bonhomme Richard; these were so punched with holes that the sea began to flood in.

The terrors of close-quarter battle between two wooden battleships in the later 18th century was described by a British prisoner aboard the Bonhomme Richard:

"The first impression was of pandemonium let loose. The thunder of the cannon, the pall of thick smoke, the crowds of men naked to the waist rushing hither and thither, their shouting, cursing and screaming, the tops manned with marksmen, the groans of the wounded as they were carried below decks strewn with wreckage and red with blood- a spectacle frightful and fiendish ..."

As the three and a half hour battle reached its bloody climax the damage done to the Bonhomme Richard was such that the ship was sinking. The master-at-arms, despite his captain's orders to the contrary, released one hundred British prisoners and told them to man the pumps to stop the ship from going under. As Jones directed grape-shot from his few remaining guns and musket fire onto the decks of the Serapis, fire broke out on both ships both aloft in the sails and below decks. With over half the American crew dead or wounded the situation

looked hopeless for Jones but he fought on stubbornly and when asked if he wished to surrender by Pearson defiantly declared: "I have not yet begun to fight."

It was then that fate intervened. According to Jones's own journal one of his crew, William Hamilton, high up on the main yard of the Bonhomme Richard, began throwing grenades down onto the deck of the Serapis below. It seems that one of these fell into an open hatchway and exploded near ammunition stacked close to the port side guns. This created a flash fire that detonated yet more explosives killing 20 British crewmen and injuring many more. With this disaster the guns of the Serapis fell silent and when the Alliance too joined in the battle against her Captain Pearson decided to surrender his ship to Jones. The Countess of Scarborough had surrendered earlier to the Pallas after a two-hour battle.

Despite the odds the Americans had prevailed against the superior British ships pitted against them. However, attempts to stop the Bonhomme Richard from sinking proved fruitless and she sank under the waters of the North Sea on the 25th September taking with her Jones's clothes, books and personal possessions. Now in control of the Serapis Jones sailed for Texel in Holland and a hero's welcome. This public adulation and the honours he received in France from King Louis XVI seemed to go to his head and his flair for self-promotion served to irritate his friends and fellow officers alike.

By his victory over the British off Flamborough Head on 23rd September 1779 Jones became a hero of the American Revolution and is considered by many to be the 'Father of the American Navy'. The legendary nature of his exploits and his against-the-odds victory over the British have meant that in the USA there has been considerable interest in locating the wreck of the Bonhomme Richard. In 1978-1979 for example the internationally famous novelist Clive Cussler was involved in attempts to search the seabed off Flamborough Head and although unsuccessful he concluded that what remains of the wreck lies between twenty-five and thirty five miles out to sea.

With so much of the North Sea to cover the search for the Bonhomme Richard has become ever more sophisticated and between 2006 and 2008 the Ocean Technology Foundation based in Connecticut made determined efforts to locate what remains of the ship using the most up-to-date technology available. In June 2008 a US navy research submarine spent twenty-one days collecting sonar images in the elusive search for a wreck that may, by now, may be little more than debris scattered across the seabed of the North Sea.

The Genealogical Services Directory

Family History Societies

British Association for Local History PO Box 6549, Somersal Herbert, Ashbourne, Derbyshire DE6 5WH T: 01283 585947 E: mail@balh.co.uk W: www.balh.co.uk

Federation of Family History Societies PO Box 8857, Lutterworth, LE17 9BJ T: 01455 203 133 E: info@ffhs.org.uk W: www.ffhs.org.uk

Institute of Heraldic & Genealogical Studies 79 - 82 Northgate, Canterbury, Kent CT1 1BA T: 01227 768664 E: ihgs@ihgs.ac.uk W: www.ihgs.ac.uk

Society of Genealogists - Library 14 Charterhouse Buildings, Goswell Road, London, EC1M 7BA T: 020-7251-8799 E: library@sog.org.uk W: www.sog.org.uk

South West Group of Family History Societies 32 Marconi Close, Weston Super Mare, Somerset BS23 3HH T: 01934 627053

Yorkshire Group of Family History Societies 101 Thornes Road, Wakefield, West Yorkshire WF2 8QD T: 01924 373014 E: cdgwelch@aol.com

England
Bedfordshire
Bedfordshire FHS PO Box 214, Bedford, MK42 9RX E: bfhs@bfhs.org.uk W: www.bfhs.org.uk

Berkshire
Berkshire FHS 161 St Peter's Road, Earley, Reading RG6 1PG T: 0118 966 3585 E: webmaster@berksfhs.org.uk W: www.berksfhs.org.uk

Birmingham
Birmingham & Midland Society for Genealogy and Heraldry 5 Sanderling Court, Spennells, Kidderminster DY10 4TS T: 01562 743912 E: jackie.cotterill1@btinternet.com W: www.bmsgh.org

Bristol
Bristol & Avon FHS 50 Russell Grove, Westbury Park, Bristol, BS6 7UF E: secretary@bafhs.org.uk W: www.bafhs.org.uk

Buckinghamshire
Buckinghamshire FHS PO Box 403, Aylesbury, Buckinghamshire HP21 7GU E: society@bucksfhs.org.uk W: www.bucksfhs.org.uk

Buckinghamshire Genealogical Society Varneys, Rudds Lane, Haddenham HP17 8JP T: 01844 291631 E: eve@varneys.org.uk W: www.bucksgs.org.uk

Cambridgeshire
Cambridge University H & G S c/o Crossfield House, Dale Road, Stanton, Bury St Edmunds, Suffolk IP31 2DY T: 01359 251050 E: derekpalgrave@btinternet.com W: www.cam.ac.uk/societies/cuhags/

Cambridgeshire FHS 43 Eachard Road, Cambridge, Cambridgeshire CB3 0HZ E: secretary@cfhs.org.uk W: www.cfhs.org.uk

East Anglian Group of Family History Societies 42 Crowhill, Godmanchester, Huntington PE29 2NR E: secretary@huntsfhs.org.uk

Fenland FHS Rose Hall, Walpole Bank, Walpole St Andrew, Wisbech, PE14 7JD E: judy.green@farming.me.uk W: www.cambridgeshirehistory.com/Societies/ffhs

Huntingdonshire FHS 42 Crowhill, Godmanchester, Huntingdon, PE29 2NR T: 01480 390476 E: secretary@huntsfhs.org.uk W: www.huntsfhs.org.uk

Peterborough & District FHS 7 Teasels, Deeping St James, Peterborough, Cambridgeshire PE6 8SJ T: 01778 341 290 E: secpdfhs@btopenworld.com W: www.peterboroughfhs.org.uk

Cheshire
Family History Society of Cheshire Little Trees, Gawsworth Road, Gawsworth, Macclesfield, Cheshire SK11 9RA T: 01625 426173 E: info@fhsc.org.uk W: www.fhsc.org.uk

North Cheshire FHS 9 Kitts Moss Lane, Bramhall, Stockport, Cheshire SK7 2BG T: 0161 439 2635 E: liz.demercado@ntlworld.com W: www.ncfhs.org.uk

South Cheshire FHS incorporating S E Cheshire Local Studies Group Little Trees, Gawsworth Road, Gawsworth, Macclesfield, Cheshire SK11 9RA T: 01625 426 173 W: www.scfhs.org.uk

Cleveland
Cleveland FHS 4 North Park North, Sedgefield, Stockton on Tees, TS21 3AH T: 01740 623 175 E: christinedunn48@yahoo.co.uk W: www.clevelandfhs.org.uk/

Cornwall
Cornwall FHS 5 Victoria Square, Truro TR1 2RS T: 01872 264044 E: secretary@cornwallfhs.com W: www.cornwallfhs.com

Fal Worldwide Family History Group 76 Chyvelah Vale, Gloweth, Truro TR1 3YL T: 01872 275599 E: angela@thorpmallard.plus.com W: http://beehive.thisiscornwall.co.uk/falwwfhg

Coventry
Coventry FHS 12 Knoll Drive, Styvechale, Coventry CV3 5BT T: 0247 669 3904 E: enquiries@covfhs.org W: www.covfhs.org

Cumberland see **Cumbria**

Cumbria
Cumbria FHS Rose Villa, 25 Eden Street, Stanwix, Carlisle, Cumbria CA3 9LS T: 01228 535 228 E: laarltrev@aol.com W: www.cumbriafhs.com

Furness FHS 64 Cowlarns Road, Hawcoat, Barrow-in-Furness LA14 4HJ T: 01229 830942 E: julia.fairbairn@furnessfhs.co.uk W: www.furnessfhs.co.uk

Derbyshire
Buxton & District U3A - FHG Yarrow, 8 Carlisle Grove, Buxton SK17 6XP T: 01298 70959 E: taylor.ian9@googlemail.com

Chesterfield & District FHS 2 Highlow Close, Loundsley Green, Chesterfield, Derbyshire S40 4PG T: 01246 231900 E: cadfhs@aol.com W: www.cadfhs.org.uk

Derbyshire Ancestral Research Group 86 High Street, Loscoe, Heanor, Derbyshire DE75 7LF T: 01773-604916

Derbyshire FHS Bridge Chapel House, St Mary's Bridge, Sowter Road, Derby, Derbyshire DE1 3AT T: 01332 363876 E: see website W: www.dfhs.org.uk

Devon
Devon FHS PO Box 9, Exeter, Devon EX2 6YP T: 01392 433212 E: enquiries@devonfhs.org.uk W: www.devonfhs.org.uk

Thorverton & District History Society Ferndale, Thorverton, Exeter, Devon EX5 5NG T: 01392 860932

Dorset
Dorset FHS Treetops Research Centre, Suite 5 Stanley House, 3 Fleets Lane, Poole, Dorset BH15 3AJ T: 01202 785623 E: contact@dorsetfhs.org.uk W: www.dorsetfhs.org.uk

Somerset & Dorset FHS PO Box 4502, Sherborne, Dorset DT9 6YL T: 01935 389611 E: society@sdfhs.org W: www.sdfhs.org

Durham
Cleveland FHS 4 North Park North, Sedgefield, Stockton on Tees, TS21 3AH T: 01740 623 175 E: christinedunn48@yahoo.co.uk W: www.clevelandfhs.org.uk/

Elvet Local & Family History Groups 37 Hallgarth Street, Durham, County Durham DH1 3AT T: 0191 386 4098

Newton Aycliffe FHS 4 Barnard Close, Woodham Village, Newton Aycliffe, County Durham DL5 4SP T: 01325 315959

Northumberland & Durham FHS 2nd Floor, Bolbec Hall, Westgate Road, Newcastle-on-Tyne, Tyne and Wear NE1 1SE T: 0191 261 2159 E: secretary@ndfhs.org.uk W: www.ndfhs.org.uk

Essex
Essex Society for Family History Research Centre, Essex Record Office, Wharf Road, Chelmsford, Essex CM2 6YT T: 01245 244670 E: secretary@esfh.org.uk W: www.esfh.org.uk

Waltham Forest FHS 49 Sky Peals Road, Woodford Green, Essex IG8 9NE E: barriefb@hotmail.co.uk

Felixstowe
Felixstowe FHS The Tree House, Maidstone Road, Felixstowe IP11 9ED T: 01394 271762 E: fxfhs@hotmail.com W: www.itgen.co.uk/ffhs/

Gloucestershire
Campden & District Branch of Gloucestershire FHS The Old Police station, High Street, Chipping Campden, Gloucestershire GL55 6HB T: 01386 840561 E: familyhistory@chippingcampdenhistory.org.uk W: www.chippingcampdenhistory.org.uk

Gloucestershire FHS Clarence Row, Alvin Street, Gloucester, GL1 3AH T: 01452 524344 (Resource Centre) E: secretary@gfhs.org.uk W: www.gfhs.org.uk

Gloucestershire - South see Bristol

Hampshire
Hampshire Genealogical Society 198A Havant Road, Drayton, Portsmouth, Hampshire PO6 2EH T: 023 9238 7000 E: secretary@hgs-online.org.uk W: www.hgs-online.org.uk

Herefordshire
Herefordshire FHS 17 Whittern Way, Tupsley, Hereford, Herefordshire HR1 1PE T: 01981-250974 E: W: www.rootsweb.com/~ukhfhs

Hertfordshire
Codicote LHS 34 Harkness Way, Hitchin, Hertfordshire SG4 0QL T: 01462 622953
Hertfordshire FHS 30 Blenheim Way, Stevenage, Hertfordshire SG2 8TE T: 01438 216785 E: secretary@hertsfhs.org.uk W: www.hertsfhs.org.uk
Letchworth & District Family History Group 60 Woodland Rise, Welwyn Garden City, Hertfordshire AL8 7LF E: secretary@ldfhg.org.uk W: www.ldfhg.org.uk
Royston & District LHS 60 Beldam Avenue, Royston, Hertfordshire SG8 9UW E: membership@roystonfhs.org.uk W: www.roystonfhs.org.uk
Welwyn & District LHS 40 Hawbush Rise, Welwyn, Hertfordshire AL6 9PP T: 01438 716415 E: paul@jiggens.net W: www.welwynhistory.org

Huntingdon
East Anglian Group of Family History Societies 42 Crowhill, Godmanchester, Huntington, Cambridgeshire PE29 2NR E: secretary@huntsfhs.org.uk

Isle of Wight
Isle of Wight FHS 13 Britannia Way, East Cowes, Isle of Wight PO32 6DG T: 01983 289 599 E: val.luter@talktalk.net W: www.isle-of-wight-fhs.co.uk

Kent
Folkestone & District FHS Kingsmill Down, Hastingleigh, Ashford, Kent TN25 5JJ T: 01233 750321 E: secretary@folkfhs.org.uk W: www.folkfhs.org.uk
Kent FHS Bullockstone Farm, Bullockstone Road, Herne Bay, Kent CT6 7NL E: secretary@kfhs.org.uk W: www.kfhs.org.uk
North West Kent FHS 51 Newbury Avenue, Allington, Maidstone, ME16 0RG E: secretary@nwkfhs.org.uk W: www.nwkfhs.org.uk
Tunbridge Wells FHS Yew Tree Byre, Yew Tree Lane, Rotherfield, TN6 3QP E: secretary@tunwells-fhs.co.uk W: www.tunwells-fhs.co.uk
Woolwich & District FHS 121 Crofton Avenue, Bexley, Kent DA5 3AU E: suhiwfhs@tiscali.co.uk

Lancashire
Bolton & District FHS see **Manchester & Lancashire FHS**
Lancashire Family History & Heraldry Society 2 Straits, Oswaldtwistle, Lancashire BB5 3LU T: 01254 239919 E: secretary@lfhhs.org.uk W: www.lfhhs.org.uk
Lancaster Family History Group 116 Bowerham Road, Lancaster, Lancashire LA1 4HL E: secretary@lfhg.org
Liverpool & S W Lancashire FHS 6 Kirkmore Road, Liverpool L18 4QN E: secretary@liverpool-genealogy.org.uk W: www.liverpool-genealogy.org.uk
Manchester & Lancashire FHS Clayton House, 59 Piccadilly, Manchester, M1 2AQ T: 0161 236 9750 E: office@mlfhs.org.uk W: www.mlfhs.org.uk
North Meols (Southport) FHS 6 Millars Pace, Marshside, Southport, PR9 9FU E: secretary@nmfhssouthport.co.uk W: www.nmfhssouthport.co.uk
North West Group of FHS - Family History Fair Liverpool & SW Lancashire FHS, 23 School Fold, Hesketh Bank, West Lancashire PR4 6RE T: 01772 816 841 E: ian.white4@virgin.net W: www.nwgfhs.org.uk
Oldham & District FHS Clayton House, 59 Piccadilly, Manchester, M1 2QA T: 0161 236 9750 E: office@mlfhs.org.uk W: www.mlfhs.org.uk
Ormskirk & District FHS PO Box 213, Aughton, Ormskirk, L39 5WT T: 01695 578780 E: secretary@odfhs.org.uk W: www.odfhs.org.uk
Rossendale Branch of Lancashire Family History & Heraldry Society c/o LFHHS, 2 The Straits, Oswaldtwistle, Lancashire BB5 3LU T: 01254 239919 E: rossendale@lfhhs.org.uk W: www.rossendale-fhhs.fsnet.co.uk
St Helens Townships FHS 6 Gainford Close, Widnes, Cheshire WA8 4UN E: townshipsFHS@googlemail.com W: www.sthelenstownshipsfhs.org.uk
Wigan FHS 7 Pearl Street, Wigan, Lancashire WN6 7HL E: anthony_haslam@sky.com W: www.wiganworld.co.uk/familyhistory/

Leicestershire
Leicestershire & Rutland FHS 37 Cyril Street, Leicester, Leicestershire LE3 2FF T: 0116 285 7211 - Research Centre E: secretary@lrfhs.org.uk W: www.lrfhs.org.uk

Lincolnshire
Fenland FHS Rose Hall, Walpole Bank, Walpole St Andrew, Wisbech PE14 7JD E: judy.green@farming.me.uk W: www.cambridgeshirehistory.com/Societies/ffhs

Isle of Axholme FHS Colywell, 43 Commonside, Westwoodside, Doncaster, South Yorkshire DN9 2AR T: 01427 752692 E: secretary@axholme-fhs.org.uk W: www.linktop.demon.co.uk/axholme/
Lincolnshire FHS 1 Elliston Street, Cleethorpes, north East Lincolnshire DN35 7HS E: secretary@lincolnshirefhs.org.uk W: www.lincolnshirefhs.org.uk
Lincolnshire FHS (Publications) Unit 6 Monks Way, Monks Road, Lincoln, Lincolnshire LN2 5LN T: 01522 528088 E: hazel.deighton14@btinternet.com W: www.lincolnshirefhs.org.uk

Liverpool
Liverpool & S W Lancashire FHS 6 Kirkmore Road, Liverpool L18 4QN E: secretary@liverpool-genealogy.org.uk W: www.liverpool-genealogy.org.uk

London
East of London FHS 46 Brights Avenue, Rainham, Essex RM13 9NW E: See Website W: www.eolfhs.org.uk
Hillingdon FHS 20 Moreland Drive, Gerrards Cross, Buckinghamshire SL9 8BB T: 01753 885602 E: gillmay@dial.pipex.com W: www.hfhs.co.uk
London, Westminster & Middlesex FHS 57 Belvedere Way, Kenton, Harrow, Middlesex HA3 9XQ T: 020 8204 5470 E: william.pyemont@virgin.net W: wwww.lnmfhs.dircon.co.uk

Manchester
Manchester & Lancashire FHS Clayton House, 59 Piccadilly, Manchester, M1 2AQ T: 0161 236 9750 E: office@mlfhs.org.uk W: www.mlfhs.org.uk

Merseyside
Liverpool & S W Lancashire FHS 6 Kirkmore Road, Liverpool L18 4QN E: secretary@liverpool-genealogy.org.uk W: www.liverpool-genealogy.org.uk
St Helens Townships FHS 6 Gainford Close, Widnes, Cheshire WA8 4UN E: townshipsFHS@googlemail.com W: www.sthelenstownshipsfhs.org.uk

Middlesex
Hillingdon FHS 20 Moreland Drive, Gerrards Cross, Buckinghamshire SL9 8BB T: 01753 885602 E: gillmay@dial.pipex.com W: www.hfhs.co.uk
London, Westminster & Middlesex FHS 57 Belvedere Way, Kenton, Harrow, Middlesex HA3 9XQ T: 020 8204 5470 E: william.pyemont@virgin.net W: www.lnmfhs.dircon.co.uk
West Middlesex FHS 1 Camellia Place, Whitton, Twickenham, Middlesex TW2 7HZ E: secretary@west-middlesex-fhs.org.uk W: www.west-middlesex-fhs.org.uk

Norfolk
East Anglian Group of Family History Societies 42 Crowhill, Godmanchester, Huntington, Cambridgeshire PE29 2NR E: secretary@huntsfhs.org.uk
Fenland FHS Rose Hall, Walpole Bank, Walpole St Andrew, Wisbech PE14 7JD E: judy.green@farming.me.uk W: www.cambridgeshirehistory.com/Societies/ffhs
Mid - Norfolk FHS 104 Norwich Road, Dereham, Norwich, Norfolk NR20 3AR E: sue.vickerage@ic24.net W: www.mnfhs.co.uk
Norfolk FHS Headquarters, Library & Registered Office, Kirby Hall, 70 St Giles Street, Norwich, Norfolk NR2 1LS T: 01603 763718 E: nfhs@paston.co.uk W: www.norfolkfhs.org.uk

North Lancashire see **Cumbria**

Northampton
Northamptonshire
Northamptonshire FHS 22 Godwin Walk, Ryehill Estate, Northampton NN5 7RW E: secretary@northants-fhs.org W: www.northants-fhs.org

Northumberland
Northumberland & Durham FHS 2nd Floor, Bolbec Hall, Westgate Road, Newcastle-on-Tyne, Tyne and Wear NE1 1SE T: 0191 261 2159 E: secretary@ndfhs.org.uk W: www.ndfhs.org.uk

Nottinghamshire
Mansfield & District FHS 15 Cranmer Grove, Mansfield, NG19 7JR
Nottinghamshire FHS 26 Acorn Bank, West Bridgford, Nottingham, Nottinghamshire NG2 7DU E: see website W: www.nottsfhs.org.uk

Oxfordshire
Oxfordshire FHS 19 Mavor Close, Woodstock, Oxford OX20 1YL T: 01993 812258 E: secretary@ofhs.org.uk W: www.ofhs.org.uk

Rutland see **Leicestershire**

Shropshire
Cleobury Mortimer Historical Society The Old Schoolhouse, Neen Savage, Cleobury Mortimer, Kidderminster, Shropshire DY14 8JU T: 01299 270319
Shropshire FHS Larkrise, 16 Glentworth Avenue, Oswestry, Shropshire SY10 9PZ T: 01691 653 316 E: secretary@sfhs.org.uk W: www.sfhs.org.uk

Somerset
Somerset & Dorset FHS PO Box 4502, Sherborne DT9 6YL T: 01935 389611 E: society@sdfhs.org W: www.sdfhs.org
South West Group of Family History Societies E: brianpam125@talktalk.net W: www.swagfhs.org.uk
Weston-Super-Mare FHS 125 Totterdown Road, Weston Super Mare BS23 4LW E: secretary@wsmfhs.org.uk W: www.wsmfhs.org.uk
Somerset - North see Bristol

South Gloucestershire
Sodbury Vale Family History Group 36 Westcourt Drive, Oldland Common, Bristol, BS30 9RU T: 0117 932 4133 E: secretary@bafhs.org.uk

Staffordshire
Ancestral Rescue Club 19 Mansfield Close, Tamworth, Staffordshire B79 7YE T: 01827 65322 E: ancestral.rescue@ntlworld.com W: www.rootsweb.com/~engarc/index.html
Audley & District FHS 20 Hillside Avenue, Endon, Stoke on Trent, Staffordshire ST9 9HH E: famhist147@hotmail.co.uk W: www.acumenbooks.co.uk/audleynet/famhist/index.htm
Birmingham & Midland Society for Genealogy and Heraldry 5 Sanderling Court, Spennells, Kidderminster DY10 4TS T: 01562 743912 E: jackie.cotterill1@btinternet.com W: www.bmsgh.org
Burntwood Family History Group 8 Peakes Road, Rugeley, WS15 2LY E: jennifer.lee1@virgin.net W: www.geocities.com/bfgh1986

Suffolk
Felixstowe FHS The Tree House, Maidstone Road, Felixstowe, Suffolk IP11 9ED T: 01394 271762 E: fxfhs@hotmail.com W: www.itgen.co.uk/ffhs/
Suffolk FHS 2 Flash Corner, Theberton, Leiston, Suffolk IP16 4RW E: admin@suffolkfhs.org.uk W: www.suffolkfhs.org.uk

Surrey
East Surrey FHS 10 Cobham Close, Wallington, Surrey SM6 9DS T: 020 8642 6789 E: secretary01@eastsurreyfhs.org.uk W: www.eastsurreyfhs.org.uk
Reigate District Family History Group St Mark's Hall, Alma Road, Reigate, Surrey T: 01737 766 135 E: johnsonjackie@hotmail.com W: www.surreycc.gov.uk/redhilllocalhistory
The Selsey Society Sugham Farm, Lingfield, Surrey RH7 6BZ E: treasurer@selseysociety.co.uk W: www.selseysociety.co.uk
West Surrey FHS 21 Sheppard Road, Basingstoke, Hampshire RG21 3HT E: secretary@wsfhs.org W: www.wsfhs.org.uk

Sussex
Eastbourne & District (Family Roots) FHS 8 Park Lane, Eastbourne, East Sussex BN212 2UT T: 01323 502 432 E: johnandvalmai@talktalk.net W: www.eastbournefhs.org.uk
Hastings & Rother FHS 355 Bexhill Road, St Leonards on Sea, East Sussex TN38 8AJ T: 01424 437493 E: enquiries@hrfhs.org.uk W: www.hrfhs.org.uk
Sussex Family History Group 8 Wythwood, Haywards Heath, West Sussex RH16 4RD E: secretary@sfhg.org.uk W: www.sfhg.org.uk

Tyne and Wear see Northumberland & Durham

Waltham Forest
Waltham Forest FHS 49 Sky Peals Road, Woodford Green, Essex IG8 9NE E: barriefb@hotmail.co.uk

Warwickshire
Birmingham & Midland Society for Genealogy and Heraldry 5 Sanderling Court, Spennells, Kidderminster DY10 4TS T: 01562 743912 E: jackie.cotterill1@btinternet.com W: www.bmsgh.org
Coventry FHS 12 Knoll Drive, Styvechale, Coventry, Warwickshire CV3 5BT T: 0247 669 3904 E: enquiries@covfhs.org W: www.covfhs.org
Nuneaton & North Warwickshire FHS 34 Falmouth Close, Nuneaton, Warwickshire CV11 6OB T: 024 7638 1090 E: nuneatonian2000@aol.com W: www.nnwfhs.org.uk
Rugby FHG Springfields, Rocheberie Way, Rugby, CV22 6EG T: 01788 813 957 E: j.chard@ntlworld.com W: www.rugbyfhg.co.uk
Warwickshire FHS 44 Abbotts Lane, Coventry, CV1 4AZ E: chairman@wfhs.org.uk W: www.wfhs.org.uk

West Midlands
Birmingham & Midland Society for Genealogy and Heraldry 5 Sanderling Court, Spennells, Kidderminster DY10 4TS T: 01562 743912 E: jackie.cotterill1@btinternet.com W: www.bmsgh.org
Sandwell FHS 10 Linden Lane, Short Heath, Willenhall, West Midlands WV12 5NX T: 01922 492 653 E: gffrywbb@aol.com

Westminster
London, Westminster & Middlesex FHS 57 Belvedere Way, Kenton, Harrow, Middlesex HA3 9XQ T: 020 8204 5470 E: william.pyemont@virgin.net W: www.lnmfhs.dircon.co.uk

Westmorland see Cumbria

Wiltshire
Wiltshire FHS Resource Centre, Unit 3 Bath Road Business entre, Devizes, Wiltshire SN10 1XA T: 01380 724 379 E: secretary@wiltshirefhs.co.uk W: www.wiltshirefhs.co.uk

Worcestershire
Malvern FHS Apartment 5 Severn Grange, Northwick Road, Bevere, Worcester WR3 7RE E: secretary@mfhs.org.uk W: www.mfhs.org.uk
see also Birmingham

Yorkshire
London Group of Yorkshire Family History Societies 1 Waverley Way, Carlshalton Beeches SM5 3LQ E: ian-taylor@blueyonder.co.uk W: www.genuki.org.uk/big/eng/YKS/Misc/FHS/index.html
Yorkshire Archaeological Society - Family History Section Claremont, 23 Clarendon Road, Leeds, LS2 9NZ E: editor@yorkshireroots.org.uk W: www.yorkshireroots.org.uk
Yorkshire - East
East Yorkshire FHS Carnegie Heritage Centre, 342 Anlaby Road,, Hull, East Yorkshire HU3 6JA E: secretary@eyfhs.org.uk W: www.eyfhs.org.uk
Yorkshire - North
Cleveland FHS 4 North Park North, Sedgefield, Stockton on Tees, County Durham TS21 3AH T: 01740 623 175 E: christinedunn48@yahoo.co.uk W: www.clevelandfhs.org.uk/
Harrogate & District FHS 16 Swinborne Close, Harrogate, North Yorkshire HG1 3LX E: info@hadfhs.co.uk W: www.hadfhs.co.uk
Ripon Historical Society & Family History Group 42 Knox Avenue, Harrogate, North Yorkshire HG1 3JB E: sec.rhs@btinternet.com W: www.riponhistoricalsociety.org.uk
Rosedale History Society Phoenix House, Rosedale Abbey, Pickering YO18 8SE T: 01751 417 071 E: rosedalehistory@hotmail.co.uk W: http://rosedale.ryedaleconnect.org.uk
Ryedale Family History Group 5 High Street, Hovingham YO62 4LA T: 01653 628952 E: info@ryedalefamilyhistory.org W: www.ryedalefamilyhistory.org
Selby & District Family History Group 9 Larkfield Road, Selby, North Yorkshire YO8 9AS E: sheila9@tiscali.co.uk
Upper Dales Family History Group - a branch of Cleveland FHS Croft House, Newbiggin in Bishopdale, Nr Leyburn, North Yorkshire DL8 3TD T: 01969 663738 E: glenys@bishopdale.demon.co.uk W: www.upperdalesfhg.org.uk
Yorkshire - North
Wharfedale Family History Group Hideaway Cottage, Middle Lane, Kettlewell, Skipton, North Yorkshire BD23 5QX T: membership@wharfedalefhg.org.uk W: www.wharfedalefhg.org.uk
Yorkshire - South
Barnsley FHS 11 Meadow Rise, Wadworthy, Barnsley, South Yorkshire DN11 9AP E: secretary@barnsleyfhs.co.uk W: www.barnsleyfhs.co.uk
Doncaster & District FHS 8 Tenter Lane, Warmsworth, Doncaster, South Yorkshire DN4 9PT T: 01302 845 809 E: honsecretary@doncasterfhs.co.uk W: www.doncasterfhs.co.uk
Grenoside & District Local History Group 4 Stepping Lane, Grenoside, Sheffield, South Yorkshire S35 8RA T: 0114 257 1929 E: info@grenosidelocalhistory.co.uk W: www.grenosidelocalhistory.co.uk
Rotherham FHS 36 Warren Hill, Rotherham, South Yorkshire S61 3SX E: brian_allott@msn.com W: www.rotherhamfhs.co.uk
Sheffield & District FHS 12 Birchitt Road, Bradway, Sheffield, S17 4QP E: secretary@sheffieldfhs.org.uk W: www.sheffieldfhs.org.uk
Yorkshire - West
Boothferry Family & Local History Group 17 Airmyn Avenue, Goole DN14 6PF E: howardrj@madasafish.com
Bradford FHS 5 Leaventhorpe Avenue, Fairweather Green, Bradford, West Yorkshire BD8 0ED E: secretary@bradfordfhs.org.uk W: www.bradfordfhs.org.uk
Calderdale FHS inc Halifax & District 15 Far View, Illingworth, Halifax, West Yorkshire HX2 0NU E: secretary@cfhsweb.co.uk W: www.cfhsweb.co.uk

Huddersfield & District FHS 33a Green's End, Meltham, Holmfirth, HD9 5NW E: secretary@hdfhs.org.uk W: www.hdfhs.org.uk

Keighley & District FHS 2 The Hallows, Shann Park, Keighley, West Yorkshire BD20 6HY T: 01535 672144 E: suedaynes@hotmail.co.uk W: www.kdfhs.org.uk

Morley & District Family History Group 1 New Lane, East Ardsley, Wakefield WF3 2DP E: carol@morleyfhg.co.uk W: www.morleyfhg.co.uk

Pontefract & District FHS Eadon House, Main Street, Hensall, Goole DN14 0QZ E: secretary@pontefractfhs.org.uk W: www.pontefractfhs.org.uk

Wakefield & District FHS 101 Thornes Road, Wakefield, West Yorkshire WF2 8QD T: 01924 373014 W: www.wdfhs.co.uk

Wharfedale Family History Group Hideaway Cottage, Middle Lane, Kettlewell, Skipton, North Yorkshire BD23 5QX E: membership@wharfedalefhg.org.uk W: www.wharfedalefhg.org.uk

Yorkshire - York

City of York & District FHS 26 Nursery Road, Nether Poppleton, York YO26 6NN T: 01904 794 973 E: secretary@yorkfamilyhistory.org.uk W: www.yorkfamilyhistory.org.uk

Isle of Man FHS

4 Eleanoa Gardens, Douglas IM2 3NR E: paminmans@manx.net W: www.isle-of-man.com/interests/genealogy/fhs

Channel Islands

Guernsey

Family History Section of La Société Guernesiaise PO Box 314, St Peter Port, Guernsey GY1 3TG E: societe@cwgsy.net W:www.societe.org.gg/sections/familyhistory.php

Jersey

Channel Islands FHS P0 Box 507, St Helier, Jersey JE4 5TN E: queenie912001@yahoo.co.uk W: www.channelislandshistory.com

Wales

Federation of Family History Societies PO Box 8857, Lutterworth, LE17 9BJ T: 01455 203 133 E: info@ffhs.org.uk W: www.ffhs.org.uk

London Branch of the Welsh Family History Societies 87 Malford Grove, South Woodford, London, E18 2DH E: annee.jones@ntworld.com

Welsh Association of Family History Societies c/o Menna Evans, Adran Casgliadau, National Library of Wales, Aberystwyth, Ceredigion SY25 3BU E: secretary@fhswales.info W: www.fhswales.info

Brecknockshire

Powys FHS 13 Swan Court, Woodchurch Road, Prenton, Birkenhead, Merseyside CH43 0RX T: 07977 631 132 E: helen.brick1@virgin.net W: www.rootsweb.com/~wlspfhs

Cardiganshire

Cardiganshire FHS c/o Menna Evans, Adran Casgliadau, National Library of Wales, Aberystwyth, Ceredigion SY25 3BU E: ymholiadau@cgnfhs.org.uk W: www.cgnfhs.org.uk

Carmarthenshire see **Dyfed**

Ceredigion see **Dyfed**

Clwyd

Clwyd FHS The Laurels, Dolydd Road, Cefn Mawr, Wrexham, LL14 3NH T: 01978 822218 E: secretary@clwydfhs.org.uk W: www.clwydfhs.org.uk

Denbighshire see **Clwyd FHS**

Dyfed

Dyfed FHS White Lodge, Deanshill Close, Stafford, Staffordshire ST16 1BW T: 01785 245 103 E: membership@dyfedfhs.org.uk W: www.dyfedfhs.org.uk

Flintshire see **Clwyd FHS**

Glamorgan

Glamorgan FHS 44 Hendrecafn Road, Penygraig, Rhondda, Mid Glamorgan CF40 1LL T: 01443 434547 E: secretary@glamfhs.org W: www.glamfhs.org

Gwent

Gwent FHS 11 Rosser Street, Wainfelin, Pontypool, Gwent NP4 6EA E: secretary@gwentfhs.info W: www.gwentfhs.info

Gwynedd

Gwynedd FHS 12 Long Street, Gerlan, Bangor, Conwy LL57 3SY T: 01248 600 102 E: david.roberts10@homecall.co.uk W: www.gwynddfhs.org

Monmouthshire see **Gwent**

Montgomeryshire

Montgomeryshire Genealogical Society 24 Dysart Terrace, Canal Road, Newtown, Powys SY16 2JL T: 01686 627916 E: monica.woosnam@btinternet.com W: http://home.freeuk.net/montgensoc

Pembrokeshire see **Dyfed**

Powys

Powys FHS 13 Swan Court, Woodchurch Road, Prenton, Birkenhead, Merseyside CH43 0RX T: 07977 631 132 E: helen.brick1@virgin.net W: www.rootsweb.com/~wlspfhs

Ystradgynlais FHS c/o Ystradgynlais Library, Temperance Lane, Ystradgynlais, Powys SA9 1JP T: 01639 845 353 E: Caryljones@talktalk.net W: www.ystradgynlaisfhs.co.uk

Radnorshire see **Powys**

Scotland

Scottish Association of Family History Societies 77 Erskine Hill, Polmont, Falkirk, FK2 0UH T: 01324 713037 E: see website W: www.safhs.org.uk

Scottish Genealogy Society 15 Victoria Terrace, Edinburgh, EH1 2JL T: 0131-220-3677 E: sales@scotsgenealogy.com W: www.scotsgenealogy.com

Aberdeenshire

Aberdeen & North East Scotland FHS 158 - 164 King Street, Aberdeen, AB24 5BD T: 01224 646323 E: enquiries@anesfhs.org.uk W: www.anesfhs.org.uk

Angus see **Tay Valley Family History Society**

Argyll

see **Glasgow & West of Scotland Family History Society**

Islay FHS Islay House Square, Bridgend, Isle of Islay, Argyll PA44 7NZ T: 01496 810 187 E: islayfhs@btconnect.com W: http://homepages.rootsweb.ancestry.com/~steve/islay/fhs/visit.htm

Ayrshire

Alloway & Southern Ayrshire FHS c/o Alloway Church Hall, Auld Nick's View, Alloway, Ayr, Ayrshire KA7 4RT W: www.asafhs.org.uk

East Ayrshire FHS c/o Dick Institute, Elmbank Avenue, Kilmarnock, KA1 3BU E: enquiries@eastayrshirefhs.org.uk W: www.eastayrshirefhs.org.uk

see **Glasgow & West of Scotland Family History Society**

Largs & North Ayrshire FHS Bogriggs Cottage, Carlung, West Kilbride, Ayrshire KA23 9PS T: 01294 823690 E: membership@largsnafhs.org.uk W: www.largsnafhs.org.uk

SW Scotland Local / Family History Maybole Historical Society 15F Campbell Court, Ayr, Ayrshire KA8 0SE T: 01292 610461 E: ayrloom@btinternet.com W: www.maybole.org

Troon @ Ayrshire FHS c/o M.E.R.C., Troon Public Library, South Beach, Troon, Ayrshire KA10 6EF T: E: info@troonayrshirefhs.org.uk W: www.troonayrshirefhs.org.uk

Berwickshire see Borders FHS

Borders

Borders FHS 30 Elliot Road, Jedburgh, Scottish Borders TD8 6HN E: see website W: www.bordersfhs.org.uk

Bute see **Glasgow & West of Scotland Family History Society**

Caithness

Caithness FHS Dwarick Park, Dunnet, Caithness KW14 8XD T: 01847 851 295 E: b.l.hiddleston@btinternet.com W: www.caithnessfhs.org.uk

Central Scotland

Central Scotland FHS 11 Springbank Gardens, Dunblane, Perthshire FK15 9JX T: 01786 823937 W: www.csfhs.org.uk

Clackmannanshire see **Central Scotland Family History Society**

Dumfrieshire

Dumfries & Galloway FHS Family History Research Centre, 9 Glasgow Street, Dumfries, DG2 9AF T: 01387-248093 E: secretary@dgfhs.org.uk W: www.dgfhs.org.uk

Clan Moffat FHS Whinney Brae, Tundergarth, Lockerbie, Dumfrieshire DG11 2PP E: geat@albasw.wanadoo.co.uk

Dunbartonshire see**Glasgow & West of Scotland FHS**

East Lothian

Lothians FHS c/o Lasswade High School Centre, Eskdale Drive, Bonnyrigg, Midlothian EH19 2LA E: lothiansfhs@hotmail.com W: www.lothiansfhs.org.uk

Edinburgh see **Lothians FHS**

Fife

Fife FHS Glenmoriston, Durie Street, Leven, Fife KY8 4HF T: 01333 425321 E: membership@fifefhs.org W: www.fifefhs.org

see **Tay Valley Family History Society**

Glasgow

Glasgow & West of Scotland FHS Unit 13, 32 Mansfield Street, Partick, Glasgow, G11 5QP T: 0141 339 8303 E: publicity@gwsfhs.org.uk W: www.gwsfhs.org.uk

Highlands

Highland FHS Highland Archive & Registration Centre, Bught Road, Inverness, IV3 5SS E: info@highlandfamilyhistorysociety.org W: www.highlandfamilyhistorysociety.org

Invernesshire see **Highland FHS**

Kinross-shire see**Tay Valley FHS**

Lanarkshire see **Glasgow & West of Scotland FHS**
Lanarkshire FHS c/o Local History Room, Motherwell Heritage
Centre, High Road, Motherwell ML1 3HU E:
society@lanarkshirefhs.org.uk W: www.lanarkshirefhs.org.uk
Midlothian see **Lothians Family History Society**
Nairnshire
Cawdor Heritage Group Family & Local History Room, Nairn
Museum, Viewfield Drive, Nairn, Nairnshire IV12 4EE T: 01667
456791 W: www.nairnmuseum.co.uk
Moray & Nairn FHS E: info@morayandnairnfhs.co.uk W:
www.morayandnairnfhs.co.uk
Orkney
Orkney FHS Orkney Library and Archives, 44 Junction Road,
Kirkwall, Orkney KW15 1AG T: 01856 879 207 E:
secretary@orkneyfhs.co.uk W: www.orkneyfhs.co.uk
Peebleshire see **Borders Family History Society**
Perthshire see **Tay Valley Family History Society**
Renfrewshire
see **Glasgow & West of Scotland FHS**
Renfrewshire FHS c/o Museum and Art Galleries, High Street,
Paisley, Renfrewshire PA1 2BA E: webmaster.rfhs@ntlworld.com W:
www.geocities.com/renfrewshirefhs
Roxburghshire see **Borders FHS**
Selkirkshire see **Borders FHS**
Shetland
Shetland FHS 6 Hillhead, Lerwick, Shetland ZE1 0EJ T: 01595
692276 E: secretary@shetland-fhs.org.uk W: www.shetland-fhs.org.uk
Stirlingshire
see **Central Scotland Family History Society**
see **Glasgow & West of Scotland FHS**
West Lothian see **Lothians FHS**

Northern Ireland
Armagh Ancestry 38a English Street, Armagh BT61 7BA T: 028 3752
1800 E: researcher@armagh.gov.uk W: www.armagh.gov.uk
Irish Heritage Association A.204 Portview, 310 Newtownards Road,
Belfast, BT4 1HE T: 028 90455325
North of Ireland FHS Graduate School of Education, Queen's
university of Belfast, 69 University Street, Belfast, BT7 1HL E:
web@nifhs.org W: www.nifhs.org
Society of Genealogists Northern Ireland (SGNI) E:
secretary@sgni.net W: www.sgni.net
Ulster Historical Foundation 49 Malone Road, Belfast, BT9 6RY T:
028 9066 1988 F: 028 9066 1977 E: enquiry@uhf.org.uk W:
www.ancestryireland.com

Ireland
Council of Irish Genealogical Organisations 31a All Saints Road,
Raheny, Dublin 5 T: +353 1 406 3542 E: info@cigo.ie W:
www.cigo.ie/
Cumann Geinealais na hÉireann : Genealogical Society of Ireland
Archive: An Daonchartlann, Carlisle Pier, Dún Laoghaire Harbour,
Co. Dublin, Ireland, Secretary: 11 Desmond Avenue, Dun Laoghaire,
Co Dublin T: 353 1 284 2711 E: eolas@familyhistory.ie W:
www.familyhistory.ie
Hugenot Society of Great Britain & Ireland - Irish Section Echo
Hall, Spa, County Down BT24 8PT E: EchoHall@aol.com W:
www.hugenotsociety.org.uk
Irish Ancestry Group Clayton House, 59 Piccadilly, Manchester, M1
2AQ T: 0161 236 9750 E: office@mlfhs.org.uk W: www.mlfhs.org.uk
Irish Family History Foundation c/o Riverbank, Newbridge, County
Kildare E: enquiries@rootsireland.ie W: www.rootsireland.ie
Irish FHS P0 Box 36, Naas, Co Kildare E: ifhs@eircom.net W:
www.ifhs.ie
Irish Genealogical Research Society 18 Stratford Avenue, Rainham,
Gillingham, Kent ME8 0EP E: info@igrsoc.org W: www.igrsoc.org
Irish Jewish Genealogical Society & Family History Centre -
Division of Irish Jewish Museum 3 Walworth Road, Portobello,
Dublin, 8 T: +353 1 677 3808 E: masterc@medianet.ie W:
www.jewishireland.org/genealogy
Irish Palatine Association Old Railway Buildings, Rathkeale, County
Limerick E: info@irishpalatines.org W: www.irishpalatines.org
Society of Genealogists Northern Ireland (SGNI) E:
secretary@sgni.net W: www.sgni.net
see **Ulster Historical Foundation**
County Cavan
Cavan Genealogy Johnston Central Library, Farnham Street, Cavan,
Tel: +353 49 436 1094 E: cavangenealogy@eircom.net
County Cork
Bandon Genealogy Group Kilbrogan House, Kilbrogan Hill,
Bandon, County Cork T: 00 353 23 88 44935 E:
badon.genealogy@gmail.com W: www.kilbrogan.com
www.bandon-genealogy.com

Cork Genealogical Society 22 Elm Drive, Shamrock Lawn, Douglas,
County Cork T: 086 8198359 W: www.corkgenealogicalsociety.com
County Dublin
Ballinteer FHS 29 The View, Woodpark, Ballinteer, Dundrum, Dublin
16 T: 01-298-8082 E: ryanct@eircom.net
Flannery Clan / Clann Fhlannabhra 81 Woodford Drive,
Clondalkin, Dublin, 22 E: oflannery@eircom.net W:
www.flanneryclan.ie
Raheny Heritage Society 101 Collins Park, Donnycarney, Dublin 9,
Dublin E: bjwray@eircom.net
County Galway
Galway East FHS Woodford Heritage Centre, Woodford, Loughrea,
County Galway T: +353 90 974 9309 F: +353 90 974 9546 E:
galwayroots@eircom.net W: www.galwaysroots.com
Galway FHS (West) Ltd Ashe Road, Shantalla, County Galway T:
+353 91 086 464 F: +353 0 91 086 432 E:
galwaywestroots@eircom.net W: www.rootsireland.ie
County Kildare
Kildare History & Family Research Centre River Bank, Main
Street, Newbridge T: +353 45 448 350 E: kildaregenealogy@iol.ie W:
http://kildare.ie/Library/KildareCollectionsandResearchServices/Genea
logy/
County Wexford
County Wexford Heritage and Genealogy Society County Wexford
Heritage and Genealogy Society, Yola Farmstead, Folk Park, Tagoat,
Rosslare, County Wexford T: +353 53 32611 E: wexgen@eircom.net
W: www.irish-roots.net
Wexford FHS 24 Parklands, Wexford, Co Wexford T: +353 53 22973
E: murphyh@tinet.ie
County Wicklow
Wicklow County Genealogical Society 55 Seafield, Wicklow Town,
County Wicklow

Specialist Family History Societies
1788-1820 Pioneer Association PO Box 57, Croydon NSW 2132 T:
(02) 9797 8107
Anglo-French FHS 31 Collingwood Walk, Andover SP10 1PU
Anglo-German FHS 82 Hillside Grove, Chelmsford, Essex CM2
9DB E: gwendolinedavis@aol.com W: www.agfhs.org.uk
Anglo-Italian FHS Yew Cottage, Shurton, Bridgewater TA5 1GF T:
01278 733874 E: see website W: www.anglo-italianfhs.org.uk
Anglo-Scottish FHS Clayton House, 59 Piccadilly, Manchester, M1
2AQ T: 0161 236 9750 E: office@mlfhs.org.uk W: www.mlfhs.org.uk
Australian Society of the Lace Makers of Calais Inc PO Box 1277,
Queanbeyan NSW 2620 T: 02 6297 2168 E:
richardlander@ozemail.com.au
gilliankelly1@bigpond.com W: www.angelfire.com/al/aslc/
British Ancestors in India - The Indiaman Magazine 2 South Farm
Avenue, Harthill, Sheffield, South Yorkshire S26 7WY T: +44 (0)
1909 774416 E: editorial@indiaman.com W: www.indiaman.com
British Association for Cemeteries in South Asia 135 Burntwood
Lane, London, SW17 0AJ T: 0208 947 9131 E: rosieljai@clara.co.uk
W: www.bacsa.org.uk/
Catholic Family History Society 9 Snows Green Road, Shotley
Bridge, Consett, DH8 0HD E: margaretbowery@aol.com W:
www.catholic-history.org.uk/cfhs
Catholic Record Society 12 Melbourne Place, Wolsingham, County
Durham DL13 3EH W: www.catholic-history.org.uk/crs/
Chapels Heritage Society - CAPEL 5 Cuffnell Close, Liddell Park,
Llandudno, LL30 1UX E: obadiah1@btinternet.com W:
www.capeli.org.uk/
Descendants of Convicts Group PO Box 12224, A'Beckett Street,
Victoria 8006 T: 03 9808 1980 W: http://vicnet.net.au/~dcginc
Families in British India Society Sentosa, Godolphin Road,
Weybridge, Surrey KT13 0PT E: fibis-chairman@fibis.org W:
www.fibis.org
Family Search - (Genealogical Society of Utah) (UK) 185 Penns
Lane, Sutton Coldfield, West Midlands B76 1JU T: 0121 384 9921 F:
0121 384 9929 E: withingtonk@familysearch.org W:
www.familysearch.org
Heraldry Society PO Box 772, Guildford, Surrey GU3 3ZX T: 01483
237 373 E: honsec_heraldry@excite.co.uk W:
www.theheraldrysociety.com/
Hugenot & Walloon Research Association Malmaison, Church St,
Great Bedwyn, Wiltshire SN8 3PE
Hugenot Society of Great Britain & Ireland Hugenot Library
University College, Gower Street, London, WC1E 6BT T: 020 7679
5199 E: secretary@hugenotsociety.org.uk W:
www.hugenotsociety.org.uk
International Soc for British Genealogy & Family History PO Box
350459, Westminster, Colorado 80035-0459 T: 801-272-2178 W:
www.isbgfh.org

Jewish Genealogical Society of Great Britain 33 Seymour Place, London, W1H 5AU T: 020 7724 4232 E: chairman@jgsgb.org.uk W: www.jgsgb.org.uk

London & North Western Railway Society - Staff History Group 34 Falmouth Close, Nuneaton, Warwickshire CV11 6GB T: 024 76 381090 E: secretary@lnwrs.org.uk W: www.lnwrs.org.uk/

North East England Family History Club 5 Tree Court, Doxford Park, Sunderland, Tyne and Wear SR3 2HR T: 0191 522 8344

Pedigree Users Group 19 Lombardy Close, Leverstock Green, Hemel Hempstead, Hertfordshire HP2 4NG E: membership@pugweb.org.uk W: www.pugweb.org.uk

Quaker Family History Society 3 Sheridan Place, Hampton, Middlesex TW12 2SB E: info@qfhs.co.uk W: www.qfhs.co.uk

Railway Ancestors Family History Society Lundy, King Edward Street, Barmouth, Gwynedd LL42 1NY T: 01341 281 601 E: rafhs@btinternet.com

Romany & Traveller Family History Society 7 Park Rise, Nonchurch, Berkhamstead, hertfordshire HP4 3RT W: www.rtfhs.org.uk

Society of Brushmakers Descendants Family History Society 13 Ashworth Place, Church Langley, Essex CM17 9PU T: 01279-629392 E: s.b.d.@lineone.net W: www.brushmakers.com

Society for Name Studies in Britain & Ireland 22 Peel Park Avenue, Clitheroe, Lancashire BB7 1ET T: 01200-423771 W: www.snsbi.org.uk/

Tennyson Society Central Library, Free School Lane, Lincoln, LN2 1EZ T: 01522-552862 E: kathleen.jefferson@lincolnshire.gov.uk W: www.tennysonsociety.org.uk

Victorian Military Society PO Box 5837, Newbury, Berkshire RG14 7FJ T: 01635 48628 E: vmsdan@msn.com W: www.victorianmilitarysociety.org.uk

One Name Societies

Guild of One Name Studies Box G, 14 Charterhouse Buildings, Goswell Rd, London, EC1M 7BA T: 0800 011 2182 E: guild@one-name.org W: www.one-name.org

Alabaster Society Tollgate Cottage, The Turnpike, Bunwell, Norwich NR16 1SR E: laraine10@btinternet.com W: www.alabaster.org.uk

Alderson FHS No Postal Contact Address, E: secretary@afhs.org W: www.afhs.org

Alderton Family 16 Woodfield Drive, Gidea Park, Romford RM2 5DH

Allsop Family Group 86 High Street, Loscoe, Heanor DE75 7LF

Armstrong Clan Association Thyme, 7 Riverside Park, Hollows, Canonbie, DG14 0UY T: 01387 371 876 E: arm.clan@sky.com W: www.armstrongclan.info

Badham One Name Society Old School House, Old Radnor, Presteigne LD8 2RH E: research@badham.org.uk W: www.badham.org.uk

Baldry FHS Art & Science, 17 Gerrard Road, Islington, London, N1 8AY T: 020 7359 6294 E: ken@art-science.com W: www.baldry.org.uk

Beresford Family Society 2 Malatia, 78 St Augustines Avenue, South Croydon, Surrey CR2 6JH T: (020) 8686 3749 E: secretary@beresfordfamilysociety.org.uk W: www.beresfordfamilysociety.org.uk

Birkbecks of Westmoreland& Others 330 Dereham Road, Norwich, Norfolk NR2 4DL E: Seosimhin@btopenworld.com W: www.jgeoghegan.org.uk

Blanchard FHS 22 Pontefract Road, Cudworth, Barnsley S72 8AY E: secretary@blanchardfamilyhistorysociety.org.uk W: www.blanshardfamilyhistorysociety.org.uk

Bliss Old Well Cottage, Washdyke Lane, Fulbeck NG32 3LB T: 01400 279050 E: bliss@one-name.org W: www.blissfhs.co.uk

Braund Society 140 Stucley Road, Bideford, Devon EX39 3EL E: braund@one-name.org W: www.braundsociety.org

Brooking FHS 22 Parkside Drive, Exmouth, Devon EX8 4LB E: marylogan22@btinternet.com W: www.brookingsociety.org.uk

Bunting Society 'Firgrove', Horseshoe Lane, Ash Vale, Aldershot, Surrey GU12 5LL T: 01252 325644 E: bunting@one-name.org W: www.buntingsociety.org.uk

Caraher FHS 142 Rexford Street, Sistersville, VA 26175

Cave FHS 45 Wisbech Road, Thorney, Peterborough PE6 0SA T: 01733 270881 E: hugh-cave@cave-fhs.org.uk W: www.cave-fhs.org.uk

Clan Davidson Association Ballynester House, 1A Cardy Road, Greyabbey, Newtownards, Co Down BT22 2LS T: 028 427-38402

Clan Gregor Society Administrative Office, 2 Braehead, Alloa, FK10 2EW T: 01259-212076 E: clangregor@sol.co.uk W: www.clangregor.com/macgregor

Cobbing FHS 89a Petherton Road, London, N5 2QT T: (020) 7226-2657

Courtenay Society Powderham Castle, Kenton, Exeter EX6 8JQ T: 01626 891554 E: courtsoc@courtsoc.co.uk W: www.courtsoc.co.uk

Cory Society 3 Bourne Close, Thames Ditton, London, KT7 0EA E: cory@one-name.org W: www.corysociety.org.uk

Dalton Genealogical Society 2 Harewood Close, Reigate, Surrey RH2 0HE E: dalton@one-name.org W: www.daltongensoc.com

East FHS 45 Windsor Road, Ealing, London, W5 3UP

Entwistle Family History Association 96 Devon Street, Barrow in furness, Cumbria LA13 9PY W: www.entwistlefamily.org.uk

Geoghegan/McGeoghegan One Name Study 5 School Close, Feltwell, Norwich IP26 4EE T: 01842 828 649 E: josi@geoghegan.org

Goddard Association of Europe 2 Lowergate Road, Huncoat, Accrington BB5 6LN T: 01254-235135 W: www.goddard-association.co.uk

Hamley, Hambly & Hamlyn FHS (International) 59 Eylewood Road, West Norwood, London, SE27 9LZ T: (020) 8670-0683 W: www.hhh-fhs.com

Hards Family Society Venusmead, 36 Venus Street, Congresbury, Bristol, BS49 5EZ T: 01934 834780

Holdich FHS 19 Park Crescent, Elstree, Hertfordshire WD6 3PT T: (020) 8953 7195 E: deborahc.taylor@btopenworld.com

Holt Ancestry 26a Avondale Road, Bath, Somerset BA1 3EG E: victoria-holt@holtancestry.co.uk W: www.holtancestry.co.uk

Hotham/Owst One Name Study 2 The Circle, Hessle, Hull, East Yorkshire HU13 0QJ E: jbresearch870@hotmail.com

International Haskell Family Society Ella Farmhouse, Appersett, Hawes, DL8 3LN E: roger.emmins@btinternet.com W: www.ihfs.co.uk

International Relf Society Chatsworth House, Sutton Road, Somerton, Somerset TA11 6QL T: 01458-274015 E: withamcornel@aol.com W: www.relfsociety.org

Kay Family Association UK 1 Rowan Way, Canewdon, Rochford, Essex SS4 3PD T: 01702 258403 E: kayuk@btinternet.com W: www.kayfamilyassociationuk.com

Krans-Buckland Family Association P0 Box 1025, North Highlands, California 95660-1025 T: (916)-332-4359

Leather FHS 134 Holbeck, Great Hollands, Bracknell, Berkshire RG12 8XG T: 01344-425092 E: s.leather@ic.ac.uk W: www.ffhs.org.uk/members/leather.htm

Lin(d)field One Name Group Southview, Maplehurst, Horsham, West Sussex RH13 6QY T: 01403-864389 E: lindfield@one-name.org W: www.lindfield.force9.co.uk/long

Mackman FHS Chawton Cottage, 22a Long Ridge Lane, Nether Poppleton, York YO26 6LX T: +44 (0)1904 781752 E: mackman@one-name.org

Marsden One Name Study W: www.marsden-ons.co.uk

Mayhew Ancestry Research 28 Windmill Road, West Croydon, Surrey CR0 2XN

Metcalfe Society 22 Webster Crescent, Kimberworth, Rotherham, South Yorkshire S61 2BP T: 01709 561 011 E: treasurer@metcalfe.org.uk W: www.metcalfe.org.uk

Morbey Family History Group 23 Cowper Crescent, Bengeo, Hertford, Hertfordshire SG14 3DZ

Morgan Society of England & Wales Elmcote, Chepstow Road, Raglan, NP15 2EN W: www.moxonsociety.org

Mower Family History Association 615 County Road 123, Bedford, Wyoming 83112 E: jmower@silverstar.com W: www.mowerfamily.org

Moxon Family Research Trust 1 Pine Tree Close, Cowes, Isle of Wight PO31 8DX T: 01983 296921 E: enquiries@moxonsociety.org W: www.moxonsociety.org.uk

Offley Family Society 39 Windmill Fields, Old Harlow, Hertfordshire CM17 0LQ T: 01438-820006 E: offleyfamilysociety@ntlworld.com W: www.offleysociety.co.uk

P*rr*tt FHS 48 Prospect Drive, Matlock, Derbyshire DE4 3TA E: webmaster@p-rr-tt.org.uk W: www.p-rr-tt.org.uk

Palgrave Society Crossfield House, Dale Road, Stanton, Bury St Edmunds, Suffolk IP31 2DY T: 01359-251050 E: palgrave@one-name.org W: www.ffhs.org.uk/members/palgrave.htm

Penty Family Name Society Kymbelin, 30 Lych Way, Horsell Village, Surrey GU21 4QG T: 01483-764904 E: pentytree@aol.com

Percy-Piercy FHS 32 Ravensdale Avenue, North Finchley, London, N12 9HT T: 020 8446 0592 E: brian.piercy@which.net

Plant Family History Group 57 Helston Close, Brookvale, Runcorn, Wirral WA7 6AA T: 01928 751 802 E: Johnson19642009@live.co.uk W: www.plant-fhg.org.uk

Polperro FHS The Crown House, Clifton on Teme, Worcestershire WR6 6EN E: jeremy.johns@polperro.org W: www.heritagepress.polperro.org/famhist.html

Rix Family Alliance 4 Acklam Close, Hedon, Hull, HU12 8NA E:

susie.rix@virgin.net W: www.rix-alliance.co.uk
Serman, Surman FHS 24 Monks Walk, Bridge Street, Evesham, WR11 4SL T: 01386 49967 E: design@johnsermon.demon.co.uk W: www.msurman.freeserve.co.uk
Silverthorne Family Association 1 Cambridge Close, Swindon, Wiltshire SN3 1JQ T: 01793 537103
Society of Cornishes 1 Maple Close, Tavistock, Devon PL19 9LL T: 01822 614613 E: cornish@one-name.org W: www.cornishsurname.mathewcornish.html
Sole Society 34 Hemwood Road, Windsor, Berkshire SL4 4YU T: 01753 675 009 E: info@sole.org.uk W: www.sole.org.uk
Spencer Family 1303 Azalea Lane, Dekalb, Illinois 60115
Stendall & Variants One Name Study PO Box 6417, Sutton in Ashfield, Nottinghamshire NG17 3LE T: 01623 406870 E: stendall@historians.co.uk W: www.genealogy-links.co.uk
Stockdill FHS 6 First Avenue, Garston, Watford, Hertfordshire WD2 6PZ T: 01923-675292 E: roy.stockdill@btinternet.com W: www.stockdillfhs.org.uk
Stockton Society The Leas, 28 North Road, Builth Wells, Powys LD2 3BU T: 01982 551667 E: cestrienne@aol.com W: www.stocktonsociety.com
Stonehewer to Stanier Society The Shires, 71 Knutsford Road, Row of Trees, Alderley Edge, Cheshire SK9 7SH E: stonehewer@one-

name.org W: http://freepages.genealogy.rootsweb.com~stanier/
Swinnerton Family Society 23 Catherine Road, Heath Park, Romford, Essex RM2 5SA T: (020) 8458-3443 E: ianswinnerton@gmail.com W: www.swinnerton.org/
Talbot Research Organisation 142 Albemarle Avenue, Elson, Gosport., Hampshire PO12 4HY T: 023 92589785 E: mjh.talbot142@btinternet.com W: www.kiamara.demon.co.uk/index.html
The Halsted Trust Box H, 14 Charterhouse Buildings, Goswell Road, London, EC1M 7BA E: secretary@halsted.org.uk
The Johns Family History Association E: JOHNS-L@rootsweb.com W: http://freepages.genealogy.rootsweb.com/~johns/njfrg
The UK FHS of Martin 63 Higher Coombe Drive, Teignmouth, Devon TQ14 9NL W: www.fhsofmartin.org.uk
Toseland Clan Society 40 Moresdale Lane, Seacroft, Leeds, West Yorkshire LS14 5SY
Tyrrell FHS 16 The Crescent, Solihull, West Midlands B91 7PE W: www.tyrrellfhs.org.uk
Watkins FHS PO Box 1698, Douglas, Georgia 31534-1698 W: www.watkins-fhs.org
Witheridge FHS Cherry Trees, Ingleden Park Road, Tenterden, Kent TN30 6NS E: witheridge1987@aol.com W: www.witheridgefhs.com

Australia
Australasian Federation of Family History Organisations Inc PO Box 3012, Weston Creek ACT 2611 E: secretary@affho.org W: www.affho.org
Genealogical Society of Victoria Level B1, 257 Collins Street, Melbourne 3000, Victoria T: +61 03 9662 4455 E: gsv@gsv.org.au W: www.gsv.org.au
Society of Australian Genealogists Richmond Villa, 120 Kent Street, Observatory Hill, Sydney 2000 NSW T: 61-02-92473953 E: info@sag.org.au W: www.sag.org.au
Australian Institute of Genealogical Studies PO Box 339, Blackburn, Victoria 3130 W: www.aigs.org.au
Capital Territory
The Heraldry & Genealogy Society of Canberra Inc GPO Box 585, Canberra, ACT 2601 T: 02 6282 9356E: hagsoc@hagsoc.org.au W: www.hagsoc.org.au
New South Wales
1788-1820 Pioneer Association PO Box 57, Croydon NSW 2132 T: (02) 9797 8107
Australian Society of the Lace Makers of Calais Inc PO Box 1277, Queanbeyan NSW 2620 T: 02 6297 2168 E: gillkell@tpg.com.auW: www.angelfire.com/al/aslc/
Bega Valley Genealogical Society Inc PO Box 19, Pambula NSW 2549 E: see website W: www.thebegavalley.org.au/bvgenealogy.0.html
Berrima District Historical & FHS Inc PO Box 131, Mittagong NSW 2575 T: 02 4872 2169 E: bdhsarchives@acenet.com.au W: www.berrimadistricthistoricalsociety.org.au
Blayney Shire Local & FHS Group Inc The Library, 48 Adelaide Street, Blayney NSW 2799 W: www.geocities.com/blayneyhistory/
Blue Mountains FHS PO Box 97, Springwood NSW NSW 2777 E: xploretree@yahoo.com.au W: www.rootsweb.ancestry.com/~nswbmfhs/
Botany Bay FHS Inc PO Box 1006, Sutherland NSW 1499 E: botanybayfhs@yahoo.co.au W: www.bbfhs.org.au
Broken Hill Family History Group PO Box 779, 75 Pell Street, Broken Hill NSW 2880 T: 08-80-881321 E: jjjcam@tadaust.org.au
Burwood Drummoyne & District FH Group Burwood Central Library, 4 Marmaduke Street, Burwood NSW 2134 T: 02 9744 9131
Cape Banks FHS PO Box 67, Maroubra NSW NSW 2035 E: mmorsch@bigpond.net.au W: www.capebanks.org.au
Casino & District Family History Group Inc PO Box 586, Casino NSW 2470 W: www.rootsweb.com/~auscdhs
Central Coast FHS Inc PO Box 4090, East Gosford NSW 2250 W: www.centralcoastfhs.org.au
Coffs Harbour Dist FHS Inc PO Box 2057, Coffs Harbour NSW 2450
Cowra FHG Inc PO Box 495, Cowra NSW 2794 W: www.cfhg.org.au
Deniliquin Family History Group Inc PO Box 144, Multi Arts Hall, Cressy Street, Deniliquin NSW 2710 T: 03 5881 3980 W: http://bordernet.com.au/~denifhd
Dubbo & District FHS Inc PO Box 868, Dubbo NSW 2830 T: 068-818635 E: ddfhs_2000@yahoo.com.au W: au.geocities.com/ddfhs_2000/
Fellowship of First Fleeters First Fleet House, 105 Cathedral Street, Woolloomooloo NSW 2000 T: 02 9360 3788 E: fffaus@optusnet.com.au W: www.geocities.com/fellowship_of_first_fleeters/
Forbes FHy Group Inc PO Box 574, Forbes NSW 2871 T: 02 6853 1139
Goulburn District Family History Society Inc PO Box 611, Goulburn NSW 2580
Griffith Genealogical & Historical Society Inc PO Box 270, Griffith NSW 2680 T: 02 6962 1650 W: http://suers.dragnet.com.au/~ggahs
GwydirFHS Inc PO Box EM61, East Moree NSW 2400 T: 02 6754 0254
Hastings Valley Family History Group Inc PO Box 1359, Port Macquarie NSW 2444
Hawkesbury FHG C/o Hawkesbury City Council Library, Dight Street, Windsor NSW 2756 W: www.hawkesbury.net.au/community/hfhg/

Hill End Family History Group Sarnia, Hill End NSW 2850 W: www.hillendfamilyhistory.com/index.php
Hornsbury Kuring-Gai FHS Inc PO Box 680, Hornsby NSW 2074
Illawarra Family History Group The Secretary, PO Box 1652, South Coast Mail Centre, Wollongong NSW 2521 T: (02)-42622212 E: researchifhg@gmail.com W: www.rootsweb.com/~ausifhg
Inverell District FHG Inc PO Box 367, Inverell NSW 2360 W: http://users.northnet.com.au/~familyhistory/
Ku-Ring-Gai Historical Society PO Box 109, Gordon NSW 2072 W: www.khs.org.au
Leeton FHS PO Box 475, Centre Point, Pine Avenue, Leeton NSW 2705 T: 02 6955 7199
Lithgow & District FHS PO Box 516, Lithgow NSW 2790 E: ldfhs@lisp.com.au W: www.lisp.com.au/~ldfhs/
Little Forest Family History Research Group PO Box 87, 192 Little Forest Road, Milton NSW 2538 T: 02 4455 4780 W: www.shoalhaven.net.au/~cathyd/groups.html
Liverpool & District FHS PO Box 830, Liverpool NSW 2170
Maitland FH Circle Inc PO Box 247, Maitland NSW 2320 W: www.rootsweb.com/~ausmfhc
Manning Wallamba FHS Greater Taree City Library, Pulteney Street, Taree NSW 2430 W: www.manningwallambafhs.com.au/index.htm
Milton Ulladulla Genealogical Soc Inc PO Box 619, Ulladulla NSW 2539 T: 02 4455 4206 W: http://au.geocities.com/miltonulladullagenies/
Moruya & District Historical Society PO Box 259, Moruya NSW 2537 W: www.sci.net.au/userpages/mgrogan/mhs/
Nepean FHS PO Box 81, Emu Plains NSW 2750 T: (02)-47-353-798 E: secretary@nepeanfhs.org.au W: www.nepeanfhs.org.au
Newcastle FHS PO Box 233, Lambton NSW 2299 E: nfhsinc@gmail.com W: www.nfhs.org.au/
NSW & ACT Association of Family History Societies PO Box 4328, Winmalee NSW 2777 T: +61 2 4754 1544 E: nswact@gmail.com or jank@eftel.com.au W: www.nswactfhs.org/
Orange FHS PO Box 35, Orange NSW 2800 E: familyhistory@orange.nsw.gov.au W: www.ofhg.org.au/
Port Stephens-Tilligerry & Districts FHS PO Box 32, Tanilba Bay NSW 2319 W: www.portstephensfamilyhistory.com.au/
Richmond River Historical Society Inc PO Box 467, 165 Molesworth Street, Lismore NSW 2480 T: 02 6621 9993
Richmond-Tweed FHS PO Box 817, Ballina NSW 2478 E: kerriea@aapt.net.au W: www.rtfhs.org.au

Ryde District Historical Society Inc Willdra, 770 Victoria Road, Ryde NSW 2112 T: 02 9807 7137 W: www.rydehistory.org
Scone & Upper Hunter Historical Society Inc PO Box 339, Kingdon Street, Upper Hunter, Scone NSW 2337 T: 02-654-51218
Shoalhaven FHS Inc PO Box 591, Nowra NSW 2541 T: 0432 474 912 E: sfhssecretary@shoalhaven.net.au W: www.shoalhaven.net.au/~sfhs
Singleton FHS Inc PO Box 422, Singleton NSW 2330 W: www.xroyvision.com.au/singleton/sfhspage.htm
Snowy Mountains FH Group PO Box 153, Cooma NSW 2630
Tweed Gold Coast FH & HA Inc PO Box 2729, Tweed Heads South NSW 2486 W: www.tweedgoldcoastfamilyhistoryheritageassociation.bravehost.com/
Wagga Wagga & District FHS Inc PO Box 307, Wagga Wagga NSW 2650 E: rivtron@bigpond.com W: www.waggafamilyhistory.org.au
Wingham FHG PO Box 72, Wingham NSW 2429
Young & District FHG Inc PO Box 586, Young NSW 2594
Northern Territory
Genealogical Society of the Northern Territory PO Box 37212, Winnellie, Northern Territory 0821 T: 08-898-17363 W: http://members.iinet.net.au/~genient/

Queensland

Beaudesert Branch, Genealogical Society of Queensland Inc PO Box 664, Beaudesert, Queensland 4285

Bundaberg Genealogical Association Inc PO Box 103, Bundaberg, Queensland 4670

Burdekin Contact Group Family Hist Assn of N Qld Inc PO Box 393, Home Hill, Queensland 4806

Caboolture FH Research Group Inc PO Box 837, Caboolture, Queensland 4510 E: cfhrg@mail.cth.com.au cfhrg@yahoo.com.au W: http://.cfhrg.tripod.com

Cairns & DistrictFHS Inc PO Box 5069, Cairns, Queensland 4870 T: 07-40537113 E: info@cdfhs.org W: www.cdfhs.org

Central Queensland Family History Inc PO Box 171, Indooroopilly, Queensland 4068 E: secretary@qfhs.org.au W: www.qfhs.org.au

Charters Towers & Dalrymple FH Association Inc PO Box 783, 54 Towers Street, Charters Towers, Queensland 4820 T: 07-4787-2124

Cooroy Noosa Genealogical & Historical Research Group Inc PO Box 792, Cooroy, Queensland 4563 E: info@genealogy-noosa.org.au W: www.genealogy-noosa.org.au

Dalby FHS inc PO Box 962, Dalby, Queensland 4405

Darling Downs FHS PO Box 2229, Toowoomba, Queensland 4350

Genealogical Society of Queensland Inc PO Box 8423, Woolloongabba, Queensland 4102 E: gsq@gsq.org.au W: www.gsq.org.au

Gladstone Branch G.S.Q. PO Box 1778, Gladstone, Queensland 4680

Gold Coast FHS Inc PO Box 2763, Southport, Queensland 4215 E: info@goldcoastfhs.org.au W: www.goldcoastfhs.org.au

Goondiwindi & District FHS PO Box 190, Goondiwindi, Queensland 4390 T: 746712156

Gympie Ancestral Research Society Inc PO Box 767, Gympie, Queensland 4570

Ipswich Genealogical Society Inc. PO Box 323, 1st Floor, Ipswich Campus Tafe, cnr. Limestone & Ellenborough Streets, Ipswich, Queensland 4304 T: (07)-3201-8770

Kingaroy Family History Centre PO Box 629, James Street, Kingaroy, Queensland 4610

Mackay Branch Genealogical Society of Queensland Inc PO Box 882, Mackay, Queensland 4740 T: (07)-49426266

Maryborough District FHS PO Box 408, Maryborough, Queensland 4650 E: mdfhs@satcom.net.au W: www.satcom.net.au/mdfhs

Mount Isa FHS Inc PO Box 1832, Mount Isa, Queensland 4825

North Brisbane Branch - Genealogical Society of Queensland Inc PO Box 353, Chermside South, Queensland 4032

Queensland FHS Inc PO Box 171, Indooroophilly, Queensland 4068 E: info@qfhs.org.au W: www.qfhs.org.au

Rockhampton Genealogical Society of Queensland Inc PO Box 992, Rockhampton, Queensland 4700

Roma & District Local & FHS PO Box 877, Roma, Queensland 4455

South Burnett Genealogical & FHS PO Box 598, Kingaroy, Qld 4610

Southern Suburbs Branch - G.S.Q. Inc PO Box 844, Mount Gravatt, Queensland 4122

Sunshine Coast Historical & Genealogical Resource Centre Inc PO Box 1051, Nambour, Queensland 4560

Toowoomba Family History Centre c/o South Town Post Office, South Street, Toowoomba, Queensland 4350 T: 0746-355895

Townsville - Family History Association of North Queensland Inc PO Box 6120, Townsville M.C., Queensland 4810

Whitsunday Branch - Genealogical Society Queensland Inc PO Box 15, Prosperpine, Queensland 4800

South Australia

Fleurieu Peninsula FH Group Inc PO Box 1078, Christies Beach North, South Australia 5165 W: www.rootsweb.com/~safpfhg

South Australian Genealogical & Heraldic Society GPO Box 592, Adelaide 5001, South Australia T: (08)-8272-4222 W: www.saghs.org.au

South East FHG Inc PO Box 758, Millicent, South Australia 5280

Southern Eyre Peninsula FHG 26 Cranston Street, Port Lincoln, South Australia 5606

Whyalla FHG PO Box 2190, Whyalla Norrie, South Australia 5608

Yorke Peninsula Family History Group - 1st Branch SAGHS PO Box 260, Kadina, South Australia 5554

Tasmania

Tasmanian FHS Inc PO Box 191, Launceston, Tasmania 7250 T: 03 6344 4034 E: secretary@tasfhs.org W: www.tasfhs.org

Tasmanian FHS Inc PO Box 191, Launceston, Tasmania 7250 E: secretary@tasfhs.org W: www.tasfhs.org

Victoria

Benalla & District FH Group Inc PO Box 268, St Andrews Church Hall, Church Street, Benalla, Victoria 3672 T: (03)-57-644258

Cobram Genealogical Group PO Box 75, Cobram, Victoria 3643

East Gippsland FH Group Inc PO Box 1104, Bairnsdale, Victoria 3875

Echuca/Moama FHG Inc PO Box 707, Echuca, Victoria 3564

Emerald Genealogy Group 62 Monbulk Road, Emerald, Victoria 3782

Euroa Genealogical Group 43 Anderson Street, Euroa, Victoria 3666

Geelong Family History Group Inc PO Box 1187, Geelong, Victoria 3220 W: www.home.vicnet.net.au/wgfamhist/index.htm

Genealogical Society of Victoria Level B1, 257 Collins Street, Melbourne 3000, Victoria T: +61 03 9662 4455 E: gsv@gsv.org.au W: www.gsv.org.au

Hamilton Family & Local History Group PO Box 816, Hamilton, Victoria 3300 T: 61-3-55-724933 W: www.freenet.com.au/hamilton

Kerang & District Family History Group PO Box 325, Kerang, Victoria 3579

Mid Gippsland FHS Inc PO Box 767, Morwell, Victoria 3840

Mildura & District Genealogical Society Inc PO Box 2895, Mildura, Victoria 3502

Mornington Peninsula FHS 16 Tavisstock Road, Frankston South, Victoria 3199 T: 61 3 9783 8773 W: www.mpfhs.org

Narre Warren & District FHG PO Box 149, Narre Warren, Victoria 3805 E: president@nwfhg.org.au W: http://home.vicnet.net.au/~nwfhg/

Nathalia Genealogical Group Inc R.M.B. 1003, Picola, Victoria 3639

Sale & District FHG Inc PO Box 773, Sale, Victoria 3850

Stawell Biarri Group for Genealogy Inc PO Box 417, Stawell, Victoria 3380

Swam Hill Genealogical & Historical Society Inc PO Box 1232, Swan Hill, Victoria 3585

The Port Fairy Genealogical Society of Victoria Inc PO Box 253 or 84 Bank Street, Port Fairy, Victoria 3284 E: portfairygenealogy@westvic.com.au W: http://www.rootsweb.ancestry.com/~auspfgs/index.html

Toora & District FHG Inc PO Box 41, Toora, Victoria 3962

Wangaratta Gen Soc Inc PO Box 683, Wangaratta, Victoria 3676

West Gippsland Gen Soc Inc PO Box 225, Old Shire Hall, Queen Street, Warragul, Victoria 3820 T: 03 5623 2612 W: www.vicnet.net.au/~wggs

Wimmera Assoc for Genealogy PO Box 880, Horsham, Victoria 3402

Wodonga FHS Inc PO Box 289, Wodonga, Victoria 3689

Yarram Genealogical Group Inc PO Box 42, 161 Commercial Road, Yarram, Victoria 3971

Western Australia

Australasian Federation of FH Organisations Inc PO Box 3012, Weston Creek, ACT 2611 E: secretary@affho.org W: www.affho.org

Australasian Federation of FH Orgs Inc 6/48 May Street, Bayswater, Western Australia 6053 W: www.affho.org

Geraldton FHS PO Box 2502, Geralton 6531, Western Australia

Goldfields Branch, West Australian Genealogical Society Inc PO Box 1462, Kalgoorlie, Western Australia 6430

Melville Family History Centre PO Box 108 (Rear of Church of Jesus Christ Latter Day Saints, 308 Preston Point Road, Attadale, Melville, Western Australia 6156

Western Australia Genealogical Society 6/48 May Street, Bayswater, Western Australia 6053 E: see website W: www.wags.org.au/

New Zealand

Bishopdale Branch, NZ Society of Genealogists Inc. c/o 19a Resolution Place, Christchurch, 8005 T: 03 351 0625

Cromwell Family History Group 3 Porcell Court, Cromwell, 9191

Fairlie Genealogy Group c/o 38 Gray Street, Fairlie , 8771

General Research Institute of New Zealand PO Box 12531, Thorndon, Wellington, 6038

Hawkes Bay Branch, NZ Society of Genealogists Inc. P O Box 7375, Taradale, Hawkes Bay,

Kapiti Branch, NZ Society of Genealogists Inc. P O Box 6, Paraparaumu, Kapiti Coast, 6450

Mercury Bay Branch, NZ Society of Genealogists Inc. 31 Catherine Cres., Whitianga, 2856 T: 0 7 866 2355

Morrinsville Branch, NZ Society of Genealogists Inc. 1 David St., Morrinsville, 2251

N.Z. Fencible Soc P O Box 8415, Symonds Street, Auckland, 1003

New Zealand FHS Inc, PO Box 13301, Armagh, New Zealand

New Zealand Society of Genealogists, P O Box 14036, Panmure, 1741 NZ T: 09 570 4248 E: exec.officer@genealogy.org.nz W: www.genealogy.org.nz

Northern Wairoa Branch, NZ Society of Genealogists Inc. 60 Gordon Street, Dargaville, 300

NZ Society of Genealogists Inc. - Alexandra Branch 21 Gregg Street, Alexandra, 9181

Palmerston North Genealogy Group PO Box 1992, Palmerston North, 5301

Panmure Branch, NZ Society of Genealogists Inc. 29 Mirrabooka Ave, Howick, Auckland, 1705

Papakura Branch, NZ Society of Genealogists Inc. P O Box 993, Papakura, Auckland,

Polish Genealogical Society of New Zealand Box 88, Urenui, Taranaki, T: 06 754 4551

Rotorua Branch, NZ Society of Genealogists Inc. 17 Sophia Street, Rotorua, 3201 T: 0 7 347 9122

Scottish Interest Group, NZ Society of Genealogists Inc. P O Box 8164, Symonds Street, Auckland, 1003

South Canterbury Branch, NZ Society of Genealogists Inc. 9 Burnett Street, Timaru, 8601

Tairua Branch, NZ Society of Genealogists Inc. c/o 10 Pepe Road, Tairua, 2853

Te Awamutu Branch, NZ Society of Genealogists Inc. Hairini, RD1, Te Awamutu, 2400

Te Puke Branch, NZ Society of Genealogists Inc. 20 Valley Road, Te Puke, 3071

The New Zealand FHS P O Box13,30, Armagh, Christchurch, T: 03 352 4506 E: ranz@xtra.co.nz

Waimate Branch, NZ Society of Genealogists Inc. 4 Saul Shrives Place, Waimate, 8791

Wairarapa Branch, NZ Society of Genealogists Inc. 34 Rugby Street, Masterton, 5901

Whakatane Branch, NZ Society of Genealogists Inc. P O Box 203, Whakatane, 3080

Whangamata Genealogy Group 116 Hetherington Road, Whangamata, 3062

Whangarei Branch, NZ Society of Genealogists Inc. P O Box 758, Whangarei, 115 T: 09 434 6508

South Africa

Genealogical Institute of South Africa, PO Box 3033, Matieland, Western Cape, 7602, South Africa, 021 887 5070 E: leon@gisa.org.za E: gisa@sun.ac.za W: www.gisa.org.za

Genological Society of South Africa Suite 143, Postnet X2600, Houghton, 2041

Human Sciences Research Council, Genealogy Information, HSRC Library & Information Service, Private Bag X41, South Africa T: (012)-302-2636

West Rand FHS The Secretary, PO Box 760, Florida 1710, W: www.geocities.com/Heartland/8256/westrand.html

Zimbabwe

Heraldry & Genealogy Society of Zimbabwe Harare Branch, 8 Renfrew Road, Eastlea, Harare

Canada

Alberta

Alberta Family Histories Society 712-16 Avenue NW, Station B, Calgary, Alberta T2M 0J8 E: afhs@afhs.ab.ca W: www.afhs.ab.ca

Alberta Gen Soc # 116, 10440-108 Avenue, Edmonton, T5H 3Z9 T: (403)-424-4429 E: abgensoc@compusmart.ab.ca W: www.abgensoc.ca/

Alberta Gen Soc Drayton Valley Branch PO Box 115, Rocky Rapids, Alberta T0E 1Z0 T: 403 542 2787 W: www.abgensoc.ca/

Alberta Gen Soc Fort McMurray Branch PO Box 6253, Fort McMurray, Alberta T9H 4W1 W: www.abgensoc.ca/

Alberta Gen Soc Grande Prairie & District Branch PO Box 1257, Grande Prairie, Alberta T8V 4Z1

Alberta Gen Soc Medicine Hat & District Branch PO Box 971, Medicine Hat, Alberta T1A 7G8 W: www.abgensoc.ca/

Alberta Gen Soc Red Deer & District Branch PO Box 922, Red Deer, Alberta T4N 5H3 W: www.abgensoc.ca/

Brooks & District Branch, Alberta Gen Soc PO Box 1538, Brooks, Alberta T1R 1C4 E: abgensoc@compusmart.ab.ca W: www.abgensoc.ca/

Ukrainian Genealogical & Historical Society of Canada R.R.2, Cochrane, Alberta T0L 0W0 T: (403) 932 6811

British Columbia

British Columbia Gen Soc PO Box 88054, Lansdowne, Richmond, British Columbia V6X 3T6 E: bcgs@bcgs.ca W: www.bcgs.ca

Campbell River Genealogy Society PO Box 884, Campbell River, V9W 6Y4 T: 250 286 8042 W: www.rootsweb.ancestry.com/~bccrgc/

Comox Valley Family History Research Group c/o Courtenay & District Museum & Archives, 360 Cliffe Street, Courtenay, British Columbia V9N 2H9 W: www.cvfamilyhistory.org/

Kamloops Family History Society Box 1162, Kamloops, British Columbia V2C 6H3 W: www.kfhs.org

Kelowna & District Gen Soc PO Box 501, Station A, Kelowna V1Y 7P1 T: 1-250-763-7159 W: www.rootsweb.ancestry.com/~bckdgs/

Nanaimo FHS PO Box 1027, Nanaimo, British Columbia V9R 5Z2 W: http://members.shaw.ca/nfhs/

Port Alberni Genealogy Club 3551, 16th Avenue, Port Alberni, V9Y 5C9 E: cmunsil@shaw.ca mmunsil@sd70.bc.ca

Powell River Genealogy Club 6792 Cranberry Street, Powell River, British Columbia V8A 3Z4 W: www.rootsweb.ancestry.com/~bcprgg/

Prince George Gen Soc PO Box 1056, Prince George, V2L 4V2 W: http://members.tripod.com/pg_genealogy_society/welcome.html

Revelstoke Genealogy Group PO Box 2613, Revelstoke, British Columbia V0E 2S0 E: flange7013@aol.com

Shuswap Lake Genealogical Society PO Box 754, Chase, British Columbia V0E 1M0 E: tish@cablelan.net

South Okanagan Genealogical Society c/o Museum, 785 Main Street, Penticton, British Columbia V2A 5E3 E: sogs@shaw.ca

Vernon & District FHS PO Box 1447, Vernon, British Columbia V1T 6N7 E: verfamhist@shaw.ca W: www.vdfhs.com/

Victoria Genealogical Society PO Box 43021, Victoria North PO, Victoria V8X 3G2 E: vgs@victoriags.org W: www.victoriags.org

Manitoba

Canadian Federation of Genealogical & Family History Societies 227 Parkville Bay, Winnipeg, Manitoba R2M 2J6 W: www.geocities.com/athens/troy/2274/index.html

East European Gen Soc PO Box 2536, Winnipeg, Manitoba R3C 4A7

La Societe Historique de Saint Boniface 220 Ave de la Cathedral, Saint Boniface, Manitoba R2H 0H7

Manitoba Gen Soc Unit A, 1045 St James Street, Winnipeg, Manitoba R3H 1B1

South West Branch of Manitoba Genealogical Society 53 Almond Crescent, Brandon, Manitoba R7B 1A2 T: 204-728-2857

Winnipeg Branch of Manitoba Genealogical Society PO Box 1244, Winnipeg, Manitoba R3C 2Y4

New Brunswick

Centre d'Etudes Acadiennes Universite de Moncton, Moncton, New Brunswick E1A 3E9

New Brunswick Genealogical Society PO Box 3235, Station B, Fredericton, New Brunswick E3A 5G9

Newfoundland

Newfoundland & Labrador Genealogical Society Colonial Building, Military Road, St John's, Newfoundland A1C 2C9 W: www3.nf.sympatico.ca/nlgs

Nova Scotia

Archelaus Smith Historical Society PO Box 291, Clarks Harbour, Nova Scotia B0W 1P0

Cape Breton Gen Soc PO Box 53, Sydney, Nova Scotia B1P 6G9

Genealogical Association of Nova Scotia PO Box 641, Station Central, Halifax, Nova Scotia B3J 2T3

Queens County Historical Society PO Box 1078, Liverpool, Nova Scotia B0T 1K0

Shelburne County Gen Soc PO Box 248 Town Hall, 168 Water Street, Shelburne, Nova Scotia B0T 1W0

Ontario

British Isles FHS of Greater Ottawa Box 38026, Ottawa, Ontario K2C 3Y7 E: recsec@bifhsgo.ca W: www.bifhsgo.ca

Bruce & Grey Branch - Ontario Gen Soc PO Box 66, Owen Sound N4K 5P1

Bruce County Gen Soc PO Box 1083, Port Elgin, Ontario N0H 2C0

Elgin County Branch Ontario Gen Soc PO Box 20060, St Thomas, Ontario N5P 4H4

Essex County Branch Ontario Gen Soc PO Box 2, Station A, Windsor, Ontario N9A 6J5

Haliburton Highlands Genealogy Group Box 834, Minden, Ontario K0M 2K0 T: (705) 286-3154

Halton-Peel Branch Ontario Genealogical Society PO Box 24, Streetsville, Ontario L5M 2B7 W: www.halinet.on.ca

Hamilton Branch Ontario Genealogical Society PO Box 904, LCD 1, Hamilton, Ontario L8N 3P6

Huron County Branch Ontario Genealogical Society PO Box 469, Goderich, Ontario N7A 4C7

Jewish Genealogical Society of Canada PO Box 446, Station A, Willowdale, Ontario M2N 5T1

Jewish Gen Soc of Canada (Toronto) PO Box 91006, 2901 Bayview Avenue, Toronto, Ontario M2K 2Y6 W: www.jgstoronto.ca

Kawartha Branch Ontario Genealogical Society PO Box 861, Peterborough, Ontario K9J 7AZ

Kent County Branch Ontario Genealogical Society PO Box 964, Chatham, Ontario N7M 5L3

Kingston Branch, Ontario Genealogical Society PO Box 1394, Kingston, Ontario K7L 5C6

Lambton County Branch Ontario Genealogical Society PO Box 2857, Sarnia, Ontario N7T 7W1

Lanark County Genealogical Society PO Box 512, Perth, Ontario K7H 3K4 W: www.globalgenealogy.com/LCGs

Marilyn Adams Genealogical Research Centre PO Box 35, Ameliasburgh, Ontario K0K 1A0 T: 613-967-6291

Niagara Peninsula Branch Ontario Genealogical Society PO Box 2224, St Catharines, Ontario L2R 7R8

Nipissing District Branch Ontario Genealogical Society PO Box 93, North Bay, Ontario P1B 8G8

Nor-West Genealogy & History Society PO Box 35, Vermilion Bay, Ontario P0V 2V0 T: 807-227-5293

Norfolk County Branch Ontario Genealogical Society PO Box 145, Delhi, Ontario N4B 2W9

Norwich & District Historical Society c/o Archives, R.R. #3, Norwich, Ontario N0J 1P0 T: (519)-863-3638

Ontario Gen Soc Suite 102, 40 Orchard View Boulevard, Toronto, Ontario M4R 1B9 T: 416-489-0734 W: www.ogs.on.ca

Ontario Genealogical Society (Toronto Branch) Box 518, Station K, Toronto, Ontario M4P 2G9 W: www.torontofamilyhistory.org

Ottawa Branch Ontario Genealogical Society PO Box 8346, Ottawa, Ontario K1G 3H8

Perth County Branch Ontario Genealogical Society PO Box 9, Stratford, Ontario N5A 6S8 T: 519-273-0399

Simcoe County Branch Ontario Genealogical Society PO Box 892, Barrie, Ontario L4M 4Y6

Sioux Lookout Gen Club PO Box 1561, Sioux Lookout Ont P8T 1C3

Societe Franco-Ontarienne D'Histoire et de Genealogie C.P.720, succursale B, Ottawa, Ontario K1P 5P8

Stormont, Dundas & Glengarry Genealogical Society PO Box 1522, Cornwall, Ontario K6H 5V5

Sudbury District Branch Ontario Gen Soc c/o Sudbury Public Library, 74 MacKenzie Street, Sudbury P3C 4X8 T: (705)-674-9991

Thunder Bay District Branch Ontario Genealogical Society PO Box 10373, Thunder Bay, Ontario P7B 6T8

Upper Ottawa Gen Group PO Box 972, Pembroke Ont K8A 7M5

Waterdown East Flamborough Heritage Society PO Box 1044,

Waterdown, Ontario L0R 2H0 T: 905-689-4074
Waterloo-Wellington Branch Ontario Genealogical Society 153 Frederick Street, Ste 102, Kitchener, Ontario N2H 2M2 W: www.dos.iwaterloo.ca/~marj/genealogy/ww.html
West Elgin Genealogical & Historical Society 22552 Talbot Line, R.R.#3, Rodney, Ontario N0L 2C0
Whitby - Oshawa Branch Ontario Genealogical Society PO Box 174, Whitby, Ontario L1N 5S1
Quebec
Brome County Historical Society PO Box 690, 130 Lakeside, Knowlton, Quebec J0E 1V0 T: 450-243-6782
Federation Quebecoise des Societies de Genealogie C.P. 9454, Sainte Foy, Quebec G1V 4B8 W: www.federationgenealogie.qc.ca/
Les Patriotes Inc 105 Prince, Sorel, Quebec J3P 4J9
Missisquoi Historical Society PO Box 186, Stanbridge East, Quebec J0J 2H0 T: (450)-248-3153
Quebec Family History Society PO Box 1026, Postal Station, Pointe Claire, Quebec H9S 4H9 E: admin@qfhs.ca W: www.qfhs.ca
Societ de Genealogie de la Maurice et des Bois Francs C.P. 901, Trois Rivieres, Quebec G9A 5K2
Societe d'Histoire d'Amos 222 1ere Avenue Est, Amos, Quebec J9T 1H3
Societe d'Histoire et d'Archeologie des Monts C.P. 1192, 675 Chemin du Roy, Sainte Anne des Monts, Quebec G0E 2G0
Societe d'Histoire et de Genealogie de Matane 145 Soucy, Matane, Quebec G4W 2E1
Societe d'Histoire et de Genealogie de Riviere du Loup 300 rue St Pierre, Riviere du Loup, Quebec G5R 3V3 T: (418)-867-4245 W: www.icrdl.net/shgrd/index.html
Societe d'Histoire et de Genealogie de Verdun 198 chemin de lÕAnce, Vaudreuil, Quebec J7V 8P3
Societe d'histoire et de genealogie du Centre-du-Quebec 34-A rue Laurier est, Victoriaville, Quebec G6P 6P7 T: (819)-357-4029 W: www.genealogie.org/
Societe d'Histoire et de Genealogie Maria Chapdeleine 1024 Place des Copains, C.P. 201,

Europe
Austria
Heraldisch-Genealogische Gesellschaft 'Adler'
Universitatsstrasse 6, Wien, A-1096, Austria
Belgium
Cercle de Genealogie Juive de Belgique, 21 Rue des Minimes, B-1000, Belgium,T: 32 0 2 512 19 63
Federation des Associations de Famille
Bruyeres Marion 10, Biez, B-1390, Belgium
Federation Genealogique et Heraldique de Belgique
Avenue Parmentier 117, Bruxelles, B-1150, Belgium
Office Genealogique et Heraldique de Belgique
Avenue C Thielemans 93, Brussels, B-1150, Belgium
Croatia
Croatian Genealogical Society
2527 San Carlos Ave, San Carlos, CA, 94070, USA
Czech Republic
Czechoslovak Genealogical Society International PO Box 16225, St Paul, MN, 55116-0225, USA E: info@cgsi.org W: www.cgsi.org
Denmark
Danish Soc. for Local History
Colbjornsensvej 8, Naerum, DK-2850, Denmark
Sammenslutningen af Slaegtshistoriske Foreninger
Klostermarker 13, Aalborg, DK-9000
Society for Danish Genealogy & Biography Grysgardsvej 2, Copenhagen NV, DK-2400, Denmark W: www.genealogi.dk
Estonia
Estonia Genealogical Society
Sopruse puiestec 214-88, Tallin, EE-0034, Estland
Finland
Genealogiska Samfundet i Finland
Fredsgatan 15 B, Helsingfors, SF-00170, Finland
Helsingfors Slaktforskare R.F.
Dragonvagen 10, Helsingfors, FIN-00330, Finland
France
Amicale des Familles d'alliance Canadiennne-Francaise
BP10, Les Ormes, 86220, France
Amities Genealogiques Bordelaises 2 rue Paul Bert, Bordeaux, Aquitaine, 33000, France T: 05 5644 8199 Fax: 05 5644 8199
Assoc. Genealogique et Historique des Yvelines Nord
Hotel de Ville, Meulan, 78250, France
Association Catalane de Genealogie
BP 1024, Perpignan Cedex, Languedoc Rousillon, 66101
Association de la Bourgeoisie Ancienne Francaise
74 Avenue Kleber, Paris, 75116, France
Association Genealogique de la Charente
Archives Departementales, 24 avenue Gambetta, Angouleme, Poitou Charentes, 16000, France
Association Genealogique de l'Anjou
75 rue Bressigny, Angers, Pays de la Loire, 49100, France

Association Genealogique de l'Oise
BP 626, Compiegne Cedex, Picardie, 60206, France
Association Genealogique des Bouches-du-Rhone
BP 22, Marseilles Cedex, Provence Alpes Cote d'Azur, 1
Association Genealogique des Hautes Alpes
Archives Departementales, route de Rambaud, Gap, Provence Alpes Cote d'Azur, 5000, France
Association Genealogique du Pas de Calais
BP 471, Arras Cedex, Nord-Pas de Calais, 62028
Association Genealogique du Pays de Bray
BP 62, Serqueux, Normandie, 76440 Fax: 02 3509 8756
Association Genealogique du Var
BP 1022, Toulon Cedex, Provence Alpes Cote d'Azur, 83051
Association Genealogique Flandre-Hainaut
BP493, Valenciennes Cedex, Nord-Pas de Calais, 59321
Association Recherches Genealogiques Historique d'Auvergne
Maison des Consuls, Place Poly, Clermont Ferrand, Auvergne, 63100
Bibliotheque Genealogique
3 Rue de Turbigo, Paris, 75001, France T: 01 4233 5821
Brive-Genealogie Maison des Associations, 11 place J M Dauaier, Brive, Limousin, 19100, France
Centre de Recherches Genealogiques Flandre-Artois
BP 76, Bailleul, Nord-Pas de Calais, 59270, France
Centre d'Entraide Genealogique de France 3 Rue de Turbigo, Paris, 75001, France T: 33 4041 9909 Fax: 33 4041 9963 E: cegf@usa.net W: www.mygale.org/04cabrigol/cegf/
Centre Departemental d'Histoire des Familles 5 place Saint Leger, Guebwiller, Alsace, 68500, France E: cdhf@telmat-net.fr W: web.telemat-net-fr~cdhf
Centre Entraide Genealogique Franche Comte
35 rue du Polygone, Besancon, Franche Comte, 25000
Cercle Genealogique du Finistere, Salle Municipale, rue du Commandant Tissot, Bretagne, 29000 W: www.karolus.org/membres/cgf.htm
Centre Genealogique de la Marne BP 20, Chalons-en-Champagne, Champagne Ardennes, 51005
Centre Genealogique de Savoie BP1727, Chambery Cedex, Rhone Alpes, 73017, France
Centre Genealogique de Touraine BP 5951, Tours Cedex, Centre, 37059, France
Centre Genealogique des Cotes d'Armor 3bis rue Bel Orient, Saint Brieuc, Bretagne, 22000, France Fax: 02 9662 8900
Centre Genealogique des Landes Societe de Borda, 27 rue de Cazarde, Dax, Aquitaine, 40100
Centre Genealogique des Pyrenees Atlantique BP 1115, Pau Cedex, Aquitaine, 64011, France
Centre Genealogique du Perche 9 rue Ville Close, Bellame, Normandie, 61130, France T: 02 3383 3789
Centre Genealogique du Sud Ouest Hotel des Societes Savantes, 1 Place Bardineau, Bordeaux, Aquitaine, 33000, France
Centre Genealogique et Heraldique des Ardennes
Hotel de Ville, Charleville Mezieres, Champagne Ardennes, 8000
Centre Genealogique Protestant 54 rue des Saints-Peres, Paris, 75007, France
Cercle de Genealogie du Calvados Archives Departementales, 61 route de Lion-sur-Mer, Caen, Normandie, 14000, France
Cercle de Genealogie et d'Heraldique de Seine et Marne BP 113, Melun Cedex, 77002, France
Cercle de Genealogie Juive (Jewish) 14 rue St Lazare, Paris, 75009, France T: 01 4023 0490
Cercle d'Etudes Genealogiques et Heraldique d'Ile-de-France 46 Route de Croissy, Le Vesinet, 78110, France
Cercle d'Histoire et Genealogique du Perigord 2 rue Roletrou, Perigueux, Aquitaine, 24000, France
Cercle Genealogique Bull rue Jean Jaures, BP 53, Les-Clayes-sous-Bois, 78340,
Cercle Genealogique d'Alsace
Archives du Bas-Rhin, 5 rue Fischart, Strasbourg, Alsace, 67000
Cercle Genealogique d'Aunis et Saintonge c/o Mr Provost, 10 ave de Metz, La Rochelle, Poitou Charentes, 17000, France
Cercle Genealogique de la Manche
BP 410, Cherbourg Cedex, Normandie, 50104, France
Cercle Genealogique de la Meurthe et Moselle
4 rue Emile Gentil, Briey, Lorraine, 54150, France
Cercle Genealogique de la Region de Belfort
c/o F Werlen, 4 ave Charles de Gaulle, Valdoie, Franche Comte, 90300
Cercle Genealogique de l'Eure Archives Departementales, 2 rue de Verdun, Evreux Cedex, Normandie, 27025, France
Cercle Genealogique de Saintonge
8 rue Mauny, Saintes, Poitou Charentes, 17100, France
Cercle Genealogique de Vaucluse
Ecole Sixte Isnard, 31 ter Avenue de la Trillade, Avignon, Provence Alpes Cote d'Azur, 84000, France
Cercle Genealogique des Deux-Sevres
26 rue de la Blauderie, Niort, Poitou Charentes, 79000
Cercle Genealogique des P.T.T. BP33, Paris Cedex 15, 75721
Cercle Genealogique d'Ille-et-Vilaine
6 rue Frederic Mistral, Rennes, Bretagne, 35200 T: 02 9953 6363

Cercle Genealogique du C.E. de la Caisse d'Epargne Ile de France-Paris 19 rue du Louvre, Paris, 75001, France
Cercle Genealogique du Finistere Salle Municipale, rue du Commandant Tissot, Brest, Bretagne, 29000 W: www.karolus.org/membres/cgf.htm
Cercle Genealogique du Haut-Berry place Martin Luther King, Bourges, Centre, 18000
Cercle Genealogique du Languedoc 18 rue de la Tannerie, Toulouse, Languedoc Rousillon, 31400, France T: 05 6226 1530
Cercle Genealogique du Loir-et-Cher 11 rue du Bourg Neuf, Blois, Centre, 41000 T: 02 5456 0711
Cercle Genealogique d'Yvetot et du Pays de Caux Pavillion des Fetes, Yvetot, Normandie, 76190, France
Cercle Genealogique et Historique du Lot et Garonne 13 rue Etienne Marcel, Villeneuve sur Lot, Aquitaine, 47340
Cercle Genealogique Poitevin 22bis rue Arsene Orillard, Poitiiers, Poitou Charentes, 86000
Cercle Genealogique Rouen Seine-Maritime Archives Departementales, Cours Clemenceau, Normandie, 76101
Cercle Genealogique Saone-et-Loire 115 rue des Cordiers, Macon, Bourgogne, 71000, France
Cercle Genealogique Vendeen Bat.H, 307bis, Cite de la Vigne aux Roses, La Roche-sur-Yon, Pays de la Loire, 85000, France
Cercle Genealogique Versailles et Yvelines Archives Departementales, 1 avenue de Paris, Versailles, 78000 T: 01 3952 7239
Cercle Genealogique du Rouergue Archives Departementales, 25 av Victor Hugo, Rodez, Midi-Pyrenees, 12000, France
Club Genealogique Air France CE Air France Roissy Exploitation, BP 10201, Roissy CDG Cedex, 95703, France
Club Genealogique Group IBM France CE IBM St Jean de Braye-Ste Marie, 50-56 ave Pierre Curie, St Jean de Braye Cedex, 45807
Confederation Internationale de Genealogie et d'Heraldique Maison de la Genealogie, 3 rue Turbigo, Paris, F - 75001
Etudes Genealogique Drome-Ardeche 14 rue de la Manutention, Valence, Rhone Alpes, 26000
Federation Francaise de Genealogie 3 Rue de Turbigo, Paris, 75001, France T: 01 4013 0088 W: www.karolus.org
France-Louisuane/Franco-Americanie Commission Retrouvailles, Centre CommercialeGatie, 80 avenue du Maine, Paris 75014 W: www.noconnet.co:80/forms/cajunews.htm
Genealogie Algerie Maroc Tunisie Maison Marechal Alphonse, Juin 28 Av. de Tubingen, Aix en Provence, 13090, France
Genealogie Entraide Recherche en Cote d'Or 97 rue d'Estienne d'Orves, Clarmart, Bourgogne, 92140
Genealogie et Histoire de la Caraibe Pavillion 23, 12 avenue Charles de Gaulle, Le Pecq 78230, France
Groupement Genealogique de la Region du Nord BP 62, Wambrechies, Nord-Pas de Calais, 59118, France
Groupement Genealogique du Havre et de Seine Maritime BP 80, Le Havre Cedex, Normandie, 76050 T: 02 3522 7633
Institut Francophone de Genealogie et d'Histoire 5 rue de l'Aimable Nanette, le Gabut, La Rochelle 17000 T: 05 4641 9032
Institut Genealogique de Bourgogne 237 rue Vendome, BP 7076, Lyon, Bourgogne, 69301
Loiret Genealogique BP 9, Orleans Cedex, Centre, 45016, France
Salon Genealogique de Vichy et du Centr48 Boulevard de Sichon, Vichy, Auvergne, 3200, France W: www.genea.com
Section Genealogique de l'Assoc. Artistique-Banque de France 2 rue Chabanais, Paris, 75002, France
Societe Genealogique du Bas-BerrMaison des Associations, 30 Espace Mendez France, Chateauroux, Centre, 36000, France
Societe Genealogique du Lyonnais 7 rue Major Martin, Lyon, Rhone Alpes, 69001, France

Germany
Arbeirkreis fur Familienforschung e.V Muhlentorturm, Muhlentortplatz 2, Lubeck, Schleswig-Holstein, D - 23552, Germany
Bayerischer Landesverein fur Familienkunde Ludwigstrasse 14/1, Munchen, Bayern, D - 80539 W: www.genealogy.com/gene/reg/BAY/BLF-d.html
Deutsche Zentalstelle fur Genealogie Schongaver str. 1, Leipzig, D - 04329, Germany
Dusseldorfer Verein fur Familienkunde e.V Krummenweger Strasse 26, Ratingen, Nordrhein Westfalen, D - 40885, Germany
Herold - Verein fur Genealogie Heraldik und Reiwandte Wissen-Scahaften Archiv Str. 12-14, Berlin, D -14195, Germany
Niedersachsischer Gesellschaft fur Familienkunde e.V Stadtarchiv, Am Bokemahle 14 - 16, Hannover, Niedersachsen, D - 30171
Oldenburgische Gesellschaft fur Familienkunde Lerigauweg 14, Oldenurg, Niedersachsen, D - 26131, Germany
Verein fur Familien u.W. Wappenkunde in Wurttemberg und Baden Postfach 105441, Stuttgart, Baden-Wuerttemberg, D - 70047
Westdeutsche Gesellschaft fur Familienkunde e.V Sitz Koln Unter Gottes Gnaden 34, Koln-Widdersdorf, Nordrhein Westfalen, D - 50859, Germany T: 49 221 50 48 88
Zentralstelle fur Personnen und Familiengeschichte Birkenweg 13, Friedrichsdorf, D - 61381, Germany

Greece
Heraldic-Genealogical Society of Greece 56 3rd Septemvriou Str., Athens, GR - 10433, Greece

Hungary
Historical Society of Hungary University of Eoetveos Lorand, Pesti Barnabas utca 1, Budapest, H - 1052, Hungary T: 267 0966

Iceland
The Genealogical Society P O Box 829, Reykjavick, 121, Iceland **Italy**
Ancetres Italien 3 Rue de Turbigo, Paris, 75001T: 01 4664 2722

Netherlands
Centraal Bureau voor Genealogie P O Box 11755, The Hague, NL - 2502 AT T: 070 315 0500 F: 070 347 8394 W: www.cbg.nl
Koninklijk Nederlandsch Genootschap voor Geslacht-en Wapen-KundeP O Box 85630, Den Haag, 2508 CH, Netherlands
Nederlandse Genealogische Vereniging Postbus 976, Amsterdam, NL - 1000 AZ, Netherlands E: info@ngu.nl W: www.ngu.nl
Stichting 'Genealogisch Centrum Zeeland' Wijnaardstraat, Goes, 4416DA T: 0113 232 895
The Caledonian Society Zuiderweg 50, Noordwolde, NL 8391 KH T: 0561 431580

Norway
Norsk Slektshistorik Forening Sentrum Postboks 59, Oslo, N - 0101, Norway T: 2242 2204 Fax: 2242 2204

Poland
Polish Genealogical Society of America, 984 N. Milwaukee Ave, IL, 60622, USA W: www.pgsa.org
Polish Genealogical Society of New Zealand Box 88, Urenui, Taranaki NZ T: 06 754 4551 E: pgs.newzealand@clear.net.nz

Slovakia
Slovak GHS At Matica Slovenska Novomeskeho, 32, 036 52 Martin
Czechoslovak Genealogical Society International PO Box 16225, St Paul, MN, 55116-0225, USA

Spain
Asociacion de Diplomados en Genealogia y Nobilaria Alcala 20, 2 Piso, Madrid, 28014 T: 34 522 3822 Fax: 34 532 6674
Asociacion de Hidalgos a Fuerto de Espana Aniceto Marinas 114, Madrid, 28008, Spain
Cercle Genealogic del Valles Roca 29, 5 2, Sabadell, Barcelona, 8208, Spain
Circulo de Estudios Genealogicos Familiares Prado 21, Ateneo de Madrid, Madrid, 28014, Spain
Instituto Aragones de Investigaciones Historiograficas Madre Sacramento 33, 1', Zaragoza, 50004, Spain
Instituto de Estudios Heraldicos y Genealogicos de Extremadura Lucio Cornelio Balbo 6, Caceres, 1004, Spain
Real Academia Matritense de Heraldica y Genealogia Quintana 28, Madrid, 28008, Spain
Sociedad Toledana de Estudios Heraldicos y Genealogicos Apartado de Correos No. 373, Toledo, Spain
Societat Catalona de Genealogia Heraldica Sigillografia Vexillologia P O Box 2830, Barcelona, 8080, Spain
Societat Valenciana de Genealogia Heraldica Sigillografia Vexillologia Les Tendes 22, Oliva, 46780, Spain

Sweden
Sveriges Slaktforskarforbund Box 30222, Stockholm, 104 25, Sweden T: 08 695 0890

Switzerland
Genealogical & Heraldry Association of Zurich Dammbodenstrasse 1, Volketswil, CH-8604, Switzerland
Swiss Genealogical Society Eggstr 46, Oberengstringen, CH 8102, Switzerland W: www.eye.ch/swissgen/SGFF.html
Swiss Society for Jewish Genealogy P O Box 876, Zurich, CH-8021, Switzerland
Zentralstelle fur Genealogie Vogelaustrasse 34, CH-8953, Switzerland Fax: 44 1 742 20 84 E: aicher@eyekon.ch

United States of America
Alaska
Alaska Gen Soc 7030 Dickerson Drive, Anchorage, Alaska 99504
Anchorage Gen Soc PO Box 212265, Anchorage, Alaska 99521-2265 T: 907-337-6377
Fairbanks Genealogical Society PO Box 60534, Fairbanks, Alaska 99706-0534 T: 907-479-2895
Gen Soc of South East Alaska PO Box 6313, Ketchikan, Alaska 99901
Arizona
Apache Genealogy Society PO Box 1084, Sierra Vista public Library, Sierra Vista, Arizona 85636-1084 T: 602-458-7770
Arizona Soc of Gen, The 6565 East Grant Road, Tucson, Arizona 85715
Arizona State Gen Soc PO Box 42075, Tucson, Arizona 85733-2075 E: ralong@ieee.org W: www.azsgs.org
FHS of Arizona PO Box 310, Glendale, Arizona 85311
Gen Soc of Arizona PO Box 27237, Tempe, Arizona 85282

Mohave County Gen Soc 400 West Beale Street, Kingman, Arizona 864014
Northern Arizona Gen Soc PO Box 695, Prescott, Arizona 86302
Arkansas
Arkansas Gen Soc PO Box 908, Hot Springs, Arkansas 71902-0908
North East Arkansas Genealogical Association PO Box 936, 314 Vine Street, Newport, Arkansas 72112
North West Arkansas Genealogical Association PO Box 796, Rogers, Arkansas 72757
Sevier County Gen Soc 717 Maple Street, De Queen, Arkansas 71832
California
British Isles FHS - USA 2531 Sawtelle Boulevard, PMB #134, Los Angeles, California CA 90064-3163 E: president@bifhsusa.org W: www.rootsweb.com/~bifhsusa
California Gen Soc Suite 200, Latham Office Building, 1611 Telegraph Avenue, Oakland, California 94612-2152 T: 510-663-1358 W: www.calgensoc.com
California State Genealogical Alliance 4808 East Garland Street, Anaheim, California 92807-1005 T: 714-777-0483
Kyle Family Society 3053 Fillmore Street, #118 , San Francisco 94123 E: kylesociety@hotmail.com W: www.kylesociety.org
Santa Barbara County Genealogical Society PO Box 1303, Goleta, Santa Barbara, California CA 93116-1303 T: 1-805-884-9909 E: sbcgs@msn.com W: www.cagenweb.com/santabarbara/sbcgs
Colorado
Colorado Genealogical Society PO Box 9218, Denver, Colorado 80209-0218
Colorado Council of Genealogical Societies PO Box 24379, Denver, Colorado 80224-0379
Wales, Ireland, Scotland, England FHS W.I.S.E. FHS, PO Box 40658, Denver, Colorado 80204-8226
Connecticut
Connecticut Society of Genealogists Inc PO Box 435, Glastonbury, Connecticut 06033-0435 T: 203-569-0002
District of Columbia
National Society Daughters of the American Revolution 1776 D Street NW, Washington, District of Columbia 20006-5392
Florida
Florida Gen Soc PO Box 18624, Tampa, Florida 33679-8624
Florida Society for Genealogical Research 8461 54th Street North, Pinellas Park, Florida 33565
Florida State Genealogical Society PO Box 10249, Tallahassee, Florida 32302-2249
Georgia
Georgia Genealogical Society PO Box 54575, Atlanta, Georgia 30308-0575 T: 404-475-4404 W: http://www.state.ga.us/SOS/Archives/
Hawaii
Sandwich Islands Genealogical Society, The Hawaii State Library, 478 South King Street, Honolulu, Hawaii 96813
Idaho
Idaho Gen Soc Inc # 204, 4620 Overland Road, Boise, Idaho 83705-2867 T: 208-384-0542
Illinois
Illinois State Gen Soc PO Box 10195, Springfield, Illinois 62791-0195 T: 217-789-1968
Indiana
Indiana Genealogical Society Inc PO Box 10507, Fort Wayne, Indiana 46852-0507 T: 219-269-1782 W: www.indgensoc.org
Iowa
Iowa Gen Soc PO Box 7735, 6000 Douglas, Des Moines, Iowa 50322-7735 T: 515-276-0287 W: www.digiserve.com/igs/igs.htm
Kansas
Jefferson County Gen Soc Box 174, Oskalobsa, Kansas 66066
Kansas Council of Genealogical Societies Inc PO Box 3858, Topeka, Kansas 66604-6858 T: 913-774-4411
Kansas Gen Soc Inc PO Box 103, 2601 Central, Dodge City, Kansas 67801-0103 T: 316-225-1951
Kentucky
Kentucky Gen Soc Inc PO Box 153, Frankfort, Kentucky 40602 T: 502-875-4452 E: kygs@aol.com W: www.kygs.org
Louisiana
Louisiana Genealogical & Historical Society PO Box 3454, Baton Rouge, Louisiana 70821
Maine
Maine Gen Soc PO Box 221, Farmington, Maine 04938-0221 W: www.maineroots.org
Maryland
Maryland Genealogical Society 201 West Monument Street, Baltimore, Maryland 21201 T: 410-685-3750
Massachusetts
Massachusetts Genealogical Council PO Box 5393, Cochituate, Massachusetts 1778
Massachusetts Soc of Gen PO Box 215, Ashland, Massachusetts 01721-0215
New England Historic Gen Soc 99 - 101 Newbury Street, Boston, Massachusetts 02116 T: 617-536-5740 E: membership@nehgs.org W: www.nehgs.org
Michigan
Michigan Genealogical Council PO Box 80953, Lansing, Michigan

48908-0953
Minnesota
Dakota County Genealogical Society PO Box 74, 347 12th Avenue North, South St Paul, Minnesota 55075 T: (651)-451-6260
Irish Genealogical Society International PO Box 16585, St Paul, Minnesota 55116-0585 T: (612)-574-1436 W: www.rootsweb.com/~irish
Minnesota Genealogical Society 5768 Olson Memorial Highway, Golden Valley, Minnesota 55422 T: 612-595-9347
Mississippi
Historical & Genealogical Association of Mississippi 618 Avalon Road, Jackson, Mississippi 39206 T: 601-362-3079
Mississippi Gen Soc PO Box 5301, Jackson, Mississippi 39296-5301
Missouri
Missouri State Genealogical Association PO Box 833, Columbia, Missouri 65205-0803
Montana
Big Horn County Gen Soc PO Box 51, Hardin, Montana 59034
Montana State Gen Soc PO Box 555, Chester, Montana 59522
Nebraska
Nebraska State Gen Soc PO Box 5608, Lincoln, Nebraska 68505-0608
Nevada
Carson City Gen Soc 1509 Sharon Drive, Carson City, Nevada 89701 T: 702-687-4810
Nevada State Gen Soc PO Box 20666, Reno, Nevada 89515
New Hampshire
New Hampshire Society of Genealogists PO Box 633, Exeter, New Hampshire 03833-0633 T: 603-432-8137
New Jersey
Gen Soc of New Jersey PO Box 1291, New Brunswick, New Jersey 8903 T: 201-356-6920
Genealogy Club of the Library of the New Jersey Historical Society 230 Broadway, Newark, New Jersey 7104 T: 201-483-3939
New Mexico
New Mexico Genealogical Society PO Box 8283, Alberquerque, New Mexico 87198-8283 T: 505-256-3217
New York
Irish Family History Forum PO Box 67, Plainview, New York 11803-0067 W: www.ifhf.org
Jewish Gen Soc (New York) PO Box 286398, New York, New York 10128-0004 E: info@jgsny.org W: www.jgsny.org
New York Genealogical & Biographical Society 122 East 58th Street, 4th Floor, New York New York 10022-1939 T: 212-755-8532 W: www.nygbs.org
North Carolina
North Carolina Gen Soc PO Box 1492, Raleigh, North Carolina 27602
Ohio
Ohio Genealogical Society 713 South Main Street, Mansfield, Ohio 44907-1644 T: 419 756 7294 E: ogs@ogs.org W: www.ogs.org/
Oklahoma
Federation of Oklahoma Genealogical Societies PO Box 26151, Oklahoma City, Oklahoma 73126
Genealogical Institute of Oklahoma 3813 Cashion Place, Oklahoma City, Oklahoma 73112
Oklahoma Genealogical Society PO Box 12986, Oklahoma City, Oklahoma 73157-2986 W: www.rootsweb.com/~okgs/fftt.htm
Oregon
Genealogical Forum of Oregon Inc Room 812, 1410 S W Morrison Street, Portland, Oregon 97205 T: 503-227-2398
Genealogical Heritage Council of Oregon Inc PO Box 628, Ashland, Oregon 97520-0021
Oregon Genealogical Society PO Box 10306, Ashland, Oregon 97440-2306 T: 503-746-7924
Pennsylvania
Bucks County Genealogical Society PO Box 1092, Doylestown, Pennsylvania 18901 T: (215)-230-9410
Genealogical Society of Pennsylvania 1300 locust Street, Philadelphia, Pennsylvania 19107-5699 E: exdir@aol.com W: www.genpa.org
Rhode Island
Rhode Island Genealogical Society 13 Countryside Drive, Cumberland, Rhode Island 02864-2601
South Carolina
South Carolina Genealogical Society PO Box 16355, Greenville, South Carolina 29606
South Dakota
South Dakota Genealogical Society Rt 2 Box 10, Burke, South Dakota 57523 T: 605-835-9364
Tennessee
Tennessee Genealogical Society, The PO Box 111249, Memphis, Tennessee 38111-1249 T: 901-327-3273
Texas
Amarillo Genealogical Society PO Box 2171, 413 East Fourth Street, Amarillo, Texas 79189-2171 T: 806-378-3054
Federation of Genealogical Societies, The PO Box 200940, Austin, Texas 78720-0940 E: office@fgs.org W: www.fgs.org
Texas State Genealogical Society 2507 Tannehill, Houston, Texas 77008-3052 T: 713-864-6862
Utah
Utah Genealogical Association PO Box 1144, Salt Lake City, Utah

84110-1144 W: www.infouga.org
Vermont
Genealogical Society of Vermont PO Box 422, Main Street, Pittsford, Vermont 5763 T: 802-483-2900
Virginia
Genealogical Research Institute of Virginia PO Box 29178, Richmond, Virginia 23242-0178
National Genealogical Society, The 3108 Columbia Pike, Ste 300, Arlington, Virginia 22204-4304 T: (703)-525-0050 E: membership@ngsgenealogy.org W: www.ngsgenealogy.org
Virginia Genealogical Society Suite 115, 5001 West Broad Street, Richmond, Virginia 23230-3023 T: 804-285-8954 W: www.vgs.org
Washington
Washington State Genealogical Society PO Box 1422, Olympia, Washington 98507 T: 206-352-0595
West Virginia
West Virginia Gen Soc Inc PO Box 249, 5236 A Elk River Road North,

Elk District, Elk View, Kanawha County, West Virginia 25071 T: 1-304-965-1179
Wisconsin
Wisconsin Genealogical Council Inc Rt 3 Box 253, Black River Falls, Wisconsin 54615-9405 T: 608-378-4388
Wisconsin State Genealogical Society PO Box 5106, Madison, Wisconsin 53705-0106 T: 608-325-2609
Wyoming
Cheyenne Gen Soc Laramie County Library Service - Ge, 2800 Central Avenue, Cheyenne, Wyoming 82001 T: 307-634-3561

Local and History Societies

Association of Local History Tutors 47 Ramsbury Drive, Earley, Reading, Berkshire RG6 7RT T: 0118 926 4729
Battlefields Trust 33 High Green, Brooke, Norwich NR15 1HR T: 01508 558145 E: BattlefieldTrust@aol.com W: www.battlefieldstrust.com
Black & Asian Studies Association 28 Russell Square, London, WC1B 5DS T: (020) 7862 8844 E: secretary@blackandasianstudies.org.uk W: www.blackandasianstudies.org.uk/
Brewery History Society Manor Side East, Mill Lane, Byfleet, West Byfleet, Surrey KT14 7RS E: membership@breweryhistory.com W: www.breweryhistory.com
British Association for Local History PO Box 6549, Somersal Herbert, Ashbourne, Derbyshire DE6 5WH T: 01283 585947 E: mail@balh.co.uk W: www.balh.co.uk
British Brick Society 19 Woodcroft Avenue, Stanmore HA7 3PT T: 020 8954 4976 E: micksheila67@hotmail.com W: www.britishbricksoc.free-online.co.uk
British Deaf History Society 288 Bedfont Lane, Feltham, Middlesex TW14 9NU
British Records Association c/o Finsbury Library, 245 St Johns Street, London, EC1V 4NB T: 020 7833 0428 F: 020 7833 0416 E: britcass@btconnect.com W: www.britishrecordsassociation.org.uk/
British Records Association c/o Finsbury Library, 245 St John Street, London, EC1V 4NB T: 020 7833 0428 E: britcassoc@hotmail.com W: www.britishrecordsassociation.org.uk
British Records Society Stone Barn Farm, Sutherland Road, Longsdon, Staffordshire ST9 9QD T: 01782 385446 W: www.britishrecordsociety.org.uk
British Society for Sports History Dept of Sports & Science, John Moore's University, Byrom Street, Liverpool, Merseyside L3 3AF
Chapels Society 47 Salisbury Drive, Midway, Swadlincote, DE11 7LD T: 01283558169 E: chapelssociety@gmail.com W: www.britarch.ac.uk/chapelsoc
Coble and Keelboat Society 19 Selwyn Avenue, Whitley Bay, Northumberland NE25 9DH T: 0191 251 4412
Costume Society St Paul's House, 8 Warwick Road, London, EC4P 4BN W: www.costumesociety.org.uk
Cross & Cockade International - The First World War Aviation Historical Society 5 Cave Drive, Downend, Bristol, BS16 2TL W: www.crossandcockade.com
Ecclesiastical History Society 6 Gallows Hill, Saffron Walden CB11 4DA
English Place Name Society c/o School of English Studies, University of Nottingham, Nottingham NG7 2RD T: 0115 951 5919 W: www.nottingham.ac.uk/english/
Family & Community Historical Society Woburn Lane, Aspley Suise, Milton Keynes, Bedfordshire MK17 8JR W: www.fachrs.com
Heraldry Society PO Box 772, Guildford, Surrey GU3 3ZX T: 01483 237 373 E: honsec_heraldry@excite.co.uk W: www.theheraldrysociety.com/
Historical Association (Local History) 59A Kennington Park Road, London, SE11 4JH T: (020) 7735-3901 E: enquiry@history.org.uk W: www..history.org.uk
Hugenot Society of Great Britain & Ireland Hugenot Library University College, Gower Street, London, WC1E 6BT T: 020 7679 5199 E: secretary@huguenotsociety.org.uk W: www.hugenotsociety.org.uk
Labour Heritage 18 Ridge Rd, Mitcham CR4 2EY T: 020 8640 1814
Local Population Studies Society LPS General Office, Faculty of Humanities & Education, University of Hertfordshire, College Lane, Hatfield AL10 9AB T: 01707 285 688 E: lps@herts.ac.uk W: www.localpopulationstudies.org.uk/

Local Studies Group of CILIP - Formerly the Library Association 25 Bromford Gardens, Edgbaston, Birmingham, West Midlands B15 3XD T: 0121 454 0935
Mercia Cinema Society 5 Arcadia Avenue, Chester le Street DH3 3UH
Museum of the Royal Pharmaceutical Society 1 Lambeth High Street, London, SE1 7JN T: (020) 7572 2210 E: museum@rpharms.com W: www.rpharms.com/museum
Parish Register Transcription Society 50 Silvester Road, Waterlooville PO8 5TL E: mail@prtsoc.org.uk W: www.prtsoc.org.uk
Postal History Society 60 Tachbrook Street, London, SW1V 2NA T: (020) 7821-6399 W: www.postalhistory.org.uk/
Pub History Society 254a Kew Road, Richmond TW9 3EG T: 020 8940 6884 E: sfowler@sfowler.force9.co.uk W: www.pubhistorysociety.co.uk
Royal Geographical Society (with IBG) 1 Kensington Gore, London, SW7 2AR T: 020 7291 3001 W: www.rgs.org
Royal Photographic Society Historical Group 7A Cotswold Road, Belmont, Sutton, Surrey SM2 5NG T: (020) 8643 2743
Royal Society 6 - 9 Carlton House Terrace, London, SW1Y 5AG T: 020 7451 2606 E: library@royalsociety.org W: royalsociety.org
Royal Society of Chemistry Library & Information Centre Burlington House, Piccadilly, London, W1J 0BA T: (020) 7440 3373 E: library@rsc.org W: www.rsc.org/library/Services/GenealogyEnquiriesSearch.asp
Society for Nautical Research Stowell House, New Pond Hill, Cross in Hand, Heathfield TN21 0LX
Society of Antiquaries Burlington House, Piccadilly, London, W1J 0BE T: (020) 7479 7080 E: admin@sal.org.uk W: www.sal.org.uk
Society of Cirplanologists 26 Roe Cross Green, Mottram, Hyde, Cheshire SK14 6LP T: 01457 763485
Society of Jewellery Historians Department of Scientific Research, The British Museum, Great Russell Street, London, WC1B 3DG E: info@societyofjewelleryhistorians.ac.uk W: www.societyofjewelleryhistorians.ac.uk
Tennyson Society Central Library, Free School Lane, Lincoln, LN2 1EZ T: 01522-552862 W: www.tennysonsociety.org.uk
The Garden History Society 70 Cowcross Street, London, EC1M 6EJ T: (020) 7608 2409 E: enquiries@gardenhistorysociety.org W: www.gardenhistorysociety.org
United Kingdom Reminiscence Network , 11 Blackheath Village, London, SE3 9LA T: 020 8318 9105
United Reformed Church History Society Westminster College, Madingley Road, Cambridge, CB3 0AA T: 01223 741300 (NOT Wednesdays)
University of London Extra-Mural Society For Genealogy and History of The Family 136 Lennard Road, Beckenham, BR3 1QT
Vernacular Architecture Group Sunnyfield, 3 Church Row, Redwick, Magor NP26 3DE E: hall.email@virgin.net W: www.vag.org.uk
Veterinary History Society 608 Warwick Road, Solihull, West Midlands B91 1AA
Victorian Society 1 Priory Gardens, Bedford Park, London, W4 1TT T: (020) 8994 1019 E: admin@victoriansociety.org.uk W: www.victoriansociety.org.uk
Voluntary Action History Society National Centre for Volunteering, Regent's Wharf, 8 All Saints Street, London, N1 9RL T: (020) 7520 8900 W: www.ivr.org.uk/vahs.htm
War Memorials Trust 42a Buckingham Palace Road, London, SW1W 0RE T: 0300 123 0764 E: info@warmemorials.org W: www.warmemorials.org
War Research Society 27 Courtway Avenue, Birmingham B14 4PP T: 0121 430 5348 E: info@battlefieldtours.co.uk W: www.battlefieldtours.co.uk

Wesley Historical Society 7 Haugh Shaw Road, Halifax HX1 3AH T: 01422 250780 E: johnahargreaves@blueyonder.co.uk W: www.wesleyhistoricalsociety.org.uk

Avon
Bristol & Avon Archaeological Society 3 Priory Avenue, Westbury on Trym, Bristol, BS9 4DA T: 0117 9620161 (evenings) W: http://www-digitalbristol.org/members/baas/

Bedfordshire
Ampthill & District Archaeological and Local History 14 Glebe Avenue, Flitwick, Bedford MK45 1HS E: petwood@waitrose.com W: www.museums.bedfordshire.gov.uk/localgroups/ampthill2/html
Ampthill & District Preservation Society Seventh House, 43 Park Hill, Ampthill, Bedfordshire MK45 2LP
Ampthill History Forum 32 Ashburnham Road, Ampthill, MK45 2RH E: forum@ampthillhistory.co.uk W: www.ampthillhistory.co.uk
Bedfordshire Archaeological and LHS 7 Lely Close, Bedford, Bedfordshire MK41 7LS T: 01234 365095 W: www.museums.bedfordshire.gov.uk/localgroups
Bedfordshire Historical Record Society 48 St Augustine's Road, Bedford, Bedfordshire MK40 2ND T: 01234 309548 E: rsmart@ntlworld.com W: www.bedfordshirehrs.org.uk
Bedfordshire Local History Association 29 George Street, Maulden, Bedford, Bedfordshire MK45 2DF T: 01525633029
Biggleswade History Society 6 Pine Close, Biggleswade, SG18 QEF
Caddington Local History Group 98 Mancroft Road, Caddington, Nr. Luton, Bedfordshire LUL 4EN W: www.caddhist.moonfruit.com
Carlton & Chellington Historical Society 3 High Street, Carlton, Bedfordshire MK43 7JX
Dunstable & District LHS 7 Castle Close, Totternhoe, Dunstable, Bedfordshire LU6 1QJ T: 01525 221963
Dunstable Historic and Heritage Studies 184 West Street, Dunstable, Bedfordshire LU6 1 NX T: 01582 609018
Harlington Heritage Trust 2 Shepherds Close, Harlington, Near Dunstable, Bedfordshire LU5 6NR
Leighton-Linslade Heritage Display Society 25 Rothschild Road, Linslade, Leighton Buzzard, Bedfordshire LU7 7SY
Luton & District Historical Society 22 Homerton Road, Luton, LU3 2UL T: 01582 584367
Social History of Learning Disability Research Group School of Health & Social Welfare, Open University, Milton Keynes, MK7 6AA
Toddington Historical Society 21 Elm Grove, Toddington, Dunstable LU5 6BJ W: www.museums.bedfordshire.gov.uk/local/toddington.htm
Wrestlingworth History Society 18 Braggs Lane, Church Lane, Wrestlingworth, Bedfordshire SG19 2ER

Berkshire
Berkshire Industrial Archaeological Group 20 Auclum Close, Burghfield Common, Reading, Berkshire RG7 DY
Berkshire Local History Association Department of History, University of Reading, Whiteknights, Reading, Berkshire RG6 6AA E: secretary@blha.org.uk W: www.blha.org.uk
Berkshire Record Society Berkshire Record Office, 9 Coley Avenue, Reading RG1 6AF T: 0118 937 5130 E: editor@berkshirerecordsociety.org.uk W: www.berkshirerecordsociety.org.uk
Blewbury Local History Group Spring Cottage, Church Road, Blewbury, Didcot, Oxfordshire OX11 9PY T: 01235 850427
Bracknell & District Historical Society 16 Harcourt Road, Bracknell, Berkshire RG12 7JD T: 01344 640341
Brimpton Parish Research Association Shortacre, Brimpton Common, Reading, Berkshire RG7 4RY T: 0118 981 3649
Chiltern Heraldry Group Magpie Cottage, Pondwood Lane, Shottesbrooke, Berkshire SL6 3SS T: 0118 934 3698
Cox Green Local History Group 29 Bissley Drive, Maidenhead, Berkshire SL6 3UX T: 01628 823890
Datchet Village Society Flat 3 Riverbank, 9 Southlea Road, Datchet, SL3 9BY T: 01273 204330 E: janet@datchet.com W: www.datchet.com
Eton Wick History Group 47 Colenorton Crescent, Eton Wick, Windsor, Berkshire SL4 6WW T: 01753 861674
Finchampstead History & Heritage Group 134 Kiln Ride, California, Wokingham, Berkshire RG40 3PB T: 0118 973 3005
Friends of Reading Museums 15 Benyon Court, Bath Road, Reading, Berkshire RG1 6HR T: 0118 958 0642
Friends of Wantage Vale & Downland Museum 19 Church Street, Wantage, Berkshire OX12 8BL T: 01235 771447 W:
Goring & Streatley LHS 45 Springhill Road, Goring On Thames, Reading, Berkshire RG8 OBY T: 01491 872625
Hare Hatch & Kiln Green Local History Group - disbanded contact Wargrave Local History
Hedgerley Historical Society 13 Coppice Way, Hedgerley, Slough, SL2 3YL T: +44 (0)1753 647 187 E: jdlovelock@btinternet.com

History of Reading Society 5 Wilmington Close, Woodley, Reading, Berkshire RG5 4LR T: 0118 961 8559
Hungerford Historical Association Westbrook Farmhouse, Smitham Bridge Road, Hungerford, Berkshire RG17 0QP T: 01488 682976 E: jaykay01@tiscali.co.uk W: www.hungerfordhistorical.org.uk
Maidenhead Archaeological & Historical Society 70 Lambourne Drive, Maidenhead, Berkshire SL6 3HG T: 01628 672196
Middle Thames Archaeological & Historical Society 1 Saffron Close, Datchet, Slough, Berkshire SL3 9DU T: 01753 543636
Mortimer Local History Group 19 Victoria Road, Mortimer, Berkshire RG7 3SH T: 0118 933 2819
Newbury & District Field Club 4 Coombe Cottages, Coombe Road, Crompton, Newbury, Berkshire RG20 6RG T: 01635 579076
Project Purley 4 Allison Gardens, Purley on Thames, Berkshire RG8 8DF T: 0118 942 2485
Sandhurst Historical Society Beech Tree Cottage, Hancombe Road, Little Sandhurst, Berkshire GU47 8NP T: 01344 777476 W: www.sandhurst-town.com/societies
Shinfield & District Local History Societies Long Meadow, Part Lane, Swallowfield, Berkshire RG7 1TB
Swallowfield LHS Kimberley, Swallowfield, Reading, Berkshire RG7 1QX T: 0118 988 3650
Thatcham Historical Society 72 Northfield Road, Thatcham, RG18 3ES T: 01635 864820 W: www.thatchamhistoricalsociety.org.uk
Twyford & Ruscombe LHS 26 Highfield Court, Waltham Road, Twyford, Berkshire RG10 0AA T: 0118 934 0109
Wargrave LHS 6 East View Close, Wargrave, Berkshire RG10 8BJ T: 0118 940 3121 E: info@wargravehistory.org.uk W: www.wargravehistory.org.uk
Windsor Local History Group 256 Dedworth Road, Windsor, Berkshire SL4 4JR T: 01753 864835 E: windlesora@hotmail.com W: www.windlesora.org.uk
Wokingham History Group 39 Howard Road, Wokingham, Berkshire RG40 2BX T: 0118 978 8519

Birmingham
Alvechurch Historical Society Bearhill House, Alvechurch, Birmingham, B48 7JX T: 0121 445 2222
Birmingham & District Local History Association 112 Brandwood Road, Kings Heath, Birmingham B14 6BX T: 0121-444-7470
Birmingham Canal Navigation Society 37 Chestnut Close, Handsacre, Rugeley, Staffordshire WS15 4TH
Birmingham War Research Society 43 Norfolk Place, Kings Norton, Birmingham, West Midlands B30 3LB T: 0121 459 9008
Small Heath LHS 381 St Benedicts Road, Small Heath, Birmingham, B10 9ND
Wythall History Society 64 Meadow Road, Wythall, Worcestershire B47 6EQ T: 01564 822 483 W: www.wythallhistory.co.uk

Bristol
Alveston LHS 6 Hazel Gardens, Alveston, Bristol BS35 3RD T: 01454 43881 E: jc1932@alveston51.fsnet.co.uk
Avon Local History Association 4 Dalkeith Avenue, Kingswood, Bristol, BS15 1HH T: 0117 967 1362
Bristol & Avon Archaeological Society 3 Priory Avenue, Westbury on Trym, Bristol, BS9 4DA T: 0117 9620161 (evenings) W: http://www-digitalbristol.org/members/baas/
Bristol & Gloucestershire Archaeological Society Stonehatch, Oakridge Lynch, Stroud, Gloucestershire GL6 7NR T: 01285 760460 E: john@loosleyj.freeserve.co.uk W: www.bgas.org.uk
Bristol Records Society Regional History Centre, Faculty of Humanities, University of the West of England, St Maththias Campus, Oldbury Court Road, Fishponds, Bristol, BS16 2JP T: 0117 344 4395 W: www.bris.ac.uk/Depts/History/bristolrecordsociety/index.htm
Congresbury History Group Venusmead, 36 Venus Street, Congresbury, Bristol, BS49 5EZ T: 01934 834780
Downend LHS 141 Overndale Road, Downend, Bristol, B516 2RN
The West of England Costume Society 4 Church Lane, Long Aston, Nr. Bristol, BS41 9LU T: 01275-543564
Whitchurch LHS 62 Nailsea Park, Nailsea, Bristol, B519 1BB
Yatton LHS 27 Henley Park, Yatton, Bristol, BS49 4JH T: 01934 832575

Buckinghamshire
Buckinghamshire Archaeological Society County Museum, Church Street, Aylesbury, Buckinghamshire HP20 2QP T: 01269 678114
Buckinghamshire Record Society Centre for Buckinghamshire Studies, County Hall, Aylesbury, Buckinghamshire HP20 1UU T: 01296 383013 E: archives@buckscc.gov.uk W: www.bucksinfo.net/brs
Chesham Society 54 Church Street, Chesham HP5 IHY
Chess Valley Archealogical & Historical Society 16 Chapmans Crescent, Chesham, Buckinghamshire NP5 2QU T: 01494 772914

Pitstone & Ivinghoe Museum Society Vicarage Road, Pitstone, Leighton Buzzard, Buckinghamshire LU7 9EY T: 01582 605464 E: pjk96tpr@hotmail.com W: http://website.lineone.net/~pitstonemus
Princes Risborough Area Heritage Society Martin's Close, 11 Wycombe Road, Princes Risborough, Buckinghamshire HP27 0EE T: 01844 343004 W: www.bucksinfonet/prahs/

Cambridgeshire
Cambridge Antiquarian Society P0 Box 376, 96 Mill Lane, Impington, Cambridge , Cambridgeshire CB4 9HS T: 01223 502974 E: liz-allan@hotmail.com
Cambridge Group for History of Population and Social History Sir William Hardy Building, Downing Place, Cambridge, CB2 3EN T: 01223 333181 W: http://www-hpss.geog.cam.ac.uk
Cambridgeshire Archaeology Castle Court, Shire Hall, Cambridge, Cambridgeshire CB3 0AP T: 01223 717312 W: http://edweb.camcnty.gov.uk/archaeology www.archaeology.freewire.co.uk
Cambridgeshire LHS 1A Archers Close, Swaffham Bulbeck, Cambridge, Cambridgeshire CB5 0NG
Cambridgeshire Records Society County Record Office, Shire Hall, Cambridge, Cambridgeshire CB3 0AP W: www.cambridgeshirehistory.com/societies/crs/index.html
Hemingfords LHS Royal Oak Corner, Hemingford Abbots, Huntingdon, Cambridgeshire PE28 9AE T: 01480 463430
Houghton & Wyton LHS Church View, Chapel Lane, Houghton, Huntingdon PE28 2AY T: 01480 469376
Huntingdonshire LHS 2 Croftfield Road, Godmanchester, Cambridgeshire PE29 2ED T: 01480 411202
Sawston Village History Society 21 Westmoor Avenue, Sawston, Cambridge, CB2 4BU T: 01223 833475
Upwood & Raveley History Group The Old Post Office, 71-73 High Street, Upwood, Huntingdon, Cambridgeshire PE17 1QE

Cheshire
Altrincham History Society 10 Willoughby Close, Sale, Cheshire M33 6PJ T: 0161 962 7658
Ashton & Sale History Society Tralawney House, 78 School Road, Sale, Cheshire M33 7XB T: 0161 9692795
Bowdon History Society 5 Pinewood, Bowdon, Altrincham, Cheshire WA14 3JQ T: 0161 928 8975
Cheshire Heraldry Society 24 Malvern Close, Congleton CW12 4PD
Cheshire Local History Association Cheshire Record Office, Duke St, Chester CH1 1RL T: 01224 602559 W: www.cheshirehistory.org.uk
Chester Archaeological Society Grosvenor Museum, 27 Grosvenor Street, Chester CH1 2DD T: 01244 402028 W: www.chesterarchaeolsoc.org.uk
Christleton Local History Group 25 Croft Close, Rowton, Cheshire CH3 7QQ T: 01244 332410
Congleton History Society 45 Harvey Road, Congleton, Cheshire CWI2 2DH T: 01260 278757 E: awill0909@aol.com
Department of History & Archaeology - University of Chester University of Chester, Department of History & Archaeology, Parkgate Road, Chester, Cheshire CH1 4BJ T: 01244 512160 E: history@chester.ac.uk W: www.chester.ac.uk/history
Disley LHS 5 Hilton Road, Disley SK12 2JU T: 01663 763346
Historic Society of Lancashire & Cheshire East Wing Flat, Arley Hall, Northwich, Cheshire CW9 6NA T: 01565 777231
Lancashire & Cheshire Antiquarian Society 59 Malmesbury Road, Cheadle Hulme, Cheshire SK8 7QL T: 0161 439 7202 W: www.lancashirehistory.co.uk www.cheshirehistory.org.uk
Lawton History Group 17 Brattswood Drive, Church Lawton, Stoke on Trent, Cheshire ST7 3EJ T: 01270 873427

Macclesfield Historical Society 42 Tytherington Drive, Macclesfield, Cheshire SK10 2HJ T: 01625 420250
Northwich & District Heritage Society 13 Woodlands Road, Hartford, Northwich, Cheshire CW8 1NS
Poynton LHS 6 Easby Close, Poynton SK12 1YG
South Cheshire Family History Society incorporating S E Cheshire Local Studies Group Little Trees, Gawsworth Road, Gawsworth SK11 9RA T: 01625 426 173 W: www.scfhs.org.uk
Stockport Historical Society 59 Malmesbury Road, Cheadle Hulme, Stockport, Cheshire SK8 7QL T: 0161 439 7202
Weaverham History Society Ashdown, Sandy Lane, Weaverham, Northwich, Cheshire CW8 3PX T: 01606 852252
Wilmslow Historical Society 4 Campden Way, Handforth, Wilmslow, Cheshire SK9 3JA T: 01625 529381

Cleveland
Cleveland & Teesside LHS 150 Oxford Road, Linthorpe, Middlesbrough, Cleveland TS5 5EL

North-East England History Institute (NEEHI) School of Arts & Media, University of Teesside, Middlesbrough, TS1 3BA T: 01642 384019 E: neehi@tees.ac.uk W: www.neehi.co.uk

Cornwall
Bodmin Local History Group 1 Lanhydrock View, Bodmin, Cornwall PL31 1BG
Cornwall Association of Local Historians St Clement's Cottage, Coldrinnick Bac, Duloe, Liskeard PL14 4QF T: 01503 220947
Cornwall Family History Society 5 Victoria Square, Truro, Cornwall TR1 2RS T: 01872 264044 E: secretary@cornwallfhs.com W: www.cornwallfhs.com
Royal Institution of Cornwall, Courtney Library & Cornish History Research Centre Royal Cornwall Museum, River St, Truro TR1 2SJ T: 01872 272205 W: www.cornwall-online.co.uk www.cornwall.gov.uk/genealogy
The Devon & Cornwall Record Soc 7 The Close, Exeter EX1 1EZ T: 01392 274727 (Ansaphone) W: www.cs.ncl.ac.uk/genuki/DEV/DCRS

County Durham
Architectural & Archaeological Society of Durham & Northumberland Broom Cottage, 29 Foundry Fielkds, Crook, DL15 9SY T: 01388 762620
Darlington Railway Preservation Society Station Rd, Hopetown, Darlington DL3 6ST T: 01325 483606
Durham County LHS 21 St Mary's Grove, Tudhoe Village, Spennymoor DL16 6LR T: 01388 816209 E: johnbanham@tiscali.co.uk W: www.durhamweb.org.uk/dclhs
Durham Victoria County History Trust Redesdale, The Oval, North Crescent, Durham DH1 4NE T: 0191 384 8305 W: www.durhampast.net
Elvet Local & Family History Groups 37 Hallgarth Street, Durham, County Durham DH1 3AT T: 0191-386-4098
Houghton & District Local History Group 20 Fenton Terrace, Houghton le Spring, County Durham DH4 7AZ T: 0191 512 0030
Lanchester LHS 11 St Margaret's Drive, Tanfield Village, Stanley, County Durham DH9 9QW T: 01207-236634
Monkwearmouth Local History Group 75 Escallond Drive, Dalton Heights, Seaham, County Durham SR7 8JZ
North-East England History Institute (NEEHI) School of Arts & Media, University of Teesside, Middlesbrough, TS1 3BA T: 01642 384019 E: neehi@tees.ac.uk W: www.neehi.co.uk
Southwick History and Preservation Society 8 St Georges Terrace, Roker, Sunderland SR6 9LX T: 0191 567 2438 W: www.southwickhistory.org.uk
Teesdale Heritage Group Wesley Terrace, Middleton in Teesdale, Barnard Castle, County Durham DL12 0Q T: 01833 641104
The Derwentdale LHS 36 Roger Street, Blackhill, Consett, County Durham DH8 5SX
Tow Law History Society 27 Attleee Estate, Tow Law, County Durham DL13 4LG T: 01388-730056 W: www.historysociety.org.uk
Wheatley Hill History Club Broadmeadows, Durham Road, Wheatley Hill DH6 3LJ T: 01429 820813 E: history.club2@btinternet.com W: www.wheatley-hill.org.uk

Cumbria
Ambleside Oral History Group 1 High Busk, Ambleside, Cumbria LA22 0AW T: 01539 431070 W: www.aohg.org.uk/
Appleby Archaeology Group Pear Tree Cottage, Kirkland Road, Skirwith, Penrith, Cumbria CA10 1RL T: 01768 388318
Appleby In Westmorland Record Society Kingstone House, Battlebarrow, Appleby-In-Westmorland, Cumbria, CA16 6XT T: 017683 52282
Caldbeck & District LHS Whelpo House, Caldbeck, Wigton, Cumbria CA7 8HQ T: 01697 478270
Cartmel Peninsula LHS Fairfield, Cartmel, Grange Over Sands, Cumbria LA11 6PY T: 015395 36503

Crosby Ravensworth LHS Brookside, Crosby Ravensworth, Penrith, Cumbria CA10 3JP T: 01931 715324
Cumberland and Westmorland Antiquarian & Archaeological Society County Offices, Kendal, Cumbria LA9 4RQ T: 01539 773431 W: www.cwaas.org.uk
Cumbria Amenity Trust Mining History Society The Rise, Alston, Cumbria CA9 3DB T: 01434 381903 W: www.catmhs.co.uk
Cumbria Industrial History Society Coomara, Carleton, Carlisle, Cumbria CA4 0BU T: 01228 537379 E: gbrooksvet@tiscali.co.uk W: www.cumbria-industries.org.uk
Cumbria Local History Federation Oakwood, The Stripes, Cumwhinton, Carlisle, Cumbria CA4 0AP
Cumbrian Railways Association Whin Rigg, 33 St Andrews Drive, Perton, Wolverhampton, West Midlands WV6 7YL T: 01902 745472 E: info@cumbria-railways.co.uk W: www.cumbria-railways.co.uk
Dalton LHS 15 Kirkstone Crescent, Barrow in Furness, Cumbria LA14 4ND T: 01229 823558

Dudden Valley Local History Group Seathwaite Lodge, Dudden Valley, Broughton in Furness, Cumbria LA20 6ED

Duddon Valley Local History Group High Cross Bungalow, Broughton in Furness, Cumbria LA20 6ES T: 01229 716196

Friends of Cumbria Archives 42 Fairfield, Flookburgh, Grange over Sands LA11 7NB T: 01539 558343 E: jc@baytsaiq.fsnet.co.uk W: www.focas1991.co.uk

Friends of The Helena Thompson Museum 24 Calva Brow, Workington, Cumbria CA14 1DD T: 01900 603312

Holme & District LHS The Croft, Tanpits Lane, Burton, Carnforth LA6 1HZ T: 01524 782121

Keswick Historical Society Windrush, Rogersfield, Keswick, Cumbria CA12 4BN T: 01768 772771

Lorton and Derwent Fells LHS Beech Cottage, High Lorton, Cockermouth CA13 9UQ T: 01900 85551 W: www.derwentfells.com

Matterdale Historical and Archaeological Society The Knotts, Matterdale, Penrith, CA11 0LD T: 01768 482358

North Pennines Heritage Trust Nenthead Mines Heritage Centre, Nenthead, Alston CA9 3PD T: 01434 382037 W: www.npht.com

Sedbergh & District History Society 72a Main Street, Sedbergh, Cumbria LA10 5AD T: 01539 620504 E: sedberghhistsoc@aol.com W: www.sedberghhistory.org

Shap LHS The Hermitage, Shap, Penrith, Cumbria CA10 3LY T: 01931 716671 W: www.shaphistorysociety.org.uk

Solway History Society 9 Longthwaite Crescent, Wigton, Cumbria CA7 9JN T: 01697 344257 E: s.l.thornhill@talk21.com

Staveley and District History Society 9 Fairfield Close, Staveley, Kendal, Cumbria LA8 9RA E: sec@sdhs.org.uk W: www.sdhs.org.uk

Upper Eden History Society Copthorne, Brough Sowerby, Kirkby Stephen, Cumbria CA17 4EG T: 01768 341007

Whitehaven LHS Cumbria Record Office & local studies Library, Scotch Street, Whitehaven, Cumbria CA28 7BJ T: 01946 852920

Derbyshire

Allestree Local Studies Group 30 Kingsley Road, Allestree, Derby, Derbyshire DE22 2JH

Arkwright Society Cromford Mill, Mill Lane, Cromford, Derbyshire DE4 3RQ T: 01629 823256 E: info@arkwrightsociety.org.uk W: www.arkwrightsociety.org.uk

Chesterfield & District LHS Melbourne House, 130 Station Rd, Bimington, Chesterfield S43 1LU T: 01246 620266

Derbyshire Archaeological Society 2 The Watermeadows, Swarkestone, Derby, Derbyshire DE73 7FX E: barbarafoster@talk21.com W: www.DerbyshireAS.org.uk

Derbyshire Local History Societies Network Derbyshire Record Office, Libraries & Heritage Dept, County Hall, Matlock, Derbyshire DE4 3AG T: 01629-580000-ext-3520-1 W: www.derbyshire.gov.uk

Derbyshire Record Society 57 New Road, Wingerworth, Chesterfield S42 6UJ T: 01246 231024 W: www.derbyshirerecordsociety.org/

Holymoorside and District History Society 12 Brook Close, Holymoorside, Chesterfield, Derbyshire S42 7HB T: 01246 566799 W: www.holymoorsidehistsoc.org.uk

Ilkeston & District LHS 16 Rigley Avenue, Ilkeston, Derbyshire DE7 5LW

New Mills LHS High Point, Cote Lane, Hayfield, High Peak, Derbyshire SK23 T: 01663-742814

Old Dronfield Society 2 Gosforth Close, Dronfield S18 INT

Pentrich Historical Society c/o The Village Hall, Main Road, Pentrich DE5 3RE E: mail@pentrich.org.uk W: www.pentrich.org.uk

Devon

Chagford LHS Footaway, Westcott, Chagford, Newton Abbott, Devon TQ13 8JF T: 01647 433698

Dulverton and District Civic Society 39 jury Road, Dulverton, Devon TA22 9EJ

Holbeton Yealmpton Brixton Society 32 Cherry Tree Drive, Brixton, Plymouth PL8 2DD W: http://beehive.thisisplymouth.co.uk/hyb

Moretonhampstead History Society School House, Moreton, Hampstead, Devon TQ13 8NX

Newton Tracey & District LHS Home Park, Lovacott , Newton Tracey, Barnstaple EX31 3PY T: 01271 858451

Tavistock & District LHS 18 Heather Close, Tavistock, PL19 9QS T: 01822 615211

The Devon & Cornwall Record Society 7 The Close, Exeter EX1 1EZ T: 01392 274727 (Ansaphone) W: www.cs.ncl.ac.uk/genuki/DEV/DCRS

The Devon History Society c/o 112 Topsham Road, Exeter, Devon EX2 4RW T: 01803 613336

The Old Plymouth Society 625 Budshead Road, Whitleigh, Plymouth, Devon PL5 4DW

Thorverton & District History Society Ferndale, Thorverton, Exeter, Devon EX5 5NG T: 01392 860932

Wembury Amenity Society 5 Cross Park Road, Wembury, Plymouth, Devon PL9 OEU

Yelverton & District LHS 4 The Coach House, Grenofen, Tavistock, Devon PL19 9ES W: www.floyds.org.uk/ylhs

Dorset

Bournemouth Local Studies Group 6 Sunningdale, Fairway Drive, Christchurch, Dorset BH23 1JY T: 01202 485903

Bridport History Society 22 Fox Close, Bradpole, Bridport, West Dorset DT6 3JF T: 01308 456876 (Home)

Dorchester Association For Research into Local History 7 Stokehouse Street, Poundbury, Dorchester, Dorset DT1 3GP

Dorset Natural History & Archaeological Society Dorset County Museum, High West Street, Dorchester, Dorset DT1 1XA T: 01305 262735

Dorset Record Society Dorset County Museum, High West Street, Dorchester, Dorset DT1 1XA T: 01305-262735

Notes and Queries for Somerset and Dorset Marston House, Marston Bigot, Frome, Somerset BA11 5DU

Verwood Historical Society 74 Lake Road, Verwood, Dorset BH31 6BX T: 01202 824175 E: trevorgilbert@hotmail.com

William Barnes Society Pippins, 58 Mellstock Avenue, Dorchester, Dorset DT1 2BQ T: 01305 265358

Essex

Barking & District Historical Society c/o 16 North Road, Chadwell Heath, Romford, Essex RM6 6XU T: 020 8597 7210 E: barkinghistorical@hotmail.com W: www.barkinghistory.co.uk

Billericay Archaeological and Historical Society 24 Belgrave Road, Billericay, Essex CM12 1TX T: 01277 658989

Brentwood & District Historical Society 51 Hartswood Road, Brentwood, Essex CM14 5AG T: 01277 221637

Burnham & District Local History & Archaeological Society The Museum, The Quay, Burnham on Crouch, Essex CM0 8AS

Chadwell Heath Historical Society Wangey Road Chapel, Wangey Road, Chadwell Heath, Romford, Essex RM6 4BW T: 020 8590 4659 or 020 8597 1225 E: chadwellheathhs@hotmail.com

Colchester Archaeological Group 172 Lexden Road, Colchester, CO3 4BZ T: 01206 575081 W: www.camulos.com//cag/cag.htm

Dunmow & District Historical and Literary Society 18 The Poplars, Great Dunmow, Essex CM6 2JA T: 01371 872496

Essex Archaeological & Historical Congress Roseleigh, Epping Rd, Epping CM16 5HW T: 01992 813725 E: pmd2@ukonline.co.uk

Essex Historic Buildings Group 12 Westfield Avenue, Chelmsford, Essex CM1 1SF T: 01245 256102 E: cakemp@hotmail.com

Essex Society for Archeaology & History 2 Landview Gardens, Ongar, Essex CM5 9EQ T: 01277 363106

Friends of Historic Essex 11 Milligans Chase, Galleywood, Chelmsford, Essex CM2 8QD T: 01245 436043

Friends of The Hospital Chapel - Ilford 174 Aldborough Road South, Seven Kings, Ilford, Essex IG3 8HF T: (020) 8590 9972

Friends of Thomas Plume's Library The Old Vicarage, Great Totham, Maldon, Essex CM9 8NP T: 01621 892261

Halstead & District LHS Magnolia, 3 Monklands Court, Halstead, Essex C09 1AB

(HEARS) Herts & Essex Architectural Research Society 18 Wellfields, Loughton, Essex IG10 1NX T: 020 8508 2512

High Country History Group Repentance Cottage, Drapers Corner, Greensted, Ongar, Essex CM5 9LS T: 01277 364305 E: rob.brooks@virgin.net

Ingatestone and Fryerning Historical and Archaeological Society 36 Pine Close, Ingatestone, Essex CM4 9EG T: 01277 354001

Loughton & District Historical Society 6 High Gables, Loughton, Essex IG10 4EZ T: (020) 8508 4974

Maldon Society 15 Regency Court, Heybridge, Maldon CM9 4EJ

Nazeing History Workshop 16 Shooters Drive, Nazeing EN9 2QD T: 01992 893264 E: d_pracy@hotmail.com W: www.eppingforestdc.gov.uk/leisure_and_culture/Museum/Nazeing_History_Workshop.asp

Newham History Society 52 Eastbourne Road, East Ham, London, E6 6AT T: (020) 8471 1171 W: www.pewsey.net/newhamhistory.htm

Romford & District Historical Society 14 Thames Close, Rainham, Essex RM13 9HP T: 01708 520673 E: jackie@arctic.eclipse.co.uk W: www.romford.org/histsoc.htm

Saffron Walden Hist Soc 9 High Street, Saffron Walden CB10 1AT

The Colne Smack Preservation Society 76 New St, Brightlingsea, CO7 0DD T: 01206 304768 W: www.colne-smack-preservation.rest.org.uk

Thurrock Heritage Forum c/o Thurrock Museum, Orsett Rd, Grays RM17 5DX T: 01375 673828 E: enquiries@thurrockheritageforum.co.uk W: www.thurrockheritageforum.co.uk

Thurrock LHS 13 Rosedale Road, Little Thurrock, Grays, Essex RM17 6AD T: 01375 377746

Waltham Abbey Historical Society 28 Hanover Court, Quaker Lane, Waltham Abbey, Essex EN9 1HR T: 01992 716830
Walthamstow Historical Society 24 Nesta Road, Woodford Green, Essex IG8 9RG T: (020) 8504 4156
Wanstead Historical Society 28 Howard Road, Ilford IG1 2EX
Westcliff High School for Girls Society Kenilworth Gardens, Westcliff on Sea, Essex SS0 0BS
Witham History Group 35 The Avenue, Witham, Essex CM8 2DN T: 01376 512566
Woodford Historical Soc 2 Glen Rise, Woodford Green IG8 0AW

Gloucestershire
Alveston LHS 6 Hazel Gardens, Alveston, Bristol BS35 3RD T: 01454 43881 E: jc1932@alveston51.fsnet.co.uk
Bristol & Gloucestershire Archaeological Society Stonehatch, Oakridge Lynch, Stroud, Gloucestershire GL6 7NR T: 01285 760460 E: john@loosleyj.freeserve.co.uk W: www.bgas.org.uk
Campden & District Historical & Archaeological Society (CADHAS) The Old Police Station, High Street, Chipping Campden, GL55 6HB T: 01386 848840 E: enquiries@chippingcampdenhistory.org.uk W: www.chippingcampdenhistory.org.uk
Charlton Kings LHS 28 Chase Avenue, Charlton Kings, Cheltenham, Gloucestershire GL52 6YU T: 01242 520492
Cheltenham LHS 1 Turkdean Road, Cheltenham, Gloucestershire GL51 6AP
Cirencester Archaeological and Historical Society 8 Tower Street, Cirencester GL7 1EF E: dviner@waitrose.com W: www.cirenhistory.org.uk
Forest of Dean LHS Patch Cottage, Oldcroft Green, Lydney, Gloucestershire GL15 4NL T: 01594 563165 W: www.forestofdeanhistory.co.uk
Frenchay Tuckett Society and Local History Museum 247 Frenchay Park Road, Frenchay, Gloucestershire BS16 ILG T: 0117 956 9324 W: www.frenchay.org/museum.html
Friends of Gloucestershire Archives Clarence Row, Alvin Street, Gloucester, Gloucestershire GL1 3DW T: 01452 425295 E: foga@gloucester.demon.co.uk W: www.foga.org.uk
Gloucestershire County Local History Committee Gloucestershire RCC, Community House, 15 College Green, Gloucester, Gloucestershire GL1 2LZ T: 01452 528491 E: glosrcc@grcc.org.uk
Lechlade History Society The Gables, High Street, Lechlade, Gloucestershire GL7 3AD T: 01367 252457
Leckhampton LHS 202 Leckhampton Road, Leckhampton, Cheltenham, GL53 OHG
Marshfield & District LHS Weir Cottage, Weir Lane, Marshfield, Chippenham SN14 8NB T: 01225 891229
Moreton-In-Marsh & District LHS Chapel Place, Longborough, Moreton in Marsh, GL56 OQR T: 01451 830531 W: www.moretonhistory.co.uk
Newent LHS Arron, Ross Rd, Newent GL18 1BE T: 01531 821398
Painswick LHS Canton House, New Street, Painswick, Gloucestershire GL6 6XH T: 01452 812419
Stroud Civic Society Blakeford House, Broad Street, Kings Stanley, Stonehouse, Gloucestershire GL10 3PN T: 01453 822498
Stroud LHS 16 Barrowfield Road, Farmhill, Stroud, Gloucestershire GL5 4DF T: 01453 766764
Swindon Village Society 3 Swindon Hall, Swindon Village, Cheltenham, GL51 9QR T: 01242 521723
Tewkesbury Historical Society 5 Stokes Court, Oldbury Road, Tewkesbury, Gloucestershire GL20 5JL T: 01684 294262
The Waterways Trust The National Waterways Museum, Llanthony Warehouse, Gloucester Docks, Gloucester, Gloucestershire GL1 2EH T: 01452 318053 W: www.nwm.org.uk

Hampshire
Aldershot Historical and Archaeological Society 10 Brockenhurst Road, Aldershot, Hampshire GU11 3HH T: 01252 26589
Andover History and Archaeology Society 140 Weyhill Road, Andover, Hampshire SPlO 3BG T: 01264 324926
Basingstoke Archaeological and Historical Society 57 Belvedere Gardens, Chineham, Basingstoke, Hampshire RG21 T: 01256 356012
Bitterne LHS Heritage Centre, 225 Peartree Avenue, Bitterne, Southampton, Hampshire T: 023 8049 0948 E: martyn.blhs@btinternet.com W: www.bitterne.net
Botley & Curdridge Local History 3 Mayfair Ct, Botley, SO30 2GT
Fareham Local History Group Wood End Lodge, Wood End, Wickham, Fareham PO17 6JZ W: www.cix.co.uk/~catisfield/farehist.htm
Farnham and District Museum Society Tanyard House, 13a Bridge Square, Farnham, Surrey GU9 7QR
Fleet & Crookham Local History Group 33 Knoll Road, Fleet, Hampshire GU51 4PT W: www.hants.gov.uk/fclhg
Fordingbridge Historical Society 26 Lyster Road,, Manor Park, Fordingbridge, Hampshire SP6 IQY T: 01425 655417

Hampshire Archives Trust 3 Scott-Paine Drive, Hythe S045 6JY
Hampshire Field Club & Archaeological Society (Local History Section) c/o Hampshire Record Office, Sussex Street, Winchester SO23 8TH
Hampshire Field Club and Archaeological Society 8 Lynch Hill Park, Whitchurch, Hampshire RG28 7NF T: 01256 893241 W: www.fieldclub.hants.org.uk/
Lymington & District Historical Society Larks Lees, Coxhill Boldre, Lymington S041 8PS T: 01590 623933 E: birchsj@clara.co.uk
Lyndhurst Historical Society - disbanded May 2003
Milford-on-Sea Historical Record Society New House, New Road, Keyhaven, Lymington, S041 0TN
Newbury & District Field Club 4 Coombe Cottages, Coombe Road, Crompton, Newbury, Berkshire RG20 6RG T: 01635 579076
North East Hampshire Historical and Archaeological Society 2 Rotherwick Court, Farnborough, Hampshire GU14 6DD T: 01252 543023 E: nehhas@netscape.net W: www.hants.org.uk/nehhas
Porchester Society Mount Cottage, Nelson Lane, Portchester PO17 6AW
Somborne & District Society The Leasow, Old Palace farm, King's Somborne, Stockbridge, Hampshire SO20 6NJ T: 01794 388107 E: mikeandeileen@fsmail.net W: www.communigate.co.uk/hants/somsoc
South of England Costume Society Bramley Cottage, 9 Vicarage Hill, Hartley Witney, Hook, Hampshire RG27 8EH
Southampton Local History Forum Local Studies & Maritime Collections, Central Library, Civic Centre, Southampton, Hampshire SO14 7LW T: 023 8083 2205 E: local.studies@southampton.gov.uk W: www.southampton.gov.uk/s-leisure/libraries/
Stubbington & Hillhead History Society 34 Anker Lane, Stubbington, Fareham, Hampshire PO14 3HE T: 01329 664554
Tadley and District History Society (TADS) PO Box 7642, Tadley, Hampshire RG26 3AF T: 0118 981 4006 W: www.tadhistorey.com
West End LHS 40 Hatch mead, West End, Southampton, Hampshire SO30 3NE T: 023 8047 1886 E: westendlhs@aol.com W: www.westendlhs.hampshire.org.uk

Herefordshire
Bromyard & District LHS Local 7 Family History Centre, 5 Sherford Street, Bromyard HR7 4DL T: 01885 488755 E: bromyard.history@virgin.net W: www.bromyardhistorysociety.org.uk
Eardisland Oral History Group W:www.eardislandhistory.co.uk
Ewyas Harold & District WEA c/o Hillside, Ewyas Harold, Hereford, Herefordshire HR2 0HA T: 01981 240529
Kington History Society Kington Library, 64 Bridge Street, Kington, Herefordshire HR5 3DJ T: 01432 260600 E: vee.harrison@virgin.net
Leominster Historical Society Fircroft, Hereford Road, Leominster, Herefordshire HR6 8JU T: 01568 612874
Weobley & District LHS and Museum Weobley Museum, Back Lane, WeobleyHR4 8SG T: 01544 340292

Hertfordshire
Abbots Langley LHS 19 High Street, Abbots Langley WD5 0AA E: info@allhs.org.uk W: www.allhs.org.uk
Abbots Langley LHS 159 Cottonmill Lane, St Albans AL1 2EX
Baptist Historical Society 60 Strathmore Avenue, Hitchin, SG5 1ST T: 01462-431816 W: www.baptisthistory.org.uk
Barnet & District LHS 31 Wood Street, Barnet EN4 9PA
Braughing LHS Pantiles, Braughing Friars, Ware SG11 2NS
Codicote LHS 34 Harkness Way, Hitchin SG4 0QL T: 01462 622953
East Herts Archaeological Society 1 Marsh Lane, Stanstead Abbots, Ware, Hertfordshire SG12 8HH T: 01920 870664
Hertford & Ware LHS 10 Hawthorn Close, SG14 2DT
Hertford Museum (Hertfordshire Regiment) 18 Bull Plain, Hertford, SG14 1DT T: 01992 582686 W: www.hertfordmuseum.org
Hertfordshire Archaeological Trust The Seed Warehouse, Maidenhead Yard, The Wash, Hertford, SG14 1PX T: 01992 558 170 W: www.hertfordshire-archaeological-trust.co.uk
Hertfordshire Association for Local History 19 Cringle Court, Thornton Road, Little Heath EN6 1JR T: 01727 856250
Hertfordshire Record Society 119 Winton Drive, Croxley Green, Rickmansworth WD3 3QS T: 01923-248581 E: info@hrsociety.org.uk W: www.hrsociety.org.uk
Hitchin Historical Society c/o Hitchin Museum, Paynes Park, Hitchin, Hertfordshire SG5 2EQ
Kings Langley Local History & Museum Society Kings Langley Library, The Nap, Kings Langley, Hertfordshire WD4 8ET T: 01923 263205 W: www.kingslangley.org.uk
London Colney LHS 6 Telford Road, London Colney, St Albans, Hertfordshire AL2 1PQ
North Mymms LHS 89 Peplins Way, Brookmans Park, Hatfield AL9 7UT T: 01707 655970 W: www.brookmans.com
Potters Bar and District Historical Society 9 Hill Rise, Potters Bar, Hertfordshire EN6 2RX T: 01707 657586
Rickmansworth Historical Society 20 West Way, Rickmansworth, Hertfordshire WD3 7EN T: 01923 774998

Royston & District LHS 8 Chilcourt, Royston, SG8 9DD T: 01763 242677 E: david.allard@ntlworld.com W: www.roystonlocalhistory.org.uk

South West Hertfordshire Archaeological and Historical Society 29 Horseshoe Lane, Garston, Watford WD25 0LN T: 01923 672482

St. Albans & Herts Architectural & Archaeological Society 24 Rose Walk, St Albans, Hertfordshire AL4 9AF T: 01727 853204

Swing Riots, Rioters & Black Sheep Search 45 Kesteven Road, Stamford PE9 1SU T: 01780 751 320 E: jillchmbrs@aol.com W: www.swingriotsriotersblacksheepresearch.com

The Berkhamsted Local History and Museum Society Rhenigidale, Ivy House Lane, Berkhamsted HP4 2PP T: 01442 865 158

The Dacorum Heritage Trust Ltd The Museum Store, Clarence Road, Berkhamsted, Hertfordshire HP4 3YL T: 01442 879525

The Harpenden & District LHS The History Centre, 19 Arden Grove, Harpenden AL5 4SJ T: 01582 713539

Watford and District Industrial History Society 79 Kingswood Road, Garston, Watford, WD25 0EF T: 01923 673253

Welwyn & District LHS 40 Hawbush Rise, Welwyn AL6 9PP T: 01438 716415 E: paul@jiggens.net W: www.welwynhistory.org

Welwyn Archaeological Society The Old Rectory, 23 Mill Lane, Welwyn AL6 9EU T: 01438 715300 E: tony.rook@virgin.net

Isle of Wight

Isle of Wight Natural History & Archaeological Society Salisbury Gardens, Dudley Road, Ventnor IOW PO38 1EJ T: 01983 855385

Newchurch Parish Register Society 1 Mount Pleasant, Newport Road, Sandown, Isle of Wight P036 OLS

St Helens Historical Society Gloddaeth, Westfield Road, St. Helens, Ryde, Isle Of Wight P033 LUZ

St Helens History Society c/o The Castle, Duver Road, St Helens, Ryde, Isle of Wight P033 1XY T: 01983 872164

Kent

Anglo-Zulu War Historical Society Woodbury House, Woodchurch Road, Tenterden, Kent TN30 7AE T: 01580-764189

Appledore LHS 72 The Street, Appledore, Ashford, Kent TN26 2AE T: 01233 758500

Ashford Archaeological and Historical Society Gablehook Farm, Bethersden, Ashford, Kent TN26 3BQ T: 01233 820679

Aylesford Society 30 The Avenue, Greenacres, Aylesford, Maidstone, Kent ME20 7LE

Bearsted & District LHS 17 Mount Lane, Bearsted, Maidstone, Kent ME14 4DD

Bexley Civic Society 58 Palmeira Road, Bexleyheath DA7 4UX

Bexley Historical Society 36 Cowper Close, Welling, Kent DAI6 2JT

Biddenden LHS Willow Cottage, Smarden Road, Biddenden, Ashford, Kent TN27 8JT

Brenchley & Matfield LHS Ashendene, Tong Road, Brenchley, Tonbridge, Kent TN12 7HT T: 01892 723476

Bridge & District History Society La Dacha, Patrixbourne Road, Bridge, Canterbury, Kent CT4 5BL

Broadstairs Society Roof Tops, 58 High Street, Broadstairs, Kent CT10 lJT T: 01843 863453

Bromley Borough LHS 62 Harvest Bank Road, West Wickham, Kent BR4 9DJ T: 020 8462 5002

Canterbury Archaeology Society Dane Court, Adisham, Canterbury, Kent CT3 3LA

Charing & District LHS Old School House, Charing, Ashford, Kent TN27 0LS

Chatham Historical Society 69 Ballens Road, Walderslade, Chatham, Kent ME5 8NX T: 01634 865176

Council for Kentish Archaeology 14 Florence House, Royal Hebbert Pavilion, Gilbert Close, London SE18 4PP E: information@the-cka.fsnet.co.uk W: www.the-cka.fsnet.co.uk

Cranbrook & District History Society 61 Wheatfield Way, Cranbrook, Kent TN17 3NE

Crayford Manor House Historical & Archaeological Society 17 Swanton Road, Erith, Kent DA8 1LP T: 01322 433480

Croydon Natural History & Scientific Society Ltd 96a Brighton Road, South Croydon, Surrey CR2 6AD T: (020) 8688 4539 W: www.grieg51.freeserve.co.uk/cnhss

Dartford History & Antiquarian Society 14 Devonshire Avenue, Dartford, Kent DA1 3DW

Deal & Walmer LHS 7 Northcote Road, Deal, Kent CT14 7BZ

Detling Society 19 Hockers Lane, Detling, Maidstone, Kent ME14 3JL T: 01622 737940

Dover History Society 2 Courtland Drive, Kearsney, Dover, Kent CT16 3BX T: 01304 824764

East Peckham Historical Society 13 Fell Mead, East Peckham, Tonbridge, Kent TNI2 5EG

Edenbridge & District History Society 17 Grange Close, Edenbridge, Kent TN8 5LT

Erith & Belvedere LHS 67 Merewood Road, Barnehurst DA7 6PF

Farningham & Eynsford LHS Lavender Hill, Beesfield Lane, Farningham, Dartford, Kent DA4 ODA

Faversham Society 10-13 Preston St, Faversham, Kent ME13 8NS T: 01795 534542 E: ticfaversham@btconnect.com W: www.faversham.org/society

Fawkham & District Historical Society The Old Rectory, Valley Road, Fawkham, Longfield, Kent DA3 8LX

Folkestone & District LHS 7 Shorncliffe Crescent, Folkestone, Kent

Friends of Lydd 106 Littlestone Road, New Romney TN28 8NH

Frittenden History Society Bobbyns, The Street, Frittenden, Cranbrook, Kent TN17 2DG T: 01580 852459

Gillingham & Rainham LHS 23 Sunningdale Road, Rainham, Gillingham, Kent ME8 9EQ

Goudhurst & Kilndown LHS 2 Weavers Cottages, Church Road, Goudhurst, Kent TN17 1BL

Gravesend Historical Society 58 Vicarage Lane, Chalk, Gravesend, Kent DA12 4TE T: 01474 363998 W: www.ghs.org.uk

Great Chart Society Swan Lodge, The Street, Great Chart, Ashford, Kent TN23 3AH

Hadlow Historical Society Spring House, Tonbridge Road, Hadlow, Tonbridge, Kent TN11 0DZ T: 01732 850214 E: billanne@hadlow12.freeserve.co.uk

Halling LHS 58 Ladywood Road, Cuxton, Rochester, Kent ME2 1EP T: 01634 716139

Hawkhurst LHS 17 Oakfield, Hawkhurst, Cranbrook, Kent TN18 4JR T: 01580 752376

Headcorn LHS Cecil Way, 2 Forge Lane, Headcorn, Kent TN27 9QQ T: 01622 890253 W: www.headcorn.org.uk

Herne Bay Historical Records Society c/o Herne Bay Museum, 12 William St, Herne Bay, Kent CT6 5EJ

Higham Village History Group Forge House, 84 Forge Lane, Higham, Rochester, Kent ME3 7AH

Horton Kirby & South Darenth LHS Appledore, Rays Hill, Horton Kirby, Dartford, Kent DA4 9DB T: 01322 862056

Hythe Civic Society 25 Napier Gardens, Hythe, Kent CT2l 6DD

Isle of Thanet Hist Soc 58 Epple Bay Avenue, Birchington on Sea

Kemsing Historical & Art Society 26 Dippers Close, Kemsing, Sevenoaks, Kent TN15 6QD T: 01732 761774

Kent Archaeological Rescue Unit Roman Painted House, New St, Dover CTl7 9AJ T: 01304 203279 W: www.the-cka.fsnet.co.uk

Kent History Federation 14 Valliers Wood Road, Sidcup DA15 8BG

Kent Mills Group Windmill Cottage, Mill Lane, Willesborough, Kent TN27 0QG

Kent Postal History Group 27 Denbeigh Dr, Tonbridge TN10 3PW

Lamberhurst LHS 1 Tanyard Cotts, The Broadway, Lamberhurst, Tunbridge Wells, Kent TN3 8DD

Lamorbey & Sidcup LHS 14 Valliers Wood Rd, Sidcup DA15 8BG

Legion of Frontiersmen of Commonwealth 4 Edwards Road, Belvedere, Kent DA17 5AL

Leigh and District History Society Elizabeths Cottage, The Green, Leigh, Tonbridge, Kent TN11 8QW T: 01732 832459

Lewisham LHS 2 Bennett Park, Blackheath Village, London, SE3 9RB

Loose Area Hist Soc 16 Bedgebury Close, Maidstone ME14 5QY

Lyminge Historical Society Ash Grove, Canterbury Road, Etchinghill, Folkestone, Kent CTl8 8DF

Maidstone Area Archaeological Group 40 Bell Meadow, Maidstone, Kent ME15 9ND

Maidstone Historical Society 37 Bower Mount Road, Maidstone, ME16 8AX T: 01622 676472

Margate Civic Society 19 Lonsdale Avenue, Cliftonville, Margate, Kent CT9 3BT

Meopham Historical Society Tamar, Wrotham Road, Meopham, Kent DA13 0EX

Orpington History Society 42 Crossway, Petts Wood, Orpington, Kent BR5 1PE

Otford & District History Society Thyme Bank, Coombe Road, Otford, Sevenoaks, Kent TNI4 5RJ

Otham Society Tudor Cottage, Stoneacre Lawn, Otham, Maidstone, Kent ME15 8RT

Paddock Wood History Society 19 The Greenways, Paddock Wood, Tonbridge, Kent TNI2 6LS

Plaxtol Local History Group Tebolds, High Street, Plaxtol, Sevenoaks, Kent TN15 0QJ

Rainham Historical Society 52 Northumberland Avenue, Rainham, Gillingham, Kent ME8 7JY

Ramsgate Society Mayfold, Park Road, Ramsgate, Kent CT11 7QH

Ringwould History Society Back Street, Ringwould, Deal, Kent CT14 8HL T: 01304 361030 W: www.ringwould-village.org.uk

Romney Marsh Research Trust 11 Caledon Terrace, Canterbury, Kent CT1 3JS T: 01227 472490 E: s.m.sweetinburgh@kent.ac.uk W: www.kent.ac.uk/mts/rmrt/

Rye Local History Group 107 Military Road, Rye TN31 7NZ

Sandgate Soc The Old Fire Station, 51 High St, Sandgate CT20 3AH

Sandwich LHS Clover Rise, 14 Stone Cross Lees, Sandwich, Kent CT13 OBZ T: 01304 613476

Sevenoaks Hist Society 10 Plymouth Park, Sevenoaks, TN13 3RR

Sheppey LHS 34 St Helens Road, Sheerness, Kent

Shoreham & District Historical Society The Coach House, Darenth Hulme, Shoreham, Kent TNI4 7TU

Shorne Local History Gp 2 Calderwood, Gravesend DAl2 4Q11

Sittingbourne Society 11 Farm Crescent, Sittingbourne, Kent ME10 4QD T: 01795 423288 E: michael@baldwin963.fslife.co.uk

Smarden LHS 7 Beult Meadow, Cage Lane, Smarden, Kent TN27 8PZ T: 01233 770 856

Snodland Historical Society 214 Malling Road, Snodland ME6 SEQ E: aa0060962@blueyonder.co.uk W: www.snodlandhistory.org.uk

St Margaret's Bay History Society Rock Mount, Salisbury Road, St Margarets Bay, Dover, Kent CT15 6DL T: 01304 852236

Staplehurst Society Willow Cottage, Chapel Lane, Staplehurst, Kent TN12 0AN T: 01580 891059

Stretford LHS 26 Sandy Lane, Stretford, Manchester, M32 9DA T: 0161 283 9434 W: www.stretfordlhs.cwc.net

Tenterden & District LHS Little Brooms, Ox Lane, St Michaels, Tenterden, Kent TN30 6NQ

Teston History Society Broad Halfpenny, Malling Road, Teston, Maidstone, Kent ME18 SAN

Thanet Retired Teachers Association 85 Percy Avenue, Kingsgate, Broadstairs, Kent CT10 3LD

The Kent Archaeological Society Maidstone Museum, St Faith's Street, Maidstone, Kent ME14 1LH E: secretary@kentarchaeology.org.uk W: www.kentarchaeology.org.uk

The Marden Society 6 Bramley Court, Marden, Tonbridge, Kent TN12 9QN T: 01622 831904 W: www.marden.org.uk

Three Suttons Society Henikers, Henikers Lane, Sutton Valence, Kent ME17 3EE

Wateringbury LHS Vine House , 234 Tonbridge Road, Wateringbury, Kent ME18 5NY

Weald History Group Brook Farm, Long Barn Road, Weald, Sevenoaks, Kent

Wealden Buildings Study Group 64 Pilgrims Way, East Otford, Sevenoaks, Kent TN14 5QW

Whitstable Hist Soc 83 Kingsdown Park, Tankerton, Whitstable, Kent

Wingham LHS 67 High Street, Wingham, Canterbury CT3 1AA

Woodchurch LHS Woodesden, 24 Front Road, Woodclnurch, Ashford, Kent TN26 3QE

Wrotham Historical Society Hillside House, Wrotham TN15 7JH

Wye Hist Soc 1 Upper Bridge Street, Wye, AshfordTN2 5 SAW

Lancashire

Aspull and Haigh Historical Society 1 Tanpit Cottages, Winstanley, Wigan, Lancashire WN3 6JY T: 01942 222769

Birkdale & Ainsdale Historical Research Society 20 Blundell Drive, Birkdale, Southport PR8 4RG W: www.harrop.co.uk/bandahrs

Blackburn Civic Society 20 Tower Road, Blackburn, Lancashire BB2 5LE T: 01254 201399

Burnley Historical Society 66 Langdale Road, Blackburn, Lancashire BB2 5DW T: 01254 201162

Chadderton Historical Society 18 Moreton Street, Chadderton, Lancashire OL9 OLP T: 0161 652 3930 E: enid@chadderton-hs.freeuk.com W: www.chadderton-hs.freeuk.com

Denton LHS 94 Edward Street, Denton, Manchester, M34 3BR

Ewecross History Society Gruskholme, Bentham, Lancaster, Lancashire LA2 7AX T: 015242 61420

Fleetwood & District Historical Society 54 The Esplanade, Fleetwood, Lancashire FY7 6QE

Friends of Smithills Hall Museum Smithills Hall, Smithills deane Road, Bolton, Lancashire BL1 7NP

Garstang Historical & Archaelogical Society 7 Rivermead Drive, Garstang PR3 1JJ T: 01995 604913 E: marian.fish@btinternet.com

Historic Society of Lancashire & Cheshire East Wing Flat, Arley Hall, Northwich, Cheshire CW9 6NA T: 01565 777231

Hyndburn LHS 20 Royds Ave, Accrington BB5 2LE T: 01254 235511

Lancashire & Cheshire Antiquarian Society 59 Malmesbury Road, Cheadle Hulme, Cheshire SK8 7QL T: 0161 439 7202 W: www.lancashirehistory.co.uk www.cheshirehistory.org.uk

Lancashire Family History & Heraldry Society 2 Straits, Oswaldtwistle, Lancashire BB5 3LU T: 01254 239919 E: secretary@lfhhs.org.uk W: www.lfhhs.org.uk

Lancashire History 4 Cork Road, Lancaster, Lancashire LA1 4AJ

Lancashire Local History Federation 25 Trinity Court, Cleminson Street, Salford M3 6DX E: secretary@lancashirehistory.org W: www.lancashirehistory.org/

Lancashire Parish Register Society 19 Churton Grove, Shevington Moor, Wigan WN6 0SZ E: akenwright@yahoo.com W: www.lprs.org

Leyland Historical Society 172 Stanifield Lane, Farington, Leyland, Preston, Lancashire PR5 2QT

Littleborough Historical and Archaeological Society 8 Springfield Avenue, Littleborough, Lancashire LA15 9JR T: 01706 377685

Maghull & Lydiate LHS 15 Brendale Avenue, Maghull, Liverpool, L31 7AX

Mourholme LHS 14 Langdale Crescent, Storth, Milnthorpe, Cumbria LA7 7JG T: 01539 564 514

Nelson LHS 5 Langholme Street, Nelson, Lancashire BB9 ORW T: 01282 699475

North West Sound Archive Old Steward's Office, Clitheroe Castle, Clitheroe BB7 1AZ T: 01200 427897 E: nwsa@ed.lancscc.gov.uk W: www.lancashire.gov.uk/education/d_lif/ro/content/sound/imdex.asp

Saddleworth Historical Society 7 Slackcote, Delph, Oldham, Lancashire OL3 5TW T: 01457 874530

Society for Name Studies in Britain & Ireland 22 Peel Park Avenue, Clitheroe, Lancashire BB7 1ET T: 01200-423771 W: www.snsbi.org.uk/

Urmston District LHS 78 Mount Drive, Urmston, Manchester, M41 9QA

Leicestershire

Desford & District Local History Group Lindridge House, Lindridge Lane, Desford, Leicestershire LE9 9FD T: 01455 824514

East Leake & District LHS 8 West Leake Road, East Leake, Loughborough, Leicestershire LE12 6LJ T: 01509 852390

Glenfield and Western Archaeological and Historical Group 50 Chadwell Road, Leicester, Leicestershire LE3 6LF T: 1162873220

Great Bowden Historical Society 14 Langdon Road, Market Harborough, Leicestershire LE16 7EZ

Leicestershire Archaeological & Historical Society The Guildhall, Leicester, Leicestershire LE1 5FQ T: 0116 270 3031 E: alan@dovedale2.demon.co.uk W: www.le.ac.uk/lahs

Sutton Bonington LHS 6 Charnwood Fields, Sutton Bonington, Loughborough, Leicestershire LE12 5NP T: 01509 673107

Vaughan Archaeological and Historical Society c/o Vaughan College, St Nicholas Circle, Leicester, Leicestershire LEl 4LB

Lincolnshire

Lincoln Record Society Lincoln Cathedral Library, Cathedral, Minster Yard, Lincoln, Lincolnshire LN2 1PX T: 01522 561640 E: secretary@lincoln-record-society.org.uk W: www.lincoln-record-society.org.uk

Long Bennington LHS Kirton House, Kirton Lane, Long Bennington, Newark, Nottinghamshire NG23 5DX T: 01400 281726

Society for Lincolnshire History & Archaeology Jews' Court, Steep Hill, Lincoln, Lincolnshire LN2 1LS T: 01522-521337 E: slha@lincolnshirepast.org.uk W: www.lincolnshirepast.org.uk

London

Acton History Group 30 Highlands Avenue, London, W3 6EU T: (020) 8992 8698

Birkbeck College Birkbeck College, Malet Street, London, London WC1E 7HU T: (020) 7631 6633 E: info@bbk.ac.uk W: www.bbl.ac.uk

Brentford & Chiswick LHS 25 Hartington Road, London, W4 3TL

British Records Association c/o Finsbury Library, 245 St Johns Street, London, EC1V 4NB T: 020 7833 0428 F: 020 7833 0416 E: britrecass@btconnect.com W: www.britishrecordsassociation.org.uk/

Brixton Society 82 Mayall Road, London, SE24 0PJ T: (020) 7207 0347 E: apiperbrix@aol.com W: www.brixtonsociety.org.uk

Bromley Borough LHS 62 Harvest Bank Road, West Wickham, Kent BR4 9DJ T: 020 8462 5002

Centre for Metropolitan History Institute of Historical Research, Senate House, Malet Street, London, WC1E 7HU T: (020) 7862 8790 E: ihrcmh@sas.ac.uk W: www.history.ac.uk/cmh

Costume Society St Paul's House, 8 Warwick Road, London, EC4P 4BN W: www.costumesociety.org.uk

Croydon Local Studies Forum c/o Local Studies Library, Catherine Street, Croydon, CR9 1ET

Croydon Natural History & Scientific Society Ltd 96a Brighton Road, South Croydon, Surrey CR2 6AD T: (020) 8688 4539 W: www.grieg51.freeserve.co.uk/cnhss

East London History Society 42 Campbell Road, Bow, London, E3 4DT T: 020 8980 5672 E: mail@eastlondonhistory.org.uk W: www.eastlondonhistory.org.uk

Edmonton Hundred Hist Society Local History Unit, Southgate Town Hall, Green Lanes, London N13 4XD T: (020) 8379 2724

Friends of Historic Essex 11 Milligans Chase, Galleywood, Chelmsford, Essex CM2 8QD T: 01245 436043

Friends of The Metropolitan Police Historical Collection PO Box 27970, London, SE7 7XY E: historicstore@met.police.uk W: www.met.police.uk/history/friends.htm

Fulham & Hammersmith Historical Society Flat 12, 43 Peterborough Road, Fulham, London, SW6 3BT T: (020) 7731 0363 E: mail@fhhs.org.uk W: www.fhhs.org.uk

Hendon & District Archaeological Society 13 Reynolds Close, London, NW11 7EA T: (020) 8458 1352 W: www.hadas.org.uk

Hornsey Historical Society The Old Schoolhouse, 136 Tottenham Lane, London, N8 7EL T: (020) 8348 8429 W: www.hornseyhistorical.org.uk

Hornsey Historical Society The Old Schoolhouse, 136 Tottenham Lane, London, N8 7EL T: (020) 8348 8429 W: www.hornseyhistorical.org.uk

Hornsey Historical Society The Old Schoolhouse, 136 Tottenham Lane, London, N8 7EL T: (020) 8348 8429 W: www.hornseyhistorical.org.uk

London & Middlesex Archaeological Society Placements Office, University of North London, 62-66 Highbury Grove, London, N5 2AD

London Record Society c/o Institute of Historical Research, Senate House, Malet Street, London, WC1E 7HU T: (020) 7862-8798 W: www.ihrinfo.ac.uk/cmh

Mill Hill Historical Society 41 Victoria Road, Mill Hill, London, NW7 4SA T: (020) 8959 7126

Newham History Society 52 Eastbourne Road, East Ham, London, E6 6AT T: (020) 8471 1171 W: www.pewsey.net/newhamhistory.htm

Paddington Waterways and Maida Vale Society (Local History) 19a Randolph Rd, Maida Vale, London, W9 1AN T: 020 7289 0950

Richmond LHS 9 Bridge Road, St Margarets, Twickenham TWI IRE

Royal Arsenal Woolwich Historical Society Main Guard House, Royal Arsenal Woolwich, Woolwich, London, SE18 6ST

The Peckham Society 6 Everthorpe Road, Peckham, London, SE15 4DA T: (020) 8693 9412

The Vauxhall Society 20 Albert Square, London, SW8 1BS

Walthamstow Historical Society 24 Nesta Road, Woodford Green, Essex IG8 9RG T: (020) 8504 4156

Wandsworth Historical Society 31 Hill Court, Putney Hill, London, SW15 6BB

Willesden LHS (London Borough of Brent) 9 Benningfield Gardens, Berkhamstead, HP4 2GW T: 01442 878477

Merseyside

Birkdale & Ainsdale Historical Research Society 20 Blundell Drive, Birkdale, Southport PR8 4RG W: www.harrop.co.uk/bandahrs

British Society for Sports History Dept of Sports & Science, John Moore's University, Byrom Street, Liverpool, Merseyside L3 3AF

Friends of Williamson's Tunnels 15-17 Chatham Place, Edge Hill, Liverpool, Merseyside L7 3HD T: 0151 475 9833 E: info@williamsontunnels.com W: www.williamsontunnels.com

Historic Society of Lancashire & Cheshire East Wing Flat, Arley Hall, Northwich, Cheshire CW9 6NA T: 01565 777231

Liverpool History Society 32 Rugby Drive, Aintree Village, Liverpool L10 8JU E: enquiries@liverpoolhistorysociety.org.uk W: www.liverpoolhistorysociety.org.uk

Maghull & Lydiate LHS 15 Brendale Avenue, Maghull, Liverpool, L31 7AX

Merseyside Archaeological Society 20 Osborne Road, Formby, Liverpool, L37 6AR T: 01704 871802

The Guild of Merseyside Historians and Tourist Guides 49 Parkhill Road, Prenton, Birkenhead L42 9JD T: 0151 608 3769

Middlesex

Borough of Twickenham LHS 258 Hanworth Rd, Hounslow, TW3 3TY

Edmonton Hundred Historical Society Local History Unit, Southgate Town Hall, Green Lanes, London N13 4XD T: (020) 8379 2724

Hounslow & District History Society 16 Orchard Avenue, Heston, Middlesex TW5 0DU T: (020) 8570 4264

London & Middlesex Archaeological Society Placements Office, University of North London, 62-66 Highbury Grove, London, N5 2AD

Middlesex Heraldry Society 4 Croftwell, Harpeden AL5 1JG T: 01582 766372

Northwood & Eastcote LHS 3 Elbridge Close, Ruislip, Middlesex HA4 7XA T: 01895 637134 W: www.rnelhs.flyer.co.uk

Pinner LHS 22 Malpas Drive, Pinner, Middlesex HA5 3DQ T: 020 8866 1677 E: enquiries@pinnerlhs.org.uk W: www.pinnerlhs.org.uk

Ruislip Northwood & Eastcote LHS 3 Elmbridge Close, Ruislip, Middlesex HA4 7XA T: 01895 637134 E: toms.susan@googlemail.com W: www.rnelhs.flyer.co.uk

Sunbury and Shepperton Local 30 Lindsay Drive, Shepperton, Middlesex TW17 88JU T: 01932 226776 W: http://users.eggconnect.net/h.l.brooking/sslhs

Norfolk

Blakeney Area Historical Society 2 Wiveton Road, Blakeney, Norfolk NR25 7NJ T: 01263 741063

Federation of Norfolk Historical and Archaeological Organisations 14 Beck Lane, Horsham St Faith, Norwich NR10 3LD

Feltwell (Historical and Archaeological) Society 16 High Street, Feltwell, Thetford, Norfolk IP26 4AF T: 01842 828448

Holt History Group 6 Kelling Close, Holt, Norfolk NR23 6RU

Narborough LHS 101 Westfields, Narborough, Kings Lynn, Norfolk PE32 ISY W: www.narboroughaerodrome.org.uk

Norfolk and Norwich Archaeological Society 30 Brettingham Avenue, Cringleford, Norwich, Norfolk NR4 6XG T: 01603 455913

Norfolk Archaeological and Historical Research Group 50 Cotman Road, Norwich, NR1 4AH T: 01603 435470

Norfolk Heraldry Society 26c Shotesham Road, Poringland, Norwich, Norfolk NR14 7LG T: 01508 493832 W: www.norfolkheraldry.co.uk

Norfolk Record Society 17 Christchurch Road, Norwich NR2 2AE

Richard III Society - Norfolk Group 20 Rowington Road, Norwich, NR1 3RR

Northamptonshire

Bozeat Historical and Archaeological Society 44 Mile Street, Bozeat, Northamptonshire NN9 7NB T: 01933 663647

Brackley & District History Society 32 Church Lane, Evenley, Brackley, Northamptonshire NN13 5SG T: 01280 703508

Higham Chichele Society 3 Bramley Close, Rushden, NN10 6RL

Houghtons & Brafield History 5 Lodge Road, Little Houghton, Northamptonshire NN7 IAE

Irchester Parish Historical Society 80 Northampton Road, Wellingborough NN8 3HT T: 01933 274880 W: www.irchester.org www.iphs.org.uk

Northamptonshire Association for Local History 6 Bakers Lane, Norton, Daventry NN11 2EL T: 01327 312850 E: dargasson@tandjassociates.co.uk W: www.northants-history.org.uk

Northamptonshire Record Society Wootton Park Hall, Northampton, Northamptonshire NN4 8BQ T: 01604 762297

Oundle Hist Soc 13 Lime Avenue, Oundle, Peterborough, PE8 4PT

Rushden & District History Society 25 Byron Crescent, Rushden, NN10 6BL E: rdhs.rushden@virgin.net W: www.rdhs.org.uk

Weedon Bec Hist Soc 35 Oak St, Weedon, Northampton, NN7 4RR

West Haddon Local History Group Bramley House, 12 Guilsborough Road, West Haddon, Northamptonshire NN6 7AD

Northumberland

Architectural & Archaeological Society of Durham & Northumberland Broom Cottage, 29 Foundry Fields, Crook, County Durham DL15 9SY T: 01388 762620

Association of Northumberland Local History Societies c/o The Black Gate, Castle Garth, Newcastle upon Tyne, Tyne and Wear NE1 1RQ T: 0191 257 3254

Felton & Swarland LHS 23 Benlaw Grove, Felton, Morpeth, Northumberland NE65 9NG T: 01670 787476

Hexham LHS Dilstone, Burswell Villas, Hexham, Northumberland NE46 3LD T: 01434 603216

Morpeth Antiquarian Society 9 Eden Grove, Morpeth, NE61 2UN T: 01670 514792 E: hudson.c@virgin.net W: www.morpethnet.co.uk

Morpeth Nothumbrian Gathering Westgate House, Dogger Bank, Morpeth, Northumberland NE61 1RF

North-East England History Institute (NEEHI) School of Arts & Media, University of Teesside, Middlesbrough, TS1 3BA T: 01642 384019 E: neehi@tees.ac.uk W: www.neehi.co.uk

Northumberland LHS 44 Alwington Terrace, Newcastle upon Tyne, Tyne and Wear NE3 1UD

Northumbrian Language Society Westgate House, Dogger Bank, Morpeth, Northumberland NE61 1RE T: 01670 513308 E: enquiries@northumbriana.org.uk W: www.northumbriana.org.uk

Prudhoe & District LHS Prudhoe Community Enterprise Office, 82 Front Street, Prudhoe, Northumberland NE42 5PU E: mail@anlhs.org.uk W: www.anlh.org.uk

Stannington LHS Glencar House, 1 Moor Lane, Stannington, Morpeth, Northumberland NE61 6EA

The Ponteland LHS Woodlands, Prestwick Village, Ponteland, Northumberland NE20 9TX T: 01661 824017 E: jmichaeltaylor@btinternet.com W: www.ponthistsoc.freeuk.com

War Memorials Trust Bilsdale, Ulgham, Morpeth, Northumberland NE61 3AR T: 01670 790465 W: www.warmemorials.com

Nottinghamshire

Basford & District LHS 44 Cherry Tree Close, Bucinsley, Nottingham, Nottinghamshire NG16 5BA T: 0115 927 2370

Beeston & District LHS 16 Cumberland Avenue, Beeston, Nottinghamshire NG9 4DH T: 0115 922 3008

Bingham & District LHS 56 Nottingham Road, Bingham, NG13 8AT T: 01949 875866

Bleasby LHS 5 Sycamore Ln, Bleasby NG14 7GJ T: 01636 830094

Bulwell Historical Society 19 Woodland Avenue, Bulwell, Nottingham, Nottinghamshire NG6 9BY T: 0115 927 9519

Burton Joyce and Bulcote LHS 9 Carnarvon Drive, Burton Joyce, Nottingham, Nottinghamshire NG14 5ER T: 0115 931 3669

Caunton LHS Beech House, Caunton, Newark, Nottinghamshire NG23 6AF T: 01636 636564

Chinemarelian Society 3 Main Street, Kimberley, Nottinghamshire NG16 2NL T: 0115 945 9306

East Leake & District LHS 8 West Leake Road, East Leake, Loughborough, Leicestershire LE12 6LJ T: 01509 852390

East Midlands Historian School of Continuing Education, Nottingham University, University Park, Nottingham, Nottinghamshire NG7 2RD T: 0115 951 4398

Eastwood Historical Society 18 Park Crescent, Eastwood , Nottinghamshire NG16 3DU T: 01773 712080

Edwalton LHS Camelot, 74 Wellin Lane, Edwalton, Nottingham, NG12 4AH T: 0115 923 3015 E: hallatcamelot@aol.com

Edwinstowe Historical Society 12 Church Street, Edwinstowe, Nottinghamshire NG21 9QA T: 01623 824455

Epperstone Hist Soc Sunny Mead, Main St, Epperstone, NG14 6AG

Farndon & District LHS 22 Brockton Avenue, Farndon, Newark, Nottinghamshire NG24 4TH T: 01636 610070

Flintham Society & Flintham Museum Inholms Rd, Flintham NG23 5LF T: 0163.6 525111 W: www.flintham-museum.org.uk

Gotham & District LHS 108A Leake Road, Gotham, Nottinghamshire NG11 0JN T: 0115 983 0494

Hucknall Heritage Society 64 Bestwood Road, Hucknall, Nottingham, Nottinghamshire NG15 7PQ E: m.newton2000@btinternet.com W: www.hucknalltorkardhistory.co.uk

Keyworth & District LHS Keyworth Library, Church Drive, Keyworth, Nottingham NG12 5FF W: www.keyworth-history.org.uk

Lambley Historical Society 11 Steeles Way, Lambley, Nottingham, Nottinghamshire NG4 4QN T: 0115 931 2588

Lenton LHS 53 Arnesby Road, Lenton Gardens, Nottingham, Nottinghamshire NG7 2EA T: 0115 970 3891

Newark Archaeological & LHS 13 Main Street, Sutton on Trent, Newark NG23 6PF T: 01636 821781 (Eves) E: jill.campbell@ic24.net

North Muskham History Group Roseacre, Village Lane, North Muskham, Nottinghamshire NG23 6ES T: 01636 705566

Nottingham Civic Society 57 Woodhedge Drive, Nottingham, NG3 6LW T: 0115 958 8247 W: www.nottinghamcivicsociety.org.uk

Nottingham Historical and Archaeological Society 9 Churchill Drive, Stapleford, Nottingham NG9 8PE T: 0115 939 7140

Nottinghamshire Industrial Archaeology Society 18 Queens Avenue, Ilkeston, Derbyshire DE7 4DL T: 0115 932 2228

Nottinghamshire Local History Association 128 Sandhill Street, Worksop, Nottinghamshire S80 1SY T: 01909 488878

Numismatic Society of Nottinghamshire T: 0115 925 7674

Nuthall & District LHS 14 Temple Drive, Nuthall, Nottingham, NG16 1BE T: 0115 927 1118 E: tony.horton@ntlworld.com

Old Mansfield Society 7 Barn Close, Mansfield NG18 3JX T: 01623 654815 E: dcrut@yahoo.com W: www.old-mansfield.org.uk

Old Mansfield Woodhouse Society Burrwells, Newboundmill Lane, Pleasley, Mansfield, Nottinghamshire NG19 7QA T: 01623 810396

Old Warsop Society 1 Bracken Close, Market Warsop, NG20 0QQ

Pentagon Society Dellary, Mill Road, Elston, Newark, Nottinghamshire NG23 5NR T: 01636 525278

Pleasley History Group 8 Cambria Road, Pleasley, Mansfield, Nottinghamshire NG19 7RL T: 01623 810201

Radford Memories Project 25 Manston Mews, Alfreton Road, Radford, Nottingham, Nottinghamshire NG7 3QY T: 0115 970 1256

Retford & District Historical & Archaeological Society Cambridge House, 36 Alma Road, Retford, Nottinghamshire DN22 6LW T: 07790212360 E: JOAN@grant.demon.co.uk

Ruddington LHS St Peter's Rooms, Church Street, Ruddington, Nottingham, Nottinghamshire NG11 6HA T: 0115 914 6645

Sherwood Archaeological Society 32 Mapperley Hall Drive, Nottingham, Nottinghamshire NG3 5EY T: 0115 960 3032

Shireoaks Local History Group 22 Shireoaks Row, Shireoaks, Worksop, Nottinghamshire S81 8LP

Sneinton Environmental Society 248 Greenwood Road, Nottingham, Nottinghamshire NG3 7FY T: 0115 987 5035

Southwell & District LHS Fern Cottage, 70 Kirklington Road, Southwell, Nottinghamshiure NG25 0AX T: 01636 812220

Stapleford & District LHS 25 Westerlands, Stapleford, Nottingham, Nottinghamshire NG9 7JE T: 0115 939 2573

Sutton Heritage Society 8 Sheepbridge Lane, Mansfield, NG18 5EA T: 01623 451179 E: lildawes@yahoo.co.uk

Sutton on Trent LHS 14 Grassthorpe Road, Sutton on Trent, Newark, Nottinghamshire NG23 6QD T: 01636 821228

Thoroton Society of Nottinghamshire 38 Stuart Close, Arnold, Nottingham, Nottinghamshire NG5 8AE T: 0115 926 6175 E: wilsonicus@hotmail.co.uk W: www.thorotonsociety.org.uk

Tuxford Heritage Society 140 lincoln Road, Tuxford, Newark, Nottinghamshire NG22 0HS

West Bridgford & District LHS 30 Repton Road, West Bridgford, Nottinghamshire NG2 7EJ T: 0115 923 3901

Whitwell Local History Group 34 Shepherds Avenue, Worksop, S81 0JB E: jandpwalker34@aol.com W: www.wlhg.freeuk.com

Wilford History Society 10 St Austell Drive, Wilford, Nottingham, Nottinghamshire NG11 7BP T: 0115 981 7061

Woodborough Local History Group The Woodpatch, 19 Sunningdale Drive, Woodborough, Nottinghamshire NG14 6EQ T: 0115 965 3103 W: www.woodborough-heritage.org.uk

Worksop Archaeological & LHS 42 Dunstan Crescent, Worksop, Nottinghamshire S80 1AF T: 01909 477575

Oxfordshire

Abingdon Area Archaeological and Historical Society 4 Sutton Close, Abingdon OX14 1ER T: 01235 529720 W: www.aaahs.org.uk

Ashbury LHS Claremont , Asbury, Swindon SN6 8LN E: marionlt@waitrose.com

Banbury Historical Society c/o Banbury Museum, Spiceball Park Road, Banbury, Oxfordshire OX16 2PQ T: 01295 672626 W: www.cherwell-dc.gov.uk/banburymuseum/banburyhistoricalsoc.cfm

Berkshire Local History Association Department of History, University of Reading, Whiteknights, Reading, Berkshire RG6 6AA E: secretary@blha.org.uk W: www.blha.org.uk

Blewbury Local History Group Spring Cottage, Church Road, Blewbury, Didcot, Oxfordshire OX11 9PY T: 01235 850427

Bloxham Village History Group 1 Hyde Grove, Bloxham, Banbury, Oxfordshire OX15 4HZ T: 01295 720037

Chadlington LHS 10 Rawlinson Close, Chadlington, Chipping Norton OX7 3LN T: 01608 676 526 E: tdgarratt@aol.com W: www.chaddingtonhistorysociety.org

Charlbury Society Chimney Cottage, Dancers Hill, Charlbury, OX7 3RZ T: 01608 819091 E: brian_murray_guide@yahoo.co.uk

Chinnor Historical & Archealogical Society 4 Beech Road, Thame, Oxfordshire OX9 2AL T: 01844 216538

Chipping Norton History Society 9 Toy Lane, Chipping Norton, Oxfordshire OX7 5FH T: 01608 642754

Cumnor and District History Society 4 Kenilworth Road, Cumnor, Nr Oxford OX2 9QP T: 01865 862965

Dorchester on Thames Historical Society 14 Herringcote, Martins Lane, Dorchester on Thames, Wallingford, Oxfordshire OX10 7RD T: 01865 341977 E: gail.thomas8@btopenworld.com

Enstone Local History Circle The Sheiling, Sibford Ferris, Banbury, Oxfordshire OX15 5RG

Eynsham History Group 11 Newland Street, Eynsham, Oxfordshire OX29 4LB T: 01865 883141

Faringdon Archaeological & Historical Society 1 Orchard Hill, Faringdon SN7 7EH T: 01367 240885 W: www.faringdon.org/hysoc

Finstock LHS 36 High Street, Finstock OX7 3DW T: 01993 868768 E: bruce768@gmail.com W: http://finstocklocalhistory.blogspot.com

Goring & Streatley LHS 45 Springhill Road, Goring On Thames, Reading, Berkshire RG8 0BY T: 01491 872625

Hanney History Group Willow Tree House, The Green, East Hanney, Wantage, Oxfordshire OX12 0HQ T: 01238 68375

Henley on Thames Archaeological and Historical Group 52 Elizabeth Road, Henley on Thames RG9 1RA T: 01491 578 530

Hook Norton Local History Group Sunnybank Farmhouse, Scotland End, Hook Norton, Banbury OX15 5NR T: 01608 737103 E: scotlandend@btinternet.com

Iffley LHS 4 Abberbury Avenue, Oxford OX4 4EU T: 01865 779257

Kidlington and District Historical Society 18 Oak Drive, Kidlington OX5 2HL T: 01865 373517 W: www.communigate.co.uk/oxford

Launton Historical Society Salamanca, Launton, Oxfordshire OX26 5DQ T: 01869 253281 E: p_tucker@tesco.net

Lechlade History Society The Gables, High Street, Lechlade, Gloucestershire GL7 3AD T: 01367 252457

Longworth LHS 7 Norwood Avenue, Southmoor, Abingdon, Oxfordshire OX13 5AD T: 01865 820522 W: www.l-h-s.org.uk

Marcham Society Prior's Corner, 2 Priory Lane, Marcham, Abingdon OX13 6NY T: 01865 391439 E: e.dunford@btinternet.com

Over Norton History Group Fountain Cottage, The Green, Over Norton, Oxfordshire OX7 5PT T: 01608 641057

Oxfordshire Architectural & Hist Soc 53 Radley Road, Abingdon, Oxford OX14 3PN T: 01235 525960 E: tony@oahs.org.uk W: www.oahs.org.uk

Oxfordshire Local History Association 12 Meadow View, Witney, Oxfordshire OX28 6TY T: 01993 778345

Oxfordshire Record Society Bodleian Library, Oxford, Oxfordshire OX1 3BG T: 01865 277164 E: secretary@oahs.org.uk

Shrivenham LHS Ridgeway, Kings Lane, Loncot, Faringdon, Oxfordshire SN7 7SS T: 01793783083

Thame Historical Society 12 Park Terrace, Thame, Oxfordshire OX9 3HZ T: 01844 212336 E: csear58229@aol.com

The Bartons History Group 18 North Street, Middle Barton, Oxfordshire OX7 7BJ T: 01869 347013

Volunteer Corps of Frontiersmen Archangels' Rest, 26 Dark Lane, Witney, Oxfordshire OX8 5LE

Wallingford Historical & Archaeological Society Wallingford Museum, Flint House, 52a High Street, Wallingford, OX1O 0DB T: 01491 835065

Whitchurch: The Ancient Parish of Whitchurch Historical Society Ashdown, Duchess Close, Whitchurch on Thames RG8 7EN

Witney & District Historical & Archaeological Society 16 Church Green, Witney, Oxfordshire OX28 4AW T: 01993 703289

Wolvercote LHS 18 Dovehouse Close, Upper Wolvercote, Oxfordshire OX2 8BG T: 01865 514033

Wootton, Dry Sandford & District History Society 46 Church Lane, Dry Sandford, Abingdon OX13 6JP T: 01865 390441

Wychwoods LHS Littlecott, Honeydale Farm, Shipton Under Wychwood, Chipping Norton, Oxfordshire OX7 6BJ T: 01993 831023

Yarnton with Begbroke Hist Soc 6 Quarry End, Begbroke, OX5 1SF

Rutland

Rutland Local History & Record Society c/o Rutland County Museum, Catmos Street, Oakham LE15 6HW T: 01572 758440

Shropshire

Cleobury Mortimer Hist Soc The Old Schoolhouse, Neen Savage, Cleobury Mortimer, Kidderminster DY14 8JU T: 01299 270319

Field Studies Council Head Office, Preston Montford, Montford Bridge, Shrewsbury, Shropshire SY4 1HW T: 01743 852100 E: fsc.headoffice@ukonline.co.uk W: www.field-studies-council.org

Shropshire Archaeological and Historical Society Lower Wallop Farm, Westbury, Shrewsbury, Shropshire SY5 9RT T: 01743 891215

Whitchurch History and Archaeology Group Smallthythe, 26 Rosemary Lane, Whitchurch, Shropshire SY13 1EG T: 01948 662120

Somerset

Avon Local History Association 4 Dalkeith Avenue, Kingswood, Bristol, BS15 1HH T: 0117 967 1362

Axbridge Archaeological and LHS King John's Hunting Lodge, The Square, Axbridge, Somerset BS26 2AR T: 01934 732012

Bathford Society 36 Bathford Hill, Bathford, Somerset BA1 7SL

Bruton Museum Society The Dovecote Building, High Street, Bruton T: 01749 812851 W: www.southsomersetmuseum.org.uk

Castle Cary & District Museum & Preservation Society Woodville House, Woodcock Street, Castle Cary BA7 7BJ T: 01963 351122 W:

Chard History Group 17 Kinforde, Chard, Somerset TA20 1DT T: 01460 62722 E: carterw@globalnet.co.uk W:

Congresbury History Group Venusmead, 36 Venus Street, Congresbury, Bristol, BS49 5EZ T: 01934 834780

Freshford & District LHS Quince Tree House, Pipehouse Lane, Freshford, Bath, Somerset BA2 7UH T: 01225 722339

Nailsea & District LHS PO Box 1089, Nailsea BS48 2YP

Notes and Queries for Somerset and Dorset Marston House, Marston Bigot, Frome, Somerset BA11 5DU

Oakhill & Ashwick LHS Bramley Farm, Bath Road, Oakhill, Somerset BA3 5AF T: 01749 840 241

Somerset Archaeological & Natural History Society Taunton Castle, Taunton, Somerset TA1 4AD T: 01823 272429 E: office@sanhs.org W: www.sanhs.org

Somerset Record Society Somerset Studies Library, Paul Street, Taunton, Somerset TA1 3XZ T: 01823-340300

South East Somerset Archaeological and Historical Society Silverlands, Combe Hill, Templecombe BA8 OLL T: 01963 371307

South Petherton Local History Crossbow, Hele Lane, South Petherton, Somerset TA13 5DY

South Petherton Local History Group Cobbetts Droveway, South Petherton, Somerset TAI3 5DA T: 01460 240252

Staffordshire

Berkswich History Society 1 Greenfield Road, Stafford, Staffordshire ST17 OPU T: 01785 662401

Birmingham Canal Navigation Society 37 Chestnut Close, Handsacre, Rugeley, Staffordshire WS15 4TH

Landor Society 38 Fortescue Lane, Rugeley, Staffordshire WS15 2AE T: 01889 582709 W:

Lawton History Group 17 Brattswood Drive, Church Lawton, Stoke on Trent, Cheshire ST7 3EJ T: 01270 873427

Mid-Trent Historical Association 36 Heritage Court, Lichfield, Staffordshire WS14 9ST T: 01543 301097

North Staffordshire Historians' Guild 14 Berne Avenue, Newcastle under Lyme, Staffordshire ST5 2QJ

Ridware History Society 8 Waters Edge, Handsacre, Nr. Rugeley, Staffordshire WS15 7HP T: 01543 307456

Stafford Historical & Civic Society 86 Bodmin Avenue, Weeping Cross, Stafford ST17 OEQ T: 01785 612194 E: esj@supanet.com

Staffordshire Archaeological & Historical Society 6 Lawson Close, Aldridge, Walsall, WS9 0RX T: 01922 452230 W: www.sahs.uk.net

Suffolk

Framlingham & District Local History & Preservation Society 28 Pembroke Road, Framlingham, Suffolk IP13 9HA T: 01728 723214

Lowestoft Archaeological and LHS 1 Cranfield Close, Pakefield, Lowestoft, Suffolk NR33 7EL T: 01502 586143

Suffolk Institute of Archaeology and History Roots, Church Lane, Playford, Ipswich, Suffolk IP6 9DS T: 01473-624556 E: brianseward@btinternet.com W: www.suffolkarch.org.uk

Suffolk Local History Council Suffolk Community Resource Centre, 2 Wharfedale Rd, Ipswich IP1 4JP W: www.suffolklocalhistorycouncil.org.uk

Surrey

Addlestone History Society 53 Liberty Lane, Addlestone, Weybridge, Surrey KT15 1NQ

Beddington & Carshalton Historical Society 57 Brambledown Road, Wallington, Surrey SM6 0TF

Beddington Carshalton & Wallington History Society 7 Mortlake Close, Beddington, Croydon, Surrey CR0 4JW T: (020) 8726 0255

Bourne Society 54 Whyteleafe Road, Caterham, Surrey CR3 5EF T: 01883 349287 W: www.bourne-society.org.uk

Carshalton Society 43 Denmark Road, Carshalton, Surrey SM5 2JE

Centre for Local History Studies Faculty of Artss & Social Sciences, Kingston University, Penrhyn Road, Kingston KT1 2EE T: 020 8417 2359 E: localhistory@kingston.ac.uk W: http://localhistory.kingston.ac.uk

Croydon Natural History & Scientific Society Ltd 96a Brighton Road, South Croydon, Surrey CR2 6AD T: (020) 8688 4539 W: www.grieg51.freeserve.co.uk/cnhss

Domestic Buildings Research Group (Surrey) The Ridings, Lynx Hill, East Horsley, Surrey KT24 5AX T: 01483 283917

Dorking Local History Group Dorking & District Museum, The Old Foundry, 62a West St, Dorking, Surrey RH4 1BS T: 01306 876591

Esher District LHS 45 Telegraph Lane, Claygate, Surrey KT10 0DT

Farnham and District Museum Society Tanyard House, 13a Bridge Square, Farnham, Surrey GU9 7QR

Friends of Public Record Office The Public Record Office, Ruskin Avenue, Kew, Richmond TW9 4DU T: (020) 8876 3444 ext 2226 W: www.pro.gov.uk/yourpro/friends.htm

Guildford Archaeology and Local History Group 6 St Omer Road, Guildford, Surrey GU1 2DB T: 01483 532201

Hayward Memorial Local History Centre The Guest House, Vicarage Road, Lingfield, Surrey RH7 6HA T: 01342 832058

History of Thursley Soc 50 Wyke Ln, Ash, Aldershot, GU12 6EA

Leatherhead and District LHS Leatherhead Museum, 64 Church Street, Leatherhead, Surrey KT22 8DP T: 01372 386348

Nonsuch Antiquarian Society 17 Seymour Avenue, Ewell, Surrey KT17 2RP T: (020) 8393 0531 W: www.nonsuchas.org.uk

Puttenham & Wanborough History Society Brown Eaves, 116 The Street, Puttenham, Guildford, Surrey GU3 1AU

Richmond LHS 9 Bridge Road, St Margarets, Twickenham TWI IRE

Send and Ripley History Society St Georges Farm House, Ripley, Surrey GU23 6AF T: 01483 222107

Shere Gomshall & Peaslake LHS Twiga Lodge, Wonham Way, Gomshall, Guildford, GU5 9NZ T: 01483 202112 W: www.gomshall.freeserve.co.uk/sglshhp.htm

Surrey Archaeological Society Castle Arch, Guildford GU1 3SX T: 01483 532454 W: www.ourworld.compuserve.com/homepages/surreyarch

Surrey Local History Council Guildford Institute, University of Surrey, Ward Street, Guildford, Surrey GU1 4LH

Surrey Record Society c/o Surrey History Centre, 130 Goldsworth Road, Woking, Surrey GU21 1ND T: 01483 594603

The RH7 History Group Bidbury House, Hollow Lane, East Grinstead, West Sussex RH19 3PS

The Woldingham History Society Picardie, High Drive, Woldingham, Surrey CR3 7ED

Walton & Weybridge LHS 67 York Gardens, Walton on Thames, Surrey KT12 3EN

Walton On The Hill District LHS 5 Russell Close, Walton On The Hill, Tadworth, Surrey KT2O 7QH T: 01737 812013

Westcott Local History Group 6 Heath Rise, Westcott, Dorking, Surrey RH4 3NN T: 01306 882624 E: info@westcotthistory.org.uk W: www.westcotthistory.org.uk

Sussex

Danehill Parish Historical Society Butchers Barn, Freshfield Lane, Danehill, Sussex RH17 7HQ T: 01825 790292

Eastbourne LHS 12 Steeple Grange, 5 Mill Road, Eastbourne, Sussex BN21 2LY

Lewes Archaeological Group Rosemary Cottage, High Street, Barcombe, near Lewes, BN8 5DM T: 01273 400878

Sussex Archaeological Society Barbican House, 169 High Street, Lewes, East Sussex BN7 1YE T: 01273 405733 E: research@sussexpast.co.uk W: www.sussexpast.co.uk

Sussex History Study Group Colstock, 43 High Street, Ditchling, Sussex BN5 8SY

Sussex Local History Forum Anne of Cleves House, 52 Southover, High Street, Lewes, Sussex BN7 1JA

Sussex - East

Blackboys & District Historical Society 18 Maple Leaf Cottages, School Lane, Blackboys, Uckfield, East Sussex TN22 5LJ E: baturner.18maple@btinternet.com

Brighton & Hove Archealogical Society 115 Braeside Avenue, Patcham, Brighton, East Sussex BN1 8SQ

Eastbourne Natural History and Archaeological Society 11 Brown Jack Avenue, Polegate, East Sussex BN26 5HN T: 01323 486014

Friends of East Sussex Record Office The Maltings, Castle Precincts, Lewes BN7 1YT T: 01273-482349 W: www.esrole.fsnet.co.uk

Maresfield Historical Society Hockridge House, London Road, Maresfield, East Sussex TN22 2EH T: 01825 765386

Peacehaven & Telscombe Historical Society 2 The Compts, Peacehaven BN1O 75Q T: 01273 588874 W: www.history-peacehaven-telscombe.org.uk

Sussex Archaeological Society & Sussex Past Barbican House, 169 High Street, Lewes, East Sussex BN7 1YE T: 01273 405738 E: library@sussexpast.co.uk W: sussexpast.co.uk

Uckfield & District Preservation Society 89 Lashbrooks Road, Uckfield, East Sussex TN22 2AZ

Warbleton & District History Group Hillside Cottage, North Road, Bodle Street Green, Hailsham BN27 4RG T: 01323 832339 E: junegeoff.hillside@tiscali.co.uk

Sussex - West

Beeding & Bramber LHS 19 Roman Road, Steyning, West Sussex BN44 3FN T: 01903 814083

Billingshurst LHS 2 Cleve Way, Billingshurst, West Sussex RH14 9RW T: 01403 782472

Bolney LHS Leacroft, The Street, Bolney, Haywards, West Sussex RH17 5PG T: 01444 881550

Chichester LHS 38 Ferndale Road, Chichester PO19 6QS

Henfield History Group Maleth, Chestnut Way, Henfield, BN5 9PA

Mid Sussex Local History Group Saddlers, Stud Farm Stables, Gainsborough Lane, Polegate BN26 5HQ T: 01323 482215

Midland Railway Society 4 Canal Road, Yapton, West Sussex BN18 0HA T: 01243-553401 E: secretary@midlandrailwaysociety.org.uk W: www.midlandrailwaysociety.org.uk

Steyning Society 30 St Cuthmans Road, Steyning BN44 3RN

Sussex Record Society West Sussex Record Office, County Hall, Chichester, West Sussex PO19 1RN T: 01243 753602 E: peter.wilkinson@westsussex.gov.uk

The Angmering Society 45 Greenwood Drive, Angmering, West Sussex BNI6 4JW T: 01903-775811 W: www.angmeringsociety.org.uk

West Sussex Archives Society c/o West Sussex Record Office, West Sussex CountyCouncil County Hall, Chichester, PO19 IRN T: 01243 753600 E: records.office@westsussex.gov.uk W: www.westsussex.gov.uk/cs/ro/rohome.htm

Wivelsfield Historical Society Wychwood, Theobalds Road, Wivelsfield, Haywards Heath, West Sussex RH15 0Sx T: 01444 236491

Tyne and Wear

Association of Northumberland Local History Societies c/o The Black Gate, Castle Garth, Newcastle upon Tyne, Tyne and Wear NE1 1RQ T: 0191 257 3254

Cullercoats LHS 33 St Georges Road, Cullercoats, North Shields, Tyne and Wear NE30 3JZ T: 0191 252 7042

North East Labour History Society Department of Historical & Critical Studies, University of Northumbria, Newcastle upon Tyne, Tyne and Wear NE1 8ST T: 0191-227-3193

North-East England History Institute (NEEHI) School of Arts & Media, University of Teesside, Middlesbrough, TS1 3BA T: 01642 384019 E: neehi@tees.ac.uk W: www.neehi.co.uk

Society of Antiquaries of Newcastle upon Tyne Great North Museum : Hancock, Barras Bridge, Newcastle upon Tyne, NE2 4PT T: 0191 231 2700 E: admin@newcastle-antiquaries.org.uk W: www.newcastle-antiquaries.org.uk

South Hylton LHS 6 North View, South Hylton, Sunderland, SR4 0LH T: 0191 534 4251 E: south.hyltonlhs@ntlworld.com W: www.shlhs.com

Southwick History and Preservation Society 8 St Georges Terrace, Roker, Sunderland SR6 9LX T: 0191 567 2438 W: www.southwickhistory.org.uk

Sunderland Antiquarian Society 22 Ferndale Avenue, East Boldon, Tyne and Wear NE36 0TN T: 0191 536 1692

The North Eastern Police History Society 1 Darley Court, Plawsworth, Chester le Street, County Durham DH2 3LQ T: 0191 371 0276 E: janicestothard@aol.com W: www.communigate.co.uk/ne/nepolicehistory/

War Memorials Trust Bilsdale, Ulgham, Morpeth, Northumberland NE61 3AR T: 01670 790465 W: www.warmemorials.com

Wesley Historical Society - North East England Branch 31 Castle Hills, Castleside, Consett DH8 9RL T: 01207 505290 E: rev.terryhurst@freezone.co.uk W: www.wesleyhistoricalsociety.org.uk

Warwickshire

Alcester & District LHS 19 Gerard Road, Kinwarton, Alcester, B49 6QG T: 01789 400 280 E: enquiries@alcesterhistory.org.uk W: www.alcesterhistory.org.uk

Kineton and District Local History Group The Glebe House, Lighthorne Road, Kineton, Warwickshire CV35 0JL T: 01926 690298

Warwickshire LHS 9 Willes Terrace, Leamington Spa CV31 1DL T: 01926 429671

West Midlands

Aldridge LHS 45 Erdington Road, Walsall, West Midlands WS9 8UU

Barr & Aston Local History 17 Booths Farm Road, Great Barr, Birmingham, West Midlands 642 2NJ

Birmingham Heritage Forum 95 Church Hill Road, Solihull, B91 3JH

Birmingham War Research Society 43 Norfolk Place, Kings Norton, Birmingham, West Midlands B30 3LB T: 0121 459 9008

Black Country Local History Consortium Canal Street, Tipton Road, Dudley, West Midlands DY1 4SQ T: 0121 522 9643 E: info@bclm.co.uk W: ww.bclm.co.uk

Black Country Society PO Box 71, Kingswinford, DY6 9YN E: editor@blackcountrysociety.co.uk W: www.blackcountrysociety.co.uk

Council for British Archaeology - West Midlands Birmingham Archaeology, University of Birmingham, Edgbaston, Birmingham, B15 2TT T: 0121 414 5513 E: cbawestmidlands@britarch.ac.uk W: www.britarch.ac.uk/cbawm/

Local History Consortium The Black Country Living Museum, Tipton Road, Dudley, West Midlands DY1 4SQ T: 0121 557 9643

Quinton LHS 15 Worlds End Avenue, Quinton, Birmingham B32 1JF T: 0121-422-1792 E: qlhs@bjt.me.uk W: www.qlhs.org.uk

Romsley & Hunnington History Society Port Erin, Green Lane, Chapmans Hill, Romsley, Halesowen, B62 0HB T: 01562 710295

Smethwick LHS 47 Talbot Road, Smethwick, Warley, West Midlands B66 4DX W: www.smethwicklocalhistory.co.uk

Wythall History Society 64 Meadow Road, Wythall, Worcestershire B47 6EQ T: 01564 822 483 W: www.wythallhistory.co.uk

Wiltshire

Amesbury Soc 34 Countess Rd, Amesbury SP4 7AS T: 01980 623123

Atworth History Group 140 The Midlands, Trowbridge BA14 6RG T: 01225 782 090 E: gemmakay@btinternet.com W: www.atworth-familyhistory.co.uk

Chiseldon Local History Group 3 Norris Close, Chiseldon, Wiltshire SN4 0LW T: 01793 740432

Devizes Local History Group 9 Hartfield, Devizes, Wiltshire SN10 5JH T: 01380 727369

Highworth Historical Society 6 Copper Beeches, Highworth, Swindon, Wiltshire SN6 7BJ T: 01793 763863

Marshfield & District LHS Weir Cottage, Weir Lane, Marshfield, Chippenham, Wiltshire SN14 8NB T: 01225 891229

Melksham & District Historical Association 13 Sandridge Road, Melksham, Wiltshire SN12 7BE T: 01225 703644

Mere Historical Society Bristow House, Castle Street, Mere, BA12 6JF T: 01747 860643

Mid Thorngate Society Yewcroft, Stoney Batter, West Tytherley, Salisbury, SP5 ILD

Pewsey Vale LHS 10 Holly Tree Walk, Pewsey, Wiltshire SN9 5DE T: 01672 562417

Purton Historical Society 1 Church Street, Purton, Wiltshire SN5 4DS T: 01793 770331

Redlynch & District LHS Fieldfare Gate, Quavey Rd, Redlynch, Salisbury SP5 2HL E: kate.crouch@hotmail.co.uk W: www.southwilts.com

Salisbury Civic Society 4 Chestnut Close, Laverstock, Salisbury, SP1 1SL

Salisbury Local History Group 67 St Edmunds Church Street, Salisbury, Wiltshire SP1 1EF T: 01722 338346

South Wiltshire Industrial Archaeology Society 2 Byways Close, Salisbury, Wiltshire SP1 2QS T: 01722 323732 E: enquiries.swias@btinternet.com W: www.southwilts.co.uk/site/south-wiltshire-industrial-archaeology-society
Swindon Society 4 Lakeside, Swindon SN3 1QE T: 01793-521910
The Hatcher Society 11 Turner Close, Harnham, Salisbury SP2 8NX
The Historical Association (West Wiltshire Branch) 24 Meadowfield, Bradford on Avon BA15 1PL T: 01225 862722
Tisbury LHS Suzay House, Court Street, Tisbury, Wiltshire SP3 6NF
Trowbridge Civic Society 43 Victoria Road, Trowbridge BA14 7LD
Warminster History Society 13 The Downlands, Warminster, Wiltshire BA12 0BD T: 01985 216022
Wilton Historical Society 3 Wiley Terrace, North Street, Wilton, Wiltshire SP2 0HN T: 01722 742856
Wiltshire Archaeological and Natural History Society Wiltshire Heritage Library, 41 Long Str, Devizes SN10 1NS T: 01380 727369 E: wanhs@wiltshireheritage.org.uk W: www.wiltshireheritage.org.uk
Wiltshire Local History Forum Tanglewood, Laverstock Park, Salisbury, Wiltshire SP1 1QJ T: 01722 328922
Wiltshire Record Society County Record Office, County Libraries HQ, Trowbridge, Wiltshire BA14 8BS T: 01225 713136
Wootton Bassett Historical Society 20 The Broadway, Rodbourne Cheney, Swindon, Wiltshire SN25 3BT
Wroughton History Group 32 Kerrs Way, Wroughton, Wiltshire SN4 9EH T: 01793 635838

Worcestershire
Alvechurch Historical Society Bearhill House, Alvechurch, Birmingham, B48 7JX T: 0121 445 2222
Bewdley Historical Research 8 Ironside Close, Bewdley, Worcestershire DY12 2HX T: 01299 403582
Dodderhill Parish History Project - Discovering Wychbol's Past 9 Laurelwood Close, Droitwich Spa, Worcestershire WR9 7SF
Droitwich History and Archaeology Society 45 Moreland Road, Droitwich Spa, Worcestershire WR9 8RN T: 01905-773420
Feckenham Forest History Society Lower Grinsty Farmhouse, Callow Hill, Redditch, Worcestershire B97 5PJ T: 01527-542063

Feckenham Parish, Worcestershire One Place Study 33c Castle Street, Astwood Park, Worcester, Worcestershire B96 6DP
Kidderminster & District Archaeological & Hist Soc 39 Cardinal Drive, Kidderminster DY10 4RZ E: kidderhist.soc@virgin.net W: www.communigate.co.uk/worcs/kidderminsterhistorysoc/index.phtml
Kidderminster Field Club 7 Holmwood Avenue, Kidderminster, Worcestershire DYL 1 6DA
Open University History Society 14 Coverdale Avenue, Bexhill on Sea, TN39 4TY T: (024) 76397668 W: www.ouhistory.org.uk/
Pershore Heritage & History Society 6 Abbey Croft, Pershore, Worcestershire WR10 1JQ T: 01386 552482
Wolverley & Cookley Historical Society 18/20 Caunsall Road, Cookley, Kidderminster, Worcestershire DYL 1 5YB
Wolverley & Cookley History Society The Elms, Drakelow Lane, Wolverley, Kidderminster DY11 5RU T: 01562 850215
Worcestershire Archaeological Society 26 Albert Park Road, Malvern, Worcestershire WR14 1HN T: 01684 565190
Worcestershire Historic Environment & Archaeological Service Woodbury Hall, University of Worcester, Henwick Grove, Worcester, WR2 6AJ T: 01905 855 455 E: archaeology@worcestershire.gov.uk W: http://worcestershire.gov.uk/archaeology
Worcestershire Industrial Archealogy & LHS 99 Feckenham Road, Headless Cross, Redditch, Worcestershire B97 5AM
Worcestershire Local History Forum 45 Moreland Road, Droitwich, Worcestershire WR9 8RN T: 01905-773420
Wythall History Society 64 Meadow Road, Wythall, Worcestershire B47 6EQ T: 01564 822 483 W: www.wythallhistory.co.uk

Yorkshire
The Yorkshire Buildings Preservation Trust c/o Elmhirst & Maxton Solicitors, 17-19 Regent Street, Barnsley, South Yorkshire S70 2HP
The Yorkshire Heraldry Society 2 Woodhall Park Grove, Pudsey, Leeds, LS28 7HB DN4 7HJ
York Georgian Society King's Manor, York, Yorkshire YO1 7EW
Yorkshire Architectural & York Archaeological Society c/o York Archaeological Trust, Cromwell House, 13 Ogleforth, York, YO1 7FG
Yorkshire Philosophical Society The Lodge, Museum Gardens, Museum Street, York, YO1 7DR T: 01904 656713 E: info@yorksphilsoc.org.uk W: www.yorksphilsoc.org.uk
Yorkshire Quaker Heritage Project Brynmore Jones Library, University of Hull, Hull, Hull HU6 7RX
Yorkshire Vernacular Buildings Study Group 18 Sycamore Terrace, Bootham, York, Yorkshire YO30 7DN T: 01904 652387 W: www.yvbsg.org.uk

Yorkshire - East
East Riding Archaeological Society 455 Chanterland Avenue, Hull, HU5 4AY T: 01482 445232
East Yorkshire LHS 13 Oaktree Drive, Molescroft, Beverley HU17 7BB
Yorkshire - North
Forest of Galtres Society c/o Crawford House, Long Street, Easingwold, York, North Yorkshire YO61 3JB T: 01347 821685
Northallerton and District LHS 17 Thistle Close, Romanby Park, Northallerton, North Yorkshire DL7 8FF T: 01609 771878
Poppleton History Society Russett House, The Green, Upper Poppleton, York YO26 6DR T: 01904 798868 W: www.poppleton.net/historysoc
Rosedale History Society Phoenix House, Rosedale Abbey, Pickering YO18 8SE T: 01751 417 071 E: rosedalehistory@hotmail.co.uk W: http://rosedale.ryedaleconnect.org.uk
Scarborough Archaeological & Hist Soc 10 Westbourne Park, Scarborough YO12 4AT T: 01723 354237 W: www.scarborough-heritage.org
Snape Local Hist Group Lammas Cottage, Snape, Bedale DL8 2TW T: 01677 470727 W: www.communigate.co.uk/ne/slhg/index.phtml
Stokesley Local History Study Group 44 Cleveland Avenue, Stokesley TS9 5HB T: 01642 711875 E: chrisbainbridge46@hotmail.co.uk W: www.historic-cleveland.co.uk
The Haxby Local History Group 14 Old Dikelands, Haxby, York, YO32 2WN T: 01904 763 937
Upper Dales Family History Group - a branch of Cleveland FHS Croft House, Newbiggin in Bishopdale, Nr Leyburn DL8 3TD T: 01969 663738 E: glenys@bishopdale.demon.co.uk W: www.upperdalesfhg.org.uk
Upper Wharfedale Field Soc (Local History Section) Brookfield, Hebden Hall Park, Grassington, Skipton BD23 5DX T: 01756-752012
Upper Wharfedale Museum Society & Folk Museum The Square, Grassington, North Yorkshire BD23 5AU
Wensleydale Railway Assoc WRA Membership Administration, PO Box 65, Northallerton DL7 8YZ T: 01969 625182 E: website@wensleydalerailway.com W: www.wensleydalerailway.com
Whitby Literary & Philosophical Society, Library and Archives Whitby Museum, Pannett Park, Whitby YO21 1RE T: 01947 602908 E: library@whitbymuseum.org.uk W: www.whitbymuseum.org.uk
Yorkshire Dialect Society 51 Stepney Ave, Scarborough YO12 5BW
Yorkshire - South
Barnscan - The Barnsdale Local History Group Old Post Cottage, High Street, Campsall, Doncaster, DN6 9AF T: 01302 7011036 E: jan.millward@btinternet.com W: www.barnscan.co.uk
Bentley with Arksey Heritage Society 45 Finkle Street, Bentley, Doncaster, South Yorkshire DN5 0RP
Chapeltown & High Green Archives The Grange, 4 Kirkstead Abbey Mews, Thorpe Hesley, Rotherham, South Yorkshire S61 2UZ T: 0114 245 1235 W: www.chgarchives.co.uk
Doncaster Archaeological Society a Group of the Yorkshire Archaeological Society The Poplars, Long Plantation, Edenthorpe, Doncaster DN3 2NL T: 01302 882840 E: d.j.croft@talk21.com
Friends of Barnsley Archives and Local Studies 30 Southgate, Barnsley, South Yorkshire S752QL
Grenoside & District Local Hist Group 4 Stepping Lane, Grenoside, Sheffield S35 8RA T: 0114 257 1929 E: info@grenosidelocalhistory.co.uk W: www.grenosidelocalhistory.co.uk
Wombwell Heritage Group 9 Queens Gardens, Wombwell, Barnsley, South Yorkshire S73 0EE T: 01226 210648
Yorkshire - West
Beeston LHS 30 Sunnyview Avenue, Leeds LS11 8QY T: 0113 271 7095
East Leeds Historical Society 10 Thornfield Drive, Cross Gates, Leeds, West Yorkshire LS15 7LS
Halifax Antiquarian Society 66 Grubb Lane, Gomersal, Cleckheaton, West Yorkshire BD19 4BU T: 01274 865418
Kippax & District History Society 8 Hall Park Croft, Kippax, Leeds, LS25 7QF T: 0113 286 4785 E: mdlbrumwell@tinyworld.co.uk W: www.kippaxhistoricalsoc.leedsnet.com
Lowertown Old Burial Ground Trust 16 South Close, Guisley, Leeds, West Yorkshire LS20 8TD
Northern Society of Costume & Textiles 43 Gledhow Lane, Leeds, West Yorkshire LS8 1RT
Olicana Historical Society 54 Kings Road, Ilkley, West Yorkshire LS29 9AT T: 01943 609206
Ossett & District Historical Society 29 Prospect Road, Ossett, West Yorkshire T: 01924 279449
Pudsey Civic Society PO Box 146, Leeds, West Yorkshire LS28 8WY
Shipley LHS 68 Wycliffe Gardens, Shipley BD18 3NH
Thoresby Society 23 Clarendon Road, Leeds, West Yorkshire LS2 9NZ T: 0113 245 7910 W: www.thoresby.org.uk

Wetherby & District Historical Society 73 Aire Road, Wetherby, West Yorkshire LS22 7UE T: 01937 584875

Yorkshire Archaeological Society - Local History Study Section Claremont, 23 Clarendon Road, Leeds, LS2 9NZ www.yas.org.uk T: 0113-245-7910

Yorkshire - York

Holgate Windmill Preservation Society 2 Murray Street, York, YO24 4JA T: 01904 799295 E: lambert49@ntlworld.com W: www.holgatewindmill.org

York Archaeological Trust 13 Ogleforth, York, YO1 7FG T: 01904 663000 E: enquiries@yorkarchaeology.co.uk W: www.yorkarchaeology.co.uk

Wales

British Association for Local History PO Box 6549, Somersal Herbert, Ashbourne, Derbyshire DE6 5WH T: 01283 585947 E: mail@balh.co.uk W: www.balh.co.uk

Chapels Heritage Society - CAPEL 5 Cuffnell Close, Liddell Park, Llandudno, LL30 1UX E: obadiah1@btinternet.com W: www.capeli.org.uk/

Hugenot Society of Great Britain & Ireland Hugenot Library University College, Gower Street, London, WC1E 6BT T: 020 7679 5199 E: secretary@huguenotsociety.org.uk W: www.hugenotsociety.org.uk

South Wales Record Society 13 St Cybi Drive, Llangybi, Usk, Monmouthshire NP15 1TU T: 01633 450353

Anglesey

The Anglesey Antiquarian Society & Field Club 1 Fronheulog, Sling, Tregarth, Bangor, Gwynedd LL57 4RD T: 01248 600083 W: www.hanesmon.btinternet.co.uk

Caernarvonshire

Federation of History Societies in Caernarvonshire 19 Lon Dinas, Cricieth, Gwynedd LL52 0EH T: 01766 522238

Cardiff

Pentyrch & District Local History Society 34 Castell Coch View, Tongwynlais, Cardiff, CF15 7LA

Carmarthenshire

Carmarthenshire Antiquarian Society 24 Hoel Beca, Carmarthen, SA31 3LS E: arfon.rees@btinternet.com W: www.carmantiqs.org.uk

Gwendraeth Val History Society 19 Grugos Avenue, Pontyberem, Llanelli, Carmarthenshire SA15 5AF

Gwendraeth Valley Hist Society 19 Grugos Avenue, Pontyberem, Llanelli, Carmarthenshire SA14 5AF

Llanelli Historical Society Gwynfryn, Mountain Road, Trimsaran, Kidwelly, Carmarthenshire SA17 4EU T: 01554 810677

Ceredigion

Ceredigion Antiquarian Society Archives Department, Ceredigion County Council, Aberystwyth, Ceredigion SY23 T: 01970 633697 E: info@ceredigion.gov.uk

Clwyd

Friends of The Clwyd Archives Bryn Gwyn, 2 Rhodea Anwyl, Rhuddlan, LL18 2SQ T: 01745 591676

Conwy

Abergele Field Club and Historical Society Rhyd y Felin, 47 Bryn Twr, Abergele, Conwy LL22 8DD T: 01745 832497

Llandudno & District Historical Society Springfield, 97 Queen's Road, Llandudno, Conwy LL30 1TY T: 01492 876337

Denbighshire

Denbighshire Historical Society 1 Green Park, Erddig, Wrexham, LL13 7YE

Flintshire Historical Society - see Flintshire

Ruthin Local History Group 27 Tan y Bryn, Llanbedr D.C., Ruthin, Denbighshire LL15 1AQ T: 01824 702632

Flintshire

Flintshire Historical Society 69 Pen y Maes Avenue, Rhyl, Denbighshire LL18 4ED T: 01745 332220

Glamorgan

Glamorgan History Society 87 Gabalfa Road, Swansea, SA2 8ND T: 01792 205 888 E: paulreynolds44@googlemail.com W: www.glamorganhistory.org

Kenfig Society Glan y Llyn, Broadlands, North Cornelly, Bridgend, CF33 4EF T: 01656 782351 W: www.kenfigsociety.org/

Llantrisant & District Local History Society 2 Shadow Wood Drive, Miskin, Pontyclun, CF72 8SX T: 01443 239 743 E: jeff_tjbrown@btinternet.com W: www.ladhs.org.uk

Merthyr Tydfil Historical Society Ronamar, Ashlea Drive, Twynyrodyn, Merthyr Tydfil CF47 0NY T: 01685 385871

Gwent

Abertillery & District Museum 5 Harcourt Terrace, Glandwr Street, Abertillery, Gwent NP3 2HR

Abertillery & District Museum Society The Metropole, Market Street, Abertillery, Gwent NP13 1AH T: 01495 211140

Gwent Local History Council 8 Pentonville, Newport, Gwent NP9 5XH T: 01633 213229

Newport Local History Society 72 Risca Road, Newport NP20 4JA

Pontypool Local History Society 24 Longhouse Grove, Henllys, Cwmbran, Gwent NP44 6HQ T: 01633 865662

Gwynedd

Abergele Field Club and Historical Society Rhyd y Felin, 47 Bryn Twr, Abergele, Conwy LL22 8DD T: 01745 832497

Caernarvonshire Historical Society Gwynedd Archives, County offices, Caernarfon, Gwynedd LL555 1SH T: 01286 679088 W: www.caernarvonshirehistoricalsociety.btinternet.co.uk

Cymdeithas Hanes a Chofnodion Sir Feirionnydd

Meirioneth Historicial and Record Society Archifdy Meirion Cae Penarlag, Dolgellau, Gwynedd LL40 2YB T: 01341 424444

Cymdeithas Hanes a Chofnodion Sir Feirionnydd

Meirioneth Historicial and Record Society Archifdy Meirion Cae Penarlag, Dolgellau, Gwynedd LL40 2YB T: 01341 424444

Cymdeithas Hanes Beddgelert - Beddgelert History Society Creua, Llanfrothen, Penrhyndeudraeth, Gwynedd LL48 6SH T: 01766770534

Pembrokeshire

The Pembrokeshire Historical Society Dolau Dwrbach, Fishguard, Pembrokeshire SA65 9RN T: 01348 873316

Pentyrch

Pentyrch & District Local History Society 34 Castell Coch View, Tongwynlais, Cardiff, CF15 7LA

Powys

Radnorshire Society Pool House, Discoed, Presteigne LD8 2NW

Wrexham- see Denbighshire

Wrexham Maelor Hist Soc 37 Park Avenue, Wrexham, LL12 7AL

Scotland

National

British Association for Local History PO Box 6549, Somersal Herbert, Ashbourne, Derbyshire DE6 5WH T: 01283 585947 E: mail@balh.co.uk W: www.balh.co.uk

Scottish Records Association Membership Secretary - Perth & Kinross Archive, AK Bell Library, York Place, Perth PH2 8EP T: 01738 477012 E: jmmerchant@pkc.gov.uk W: www.scottishrecordsassociation.org/

Society of Antiquaries of Scotland Royal Museum of Scotland, Chambers Street, Edinburgh, EH1 1JF T: 0131 247 4115 W: www.socantscot.org

Airdrie

Monklands Heritage Society 141 Cromarty Road, Cairnhill, Airdrie, ML6 9RZ T: 01236 764192

Angus

Abertay Historical Society c/o Museum Services, University of Dundee DD1 4HN T: 01382 384310 E: museum@dundee.ac.uk W: www.abertay.org.uk

Ayrshire

Ayrshire Federation of Historical Societies 11 Chalmers Road, Ayr, Ayrshire KA7 2RQ

SW Scotland Local / Family History Maybole Historical Society 15F Campbell Court, Ayr, Ayrshire KA8 0SE T: 01292 610461 E: david.kiltie@virgin.net W: www.maybole.org

Dundee

Friends of Dundee City Archives 21 City Square, Dundee, DD1 3BY T: 01382 434494 E: richard.cullen@dundeecity.gov.uk W: www.fdca.org.uk

East Ayrshire

Stewarton Library Cunningham Institute, Stewarton, East Ayrshire KA3 5AB T: 01560 484385

Falkirk

Falkirk Local History Society 11 Neilson Street, Falkirk, FK1 5AQ

Fife

Abertay Historical Society c/o Museum Services, University of Dundee DD1 4HN T: 01382 384310 E: museum@dundee.ac.uk W: www.abertay.org.uk

Glasgow

Glasgow Hebrew Burial Society 222 Fenwick Road, Griffnock, Glasgow, G46 6UE T: 0141 577 8226

Perthshire

Abertay Historical Society c/o Museum Services, University of Dundee, Dundee, DD1 4HN T: 01382 384310 E: museum@dundee.ac.uk W: www.abertay.org.uk

Dunning Parish Historical Society The Old Schoolhouse, Newtown of Pitcairns, Dunning, Perth, Perthshire PH2 0SL T: 01764 684448 E: postman@dunning.uk.net W: www.dunning.uk.net

Police

Glasgow Police Heritage Society c/o The Glasgow Police Museum, 1/1 30 Bell Street, Merchant City, Glasgow, G1 1LG T: 0141 552 1818 E: curator@policemuseum.org.uk W: www.policemuseum.org.uk

Renfrewshire
Bridge of Weir History Society 41 Houston Road, Bridge Of Weir, Renfrewshire PA11 3QR
Paisley Philosophical Institution 26 Thornly Park Drive, Paisley, Renfrewshire PA2 7RP T: 0141 884 4690
Renfrewshire Local History Forum 15 Victoria Crescent, Clarkston, Glasgow, G76 8BP T: 0141 644 2522 W: www.rlhf.info
Stirling
Drymen Library The Square, Drymen, Stirlingshire G63 0BL T: 01360 660751 E: drymenlibrary@stirling.gov.uk
West Lothian
Linlithgow Union Canal Society Manse Road Basin, Linlithgow, West Lothian EH49 6AJ T: 01506-671215 (Answering Machine) E: info@lucs.org.uk W: www.lucs.org.uk
Scottish Local History Forum 45 High Street, Linlithgow, West Lothian EH54 6EW T: 01506 844649

Northern Ireland
Archives & Records Association (UK & Ireland) Prioryfield House, 20 Canon Street, Taunton, Somerset TA1 1SW T: 01823 327030 E: ara@archives.org.uk W: www.archives.org.uk
British Association for Local History PO Box 6549, Somersal Herbert, Ashbourne, Derbyshire DE6 5WH T: 01283 585947 E: mail@balh.co.uk W: www.balh.co.uk
Federation for Ulster Local Studies 18 May Street, Belfast, BT1 4NL T: (028) 90235254 E: vherbert@clonaog.freeserve.co.uk W: http://ulht.org.uk/
Hugenot Society of Great Britain & Ireland Hugenot Library University College, Gower Street, London, WC1E 6BT T: 020 7679 5199 E: secretary@huguenotsociety.org.uk W: www.hugenotsociety.org.uk
Wesley Historical Society Methodist Study Centre, Edgehill College, 9 Lennoxvale, Belfast, BT9 5BY T: 028 9068 6936 E: libr@edgehillcollege.org W: www.edgehillcollege.org/library
Co Tyrone
Centre for Migration Studies Ulster American Folk Park, Mellon Road, Castletown, Omagh, Co Tyrone BT78 5QY T: 028 82 256315 E: cms@librariesni.org.uk W: www.folkpark.com
County Londonderry
Roe Valley Historical Society 36 Drumachose Park, Limavady, County Londonderry BT49 0NZ
Co Tyrone
Centre for Migration Studies Ulster American Folk Park, Mellon Road, Castletown, Omagh, Co Tyrone BT78 5QY T: 028 82 256315 E: cms@librariesni.org.uk W: www.folkpark.com

Ireland
Federation of Local History Societies - Ireland Winter's Hill, Kinsale, County Cork E: historyfed@eircom.net W: http://homepage.eircom.net/~localhist/index.html

Hugenot Society of Great Britain & Ireland Hugenot Library University College, Gower Street, London, WC1E 6BT T: 020 7679 5199 E: secretary@huguenotsociety.org.uk W: www.hugenotsociety.org.uk
Hugenot Society of Great Britain & Ireland Hugenot Library University College, Gower Street, London, WC1E 6BT T: 020 7679 5199 E: secretary@huguenotsociety.org.uk W: www.hugenotsociety.org.uk
Hugenot Society of Great Britain & Ireland - Irish Section Echo Hall, Spa, County Down BT24 8PT E: EchoHall@aol.com W: www.hugenotsociety.org.uk
Presbyterian Historical Society of Ireland 26 College Green, Belfast, BT1 1LN T: 028 9072 7330 E: phsilibrarian@pcinet.org W: www.presbyterianhistoryireland.com
Wesley Historical Society Methodist Study Centre, Edgehill College, 9 Lennoxvale, Belfast, BT9 5BY T: 028 9068 6936 E: libr@edgehillcollege.org W: www.edgehillcollege.org/library
County Carlow
Carlow Historical & Archaeological Society 38 Kennedy Street, Carlow, County Carlow
County Cork
Bandon Genealogy Group Kilbrogan House, Kilbrogan Hill, Bandon, County Cork T: 00 353 23 88 44935 E: badon.genealogy@gmail.com W: www.kilbrogan.com www.bandon-genealogy.com
County Dublin
Ballyfermot Heritage Group c/o Ballyfermot Library, Ballyfermot Road, Dublin, 10 T: Please Update E: heritagegroup@ballyfermot.ie W: Please Update
County Londonderry
Roe Valley Historical Society 36 Drumachose Park, Limavady, County Londonderry BT49 0NZ
County Mayo
Mayo North Family History Research Centre Enniscoe, Castlehill, Ballina, County Mayo T: + 353 96 31809 E: normayo@iol.ie W: www.mayo.irish-roots.net
Mayo South Family Research Centre Main Street, Ballinrobe, County Mayo T: +353 94 954 1214 E: soumayo@iol.ie W: http://mayo.irishroots.net/
County Wexford
Wexford Historical Society c/o Melford House, Ballyhealy, Kilmore, County Wexford E: chair@wexfordhistoricalsociety.com W: www.wexfordhistoricalsociety.com
Dublin
Raheny Heritage Society 101 Collins Park, Donnycarney, Dublin 9, Dublin E: bjwray@eircom.net
Police
Garda Historical Society 8 Aisling Close, Ballincollig, County Cork T: +353 86 806 0385 E: J_herlihy@esatclear.ie W: www.esatclear.ie/~ric

Libraries

National
British Film Institute - Library & Film Archive 21 Stephen Street, London, W1T 1LN T: 020 7957 4824 W: www.bfi.org.uk
British Geological Survey Library Kingsley Dunham Centre, Keyworth, Nottingham, Nottinghamshire NG12 5GG T: 0115 936 3205 E: libuser@bgs.ac.uk W: www.bgs.ac.uk
British Library Boston Spa, Wetherby, West Yorkshire LS23 7BY
British Library British Library Building, 96 Euston Road, London, NW1 2DB T: (020) 7412 7000 W: www.portico.bl.uk
British Library - Rare Books Reference Service 96 Euston Road, London, NW1 2DB T: (020) 7412 7564 E: rare-books@bl.uk W: www.bl.uk
British Library Newspapers 130 Colindale Avenue, London, NW9 5HE T: 020 7412 7353 E: newspaper@bl.uk W: www.bl.uk/reshelp/bidept/news/index.html
British Library of Political and Economic Science London School of Economics, 10 Portugal Street, London, WC2A 2HD T: 020 7955 7223 W: www.lse.ac.uk
Cambridge University Library - Department of Manuscripts & University Archives West Road, Cambridge CB3 9DR T: 01223 333000 ext 33143 (Manuscripts) W: www.lib.cam.ac.uk/MSS/
Catholic National Library St Michael's Abbey, Farnborough Road, Farnborough GU14 7NQ T: 01252 543818 E: library@catholic-library.org.uk W: www.catholic-library.org.uk
Centre for South Asian Studies Cambridge University, Laundress Lane, Cambridge CB2 1SD T: 01223 338094 W: www.s-asian.cam.ac.uk

Dr Williams's Library 14 Gordon Square, London, WC1H 0AR T: (020) 7387-3727 E: enquiries@dwlib.co.uk W: www.dwlib.co.uk
Evangelical Library 78a Chiltern Street, London, W1M 2HB
House of Commons Library House of Commons, 1 Derby Gate, London, SW1A 2DG T: (020) 7219-5545
Huguenot Library University College, Gower Street, London, WC1E 6BT T: (020) 7679 7094 W: www.ucl.ac.uk/ucl-info/divisions/library/hugenot.htm
Institute of Heraldic & Genealogical Studies 79 - 82 Northgate, Canterbury CT1 1BA T: 01227 768664 E: ihgs@ihgs.ac.uk W: www.ihgs.ac.uk
Jewish Studies Library University College, Gower Street, London, WC1E 6BT T: (020) 7387 7050
Lambeth Palace Library Lambeth Palace Road, London, SE1 7JU T: 020 7898 1400 E: lpl.staff@c-of-e.org.uk W: www.lambethpalacelibrary.org
Library of Primitive Methodism Englesea Brook Chapel & Museum, Englesea Brook, Crewe CW2 5QW T: 01270 820836 E: engleseabrook-methodist-museum@supanet.com W: www.engleseabrook-museum.org.uk
Library of the Religious Society of Friends (Quakers) Friends House, 173 - 177 Euston Rd, London, NW1 2BJ T: 0207 663 1135 E: library@quaker.org.uk W: www.quaker.org.uk/library
Library of the Royal College of Surgeons of England 35-43 Lincoln's Inn Fields, London, WC2A 3PE T: (020) 7869 6555 E: archives@rcseng.ac.uk W: www.rcseng.ac.uk
Linnean Society of London Burlington House, Piccadilly, London, W1J 0BF T: 020 7437 4479 W: www.linnean.org

Methodist Archives and Research Centre John Rylands University Library, 150 Deansgate, Manchester, M3 3EH T: 0161 834 5343
Modern Records Centre University of Warwick Library, Coventry, Warwickshire CV4 7AL T: 024 7652 4219 E: archives@warwick.ac.uk W: http://modernrecords.warwick.ac.uk
Museum of the Order of St John St John's Gate, St John's Lane, Clerkenwell, London, EC1M 4DA T: (020) 7253-6644 E: juliet.barclay@nhq.sja.org.uk W: www.sja.org.uk/history
National Gallery Library and Archive Trafalgar Square, London, WC2N 5DN T: 020 7747 2542 W: www.nationalgallery.org.uk
National Maritime Museum Romney Road, Greenwich, London, London SE10 9NF T: 020 8858 4422 E: library@nmm.ac.uk manuscripts@nmm.ac.uk W: www.nmm.ac.uk
National Maritime Museum - Caird Library Park Row, Greenwich, London, London SE10 9NF T: (020) 8312 6673 E: pkelvin@nmm.ac.uk W: www.nmm.ac.uk
Royal Armouries H.M Tower Of London, Tower Hill, London, EC3N 4AB T: (020) 7480 6358 ext 30 W: www.armouries.org.uk
Royal Commonwealth Society Library West Road, Cambridge, CB3 9DR T: 01223 333198 W: www.lib.cam.ac.uk/MSS/
Royal Institute of British Architects' Library Manuscripts & Archives Collection, 66 Portland Place, London, W1N 4AD T: 020 7307 3615
Royal Society of Chemistry Library & Information Centre Burlington House, Piccadilly, London, W1J 0BA T: (020) 7440 3373 E: library@rsc.org W: www.rsc.org/library/Services/GenealogyEnquiriesSearch.asp
School of Oriental and African Studies library Thornhaugh Street, Russell Square, London, WC1H 0XG T: 020 7323 6112 W: www.soas.ac.uk/library/
Society of Antiquaries of London Burlington House, Piccadilly, London, W1J 0BE T: 020 7479 7084 E: library@sal.org.uk W: www.sal.org.uk
Society of Genealogists - Library 14 Charterhouse Buildings, Goswell Road, London, EC1M 7BA T: 020-7251-8799 E: library@sog.org.uk W: www.sog.org.uk
The Kenneth Ritchie Wimbledon Library The All England Lawn Tennis & Croquet Club, Church Road, Wimbledon, London, SW19 5AE T: (020) 8946 6131 W: www.wimbledon.org
The Library & Museum of Freemasonry Freemasons' Hall, 60 Great Queen Street, London, WC2B 5AZ T: (020) 7395 9257 W: www.grandlodge-england.org
The National Coal Mining Museum for England Caphouse Colliery, New Road, Overton, Wakefield, West Yorkshire WF4 4RH T: 01924 848806 E: info@ncm.org.uk W: www.ncm.org.uk
The Science Museum Library Imperial College Road, South Kensington, London, SW7 5NH T: 020 7942 4242 E: smlinfo@sciencemuseum.org.uk W: www.sciencemuseum.org.uk/library/
The Science Museum Library & Archives - Wroughton Science Museum at Wroughton, Hackpen Lane, Wroughton, Swindon, SN4 9NS T: (0)1793 846 222 E: smlwroughton@sciencemuseum.org.uk W: www.sciencemuseum.org.uk/library/
The Wellcome Library (Wellcome Trust) 183 Euston Road, London, NW1 2BE T: (020) 7611 8722 E: library@wellcome.ac.uk W: http://library.wellcome.ac.uk
The Women's Library Old Castle Street, London, E1 7NT T: 020 7320 1189 W: www.lgu.ac.uk./fawcett
Trades Union Congress Library - University of North London 236 - 250 Holloway Road, London, N7 6PP W: www.unl.ac.uk/library/tuc
Trinity College Library Cambridge Trinity College Library, Cambridge, Cambridgeshire CB1 1TQ T: 01223 338488 E: wren.library@trin.cam.ac.uk W: www.trin.cam.ac.uk/index
United Reformed Church History Society Westminster College, Madingley Road, Cambridge, CB3 0AA T: 01223 741300 (NOT Wednesdays)
Victoria & Albert Museum - National Art Library Cromwell Road, South Kensington, London, SW7 2RL T: (020) 7938 8315 W: www.nal.vam.ac.uk
Victoria & Albert Museum - Word & Image Department - Archive of Art & Design Victoria & Albert Museum Archives, Blythe House, 23 Blythe Road, London, W14 0QF T: 020 7603 7493 E: archive@vam.ac.uk W: www.vam.ac.uk/resources/archives
Wellcome Library 183 Euston Road, London, NW1 2BE T: (020) 7611 8722 E: library@wellcome.ac.uk W: http://library.wellcome.ac.u

England
Bedfordshire
Bedford Central Library Harpur Street, Bedford, Bedfordshire MK40 1PG T: 01234-350931 W: www.bedfordshire.gov.uk
Biggleswade Library Chestnut Avenue, Biggleswade SG18 0LL T: 01767 312324

Dunstable Library Vernon Place, Dunstable LU5 4HA T: 01582 608441
Leighton Buzzard Library Lake Street, Leighton Buzzard, Bedfordshire LU7 1RX T: 01525 371788
Local Studies Library Luton Central Library, St George's Square, Luton, Bedfordshire LU1 2NG T: 01582-547420 W: www.luton.gov.uk

Berkshire
Ascot Heath Library Fernbank Road, North Ascot, Berkshire SL5 8LA T: 01344 884030
Berkshire Medical Heritage Centre Level 4, Main Entrance, Royal Berkshire Hospital, London Road, Reading, Berkshire RG1 5AN T: 0118 987 7298 W: www.bmhc.org
Binfield Library Benetfeld Road, Binfield, Berkshire RG42 4HD T: 01344 306663
Bracknell Library - Local Studies Town Square, Bracknell, Berkshire RG12 1BH T: 01344 352515
Crowthorne Library Lower Broadmoor Road, Crowthorne, Berkshire RG45 7LA T: 01344 776431
Eton College College Library, Eton College, Windsor, Berkshire SL4 6DB T: 01753 671269 E: archivist@etoncollege.org.uk W: www.etoncollege.com
Maidenhead Library - Royal Borough of Windsor and Maidenhead Maidenhead Library, St Ives Road, Maidenhead, Berkshire SL6 1QU T: 01628 796968 E: libraries@rbwm.gov.uk W: www.rbwm.gov.uk
Newbury Reference Library Newbury Central Library, The Wharf, Newbury, Berkshire RG14 5AU T: 01635 519900 W: www.westberks.gov.uk
Reading Local Studies Library 3rd Floor, Central Library, Abbey Square, Reading, Berkshire RG1 3BQ T: 0118 901 5965 E: info@readinglibraries.org.uk W: www.readinglibraries.org.uk
Reading Local Studies Library Reading Central Library, Abbey Square, Reading, Berkshire RG1 1QH T: 0118 901 5965
Reading University Library University of Reading, Whiteknights PO Box 223, Reading, RG6 6AE T: 0118-931-8776 W: www.reading.ac.uk/
Sandhurst Library The Broadway, Sandhurst, Berkshire GU47 9BL T: 01252 870161
Slough Local Studies Library Top Floor, Slough Library, High Street, Slough, Berkshire SL1 1EA T: 01753 787511 W: www.slough.gov.uk/libraries
Whitegrove Library 5 County Lane, Warfield, Berkshire RG42 3JP T: 01344 424211
Wokingham Library Local Studies The Library, Denmark Street, Wokingham, Berkshire RG40 2BB T: 0118 978 1368 E: libraries@wokingham.gov.uk W: www.wokingham.gov.uk/libraries

Bristol
Bristol Central Library Reference Section, College Green, Bristol, BS1 5TL T: 0117 903 7202
Bristol University Library - Special Collections Tyndall Avenue, Bristol, BS8 1TJ T: 0117 928 8014 E: special-collections@bris.ac.uk W: www.bris.ac.uk/is/services/specialcollections/

Buckinghamshire
County Reference Library Walton Street, Aylesbury, Buckinghamshire HP20 1UU T: 01296-382250
High Wycombe Reference Library Queen Victoria Road, High Wycombe, Buckinghamshire HP11 1BD T: 01494-510241 W: www.buckscc.gov.uk
Milton Keynes Reference Library 555 Silbury Boulevard, Milton Keynes, Buckinghamshire MK9 3HL T: 01908 254160 E: mklocal@milton-keynes.gov.uk W: www.milton-keynes.gov.uk/library_services/home.asp

Cambridgeshire
Cambridgeshire Collection Central Library, Lion Yard, Cambridge, CB2 3QD T: 0345 045 5225 E: cambs.archives@cambridgeshire.gov.uk W: www.cambridgeshire.gov.uk/archives/
Fenland Collection Wisbech Library, 1 Ely Place, Wisbech, Cambridgeshire PE13 EU T: 0345 045 5225 F: 01945 589 240 E: cambs.archives@cambridgeshire.gov.uk W: www.cambridgeshire.gov.uk/archives/
Homerton College Library The New Library, Hills Road, Cambridge, Cambridgeshire CB2 2PH
Norris Library and Museum The Broadway, St Ives, Cambridgeshire PE27 5BX T: 01480 497314 E: bob@norrismuseum.org.uk W: www.norrismuseum.org.uk
Peterborough Archives Service and Local Studies Collection Central Library, Broadway, Peterborough, PE1 1RX T: 01733 742700 W: www.peterborough.gov.uk

Cheshire

Alderley Edge Library Heys Lane, Alderley Edge, Cheshire SK9 7JT T: 01625 584487 W: www.cheshire.gov.uk

Alsager Library Sandbach Road North, Alsager, Cheshire ST7 2QH T: 01270 873552 E: alsager.infopoint@cheshire.gov.uk W: www.cheshire.gov.uk

Barnton Library Townfield Lane, Barnton, Cheshire CW8 4LJ T: 01606 77343 W: www.cheshire.gov.uk

Bishops' High School Library Vaughans Lane, Chester, Cheshire CH3 5XF T: 01244 313806 W: www.cheshire.gov.uk

Blacon Library Western Avenue, Blacon, Chester, Cheshire CH1 5XF T: 01244 390628 W: www.cheshire.gov.uk

Bollington Library Palmerston Street, Bollington, Cheshire SK10 5JX T: 01625 573058 W: www.cheshire.gov.uk

Chester Library Northgate Street, Chester, Cheshire CH1 2EF T: 01244 977 380 E: chester.infopoint@cheshirewestandchester.gov.uk W: www.cheshire.gov.uk

Congleton Library Market Square, Congleton, Cheshire CW12 1ET T: 01260 375550 E: congleton.infopoint@cheshireeast.gov.uk W: www.cheshireeast.gov.uk

Crewe Library Prince Albert Street, Crewe, Cheshire CW1 2DH T: 01270 375295 E: crewe.infopoint@cheshireeast.gov.uk W: www.cheshireeast.gov.uk/

Ellesmere Port Library Civic Way, Ellesmere Port, South Wirral, Cheshire CH65 0BG T: 0151 337 4684 E: ellesmereportreferencelibrary@cheshirewestandchester.gov.uk W: www.cheshirewestandchester.gov.uk

Frodsham Library Rock Chapel, Main Street, Frodsham, Cheshire WA6 7AN T: 01928 732775

Golborne Library Tanners Lane, Golborne, Warrington, Cheshire WA3 3AW T: 01942 777800

Great Boughton Library Green Lane, Vicars Cross, Chester, Cheshire CH3 5LB T: 01244 320709 W: www.cheshire.gov.uk

Halton Lea Library Halton Lea, Runcorn, Cheshire WA7 2PF T: 01928-715351 W: www.cheshire.gov.uk

Handforth Library The Green, Wilmslow Road, Handforth, Cheshire SK9 3ES T: 01625 528062 W: www.cheshire.gov.uk

Helsby Library Lower Robin Hood Lane, Helsby, Cheshire WA5 0BW T: 01928 724659 W: www.cheshire.gov.uk

Holmes Chapel Library London Road, Holmes Chapel, Cheshire CW4 7AP T: 01477 535126 W: www.cheshire.gov.uk

Hoole Library 91 Hoole Road, Chester, Cheshire CH2 3NG T: 01244 347401 W: www.cheshire.gov.uk

Hope Farm Library Bridge Meadow, Great Sutton, Cheshire CH66 2LE T: 0151 355 8923 W: www.cheshire.gov.uk

Hurdsfield Library 7 Hurdsfield Green, Macclesfield, Cheshire SK10 2RJ T: 01625 423788 W: www.cheshire.gov.uk

Knutsford Library Toft Road, Knutsford WA16 0PG T: 01565 632909 E: knutsford.infopoint@cheshire.gov.uk W: www.cheshire.gov.uk

Lache Library Lache Park Avenue, Chester, Cheshire CH4 8HR T: 01244 683385 W: www.cheshire.gov.uk

Little Sutton Library Chester Road, Little Sutton, Cheshire CH66 1QQ T: 0151 339 3373 W: www.cheshire.gov.uk

Local Heritage Library Central Library, Wellington Road South, Stockport, Cheshire SK1 3RS T: 0161-474-4530 E: localheritage.library@stockport.gov.uk W: www.stockport.gov.uk

Macclesfield Library 2 Jordongate, Macclesfield, Cheshire SK10 1EE T: 01625 374000 E: macclesfield.infopoint@cheshireeast.gov.uk W: www.cheshireeast.gov.uk

Macclesfield Silk Museums Paradise Mill, Park Lane, Macclesfield, Cheshire SK11 6TJ T: 01625 612045 W: www.silk-macclesfield.org

Malpas Library Bishop Herber High School, Malpas, Cheshire SY14 8JD T: 01948 860571 W: www.cheshire.gov.uk

Middlewich Library Lewin Street, Middlewich, Cheshire CW10 9AS T: 01606 832801 W: www.cheshire.gov.uk

Nantwich Library Beam Street, Nantwich CW5 5LY T: 01270 375361 E: nantwich.infopoint@cheshireeast.gov.uk W: www.cheshireeast.gov.uk

Northwich Library Witton Street, Northwich CW9 5DR T: 01606 44221 E: northwich.infopoint@cheshirewestandcheshire.gov.uk W: www.cheshire.gov.uk

Poynton Library Park Lane, Poynton SK12 1RB T: 01625 876257 E: poynton.infopoint@cheshireeast.gov.uk W: www.cheshireeast.gov.uk

Prestbury Library The Reading Room, Prestbury, Cheshire SK10 4AD T: 01625 827501 W: www.cheshire.gov.uk

Sandbach Library The Common, Sandbach, Cheshire CW11 1FJ T: 01270 375355 E: sandbach.infopoint@cheshireeast.gov.uk W: www.cheshire.gov.uk

Sandiway Library Mere Lane, Cuddington, Northwich, Cheshire CW8 2NS T: 01606 888065 W: www.cheshire.gov.uk

Stockport MBC Bibliographical Services Unit Phoenix House, Bird Hall Lane, Stockport, Cheshire SK3 0RA

Tameside Local Studies Library Stalybridge Library, Trinity Street, Stalybridge, Cheshire SK15 2BN T: 0161-338-2708 W: www.tameside.gov.uk

Tarporley Library High School, Eaton Road, Tarporley, Cheshire CW6 0BJ T: 01829 732558 W: www.cheshire.gov.uk

Upton Library Wealstone Lane, Upton by Chester, Cheshire CH2 1HB T: 01244 380053 W: www.cheshire.gov.uk

Weaverham Library Russett Road, Weaverham, Northwich, Cheshire CW8 3HY T: 01606 853359 W: www.cheshire.gov.uk

Weston Library Heyes Hall, Weston, Macclesfield, Cheshire SK11 8RL T: 01625 614008 W: www.cheshire.gov.uk

Wharton Library Willow Square, Wharton, Winsford, Cheshire CW7 3HP T: 01606 593883 W: www.cheshire.gov.uk

Wilmslow Library South Drive, Wilmslow, Cheshire SK9 1NW T: 01625 374060 E: wilmslow.infopoint@cheshireeast.gov.uk W: www.cheshireeast.gov.uk

Winsford Library High Street, Winsford, Cheshire CW7 2AS T: 01606 552065 E: winsford.infopoint@cheshirewestandchester.gov.uk W: www.cheshirewestandchester.gov.uk

Cleveland

Hartlepool Central Library 124 York Road, Hartlepool, Cleveland TS26 9DE T: 01429 263778

Middlesbrough Libraries Central Library, Victoria Square, Middlesbrough TS1 2AY T: 01642 729001 E: reference_library@middlesbrough.gov.uk W: www.middlesbrough.gov.uk

Redcar Reference Library Coatham Road, Redcar, Cleveland TS10 1RP T: 01642 489292 E: reference_library@redcar-cleveland.gov.uk

Stockton Reference Library Church Road, Stockton on Tees, TS18 1TU T: 01642 528079 E: reference.library@stockton.gov.uk W: www.stockton.gov.uk

Cornwall

Cornish Studies Library The Cornwall Centre, Alma Place, Redruth, Cornwall TR15 2AT T: 01209 216 760 E: cornishstudies.library@cornwall.gov.uk W: www.cornwall.gov.uk/cornwallcentre

Royal Institution of Cornwall, Courtney Library & Cornish History Research Centre Royal Cornwall Museum, River Street, Truro, Cornwall TR1 2SJ T: 01872 272205 W: www.cornwall-online.co.uk/genealogy

County Durham

Darlington Local Studies Centre The Library, Crown Street, Darlington, County Durham DL1 1ND T: 01325-349630 E: local.studies@darlington.gov.uk W: www.darlington.gov.uk/library/localstudies

Durham City Reference & Local Studies Library Durham Clayport Library, Millennium Place, Durham, County Durham DH1 1WA T: 0191 386 4003 W: www.durham.gov.uk

Durham University Library Archives and Special Collections Durham University Library, Palace Green, Durham, DH1 3RN T: 0191 334 2972 E: pg.library@durham.ac.uk W: www.dur.ac.uk/library/asc

The Oriental Museum University of Durham Museums, Elvet Hill, Durham, DH1 3TH T: 0191 334 5694 E: oriental.museum@durham.ac.uk W: www.dur.ac.uk/oriental.museum/

Cumbria

Barrow in Furness - Cumbria Record Office & Local Studies Library 140 Duke St, Barrow in Furness LA14 1XW T: 01229 407363 E: barrow.record.office@cumbriacc.gov.uk W: www.cumbria.gov.uk/archives

Carlisle Library 11 Globe Lane, Carlisle, Cumbria CA3 8NX T: 01228-607310 E: carlisle.library@cumbriacc.gov.uk W: www.cumbria.gov.uk/libraries

Kendal Library Stricklandgate, Kendal LA9 4PY T: 01539 713 520 E: kendal.library@cumbriacc.gov.uk W: www.cumbriacc.gov.uk

Penrith Library St Andrews Churchyard, Penrith, Cumbria CA11 7YA T: 01768-242100 W: www.cumbria.gov.uk

Whitehaven - Cumbria Record Office & Local Studies Library Scotch Street, Whitehaven CA28 7NL T: 01946 506420 E: whitehaven.record.office@cumbriacc.gov.uk W: www.cumbria.gov.uk/archives

Workington Library Vulcans Lane, Workington CA14 2ND T: 01900-325170 E: workington.library@cumbriacc.gov.uk W: www.cumbriacc.gov.uk

Derbyshire

Chesterfield Library, Local Studies Chesterfield Library, New Beetwell Street, Chesterfield, Derbyshire S40 1QN T: 01629 533 400 E: chesterfield.library@derbyshire.gov.uk W: www.derbyshire.gov.uk

Derby Local Studies Library 25b Irongate, Derby, Derbyshire DE1 3GL T: 01332 642240 E: localstudies.library@derby.gov.uk W: www.derby.gov.uk/libraries/about/local_studies.htm

Local Studies Library - Matlock County Hall, Smedley Street, Matlock DE4 3AG T: 01629 536 579 E: localstudies@derbyshire.gov.uk W: www.derbyshire.gov.uk/leisure/local_studies

Devon

Devon & Exeter Institution Library 7 The Close, Exeter, Devonshire EX1 1EZ T: 01392 251017 W: www.ex.ac.uk/library/devonex.html

Exeter University Library Stocker Road, Exeter, Devon EX4 4PT T: 01392 263872 E: library@exeter.ac.uk W: www.library.exeter.ac.uk

The History Room, Plymouth Central Library Plymouth Central Library, Drake Circus, Plymouth, PL4 8AL T: 01752 305 907/08 E: library@plymouth.gov.uk W: www.plymouth.gov.uk/libraries

Torquay Library Lymington Road, Torquay, Devon TQ1 3DT T: 01803 208305

West Country Studies Library Exeter Central Library, Castle Street, Exeter, Devon EX4 3PQ T: 01392 384216 W: www.devon-cc.gov.uk/library/locstudy

Dorset

Dorchester Reference Library Colliton Park, Dorchester, Dorset DT1 1XJ T: 01305-224448

Dorset County Museum High West Street, Dorchester, Dorset DT1 1XA T: 01305 262735 E: enquiries@dorsetcountymuseum.org W: www.dorsetcountymuseum.org

Poole Central Library Dolphin Centre, Poole, Dorset BH15 1QE T: 01202 262424 E: centrallibrary@poole.gov.uk W: www.boroughofpoole.com/libraries

Weymouth Reference Library Great George Street, Weymouth, Dorset DT4 8NN T: 01305 762418 E: weymouthlibrary@dorsetcc.gov.uk W: www.dorsetcc.gov.uk

Essex

Essex County Council Libraries - Answers Direct PO Box 882, Market Road, Chelmsford, Essex CM1 1LH T: 0845 603 7628 E: answers.direct@essex.gov.uk W: www.essex.gov.uk/libraries http://elan.essexcc.gov.uk (Online Catalogue) www.answersdirect.info

Ilford Local Studies and Archives, London Borough of Central Library, Clements Road, Ilford, Essex IG1 1EA T: 020 8708 2417

Redbridge Library Central Library, Clements Road, Ilford, Essex IG1 1EA T: (020) 8708 2417 W: www.redbridge.gov.uk

Southend Library and Local Studies Central Library, Victoria Avenue, Southend on Sea, Essex SS2 6EX T: 01702 215011 E: library@southend.gov.uk W: www.southend.gov.uk/libraries/

Thomas Plume Library Market Hill, Maldon, Essex CM9 4PZ

Gloucestershire

Cheltenham Local Studies Centre Cheltenham Library, Clarence Street, Cheltenham, Gloucestershire GL50 3JT T: 01242-532678

Gloucester Library, Arts & Museums County Library, Quayside, Shire Hall, Gloucester GL1 1HY T: 01452-425037 W: www.gloscc.gov.uk

Gloucestershire County Library Brunswick Road, Gloucester, GL1 1HT T: 01452-426979 W: www.gloscc.gov.uk

Gloucestershire Family History Society Clarence Row, Alvin Street, Gloucester, Gloucestershire GL1 3AH T: 01452 524344 (Resource Centre) E: secretary@gfhs.org.uk W: www.gfhs.org.uk

Yate Library 44 West Walk, Yate BS37 4AX T: 01454 868006 E: yate_library@southglos.gov.uk W: www.southglos.gov.uk

Gloucestershire - South

Thornbury Library St Mary Street, Thornbury, South Gloucestershire BS35 2AA T: 01454 868006 E: thornbury.library@southglos.gov.uk W: www.southglos.gov.uk

Hampshire

Aldershot Library 109 High Street, Aldershot GU11 1DQ T: 01252 322456

Andover Library Chantry Centre, Andover, Hampshire SP10 1LT T: 01264 352807 E: clceand@hants.gov.uk W: www.hants.gov.uk

Basingstoke Library North Division Headquarters, 19 - 20 Westminster House, Potters Walk, Basingstoke, Hampshire RG21 7LS T: 01256-473901 W: www.hants.gov.uk

Bournemouth Library 22 The Triangle, Bournemouth, Hampshire BH2 5RQ T: 01202 454817

Eastleigh Library The Swan Centre, Eastleigh, Hampshire SO50 5SF T: 023 8061 2513 E: clweeas@hants.gov.uk W: www.hants.gov.uk

Fareham Library Osborn Road, Fareham, Hampshire PO16 7EN T: 01329 284902 W: www.hants.gov.uk

Farnborough Library Pinehurst, Farnborough GU14 7JZ T: 0845 603 5631 E: clnoref@hants.gov.uk W: www.brit-a-r.demon.co.uk

Fleet Library 236 Fleet Road, Fleet, Hampshire GU51 4BX T: 0845 603 5631 E: clnofle@hants.gov.uk W: www.hants.gov.uk

Gosport Library High Street, Gosport, Hampshire PO12 1BT T: (023) 9252 3431 W: www.hants.gov.uk

Hampshire Archives & Local Studies Hampshire Record Office, Sussex Street, Winchester, Hampshire SO23 8TH T: 01962 846154 E: enquiries.archives@hants.gov.uk W: www.hants.gov.uk/archives

Hampshire County Library West Division Headquarters, The Old School, Cannon Street, Lymington, Hampshire SO41 9BR T: 01590-675767 W: www.hants.gov.uk

Lymington Library North Close, Lymington SO41 9BW T: 0845 603 5631 E: clwelym@hants.gov.uk W: www.hants.gov.uk/library

Portsmouth City Libraries Central Library, Guildhall Square, Portsmouth, Hampshire PO1 2DX T: 023 9268 8046 (Bookings & Enquiries) E: reference.library@portsmouthcc.gov.uk W: www.portsmouth.gov.uk/learning/15605.html

Southampton City Libraries - Local Studies & Maritime Collections Central Library, Civic Centre, Southampton, Hampshire SO14 7LW T: 023 8083 2205 E: local.studies@southampton.gov.uk W: www.southampton.gov.uk/s-leisure/libraries/

Southampton University Library Highfield, Southampton, Hampshire SO17 1BJ T: 023 8059 3724

Waterlooville Library The Precinct, Waterlooville PO7 7DT T: (023) 9225 2608 E: clsowvl@hants.gov.uk W: www.hants.gov.uk

Winchester Discovery Centre Jewry Street, Winchester SO23 8RX T: 01962 873600 E: winchesterdiscoverycentre@hants.gov.uk W: www.discoverycentres.co.uk/winchester

Herefordshire

Bromyard Library 34 Church Street, Bromyard HR7 4DP T: 01885 482657

Colwall Library Humphrey Walwyn Library, Colwall, Malvern, Herefordshire WR13 6QT T: 01684 540642

Hereford Cathedral Library & Archives 5 College Cloisters, Cathedral Close, Hereford HR1 2NG T: 01432 374225/6 E: library@herefordcathedral.org W: www.herefordcathedral.org

Hereford Library Broad Street, Hereford HR4 9AU T: 01432 383600 E: herefordlibrary@herefordshire.gov.uk W: www.herefordshire.gov.uk/libraries

Ledbury Library The Homend, Ledbury HR8 1BT T: 01531 632133

Leominster Library 8 Buttercross, Leominster HR6 8BN T: 01568-612384

Ross Library Cantilupe Road, Ross on Wye HR9 7AN T: 01989 567937

Hertfordshire

Bushey Museum, Art Gallery and Local Studies Centre Rudolph Road, Bushey, Hertfordshire WD23 3HW T: 020 8420 4057 E: busmt@bushey.org.uk W: www.busheymuseum.org

Hertfordshire Archives and Local Studies County Hall, Pegs Lane, Hertford, Hertfordshire SG13 8EJ T: 0300 123 4049 E: hertsdirect@hertscc.gov.uk W: www.hertsdirect.org/Hals

Welwyn Garden City Central Library Local Studies Section, Campus West, Welwyn Garden City AL8 6AJ T: 01438 737333

Hull

Brynmor Jones Library - University of Hull Cottingham Road, Hull, HU6 7RX T: 01482 465265 W: www.hull.ac.uk/lib www.hull.ac.uk/lib/archives

Hull Central Library Family & Local History Unit Central Library, Albion Street, Kingston upon Hull, HU1 3TF T: 01482 616828 W: www.hullcc.gov.uk/genealogy

Hull College - Local History Unit James Reckitt Library, Holderness Road, Hull, HU9 1EA T: 01482 331551 W: www.historyofhull.co.uk

Hull Local Studies Library Central Library, Albion Street Hull, HU1 3TF T: 01482 210077 E: local.studies@hullcc.gov.uk W: www.historycentrehull.org.uk

Isle of Wight

Isle of Wight County Library Lord Louis Library, Orchard Street, Newport, Isle of Wight PO30 1LL T: 01983-823800 W: www.iwight.com/thelibrary

Kent

Ashford Library Church Road, Asford, Kent TN23 1QX T: 01233 620649 W: www.kent.gov.uk

Broadstairs Library The Broadway, Broadstairs, Kent CT10 2BS T: 01843-862994 W: www.kent.gov.uk

Canterbury Cathedral Library The Precincts, Canterbury, Kent CT1 2EH T: 01227-865287 E: library@canterbury-cathedral.org W: www.canterbury-cathedral.org/history/libraries.htm

Canterbury Library & Local Studies Collection 18 High Street, Canterbury, Kent CT1 2JF T: 01227-463608 W: www.kent.gov.uk

Dartford Central Library - Reference Department Market Street, Dartford, Kent DA1 1EU T: 01322-221133 W: www.kent.gov.uk

Deal Library Broad Street, Deal, Kent CT14 6ER T: 01304 374726 W: www.kent.gov.uk

Dover Library Maison Dieu House, Biggin Street, Dover, Kent CT16 1DW: T: 01304 204241 W: www.kent.gov.uk
Faversham Library Newton Road, Faversham, Kent ME13 8DY T: 01795 532448 W: www.kent.gov.uk
Folkestone Library & Local Heritage Studies 2 Grace Hill, Folkestone, Kent CT20 1HD T: 01303-256710 W: www.kent.gov.uk
Gillingham Library High St, Gillingham ME7 1BG T: 01634 337340 E: Gillingham.Library@medway.gov.uk W: www.medway.gov.uk
Gravesend Library Windmill Street, Gravesend, Kent DA12 1BE T: 01474 352758 W: www.kent.gov.uk
Greenhill Library Greenhill Road, Herne Bay, Kent CT6 7PN T: 01227 374288 W: www.kent.gov.uk
Herne Bay Library 124 High Street, Herne Bay, Kent CT6 5JY T: 01227-374896 W: www.kent.gov.uk
Maidstone Reference Library St Faith's Street, Maidstone, Kent ME14 1LH T: 01622 701943 W: www.kent.gov.uk
Margate Library Local History Collection Cecil Square, Margate, Kent CT9 1RE T: 01843-223626 W: www.kent.gov.uk
Medway Archives & Local Studies Centre Civic Centre, Strood, Rochester, Kent ME2 4AU T: 01634 332 714 E: malsc@medway.gov.uk W: http://cityark.medway.gov.uk
Ramsgate Library and Museum Guildford Lawn, Ramsgate, Kent CT11 9QY T: 01843-593532 W: www.kent.gov.uk
Ramsgate Library Local Strudies Collection & Thanet Branch Archives Ramsgate Library, Guildford Lawn, Ramsgate, Kent CT11 9AY T: 01843-593532 W: www.kent.gov.uk
Sevenoaks Library Buckhurst Lane, Sevenoaks, Kent TN13 1LQ T: 01732-453118 W: www.kent.gov.uk
Sheerness Library Russell Street, Sheerness, Kent ME12 1PL T: 01795-662618 W: www.kent.gov.uk
Sittingbourne Library Central Avenue, Sittingbourne, Kent ME10 4AH T: 01795-476545 W: www.kent.gov.uk
Sturry Library Chafy Crescent, Sturry, Canterbury, Kent CT2 0BA T: 01227 711479 W: www.kent.gov.uk
Swalecliffe Library 78 Herne Bay Road, Chestfield, Kent CT5 2LX T: 01227 792645
Tonbridge Library Avenbury Avenue, Tonbridge, Kent TN9 1TG T: 01732 352754 W: www.kent.gov.uk
Tunbridge Wells Library Mount Pleasant, Tunbridge Wells, Kent TN1 1NS T: 01892-522352 W: www.kent.gov.uk
University of Kent at Canterbury Library Canterbury, Kent CT2 7NU T: 01227 764000 W:
Whitstable Library 31-33 Oxford Street, Whitstable, Kent CT5 1DB T: 01227-273309

Lancashire
Bacup Library St James's Square, Bacup OL13 9AH T: 01706 873324
Barnoldswick Library Fernlea Avenue, Barnoldswick BB18 5DW T: 01282-812147
Barnoldswick Library Fernlea Avenue, Barnoldswick, Colne, Lancashire BB8 5DW T: 01282 812147
Blackburn Central Library - Community History Dept Town Hall Street, Blackburn BB2 1AG T: 01254 587919 E: community.history@blackburn.gov.uk W: www.blackburn.gov.uk/library www.cottontown.org
Burnley Central & Local Studies Library Grimshaw Street, Burnley, Lancashire BB11 2BD T: 01282-437115 E: burnley.reference@lcl.lancscc.gov.uk W: www.lancscc.gov.uk
Bury Central Library - References & Information Services Bury Central Library, Manchester Rd, Bury BL9 0DG T: 0161 253 5871 E: information@bury.gov.uk W: www.bury.gov.uk/libraries
Central Library Civic Centre, Le Mans Crescent, Bolton, BL1 1SE T: 01204 333185
Chethams Library Long Millgate, Manchester, M3 1SB T: 0161 834 7961 W: www.chethams.org.uk
Chorley Central Library Union St, Chorley PR7 1EB T: 01257 277222
Clitheroe Library Church St, Clitheroe BB7 2DG T: 01200 428788
Colne Library Market Street, Colne BB8 0AP T: 01282-871155
Haslingden Library Higher Deardengate, Haslingden, Rossendale, Lancashire BB4 5QL T: 01706 215690
Heywood Local Studies Library Heywood Library, Church Street, Heywood, Lancashire OL10 1LL T: 01706 360947
Hyndburn Central Library St James Street, Accrington, Lancs, BB5 1NQ T: 01254-872385 W: www.lancscc.gov.uk
John Rylands University Library Special Collections Division, 150 Deansgate, Manchester, M3 3EH T: 0161-834-5343 W: www.library.manchester.ac.uk
Lancashire Record Office Bow Lane, Preston PR1 2RE T: 01772 533039 E: record.office@lancashire.gov.uk W: www.archives.lancashire.gov.uk

Leyland Library Lancastergate, Leyland PR25 2EX T: 01771 458500 E: leyland.library@lcl.lancscc.gov.uk W: www.lancashire.gov.uk/libraries
Manchester Central Library - Archives & Local Studies Manchester Central Library, St Peter's Square, Manchester, M2 5PD T: 0161-234-1979 W: www.manchester.gov.uk/libraries/index.htm
Middleton Local Studies Library Middleton Library, Long Street, Middleton, Lancashire M24 6DU T: 0161-643-5228
Morecambe Library Central Drive, Morecambe LA4 5DL T: 01524 402110
Nelson Library & Information Service : Community History Department Market Square, Nelson, Lancashire BB9 7PU T: 01282 449 586 E: nelson.ch@lancashire.gov.uk W: www.lancashire.gov.uk/libraries
Oldham Local Studies and Archives 84 Union Street, Oldham, Lancashire OL1 1DN T: 0161-911-4654 E: archives@oldham.gov.uk W: www.oldham.gov.uk/archives www.oldham.gov.uk/local_studies
Ormskirk Library Burscough Street, Ormskirk, Lancashire L39 2EN T: 01695 573448
Preston Harris Library Market Square, Preston PR1 2PP T: 01772 532 668 E: Harris.CH@lancashire.gov.uk W: www.lancashire.gov.uk/libraries
Prestwich Library Longfield Centre, Prestwich M25 1AY T: 0161 253 7214 E: Prestwich.lib@bury.gov.uk W: www.bury.gov.uk
Radcliffe Library Stand Lane, Radcliffe, Lancashire M26 9WR T: 0161 253 7160 W: www.bury.gov.uk
Ramsbottom Library Carr Street, Ramsbottom BL0 9AE T: 0161 253 5352 E: Ramsbottom.lib@bury.gov.uk W: www.bury.gov.uk
Rawtenstall Library Haslingden Road, Rawtenstall, Rossendale, Lancashire BB4 6QU T: 01706 227911 E: Rawtenstall.ch@lancashire.gov.uk W: www.lancashire.gov.uk/libraries
Rochdale Local Studies Centre Touchstones Rochdale, The Esplanade, Rochdale, Lancashire OL16 1AQ T: 01706 924915 E: localstudies@link4life.org W: www.link4life.org/localstudies
Salford Local History Library Peel Park, The Crescent, Salford, Lancashire M5 4WU T: 0161 778 0814 E: local.history@salford.gov.uk W: www.salford.gov.uk/lhlibrary.htm
Salford Museum & Art Gallery Peel Park, Salford, Lancashire M5 4WU T: 0161 736 2649 W: www.salford.gov.uk/salfordmuseum
Skelmersdale Central Library Southway, Skelmersdale, Lancashire WN8 6NL T: 01695 720312
St Anne's Library 254 Clifton Drive, St Anne's on Sea, Lancashire FY8 1NR T: 01253 643900
Working Class Movement Library Jubilee House, 51 The Crescent, Salford, Lancashire M5 4WX T: 0161 736 3601 E: enquiries@wcml.org.uk W: www.wcml.org.uk

Leicestershire
Coalville Library High Street, Coalville LE67 3EA T: 116 305 3565 E: coalvillelibrary@leics.gov.uk W: www.leics.gov.uk/coalville_library
Hinckley Library Local Studies Collection Hinckley Library, Lancaster Road, Hinckley LE10 0AT T: 0116 305 2500 E: hinckleylibrary@leics.gov.uk W: www.leics.gov.uk/hinckley_library
Leicester Reference and Information Library Bishop Street, Leicester, Leicestershire LE1 6AA T: 0116 299 5401
Leicestershire Libraries & Information Service 929 - 931 Loughborough Road, Rothley, Leicestershire LE7 7NH T: 0116 305 3801 E: libraries@leics.gov.uk W: www.leicestershire.gov.uk/libraries
Loughborough Library Local Studies Collection Granby Street, Loughborough LE11 3DZ T: 0116 305 2420 E: loughboroughlibrary@leics.gov.uk W: www.leics.gov.uk/loughborough_library
Market Harborough Library Pen Lloyd Library, Adam and Eve Street, Market Harborough, Leicestershire LE16 7LT T: 0116 305 3627 E: marketharboroughlibrary@leics.gov.uk W: www.leics.gov.uk/marketharborough_library
Melton Mowbray Library Wilton Road, Melton Mowbray, LE13 0UJ T: 0116 305 3646 E: meltonmowbraylibrary@leics.gov.uk W: www.leics.gov.uk/meltonmowbray_library
Southfields Library Reader Development Services, Saffron Lane, Leicester, Leicestershire LE2 6QS

Lincolnshire
Boston Library County Hall, Boston PE21 6LX T: 01205 310010 ext 2874
Gainsborough Library Cobden Street, Gainsborough DN21 2NG T: 01522 782010 E: gainsborough.library@lincolnshire.gov.uk
Grantham Library Issac Newton Centre, Grantham, Lincolnshire NG1 9LD T: 01476 591411
Lincoln Cathedral Library Lincoln Cathedral Library, Minster Yard, Lincoln, Lincolnshire LN2 1PZ T: 01522 561640 E: librarian@lincolncathedral.com W: www.lincolncathedral.com
Lincolnshire County Library Local Studies Section, Lincoln Central Library, Free School Lane, Lincoln LN2 1EZ T: 01522 782010 E: lincoln_library@lincolnshire.gov.uk W: www.lincolnshire.gov.uk

Stamford Library High Street, Stamford PE9 2BB T: 01780 763442
Lincolnshire - North
Scunthorpe Central Library Carlton Street, Scunthorpe DN15 6TX
T: 01724-860161 W: www.nothlincs.gov.uk/library
Lincolnshire - North East
Grimsby Central Library Reference Department Central Library,
Town Hall Square, Great Grimsby DN31 1HG T: 01472 323628 E:
jennie.mooney@nelincs.gov.uk W: www.nelincs.gov.uk

Liverpool
**Liverpool Central Library - The Liverpool Central Library and
Archive in the City Centre is undergoing redevelopment** Central
Library, William Brown Street, Liverpool, L3 8EW T: 0151 233 5817 E:
library.enquiries@liverpool.gov.uk W: www.liverpool.gov.uk/libraries
Liverpool Libraries & Archive Service Unit 33, Wellington
Employment Park South, Dunes Way (off Sandhills Lane), Liverpool,
L5 9ZS T: 0151 233 5817 E: archives@liverpool.gov.uk W:
www.liverpool.gov.uk/archives
Liverpool University Special Collections & Archives University of
Liverpool Library, PO Box 123, Liverpool, L69 3DA T: 0151-794-
2696 W: www.sca.lib.liv.ac.uk/collections/index.html

London
Bancroft Library 277 Bancroft Road, London, E1 4DQ T: 020 7364 1290
Barking & Dagenham Archives & Local Studies Centre - LB
Valence House, Beacontree Avenue, Dagenham, Essex RM8 3HT T:
020 8227 2033 E: localstudies@lbbd.gov.uk W:
www.lbbd.gov.uk/heritage
Barnet - Local Studies - LB Hendon Library, The Burroughs,
London, NW4 4BQ T: (020) 8359 3960 E:
library.archives@barnet.gov.uk W: www.barnet.gov.uk/archives
Bishopsgate Institute 230 Bishopsgate, London, EC2M 4QH T: (020)
7392 9270 E: library@bishopsgate.org.uk W:
www.bishopsgate.org.uk/library
Brent Archive - LB 152 Olive Road, Cricklewood, London, NW2
6UY T: (020) 8937 3541 E: archive@brent.gov.uk W:
www.brent.gov.uk/archive
Bromley Local Studies Library - LB Central Library, High Street,
Bromley BR1 1EX T: 020 8461 7170 E:
localstudies.library@bromley.gov.uk W: www.bromley.gov.uk/libraries
Camden Local Studies & Archive Centre - LB Holborn Library, 32
- 38 Theobalds Road, London, WC1X 8PA T: 020 7974 6342 E:
localstudies@camden.gov.uk W: www.camden.gov.uk/localstudies
Chelsea Public Library - LB Old Town Hall, King's Road, London,
SW3 5EZ T: (020) 7352-6056
Chiswick & Brentford Local Studies Collection - LB Chiswick
Public Library, Dukes Avenue, Chiswick, London, W4 2AB T: (020)
8994-5295
Croydon Local Study and Archives Service - LB Central Library,
Katharine Street, Croydon, CR9 1ET T: 020 8726 6900 x 61112 E:
localstudies@croydon.gov.uk W: www.croydon.gov.uk/
Ealing Local History Centre Central Library, 103 Broadway Centre,
Ealing, London, W5 5JY T: (020) 8567-3656-ext-37 E:
localhistory@hotmail.com W: www.ealing.gov.uk/libraries
Enfield Libraries - LB Southgate Town Hall, Green Lanes, Palmers
Green, N13 4XD T: (020) 8379-2724
Fawcett Library London Guildhall University, Old Castle Street,
London, E1 7NT T: (020) 7320-1189 W: www.lgu.ac.uk/.fawcett
Finsbury Library - Islington - LB 245 St John Street, London,
EC1V 4NB T: (020) 7527 7994 W: www.islington.gov.uk/htm
Greenwich Heritage Centre - LB Artillery Square, Royal Arsenal,
Woolwich, London, SE18 4DX T: (020) 8854 2452 E:
info@greenwichheritage.org W: www.greenwich.gov.uk
**Guildhall Library, Manuscripts Section - Closed permanently and
merged with London Metropolitan Archive** 40 Northampton Row,
London, EC1R 0HB T: 020 7332 3820 E:
ask.lma@cityoflondon.gov.uk W: www.cityoflondon.gov.uk/lma
Hammersmith Central Library, London Borough of Shepherds
Bush Road, London, W6 7AT T: 020 8753 3816 W: www.lbhf.gov.uk
Havering Central Reference Library - LB Reference Library, St
Edward's Way, Romford, Essex RM1 3AR T: 01708 432393
Hillingdon Libraries - LB Central Library, High Street, Uxbridge,
Middlesex UB8 1HD T: 01895 250702 W: www. hillingdon.gov.uk
Hounslow Library (Local Studies & Archives) - LB Centrespace,
Treaty Centre, High Street, Hounslow, London TW3 1ES T: 0845 456
2800 W: www.cip.com
Imperial College Archives Room 455 Sherfield Building, Imperial
College, London, SW7 2AZ T: 020 7594 8850 E:
a.barrett@imperial.ac.uk W: www3.imperial.ac.uk/recordsandarchives
Institute of Commonwealth Studies , University of London 28
Russell Square, London, WC1B 5DS T: (020) 7862 8844 E:
icommlib@sas.ac.uk W: http://sas.ac.uk/commonwealthstudies

Islington Local History Centre - LB Finsbury library, 245 St John
Street, London, EC1V 4NB T: (020) 7527 7988 E:
local.history@islington.gov.uk W: www.islington.gov.uk/heritage
James Clavell Library Royal Arsenal (West), Warren Lane,
Woolwich, London, SE18 6ST T: 020 8312 7125 W:
www.firepower.org.uk
Jewish Museum The Sternberg Centre for Judaism, 80 East End
Road, Finchley, London, N3 2SY T: 020 8349 1143 E:
admin@jewishmuseum.org.uk W: www.jewishmuseum.org.uk
**Kensington and Chelsea Libraries, Local Studies & Archives
Department - Royal Borough of** Central Library, Phillimore Walk,
Kensington, London, W8 7RX T: 020 7361 3038 E:
information.services@rbkc.gov.uk W: www.rbkc.gov.uk/libraries
Lambeth Archives Department - LB Minet Library, 52 Knatchbull
Road, Lambeth, London, SE5 9QY T: (020) 7926 6076 W:
www.lambeth.gov.uk
Lewisham Local History & Archives Centre - LB Lewisham
Library, 199 - 201 Lewisham High Street, London, SE13 6LG T: 020
8314 8501 E: local.studies@lewisham.gov.uk W: www.lewisham.gov.uk
London Metropolitan Archives 40 Northampton Road, London,
EC1R 0HB T: 020 7332 3820 E: ask.lma@cityoflondon.gov.uk W:
www.lma.gov.uk/
London University - Institute of Advanced Legal Studies Charles
Clore House, 17 Russell Square, London, WC1B 5DR T: (020) 7862
5800 E: ials@sas.ac.uk W: http://ials.sas.ac.uk
Merton Local Studies Centre - LB Merton Civic Centre, London
Road, Morden, Surrey SM4 5DX T: (020) 8545-3239 E:
local.studies@merton.gov.uk W: www.merton.gov.uk/libraries
Minet Library 52 Knatchbull Road, Lambeth, London, SE5 9QY T:
(020) 7926 6076 W: www.lambeth.gov.uk
Museum in Docklands Library & Archives Library & Archive, No
1 Warehouse, West India Quay, Hertsmere Road, London, E14 4AL T:
020 7001 9825 (Librarian) E:
info.docklands@museumoflondon.org.uk W:
www.museumindocklands.org.uk
Museum of London Library 150 London Wall, London, EC2Y 5HN
T: 020 7814 5588 E: library@museumoflondon.org.uk W:
www.museumoflondon.org.uk
Newham Archives & Local Studies Library - LB Stratford Library,
3 The Grove, London, E15 1EL T: (020) 8430 6881 W:
www.newham.gov.uk
Richmond upon Thames Local Studies Library - LB Old Town
Hall, Whittaker Avenue, Richmond upon Thames TW9 1TP T: (020)
8332 6820 E: localstudies@richmond.gov.uk W:
www.richmond.gov.uk
Royal Botanic Gardens Library & Archives, Kew, Richmond, Surrey
TW9 3AE T: 020 8332 5414
Senate House Library - Special Collections University of London,
Senate House Library, Malet Street, London, WC1 7HU T: 020 7862
8470 E: shl.specialcollections@london.ac.uk W: www.shl.lon.ac.uk :
www.shl.lon.ac.uk/specialcollections/archives/studentrecords.shtml
Southwark Local History Library - LB 211 Borough High Street,
Southwark, London, SE1 1JA T: 020 7525 0232 E:
local.history.library@southwark.gov.uk W: www.southwark.gov.uk
Sutton Central Library St Nicholas Way, Sutton, Surrey SM1 1EA
T: 020 8770 4747 E: local.studies@sutton.gov.uk W:
www.sutton.gov.uk
Tower Hamlets Local History Library & Archives - LB Bancroft
Library, 277 Bancroft Road, London, E1 4DQ T: (020) 7364 1290 E:
localhistory@towerhamlets.gov.uk W: www.ideastore.co.uk
**Twickenham Library - collection transferred to Richmond Local
Studies Library** Twickenham Library, Garfield Road, Twickenham,
Middlesex TW1 3JS T: (020) 8891-7271 W: www.richmond.gov.uk
UCL Library Services - Special Collections Library Services,
University College, Gower Street, London, WC1E 6BT T: 020 7679
5197 E: spec.coll@ucl.ac.uk W: www.ucl.ac.uk/library/special-coll/
University of Westminster Archive Information Systems & Library
Services, 4-12 Little Titchfield Street, London, W1W 7UW T: 020
7911 5000 ext 2524 E: archive@westminster.ac.uk W:
www.westminster.ac.uk/about/archive-services
Waltham Forest Local Studies Library, London Borough of Vestry
House Museum, Vestry Road, Walthamstow, London E17 9NH T: 020
8496 4381 E: vhm.enquiries@walthamforest.gov.uk W:
www.walthamforest.gov.uk/index/leisure/museums-galleries/vestry-
house/local-studies-library-3.htm
Wandsworth Heritage Service - LB Wandsworth Battersea Library,
265 Lavender Hill, London, SW11 1JB T: (020) 8871 7753 E:
heritage@wandsworth.gov.uk W: www.wandsworth.gov..uk/heritage
Westminster Abbey Library & Muniment Room Westminster
Abbey, London, SW1P 3PA T: 020 7654 4830 E:
library@westminster-abbey.org W: www.westminster-abbey.org

Merseyside
Crosby Library (South Sefton Local History Unit) Crosby Road North, Waterloo, Liverpool, Merseyside L22 0LQ T: 0151 257 6401 E: local-history.south@leisure.sefton.gov.uk W: www.sefton.gov.uk
Huyton Central Library Huyton Library, Civic Way, Huyton, Knowsley, Merseyside L36 9GD T: 0151-443-3738 W: www.knowsley.gov.uk/leisure/libraries/huyton/index.html
Southport Library (North Sefton Local History Unit) - Closed for Refurbishment until 2013
St Helen's Local History & Archives Library Central Library, Gamble Institute, Victoria Square, St Helens WA10 1DY T: 01744-456952
Middlesex
Harrow Local History Collection - Civic Centre Library - LB PO Box 4, Civic Centre, Harrow HA1 2UU T: 020 8424 1055 F: 020 8424 1971 E: localhistory.library@harrow.gov.uk W: www.harrow.gov.uk

Military
Catterick Garrison Library Gough Road, Catterick Garrison, North Yorkshire DL9 3EL T: 01748 833543 W: www.northyorks.gov.uk
National Museum of the Royal Navy HM Naval Base (PP66), Portsmouth, Hampshire PO1 3NH T: 023 9272 3795 E: library@nmrm.org.uk W: www.royalnavalmuseum.org
Royal Marines Museum Eastney, Southsea PO4 9PX T: (023) 9281 9385 Exts 224 E: info@royalmarinesmuseum.co.uk W: www.royalmarinesmuseum.co.uk

Mining
North of England Institute of Mining and Mechanical Engineers The Nicholas Wood Memorial Library, Neville Hall, Westgate Road, Newcastle upon Tyne, Tyne & Wear NE1 1SE T: 0191 233 2459 E: librarian@mininginstitute.org.uk W: www.mininginstitute.org.uk

Norfolk
Great Yarmouth Central Library Tolhouse Street, Great Yarmouth, Norfolk NR30 2SH T: 01493-844551 E: yarmouth.lib@norfolk.gov.uk W: www.library.norfolk.gov.uk
Kings Lynn Library London Road, King's Lynn PE30 5EZ T: 01553-772568 E: kings.lynn.lib@norfolk.gov.uk W: www.norfolk.gov.uk
Norfolk Heritage Centre, Norfolk and Norwich Millennium Library The Forum, Millennium Plain, Norwich, Norfolk NR2 1AW T: 01603 774740 E: norfolk.studies.lib@norfolk.gov.uk W: www.norfolk.gov.uk/heritagecentre
Thetford Public Library Raymond Street, Thetford, Norfolk IP24 2EA T: 01842-752048 E: thetford.lib@norfolk.gov.uk W: www.culture.norfolk.gov.uk

Northumberland
Alnwick Library Green Batt, Alnwick, Northumberland NE66 1TU T: 01665-602689 W: www.northumberland.gov.uk
Berwick upon Tweed Library Church Street, Berwick upon Tweed, Northumberland TD15 1EE T: 01289-307320 W: www.northumberland.gov.uk
Blyth Library Bridge Street, Blyth, Northumberland NE24 2DJ T: 01670-361352 W: www.northumberland.gov.uk
Border Library Hexham Old Gaol, Hallgate, Hexham, Northumberland NE46 3NH T: 01434 600910 E: museum@tynedale.gov.uk W: www.tynedaleheritage.org
Hexham Library Queens Hall, Beaumont Street, Hexham, NE46 3LS T: 01434 652491 E: mbenjamin@northumberland.gov.uk W: www.northumberlandlibraries.com
Morpeth Library Gas House Lane, Morpeth, NE61 1TA

Nottinghamshire
Arnold Library Front Street, Arnold NG5 7EE T: 0115-920-2247 W: www.nottscc.gov.uk
Beeston Library Foster Avenue, Beeston NG9 1AE T: 0115-925-5168 W: www.nottscc.gov.uk
Eastwood Library Wellington Place, Eastwood NG16 3GB T: 01773-712209 W: www.nottscc.gov.uk
Mansfield Library Four Seasons Centre, Westgate, Mansfield, NG18 1NH T: 01623 627591 E: mansfield.library@nottscc.gov.uk W: www.nottinghamshire.gov.uk
Manuscripts and Special Collections The University of Nottingham, King's Meadow Campus, Lenton Lane, Nottingham NG7 2NR T: 0115 951 4565 E: mss-library@nottingham.ac.uk W: www.nottingham.ac.uk/mss/
Newark Library Beaumont Gardens, Newark,NG24 1UW T: 01636-703966 W: www.nottscc.gov.uk
Nottingham Central Library : Local Studies Centre Angel Row, Nottingham NG1 6HP T: 0115 915 2873 W: www.nottinghamcity.gov.uk/libraries
Retford Library Denman Library, Churchgate, Retford, DN22 6PE T: 01777-708724 W: www.nottscc.gov.uk

Southwell Minster Library Minster Office, Trebeck Hall, Bishop's Drive, Southwell, Nottinghamshire NG25 0JP T: 01636-812649 W: www.southwellminster.org.uk
Sutton in Ashfield Library Devonshire Mall, Sutton in Ashfield, Nottinghamshire NG17 1BP T: 01623-556296 W: www.nottscc.gov.uk
University of Nottingham Hallward Library, University Park, Nottingham, NG7 2RD T: 0115-951-4514 W: www.nottingham.ac.uk/library/
West Bridgford Library Bridgford Road, West Bridgford, Nottinghamshire NG2 6AT T: 0115-981-6506 W: www.nottscc.gov.uk

Oxfordshire
Abingdon Library The Charter, Abingdon, Oxfordshire OX14 3LY T: 01235-520374 W: www.oxfordshire.gov.uk
Angus Library Regent's Park College, Pusey Street, Oxford, Oxfordshire OX1 2LB T: 01865 288142
Banbury Library Marlborough Rd, Banbury OX16 8DF T: 01295-262282
Henley Library Ravenscroft Road, Henley on Thames, Oxfordshire RG9 2DH T: 01491-575278
Middle East Centre St Anthony's College, Pusey Street, Oxford, Oxfordshire OX2 6JF T: 01865 284706
Nuffield College Library Oxford, Oxfordshire OX1 1NF T: 01865 278550 W: www.nuff.ox.ac.uk/library
Oxfordshire Studies Central Library, Westgate, Oxford OX1 1DJ T: 01865 815 749 E: oxfordshire.studies@oxfordshire.gov.uk W: www.oxfordshire.gov.uk/oxfordshirestudies
Puysey House Library Pusey House, 61 St Giles, Oxford, Oxfordshire OX1 1LZ T: 01865 278415 E: pusey.house@ic24.net
Rhodes House Library Bodleian Library, South Parks Road, Oxford, Oxfordshire OX1 3RG T: 01865 270909
River & Rowing Museum Mill Meadows, Henley on Thames, RG9 1BF T: 01491 415600 E: museum@rrm.co.uk W: www.rrm.co.uk
The Bodleian Library Broad Street, Oxford, Oxfordshire OX1 3BG T: 01865 277000 W: www.bodley.ox.ac.uk
Wantage Library Stirlings Rd, Wantage OX12 7BB T: 01235 762291
Witney Library Welch Way, Witney OX8 7HH T: 01993-703659

Rutland
Oakham Library Catmos Street, Oakham LE15 6HW T: 01572 722918

Shropshire
Wrekin Local Studies Forum Madeley Library, Russell Square, Telford TF7 5BB T: 01952 586575 W: www.madeley.org.uk

Somerset
Bath Central Library 19 The Podium, Northgate Street, Bath, BA1 5AN T: 01225 394041 E: council_connect@bathnes.gov.uk W: www.bathnes.gov.uk/libraries
Nailsea Library Somerset Sq, Nailsea BS19 2EX T: 01275-854583
Reference Library Binford Place, Bridgewater, Somerset TA6 3LF T: 01278-450082 W: www.somerset.gov.uk
Reference Library Justice Lane, Frome BA11 1BA T: 01373-462215
Somerset Studies Paul Street, Taunton, Somerset TA1 3XZ T: 01823-340300 E: somstud@somerset.gov.uk W: www.somerset.gov.uk/libraries
Weston Library The Boulevard, Weston Super Mare BS23 1PL T: 01934 426 861 E: weston.library@n-somerset.gov.uk W: www.n-somerset.gov.uk
Yeovil Library King George Street, Yeovil, Somerset BA20 1PY T: 01935-421910 W: www.somerset.gov.uk

Staffordshire
Barton Library Dunstall Road, Barton under Needwood, DE13 8AX T: 01283 713753 W: www.staffordshire.gov.uk
Biddulph Library Tunstall Road, Biddulph, Stoke on Trent, ST8 6HH T: 01782-512103 W: www.staffordshire.gov.uk
Brewood Library Newport Street, Brewood, Staffordshire ST19 9DT T: 01902-850087 W: www.staffordshire.gov.uk
Burton Library Burton Library, Riverside, High St, Burton on Trent DE14 1AH T: 01283 239556 E: burton.library@staffordshire.gov.uk W: www.staffordshire.gov.uk/leisure
Cannock Library Manor Ave, Cannock WS11 1AA T: 01543 510365 E: cannock.library@staffordshire.gov.uk W: www.staffordshire.gov.uk
Cheslyn Hay Library Cheslyn Hay, Walsall, Staffordshire WS56 7AE T: 01922-413956 W: www.staffordshire.gov.uk
Codsall Library Histons Hill, Codsall, Staffordshire WV8 1AA T: 01902-842764 W: www.staffordshire.gov.uk
Great Wyrley Library John's Lane, Great Wyrley, Walsall, WS6 6BY T: 01922-414632 W: www.staffordshire.gov.uk
Keele University Library - Special Collections & Archives Keele, Staffordshire ST5 5BG T: 01782 733237 E: h.burton@lib.keele.ac.uk W: www.keele.ac.uk/library/specarc/

Kinver Library Vicarage Drive, Kinver, Stourbridge, Staffordshire DY7 6HJ T: 01384-872348 W: www.staffordshire.gov.uk

Leek Library Nicholson Institute, Stockwell Street, Leek, ST13 6DW T: 01538 483 209 E: leek.library@staffordshire.gov.uk W: www.staffordshire.gov.uk

Lichfield Library (Local Studies Section) Lichfield Library, The Friary, Lichfield, Staffordshire WS13 6QG T: 01543 510720

Newcastle Library Ironmarket, Newcastle under Lyme, Staffordshire ST5 1AT T: 01782-297310 E: newcastle.library@staffordshire.gov.uk W: www.staffordshire.gov.uk

Penkridge Library Bellbrock, Penkridge, Staffordshire ST19 9DL T: 01785-712916 W: www.staffordshire.gov.uk

Perton Library Severn Drive, Perton WV6 7QU T: 01902-755794 E: perton.library@staffordshire.gov.uk W: www.staffordshire.gov.uk

Rugeley Library Anson Street, Rugeley, Staffordshire WS16 2BB T: 01889-583237 W: www.staffordshire.gov.uk

Staffordshire & Stoke on Trent Archive Service - Stoke on Trent City Archives City Central Library, Bethesda Street, Hanley, Stoke on Trent, Staffordshire ST1 3RS T: 01782 238 420 F: 01782 238 499 E: stoke.archives@stoke.gov.uk W: www.staffordshire.gov.uk/archives

Tamworth Library Corporation Street, Tamworth B79 7DN T: 01827 475645 E: tamworth.library@staffordshire.gov.uk W: www.staffordshire.gov.uk/leisure/librariesnew/doforyou/discover/local familyhistory/

Uttoxeter Library High Street, Uttoxeter, Staffordshire ST14 7JQ T: 01889-256371 W: www.staffordshire.gov.uk

William Salt Library 19 Eastgate Street, Stafford, Staffordshire ST16 2LZ T: 01785 278372 E: william.salt.library@staffordshire.gov.uk W: www.staffordshire.gov.uk/salt

Wombourne Library Windmill Bank, Wombourne, Staffordshire WV5 9JD T: 01902-892032 W: www.staffordshire.gov.uk

Suffolk

Chantry Library Chantry library, Hawthorne Drive, Ipswich, Suffolk IP2 0QY T: 01473 686117

Surrey

Bourne Hall Library Bourne Hall, Spring Street, Ewell, Epsom, Surrey KT17 1UF T: 020 8394 0372 W: www.surrey.gov.uk

Caterham Valley Library Caterham Valley Library, Stafford Road, Caterham, Surrey CR3 6JG T: 01883 343580 W: www.surrey.gov.uk

Cranleigh Library and Local History Centre High Street, Cranleigh, Surrey GU6 8AE T: 01483 272413 W: www.surrey.gov.uk

Epsom and Ewell Local History Centre Bourne Hall, Spring Street, Ewell, Epsom KT17 1UF T: 020 8394 0372 W: www.surrey.gov.uk

Horley Library Horley Library, Victoria Road, Horley, Surrey RH6 7AG T: 01293 784141 W: www.surrey.gov.uk

Lingfield Library The Guest House, Vicarage Road, Lingfield, Surrey RH7 6HA T: 01342 832058 W: www.surrey.gov.uk

Minet Library 52 Knatchbull Road, Lambeth, London, SE5 9QY T: (020) 7926 6076 W: www.lambeth.gov.uk

Redhill Library Warwick Quadrant, Redhill, Surrey RH1 1NN T: 01737 763332 W: www.surrey.gov.uk

Surrey Heath Museum Knoll Road, Camberley, Surrey GU15 3HD T: 01276 707284 E: museum@surreyheath.gov.uk W: www.surreyheath.gov.uk/leisure

Surrey History Centre Surrey History Centre, 130 Goldsworth Road, Woking, Surrey GU21 6ND T: 01483 518737 E: shs@surreycc.gov.uk W: www.surreycc.gov.uk/surreyhistorycentre

Sutton Central Library St Nicholas Way, Sutton, Surrey SM1 1EA T: 020 8770 4747 E: local.studies@sutton.gov.uk W: www.sutton.gov.uk

Sussex

Sussex University Library Manuscript Collections, Falmer, Brighton, Sussex BN1 9QL T: 01273 606755

Sussex - East

Brighton History Centre Brighton Museum & Art Gallery, Royal Pavilion Gardens, Brighton BN1 1EE T: 01273 296972 E: localhistory@brighton-hove.gov.uk W: www.brighton-hove-rpml.org.uk

Hove Reference Library 182 - 186 Church Road, Hove, East Sussex BN3 2EG T: 01273 296937 E: hovelibrary@brighton-hove.gov.uk W: www.brighton-hove.gov.uk

Sussex - West

Worthing Reference Library Richmond Road, Worthing BN11 1HD T: 01903 704824 E: worthing.library@westsussex.gov.uk W: www.westsussex.gov.uk/libraries

Tyne and Wear

City Library & Arts Centre 28 - 30 Fawcett Street, Sunderland, SR1 1RE T: 0191 561 8413 W: www.sunderland.gov.uk

Gateshead Central Library & Local Studies Department Prince Consort Road, Gateshead NE8 4LN T: 0191 433 8430 W: www.gateshead.gov.uk/ls

Local Studies - North Tyneside Libraries Northumberland Square, North Shields NE30 1QU T: 0191 643 5270 E: central.library@northtyneside.gov.uk W: www.northtyneside.gov.uk/libraries/index.htm

Newcastle Libraries & Information Service City Library, Charles Avison Building, 33 New Bridge Street West, Newcastle upon Tyne, NE1 8AX T: 0191 277 4100 E: information@newcastle.gov.uk W: www.newcastle.gov.uk/libraries

Robinson Library Newcastle University, Newcastle Upon Tyne NE2 4HQ T: 0191 222 7662 W: www.ncl.ac.uk/library/

South Tyneside Central Library - Local Studies Prince Georg Street, South Shields NE33 2PE T: 0191 424 7860 E: localstudies.library@southtyneside.gov.uk W: www.southtyneside.gov.uk

Warrington

Warrington Library, Archives & Local Studies Museum Street, Cultural Quarter, Warrington, Cheshire WA1 1JB T: 01925 442 889 E: library@warrington.gov.uk W: www.warrington.gov.uk

Warwickshire

Atherstone Library Long Street, Atherstone, Warwickshire CV9 1AX T: 01827 712395 E: libraryenquiryteam@warwickshire.gov.uk W: www.warwickshire.gov.uk/libraries

Bedworth Library 18 High Street, Bedworth, Nuneaton, Warwickshire CV12 8NF T: 024 7631 2267 E: bedworthlibrary@warwickshire.gov.uk W: www.warwickshire.gov.uk

Kenilworth Library Smalley Place, Kenilworth, Warwickshire CV8 1QG T: 01926 748900 E: kenilworthlibrary@warwickshire.gov.uk W: www.warwickshire.gov.uk

Nuneaton Library Church Street, Nuneaton, Warwickshire CV11 4DR T: 024 7638 4027 E: lesleykirkwood@warwickshire.gov.uk nuneatonlibrary@warwickshire.gov.uk W: www.warwickshire.gov.uk

Rugby Library Little Elborow Street, Rugby, Warwickshire CV21 3BZ T: 01788 533250 E: librarylocalstudies@warwickshire.gov.uk W: www.warwickshire.gov.uk/localstudies

Shakespeare Centre Library & Archive Shakespeare Birthplace Trust, Henley Street, Stratford upon Avon, Warwickshire CV37 6QW T: 01789 201816 E: records@shakespeare.org.uk W: www.shakespeare.org.uk

Stratford on Avon Library 12 Henley Street, Stratford on Avon CV37 6PZ T: 01789 292209 E: stratfordlibrary@warwickshire.gov.uk W: www.warwickshire.gov.uk

Warwick Library - Warwickshire Local Collection (County Collection) Warwick Library, Barrack Street, Warwick CV34 4TH T: 01926 412 189 E: warwicklibrary@warwickshire.gov.uk W: www.warwickshire.gov.uk

Warwickshire County Library Leamington Library, Royal Pump Rooms, The Parade, Leamington Spa CV32 4AA T: 01926 742721 E: leamingtonlibrary@warwickshire.gov.uk W: www.warwickshire.gov.uk

West Midlands

Birmingham Central Library - The Genealogist, Local Studies & History Service Floor 6, Central Library, Chamberlain Square, Birmingham, West Midlands B3 3HQ T: 0121 303 4549 W: www.birmingham.gov.uk

Birmingham University Library Services - Special Collections Cadbury Research Library, Muirhead Tower, University of Birmingham, Edgbaston, Birmingham B15 2TT T: 0121 414 5838 E: special-collections@bham.ac.uk W: www.special-coll.bham.ac.uk

Coventry History Centre & Museum Herbert Art Gallery & Museum, Jordan Well, Coventry CV1 5QP T: 024 7683 4060 E: historycentre@theherbert.org W: www.coventry.gov.uk

Dudley Archives & Local History Service Mount Pleasant Street, Coseley, Dudley WV14 9JR T: 01384-812770 W: www.dudley.gov.uk

Dudley Library & Information Services St James's Road, Dudley, DY1 1HR T: 01384-814103 W: http://dudleygov.uk/council/library/archives/archive1.htm

MLA West Midlands: the Regional Council for Museums, Libraries and archives 2nd Floor, Grosvenor House, 14 Bennetts Hill, Worcestershire B2 5RS T: 01527 872258

Sandwell Community History & Archives Service Smethwick Library, High Street, Smethwick B66 1AA T: 0121 558 2561 E: archives_service@sandwell.gov.uk W: www.archives.sandwell.gov.uk

Solihull Heritage and Local Studies service Solihull Central Library, Homer Road, Solihull B91 3RG T: 0121-704-6977 W: www.solihull.gov.uk/wwwlib/#local

Sutton Coldfield Reference Library - Local Studies Section 45 Lower Parade, Sutton Coldfield B72 1XX T: 0121 464 0164 E: sutton.coldfield.reference.lib@birmingham.gov.uk W: www.birmingham.gov.uk

Walsall Local History Centre Essex Street, Walsall WS2 7AS T: 01922-721305 W: www.walsall.gov.uk/index/leisure_and_culture/localhistorycentre
Wolverhampton Archives & Local Studies Molineux Hotel Building, Whitmore Hill, Wolverhampton WV1 1SF T: 01902 552 480 F: 01902 552 481 E: archives@wolverhampton.gov.uk W: www.wolverhampton.gov.uk/archives

Wigan
Ashton Library Wigan Road, Ashton in Makerfield, Wigan, WN2 9BH T: 01942 727119 E: ashton.library@wlct.org W: www.wlct.org/libraries
Aspull Library Oakfield Crescent, Aspull, Wigan WN2 1XJ T: 01942 831303 E: aspull.library@wlct.org W: www.wlct.org/libraries
Atherton Library York Street, Atherton, Manchester M46 9JH T: 01942 404817 E: atherton.library@wlct.org W: www.wlct.org/libraries
Beech Hill Library Buckley Street West, Beech Hill, Wigan, WN6 7PQ E: beechhill.library@wlct.org W: www.wlct.org/libraries
Golborne Library Tanners Lane, Golborne, Warrington, WA3 3AW T: 01942 777 800 E: golborne.library@wlct.org W: www.wlct.org/libraries
Hindley Library Market Street, Hindley, Wigan, WN2 3AN T: 01942 255287 E: hindley.library@wlct.org W: www.wlct.org/libraries
Ince Library Smithy Green, Ince, Wigan, WN2 2AT T: 01942 255287 E: ince.library@wlct.org W: www.wlct.org/libraries
Leigh Library & Local Studies Turnpike Centre, Civic Square, Leigh, WN7 1EB T: 01942 404557 E: heritage@wlct.org W: www.wlct.org/libraries
Marsh Green Library Harrow Road, Marsh Green, Wigan, WN5 0QL T: 01942 760041 E: marshgreen.library@wlct.org W: www.wlct.org/libraries
Orrell Library Orrell Post, Orrell, Wigan, WN5 8LY T: 01942 705060 E: orrell.library@wlct.org W: www.wlct.org/libraries
Platt Bridge Community Library Community First, Rivington Avenue, Platt bridge, Wigan, Lancashire WN2 5NG T: 01942 487 997 E: plattbridge.library@wlct.org W: www.wlct.org/libraries
Shevington Library Gathurst Lane, Shevington, Wigan, WN6 8HA T: 01257 252618 E: shevington.library@wlct.org W: www.wlct.org/libraries
Standish Library Cross Street, Standish, Wigan, WN6 0HQ T: 01257 400496 E: standish.library@wlct.org W: www.wlct.org/libraries
Tyldesley Library Stanley Street, Tyldesley, Manchester, M29 8AH T: 01942 404 738 E: tyldesley.library@wlct.org W: www.wlct.org/libraries
Wigan Library College Avenue, Wigan, WN1 1NN T: 01942 827619 E: wigan.library@wlct.org W: www.wlct.org/libraries 827619 E: wigan.library@wlct.org W: www.wlct.org/libraries

Wiltshire
Salisbury Reference and Local Studies Library Market Place, Salisbury SP1 1BL T: 01722 411098 W: www.wiltshire.gov.uk
The Science Museum Library & Archives - Wroughton Science Museum at Wroughton, Hackpen Lane, Wroughton, Swindon, SN4 9NS T: (0)1793 846 222 F: 0)1793 815 413 E: smlwroughton@sciencemuseum.org.uk W: www.sciencemuseum.org.uk/library/
The Swindon Collection Local Studies & Family History, Swindon Central Library, Regent Circus, Swindon SN1 1QG T: 01793 463238 E: central.library@swindon.gov.uk W: www.swindon.gov.uk/libraries
Wiltshire Archaeological and Natural Hist Soc Wiltshire Heritage Library, 41 Long Street, Devizes SN10 1NS T: 01380 727369 E: wanhs@wiltshireheritage.org.uk W: www.wiltshireheritage.org.uk
Wiltshire Buildings Record The Wiltshire & Swindon History Centre, Cocklebury Road, Chippenham SN15 3QN T: 01249 705 508 F: 01249 705 527 E: wbr@wiltshire.gov.uk W: www.wiltshire.gov.uk
Wiltshire Heritage Museum Library Wiltshire Archaeological & Natural Hist Soc, 41 Long Street, Devizes SN10 1NS T: 01380 727369 E: wanhs@wiltshireheritage.org.uk W: www.wiltshireheritage.org.uk
Wiltshire Studies Library Library & heritage HQ, Bythesea Road, Trowbridge BA14 8BS T: 01225-713732 W: www.wiltshire.gov.uk/community/

Wirral
Wirral Central Library Borough Road, Birkenhead, CH41 2XB T: 0151 652 6106

Worcestershire
Bewdley Museum Research Library Load Street, Bewdley, DY12 2AE T: 01229 403573 E: bewdley.museum@wyreforestdc.gov.uk W: www.wyreforestdc.gov.uk/museum
Bromsgrove Library Stratford Road, Bromsgrove, Worcestershire B60 1AP T: 01527-575855 W: www.worcestershire.gov.uk

Evesham Library Oat Street, Evesham WR11 4PJ T: 01905 822 722 E: eveshamlib@worcestershire.gov.uk W: www.worcestershire.gov.uk
Kidderminster Library Market Street, Kidderminster, Worcestershire DY10 1AD T: 01562-824500 W: www.worcestershire.gov.uk
Malvern Library Graham Road, Malvern, Worcestershire WR14 2HU T: 01684-561223 W: www.worcestershire.gov.uk
Redditch Library 15 Market Place, Redditch, B98 8AR T: 01527-63291 W: www.worcestershire.gov.uk
Worcester Library Foregate Street, Worcester WR1 1DT T: 01905 822 722 E: worcesterlib@worcestershire.gov.uk W: www.worcestershire.gov.uk/libraries
Worcesterhire History Centre History Centre, Trinity Street, Worcester, Worcestershire WR1 2PW T: 01905 765922 E: wlhc@worcestershire.gov.uk W: www.worcestershire.gov.uk/records

Yorkshire - East
Bridlington Local Studies Library Bridlington Library, King Street, Bridlington, East Yorkshire YO15 2DF T: 01262 672917 E: bridlingtonref.library@eastriding.gov.uk W: www.eastriding.gov.uk
East Riding Heritage Library & Museum Sewerby Hall, Church Lane, Sewerby, Bridlington YO15 1EA T: 01262 677874 E: sewerby.hall@eastriding.gov.uk W: www.sewerby-hall.co.uk
East Yorkshire Archive and Local Studies Service The Treasure House, Champney Road, Beverley HU17 8HE T: 01482 392 790 E: archives.service@eastriding.gov.uk W: www.eastriding.gov.uk/cs/culture-and-information/archives/archivesloc/
Goole Local Studies Library Goole Library, Carlisle Street, Goole, DN14 5DS T: 01405-762187 E: gooleref.library@eastriding.gov.uk W: www.eastriding.gov.uk

Yorkshire - North
Catterick Garrison Library Gough Road, Catterick Garrison, DL9 3EL T: 01748 833543 W: www.northyorks.gov.uk
Harrogate Reference Library Victoria Avenue, Harrogate, North Yorkshire HG1 1EG T: 01423-502744 W: www.northyorks.gov.uk
Malton Library St Michael's Street, Malton, North Yorkshire YO17 7LJ T: 01653 692714 W: www.northyorks.gov.uk
Northallerton Reference Library 1 Thirsk Road, Northallerton, North Yorkshire DL6 1PT T: 0845 034 9507 E: northallerton.library@northyorks.gov.uk W: www.northyorks.gov.uk
Pickering Reference Library The Ropery, Pickering YO18 8DY T: 01751-472185 W: www.northyorks.gov.uk
Richmond Library Queen's Road, Richmond, North Yorkshire DL10 4AE T: 01748 823120 W: www.northyorks.gov.uk
Ripon Library The Arcade, Ripon, North Yorkshire HG4 1AG T: 01765 792926 W: www.northyorks.gov.uk
Scarborough Reference Library Vernon Road, Scarborough YO11 2NN T: 0845 034 9517 E: scarborough.library@northyorks.gov.uk W: www.northyorks.gov.uk
Selby Reference Library 52 Micklegate, Selby, North Yorkshire YO8 4EQ T: 01757-702020 W: www.northyorks.gov.uk
Skipton Reference Library High Street, Skipton, North Yorkshire BD23 1JX T: 01756-794726 W: www.northyorks.gov.uk
Whitby Library Windsor Terrace, Whitby YO21 1ET T: 01947-602554

Yorkshire - South
Barnsley Archives and Local Studies Department Central Library, Shambles Street, Barnsley S70 2JF T: 01226 773950 E: Archives@barnsley.gov.uk W: www.barnsley.gov.uk
Doncaster & District Family History Society 8 Tenter Lane, Warmsworth, Doncaster, South Yorkshire DN4 9PT T: 01302 845 809 E: honsecretary@doncasterfhs.co.uk W: www.doncasterfhs.co.uk
Doncaster Libraries - Local Studies Section Central Library, Waterdale, Doncaster DN1 3JE T: 01302-734307 E: central.localhistory@doncaster.gov.uk W: www.doncaster.gov.uk/localstudies
Rotherham Archives & Local Studies Central Library, Walker Place, Rotherham, South Yorkshire S65 1JH T: 01709 823616 E: archives@rotherham.gov.uk W: www.rotherham.gov.uk
Sheffield Libraries, Archives & Information Surrey Street, Sheffield S1 1XZ T: 0114 273 4753 E: localstudies.library@sheffield.gov.uk W: www.sheffield.gov.uk/libraries/archives-and-local-studies www.picturessheffield.com
Sheffield University Library Special Collections & Library Archives, Western Bank, Sheffield, South Yorkshire S10 2TN T: 0114 222 7230 E: lib-special@sheffield.ac.uk W: www.shef.ac.uk/library/special

Yorkshire - West
Batley Library Market Place, Batley WF17 5DA T: 01924 326021 E: batley.library@kirklees.gov.uk W: www.kirklees.gov.uk
British Library Acquisitions Unit - Monograph Ordering The British Library, Boston Spa, Wetherby, LS23 7BQ T: 01937-546212

Brotherton Library Department of Special Collections, Leeds University, Leeds LS2 9JT T: 0113 233 55188 E: specialcollections@library.leeds.ac.uk W: www.leeds.ac.uk/library/spcoll

Calderdale Central Library Northgate House, Northgate, Halifax, HX11 1UN T: 01422392631 W: www.calderdale.co.uk

Cleckheaton Library Whitcliffe Road, Cleckheaton, West Yorkshire BD19 3DX T: 01274 335170

Dewsbury Library Dewsbury Retail Park, Railway Street, Dewsbury, West Yorkshire WF12 8EQ T: 01924 325080

Huddersfield Local History Library Library & Art Gallery, Princess Alexandra Walk, Huddersfield HD1 2SU T: 01484-221965 E: Huddersfield.localhistory@kirklees.gov.uk W: www.kirklees.gov.uk

Keighley Reference Library North Street, Keighley BD21 3SX T: 01535-618215 E: keighleylocalstudies@bradford.gov.uk W: www.bradford.gov.uk

Local and Family History Library Leeds Central Library, Calverley Street, Leeds, West Yorkshire LS1 3AB T: 0113 247 8290 E: localstudies@leedslearning.net W: www.leeds.gov.uk/localstudies

Local Studies Reference Library Central Library, Prince's Way, Bradford, West Yorkshire BD1 1NN T: 01274 433661 E: local.studies@bradford.gov.uk W: www.bradford.gov.uk

Mirfield Library East Thorpe Lodge, Mirfield, West Yorkshire WF14 8AN T: 01924 326470

Olicana Historical Society 54 Kings Road, Ilkley, West Yorkshire LS29 9AT T: 01943 609206

Pontefract Library & Local Studies Centre Pontefract library, Shoemarket, Pontefract, West Yorkshire WF8 1BD T: 01977-727692

Wakefield Library Headquarters - Local Studies Department Balne Lane, Wakefield, West Yorkshire WF2 0DQ T: 01924-302224 W: www.wakefield.gov.uk

Wakefield Metropolitan District Libraries & Information Services Castleford Library & Local Studies Dept, Carlton Street, Castleford, West Yorkshire WF10 1BB T: 01977-722085

Yorkshire Archaeological Society Claremont, 23 Clarendon Rd, Leeds, West Yorkshire LS2 9NZ T: 0113-245-6342 W: www.yas.org.uk

Yorkshire - York

York Archives & Local History Department York explore, Library Square, Museum Street, York, YO1 7DS T: 01904 552800 E: archives@york.gov.uk W: www.york.gov.uk/libraries

York Minster Library : **Yorkshire Family History - Biographical Database** York Minster Library & Archives, Dean's Park, York, YO1 7JQ T: 01904 625308 Library E: antonioj@yorkminster.org W: www.yorkminster.org/learning/library-archives-conservation Library W: www.yorkminster.org

Wales
National
South Wales Miners' Library - Swansea University Hendrefoelan Campus, Gower Road, Swansea, SA2 7NB T: 01792 518603 E: miners@swansea.ac.uk W: www.swan.ac.uk/lis/librafry/libraries/swml

The National Library of Wales Penglais, Aberystwyth SY23 3BU T: 01970 632800 E: www.llgc.org.uk/enquire W: www.llgc.org.uk/

University of Walwes Swansea library Library & Information Centre, Singleton Park, Swansea, SA2 8PP T: 01792 295021

Blaenau Gwent
Ebbw Vale Library Ebbw Vale Library, 21 Bethcar Street, Ebbw Vale, Gwent NP23 6HH T: 01495-303069

Tredegar Library The Circle, Tredegar, Gwent NP2 3PS T: 01495-722687

Brecon
Brecon Area Library Ship Street, Brecon, Powys LD3 9AE T: 01874-623346 E: breclib@mail.powys.gov.uk W: www.powys.gov.uk

Caerphilly
Bargoed Library The Square, Bargoed, Caerphilly CF81 8QQ T: 01443-875548 E: 9e465@dial.pipex.com

Caerphilly Library HQ Unit 7 Woodfieldside Business Park, Penmaen Road, Pontllanfraith, Blackwood, Caerphilly NP12 2DG T: 01495 235584 E: cael.libs@dial.pipex.com

Cardiff
Cardiff Central Library (Local Studies Department) St Davids Link, Frederick Street, Cardiff, CF1 4DT T: (029) 2038 2116 W: www.cardiff.gov.uk

Carmarthenshire
Carmarthen Library St Peters Street, Carmarthen SA31 1LN T: 01267 230873

Llanelli Public Library Vaughan Street, Lanelli SA15 3AS T: 01554 773538

Ceredigion
Aberystwyth Reference Library Corporation Street, Aberystwyth, SY23 2BU T: 01970-617464 E: llyfrygell.library@ceredigion.gov.uk W: www.ceredigion.gov.uk/libraries

Flintshire
Flintshire Reference Library Headquarters County Hall, Mold, Flintshire CH7 6NW T: 01352 704411 E: libraries@flintshire.gov.uk W: www.flintshire.gov.uk

Glamorgan
Bridgend Library & Information Service Coed Parc, Park Street, Bridgend, Glamorgan CF31 4BA T: 01656 767451 W: www.bridgend.gov.uk

Dowlais Library Church Street, Dowlais, Merthyr Tydfil, Glamorgan CF48 3HS T: 01985-723051

Merthyr Tydfil Central Library (Local Studies Department) Merthyr Library, High Street, Merthyr Tydfil, Glamorgan CF47 8AF T: 01685-723057 E: library@merthyr.gov.uk W: www.merthyr.gov.uk

Pontypridd Library Library Road, Pontypridd, Rhondda Cynon Taff CF37 2DY T: 01443-486850 E: hywel.w.matthews@rhondda-cynon-taff.gov.uk W: www.rhondda-cynon-taff.gov.uk/libraries/pontypri

Port Talbot Library 1st Floor Aberafan Shopping Centre, Port Talbot, Glamorgan SA13 1PB T: 01639-763490 W: www.neath-porttalbot.gov.uk

Treorchy Library Station Road, Treorchy, Glamorgan CF42 6NN T: 01443-773204

Glamorgan - West
Neath Central Library (Local Studies Department) 29 Victoria Gardens, Neath, Glamorgan SA11 3BA T: 01639-620139 W: www.neath-porttalbot.gov.uk

Swansea Central Library Civic Centre, Oystermouth Road, Swansea, SA1 3SN T: 01792 636464 E: libraryline@swansea.gov.uk W: www.swansea.gov.uk/libraries

Gwent
Abertillery Library Station Hill, Abertillery, Gwent NP13 1TE T: 01495-212332

Chepstow Library & Information Centre Manor Way, Chepstow, Monmoputhshire NP16 5HZ T: 01291-635730 E: chepstowlibrary@monmouthshire.gov.uk W: www.monmouthshire.gov.uk/leisure/libraries

Newport Community Learning and Libraries Newport Central Library, John Frost Square, Newport, South Wales NP20 1PA T: 01633 656656 E: reference.library@newport.gov.uk W: www.newport.gov.uk

Gwynedd
Canolfan Llyfrgell Dolgellau Library FforddBala, Dolgellau, Gwynedd LL40 2YF T: 01341-422771 W: www.gwynedd.gov.uk

Gwynedd Library & Information Service Allt Pafiliwn, Caernafon, Gwynedd LL55 1AS T: 01286 679465 E: library@gwynedd.gov.uk W: www.gwynedd.gov.uk/library

Merthyr Tydfil
Treharris Library Perrott Street, Treharris, Merthyr Tydfil, CF46 5ET T: 01443-410517

Monmoputhshire
Chepstow Library & Information Centre Manor Way, Chepstow, Monmoputhshire NP16 5HZ T: 01291-635730 E: chepstowlibrary@monmouthshire.gov.uk W: www.monmouthshire.gov.uk/leisure/libraries

Neath Port Talbot
Lifelong Learning Service Theodore Road, Port Talbot, SA13 1SP T: 01639-898581 E: lls@neath-porttalbot.gov.uk W: www.neath-porttalbot.gov.uk

Pembrokeshire
Pembrokeshire Libraries The County Library, Dew Street, Haverfordwest, Pembrokeshire SA61 1SU T: 01437 775248 E: george.edwards@pembrokeshire.gov.uk W: www.pembrokeshire.gov.uk

Powys
Brecon Area Library Ship Street, Brecon, Powys LD3 9AE T: 01874-623346 E: breclib@mail.powys.gov.uk W: www.powys.gov.uk

Llandrindod Wells Library Cefnllys Lane, Llandrindod Wells, Powys LD1 5LD T: 01597-826870 E: llandod.library@powys.gov.uk W: www.powys.gov.uk

Newtown Area Library Park Lane, Newtown, Powys SY16 1EJ T: 01686-626934 E: nlibrary@powys.gov.uk W: www.powys.gov.uk

Rhondda Cynon Taff
Aberdare Library Green Street, Aberdare, Rhondda Cynon Taff CF44 7AG T: 01685 880053 E: alun.r.prescott@rhondda-cynon-taff.gov.uk W: www.rhondda-cynon-taff.gov.uk/libraries/aberdare.htm

Pontypridd Library Library Road, Pontypridd, Rhondda Cynon Taff CF37 2DY T: 01443-486850 E: hywel.w.matthews@rhondda-cynon-taff.gov.uk W: www.rhondda-cynon-taff.gov.uk/libraries/pontypri.htm

Treorchy Library Station Road, Treorchy, Glamorgan CF42 6NN T: 01443-773204

Vale of Glamorgan
Barry Library King Square, Holton Road, Barry, Glamorgan CF63 4RW T: 01446-735722

West Glamorgan
West Glamorgan Archive Service - Port Talbot Access Point Port Talbot Library, 1st Floor, Aberavon Shopping Centre, Port Talbot, West Glamorgan SA13 1PB T: 01639 763430 W: www.swansea.gov.uk/archives
Wrexham CBC
Wrexham Library & Arts Centre Rhosddu Road, Wrexham, LL11 1AU T: 01978 292091 E: reference@wrexham.gov.uk W: www.wrexham.gov.uk/libraries

Scotland
National
Edinburgh University Library, Special Collections Department George Square, Edinburgh, EH8 9LJ T: 0131 650 3412 E: special.collections@ed.ac.uk W: www.lib.ed.ac.uk
Edinburgh University New College Library Mound Place, Edinburgh, EH1 2UL T: 0131 650 8957 E: New.College.Library@ed.ac.uk W: www.lib.ed.ac.uk
National Library of Scotland George IV Bridge, Edinburgh, EH1 1EW T: 0131 623 3700 E: enquiries@nls.uk W: www.nls.uk
National Museums Scotland Library Chambers Street, Edinburgh, EH1 1JF T: 0131 247 4137 E: library@nms.ac.uk W: www.nms.ac.uk
National War Museum Scotland Library The Castle, Museum Square, Edinburgh, EH1 2NG T: 0131 247 4409 E: library@nms.ac.uk W: www.nms.ac.uk
Royal Botanic Garden The Library, 20a Inverleith Row, Edinburgh, EH3 5LR T: 0131 552 7171
Royal Commission on the Ancient & Historical Monuments of Scotland John Sinclair House, 16 Bernard Terrace, Edinburgh, EH8 9NX T: 0131 662 1456 E: info@rcahms.gov.uk W: www.rcahms.gov.uk
Scottish Genealogy Society & Library 15 Victoria Terrace, Edinburgh, EH1 2JL T: 0131-220-3677 E: info@scotsgenealogy.com & sales@scotsgenealogy.com W: www.scotsgenealogy.com
St Andrews University Library - Special Collections Department North Street, St Andrews, Fife KY16 9TR T: 01334 462339 E: speccoll@st-and.ac.uk W: www.st-andrews.ac.uk/specialcollections
Strathclyde University Archives McCance Building, 16 Richmond Street, Glasgow, G1 1XQ T: 0141 548 2397
Aberdeenshire
Aberdeen City Libraries - Local Studies Rosemount Viaduct, Aberdeen, AB25 1GW T: 01224 652512 E: localstudieslibrary@aberdeencity.gov.uk W: www.aberdeencity.gov.uk/libraries
Aberdeenshire Library & Information Service The Meadows Industrial Estate, Meldrum Meg Way, Oldmeldrum, Aberdeenshire AB51 0GN T: 01651 871219 E: ALIS@aberdeenshire.gov.uk W: www.aberdeenshire.gov.uk
University of Aberdeen DISS: Heritage Division Special Collections & Archives Kings College, Aberdeen, AB24 3SW T: 01224-272598 E: speclib@abdn.ac.uk W: www.abdn.ac.uk/diss/heritage
Angus
Angus Archives Hunter Library, Restenneth Priory, By Forfar, Angus DD8 2SZ T: 01307 468644 E: angus.archives@angus.gov.uk W: www.angus.gov.uk/history/default.htm
Montrose Library - Angus District Montrose Library, 214 High Street, Montrose, MO10 8PH T: 01674-673256
Argyll
Argyll & Bute Library Service Library Headquarters, Highland Avenue, Sandbank, Dunoon, Argyll PA23 8PB T: 01369-703214 W: www.argyll-bute.gov.uk
Argyll & Bute Council Library Service - Local Studies Highland Avenue, Sandbank, Dunoon, Argyll PA23 8PB T: 01369 703214 E: eleanor.harris@argyll-bute.gov.uk W: www.argyll-bute.gov.uk
Campbeltown Library & Museum Hall St, Campbeltown, Argyll PA28 6BU T: 01586 552366 E: mary.vanhelmond@argyll-bute.gov.uk W: www.argyle-bute.gov.uk/content/leisure/museums
Ayrshire
East Ayrshire Council District History Centre & Museum Baird Institute, 3 Lugar Street, Cumnock KA18 1AD T: 01290 421701 E: Baird.institute@east-ayrshire.gov.uk W: www.east-ayrshire.gov.uk
North Ayrshire Libraries Library Headquarters, 39 - 41 Princes Street, Ardrossan KA22 8BT T: 01294 469137 W: www.north-ayrshire.gov.uk
South Ayrshire Library Carnegie Library, 12 Main Street, Ayr, KA8 8ED T: 01292 272231 E: localhistory@south-ayrshire.gov.uk W: www.south-ayrshire.gov.uk/libraries/localhistory.htm
Ayrshire - East
Auchinleck Library Community Centre, Well Road, Auchinleck, KA18 2LA T: 01290 422829 W: www.east-ayrshire.gov.uk

Bellfield Library 79 Whatriggs Road, Kilmarnock, East Ayrshire KA1 3RB T: 01563 534266 E: libraries@east-ayrshire.gov.uk W: www.east-ayrshire.gov.uk
Catrine Library A M Brown Institute, 2 Institute Avenue, Catrine, KA5 6RT T: 01290 551717 E: libraries@east-ayrshire.gov.uk W: www.east-ayrshire.gov.uk
Crosshouse Library 11-13 Gatehead Road, Crosshouse,KA2 0HN T: 01563 573640 E: libraries@east-ayrshire.gov.uk W: www.east-ayrshire.gov.uk
Dalmellington Library Townhead, Dalmellington KA6 7QZ T: 01292 550159 E: libraries@east-ayrshire.gov.uk W: www.east-ayrshire.gov.uk
Dalrymple Library Barbieston Road, Dalrymple, East Ayrshire KA6 6DZ E: libraries@east-ayrshire.gov.uk W: www.east-ayrshire.gov.uk
Darvel Library Town Hall, West Main Street, Darvel KA17 0AQ T: 01560 322754 E: libraries@east-ayrshire.gov.uk W: www.east-ayrshire.gov.uk
Drongan Library Mill O'Shield Road, Drongan KA6 7AY T: 01292 591718 E: libraries@east-ayrshire.gov.uk W: www.east-ayrshire.gov.uk
East Ayrshire Libraries Dick Institute, Elmbank Ave, Kilmarnock KA1 3BU T: 01563 554310 E: baird.institute@east-ayrshire.gov.uk W: www.east-ayrshire.gov.uk
East Ayrshire Libraries - Cumnock 25-27 Ayr Road, Cumnock, East Ayrshire KA18 1EB T: 01290-422804 W: www.east-ayrshire.gov.uk
Galston Library Henrietta Street, Galston KA4 8HQ T: 01563 821994 E: libraries@east-ayrshire.gov.uk W: www.east-ayrshire.gov.uk
Hurlford Library Blair Road, Hurlford KA1 5BN T: 01563 539899 E: libraries@east-ayrshire.gov.uk W: www.east-ayrshire.gov.uk
Kilmaurs Library Irvine Road, Kilmaurs, East Ayrshire KA3 2RJ T: 01563 539895 E: libraries@east-ayrshire.gov.uk W: www.east-ayrshire.gov.uk
Mauchline Library 2 The Cross, Mauchline T: 01290 550824 E: libraries@east-ayrshire.gov.uk W: www.east-ayrshire.gov.uk
Muirkirk Library Burns Avenue, Muirkirk KA18 3RH T: 01290 661505 E: libraries@east-ayrshire.gov.uk W: www.east-ayrshire.gov.uk
New Cumnock Library Community Centre, The Castle, New Cumnock KA18 4AH T: 01290 338710 E: libraries@east-ayrshire.gov.uk W: www.east-ayrshire.gov.uk
Newmilns Library Craigview Road, Newmilns KA16 9DQ T: 01560 322890 E: libraries@east-ayrshire.gov.uk W: www.east-ayrshire.gov.uk
Ochiltree Library Main Street, Ochiltree KA18 2PE T: 01290 700425 E: libraries@east-ayrshire.gov.uk W: www.east-ayrshire.gov.uk
Patna Library Doonside Avenue, Patna KA6 7LX T: 01292 531538 E: libraries@east-ayrshire.gov.uk W: www.east-ayrshire.gov.uk
Clackmannanshire
Clackmannanshire Archives Alloa Library, 26/28 Drysdale Street, Alloa, Clackmannanshire FK10 1JL T: 01259 722262 E: libraries@clacks.gov.uk W: www.clacksweb.org.uk/dyna/archives
Clackmannanshire Libraries Alloa Library, 26/28 Drysdale Street, Alloa, Clackmannanshire FK10 1JL T: 01259-722262 E: clack.lib@mail.easynet.co.uk
Dumfries & Galloway
Ewart Library Catherine Street, Dumfries, DG1 1JB T: 01387 260285 E: ericaj@dumgal.gov.uk W: www.dgc.gov.uk/service/depts/comres/library/gresearch
Dunbartonshire
Dumbarton Public Library Strathleven Place, Dumbarton, G82 1BD T: 01389-733273 E: wdlibs@hotmail.com W: www.wdcweb.info
Dundee
Dundee Central Library - Local History Centre The Wellgate, Dundee, DD1 1DB T: 01382 431550 E: local.history@dundeecity.gov.uk W: www.dundeecity.gov.uk/centlibd/loc_stud.htm
Tay Valley Family History Society Family History Research Centre, 179 – 181 Princes Street, Dundee, DD4 6DQ T: 01382 461845 E: tvfhs@tayvalleyfhs.org.uk W: www.tayvalleyfhs.org.uk
East Dunbarton
Bishopbriggs Library 170 Kirkintilloch Road, Bishopbriggs G64 2LX T: 0141 772 4513 W: www.eastdunbarton.gov.uk
Brookwood Library 166 Drymen Road, Bearsden, Glasgow, East Dunbarton G61 3RJ T: 0141-942 6811 W: www.eastdunbarton.gov.uk
Craighead Library Milton of Campsie, East Dunbarton G66 8Dl T: 01360 311925 W: www.eastdunbarton.gov.uk
East Dunbartonshire Information & Archives William Patrick Library, 2 West High Street, Kirkintilloch G66 1AD T: 0141 777 3142 E: libraries@eastdunbarton.gov.uk W: www.eastdunbarton.gov.uk
Lennoxtown Library Main Street, Lennoxtown G66 7HA T: 01360 311436

Lenzie Library 13 - 15 Alexandra Avenue, Lenzie, East Dunbarton G66 5BG T: 0141 776 3021 W: www.eastdunbarton.gov.uk

Milgarvie Library Allander Road, Milngarvie, East Dunbarton G62 8PN T: 0141 956 2776 W: www.eastdunbarton.gov.uk

Westerton Library 82 Maxwell Avenue, Bearsden, East Dunbarton G61 1NZ T: 0141 943 0780

East Renfrewshire
Giffnock Library Station Road, Giffnock, Glasgow, East Renfrewshire G46 6JF T: 0141-577-4976 W: www.eastrenfrewshire.gov.uk/leisure/libraries/your_local_library/giffnock_library_page.htm

Edinburgh
Edinburgh Central Library Edinburgh Room, George IV Bridge, Edinburgh, EH1 1EG T: 0131-242 8030 E: eclis@edinburgh.gov.uk W: www.edinburgh.gov.uk

Falkirk
Falkirk Library Hope Street, Falkirk, FK1 5AU T: 01324 503605 W: www.falkirk.gov.uk

Falkirk Museum History Research Centre Callendar House, Callendar Park, Falkirk, FK1 1YR T: 01324 503778 E: callendar.house@falkirk.gov.uk W: www.falkirk.gov.uk/services/community/cultural_services/museums/museums_and_archives.aspx

Fife
Dunfermline Library - Local History Department Abbot Street, Dunfermline, Fife KY12 7NL T: 01383-312994 W: www.fife.gov.uk

Fife Council Central Area Libraries Central Library, War Memorial Grounds, Kirkcaldy, Fife KY1 1YG T: 01592-412878 W: www.fife.gov.uk

St Andrews Library Church Square, St Andrews, Fife KY16 9NN T: 01334-412685 W: www.fife.gov.uk

St Andrews University Library North Street, St Andrews, Fife KY16 9TR T: 01334-462281 W: www.library.st-and.ac.uk

Tay Valley Family History Society Family History Research Centre, 179 – 181 Princes Street, Dundee, DD4 6DQ T: 01382 461845 E: tvfhs@tayvalleyfhs.org.uk W: www.tayvalleyfhs.org.uk

Glasgow
Brookwood Library 166 Drymen Road, Bearsden, Glasgow, East Dunbarton G61 3RJ T: 0141-942 6811 W: www.eastdunbarton.gov.uk

Glasgow City Libraries & Archives Mitchell Library, North Street, Glasgow, G3 7DN T: 0141 287 2937 W: www.glasgow.gov.uk/html/council/cindex.htm

Glasgow University Library & Special Collections Department Hillhead Street, Glasgow, G12 8QE T: 0141 330 6704 E: library@lib.gla.ac.uk W: www.gla.ac.uk/library

Social Sciences Department - History & Glasgow Room The Mitchell Library, North Street, Glasgow, G3 7DN T: 0141-227-2935 W: www.libarch.glasgow

Highland
North Highland Archive Wick Library, Sinclair Terrace, Wick, KW1 5AB T: 01955 606432

Isle of Barra
Castlebay Community Library Community School, Castlebay, Isle of Barra HS95XD T: 01871-810471

Isle of Benbecula
Community Library Sgoil Lionacleit, Liniclate, Isle of Benbecula HS7 5PJ T: 01870-602211

Isle of Lewis
Stornoway Library 19 Cromwell Street, Stornoway, Isle of Lewis HS1 2DA T: 01851 708631

Kinross-shire
Perth & Kinross Libraries A K Bell Library, 2 - 8 York Place, Perth, PH2 8EP T: 01738-477062 E: jaduncan@pkc.gov.uk W: www.pkc.gov.uk

Tay Valley Family History Society Family History Research Centre, 179 – 181 Princes Street, Dundee, DD4 6DQ T: 01382 461845 E: tvfhs@tayvalleyfhs.org.uk W: www.tayvalleyfhs.org.uk

Lanarkshire
Airdrie Library Wellwynd, Airdrie, Lanarkshire ML6 0AG T: 01236-763221 W: www.northlan.gov.uk/

Cumbernauld Central Library 8 Allander Walk, Cumbernauld, Lanarkshire G67 1EE T: 01236-735964 W: www.northlan.gov.uk

Leadhills Miners' Library 15 Main Street, Leadhills ML12 6XP T: 01659-74326 E: anne@leadshilllibrary.co.uk W: www.lowtherhills.fsnet.co.uk

Lanarkshire - North
Kilsyth Library Burngreen, Kilsyth G65 0HT T: 01236-823147 W: www.northlan.gov.uk

Motherwell Heritage Centre High Road, Motherwell, North ML1 3HU T: 01698-251000 E: heritage@mhc158.freeserve.co.uk W: www.northlan.gov.uk

Shotts Library Benhar Road, Shotts, North Lanarkshire ML7 5EN T: 01501-821556 W: www.northlan.org.uk

Midlothian
Midlothian Archives and Local Studies Centre 2 Clerk Street, Loanhead, Midlothian EH20 9DR T: 0131 271 3976 E: local.studies@midlothian.gov.uk W: www.midlothian.gov.uk

Morayshire
Buckie Library Clunu Place, Buckie AB56 1HB T: 01542-832121 E: buckie.lib@techleis.moray.gov.uk W: www.moray.gov.uk

Forres Library Forres House, High Street, Forres, Moray IV36 0BJ T: 01309-672834 W: www.moray.gov.uk

Keith Library Union Street, Keith, Morayshire AB55 5DP T: 01542-882223 W: www.moray.gov.uk

Moray Local Heritage Centre Old East End School, Institution Road, Elgin, Moray IV30 1HS T: 01343 569011 E: heritage@moray.gov.uk W: www.morray.org/localheritage/index

Orkney
Orkney Library The Orkney Library, Laing Street, Kirkwall, Orkney KW15 1NW T: 01856-873166 W: www.orkney.gov.uk

Perthshire
Perth & Kinross Libraries A K Bell Library, 2 - 8 York Place, Perth, PH2 8EP T: 01738-477062 E: jaduncan@pkc.gov.uk W: www.pkc.gov.uk

Tay Valley Family History Society Family History Research Centre, 179 – 181 Princes Street, Dundee, DD4 6DQ T: 01382 461845 E: tvfhs@tayvalleyfhs.org.uk W: www.tayvalleyfhs.org.uk

Renfrewshire
Renfrewshire Council Library & Museum Services Central Library & Museum Complex, High Street, Paisley, Renfrewshire PA1 2BB T: 0141-889-2350 E: local_studies.library@renfrewshire.gov.uk W: www.renfrewshire.gov.uk

Watt Library 9 Union Street, Greenock, PA16 8JH T: 01475 715628 E: library.watt@inverclyde.gov.uk W: www.inverclyde-libraries.info

Scottish Borders
Scottish Borders Archive & Local History Centre Heritage Hub, Kirkstile, Hawick, Roxburghshire TD9 0AE T: 01750 20842 E: archives@scotborders.gov.uk W: www.heartofhawick.co.uk/heritagehub

Shetland
Shetland Library Lower Hillhead, Lerwick, Shetland ZE1 0EL T: 01595 743868 E: ShetlandLibrary@sic.shetland.gov.uk W: www.shetland-library.gov.uk

Stirling
Stirling Council Libraries: Bridge of Allan Fountain Road, Bridge of Allan, Stirlingshire FK9 4AT T: 01786 833680 W: www.stirling.gov.uk

Stirling Council Libraries: Central Library Central Library, Corn Exchange Road, FK8 2HX T: 01786 432106 E: centrallibrary@stirling.gov.uk W: www.stirling.gov.uk

Stirling Council Libraries: Dunblane Library High Street, Dunblane, Stirlingshire FK15 0ER T: 01786 823125 E: dunblanelibrary@stirling.gov.uk W: www.stirling.gov.uk

Stirling Council Libraries: St Ninians Library Mayfield Centre, St Ninians, Stirlingshire FK7 0DB T: 01786 472069 E: stninlibrary@stirling.gov.uk W: www.stirling.gov.uk

Tayside
Dundee University Archives , Records Management and Museum Services (ARMMS) Centre for Archive and Information Studies (CAIS), Tower Building, Nethergate, Dundee, DD1 4HN T: 01382 385543 E: armtraining@dundee.ac.uk W: www.dundee.ac.uk/cais

West Lothian
West Lothian Council Libraries Connolly House, Hopefield Road, Blackburn, West Lothian EH47 7HZ T: 01506-776331 E: localhistory@westlothian.gov.uk W: www.wlonline.org

Northern Ireland
National
Centre for Migration Studies Ulster American Folk Park, Mellon Road, Castletown, Omagh, Co Tyrone BT78 5QY T: 028 82 256315 E: cms@librariesni.org.uk W: www.folkpark.com

Linen Hall Library 17 Donegall Square North, Belfast, BT1 5GB T: 028 9032 1707 E: info@linenhall.com W: www.discovernorthernireland.com/The-Linen-Hall-Library-Belfast-P3057

Antrim
North Eastern Library Board & Local Studies Area Reference Library, Demesne Avenue, Ballymena, Antrim BT43 7BG T: (028) 25 6641212 E: yvonne_hirt@hotmail.com W: www.neelb.org.uk

Belfast
Belfast Central Library Belfast Ulster Irish Studies, Royal Avenue, Belfast, BT1 1EA T: (028) 9024 3233 E: sheila.mcclean@librariesni.org.uk W: www.librariesni.org.uk

County Armagh
Armagh Public Library 43 Abbey Street, Armagh, County Armagh
BT61 1DY T: 028 37 523 142 E: admin@armaghpubliclibrary.co.uk
W: www.armaghrobinsonlibrary.org
County Antrim
NEELB Local Studies Service Ballymena Central Library, 5 Pat's
Brae, Ballymena, Co Antrim BT43 5AX T: (028) 2563 3960 E:
localstudies.neelb@ni-libraries.net W: www.neelb.org.uk
see also - South Eastern Library Board & Local Studies
County Down
South Eastern Library Board & Local Studies Library HQ,
Windmill Hill, Ballynahinch, County Down BT24 8DH T: (028) 9756
6400 E: ballynahinchlibrary@librariesni.org.uk
County Fermanagh
Enniskillen Library Irish and Local Studies, Halls Lane, Enniskillen,
Co Fermanagh BT74 7DR T: 028 6632 2886 E:
enniskillenlibrary@librariesni.org.uk
County Londonderry
Central and Reference Library 35 Foyle Street, Londonderry,
County Londonderry BT24 6AL T: (028) 71272300 E:
derrycentrallibrary@librariesni.org.uk
Irish Room Coleraine County Hall, Castlerock Road, Ballymena,
County Londonderry BT1 3HP T: (028) 705 1026 E:
educationlibraryservice@librariesni.org.uk W: www.neelb.org.uk
County Tyrone
Omagh Library 1 Spillars Place, Omagh, County Tyrone BT78 1HL
T: 028 8224 4821 E: omaghlibrary@librariesni.org.uk W:
www.librariesni.org.uk
Derry
Derry Central Library 35 Foyle Street, Derry, BT48 6AL T: 028
7127 2300 E: derrycentrallibrary@librariesni.org.uk

Ireland
National
National Library of Ireland Kildare Street, Dublin, 2 T: +353 1 603
0200 E: info@nli.ie W: www.nli.ie
Society of Friends (Quakers) in Ireland Quaker House, Stocking
Lane, Dublin, 16 T: +353 1 495 6890 E: office@quakers-in-ireland.ie
W: www.quakers.ie
Dublin
Dublin City Library & Archive 138 - 142 Pearse Street, Dublin, 2 T:
353 1 674 4999 E: dublinstudies@dublincity.ie
cityarchives@dublincity.ie W:
www.dublincity.ie/living_in_the_city/libraries/heritage_and_history/
County Carlow
Carlow County Library Tullow Street, Carlow, County Carlow T:
+353 0 59 917 0094 E: library@carlowcoco.ie
County Cavan
Cavan County Library & Archives Farnham Centre, Farnham
Street, Cavan, County Cavan T: +3530 49 437 8500 E:
library@cavancoco.ie archives@cavancoco.ie
County Clare
Clare County Library The Manse, Harmony Row, Ennis, County
Clare T: +353 65 684 6271 E: mailbox@clarelibrary.ie W:
www.iol.ie/~clarelib
County Cork
Cork City Library 57 - 61 Grand Parade, Cork, Co Cork T: +353 21
492 4900 E: libraries@corkcity.ie W: www.corkcitylibraries.ie/
Cork County Library Carrigrohane Road, Cork, County Cork T:
+353 21 454 6499 E: corkcountylibrary@corkcoco.ie W:
www.corkcoco.ie/library
Mallow Heritage Centre 27/28 Bank Place, Mallow, County Cork T:
+353 22 50302 E: mallowheritagecentre@gmail.com W:
www.rootsireland.ie/
County Donegal
Donegal Central Library Oliver Plunkett Road, Letterkenny, County
Donegal T: +353 74 912 4950 E: central@donegallibrary.ie
Donegal Local Studies Centre Central Library & Arts Centre, Oliver
Plunkett Road, Letterkenny, County Donegal T: 00353 74 24950 E:
Portal@donegalcoco.ie W: www.donegal.ie/library
County Down
South Eastern Library Board & Local Studies Library HQ,
Windmill Hill, Ballynahinch, County Down BT24 8DH T: (028) 9756
6400 E: ballynahinchlibrary@librariesni.org.uk
County Dublin
Ballyfermot Public Library Ballyfermot Road, Dublin, 10 T: +353 1
626 9324 E: ballyfermotlibrary@dublincity.ie W: www.dublincity.ie
Dun Laoghaire Library Lower George's Street, Dun Laoghaire,
County Dublin T: 2801147 E: localhistory@dlrcoco.ie W:
www.dlrcoco.ie/library/lhistory.htm

Fingal Local Studies & Archives Clonmel House, Forster Way,
Swords, County Dublin T: +353 1 870 4495 E:
local.studies@fingalcoco.ie
County Galway
Galway County library Island House, Cathedral square, Galway,
County Galway T: +353 91 562 471 E: info@galwaylibrary.ie
County Kerry
Kerry County Library Genealogical Centre Cathedral Walk,
Killarney, Co Kerry T: +353 64 359 946 E: culture@kerrycoco.ie
Kerry Library Moyderwell, Tralee, County Kerry T: +353 66 712
1200 E: info@kerrylibrary.ie localhistory@kerrylibrary.ie
archivist@kerrylibrary.ie W: www.kerrylibrary.ie
County Kidare
Kildare Heritage & Genealogy Riverbank, Main Street, Newbridge,
County Kidare T: +353 45 118 350 E: kildaregenealogy@iol.ie
Kidare Library & Arts Centre Riverbank Arts Centre, Main Street,
Newbridge, County Kildare T: +353 45 431 109 E:
colibrary@kildarecoco.ie
County Kilkenny
Kilkenny County Library John Green's House, John's Green,
Kilkenny, County Kilkenny T: +353 56 779 4160 E:
info@kilkennylibrary.ie
County Laois
Laois County Library J.F.L. Avenue, Portlaoise, County Laois T:
+353 57 867 4315 E: laoislibrary@laoiscoco.ie
County Leitrim
Leitrim County Library Main Street, Ballinamore, County Leitrim
T: +353 71 964 5582 E: leitrimlibrary@leitrimcoco.ie
County Limerick
Limerick City Library & Archives The Granary, Michael Street,
Limerick, County Limerick T: +353 61 314668 E:
archives@limerickcity.ie W: www.limerickcity.ie/
Limerick County library Lissanalta House, Dooradoyle Road,
Limericl, County Limerick T: +353 61 496 526 E:
libinfo@limerickcoco.ie
Longford County Library Town Centre, Longford, County Longford
T: +353 43 334 1124 E: library@longfordcoco.ie
County Louth
Louth County Library Roden Place, Dundalk, County Louth T:
+353 42 935 3190 E: libraryhelpdesk@louthcoco.ie W:
www.louthcoco.ie
Louth County Reference Library Roden Place, Dundalk, County
Louth T: +353 42 933 5457 E: referencelibary@louthcoco.ie
County Mayo
Mayo Central Library John Moore Road, Catslebar, County Mayo
T: +353 94 904 7953 E: librarymayo@mayococo.ie W:
www.mayolibrary.ie
County Meath
Meath County Library Railway Street, Navan, County Meath T:
+353 46 902 1134 E: colibrarian@meathcoco.ie
County Monaghan
Monaghan County Library 98 Avenue, Clones, Couny Monaghan T:
+353 47 74712 or +353 47 74713 E: clennon@monaghancoco.ie
County Offaly
Offaly County Library O'Connor Square, Tullamore, County Offaly
T: +353 57 934 6832 E: libraryhq@offalycoco.ie
County Roscommon
Roscommon County Library Abbey Street, Roscommon, County
Roscommon T: +353 90 663 7275 E: roslib@roscommoncoco.ie
County Sligo
Sligo Reference & Local Studies Library Westward Town Centre,
Bridge Street, Sligo, County Sligo T: +353 71 911 1858 E:
sligolib@sligococo.ie W: www.sligolibrary.ie
County Tipperary
Tipperary Studies Source Library, Cathedral Street, Thurles, County
Tipperary T: +353 504 292 78 E: studies@tipperarylibraries.ie
County Tyrone
Omagh Library 1 Spillars Place, Omagh, County Tyrone BT78 1HL
T: 028 8224 4821 E: omaghlibrary@librariesni.org.uk W:
www.librariesni.org.uk
County Waterford
Waterford County Library Dungarvan Central Library, Davitt's
Quay, Dungarvan, County Waterford T: +353 58 412 31 E:
dungarvanlibrary@waterfordcoco.ie W: www.waterfordcoco.ie/
County Westmeath
Athlone - Westmeath County Library - Local Studies Athlone
Civic offices, Church Avenue, Athlone, County Westmeath T: +353 90
644 2157 E: athlib@westmeathcoco.ie W: www.westmeathcoco.i
Mullingar - Westmeath County Library - Local Studies County
Buildings, Mount Street, Mullingar, County Westmeath T: +353 44
933 2161 E: mgarlib@westmeathcoco.ie

County Wexford
Enniscorthy Branch Library Lymington Road, Enniscorthy, County Wexford T: +353 53 923 6055 E: enniscorthylib@wexfordcoco.ie W: www.wexford.ie/library
New Ross Branch Library Barrack Lane, New Ross, Co Wexford T: +353 51 21877 E: newrosslib@wexfordcoco.ie
Wexford Library McCauley's Car Park, Off Redmond Square, Wexford, County Wexford T: +353 53 912 1637 E: wexfordlib@wexfordcoco.ie W: www.wexford.ie/
County Wicklow
Wicklow County Library Boghall Road, Bray, County Wicklow T: +353 1 286 6566 E: library@wicklowcoco.ie W: www.wicklow.ie

Isle of Man
Manx National Heritage Library Manx Museum, Douglas IM1 3LY T: 01624 648000 E: enquiries@mnh.gov.im W: www.gov.im/mnh

Channel Islands
Guernsey
Priaulx Library Candie Road, St Peter Port, Guernsey GY1 1UG T: 01481 721998 F: 01481 713804 W: www.priaulx.gov.gg
Jersey
Lord Coutanche Library Societe Jersiaise, 7 Pier Road, St Helier, Jersey JE2 4XW T: 01534-30538 F: 01534-888262 E: library@societe-jersiaise.org W: www.societe-jersiaise.org

Australia
Capital Territory
National Library of Australia Canberra, ACT 2600 T: 02-6262-1111 W: www.nla.gov.au
New South Wales
Mitchell Library, The Macquarie Street, Sydney NSW 2000 T: 02-9230-1693 F: 02-9235-1687 W: www.sl.nsw.gov.au
State Library of New South Wales Macquarie Street, Sydney NSW 2000 T: 02-9230-1414 W: www.slsw.gov.au
Queensland
State Library of Queensland, The PO Box 3488, Cnr Peel and Stanley Streets, South Brisbane, Brisbane, Queensland 4101 T: 07-3840-7775 F: 07-3840-7840 E: genie@slq.qld.gov.au W: www.slq.qld.gov.au/subgenie/htm
South Australia
South Australia State Library PO Box 419, Adelaide, South Australia 5001 T: (08)-8207-7235 F: (08)-8207-7247 E: famhist@slsa.sa.gov.au W: www.slsa.sa.gov.au/library/collres/famhist
Victoria
State Library of Victoria 328 Swanston Street Walk, Melbourne, Victoria 3000 T: 03-9669-9080 W: www.slv.vic.gov.au/slv/genealogy/index
Western Australia
State Library Alexander Library, Perth Cultural Centre, Perth, Western Australia 6000 T: 09-427-3111 F: 09-427-3256 W: www.wa.gov.au/

New Zealand
Alexander Turnbull Library PO Box 12-349, Wellington, 6038 T: 04-474-3050 F: 04-474-3063
Auckland Research Centre, Auckland City Libraries PO Box 4138, 44-46 Lorne Street, Auckland, T: 64-9-377-0209 W: www.auckland-library.gov.nz
Canterbury Public Library PO Box 1466, Christchurch, T: 03-379-6914 F: 03-365-1751
Dunedin Public Libraries PO Box 5542, Moray Place, Dunedin, T: 03-474-3651 F: 03-474-3660 W: www.dcc.gov.nz
Fielding Public Library PO Box 264, Fielding, 5600 T: 06-323-5373
Hamilton Public Library PO Box 933, Garden Place, Hamilton, 2015 T: 07-838-6827 F: 07-838-6858
Hocken Library PO Box 56, Dunedin, T: 03-479-8873
National Library of New Zealand PO Box 1467, Thorndon, Wellington, T: (0064)4-474-3030 W: www.natlib.gov.nz
Porirua Public Library PO Box 50218, Porirua, 6215 T: 04-237-1541 F: 04-237-7320
Takapuna Public Library Private Bag 93508, Takapuna, 1309 T: 09-486-8466 F: 09-486-8519
Wanganui District Library Private Bag 3005, Alexander Building, Queens Park, Wanganui, 5001 T: 06-345-8195 F: 06-345-5516 W: www.wanganuilibrary.com/sec_contact/contact_index.html

South Africa
South African Library PO Box 496, Cape Town, 8000 T: 021-246320 F: 021-244848

Canada
Alberta
Calgary Public Library 616 MacLeod Tr SE, Calgary, Alberta T2G 2M2 T: 260-2785
Glenbow Library & Archives 130-9th Avenue SE, Calgary, Alberta T2G 0P3 T: 403-268-4197 F: 403-232-6569
British Columbia
British Columbia Archives 865 Yates Street, Victoria, British Columbia V8V 1X4 T: 604 387 1952 E: access@bcarchives.bc.ca W: www.bcarchives.bc.ca/
Cloverdale Library (Branch of Surrey Public Library) 5642 - 176a Street, Surrey, British Columbia V3S 4G9 T:604 598 7320 E: genealogy@city.surrey.bc.ca W: www.spl.surrey.bc.ca
New Brunswick
Harriet Irving Library PO Box 7500, Fredericton, New Brunswick E3B 5H5 T: 506-453-4748 F: 506-453-4595
Loyalist Collection & Reference Library PO Box 7500, Fredericton, New Brunswick E3B 5H5 T: 506-453-4749 F: 506-453-4596
Newfoundland
Newfoundland Provincial Resource Library Arts and Cultural Centre, Allandale Road, St Johns, Newfoundland A1B 3A3 T: 709-737-3955 F: 709-737-2660

Ontario
James Gibson Reference Library 500 Glenridge Avenue, St Catherines, Ontario L2S 3A1 T: 905-688-5550 F: 905-988-5490
National Library 395 Wellington Street, Ottawa, Ontario K1A 0N4 T: 613-995-9481 F: 613-943-1112 W: www.collectionscanada.gc.ca/
Public Library PO Box 2700, Station LCD 1, Hamilton, Ontario L8N 4E4 T: 546-3408 F: 546-3202
Public Library, The 85 Queen Street North, Kitchener, Ontario N2H 2H1 T: 519-743-0271 F: 519-570-1360
Public Library, The 305 Queens Avenue, London, Ontario N6B 3L7 T: 519-661-4600 F: 519-663-5396
Public Library, The 301 Burnhamthorpe Road West, Mississauga, Ontario L5B 3Y3 T: 905-615-3500 E: library.info@city.mississauga.on.ca W: www.city.mississauga.on.ca/library
Public Library, The 74 Mackenzie Street, Sudbury, Ontario P3C 4X8 T: 673-1155 F: 673-9603
St Catharines Public Library 54 Church Street, St Catharines, Ontario L2R 7K2 T: 905-688-6103 F: 905-688-2811 E: scpublib@stcatharines.library.on.ca W: www.stcatharines.library.on.ca
Toronto Public Library North York (Entral Library) Canadiana Department, 5120 Yonge Street, North York, Ontario M2N 5N9 T: 416-395-5623 W: www.tpl.tor.on.ca
Toronto Reference Library 789 Yonge Street, Toronto, Ontario M4W 2G8 T: 416-393-7155 F: 416-393-7229
Quebec
Bibliotheque De Montreal 1210, Rue Sherbrooke East Street, Montreal, Quebec H2L 1L9 T: 514-872-1616 F: 514-872-4654 E: daniel_olivier@ville.montreal.qc.ca W: www.ville.montreal.qc.ca/biblio/pageacc.htm
Saskatchewan
Public Library, The PO Box 2311, Regina, Saskatchewan S4P 3Z5 T: 306-777-6011 F: 306-352-5550
Public Library, The 311 - 23rd Street East, Saskatoon, Saskatchewan S7K 0J6 T: 306-975-7555 F: 306-975-7542

Record Offices and Archives

National

Archive Centre (King's College Library, Cambridge University) King's College, Cambridge CB2 1ST T: 01223 331444 E: archivist@kings.cam.ac.uk W: www.kings.cam.ac.uk/library/archives

Archives of the Independent Methodist Churches Independent Methodist Resource Centre, Fleet St, Pemberton, Wigan, WN5 0DS T: 01942 223526 E: archives@imcgb.org.uk W: www.imcgb.org.uk

Archives of The Institution of Civil Engineers Great George Street, London, SW1P 3AA T: (020) 7222 7722 W: www.ice.org.uk

Bank of England Archive Archive Section HO-SV, The Bank of England, Threadneedle Street, London, EC2R 8AH T: 020 7601 4810/4889/5096 E: archive@bankofengland.co.uk W: www.bankofengland.co.uk/archive

Barnardo's Film & Photographic Archive Aftercare Section - Barnardo's, Tanner Lane, Barkingside, Ilford, IG6 1QG T: (020) 8550-8822

BBC Written Archives Centre Caversham Park, Reading RG4 8TZ T: 0118 948 6281 E: heritage@bbc.co.uk W: www.bbc.co.uk/historyofthebbc/contacts/wac.html

Black Cultural Archives 1 Othello Close, Kennington, London, SE11 4RE T: 020 7582 8516 E: info@bcaheritage.org.uk W: www.bcaheritage.org.uk

Brassworkers Index 29 Gilda Court, Watford Way, Mill Hill, London, NW7 2QN

British Airways Archives Trident House - Block E S583, London heathrow airport, Hounslow, Middlesex TW6 2JA

British Brick Society 19 Woodcroft Avenue, Stanmore HA7 3PT T: 020 8954 4976 E: micksheila67@hotmail.com W: www.britishbricksoc.free-online.co.uk

British Deaf History Society 288 Bedfont Lane, Feltham TW14 9NU

British Empire & Commonwealth Museum (Bristol) - closed relocating to London in 2012 E: admin@empiremuseum.co.uk W: www.empiremuseum.co.uk

British Film Institute - Library & Film Archive 21 Stephen Street, London, W1T 1LN T: 020 7957 4824 W: www.bfi.org.uk

British Library - Asia, Pacific and Africa Collections 96 Euston Road, London, NW1 2DB T: (020) 7412 7873 E: apac-enquiries@bl.uk W: www.bl.uk/collections/oriental

British Library Newspapers 130 Colindale Avenue, London, NW9 5HE T: 020 7412 7353 E: newspaper@bl.uk W: www.bl.uk/reshelp/bidept/news/index.html

British Library of Political and Economic Science London School of Economics, 10 Portugal Street, London, WC2A 2HD T: 020 7955 7223 W: www.lse.ac.uk

British Library Oral History Department British Library, 96 Euston Road, London, NW1 2DB T: (020) 7412 7405 E: rob.perks@bl.uk W: www.bl.uk/oralhistory

British Library Western Manuscripts Collections 96 Euston Road, London, NW1 2DB T: (020) 7412 7513 E: mss@bl.uk W: www.bl.uk/

British Pathe Plc c/o ITN Archive, 200 Gray's Inn Road, London, WC1X 8XZ T: 0207 430 4480 E: pathe@itnarchive.com W: www.britishpathe.com

British Red Cross Museum & Archives UK Office, 44 Moorfields, London, EC2Y 9AL T: 020 7877 7058 E: enquiry@redcross.org.uk W: www.redcross.org.uk/museumandarchives

British Universities Film and Video Council 77 Wells Street, London, W1T 3QJ T: 020 7393 1500 W: www.bufvc.ac.uk

British Waterways Archives & The Waterways Trust Llanthony Warehouse, Gloucester Docks, Gloucester, Gloucestershire GL1 2EJ T: 01452 318041 W: www.britishwaterways.org.uk

Cambridge University Library - Department of Manuscripts & University Archives West Road, Cambridge CB3 9DR T: 01223 333000 ext 33143 (Manuscripts) W: www.lib.cam.ac.uk/MSS/

Canonbury Masonic Research Centre Canonbury Tower, London, N1 2NQ W: www.canonbury.ac.uk

Catholic Record Society 12 Melbourne Place, Wolsingham, County Durham DL13 3EH W: www.catholic-history.org.uk/crs/

Centre for South Asian Studies Cambridge University, Laundress Lane, Cambridge CB2 1SD T: 01223 338094 W: www.s-asian.cam.ac.uk

Church of England Record Centre 15 Galleywall Road, South Bermondsey, London, SE16 3PB T: 020 7898 1030 W: www.church-of-england.org

Churchill Archives Centre Churchill College, Cambridge, CB3 0DS T: 01223 336087 E: archives@chu.cam.ac.uk W: www.chu.cam.ac.uk/archives/home.htm

Coal Miners Records Cannock Record Centre, Old Mid-Cannock (Closed) Colliery Site, Rumer Hill Road, Cannock, Staffordshire WS11 3EX T: 01543-570666

College of Arms 130 Queen Victoria Street, London, EC4V 4BT T: 020 7248 2762 E: enquiries@college-of-arms.gov.uk W: www.college-of-arms.gov.uk

Commonwealth War Graves Commission 2 Marlow Road, Maidenhead, Berkshire SL6 7DX T: 01628 634221 E: casualty.enq@cwgc.org W: www.cwgc.org

Connexional Archives for the Methodist Church 33 Harrow View, Harrow, Middlesex HA1 1RE

Customs Officers Index 174a Wendover Road, Weston Turville, Aylesbury, Buckinghamshire HP22 5TG

Deed Poll Records Section Room E 15 Royal Courts of Justice, Strand, London, WC2A 2LL T: (020) 7947 6528

Dr Williams's Library 14 Gordon Square, London, WC1H 0AR T: (020) 7387-3727 E: enquiries@dwlib.co.uk W: www.dwlib.co.uk

Entertainers Index 2 Summer Lane, Sheffield S17 4AJ

Evangelical Library 78a Chiltern Street, London, W1M 2HB

Gas Industry Genealogical Index (GIGI) Old Barnshaw Cottage, Pepper Street, Mobberley WA16 6JH E: tmm@tinyworld.co.uk

Gunmakers and Allied Trades Index 20 Cautley Close, Quainton, Aylesbury, Buckinghamshire HP22 4BN

HM Land Registry HM Land Registry, Lincoln's Inn Fields, London, WC2A 3PH T: 0844 892 1111 E: customersupport@landregistry.gsi.gov.uk W: www.landreg.gov.uk

Huguenot Library University College, Gower Street, London, WC1E 6BT T: (020) 7679 7094 W: www.ucl.ac.uk/ucl-info/divisions/library/hugenot.htm

Images of England Project National Monuments Records Centre, Kemble Drive, Swindon, Wiltshire SN2 2GZ T: 01793 414779 W: www.imagesofengland.org.uk

Imperial War Museum - Documents & Sound Section Documents and Sound T: (020) 7416 5221/2/3/6 E: docs@iwm.org.uk W: www.iwm.org.uk **Imperial War Museum Film & Video Archive** Lambeth Road, London, SE1 6HZ T: 020 7416 5289 W: www.iwm.org.uk/collections/film.htm

Institute of Heraldic & Genealogical Studies 79 - 82 Northgate, Canterbury CT1 1BA T: 01227 768664 E: ihgs@ihgs.ac.uk W: www.ihgs.ac.uk

Institution of Electrical Engineers Savoy Place, London, WC2R 0BL T: (020) 7240 1871 W: www.iee.org.uk

Institution of Mechanical Engineers 1 Birdcage Walk, Westminster, London, SW1H 9JJ T: (020) 7973 1274 E: archive@imeche.org.uk W: www.imeche.org

Institution of Mining & Metallurgy Hallam Court, 77 Hallam Street, London, W1N 5LR

Labour History Archive & Study Centre People's History Museum & Study Centre, 103 Princess Street, Manchester, M1 6DD T: 0161 228 7212 E: archives@phm.org.uk W: www.phm.org.uk

Lambeth Palace Library Lambeth Palace Road, London, SE1 7JU T: 020 7898 1400 E: lpl.staff@c-of-e.org.uk W: www.lambethpalacelibrary.org

Library of the Religious Society of Friends (Quakers) Friends House, 173 - 177 Euston Rd, London, NW1 2BJ T: 0207 663 1135 E: library@quaker.org.uk W: www.quaker.org/library

Library of the Royal College of Surgeons of England 35-43 Lincoln's Inn Fields, London, WC2A 3PE T: (020) 7869 6555 E: archives@rcseng.ac.uk W: www.rcseng.ac.uk

Linnean Society of London Burlington House, Piccadilly, London, W1J 0BF T: 020 7437 4479 W: www.linnean.org

Lloyds Register of Shipping Information Services, 71 Fenchurch Street, London, EC3M 4BS T: (020) 7423 2531 W: www.lr.org

Manorial Documents Register The National Archives, Kew, Richmond TW9 4DU T: (020) 8876 3444 E: nas@nationalarchives.gov.uk W: www.nationalarchives.gov.uk/nra/default.asp

Maritime History Archive Memorial University of Newfoundland, St Johns, Newfoundland A1C 5S7 T: ++709-737-8428 W: www.mun.ca/mha/

Marks & Spencer Company Archive Company Archive Box 10.11 Waterside House, 35 North Wharf Road, London, W2 1NW T: 020 8718 2800 E: companyarchive@marks-and-spencer.com W: http://marksintime.marksandspencer.com

Marks in Time Centenary Gallery, Parkinson Buiding, University of Leeds, Woodhouse Lane, Leeds, West Yorkshire LS2 9JT T: 0208 718 2800 (Bookings) E: exhibitionbookings@marks-and-spencer.com W: http://marksintime.marksandspencer.com

Methodist Archives and Research Centre John Rylands University Library, 150 Deansgate, Manchester, M3 3EH T: 0161 834 5343

Ministry of Defence - Fleet Air Arm Records Service CS(R)2, Bourne Avenue, Hayes, Middlesex UB3 1RF

Ministry of Defence - Joint Personnel Administration Centre JPAC Enquiry Centre, Mail Point 465, Kentigern House, 65 Brown Street , Glasgow G2 8EX, G2 8EX W: www2.army.mod.uk/contacts/divisions/records.htm

Modern Records Centre University of Warwick Library, Coventry, Warwickshire CV4 7AL T: 024 7652 4219 E: archives@warwick.ac.uk W: http://modernrecords.warwick.ac.uk

Museum of the Order of St John St John's Gate, St John's Lane, Clerkenwell, London, EC1M 4DA T: (020) 7253-6644 E: juliet.barclay@nhq.sja.org.uk W: www.sja.org.uk/history

Museum of the Royal Pharmaceutical Society Museum of the Royal Pharmaceutical Society, 1 Lambeth High Street, London, SE1 7JN T: (020) 7572 2210 E: museum@rpharms.com W: www.rpharms.com/museum

National Army Museum Department of Archives, Photographs, Film & Sound Royal Hospital Road, London, SW3 4HT T: 020 7730 0717 E: apfs@nam.ac.uk W: www.nam.ac.uk

National Gallery Library and Archive Trafalgar Square, London, WC2N 5DN T: 020 7747 2542 W: www.nationalgallery.org.uk

National Media Museum Bradford, West Yorkshire BD1 1NQ T: 01274-202030 W: www.nmpft.org.uk

National Monuments Record Enquiry and Research Services 55 Blandford Street, London, W1H 3AF T: 020 7208 8200 W: www.english-heritage.org.uk/knowledge/nmr

National Portrait Gallery Heinz Archive & library, 2 St. Martins Place, London, WC2H 0HE T: (020) 7306 0055 W: www.npg.org.uk

National Railway Museum Leeman Road, York, YO26 4XJ T: 0844 815 3139 E: nrm@nrm.org.uk W: www.nrm.org.uk

National Register of Archives The National Archives, Kew, Richmond, Surrey TW9 4DU T: (020) 8876 3444 E: nas@nationalarchives.gov.uk W: www.nationalarchives.gov.uk/nra/default.asp

National Sound Archive British Library Building, 96 Euston Road, London, NW1 2DB T: (020) 7412-7440 W: www.bl.uk

National Waterways Museum South Pier Road, Ellesmere Port, Cheshire CH65 4FW T: 0151 355 5017 E: ellesmereport@thewaterwaystrust.org.uk W: http://nwm.org.uk

NEEMARC - (North East of England Mining Archive & Resource Centre) Special Collections Room, Umiversity of Sunderland, The Murray Library, Sunderland SR1 3SD T: 0191 515 2905 E: collections.murray@sunderland.ac.uk W: www.neemarc.com

Parliamentary Archives Houses of Parliament, London, SW1A 0PW T: (020) 7219 3074 E: archives@parliament.uk W: www.parliament.uk/archives

Pilkington Group - Archives & Record Service Unit 2b Delphwood, Sherdley Industrial Estate, St Helens, Lancashire WA9 5JE T: 01744 453 555

Royal College of Obstetricians and Gynaecologists College Archives, 27 Sussex Place, Regents Park, London, NW1 4RG T: 020 7772 6277 E: archives@rcog.org.uk W: www.rcog.org.uk

Royal Commission on Historical Manuscripts Quality House, Quality Court, Chancery Lane, London, WC2A 1HP T: (020) 7242-1198 E: nra@hmc.gov.uk W: www.hmc.gov.uk

Royal Commonwealth Society Library West Road, Cambridge, Cambridgeshire CB3 9DR T: 01223 333198 W: www.lib.cam.ac.uk/MSS/

Royal Greenwich Observatory Archives West Road, Cambridge, Cambridgeshire CB3 9DR T: 01223 333056 W: www.lib.cam.ac.uk/MSS/

Royal Institution of Great Britain 21 Albemarle Street, London, W1X 4BS T: 020 7409 2992

Royal Society 6 - 9 Carlton House Terrace, London, SW1Y 5AG T: 020 7451 2606 E: library@royalsociety.org W: royalsociety.org

School of Oriental and African Studies library Thornhaugh Street, Russell Square, London, WC1H 0XG T: 020 7323 6112 W: www.soas.ac.uk/library/

Society of Antiquaries of London Burlington House, Piccadilly, London, W1J 0BE T: 020 7479 7084 E: library@sal.org.uk W: www.sal.org.uk

Society of Genealogists - Library 14 Charterhouse Buildings, Goswell Road, London, EC1M 7BA T: 020-7251-8799 E: library@sog.org.uk W: www.sog.org.uk

Southern Courage Archives Southern Accounting Centre, PO Box 85, Counterslip, Bristol, BS99 7BT

Tate Archive Collection Tate Britain, Millbank, London, SW1P 4RG T: 020 7887 8831

Tennyson Research Centre Central Library, Free School Lane, Lincoln, Lincolnshire LN2 1EZ T: 01522-552862 E: k W: www.lincolnshire.gov.uk

The Archives of Worshipful Company of Brewers Brewers' Hall, Aldermanbury Square, London, EC2V 7HR T: 020 7600 1801 E: archivist@brewershall.co.uk W: www.brewershall.co.uk

The British Postal Museum & Archive Freeling House, Phoenix Place, London, WC1X 0DL T: (020) 7239 2570 E: info@postalheritage.org.uk W: www.postalheritage.org.uk

The Council for British Archaeology St Mary's House, 66 Bootham, York, YO30 7BZ T: 01904 671 417 E: info@britarch.ac,uk W: www.britarch.ac.uk

The Historical Diving Society Little Gatton Lodge, 25 Gatton Road, Reigate, Surrey RH2 0HB E: enquiries@thehds.com W: www.thehds.com

The Kings College London Archives and Liddell Hart Centre for Military Archives King's College London, Strand, London, WC2R 2LS T: 020 7848 2015 E: archives@kcl.ac.uk W: www.kcl.ac.uk/iss/archives

The Library & Museum of Freemasonry Freemasons' Hall, 60 Great Queen Street, London, WC2B 5AZ T: (020) 7395 9257 W: www.grandlodge-england.org

The Mills Archive Trust Watlington House, 44 Watlington Street, Reading , Berkshire RG1 4RJ T: 0118 952 052 E: info@millarchive.com W: www.millsarchive.com

The National Archive of Memorial Inscriptions (NAOMI) E: naomi@memorialinscriptions.org.uk W: www.memorialinscriptions.org.uk

The National Archives Kew, Richmond, Surrey TW9 4DU T: (020) 8876 3444 E: Online contact Form W: www.nationalarchives.gov.uk/

The National Football Museum Sir Tom Finney Way, Deepdale, Preston, Lancashire PR1 6RU T: 01772 908 400 E: enquiries@nationalfootballmuseum.com W: www.nationalfootballmuseum.com

The Piano Archive Walnut Cottage, 255 Raglan Street, Lowestoft, Suffolk NR32 2LA T: 01502 531178 W: www.uk-piano.org/piano-gen

The Royal College of Physicians of London Heritage Centre, 11 St Andrews Place, Regents Park, London, NW1 4LE T: 020 7935 1543 E: heritage@rcplondon.ac.uk W: www.rcplondon.ac.uk/heritage

The United Grand Lodge of England Freemasons' Hall, 60 Great Queen Street, London, WC2B 5AZ T: (020) 7831 9811 W: www.grandlodge.org

The Wellcome Library (Wellcome Trust) 183 Euston Road, London, NW1 2BE T: (020) 7611 8722 E: library@wellcome.ac.uk W: http://library.wellcome.ac.uk

Traceline - Tel: 0151 471 4811 PO Box 106, Southport, Lancashire PR8 2HH T: 0151 471 4811

Trinity College Library Cambridge Trinity College Library, Cambridge, Cambridgeshire CB1 1TQ T: 01223 338488 E: wren.library@trin.cam.ac.uk W: www.trin.cam.ac.uk/index

United Reformed Church History Society Westminster College, Madingley Road, Cambridge, CB3 0AA T: 01223 741300 (NOT Wednesdays)

Victoria & Albert Museum - Word & Image Department - Archive of Art & Design Victoria & Albert Museum Archives, Blythe House, 23 Blythe Road, London, W14 0QF T: 020 7603 7493 E: archive@vam.ac.uk W: www.vam.ac.uk/resources/archives

Wellcome Library 183 Euston Road, London, NW1 2BE T: (020) 7611 8722 E: library@wellcome.ac.uk W: http://library.wellcome.ac.uk

Brewing

Brewery History Society Manor Side East, Mill Lane, Byfleet, West Byfleet KT14 7RS E: membership@breweryhistory.com W: www.breweryhistory.com

Guinness Archive Park Royal Brewery, London, NW10 7RR

Pub History Society 254a Kew Road, Richmond, Surrey TW9 3EG T: 020 8940 6884 E: sfowler@sfowler.force9.co.uk W: www.pubhistorysociety.co.uk

The Archives of Worshipful Company of Brewers Brewers' Hall, Aldermanbury Square, London, EC2V 7HR T: 020 7600 1801 E: archivist@brewershall.co.uk W: www.brewershall.co.uk

The Institute of Brewing & Distilling 33 Clarges Street, London, W1J 7EE T: 020 7499 8144 E: enquiries@ibd.org.uk W: www.ibd.org.uk

The National Brewery Centre Horninglow Street, Burton on Trent, DE14 1YQ T: 0845 6000598 E: info@nationalbrewerycentre.co.uk W: www.nationalbrewerycentre.co.uk

Young's & Co's Brewery Archives Ram Brewery, High Street, Wandsworth, London, SW18 4JD

Film Archives

Barnardo's Film & Photographic Archive Aftercare Section - Barnardo's, Tanner Lane, Barkingside, Ilford IG6 1QG T: (020) 8550-8822

BBC Sound and Film Archives BBC Research Central, T: 020 7557 2452 E: see website W: www.bbc.co.uk/archive/index.shtml

Bill Douglas Centre for the History of Cinema and Popular Culture University of Exeter, Queen's Building, Queen's Drive, Exeter EX4 4QH T: 01392 264321 W: www.ex.ac.uk/bill.douglas
British Film Institute 21 Stephen Street, London, W1T 1LN T: 020 7255 1444 E: library@bfi.org.uk W: www.bfi.org.uk
British Film Institute - Library & Film Archive 21 Stephen Street, London, W1T 1LN T: 020 7957 4824 W: www.bfi.org.uk
British Pathe Plc c/o ITN Archive, 200 Gray's Inn Road, London, WC1X 8XZ T: 0207 430 4480 E: pathe@itnarchive.com W: www.britishpathe.com
British Universities Film and Video Council 77 Wells Street, London, W1T 3QJ T: 020 7393 1500 W: www.bufvc.ac.uk
East Anglian Film Archive The Archive Centre, Martineau Lane, Norwich, Norfolk NR1 2DQ T: 01603 592664 W: www.uea.ac.uk/eafa
Imperial War Museum Film and Video Archive Lambeth Road, London, SE1 6HZ T: 020 7416 5289 W: www.iwm.org.uk/collections/film.htm
Media Archive for Central England Institute of Film Studies, University of Nottingham, Nottingham, Nottinghamshire NG7 2RD T: 0115 846 6448 W: www.nottingham.ac.uk/film/mace
National Army Museum Department of Archives, Photographs, Film & Sound Royal Hospital Road, London, SW3 4HT T: 020 7730 0717 E: apfs@nam.ac.uk W: www.nam.ac.uk
National Media Museum Bradford, West Yorkshire BD1 1NQ T: 01274-202030 W: www.nmpft.org.uk
North West Film Archive Manchester Metropolitan University, Minshull House, 47-49 Chorlton Street, Manchester, M1 3EU T: 0161 247 3097 W: www.nwfa.mmu.ac.uk
Northern Region Film & Television Archive School of Law, Arts and Humanities, Room M 616 Middlesbrough Tower, University of Teeside, Middlesbrough TS1 3BA T: 01642 384022 W: www.tees.ac.uk
South East Film & Video Archive University of Brighton, Grand Parade, Brighton, Sussex BN2 2JY T: 01273 643213 W: www.bton.ac.uk/sefva
South West Film & Television Archive Melville Building, Royal William Yard, Stonehouse, Plymouth PL1 3RP T: 01752 202650 W: www.tswfta.co.uk
Wessex Film & Sound Archive Hampshire Record Office, Sussex Street, Winchester SO23 8TH T: 01962 847742 W: www.hants.gov.uk/record-office/film.html
Yorkshire Film Archive York St John University, Lord Mayor's Walk, York, North Yorkshire YO31 7EX T: 01904 876550 E: yfa@yorksj.ac.uk W: www.yorkshirefilmarchive.com

Romany Traveller & Gypsy

Gypsy
Gordon Boswell Romany Museum Hawthorns Clay Lake, Spalding, Lincolnshire PE12 6BL T: 01775 710599 W:
Romany & Traveller Family History Society 7 Park Rise, Nonchurch, Berkhamstead HP4 3RT W: www.rtfhs.org.uk
The Gypsy Collections University of Liverpool, PO Box 229, Liverpool, L69 3DA T: 0151 794 2696 W: www.sca.lib.liv.ac.uk/collections/index.html
The Robert Dawson Romany Collection Rural History Centre, University of Reading, Whiteknights PO Box 229, Reading, RG6 6AG T: 0118 378 8660 E: merl@reading.ac.uk W: www.reading.ac.ukmerl
The Romany Collections Brotherton Library, Leeds University, Leeds LS2 9JT T: 0113 343 55188 E: special-collections@library.leeds.ac.uk W: http://leeds.ac.uk/library/spcoll/

England

Bedfordshire
Bedfordshire & Luton Archives & Record Service Riverside Building, County Hall, Cauldwell Street, Bedford MK42 9AP T: 01234-228833 E: archive@bedford.gov.uk W: www.bedford.gov.uk/archive

Berkshire
Berkshire Medical Heritage Centre Level 4, Main Entrance, Royal Berkshire Hospital, London Road, Reading RG1 5AN T: 0118 987 7298 W: www.bmhc.org
Berkshire Record Office 9 Coley Avenue, Reading, RG1 6AF T: 0118 937 5132 E: arch@reading.gov.uk W: www.berkshirerecordoffice.org.uk
Eton College College Library, Eton College, Windsor, SL4 6DB T: 01753 671269 E: archivist@etoncollege.org.uk W: www.etoncollege.com
Museum of English Rural Life University of Reading, Redlands Road, Reading, Berkshire RG1 5EX T: 0118 378 8660 E: merl@reading.ac.uk W: www.reading.ac.uk/merl/

The Museum of Berkshire Aviation Trust Mohawk Way, Bader Way, Woodley, Reading RG5 4UE T: 0118 944 8089 E: museumofberkshireaviation@fly.to W: http://fly.to/museumofberkshireaviation
West Berkshire Museum - Newbury - closed for refurbishment until 2014 - See website: **www.westberkshiremuseum.org.uk**

Bristol
Bristol Records Office B Bond Warehouse, Smeaton Road, Bristol, BS1 6XN T: 0117 922 4224 E: bro@bristol.gov.uk W: www.bristol.gov.uk/recordsoffice
Bristol University Library - Special Collections Tyndall Avenue, Bristol, BS8 1TJ T: 0117 928 8014 E: special-collections@bris.ac.uk W: www.bris.ac.uk/is/services/specialcollections/

Buckinghamshire
Centre for Buckinghamshire Studies County Offices, Walton Street, Aylesbury, Buckinghamshire HP20 1UU T: 01296 382587 (Archives) E: archives@buckscc.gov.uk W: www.buckscc.gov.uk/archives

Cambridgeshire
Cambridgeshire Archives Box RES 1009, Shire Hall, Cambridge, CB3 0AP T: 01223 699 399 E: cambs.archives@cambridgeshire.gov.uk W: www.cambridgeshire.gov.uk/archives/
Cambridgeshire Collection Central Library, Lion Yard, Cambridge, Cambridgeshire CB2 3QD T: 0345 045 5225 E: cambs.archives@cambridgeshire.gov.uk W: www.cambridgeshire.gov.uk/archives/
Centre for Regional Studies Anglia Polytechnic University, East Rd, Cambridge CB1 1PT T: 01223-363271 ext 2030 W: www.anglia.ac.uk
Fenland Collection Wisbech Library, 1 Ely Place, Wisbech, PE13 EU T: 0345 045 5225 E: cambs.archives@cambridgeshire.gov.uk W: www.cambridgeshire.gov.uk/archives/
Huntingdonshire Archives Library & Archives, Princes Street, Huntingdon PE29 3PA T: 01480 372 738 E: hunts.archives@cambridgeshire.gov.uk W: www.cambridgeshire.gov.uk/leisure/archives
Peterborough Archives Service and Local Studies Collection Central Library, Broadway, Peterborough, PE1 1RX T: 01733 742700 W: www.peterborough.gov.uk

Cheshire
Cheshire & Chester Archives & Local Studies Duke Street, Chester CH1 1RL T: 01244 972574 E: recordoffice@cheshire.gov.uk W: www.cheshire.gov.uk/recoff/home.htm
Chester History & Heritage St Michaels Church, Bridge Street Row, Chester, Cheshire CH1 1NW T: 01244 402110 E: cheshiremuseums@cheshire.gov.uk W: www.cheshire.gov.uk/TourismLeisureAndCulture/museums/museumshome.htm
Macclesfield Silk Museums Paradise Mill, Park Lane, Macclesfield, Cheshire SK11 6TJ T: 01625 612045 W: www.silk-macclesfield.org
Stockport Local Heritage library Central Library, Wellington Road South, Stockport, Cheshire SK1 3RS T: 0161-474-4530 E: localheritagelibrary@stockport.gov.uk W: www.stockport.gov.uk
Tameside Local Studies Library Stalybridge Library, Trinity Street, Stalybridge SK15 2BN T: 0161-338-2708 W: www.tameside.gov.uk
Trafford Local Studies Centre Public Library, Tatton Road, Sale, M33 1YH T: 0161-912-3013

Cleveland
Friends of Teesside Archives 9 Killing Close, Billingham TS23 3UJ
Tees Archaeology - The Archaeological Service for Teesside Sir William Gray, Clarence Road, Hartlepool, TS24 8BT T: 01429 523455 E: tees-archaeology@hartlepool.gov.uk W: www.hartlepool.gov.uk

Cornwall
Cornish Studies Library The Cornwall Centre, Alma Place, Redruth, TR15 2AT T: 01209 216 760 E: cornishstudies.library@cornwall.gov.uk W: www.cornwall.gov.uk/cornwallcentre
Cornish-American Connection Murdoch House, Cross Street, Redruth, Cornwall TR15 2BU T: 01209 216333 W: www.ex.ac.uk/~cnfrench/ics/welcome.htm
Cornwall Record Office County Hall, Truro, Cornwall TRI 3AY T: 01872 323127 E: cro@cornwall.gov.uk W: www.cornwall.gov.uk
Porthcurno Telegraph Museum and Archive Eastern House, Porthcurno, Penzance, Cornwall TR19 6JX T: 01736 810478 E: caroline.seats@porthcurno.org.uk W: www.porthcurno.org.uk
Royal Institution of Cornwall, Courtney Library & Cornish History Research Centre Royal Cornwall Museum, River Street, Truro, Cornwall TR1 2SJ T: 01872 272205 W: www.cornwall-online.co.uk/genealogy

County Durham

Darlington Local Studies Centre The Library, Crown St, Darlington
DL1 1ND T: 01325-349630 E: local.studies@darlington.gov.uk W:
www.darlington.gov.uk/library/localstudies
Durham County Record Office County Hall, Durham DH1 5UL T:
0191 383 3253 E: record.office@durham.gov.uk W:
www.durhamrecordoffice.org.uk
Durham University Library Archives and Special Collections
Durham University Library, Palace Green, Durham, DH1 3RN T:
0191 334 2972 E: pg.library@durham.ac.uk
 W: www.dur.ac.uk/library/asc
North East War Memorials Project 14 Park Road North, Chester le
Street, Co Durham DH3 3SD T: 0191 388 3667 E:
john@newmp.org.uk W: www.newmp.org.uk
The Oriental Museum University of Durham Museums, Elvet Hill,
Durham, DH1 3TH T: 0191 334 5694 E:
oriental.museum@durham.ac.uk W: www.dur.ac.uk/oriental.museum/

Cumbria

**Barrow in Furness - Cumbria Record Office & Local Studies
Library** 140 Duke St, Barrow in Furness, Cumbria LA14 1XW T:
01229 407363 E: barrow.record.office@cumbriacc.gov.uk W:
www.cumbria.gov.uk/archives
Carlisle - Cumbria Archive Centre Cumbria Archive Centre, Lady
Gillford's House, Petteril Bank Road, Carlisle, Cumbria CA1 3AJ T:
01227 27 285 E: carlisle.record.office@cumbriacc.gov.uk W:
www.cumbriacc.gov.uk/archives
Heritage First - formerly Ulverston Heritage Centre Lower Brook St,
Ulverston LA12 7EE T: 01229 580820 W:
www.rootsweb.com/~ukuhc/
Kendal - Cumbria Record Office County Offices, Stricklandgate,
Kendal LA9 4RQ T: 01539 773540 E:
kendal.record.office@cumbriacc.gov.uk W:
www.cumbria.gov.uk/archives
Whitehaven - Cumbria Record Office & Local Studies Library
Scotch Street, Whitehaven, Cumbria CA28 7NL T: 01946 506420 E:
whitehaven.record.office@cumbriacc.gov.uk W:
www.cumbria.gov.uk/archives

Derbyshire

Derby Local Studies Library 25b Irongate, Derby, Derbyshire DE1
3GL T: 01332 642240 E: localstudies.library@derby.gov.uk W:
www.derby.gov.uk/libraries/about/local_studies.htm
Derbyshire Record Office County Hall, Matlock, Derbyshire DE4
3AG T: 01629-580000-ext-35207
Erewash Museum The Museum, High Street, Ilkeston DE7 5JA T:
0115 907 1141 E: museum@erewash.gov.uk W: www.erewash.gov.uk

Devon

Beaford Photograph Archive Barnstaple EX32 7EJ T: 01271 288611
Devon Record Office Great Moor House, Bittern Road, Sowton,
Exeter, Devon EX2 7NL T: 01392 384253 E: devrec@devon.gov.uk
W: www.devon.gov.uk/record_office.htm
North Devon Record Office Tuly Street, Barnstaple, Devon EX31
1EL T: 01271 388607 E: ndevrec@devon.gov.uk W:
www.devon.gov.uk/dro/homepage
The Devonshire & Dorset Regiment (Archives) RHQ, Wyvern
Barracks, Barrack Road, Exeter, Devon EX2 6AR T: 01392 492436

Dorset

Bridport Museum Trust - Local History Centre The Coach House,
Gundry Lane, Bridport, Dorset DT6 3RJ T: 01308 458703 E:
office@bridportmuseum.co.uk W: www.bridportmuseum.co.uk
Dorset History Centre 9 Bridport Road, Dorchester, Dorset DT1
1RP T: 01305 250550 E: archives@dorsetcc.gov.uk W: www.dorset-
cc.gov.uk/dorsethistorycentre
Poole Central Library Dolphin Centre, Poole, Dorset BH15 1QE T:
01202 262424 E: centrallibrary@poole.gov.uk W:
www.boroughofpoole.com/libraries
Poole Museum and Poole History Centre 4 High Street, Poole,
Dorset BH15 1BW T: 01202 262 600 E: museums@poole.gov.uk
 W: www.boroughofpoole.gov.uk/museums

Essex

Essex County Council Libraries - Answers Direct PO Box 882,
Market Road, Chelmsford, Essex CM1 1LH T: 0845 603 7628 E:
answers.direct@essex.gov.uk W: www.essex.gov.uk/libraries
http://elan.essexcc.gov.uk (Online Catalogue)
www.answersdirect.info
Essex Record Office Wharf Road, Chelmsford, Essex CM2 6YT T:
01245 244644 W: www.essexcc.gov.uk/ero
Colchester & NE Essex Branch - closed moved to Chelmsford
Havering Central Reference Library - L B of Reference Library, St
Edward's Way, Romford, Essex RM1 3AR T: 01708 432393

Redbridge Library Central Library, Clements Road, Ilford, Essex
IG1 1EA T: (020) 8708 2417 W: www.redbridge.gov.uk
Southend Library and Local Studies Central Library, Victoria
Avenue, Southend on Sea, Essex SS2 6EX T: 01702 215011 E:
library@southend.gov.uk W: www.southend.gov.uk/libraries/
Valence House Museum Valence House Museum, Becontree Avenue,
Dagenham, Essex RM8 3HT T: 020 8270 6866 E:
valencehousemuseum@lbbd.gov.uk W: www.lbbd.gov.uk/valence

Gloucestershire

Gloucestershire Archives Clarence Row, Alvin Street, Gloucester,
GL1 3DW T: 01452 425295 E: archives@gloucestershire.gov.uk W:
www.gloucestershire.gov.uk/archives

Greater Manchester

Greater Manchester County Record Office 56 Marshall St, New
Cross, Manchester, Greater Manchester M4 5FU T: 0161-832-5284 E:
archives@gmcro.co.uk W: www.gmcro.co.uk

Hampshire

Hampshire Archives & Local Studies Hampshire Record Office,
Sussex Street, Winchester, Hampshire SO23 8TH T: 01962 846154 E:
enquiries.archives@hants.gov.uk W: www.hants.gov.uk/archives
Hampshire Archives and Local Studies Sussex Street, Winchester,
SO23 8TH T: 01962 846151 E: enquiries.archives@hants.gov.uk W:
www.hants.gov.uk/record-office
Portsmouth City Libraries Central Library, Guildhall Square,
Portsmouth, Hampshire PO1 2DX T: 023 9268 8046 (Bookings &
Enquiries) E: reference.library@portsmouthcc.gov.uk W:
www.portsmouth.gov.uk/learning/15605.html
Portsmouth City Museum & Record Office Museum Road,
Portsmouth PO1 2LJ T: (023) 92827261 E:
Searchroom@portsmouthcc.gov.uk W:
www.portsmouthmuseums.co.uk/
Portsmouth Roman Catholic Diocesan Archives St Edmund House,
Edinburgh Road, Portsmouth, Hampshire PO1 3QA T: 023 9282 5430
Southampton Archive Service Civic Centre, Southampton SO14
7LY T: (023) 80832251 E: city.archives@southampton.gov.uk W:
www.southampton.gov.uk
**Southampton City Libraries - Local Studies & Maritime
Collections** Central Library, Civic Centre, Southampton, SO14 7LW
T: 023 8083 2205 E: local.studies@southampton.gov.uk W:
www.southampton.gov.uk/s-leisure/libraries/

Herefordshire

Hereford Cathedral Library & Archives 5 College Cloisters,
Cathedral Close, Hereford HR1 2NG T: 01432 374225/6 E:
library@herefordcathedral.org W: www.herefordcathedral.org
Herefordshire Archive Service Herefordshire Record Office, Harold
Street, Hereford HR1 2QX T: 01432 260750 E:
archives@herefordshire.gov.uk W: www.herefordshire.gov.uk/archives

Hertfordshire

Ashwell Education Services 59 High Street, Ashwell SG7 5NP T:
01462 742385 E: aes@ashwell-education-services.co.uk W:
www.ashwell-education-services.co.uk
Bushey Museum, Art Gallery and Local Studies Centre Rudolph
Road, Bushey, Hertfordshire WD23 3HW T: 020 8420 4057 E:
busmt@bushey.org.uk W: www.busheymuseum.org
Hertfordshire Archives and Local Studies County Hall, Pegs Lane,
Hertford, Hertfordshire SG13 8EJ T: 0300 123 4049 E:
hertsdirect@hertscc.gov.uk W: www.hertsdirect.org/Hals

Hull

Brynmor Jones Library - University of Hull Cottingham Road,
Hull, HU6 7RX T: 01482 465265 W: www.hull.ac.uk/lib
www.hull.ac.uk/lib/archives
Hull History Centre and Local Studies Library Worship Street,
Hull HU2 8BG T: 01482 317 500 E: hullhistorycentre@hullcc.gov.uk

Isle of Wight

Isle of Wight Record Office 26 Hillside, Newport, Isle of Wight
PO30 2EB T: 01983-823820/1 E: record.office@iow.gov.uk W:
www.iwight.com/library/record_office/default.asp

Kent

Bexley Local Studies and Archive Centre - L B of Central Library,
Townley Road, Bexleyheath DA6 7HJ T: (020) 8836 7369 E:
archives@bexley.gov.uk W: www.bexley.gov.uk/archives
Canterbury Cathedral Archives The Precincts, Canterbury, Kent
CT1 2EH T: 01227 865330 E: archives@canterbury-cathedral.org W:
www.canterbury-cathedral.org
Canterbury Library & Local Studies Collection 18 High Street,
Canterbury, Kent CT1 2JF T: 01227-463608 W: www.kent.gov.uk

Centre for Kentish Studies / Kent Archives Service Sessions House, County Hall, Maidstone, Kent, ME141XQ T: 01622-694363 E: archives@kent.gov.uk W: www.kent.gov.uk/archives
East Kent Archives Centre East Kent Archives Centre, Enterprise Zone, Honeywood Road, Whitfield, Dover, Kent CT16 3EH T: 01304 829306 E: eastkentarchives@kent.gov.uk W: www.kent.gov.uk/leisure_and_culture/archives_and_local_history/archive_and_local_history/east_kent_archives_centre.aspx
Margate Library Local History Collection Cecil Square, Margate, Kent CT9 1RE T: 01843-223626 W: www.kent.gov.uk
Medway Archives & Local Studies Centre Civic Centre, Strood, Rochester, Kent ME2 4AU T: 01634 332 714 E: malsc@medway.gov.uk W: http://cityark.medway.gov.uk
Ramsgate Library Local Strudies Collection & Thanet Branch Archives Ramsgate Library, Guildford Lawn, Ramsgate, Kent CT11 9AY T: 01843-593532 W: www.kent.gov.uk
Sevenoaks Archives Office Central Library, Buckhurst Lane, Sevenoaks, Kent TN13 1LQ T: 01732-453118

Lancashire
Blackburn Cathedral & Archives Cathedral Close, Blackburn, Lancashire BB1 5AA T: 01254 503 090 E: cathedral@blackburncathedral.co.uk W: www.blackburncathedral.com
Blackburn Central Library - Community History Department Town Hall Street, Blackburn, Lancashire BB2 1AG T: 01254 587919 E: community.history@blackburn.gov.uk W: www.blackburn.gov.uk/library www.cottontown.org
Bolton Museum & Archive Service Bolton History Centre, Civic Centre, Le Mans Crescent, Bolton BL1 1SE T: 01204 332 185 F: 01204 332 241 E: archives@bolton.gov.uk W: www.boltonmuaseums.org.uk/bolton-archives
Bury Archives Service Bury Museum and Archives, Moss Street, Bury, Greater Manchester BL9 0DR T: 0161 253 6782 E: archives@bury.gov.uk W: www.bury.gov.uk/archives
Centre for North West Regional Studies Fylde College, Lancaster University, Lancaster, Lancashire LA1 4YF T: 01524 593770 E: sam.riches@lancaster.ac.uk W: www.lancs.ac.uk/users/cnwrs
Lancashire Record Office Bow Lane, Preston PR1 2RE T: 01772 533039 E: record.office@lancashire.gov.uk W: www.archives.lancashire.gov.uk
North West Sound Archive Old Steward's Office, Clitheroe Castle, Clitheroe BB7 1AZ T: 01200 427897 E: nwsa@ed.lancscc.gov.uk W: www.lancashire.gov.uk/education/d_lif/ro/content/sound/imdex.asp
Oldham Local Studies and Archives 84 Union Street, Oldham, OL1 1DN T: 0161-911-4654 E: archives@oldham.gov.uk W: www.oldham.gov.uk/archives www.oldham.gov.uk/local_studies
Rochdale Local Studies Centre Touchstones Rochdale, The Esplanade, Rochdale, Lancashire OL16 1AQ T: 01706 924915 E: localstudies@link4life.org W: www.link4life.org/localstudies
Salford City Archives Salford Archives Centre, 658/662 Liverpool Rd, Irlam, Manchester, M44 5AD T: 0161 775-5643
Salford Local History Library Peel Park, The Crescent, Salford, Lancashire M5 4WU T: 0161 778 0814 E: local.history@salford.gov.uk W: www.salford.gov.uk/lhlibrary.htm
The Documentary Photography Archive - Manchester c/o 7 Towncroft Lane, Bolton, Lancashire BL1 5EW T: 0161 832 5284
The Museum of Wigan Life Wigan Leisure and Culture Trust, Library Street, Wigan, Greater Manchester WN1 1NU T: 01942 828128 E: heritage@wlct.org W: www.wlct.org/culture/heritage
Wigan Archive Service Town Hall, Civic Square, Market Street, Leigh, Wigan, Greater Manchester WN7 1DY T: 01942 404 430 E: heritage@wict.org W: www.wiganmbc.gov.uk

Land Registries
Coventry District Land Registry Leigh Court, Torrington Avenue, Tile Hill, Coventry, CV4 9XZ T: 024 7686 0860 E: customersupport@landregistry.gsi.gov.uk W: www.landreg.gov.uk
Croydon District Land Registry Traflagar House, 1 Bedford Park, Croydon, CR9 2AQ T: 020 8781 9100 E: customersupport@landregistry.gsi.gov.uk W: www.landreg.gov.uk
Durham District Land Registry Southfield House, Southfield Way, Durham, County Durham DH1 5TR T: 0191 301 3500 E: customersupport@landregistry.gsi.gov.uk W: www.landreg.gov.uk
Flyde District Land Registry Wrea Brook Court, Lytham Road, Warton, Lancashire PR4 1TE T: 01772 836700 E: customersupport@landregistry.gsi.gov.uk W: www.landreg.gov.uk
Gloucester District Land Registry Twyver House, Bruton Way, Gloucester, Gloucestershire GL1 1DQ T: 01452 511111 E: customersupport@landregistry.gsi.gov.uk W: www.landreg.gov.uk
Kingston Upon Hull District Land Registry Earle House, Portland Street, Hull, HU2 8JN T: 01482 223244 E: customersupport@landregistry.gsi.gov.uk W: www.landreg.gov.uk

Leicester District Land Registry Westbridge Place, Leicester, Leicestershire LE3 5DR T: 0116 265 4000 E: customersupport@landregistry.gsi.gov.uk W: www.landreg.gov.uk
Nottingham District Land Registry Chalfont Drive, Nottingham, Nottinghamshire NG8 3RN T: 0115 935 1166 E: customersupport@landregistry.gsi.gov.uk W: www.landreg.gov.uk
Peterborough District Land Registry Touthill Close, City Road, Peterborough, PE1 1XN T: 01733 288288 E: customersupport@landregistry.gsi.gov.uk W: www.landreg.gov.uk
Plymouth District Land Registry Plumer House, Tailyour Road, Crownhill, Plymouth, Devon PL6 5HY T: 01752 636000 E: customersupport@landregistry.gsi.gov.uk W: www.landreg.gov.uk
Portsmouth District Land Registry St Andrews Court, St Michael's Road, Portsmouth, Hampshire PO1 2JH T: (023) 9276 8888 E: customersupport@landregistry.gsi.gov.uk W: www.landreg.gov.uk
Stevenage District Land Registry Brickdale House, Swingate, Stevenage, Hertfordshire SG1 1XG T: 01438 788 888 E: customersupport@landregistry.gsi.gov.uk W: www.landreg.gov.uk
Telford District Land Registry Parkside Court, Hall Park Way, Telford, Shropshire TF3 4LR T: 01952 290355 E: customersupport@landregistry.gsi.gov.uk W: www.landreg.gov.uk
Tunbridge Wells District Land Registry Forest Court, Forest Road, Tunbridge Wells, Kent TN2 5AQ T: 01892 510015 E: customersupport@landregistry.gsi.gov.uk W: www.landreg.gov.uk
Wales District Land Registry Ty Bryn Glas, High Street, Swansea, SA1 1PW T: 01792 355000 E: customersupport@landregistry.gsi.gov.uk W: www.landreg.gov.uk
Weymouth District Land Registry Melcombe Court, 1 Cumberland Drive, Weymouth, Dorset DT4 9TT T: 01305 363636 E: customersupport@landregistry.gsi.gov.uk W: www.landreg.gov.uk

Leicestershire
East Midlands Oral History Archive Centre for Urban History, University of Leicester, Leicester, Leicestershire LE1 7RH T: 0116 252 5065 E: emoha@le.ac.uk W: www.le.ac.uk/emoha
Melton Mowbray Library Wilton Road, Melton Mowbray, LE13 0UJ T: 0116 305 3646 E: meltonmowbraylibrary@leics.gov.uk W: www.leics.gov.uk/meltonmowbray_library
Record Office for Leicestershire, Leicester and Rutland Long Street, Wigston Magna, Leicestershire LE18 2AH T: 0116 257 1080 E: recordoffice@leics.gov.uk W: www.leics.gov.uk

Lincolnshire
Lincolnshire Archives St Rumbold Street, Lincoln, Lincolnshire LN2 5AB T: 01522-526204 W: www.lincolnshire.gov.uk/archives
Lincolnshire County Library Local Studies Section, Lincoln Central Library, Free School Lane, Lincoln LN2 1EZ T: 01522 782010 E: lincoln_library@lincolnshire.gov.uk W: www.lincolnshire.gov.uk
Lincolnshire - North
North East Lincolnshire Archives Town Hall, Town Hall Square, Grimsby, North East Lincolnshire DN31 1HX T: 01472-323585 E: john.wilson@nelincs.gov.uk W: www.nelincs.gov.uk

Liverpool
Liverpool Libraries & Archive Service Unit 33, Wellington Employment Park South, Dunes Way (off Sandhills Lane), Liverpool, L5 9ZS T: 0151 233 5817 E: archives@liverpool.gov.uk W: www.liverpool.gov.uk/archives
Liverpool University Special Collections & Archives University of Liverpool Library, PO Box 123, Liverpool, L69 3DA T: 0151-794-2696 W: www.sca.lib.liv.ac.uk/collections/index.html

London
Alexander Fleming Laboratory Museum / Imperial College Healthcare NHS Trust Archives St Mary's Hospital, Praed Street, Paddington, London, W2 1NY T: 020 331 26528 E: kevin.brown@imperial.nhs.uk W: www.imperial.nhs.uk
Barking & Dagenham Archives & Local Studies Centre - L B of Valence House, Beacontree Avenue, Dagenham, Essex RM8 3HT T: 020 8227 2033 E: localstudies@lbbd.gov.uk W: www.lbbd.gov.uk/heritage
Barnet - Local Studies - L B of Hendon Library, The Burroughs, London, NW4 4BQ T: (020) 8359 3960 E: library.archives@barnet.gov.uk W: www.barnet.gov.uk/archives
Bethlem Royal Hospital Archives and Museum, Monks Orchard Road, Beckenham, Kent BR3 3BX T: (020) 8776 4307 E: colin.gale@slam.nhs.uk JMichael.Phillips@slam.nhs.uk W: www.bethlemheritage.org.uk/
Bexley Local Studies and Archive Centre - L B of Central Library, Townley Road, Bexleyheath, Kent DA6 7HJ T: (020) 8836 7369 E: archives@bexley.gov.uk W: www.bexley.gov.uk/archives
Brent Archive - L B of 152 Olive Road, Cricklewood, London, NW2 6UY T: (020) 8937 3541 E: archive@brent.gov.uk W: www.brent.gov.uk/archive

Bromley Local Studies Library - L B of Central Library, High Street, Bromley, Kent BR1 1EX T: 020 8461 7170 E: localstudies.library@bromley.gov.uk W: www.bromley.gov.uk/libraries

Camden Local Studies & Archive Centre - L B of Holborn Library, 32 - 38 Theobalds Road, London, WC1X 8PA T: 020 7974 6342 E: localstudies@camden.gov.uk W: www.camden.gov.uk/localstudies

Chelsea Public Library - L B of Old Town Hall, King's Road, London, SW3 5EZ T: (020) 7352-6056

Chiswick & Brentford Local Studies Collection - L B of Chiswick Public Library, Dukes Avenue, Chiswick, London, W4 2AB T: (020) 8994-5295

City of Westminster Archives Centre 10 St Ann's Street, London, SW1P 2DE T: (020) 7641-5180 W: www.westminster.gov.uk

Corporation of London Records Office transferred to London Metropolitan Archives 40 Northampton Road, London, EC1R 0HB T: 020 7332 3820 E: ask.lma@cityoflondon.gov.uk W: www.lma.gov.uk

Croydon Local Study and Archives Service - L B of Central Library, Katharine Street, Croydon, CR9 1ET T: 020 8726 6900 x 61112 E: localstudies@croydon.gov.uk W: www.croydon.gov.uk/

Ealing Local History Centre Central Library, 103 Broadway Centre, Ealing, London, W5 5JY T: (020) 8567-3656-ext-37 E: localhistory@hotmail.com W: www.ealing.gov.uk/libraries

Enfield Archives & Local History Unit - L B of Southgate Town Hall, Green Lanes, Palmers Green, London, N13 4XD T: (020) 8379-2724

Greenwich Heritage Centre - L B of Artillery Square, Royal Arsenal, Woolwich, London, SE18 4DX T: (020) 8854 2452 E: info@greenwichheritage.org W: www.greenwich.gov.uk

Grenadier Guards Record Office Wellington Barracks, Birdcage Walk, London, London SW1E 6HQ E: grenadierenquiries@grengds.com - email requests not accepted written enquiries only. Access is by appointment made in advance.

Guildhall Library, Manuscripts Section - Closed permanently and merged with London Metropolitan Archive 40 Northampton Row, London, EC1R 0HB T: 020 7332 3820 E: ask.lma@cityoflondon.gov.uk W: www.cityoflondon.gov.uk/lma

Hackney Archives Department - L B of London Borough of Hackney, 43 De Beauvoir Road, London, N1 5SQ T: (020) 7241 2886 E: archives@hackney.gov.uk W: www.hackney.gov.uk/ca-history

Hammersmith & Fulham Archives & Local History Centre - L B of The Lilla Huset, 191 Talgarth Road, London, W6 8BJ T: 0208 741 5159 W: www.lbhf.gov.uk

Haringey Archives & Local Studies Library - L B of Bruce Castle Museum, Lordship Lane, Tottenham, London, N17 8NU T: 020 8808 8772 E: museum.services@haringey.gov.uk W: www.haringey.gov.uk

Hillingdon Local Studies & Archives Central Library, High Street, Uxbridge, London, Middlesex UB8 1HD T: 01895 250702 W: www.hillingdon.gov.uk/goto/libraries

Hounslow Library (Local Studies & Archives) - L B of Centrespace, Treaty Centre, High Street, Hounslow, London TW3 1ES T: 0845 456 2800 W: www.cip.com

Imperial College Archives Room 455 Sherfield Building, Imperial College, London, SW7 2AZ T: 020 7594 8850 E: a.barrett@imperial.ac.uk W: www3.imperial.ac.uk/recordsandarchives

Institute of Commonwealth Studies , University of London 28 Russell Square, London, WC1B 5DS T: (020) 7862 8844 E: icommlib@sas.ac.uk W: http://sas.ac.uk/commonwealthstudies

Institute of Historical Research University of London , Senate House, Malet Street, London, WC1E 7HU T: 020 7862 8740 E: ihr.library@sas.ac.uk W: www.history.ac.uk

Islington Local History Centre - L B of Finsbury library, 245 St John Street, London, EC1V 4NB T: (020) 7527 7988 E: local.history@islington.gov.uk W: www.islington.gov.uk/heritage

Kensington and Chelsea Libraries, Local Studies & Archives Department - Royal Borough of Central Library, Phillimore Walk, Kensington, London, W8 7RX T: 020 7361 3038 E: information.services@rbkc.gov.uk W: www.rbkc.gov.uk/libraries

Kingston Museum & Heritage Service - L B of North Kingston Centre, Richmond Road, Kingston upon Thames, Surrey KT2 5PE T: (020) 8547-6738 E: local.history@rbk.kingston.gov.uk W: www.kingston.gov.uk/museum/

Lambeth Archives Department - L B of Minet Library, 52 Knatchbull Road, Lambeth, London, SE5 9QY T: (020) 7926 6076 W: www.lambeth.gov.uk

Lewisham Local History & Archives Centre - L B of Lewisham Library, 199 - 201 Lewisham High Street, London, SE13 6LG T: 020 8314 8501 E: local.studies@lewisham.gov.uk W: www.lewisham.gov.uk

London Metropolitan Archives 40 Northampton Road, London, EC1R 0HB T: 020 7332 3820 E: ask.lma@cityoflondon.gov.uk W: www.lma.gov.uk/

London University - Institute of Advanced Legal Studies Charles Clore House, 17 Russell Square, London, WC1B 5DR T: (020) 7862 5800 E: ials@sas.ac.uk W: http://ials.sas.ac.uk

London University - Institute of Education 20 Bedford Way, London, WC1H 0AL T: 020 7612 6063 E: info@ioe.ac.uk W: www.ioe.ac.uk/library/

Merton Local Studies Centre - L B of Merton Civic Centre, London Road, Morden, Surrey SM4 5DX T: (020) 8545-3239 E: local.studies@merton.gov.uk W: www.merton.gov.uk/libraries

Museum of London Library 150 London Wall, London, EC2Y 5HN T: 020 7814 5588 E: library@museumoflondon.org.uk W: www.museumoflondon.org.uk

Newham Archives & Local Studies Library - L B of Stratford Library, 3 The Grove, London, E15 1EL T: (020) 8430 6881 W: www.newham.gov.uk

Royal Air Force Museum - Department of Research & Information Services Grahame Park Way, Hendon, London, NW9 5LL T: (020) 83584873 E: research@rafmuseum.org W: www.rafmuseum.org

Royal Botanic Gardens Library & Archives, Kew, Richmond, Surrey TW9 3AE T: 020 8332 5414

Royal London Hospital Archives and Museum Royal London Hospital Archives, 9 Prescot Street, Aldgate, London, E1 8PR T: (020) 7377 7608 E: rlharchives@bartsandthelondon.nhs.uk W: www.bartsandthelondon.nhs.uk/museums

Senate House Library - Special Collections University of London, Senate House Library, Malet Street, London, WC1 7HU T: 020 7862 8470 E: shl.specialcollections@london.ac.uk W: www.shl.lon.ac.uk : www.shl.lon.ac.uk/specialcollections/archives/studentrecords.shtml

Southwark Local History Library - L B of 211 Borough High Street, Southwark, London, SE1 1JA T: 020 7525 0232 E: local.history.library@southwark.gov.uk W: www.southwark.gov.uk

St Bartholomew's Hospital Archives & Museum North Wing, St Bartholomew's Hospital , West Smithfield, London, EC1A 7BE T: 020 3465 5798 E: barts.archives@bartsandthelondon.nhs.uk W: www.bartsandthelondon.nhs.uk/museums

Sutton Archives - L B of Central Library, St Nicholas Way, Sutton, Surrey SM1 1EA T: (020) 8770-4747 E: local.studies@sutton.gov.uk W: www.sutton.gov.uk

The Galton Institute 19 Northfields Prospect, London, SW18 1PE

Tower Hamlets Local History Library & Archives - L B of Bancroft Library, 277 Bancroft Road, London, E1 4DQ T: (020) 7364 1290 E: localhistory@towerhamlets.gov.uk W: www.ideastore.co.uk

Twickenham Library - collection transferred to Richmond Local Studies Library Twickenham Library, Garfield Road, Twickenham, Middlesex TW1 3JS T: (020) 8891-7271 W: www.richmond.gov.uk

UCL Library Services - Special Collections Library Services, University College, Gower Street, London, WC1E 6BT T: 020 7679 5197 E: spec.coll@ucl.ac.uk W: www.ucl.ac.uk/library/special-coll/

University of Westminster Archive Information Systems & Library Services, 4-12 Little Titchfield Street, London, W1W 7UW T: 020 7911 5000 ext 2524 E: archive@westminster.ac.uk W: www.westminster.ac.uk/about/archive-services

Waltham Forest Archives - L B of Vestry House Museum, Vestry Road, Walthamstow, London, E17 9NH T: 020 8496 4381 E: vhm@walthamforest.gov.uk W: www.walthamforest.gov.uk/archives-local-studies

Wandsworth Heritage Service - L B of Wandsworth Battersea Library, 265 Lavender Hill, London, SW11 1JB T: (020) 8871 7753 E: heritage@wandsworth.gov.uk W: www.wandsworth.gov.uk/heritage

Westminster Abbey Library & Muniment Room Westminster Abbey, London, SW1P 3PA T: 020 7654 4830 E: library@westminster-abbey.org W: www.westminster-abbey.org

Westminster Diocesan Archives 16a Abingdon Road, Kensington, London, W8 6AF T: (020) 7938-3580

Manchester
John Rylands University Library Special Collections Division, 150 Deansgate, Manchester, M3 3EH T: 0161-834-5343 W: www.library.manchester.ac.uk

Manchester Central Library - Archives & Local Studies Manchester Central Library, St Peter's Square, Manchester, M2 5PD T: 0161-234-1979 W: www.manchester.gov.uk/libraries/index.htm

Merseyside
Crosby Library (South Sefton Local History Unit) Crosby Road North, Waterloo, Liverpool, Merseyside L22 0LQ T: 0151 257 6401 E: local-history.south@leisure.sefton.gov.uk W: www.sefton.gov.uk

Huyton Central Library Huyton Library, Civic Way, Huyton, Knowsley, Merseyside L36 9GD T: 0151-443-3738 W: www.knowsley.gov.uk/leisure/libraries/huyton/index.html

Merseyside Maritime Museum Maritime Archives and Library, Albert Dock, Liverpool, Merseyside L3 4AQ T: 0151 478 4424 E: maritime.archives@liverpoolmuseums.org.uk W: www.liverpoolmuseums.org.uk/maritime

Southport Library (North Sefton Local History Unit) - Closed for Refurbishment until 2013 E: local-history.north@leisure.sefton.gov.uk

St Helen's Local History & Archives Library Gamble Institute, Victoria Square, St Helens WA10 1DY T: 01744-456952

Wirral Archives Service Lower Ground Floor, Cheshire Lines Building, Canning Street, Birkenhead, Merseyside CH41 1ND T: 0151 606 2929 E: archives@wirral.gov.uk W: www.wirral.gov.uk/my-services/leisure-and-culture/wirral-archives-service

Methodist

Archives of the Independent Methodist Churches Independent Methodist Resource Centre, Fleet Street, Pemberton, Wigan, WN5 0DS T: 01942 223526 E: archives@imcgb.org.uk W: www.imcgb.org.uk

Connexional Archives for the Methodist Church 33 Harrow View, Harrow, Middlesex HA1 1RE

Methodist - Central Hall Westminster Archives Central Hall Westminster, Storey's Gate, Westminster, London, SW1H 9NH T: 020 7654 3870 W: www.c-h-w.co.uk

Methodist Archives and Research Centre John Rylands University Library, 150 Deansgate, Manchester, M3 3EH T: 0161 834 5343

Middlesbrough

Teesside Archives Exchange House, 6 Marton Rd, Middlesbrough, TS1 1DB T: 01642 248321 E: teesside_archives@middlesbrough.gov.uk W: www.middlesbrough.gov.uk/teessidearchives

Middlesex

Harrow Local History Collection - Civic Centre Library - L B of PO Box 4, Civic Centre, Harrow, Middlesex HA1 2UU T: 020 8424 1055 F: 020 8424 1971 E: localhistory.library@harrow.gov.uk W: www.harrow.gov.uk

Military

National Army Museum Royal Hospital Road, Chelsea, London, SW3 4HT T: 020 7730 0717 E: info@nam.ac.uk W: www.nam.ac.uk

Royal Dragoon Guards Military Museum (4th/7th Royal Dragoon Guards & 5th Royal Inniskilling Dragoon Guards) 3A Tower Street, York YO1 9SB T: 01904 461010 E: hhq@rdgmuseum.org.uk W: www.rdgmuseum.org.uk/

Royal Marines Museum Eastney, Southsea PO4 9PX T: (023) 9281 9385 Exts 224 E: info@royalmarinesmuseum.co.uk W: www.royalmarinesmuseum.co.uk

Suffolk Regiment Archive - closed to the public E: bury.ro@libher.suffolkcc.gov.uk W: www.suffolkcc.gov.uk/sro/

The Kings College London Archives and Liddell Hart Centre for Military Archives King's College London, Strand, London, WC2R 2LS T: 020 7848 2015 E: archives@kcl.ac.uk W: www.kcl.ac.uk/iss/archives

WFR Museum (Sherwood Foresters Collection) Archives RHQ Mercian(Nottingham), Foresters House, Chetwynd Barracks, Chilwell, Nottingham, Nottinghamshire NG9 5HA T: 0115 946 5415 E: curator@wfrmuseum.org.uk W: www.wfrmuseum.org.uk

Norfolk

Kings Lynn Borough Archives The Old Gaol House, Saturday Market Place, Kings Lynn, Norfolk PE30 5DQ T: 01553 774297 E: norfrec@norfolk.gov.uk W: http://archives.norfolk.gov.uk

Norfolk Record Office The Archive Centre, Martineau Lane, Norwich, Norfolk NR1 2DQ T: 01603222599 E: norfrec@norfolk.gov.uk W: http://archives.norfolk.gov.uk

Northamptonshire

Northamptonshire Central Library Abington Street, Northampton, Northamptonshire NN1 2BA T: 01604-462040 E: ns-centlib@northamptonshire.gov.uk W: www.northamptonshire.gov.uk

Northamptonshire Record Office Wootton Hall Park, Northampton, NN4 8BQ T: 01604-762129 W: www.northamptonshire.gov.uk

Northumberland

Berwick upon Tweed Record Office Council Offices, Wallace Green, Berwick-Upon-Tweed TD15 1ED T: 01289 301 865 E: lbankier@woodhorn.org.uk W: www.experiencewoodhorn.com/berwick-record www.northumberland.gov.uk/collections

Friends of Northumberland Archives 6 Brecon Close, Ashington, Northumberland NE63 0HT T: 01670 520350

Northumberland Archives Woodhorn, Northumberland Museum and Archives, Queen Elizabeth II Country Park, Ashington, NE63 9YF T: 01670 528 080 E: collections@woodhorn.org.uk W: www.northumberland.gov.uk/collections www.experiencewoodhorn.com

Nottinghamshire

Manuscripts and Special Collections The University of Nottingham King's Meadow Campus, Lenton Lane, Nottingham, NG7 2NR T: 0115 951 4565 E: mss-library@nottingham.ac.uk W: www.nottingham.ac.uk/mss/

Nottingham Catholic Diocesan Archives Willson House, Derby Road, Nottingham, Nottinghamshire NG1 5AW T: 0115 953 9803 E: archives@nrcdt.org.uk W: www.nottingham-diocese.org.uk

Nottingham Central Library : Local Studies Centre Angel Row, Nottingham, NG1 6HP T: 0115 915 2873 W: www.nottinghamcity.gov.uk/libraries

Nottinghamshire Archives Castle Meadow Road, Nottingham, Nottinghamshire NG2 1AG T: 0115 950 4524 Admin E: archives@nottscc.gov.uk W: www.nottinghamshire.gov.uk/archives

Southwell Minster Library Minster Office, Trebeck Hall, Bishop's Drive, Southwell NG25 0JP T: 01636-812649 W: www.southwellminster.org.uk

Oxfordshire

Oxfordshire Record Office St Luke's Church, Temple Road, Cowley, Oxford OX4 2HT T: 01865 398200 E: archives@oxfordshire.gov.uk W: www.oxfordshire.gov.uk

Plymouth

Plymouth & West Devon Record Office Unit 3, Clare Place, Coxside, Plymouth, Devon PL4 0JW T: 01752-305940 E: pwdro@plymouth.gov.uk W: www.plymouth.gov.uk/archives

Shropshire

Ironbridge Gorge Museum, Library & Archives Coach Road, Coalbrookdale, Telford, TF8 7DQ T: 01952 432141 E: library@ironbridge.org.uk W: www.ironbridge.org.uk

Shropshire Archives Castle Gates, Shrewsbury, Shropshire SY1 2AQ T: 01743 255350 E: archives@shropshire.gov.uk W: www.shropshirearchives.org.uk

Wrekin Local Studies Forum Madeley Library, Russell Square, Telford, Shropshire TF7 5BB T: 01952 586575 W: www.madeley.org.uk

Somerset

Bath & North East Somerset Record Office Guildhall, High Street, Bath, Somerset BA1 5AW T: 01225 477421 E: archives@bathnes.gov.uk W: www.batharchives.co.uk

Somerset Heritage Service: Archives & Local Studies Somerset Heritage Centre, Brunel Way, North Fitzwarren, Taunton, Somerset TA2 6SF T: 01823-337600 Appointments E: archives@somerset.gov.uk W: www.somerset.gov.uk/archives

Staffordshire

Keele University Special Collections & Archives Keele, Staffordshire ST5 5BG T: 01782 583237 E: h.burton@lib.keele.ac.uk W: www.keele.ac.uk/library/specarc/

Lichfield Record Office Lichfield Library, The Friary, Lichfield, Staffordshire WS13 6QG T: 01543 510720 E: lichfield.record.office@staffordshire.gov.uk W: www.staffordshire.gov.uk/archives/

Staffordshire & Stoke on Trent Archive Service - Stoke on Trent City Archives City Central Library, Bethesda Street, Hanley, Stoke on Trent, Staffordshire ST1 3RS T: 01782 238 420 F: 01782 238 499 E: stoke.archives@stoke.gov.uk W: www.staffordshire.gov.uk/archives

Staffordshire Record Office Eastgate Street, Stafford, Staffordshire ST16 2LZ T: 01785 278373 (Bookings) E: staffordshire.record.office@staffordshire.gov.uk W: www.staffordshire.gov.uk/archives

Tamworth Library Corporation Street, Tamworth, Staffordshire B79 7DN T: 01827 475645 E: tamworth.library@staffordshire.gov.uk W: www.staffordshire.gov.uk/leisure/librariesnew/doforyou/discover/local familyhistory/

William Salt Library 19 Eastgate Street, Stafford, Staffordshire ST16 2LZ T: 01785 278372 E: william.salt.library@staffordshire.gov.uk W: www.staffordshire.gov.uk/salt

Suffolk

Bury St Edmunds 77 Raingate Street, Bury St Edmunds IP33 2AR T: 01284 352352 E: bury.ro@libher.suffolkcc.gov.uk W: www.suffolk.gov.uk/LeisureAndCulture/LocalHistoryAndHeritage/SuffolkRecordOffice

Ipswich Gatacre Road, Ipswich IP1 2LQ T: 01473 584541 E: ipswich.ro@libher.suffolkcc.gov.uk W: www.suffolk.gov.uk/LeisureAndCulture/LocalHistoryAndHeritage/SuffolkRecordOffice

Lowestoft The Library, Clapham Road, Lowestoft NR32 1DR T: 01502 405357 W: www.suffolk.gov.uk/LeisureAndCulture/LocalHistoryAndHeritage/SuffolkRecordOffice

Suffolk Regiment Archive - closed to the public E: bury.ro@libher.suffolkcc.gov.uk W: www.suffolkcc.gov.uk/sro/

Surrey
Cranleigh Library and Local History Centre High Street, Cranleigh, Surrey GU6 8AE T: 01483 272413 W: www.surrey.gov.uk
Domestic Buildings Research Group (Surrey) The Ridings, Lynx Hill, East Horsley, Surrey KT24 5AX T: 01483 283917
Epsom and Ewell Local History Centre Bourne Hall, Spring Street, Ewell, Epsom KT17 1UF T: 020 8394 0372 W: www.surrey.gov.uk
Horley Local History Centre Horley Library, Victoria Road, Horley, Surrey RH6 7AG T: 01293 784141 W: www.surrey.gov.uk
North Tandridge Local History Centre Caterham Valley Library, Stafford Rd, Caterham CR3 6JG T: 01883 343580 W: www.surrey.gov.uk
Redhill Centre for Local & Family History Redhill Library, Warwick Quadrant, Redhill, RH1 1NN T: 01737 763332 W: www.surrey.gov.uk
Surrey History Centre Surrey History Centre, 130 Goldsworth Road, Woking, Surrey GU21 6ND T: 01483 518737 E: shs@surreycc.gov.uk W: www.surreycc.gov.uk/surreyhistorycentre

Sussex - East
Brighton History Centre Brighton Museum and Art Gallery, Royal Pavilion Gardens, Brighton, East Sussex BN1 1EE T: 01273 296972 (Enquiries) E: localhistory@brighton-hove.gov.uk W: www.brighton-hove-rpml.org.uk
East Sussex Record Office The Maltings, Castle Precincts, Lewes, East Sussex BN7 1YT T: 01273 482349 E: archives@eastsussex.gov.uk W: www.eastsussex.gov.uk/useourarchives

Sussex - West
West Sussex Record Office County Hall, Chichester, West Sussex PO19 1RN T: 01243 753600 E: records.office@westsussex.gov.uk W: www.westsussex.gov.uk/ro/
Worthing Reference Library Worthing Library, Richmond Road, Worthing, West Sussex BN11 1HD T: 01903 704824 E: worthing.library@westsussex.gov.uk W: www.westsussex.gov.uk/libraries

Tyne and Wear
Gateshead Central Library & Local Studies Department Prince Consort Road, Gateshead, Tyne & Wear NE8 4LN T: 0191 433 8430 E: anthealang@gateshead.gov.uk W: www.gateshead.gov.uk/ls
Newcastle Libraries & Information Service City Library, Charles Avison Building, 33 New Bridge Street West, Newcastle upon Tyne, NE1 8AX T: 0191 277 4100 E: information@newcastle.gov.uk W: www.newcastle.gov.uk/libraries
South Tyneside Central Library - Local Studies Prince Georg Street, South Shields NE33 2PE T: 0191 424 7860 E: localstudies.library@southtyneside.gov.uk W: www.southtyneside.gov.uk
Tyne & Wear Archives Service Blandford House, Blandford Square, Newcastle upon Tyne, Tyne and Wear NE1 4JA T: 0191-232-6789 W: www.tyneandweararchives.org.uk/

Warrington
Warrington Library, Archives & Local Studies Museum Street, Cultural Quarter, Warrington, Cheshire WA1 1JB T: 01925 442 889 E: library@warrington.gov.uk W: www.warrington.gov.uk

Warwickshire
Rugby School Archives Temple Reading Room, Rugby School, Barby Road, Rugby CV22 5DW T: 01788 556227 W: www.rugby-school.warwks.sch.uk
Shakespeare Centre Library & Archive Shakespeare Birthplace Trust, Henley Street, Stratford upon Avon CV37 6QW T: 01789 201816 E: records@shakespeare.org.uk W: www.shakespeare.org.uk
Warwickshire County Record Office Priory Park, Cape Road, Warwick, Warwickshire CV34 4JS T: 01926 738959 E: recordoffice@warwickshire.gov.uk W: www.warwickshire.gov.uk

West Midlands
Birmingham City Archives Floor 7, Central Library, Chamberlain Square, Birmingham, West Midlands B3 3HQ T: 0121 303 4217 E: archives@birmingham.gov.uk W: www.birmingham.gov.uk/archives
Birmingham Roman Catholic Archdiocesan Archives Cathedral House, St Chad's Queensway, Birmingham B4 6EU T: 0121-236-2251 E: archives@rc-birmingham.org W: www.rc-birmingham.org
Birmingham University Library Services - Special Collections Cadbury Research Library, Muirhead Tower, University of Birmingham, Edgbaston, Birmingham B15 2TT T: 0121 414 5838 E: special-collections@bham.ac.uk W: www.special-coll.bham.ac.uk

Coventry City Archives Mandela House, Bayley Lane, Coventry, CV1 5RG T: (024) 7683 2418 W: www.coventry.gov.uk
Dudley Archives & Local History Service Mount Pleasant Street, Coseley, Dudley WV14 9JR T: 01384-812770 W: www.dudley.gov.uk
MLA West Midlands: the Regional Council for Museums, Libraries and archives 2nd Floor, Grosvenor House, 14 Bennetts Hill, Worcestershire B2 5RS T: 01527 872258
Sandwell Community History & Archives Service Smethwick Library, High Street, Smethwick B66 1AA T: 0121 558 2561 E: archives_service@sandwell.gov.uk W: www.archives.sandwell.gov.uk
Solihull Heritage and Local Studies service Solihull Central Library, Homer Road, Solihull B91 3RG T: 0121-704-6977 W: www.solihull.gov.uk/wwwlib/#local
Sutton Coldfield Reference Library - Local Studies Section 45 Lower Parade, Sutton Coldfield B72 1XX T: 0121 464 0164 E: sutton.coldfield.reference.lib@birmingham.gov.uk W: www.birmingham.gov.uk
Walsall Local History Centre Essex Street, Walsall WS2 7AS T: 01922-721305 W: www.walsall.gov.uk/index/leisure_and_culture/localhistorycentre
Wolverhampton Archives & Local Studies Molineux Hotel Building, Whitmore Hill, Wolverhampton, WV1 1SF T: 01902 552 480 E: archives@wolverhampton.gov.uk W: www.wolverhampton.gov.uk/archives

Wiltshire
Salisbury Reference and Local Studies Library Market Place, Salisbury, SP1 1BL T: 01722 411098 W: www.wiltshire.gov.uk
The Swindon Collection Local Studies & Family History, Swindon Central Library, Regent Circus, Swindon SN1 1QG T: 01793 463238 E: central.library@swindon.gov.uk W: www.swindon.gov.uk/libraries
Wiltshire and Swindon Archives Wiltshire & Swindon History Centre, Cocklebury Road, Chippenham SN15 3QN T: 01249 705 513 F: 01249 705 527 E: archives@wiltshire.gov.uk W: www.wshc.eu
Wiltshire Buildings Record The Wiltshire & Swindon History Centre, Cocklebury Road, Chippenham, SN15 3QN T: 01249 705 508 F: 01249 705 527 E: wbr@wiltshire.gov.uk W: www.wiltshire.gov.uk
Wiltshire Studies Library Library & heritage HQ, Bythesea Road, Trowbridge BA14 8BS T: 01225-713732 W: www.wiltshire.gov.uk/community/

Worcestershire
Worcesterhire History Centre History Centre, Trinity Street, Worcester, Worcestershire WR1 2PW T: 01905 765922 E: wlhc@worcestershire.gov.uk W: www.worcestershire.gov.uk/records
Worcestershire Regimental Archives RHQ The Worcestershire & Sherwood Foresters Regiment, Norton Barracks, Worcester, Worcestershire WR5 2PA T: 01905-354359 W: www.wfrmuseum.org.uk

Yorkshire - East
Carnegie Heritage Centre 342 Anlaby Road, Hull, HU3 6JA T: 01482 561 216 E: carnegiehull@hotmail.co.uk W: www.carniegiehull.co.uk
East Yorkshire Archive & Local Studies Service The Treasure House, Champney Road, Beverley HU17 8HE T: 01482 392 790 E: archives.service@eastriding.gov.uk W: www.eastriding.gov.uk/cs/culture-and-information/archives/archivesloc/
Yorkshire - North
North Yorkshire County Record Office Malpas Road, Northallerton, DL7 8TB T: 01609 777585 E: archives@northyorks.gov.uk W: www.northyorks.gov.uk/archives
Ripon Local Studies Centre 42 Market Place, Ripon, North Yorkshire HG4 1BZ T: 01765 692200 W: www.riponlocalstudies.org
Whitby Literary & Philosphical Society, Library and Archives Whitby Museum, Pannett Park, Whitby YO21 1RE T: 01947 602908 E: library@whitbymuseum.org.uk W: www.whitbymuseum.org.uk
Whitby Pictorial Archives Trust Whitby Archives & Heritage Centre, Flowergate, Whitby YO21 3BA T: 01947 821364 W: www.whitbyarchives.org.uk
Yorkshire - South
Barnsley Archives and Local Studies Department Central Library, Shambles Street, Barnsley S70 2JF T: 01226 773950 E: Archives@barnsley.gov.uk W: www.barnsley.gov.uk
Doncaster Archives King Edward Road, Balby, Doncaster, DN4 0NA T: 01302 859811 E: doncaster.archives@doncaster.gov.uk W: www.doncaster.gov.uk
Northern General Hospital Project Clock Tower Reception, Herries Road, Sheffield S5 7AU E: ngh.archives@blueyonder.co.uk
Rotherham Archives & Local Studies Central Library, Walker Place, Rotherham, South Yorkshire S65 1JH T: 01709 823616 E: archives@rotherham.gov.uk W: www.rotherham.gov.uk

Sheffield Archives 52 Shoreham Street, Sheffield S1 4SP T: 0114 203 9395 E: archives@sheffield.gov.uk W: www.sheffield.gov.uk/libraries/archives-and-local-studies
Sheffield Libraries, Archives & Information Surrey Street, Sheffield S1 1XZ T: 0114 273 4753 E: localstudies.library@sheffield.gov.uk W: www.sheffield.gov.uk/libraries/archives-and-local-studies www.picturesheffield.com

Yorkshire - West
John Goodchild Collection Local History Study Centre Below Central Library, Drury Lane, Wakefield WF1 2DT T: 01924-298929
Local & Family History Library Leeds Central Library, Calverley Street, Leeds LS1 3AB T: 0113 247 8290 E: localstudies@leedslearning.net W: www.leeds.gov.uk/localstudies
Wakefield Library Headquarters - Local Studies Department Balne Lane, Wakefield WF2 0DQ T: 01924-302224 W: www.wakefield.gov.uk
West Yorkshire Archive Service - Calderdale Central Library, Northgate, Halifax HX1 1UN T: 01422 392636 E: calderdale@wyjs.org.uk W: www.archives.wyjs.org.uk
West Yorkshire Archive Service - Leeds 2 Chapeltown Road, Sheepscar, Leeds LS7 3AP T: 0113 214 5814 E: leeds@wyjs.org.uk W: www.archives.wyjs.org.uk
West Yorkshire Archive Service - Wakefield Registry of Deeds, Newstead Road, Wakefield, WF1 2DE T: 01924 305980 E: wakefield@wyjs.org.uk W: www.archives.wyjs.org.uk
West Yorkshire Archive Service - Kirklees Central Library, Princess Alexandra Walk, Huddersfield HD1 2SU T: 01484 221966 E: kirklees@wyjs.org.uk W: www.archives.wyjs.org.uk
West Yorkshire Archives - Bradford Bradford Central Library, Princes Way, Bradford BD1 1NN T: 01274 435099 E: bradford@wyjs.org.uk W: www.archives.wyjs.org.uk
Yorkshire Archaeological Society Claremont, 23 Clarendon Rd, Leeds LS2 9NZ T: 0113-245-6342 W: www.yas.org.uk

Yorkshire - York
Borthwick Institute of Historical Research University of York, Heslington, York, YO10 5DD T: 01904 321166 - archives W: www.york.ac.uk/inst/bihr www.york.ac.uk/borthwick
Yorkshire Family History - Biographical Database York Minster Library & Archives, Dean's Park, York, Yorkshire YO1 7JQ T: 01904 625308 Library W: www.yorkminster.org
York Archives & Local History Department York explore, Library Square, Museum Street, York, YO1 7DS T: 01904 552800 E: archives@york.gov.uk W: www.york.gov.uk/libraries

Wales

National
Department of Manuscripts Main Library, University of Wales, College Road, Bangor, Gwynedd LL57 2DG T: 01248-382966
National Monuments Record of Wales Royal Commission on the Ancient & Historical Monuments of Wales, Crown Building, Plas Crug, Aberystwyth T: 01970-621200 E: nmr.wales@rcahmw.org.uk W: www.rcahmw.org.uk
National Monuments Record of Wales Royal Commission - Ancient & Historical Monuments Wales, Crown Building, Plas Crug, Aberystwyth, SY23 1NJ T: 01970 621200 E: nmr.wales@rcahmw.org.uk W: www.rcahmw.org.uk
The National Library of Wales Penglais, Aberystwyth, Ceredigion SY23 3BU T: 01970 632800 E: Enquiries: www.llgc.org.uk/enquire W: www.llgc.org.uk/
National Screen and Sound Archive of Wales Unit 1, Science Park, Aberystwyth SY23 3AH T: 01970 626007 W: http://screenandsound.llgc.org.uk

Anglesey
Anglesey County Archives Service Shirehall, Glanhwfa Road, Llangefni LL77 7TW T: 01248-752080 W: www.anglesey.gov.uk
Carmarthenshire
Carmarthenshire Archive Service Parc Myrddin, Richmond Terrace, Carmarthen, Carmarthenshire SA31 1DS T: 01267 228232 E: archives@carmarthenshire.gov.uk W: www.carmarthenshire.gov.uk
Ceredigion
Archifdy Ceredigion Swyddfa'r Sir, County Offices, Glan y Mor, Marine Terrace, Aberystwyth, SY23 2DE T: 01970-633697 E: archives@ceredigion.gov.uk W: www.archifdy-ceredigion.gov.uk
Conwy
Conwy Archive Service Old Board school, Lloyd Street, Llandudno, Conwy LL30 2YG T: 01492 577 550 E: archifau.archives@conwy.gov.uk W: www.conwy.gov.uk/archives
Denbighshire
Denbighshire Record Office 46 Clwyd Street, Ruthin LL15 1HP T: 01824-708250 E: archives@denbighshire.gov.uk W: www.denbighshire.gov.uk

Flintshire
Flintshire Record Office The Old Rectory, Rectory Lane, Hawarden, Flintshire CH5 3NR T: 01244 532 364 E: archives@flintshire.gov.uk W: www.flintshire.gov.uk/archives
Glamorgan
Aberkenfig Resource Centre Pensioners Hall, Heol Persondy, Aberkenfig, Glamorgan CF32 9RF T: 01656 728 531 E: arc@glamfhs.info W: www.glamfhs.info
Glamorgan Record Office Glamorgan Building, King Edward VII Avenue, Cathays Park, Cardiff, CF10 3NE T: (029) 2078 0282 E: GlamRO@cardiff.ac.uk W: www.glamro.gov.uk
Neath Central Library (Local Studies Department) 29 Victoria Gardens, Neath SA11 3BA T: 01639-620139 W: www.neath-porttalbot.gov.uk
Swansea Central Library Civic Centre, Oystermouth Road, Swansea, SA1 3SN T: 01792 636464 E: libraryline@swansea.gov.uk W: www.swansea.gov.uk/libraries
Gwent
Blaenavon Ironworks Blaenavon Tourist Information Office, North Street, Blaenavon, Gwent NP4 9RQ T: 01495 792615 W: www.btinternet.com~blaenavon.ironworks/pages/genealogy.htm
Gwent Archives Address from May 2011 - see website for details, Steelworks Road, Ebbw Vale, Gwent T: 01633 644886 E: gwent.records@torfaen.gov.uk W: www.gwentarchives.gov.uk
Newport Community Learning and Libraries Newport Central Library, John Frost Square, Newport NP20 1PA T: 01633 656656 E: reference.library@newport.gov.uk W: www.newport.gov.uk
Gwynedd
Archifdy Meirion Swyddfeydd y Cyngor, Cae Penarlag, Dolgellau LL40 2YB T: 01341-424444 W: www.gwynedd.gov.uk/archives/
Caernarfon Area Record Office, Gwynedd Archives Caernarfon Area Record Office, Victoria Dock, Caernarfon, Gwynedd LL55 1SH T: 01286 679095 W: www.gwynedd.gov.uk/adrannau/addysg/archifau
Pembrokeshire
Pembrokeshire Libraries The County Library, Dew Street, Haverfordwest SA61 1SU T: 01437 775248 E: george.edwards@pembrokeshire.gov.uk W: www.pembrokeshire.gov.uk
Pembrokeshire Record Office The Castle, Haverfordwest, SA61 2EF T: 01437 763707 E: record.office@pembrokeshire.gov.uk W: www.pembrokeshire.gov.uk
Tenby Museum Tenby Museum & Art Gallery, Castle Hill, Tenby, SA70 7BP T: 01834-842809 E: info@tenbymuseum.org.uk W: www.tenbymuseum.org.uk
Powys
Crickhowell District Archive Centre CRiC Building, Ty y fro, Beaufort Street, Crickhowell, Powys NP8 1BN T: 01873 810 922 E: archive@crickhowellinfo.org.uk
Powys County Archives Office County Hall, Llandrindod Wells, LD1 5LG T: 01597 826088 E: archives@powys.gov.uk W: http://archives.powys.gov.uk
West Glamorgan
West Glamorgan Archive Service Civic Hall, Oystermouth Road, Swansea SA1 3SN T: 01792-636589 E: westglam.archives@swansea.gov.uk W: www.swansea.gov.uk/westglamorganarchives
West Glamorgan Archive Service - Neath Archives Access Point Neath Mechanics Institute, Church Place, Neath SA11 3BA T: 01639-620139 W: www.swansea.gov.uk/archives
West Glamorgan Archive Service - Port Talbot Access Point Port Talbot Library, 1st Floor, Aberavon Shopping Centre, Port Talbot, SA13 1PB T: 01639 763430 W: www.swansea.gov.uk/archives
Wrexham
Wrexham Archives and Local Studies Service A N Palmer Centre, County Buildings, Regent Street, Wrexham, LL11 1RB T: 01978 317973 E: archives@wrexham.gov.uk localstudies@wrexham.gov.uk W: www.wrexham.gov.uk/archives

Channel Islands
Guernsey Island Archives 29 Victoria Road, St Peter Port, Guernsey GY1 1HU T: 01481 724512
Jersey Archives Service - Jersey Heritage Trust Clarence Road, St Helier, Jersey JE2 4JY T: 01534 833303
Judicial Greffe Morier House, Halkett Place, St Helier, Jersey JE1 1DD T: 01534-502300 E: jgreffe@super.net.uk W: www.jersey.gov.uk

Isle of Man
Manx National Heritage Library Manx Museum, Douglas IM1 3LY T: 01624 648000 E: enquiries@mnh.gov.im W: www.gov.im/mnh

Scotland

National

General Register Office for Scotland New Register House, Edinburgh, EH1 3YT T: 0131 314 4300 (Family History) E: enquiries@scotlandspeoplehub.gov.uk records@gro-scotland.gsi.gov.uk W: www.gro-scotland.gov.uk www.scotlandpeople.gov.uk

Grand Lodge of Scotland Freemasons' Hall, 96 George Street, Edinburgh, EH2 3DH T: 0131 225 5304 E: curator@grandlodgescotland.com W: www.grandlodgescotland.com

National Archives of Scotland HM General Register House, 2 Princes Street, Edinburgh, EH1 3YY T: 0131 535 1334 E: enquiries@nas.gov.uk W: www.nas.gov.uk

National Archives of Scotland - West Search Room West Register House, Charlotte Square, Edinburgh, EH2 4DJ T: 0131 535 1413 E: wsr@nas.gov.uk W: www.nas.gov.uk

National Library of Scotland - Manuscript Collections National Library of Scotland, George IV Bridge, Edinburgh, EH1 1EW T: 0131 623 3876 E: manuscripts@nls.uk W: www.nls.uk

National Register of Archives for Scotland H M General Register House, 2 Princes Street, Edinburgh, EH1 3YY T: 0131 535 1405 E: nra@nas.gov.uk W: www.nas.gov.uk/nras

Royal Commission on the Ancient & Historical Monuments of Scotland John Sinclair House, 16 Bernard Terrace, Edinburgh, EH8 9NX T: 0131 662 1456 E: info@rcahms.gov.uk W: www.rcahms.gov.uk

Scottish Archive Network The National archives of scotland, HM General register House, 2 princes Street, Edinburgh, EH1 3YY T: 0131 535 1314 E: enquiries@scan.org.uk W: www.scan.org.uk www.scottishhandwriting.com

Scottish Brewing Archive Glasgow University Archive Services, 13 Thurso Street, Glasgow, G11 6PE T: 0141 330 5515 E: enquiries@archives.gla.ac.uk W: www.archives.gla.ac.uk/sba/

Scottish Catholic Archives Columba House, 16 Drummond Place, Edinburgh, EH3 6PL T: 0131-5563661 W: www.scottishcatholicarchives.org

Scottish Genealogy Society 15 Victoria Terrace, Edinburgh, EH1 2JL T: 0131-220-3677 E: sales@scotsgenealogy.com W: www.scotsgenealogy.com

Scottish Genealogy Society - Library 15 Victoria Terrace, Edinburgh, EH1 2JL T: 0131-220 3677 E: info@scotsgenealogy.com W: www.scotsgenealogy.com

Scottish Screen Archive Scottish Screen, 1 Bowmont Gardens, Glasgow, G12 9LR T: 0141 337 7400 W: www.scottishscreen.com

Scottish Jewish Archives Centre Garnethill Synagogue, 129 Hill Street, Garnethill, Glasgow, G3 6UB T: 0141 332 4911 W: www.sjac.org.uk

St Andrews University Library - Special Collections Department North Street, St Andrews, Fife KY16 9TR T: 01334 462339 E: speccoll@st-and.ac.uk W: www.st-andrews.ac.uk/specialcollections

Strathclyde University Archives McCance Building, 16 Richmond Street, Glasgow, G1 1XQ T: 0141 548 2397

Heriot-Watt University Museum & Archives Mary Burton Centre, Heriot-Watt University, Edinburgh, EH14 4AS T: 0131 451 3218 E: archive@hw.ac.uk W: www.hw.ac.uk/archive

Aberdeen City

Aberdeen City and Aberdeenshire Archives Aberdeen City Council, Town House, Broad Street, Aberdeen, AB10 1AQ T: 01224 522 513 E: archives@aberdeencity.gov.uk W: www.aberdeencity.gov.uk/archives

Aberdeen City & Aberdeenshire Archives Old Aberdeen House, Dunbar Street, Aberdeen, AB24 3UJ T: 01224 481 775 E: archives@aberdeencity.gov.uk W: www.aberdeencity.gov.uk/archives

Aberdeen Synagogue 74 Dee Street, Aberdeen, AB11 6DS T: 01224 582135

Angus

Angus Archives Hunter Library, Restenneth Priory, By Forfar, Angus DD8 2SZ T: 01307 468644 E: angus.archives@angus.gov.uk W: www.angus.gov.uk/history/default.htm

Argyll

Argyll & Bute District Archives Manse Brae, Lochgilphead, Argyll PA31 8QU T: 01546 604120

Ayrshire

Ayrshire Archives Ayrshire Archives Centre, Craigie Estate, Ayr, Ayrshire KA8 0SS T: 01292 287584 E: archives@south-ayrshire.gov.uk W: www.ayrshirearchives.org.uk

East Ayrshire Council District History Centre & Museum Baird Institute, 3 Lugar Street, Cumnock, Ayrshire KA18 1AD T: 01290 421701 E: Baird.institute@east-ayrshire.gov.uk W: www.east-ayrshire.gov.uk

North Ayrshire Libraries Library Headquarters, 39 - 41 Princes Street, Ardrossan, Ayrshire KA22 8BT T: 01294 469137 W: www.north-ayrshire.gov.uk

Clackmannanshire

Clackmannanshire Archives Alloa Library, 26/28 Drysdale Street, Alloa, Clackmannanshire FK10 1JL T: 01259 722262 E: libraries@clacks.gov.uk W: www.clacksweb.org.uk/dyna/archives

Registrar of Births, Deaths and Marriages - Clackmannanshire Marshill House, Marshill, Alloa FK10 1AB T: 01259 723850

Dumfries & Galloway

Ewart Library Catherine Street, Dumfries, DG1 1JB T: 01387 260285 E: ericaj@dumgal.gov.uk W: www.dgc.gov.uk/service/depts/comres/library/gresearch

Dumfries & Galloway Library and Archives Archive Centre, 33 Burns Street, Dumfries, DG1 1PS T: 01387 269254 W: www.dumgal.gov.uk

Dundee

Dundee City Archives 21 City Square, (callers should first report to City Chambers reception at 18 City Square), Dundee, DD1 3BY T: 01382 434494 E: archives@dundeecity.gov.uk W: www.fdca.org.uk www.dundeecity.gov.uk/archive/routestoyourroots

Dundee City Council - Scottish Family History Centre Wellgate Library, Dundee, DD1 1DB T: 01382 435222 & 01382 431516 E: registrars@dundeecity.gov.uk W: www.dundeecity.gov.uk/supportservs/registrar

Dundee Synagogue St Mary Place, Dundee, DD1 5RB

East Dunbartonshire

East Dunbartonshire Information & Archives William Patrick Library, 2 West High Street, Kirkintilloch G66 1AD T: 0141 777 3142 E: libraries@eastdunbarton.gov.uk W: www.eastdunbarton.gov.uk

East Renfrewshire

East Renfrewshire Record Offices East Renfrewshire District Council, Rouken Glen Road, Glasgow G46 6JF T: 0141 577 4976

Edinburgh

Edinburgh City Archives City Chambers, High St, Edinburgh, EH1 1YJ T: 0131 529 4616

Edinburgh Synagogue 4 Salisbury Road, Edinburgh, EH16 5AB Scotland

Falkirk

Falkirk Library Hope Street, Falkirk, FK1 5AU T: 01324 503605 W: www.falkirk.gov.uk

Falkirk Museum History Research Centre Callendar House, Callendar Park, Falkirk, FK1 1YR T: 01324 503778 E: callendar.house@falkirk.gov.uk W: www.falkirk.gov.uk/services/community/cultural_services/museums/museums_and_archives.aspx

Fife

Fife Council Archive Centre Carleton House, Haig Business Park, Balgonie Road, Markinch, Glenrothes, Fife KY7 6AQ T: 01592 583 352 E: archive.enquiries@fife.gov.uk W: www.fifedirect.org.uk

Glasgow

Glasgow City Archives Mitchell Library, North Street, Glasgow, G3 7DN T: 0141-287-2913 E: archives@cls.glasgow.gov.uk W: www.glasgow.gov.uk/en/Residents/Leisure_Culture/Libraries/Collections/ArchivesandSpecialCollections

Glasgow Jewish Representative Council 222 Fenwick Road, Giffnock, Glasgow, G46 6UE T: 0141 577 8200 E: jrepcouncil@aol.com W: www.j-scot.org/glasgow

Glasgow University Archive Services 13 Thurso Street, Glasgow, G11 6PE T: 0141 330 4159 E: enquiries@archives.gla.ac.uk W: www.archives.gla.ac.uk

Glasgow University Library & Special Collections Department Hillhead Street, Glasgow, G12 8QE T: 0141 330 6704 E: library@lib.gla.ac.uk W: www.gla.ac.uk/library

Royal College of Physicians and Surgeons of Glasgow - Archives 232 - 242 St Vincent Street, Glasgow, G2 5RJ T: 0141 221 6072 E: carol.parry@rcpsg.ac.uk W: www.rcpsg.ac.uk

Highland

North Highland Archive Wick Library, Sinclair Terrace, Wick, KW1 5AB T: 01955 606432

Invernesshire

Highland Archive Service Highland Archive & Registration Centre, Bught Road, Inverness, IV3 5SS T: 01463 265444 E: archives@highland.gov.uk W: www.highlandarchives.org.uk/

Isle of Lewis

Stornoway Record Office Town Hall, 2 CromwellStreet, Stornoway, HS1 2BD T: 01851-709438 E: emacdonald@cne-siar.gov.uk

Lanarkshire

North Lanarkshire - Lenziemill Archives 10 Kelvin Road, Cumbernauld G67 2BA T: 01236 737114 W: www.northlan.gov.uk

South Lanarkshire Council Archives 30 Hawbank Road, College Milton, East Kilbride, South Lanarkshire G74 5EX T: 01355 239193

Midlothian
Midlothian Archives and Local Studies Centre 2 Clerk Street, Loanhead, Midlothian EH20 9DR T: 0131 271 3976 E: local.studies@midlothian.gov.uk W: www.midlothian.gov.uk
Military
Dunkeld Cathedral Chapter House Museum Dunkeld, PH8 0AW T: 01350 728732 E: webmaster@dunkeldcathedral.org.uk W: www.dunkeldcathedral.org.uk
Regimental Museum and Archives of Black Watch Balhousie Castle, Hay Street, Perth, Perthshire PH1 5HR T: 0131 310 8530 E: archives@theblackwatch.co.uk W: www.theblackwatch.co.uk
Scottish Horse Regimental Archives - Dunkeld Cathedral Dunkeld, PH8 0AW T: 01350 727614 E: webmaster@dunkeldcathedral.org.uk
Morayshire
Moray Local Heritage Centre Old East End School, Institution Road, Elgin, Moray IV30 1HS T: 01343 569011 E: heritage@moray.gov.uk W: www.morray.org/localheritage/index
Orkney
Orkney Archives The Orkney Library, Laing Street, Kirkwall, Orkney KWI5 1NW T: 01856-873166 W: www.orkney.gov.uk
Orkney Library The Orkney Library, Laing Street, Kirkwall, Orkney KWI5 1NW T: 01856-873166 W: www.orkney.gov.uk
Perthshire
Perth and Kinross Council Archives A K Bell Library, 2 - 8 York Place, Perth, Perthshire PH2 8EP T: 01738 477012 E: archives@pkc.gov.uk W: www.pkc.gov.uk/archives
Renfrewshire
Renfrewshire Archives Central Library & Museum Complex, High Street, Paisley, Renfrewshire PA1 2BB T: 0141-889-2350 W: www.renfrewshire.gov.uk
Scottish Borders
Scottish Borders Archive & Local History Centre Heritage Hub, Kirkstile, Hawick, Roxburghshire TD9 0AE T: 01750 20842 E: archives@scotborders.gov.uk W: www.heartofhawick.co.uk/heritagehub
Shetland
Shetland Museum & Archives Shetland Museum & Archives, Hay's Dock, Lerwick, Shetland ZE1 0WP T: 01595 695057 W: www.shetlandmuseumandarchives.org.uk
Unst Heritage Centre Haroldswick, Unst, Shetland ZE2 9ED T: 01957 711528
Stirlingshire
Stirling Council Archives 5 Borrowmeadow Road, Stirling, FK7 7UW T: 01786 450745 E: archive@stirling.gov.uk W: www.stirling.gov.uk
West Lothian
West Lothian Council Archives - Archives & Records Centre 9 Dunlop Square, Deans Industrial Esatte, Livingston EH54 8SB T: 01506 773 770 F: 01506 773 775 E: archive@westlothian.gov.uk W: www.westlothian.gov.uk/torism/LibsArch/archives

Northern Ireland
General Register Office of Northern Ireland Oxford House, 49 - 55 Chichester Street, Belfast, BT1 4HL T: (028) 90 252000 E: gro.nisra@dfpni.gov.uk W: www.nidirect.gov.uk
Irish World Heritage Centre 51 Dungannon Road, Coalisland, BT71 4HP T: 028 877 46055 E: info@irish-world.com
Presbyterian Historical Society of Ireland 26 College Green, Belfast, BT1 1LN T: 028 9072 7330 E: phsilibrarian@pcinet.org W: www.presbyterianhistoryireland.com
Public Record Office of Northern Ireland 66 Balmoral Avenue (Please Update), Belfast, BT9 6NY (Please Update) T: 028 9025 5905 (Please Update) E: Ann.McVeigh@dcalni.gov.uk W: www.proni@dcalni.gov.uk
Belfast
Belfast Central Library Belfast Ulster Irish Studies, Royal Avenue, Belfast, BT1 1EA T: (028) 9024 3233 E: sheila.mcclean@librariesni.org.uk W: www.librariesni.org.uk
Belfast Family History & Cultural Heritage Centre 64 Wellington Place, Belfast, BT1 6GE T: (028) 9023 5392 E: office@iwhc.com
County Antrim
Belfast Central Library Belfast Ulster Irish Studies, Royal Avenue, Belfast, BT1 1EA T: (028) 9024 3233 E: sheila.mcclean@librariesni.org.uk W: www.librariesni.org.uk
County Armagh
Armagh Public Library 43 Abbey Street, Armagh, County Armagh BT61 1DY T: 028 37 523 142 E: admin@armaghpubliclibrary.co.uk W: www.armaghrobinsonlibrary.org
County Down
Banbridge Genealogy Services Gateway Tourist Information Centre, 200 Newry Road, Banbridge BT32 3NB T: 028 4062 6369 E: info@banbridgegenealogy.com W: www.banbridgegenealogy.com/

County Londonderry
Derry City Council Heritage & Museum Service Archive & Genealogical Service, Harbour Museum, Harbour Square, Derry, Co Londonderry BT48 6AF T: 028 7137 7331 E: bernadette.walsh@derrycity.gov.uk
Derry Genealogy Centre Harbour Museum, Harbour Square, Londonderry, County Londonderry BT48 6AF T: 028 7137 7331 E: genealogy@derrycity.gov.uk W: www.derry.rootsireland.ie

Ireland
National
Church of Ireland Representative Church Body - Library Representative Church Body Library, Braemor Park, Churchtown, Dublin 14, T: 01 492 3979 E: library@ireland.anglican.org W: www.library@ireland.anglican.org
Garda Historical Society 8 Aisling Close, Ballincollig, County Cork T: +353 86 806 0385 E: J_herlihy@esatclear.ie W: www.esatclear.ie/~ric
Garda Siochana Museum & Archives The Records Tower, Dublin, 2 T: +353 1 6719 597 E: j_herlihy@esatclear.ie W: www.esatclear.ie/~garda/museum.html
Grand Lodge of Ireland Freemasons' Hall, 17 Molesworth Street, Dublin 2, T: +353 01 6760 1337 E: office@freemason.ie W: www.irish-freemasons.org/
Irish Roots Magazine Blackrock, Blessington, County Wicklow T: +353 87 942 7815 E: editor@irishrootsmagazine.com W: www.irishrootsmedia.com
National Archives of Ireland Bishop Street, Dublin 8, T: 353-1-407-2300 E: mail@nationalarchives.ie W: www.nationalarchives.ie
Office of the Chief Herald of Ireland Kildare Street, Dublin 2, Co Dublin T: +353 1 603 0200 E: herald@nli.ie W: www.nli.ie
Registrar General for Ireland Convent Road , Roscommon, Coounty Roscommon T: +353 9 0663 2900 E: gro.groireland.ie W: www.groireland.ie
Registry of Deeds Henrietta Street, Dublin 1, T: +353 1 804 8417 E: declan.ward@prai.ie W: www.landregistry.ie
Valuation Office Irish Life Centre, Lower abbey Street, Dublin 1, T: +353 1 817 1000 E: info@valoff.ie W: www.valoff.ie
County Carlow
Carlow County Library Tullow Street, Carlow, County Carlow T: +353 0 59 917 0094 E: library@carlowcoco.ie
County Cavan
Cavan County Library & Archives Farnham Centre, Farnham Street, Cavan, County Cavan T: +3530 49 437 8500 E: library@cavancoco.ie archives@cavancoco.ie
County Clare
Clare County Archives Clare County Council - Áras Contae an Chláir, New Road, Ennis, Co Clare T: +353 65 684 6414 E: archivesrecords@clarecoco.ie W: www.clarelibrary.ie/eolas/archives/archives_index.htm
Clare Heritage and Genealogical Centre Church Street, Corofin, County Clare T: + 353 65 6837955 E: clareroots@gmail.com W: www.clareroots.com
County Cork
Cork City & County Archives 33a Great William O'Brien Strdeet, Blackpool, Cork City, County Cork T: + 353 (0) 21 450 5876 E: archivist@corkcity.ie W: www.corkarchives.ie
Cork City Ancestral project c/o Cork County Library, Carrigrohane Road, Cork, County Cork T: +353 21 428 5648 E: corkancestry@ireland.com
Mallow Heritage Centre 27/28 Bank Place, Mallow, County Cork T: +353 22 50302 E: mallowheritagecentre@gmail.com W: www.rootsireland.ie/
County Donegal
Donegal Ancestry Centre The Quay, Ramleton, County Donegal T: +353 74 915 1266 E: info@donegalancestry.com W: www.donegalancestry.com
Donegal County Archives Cultural Services, 3 Rivers Centre, Lifford, County Donegal T: + 00353 74 72490 E: archivist@donegalcoco.ie W: www.donegal.ie
Donegal Local Studies Centre Central Library & Arts Centre, Oliver Plunkett Road, Letterkenny, County Donegal T: 00353 74 24950 E: Portal@donegalcoco.ie W: www.donegal.ie/library
County Dublin
Dun Laoghaire Heritage & Genealogy Centre Craft Courtyard, Marlay Park, Rathfarnham, County Dublin T: +353 1 204 7264 E: cmalone@dlrcoco.ie W: www.dlrcoco.ie/library/lhistory.htm
Fingal Genealogy / North Dublin - Swords Historical Society Ltd Carnegie Library, North Street, Swords, County Dublin T: +353 1 840 3629 E: swordsheritage@eircom.net fingalgenealogy@gmail.com W: www.rootsireland.ie

County Limerick
Limerick City Archives Limerick City Council, Merchant's Quay, Limerick, County Limerick T: +353 61 407293 E: archives@limerickcity.ie W: www.limerickcity.ie/
Limerick Genealogy Lissanalta House, Dooradoyle Road, Limerick, County Limerick T: +353 61 496 542 E: research@limerickgenealogy.com W: www.limerickgenealogy.com
Limerick Studies Lissanalta House, Dooradoyle Road, Limerick, T: +353 61 496 526 E: limerickstudies@limerickcoco.ie W: www.limerickcoco.ie
County Longford
Longford Genealogy 17 Dublin Street, Longford, County Longford T: +353 43 334 1235 E: longroot@iol.ie
County Louth
Louth County Archive Service Old Gaol, Ardee Road, Dundalk, County Louth T: + 353 (0)42 933 9387 E: archive@louthcoco.ie W: www.louthcoco.ie/
Louth County Reference Library Roden Place, Dundalk, County Louth T: +353 42 933 5457 E: referencelibary@louthcoco.ie
County Mayo
Local Record Offices The Registration Office, New Antrim Street, Castlebar, Co Mayo T: 094-23249
Mayo North Family History Research Centre Enniscoe, Castlehill, Ballina, County Mayo T: + 353 96 31809 E: normayo@iol.ie W: www.mayo.irish-roots.net
Mayo South Family Research Centre Main Street, Ballinrobe, County Mayo T: +353 94 954 1214 E: soumayo@iol.ie W: http://mayo.irishroots.net/
County Meath
Meath Heritage Town Hall, Castle Street, Trim, County Meath T: +353 46 943 6633 E: meathhc@iol.ie
County Offaly
Irish Midlands Ancestry Bury Quay, Tullamore, County Offaly T: +353 506 21421 E: info@offalyhistory.com
County Roscommon
Roscommon Heritage & Genealogical Centre Church Street, Strokestown, County Roscommon T: +353 71 963 3380 E: info@roscommonroots.com W: www.roscommonroots.com
County Sligo
Sligo Heritage & Genealogy Society Aras Reddan, Temple Street, Sligo, County Sligo T: +353 71 914 3728 E: heritagesligo@eircom.net
County Tipperary
Excel Heritage Centre Mitchell Street, Tipperary Town, County Tipperary T: +353 628 0555/6 E: See website W: www.tfhr.org
Tipperary North Genealogy Centre The Governor's House, Kickham Street, Nenagh, County Tipperary T: +353 673 3850 E: tipperarynorthgenealogy@eircom.net
Tipperary South Bru Boru Cultural Centre Rock of Cashel, Cashel, County Tipperary T: +353 62 61122 E: info@bruboru.ie
County Waterford
Waterford Archives & Local Records St Joseph's Hospital, Dungarvan, County Waterford T: 058-42199 E: dungarvanlibrary@waterfordcoco.ie
Waterford Heritage Services St Patrick's Church, Jenkin's Lane, Waterford, County Waterford T: +353 51 876 123 E: mnoc@iol.ie
County Westmeath
Athlone - Westmeath County Library - Local Studies Athlone Civic offices, Church Avenue, Athlone, County Westmeath T: +353 90 644 2157 E: athlib@westmeathcoco.ie W: www.westmeathcoco.i
Dun na Si Heritage Centre Knockdomney, Moate, County Westmeath T: +353 90 648 1183 E: dunnasimoate@eircom.net
Mullingar - Westmeath County Library - Local Studies County Buildings, Mount Street, Mullingar, County Westmeath T: +353 44 933 2161 E: mgarlib@westmeathcoco.ie
County Wicklow
Wicklow Family History Centre Wicklow Historic Gaol, Kilmantin Hill, Wicklow, County Wicklow T: +353 404 20126 E: wfh@eircom.net W: www.wicklow.ie/familyhistorycentre
Dublin
Dublin City Archives City Assembly House, 58 South William Street, Dublin, 2 T: (01)-677-5877 E: cityarchives@dublincity.ie
Dublin City Library & Archive 138 - 142 Pearse Street, Dublin, 2 T: 353 1 674 4999 E: dublinstudies@dublincity.ie cityarchives@dublincity.ie W: www.dublincity.ie/living_in_the_city/libraries/heritage_and_history/

Australia
Australian Capital Territory
National Archives of Australia PO Box 7425, Canberra Business Centre, Canberra, ACT 2610 T: 61 2 6212 3900 E: ref@naa.gov.au W: www.naa.gov.au
New South Wales
National Archives of Australia - Sydney Office 120 Miller Road, Chester Hill, Sydney, NSW 2162 T: 02-96450-100 W: www.naa.gov.uk
State Archives Office 2 Globe Street, Sydney NSW 2000 T: 02-9237-0254
State Library of New South Wales Macquarie Street, Sydney NSW 2000 T: 02-9230-1414 W: www.slsw.gov.au
Northern Territories
Australian Archives - Northern Territories Kelsey Crescent, Nightcliffe, Northern Territories 810 T: 08-8948-4577
Queensland
National Archives of Australia - Queensland 996 Wynnum Road, Cannon Hill, QLD 4170 T: 07-3249-4226 W: www.naa.gov.au
Queensland State Archives PO Box 1397, Sunnybanks Hills, Brisbane QLD 4109 T: 61-7-3875-8755 W: www.archives.qld.gov.au
South Australia
Australian Archives - South Australia 11 Derlanger Avenue, Collingwood, South Australia 5081 T: 08-269-0100
South Australia State Archives PO Box 1056, Blair Athol West, South Australia 5084 T: 08-8226-8000
Tasmania
National Archives of Australia - Hobart Office 4 Rosny Hill Road, Rosny Park, Tasmania 7018 T: 03-62-440101 W: www.naa.gov.au
State Archives, The Archives Office of Tasmania, 77 Murray Street, Hobart, Tasmania 7000 T: (03)-6233-7488 W: www.tased.edu.au/archives
Victoria
Bendigo Regional Genealogical Society Inc PO Box 1049, Bendigo, Victoria 3552
National Archives of Australia - Victoria PO Box 8005, Burwood Heights, Victoria 3151 T: 03-9285-7900
Victoria State Archives 57 Cherry Lane, Laverton North, Victoria 3028 T: 03-9360-9665
Victoria State Archives Level 2 Casselden Place, 2 Lonsdale Street, Melbourne, Victoria 3000 T: 03-9285-7999
Victoria State Archives State Offices, Corner of Mair & Doveton Streets, Ballarat, Victoria 3350 T: 03-5333-6611
Western Australia
Australian Archives - Western Australia 384 Berwick Street East, Victoria Park, Western Australia 6101 T: 09-470-7500
State Archives and Public Record Office Alexander Library, Perth Cultural Centre, Perth, Western Australia 6000 T: 09-427-3360
New Zealand
Archives New Zealand PO Box 12-050, 10 Mulgrave St Thorndon, Wellington, T: 04 499 5595 E: reference@archives.govt.nz W: www.archives.govt.nz
Canada
Maritime History Archive Memorial University of Newfoundland, St Johns, Newfoundland A1C 5S7 T: ++709-737-8428W: www.mun.ca/mha/
National Archives of Canada 395 Wellington Street, Ottawa, Ontario K1A 0N3 T: 613-996-7458 W: http://www.archives.ca
Manitoba
Hudson's Bay Company Archives 200 Vaughan Street, Winnipeg, Manitoba R3C 1T5 T: 204-945-4949 W: www.gov.mb.ca/chc/archives/hbca/index.html
Manitoba Provincial Archives 200 Vaughan Street, Winnepeg, Manitoba R3C 1T5 T: 204-945-4949
New Brunswick
Archives & Special Collections PO Box 7500, Fredericton, New Brunswick E3B 5H5 T: 506-453-4748
Loyalist Collection & Reference Department PO Box 7500, Fredericton, New Brunswick E3B 5H5 T: 506-453-4749
New Brunswick Provincial Archives PO Box 6000, Fredericton, New Brunswick E3B 5H1 T: 506-453-2122 W: www.gov.nb.ca/supply/archives
Newfoundland
Newfoundland & Labrador Archives Colonial Building, Military Road, St Johns, Newfoundland A1C 2C9 T: 709-729-0475
Nova Scotia
Nova Scotia State Archives 6016 University Avenue, Halifax, Nova Scotia B3H 1W4 T: 902-424-6060
Yarmouth County Museums & Archives 22 Collins Street, Yarmouth, Nova Scotia B5A 3C8 T: (902)-742-5539 W: www.ycn.library.ns.ca/museum/yarcomus.htm
Ontario
Archives of Ontario Unit 300, 77 Grenville Street, Toronto, Ontario M5S 1B3 T: 416 327 1582 E: reference@archives.gov.on.ca W: www.gov.on.ca/MCZCR/archives
Prince Edward Island
Public Archives & Record Office PO Box 1000, Charlottetown, Prince Edward Island C1A 7M4 T: 902 368 4290 E: archives@gov.pe.ca W: www.gov.pe.ca/cca/
Quebec
Archives Nationales PO Box 10450, Sainte Foy, Quebec G1V 4N1 T: 418-643-8904
Saskatchewan
Saskatchewan Archives Board - Regina 3303 Hillsdale Street, Regina, Saskatchewan S4S 0A2 T: 306-787-4068 W: www.gov.sk.ca/govt/archives
Saskatchewan Archives Board - Saskatoon Room 91, Murray Building, University of Saskatchewan, 3 Campus Drive, Saskatoon, Saskatchewan S7N 5A4 T: 306-933-5832 W: www.gov.sk.ca/govt/archives
South Africa
National Archives Private Bag X236, Pretoria, 1 T: ++ 323 5300

Cape Town Archives Repository Private Bag X9025, Cape Town, 8000 T: 021-462-4050

Dutch Reformed Church Archive PO Box 398, Bloemfontein, 9301 T: 051-448-9546

Dutch Reformed Church Records Office PO Box 649, Pietermaritzburg, 3200 T: 0331-452279 F: 0331-452279

Free State Archives Repository Private Bag X20504, Bloemfontein, 9300 T: 051 522 6762 F: 051 522 6765

South African Library-National Reference & Preservation P O Box 496, Cape Town, 8000 T: 021 246320 F: 021 244848

Namibia

National Archives of Namibia Private Bag, Windhoek, 13250 T: 061 293 4386 W: http://www.grnnet.gov.na/

Zimbabwe

National Archives of Zimbabwe Hiller Road, off Borrowdale Road, Gunhill, Harare, T: 792741/3

Europe

Belgium

In Flanders Fields Museum Lakenhallen, Grote Markt 34, Ieper, B-8900 T: 00-32-(0)-57-22-85-84 W: www.inflandersfields.be

Archives de l'Etat a Liege 79 rue du Chera, Liege, B-4000 T: 04 252 0393

De Kerk van Jezus Christus van den Heiligen Der Laaste Dagen, Kortrijkse Steenweg 1060, Sint-Deniss-Westrem, B-9051 T: 09 220 4316

Provinciebestuur Limburg Universititslaan 1, Afdeling 623 Archief, Hasselt, B-3500

Rijks Archief te Brugge Academiestraat 14, Brugge, 8000 T: 050 33 7288

Rijksarchief Kruibekesteenweg 39/1, Beveren, B-9210 T: 03 775 3839

Staatsarchiv in Eupen Kaperberg 2-4, Eupen, B-4700 T: 087 55 4377

Stadsarchief te Veurne Grote Markt 29, Veurne, B-8630 T: 058 31 4115

The Passchendaele Archives Jan Van der Fraenen, Ieperstraat 5, Zonnebeke, B - 8980 E: archives@passchendaele.be W: www.passchendaele.be

Cyprus

Cyprus Center of Medievalism & Heraldry P O Box 80711, Piraeus,Greece 185 10 T: 42 26 356

Denmark

Association of Local History Archives P O Box 235, Enghavevej 2, Vejle, DK-7100 W: www.lokalarkiver.dk

Cadastral Archives Rentemestervej 8, Copenhagen NV, DK-2400 W: www.kms.min.dk

Danish Data Archive Islandsgade 10, Odense C, DK-5000 W: www.dda.dk

Danish Emigration Archives P O Box 1731, Arkivstraede 1, Aalborg, DK-9100 T: 045 9931 4221 W: www.cybercity.dk/users/ccc13656

Danish National Archives Rigsdagsgaarden 9, Copenhagen, DK-1218 T: 45 3392 3310 W: www.sa.dk/ra/uk/uk.htm

Danish Society for Local History Colbjornsensvej 8, Naerum, DK-2850

Det Kongelige Bibliotek POB 2149, Copenhagen K, DK-1016 T: 045 3393 0111

Frederiksberg Municipal Libraries Solbjergvej 21-25, Frederiksberg, DK-2000 W: www.fkb.dk

Kobenhavns Stadsarkiv Kobenhavns Radhus, Kobenhavn, DK01599 T: 3366 2374

National Business Archives Vester Alle 12, Aarhus C, DK-8000 T: 45 8612 8533 E: mailbox@ea.sa.dk W: www.sa.dk/ea/engelsk.htm

Provincial Archives for Funen Jernbanegade 36, Odense C, DK-5000 T: 6612 5885 W: www.sa.dk/lao/default.htm

Provincial Archives for Nth Jutland Lille Sct. Hansgade 5, Viborg, DK-8800 T: 45 8662 1788 W: www.sa.dk/lav/default.htm

Provincial Archives for Southern Jutland Haderslevvej 45, Aabenraa, DK-6200 T: 45 7462 5858 W: www.sa.dk/laa/default.htm

Provincial Archives for Zealand etc Jagtvej 10, Copenhagen, DK-2200 W: www.sa.dk/lak.htm

Royal Library Christains Brygge 8, Copenhagen K, DK-1219 W: www.kb.dk

State Library Universitetsparken, Aarhus C, DK-8000 T: 45 8946 2022 W: www.sb.aau.dk/english

Finland

Institute of Migration Piispankatu 3, Turku, 20500 T: 2 231 7536 W: www.utu.fi/erill/instmigr/

France

Centre d'Accueil et de Recherche des Archives Nationales 60 rue des Francs Bourgeois, Paris Cedex, 75141 T: 1 40 27 6000

Centre des Archives d'Outre-Mer 29 Chemin du Moulin de Testas, Aix-en-Provence, 13090

Service Historique de l'Armee de l'Air Chateau de Vincennes, Vincennes Cedex, 94304

Service Historique de l'Armee de Terre BP 107, Armees, 481

Service Historique de la Marine Chateau de Vincennes, Vincennes Cedex, 94304

France Military (Army)

Service Historique De L'Armee De Terre Fort de Vincennes, Boite Postale 107, 00481 ARMEES T: 01 4193 34 44

France Military (Navy)

Service Historique De La Marine Chateau de Vincennes, Boite Postale 2, 00300 ARMEES T: 01 43 28 81 50

Germany

Herold - Verein fur Genealogie Heraldik und Reiwandte Wissen-Scahaften Archiv Str. 12-14, Berlin, D -14195

Historic Emigration Office Steinstr. 7, Hamburg, (D) 20095 T: 4940 300 51 282 W: users.cybercity.dk/gccc13652/addr/ger_heo.htm

Research Centre Lower Saxons in the USA Postfach 2503, Oldenburg, D-2900 T: 0441 798 2614 W: www.uni-oldenburg.de/nausa

The German Emigration Museum Inselstrasse 6, Bremerhaven, D-2850 T: 0471 49096

Zentralstelle fur Personen und Familiengeschichte Birkenweg 13, Friedrichsdorf, D-61381 T: 06172 78263 W: www.genealogy.com/gene/genealogy.html

Zentralstelle fur Personnen und Familiengeschichte Birkenweg 13, Friedrichsdorf, D - 61381

Greece

Cyprus Center of Medievalism & Heraldry P O Box 80711, Piraeus, Greece 185 10 T: 42 26 356

Liechtenstein

Major Archives, Record Offices & Libraries W: www.genealogy.com/gene/reg/CH/lichts.html

Netherlands

Amsterdam Municipal Archives P O 51140, Amsterdam, 1007 EC

Brabant-Collectie Tilburg University Library, P O Box 90153, Warandelaan, Tilburg, NL-5000 LE T: 0031 134 662127

Gemeentelijke Archiefdienst Amersfoort P O Box 4000, Amersfoort, 3800 EA T: 033 4695017

Het Utrechts Archief Alexander Numankade 199/201, Utrecht, 3572 KW T: 030 286 6611

Rijksarchief in Drenthe P O Box 595, Assen, 9400 AN T: 0031 592 313523 W: obd-server.obd.nl/instel/enderarch/radz.htm

Rijksarchief in Overijssel Eikenstraat 20, Zwolle, 8021 WX T: 038 454 0722 W: www.obd.nl/instel/arch/rkarch.htm

Zealand Documentation CTR P O Box 8004, Middelburg, 4330 EA

Norway

Norwegian Emigration Centre Strandkaien 31, Stavanger, 4005 T: 47 51 53 88 63 W: www.emigrationcenter.com

Poland

Head Office, State Archives Ul Dluga6 Skr, Poczt, Warsaw, 1005 00-950

Russia

Russian State Military Historical Archive 2 Baumanskaya 3, 107864, Moscow, T: 7 (095) 261-20-70

St Petersburg

Russian State Historical Archive (RGIA) Naberejnaya 4 (English Embankment), 1900000 St Petersburg, T: 7 (812) 315-54-35

Spain

Archivo Historico National Serrano 115, Madrid 28006 T: 261 8003

Instituucion Fernando el Catolico Plaza de Espagna 2, Zaragoza, Spain 50071 T: 09 7628 8878

Sweden

City & Provincial Archives Box 22063, Stockholm, S-104 22 T: 8 508 283 00

House of Emigrants Box 201, Vaxjo, S-351 04 T: 470 201 20

Kinship Centre Box 331, Karlstad, S-651 08 T: 54 107720

Military Archives Banergatan 64, Stockholm, S-115 88 T: 8 782 41 00

National Archives Box 12541, Stockholm, S-102 29 T: 8 737 63 50

Orebro Stadsarkiv Box 300, Orebro, S-701 35 T: 19 21 10 75

Provincial Archive Arkivvagen 1, Ostersund, S-831 31 T: 63 77 64 00 E: landsarkivet@landsarkivet-ostersund.ra.se W: www.statensarkiv.se/ola/

Provincial Archive Visborgsgatan 1, Visby, 621 57 T: 498 2129 55

Provincial Archive Box 126, Vadstena, S-592 23 T: 143 130 30

Provincial Archive Box 135, Uppsala, SE-751 04 T: 18 65 21 00

Provincial Archive Box 2016, Lund, S-220 02 T: 046 197000 E: landsarkivet@landsarkivet-lund.ra.se

Provincial Archive Box 161, Harnosand, S-871 24 T: 611 835 00 E: landsarkivet@landsarkivet-harnosand.ra.se W: www.ra.se/hla

Provincial Archive Box 19035, Goteborg, S-400 12 T: 31 778 6800

Switzerland

Archives Canonales Vaudoises Rue de la Mouline 32, Chavannes-pres-Renens, CH 1022 T: 021 316 37 11

Staatsarchiv Appenzell Ausserhoden Obstmarkt 1, Regierungsgebaede, Herisau, CH-9100 T: 071 353 6111 W: www.ar.ch/staatsarchiv

Staatsarchiv des Kantons Basel-Landschaft Wiedenhubstrasse 35, Liestal, 4410 T: 061 921 44 40 W: www.baselland.ch

Staatsarchiv des Kantons Solothurn Bielstrasse 41, Solothurn, CH-4509 T: 032 627 08 21

Staatsarchiv Luzern Postfach 7853, Luzern, 6000 T: 41 41 2285365 W: www.staluzern.ch

Geneva

Archives d'Etat 1 Rue de l'Hotel de Ville, Case Postale 164, Geneve 3, T: 41 21 319 33 95

Lausanne

Archives De La Ville De Lausanne Rue de Maupas 47, Case Postale CH-1000, Lausanne 9, T: 41 21 624 43 55

Ukraine

Odessa

Odessa State Archive 18 Shukovskovo Street, Odessa, 270001

Registrars of Births Marriages and Deaths

In previous editions of *The Family and Local History Handbook* these listings have been created using the traditional County names. However many Unitary Authorities insist that listings are alphabetical in accordance with their names. These lists has been compiled from Official Listing Information. With Local Government Reorganisation in 2010 it is noticeable that many Local Authorities have amalgamated and centralised their Registration Services since our last edition.

The General Register Office Room E201, Trafalgar Road, Birkdale, Southport, PR8 2HH T: 0845 603 7788 W: www.direct.gov.uk/gro

England

Barnsley Bernslai Close, Barnsley, South Yorkshire S70 2HS T: 01226 773 090

Bath & North East Somerset The Register Office, The Guildhall, High Street, Bath, BA1 5AW T: 01225 477234

Bedfordshire
Bedfordshire Pilgrim Centre, 20 Brickhill Drive, Bedford, Bedfordshire MK41 7PZ T: 01234 290450

Luton The Register Office, 6 George Street West, Luton, LU1 2BJ T: 01582 722603

Berkshire
Bracknell Forest Easthampstead House, Town Square, Bracknell, Berkshire RG12 1AQ T: 01344 352027

Reading The Register Office, Yeomanry House, 131 Castle Hill, Reading, Berkshire RG1 7TA T: 0118 901 5120

Slough Slough Register Office, The Centre, Farnham Road, Slough, Berkshire SL1 4UT T: 01753 787600

Windsor & Maidenhead Town Hall, St Ives Road, Maidenhead, Berkshire SL6 1RF T: 01628 796422

Wokingham The Old School, Reading Road, Wokingham, Berkshire RG41 1RJ T: 0118 978 2514

Birmingham Birmingham Register Office, Holliday Wharf, Holliday Street, Birmingham, B1 1TJ T: 0121 675 1000

Blackburn with Darwen The Register Office, King George's Hall, Northgate, Blackburn, Lancashire BB2 1AA T: 01254 588660

Blackpool The Register Office, South King Street, Blackpool, Lancashire FY1 4AX T: 01253 477177

Bolton The Register Office, Mere Hall, Merehall Street, Bolton, Lancashire BL1 2QT T: 01204 331185

Bournemouth The Register Office, The Town Hall, Bourne Avenue, Bournemouth, BH2 6DY T: 01202 454945

Bracknell Forest Easthampstead House, Town Square, Bracknell, Berkshire RG12 1AQ T: 01344 352027

Bradford & Keighley The Register Office, 22 Manor Row, Bradford, West Yorkshire BD1 4QR T: 01274 432151

Brighton & Hove Brighton Town Hall, Bartholomews, Brighton, BN1 1JA T: 01273 292016

Bristol The Register Office, The Old Council House, Corn Street, Bristol, BS1 1JG T: 0117 903 8888

Buckinghamshire Buckinghamshire Registration Office, County Offices, Walton Street, Aylesbury, Buckinghamshire HP20 1XF T: 0845 370 8090

Bury Town Hall, Manchester Road, Bury, Lancashire BL9 0SW T: 0161 253 6026

Calderdale The Register Office, Spring Hall, Huddersfield Road, Halifax, West Yorkshire HX3 0AQ T: 01484 221 030

Cambridgeshire Shire Hall, Castle Hill, Cambridgeshire, Cambridgeshire CB3 0AP T: 034 5045 5200

Cambridgeshire - Cambridge Castle Lodge, Shire Hall, Castle Hill, Cambridge, Cambridgeshire CB3 0AP T: 01223 717401

Cambridgeshire - Peterborough The Lawns, 33 Thorpe Road, Peterborough, Cambridgeshire PE3 6AB T: 01733 566323

Cheshire
Chester West Goldsmith House, Goss Street, Chester, Cheshire CH1 2BG T: 01244 602668

Halton The Register Office, Heath Road, Runcorn, Cheshire WA7 5TN T: 0151 471 7635

Warrington The Register Office, Museum Street, Warrington, Cheshire WA1 1JX T: 01925 442762

Cheshire East The Register Office, Delamere House, Chester Street, Crewe, Cheshire CW1 2LL T: 0800 387491

City of Bristol The Register Office, The Old Council House, Corn Street, Bristol, BS1 1JG T: 0117 903 8888

City of London The Register Office, Islington Town Hall, Upper Street, Islington, London, N1 2UD T: (020) 7527 6347

Cornwall
Cornwall Dalvenie House, New County Hall, Truro, Cornwall TR1 3AY T: 01872 322007

County Durham Cockton House, 35 Cockton Hill Road, Bishop Auckland, Durham DL14 6HS T: 01388 607277

Coventry The Register Office, Cheylesmore Manor House, Manor House Drive, Coventry CV1 2ND T: (024) 7683 3141

Cumbria
Barrow-in-Furness Nan Tait Centre, Abbey Road, Barrow-in-Furness, Cumbria LA14 1LG T: 01229 894510

Carlisle The Register Office, 23 Portland Square, Carlisle, Cumbria CA1 1PE T: 01228 607432

Cockermouth The Register Office, Fairfield, Station Road, Cockermouth, Cumbria CA13 9PT T: 01900 325960

Kendal The Register Office, County Offices, Kendal, Cumbria LA9 4RQ T: 01539 773567

Millom The Millom Council Centre, St Georges Road, Millom, Cumbria LA18 4DD T: 01229 772357

Penrith The Register Office, Friargate, Penrith, Cumbria CA11 7XR T: 01768 242120

Ulverston Town Hall, Queen Street, Ulverston, Cumbria LA12 7AR T: 01229 894170

Whitehaven College House, Flatt Walks, Whitehaven, Cumbria CA28 7RW T: 01946 852690

Wigton Wigton Registry Office, Station Road, Wigton, Cumbria CA7 9AH T: 016973 66117

Darlington The Register Office, Backhouse Hall, Bull Wynd, Darlington, County Durham DL1 5RG T: 01325 346604

Derby The Register Office, Royal Oak House, Market Place, Derby, Derbyshire DE1 3AR T: 01332 256526

Derbyshire
Amber Valley The Register Office, Market Place, Ripley, Derbyshire DE5 3BT T: 01773 841380

Ashbourne Town Hall, Market Place, Ashbourne, Derbyshire DE6 1ES T: 01335 300575

Bakewell The Register Office, Town Hall, Bakewell, Derbyshire DE45 1BW T: 01629 812261

Chesterfield The Register Office, New Beetwell Street, Chesterfield, Derbyshire S40 1QJ T: 01246 234754

Erewash The Register Office, 87 Lord Haddon Road, Ilkeston, Derbyshire DE7 8AX T: 0115 932 1014

South Derbyshire The Register Office, Royal Oak House, Market Place, Derby, DE1 3AR T: 01332 256526

Derbyshire - High Peak Town Hall, New Mills, High Peak, Derbyshire SK22 4AT T: 01457 852 425

Devon The Register Office, Castle Street, Exeter, Devon EX4 3PQ T: 0845 155 1002

Doncaster The Register Office, Elmfield Park, Doncaster, South Yorkshire DN1 2EB T: 01302 364922

Dorset Dorset Register Office, Colliton Annexe, County Hall, Dorchester, Dorset DT1 1XJ T: 01305 225 153

Dudley Priory Hall, Priory Park, Dudley, West Midlands DY1 4EU T: 01384 815373

East Sussex Eastbourne Town Hall, Grove Road, Eastbourne, East Sussex BN21 4UG T: 01323 415051

Essex
Brentwood The Register Office, 1 Seven Arches Road, Brentwood, Essex CM14 4JG T: 01277 233565

Southend-on-Sea Civic Centre, Victoria Avenue, Southend-on-Sea, Essex SS2 6ER T: 01702 534351

Thurrock The Register Office, Thameside Complex, Orsett Road, Grays, Essex RM17 5DX T: 01375 375245

Gateshead Civic Centre, Regent Street, Gateshead, Tyne and Wear NE8 1HH T: 0191 433 3000

Gloucestershire The Register Office, St Georges Road, Cheltenham, Gloucestershire GL50 3EW T: 01242 532455

Hampshire -Winchester The Register Office, 6Station Hill, Winchester, Hampshire SO23 8TJ T: 01962 869608

Hartlepool
Hartlepool The Register Office, Raby Road, Hartlepool, TS24 8AF T: 01429 236369 E: registrar@hartlepool.gov.uk

Herefordshire - Hereford Town Hall, St Owen Street, Hereford, Herefordshire HR1 2PJ T: 01432 260565

Hertfordshire - Hatfield The Register Office, 19b St Albans Road East, Hatfield, Hertfordshire AL10 0NG T: 01707 283920

Isle of Wight Seaclose Offices, Fairlee Road, Newport, Isle of Wight PO30 2QS T: 01983 823233

Kent - Medway Medway Register Office, Northgate, Rochester, Kent ME1 1LS T: 01634 338899

Kent The Archbishop's Palace, Palace Gardens, Mill Street, Maidstone, Kent ME15 6YE T: 01622 701922

Kingston-upon-Hull - Hull Municipal Offices, 181-191 George Street, Kingston Upon Hull, HU1 3BY T: 01482 615401
Kingston-upon-Thames - London Borough
Kingston upon Thames The Register Office, 35 Coombe Road, Kingston upon Thames, Surrey KT2 7BA T: (020) 8547 4600
Kirklees - Dewsbury The Register Office, Wellington Street, Dewsbury, West Yorkshire WF13 1LY T: 01924 324808
Kirklees - Huddersfield Town Hall, Ramsden Street, Huddersfield, West Yorkshire HD1 2TA T: 01484 221030
Knowsley District Council Offices, High Street, Prescot, Merseyside L34 3LH T: 0151 443 5210
Lancashire
Blackburn with Darwen The Register Office, King George's Hall, Northgate, Blackburn, Lancashire BB2 1AA T: 01254 588660
Blackpool The Register Office, South King Street, Blackpool, Lancashire FY1 4AX T: 01253 477177
Lancashire The Register Office, PO Box 24, Bow Lane, Preston, Lancashire PR1 8SE T: 0845 053 0021
Lancashire - Bolton The Register Office, Mere Hall, Merehall Street, Bolton, Lancashire BL1 2QT T: 01204 331185
Lancashire - Bury Town Hall, Manchester Road, Bury, Lancashire BL9 0SW T: 0161 253 6026
Lancashire - Oldham Chadderton Town Hall, Middleton Road, Chadderton, Oldham, Lancashire OL9 6PP T: 0161 678 0137
Lancashire - Rochdale Town Hall, The Esplanade, Rochdale, Lancashire OL16 1AB T: 01706 924783
Leeds Leeds Register Office, Leeds Town Hall, The Headrow, Leeds, West Yorkshire LS1 3AD T: 0113 224 3603
Leicester The Town Hall, Leicester, Leicestershire LE1 9BG T: 0845 045 0901
Leicestershire Leicestershire Register Office, County Hall, Glenfield, Leicester, Leicestershire LE3 8RN T: 0116 265 6565
Lincolnshire The Register Office, 4 Lindum Road, Lincoln, Lincolnshire LN2 1NN T: 01522 782 244
Liverpool Liverpool Register Office, The Cotton Exchange, Old Hall Street, Liverpool, L3 9UF T: 0151 233 3004
London
Barking & Dagenham Arden House, 198 Longbridge Road, Barking, Essex IG11 8SY T: (020) 8270 4743
Bexley Manor House, The Green, Sidcup, Kent DA14 6BW T: (020) 8308 7151
Brent Brent Town Hall, Forty Lane, Wembley, Middlesex HA9 9EZ T: (020) 8937 1010
Bromley Room S101, Bromley Civic Centre, Stockwell Close, Bromley, BR1 3UH T: (020) 8313 4666
Camden Camden Register Office, Camden Town Hall, Judd Street, London, WC1H 9JE T: (020) 7974 1900
City of London The Register Office, Islington Town Hall, Upper Street, Islington, London, N1 2UD T: (020) 7527 6347
Croydon The Town Hall, Fell Road, Croydon, CR0 1NX T: 020 8686 4433
Ealing Ealing Town Hall, New Broadway, Ealing, London W5 2BY T: (020) 8825 7272
Enfield Public Offices, 1 Gentlemen's Row, Enfield, Middlesex EN2 6PS T: (020) 8367 5757
Greenwich The Register Office, Town Hall, Wellington Street, Greenwich, London, SE18 6PW T: (020) 8854 8888
Hackney The Register Office, Town Hall, Mare Street, London, E8 1EA T: (020) 8356 3365
Hammersmith and Fulham Hammersmith & Fulham Register Office, Fulham Town Hall, Harwood Road, Fulham, London, SW6 1ET T: (020) 8753 2140
Haringey The Register Office, Civic Centre, High Road, Wood Green, London, N22 4LE T: (020) 8489 2605
Harrow The Civic Centre, Station Road, Harrow, Middlesex HA1 2UX T: (020) 8424 1618
Havering Langtons, Billet Lane, Hornchurch, Essex RM11 1XL T: 01708 433481
Hillingdon The Register Office, Hillingdon Civic Centre, Uxbridge, Middlesex UB8 1UW T: 01895 250418
Hounslow The Register Office, 88 Lampton Road, Hounslow, Middlesex TW3 4DW T: (020) 8583 2090
Islington The Register Office, Islington Town Hall, Upper Street, London, N1 2UD T: (020) 7527 6347
Kensington & Chelsea The Kensington & Chelsea Register Office, Chelsea Old Town Hall, Kings Road, London, SW3 5EE T: (020) 7361 4100
Kingston upon Thames The Register Office, 35 Coombe Road, Kingston upon Thames, Surrey KT2 7BA T: (020) 8547 4600
Lambeth The Register Office, Lambeth Town Hall, Brixton Hill, Lambeth, London, SW2 1RW T: (020) 7926 9859

Lewisham The Register Office, 368 Lewisham High Street, London, SE13 6LQ T: (020) 8690 2128
Merton Morden Park House, Morden Hall, London Road, Morden, Surrey SM4 5QU T: (020) 8274 5777
Newham The Register Office, Passmore Edwards Building, 207 Plashet Grove, East Ham, London, E6 1BT T: (020) 8430 2000
Redbridge Queen Victoria House, 794 Cranbrook Road, Barkingside, Ilford, Essex IG6 1JS T: (020) 8708 7160
Richmond upon Thames The Register Office, 1 Spring Terrace, Richmond, Surrey TW9 1LW T: (020) 8940 2853
Southwark The Register Office, 34 Peckham Road, Southwark, London, SE5 8QA T: (020) 7525 7651
Sutton Russettings, 25 Worcester Road, Sutton, Surrey SM2 6PR T: (020) 8770 6790
Tower Hamlets The Register Office, Bromley Public Hall, Bow Road, London E3 3AA T: (020) 7364 7880
Waltham Forest The Register Office, 106 Grove Road, Walthamstow, London E17 9BY T: (020) 8496 2716
Wandsworth The Register Office, The Town Hall, Wandsworth High Street, London, SW18 2PU T: (020) 8871 6120
London - City of Westminster The Register Office, Westminster Council House, Marylebone Road, London, NW1 5PT T: (020) 7641 1161
Luton The Register Office, 6 George Street West, Luton, LU1 2BJ T: 01582 722603
Manchester Heron House, 47 Lloyd Street, Manchester, M2 5LE T: 0161 234 5504
Merseyside
Knowsley District Council Offices, High Street, Prescot, Merseyside L34 3LH T: 0151 443 5210
Liverpool Liverpool Register Office, The Cotton Exchange, Old Hall Street, Liverpool, L3 9UF T: 0151 233 3004
St Helens The Register Office, Central Street, St Helens, Merseyside WA10 1UJ T: 01744 456789
Wirral Town Hall, Mortimer Street, Birkenhead, Merseyside L41 5EU T: 0151 666 4096
Merseyside - Sefton
Sefton North Town Hall, Corporation Street, Southport, Merseyside PR8 1DA T: 0151 934 2013
Sefton South Crosby Town Hall, Great Georges Road, Waterloo, Liverpool, L22 1RB T: 0151 934 3045
Middlesbrough The Register Office, Corporation Road, Middlesbrough, TS1 2DA T: 01642 729004
Milton Keynes Bracknell House, Aylesbury Street, Bletchley, Milton Keynes MK2 2BE T: 01908 372101
Newcastle-upon-Tyne Civic Centre, Barras Bridge, Newcastle-upon-Tyne, Tyne and Wear NE1 8PS T: 0191 232 8520
Norfolk
Depwade Council Offices, 11-12 Market Hill, Diss, Norfolk IP22 3JX T: 01379 643915
Downham The Register Office, 15 Paradise Road, Downham Market, Norfolk PE38 9HS T: 01366 387104
East Dereham The Breckland Business Centre, St Withburga Lane, Dereham, Norfolk NR19 1FD T: 01362 698021
Fakenham The Register Office, Fakenham Connect, Oak Street, Fakenham, Norfolk NR21 9SR T: 01328 850111
Great Yarmouth Ferryside, High Road, Southtown, Great Yarmouth, Norfolk NR31 0PH T: 01493 662313
King's Lynn Hanse House, St Margaret's Place, King's Lynn, Norfolk PE30 5DW T: 01553 669251
North Walsham The Register Office, 18 Kings Arms Street, North Walsham, Norfolk NR28 9JX T: 01692 406220
Norwich Churchman House, 71 Bethel Street, Norwich, NR2 1NR T: 01603 767600
Wayland Kings House, Kings Street, Thetford, Norfolk IP24 2AP T: 01842 766848
North-East Lincolnshire The Register Office, Town Hall Square, Grimsby, North East Lincolnshire DN31 1HX T: 01472 324860
North Lincolnshire Register Office, 92 Oswald Road, Scunthorpe, North Lincolnshire DN15 7PA T: 01724 843915
North Somerset The Register Office, 41 The Boulevard, Weston-super-Mare, North Somerset BS23 1PG T: 01934 627552
North Tyneside Maritime Chambers, 1 Howard Street, North Shields, Tyne and Wear NE30 1LZ T: 0191 200 6164
Northamptonshire The Guildhall, St Giles Square, Northampton, Northamptonshire NN1 1DE T: 01604 745390
Northumberland The Register Office, 94 Newgate Street, Morpeth, Northumberland NE61 1BU T: 01670 513232
Nottinghamshire
Basford The Register Office, Highbury Road, Bulwell, Nottinghamshire NG6 9DA T: 0115 927 1294

Bassetlaw Notts County Council Offices, Chancery Lane, Retford, Nottinghamshire DN22 6DG T: 01777 708631

Mansfield County House, 100 Chesterfield Road South, Mansfield, Nottinghamshire NG19 7DN T: 01623 476564

Newark County Offices, Balderton Gate, Newark, Nottinghamshire NG24 1UW T: 01636 705455

Nottingham The Register Office, 50 Shakespeare Street, Nottingham, Nottinghamshire NG1 4FP T: 0115 947 5665

Rushcliffe The Hall, Bridgford Road, West Bridgford, Nottinghamshire NG2 6AQ T: 0115 981 5307

Oldham Chadderton Town Hall, Middleton Road, Chadderton, Oldham, Lancashire OL9 6PP T: 0161 678 0137

Oxfordshire The Register Office, Tidmarsh Lane, Oxford, Oxfordshire OX1 1NS

Plymouth The Register Office, Lockyer Street, Plymouth, Devon PL1 2QD T: 01752 268331

Poole The Guildhall, Market Street, Poole, Dorset BH15 1NP T: 01202 633744

Portsmouth The Register Office, Milldam House, Burnaby Road, Portsmouth, Hampshire PO1 3AF T: (023) 9282 9041

Redcar & Cleveland The Register Office, 88 Westgate, Guisborough, Cleveland TS14 6AP T: 01287 632564

Rochdale Town Hall, The Esplanade, Rochdale, Lancashire OL16 1AB T: 01706 924783

Rotherham Bailey House, Rawmarsh Road, Rotherham, South Yorkshire S60 1TX T: 01709 382121

Rutland Catmose, Oakham, Rutland LE15 6JU T: 01572 758370

Salford Town Hall, Chorley Road, Swinton, Manchester M27 5DA T: 0161 909 6501

Sandwell - West Midlands Highfields, High Street, West Bromwich, Sandwell, West Midlands B70 8RJ T: 0121 569 2480

Sheffield The Town Hall, Sheffield, S1 2HH T: 0114 203 9423

Sheffield Register Office The Town Hall, Pinstone Street, Sheffield, South Yorkshire S1 2HH T: 0114 273 9423 E: registeroffice@sheffield.gov.uk

Shropshire The Register Office, Column Lodge, Preston Street, Shrewsbury, Shropshire SY2 5NY T: 01743 251921

Telford & Wrekin The Beeches, 29 Vineyard Road, Wellinton, Telford, Shropshire TF1 1HB T: 01952 382444

Solihull The Register Office, Homer Road, Solihull, West Midlands B91 3QZ T: 0121 704 6099

Somerset The Old Municipal Building, Corporation Street, Taunton, Somerset TA1 4AQ T: 01984 633116

South Gloucestershire Poole Court, Poole Court Drive, Yate, Bristol, South Gloucestershire BS37 5PT T: 01454 863 140

South Tyneside The Register Office, 10 Broughton Road, South Shields, Tyne and Wear NE33 2RN T: 0191 455 3915

Southampton The Register Office, 6A Bugle Street, Southampton, SO14 2LX T: (023) 8063 1422

St Helens The Register Office, Central Street, St Helens, Merseyside WA10 1UJ T: 01744 456789

Staffordshire Eastgate House, 79 Eastgate Street, Stafford, Staffordshire ST16 2NG T: 01785 277880

Stockport Town Hall - John Street Entrance, Stockport, Cheshire SK1 3XE T: 0161 474 3399

Stockton-on-Tees Nightingale House, Balaclava Street, Stockton-on-Tees, TS18 2AL T: 01642 527720

Stoke-on-Trent Town Hall, Albion Street, Hanley, Stoke on Trent, Staffordshire ST1 1QQ T: 01782 235260

Suffolk - Ipswich St Peter House, 16 Grimwade Street, Ipswich, Suffolk IP4 1LP T: 01473 583050

Sunderland Town Hall & Civic Centre, PO Box 108, Sunderland, SR2 7DN T: 0191 553 7931

Surrey Rylston, 81 Oatlands Drive, Weybridge, Surrey KT13 9LN T: 01932 794704

Sussex - East Eastbourne Town Hall, Grove Road, Eastbourne, East Sussex BN21 4UG T: 01323 415051

Sussex - West Crawley Southgate Avenue, Crawley, West Sussex RH10 6HG T: 01293 438000

Swindon 1st Floor, Aspen House, Temple Street, Swindon, SN1 1SQ T: 01793 521734

Tameside Tameside Register Office, Town Hall, King Street, Dukinfield, Cheshire SK16 4LA T: 0161 342 5032

Telford & Wrekin The Beeches, 29 Vineyard Road, Wellinton, Telford, Shropshire TF1 1HB T: 01952 382444

Torbay The Register Office, Oldway Mansion, Paignton, Devon TQ3 2TU T: 01803 207130

Trafford Sale Town Hall, School Road, Sale, Cheshire M33 7ZF T: 0161 912 3026

Wakefield The Register Office, 71 Northgate, Wakefield, West Yorkshire WF1 3BS T: 01924 302185

Walsall The Register Office, Civic Centre, Hatherton Road, Walsall, West Midlands WS1 1TN T: 01922 652260

Warwickshire Shire Hall, PO Box 9, Warwick CV34 4RR T: 01926 494269

West Berkshire Shaw House, Church Road, Shaw, Newbury, Berkshire RG14 2DR T: 01635 279230

Wigan & Leigh Town Hall, Library Street, Wigan, Lancashire WN1 1YD T: 01942 705000

Wiltshire

Swindon 1st Floor, Aspen House, Temple Street, Swindon, SN1 1SQ T: 01793 521734

Trowbridge East Wing Block, County Hall, Trowbridge, Wiltshire BA14 8EZ T: 01225 713000

Windsor & Maidenhead Town Hall, St Ives Road, Maidenhead, Berkshire SL6 1RF T: 01628 796422

Wirral Town Hall, Mortimer Street, Birkenhead, Merseyside L41 5EU T: 0151 666 4096

Wokingham The Old School, Reading Road, Wokingham, Berkshire RG41 1RJ T: 0118 978 2514

Wolverhampton Civic Centre, St Peters Square, Wolverhampton, WV1 1RU T: 01902 554989

Worcestershire The Register Office, County Hall, Spetchley Road, Worcester, Worcestershire WR5 2NP T: 01905 768388

York The Register Office, 56 Bootham, York, YO30 7DA T: 01904 654477

Yorkshire - East

East Riding of Yorkshire The Register Office, Walkergate House, Walkergate, Beverley, East Yorkshire HU17 9EJ T: 01482 393600

Yorkshire - North

North Yorkshire Registration Service - North Yorkshire Bilton House, 31 Park Parade, Harrogate, North Yorkshire HG1 5AG T: 01423 506949

Yorkshire - South

Barnsley Bernslai Close, Barnsley, South Yorkshire S70 2HS T: 01226 773 090

Sheffield Register Office The Town Hall, Pinstone Street, Sheffield, South Yorkshire S1 2HH T: 0114 273 9423 E: registeroffice@sheffield.gov.uk

Yorkshire - West

Bradford & Keighley The Register Office, 22 Manor Row, Bradford, West Yorkshire BD1 4QR T: 01274 432151

Calderdale The Register Office, Spring Hall, Huddersfield Road, Halifax, West Yorkshire HX3 0AQ T: 01484 221 030

Dewsbury The Register Office, Wellington Street, Dewsbury, West Yorkshire WF13 1LY T: 01924 324880

Huddersfield Town Hall, Ramsden Street, Huddersfield, West Yorkshire HD1 2TA T: 01484 221030

Leeds Leeds Register Office, Leeds Town Hall, The Headrow, Leeds, West Yorkshire LS1 3AD T: 0113 224 3603

Wakefield The Register Office, 71 Northgate, Wakefield, West Yorkshire WF1 3BS T: 01924 302185

Wales
National

The General Register Office Room E201, Trafalgar Road, Birkdale, Southport, PR8 2HH T: 0845 603 7788 W: www.direct.gov.uk/gro

Bridgend County Borough Offices, Sunnyside, Bridgend, Glamorgan CF31 4AR T: 01656 642391

Caerphilly The Council Offices, Ystrad Fawr, Caerphilly Road, Ystrad Mynach, Hengoed, CF82 7SF T: 01443 863478

Cardiff The Register Office, City Hall, Cathays Park, Cardiff, CF10 3ND T: 029 2087 1736

Carmarthenshire Carmarthen Register Office, Parc Myrddin, Richmond Terrace, Carmarthen, Carmarthenshire SA31 1DS T: 01267 228210

Ceredigion

Cardiganshire Central The Register Office, 21 High Street, Lampeter, Ceredigion SA48 7BG T: 01570 422558

Cardiganshire North Canolfan Rheidol, Rhodfa Padarn, Llanbadarn Fawr, Aberystwyth, Ceredigion SY23 3UE T: 01970 633582

Cardiganshire South Glyncoed Chambers, Priory Street, Cardigan, Ceredigion SA43 1BX T: 01239 612684

Conwy The Town Hall, Lloyd Street, Llandudno, Gwynedd LL30 2UP T: 01492 576624

Denbighshire

Denbighshire North Morfa Clwyd, Marsh Road, Rhyl, Denbighshire LL18 2AF T: 01745 366610

Denbighshire South The Town Hall, Wynnstay Road, Ruthin, Denbighshire LL15 1YN T: 01824 706174

Flintshire Register Office, Llwynegrin Hall, Mold, Flintshire CH7 6NR T: 01352 703333

Glamorgan
Merthyr Tydfil TY Penderyn, 26 High Street, Merthyr Tydfil, Glamorgan CF47 8DP T: 01685 723318
Gwent
Blaenau Gwent The Grove, Church Street, Tredegar, Gwent NP2 3DS T: 01495 722305
Gwynedd
Bangor The Register Office, Town Hall, Bangor, Gwynedd LL55 1SH T: 01248 362418
Conwy The Town Hall, Lloyd Street, Llandudno, Gwynedd LL30 2UP T: 01492 576624
Isle of Anglesey - Ynys Môn Shire Hall, Glanhwfa Road, Llangefni, Anglesey LL77 7TW T: 01248 752564
Merthyr Tydfil Ty Penderyn, 26 High Street, Merthyr Tydfil, Glamorgan CF47 8DP T: 01685 723318
Monmouthshire Monmouth The Register Office, Coed Glas, Coed Glas Lane, Abergavenny, Monmouthshire NP7 5LE T: 01873 735435
Neath Port Talbot The Register Office, 119 London Road, Neath, Port Talbot, SA11 1HL T: 01639 760020
Newport The Register Office, 8 Gold Tops, Newport, Gwent NP20 4PH T: 01633 265547
Pembrokeshire Pembrokeshire The Register Office, Tower Hill, Haverfordwest, Pembrokeshire SA61 1SS T: 01437 775176
Powys The Gwalia, Ithon Road, Llandrindod Wells, Powys LD1 6AA T: 01597 826020
Rhonda Cynon Taff The Register Office, Municipal Buildings, Gelliwastad Road, Pontypridd, CF37 2DP T: 01443 486869
Swansea The Swansea Register Office, Civic Centre, Swansea, SA1 3SN T: 01792 636188
Torfaen The Civic Centre, Pontypool, Torfaen NP4 6YB T: 01495 762937
Vale of Glamorgan The Register Office, Civic Offices, Holton Road, Barry, Glamorgan CF63 4RU T: 01446 709490
Wrexham Ty Dewi Sant, Rhosddu Road, Wrexham, LL11 1NF T: 01978 292027
Ynys Môn Shire Hall, Glanhwfa Road, Llangefni, Anglesey LL77 7TW T: 01248 752564

Isle of Man
Civil Registry Registries Building, Deemster's Walk, Bucks Road, Douglas IM1 3AR T: 01624 687039 E: civil@registry.gov.im W: www.gov.im/registries/general/civilregistry/birth.xml

Channel Islands
Guernsey
HM Greffier Royal Court House, St Peter Port, Guernsey GY1 2PB T: 01481 725277 W: www.gov.gg/ccm/portal/
Jersey
Judicial Greffe Morier House, Halkett Place, St Helier, Jersey JE1 1DD T: 01534-502300 E: jgreffe@super.net.uk W: www.gov.je/
Jersey 10 Royal Square, St Helier, Jersey JE2 4WA T: 01534 502335

Isles of Scilly
The Register Office, Porthcressa Bank, St Marys, Isles of Scilly TR21 0JL T: 01720 423751

Northern Ireland
General Register Office of Northern Ireland Oxford House, 49 - 55 Chichester Street, Belfast, BT1 4HL T: (028) 90 252000 E: gro.nisra@dfpni.gov.uk W: www.groni.gov.uk

Ireland
Registration Records in The Republic of Ireland The General Register Office (Oifig An Ard-Chláraitheora), Government Offices,, Convent Road, Roscommon T: +353 (0) 90 663 2900 W: www.groireland.ie/ Email certificate application (must be sent with appropriate downloadable form) The General Register Office also maintains a family history research facility at 3rd Floor, Block 7, Irish Life Centre, Lower Abbey Street, Dublin 1 This is the central repository for all records relating to life events (Births, Deaths, Marriages, Legal Domestic Adoptions, Stillbirths) in the Irish State. The General Register Office (Oifig An Ard-Chláraitheora) maintains a genealogical/family history research facility at 3rd Floor, Block 7, Irish Life Centre, Lower Abbey Street, Dublin 1.

Registrars of Births Marriages & Deaths - Scotland

Scotland
Aberdeenshire
Bucksburn Area Office, 23 Inverurie Road, Bucksburn, AB21 9LJ T: 01224 712866 F: 01224 716997 E: mitosh@aberdeencity.gov.uk
Peterculter Lilydale, 102 North Deeside Road, Peterculter, AB14 0QB T: 01224 732648 F: 01224 734637
Aberdeen St Nicholas House, Upperkirkgate, Aberdeen, AB10 1EY T: 01224 522616 Search Room: 01224 522 033 E: registrars@aberdeencity.gov.uk
Aboyne and Torphins District Council Offices, Bellwood Road, Aboyne, AB34 5HQ T: 01339 886109 F: 01339 86798 E: esther.halkett@aberdeenshire.gov.uk
Alford, Sauchen and Strathdo Council Office, School Road, Alford, AB33 8PY T: 01975 562421 F: 01975 563286 E: anne.shaw@aberdeenshire.gov.uk
Ballater An Creagan, 5 Queens Road., Ballater, AB35 5NJ T: 01339 755535
Banchory Aberdeenshire Council, The Square, High Street, Banchory, AB31 5RW T: 01330 822878 F: 01330 822243 E: christine.handsley@aberdeenshire.gov.uk
Banff Seafield House, 37 Castle Street, Banff, AB45 1DQ T: 01261 813439 E: kate.samuel@aderdeenshire.gov.uk
Braemar The Braemar Royal Highland Society, Hillside Road, Braemar, AB35 5YU T: 01339 741349
Ellon Area Office, Neil Ross Square, 29 Bridge Street, Ellon, AB41 9AA T: 01358 720295 F: 01358 726410 E: gail.duthie@aberdeenshire.gov.uk
Fraserburgh The Register Office, 14 Saltoun Square, Fraserburgh, AB43 9DA T: 01346 513281 E: eleanor.young@aberdeenshire.gov.uk
Huntly The Register Office, 25 Gordon Street, Huntly, AB54 8AN T: 01466 794488
Insch Marbert, George Street, Insch, AB52 6JL T: 01464 820964
Inverurie, Oldmeldrum, Skere and Echt Gordon House, Blackhall Road, Inverurie, AB51 3WA T: 01467 620981 F: 01467 628012 E: isobel.ross@aberdeenshire.gov.uk
Maud County Offices, Nethermuir Road, Maud, Aberdeenshire AB42 4ND T: 01771 613667 F: 01771 613204 E: maureen.stephen@aberdeenshire.gov.uk
Peterhead Aberdeenshire Council, Broad Street, Peterhead, AB42 1DA T: 01779 483244 F: 01779 483246 E: peterhead.registrars@aberdeenshire.gov.uk

Stonehaven, East Kinkardine & Inverbervie Viewmount, Arduthie Road, Stonehaven, AB39 2DQ T: 01569 768360 F: 01569 765455 E: cressida.coates@aberdeenshire.gov.uk
Turriff Towie House, Manse Road, Turriff, AB53 4AY T: 01888 562427 F: 01888 568559 E: diane.duncan@aberdeenshire.gov.uk
Angus
Arbroath The Register Office, 69/71 High Street, Arbroath, DD11 1AN T: 01241 873752 E: macpherson@angus.gov.uk
Arrochar The Register Office, 1 Cobbler View, Arrochar, G83 7AD T: 01301 702289
Brechin Contact Arbroath, **Carnoustie** Contact Arbroath,
Forfar The Register Office, 9 West High Street, Forfar, DD8 1BD T: 01307 464973 E: regforfar@angus.gov.uk
Kirriemuir Contact Arbroath,
Montrose The Register Office, 51 John Street, Montrose, Angus DD10 8LZ T: 01674 672351 E: regmontrose@angus.gov.uk
Argyll & Bute
Campbeltown Campbeltown Servicepoint, Burnet Building, St John Street, Campbeltown PA28 6BJ T 01586 559017 E: julie.mclellan@argyll-bute.gov.uk W: www.argyll-bute.gov.uk
Coll The Register Office, 9 Carnan Road, Isle of Coll, Argyll & Bute PA78 6TA T: 01879 230329
Colonsay & Oronsay Colonsay Service Point, Village Hall, Colonsay, Argyll & Bute PA61 7YW T: 01951 200263
Dunoon Council Offices, Hill Street, Dunoon, PA23 7AP T: 01369 704374 F: 01369 705948 E: ann.saidler@argyll-bute.gov.uk
Gigha 10 Ardminish, Gigha, PA41 7AB T: 01583 505249
Helensburgh Scotcourt House, 45 West Princes Street, Helensburgh, Argyll & Bute G84 8BP T: 01436 658822 F: 01436 658821
Inveraray Operating from Lochgilphead, Argyll & Bute PA32 8UZ T: 01546 604511
Islay Council Office, Jamieson Street, Bowmore, Islay, Argyll & Bute PA43 7HL T: 01496 301301 E: sharon.mcharrie@argyll-bute.gov.uk
Isle of Bute Council Office, Mount Pleasant Road, Rothesay, Isle of Bute PA20 9HH T: 01700 503331/551
Jura Forestry Cottage, Craighouse, Jura, PA60 7XG T: 01496 820326
Kilbrandon and Kilchattan Dalamasaig, Isle of Seil, By Oban, Argyll & Bute PA34 4TJ T: 01852 300380
Kilfinichen & Kilvickeon The Anchorage, Fionnphort, Isle Of Mull, Argyll & Bute PA66 6BL T: 01681 700241
Lochgilphead Dalriada House, Lochnell Street, Lochgilphead, PA31 8ST T: 01546 604511 E: shona.brechin@argyll-bute.gov.uk

Lochgoilhead Council Offices, Hill Street, Dunoon, PA23 7AP T: 01369 704374

Lismore Operating from Oban, Argyle & Bute T: 01631 567930

Oban Lorn House, Albany Street, Oban, Argyll & Bute PA34 4AW T: 01631 567930 E: gemma.cummins@argyll-bute.gov.uk

Rosneath operating from Scotcourt House, 45 West Princes Street, Helensburgh, Argyll & Bute G84 8BP T: 01436 658822

South Cowal Copeswood, Auchenlochan High Road, Tighnabruaich, Argyll & Bute PA21 2BE T: 01700 811601

Strachur Council Offices, Hill Street, Dunoon, PA23 7AP T: 01369 704374

Tarbert Argyll House, Harbour Street, Tarbert, PA29 6UA T: 01880 821300

Tayinloan Operating from Dell Road, Campbeltown, PA28 6JG T: 01586 552366

Tobermory County Buldings, Breadalbane Street, Tobermory, Argyll & Bute PA75 6PX T: 01688 302051

Tyree The Register Office, Crossapol, Isle Of Tyree, PA77 6UP T: 01879 220349

Clackmannanshire

Clackmannanshire Marshill House, Marshill, Alloa, Clackmannanshire FK10 1AB T: 01259 723850 W:

Dumfries & Galloway

Annan Council Offices, 15 Ednam Street, Annan, DG12 5EF T: 01461 204914

Castle Douglas 4 Market Street, Castle Douglas DG7 1BE T: 01556 505264

Dalbeattie Town Hall Buildings, Water Street, Dalbeattie, DG5 4JX T: 01557 330291 Ext 323

Dalry 42 Main Street, Dalry, Castle Douglas, DG7 3UW T: 01644 430310

Dumfries Municipal Chambers, Buccleuch Street, Dumfries, DG1 2AD T: 01387 245906

Girthon 63 High Street, Gatehouse of Fleet, DG7 2HS T: 01557 814646

Gretna Registration Office, Central Avenue, Gretna, DG16 5AQ T: 01461 337648

Kirkconnell Nith Buildings, Greystone Avenue, Kelloholm, Kirkconnel, DG4 6RX T: 01659 66052

Kirkcudbright District Council Offices, Daar Road, Kirkcudbrigbt, DG6 4JG T: 01557 332534

Kirkmabreck The Bogue, Creetowm, Newton Stewart, DG8 7JW T: 01671 820266

Langholm Town Hall, Langholm, DG13 0JQ T: 01387 380255

Lockerbie Town Hall, High Street, Lockerbie DG11 2ES T: 01576 204267

Mochrum The Library, Main Street, Port William, DG8 9JQ T: 07709 479 664

Moffat Town Hall, High Street, Moffat, DG10 9HF T: 01683 220536

Newton Stewart Area McMillan Hall, Dashwood Square, Newton Stewart, DG8 6EQ T: 01671 404187

Sanquhar Council Offices, 100 High Street, Sanquhar, DG4 6DZ T: 01659 50697

Stranraer Area The Register Office, Council Offices, Sun Street, Stranraer, DG9 7JJ T: 01776 888439

Thornhill One Stop Shop, Manse Road, Thornhill, DG3 5DR T: 01848 330303

Whithorn Area The Register Office, 75 George Street, Whithorn, DG8 8NU T: 01988 500458

Wigtown Area Council Sub-office, County Buildings, Wigtown, DG8 9JH T: 0770 947 9664

Dundee

Dundee City Council - Scottish Family History Centre Wellgate Library, Dundee, DD1 1DB T: 01382 435222 & 01382 431516 E: registrars@dundeecity.gov.uk W: www.dundeecity.gov.uk/supportservs/registrar

East Ayrshire

Auchinleck The Register Office, 28 Well Road, Auchlinleck, Cummock, East Ayrshire KA18 2LA T: 01290 420582

Dalmellington Dalmellington Area Centre, 33 Main Street, Dalmellington, East Ayrshire KA6 7QL T: 01292 552 880

Darvel, Galston, Newmilns The Register Office, 11 Cross Street, Galston, East Ayrshire KA4 8AA T: 01563 820218

Kilmarnock Civic Centre, John Dickie Street, Kilmarnock, East Ayrshire KA1 1HW T: 01563 576695

Mauchline 2 The Cross, Mauchline, East Ayrshire KA5 5DA T: 01290 550231

Muirkirk 44 Main Street, Muirkirk, East Ayrshire KA18 3RD T: 01290 661227

Old Cumnock Council Office Millbank, 14 Lugar Street, Cumnock, East Ayrshire KA18 1AB T: 01290 420666

East Dunbartonshire

Bishopbriggs Council Offices, The Triangle, Kirkintilloch Road, Bishopbriggs, East Dunbartonshire G64 2TR T: 0141 578 8557

Kirkintilloch & Lennoxtown Council Office, 21 Southbank Road, Kirkintilloch, G66 1NH T: 0141 578 8020

New Kilpatrick Council Office, 38 Roman Road, Bearsden, East Dunbartonshire G61 2SH T: 0141 578 8669

East Lothian

Dunbar Town House, 48 High Street, Dunbar EH42 1JH T: 01368 863434

Haddington The Register Office, John Muir House, Brewery Park, Haddington, East Lothian EH41 3HA T: 01620 827308

Musselburgh Brunton Hall, Ladywell Way, Musselburgh, East Lothian EH21 6AF T: 0131 653 5225

North Berwick The Register Office, 2 Quality Street, North Berwick, East Lothian EH39 4HW T: 01620 895647

Prestonpans Aldhammer House, High Street, Prestonpans, East Lothian EH32 9SH T: 01875 810232

Tranent The Register Office, 8 Civic Square, Tranent, East Lothian EH33 1LH T: 01875 610278

East Renfrewshire

Barrhead Council Office, 13 Lowndes Street, Barrhead, East Renfrewshire G78 2QX T: 0141 577 3551

Giffnock Council Offices, Eastwood Park, Roukenglen Road, Giffnock, East Renfrewshire G46 6UG T: 0141 577 3100

Edinburgh

Edinburgh (Currie) The Register Office, 138 Lanark Road West, Currie, Edinburgh EH14 5NY T: 0131 449 5318

Edinburgh (Kirkliston) 19 Station Road, Kirkliston, Edinburgh EH29 9BB T: 0131 333 3210

Edinburgh (Leith) The Register Office, 30 Ferry Road, Edinburgh, EH6 4AE T: 0131 554 8452

Edinburgh (Queensferry) Council Office, 53 High Street, South Queensferry, Edinburgh EH30 9HP T: 0131 331 1590

Edinburgh Central Lothian Chambers, 59 - 63 George IV Bridge, Edinburgh, EH1 1RN T: 0131 529 2600

Eileanan Siar

Barra Council Offices, Castlebay, Barra HS9 5XD T: 01871 810431

Benbecula Council Offices, Balivanich, Benbecula, South Uist, Eileanan Siar HS7 5LA T: 01870 602425

Boisdale Post Office House, Daliburgh, South Uist, Eileanan Siar HS8 5SS T: 01878 700300

Harris Council Offices, Tarbert, Harris HS3 3DJ T: 01859 502367

North Uist Fairview, Lochmaddy, North Uist HS6 5AW T: 01876 500239

Stornoway & South Lochs Town Hall, 2 Cromwell Street, Stornoway HS1 2DB T: 01851 709438 E: emacdonald@cne-siar.gov.uk

Falkirk

Bo'ness and Carriden Registration Office, 15a Seaview Place, Bo'ness, Falkirk EH51 0AJ T: 01506 778992

Denny Carronbank House, Carronbank Crescent, Denny, Falkirk FK6 6GA T: 01324 504280

Falkirk (Falkirk) Old Burgh Buildings, Newmarket Street, Falkirk, Falkirk FK1 1JE T: 01324 506580

Grangemouth Municipal Chambers, Bo'ness Road, Grangemouth, Falkirk FK3 8AY T: 01324 504499

Larbert The Register Office, 318 Main Street, Stenhousemuir, Falkirk FK5 3BE T: 01324 503580

Polmont & Muiravonside Council Offices, Redding Road, Brightons, Falkirk, Falkirk FK2 0HG T: 01324 503990

Fife

Fife (Auchtermuchty) Local Office, 15 High Street, Auchtermuchty, Fife KY14 7AP T: 08451 555555

Fife (Benarty) Benarty Local Office, 6 Benarty Square, Ballingry, Fife KY5 8NR T: 08451 555555

Fife (Buckhaven) Local Office, Municipal Buildings, College Street, Buckhaven, Fife KY8 1AB T: 08451 555555

Fife (Cowdenbeath) The Register Office, 123 High Street, Cowdenbeath, Fife KY4 9QB T: 08451 555555

Fife (Cupar) County Buildings, St Catherine Street, Cupar, Fife KY15 4TA T: 08451 555555

Fife (Dunfermline) City Chambers, Kirkgate, Dunfermline, Fife KY12 7ND T: 08451 555555

Fife (East Neuk) Anstruther Local Office, Ladywalk, Anstruther, Fife KY10 3EX T: 08451 555555

Fife (Glenrothes) Albany House, Albany Gate Kingdom Centre, Glenrothes, Fife KY7 5NX T: 08451 555555

Fife (Inverkeithing) Contact Dunfermline, Fife T: 08451 555555

Fife (Kelty) Kelty Local Services, Sanjana Court, 51 Main Street, Kelty, Fife KY4 0AA T: 08451 555555

Fife (Kirkcaldy) District Office, Town Hall, Kirkcaldy, Fife KY1 1XW T: 08451 555555

Fife (Leven) Carberry House, Scoonie Road, Leven, Fife KY8 4JS T: 08451 555555

Fife (Lochgelly) Lochgelly Local Office, Town House, Hall Street, Lochgelly, Fife KY5 9JN T: 08451 555555

Fife (Newburgh) Tayside Institute, 90-92 High Street, Newburgh, Fife KY14 6DA T: 08451 555555

Fife (St Andrews) Area Office, St Mary's Place, St Andrews, Fife KY16 9UY T: 08451 555555

Fife (Tayport) Burgh Chambers, Tayport, Fife DD6 9JY T: 08451 555555

Gairloch

Gairloch The Service Point, Achtercairn, Gairloch, IV22 2BP T: 01445 712572

Glasgow

Glasgow The Register Office, 22 Park Circus, Glasgow, G3 6BE T: 0141 287 8350 F: 0141 287 8357

Glasgow (Martha Street) The Register Office, 1 Martha Street, Glasgow, G1 1JJ T: 0141 287 7677

Glasgow (Park Circus) The Register Office, 22 Park Circus, Glasgow, G3 6BE T: 0141 287 8350

Highland

Black Isle Black Isle Leisure Centre Service office, Deans Road, Fortrose, Highland IV10 8TJ T: 01381 620797

Ardgour The Register Office, 9 Clovullin, Ardgour, by Fort William, Highland PH33 7AB T: 01855 841261

Assynt Post Office House, Lochinver, Lochinver by Lairg, Highland IV27 4JY T: 01571 844201

Aviemore Service point, School House, Milton Road, Aviemore, Highland PH22 1RR T: 01479 811990

Black Isle Black Isles Leisure Centre, Deans Road, Fortrose, Highland IV10 8TJ T: 01381 620797

Bonar and Kincardine Post Office, Bonar Bridge, Ardgay, Highland IV24 3EA T: 01863 766219

Broadford Service Point, Industrial Estate, Old Corry Road, Broadford, Skye IV49 9AB T: 01471 822195

Clyne Brora Service Point, Gower Street, Brora, Highland KW9 6PD T: 01408 622646 E: margaret.mackintosh@highland.gov.uk

Dingwall & Carnoch Council Offices, Ferry Road, Dingwall, Highland IV15 9QR T: 01349 863113

Dingwall & Carnoch Council Offices, Ferry Road, Dingwall, IV15 9QR T: 01349 863113

Dornoch Service Point Office, The Court House, Castle Street, Dornoch, Highland IV25 3FD T: 01862 810594

Dunvegan Tigh-na-Bruaich, Dunvegan, Isle Of Skye IV55 8WA T: 01470 521296

Durness Service Point, Highlands of Scotland Tourist Board, Sangomore, Durness IV27 4PZ T: 01971 511773

Fort Augustus Highland Council Service Point, Memorial Hall, Oich Road, Fort Augustus, Highland PH32 4DJ T: 01320 366733 E: heather.smart@highland.gov.uk

Fort William & Ballachulish An Aird, Fort William, Highland PH33 6FF T: 01397 704583 E: fortwilliamregistrars@highland.gov.uk W: www.highland.gov.uk

Gairloch The Service Point, Achtercairn, Gairloch, Ross-shire IV21 2BP T: 01445 712769 E: trudy.mackenzie@highland.gov.uk

Glenelg Taobh na Mara, Na Mara, Glenelg Kyle, Ross-shire IV40 8JT T: 01599 522310

Golspie Council Offices, Main Street, Golspie, KW10 6RB T: 01408 635218 E: moira.macdonald@highland.gov.uk

Grantown-on-Spey & Nethyridge Council Offices, The Square, Grantown On Spey, Highland PH26 3HF T: 01479 872539 F: 01479 872942 E: diane.brazier@highland.gov.uk

Helmsdale Helmsdale Library Service Point, Dunrobin Street, Helmsdale, Highland KW8 6JX T: 01431 821690

Inverness Moray House, 16/18 Bank Street, Inverness, Highland IV1 1QY T: 01463 239792 E: margaret.straube@highland.gov.uk W: www.highland.gov.uk

Kingussie Council Offices, Ruthven Road, Kingussie, Inverness-shire PH21 1EJ T: 01540 664529 E: lorna.mcgregor@highland.gov.uk

Kinlochbervie North & West Sutherland Advice & Information Service, The Harbour, Kinlochbervie, Highland IV27 4RHR T: 01971 521730

Kirkton & Tongue The Service Point, Naver Teleservice Centre, Bettyhill, Caithness KW14 7SS T: 01641 521754 E: mary.cook@highland.gov.uk

Lairg Contact Dingwall Registrar, T: 01349 863113

Latheron Post Office, Latheron, Highland KW5 6DG T: 01593 741201

Lochalsh The Service Point, Main Street, Kyle of Lochalsh, Highland IV40 8AB T: 01599 534956

Lochbroom & Coigach Service Point, North Road, Ullapool, Highland IV26 2XL T: 01854 612426

Lochcarron & Shieldaig Lochcarron Service Point, Main Street, Lochcarron, Highland IV54 8YB T: 01520 722970

Mallaig & Knoydart Mallaig & Morar Community Centre, Mallaig, Inverness-shire PH40 4PY T: 01687 462798

Nairn The Court House, Nairn, Highland IV12 4AU T: 01667 458559 E: anthea.lindsay@highland.gov.uk

Portree & Raasay Registrars Office, Tigh na Sgire, Park Lane, Portree, Highland IV51 9GP T: 01478 613277 E: meg.gillies@highland.gov.uk

Rosskeen Invergordon Service Point, 62 High Street, Invergordon, Highland IV18 0DH T: 01349 853778

Small Isles Kildonan House, Isle Of Eigg, Highland PH42 4RL T: 01687 482446

Strontian Easgadail, Longrigg Road, Strontian, Acharacle, Argyll PH36 4HY T: 01967 402037

Tain Highland Service Point, 24 High Street, Tain, Highland IV19 1AE T: 01349 886644

Tarradale Service Point Office, Seaforth Road, Muir Of Ord, Highland IV6 7TA T: 01463 8702147

Thurso, Strathy & Mey Library Buildings, Davidsons Lane, Thurso, Caithness KW14 7AF T: 01847 892786 F: 01847894611 E: pauline.edmunds@highland.gov.uk

Thurso, Strathy & Mey District Office, Library Buildings, Davidson's Lane, Thurso, Highland KW14 7AF T: 01847 892786

Wick Town Hall, Bridge Street, Wick KW1 4AJ T: 01955 605713

Inverclyde

Inverclyde The Register Office, 40 West Stewart Street, Greenock, Inverclyde PA15 1YA T: 01475 714250

Midlothian

Dalkeith The Register Office, 2-4 Buccleuch Street, Dalkeith, EH22 1HA T: 0131 271 3281 E: dkregistrars@midlothian.gov.uk

Moray

Buckie Town House West, Cluny Place, Buckie, Moray AB56 1HB T: 01542 832691

Elgin inc Tomintoul The Register Office, 240 High Street, Elgin, Moray IV30 1BA T: 01343 554600

Forres 153 High Street, Forres, Moray IV36 1DX T: 01309 694070 E: forres.registrar@chief.moray.gov.uk

Keith & Upper Speyside Area Office, Mid Street, Keith, Moray AB55 5BJ T: 01542 885525 E: keith.registrar@chief.moray.gov.uk

North Ayrshire

Irvine The Register Office, 106-108 Bridgegate House, Irvine, North Ayrshire KA12 8BD T: 01294 324988

Isle of Arran District Council Office, Lamlash, Isle Of Arran KA27 8LB T: 01770 600338

Kilbirnie, Beith & Dalry 19 School Wynd, Kilbirnie, KA25 7AY T: 01505 682416

Largs Moorburn, 24 Greenock Road, Largs, North Ayrshire KA30 8NE T: 01475 676552 W: www.north-ayrshire.gov.uk

Saltcoats The Register Office, 45 Ardrossan Road, Saltcoats, KA21 5BS T: 01294 463312 W: www.north-ayrshire.gov.uk

North Lanarkshire

Airdrie 37 Alexander Street, Airdrie, North Lanarkshire ML6 0BA T: 01236 758080

Bellshill The Register Office, 20/22 Motherwelt Road, Bellshill, ML4 1RB T: 01698 346780

Chryston Moodiesburn First Stop Shop, Blackwoods Crescent, Moodiesburn, North Lanarkshire G69 OEN T: 01236 638666

Coatbridge The Register Office, 183 Main Street, Coatbridge, North Lanarkshire ML5 3HH T: 01236 812647 W: www.northlan.gov.uk

Cumbernauld Council Offices, Bron Way, Cumbernauld, North Lanarkshire G67 1DZ T: 01236 616390

Kilsyth Health Centre, Burngreen Park, Kilsyth, North Lanarkshire G65 0HU T: 01236 826813

Motherwell & Wishaw Civic Centre, Windmillhill Street, Motherwell, ML1 1TW T: 01698 302206

Shotts Council Offices, 106 Station Road, Shotts, North Lanarkshire ML7 4BH T: 01501 824740

Orkney Islands

Birsay Cumlaquoy, Mafwick, Birsay, Orkney KW17 2ND T: 01856 721296

Eday & Pharay Redbanks, Eday, Orkney KW17 2AA T: 01857 622219

Flotta Post Office, Flotta , Stromness, Orkney KW16 3NP T: 01856 701252

Harray New Breckan, Harray, Orkney KW17 2JR T: 01856 771233

Holm & Paplay The Register Office, Netherbreck , Holm, Orkney KW17 2RX T: 01856 781231

Hoy Laundry House, Melsetter, Longhope, Orkney KW16 3NZ T: 01856 791337

Kirkwall Council Offices, School Place, Kirkwall, Orkney KW15 1NY T: 01856 873535 ext 2109 E: chief.registrar@orkney.gov.uk W: www.orkney.gov.uk

North Ronaldsay Hooking, North Ronaldsay, Orkney KW17 2BE T: 01857 633257

Orphir The Bu, Orphir, Kirkwall, KW17 2RD T: 01856 811319

Papa Westray Bewan, Papa Westray, Orkney KW17 2BU T: 01857 644245

Rousay Braehead , Rousay, Kirkwall, Orkney KW17 2PT T: 01856 821222

Sanday Neigarth, Sanday, Orkney KW17 2BW T: 01857 600327

Sandwick The Register Office, Lee Cottage, Sandwick, Stromness, Shetland KW16 3JF T: 01856 841518

Shapinsay The Register Office, Girnigoe, Shapinsay, Orkney KW17 2EB T: 01856 711256

South Ronaldsay The Register Office, West Cara, Grimness, South Ronaldsay KW17 2TH T: 01856 831323

Stenness The Register Office, Langbigging, Stenness, Orkney KW16 3LB T: 01856 850320

Stromness The Register Office, Ferry Terminal Building, Ferry Road, Stromness, Orkney KW16 3AE T: 01856 850854

Stronsay The Register Office, Strynie, Stronsay, Kirkwall, Orkney KW17 2AR T: 01857 616239

Westray Myrtle Cottage, Pierowall, Westray, Orkney KW17 2DH T: 01857 677278

Perth & Kinross

Aberfeldy Duntaggart, Crieff Road, Aberfeldy, Perth & Kinross PH15 2EN T: 01887 829218

Auchterarder The Ayton Hall, 91 High Street, Auchterarder, Perth & Kinross PH3 1BJ T: 01764 662155

Blairgowrie Council Buildings, 46 Leslie Street, Blairgowrie, PH10 6AW T: 01250 872051

Coupar-Angus Union Bank Buildings, Coupar Angus, Perth & Kinross PH13 9AJ T: 01828 628395

Crieff Crieff Area Office, 32 James Square, Crieff, PH7 3EY T: 01764 657550

Kinross Kinross Area Office, 21/25 High Street, Kinross, Perth & Kinross KY13 8AP T: 01577 867602

Milnathort Rowallan, 21 Church Street, Milnathort, Perth & Kinross KY13 9XH T: 01577 862536

Perth The Register Office, 3 High Street, Perth, Perth & Kinross PH1 5JS T: 01738 475122

Pitlochry District Area Office, 26 Atholl Road, Pitlochry, Perth & Kinross PH16 5BX T: 01796 472323

Rannoch & Foss Kinloch Rannoch Medical Practice, The Surgery, Kinloch Rannoch, Pitlochry, Perth & Kinross PH16 5PR T: 01882 632277

Renfrewshire

Johnstone The Register Office, 16-18 McDowall Street, Johnstone, Renfrewshire PA5 8QL T: 01505 320012 W: www.renfrewshire.gov.uk

Paisley Registration Office, 1 Cotton Street, Paisley, PA1 1BU T: 0141 840 3388 W: www.renfrewshire.gov.uk

Renfrew Town Hall, Renfrew, Renfrewshire PA4 8PF T: 0141 886 3589

Scottish Borders

Castleton 10 Douglas Square, Newcastleton, TD9 0QD T: 01387 375606

Coldstream 73 High Street, Coldstream, TD12 4AE T: 01890 883156

Duns The Register Office, 8 Newtown Street, Duns, Scottish Borders TD11 3DT T: 01361 886110

Eyemouth Community Centre, Albert Road, Eyemouth, Scottish Borders TD14 5DE T: 01890 750690

Galashiels Library Buildings, Lawyers Brae, Galashiels, Scottish Borders TD1 3JQ T: 01896 752822

Hawick Council Offices, Town Hall, Hawick, Scottish Borders TD9 9EF T: 01450 364710

Jedburgh Library Building, Castlegate, Jedburgh, TD8 6AS T: 01835 863670 W: www.scotborders.gov.uk

Kelso Town House, Kelso, Scottish Borders TD5 7HF T: 01573 225659

Lauder The Old Jail, Mid Row, Lauder, TD2 6SZ T: 01578 722795

Melrose Ormiston Institute, Market Square, Melrose, Scottish Borders TD6 9PN T: 01896 823114 E: jnorman@scotborders.gsx.gov.uk

Peebles Chambers Institute, High Street, Peebles, Scottish Borders EH45 8AG T: 01721 723817

Selkirk Municipal Buildings, High Street, Selkirk, TD7 4JX T: 01750 23104 E: jstock@scotborders.gsx.gov.uk

West Linton Council Office, West Linton, Borders EH46 7ED T: 01968 660267

Shetland Island

Fair Isle Field, Fair Isle, Shetland ZE2 9JU T: 01595 760224

Sandsting & Aithsting The Register Office, Modesty, West Burrafirth, Aithsting, Shetland ZE2 9NT T: 01595 809428

Shetland Islands

Bressay The Register Office, No 2 Roadside Bressay, Lerwick, Shetland ZE2 9EL T: 01595 820356

Burra Isles Roadside, Hannavoe, Lerwick, Shetland ZE2 9LA T: 01595 859201

Delting North Mainland Community Office, 4 Havragord, Brae, Shetland ZE2 9SZ T: 01595 840691

Dunrossness Wayland, Quendale, Shetland ZE2 9JD T: 01950 460792

Fetlar Lower Toft Funzie, Fetlar, Shetland ZE2 9DJ T: 01957 733273

Foula Magdala, Foula, Shetland ZE2 9PN T: 01595 753236

Lerwick County Buildings, Lerwick, Shetland ZE1 0HD T: 01595 744562 E: registrar@shetland.gov.uk

Lunnasting Vidlin Farm, Vidlin, Shetland ZE2 9QB T: 01806 577204

Mid & South Yell Schoolhouse, Ulsta, Yell, Shetland Islands ZE2 9BD T: 01957 722260

Nesting Laxfirth Brettabister, North Nesting, Shetland ZE2 9PR T: 01595 890260

North Yell Breckon, Cullivoe, Yell, Shetland Islands ZE2 9DD T: 01957 744244

Northmaven Uradell, Eshaness, Shetland ZE2 9RS T: 01806 503362

Sandness grindidale, Sandness, Shetland ZE2 9PL T: 01595 870205

Sandwick The Register Office, Pytaslee Leebitton, Sandwick, Shetland ZE2 9HP T: 01950 431367

Tingwall Vindas, Laxfirth, Tingwall, Shetland ZE2 9SG T: 01595 840450

Unst New Hoose, Baltasound, Unst, Shetland Islands ZE2 9DX T: 01957 711348

Walls Modesty, West Burrafirth, Aithsting, Shetland ZE2 9HP T: 01595 890428

Whalsay Conamore, Brough, Whalsay, Shetland ZE2 9AL T: 01806 566544

Whalsay-Skerries Fairview, East Isle, Skerries, Lerwick ZE2 9AR T: 01806 515255

Whiteness & Weisdale Vista, Whiteness, Shetland ZE2 9LJ T: 01595 830332

South Ayrshire

Ayr Registration Office, 5 - 9 High Street, Ayr, South Ayrshire KA7 1LU T: 01292 617617

Girvan Registration Office, 22 Dalrymple Street, Girvan, KA26 9AE T: 01465 712894

Maybole Council Office, 64 High Street, Maybole, KA19 7BZ T: 01655 882124

Troon Municipal Buildings, 8 South Beach, Troon, South Ayrshire KA10 6EF T: 01292 313555 F: 01292 318009

South Lanarkshire

Biggar The Register Office, 4 Ross Square, Biggar, South Lanarkshire ML12 6DH T: 01899 220997

Blantyre Local Office, 45 John Street, Blantyre, South Lanarkshire G72 0JG T: 01698 527901

Cambuslang Cambuslang Gate, 27 Main Street, Cambuslang, South Lanarkshire G72 7EX T: 0141 584 2577 W: www.southlanarkshire.gov.uk

Carluke The Register Office, 9 Kirkton Street, Carluke, ML8 4AB T: 01555 777844

Coalburn 42 Coalburn Road, Coalburn, ML11 0LH T: 01555 673242

Crawford Raggengill, 45 Carlisle Road, Crawford, Biggar, ML12 6TP T: 01864 502633

Douglas Post Office, Ayr Road, Douglas, South Lanarkshire ML11 0PU T: 01555 851227

East Kilbride Civic Centre, Cornwall Street, East Kilbride, South G74 1AF T: 01355 806474 E: registration@southlanarkshire.gov.uk W: www.southlanarkshire.gov.uk

Forth South Lanarkshire Community Flat, Forth, South Lanarkshire ML11 8EY T: 01555 673242

Hamilton The Town Hall, 102 Cadzow Street, Hamilton, Lanarkshire ML3 6HH T: 01698 452108

Lanark The Register Office, South Vennel, Lanark, South Lanarkshire ML11 7JT T: 01555 673242

Larkhall Council Office, 55 Victoria Street, Larkhall, ML9 2BN T: 01698 882864

Leadhills Operating from Lanark Temporarily, Leadhills, ML12 6XS T: 01555 673242

Lesmahagow The Register Office, 40/42 Abbeygreen, Lesmahagow, ML11 0EQ T: 01555 893812

Rutherglen 139 Main Street, Rutherglen, South Lanarkshire G73 2JJ T: 0141 613 5731

Strathaven Royal Bank of Scotland Buildings, 34 Common Green, Strathaven, South Lanarkshire ML10 6AQ T: 01357 520316

Stirling

Aberfoyle Aberfoyle Local Office, Main Street, Aberfoyle, Stirling FK8 3UQ T: 01877 382986

Balfron Balfron Local Office, 32 Buchanan Street, Balfron, Stirling G63 0TR T: 01360 440315

Callander The Register Office, 1 South Church Street, Callander, Stirling FK17 8BN T: 01877 330166

Dunblane Municipal Buildings, Dunblane, Stirling FK15 0AG T: 01786 823300

Killin 8 Lyon Villas, Killin, Stirling FK21 8TF T: 01567 820655

Stirling Municipal Buildings, 8 - 10 Corn Exchange Road, Stirling, FK8 2HU T: 01786 432343 E: registrar@stirling.gov.uk

West Dunbartonshire

Alexandria The Register Office, 77 Bank Street, Alexandria, West Dunbartonshire G83 0LE T: 01389 608980

Dumbarton 18 College Street, Dumbarton, West Dunbartonshire G82 1NR T: 01389 738350

Old Kilpatrick Council Offices, Rosebery Place, Clydebank, West Dunbartonshire G81 1TG T: 01389 738770

West Lothian

Bathgate The Register Office, 76 Mid Street, Bathgate, West Lothian EH48 1QD T: 01506 776192

East Calder East Calder Library, 200 Main Street, East Calder, West Lothian EH53 0EJ T: 01506 884680

Linlithgow The Register Office, High Street, Linlithgow, West Lothian EH49 7EZ T: 01506 775373

Livingston Lammermuir House, Owen Square, Avondale, Livingston, West Lothian EH54 6PW T: 01506 773754

Uphall Strathbrock Partnership, 189a West Main Street, Broxburn, West Lothian EH52 5LH T: 01506 775509

West Calder The Register Office, 24 - 26 Main Street, West Calder, West Lothian EH55 8DR T: 01506 874704

Whitburn The Register Office, 5 East Main Street, Whitburn, West Lothian EH47 0RA T: 01501 678005

Probate Records

Information from Probate records can provide vital pieces of the genealogical puzzle. Although often not as useful as records of births, marriages and deaths, which can evidence crucial links to previous generations, they can provide evidence of relatedness within generations, and often contain fascinating insights into the financial affairs of people in times past.

Probate is a process whereby some person or persons, usually the executor(s) of a Will if there was one, or one or more of the next-of-kin if there was no Will, are appointed in law to administer the estate of someone who has died. This is usually only necessary if the deceased person left fairly substantial assets, so don't expect to find any Probate record relating to the estate of a person who had little or no estate of their own. The Probate concept of 'estate' refers just to assets held in the sole name of the person who has died, and so Probate isn't necessary for the release of assets held jointly with another person. When an application for Probate is made, any Will that the deceased person left must be submitted to the Probate Registry. The Will, if judged to be valid, is thereafter kept on file, and it is normally possible for anyone to obtain a copy of it. There are exceptions, however, such as the Wills of members of the Royal family. The important point is that Wills are available from the Probate Registries only as a by-product of the Probate process: if Probate wasn't needed, then the Probate Registries have no record of the estate at all.

You should bear in mind that the Probate record, if any, will be dated some time after the date of death of the person concerned, so start searching from the year of death, or the year in which you think the person died. You should normally expect to find the Probate record within the first year or two after the date of death, and, if you have not found it within three, you can usually assume that Probate wasn't necessary. However, in a very small number of cases, Probate is granted many years after the person in question died. Take a tip from the professionals: if you don't find a probate record within the first few years, the next most likely time to search is the year in which their heir(s) died. This is because unadministered estate is most likely to come to light at that time. How far you want to go with the search will probably depend on how crucial the person in question is to your research, but there is as yet no shortcut: you will have to search the index for each year separately.

Control of Probate record-keeping passed from the Church to the state in 1858, at which point the records were unified into one Calendar index. These indexes, which summarise all Probate grants for England and Wales during a given year, act as a table of contents for the vast store of records held by the Probate Registries. If the subject of your research died before 1858, it will be more difficult to trace their Will. However, if they were very wealthy or owned a lot of land, consult the indexes of the Prerogative Court of Canterbury (PCC) first, and then those of the lesser ecclesiastical courts of the region in which they lived. PCC records are held by the Family Records Centre in London (T: 020 8392 5300), but records of the lesser ecclesiastical Probate courts are highly dispersed. Try the local authority archives, such as public libraries and County Record Offices of the appropriate region, and also any local historical research institutes. Major ecclesiastical centres are also likely to have their own archives.

The table below lists the Calendar indexes held by the various Probate Registries in England and Wales. You can usually call in to consult the indexes, but check with the Registry concerned first, especially if you intend to travel any distance. Probate grants for each year are listed alphabetically by surname. The crucial parts of the Probate record are the Grant type, which is usually 'Probate', 'Administration' or 'Administration with Will', the issuing Registry, and the grant issue date. They are normally written in sequence towards the end of the index entry, but the older books give the grant date first and highlight the issuing Registry in the text of the entry. The grant type can be inferred from the text, but note that the indexes prior to 1871 listed the 'Administration' grants in a separate part of the book from the 'Probate' and 'Administration with Will' grants, so be sure to search in both places for years prior to this. In addition, there may be a handwritten number next to entries for Wills proved in the Principal Probate Registry (London) between 1858 and 1930. This is the Folio number, which is used by the Probate Registries when obtaining copies of the Will. Always make a note of this if applicable.

If the grant type is 'Administration', this tells you that the person in question did not leave a valid Will. However, the Probate Registries can still supply a copy of the grant, which is the document naming the person appointed in law as the administrator of the estate. This can provide genealogical information, especially in older grants where the relationship of the applicant to the deceased was stated. It also gives the value of the estate, although in most cases this is stated as 'not exceeding' a certain figure rather than quoting an exact amount. In fact, the Probate record contains very little information about the estate at all, and no information about its composition. Don't expect to find inventories on file for records after 1858, although they sometimes form part of the Probate record prior to this.

In many cases you can save a lot of time and money by making the search yourself, but there is a postal service by which a search is made on your behalf for a period of four years. There is a fee of £5 for this, but this includes copies of the Will and/or grant if a record is found. It also gives you the benefit of the experience of Probate staff, for instance in knowing when to search and judging under which name the record is likely to be listed. If you want the Probate Registry to conduct a search for a period longer than the standard four years, there is an additional fee of £3 for each 4-year period after the first four. Thus, an 8-year search will cost £8, a 12-year search £11, and so on.

If you want to make a postal search, contact **The Postal Searches and Copies Department,** York Probate Sub-Registry, 1st Floor, Castle Chambers, Clifford Street, York YO1 9RG UK Tel: +44 (1904) 666777

Applications for searches must be made in writing, and give the full name, last known address and date of death of the person concerned. A search can normally be made using less detail, but if the date of death is not known, you must state the year from which you want the search to be made, or give some other evidence that might indicate when the person died. If you have information about legal actions related to Probate or the disposition of assets, include that on your application. Many people find it convenient to order copies in this way even if they have already made a search of the Probate indexes and located a record relating to the subject of their research, but if this is the case, please include the grant type, issuing Registry and grant issue date on your application, as well as the Folio number if applicable (see above) as this can speed up the supply of copies considerably. The fee should be payable to "HMCS", and if it is paid from abroad, must be made by International Money Order or bank draft, payable through a United Kingdom bank and made out in £ sterling. If you are applying for a search as well, you can request a search of any length, and fees for this are outlined above.

The records referred to here relate only to estates in England and Wales.

Most Registries will have had indexes dating back to 1858, but are not required to keep them for more than fifty years. Usually, the older indexes will have been donated to local authority archives. Contact your local public library or County/City Record Office to see what Probate records they have. If you know of any historical research institute in your area, find out if they have any Probate records.

Please note that, since the York Probate Registry serves as a national centre for postal requests for searches and copies, it is not possible to inspect the Probate indexes in person there. The Service has undergone a process of computerisation, but as yet this covers only recently-issued grants, which will be of limited interest to genealogists. However, anyone who is interested in checking up on grants since 1996 can search the Probate Service database themselves. To date, workstations for public use have been installed at the Principal Probate Registry and Manchester District Probate Registry. The Postal Searches and Copies Department at York is also completing a long period of computerisation, which should see a much-improved service to family history researchers, with clearer and more comprehensive

information and quicker supply of documents.

This information is based on details supplied by the Probate Service. The details are liable to change without notice. Always telephone the Registry before visiting, to check opening times and the availability of records. While every effort is made to ensure the accuracy of these details, the Probate Service cannot be held responsible for any consequence of errors.

Please check our website at www.courtservice.gov.uk before applying for searches or copy documents by post.

Probate Registries & Sub-Registries

Principal Probate Registry T: 020 7947 6939 First Avenue House, 42-49 High Holborn, London WC1
Probate Registry of Wales - Cardiff T: 02920 474373 3rd Floor, Cardiff Magistrates Court, Fitzalan Place, Cardiff CF24 0RZ
Bangor Probate Sub-Registry T: 01248 362410Council Offices, FFord, Bangor LL57 1DT
Birmingham District Probate Registry T: 0121 681 3400 The Priory Courts, 33 Bull Street, Birmingham B4 6DU
Bodmin Probate Sub-Registry T: 01208 261581
Launceston Road, Bodmin PL31 2AL
Brighton District Probate Registry T: 01273 573510
William Street, Brighton BN2 2LG
Bristol District Probate Registry T: 0117 366 4960 / 4961
2 Redcliff Street, Bristol BS1 6GR
Carlisle Probate Sub- Registry T: 01228 521751
Courts of Justice, Earl Street, Carlisle CA1 1DJ
Carmarthen Probate Sub-Registry T: 01267 242560
14 King Street, Carmarthen SA31 1BL
Chester Probate Sub-Registry T: 0151 236 8264 Chester Civil Justice Centre, Trident House, Little John Styreet, Chester CH1 1SN
Exeter Probate Sub-Registry T: 01392 415370 2nd Floor, Exeter Crown & County Courts, Southernhay Gardens, Exeter EX1 1UH
Gloucester Probate Sub-Registry T: 01452 834966 2nd Floor, Combined Court Building, Kimbrose Way, Gloucester GL1 2DG
Ipswich District Probate Registry T: 01473 284260
Ground Floor, 8 Arcade Street, Ipswich IP1 1EJ
Lancaster Probate Sub-Registry T: 0151 236 8264 Room 111, Mitre House, Church St, Lancaster LA1 1HE
Leeds District Probate Registry T: 0113 386 3540 3rd Floor, Coronet House, Queen Street, Leeds LS1 2BA

Leicester Probate Sub-Registry T: 0116 285 3380
Crown Court Building, 90 Wellington St, Leicester LE1 6HG
Lincoln Probate Sub-Registry T: 01522 523 648. 360 High Street, Lincoln LN5 7PS
Liverpool District Probate Registry T: 0151 236 8264 Queen Elizabeth II Law Courts, Derby Square, Liverpool L2 1XA
Maidstone Probate Sub-Registry (01622) 202048
The Law Courts, Barker Road, Maidstone ME16 8EQ
Manchester District Probate Registry T: 0161 837 6070
Manchester Civil Justice Centre, Ground Floor, 1 Bridge Street West, PO Box 4240, Manchester M60 1WJT
Middlesbrough Probate Sub-Registry T: 0191 211 2170 Teesside Combined Court Centre, Russell Street, Middlesbrough TS1 2AE
Newcastle-upon-Tyne District Probate Registry T: 0191211 2170 1 Waterloo Square, Newcastle-upon-Tyne NE1 4DR
Norwich Probate Sub-Regsitry T: 01603) 728267 Combined Court Building, The Law Courts, Bishopgate, Norwich NR3 1UR
Nottingham Probate Sub-Registry T: 0115 941 4288. 33 Park Row, Nottingham NG1 6GR
Oxford District Probate Registry T: 01865 793055
Combined Court Building, St.Aldates, Oxford OX1 1LY
Peterborough Probate Sub-Registry T: 01733 562802, Crown Building, Rivergate, Peterborough PE1 1EJ
Sheffield Probate Sub-Registry T: 0114 281 2596
PO Box 832, The Law Courts, 50 West Bar Sheffield S3 8YR
Stoke-on-Trent Probate Sub-Registry T: 01782 854065 Combined Court Centre, Bethesda Street, Hanley, Stoke-on-Trent ST1 3BP
Winchester District Probate Registry T: 01962 897029 4th Floor, Cromwell House, Andover Road, Winchester SO23 7EW
York Probate Sub-Registry, 1st Floor, Castle Chambers, Clifford St, York YO1 9RG UK T: +44 (1904) 666 777 F: +44 (1904) 666 776

Cemeteries & Crematoria

England

Avon

Bristol General Cemetery East Lodge, Bath Rd, Arnos Vale, Bristol, Avon BS4 3EW T: 0117 971 3294

Canford Crematorium & Cemetery Canford Lane, Westbury On Trym, Bristol, Avon BS9 3PQ T: 0117 903 8280 F: 0117 903 8287

Cemetery of Holy Souls Bath Rd, Bristol, Avon BS4 3EW T: 0117 977 2386

Haycombe Crematorium & Cemetery Whiteway Rd, Bath, Avon BA2 2RQ T: 01225 423682

South Bristol Crematorium & Cemetery Bridgwater Rd, Bristol, Avon BS13 7AS T: 0117 963 4141

Westerleigh Crematorium Westerleigh Rd, Westerleigh, Bristol, Avon BS37 8QP T: 0117 937 4619

Weston Super Mare Crematorium Ebdon Rd, Worle, Weston-Super-Mare, Avon BS22 9NY T: 01934 511717

Bedfordshire

Church Burial Ground 26 Crawley Green Rd, Luton, Bedfordshire LU2 0QX T: 01582 722874 W: www.stmarysluton.org

Dunstable Cemetery West St, Dunstable LU6 1PB T: 01582 662772

Kempston Cemetery Cemetery Lodge, 2 Green End Rd, Kempston, Bedford, Bedfordshire MK43 8RJ T: 01234 851823

Luton Crematorium The Vale, Butterfield Green Rd, Stopsley, Luton, Bedfordshire LU2 8DD T: 01582 723700 F: 01582 723700

Luton General Cemetery Rothesay Rd, Luton LU1 1QX T: 01582 727480

Norse Rd Crematorium 104 Norse Rd, Bedford, Bedfordshire MK41 0RL T: 01234 353701

Kempston Cemetery Cemetery Lodge, 2 Green End Rd, Kempston, Bedford, Bedfordshire MK43 8RJ T: 01234 851823

Berkshire

Easthampstead Park Cemetry & Crematorium Nine Mile Ride, Wokingham, Berkshire RG40 3DW T: 01344 420314

Henley Rd Cemetery & Reading Crematorium All Hallows Rd, Henley Rd, Caversham, Reading RG4 5LP T: 0118 947 2433

Larges Lane Cemetery Larges Lane, Bracknell, Berkshire RG12 9AL T: 01344 450665

Newbury Cemetery Shaw Hill, Shaw Fields, Shaw, Newbury, Berkshire RG14 2EQ T: 01635 40096

Slough Cemetery & Crematorium Stoke Rd, Slough SL2 5AX T: 01753 523127 (Cemetery)E: sloughcrem@hotmail.com W: www.slough.gov.uk

Bristol

South Bristol Crematorium and Cemetery Bridgwater Rd, Bedminster Down, Bristol, BS13 7AS T: 0117 903 8330

Buckinghamshire

Chilterns Crematorium Whielden Lane, Winchmore Hill, Amersham, Buckinghamshire HP7 0ND T: 01494 724263

Crownhill Crematorium Dansteed Way, Crownhill, Milton Keynes, Buckinghamshire T: 01908 568112

Cambridgeshire

American Military Cemetery Madingley Rd, Coton, Cambridge, CB3 7PH T: 01954 210350 E: info@abmc.gov W: www.abmc.gov

Cambridge City Crematorium Huntingdon Rd, Girton, Cambridge, Cambridgeshire CB3 0JJ T: 01954 780681

City of Ely Council Ely Cemetery, Beech Lane, Ely, Cambridgeshire CB7 4QZ T: 01353 669659

Marholm Crematorium Mowbray Rd, Peterborough, PE6 7JE T: 01733 262639

Cheshire

Altrincham Cemetery Hale Rd, Altrincham, Cheshire WA14 2EW T: 0161 980 4441

Altrincham Crematorium White House Lane, Dunham Massey, Altrincham, Cheshire WA14 5RH T: 0161 928 7717

Chester Cemetries & Crematorium Blacon Avenue, Blacon, Chester, Cheshire CH1 5BB T: 01244 372428

Dukinfield Crematorium Hall Green Rd, Dukinfield, Cheshire SK16 4EP T: 0161 330 1901

Macclesfield Cemetery Cemetery Lodge, 87 Prestbury Rd, Macclesfield, Cheshire SK10 3BU T: 01625 422330

Middlewich Cemetery 12 Chester Rd, Middlewich, Cheshire CW10 9ET T: 01606 737101

Overleigh Rd Cemetery The Lodge, Overleigh Rd, Chester, Cheshire CH4 7HW T: 01244 682529

Walton Lea Crematorium Chester Rd, Higher Walton, Warrington, Cheshire WA4 6TB T: 01925 267731

Widnes Cemetery & Crematorium Birchfield Rd, Widnes, Cheshire WA8 9EE T: 0151 471 7332

Cleveland

Teesside Crematorium Acklam Rd, Middlesbrough, Cleveland TS5 7HE T: 01642 817725 E: peter_gitsham@middlesbrough.gov.uk W: www.middlesbrough.gov.uk

Cornwall

Glynn Valley Crematorium Turfdown Rd, Fletchers Bridge, Bodmin, Cornwall PL30 4AU T: 01208 73858

Penmount Crematorium Penmount, Truro, Cornwall TR4 9AA T: 01872 272871 F: 01872 223634 E: mail@penmount-crematorium.org.uk W: www.penmount-crematorium.org.uk

County Durham

Birtley Cemetery & Crematorium Windsor Rd, Birtley, Chester Le Street, County Durham DH3 1PQ T: 0191 4102381

Chester Le Street Cemetery Chester Le Street District Council Civic Centre, Newcastle Rd, Chester Le Street, County Durham DH3 3UT T: 0191 3872117

Horden Parish Council Horden Cemetery Lodge, Thorpe Rd, Horden, Peterlee, County Durham SR8 4TP T: 0191 5863870

Mountsett Crematorium Ewehurst Rd, Dipton, Stanley, County Durham DH9 0HN T: 01207 570255

Murton Parish Council Cemetery Lodge, Church Lane, Murton, Seaham, County Durham SR7 9RD T: 0191 5263973

Newton Aycliffe Cemetery Stephenson Way, Newton Aycliffe, County Durham DL5 7DF T: 01325 312861

Princess Rd Cemetery Princess Rd, Seaham, County Durham SR7 7TD T: 0191 5812943

Trimdon Foundry Parish Council Cematery Lodge, Thornley Rd, Trimdon Station, County Durham TS29 6NX T: 01429 880592

Trimdon Parish Council Cemetery Lodge, Northside, Trimdon Grange, Trimdon Station, County Durham TS29 6HN T: 01429 880538

Wear Valley District Council Cemetery Lodge, South Church Rd, Bishop Auckland, County Durham DL14 7NA T: 01388 603396

Cumbria

Carlisle Cemetery Richardson St, Carlisle, Cumbria CA2 6AL T: 01228 625310 F: 01228 625313 E: junec@carlisle-city.gov.uk

Penrith Cemetery Beacon Edge, Penrith, Cumbria CA11 7RZ T: 01768 862152

Wigton Burial Joint Committee Cemetery House, Station Hill, Wigton, Cumbria CA7 9BN T: 016973 42442

Derbyshire

Bretby Crematorium Geary Lane, Bretby, Burton-On-Trent, Staffordshire DE15 0QE T: 01283 221505 F: 01283 224846 E: bretby.crematorium@eaststaffsbc.gov.uk W: www.eaststaffsbc.gov.uk

Castle Donington Parish Council Cemetery House, The Barroon, Castle Donington, Derby, Derbyshire DE74 2PF T: 01332 810202

Chesterfield & District Joint Crematorium Chesterfield Rd, Brimington, Chesterfield, Derbyshire S43 1AU T: 01246 345888 F: 01246 345889

Clay Cross Cemetery Cemetery Rd, Danesmoor, Chesterfield, Derbyshire S45 9RL T: 01246 863225

Dronfield Cemetery Cemetery Lodge, 42 Cemetery Rd, Dronfield, Derbyshire S18 1XY T: 01246 412373

Glossop Cemetery Arundel House, Cemetery Rd, Glossop, Derbyshire SK13 7QG T: 01457 852269

Markeaton Crematorium Markeaton Lane, Derby, Derbyshire DE22 4NH T: 01332 341012 F: 01332 331273

Melbourne Cemetery Pack Horse Rd, Melbourne, Derby, Derbyshire DE73 1BZ T: 01332 863369

Shirebrook Town Council Common Lane, Shirebrook, Mansfield, Nottinghamshire NG20 8PA T: 01623 742509

Devon

Drake Memorial Park Ltd The Haye Rd, Plympton, Plymouth, Devon PL7 1UQ T: 01752 337937

Exeter & Devon Crematorium Topsham Rd, Exeter, Devon EX2 6EU T: 01392 496333

Exeter Higher Cemetery, St Mark's Avenue, Heavitree, Exeter EX1 2PX E:kelly.james@exeter.gov.uk

Exwick Cemetery, Exwick Road, Exeter EX4 2BT E: kelly.james@exeter.gov.uk

Ford Park Cemetery Trust Ford Park Rd, Plymouth, Devon PL4 6NT T: 01752 665442 F: 01752 601177 E: trustees@ford-park-cemetery.org W: www.ford-park-cemetery.org

Littleham Church Yard Littleham Village, Littleham, Exmouth, Devon EX8 2RQ T: 01395 225579

Mole Valley Green Burial Ground Woodhouse Farm, Queens Nympton, South Molton, Devon EX36 4JH T: 01769 574512 F: 01769 574512 E: woodhouse.org.farm@farming.co.uk

North Devon Crematorium Old Torrington Rd, Barnstaple, Devon EX31 3NW T: 01271 345431

Tavistock Cemetery Cemetery Office, Plymouth Rd, Tavistock, Devon PL19 8BY T: 01822 612799 F: 01822 618300 E: tavistocktc@aol.com W: www.tavistock.gov.uk

Topsham Cemetery, Elm Grove Road, Topsham, Exeter EX3 0BW T: kelly.james@exeter.gov.uk

Torquay Crematorium & Cemetery Hele Rd, Torquay, Devon TQ2 7QG T: 01803 327768

Dorset

Dorchester Cemetery Office 31a Weymouth Avenue, Dorchester, Dorset DT1 2EN T: 01305 263900

Parkstone Cemetery 134 Pottery Rd, Parkstone, Poole, Dorset

BH14 8RD T: 01202 741104
Poole Cemetery Dorchester Rd, Oakdale, Poole, Dorset BH15 3RZ T: 01202 741106
Poole Crematorium Gravel Hill, Poole, Dorset BH17 9BQ T: 01202 602582
Sherborne Cemetery Lenthay Rd, Sherborne, Dorset DT9 6AA T: 01935 812909
Weymouth Crematorium Quibo Lane, Weymouth, Dorset DT4 0RR T: 01305 786984
Essex
Basildon & District Crematorium Church Rd, Bowers Gifford, Basildon, Essex SS13 2HG T: 01268 584411
Chadwell Heath Cemetery Whalebone Lane, North Chadwell Heath, Romford, Essex RM6 5QX T: 0208 590 3280
Chelmsford Crematorium Writtle Rd, Chelmsford, Essex CM1 3BL T: 01245 256946
Chigwell Cemetery Frog Hall LaneChapman, Manor Rd, Chigwell, Essex IG7 4JX T: 020 8501 4275 F: 020 8501 2045 E: chigwell@tesco.net
Colchester Cemetery & Crematorium Mersea Rd, Colchester, Essex CO2 8RU T: 01206 282950
Eastbrookend Cemetery Dagenham Rd, Dagenham, Essex RM10 7DR T: 01708 447451
Federation of Synagogues Burial Society 416 Upminster Rd North, Rainham, Essex RM13 9SB T: 01708 552825
Great Burstead Cemetery Church St, Great Burstead, Billericay, Essex CM11 2TR T: 01277 654334
Parndon Wood Crematorium and Cemetery Parndon Wood Rd, Harlow, Essex CM19 4SF T: 01279 446199 E: chris.brown@harlow.gov.uk
Pitsea Cemetery Church Rd, Pitsea, Basildon, Essex SS13 2EZ T: 01268 552132
Romford Cemetery Crow Lane, Romford, Essex RM7 0EP T: 01708 740791
Sewardstone Rd Cemetery Sewardstone Rd, Waltham Abbey, Essex EN9 1NX T: 01992 712525
South Essex Crematorium Ockendon Rd, Corbets Tey, Upminster, Essex RM14 2UY T: 01708 222188
Sutton Rd Cemetery The Lodge, Sutton Rd, Southend-On-Sea, Essex SS2 5PX T: 01702 603907 F: 01702 603906
Weeley Crematorium Colchester Rd, Weeley, Clacton-On-Sea, Essex CO16 9JP T: 01255 831108 F: 01255 831440
Wickford Cemetery Park Drive, Wickford SS12 9DH T: 01268 733335
Gloucestershire
Cheltenham Cemetery & Crematorium Bouncers Lane, Cheltenham, Gloucestershire GL52 5JT T: 01242 244245 F: 01242 263123 E: cemetery@cheltenham.gov.uk W: www.cheltenham.gov.uk
Coney Hill Crematorium Coney Hill Rd, Gloucester, Gloucestershire GL4 4PA T: 01452 523902
Forest of Dean Crematorium Yew Tree Brake, Speech House Rd, Cinderford, Gloucestershire GL14 3HU T: 01594 826624
Mile End Cemetery Mile End, Coleford, Gloucestershire GL16 7DB T: 01594 832848
Hampshire
Aldershot Crematorium 48 Guildford Rd, Aldershot GU12 4BP T: 01252 321653
Anns Hill Rd Cemetery Anns Hill Rd, Gosport PO12 3JX T: 023 9258 0181 F: 023 9251 3191 W: www.gosport.gov.uk
Basingstoke Crematorium Manor Farm, Stockbridge Rd, North Waltham, Basingstoke RG25 2BA T: 01256 398784
Magdalen Hill Cemetery Magdalen Hill, Arlesesford Rd, Winchester, Hampshire SO21 1HE T: 01962 854135
Portchester Crematorium Upper Cornaway Lane, Portchester, Fareham PO16 8NE T: 01329 822533
Portsmouth Cemeteries Office Milton Rd, Southsea, Hampshire PO4 8 T: 023 9273 2559
Southampton City Council 6 Bugle St, Southampton SO14 2AJ T: 023 8022 8609
Warblington Cemetery Church Lane, Warblington, Havant PO9 2TU
Worting Rd Cemetery 105 Worting Rd, Basingstoke, Hampshire RG21 8YZ T: 01256 321737
Herefordshire
Hereford Cemetery & Crematorium Bereavement Services office, Westfaling Street, HerefordHR4 0JE T: 01432 383200
Hertfordshire
Almonds Lane Cemetery Almonds Lane, Stevenage SG1 3RR T: 01438 350902
Bushey Jewish Cemetery Little Bushey Lane, Bushey, Watford WD2 3TP T: 0208 950 6299
Chorleywood Rd Cemetery Chorleywood Rd, Rickmansworth WD3 4EH T: 01923 772646
Dacorum Borough Council Woodwells Cemetery, Buncefield Lane, Hemel Hempstead HP2 7HY T: 01442 252856
Harwood Park Crematorium Ltd Watton Rd, Stevenage SG2 8XT T: 01438 815555
Hatfield Rd Cemetery Hatfield Rd, St. Albans AL1 4LU T: 01727 819362 F: 01727 819362
North Watford Cemetery North Western Avenue, Watford WD25

0AW T: 01923 672157 F: 01923 672157
Tring Cemetery Aylesbury Rd, Aylesbury, Tring HP23 4DH T: 01442 822248
Vicarage Rd Cemetery Vicarage Rd, Watford WD18 0EJ T: 01923 672157 F: 01923 672157
Vicarage Rd Cemetery Vicarage Rd, Watford WD1 8EJ T: 01923 225147
Watton Rd Cemetery Watton Rd, Ware SG12 0AX T: 01920 463261
West Herts Crematorium High Elms Lane, Watford WD25 0JS T: 01923 673285 W: www.westhertscrem.org
Western Synagogue Cemetery Cheshunt Cemetery, Bulls Cross Ride, Waltham Cross EN7 5HT T: 01992 717820
Weston Rd Cemetery Weston Rd, Stevenage SG1 4DE T: 01438 367109
Woodcock Hill Cemetery Lodge, Woodcock Hill, Harefield Rd, Rickmansworth WD3 1PT T: 01923 775188
Isle Of Wight
Shanklin Cemetery 1 Cemetery Rd, Lake Sandown, Sandown, Isle Of Wight PO36 9NN T: 01983 403743
Kent
Barham Crematorium Canterbury Rd, Barham, Canterbury, Kent CT4 6QU T: 01227 831351 F: 01227 830258
Beckenham Crematorium & Cemetery Elmers End Rd, Beckenham, Kent BR3 4TD T: 0208 650 0322
Chartham Cemetery Lodge Ashford Rd, Chartham, Canterbury, Kent CT4 7NY T: 01227 738211 F: 01227 738211
Gravesham Borough Council Old Rd West, Gravesend, Kent DA11 0LS T: 01474 337491
Hawkinge Cemetery & Crematorium Aerodrome Rd, Hawkinge, Folkestone, Kent CT18 7AG T: 01303 892215
Kent & Sussex Crematorium Benhall Mill Rd., Tunbridge Wells, Kent TN2 5JH T: 01892 523894
Kent County Crematorium plc Newcourt Wood, Charing, Ashford, Kent TN27 0EB T: 01233 712443 F: 01233 713501
Medway Crematorium Robin Hood Lane, Blue Bell Hill, Chatham, Kent ME5 9QU T: 01634 861639 F: 01634 671206 E: paul.edwards@medway.gov.uk
Northfleet Cemetery Springhead Rd, Northfleet, Gravesend, Kent DA11 8HW T: 01474 533260
Snodland Cemetery Cemetery Cottage, Cemetery Rd, Snodland, Kent ME6 5DN T: 01634 240764
Thanet Crematorium Manston Rd, Margate, Kent CT9 4LY T: 01843 224492 F: 01843 292218
The Cremation Society 2nd Floor Brecon House, 16/16a Albion Place, Maidstone, Kent ME14 5DZ T: 01622 688292/3 F: 01622 686698 E: cremsoc@aol.com W: www.cremation.org.uk
Vinters Park Crematorium Bearstead Rd, Weavering, Maidstone, Kent ME14 5LG T: 01622 738172 F: 01622 630560
Lancashire
Accrington Cemetery & Crematorium Burnley Rd, Accrington, Lancashire BB5 6HA T: 01254 232933 F: 01254 232933
Atherton Cemetery Leigh Rd, Atherton, Lancashire
Audenshaw Cemetery Cemetery Rd, Audenshaw, Manchester, Lancashire M34 5AH T: 0161 336 2675
Blackley Cemetery & Crematorium Victoria Avenue, Manchester, Lancashire M9 8 T: 0161 740 5359
Burnley Cemetery Rossendale Rd, Burnley, Lancashire BB11 5DD T: 01282 435411 F: 01282 458904 W: www.burnley.gov.uk
Carleton Crematorium Stocks Lane, Carleton, Poulton-Le-Fylde, Lancashire FY6 7QS T: 01253 882541
Central & North Manchester Synagogue Jewish Cemetery Rainsough Brow, Prestwich, Manchester, Lancashire M25 9XW T: 0161 773 2641
Central & North Manchester Synagogue Jewish Cemetery Rochdale Rd, Manchester, Lancashire M9 6FQ T: 0161 740 2317
Chadderton Cemetery Cemetery Lodge, Middleton Rd, Chadderton, Oldham, Lancashire OL9 0JZ T: 0161 624 2301
Gidlow Cemetery Gidlow Lane, Standish, Wigan, Lancashire WN6 8RT T: 01257 424127
Greenacres Cemetery Greenacres Rd, Oldham, Lancashire OL4 3HT T: 0161 624 2294
Hindley Cemetery Castle Hill Rd Rd, Ince, Wigan, Lancashire WN3
Hollinwood Cemetery (incorporating Oldham Crematorium) Central Cemeteries Office, Roman Rd, Hollinwood, Oldham, Lancashire OL8 3LU T: 0161 681 1312 F: 0161 683 5233 E: oper.cemeteries@oldham.gov.uk W: www.oldham.gov.uk
Howe Bridge Crematorium Crematorium Management Ltd, Lovers Lane, Atherton, Manchester, Lancashire M46 0PZ T: 01942 870811
Howebridge Cemetery Lovers Lane, Atherton, Lancashire
Ince in Makerfield Cemetery Warrington Rd, Lower Ince, Wigan
Leigh Cemetery Manchester Rd, Leigh, Lancashire WN7 2 T: 01942 671560 F: 01942 828877 W: www.wiganbc.gov.uk
Lower Ince Cemetery and Crematorium Cemetery Rd, Lower Ince, Wigan, Lancashire WN3 4NH T: 01942 866455 F: 01942 828855 E: t.bassett@wiganmbc.gov.uk
Lytham Park Cemetery & Cremarotium Regent Avenue, Lytham St. Annes, Lancashire FY8 4AB T: 01253 735429 F: 01253 731903
Manchester Crematorium Ltd Barlow Moor Rd, Manchester,

Lancashire M21 7GZ T: 0161 881 5269
Middleton New Cemetery Boarshaw Rd, Middleton, Manchester, Lancashire M24 6 T: 0161 655 3765
New Manchester Woodland Cemetery City Rd, Ellenbrook, Worsley, Manchester, Lancashire M28 1BD T: 0161 790 1300
Overdale Crematorium Overdale Drive, Chorley New Rd, Heaton, Bolton, Lancashire BL1 5BU T: 01204 840214
Padiham Public Cemetery St. Johns Rd, Padiham, Burnley, Lancashire BB12 7BN T: 01282 778139
Preston Cemetery New Hall Lane, Preston PR1 4SY T: 01772 794585 F: 01772 703857 E: m.birch@preston.gov.uk W: www.preston.gov.uk
Preston Crematorium Longridge Rd, Ribbleton, Preston, Lancashire PR2 6RL T: 01772 792391 F: 01772 703857 E: m.birch@preston.gov.uk W: www.preston.gov.uk
Rochdale Cemetery Bury Rd, Rochdale, Lancashire OL11 4DG T: 01706 645219
Southern Cemetery Barlow Moor Rd, Manchester, Lancashire M21 7GL T: 0161 881 2208
St Joseph's Cemetery Moston Lane, Manchester, Lancashire M40 9QL T: 0161 681 1582 E: cemeteries@salforddiocese.org
St. Mary's Catholic Cemetery Manchester Rd, Wardley, Manchester, M28 2UJ T: 0161 794 2194 E: cemeteries@salforddiocese.org
Tyldesley Cemetery Hough Lane, Tyldesley, Lancashire
United Synagogue Burial Ground Worsley Hill Farm, Phillips Park Rd, Whitefield, Manchester, Lancashire M45 7ED T: 0161 766 2065
Westwood Cemetery Westwood Lane, Lower Ince, Wigan, Lancashire
Whitworth Cemetery Edward St, Whitworth, Rochdale, Lancashire OL16 2EJ T: 01706 217777
Wigan Council Cemeteries & Crematorium Section 1 - 3 Worsley Terrace, Standishgate, Wigan, Lancashire WN1 1XW T: 01942 828993 F: 01942 828877 E: t.boussele@wiganmbc.gov.uk
Leicestershire
Cemetery Lodge Thorpe Rd, Melton Mowbray, Leicestershire LE13 1SH T: 01664 562223
Loughborough Crematorium Leicester Rd, Loughborough, Leicestershire LE11 2AF T: 01743 353046
Saffron Hill Cemetery Stonesby Avenue, Leicester, Leicestershire LE2 6TY T: 0116 222 1049
Lincolnshire
Boston Cemetery & Crematorium Cemeteries and Crematorium Office, Marian Rd, Boston, Lincolnshire PE21 9HA T: 01205 364612 E: martin.potts@boston.gov.uk W: www.boston.gov.uk
Bourne Town Cemetery South Rd, Bourne, Lincolnshire PE10 9JB T: 01778 422796
Grantham Cemetery & Crematorium Harrowby Rd, Grantham, Lincolnshire NG31 9DT T: 01476 563083 F: 01476 576228
Horncastle Cemetery Boston Rd, Horncastle, Lincolnshire LN9 6NF T: 01507 527118
Stamford Cemetery Wichendom, Little Casterton Rd, Stamford, Lincolnshire PE9 1BB T: 01780 762316
Tyler Landscapes Newport Cemetery, Manor Rd, Newport, Lincoln, Lincolnshire LN4 1RT T: 01522 525195
London
Abney Park Cemetery Trust The South Lodge, Abney Park Cemetery, High Street, Stoke Newington, London, N16 0LN T: 020 7278 7557 F: 020 7275 7557 E: abneypark@geo2.poptel.org.uk W: www.abney-park.org.uk
Brockley Ladywell Hithergreen & Grove Park Cemeteries Verdant Lane, Catford, London , SE6 1TP T: 0208 697 2555
Brompton Cemetery Fulham Rd, London, SW10 9UG T: 0207 352 1201
Cemetery Management Ltd The City of Westminster Office, 38 Uxbridge Rd, London, W7 3PP T: 0208 567 0913
Charlton Cemetery Cemetery Lane, London, SE7 8DZ T: 0208 854 0235
Chingford Mount Cemetery LB Waltham Forest, Old Church Rd, London, E4 6ST T: 020 8524 5030
City of London Cemetery & Crematorium Aldersbrook Rd, London, E12 5DQ T: 0208 530 2151
Coroners Court 8 Ladywell Rd, Lewisham, London, SE13 7UW T: 0208 690 5138
East London Cemetery Co.Ltd Grange Rd, London, E13 0HB T: 020 7476 5109 E: enquiries@eastlondoncemetery.co.uk W: www.eastlondoncemetery.co.uk
Edmonton Cemetery Church St, Edmonton, London, N9 9HP T: 0208 360 2157
Eltham Cemetery & Crematorium Crown Woods Way, Eltham, London, SE9 2RF T: 0208 850 2921 (Cemetery)
Gap Rd Cemetery Gap Rd, London, SW19 8JF T: 0208 879 0701
Golders Green Crematorium 62 Hoop Lane, London, NW11 7NL T: 0208 455 2374
Greenwich Cemetery Well Hall Rd, London, SE9 6TZ T: 0208 856 8666
Hackney Archives Department - LB of Hackney, 43 De Beauvoir Rd, London, N1 5SQ T: (020) 7241 2886 F: (020) 7241-6688 E: archives@hackney.gov.uk W: www.hackney.gov.uk/ca-history
Hendon Cemetery & Crematorium Holders Hill Rd, London, NW7 1NB T: 0208 346 0657

Highgate Cemetery Swains Lane, London, N6 6PJ T: 0208 340 1834
Honor Oak Crematorium Brenchley Gardens, London, SE23 3RB T: 020 7639 3121 F: 020 7732 3557 E: terry.connor@southwark.gov.uk
Islington Cemetery & Crematorium High Rd, East Finchley, London, N2 9AG T: 0208 883 1230
Kensal Green Cemetery Harrow Rd, London, W10 4RA T: 020 8969 0152 F: 020 8960 9744
L B S Cemeteries Brenchley Gardens, London, SE23 3RD T: 020 7639 3121 F: 020 7732 3557 E: terry.connor@southwark.gov.uk
Lambeth Cemetery and Crematorium Cemetary Lodge, Blackshaw Rd, Tooting, London, SW17 0BY T: 0208 672 1390
Lewisham Crematorium Verdant Lane, London, SE6 1TP T: 0208 698 4955
Liberal Jewish Cemetery The Lodge, Pound Lane, London, NW10 2HG T: 0208 459 1635
London Borough of Hackney Mortuary Lower Clapton Rd, London, E5 8EQ T: 0208 985 2808
Manor Park Cemetery Co.Ltd Sebert Rd, Forest Gate, London, E7 0NP T: 020 8534 1486 F: 020 8519 1348 W: www.mpark.co.uk
New Southgate Cemetery & Crematorium Ltd 98 Brunswick Park Rd, London, N11 1JJ T: 0208 361 1713
Newham London Borough of, High St South, London, E6 6ET T: 0208 472 9111
Plumstead Cemetery Wickham Lane, London, SE2 0NS T: 0208 854 0785
Putney Vale Cemetery & Crematorium Kingston Rd, London, SW15 3SB T: 0208 788 2113
South London Crematorium & Streatham Park Cemetery Rowan Rd, London, SW16 5JG T: 0208 764 2255
St. Marylebone Crematorium East End Rd, Finchley, London, N2 0RZ T: 0208 343 2233
St. Pancras Cemetery (LB Camden) High Rd, East Finchley, London, N2 9AG T: 0208 883 1231
St. Patrick's Catholic Cemetery Langthorne Rd, London, E11 4HL T: 020 8539 2451
St.Mary's Catholic Cemetery Harrow Rd, London, NW10 5NU T: 0208 969 1145
Tottenham Park Cemetery Montagu Rd, Edmonton, London N18 2NF T: 0208 807 1617
United Synagogue Beaconsfield Rd, Willesden, London, NW10 2JE T: 0208 459 0394
West End Chesed V'Ameth Burial Society 3 Rowan Rd, London, SW16 5JF T: 0208 764 1566
West Ham Cemetery Cemetery Rd, London, E7 9DG T: 0208 534 1566
West London Synagogue Hoop Lane, London, NW11 7NJ T: 0208 455 2569
West Norwood Cemetery & Crematorium Norwood Rd, London, SE27 9AJ T: 0207926 7900
Woodgrange Park Cemetery Romford Rd, London, E7 8AF T: 0208 472 3433
Woolwich Cemetery Kings Highway, London, SE18 2BJ T: 0208 854 0740
Merseyside
Anfield Crematorium Priory Rd, Anfield, Liverpool, Merseyside L4 2SL T: 0151 263 3267
Southport Cemeteries & Crematoria Southport Rd, Scarisbrick, Southport, Merseyside PR8 5JQ T: 01704 533443
St. Helens Cemetery & Crematorium Rainford Rd, Windle, St. Helens, Merseyside WA10 6DF T: 01744 677406 F: 01744 677411
Thornton Garden Of Rest Lydiate Lane, Thornton, Liverpool, Merseyside L23 1TP T: 0151 924 5143
Middlesex
Adath Yisroel Synagogue & Burial Society Carterhatch Lane, Enfield, Middlesex EN1 4BG T: 0208 363 3384
Breakspear Crematorium Breakspear Rd, Ruislip, Middlesex HA4 7SJ T: 01895 632843 F: 01895 624209
Enfield Crematorium Great Cambridge Rd, Enfield, Middlesex EN1 4DS T: 0208 363 8324
Heston & Isleworth Borough Cemetry 190 Powder Mill Lane, Twickenham, Middlesex TW2 6EJ T: 0208 894 3830
Richmond Cemeteries LBRichmond upon Thames, Sheen Rd, Richmond, Surrey TW10 5BJ T: 020 8876 4511 F: 020 8878 8118 E: cemeteries@richmond.gov.uk
South West Middlesex Crematorium Hounslow Rd, Hanworth, Feltham, Middlesex TW13 5JH T: 0208 894 9001
Spelthorne Borough Council Green Way, Sunbury-On-Thames, Middlesex TW16 6NW T: 01932 780244
Norfolk
Colney Wood Memorial Park Colney Hall, Watton Rd, Norwich, Norfolk NR4 7TY T: 01603 811556
Mintlyn Crematorium Lynn Rd, Bawsey, King's Lynn, Norfolk PE32 1HB T: 01553 630533 F: 01553 630998 E: creminfo@west-norfolk.gov.uk W: www.west-norfolk.gov.uk
Norwich & Norfolk Crematoria - St. Faiths & Earlham 75 Manor Rd, Horsham St. Faith, Norwich, Norfolk NR10 3LF T: 01603 898264
Sprowston Cemetery Church Lane, Sprowston, Norwich, Norfolk NR7 8AU T: 01603 425354

North East Lincolnshire
Cleethorpes Cemetery Beacon Avenue, Cleethorpes, North Lincolnshire DN35 8EQ T: 01472 324869 F: 01472 324870
N E Lincolnshire Crematorium & Cemeteries Department Weelsby Avenue, Grimsby, North East Lincolnshire DN32 0BA T: 01472 324869 F: 01472 324870
North Lincolnshire
Bereavement Services - North Lincolnshire Council Brumby Wood Lane, Scunthorpe, North Lincolnshire DN17 1SP T: 01724 747555 E: crematorium@northlincs.gov.uk W: www.northlincs.gov.uk/environmentalhealth/cemetery.htm
North Tyneside
North Tyneside Metropolitan Borough Council Whitley Bay Cemetery, Blyth Rd, Whitley Bay, Tyne And Wear NE26 4NH T: 0191 200 5861 F: 0191 200 5860
North Tyneside Metropolitan Borough Council Earsdon Cemetery, Earsdon, Whitley Bay, Tyne And Wear NE25 9LR T: 0191 200 5861 F: 0191 200 5860
Northamptonshire
Counties Crematorium Towcester Rd, Milton Malsor, Northampton, Northamptonshire NN4 9RN T: 01604 858280
Dallington Cemetery Harlstone Rd, Dallington, Northampton, Northamptonshire NN5 7 T: 01604 751589
Northumberland
Alnwick Cemetary Cemetary Lodge Office, South Rd, Alnwick, Northumberland NE66 2PH T: 01665 602598 F: 01665 579272 W: www.alnwicktown.com
Blyth Cemetery Links Rd, Blyth, Northumberland NE24 3PJ T: 01670 369623
Cowpen Cemetery Cowpen Rd, Blyth, Northumberland NE24 5SZ T: 01670 352107
Embleton Joint Burial Committee Spitalford, Embleton, Alnwick, Northumberland NE66 3DW T: 01665 576632
Haltwhistle & District Joint Burial Committee Cemetery Lodge, Haltwhistle NE49 0LF T: 01434 320266 F: 01434 320266
Rothbury Cemetery Cemetery Lodge, Whitton Rd , Rothbury, Morpeth, Northumberland NE65 7RX T: 01669 620451
Nottinghamshire
Bramcote Crematorium Coventry Lane, Beeston, Nottingham, Nottinghamshire NG9 3GJ T: 0115 922 1837
Mansfield & District Crematorium Derby Rd, Mansfield, Nottinghamshire NG18 5BJ T: 01623 621811
Northern Cemetery Hempshill Lane, Bulwell, Nottingham, Nottinghamshire NG6 8PF T: 0115 915 3245 F: 0115 915 3246 E: alec.thomson@nottinghamcity.gov.uk W: www.nottinghamcity.gov.uk/bereavement
Southern Cemetery & Crematoria Wilford Hill, West Bridgford, Nottingham, Nottinghamshire NG2 7FE T: 0115 915 2340
Tithe Green Woodland Burial Ground Salterford Lane, Calverton, Nottingham, Nottinghamshire NG14 6NZ T: 01623 882210
Oxfordshire
Oxford Crematorium Ltd Bayswater Rd, Headington, Oxford, Oxfordshire OX3 9RZ T: 01865 351255
Sheffield
Sheffield Central Cemetery The Cemetery Gatehouse, Cemetery Avenue, Sheffield S11 8NT T: 0114 268 3486 W: www.gencem.org
Shropshire
Bridgnorth Cemetery Mill St, Bridgnorth, Shropshire WV15 5NG T: 01746 762386
Emstrey Crematorium London Rd, Shrewsbury, Shropshire SY2 6PS T: 01743 359883
Hadley Cemetery 85 Hadley Park Rd, Hadley, Telford, Shropshire TF1 4PY T: 01952 223418
Longden Rd Cemetery Longden Rd, Shrewsbury, Shropshire SY3 7HS T: 01743 353046
Market Drayton Burial Committee Cemetery Lodge, Cemetery Rd, Market Drayton, Shropshire TF9 3BD T: 01630 652833
Oswestry Cemetery Cemetery Lodge, Victoria Rd, Oswestry, Shropshire SY11 2HU T: 01691 652013 E: objc@btinternet.com
Whitchurch Joint Cemetery Board The Cemetery Lodge, Mile Bank Rd, Whitchurch, Shropshire SY13 4JY T: 01948 665477
Somerset
Burnham Area Burial Board The Old Courthouse, Jaycroft Rd, Burnham-On-Sea, Somerset TA8 1LE T: 01278 795111
Chard Town Council Holyrood Lace Mill, Hoilyrood Street, Chard, Somerset TA20 12YA T: 01460 260370 F: 01460 260372
Minehead Cemetery Porlock Rd, Woodcombe, Minehead, Somerset TA24 8RY T: 01643 705243
Sedgemoor District Council The Cemetery, Quantock Rd, Bridgwater, Somerset TA6 7EJ T: 01278 423993
Taunton Deane Cemeteries & Crematorium Wellington New Rd, Taunton, Somerset TA1 5NE T: 01823 284811 F: 01823 323152 W: www.tauntondeane.gov.uk/TDBCsites/crem
Wells Burial Joint Committee 127 Portway, Wells, Somerset BA5 1LY T: 01749 672049
Yeovil Cemetery Preston Rd, Yeovil BA21 3AG T: 01935 423742
Yeovil Crematorium Bunford Lane, Yeovil BA20 2EJ T: 01935 476718
Staffordshire

Bretby Crematorium Geary Lane, Bretby, Burton-On-Trent, Staffordshire DE15 0QE T: 01283 221505 F: 01283 224846 E: bretby.crematorium@eaststaffsbc.gov.uk W: www.eaststaffsbc.gov.uk
Cannock Cemetery Cemetery Lodge, 160 Pye Green Rd, Cannock, Staffordshire WS11 2SJ T: 01543 503176
Carmountside Cemetery and Crematorium Bereavement Care Services, Leek Rd, Milton, Stoke-On-Trent ST2 7AB T: 01782 235050 F: 01782 235050 E: karendeaville@civic2.stoke.gov.uk
Leek Cemetery Condlyffe Rd, Leek ST13 5PP T: 01538 382616
Newcastle Cemetery Lymewood Grove, Newcastle ST5 2EH T: 01782 616379 E: jeanette.hollins@newcastle-staffs.gov.uk
Newcastle Crematorium Chatterley Close, Bradwell, Newcastle, Staffordshire ST5 8LE T: 01782 635498 F: 01782 710859
Stafford Crematorium Tixall Rd, Stafford ST18 0XZ T: 01785 242594
Stapenhill Cemetery 38 Stapenhill Rd, Burton-On-Trent, Staffordshire DE15 9AE T: 01283 508572 F: 01283 566586 E: cemetery@eaststaffsbc.gov.uk W: www.eaststaffsbc.gov.uk
Stilecop Cematary Stilecop Rd, Rugeley, Staffordshire WS15 1ND T: 01889 577739
Uttoxeter Town Council Cemetery Lodge, Stafford Rd, Uttoxeter , Staffordshire ST14 8DS T: 01889 563374
Stockton on Tees
Tees Cemetery Records Registrar of Births, Deaths & Marriages - Stockton-on-Tees, Nightingale House, Balaclava Street, Stockton-on-Tees, TS18 2AL T: 01642 527720 W: www.stockton.gov.uk
Suffolk
Brinkley Woodland Cemetery 147 All Saints Rd, Newmarket, Suffolk CB8 8HH T: 01638 600693
Bury St. Edmunds Cemetery 91 Kings Rd, Bury St. Edmunds, Suffolk IP33 3DT T: 01284 754447
Hadleigh Town Council Friars Rd, Hadleigh, Ipswich, Suffolk IP7 6DF T: 01473 822034
Haverhill Cemetery Withersfield Rd, Haverhill, Suffolk CB9 9HF T: 01440 703810
Ipswich Cemetery & Crematorium Cemetery Lane, Ipswich, Suffolk IP4 2TQ T: 01473 433580 F: 01473 433588
Leiston Cemetery Waterloo Avenue, Leiston, Suffolk IP16 4EH T: 01728 831043
West Suffolk Crematorium Risby, Bury St. Edmunds, Suffolk IP28 6RR T: 01284 755118 F: 01284 755135
Surrey
American Cemetery Cemetery Pales, Brookwood, Woking, Surrey GU24 0BL T: 01483 473237
Bandon Hill Cemetery Joint Committee Plough Lane, Wallington, Surrey SM6 8JQ T: 0208 647 1024
Brookwood Cemetery Cemetery Pales, Brookwood, Woking, Surrey GU24 0BL T: 01483 472222
Confederation of Burial Authorities The Gate House, Kew Meadow Path, Richmond, Surrey TW9 4EN T: 0208 392 9487
Dorking Cemetery Reigate Rd, Dorking, Surrey RH4 1QF T: 01306 879299 F: 01306 876821 E: carole.brough@mole-valley.gov.uk W: www.mole-valley.gov.uk
Guildford Crematorium & Cemetaries Brdwater, New Pond Rd, Goldaming, Godalming, Surrey GU7 3DB T: 01483 444711
Kingston Cemetary & Crematorium Bonner Hill Rd, Kingston Upon Thames, Surrey KT1 3EZ T: 020 8546 4462 F: 020 8546 4463
London Rd Cemetery Figs Marsh, London Rd, Mitcham, Surrey CR4 3 T: 0208 648 4115
Merton & Sutton Joint Cemetery Garth Rd, Morden, Surrey SM4 4LL T: (020) 8337 4420 F: (020) 8337 4420
Mortlake Crematorium Board Kew Meadow Path, Town Mead Rd, Richmond, Surrey TW9 4EN T: 0208 876 8056
Mount Cemetery Weyside Rd, Guildford, Surrey GU1 1HZ T: 01483 561927
North East Surrey Crematorium Board Lower Morden Lane, Morden, Surrey SM4 4NU T: 020 8337 4835 F: 020 8337 8745 E: nescb.crematorium@talk21.com W: www.nes-crematorium.org.uk
Randalls Park Crematorium Randalls Rd, Leatherhead, Surrey KT22 0AG T: 01372 373813
Redstone Cemetery Philanthropic Rd, Redhill, Surrey RH1 4DN T: 01737 761592
Richmond Cemeteries LBRichmond upon Thames, Sheen Rd, Richmond, Surrey TW10 5BJ T: 020 8876 4511 F: 020 8878 8118 E: cemeteries@richmond.gov.uk
Surbiton Cemetery Lower Marsh Lane, Kingston Upon Thames, Surrey KT1 3BN T: 0208 546 4463
Sutton & Cuddington Cemeteries Alcorn Close, off Oldfields Rd, Sutton, Surrey SM3 9PX T: 020 8644 9437 F: 020 8644 1373
The Godalming Joint Burial Committee New Cemetery Lodge, Ockford Ridge, Godalming, Surrey GU7 2NP T: 01483 421559
Woking Crematorium Hermitage Rd, Woking, Surrey GU21 8TJ T: 01483 472197
Sussex - East
Afterthoughts Grave Care 16 Derwent Rd, Eastbourne , East Sussex BN20 7PH T: 01323 730029
Brighton Borough Mortuary Lewes Rd, Brighton, East Sussex BN2 3QB T: 01273 602345
Downs Crematorium Bear Rd, Brighton, BN2 3PL T: 01273 601601

Eastbourne Cemeteries & Crematorium Hide Hollow, Langney, Eastbourne, East Sussex BN23 8AE T: 01323 766536 (Cemetery) F: 01323 761093 (Crematorium)

Woodvale Crematorium Lewes Rd, Brighton, East Sussex BN2 3QB T: 01273 604020

Sussex - West

Chichester Crematorium Westhampnett Rd, Chichester, West Sussex PO19 4UH T: 01243 787755

Midhurst Burial Authority Cemetery Lodge, Carron Lane, Midhurst, West Sussex GU29 9LF T: 01730 812758

Surrey & Sussex Crematorium Balcombe Rd, Crawley, West Sussex RH10 3NQ T: 01293 888930

Worthing Crematorium & Cemeteries Horsham Rd, Findon, Worthing, West Sussex BN14 0RG T: 01903 872678 F: 01903 872051 E: crematorium@worthing.gov.uk

Tyne and Wear

Byker & Heaton Cemetery 18 Benton Rd, Heaton, Newcastle Upon Tyne, Tyne And Wear NE7 7DS T: 0191 2662017

Gateshead East Cemetery Cemetery Rd, Gateshead, Tyne And Wear NE8 4HJ T: 0191 4771819

Heworth Cemetery Sunderland Rd, Felling, Gateshead, Tyne And Wear NE10 0NT T: 0191 4697851

North Tyneside MBC Longbenton Cemetery, Longbenton, Newcastle Upon Tyne NE12 8EY T: 0191 2661261

Preston Cemetery & Tynemouth Crematorium Walton Avenue, North Shields, Tyne And Wear NE29 9NJ T: 0191 2005861

Saltwell Crematorium Saltwell Rd South, Gateshead, Tyne And Wear NE8 4TQ T: 0191 4910553

St. Andrews Cemetery Lodges 1-2, Great North Rd, Jesmond, Newcastle Upon Tyne, Tyne And Wear NE2 3BU T: 0191 2810953

St. Johns & Elswick Cemetery Elswick Rd, Newcastle Upon Tyne, Tyne And Wear NE4 8DL T: 0191 2734127

St. Nicholas Cemetery Wingrove Avenue Back, Newcastle Upon Tyne, Tyne And Wear NE4 9AP T: 0191 2735112

Union Hall Cemetery Union Hall Rd, Newcastle Upon Tyne, Tyne And Wear NE15 7JS T: 0191 2674398

West Rd Cemetery West Rd, Newcastle Upon Tyne NE5 2JL T: 0191 2744737

Warwickshire

Mid-Warwickshire Crematorium & Cemeteries Oakley Wood, Bishops Tachbrook, Leamington Spa, Warwickshire CV33 9QP T: 01926 651418

Nuneaton Cemetery Oaston Rd, Nuneaton, Warwickshire CV11 6JZ T: 024 7637 6357 F: 024 7637 6485

Stratford-on-Avon Cemetery Evesham Rd, Stratford-Upon-Avon, Warwickshire CV37 9AA T: 01789 292676

West Midlands

Beacon Hill Cemetery, Dovedale Road, Coseley, Bilston, Wolverhampton WV14 9BB T: 01902 554 992 E: bereavement.services@wolverhampton.gov.uk Correspondence address: Bereavement Centre, Wolverhampton City Council, Civic Centre, St. Peter's Square, Wolverhampton, WV1 1SD

Bilston Cemetery, Cemetery Street, Bilston, Wolverhampton T: 01902 554 992 E: bereavement.services@wolverhampton.gov.uk

Birmingham Crematorium 1973 389 Walsall Rd, Perry Barr, Birmingham, West Midlands B42 2LR T: 0121 356 9476

Birmingham Hebrew Congregation Cemetery The Ridgeway, Erdington, Birmingham, West Midlands B23 7TD T: 0121 356 4615

Bushbury Cemetery, Underhill Lane, Wolverhampton WV10 8BR T: 01902 554 992 E: bereavement.services@wolverhampton.gov.uk Correspondence address: Bereavement Centre, Wolverhampton City Council, Civic Centre, St. Peter's Square, Wolverhampton, WV1 1SD

Brandwood End Cemetery Woodthorpe Rd, Kings Heath, Birmingham, West Midlands B14 6EQ T: 0121 444 1328

Coventry Bereavement Services The Cemeteries & Crematorium Office, Cannon Hill Rd, Canley, Coventry, West Midlands CV4 7DF T: 024 7641 8055

Danescourt Cemetery, Wergs Road, Tettenhall, WV6 9BS Wolverhampton T: 01902 554 992 E: bereavement.services@wolverhampton.gov.uk Correspondence address: Bereavement Centre, Wolverhampton City Council, Civic Centre, St. Peter's Square, Wolverhampton, WV1 1SD

Hall Green Cemetery, Hall Green Street, Bradley, Bilston, Wolverhamptonyon WV14 8TH T: 01902 554 992 E: bereavement.services@wolverhampton.gov.uk

Handsworth Cemetery Oxhill Rd, Birmingham, West Midlands B21 8JT T: 0121 554 0096

Lodge Hill Cemetery & Cremetorium Weoley Park Rd, Birmingham, West Midlands B29 5AA T: 0121 472 1575

Merridale Cemetery Jeffcock Road, Merridale, Bradmore, Wolverhampton WV3 7AE T: 01902 554 992 E: bereavement.services@wolverhampton.gov.uk Correspondence address: Bereavement Centre, Wolverhampton City Council, Civic Centre, St. Peter's Square, Wolverhampton, WV1 1SD

Penn Cemetery Vicarage Road, Penn, Wolverhampton WV 4 5HR T: 01902 554 992 E: bereavement.services@wolverhampton.gov.uk Correspondence address: See Meridale Cemetery above

Quinton Cemetery Halesowen Rd, Halesowen, West Midlands B62 9AF T: 0121 422 2023

Robin Hood Cemetery and Crematorium Sheetsbrook Rd, Shirley, Solihull, West midlands B90 3NL T: 0121 744 1121 F: 0121 733 8674

Stourbridge Cemetry & Crematorium South Rd, Stourbridge, West Midlands DY8 3RQ T: 01384 813985

Streetly Cemetery & Crematorium Walsall Metropolitan Borough Council - Bereavement Services Division, Little Hardwick Rd, Aldridge, Walsall, West Midlands WS9 0SG T: 0121 353 7228 E: bereavementservices@walsall.gov.uk W: www.walsall.gov.uk

Sutton Coldfield Cemetery Rectory Rd, Sutton Coldfield, West Midlands B75 7RP T: 0121 378 0224

Sutton Coldfield Cremetorium Tamworth Rd, Four Oaks, Sutton Coldfield, West Midlands B75 6LG T: 0121 308 3812

West Bromwich Crematorium Forge Lane, West Bromwich, West Midlands B71 3SX T: 0121 588 2160

Widney Manor Cemetery Widney Manor Rd, Bentley Heath, Solihull, West Midlands B93 3LX

Willenhall Lawn Cemetery Bentley Lane, Willenhall, West Midlands WV12 4AE T: 01902 368621

Witton Cemetery Moor Lane Witton, Birmingham, West Midlands B6 7AE T: 0121 356 4363 F: 0121 331 1283 E: wittoncem@birmingham.gov.uk

Woodlands Cemetery and Crematorium Birmingham Rd, Coleshill, Birmingham, West Midlands B46 2ET T: 01675 464835

West Yorkshire

Brighouse Cemetery Cemetery Lodge, 132 Lightcliffe Rd, Brighouse, West Yorkshire HD6 2HY T: 01484 715183

Cottingly Hall Elland Rd, Leeds, West Yorkshire LS11 0 T: 0113 271 6101

Dewsbury Moor Crematorium Heckmondwike Rd, Dewsbury, West Yorkshire WF13 3PL T: 01924 325180

Exley Lane Cemetery Exley Lane, Elland, West Yorkshire HX5 0SW T: 01422 372449

Killingbeck Cemetery York Rd, Killingbeck, Leeds, West Yorkshire LS14 6AB T: 0113 264 5247

Lawnswood Cemetery & Crematorium Otley Rd, Adel, Leeds, West Yorkshire LS16 6AH T: 0113 267 3188

Leeds Jewish Workers Co-Op Society 717 Whitehall Rd, New Farnley, Leeds, West Yorkshire LS12 6JL T: 0113 285 2521

Moorthorpe Cemetery Barnsley Rd, Moorthorpe, Pontefract, West Yorkshire WF9 2BP T: 01977 642433

Nab Wood Crematorium Bingley Rd, Shipley, West Yorkshire BD18 4BG T: 01274 584109 F: 01274 530419

Oakworth Crematorium Wide Lane, Oakworth, Keighley, West Yorkshire BD22 0RJ T: 01535 603162

Park Wood Crematorium Park Rd, Elland, West Yorkshire HX5 9HZ T: 01422 372293

Pontefract Crematorium Wakefield Rd, Pontefract, West Yorkshire WF8 4HA T: 01977 723455

Rawdon Crematorium Leeds Rd, Rawdon, Leeds, West Yorkshire LS19 6JP T: 0113 250 2904

Scholemoor Cemetery & Crematorium Necropolis Rd, Bradford, West Yorkshire BD7 2PS T: 01274 571313

Sowerby Bridge Cemetery Sowerby New Rd, Sowerby Bridge, West Yorkshire HX6 1LQ T: 01422 831193

United Hebrew Congregation Leeds Jewish Cemetery, Gelderd Rd, Leeds, West Yorkshire LS7 4BU T: 0113 263 8684

Wakefield Crematorium Standbridge Lane, Crigglestone, Wakefield, West Yorkshire WF4 3JA T: 01924 303380

Wetherby Cemetery Sexton House, Hallfield Lane, Wetherby, West Yorkshire LS22 6JQ T: 01937 582451

Wiltshire

Box Cemetery Bath Rd, Box, Corsham, Wiltshire SN13 8AA T: 01225 742476

Devizes & Roundway Joint Burial Committee Cemetry Lodge, Rotherstone, Devizes, Wiltshire SN10 2DE T: 01380 722821

Salisbury Crematorium Barrington Rd, Salisbury, Wiltshire SP1 3JB T: 01722 333632

Swindon Crematorium Kingsdown, Swindon, Wiltshire SN25 6SG T: 01793 822259

The Cemetery Chippenham London Rd, Chippenham, Wiltshire SN15 3RD T: 01249 652728

West Wiltshire Crematorium Devizes Rd, Semington, Trowbridge, Wiltshire BA14 7QH T: 01380 871101

Wirral

Landican Cemetery Arrowe Park Rd, Birkenhead, Wirral CH49 5LW T: 0151 677 2361

Worcestershire

Pershore Cemetery Defford Rd, Pershore, Worcestershire WR10 3BX T: 01386 552043

Redith Crematorium & Abbey Cemetary Bordesley Lane, Redditch, Worcestershire B97 6RR T: 01527 62174

Westall Park Woodland Burial Holberrow Green, Redditch, Worcestershire B96 6JY T: 01386 792806

Worcester Crematorium Astwood Rd, Tintern Avenue, Worcester, Worcestershire WR3 8HA T: 01905 22633

Yorkshire - East
East Riding Crematorium Ltd Octon Cross Rd, Langtoft, Driffield, East Yorkshire YO25 3BL T: 01377 267604
East Riding of Yorkshire Council Cemetery Lodge, Sewerby Rd, Bridlington, East Yorkshire YO16 7DS T: 01262 672138
Goole Cemetery Hook Rd, Goole, East Yorkshire DN14 5LU T: 01405 762725
Yorkshire - North
Fulford New Cemetery Cemetery Lodge, Fordlands Rd, Fulford, York, North Yorkshire YO19 4QG T: 01904 633151
Mowthorpe Garden of Rest Southwood Farm, Terrington, York, North Yorkshire YO60 6QB T: 01653 648459 F: 01653 648225 E: robert@robertgoodwill.co.uk
Stonefall Cemetery & Crematoria Wetherby Rd, Harrogate, North Yorkshire HG3 1DE T: 01423 883523
Waltonwrays Cemetery The Gatehouse, Carlton Rd, Skipton, North Yorkshire BD23 3BT T: 01756 793168
York Cemetery Gate House, Cemetery Rd, York, North Yorkshire YO10 5AF T: 01904 610578
Yorkshire - South
South Yorkshire
Barnsley Crematorium & Cemetery Doncaster Rd, Ardsley, Barnsley, South Yorkshire S71 5EH T: 01226 206053
City Rd Cemetery City Rd, Sheffield, South Yorkshire S2 1GD T: 0114 239 6068
Ecclesfield Cemetery Priory Lane, Ecclesfield, Sheffield, South Yorkshire S35 9XZ T: 0114 239 6068 F: 0114 239 3757
Eckington Cemetery Sheffield Rd, Eckington, Sheffield, South Yorkshire S21 9FP T: 01246 432197
Grenoside Crematorium 5 Skew Hill Lane, Grenoside, Sheffield, South Yorkshire S35 8RZ T: 0114 245 3999
Handsworth Cemetery 51 Orgreave Lane, Handsworth, Sheffield, South Yorkshire S13 9NE T: 0114 254 0832
Hatfield Cemetery Cemetery Rd, Hatfield, Doncaster, South Yorkshire DN7 6LX T: 01302 840242
Mexborough Cemetery Cemetery Rd, Mexborough, S64 9PN T: 01709 585184
Rose Hill Crematorium Cantley Lane, Doncaster DN4 6NE T: 01302 535191
Rotherham Cemeteries & Crematorium Ridgeway East, Herringthorpe, Rotherham S65 3NN T: 01709 850344
Sheffield Cemeteries City Rd, Sheffield, South Yorkshire S2 1GD T: 0114 253 0614
Sheffield Central Cemetery The Cemetery Gatehouse, Cemetery Avenue, Sheffield, South Yorkshire S11 8NT T: 0114 268 3486 W: www.gencem.org
Stainforth Town Council Cemetery Office, Church Rd, Stainforth, Doncaster, South Yorkshire DN7 5AA T: 01302 845158
Yorkshire -West
Undercliffe Cemetery 127 Undercliffe Lane, Bradford, West Yorkshire BD3 0QD T: 01274 631445 W: www.undercliffe.org

Wales
Bridgend
Bridgend County Borough Council Cemeteries Civic Offices, Angel Street, Bridgend, Glamorgan CF31 1LX T: 01656 643422
Caerphilly
Caerphilly County Borough Council Cemeteries Council Offices, Pontllanfraith, Blackwood, NP2 2YW
Clwyd
Golden Memorial Care 5 Golden Grove, Rhyl, Clwyd LL18 2RR T: 0800 9178281
Mold Town Cemetery Cemetery Lodge, Alexandra Rd, Mold, Clwyd CH7 1HJ T: 01352 753820
Wrexham Cemeteries & Crematorium Pentre Bychan, Wrexham, Clwyd LL14 4EP T: 01978 840068
Wrexham Cemetery Lodge Ruabon Rd, Wrexham, Clwyd LL13 7NY T: 01978 263159
Conwy County
Colwyn Bay Crematorium Bron y Nant, Dinerth Rd, Colwyn Bay, Conwy County LL28 4YN T: 01492 544677
Dyfed
Aberystwyth Crematorium Clarach Rd, Aberystwyth, Dyfed SY23 3DG T: 01970 626942
Carmarthen Cemetery Elim Rd, Carmarthen, Dyfed SA31 1TX T: 01267 234134
Llanelli District Cemetery Swansea Rd, Llanelli, Dyfed SA15 3EX T: 01554 773710
Milford Haven Cemetery The Cemetery, Milford Haven, Dyfed SA73 2RP T: 01646 693324
Glamorgan
Barry Town Council Cemetery Barry Town Council, 7 Gladstone Road, Barry, Glamorgan CF62 8NA T: 01446 738663
Cowbridge (The Limes Cemetery (1925) Cemetery Cowbridge Town Council, Town Hall, Cowbridge, Glamorgan CF71 7AD T: 01446 772901
Llantwit Major Cemetery Llantwit Major Town Council, Llantwit Major, Glamorgan CF61 1SD T: 01446 793707

Merthyr Tydfil County Borough Council Cemeteries Civic Centre, Merthyr Tydfil, Glamorgan CF47 8AN T: 01685 725146
Penarth Cemetery Penarth Town Council, West House, Stanwell Road, Penarth, Glamorgan CF64 2YG T: 029 2070 0721
Penrhys Cemetery Cemetery Offices, PenrhysRoad, Tylorstown, Glamorgan CF43 3BA T: 01443 730465
Rhondda Cynon Taff CBC Cemeteries Crematorium and Cemeteries Section, Cemetery Road, Glyntaff, Pontypridd, Glamorgan CF37 4BE T: 01443 402810
Trealaw Cemetery Cemetery Offices, Brithweunydd Road, Trealaw, Glamorgan CF40 2UQ T: 01443 682829
Gwent
Ebbw Vale Cemetery Waun-y-Pound Rd, Ebbw Vale, Gwent NP23 6LE T: 01495 302187
Gwent Crematorium Treherbert Rd, Croesyceiliog, Cwmbran, Gwent NP44 2BZ T: 01633 482784
Gwynedd
Bangor Crematorium Llandygai Rd, Bangor, Gwynedd LL57 4HP T: 01248 370500
Mid Glamorgan
Cemetery Section - Rhondda Cynon Taff County Borough Council Monks St, Aberdare, Mid Glamorgan CF44 7PA T: 01685 885345
Ferndale Cemetery Cemetery Lodge, Highfield, Ferndale, Mid Glamorgan CF43 4TD T: 01443 730321
Llwydcoed Crematorium Llwydcoed, Aberdare, Mid Glamorgan CF44 0DJ T: 01685 874115 F: 01685 874115 E: enquiries@crematorium.org.uk W: www.crematorium.org.uk
Maesteg Cemetery Cemetery Rd, Maesteg, Mid Glamorgan CF34 0DN T: 01656 735485
Penrhys Cemetery Cemetery Lodge, Penrhys Rd, Tylorstown, Ferndale, Mid Glamorgan CF43 3PN T: 01443 730465
Trane Cemetery Gilfach Rd, Tonyrefail, Porth, Mid Glamorgan CF39 8HL T: 01443 670280 F: 01443 676916
Treorchy Cemetery The Lodge, Cemetery Rd, Treorchy, Mid Glamorgan CF42 6TB T: 01443 772336
Ynysybwl Cemetery 37 Heol Y Plwyf, Ynysybwl, Pontypridd, Mid Glamorgan CF37 3HU T: 01443 790159
South Glamorgan
Cardiff Crematorium and Thornhill Cemetery Bereavement Services, Thornhill Road, Cardiff, South Glamorgan CF14 9UA T: 029 2062 3294 F: 029 20692904 W: www.cardiff.gov.uk
Cathays Cemetery Fairoak Rd, Cathays, Cardiff, South Glamorgan CF24 4PY T: 029 2062 3294 W: www.cardiff.gov.uk
Western Cemetery Cowbridge Road West, Ely, Cardiff, South Glamorgan CF5 5TF T: 029 2059 3231 W: www.cardiff.gop.uk
West Glamorgan
Goytre Cemetery Neath Port Talbot CBC, Abrafan House, Port Talbot, West Glamorgan SA13 1PJ T: 01639 763415
Margam Crematorium Longland Lane, Margam, Port Talbot, West Glamorgan SA13 2PP T: 01639 883570
Oystermouth Cemetery Newton Road, Oystermouth, Swansea, West Glamorgan SA3 4GW T: 07980 721 559
Gwent
Christchurch Cemetery Christchurch, Newport, Gwent NP18 1JJ T: 01633 277566
Wrexham
Coedpoeth Cemetery The Lodge, Cemetery Rd, Coedpoeth, Wrexham LL11 3SP T: 01978 755617

Scotland
Aberdeenshire
Aberdeen Cemeteries St Nicholas House, Brd Street, Aberdeen, AB10 1BX T: 01224 523 155
Aberdeenshire (except Aberdeen City) Cemeteries (North) 1 Church Street, Macduff, AB44 1UR T: 01261 813387
Springbank Cemetery Countesswells Rd, Springbank, Aberdeen, Aberdeenshire AB15 7YH T: 01224 317323
St. Peter's Cemetery King St, Aberdeen, AB24 3BX T: 01224 638490
Trinity Cemetery Erroll St, Aberdeen, AB24 5PP T: 01224 633747
Angus
Angus (except Dundee City) Cemeteries County Buildings, Market Street, Forfar, ANGUS DD8 3WA T: 01307 461 460
Barnhill Cemetery 27 Strathmore St, Broughty Ferry, Dundee, Angus DD5 2NY T: 01382 477139
Dundee Crematorium Ltd Crematorium, Macalpine Rd, Dundee, Angus DD3 8 T: 01382 825601
Park Grove Crematorium Douglasmuir, Friocheim, Arbroath, Angus DD11 4UN T: 01241 828959
Argyll
Argyll & Bute Council Cemeteries Amenity Services, Kilmory, Lochgilphead, Argyll PA31 8RT T: 01546 604 360E: alison.mcilroy@argyll-bute.gov.uk W: www.argyll-bute.gov.uk
Arran & Cumbrae Cemeteries 43 Ardrossan Rd, Saltcoats, Bute KA21 5BS T: 01294 605 436 E: CemeteriesOffice@north-ayrshire.gov.uk
Ayrshire
Ardrossan Cemetery Sorbie Rd, Ardrossan KA22 8AQ T: 01294 463133

Dreghorn Cemetery Station Rd, Dreghorn, Irvine, Ayrshire KA11 4AJ T: 01294 211101

Hawkhill Cemetery Kilwinning Rd, Saltcoats, Stevenston, Ayrshire KA20 3DE T: 01294 465241

Holmsford Bridge Crematorium Dreghorn, Irvine, Ayrshire KA11 4EF T: 01294 214720

Kilwinning Cemetery Bridgend, Kilwinning, Ayrshire KA13 7LY T: 01294 552102

Largs Cemetery Greenock Rd, Largs, Ayrshire KA30 8NG T: 01475 673149

Maybole Cemetery - Records held at Girvan Crosshill Rd, Maybole, KA19 7BN T: 01465 712894 E: maybole.registrars@south-ayrshire.gov.uk

Newmilns Cemetery Dalwhatswood Rd, Newmilns, Ayrshire KA16 9LT T: 01560 320191

North Ayrshire Cemeteries 43 Ardrossan Rd, Saltcoats, AYRSHIRE KA21 5BS T: 01294 605 436 F: 01294 606 416 E: CemeteriesOffice@north-ayrshire.gov.uk

Prestwick Cemetery Shaw Rd, Prestwick, Ayrshire KA9 2LP T: 01292 477759

South Ayrshire Cemeteries Masonhill Crematorium, By Ayr, Ayrshire KA6 6EN T: 01292 266 051 F: 01292 610 096

Stewarton Cemetery Dalry Rd, Stewarton, Kilmarnock, Ayrshire KA3 3DY T: 01560 482888

West Kilbride Cemetery Hunterston Rd, West Kilbride, Ayrshire KA23 9EX T: 01294 822818

Banffshire

Moray Crematorium Clochan, Buckie, Banffshire AB56 5HQ T: 01542 850488

Scottish Borders Council Cemeteries Council Offices, 8 Newtown Street, Duns TD11 3DT T: 01361 882 600

Caithness

Caithness Cemeteries Wick, CaithnessKW1 4AB T: 01955 607 737 F: 01955 606 376

Clackmannanshire

Alva Cemetery The Glebe, AlvaFK12 5HR T: 01259 760354

Sunnyside Cemetery Sunnyside Rd, Alloa FK10 2AP T: 01259 723575

Tillicoultry Cemetery Dollar Rd, Tillicoultry, Clackmannanshire FK13 6PF T: 01259 750216

Dumfries & Galloway

Annan & Eskdale Cemeteries Dumfries and Galloway Council, Dryfe Rd, Lockerbie DG11 2AP T: 01576 205 000

Dumfrieshire Cemeteries Kirkbank, English Street, Dumfries, DG1 2HS T: 01387 260042 F: 01387 260188

Wigtown Cemeteries Dunbae House, Church Street, Stranraer, Dumfries DG9 7JG T: 01776 888 405

Dunbartonshire

Cardross Crematorium Main Rd, Cardross, Dumbarton, Dunbartonshire G82 5HD T: 01389 841313

Dumbarton Cemetery Stirling Rd, Dumbarton G82 2PF T: 01389 762033

East Dunbartonshire Cemeteries Broomhill Industrial Estate, Kilsyth Rd, Kirkintilloch, DUNBARTONSHIRE G66 1TF T: 0141 574 5549 E: Alan-Copeland@EastDunbarton.gov.uk

Vale Of Leven Cemetery Overton Rd, Alexandria G83 0LJ T: 01389 752266

West Dumbartonshire Crematorium North Dalnottar, Clydebank, Dunbartonshire G81 4SL T: 01389 874318

West Dunbartonshire Cemeteries Roseberry Place, Clydebank, G81 1TG T: 01389 738 709 F: 01389 733 493

West Dunbartonshire Crematorium Richmond Street, Clydebank, Dunbartonshire G81 1RF T: 01389 738709 F: 01389 738690 E: helen.murray@westdunbarton.gov.uk

Dundee

Dundee City Cemetery Administration Section Central Library, Wellgate Centre, Dundee, DD1 1DB T: 01382 301 536 E: parks.burial@dundeecity.gov.uk

East Dunbartonshire

Cadder Cemetery Kirkintilloch Rd, Bishopbriggs, Glasgow, Lanarkshire G64 2QG T: 0141 772 1977 F: 0141 775 0696

Fife

Central Fife Cemeteries Rosemount Avenue, Dunnikier, Kirkcaldy, KY1 3PL T: 01592 260 277 F: 01592 203 438

Dunfermline Cemetery Halbeath Rd, Dunfermline, Fife KY12 7RA T: 01383 724899

Dunfermline Crematorium Masterton Rd, Dunfermline, Fife KY11 8QR T: 01383 724653

East Fife Cemeteries St Catherine Street, Cupar, FIFE KY15 4TA T: 01334 412 818 F: 01334 412 896

East Fife Cemeteries Masterton Rd, Dunfermline, FIFE KY11 8QR T: 01383 724 653

Kirkcaldy Crematorium Rosemount Avenue, Dunnikier, Kirkcaldy, Fife KY1 3PL T: 01592 260277 F: 01592 203438

Glasgow

Glasgow Cemeteries 20 Trongate, Glasgow, Lanarkshire G1 5ES T: 0141 287 3961

Inverness-shire

Badenoch & Strathspey Cemeteries Ruthven Rd, Kingussie, PH21 1EJ T: 01540 664 500 F: 01540 661 004

Highland Council Cemeteries T.E.C. Services, Broom Place, Portree, Isle of SkyeIV51 9HF T: 01478 612717

Inverness Cemeteries Administration Office, Kilvean Cemetery, Kilvean Rd, InvernessIV3 8JN T: 01463 717849 E: W: www.highland.gov.uk

Inverness Crematorium Kilvean Rd, Kilvean, InvernessIV3 8JN T: 01463 717849

Invernessshire Cemeteries Fulton House, Gordon Square, Fort William PH33 6XY T: 01397 707 008

Isle Of Cumbrae

Millport Cemetery Golf Rd, Millport, Isle Of Cumbrae KA28 0HB T: 01475 530442

Kirkcudbright

Kirkcudbright Cemeteries Daar Rd, Kirkcubright, DG6 4JG T: 01557 330 291

Lanarkshire

Airbles Cemetery Airbles Rd, Motherwell ML1 3AW T: 01698 263986

Bedlay Cemetery Bedlay Walk, Moodiesburn, Glasgow G69 0QG T: 01236 872446

Bothwellpark Cemetery New Edinburgh Rd, Bellshill ML4 3HH T: 01698 748146

Cambusnethan Cemetery Kirk Rd, Wishaw ML2 8NP T: 01698 384481

Campsie Cemetery High Church of Scotland, Main Street, Lennoxtown, Glasgow G66 7DA T: 01360 311127

Cardonald Cemetery 547 Mosspark Boulevard, Glasgow G52 1SB T: 0141 882 1059

Daldowie Crematorium Daldowie Estate, Uddingston, Glasgow G71 7RU T: 0141 771 1004

Glasgow Crematorium Western Necropolis, Tresta Rd, Glasgow G23 5AA T: 0141 946 2895

Glebe Cemetery Vicars Rd, Stonehouse, Larkhall ML9 3EB T: 01698 793674

Glenduffhill Cemetery 278 Hallhill Rd, Glasgow G33 4RU T: 0141 771 2446

Kilsyth Parish Cemetery Howe Rd, Kirklands, Glasgow G65 0LA T: 01236 822144

Larkhall Cemetery The Cemetery Lodge, Duke St, Larkhall ML9 2AL T: 01698 883049

North Lanarkshire Cemeteries Old Edinburgh Rd, Bellshill ML4 3JS T: 01698 506 301 F: 01698 506 309

Old Aisle Cemetery Old Aisle Rd, Kirkintilloch, Glasgow G66 3HH T: 0141 776 2330

St. Conval's Cemetery Glasgow Rd, Barrhead, Glasgow G78 1TH T: 0141 881 1058

St. Patrick's Cemetery Kings Drive, New Stevenston, Motherwell ML1 4HY T: 01698 732938

St. Peters Cemetery 1900 London Rd, Glasgow G32 8RD T: 0141 778 1183

The Necropolis 50 Cathedral Square, Glasgow G4 0UZ T: 0141 552 3145

Lanarkshire - South

South Lanarkshire Cemeteries Atholl House, East Kilbride G74 1LU T: 01355 806 980 F: 01355 806 983

Midlothian

City of Edinburgh Council Cemeteries Howdenhall Rd, Edinburgh, Midlothian EH16 6TX T: 0131 664 4314 F: 0131 664 2031 E: sfc@edinburgh.gov.uk

Dean Cemetery Dean Path, Edinburgh, Midlothian EH4 3AT T: 0131 332 1496

Edinburgh Crematorium Ltd 3 Walker St, Edinburgh EH3 7JY T: 0131 225 7227

Midlothian Council Cemeteries Dundas Buildings, 62A Polton Street, Bonnyrigg, Midlothian EH22 3YD T: 0131 561 5280 F: 0131 654 2797 E: nancy.newton@midlothian.gov.uk

Seafield Cemetery & Crematorium Seafield Rd, Edinburgh, Midlothian EH6 7LQ T: 0131 554 3496

Warriston Crematorium 36 Warriston Rd, Edinburgh, Midlothian EH7 4HW T: 0131 552 3020

Morayshire

Morayshire Cemeteries Cooper Park, Elgin, Morayshire IV30 1HS T: 01343 544 475 F: 01343 549 050 E: graeme.wilson@moray.gov.uk W: www.moray.org/heritage/roots.html

Peebles-shire

Scottish Borders Council Burial Grounds Department Council Offices, Rosetta Rd, Peebles, Peebles-shire EH45 8HG T: 01721 726306 F: 01721 726304

Renfrewshire

Cemeteries Division - Renfrewshire Council Environmental Services Department, Cotton Street, South Building, Paisley, Renfrewshire PA1 1BR T: 0141 840 3504 F: 0141 842 1179

East Renfrewshire - including Cathcart, Neilston, Newton Mearns and Eaglesham Cemeteries Rhuallan House, 1 Montgomery Drive, Giffnock, Renfrewshire G46 6PY T: 0141 577 3913 F: 0141 577 3919 E: sandra.donnelly@eastrenfrewshire.gov.uk

Hawkhead Cemetery 133 Hawkhead Rd, Paisley, Renfrewshire PA2 7BE T: 0141 889 3472
Paisley Cemetery Co.Ltd 46 Broomlands St, Paisley, Renfrewshire PA1 2NP T: 0141 889 2260
Renfrew Cemeteries 3 Longcroft Drive, Renfrew, Renfrewshire PA4 8NF T: 0141 848 1450 F: 0141 886 2807
Renfrewshire Cemeteries Tweedie Halls, Ardlamont Square, Linwood, Renfrewshire PA3 3DE T: 01505 322 135 F: 01505 322135
Roxburghshire
Roxburghshire Environmental Health - Burials High Street, Hawick, Roxburghshire TD9 9EF T: 01450 375 991
Scottish Borders
Scottish Borders Council - Burials Paton Street, Galashiels, Selkirkshire TD1 3AS T: 01896 662739 F: 01896 750329
Shetland
Shetland Burial Ground Management Grantfield, Lerwick, Shetland ZE1 0NT T: 01595 744 871 F: 01595 744869 E: jim.grant@sic.shetland.gov.uk W: www.shetland.gov.uk
Stirlingshire
Falkirk Cemeteries and Crematorium Dorrator Rd, Camelon, Falkirk, Stirlingshire FK2 7YJ T: 01324 503 654 F: 01324 503 651 E: billbauchope@falkirk.gov.uk
Larbert Cemetery 25 Muirhead Rd, Larbert, Stirlingshire FK5 4HZ T: 01324 557867
Stirlingshire Cemeteries Viewforth, Stirling, Stirlingshire FK8 2ET T: 01786 442 559 F: 01786 442 558 E: mcbrier@stirling.gov.uk W: www.stirling.gov.uk
West Lothian
West Lothian Cemeteries County Buildings, High Street, Linlithgow EH49 7EZ T: 01506 775 300 F: 01506 775 412

Northern Ireland
County Antrim
Ballymena Cemetery Cushendall Rd, Ballymena, County Antrim BT43 6QE T: 01266 656026
Ballymoney Cemetery 44 Knock Rd, Ballymoney, County Antrim BT53 6LX T: 012656 66364
Blaris New Cemetery 25 Blaris Rd, Lisburn, County Antrim BT27 5RA T: 01846 607143
Carnmoney Cemetery 10 Prince Charles Way, Newtownabbey, County Antrim BT36 7LG T: 01232 832428
City Cemetery 511 Falls Rd, Belfast, County Antrim BT12 6DE T: 028 90323112
Greenland Cemetery Upper Cairncastle Rd, Larne, County Antrim BT40 2EG T: 01574 272543
Milltown Cemetery Office 546 Falls Rd, Belfast, County Antrim BT12 6EQ T: 01232 613972

County Armagh
Kernan Cemetery Kernan Hill Rd, Portadown, Craigavon, County Armagh BT63 5YB T: 028 38339059
Lurgan Cemetery 57 Tandragee Rd, Lurgan, Craigavon, County Armagh BT66 8TL T: 028 38342853
County Down
Ballyvestry Cemetery 6 Edgewater Millisle, Newtownards, County Down BT23 5 T: 01247 882657
Banbridge Public Cemetery Newry Rd, Banbridge, County Down BT32 3NB T: 018206 62623
Bangor Cemetery 62 Newtownards Rd, Bangor, County Down BT20 4DN T: 028 91271909
City of Belfast Crematorium 129 Ballgowan Road, Crossacreevy, Belfast, County Down BT5 7TZ T: 028 9044 8342 F: 028 9044 8579 E: crematorium@belfastcity.gov.uk W: www.belfastcrematorium.co.uk
Clandeboye Cemetery 300 Old Belfast Rd, Bangor, County Down BT19 1RH T: 028 91853246
Comber Cemetery 31 Newtownards Rd, Comber, Newtownards, County Down BT23 5AZ T: 01247 872529
Down District Council Struell Cemetery, Old Course Rd, Downpatrick, County Down BT30 8AQ T: 01396 613086
Down District Council - Lough Inch Cemetery Lough Inch Cemetery, Riverside Rd, Ballynahinch, County Down BT24 8JB T: 01238 562987
Kirkistown Cemetary Main Rd, Portavogie, Newtownards, County Down BT22 1EL T: 012477 71773
Movilla Cemetary Movilla Rd, Newtownards, County Down BT23 8EY T: 01247 812276
Redburn Cemetery Old Holywood Rd, Holywood, County Down BT18 9QH T: 01232 425547
Roselawn Cemetery 127 Ballygowan Rd, Crossnacreevy, Belfast, County Down BT5 7TZ T: 01232 448288
Whitechurch Cemetary 19 Dunover Rd, Newtownards, County Down BT22 2LE T: 012477 58659
County Londonderry
Altnagelvin Cemetery Church Brae, Altnagelvin, Londonderry, County Londonderry BT47 3QG T: 01504 343351
City Cemetery Lone Moor Rd, Londonderry, County Londonderry BT48 9LA T: 02871 362615 F: 02871 362085
County Tyrone
Greenhill Cemetery Mountjoy Rd, Omagh, County Tyrone BT79 7BL T: 028 8224 4918
Westland Road Cemetery Westland Rd, Cookstown, County Tyrone BT80 8BX T: 016487 66087

Email and Internet or Web Addresses
Email and Web addresses shown in this book have been notified to us by the Organisation or advertiser. Unlike a normal postal address these addresses are subject to frequent change. In the case of businesses Email forwarding and Website transfer are usually provided by links to the original address. This does not always happen and the only solution is to use the various search engines available on the internet. However because of the increasing amount of spam many organisations are using website based emailers and scripts to avoid the harvesting of email addresses by spammers. In instances where an email is not listed or if listed is rejected please visit the organisations website for contact details.

Disclaimer
The Editors and Publishers of The Family & Local History Handbook make every effort to verify all information published. The majority of the organisations listed in this handbook has been contacted and asked to confirm that our information is correct. We are grateful to those organisations who took the time to reply. We must express our disappointment that there were some organisations who did not reply. We cannot accept responsibilty for any errors or omissions or for any losses that may arise.

Advertisers are expected to provide a high standard of service to our readers. If there is a failure to provide such a service the Editor and Publishers reserve the right to refuse to accept advertising in future editions.

The Editors and Publishers cannot be held responsible for the errors, omissions or non performance by advertisers. Where an advertiser's performance falls below an acceptable level readers are asked to notify the Publisher in writing.

The views and opinions expressed in each of the articles are those of the author and do not necessarily reflect the opinions of the Editors.

Museums

National

Bank of England Museum Bartholomew Lane, Threadneedle Street, London, EC2R 8AH T: 020 7601 5545 E: museum@bankofengland.co.uk W: www.bankofengland.co.uk/museum

Black Cultural Archives 1 Othello Close, Kennington, London, SE11 4RE T: 020 7582 8516 E: info@bcaheritage.org.uk W: www.bcaheritage.org.uk

British Empire & Commonwealth Museum (Bristol) - closed relocating to London 2012 W: www.empiremuseum.co.uk

British Museum The Secretariat, Great Russell St, London, WC1B 3DG T: (020) 7323 8768 E: jwallace@thebritishmuseum.ac.uk W: www.thebritishmuseum.ac.uk

British Red Cross Museum & Archives UK Office, 44 Moorfields, London, EC2Y 9AL T: 020 7877 7058 E: enquiry@redcross.org.uk W: www.redcross.org.uk/museumandarchives

Imperial War Museum - Duxford Imperial War Museum, The Airfield, Duxford, Cambridge, Cambridgeshire CB2 4QR T: 01223 835 000 E: duxford@iwm.org.uk

Kensington Palace State Apartments Kensington Palace, London, W8 4PX T: (020) 7937 9561

Labour History Archive and Study Centre People's History Museum & study Centre, 103 Princess Street, Manchester, M1 6DD T: 0161 228 7212 E: archives@phm.org.uk W: www.phm.org.uk

Locomotion - The National Railway Museum @ Shildon Shildon, County Durham DL4 1PQ T: 01388 777 999 E: shildon@nrm.org.uk W: www.nrm.org.uk/shildon

Marks in Time Centenary Gallery, Parkinson Buiding, University of Leeds, Woodhouse Lane, Leeds, West Yorkshire LS2 9JT T: 0208 718 2800 (Bookings) E: exhibitionbookings@marks-and-spencer.com W: http://marksintime.marksandspencer.com

Museum of the Order of St John St John's Gate, St John,Äôs Lane, Clerkenwell, London, EC1M 4DA T: (020) 7253-6644 E: juliet.barclay@nhq.sja.org.uk W: www.sja.org.uk/history

Museum of the Royal Pharmaceutical Society Museum of the Royal Pharmaceutical Society, 1 Lambeth High Street, London, SE1 7JN T: (020) 7572 2210 E: museum@rpharms.com W: www.rpharms.com/museum

Museums Association 42 Clerkenwell Close, London, EC1R 0PA T: (020) 7250 1789

National Army Museum Department of Archives, Photographs, Film & Sound Royal Hospital Road, London, SW3 4HT T: 020 7730 0717 E: apfs@nam.ac.uk W: www.nam.ac.uk

National Army Museum Royal Hospital Road, Chelsea, London, SW3 4HT T: 020 7730 0717 E: info@nam.ac.uk W: www.nam.ac.uk

National Maritime Museum Romney Road, Greenwich, London, London SE10 9NF T: 020 8858 4422 E: library@nmm.ac.uk manuscripts@nmm.ac.uk W: www.nmm.ac.uk

National Media Museum Bradford, West Yorkshire BD1 1NQ T: 01274-202030 W: www.nmpft.org.uk

National Motorboat Museum Wattyler Country Park, Pitsea Hall Lane, Pitsea, Basildon, Essex SS16 4UH T: 01268 550077

National Portrait Gallery 2 St. Martins Place, London, WC2H 0HE T: (020) 7306 0055 W: www.npg.org.uk

National Railway Museum Leeman Road, York, YO26 4XJ T: 0844 815 3139 E: nrm@nrm.org.uk W: www.nrm.org.uk

National Tramway Museum Crich Tramway Village, Crich, Matlock, Derbyshire DE4 5DP T: 01773 852565 E: info@tramway.co.uk W: www.tramway.co.uk

National Waterways Museum South Pier Road, Ellesmere Port, Cheshire CH65 4FW T: 0151 355 5017 E: ellesmereport@thewaterwaystrust.org.uk W: http://nwm.org.uk

National Waterways Museum, The Llanthony Warehouse, Gloucester Docks, Gloucester, Gloucestershire GL1 2EH T: 01452 318054 W: www.nwm.org.uk

Natural History Museum Cromwell Rd, London, SW7 5BD T: (020) 7938 9238 W: www.nhm.ac.uk

River & Rowing Museum Mill Meadows, Henley on Thames, Oxfordshire RG9 1BF T: 01491 415600 E: museum@rrm.co.uk W: www.rrm.co.uk

Royal Air Force Museum Grahame Park Way, Hendon, London, NW9 5LL T: (020) 8200 1763 E: london@rafmuseum.org W: www.rafmuseum.org.uk

Royal Armouries H.M Tower Of London, Tower Hill, London, EC3N 4AB T: (020) 7480 6358 ext 30 W: www.armouries.org.uk

Royal Observatory Greenwich Romney Road, Greenwich, London, London SE10 9NF T: (020) 8858-4422 W: www.nmm.ac.uk

Science Museum Exhibition Road, South Kensington, London, SW7 2DD T: 0870 870 4771 W: www.sciencemuseum.org.uk

Sherlock Holmes Museum 221b Baker St, London, NW1 6XE T: (020) 7935 8866 E: sherlock@easynet.co.uk W: www.sherlock-holmes.co.uk

The Library & Museum of Freemasonry Freemasons' Hall, 60 Great Queen Street, London, WC2B 5AZ T: (020) 7395 9257 W: www.grandlodge-england.org

The Museum of Brands, Packaging and Advertising 2 Colville Mews, Lonsdale Road, Notting Hill, London, W11 2AR T: 020 7908 0880 E: info@museumofbrands.com W: www.museumofbrands.com

The National Brewery Centre Horninglow Street, Burton on Trent, DE14 1YQ T: 0845 6000598 E: info@nationalbrewerycentre.co.uk W: www.nationalbrewerycentre.co.uk

The National Coal Mining Museum for England Caphouse Colliery, New Road, Overton, Wakefield, West Yorkshire WF4 4RH T: 01924 848806 E: info@ncm.org.uk W: www.ncm.org.uk

The National Football Museum Sir Tom Finney Way, Deepdale, Preston PR1 6RU T: 01772 908 400 E: enquiries@nationalfootballmuseum.com W: www.nationalfootballmuseum.com

The Natural History Museum Cromwell Road, London, SW7 5BD T: (020) 7942 5000 W: www.nhm.ac.uk

The Science Museum Exhibition Road, London, SW7 2DD T: 0207 7942 4000 W: www.sciencemuseum.org.uk/library/

Victoria & Albert Museum South Kensington, London, SW7 2RL T: (020) 7638 8500 W: www.nal.vam.ac.uk

England

Bath

Roman Baths Museum Abbey Churchyard, Bath, BA1 1LZ T: 01225 477773

Bedfordshire

Cecil Higgins Art Gallery Castle Close, Castle Lane, Bedford, Bedfordshire MK40 3RP T: 01234 211222 W:

Cecil Higgins Art Gallery & Bedford Museum Castle Lane, Bedford, Bedfordshire MK40 3XD T: 01234 353 323 F: Bedford Museum is closed for redevelopment. Due to reopen at the end of 2012 or early 2013 E: bmuseum@bedford.gov.uk W: www.bedfordmuseum.org

Elstow Moot Hall Elstow, Bedford, Bedfordshire MK42 9XT T: 01234 266889 W: www.bedfordshire.gov.uk

Luton Museums Service Wardown Park, Luton, Bedfordshire LU2 7HA T: 01582 546725 E: adeye@luton.gov.uk

Museum of Defence Intelligence Chicksands, Shefford, Bedfordshire SG17 5PR T: 01462 752340

Station X - Bletchley Park Bletchley Park Trust, The Mansion, Bletchley, Milton Keynes, Bedfordshire MK3 6EB T: 01908 640404 W: www.bletchelypark.org.uk

Bedfordshire

John Dony Field Centre Hancock Drive, Bushmead, Luton, Bedfordshire LU2 7SF T: 01582 486983

Berkshire

Blake's Lock Museum Gasworks Rd, Reading, Berkshire RG1 3DS T: 0118 939 0918

Maidenhead Heritage Centre 41 Nicholsons Centre, Maidenhead, Berkshire SL6 1LL T: 01628 780555

Museum of English Rural Life University of Reading, Redlands Road, Reading, Berkshire RG1 5EX T: 0118 378 8660 E: merl@reading.ac.uk W: www.reading.ac.uk/merl/

Royal Borough Collection - Windsor, Friends of 14 Park Avenue, Wraysbury, TW19 5ET T: 01784 482771

Royal Borough Museum (Windsor & Maidenhead) Tinkers Lane, Windsor, Berkshire SL4 4LR T: 01628 796829 E: olivia.gooden@rbwm.gov.uk

Slough Museum 278-286 High St, Slough, Berkshire SL1 1NB T: 01753 526422

The Museum of Reading Town Hall, Blagrave Street, Reading, Berkshire RG1 1QH T: 0118-939-9800 E: info@readingmuseum.org.uk W: www.readingmuseum.org.uk

Wantage Vale & Downland Museum Church Street, Wantage, Berkshire OX12 8BL T: 01235 771447

Wellington Exhibition Stratfield Saye House, Reading, Berkshire RG7 2BT T: 01256 882882 W: www.stratfield-saye.co.uk

West Berkshire Museum The Wharf, Newbury, Berkshire RG14 5AS T: 01635 30511 E: museum@westberks.gov.uk www.westberkshiremuseum.org.uk

West Berkshire Museum - Newbury - closed for refurbishment until 2014 - see website: www.westberkshiremuseum.org.uk

Bristol
Ashton Court Visitor Centre Ashton Court, Long Ashton, Bristol, BS41 8JN T: 0117 963 9174
Blaise Castle House Museum Henbury, Bristol, BS10 7QS T: 0117 903 9818 E: general_museum@bristol-city.gov.uk W: www.bristol-city.gov.uk/museums
Bristol Industrial Museum Princes Wharf, Wapping Road, Bristol, BS1 4RN T: 0117 925 1470
City Museum & Art Gallery Queens Road, Bristol, BS8 1RL T: 0117 921 3571 E: general.museum@bristol-city.gov.uk W: www.bristol-city.gov.uk/museums
Clevedon Story Heritage Centre Waterloo House, 4 The Beach, Clevedon, BS21 7QU T: 01275 341196 W:
Clifton Suspension Bridge Visitor Centre Leigh Woods, Bristol, BS8 3PA T: 0117 974 4664 E: visitinfo@cliftonbridge.org.uk W: www.cliftonbridge.org.uk
Georgian House 7 Great George Street, Bristol, BS1 5RR T: 0117 921 1362 E: general.museum@bristol.gov.uk
Harveys Wine Museum 12 Denmark St, Bristol, BS1 5DQ T: 0117 927 5036
Red Lodge Park Row, Bristol, BS1 5LJ T: 0117 921 1360 W: www.bristol-city.gov.uk/museums
SS Great Britain and Maritime Heritage Centre Wapping Wharf, Gasferry Road, Bristol, BS1 6TY T: 0117 926 0680
Buckinghamshire
Amersham Local History Museum 49 High Street, Amersham, Buckinghamshire HP7 0DP T: 01494 725754 E: info@amershammuseum.org/ W: www.amershammuseum.org/
Buckinghamshire County Museum Church Street, Aylesbury, Buckinghamshire HP20 2QP T: 01296 331441 E: museum@buckscc.gov.uk
Chesham Town Museum Project Chesham Library, Elgiva Lane, Chesham, Buckinghamshire HP5 2JD T: 01494 783183 E: info@cheshammuseum.org.uk/ W: www.cheshammuseum.org.uk/
Chiltern Open Air Museum Ltd Newland Park, Gorelands Lane, Chalfont St. Giles, Buckinghamshire HP8 4AB T: 01494 871117
Milton Keynes Museum Stacey Hill Farm, Southern Way, Wolverton, Milton Keynes, Buckinghamshire MK12 5EJ T: 01908 316222
Pitstone & Ivinghoe Museum Society Vicarage Road, Pitstone, Leighton Buzzard, Buckinghamshire LU7 9EY T: 01582 605464 E: pjk96tpr@hotmail.com W: http://website.lineone.net/~pitstonemus
Wycombe Museum Priory Avenue, High Wycombe, Buckinghamshire HP13 6PX T: 01494 421895 E: museum@wycombe.gov.uk W: www.wycombe.gov.uk/museum

Cambridgeshire
Bell View (Belford) The Bell View Resource Centre - Belford, 33 West Street, Belford, Northumberland NE70 7QB T: 01668 219220 E: bellview-belford@tiscali.co.uk W: www.northumberlandlife.org/bellviewproject
Cambridge and County Folk Museum 2 - 3 Castle St, Cambridge, CB3 0AQ T: 01223 355159 E: info@folkmuseum.org.uk W: www.folkmuseum.org.uk
Cambridge Brass Rubbing The Round Church, Bridge St, Cambridge, Cambridgeshire CB2 1UB T: 01223 871621
Cambridge Museum of Technology Old Pumping Station, Cheddars Lane, Cambridge, Cambridgeshire CB5 8LD T: 01223 368650
Cromwell Museum The Cromwell Museum, Huntingdon, T: 01480 375830 E: cromwellmuseum@cambridgeshire.gov.uk W: www.cambridgeshire.gov.uk/cromwell
Ely Museum The Old Goal, Market Street, Ely, Cambridgeshire CB7 4LS T: 01353-666655 E: info@elymuseum.org.uk W: www.elymuseum.org.uk
Farmland Museum Denny Abbey, Ely Rd, Waterbeach, Cambridge, CB25 9PQ T: 01223 860988 E: admin@farmlandmuseum.org.uk W: www.dennyfarmlandmuseum.org.uk
Fenland & West Norfolk Aviation Museum Lynn Rd, West Walton, Wisbech, Cambridgeshire PE14 7 T: 01945 584440
March & District Museum Society Museum, High St, March, Cambridgeshire PE15 9JJ T: 01354 655300
Museum of Classical Archaeology Sidgwick Avenue, Cambridge, Cambridgeshire CB3 9DA T: 01223 335153 W: www.classics.cam.ac.uk/ark.html/
Nene Valley Railway Wansford Station, Peterborough, Cambridgeshire PE8 6LR T: 01780 782833
Norris Library and Museum The Broadway, St Ives, Cambridgeshire PE27 5BX T: 01480 497314 E: bob@norrismuseum.org.uk W: www.norrismuseum.org.uk
Octavia Hill Birthplace Museum Trust 1 South Brink Place, Wisbech, Cambridgeshire PE13 1JE T: 01945 476358
Peterborough Museum & Art Gallery Priestgate, Peterborough,

Cambridgeshire PE1 1LF T: 01733 343329 E: museum@vivacity-peterborough.com W: www.vivacity-peterborough.com
Prickwillow Drainage Engine Museum Main St, Prickwillow, Ely, Cambridgeshire CB7 4UN T: 01353 688360 W:
Railworld Museum - Nene Valley Railway Oundle Road, Peterborough, Cambridgeshire PE2 9NR T: 01733 344240 W: www.railworld.net
Ramsey Rural Museum The Woodyard, Wood Lane, Ramsey, Huntingdon, Cambridgeshire PE17 1XD T: 01487 815715
Sedgwick Museum University of Cambridge, Downing St, Cambridge, Cambridgeshire CB2 3EQ T: 01223 333456 E: mgd2@esc.cam.ac.uk
Soham Community History Museum PO Box 21, The Pavilion, Fountain Lane, Soham, Cambridgeshire CB7 5PL
Wisbech and Fenland Museum Museum Square, Wisbech, Cambridgeshire PE13 1ES T: 01945-583817 E: info@wisbechmuseum.org.uk W: www.wisbechmuseum.org.uk

Cheshire
Catalyst Gossage Building, Mersey Road, Widnes, Cheshire WA8 0DF T: 0151 420 1121 W:
Deva Roman Experience Pierpoint Lane , off Bridge Street, Chester, Cheshire CH1 2BJ T: 01244 343407
Griffin Trust The Hangars, West Road, Hutton Park airfield, Ellesmere Port, Cheshire CH65 1BQ T: 0151 350 2598
Grosvenor Museum 27 Grosvenor St, Chester CH1 2DD T: 01244 402008 W: www.cheshire.gov.uk/TourismLeisureAndCulture/museums/museums home.htm
Hack Green Secret Nuclear Bunker PO Box 127, Nantwich, Cheshire CW5 8AQ T: 01270 623353 E: coldwar@dial.pipex.com W: www.hackgreen.co.uk
Lion Salt Works Trust Ollershaw Lane, Marston, Northwich, Cheshire CW9 6ES T: 01606 41823 W: www.lionsaltworkstrust.co.uk
Macclesfield Museums Heritage Centre, Roe St, Macclesfield, K11 6UT T: 01625 613210 E: postmaster@silk-macc.u-net.com W:
Macclesfield Silk Museums Paradise Mill, Park Lane, Macclesfield, Cheshire SK11 6TJ T: 01625 612045 W: www.silk-macclesfield.org
Miniature AFV Association (MAFVA) 45 Balmoral Drive, Holmes Chapel, Cheshire CW4 7JQ T: 01477 535373 E: MAFVAHQ@aol.com W: www.mafva.net
Nantwich Museum Pillory St, Nantwich, Cheshire CW5 5BQ T: 01270 627104
Norton Priory Museum Trust Ltd Tudor Road, Manor Park, Runcorn, Cheshire WA7 1SX T: 01928 569895 E: info@nortonpriory.org W: www.nortonpriory.org
Stockport Air Raid Shelters 61 Chestergate, Stockport, Cheshire SK1 1NG T: 0161 474 1942
West Park Museum Prestbury Rd, Macclesfield, Cheshire SK10 3BJ T: 01625 619831 W:

Cleveland
Captain Cook & Staithes Heritage Centre High St, Staithes, Saltburn-By-The-Sea, Cleveland TS13 5BQ T: 01947 841454
Captain Cook Birthplace Museum Stewart Park, Marton, Middlesbrough, Cleveland TS7 6AS T: 01642 311211 W: www.aboutbritain.com/CaptainCookBirthplaceMuseum
Dorman Museum Linthorpe Rd, Middlesbrough, Cleveland TS5 6LA T: 01642 813781 E: dormanmuseum@middlesbrough.gov.uk W: www.dormanmuseum.org.uk
Green Dragon Museum Theatre Yard, High Street, Stockton-On-Tees, Cleveland TS18 1AT T: 01642 393938
Hartlepool Historic Quay Maritime Avenue, Hartlepool Marina, Hartlepool, Cleveland TS24 0XZ T: 01429 860077 E: arts-museum@hartlepool.gov.uk W: www.thisishartlepool.com
HMS Trincomalee Maritime Avenue, Hartlepool Marina, Hartlepool, Cleveland TS24 0XZ T: 01429 223193 W: www.thisishartlepool.com
Margrove Heritage Centre Margrove Park, Boosbeck, Saltburn-By-The-Sea, Cleveland TS12 3BZ T: 01287 610368
Preston Hall Museum Yarm Road, Stockton-On-Tees, Cleveland TS18 3RH T: 01642 781184
Stockton Museums Service Education, Leisure & Cultural Services, PO Box 228, Municipal Buildings, Church Road, Stockton on Tees, Cleveland TS18 1XE T: 01642 415382 E: rachel.mason@stockton.gov.uk W: www.stockton.gov.uk
The Tom Leonard Mining Experience Deepdale, Skinningrove, Saltburn, Cleveland TS13 4AA T: 01287 642877

Cornwall
Automobilia The Old Mill, Terras Rd, St. Austell, Cornwall PL26 7RX T: 01726 823092
Bodmin Museum Mount Folly, Bodmin, Cornwall PL31 2DB T: 01208 77067

Charlestown Shipwreck & Heritage Centre Quay Rd, Charlestown, St. Austell, Cornwall PL25 3NX T: 01726 69897

Flambards Village and Cornwall Aircraft Park Flambards Village Theme Park, Culdrose Manor, Helston, Cornwall TR13 0GA T: 01326 573404 E: info@flambards.co.uk W: www.flambards.co.uk

Helston Folk Museum Market Place, Helston, Cornwall TR13 8TH T: 01326 564027 E: enquiries@helstonmuseum.org.uk W: www.helstonmuseum.org.uk

John Betjeman Centre Southern Way, Wadebridge PL27 7BX T: 01208 812392

Lanreath Farm & Folk Museum Lanreath Farm, Near Looe, Cornwall PL13 2NX T: 01503 220321 W:

Lawrence House Museum 9 Castle St, Launceston, Cornwall PL15 8BA T: 01566 773277

Maritime Museum 19 Chapel Street, Penzance TR18 4AF T: 01736 68890

Merlin's Cave Crystal Mineral & Fossil Museum & Shop Molesworth St, Tintagel, Cornwall PL34 0BZ T: 01840 770023 W:

Mevagissey Museum Society Frazier House, The Quay, Mevagissey, St. Austell, Cornwall PL26 6QU T: 01726 843568 E: haycas02@yahoo.co.uk W: www.geocities.com/mevamus

National Maritime Museum (Falmouth, Cornwall) 48 Arwenack St, Falmouth, Cornwall TR11 3SA T: 01326 313388

National Maritime Museum (Saltash, Cornwall) Cotehele Quay, Cotehele, Saltash, Cornwall PL12 6TA T: 01579 350830 W:

Penryn Museum Town Hall, Higher Market St, Penryn, Cornwall TR10 8LT T: 01326 372158

Penzance Maritime Museum 19 Chapel St, Penzance, Cornwall TR18 4AW T: 01736 368890

Porthcurno Telegraph Museum and Archive Eastern House, Porthcurno, Penzance, Cornwall TR19 6JX T: 01736 810478 E: caroline.seats@porthcurno.org.uk W: www.porthcurno.org.uk

Potter's Museum of Curiosity Jamaica Inn Courtyard, Bolventor, Launceston, Cornwall PL15 7TS T: 01566 86838

Royal Cornwall Museum River St, Truro, Cornwall TR1 2SJ T: 01872 272205

Trinity House National Lighthouse Centre Wharf Road, Penzance, Cornwall TR18 4BN T: 01736 60077

County Durham

Beamish Museum Ltd - The Living Museum of the North Beamish, County Durham DH9 0RG T: 0191 370 4000 F: 0191 370 4001 E: paulcastrey@beamish.org.uk W: www.beamish.org.uk

Darlington Railway Centre & Museum North Road Station , Station Rd, Darlington, County Durham DL3 6ST T: 01325 460532

Darlington Railway Preservation Society Station Rd, Hopetown, Darlington, County Durham DL3 6ST T: 01325 483606

Discovery Centre Grosvenor House, 29 Market Place, Bishop Auckland, County Durham DL14 7NP T: 01388-662666 E: west.durham@groundwork.org.uk

Durham Heritage Centre St Mary le Bow, North Bailey, Durham, County Durham DH1 5ET T: 0191-384-5589

Durham Mining Museum 43 Primrose Crescent, Fulwell, Sunderland, Tyne & Wear SR6 9RJ T: 07931 421709 E: webmaster@dmm.org.uk W: www.dmm.org.uk

Durham University Library Archives and Special Collections Durham University Library, Palace Green, Durham, DH1 3RN T: 0191 334 2972 E: pg.library@durham.ac.uk W: www.dur.ac.uk/library/asc

Fulling Mill Museum of Archaeology The Banks, Durham, County Durham T: 0191 374 3623

Killhope Lead Mining Centre Cowshill, Weardale, County Durham DL13 1AR T: 01388-537505 E: info@killhope.org.uk W: www.killhope.org.uk

The Bowes Museum Barnard Castle, County Durham DL12 8NP T: 01833 690606 E: info@thebowesmuseum.org.uk W: www.thebowesmuseum.org.uk

The Oriental Museum University of Durham Museums, Elvet Hill, Durham, DH1 3TH T: 0191 334 5694 E: oriental.museum@durham.ac.uk W: www.dur.ac.uk/oriental.museum/

Weardale Museum South View, 2 Front Street, Ireshopeburn, County Durham DL13 1EY T: 01388-537417

Cumbria

Aspects of Motoring Western Lakes Motor Museum The Maltings, The Maltings, Brewery Lane, Cockermouth, Cumbria CA13 9ND T: 01900 824448

Birdoswald Roman Fort Gilsland, Brampton, Cumbria CA6 7DD T: 01697 747602

Dove Cottage & The Wordsworth Museum Town End, Grasmere, Ambleside, Cumbria LA22 9SH T: 015394 35544 W:

Friends of The Helena Thompson Museum 24 Calva Brow, Workington, Cumbria CA14 1DD T: 01900 603312

Haig Colliery Mining Museum Solway Road, Kells, Whitehaven, Cumbria CA28 9BG T: 01946 599949 W: www.haigpit.com

Heritage First - formerly Ulverston Heritage Centre Lower Brook St, Ulverston, Cumbria LA12 7EE T: 01229 580820 W: www.rootsweb.com/~ukuhc/

Keswick Museum & Art Gallery Station Rd, Keswick, Cumbria CA12 4NF T: 017687 73263 E: hazel.davison@allerdale.gov.uk

Lakeland Motor Museum Holker Hall, Cark In Cartmel, Grange-Over-Sands, Cumbria LA11 7PL T: 015395 58509 W:

Lakeside & Haverthwaite Railway Haverthwaite Station, Ulverston, Cumbria LA12 8AL T: 01539 531594

Laurel & Hardy Museum 4c Upper Brook St, Ulverston, Cumbria LA12 7BH T: 01229 582292 W:

Maritime Museum 1 Senhouse Street, Maryport, Cumbria CA15 6AB T: 01900 813738

Maryport Steamship Museum Elizabeth Dock South Quay, Maryport, Cumbria CA15 8AB T: 01900 815954 W:

North Pennines Heritage Trust Nenthead Mines Heritage Centre, Nenthead, Alston CA9 3PD T: 01434 382037 W: www.npht.com

Roman Army Museum Carvoran House, Greenhead, Carlisle, Cumbria CA6 7JB T: 016977 47485 W:

Ruskin Museum Yewdale Rd, Coniston, Cumbria LA21 8DU T: 015394 41164 W: www.coniston.org.uk

Senhouse Roman Museum The Battery, Sea Brows, Maryport, Cumbria CA15 6JD T: 01900 816168 E: romans@senhouse.freeserve.co.uk W: www.senhousemuseum.co.uk

Solway Aviation Museum Carlisle Airport, Carlisle, Cumbria CA6 4NW T: 01228 573823

Solway Aviation Museum Aviation House, Carlisle Airport, Carlisle , CA6 4NW T: 01227 573823 W: www.solway-aviation-museum.org.uk

The Guildhall Museum Green Market, Carlisle, Cumbria CA3 8JE T: 01228 819925 W:

The Penrith & Eden Museum Middlegate, Penrith CA11 7PT T: 01768 865105 E: museum@eden.gov.uk W: www.eden.gov.uk/museum

The Rum Story - The Dark Spirit of Whitehaven 27 Lowther Street, Whitehaven, Cumbria CA28 7DN T: 01946 592933 E: info@rumstory.co.uk W: www.rumstory.co.uk

Tullie House Museum and Art Gallery Castle Street, Carlisle, Cumbria CA3 8TP T: 01228-534781 E: enquiries@tulliehouse.co.uk W: www.tulliehouse.co.uk/

William Creighton Mineral Museum & Gallery 2 Crown St, Cockermouth, Cumbria CA13 0EJ T: 01900 828301 W:

Windermere Steamboat Museum Rayrigg Rd, Windermere, Cumbria LA23 1BN T: 015394 45565 W: www.steamboat.co.uk

Derbyshire

Chesterfield Museum & Art Gallery St Mary‚Äôs Gate, Chesterfield, Derbyshire S41 7TY T: 01246 345727 W: www.chesterfield.gov.uk

Derby Industrial Museum Silk Mill Lane, Off Full Street, Derby, Derbyshire DE1 3AF T: 01332 255308 W: www.derby.gov.uk/museums

Derby Museum & Art Gallery The Strand, Derby, Derbyshire DE1 1BS T: 01332-716659 W: www.derby.gov.uk/museums

Derwent Valley Visitor Centre Belper North Mill, Bridge Foot, Belper, Derbyshire DE56 1YD T: 01773 880474

Donington Park Racing Ltd Donington Park, Castle Donnington, Derby, Derbyshire DE74 2RP T: 01332 814697

Elvaston Castle Estate Museum Elvaston Castle Country Park, Borrowash Road, Elvaston, Derby DE72 3EP T: 01332 573799 W:

Erewash Museum The Museum, High Street, Ilkeston, DE7 5JA T: 0115 907 1141 E: museum@erewash.gov.uk W: www.erewash.gov.uk

Eyam Museum Eyam, Derbyshire S32 5QP T: 01433 631371 E: johnbeck@classicfm.net W: www.eyam.org.uk

Glossop Heritage Centre Bank House, Henry St, Glossop, Derbyshire SK13 8BW T: 01457 869176 W:

High Peak Junction Workshop High Peak Junction, Cromford, Matlock, Derbyshire DE4 5HN T: 01629 822831 W:

High Peak Trail Middleton Top, Rise End, Middleton, Matlock, Derbyshire DE4 4LS T: 01629 823204 W:

Midland Railway Centre Butterley Station, Ripley, Derbyshire DE5 3QZ T: 01773 570140

National Stone Centre Porter Lane, Wirksworth, Matlock, Derbyshire DE4 4LS T: 01629 824833

Peak District Mining Museum The Pavilion, South Parade, Matlock Bath, DE4 3NR T: 01629 583834 E: mail@peakmines.co.uk W: www.peakmines.co.uk

Pickford's House Museum 41 Friar Gate, Derby, Derbyshire DE1 1DA T: 01332 255363 W: www.derby.gov.uk/museums

Devon

Allhallows Museum of Lace & Antiquities High St, Honiton EX14 1PG T: 01404 44966 E: dyateshoniton@msn.com W: www.honitonlace.com

Brixham Heritage Museum Bolton Cross, Brixham, Devon TQ5 8LZ T: 01803 856267 E: mail@brixhamheritage.org.uk W: www.brixhamheritage.org.uk

Century of Playtime 30 Winner St, Paignton, Devon TQ3 3BJ T: 01803 553850

Crownhill Fort Crownhill Fort Road, Plymouth, Devon PL6 5BX T: 01752 793754

Dunkeswell Memorial Museum Dunkeswell Airfield, Dunkeswell Ind Est, Dunkeswell, Honiton, Devon EX14 0RA T: 01404 891943

Fairlynch Art Centre & Museum 27 Fore St, Budleigh Salterton, Devon EX9 6NP T: 01395 442666

Finch Foundary Museum of Rural Industry Sticklepath, Okehampton, Devon EX20 2NW T: 01837 840046

Ilfracombe Museum Wilder Rd, Ilfracombe, Devon EX34 8AF T: 01271 863541 E: ilfracombe@devonmuseums.net W: www.ilfracombemuseum.co.uk

Museum of Barnstaple & North Devon incorporating Royal Devon Yeomanry Museum Peter A Boyd, The Square, Barnstaple, Devon EX32 8LN T: 01271 346 747

Newton Abbot Town & Great Western Railway Museum 2A St. Pauls Rd, Newton Abbot, Devon TQ12 2HP T: 01626 201121

Newhall Visitor & Equestrian Centre Newhall, Budlake, Exeter, Devon EX5 3LW T: 01392 462453

North Devon Maritime Museum Odun House, Odun Rd, Appledore, Bideford, Devon EX39 1PT T: 01237 422064 W: www.devonmuseums.net/appledore

North Devon Museum Service St.Anne's Chapel, Paternoster Row, Barnstaple, Devon EX32 8LN T: 01271 378709 W:

Otterton Mill Otterton, Budleigh Salterton, Devon EX9 7HG T: 01395 568521 E: escape@ottertonmill.com W: www.ottertonmill.com

Plymouth City Museum & Art Gallery Drake Circus, Plymouth, Devon PL4 8AJ T: 01752 304774 E: museum@plymouth.gov.uk W: www.plymouthmuseum.gov.uk www.cottoniancollection.org.uk

Royal Albert Memorial Museum Queen Street, Exeter, Devon EX4 3RX T: 01392 265858

Seaton Tramway Harbour Road, Seaton , Devon EX12 2NQ T: 01297 20375 E: info@tram.co.uk W: www.tram.co.uk

Sidmouth Museum Hope Cottage, Church St, Sidmouth, Devon EX10 8LY T: 01395 516139 W:

Tavistock Museum Court Gate, Guildhall square, Tavistock, Devon PL19 0EA T: 01822 616503 E: rodmartin45@hotmail.com W: www.tavistockhistory.ik.com/

Teignmouth Museum 29 French St, Teignmouth, Devon TQ14 8ST T: 01626 777041 W:

The Dartmouth Museum The Butterwalk, Dartmouth, Devon TQ6 9PZ T: 01803 832923 W:

The Devonshire and Dorset Regiment (Archives) RHQ, Devonshire and Dorset Regiment, Wyvern Barracks, Barrack Road, Exeter, Devon EX2 6AR T: 01392 492436

The Museum of Dartmoor Life West Street, Okehampton, Devon EX20 1HQ T: 01837 52295 E: dartmoormuseum@eclipse.co.uk W: www.museumofdartmoorlife.eclipse.co.uk

Tiverton Museum of Mid Devon Life Beck‚Äôs Square, Tiverton, Devon EX16 6PJ T: 01884 256295 E: curator04@tivertonmuseum.org.uk W: www.tivertonmuseum.org.uk

Dorset

Bournemouth Aviation Museum Hanger 600, Bournemouth International Airport, Christchurch BH23 6SE T: 01202 580858 E: admin@aviation-museum.co.uk W: www.aviation-museum.co.uk

Bridport Harbour Museum West Bay, Bridport, Dorset DT6 4SA T: 01308 420997 W:

Bridport Museum Trust - Local History Centre The Coach House, Gundry Lane, Bridport, Dorset DT6 3RJ T: 01308 458703 E: office@bridportmuseum.co.uk W: www.bridportmuseum.co.uk

Cavalcade of Costume Lime Tree House, The Plocks, Blandford Forum, Dorset DT11 7AA T: 01258 453006 W: www.cavalcadeofcostume.com

Christchurch Motor Museum Matchams Lane, Hurn, Christchurch, Dorset BH23 6AW T: 01202 488100

Crewkerne & District Museum The Heritage Centre, Market Square, Crewkerne TA18 7JU T: +44 (0) 1460 77079 F: +44 (0) 1460 78790 E: crewkernemuseum@hotmail.co.uk W: www.crewkernemuseum.co.uk

Dinosaur Land Coombe St, Lyme Regis DT7 3PY T: 01297 443541

Dinosaur Museum, The Icen Way, Dorchester, DT1 1EW T: 01305 269880

Dorset County Museum High West Street, Dorchester, Dorset DT1 1XA T: 01305 262735 E: enquiries@dorsetcountymuseum.org W: www.dorsetcountymuseum.org

Lyme Regis Philpot Museum Bridge St, Lyme Regis, Dorset DT7 3QA T: 01297 443370 E: info@lymeregismuseum.co.uk W: www.lymeregismuseum.co.uk

Nothe Fort Barrack Rd, Weymouth, Dorset DT4 8UF T: 01305 766626 E: fortressweymouth@btconnect.com W: www.fortressweymouth.co.uk

Poole Museum and Poole History Centre 4 High Street, Poole, Dorset BH15 1BW T: 01202 262 600 E: museums@poole.gov.uk W: www.boroughofpoole.gov.uk/museums

Portland Museum Wakeham, Portland, Dorset DT5 1HS T: 01305 821804 W:

Priest's House Museum 23-27 High St, Wimborne, Dorset BH21 1HR T: 01202 882533 W:

Red House Museum & Gardens Quay Rd, Christchurch, Dorset BH23 1BU T: 01202 482860

Russell-Cotes Art Gallery & Museum East Cliff, Bournemouth, BH1 3AA T: 01202 451858 E: diane.edge@bournemouth.gov.uk

Shaftesbury Abbey Museum & Garden Park Walk, Shaftesbury, Dorset SP7 8JR T: 01747 852910

Shaftesbury Town Museum Gold Hill, Shaftesbury, Dorset SP7 8JW T: 01747 852157**Sherborne Museum Association** Abbey Gate House, Church Avenue, Sherborne, Dorset DT9 3BP T: 01935 812252

The Nothe Fort Museum of Coastal Defence Barrack Road, Weymouth , Dorset DT4 5UF T: 01305 787243

Tolpuddle Martyrs Museum TUC Memorial Cottages, Tolpuddle, Dorset DT2 7EH T: 01305 848237 W: www.tolpuddlemartyrs.org.uk

Wareham Town Museum 5 East St, Wareham, Dorset BH20 4NS T: 01929 553448 W:

Weymouth & Portland Museum Service The Esplanade, Weymouth, Dorset DT4 8ED T: 01305 765206 W:

Weymouth Museum Brewers Quay, Hope Square, Weymouth, Dorset DT4 8TR T: 01305 777622 E: admin@brewers-quay.co.uk W: www.brewers-quay.co.uk

Essex

Barleylands Farm Museum & Visitors Centre Barleylands Farm, Billericay, Essex CM11 2UD T: 01268 282090

Battlesbridge Motorcycle Museum Muggeridge Farm, Maltings Road, Battlesbridge, Wickford, Essex SS11 7RF T: 01268 560866

Castle Point Transport Museum Society 105 Point Rd, Canvey Island, Essex SS8 7TJ T: 01268 684272 W:

Chelmsford Museum Oaklands Park, Moulsham Street, Chelmsford, Essex CM2 9AQ T: 01245 605700 E: oaklands@chelmsfordbc.gov.uk W: www.chelmsford.gov.uk/museums

East England Tank Museum Oak Business Park, Wix Rd, Beaumont, Clacton-On-Sea, Essex CO16 0AT T: 01255 871119 W:

East Essex Aviation Society & Museum Martello Tower, Point Clear, Clacton on Sea, Essex T: 01255 428020

Epping Forest District Museum 39-41 Sun St, Waltham Abbey, Essex EN9 1EL T: 01992 716882 W:

Essex Secret Bunker Crown Building, Shrublands Road, Mistley, Essex CO11 1HS T: 01206 392271 (24 hour information line)

Essex Volunteer Units Colchester Museums, 14 Ryegate Road, Colchester, Essex CO1 1YG T: 01206 282935

Essex Yeomanry Collection Springfield Lyons TA Centre, Colchester Road, Chelmsford , Essex CM2 5TA T: 01245 462298

Great Dunmow Maltings Museum The Maltings, Mill Lane, Great Dunmow, Essex CM6 1BG T: 01371 878979

Harwich Maritime Museum Low Lightouse, Harbour Crescent, Harwich, Essex T: 01255 503429 W: www.harwich-society.com

Harwich Redoubt Fort Behind 29 Main Road, Harwich, Essex T: 01255 503429 W: www.harwich-society.com

Hollytrees Museum High St, Colchester, Essex CO1 1DN T: 01206 282940

Kelvedon Hatch Secret Nuclear Bunker Kelvedon Hall Lane, Kelvedon Common, Kelvedon Hatch, Brentwood, Essex CM15 0LB T: 01277 364883 E: bunker@japar.demon.co.uk W: www.secretnuclearbunker.co.uk

Leigh Heritage Centre & Museum 13a High St, Leigh-On-Sea, Essex SS9 2EN T: 01702 470834

Maldon District Museum 47 Mill Rd, Maldon, Essex CM9 5HX T: 01621 842688

Royal Gunpowder Mills administrative Office, Beaulieu drive, Powdermill Lane, Waltham Abbey, Essex EN9 1JY T: 01992 767022 W: www.royalgunpowder.co.uk

Saffron Walden Museum Museum Street, Saffron Walden, Essex CB10 1JL T: 01799 510333 E: museum@uttlesford.gov.uk W: www.saffronwaldenmuseum.org

Southend Central Museum Museum Victoria Avenue, Southend-On-Sea, Essex SS2 6EW T: 01702 434449

Stow Maries Aerodrome Hackmans Lane, Cold Norton, Essex CM3 6RN T: 01245 808 744 E: curator@stowmaries.com W: www.stowmaries.com

The Cater Museum 74 High St, Billericay, Essex CM12 9BS T: 01277 622023 W:

The Museum of Harlow Muskham Rd, Harlow, Essex CM20 2LF T: 01279 4549569 W: www.tmoh.com

Thurrock Museum Ossett Road, Grays, Essex RM17 5DX

Valence House Museum Valence House Museum, Becontree Avenue, Dagenham, Essex RM8 3HT T: 020 8270 6866 E: valencehousemuseum@lbbd.gov.uk W: www.lbbd.gov.uk/valence

Gloucestershire

Campden & District Historical & Archaeological Society (CADHAS) The Old Police Station, High Street, Chipping Campden, GL55 6HB T: 01386 848840 E: enquiries@chippingcampdenhistory.org.uk W: www.chippingcampdenhistory.org.uk

Dean Heritage Centre Soudley, Cinderford, Forest of dean, Gloucestershire GL14 2UB T: 01594 822170 E: info@deanheritagemuseum.com W: www.deanheritagemuseum.com

Frenchay Tuckett Society and Local History Museum 247 Frenchay Park Road, Frenchay, Gloucestershire BS16 ILG T: 0117 956 9324 W: www.frenchay.org/museum.html

Gloucester City Museum & Art Gallery Brunswick Rd, Gloucester, Gloucestershire GL1 1HP T: 01452 524131 W:

Gloucester Folk Museum 99-103 Westgate St, Gloucester, GL1 2PG T: 01452 526467 E: christopherm@glos-city.gov.uk

Holst Birthplace Museum 4 Clarence Rd, Cheltenham, Gloucestershire GL52 2AY T: 01242 524846 W:

Jet Age Museum Hangar 7 Meteor Business Park, Gloucestershire Airport, Cheltenham Road East, Gloucester, Gloucestershire GL2 9QY T: 01452 715100 W: www.aboutbritain.com/JetAgeMuseum.htm

John Moore Countryside Museum 42 Church St, Tewkesbury, Gloucestershire GL20 5SN T: 01684 297174

Nature In Art Wallsworth Hall, Tewkesbury Rd, Twigworth, Gloucester, Gloucestershire GL2 9PG T: 01452 731422 E: rinart@globalnet.co.uk W: www.nature-in-art.org.uk

Shambles Museum Church Street, Newent, Gloucestershire GL18 1PP T: 01531 822144 W:

The Edward Jenner Museum Church Lane, Berkeley, Gloucestershire GL13 9BN T: 01453 810631 E: manager@jennermuseum.com W: www.jennermuseum.com

The Great Western Railway Museum (Coleford) The Old Railway Station, Railway Drive, Coleford, Gloucestershire GL16 8RH T: 01594 833569

The Guild Of Handicraft Trust Silk Mill, Sheep Street, Chipping Campden, Gloucestershire GL55 6DS T: 01386 841417

Wellington Aviation Museum Broadway Road, Moreton in the Marsh, Gloucestershire GL56 0BG T: 01608 650323 W: www.wellingtonaviation.org

Hampshire

Action Stations Boathouse No 6, HM Naval Base, Portsmouth, Hampshire PO1 3LR T: 023 9286 1512

Andover Museum & Iron Age Museum 6 Church Close, Andover, Hampshire SP10 1DP T: 01264 366283 W: www.hants.gov.uk

Balfour Museum of Hampshire Red Cross History Red Cross House, Weeke, Winchester, Hampshire SO22 5JD T: 01962 865174

Bishops Waltham Museum Brookstreet, Bishop's Waltham, Southampton, Hampshire S032 1EB

Broadlands Romsey, Hampshire SO51 9ZD T: 01794 505010 E: admin@broadlands.net W: www.broadlands.net

Bursledon Brickworks Industrial Museum Coal Park Lane, Swanwick, Southampton, Hampshire SO31 7GW T: 01489 576248 E: enquiries@hampshirebuildings.org.uk W: www.bursledonbrickworks.co.uk

D-Day Museum and Overlord Museum Clarence Esplanade, Southsea, Hampshire PO5 3NT T: 023 9282 7261

Dockyard Apprentice Exhibition Portsmouth Royal Dockyard Historical Trust, 19 College Road, HM Naval Base, Portsmouth, Hampshire PO1 3LJ

Eastleigh Museum 25 High St, Eastleigh SO50 5LF T: (023) 8064 3026 E: musmst@hants.gov.uk W: www.hants.gov.uk/eastleigh-museum

Eling Tide Mill Trust Ltd The Tollbridge, Eling Hill, Totton, Southampton, Hampshire SO40 9HF T: (023) 80869575

Gosport Museum Walpole Rd, Gosport PO12 1NS T: (023) 9258 8035

Hampshire County Museums Service Chilcomb House, Chilcomb Lane, Winchester, Hampshire SO23 8RD T: 01962 846304

Havant Museum Havant Museum, 56 East Street, Havant, Hampshire P09 1BS T: 023 9245 1155 E: musmop@hants.gov.uk W: www.hants.gov.uk/museums

Historic Ships and The Naval Dockyard HM Naval Base, Portsmouth, Hampshire PO1 3LR T: 023 9286 1512 E: wnquiries@historicadockyard.co.uk W: www.flagship.org.uk

HMS Victory Victory Gate, HM Naval Base, Portsmouth, Hampshire PO1 3LR T: (023) 9277 8600 E: info@hmswarrior.org W: www.hmswarrior.org

HMS Warrior (1860) Victory Gate, HM Naval Base, Portsmouth, Hampshire PO1 3LR T: (023) 9277 8600 E: info@hmswarrior.org W: www.hmswarrior.org

Hollycombe Steam Collection Iron Hill, Midhurst Rd, Liphook, Hampshire GU30 7LP T: 01428 724900 W:

New Forest Museum & Visitor Centre High St, Lyndhurst, Hampshire SO43 7NY T: (023) 8028 3914 E: nfmuseum@lineone.net

Portsmouth City Museum and Record Office Museum Road, Portsmouth, Hampshire PO1 2LJ T: (023) 92827261 E: Searchroom@portsmouthcc.gov.uk W: www.portsmouthmuseums.co.uk/

Priddy's Hard Armament Museum Priory Rd, Gosport, Hampshire PO12 4LE T: (023) 92502490

Rockbourne Roman Villa Rockbourne, Fordingbridge, Hampshire SP6 3PG T: 01725 518541 W:

Royal Armouries - Fort Nelson Fort Nelson , Down End Roadd, Fareham , Hampshire PO17 6AN T: 01329 233734 E: enquiries@armouries.org.uk W: www.armouries.org.uk

Sammy Miller Motor Cycle Museum Bashley Manor Farm, Bashley Cross Rd, New Milton, Hampshire BH25 5SZ T: 01425 620777 W: www.sammymiller.co.uk

Search 50 Clarence Rd, Gosport, Hampshire PO12 1BU T: (023) 92501957

Southampton Hall of Aviation Albert Road South, Southampton, Hampshire SO1 1FR T: 01703 635830

Southampton Maritime Museum Bugle St, Southampton , Hampshire SO14 2AJ T: (023) 80223941

The Bear Museum 38 Dragon St, Petersfield, Hampshire GU31 4JJ T: 01730 265108 E: judy@bearmuseum.freeserve.co.uk W: www.bearmuseum.co.uk

The Mary Rose Trust 1-10 College Road, HM Naval Base, Portsmouth, Hampshire PO1 3LX T: (023) 92750521

The Willis Museum Of Basingstoke Town & Country Life Old Town Hall, Market Place, Basingstoke, Hampshire RG21 7QD T: 01256 465902 E: willismuseum@hotmail.com W: www.hants.gov.uk/leisure/museums/willis/index.html

West End Local History Society 40 Hatch mead, West End, Southampton, Hampshire SO30 3NE T: 023 8047 1886 E: westendlhs@aol.com W: www.westendlhs.hampshire.org.uk

Westbury Manor Museum West St, Fareham, Hampshire PO16 0JJ T: 01329 824895 W: www.hants.gov.uk/museum/westbury/

Whitchurch Silk Mill 28 Winchester St, Whitchurch, Hampshire RG28 7AL T: 01256 892065 W:

Winchester Museums Service 75 Hyde St, Winchester, Hampshire SO23 7DW T: 01962 848269 E: museums@winchester.gov.uk W: www.winchester.gov.uk/heritage/home.htm

Herefordshire

Churchill House Museum Venns Lane, Hereford, Herefordshire HR1 1DE T: 01432 260693

Cider Museum & King Offa Distillery 21 Ryelands St, Hereford, Herefordshire HR4 0LW T: 01432 354207 E: thompson@cidermuseum.co.uk W: www.cidermuseum.co.uk

Leominster Museum Etnam St, Leominster, Herefordshire HR6 8 T: 01568 615186 W:

Teddy Bears of Bromyard 12 The Square, Bromyard, Herefordshire HR7 4BP T: 01885 488329 W:

Waterworks Museum 86 Park Street, Broomy Hill, Hereford, HR1 2RE T: 01432-356653 E: info@www.waterworksmuseum.org.uk W: www.waterworksmuseum.org.uk/

Weobley & District Local History Society and Museum Weobley Museum, Back Lane, Weobley HR4 8SG T: 01544 340292

Hertfordshire

Bushey Museum, Art Gallery and Local Studies Centre Rudolph Road, Bushey, Hertfordshire WD23 3HW T: 020 8420 4057 E: busmt@bushey.org.uk W: www.busheymuseum.org

De Havilland Heritage Centre inc The Mosquito Aircraft Museum PO Box 107, Salisbury Hall, London Colney, Hertfordshire AL10 1EX T: 01727 822051 W: www.hertsmuseums.org

First Garden City Heritage Museum 296 Norton Way South, Letchworth Garden City, Hertfordshire SG6 1SU T: 01462 482710 E: fgchm@letchworth.com

Hertford Museum (Hertfordshire Regiment) 18 Bull Plain, Hertford, Hertfordshire SG14 1DT T: 01992 582686 W: www.hertfordmuseum.org

Hitchin British Schools 41-42 Queen St, Hitchin, Hertfordshire SG4 9TS T: 01462 420144 E: brsch@britishschools.freeserve.co.uk W: www.hitchinbritishschools.org.uk

Hitchin Museum Paynes Park, Hitchin, Hertfordshire SG5 1EQ T: 01462 434476 E: hitchin.museum@north-herts.gov.uk W: www.north-herts.gov.uk/index/discover_nhdc/art_museums_and_heritage/hitchin_museum_and_art_gallery.htm

Kingsbury Water Mill Museum St. Michaels Street, St. Albans, Hertfordshire AL3 4SJ T: 01727 853502

Letchworth Museum & Art Gallery Broadway, Letchworth Garden City SG6 3PF T: 01462 685647 W: www.north-herts.gov.uk

Mill Green Museum & Mill Mill Green, Hatfield, Hertfordshire AL9 5PD T: 01707 271362

Natural History Museum at Tring Akeman St, Tring HP23 6AP T: 020 7942 6171 E: tring-enquiries@nhm.ac.uk W: www.nhm.ac.uk/tring

Rhodes Memorial Museum & Commonwealth Centre South Rd, Bishop's Stortford, Hertfordshire CM23 3JG T: 01279 651746 E: rhodesmuseum@freeuk.com W: www.hertsmuseums.org.uk

Royston & District Museum 5 Lower King St, Royston, Hertfordshire SG8 5AL T: 01763 242587

Stondon Transport Museum Station Road, Lower Stondon, Hertfordshire SG16 6JN T: 01462 850339 E: info@transportmuseum.co.uk W: www.transportmuseum.co.uk

The De Havilland Aircraft Museum Trust P.O Box 107, Salisbury Hall, London Colney, St. Albans AL2 1EX T: 01727 822051 W:

The Environmental Awareness Trust 23 High St, Wheathampstead, St. Albans, Hertfordshire AL4 8BB T: 01582 834580

The Forge Museum High St, Much Hadham, Hertfordshire SG10 6BS T: 01279 843301

Verulamium Museum St. Michaels St, St. Albans, Hertfordshire AL3 4SW T: 01727 751810 E: museums@stalbans.gov.uk W: www.stalbansmuseums.org.uk/verulamium.htm

Ware Museum Priory Lodge, 89 High St, Ware, Hertfordshire SG12 9AD T: 01920 487848

Watford Museum 194 High St, Watford, Hertfordshire WD1 2DT T: 01923 232297

Welwyn Hatfield Museum Service Welwyn Roman Baths, By-Pass-Road, Welwyn, Hertfordshire AL6 0 T: 01438 716096

Hull

Ferens Art Gallery Kingston upon Hull City Museums, Queen Victoria Square, Kingston upon Hull, HU1 3RA T: 01482 613902

Wilberforce House Kingston upon Hull City Museums, 23-25 High Street, Kingston upon Hull, HU1 T: 01482 613902

Isle Of Wight

Bembridge Maritime Museum & Shipwreck Centre Providence House, Sherborne St, Bembridge PO35 5SB T: 01983 872223

Calbourne Water Mill Calbourne Mill, Newport PO30 4JN T: 01983 531227

Carisbroke Castle Newport PO30 1XL W: www.english-heritage.org.uk

Carisbrooke Castle Museum Carisbrooke Castle, Newport, Isle Of Wight PO30 1XY T: 01983 523112

East Cowes Heritage Centre 8 Clarence Rd, East Cowes, Isle Of Wight PO32 6EP T: 01983 280310

Guildhall Museum Newport Museum of Island History High St, Newport, Isle Of Wight PO30 1TY T: 01983 823366 E: museums@iow.gov.uk W: www.iwight.com/museums

Natural History Centre High St, Godshill, Ventnor, Isle Of Wight PO38 3HZ T: 01983 840333

Needles Old Battery West High Down, Totland Bay, Isle of Wight PO39 0JH T: 01983 754772

The Classic Boat Museum Seaclose Wharf, Town Quay, Newport, Isle Of Wight PO30 2EF T: 01983 533493 E: ebmiow@fsmail.net

The Island Aeroplane Company Ltd Embassy Way, Sandown Airport, Sandown, Isle of wight PO36 9PJ T: 01983 404448

The Lilliput Museum of Antique Dolls & Toys High St Brading, Sandown, isle Of Wight PO36 0DJ T: 01983 407231 E: lilliput.museum@btconnect.com W: lilliputmuseum.co.uk

Ventnor Heritage Museum 11 Spring Hill, Ventnor, Isle Of Wight PO38 1PE T: 01983 855407

Kent

Brenzett Aeronautical Museum Ivychurch Road, Brenzett, Romney Marsh, Kent TN29 0EE T: 01233 627911 W: www.aboutbritain.com/renzettAeronauticalMuseum

Canterbury Roman Museum Butchery Lane, Canterbury, Kent CT1 2JR T: 01227 785575

Chartwell House Chartwell, Westerham, Kent TN16 1PS T: 01732 866368 E: chartwell@nationaltrust.org.uk W: www.nationaltrust.org.uk

Chatham Dockyard Historical Society Museum Cottage Row, Barrack Rd, Chatham Dockyard, Chatham, Kent ME4 4TZ T: 01634 844897(museum)

Chatham Historic Dockyard Trust Old Surgery, The Historic Dockyard, Chatham, Kent ME4 4TZ T: 01634 823813 E: info@chdt.org.uk W: www.thedockyard.co.uk

Cobham Hall Cobham, Kent DA12 3BL T: 01474 823371

Dickens House Museum 2 Victoria Parade, Broadstairs, Kent CT10 1QS T: 01843 861232

Dolphin Sailing Barge Museum Crown Quay Lane, Sittingbourne, Kent ME10 3SN T: 01795 423215

Dover Castle Dover, Kent CT16 1HU T: 01304 201628 W: www.english-heritage.org.uk

Dover Museum Market Square, Dover, Kent CT16 1PB T: 01304 201066 E: museum@dover.gov.uk W: www.dovermuseum.co.uk

Dover Transport Museum Old Park Barracks, Whitfield, Dover, Kent CT16 2HQ T: 01304 822409

Fleur De Lis Heritage Centre 13 Preston Street, Faversham, Kent ME13 8NS T: 01795 534542 E: faversham@btinternet.com W: www.faversham.org

Fort Armherst Dock Road, Chatham, Kent ME4 4UB T: 01634 847747 W: www.fortamhurst.org.uk

Fort Luton Museum Magpie Hall Road, Chatham, Kent ME4 5XJ T: 01634 813969

Guildhall Museum Guildhall Museum, High Street, Rochester, kent ME1 1PY T: 01634 848717 E: guildhall@medway.gov.uk W: www.medway.gov.uk

Gunpowder Chart Mills Off Stonebridge Way, Faversham, Kent ME13 7SE T: 01795 534542 E: faversham@btinternet.com W: www.faversham.org

Herne Bay Museum Centre 12 William St, Herne Bay, Kent CT6 5EJ T: 01227 367368 E: museum@canterbury.gov.uk W: www.hernebay-museum.co.uk

Kent and Sharpshooters Yeomanry Museum Hever Castle, Edenbridge, Kent TN8 7DB T: 020 8688 2138

Kent Battle of Britain Museum Aerodrome Rd, Hawkinge, Folkestone, Kent CT18 7AG T: 01303 893140

Kent Battle of Britain Museum Aerodrome Road, Hawkinge, Folkestone, Kent CT18 7AG T: 01303 893140

Kent Police Museum The Historic Dockyard, Chatham, Kent ME4 4TZ T: 01634 403260 E: info@kent-police-museum.co.uk W: www.kent-police-museum.co.uk

Lashenden Air Warfare Museum Headcorn Aerodrome, Headcorn, Nr Ashford, Kent TN27 9HX T: 01622 890226

Maidstone Museum & Art Gallery St. Faith St, Maidstone, Kent ME14 1LH T: 01622 754497

Margate Old Town Hall Museum Old Town Hall, Market Place, Margate, Kent CT9 1AH T: 01843 231213

Masonic Library & Museum St. Peters Place, Canterbury, Kent CT1 2DA T: 01227 785625

Minster Abbey Gatehouse Museum Union Rd, Minster On Sea, Sheerness, Kent ME12 2HW T: 01795 872303

Minster Museum Craft & Animal Centre Bedlam Court Lane, Minster, Ramsgate, Kent CT12 4HQ T: 01843 822312

Museum of Kent Life Cobtree, Lock Lane, Sandling, Maidstone, Kent ME14 3AU T: 01622 763936 E: enquiries@museum-kentlife.co.uk W: www.museum-kentlife.co.uk

Penshurst Place & Gardens Penshurst, Tonbridge, Kent TN11 8DG T: 01892 870 307 E: enquiries@penshurstplace.com W: www.penshurstplace.com

Powell-Cotton Museum, Quex House and Gardens Quex Park, Birchington, Kent CT7 0 T: 01843 842168 E: powell-cotton.museum@virgin.net W: www.powell-cottonmuseum.co.uk

Quebec House Quebec Square, Westerham TN16 1TD T: 01892 890651

Ramsgate Maritime Museum The Clock House, Pier Yard, Royal Harbour, Ramsgate, Kent CT11 8LS T: 01843 570622 W: www.ekmt.fogonline.co.uk

Rochester Cathedral Militia Museum Guildhall Museum, High Street, Rochester, kent ME1 1PY T: 01634 848717

Roman Dover Tourist Centre Painted House, New street, Dover, Kent CT17 9AJ T: 01304 203279

Roman Museum Butchery Lane, Canterbury, Kent CT1 2JR T: 01227 785575 W: www.aboutbritain.com/CanterburyRomanMuseum

Romney Toy & Model Museum New Romney Station, Romney, Kent TN28 8PL T: 01797 362353

Royal Museum & Art Gallery 18 High St, Canterbury, Kent CT1 2RA T: 01227 452747

Sheerness Heritage Centre 10 Rose St, Sheerness, ME12 1AJ T: 01795 663317

Shoreham Aircraft Museum High Street, Shoreham, Sevenoaks, Kent TN14 7TB T: 01959 524416 W: www.s-a-m.freeserve.co.uk

Spitfire and Hurricane Memorial Building The Airfield, Manston Road, Ramsgate, Kent CT11 5DF T: 01843 821940 W: www.spitfire-museum.com

St Margaret's Museum Beach Road, St Margaret's Bay, Dover, Kent CT15 6DZ T: 01304 852764

Tenterden Museum Station Rd, Tenterden, Kent TN30 6HN T: 01580 764310

The C.M Booth Collection Of Historic Vehicles 63-67 High St, Rolvenden, Cranbrook, Kent TN17 4LP T: 01580 241234

The Charles Dickens Centre Eastgate House, High St, Rochester, Kent ME1 1EW T: 01634 844176

The Grand Shaft Snargate Street, Dover CT16 T: 01304 201066

The Romney, Hythe & Dymchurch Railway New Romney Station, Romney, Kent TN28 8PL T: 01797 362353

The West Gate St Peters Street, Canterbury, Kent T: 01227 452747

Timeball Tower Victoria Parade, Deal CT14 7BP T: 01304 360897

Victoriana Museum Deal Town Hall, High St, Deal, Kent CT14 6BB T: 01304 380546

Walmer Castle and Gardens Kingsdown Road, Walmer, Deal, Kent CT14 7LJ T: 01304 364288 W: www.english-heritage.org.uk

Watts Charity Poor Travellers House, 97 High St, Rochester, Kent ME1 1LX T: 01634 845609

Whitstable Museum & Gallery 5a Oxford St, Whitstable, Kent CT5 1DB T: 01227 276998 W: www.whitstable-museum.co.uk

Lancashire

Blackburn Museum and Art Gallery Museum Street, Blackburn, Lancashire BB1 7AJ T: 01254 667130 E: paul.flintoff@blackburn.gov.uk W: www.blackburnworld.com

Bolton Museum & Art Gallery Le Mans Crescent, Bolton, Lancashire BL1 1SE T: 01204 332190 E: bolwg@gn.apc.org

British in India Museum Newton Street, Colne, Lancashire BB8 0JJ T: 01282 870215

Duke of Lancaster's Own Yeomanry Stanley St, Preston, Lancashire PR1 4AT T: 01772 264074

East Lancashire Railway Bolton Street Station, Bolton Street, Bury, Lancashire BL9 0EY T: 0161 764 7790 E: admin@east-lancs-rly.co.uk W: www.east-lancs-rly.co.uk

Ellenroad Trust Ltd Ellenroad Engine House, Elizabethan Way, Milnrow, Rochdale, Lancashire OL16 4LG T: 01706 881952 E: ellenroad@aol.com W: http:\\ellenroad.homepage.com

Fleetwood Museum Queens Terrace, Fleetwood, Lancashire FY7 6BT T: 01253 876621 E: fleetwood.museum@mus.lancscc.gov.uk W: www.lancsmuseums.co.uk

Gawthorpe Hall Habergham Drive, Padiham, Burnley, Lancashire BB12 8UA T: 01282 771004 W: www.museumsoflancs.org.uk

Hall I'Th' Wood Museum Hall I Th Wood, Tonge Moor, Bolton, Lancashire BL1 8UA T: 01204 301159

Harris Museum & Art Gallery Market Square, Preston, Lancashire PR1 2PP T: 01772 258 248 E: harris.museum@preston.gov.uk W: www.harrismuseum.org.uk

Heaton Park Tramway (Transport Museum) Tram Depot, Heaton Park, Prestwich, Manchester, Lancashire M25 2SW T: 0161 740 1919

Helmshore Textile Museums Holcombe Road, Helmshore, Rossendale, Lancashire BB4 4NP T: 01706 226459

Heritage Trust for the North West within Pendle Heritage Centre, Colne Rd, Barrowford, Nelson, Lancashire BB9 6JQ T: 01282 661704

Judge's Lodgings Museum Church St, Lancaster, Lancashire LA1 1LP T: 01524 32808

Kippers Cats 51 Bridge St, Ramsbottom, Bury, Lancashire BL0 9AD T: 01706 822133

Lancaster City Museum Market Square, Lancaster, Lancashire LA1 1HT T: 01524 64637 E: awhite@lancaster.gov.uk

Lancaster Maritime Museum Custom House, St George,Äôs Quay, Lancaster, Lancashire LA1 1RB T: 01524 64637

Lytham Heritage Group 2 Henry St, Lytham St. Annes, Lancashire FY8 5LE T: 01253 730767

Manchester Museum Education Service University of Manchester, Oxford Rd, Manchester, Lancashire M13 9PL T: 0161 275 2630 E: education@man.ac.uk W: http://museum.man.ac.uk

Museum of Lancashire Stanley Street, Preston, Lancashire, PR1 4YP T: 01772 264079 E: museum@lancs.co.uk

North West Sound Archive Old Steward's Office, Clitheroe Castle, Clitheroe, Lancashire BB7 1AZ T: 01200 427897 E: nwsa@ed.lancscc.gov.uk W: www.lancashire.gov.uk/education/d_lif/ro/content/sound/imdex.asp

Oldham Museum Greaves St, Oldham OL1 1 T: 0161 911 4657 W:

Ordsall Hall Museum Taylorson St, Salford, M5 3HT T: 0161 872 0251

Pendle Heritage Centre Park Hill, Colne Rd, Barrowford, Nelson, Lancashire BB9 6JQ T: 01282 661702

Portland Basin Museum Portland Place, Ashton-Under-Lyne, Lancashire OL7 0QA T: 0161 343 2878

Queen St Mill Harle Syke, Queen St, Briercliffe, Burnley, Lancashire BB10 2HX T: 01282 459996

Rawtenstall Museum Whitaker Park, Haslingden Road, Rawtenstall, Lancashire T: 01706 244682

Ribchester Museum of Roman Antiquities Riverside, Ribchester, Preston, Lancashire PR3 3XS T: 01254 878261 W: www.aboutbritain.com/Ribchester Roman Museum.htm

Rochdale Museum Service The Arts & Heritage Centre, The Esplanade, Rochdale, Lancashire OL16 1AQ T: 01706 641085

Rochdale Pioneers Museum Toad Lane, Rochdale, Lancashire OL12 0NU T: 01706 524920

Saddleworth Museum & Art Gallery High St, Uppermill, Oldham, Lancashire OL3 6HS T: 01457 874093

Salford Museum & Art Gallery Peel Park, Salford, Lancashire M5 4WU T: 0161 736 2649 W: www.salford.gov.uk/salfordmuseum

Slaidburn Heritage Centre 25 Church St, Slaidburn, Clitheroe, Lancashire BB7 3ER T: 01200 446161 E: slaidburn.heritage@htnw.co.uk W: www.slaidburn.org.uk

Smithills Hall Museum Smithills Hall, Dean Road, Bolton, Lancashire BL1 7NP T: 01204 841265

The Museum of Science and Industry In Manchester Liverpool Rd, Castlefield, Manchester, Lancashire M3 4JP T: 0161 832 2244 E: marketing@msim.org.uk W: www.msim.org.uk

The Museum of Wigan Life Wigan Leisure and Culture Trust, Library Street, Wigan, Greater Manchester WN1 1NU T: 01942 828128 E: heritage@wlct.org W: www.wlct.org/culture/heritage

The Rochdale Pioneers' Museum 31 Toad Lane, Rochdale, Lancashire T: 01706-524920

Weavers Cottage Heritage Centre Weavers Cottage, Bacup Rd, Rawtenstall, Rossendale, Lancashire BB4 7NW T: 01706 229828

Whitworth Museum North Street, Whitworth, Lancashire T: 01706 343231 E: rossendale_leisure@compuserve.com

Leicester

New Walk Museum New Walk Museum, 53 New Walk, Leicester, LE1 7AE T: 0116 247 3220 E: hide001@leicester.gov.uk W: www.leicestermuseums.co.uk

Leicestershire

Abbey Pumping Station Corporation Rd, Abbey Lane, Leicester, LE4 5PX T: 0116 299 5111 W: www.leicestermuseums.ac.uk

Ashby De La Zouch Museum North St, Ashby-De-La-Zouch, Leicestershire LE65 1HU T: 01530 560090

Belgrave Hall & Gardens Church Rd, Belgrave, Leicester, Leicestershire LE4 5PE T: 0116 266 6590 E: marte001@leicester.gov.uk W: www.leicestermuseums.org.uk

Bellfoundry Museum Freehold St, Loughborough, Leicestershire LE11 1AR T: 01509 233414

Bosworth Battlefield Visitor Centre Sutton Cheney, Market Bosworth, Nuneaton, Warwickshire CV13 0AD T: 01455 290429 E: bosworth@leics.gov.uk W: www.leics.gov.uk

British Aviation Heritage Bruntingthorpe Aerodrome, Bruntingthorpe, Lutterworth, Leicestershire LE17 5QH T: 0116 221 8426 W: www.jetman.dircon.co.uk/brunty

Charnwood Museum Granby St, Loughborough LE11 3DU T: 01509 233754 W: www.leics.gov.uk/museums/musinliecs.htm#charnwood

Foxton Canal Museum Middle Lock, Gumley Rd, Foxton, Market Harborough, Leicestershire LE16 7RA T: 0116 279 2657 W:

Harborough Museum Adam and Eve Street, Market Harborough LE16 7AG T: 01858 821 085 E: harboroughmuseum@leics.gov.uk W: www.leics.gov.uk/harboroughmuseum

Hinckley & District Museum Ltd Framework Knitters Cottage, Lower Bond St, Hinckley LE10 1QU T: 01455 251218 W:

Jewry Wall Museum St. Nicholas Circle, Leicester, Leicestershire LE1 4LB T: 0116 247 3021 W:

Leicester City Museum & Art Gallery 53 New Walk, Leicester, Leicestershire LE1 7EA T: 0116 255 4100 W:

Leicestershire Ecology Centre Holly Hayes Environmental Resources Centre, 216 Birstall Rd, Birstall, Leicester, Leicestershire LE4 4DG T: 0116 267 1950 E: dlott@leics.gov.uk

Melton Carnegie Museum Thorpe End, Melton Mowbray, Leicestershire LE13 1RB T: 01664 569946 E: museums@leics.gov.uk W: www.leics.gov.uk/museums/#melton

Newarke Houses Museum The Newarke, Leicester, Leicestershire LE2 7BY T: 0116 225 4980 E: museums@leicester.gov.uk W: www.leicester.gov.uk/museums

Snibston Discovery Park Ashby Road, Coalville LE67 3LN T: 01530 278444 E: snibston@leics.gov.uk W: www.snibston.com

The Guildhall Guildhall Lane, Leicester LE1 5FQ T: 0116 253 2569

The Manor House Manor Rd, Donington Le Heath, Coalville, Leicestershire LE67 2FW T: 01530 831259 E: museums@leics.gov.uk W: www.leics.gov.uk/museums/musinliecs.htm#manor

Lincolnshire

Alford Civic Trust Manor House Museum, West Street, Alford, Lincolnshire LN13 9DJ T: 01507 463073

Ayscoughfee Hall Museum & Gardens Churchgate, Spalding, Lincolnshire PE11 2RA T: 01775 725468

Boston Guildhall Museum South Street, Boston, Lincolnshire PE21 6HT T: 01205 365954

Church Farm Museum Church Rd South, Skegness, Lincolnshire PE25 2HF T: 01754 766658

Cranwell Avation Heritage Centre Heath Farm, North Raunceby, Near Cranwell, Sleaford, Lincolnshire NG34 8QR T: 01529 488490
Gainsborough Old Hall Parnell St, Gainsborough, Lincolnshire DN21 2NB T: 01427 612669 W:
Gordon Boswell Romany Museum Hawthorns Clay Lake, Spalding, Lincolnshire PE12 6BL T: 01775 710599 W:
Grantham Museum St. Peters Hill, Grantham, Lincolnshire NG31 6PY T: 01476 568783
Lincolnshire Aviation Heritage Centre East Kirkby Airfield, East Kirkby, Spilsby, Lincolnshire PE23 4DE T: 01790 763207 E: enquiries@lincsaviation.co.uk W: www.lincsaviation.co.uk
Lincs Vintage Vehicle Society Whisby Rd, North Hykeham, Lincoln, Lincolnshire LN6 3QT T: 01522 500566 W:
Louth Naturalists Antiquarian & Literary Society 4 Broadbank, Louth, Lincolnshire LN11 0EQ T: 01507 601211 W:
Metheringham Airfield Visitor Centre Westmoor Farm, Martin Moor, Metheringham, Lincolnshire LN4 3BO T: 01526 378270
Museum of Lincolnshire Life Old Barracks, Burton Road, Lincoln, Lincolnshire LN1 3LY T: 01522-528448 E: lincolnshirelife_museum@lincolnshire.gov.uk W: www.lincolnshire.gov.uk/museumoflincolnshirelife
National Fishing Heritage Centre Alexander Dock, Great Grimsby, Lincolnshire DN31 1UZ T: 01472-323345 W: www.nelincs.gov.uk
RAF Digby Ops Room Museum RAF Digby, Scopwick, Lincoln, Lincolnshire LN4 3LH T: 01526 327503 W: www.airops.freeserve.co.uk
The Incredibly Fantastic Old Toy Show 26 Westgate, Lincoln, Lincolnshire LN1 3BD T: 01522 520534 W:
Thorpe Camp Visitor Centre Tattersall Thorpe, Lincoln, Lincolnshire LN4 4PE T: 01526 342249 E: mjhodgson@lancfile.demon.co.uk W: www.thorpecamp.org.uk
Lincolnshire - North
Baysgarth House Museum Caistor Rd, Barton-Upon-Humber, North Lincolnshire DN18 6AH T: 01652 632318
Immingham Museum Immingham Resorce Centre, Margaret St, Immingham, North Lincolnshire DN40 1LE T: 01469 577066 W:
North Lincolnshire Museum Oswald Rd, Scunthorpe, North Lincolnshire DN15 7BD T: 01724 843533 E: David.Williams@northlincs.gov.uk W: www.northlincs.gov.uk/museums

Liverpool
Museum of Liverpool - expected to open in 2011 see W: www.liverpoolmuseums.org.uk/mol/

London
Alexander Fleming Laboratory Museum / Imperial College Healthcare NHS Trust Archives St Mary‚Äôs Hospital, Praed Street, Paddington, London, W2 1NY T: 020 331 26528 E: kevin.brown@imperial.nhs.uk W: www.imperial.nhs.uk
Bethlem Royal Hospital Archives and Museum, Monks Orchard Road, Beckenham, Kent BR3 3BX T: (020) 8776 4307 E: colin.gale@slam.nhs.uk JMichael.Phillips@slam.nhs.uk W: www.bethlemheritage.org.uk/
British Dental Association Museum 64 Wimpole Street, London, W1G 8YS T: 0207 935 0875 E: museum@bda.org W: www.bda.org/museum/
Cabinet War Rooms Clive Steps, King Charles Street, London SW1A 2AQ T: (020) 7930 6961 E: cwr@iwm.org.uk W: www.iwm.org.uk
Church Farmhouse Museum Greyhound Hill, Hendon, London NW4 4JR T: (020) 8203 0130 W: www.earl.org.uk/partners/barnet/churchf.htm
Crystal Palace Museum Anerley Hill, London, SE19 2BT: 020 8676 0700
Cutty Sark King William Walk, Greenwich, London, SE10 9HT T: 020 8858 2698 E: enquiries@cuttysark.org.uk W: www.cuttysark.org.uk
Design Museum Butlers Wharf 28, Shad Thames, London, SE1 2YD T: (020) 7940 8791 E: enquiries@designmuseum.org.uk W: www.designmuseum.org
Dickens House Museum 48 Doughty St, London, WC1N 2LF T: (020) 7405 2127 E: DHmuseum@rmplc.co.uk W: www.dickensmuseum.com
Doctor Johnson's House 17 Gough Square, London, EC4A 3DE T: (020) 7353 3745
Florence Nightingale Museum 2 Lambeth Palace Road, London, SE1 7EW T: (020) 7620-0374 E: curator@florence-nightingale.co.uk W: www.florence-nightingale.co.uk
Freud Museum 20 Maresfield Gardens, London, NW3 5SX T: (020) 735-2002 E: freud@gn.apc.org W: www.freud.org.uk
Geffrye Museum Kingsland Rd, London, E2 8EA T: (020) 7739 9893 W: www.geffrye-museum.org.uk

Golden Hinde Living History Museum St. Mary Overie Dock, Cathedral St, London SE1 9DE T: 08700 118700 W: www.goldenhinde.co.uk
Grange Museum of Community History The Grange, Neasden Lane, Neasden, London, NW10 1QB T: (020) 8452 8311
Greenwich Heritage Centre - LB of Artillery Square, Royal Arsenal, Woolwich, London, SE18 4DX T: (020) 8854 2452 E: info@greenwichheritage.org W: www.greenwich.gov.uk
Gunnersbury Park Museum Gunnersbury Park, Popes Lane, London W3 8LQ T: (020) 8992 1612 E: gp-museum@cip.org.uk
H.M.S. Belfast Morgans Lane, Tooley Street, London, SE1 2JH T: (020) 7940 6300 W: www.iwm.org.uk
Hackney Museum, - LB of Technology & learning centre, 1 Reading Lane, Hackney, London, E8 1GQ T: 020 8356 3500 E: hmuseum@hackney.gov.uk W: www.hackney.gov.uk
Handel House Museum 25 Brook Street, London, W1K 4HB T: (020) 7495 1685 E: mail@handelhouse.org W: www.handelhouse.org
Hogarth's House Hogarth Lane, Chiswick, London, W4 2QN T: (020) 8994 6757
Honourable Artillery Company Armoury House, City Road, London, EC1Y 2BQ T: 020 7382 1537 E: hac@hac.org.uk W: www.hac.org.uk
Horniman Museum 100 London Rd, Forest Hill, London, SE23 3PQ T: 020 8699 1872 W: www.horniman.ac.uk
House Mill River Lea Tidal Mill Trust , Three Mills Island, Three Mill Lane, Bromley by Bow, London, E3 3DU T: (020) 8980-4626
Inns of Court and City Yeomanry Museum 10 Stone buildings, Lincoln's Inn, London, WC2A 3TG T: 020 7405 8112
Island History Trust St. Matthias Old Church, Woodstock Terrace, Poplar High St, London, E14 0AE T: (020) 7987 6041
Islington Museum Foyer Gallery, Town Hall, Upper St, London N1 2UD T: (020) 7354 9442
Jewish Museum The Sternberg Centre for Judaism, 80 East End Road, Finchley, London, N3 2SY T: 020 8349 1143 E: admin@jewishmuseum.org.uk W: www.jewishmuseum.org.uk
Keats House Museum Wentworth Place, Keats Grove, London NW3 2RR T: (020) 7435 2062
Kingston Museum & Heritage Service - LB of North Kingston Centre, Richmond Rd, Kingston upon Thames KT2 5PE T: (020) 8547-6738 E: local.history@rbk.kingston.gov.uk W: www.kingston.gov.uk/museum/
Leighton House Museum 12 Holland Park Rd, London, W14 8LZ T: 020 7602 3316 E: museums@rbkc.gov.uk W: www.rbkc.gov.uk/leightonhousemuseum
Livesey Museum for Children 682 Old Kent Rd, London, SE15 1JF T: (020) 7639 5604 E: livesley.museum@southwark.gov.uk
Lloyds Nelson Collection Lloyds of London, Lime Street, London, EC3M 7HA T: 020 7327 6260
London Canal Museum 12-13 New Wharf Rd, London, N1 9RT T: (020) 7713 0836 W: www.charitynet.org/~LCanalMus/
London Fire Brigade Museum 94a Southwark Bridge Rd, London, SE1 0EG T: 020 8555 1200 Ext 39894 E: museum@london-fire.gov.uk. W: www.london-fire.gov.uk/OurMuseum.asp
London Gas Museum Twelvetrees Crescent, London, E3 3JH T: (020) 7538 4982
London Irish Rifles Regimental Museum Duke of York‚Äôs Headquarters, Kings Road, Chelsea, London, SW3 4SA
London Toy & Model Museum 21-23 Craven Hill, London, W2 3EN T: (020) 7706 8000
London Transport Museum Covent Garden Piazza, London, WC2E 7BB T: (020) 7379 6344 E: enquiry@ltmuseum.co.uk W: www.ltmuseum.co.uk
Mander & Mitchenson Theatre Collection c/o Salvation Army Headquarters, PO BOx 249, 101 Queen Victoria Street, London, EC49 4EP T: (020) 7236 0182
Markfield Beam Engine & Museum Markfield Rd, London, N15 4RB T: (020) 8800 7061 E: alan@mbeam.org W: www.mbeam.org
Museum in Docklands Library & Archives No 1 Warehouse, West India Quay, Hertsmere Road, London, E14 4AL T: 020 7001 9844 E: info@museumoflondon.org.uk W: www.museumindocklands.org.uk
Museum of London London Wall, London, EC2Y 5HN E: info@museumoflondon.org.uk
National Gallery St. Vincent House, 30 Orange St, London, WC2H 7HH T: (020) 7747 5950
Newham Museum Service The Old Town Hall, 29 The Broadway, Stratford, London E15 4BQ T: (020) 8534 2274
North Woolwich Old Station Museum Pier Rd, North Woolwich, London, E16 2JJ T: (020) 7474 7244
Percival David Foundation of Chinese Art 53 Gordon Square, London, WC1H 0PD T: (020) 7387 3909

Petrie Museum of Egyptian Archaeology University College London, Malet Place, London, WC1E 6BT T: (020) 7679 2884 E: petrie.museum@ucl.ac.uk W: www.petrie.ucl.ac.uk

Pitshanger Manor & Gallery Mattock Lane, London , W5 5EQ T: (020) 8567 1227 E: pitshanger@ealing.gov.uk

Polish Institute & Sikorski Museum 20 Princes Gate, London, SW7 1PT T: (020) 7589 9249

Pollock's Toy Museum 1 Scala St, London, W1P 1LT T: (020) 7636 3452

Pump House Educational Museum Lavender Pond & Nature Park, Lavender Rd, Rotherhithe, London SE16 1DZ T: (020) 7231 2976

Ragged School Museum Trust 46-50 Copperfield Rd, London, E3 4RR T: (020) 8980 6405 W: www.ics-london.co.uk/rsm

Royal London Hospital Archives and Museum Royal London Hospital Archives, 9 Prescot Street, Aldgate, London, E1 8PR T: (020) 7377 7608 E: rlharchives@bartsandthelondon.nhs.uk W: www.bartsandthelondon.nhs.uk/museums

Sam Uriah Morris Society 136a Lower Clapton Rd, London, E5 0QJ T: (020) 8985 6449

Sir John Soane's Museum 13 Lincolns Inn Fields, London, WC2A 3BP T: (020) 7430 0175 W: www.soane.org

St Bartholomew's Hospital Archives & Museum Archives and Museum, North Wing, St Bartholomew's Hospital , West Smithfield, London, EC1A 7BE T: 020 3465 5798 E: barts.archives@bartsandthelondon.nhs.uk W: www.bartsandthelondon.nhs.uk/museums

The Association of Jewish Ex-Service Men and Women Military Museum AJEX House, East Bank, Stamford, London, N16 5RT T: 020 8800 2844 W: www.ajex.org.uk

The Clink Prison Museum 1 Clink St, London, SE1 9DG T: (020) 7403 6515

The Fan Museum 12 Crooms Hill, London, SE10 8ER T: (020) 8858 7879 E: admin@fan-museum.org W: www.fan-museum.org

The Foundling Museum 40 Brunswick Square, Bloomsbury, London, WC1N 1AZ T: 020 7841 3600 F: 020 7841 3601 W: www.foundlingmuseum.org.uk

The Iveagh Bequest Kenwood House, Hampstead Lane, London, NW3 7JR T: (020) 8348 1286

The Museum of Brands, Packaging and Advertising 2 Colville Mews, Lonsdale Road, Notting Hill, London, W11 2AR T: 020 7908 0880 E: info@museumofbrands.com W: www.museumofbrands.com

The Museum of Women's Art 3rd Floor, 11 Northburgh St, London, EC1V 0AN T: (020) 7251 4881

The Old Operating Theatre Museum & Herb Garret 9a St. Thomas's St, London, SE1 9RY T: 020 7188 2679 E: curator@thegarret.org.uk W: www.thegarret.org.uk

The Polish Institute and Sikorski Museum 20 Princes Gate, London, SW7 1QA T: 020 7589 9249

The Wellcome Trust 183 Euston Rd, London, NW1 2BE T: (020) 7611 8888 E: infoserv@wellcome.ac.uk W: www.wellcome.ac.uk

V&A Museum of Childhood Cambridge Heath Road, London, E2 9PA T: 020 8983 5200 E: moc@vam.ac.uk W: www.museumofchildhood.org.uk

Vestry House Museum Vestry Road, Walthamstow, London, E17 9NH T: (020) 8509 1917 E: vestry.house@walthamforeest.gov.uk W: www.lbwf.gov.uk/leisure/museum-galleries/vestry-house-museum.htm

Veterinary Archives Royal Veterinary College, Royal College Street, London, NW1 0TU T: (020) 768 5165 E: fhouston@rvc.ac.uk W: www.rvc.ac.uk

Wallace Collection Hertford House, Manchester Square, London, W1U 3BN T: 020 7563 9500 E: enquiries@wallacecollection.org W: www.wallacecollection.org

Wellington Museum - Apsley House Apsley House, 149 Piccadilly, Hyde Park Corner, London, W1J 7NT T: 020 7499 5676 W: www.apsleyhouse.org.uk

Westminster Abbey Museum Westminster Abbey, Deans Yard, London SW1P 3PA T: (020) 7233 0019

Wimbledon Lawn Tennis Museum The All England Lawn Tennis & Croquet Club, Church Road, Wimbledon SW19 5AE T: (020) 8946 6131 E: museum@aeltc.com W: www.wimbledon.org/museum

Wimbledon Museum of Local History 22 Ridgeway, London, SW19 4QN T: (020) 8296 9914

Winston Churchill‚Äôs Britain at War Experience Winston Churchill, 64-66 Tooley Street, London Bridge, London, SE1 2TF T: 020 7403 3171 E: britainatwar@dial.pipex.com W: www.britainatwar.co.uk

Manchester

Manchester Museum of Science and Industry Liverpool Road, Castlefield, Manchester, M3 4FP T: 0161 832 2244 E: n.forder@msim.org.uk W: www.msim.org.uk

Manchester Jewish Museum 190 Cheetham Hill Road, Manchester, M8 8LW T: 0161 834 9879 E: curator@manchesterjewishmuseum.com W: www.machesterjewishmuseum.com

Merseyside

Beatle Story Ltd Britannia Vaults, Albert Dock, Liverpool, Merseyside L3 4AA T: 0151 709 1963

Botanic Gardens Museum Churchtown, Southport, Merseyside PR9 7NB T: 01704 227547

Merseyside Maritime Museum Maritime Archives and Library, Albert Dock, Liverpool, Merseyside L3 4AQ T: 0151 478 4424 E: maritime.archives@liverpoolmuseums.org.uk W: www.liverpoolmuseums.org.uk/maritime

National Museums & Galleries on Merseyside 127 Dale St, Liverpool, Merseyside L2 2JH T: 0151 207 0001 E: karen.orourke@liverpoolmuseums.org.uk W:

Prescot Museum 34 Church St, Prescot, Merseyside L34 3LA T: 0151 430 7787

Shore Road Pumping Station Shore Rd, Birkenhead, CH41 1AG T: 0151 650 1182 W:

The World of Glass Chalon Way East, St Helens, Merseyside WA10 1BX T: 01744 22766 E: info@worldofglass.com W: www.worldofglass.com

Western Approaches 1 Rumford St, Liverpool, Merseyside L2 8SZ T: 0151 227 2008 W:

Middlesex

Forty Hall Museum Forty Hill, Enfield, Middlesex EN2 9HA T: (020) 8363 8196

Harrow Museum & Heritage Centre Headstone Manor, Pinner View, Harrow, Middlesex HA2 6PX T: 020 8861 2626 W:

Kew Bridge Steam Museum Green Dragon Lane, Brentford, Middlesex TW8 0EN T: (020) 8568 4757 E: info@kbsm.org W: www.kbsm.org

The Musical Museum 368 High St, Brentford, Middlesex TW8 0BD T: (020) 8560 8108

Norfolk

Bressingham Steam & Gardens Bressingham, Diss, Norfolk IP22 2AB T: 01379 687386

Bridewell Museum Bridewell Alley, Norwich, Norfolk NR2 1AQ T: 01603 614018 E: museums@norfolk.gov.uk W: www.museums.norfolk.gov.uk

Bure Valley Railway Norwich Road, Aylsham, Norfolk NR11 6BW T: 01263 733858

Castle Museum Castle Hill, Norwich, Norfolk NR1 3JU T: 01603 493624 E: museums@norfolk.gov.uk

Cholmondeley Collection of Model Soldiers Houghton Hall, Houghton, Kings Lynn, Norfolk PE31 6UE T: 01485 528569 E: administrator@houghtonhall.com W: www.houghtonhall.com

City of Norwich Aviation Museum Hosham St Faith, Norwich, Norfolk NR10 3JF T: 01603 893080

Diss Museum The Market Place, Diss, Norfolk IP22 3JT T: 01379 650618

EcoTech Swaffham, Norfolk PE37 7HT T: 01760 726100 E: info@ecotech.rmplc.co.uk W: www.ecotech.org.uk

Elizabethan House Museum 4 South Quay, Great Yarmouth, Norfolk NR30 2QH T: 01493 855746 W:

Feltwell (Historical and Archaeological) Society 16 High Street, Feltwell, Thetford, Norfolk IP26 4AF T: 01842 828448

Glandford Shell Museum Church House, Glandford, Holt, Norfolk NR25 7JR T: 01263 740081

Gressenhall Farm & Workhouse Gressenhall, Dereham, Norfolk NR20 4DR T: 01362 860563 E: museums@norfolk.gov.uk W: www.norfolk.gov.uk

Iceni Village & Museums Cockley Cley, Swaffham, Norfolk PE37 8AG T: 01760 721339 W:

Inspire Hands On Science Centre Coslany St, Norwich, Norfolk NR3 3DJ T: 01603 612612 W:

Lynn Museum Old Market St, King's Lynn PE30 1NL T: 01553 775001 E: museums@norfolk.gov.uk W: www.norfolk.gov.uk/tourism/museums

Maritime Museum for East Anglia 25 Marine Parade, Great Yarmouth, Norfolk NR30 2EN T: 01493 842267 W:

Norfolk Motorcycle Museum Station Yard, Norwich Rd, North Walsham, Norfolk NR28 0DS T: 01692 406266

Norfolk Rural Life Museum & Union Farm Beach House, Gressenhall, East Dereham, Norfolk NR20 4DR T: 01362 860563 E: museums@norfolk.gov.uk W: www.norfolk.gov.uk

Sheringham Museum Station Rd, Sheringham, Norfolk NR26 8RE T: 01263 821871

Shirehall Museum Common Place, Walsingham, Norfolk NR22 6BP T: 01328 820510 E: walsinghammuseum@farmline.com

The Air Defence Battle Command & Control Museum Neatishead, Norwich, Norfolk NR12 8YB T: 01692 633309

The Muckleburgh Collection Weybourne, Holt, Norfolk NR25 7EG T: 01263 588210 W: www.muckleburgh.co.uk

The North Norfolk Railway The Station, Sheringham, Norfolk NR26 8RA T: 01263 822045 W: www.nnrailway.co.uk

Northamptonshire
Abington Museum and Museum of The Northamptonshire Regiment Abington Park Museum, Abington, Northamptonshire NN1 5LW T: 01604 635412 W: www.northampton.gov.uk/museums
Canal Museum Stoke Bruerne, Towcester, Northamptonshire NN12 7SE T: 01604 862229
Naseby Battle Museum Purlieu Farm, Naseby, Northampton, Northamptonshire NN6 7DD T: 01604 740241
National Dragonfly Museum Ashton Mill, Ashton, Peterborough, Northamptonshire PE8 5LB T: 01832 272427 E: ndmashton@aol.com W: natdragonflymuseum.org.uk
Northampton & Lamport Railway Preservation Society Pitsford & Brampton Station, Pitsford Road, Chapel Brampton, Northampton, Northamptonshire NN6 8BA T: 01604 820327
Northampton Iron Stone Railway Trust Hunsbury Hill Country Park, Hunsbury Hill Rd, West Hunsbury, Northampton, Northamptonshire NN4 9UW T: 01604 702031 E: bnile98131@aol.com
Rushden Historical Transport Society The Station, Station Approach, Rushden, Northamptonshire NN10 0AW T: 01933 318988
Wellingborough Heritage Centre Croyland Hall, Burystead Place, Wellingborough, Northamptonshire NN8 1AH T: 01933 276838

Northumberland
Berwick Borough Museum The Barracks, The Parade, Berwick-Upon-Tweed, Northumberland TD15 1DG T: 01289 330933
Bewick Studios Mickley Square, Mickley, Stocksfield, Northumberland NE43 7BL T: 01661 844055
Border Library Hexham Old Gaol, Hallgate, Hexham, NE46 3NH T: 01434 600910 E: museum@tynedale.gov.uk W: www.tynedaleheritage.org
Chesterholm Museum Vindolanda Trust, Bardon Mill, Hexham, NE47 7JN T: 01434 344 277 E: info@vindolanda.com W: www.vindolanda.com
Chesters Roman Fort and Clayton Collection Museum Vindolanda Trust, Chollerford, Humshaugh, Hexham, Northumberland NE46 4EP T: 01434 681 379 W: www.english-heritage.org.uk
Corbridge Roman Site Corbridge, Northumberland NE45 5NT T: 01434 632349 W: www.english-heritage.org.uk
Housteads Roman Fort Museum Haydon Bridge, Hexham, Northumberland NE47 6NN T: 01434 344363
Marine Life Centre & Fishing Museum 8 Main St, Seahouses, Northumberland NE68 7RG T: 01665 721257 W:
The Heritage Centre Station Yard, Woodburn Road, Bellingham, Hexham, Northumberland NE48 2DF T: 01434 220050 E: bell.heritage@btopenworld.com W: www.bellingham-heritage.org.uk
The Vindolanda Trust Chesterholm Museum, Bardon Mill, Hexham, Northumberland NE47 7JN T: 01434 344277 E: info@vindolanda.com W: www.vindolanda.com
Tynedale Council Museums Service Department of Tourism, Culture & Communications, Prospect House, Hexham, NE46 3NH T: 01434 652351 E: janet.goodridge@northumberland.gov.uk W: www.tynedaleheritage.org
Vindolanda Trust Chesterholm Museum Bardon Mill, Hexham, Northumberland NE47 7JN T: 01434 344 277 E: info@vindolanda.com W: www.vindolanda.com

Nottinghamshire
D.H Lawrence Heritage Durban House Heritage Centre, Mansfield Rd, Eastwood, NottinghamNG16 3DZ T: 01773 717353
Flintham Society & Flintham Museum Inholms Road, Flintham NG23 5LF T: 0163.6 525111 W: www.flintham-museum.org.uk
Greens Mill & Science Museum Windmill Lane, Sneinton, Nottingham, NG2 4QB T: 0115 915 6878
Harley Gallery Welbeck, Worksop, Nottinghamshire S80 3LW T: 01909 501700
Mansfield Museum & Art Gallery Leeming Street, Mansfield, NG18 1NG T: 01623-463088 E: mansfieldmuseum@mansfield.gov.uk W: www.mansfield.gov.uk/museum/
Millgate Museum of Folk Life 48 Millgate, Newark, Nottinghamshire NG24 4TS T: 01636 655730 E: museum@nsdc.info
Natural History and Industrial Museum Wollaton Hall, Wollaton Park, Nottingham, Nottinghamshire NG8 2AE T: 0115 915 3910 W:
Newark and Sherwood Museum Service Block D, NSDC Depot, Brunel Drive, Newark, Nottinghamshire NG24 2EG T: 01636 655777 E: museums@nsdc.info W: www.nsdc.gov.uk
Newark Town Hall Museum and Art Gallery The Town Hall, Market Place, Newark, Nottinghamshire NG24 1DU T: 01636 680333 E: post@newark.gov.uk W: www.newarktownhallmuseum.co.uk

Newstead Abbey Historic House & Gardens Newstead Abbey Park, Nottingham, Nottinghamshire NG15 8NA T: 01623 455900 E: sally.winfield@nottinghamcity.gov.uk W: www.newsteadabbey.org.uk
Nottingham Castle Museum & Art Gallery Castle Rd, Nottingham, Nottinghamshire NG1 6EL T: 0115 915 3700
Ruddington Framework Knitters' Museum Chapel St, Ruddington, Nottingham NG11 6HE T: 0115 984 6914 W: www.rfkm.org
Ruddington Village Museum St. Peters Rooms, Church St, Ruddington, Nottingham NG11 6HD T: 0115 914 6645
The Galleries of Justice Shire Hall, High Pavement, Lace Market, Nottingham, Nottinghamshire NG1 1HN T: 0115-952-0555 E: info@galleriesofjustice.org.uk W: www.galleriesofjustice.org.uk
The Museum of Nottingham Lace 3-5 High Pavement, The Lace Market, Nottingham, Nottinghamshire NG1 1HF T: 0115 989 7365
The Tales of Robin Hood 30 - 38 Maid Marian Way, Nottingham, NG1 6GF T: 0115 948 3284 W: www.robinhood.uk.com
The Vina Cooke Museum Dolls & Bygone Childhood The Old Rectory, Cromwell, Newark NG23 6JE T: 01636 821364
The Workhouse - Southwell Upton Road, Southwell, NG25 0PT T: 01636 817250 E: theworkhouse@nationaltrust.org.uk
Whaley Thorn Heritage & Environment Centre Portland Terrace, Langwith, Mansfield, Nottinghamshire NG20 9HA T: 01623 742525

Oxfordshire
Abingdon Museum County Hall, Market Place, Abingdon, Oxfordshire OX14 3HG T: 01235 523703
Ashmolean Museum University of Oxford, Beaumont Street, Oxford, Oxfordshire OX1 2PH T: 01865 278000
Chipping Norton Museum 4 High Street, Chipping Norton, Oxfordshire OX7 5AD E: museum@cn2001.fsnet.co.uk
Edgehill Battle Museum The Estate Yard, Farnborough Hall, Farnborough, Banbury, Oxfordshire OX17 1DU T: 01926 332213
Great Western Society Ltd Didcot Railway Centre, Station Rd, Didcot, Oxfordshire OX11 7NJ T: 01235 817200 W:
Oxfordshire and Buckinghamshire Light Infantry Regimental Museum Slade Park, Headington, Oxford OX3 7JL T: 01865 780128
Pitt Rivers Museum South Parks Rd, Oxford, OX1 3PP T: 01865 270927 E: prm@prm.ox.ac.uk W: www.prm.ox.ac.uk
The Oxfordshire Museum Fletchers House, Park St, Woodstock, OX20 1SN T: 01993 811456 E: oxon.museum@oxfordshire.gov.uk W: www.tomocc.org.uk
Vale & Downland Museum 19 Church St, Wantage OX12 8BL T: 01235 771447 E: museum@wantage.com W: www.wantage.com/museum
Wallingford Museum Flint House, High St, Wallingford, Oxfordshire OX10 0DB T: 01491 835065
Witney & District Museum Gloucester Court Mews, High St, Witney OX8 6LX T: 01993 775915 E: janecavell@aol.com

Rutland
Rutland County Museum Catmose Street, Oakham, Rutland LE15 6HW T: 01572-723654 E: enquiries@rutland.gov.uk W: www.rutland.gov.uk/
Rutland Railway Museum Iron Ore Mine Sidings, Ashwell Rd, Cottesmore, Oakham, Rutland LE15 7BX T: 01572 813203

Shropshire
Acton Scott Historic Working Farm Wenlock Lodge, Acton Scott, Church Stretton, Shropshire SY6 6QN T: 01694 781306
Blists Hill Open Air Museum Ironbridge Gorge Museum Trust Ltd, Legges Way, Madeley, Telford, Shropshire TF7 5DU T: 01952 586063
Coalport China Museum Ironbridge Gorge Museum Trust Ltd, High St, Coalport, Telford, Shropshire TF8 7AW T: 01952 580650
Ironbridge Gorge Museum, Library & Archives Coach Road, Coalbrookdale, Telford, TF8 7DQ T: 01952 432141 E: library@ironbridge.org.uk W: www.ironbridge.org.uk
Jackfield Tile Museum Ironbridge Gorge Museum Trust Ltd, Jackfield, Telford, Shropshire TF8 7AW T: 01952 882030
Ludlow Museum Castle St, Ludlow SY8 1AS T: 01584 875384
Midland Motor Museum Stanmore Hall, Stourbridge Rd, Stanmore, Bridgnorth, Shropshire WV15 6DT T: 01746 762992
Museum Of Iron Ironbridge Gorge Museum Trust Ltd, Coach Rd, Coalbrookdale, Telford, Shropshire TF8 7EZ T: 01952 433418 W:
Museum Of The River Visitor Centre The Wharfage, Ironbridge, Telford TF8 7AW T: 01952 432405
Oswestry Transport Museum Oswald Rd, Oswestry, Shropshire SY11 1RE T: 01691 671749 E: lignetts@enterprise.net W: www.cambrian-railways-soc.co.uk
Rosehill House Ironbridge Gorge Museum Trust Ltd, Telford, Shropshire TF8 7AW T: 01952 432141 W:
Rowley's House Museum Barker Street, Shrewsbury, Shropshire SY1 1QH T: 01743 361196

Somerset

Abbey Barn - Somerset Rural Life Museum Abbey Barn, Chilkwell St, Glastonbury, Somerset BA6 8DB T: 01458 831197 E: county-museum@somerset.gov.uk W: www.somerset.gov.uk/museums

American Museum Claverton Manor, Bath BA2 7BD T: 01225 460503

Bakelite Museum Orchard Mill, Bridge St Williton, Taunton, Somerset TA4 4NS T: 01984 632133

Bath Postal Museum 27a Northgate Street, Bath, Somerset BA1 1AJ T: 01225 460333 E: info@bathpostalmuseum.org W: www.bathpostalmuseum.org

Bath Royal Literary & Scientific Institution 16-18 Queen Square, Bath, Somerset BA1 2HN T: 01225 312084

Blake Museum Blake Street, Bridgwater TA6 3NB T: 01278 456127 E: museums@sedgemoor.gov.uk W: www.blakemuseum.org.uk

Blazes Fire Museum Sandhill Park, Bishops Lydeard, Taunton, Somerset TA4 3DE T: 01823 433964

Bruton Museum Society The Dovecote Building, High Street, Bruton T: 01749 812851 W: www.southsomersetmuseum.org.uk

Chard & District Museum Godworthy House, High St, Chard, Somerset TA20 1QB T: 01460 65091

Fashion Museum Bennett Street, Bath, Somerset BA1 2QH T: 01225 477 789 E: fashion_enquiries@bathnes.gov.uk W: www.fashionmuseum.co.uk

Glastonbury Lake Village Museum The Tribunal, 9 High St, Glastonbury, Somerset BA6 9DP T: 01458 832949 W:

Holburne Museum of Art Great Pulteney St, Bath, BA2 4DB T: 01225 466669 W: www.bath.ac.uk/holbourne

Lambretta Scooter Museum 77 Alfred St, Weston-Super-Mare, BS23 1PP T: 01934 614614

Museum of Bath at Work Camden Works, Julian Road, Bath, Somerset BA1 2RH T: 01225 318348 E: mobaw@hotmail.com W: www.bath-at-work.org.uk

Museum of South Somerset Henford, Yeovil, Somerset T: 01935 462855 E: heritage.services@southsomerset.gov.uk W: www.southsomerset.gov.uk

No.1 Royal Crescent 1 Royal Crescent, Bath, BA1 2LR T: 01225 428126 W: www.bath-preservation-trust.org.uk

North Somerset Museum Service Burlington St, Weston-Super-Mare, BS23 1PR T: 01934 621028 E: museum.service@n-somerset.gov.uk W: www.n-somerset.gov.uk/museum

Radstock, Midsomer Norton & District Museum Waterloo Road, Radstock, Bath, Somerset BA3 3EP T: 01761 437722 E: info@radstockmuseum.co.uk W: www.radstockmuseum.co.uk

Somerset & Dorset Railway Trust Washford Station, Washford, Watchet, Somerset TA23 0PP T: 01984 640869 E: info@sdrt.org W: www.sdrt.org

Somerset County Museum Service Taunton Castle, Taunton, Somerset TA1 4AA T: 01823 320200

Somerset Military Museum (Somerset Light Infantry, The Building of Bath Museum The Countess of Huntingdon‚Äôs Chapel, The Vineyards, Bath, Somerset BA1 5NA T: 01225 333 895 E: admin@bptrust.org.uk W: www.bath-preservation-trust.org.uk

The Haynes Motor Museum Castle Cary Rd, Sparkford, Yeovil, Somerset BA22 7LH T: 01963 440804 W: www.haynesmotormuseum.co.uk

The Helicopter Museum The Heliport, Locking Moor Road, Weston-Super-Mare, BS24 8PP T: 01934 635227 E: office@helimuseum.fsnet.co.uk W: www.helicoptermuseum.co.uk

The Jane Austen Centre 40 Gay Street, Bath, Somerset BA1 2NT T: 01225 443000 E: info@janeausten.co.uk

The John Judkyn Memorial Garden Thorpe, Freshford, Bath, BA3 6BX T: 01225 723312 W:

The Museum Of East Asian Art 12 Bennett St, Bath, BA1 2QL T: 01225 464640 E: info@meaa.org.uk W: www.east-asian-art.co.uk

The South West Museums Council Hestercombe House, Cheddon Fitzpaine, Taunton, Somerset TA2 8LQ T: 01823 259696 E: general@mlasouthwest.org.uk W: www.mlasouthwest.org.uk

Wells Museum 8 Cathedral Green, Wells BA5 2UE T: 01749 673477

West Somerset Museum The Old School, Allerford, Minehead, Somerset TA24 8HN T: 01643 862529

William Herschel Museum 19 New King St, Bath, BA1 2BL T: 01225 311342 W:

Specialist Museums

Bursledon Brickworks Industrial Museum Coal Park Lane, Swanwick, Southampton, Hampshire SO31 7GW T: 01489 576248 E: enquiries@hampshirebuildings.org.uk W: www.bursledonbrickworks.co.uk

International Slavery Museum Albert Dock, Liverpool L3 4AQ T: 0151 478 4499 E: karen.orourke@liverpoolmuseums.org.uk W: www.liverpoolmuseums.org.uk/ism

The Foundling Museum 40 Brunswick Square, Bloomsbury, London, WC1N 1AZ T: 020 7841 3600 F: 020 7841 3601 W: www.foundlingmuseum.org.uk

The Rum Story - The Dark Spirit of Whitehaven 27 Lowther Street, Whitehaven, Cumbria CA28 7DN T: 01946 592933 E: info@rumstory.co.uk W: www.rumstory.co.uk

Staffordshire

Borough Museum & Art Gallery Brampton Park, Newcastle, Staffordshire ST5 0QP T: 01782 619705

Clay Mills Pumping Engines Trust Ltd Sewage Treatment Works, Meadow Ln, Stretton, Burton-On-Trent DE13 0DB T: 01283 509929

Etruria Industrial Museum Lower Bedford St, Etruria, Stoke-On-Trent, Staffordshire ST4 7AF T: 01782 233144 E: etruria@swift.co.uk W: www.stoke.gov.uk/museums

Gladstone Pottery Museum Uttoxeter Rd, Longton, Stoke-On-Trent, Staffordshire ST3 1PQ T: 01782 319232 W:

Hanley Museum & Art Gallery Bethesda St, Hanley, Stoke-On-Trent, Staffordshire ST1 3DW T: 01782 232323 W:

Samuel Johnson Birthplace Museum Breadmarket St, Lichfield, Staffordshire WS13 6LG T: 01543 264972 W: www.lichfield.gov.uk

The Potteries Museum & Art Gallery Bethesda Street, Hanley, Stoke-On-Trent, Staffordshire ST1 3DW T: 01782 232323 E: museums@stoke.gov.uk W: www.stoke.gov.uk/museum

Uttoxeter Heritage Centre 34-36 Carter St, Uttoxeter, Staffordshire ST14 8EU T: 01889 567176 W:

Suffolk

British Resistance Organisation Museum Parham Airfield, Parham, Framlingham, Suffolk T: 01743 711275 W: www.auxunit.org.uk

Christchurch Mansion & Wolsey Art Gallery Christchurch Park, Soane St, Ipswich, Suffolk IP4 2BE T: 01473 253246 W:

Dunwich Museum St. James's Street, Dunwich, Saxmundham, Suffolk IP17 3DT T: 01728 648796

East Anglia Transport Museum Chapel Rd, Carlton Colville, Lowestoft, Suffolk NR33 8BL T: 01502 518459 W:

Felixstowe Museum Landguards Fort, Felixstowe, Suffolk IP11 8TW T: 01394 674355 W:

Gainsborough‚Äôs House Society Gainsborough Street, Sudbury, Suffolk CO10 2EU T: 01787 372958 E: mail@gainsborough.org W: www.gainsborough.org

International Sailing Craft Association Maritime Museum Caldecott Rd, Oulton Broad, Lowestoft NR32 3PH T: 01502 585606

Ipswich Museum & Exhibition Gallery High St, Ipswich, Suffolk IP1 3QH T: 01473 213761 W:

Ipswich Transport Museum Ltd Old Trolley Bus Depot, Cobham Rd, Ipswich, Suffolk IP3 9JD T: 01473 715666 W:

Long Shop Steam Museum Main St, Leiston, Suffolk IP16 4ES T: 01728 832189 W: www.suffolkcc.gov.uk/libraries_and_heritage/sro/garrett/index.html

Lowestoft Museum Broad House, Nicholas Everitt Park, Oulton Broad, Lowestoft, Suffolk NR33 9JR T: 01502 511457

Maritime Museum Sparrows Nest The Museum, Whapload Rd, Lowestoft, Suffolk NR32 1XG T: 01502 561963 W:

Mid Suffolk Light Railway Brockford Station, Wetheringsett, Stowmarket, Suffolk IP14 5PW T: 01449 766899

Mildenhall and District Museum 6 King Street, Mildenhall, Bury St Edmunds, Suffolk IP28 7EX T: 01638 716970

The National Horseracing Museum & Tours 99 High St, Newmarket, Suffolk CB8 8JH T: 01638 667333

Norfolk and Suffolk Aviation Museum - East Anglia's Aviation Heritage Centre Buckeroo Way, The Street, Flixton, Bungay NR35 1NZ T: 01986 896644 E: nsam.flixton@virgin.net W: www.aviationmuseum.net

Rougham Control Tower Rougham Industrial Estate, Rougham, Bury St. Edmunds, Suffolk IP30 9LZ T: 01359 271 471 E: tower@rougham.org W: www.rougham.org/index.html

Royal Naval Patrol Association Museum Sparrows Nest, Lowestoft, Suffolk NR32 1XG T: 01502 586250

The Martlesham Heath Aviation Society & Control Tower Museum 341 Main Road, Martlesham, Suffolk IP5 2QU T: 01473 624510 E: control.tower@mhas.org.uk W: www.mhas.org.uk

West Stow Country Park & Anglo-Saxon Village The Visitor Centre, Icklingham Road, West Stow, Buet ST edmunds, Suffolk IP28 6HG T: 01284 728718

Surrey

Bourne Hall Museum Bourne Hall, Spring St, Ewell, Epsom, Surrey KT17 1UF T: (020) 8394 1734 W: www.epsom.townpage.co.uk

Chertsey Museum The Cedars, 33 Windsor St, Chertsey, Surrey KT16 8AT T: 01932 565764 E: enquiries@chertseymuseum.org.uk W:

Dorking & District Museum Dorking & District Museum, The Old Foundry, 62a West St, Dorking, Surrey RH4 1BS T: 01306 876591

East Surrey Museum 1 Stafford Rd, Caterham CR3 6JG T: 01883 340275
Elmbridge Museum Church St, Weybridge, Surrey KT13 8DE T: 01932 843573 E: info@elm-mus.datanet.co.uk W: www.surrey-online.co.uk/elm-mus
Godalming Museum 109a High St, Godalming, Surrey GU7 1AQ T: 01483 426510 E: godalming.museum@waverley.gov.uk W: www.waverley.gov.uk/godalmingmuseum
Guildford Museum Castle Arch, Quarry St, Guildford, Surrey GU1 3SX T: 01483 444750 E: museum@remote.guildford.gov.uk W:
Haslemere Educational Museum 78 High St, Haslemere GU27 2LA T: 01428 642112 E: haslemere_museum@compuserve.com
Kingston Upon Thames Museum North Kingston Centre, Richmond Road, New Malden, Surrey KT3 3UQ T: 020 8547 6738
Merton Heritage Centre The Cannons, Madeira Rd, Mitcham, Surrey CR4 4HD T: (020) 8640 9387
Reigate Priory Museum Reigate Priory, Bell St, Reigate, Surrey RH2 7RL T: 01737 222550
Rural Life Centre Old Kiln Museum, The Reeds, Tilford, Farnham, Surrey GU10 2DL T: 01252 795571 E: rural.life@argonet.co.uk W:
Sandhurst Collection Royal Military Academy Sandhurst, Camberley, Surrey GU15 4PQ T: 01276 412489
Staff College Museum Old Staff College Building, Camberley, Surrey GU15 4NP T: 01276 412719
Surrey Heath Museum Knoll Road, Camberley, Surrey GU15 3HD T: 01276 707284 E: museum@surreyheath.gov.uk W: www.surreyheath.gov.uk/leisure
Wandle Industrial Museum Vestry Hall Annex, London Rd, Mitcham, Surrey CR4 3UD T: (020) 8648 0127 W: www.wandle.org
Woking Museum & Arts & Craft Centre The Galleries, Chobham Rd, Woking , Surrey GU21 1JF T: 01483 725517 E: the.galleries@dial.pipex.com

Sussex

Brighton Fishing Museum 201 Kings Road, Arches, Brighton, Sussex BN1 1NB T: 01273-723064 E: Alexia.Lazou@brighton-hove.gov.uk
Museum of The Royal National Lifeboat Institution King Edward Parade, Eastbourne, Sussex BN T: 01323 730717
Tangmere Military Aviation Museum Tangmere, Chichester, Sussex PO20 2ES T: 01243 775223 W: www.tangmere-museum.org.uk
Sussex - East
Anne of Cleves House Museum 52 Southover, High St, Lewes, East Sussex BN7 1JA T: 01273 474610
Battle Museum Langton Memorial Hall, High St, Battle, East Sussex TN33 0AQ T: 01424 775905
Bexhill Museum of Costume & Social History Association Manor Gardens, Upper Sea Rd, Bexhill-On-Sea, East Sussex TN40 1RL T: 01424 210045
BN1 Visual Arts Project Brighton Media Centre, 9-12 Middle St, Brighton, East Sussex BN1 1AL T: 01273 384242
Booth Museum 194 Dyke Rd, Brighton, East Sussex BN1 5AA T: 03000 290 900 E: museums.marketing@brighton-hove.gov.uk W: www.brighton-hove-museums.org.uk
Ditchling Museum Church Lane, Ditchling, Hassocks, West Sussex BN6 8TB T: 01273 844744 E: info@ditchling-museum.com
Eastbourne Heritage Centre 2 Carlisle Rd, Eastbourne, East Sussex BN21 4BT T: 01323 411189
Filching Manor Motor Museum Filching Manor, Jevington Rd, Polegate, East Sussex BN26 5QA T: 01323 487838 W:
Fishermans Museum Rock A Nore Rd, Hastings, East Sussex TN34 3DW T: 01424 461446 W:
Hastings Museum & Art Gallery Johns Place, Bohemia Rd, Hastings, TN34 1ET T: 01424 451052 E: museum@hastings.gov.uk W: www.hmag.org.uk
Hove Museum & Art Gallery 19 New Church Road, Hove BN3 4AB T: 03000 290 900 E: museums.marketing@brighton-hove.gov.uk W: www.brighton-hove-museums.org.uk
How We Lived Then Museum of Shops 20 Cornfield Terrace, Eastbourne, East Sussex BN21 4NS T: 01323 737143
Michelham Priory Upper Dicker, Hailsham BN27 3QS E: adminmich@sussexpast.co.uk W: www.sussexpast.co.uk/property/site.php?site_id=15
Newhaven Fort Fort Road, Newhaven, East Sussex BN9 9DL T: 01273 517622 W: www.newhavenfort.org.uk
Newhaven Local & Maritime Museum Garden Paradise, Avis Way, Newhaven, East Sussex BN9 0DH T: 01273 612530 W:
Preston Manor Museum Preston Drove, Brighton, East Sussex BN1 6SD T: 03000 290 900 E: museums.marketing@brighton-hove.gov.uk W: www.brighton-hove-museums.org.uk
Rye Castle Museum East St, Rye TN31 7JY T: 01797 226728 W:
Seaford Museum of Local History Martello Tower, The Esplanade, Seaford BN25 1NP T: 01323 898222 E: museumseaford@tinyonline.co.uk W: www.seaforedmuseum.org

Society of Bexhill Museum Ltd The Lodge, Turkey Road, Bexhill-On-Sea, East Sussex TN39 5 HT T: 01424 787950 F: Bexhill Museum, Egerton Road, Bexhill on Sea, East Sussex, TN39 3HL E: museum@rother.gov.uk W: www.bexhill-museum.co.uk
The Engineerium The Droveway, Nevill Rd, Hove, East Sussex BN3 7QA T: 01273 554070 E: info@britishengineerium.com W:
Wish Tower Puppet Museum Tower 73, King Edwards Parade, Eastbourne, East Sussex BN21 4BY T: 01323 411620 E: puppet.workshop@virgin.net W: www.puppets.co.uk
Sussex - West
Amberley Museum and Heritage Centre Station Rd, Amberley, Arundel, West Sussex BN18 9LT T: 01798 831370 E: office@amberleymuseum.co.uk W: www.amberleymuseum.co.uk
Chichester District Museum 29 Little London, Chichester, West Sussex PO19 1PB T: 01243 784683 E: chichmus@breathemail.net
Fishbourne Roman Palace Roman Way, Salthill Rd, Fishbourne, Chichester, West Sussex PO19 3QR T: 01243 785859 E: adminfish@sussexpast.co.uk W: www.sussexpast.co.uk
Horsham Museum 9 Causeway, Horsham RH12 1HE T: 01403 254959 E: museum@horsham.gov.uk W: www.horshammuseum.org
Marlipins Museum High St, Shoreham-By-Sea BN43 5DA T: 01273 462994 E: smermich@sussexpast.co.uk W: www.sussexpast.co.uk
Petworth Cottage Museum 346 High St, Petworth, West Sussex GU28 0AU T: 01798 342100 W: www.sussexlive.co.uk
The Mechanical Music & Doll Collection Church Rd, Portfield, Chichester, West Sussex PO19 4HN T: 01243 372646
Weald & Downland Open Air Museum Singleton, Chichester, West Sussex PO18 0EU T: 01243-811363 E: wealddown@mistral.co.uk W: www.wealddown.co.uk

Tyne & Wear

Arbeia Roman Fort and Museum Baring Street, South Shields, Tyne and Wear NE33 2BB T: 0191 456 1369 W: www.aboutbritain.com/ArbeiaRomanFort.htm
Bede's World Museum Church Bank, Jarrow NE32 3DY T: 0191 4892106
Beamish Museum Ltd - The Living Museum of the North Beamish DH9 0RG T: 0191 370 4000 F: 0191 370 4001 E: paulcastrey@beamish.org.uk W: www.beamish.org.uk
Castle Keep Castle Garth, St. Nicholas St, Newcastle Upon Tyne, Tyne And Wear NE1 1RE T: 0191 2327938 W:
Fulwell Windmill Newcastle Road, Sunderland SR5 1EX T: 0191 516 9790 E: fulwell.windmill@sunderland.gov.uk W: www.fulwell-windmill.com
Hancock Museum Barras Bridge, Newcastle Upon Tyne, Tyne And Wear NE2 4PT T: 0191 2227418 E: hancock.museum@ncl.ac.uk
Newburn Motor Museum Townfield Gardens, Newburn, Newcastle Upon Tyne NE15 8PY T: 0191 2642977 W:
North East Aircraft Museum Old Washington Road, Sunderland, SR5 3HZ T: 0191 519 0662
Ryhope Engines Trust Pumping Station, Stockton Rd, Ryhope, Sunderland SR2 0ND T: 0191 5210235 W: www.g3wte.demon.co.uk
Segedunum Roman Fort, Baths and Museum Wallsend, Tyne and Wear NE T: 0191 236 9347 W: www.twmuseums.org.uk
South Shields Museum & Art Gallery Ocean Road, South Shields, Tyne and Wear NE33 2JA T: 0191-456-8740
Stephenson Railway Museum Middle Engine Lane, North Shields, Tyne And Wear NE29 8DX T: 0191 200 7146
Sunderland Maritime Heritage 1st Floor Office, North East Side, South Dock, Port of Sunderland, Sunderland, Tyne and Wear SR1 2EE T: 0191 510 2055 W: www.sunderlandmaritimeheritage.com
Sunderland Museum & Art Gallery and Monkwearmouth Station Museum Borough Road, Sunderland, SR1 1PP T: 0191 565 0723
The Bowes Railway Co Ltd Springwell Rd, Springwell Village, Gateshead, Tyne And Wear NE9 7QJ T: 0191 4161847 E: alison_gibson77@hotmail.com W: www.bowesrailway.co.uk
The National Glass Centre Liberty Way, Sunderland SR6 0GL T: 0191 515 5555 E: info@nationalglasscentre.com W: www.nationalglasscentre.com

Warrington

Warrington Museum & Art Gallery Museum Street, Cultural Quarter, Warrington, Cheshire WA1 1JB T: 01925 442733 E: museum@warrington.gov.uk W: www.warrington.gov.uk/museum

Warwickshire

Heritage Motor Museum Banbury Road, Gaydon CV35 0BJ T: 01926 641188 E: enquiries@heritage-motor-centre.co.uk W: www.heritage-motor-centre.co.uk
Leamington Spa Art Gallery & Museum Royal Pump Rooms, The Parade, Leamington Spa CV32 4AA T: 01926 742700 W: www.royal-pump-rooms.co.uk
Lunt Roman Fort Coventry Road, Baginton, Coventry T: 024 7683 2381

Midland Air Museum Coventry airport, Baginton, Warwickshire CV8 3AZ T: 024 7630 1033 W: www.discover.co.uk/~mam/
Nuneaton Museum & Art Gallery Riversley Park, Nuneaton, Warwickshire CV11 5TU T: (024) 76376473
Shakespeare Birthplace Trust - Museum Henley Street, Stratford upon Avon, Warwickshire CV37 6QW T: 01789 201827 E: museums@shakespeare.org.uk W: www.shakespeare.org.uk
Warwick Castle Warwick CV34 4QU T: 0870 442 2393 E: customer.information@warwick-castle.com W: www.warwick-castle.com
Warwick Doll Museum Okens House, Castle St, Warwick, Warwickshire CV34 4BP T: 01926 495546
Warwickshire Market Hall Museum Market Place, Warwick, CV34 4SA T: 01926 412500 E: museum@warwickshire.gov.uk W: www.warwickshire.gov.uk/museum
Wellesborough Aviation Museum Control Tower Entrance, Wellesborough, Warwick, Warwickshire CV34 4EW

West Midlands
Aston Manor-Road Transport Museum Ltd 208-216 Witton Lane, Birmingham, West Midlands B6 6QE T: 0121 322 2298
Bantock House & Park Bantock Park,, Finchfield Rd, Wolverhampton, West Midlands WV3 9LQ T: 01902 552195
Birmingham Museum & Art Gallery Chamberlain Square, Birmingham B3 3DH T: 0121 235 2834 W: www.birmingham.gov.uk/bmag
Birmingham Railway Museum 670 Warwick Rd, Tyseley, Birmingham, West Midlands B11 2HL T: 0121 707 4696
Black Country Museum Canal St, Tipton Rd, Dudley DY1 4SQ T: 0121 522 9643 E: info@bclm.co.uk W: ww.bclm.co.uk
Blakesley Hall Blakesley Rd, Yardley, Birmingham, West Midlands B25 8RN T: 0121 783 2193
Coventry Transport Museum Millennium Place, Hales Street, Coventry, West Midlands CV1 1JD T: 024 7623 4270 E: enquiries@transport-museum.co.uk W: www.transport-museum.com
Haden Hall & Haden Hill House Haden Hill Park, Barrs Road, Cradley Heath, B64 7JX T: 01384 569444
Herbert Art Gallery & Museum Jordan Well, Coventry, West Midlands CV1 5QP T: 024 76832381 W:
Midland Air Museum Coventry Airport, Coventry Rd, Baginton, Coventry, West Midlands CV8 3AZ T: (024) 76301033
Museum of the Jewellery Quarter 75-79 Vyse St, Hockley, Birmingham, West Midlands B18 6HA T: 0121 554 3598 E: bmag_enquiries@birmingham.gov.uk W: www.bmag.org.uk
Oak House Museum Oak Rd, West Bromwich, B70 8HJ T: 0121 553 0759
Selly Manor Museum Maple Rd, Birmingham, West Midlands B30 2AE T: 0121 472 0199
Soho House Museum Soho Avenue, Handsworth, Birmingham, West Midlands B18 5LB T: 0121 554 9122 E: Soho.House@birmingham.gov.uk W: www.bmag.org.uk
The Broadfield House Glass Museum Compton Drive, Kingswinford, West Midlands DY6 9NS T: 01384 812 745 E: glassmuseum@dudley.gov.uk W: www.glassmuseum.org.uk
The Lock Museum 55 New Rd, Willenhall, West Midlands WV13 2DA T: 01902 634542 W: http://members.tripod.co.uk/lock_museum/
The Transport Museum Birmingham & Midland Motor Omnibus Trust, Chapel Lane, Wythall, Worcestershire B47 6JX T: 01564 826 471 E: enquiries@wythall.org.uk W: www.wythall.org.uk
Walsall Leather Museum Littleton St West, Walsall, West Midlands WS2 8EN T: 01922 721153 E: leather.museum@walsall.gov.uk W:
West Midlands Police Museum Sparkhill Police Station, Stratford Rd, Sparkhill, Birmingham B11 4EA T: 0121 626 7181
Whitlocks End Farm Bills Lane, Shirley, Solihull, West Midlands B90 2PL T: 0121 745 4891 W:

Wiltshire
Alexander Keiller Museum High St, Avebury, Marlborough, Wiltshire SN8 1RF T: 01672 539250 E: avebury@nationaltrust.org.uk
Atwell-Wilson Motor Museum Trust Stockley Lane, Calne, Wiltshire SN11 0 T: 01249 813119
Lydiard House Lydiard Park, Lydiard Tregoze, Swindon, Wiltshire SN5 9PA T: 01793 770401 W:
RGBW (Salisbury) Museum The Wardrobe, 58 The Close, Salisbury, Wiltshire SP1 2EX T: 01722 419419 E: curator@thewardrobe.org.uk W: www.thewardrobe.org.uk
Salisbury & South Wiltshire Museum The King's House, 65 The Close, Salisbury, Wiltshire SP1 2EN T: 01722 332151
Sevington Victorian School Sevington, Grittleton, Chippenham, Wiltshire SN14 7LD T: 01249 783070
Steam: Museum of the Great Western Railway Kemble Drive, Swindon SN2 2TA T: 01793 466646 E: tbryan@swindon.gov.uk
The Science Museum Wroughton, Wroughton, Swindon, Wiltshire SN4 9NS T: 01793 814466 E: enquiries.wroughton@nmsi.ac.uk W: www.sciencemuseum.org.uk/wroughton

Wiltshire Heritage Museum Library Wiltshire Archaeological & Natural Hist Soc, 41 Long Street, Devizes SN10 1NS T: 01380 727369 E: wanhs@wiltshireheritage.org.uk W: www.wiltshireheritage.org.uk
Yelde Hall Museum Market Place, Chippenham SN15 3HL T: 01249 651488

Wirral
Historic Warships at Birkenhead East Float Dock, Dock Road, Birkenhead L41 1DJ T: 0151 6501573

Worcestershire
Avoncroft Museum of Historic Buildings Redditch Rd, Stoke Heath, Bromsgrove, Worcestershire B60 4JR T: 01527 831363 E: admin@avoncroft.org.uk W: www.avoncroft.org.uk
Bewdley Museum Research Library Load Street, Bewdley, DY12 2AE T: 01229 403573 E: bewdley.museum@wyreforestdc.gov.uk W: www.wyreforestdc.gov.uk/museum
Kidderminster Railway Museum Station Drive, Kidderminster, Worcestershire DY10 1QX T: 01562 825316
Malvern Museum Priory Gatehouse, Abbey Road, Malvern, Worcestershire WR14 3ES T: 01684 567811 W:
Museum of Worcester Porcelain The Royal Porcelain Works, Severn Street, Worcester WR1 2NE E: rwgeneral@royal-worcester.co.uk
The Almonry Heritage Centre Abbey Gate, Evesham, WR11 4BG T: 01385 446944 W: www.almonry.ndo.co.uk
The Commandery Civil War Museum Sidbury, Worcester, WR1 2HU T: 01905 361821 E: thecommandery@cityofworcester.gov.uk W: www.worcestercitymuseums.org.uk
The Elgar Birthplace Museum Crown East Lane, Lower Broadheath, Worcester WR2 6RH T: 01905 333224 W: www.elgarfoundation.org
Tudor House Heritage Centre Tudor House, Friar Street, Worcester, Worcestershire WR1 2NA T: 01905 612 309 or 01905 426 402 E: manager@tudorhouse.org.uk W: www.tudorhouse.org.uk/
Worcester City Museum & Art Gallery Foregate Street, Worcester, WR1 1DT T: 01905 25371 E: gallerymuseum@worcestershire.gov.uk W: www.worcestercitymuseums.org.uk
Worcestershire County Museum Hartlebury Castle, Hartlebury, DY11 7XZ T: 01229 250416 E: museum@worcestershire.gov.uk W: www.worcestershire.gov.uk/museum

Yorkshire - East
East Riding Heritage Library & Museum Sewerby Hall, Church Lane, Sewerby, Bridlington YO15 1EA T: 01262 677874 E: sewerby.hall@eastriding.gov.uk W: www.sewerby-hall.co.uk
The Hornsea Museum Burns Farm, 11 Newbegin, Hornsea HU18 1AB T: 01964 533 443 W: www.hornseamuseum.com
Withernsea Lighthouse Museum Hull Rd, Withernsea, East Yorkshire HU19 2DY T: 01964 614834 W:

Yorkshire - North
Aysgarth Falls Carriage Museum Yore Mill , Asgarth Falls, Leyburn, North Yorkshire DL8 3SR T: 01969 663399
Beck Isle Museum of Rural Life Pickering, North Yorkshire YO18 8DU T: 01751 473653
Captain Cook Memorial Museum Grape Lane, Whitby, North Yorkshire YO22 4BA T: 01947 601900 E: cookmuseum@tiscali.co.uk W: www.cookmuseumwhitby.co.uk
Captain Cook Schoolroom Museum 10 High Street, Great Ayton, North Yorkshire TS9 7HB T: 01642 723358
Dales Countryside Museum Station Yard, Burtersett Rd, Hawes, North Yorkshire DL8 3NT T: 01969 666 210 E: dcm@yorkshiredales.org.uk
Eden Camp Museum Malton, North Yorkshire YO17 6RT T: 01653 697777 E: admin@edencamp.co.uk W: www.edencamp.co.uk
Life In Miniature 8 Sandgate, Whitby, North Yorkshire YO22 4DB T: 01947 601478 W:
Malton Museum The Old Town Hall, Market Place, Malton, North Yorkshire YO17 7LP T: 01653 695136 W: www.maltonmuseum.co.uk/
Micklegate Bar Museum Micklegate, York, North Yorkshire YO1 6JX T: 01904 634436 W:
Nidderdale Museum King Street, Pateley Bridge, North Yorkshire HG3 5LE T: 01423 711225 E: info@nidderdalemuseum.com W: www.nidderdalemuseum.com
Old Courthouse Museum Castle Yard, Knaresborough, North Yorkshire T: 01423 556188 E: CustomerServices@harrogate.gov.uk W: www.harrogate.gov.uk/museums
Richard III Museum Monk Bar, York, North Yorkshire YO1 2LH T: 01904 634191 W: www.richardiiimuseum.co.uk
Richmondshire Museum Ryder's Wynd, Richmond, North Yorkshire DL10 4JA T: 01748 825611
Ripon Workhouse - Museum of Poor Law Allhallowgate, Ripon, North Yorkshire HG4 1LE T: 01765 690799 E: info@riponmuseums.co.uk W: www.riponmuseums.co.uk

Rotunda Museum Vernon Rd, Scarborough, North Yorkshire YO11 2NN T: 01723 374839 W:

Royal Pump Room Museum Crown Place, Harrogate, North Yorkshire T: 01423-556188 E: museums@harrogate.gov.uk W: www.harrogate.gov.uk/royalpumproommuseum

Ryedale Folk Museum Hutton le Hole, North Yorkshire YO62 6UA T: 01751 417367 E: info@ryedalefolkmuseum.co.uk W: www.ryedalefolkmuseum.co.uk

The North Yorkshire Moors Railway Pickering Station, Pickering, North Yorkshire YO18 7AJ T: 01751 472508 E: info@northyorkshiremoorsrailway.com W: www.northyorkshiremoorsrailway.com

The Real Aeroplane Museum The Aerodrome, Breighton, Selby, North Yorkshire YO8 7DH T: 01757 289065

The World of James Herriott 23 Kirkgate, Thirsk, North Yorkshire YO7 1PL T: 01845 524234 E: james.herriot@hambleton.gov.uk W: www.worldofjamesherriot.org/

Upper Wharfedale Museum Society & Folk Museum The Square, Grassington, North Yorkshire BD23 5AU

War Room and Motor House Collection 30 Park Parade, Harrogate, North Yorkshire HG1 5AG T: 01423 500704

Whitby Lifeboat Museum Pier Rd, Whitby, North Yorkshire YO21 3PU T: 01947 602001

Whitby Literary & Philosphical Society, Library and Archives Whitby Museum, Pannett Park, Whitby YO21 1RE T: 01947 602908 E: library@whitbymuseum.org.uk W: www.whitbymuseum.org.uk

Yorkshire Museum of Farming Murton Park, Murton Lane, York, YO19 5UF T: 01904 489966 E: enquiries@murtonpark.co.uk W: www.murtonpark.co.uk/enquiries@murtonpark.co.uk

Yorkshire - South

Abbeydale Industrial Hamlet Abbeydale Road South, Sheffield, South Yorkshire S7 2 T: 0114 236 7731

Bishops House Norton Lees Lane, Sheffield, South Yorkshire S8 9BE T: 0114 278 2600 W: www.sheffieldgalleries.org.uk

Cannon Hall Museum Cannon Hall, Cawthorne, Barnsley, South Yorkshire S75 4AT T: 01226 790270 W:

Clifton Park Museum Clifton Lane, Rotherham, South Yorkshire S65 2AA T: 01709 823635 E: guy.kilminster@rotherham.gov.uk W: www.rotherham.gov.uk

Doncaster AeroVenture - The South Yorkshire Air Museum Aero Venture, Lakeside, Doncaster, South Yorkshire T: 01302 761616

Fire Museum (Sheffield) Peter House, 101-109 West Bar, Sheffield, S3 8PT T: 0114 249 1999 W: www.hedgepig.freeserve.co.uk

Kelham Island Museum Alma St, Kelham Island, Sheffield, South Yorkshire S3 8RY T: 0114 272 2106 W:

Magna Sheffield Road, Templeborough, Rotherham S60 1DX T: 01709 720002 E: info@magnatrust.org.uk W: www.magnatrust.org.uk

Sandtoft Transport Centre Ltd Belton Rd, Sandtoft, Doncaster, South Yorkshire DN8 5SX T: 01724 711391 W:

Sheffield City Museum Weston Park, Sheffield, South Yorkshire S10 2TP T: 0114 278 2600 W: www.sheffieldgalleries.org.uk

Sheffield Industrial Museums Trust Alma Street, off Corporation Road, Sheffield S3 8RY T: 0114 272 2106 W: www.simt.co.uk

Sheffield Police and Fire Museum 101-109 West Bar, Sheffield, S3 8TP T: 0114 249 1999 W: www.hedgepig.freeserve.co.uk

Yorkshire - West

Armley Mills Canal Rd, Leeds LS12 2QF T: 0113 263 7861

Bagshaw Museum Wilton Park, Batley, West Yorkshire WF17 0AS T: 01924 326 155 E: bagshaw.museum@kirklees.gov.uk W: www.kirklees.gov.uk/museums

Bankfield Museum & Gallery Boothtown Rd, Halifax HX3 6HG T: 01422 354823 E: bankfield-museum@calderdale.gov.uk W: www.calderdale.gov.uk

Bolling Hall Museum Bowling Hall Rd, Bradford, West Yorkshire BD4 7 T: 01274 723057

Bracken Hall Countryside Centre Glen Rd, Baildon, Shipley, West Yorkshire BD17 5ED T: 01274 584140

Bradford Industrial Museum & Horses at Work Moorside Rd, Eccleshill, Bradford BD2 3HP T: 01274 435900 E: eugene.nicholson@bradford.gov.uk W: www.bradfordmuseums.org

Calderdale Museums & Arts Piece Hall, Halifax, West Yorkshire HX1 1RE T: 01422 358087 W:

Castleford Museum Room Carlton St, Castleford WF10 1BB T: 01977 722085

Cliffe Castle Museum Spring Gardens Lane, Keighley, West Yorkshire BD20 6LH T: 01535 618231 W:

Dewsbury Museum Heckmondwike Road, Dewsbury WF13 2SG T: 01924 325100 E: dewsbury.museum@kirklees.gov.uk W: www.kirklees.gov.uk/museums

Eureka The Museum For Children Discovery Road, Halifax, West Yorkshire HX1 2NE T: 01422 330069 W:

Keighley Bus Museum Trust 47 Brantfell Drive, Burnley, Lancashire

BB12 8AW T: 01282 413179 W: www.kbmt.freeuk.com

Kirkstall Abbey and Abbey House Museum Abbey Walk, Kirkstall, Leeds, WEst Yorkshire LS5 3EH T: 0113 230 5492 E: abbeyhouse.museum@virgin.net W: www.leeds.gov.uk

Leeds Museums Resource Centre Moorfield Industrial Estate, Moorfield Road, Yeadon, Leeds, West Yorkshire LS19 7BN T: 0113 214 6526 W: www.leeds.gov.uk

Lotherton Hall Lotherton Lane, Aberford, Leeds, West Yorkshire LS25 3EB T: 0113 281 3259

Manor House Art Gallery & Museum Castle Yard, Castle Hill, Ilkley, West Yorkshire LS29 9D T: 01943 600066 W:

Marks in Time Centenary Gallery, Parkinson Buiding, University of Leeds, Woodhouse Lane, Leeds, West Yorkshire LS2 9JT T: 0208 718 2800 (Bookings) E: exhibitionbookings@marks-and-spencer.com W: http://marksintime.marksandspencer.com

Middleton Railway The Station, Moor Road, Hunslet, Leeds, West Yorkshire LS10 2JQ T: 0113 271 0320 E: howhill@globalnet.co.uk W: www.personal.leeds.ac.uk/mph6mip/mrt/mrt.htm

Oakwell Hall Nutter Lane, Birstall, Batley WF17 9LG T: 01924 326 240 E: oakwell.hall@kirklees.gov.uk W: www.kirklees.gov.uk/museums

Redhouse Museum Oxford Road, Gomersal, Cleckheaton, West Yorkshire BD19 4JP T: 01274 335 100 W: www.kirklees.gov.uk/museums

Royal Armouries Armouries Drive, Leeds, West Yorkshire LS10 1LT T: 0990 106666

Shibden Hall Lister Rd, Shibden, Halifax, West Yorkshire HX3 6AG T: 01422 352246 E: shibden.hall@calderdale.gov.uk W: www.calderdale.gov.uk

Skopos Motor Museum Alexandra Mills, Alexandra Rd, Batley, West Yorkshire WF17 6JA T: 01924 444423 W:

Temple Newsham House Temple Newsham Road, off Selby Road, Leeds, West Yorkshire LS15 0AE T: 0113 264 7321

Thackray Medical Museum Beckett Street, Leeds, West Yorkshire LS9 7LN T: 0113-244-4343 E: info@thackraymuseum.org W: www.thackraymuseum.org

The Colour Museum 1 Providence Street, Bradford BD1 2PW T: 01274 390955 E: museums@sdc.org.uk W: www.sdc.org.uk

The Launds Inn Museum 23 Launds, Rochdale Road, Golcar, Huddersfiled, West Yorkshire HD7 4NN T: 01484 645961 E: robert@laundsinnmuseum.co.uk W: www.laundsinnmuseum.co.uk

Thwaite Mills Watermill Thwaite Lane, Stourton, Leeds, West Yorkshire LS10 1RP T: 0113 249 6453

Tolson Museum Ravensknowle Park, Wakefield Road, Huddersfield, HD5 8DJ T: 01484 223 830 E: tolson.museum@kirklees.gov.uk W: www.kirklees.gov.uk/museums

Vintage Carriages Trust Station Yard, Ingrow, Keighley BD21 5AX T: 01535 680425 E: admin@vintagecarriagestrust.org W: www.vintagecarriagestrust.org

Wakefield Museum Wood Street, Wakefield, West Yorkshire WF1 2EW T: 01924 305356 E: cjohnstone@wakefield.gov.uk W: www.wakefieldmuseums.org

Yorkshire - York

Archaeoligical Resource Centre St Saviourgate, York, YO1 8NN T: 01904 654324 E: jorvik@yorkat.co.uk W: www.jorvik-viking-centre.co.uk

Bar Convent 17 Blossom Street, York, YO24 1AQ T: 01904 643238 E: info@bar-convent.org.uk W: www.bar-convent.org.uk

York Archaeological Trust 13 Ogleforth, York, YO1 7FG T: 01904 663000 E: enquiries@yorkarchaeology.co.uk W: www.yorkarchaeology.co.uk

York Castle Museum The Eye of York, York, YO1 9RY T: 01904 687687 W: www.yorkcastlemuseum.org.uk/

Yorkshire Museum Museum Gardens, York, YO1 7FR T: 01904 629745 W: www.york.gov.uk

Wales

National Slate Museum Llanberis, Gwynedd LL55 4TY T: 01286 870630 E: slate@museumwales.ac.uk W: www.museumwales.ac.uk

National Collection

St Fagans National History Museum St Fagans, Cardiff, CF5 6XB T: (029) 2057 3500 E: post@museumwales.ac.uk W: www.museumwales.ac.uk

Anglesey

Beaumaris Gaol Museum Bunkers Hill, Beaumaris, Anglesey LL58 8EP T: 01248 810921

The Maritime Museum Beach Rd, Newry Beach, Holyhead, Anglesey LL65 1YD T: 01407 769745

Caernarfon

National Slate Museum Padarn Country Park, LlanberisLL55 4TY T: 01286 870630 E: wsmpost@btconnect.com W: www.nmgw.ac.uk/en/slate

Cardiff

Cardiff Castle Castle Street, Cardiff, CF10 3RB T: 029 2087 8100 E: cardiffcastle@cardiff.gov.uk W: www.cardiffcastle.com

Techniquest Stuart St, Cardiff, CF10 5BW T: (029) 20475475

Carmarthenshire

Carmarthenshire County Museum Abergwili, Carmarthen, SA31 2JG T: 01267 228696 E: museums@carmarthenshire.gov.uk W: www.en.wikipedia.org/wiki/Carmarthenshire _County_Museum

Kidwelly Industrial Museum Broadford, Kidwelly SA17 4UF T: 01554 891078

Parc Howard Museum & Art Gallery Mansion House, Parc Howard, Llanelli, Carmarthenshire SA15 3LJ T: 01554 772029

Ceredigion

Cardigan Heritage Centre Teifi Wharf, Castle St, Cardigan, Ceredigion SA43 3AA T: 01239 614404

Ceredigion Museum Coliseum, Terrace Rd, Aberystwyth, Ceredigion SY23 2AQ T: 01970 633088 E: museum@ceredigion.gov.uk W: museum.ceridigion.gov.uk amgueddfa.ceridigion.gov.uk

Mid-Wales Mining Museum - Silver River Mines Ltd Llywernog Mine, Ponterwyd, Aberystwyth, Ceredigion SY23 3AB T: 01970 890620 E: silverrivermine@aol.com W: www.silverminetours.co.uk

Conwy

Great Orme Tramway Tramffordd Y Gogarth Goprsaf Victoria, Church Walks, Llandudno, Conwy LL30 1AZ T: 01492 575350 E: enq@greatormetramway.com W: www.greatormetramway.com

Sir Henry Jones Museum Y Cwm, Llangernyw, Abergele, Conwy LL22 8PR T: 01492 575371 E: syrhenryjones@hotmail.com W: www.sirhenryjones-museums.org

Denbighshire

Cae Dai Trust Cae Dai Lawnt, Denbigh LL16 4SU T: 01745 812107

Llangollen Motor Museum Pentrefelin, Llangollen, Denbighshire LL20 8EE T: 01978 860324 W:

Dyfed

Wilson Museum of Narberth Market Square, Narberth, Pembrokeshire SA67 7AX T: 01834 861719 W:

Pembrokeshire Motor Museum Keeston Hill, Haverfordwest, Dyfed SA62 6EH T: 01437 710950 W:

Glamorgan

Brecon Mountain Railway Co Ltd Pant Station, Merthyr Tydfil, CF48 2UP T: 01685 722988 E: enquiries@breconmountainrailway.co.uk W: www.breconmountainrailway.co.uk

Gwent

Abergavenny Museum The Castle, Castle St, Abergavenny, Gwent NP7 5EE T: 01873 854282

Big Pit Mining Museum Blaenavon, Torfaen NP4 9XP T: 01495-790311

Castle & Regimental Museum Monmouth Castle, Monmouth, NP25 3BS T: 01600 772175 W: www.monmouthshirecastlemuseum.org.uk

Drenewydd Museum 26-27 Lower Row, Bute Town, Tredegar, Gwent NP22 5QH T: 01685 843039 E: morgac1@caerphilly.gov.uk

Newport Museum & Art Gallery John Frost Square, Newport, Gwent NP20 1PA T: 01633-840064 E: museum@newport.gov.uk

Pillgwenlly Heritage Community Project within Baptist Chapel, Alexandra Rd, Newport, Gwent NP20 2JE T: 01633 244893 W:

Roman Legionary Museum High Street, Caerleon, Gwent NP6 1AE T: 01633 423134 W: www.nmgw.ac.uk

Valley Inheritance Park Buildings, Pontypool, Torfaen, Gwent NP4 6JH T: 01495-752036 E: info@torfaen.gov.uk W: www.torfaen.gov.uk

Gwynedd

Bala Lake Railway   Rheilffordd Llyn Tegid The Station, Yr Orsaf, Llanuwchllyn, Gwynedd LL23 7DD T: 01678 540666 E: info@bala-lake-railway.co.uk W: www.bala-lake-railway.co.uk

Betws-y-Coed Motor Museum Museum Cottage, Betws-Y-Coed, Gwynedd LL24 0AH T: 01690 710760

Caernarfon Air World Caernarfon Airport, Dinas Dinlle, Caernarfon, Gwynedd LL54 5TP

Gwynedd Museums Service Victoria Dock, Caernarvon LL55 1SH T: 01286 679098 E: museums@gwynedd.gov.uk W: www.gwynedd.gov.uk/

Home Front Experience New Street, Llandudno, Gwynedd LL30 2YF T: 01492 871032 W: www.homefront-enterprises.co.uk

Llanberis Lake Railway Rheilffordd Llyn Padarn LLanberis, Caernarfon LL55 4TY T: 01286 870549 E: info@lake-railway.co.uk W: www.lake-railway.co.uk

Llandudno & Conwy Valley Railway Society Welsh Slate Museum, Llanberis, Gwynedd T: 01492 874590 E: mazeppa@btopenworld.com W: www.lcvrs.org.uk

Llandudno Royal Artillery Llandudno Museum, 17-19 Gloddaeth Street, Llandudno, Gwynedd LL30 2DD T: 01492 876517

Lloyd George Museum Llanstumdwy, Criccieth LL52 0SH T: 01766 522071 W: www.gwynedd.gov.uk/adrannau/addysg/amgueddfeydd/english/lg_1.htm

Porthmadog Maritime Museum Oakley Wharf 1, The Harbour, Porthmadog, Gwynedd LL49 9LU T: 01766 513736 W:

Segontium Roman Museum Beddgelert Road, Caernarfon, Gwynedd LL55 2LN T: 01286 675625 W: www.nmgw.ac.uk

Snowdon Mountain Railway LlanberisLL55 4TY T: 0870 4580033 E: info@snowdonrailway.co.uk W: www.snowdonrailway.co.uk

Teapot Museum 25 Castle St, Conwy,LL32 8AY T: 01492 596533

Welsh Highland Railway Tremadog Road, Porthmadog, LL49 9DY T: 01766 513402 E: webmaster@whr.co.uk W: www.whr.co.uk

Merthyr Tydfil

Cyfartha Castle Museum Cyfartha Park, Brecon Road, Merthyr Tydfil, Mid Glamorgan CF47 8RE T: 01685 723112

Joseph Parrys Cottage 4 Chapel Row, Merthyr Tydfil, Mid Glamorgan CF48 1BN T: 01685 383704

Mid Glamorgan

Cyfartha Castle Museum Cyfartha Park, Brecon Road, Merthyr Tydfil, Mid Glamorgan CF47 8RE T: 01685 723112

Joseph Parrys Cottage 4 Chapel Row, Merthyr Tydfil, Mid Glamorgan CF48 1BN T: 01685 383704

Pontypridd Historical & Cultural Centre Bridge St, Pontypridd, Mid Glamorgan CF37 4PE T: 01443 409512

Ynysfach Iron Heritage Centre Merthyr Tydfil Heritage Trust, Ynysfach Rd, Merthyr Tydfil CF48 1AG T: 01685 721858

Monmouthshire

Nelson Museum & Local History Centre Priory St, Monmouth, NP5 3XA T: 01600 710630 E: nelsonmuseum@monmouthshire.gov.uk

Chepstow Museum Bridge St, Chepstow, Monmouthshire NP16 5EZ T: 01291 625981 E: chepstowmuseum@monmouthshire.gov.uk

The Royal Monmouthshire Royal Engineers (Militia) Castle and Regimental Museum, The Castle, Monmouth NP25 3BS T: 01600-712935 E: curator@monmouthcastlemuseum.org.uk W: www.monmouthcastlemuseum.org.uk

Usk Rural Life Museum The Malt Barn, New Market Street, Usk, NP15 1AU T: 01291-673777 E: uskrurallife.museum@virgin.net W: www.uskmuseum.members.easyspace.com

Pembrokeshire

Haverfordwest Town Museum Castle St, Haverfordwest, Pembrokeshire SA61 2EF T: 01437 763087 W: www.haverfordwest-town-museum.org.uk

Milford Haven Museum Old Customs House, The Docks, Milford Haven, Pembrokeshire SA73 3AF T: 01646 694496 W:

Pembrokeshire Museum Service Castle Gallery, Castle St, Haverfordwest, Dyfed SA61 2EF T: 01437 775246 W:

Tenby Museum Tenby Museum & Art Gallery, Castle Hill, Tenby, Pembrokeshire SA70 7BP T: 01834-842809 E: info@tenbymuseum.org.uk W: www.tenbymuseum.org.uk

Powys

Brecknock Militia Howell Harris Museum, Coleg Trefeca, Brecon, Powys LD3 0PP T: 01874 711423 E: colegtrefeca@ebcpcw.org.uk W: www.trefeca.org.uk

Llanidloes Museum The Town Hall, Great Oak Street, Llanidloes, Powys SY18 6BN T: 01686 413777 W: http://powysmuseums.powys.gov.uk

Powysland Museum & Montgomery Canal Centre The Canal Wharf, Welshpool, Powys SY21 7AQ T: 01938 554656 W: http://powysmuseums.powys.gov.uk

Radnorshire Museum Temple St, Llandrindod Wells, Powys LD1 5DL T: 01597 824513 E: radnorshire.museum@powys.gov.uk W: www.powys.gov.uk/radnorshiremuseum

The Judge's Lodging Broad St, Presteigne, Powys LD8 2AD T: 01544 260650 W: www.judgeslodging.org.uk

Water Folk Canal Centre Old Store House, Llanfrynach, Brecon, Powys LD3 7LJ T: 01874 665382 W:

South Glamorgan

Firing Line - The Cardiff Castle Museum of the Welsh Soldier Interpretation Centre, Cardiff Castle, Cardiff, South Glamorgan CF10 3RB T: 029 2022 9367 E: director@cardiffcastlemuseum.org.uk W: www.cardiffcastlemuseum.org.uk

National Museum & Galleries of Wales Cathays Park, Cardiff, South Glamorgan CF10 3NP T: (029) 20397951

West Glamorgan

Cefn Coed Colliery Museum Blaenant Colliery, Crynant, Neath, West Glamorgan SA10 8SE T: 01639 750556 W:

Glynn Vivian Art Gallery Alexandra Rd, Swansea, West Glamorgan SA1 5DZ T: 01792 655006 E: glynn.vivian.gallery@business.ntl.com W: www.sawnsea.gov.uk

Neath Museum The Gwyn Hall, Orchard Street, Neath, West Glamorgan SA11 1DT T: 01639 645726 W:
Wrexham
Wrexham County Borough Museum County Buildings, Regent Street, Wrexham, LL11 1RB T: 01978-317970 E: museum@wrexham.gov.uk W: www.wrexham.gov.uk/heritage

Scotland

Clan Cameron Museum Achnacarry , Spean Bridge PH34 4EJ T: 01397 712090 W: www.clan-cameron.org
Heriot-Watt University Museum and Archives Mary Burton Centre, Heriot-Watt University, Edinburgh, EH14 4AS T: 0131 451 3218 E: archive@hw.ac.uk W: www.hw.ac.uk/archive
National War Museum of Scotland The Castle, Museum Square, Edinburgh, EH1 2NG T: 0131 225 7534 E: library@nms.ac.uk W: www.nms.ac.uk/war
Regimental Museum and Archives of Black Watch Balhousie Castle, Hay Street, Perth, Perthshire PH1 5HR T: 0131 310 8530 E: archives@theblackwatch.co.uk W: www.theblackwatch.co.uk
Royal Museum and Museum of Scotland Chambers Street, Edinburgh, EH1 1JF T: 0131 247 4115 E: info@nms.ac.uk. W: www.nms.ac.uk

Aberdeenshire
Aberdeen Maritime Museum 52-56 Shiprow, Aberdeen, AB11 5BY T: 01224 337700 E: info@aagm.co.uk W: www.aagm.co.uk
Alford Heritage Centre Alford & Donside Heritage Association, Mart Road, Alford, Aberdeenshire AB33 8BZ T: 019755 62906
Arbuthnot Museum St. Peter St, Peterhead,AB42 1DA T: 01779 477778
Fraserburgh Heritage Society Heritage Centre, Quarry Rd, Fraserburgh AB43 9DT T: 01346 512888 W: www.fraserburghheritage.com
Grampian Transport Museum Alford AB33 8AE T: 019755-62292
Hamilton T.B Northfield Farm, New Pitsligo, Fraserburgh, Aberdeenshire AB43 6PX T: 01771 653504
Provost Skene's House Guestrow, Aberdeen AB10 1AS T: 01224 641086
Satrosphere The Tramsheds, 179 Constitution Street, Aberdeen, AB11 6LU T: 01224 640340 E: info@satrosphere.net W: www.satrosphere.net
The Museum of Scottish Lighthouses Kinnaird Head, Fraserburgh, Aberdeenshire AB43 9DU T: 01346-511022

Angus
Arbroath Museum Signal Tower, Ladyloan, Arbroath, Angus DD11 1PY T: 01241 875598 W: www.angus.gov.uk/history
Glenesk Folk Museum The Retreat, Glenesk, Brechin, Angus DD9 7YT T: 01356 670254 E: retreat@angusglens.co.uk W: www.angusglens.co.uk
Montrose Air Station Heritage Centre Waldron Road, Montrose, Angus DD10 9BB T: 01674 678 222 E: rafmontrose@aol.com W: www.rafmontrose.org.uk
The Meffan Institute 20 High St., West, Forfar, Angus DD8 1BB T: 01307 464123 E: the.meffan@angus.gov.uk

Argyll
Campbeltown Heritage Centre Big Kiln, Witchburn Rd, Campbeltown, Argyll PA28 6JU T: 01586 551400
Campbeltown Library & Museum Hall St, Campbeltown, Argyll PA28 6BU T: 01586 552366 E: mary.vanhelmond@argyll-bute.gov.uk W: www.argyle-bute.gov.uk/content/leisure/museums
Castle House Museum Castle Gardens, Argyll St, Dunoon, Argyll PA23 7HH T: 01369 701422 E: info@castlehousemuseum.org.uk W: www.castlehousemuseum.org.uk
Kilmartin House Trust Kilmartin House, Kilmartin, Lochgilphead, Argyll PA31 8RQ T: 01546 510278 E: museum@kilmartin.org W: www.kilmartin.org

Ayrshire
Culzean Castle & Country Park Culzean Castle, Maybole, Ayrshire KA19 8LE T: +44 (0)1655 884455 or 0844 493 2149 E: culzean@nts.org.uk W: www.culzeanexperience.org
Dalgarven Mill Dalry Rd, Dalgarven, Kilwinning, Ayrshire KA13 6PL T: 01294 552448
East Ayrshire Council District History Centre & Museum Baird Institute, 3 Lugar Street, Cumnock, Ayrshire KA18 1AD T: 01290 421701 E: Baird.institute@east-ayrshire.gov.uk W: www.east-ayrshire.gov.uk
Glasgow Vennel Museum 10 Glasgow, Vennel, Irvine, Ayrshire KA12 0BD T: 01294 275059
Irvine Burns Club & Burgh Museum 28 Eglinton St, Irvine, Ayrshire KA12 8AS T: 01294 274511
McKechnie Institute Dalrymple St, Girvan, Ayrshire KA26 9AE T: 01465 713643 E: mkigir@ukgateway.net

North Ayrshire Museum Manse St, Saltcoats, Ayrshire KA21 5AA T: 01294 464174 E: namuseum@globalnet.co.uk
Rozelle House Rozelle Park, Ayr, Ayrshire KA7 4NQ T: 01292 445447
The Largs Museum Kirkgate House, Manse Court, Largs, Ayrshire KA30 8AW T: 01475 687081
The Scottish Maritime Museum Gottries Road, Irvine, Ayrshire KA12 3QE T: 01294 278283 E: jgrant5313@aol.com W: WWW:

Banffshire
The Buckie Drifter Maritime Heritage Centre Freuchny Rd, Buckie, Banffshire AB56 1TT T: 01542 834646
Berwickshire
The Jim Clark Room 44 Newtown St, Duns, Berwickshire TD11 3DT T: 01361 883960

Caithness
Clangunn Heritage Centre & Museum Old Parish Kirk, Latheron, Caithness KW5 6DL T: 01593 741700
Dunbeath Preservation Trust Old School, Dunbeath, Caithness KW6 6EG T: 01593 731233 E: info@dunbeath-heritage.org.uk W: www.dunbeath-heritage.org.uk
The Last House John O'Groats, Wick, Caithness KW1 4YR T: 01955 611250

Dumfriesshire
Dumfries Museum & Camera Obscura The Observatory, Dumfries, Dumfriesshire DG2 7SW T: 01387 253374 E: info@dumgal.gov.uk W: www.dumfriesmuseum.demon.co.uk
Ellisland Trust Ellisland Farm, Dumfries DG2 0RP T: 01387 740426
Gretna Museum & Tourist Services Headless Cross, Gretna Green, Dumfriesshire DG16 5EA T: 01461 338441 E: info@gretnagreen.com W: www.gretnagreen.com
John Paul Jones Birthplace Museum Arbigland, Kirkbean, Dumfries DG2 8BQ T: 01387 880613 W: www.jpj.demon.co.uk
Old Bridge House Museum Old Bridge House, Mill Rd, Dumfries, DG2 7BE T: 01387 256904 W: www.dumfriesmuseum.demon.co.uk
Robert Burns Centre Mill Road, Dumfries DG2 7BE T: 01387 264808 E: dumfries.museum@dumgal.gov.uk W: www.dumgal.gov.uk/museums
Sanquhar Tolbooth Museum High St, Sanquhar, Dumfriesshire DG4 6BL T: 01659 50186
Savings Banks Museum Ruthwell, Dumfries, Dumfriesshire DG1 4NN T: 01387 870640 E: tsbmuseum@btinternet.com
Shambellie House Museum of Costume Shambellie House, New Abbey, Dumfries DG2 8HQ T: 01387 850375 E: info@nms.ac.uk W: www.nms.ac.uk/museumofcostumehomepage.aspx

Dundee
Dundee Heritage Trust Verdant Works, West Henderson's Wynd, Dundee, DD1 5BT T: 01382-225282 E: info@dundeeheritage.sol.co.uk W: www.verdant-works.co.uk
Royal Research Ship Discovery Discovery point, Discovery Quay, Dundee, DD1 4XA T: 01382 201245 E: info@dundeeheritage.sol.co.uk W: www.rrs-discovery.co.uk

Dunkeld
Dunkeld Cathedral Chapter House Museum Dunkeld, PH8 0AW T: 01350 728732 E: webmaster@dunkeldcathedral.org.uk W: www.dunkeldcathedral.org.uk

East Lothian
Dunbar Museum High St, Dunbar EH42 1ER T: 01368 863734
John Muir House Museum 126-128 High St, Dunbar, East Lothian EH42 1JJ T: 01368 862585
Myreton Motor Museum Aberlady, EH32 0PZ T: 01875 870288
North Berwick Museum School Rd, North Berwick, East Lothian EH39 4JU T: 01620 895457

Edinburgh
Heritage Projects (Edinburgh) Ltd Castlehill, Royal Mile, Edinburgh Midlothian EH1 2NE T: 0131 225 7575
Museum of Edinburgh Huntly House, 142 Canongate, Edinburgh, EH8 8DD T: 0131 529 4143 W: www.cac.org.uk
Royal Yatch Britannia & Visitor Centre OceanTerminal, Leith, edinburgh, EH6 6JJ T: 0131 555 5566 E: enquiries@tryb.co.uk W: www.royalyatchbritannia.co.uk
Scottish Museum Council County House, 20-22 Torphichen Street, Edinburgh, EH3 8JB T: 0131 229 7465
The Real Mary King's Close 2 Warriston's Close, Writers' Court, Edinburgh, EH1 1PG T: 08702 430160 W: www.realmarykingsclose.com

Falkirk

Falkirk Museum History Research Centre Callendar House, Callendar Park, Falkirk, FK1 1YR T: 01324 503778 E: callendar.house@falkirk.gov.uk W: www.falkirk.gov.uk/services/community/cultural_services/museums/museums_and_archives.aspx

Fife

Andrew Carnegie Birthplace Museum Moodie St, Dunfermline, Fife KY12 7PL T: 01383 724302

Dunfermline Museum Viewfield, Dunfermline, Fife KY12 7HY T: 01383 313838

Inverkeithing Museum The Friary, Queen St, Inverkeithing, Fife KY11 1 T: 01383 313595

John McDouall Stuart Museum Rectory Lane, Dysart, Kirkcaldy, Fife KY1 2TP T: 01592 653118

Kirkcaldy Museum and Art Gallery War Memorial Gardens, Kirkcaldy, Fife KY1 1YG T: 01592 412860 E: museums@fife.gov.uk info@fife.gov.uk W: www.fife.gov.uk

Methil Heritage Centre 272 High St, Methil, Leven, Fife KY8 3EQ T: 01333 422100

Pittencrieff House Museum Pittencrieff Park, Dunfermline, Fife KY12 8QH T: 01383 722935

Scotland's Secret Bunker Underground Nuclear Command Centre, Crown Buildings (Nr St Andrews), Fife KY16 8QH T: 01333-310301

Scottish Fisheries Museum St. Ayles, Harbourhead, Anstruther, Fife KY10 3AB T: 01333 310628 W: www.scottish-fisheries-museum.org

The Fife Folk Museum High St, Ceres, Cupar, Fife KY15 5NF T: 01334 828180

Verdant Works - A Working Jute mill West Henderson's Wynd, Dundee, DD1 5BT T: 01382-225282 E: info@dundeeheritage.sol.co.uk W: www.verdantworks.co.uk

Glasgow

Fossil Grove Victoria Park, Glasgow, G14 1BN T: 0141 287 2000 W: www.glasgowmuseums.com

Glasgow Museum of Transport 1 Burnhouse Road, Glasgow, G3 8DP T: 0141 287 2720 W: www.glasgowmuseums.com

Heatherbank Museum Glasgow Caledonian University, Cowcaddens Road, Glasgow, G4 0BA T: 0141 331 8637 W: www.lib.gcal.ac.uk/heatherbank

Kelvingrove Art Gallery and Museum Kelvingrove, Glasgow, G3 8AG T: 0141 287 2699 W: www.cis.glasgow.gov.uk

Martyrs School Parson street, Glasgow, G4 0PX T: 0141 552 2356 W: www.glasgowmuseums.com

McLellan Galleries 270 Sauchiehall Street, Glasgow, G2 3EH T: 0141 565 4100 W: www.glasgowmuseums.com

Museum of Piping The Piping Centre, 30-34 McPhater Street, Cowcaddens, Glasgow, T: 0141-353-0220

Open Museum 161 Woodhead Road, South Nitshill Industrial Estate, Glasgow, G53 7NN T: 0141 552 2356 W: www.glasgowmuseums.com

Pollok House Pollok Country Park, 2060 Pollokshaws Road, Glasgow, G43 1AT T: 0141 616 6410 W: www.cis.glasgow.gov.uk

Provand's Lordship 3 Castle Street, Glasgow, G4 0RB T: 0141 552 8819 W: www.glasgowmuseums.com

Scotland Street School Museum 225 Scotland St, Glasgow, G5 8QB T: 0141 287 0500 W: www.glasgowmuseums.com

St Mungo Museum of Religious Life and Art 2 Castle Street, Glasgow, G4 0RH T: 0141 553 2557 W: www.glasgowmuseums.com

The Burrell Collection Pollok Country Park, 2060 Pollokshaws Road, Glasgow, G43 1AT T: 0141 287 2550 W: www.glasgowmuseums.com

The Hunterian Museum Glasgow University, Glasgow, G12 8QQ T: 0141 330 3711 E: e.smith@admin.gla.ac.uk

The Lighthouse 11 Mitchell Lane, Glasgow, Lanarkshire G1 3NU T: 0141 221 6362 E: enquiries@thelighthouse.co.uk W: www.thelighthouse.co.uk

Inverness-shire

Clan Cameron Museum Achnacarry , Spean Bridge, Invernesshire PH34 4EJ T: 01397 712090 W: www.clan-cameron.org

Culloden Battlefield and Visitor Centre National Trust for Scotland, Culloden Moor, Inverness, inverness-shire IV2 5EU T: 0844 4932159 E: dsmyth@nts.org.uk W: www.nts.org.uk

Highland Folk Museum Kingussie Road, Kingussie PH21 1AY T: 01540 661307 E: rachel.chisholm@highland.gov.uk

Highland Folk Museum Aultlarie Croft, Kingussie Rd, Newtonmore, Inverness-Shire PH20 1AY T: 01540 673 551 E: highland.folk@highland.gov.uk W: www.highlandfolk.com

Highland Railway Museum 5 Druimlon, Drumnadrochit, Inverness, Inverness-Shire IV63 6TY T: 01456 450527

Inverness Museum & Art Gallery Castle Wynd, Inverness, Inverness-Shire IV2 3ED T: 01463 237114

Mallaig Heritage Centre Station Rd, Mallaig, Inverness-Shire PH41 4PY T: 01687 462085 E: curator@mallaigheritage.org.uk W: www.mallaigheritage.org.uk

The Clansman Centre Canalside, Fort Augustus, Inverness-Shire PH32 4AU T: 01320 366444

West Highland Museum Cameron Square, Fort William PH33 6AJ T: 01397 702169 E: info@westhighlandmuseum.org.uk W: www.westhighlandmuseum.org.uk

Isle Of Arran

Arran Heritage Museum Rosaburn House, Brodick, Isle Of Arran KA27 8DP T: 01770 302636

Isle Of Islay

Finlaggan Trust The Cottage, Ballygrant, Isle Of Islay PA45 7QL T: 01496 840644 E: lynmags@aol.com W: www.islay.com

Isle Of Mull

The Columba Centre Fionnphort PA66 6BN T: 01681 700660

Isle Of North Uist

Taigh Chearsabhagh Trust Taigh Chearsabhagh, Lochmaddy, Isle Of North Uist HS6 5AE T: 01876 500293 E: taighchearsabhagh@zetnet.co.uk W: www.taighchearsabhagh.org.uk

Isle Of South Uist

Kildonan Museum Kildonan, Lochboisdale, Isle Of South Uist HS8 5RZ T: 01878 710343

Kinross-shire

Perth Museum & Art Gallery Perth Museum & Art Gallery, George Street, Perth, Tayside PH1 5LB T: 01738-632488 E: museum@pkc.gov.uk W: www.pkc.gov.uk/education+and+learning

Kirkcudbrightshire

The Stewartry Museum St Mary Street, Kirkcudbright, Kirkcudbrightshire DG6 4AQ T: 01557 331643 E: david@dumgal.gov.uk W: www.dumgal.gov.uk/museums

Lanarkshire

Auld Kirk Museum The Cross, Kirkintilloch, Glasgow G66 1 T: 0141 578 014

Biggar Museum Trust Moat Park Kirkstyle, Biggar ML12 6DT T: 01899 221050

Discover Carmichael Visitors Centre Warrenhill Farm, Warrenhill Road, Thankerton, Biggar, Lanarkshire ML12 6PF T: 01899 308169

Greenhill Covenanters House Museum Kirkstyle, Biggar, Lanarkshire ML12 6DT T: 01899 221572

Heritage Engineering 22 Carmyle Avenue, Glasgow, Lanarkshire G32 8HJ T: 0141 763 0007

Hunter House Maxwellton Rd, East Kilbride, Glasgow, Lanarkshire G74 3LW T: 01355 261261

John Hastie Museum Threestanes Rd, Strathaven ML10 6EB T: 01357 521257

Lanark Museum 8 West Port, Lanark, Lanarkshire ML11 9HD T: 01555 666680 E: lanarkmuseum@hotmail.com W: www.lanarkmuseum.org

Low Parks Museum 129 Muir St, Hamilton, Lanarkshire ML3 6BJ T: 01698 283981

New Lanark Trust Visitors Centre Mill No 3, New Lanark Mills, Lanark, Lanarkshire ML11 9DB T: 01555 661345 E: visit@newlanark.org W: www.newlanark.org

The People's Palace Glasgow Green, Glasgow, G40 1AT T: 0141 554 0223 W: www.glasgowmuseums.com

Weavers' Cottages Museum 23-25 Wellwynd, Airdrie, Lanarkshire ML6 0BN T: 01236 747712

Midlothian

History of Education Centre East London St, Edinburgh, Midlothian EH7 4BW T: 0131 556 4224

Lauriston Castle 2a Cramond Rd South, Edinburgh, Midlothian EH4 5QD T: 0131 336 2060

Newhaven Heritage Museum 24 Pier Place, Edinburgh, Midlothian EH6 4LP T: 0131 551 4165 W: www.cac.org.uk

Scottish Mining Museum Trust Lady Victoria Colliery, Newtongrange, Dalkeith, Midlothian EH22 4QN T: 0131 663 7519 E: enwuiries@scottishminingmuseum.com W: www.scottishminingmuseum.com

Morayshire

Elgin Museum 1 High St, Elgin, Morayshire IV30 1EQ T: 01343 543675 W: www.elginmuseum.org.uk

Falconer Museum Tolbooth St, Forres, Morayshire IV36 1PH T: 01309 673701 E: alasdair.joyce@techleis.moray.gov.uk W: www.moray.gov.uk

Grantown Museum & Heritage Trust Burnfield House, Burnfield Avenue, Grantown-On-Spey, Morayshire PH26 3HH T: 01479 872478 E: Molly.Duckett@btinternet.com W: www.grantown-on-spey.co.uk

Lossiemouth Fisheries Museum Pitgaveny St, Lossiemouth, Morayshire IV31 6TW T: 01343 813772

Nairnshire
Nairn Museum Viewfield House, King St, Nairn, Nairnshire IV12 4EE T: 01667 456791

Orkney
Orkney Farm & Folk Museum Corrigall Farm Museum, Harray, Orkney KW17 2LQ T: 01856 771411

Orkney Farm & Folk Museum Kirbister Farm, Birsay, Orkney KW17 2LR T: 01856 771268

Orkney Fossil & Vintage Centre Viewforth Burray, Orkney KW17 2SY T: 01856 731255

Orkney Museum Tankerness House, Broad Street, Kirkwall, Orkney KW15 1DH T: 01856 873 535 or 01856 873 191 E: museum@orkney.gov.uk W: www.orkney.gov.uk/

Orkney Wireless Museum Kiln Corner, Kirkwall, Orkney KW15 1LB T: 01856-871400

Scapa Flow Visitor Centre Lyness, Stromness, Orkney KW16 3NT T: 01856 791300 W: www.scapaflow.co.uk

Stromness Museum 52 Alfred Street, Stromness, Orkney T: 01856 850025 W: www.orkneycommunities.co.uk/STROMNESSMUSEUM/

Perthshire
Atholl Country Collection The Old School, Blair Atholl, Perthshire PH18 5SP T: 01796-481232 E: john.museum@virgin.net

Clan Donnachaidh (Robertson) Museum Clan Donnachaidh Centre, Bruar, Pitlochry, Perthshire PH18 5TW T: 01796 483338 E: donkey3@freenetname.co.uk

Clan Menzies Museum Castle Menzies, Weem, by Aberfeldy, Perthshire PH15 2JD T: 01887-820982 E: castlemenziesmanager@gmail.com W: www.menzies.org/

Meigle Museum Dundee Rd, Meigle, Blairgowrie, Perthshire PH12 8SB T: 01828 640612

The Hamilton Toy Collection 111 Main St, Callander, Perthshire FK17 8BQ T: 01877 330004

Renfrewshire
Mclean Museum & Art Gallery 15 Kelly St, Greenock, Renfrewshire PA16 8JX T: 01475 715624

Old Paisley Society George Place, Paisley, Renfrewshire PA1 2HZ T: 0141 889 1708

Paisley Museum Paisley Museum & Art Galleries, High Street, Paisley, Renfrewshire PA1 2BA T: 0141-889-3151

Ross-Shire
Dingwall Museum Trust Town Hall, High St, Dingwall, Ross-Shire IV15 9RY T: 01349 865366

Highland Museum of Childhood The Old Station, Strathpeffer, Ross-Shire IV14 9DH T: 01997 421031 W: www.hmoc.freeserve.co.uk

Tain Through Time Tower St, Tain, Ross-Shire IV19 1DY T: 01862 894089

The Groam House Museum High St, Rosemarkie, Fortrose, Ross-Shire IV10 8UF T: 01381 620961

Ullapool Museum & Visitor Centre 7 & 8 West Argyle St, Ullapool, Ross-Shire IV26 2TY T: 01854 612987 E: info@ullapoolmuseum.co.uk W: www.ullapoolmuseum.co.uk

Roxburghshire
Borders Museum of Arms Henderson's Knowe, Teviot, Hawick, Roxburghshire TD9 0LF T: 01450 850237

Hawick Museum & Scott Gallery Wilton Lodge Park, Hawick, Roxburghshire TD9 7JL T: 01450 373457 E: hawickmuseum@hotmail.com

Jedburgh Castle Jail Museum Castlegate, Jedburgh, Roxburghshire TD8 6BD T: 01835 863254

Mary Queen of Scots House and Visitor Centre Queens St, Jedburgh, Roxburghshire TD8 6EN T: 01835 863331

Scottish Borders
Mary Queen of Scots House and Visitor Centre Queens St, Jedburgh, Roxburghshire TD8 6EN T: 01835 863331

Selkirkshire
Halliwells House Museum Halliwells Close, Market Place, Selkirk, TD7 4BL T: 01750 20096 E: museums@scotborders.gov.uk

Shetland
Fetlar Interpretive Centre Beach Of Houbie, Fetlar, Shetland ZE2 9DJ T: 01957 733206 E: fic@zetnet.co.uk W: www.zetnet.co.uk/sigs/centre/

Old Haa Museum Burravoe Yell, ShetlandZE2 9AY T: 01957 722339

Shetland Museum & Archives Shetland Museum & Archives, Hay's Dock, Lerwick, Shetland ZE1 0WP T: 01595 695057 E: tommy@shetland.museum.org.uk W: www.shetland-museum.org.uk

Tangwick Haa Museum Tangwick, Eshaness, Shetland, ZE2 9RS T: 01806 503389

The Shetland Textile Working Museum Weisdale Mill, Weisdale, Shetland, Shetland Islands ZE2 9LW T: 01595 830419

Stirling
Stirling Smith Art Gallery & Museum Dumbarton Road, Stirling, FK8 2RQ T: 01786 471917 E: museum@smithartgallery.demon.co.uk W: www.smithartgallery.demon.co.uk

Stranraer
Stranraer Museum 55 George Street, Stranraer, DG9 7JP T: 01776 705088 E: JohnPic@dumgal.gov.uk W: www.dumgal.gov/museums

Sutherland
Strathnaver Museum Bettyhill, Sutherland KW14 7SS T: 01641 521 418 E: projectmanager@strathnavermuseum.org.uk W: www.strathnavermuseum.org.uk

Tayside
Perth Museum & Art Gallery Perth Museum & Art Gallery, George Street, Perth, Tayside PH1 5LB T: 01738-632488 E: museum@pkc.gov.uk W: www.pkc.gov.uk/education+and+learning

West Lothian
Almond Valley Heritage Trust Livingston Mill Farm, Millfield, Livingston, West Lothian EH54 7AR T: 01506 414957

Bennie Museum Mansefield St, Bathgate, West Lothian EH48 4HU T: 01506 634944 W: www.benniemuseum.homestead.co.uk

Kinneil Museum Kinneil Estate, Bo'Ness, West Lothian EH51 0AY T: 01506 778530

Queensferry Museum 53 High St, South Queensferry, West Lothian EH30 9HP T: 0131 331 5545 W: www.cac.org.uk

The Linlithgow Story Annet House, 143 High St, Linlithgow, West Lothian EH49 7EJ T: 01506 670677 E: enquiries@linlithgowstory.fsnet.co.uk W: www.linlithgowstory.org.uk

Wigtownshire
Taylor's Farm Tradition Barraer, Newton Stewart, Wigtownshire DG8 6QQ T: 01671 404890 E: info@iwtaylor.com W: http://iwtaylor.com/Galloway_Holidays/Museum/Museum.html

Northern Ireland
Ulster Aviation Heritage Centre The Maze Regeneration Site, Halftown Road, Lisburn, BT27 5RF E: info@ulsteraviationsociety.org W: www.ulsteraviationsociety.org

Belfast
Ulster Museum Botanic Gardens Botanic Gardens, Stranmillis Road, Belfast, BT9 5AB T: (028) 90381251 E: info@nmni.com/ W: www.nmni.com/

County Antrim
Ballymoney Museum Ballymoney Town Hall, 1 Townhead Street, Ballymoney, County Antrim BT53 6BE T: 028 2766 0230 E: museum@ballymoney.gov.uk W: www.ballymoneyancestry.com

Friends of the Ulster Museum 12 Malone Road, Belfast, County Antrim BT9 5BN T: (028) 90681606

Irish Linen Centre & Museum Market Square, Lisburn BT28 1AG T: 028 9266 3377 E: ilreception@lisburn.gov.uk W: www.lisburncity.gov.uk

NI Museums Council 66 Donegall Pass, Belfast, County Antrim BT7 1BU T: (028) 90550215 W: www.nimc.co.uk

The Museum Of The Royal Irish Regiment St. Patricks Barracks, Demesne Avenue, Ballymena, County Antrim BT43 7BH T: (028) 2566 1386 E: hqrirish@royalirishregiment.co.uk W: www.royalirishregiment.co.uk

Ulster American Folk Park Project Team Belfast 4 The Mount Albert Bridge Rd, Belfast, County Antrim BT5 4NA T: (028) 90452250

County Armagh
Armagh County Museum The Mall East, Armagh, County Armagh BT61 9BE T: (028) 37523070 E: info@nics.gov.uk W: www.nmni.com/acm

County Down
Down County Museum The Mall, Downpatrick, County Down BT30 6AH T: (028) 44615218 E: madeleine.mcallister@downdc.gov.uk W: www.downcountymuseum.com

Downpatrick Railway Museum Railway Station, Market St, Downpatrick, County Down BT30 6LZ T: (028) 44615779
The Ferguson Linen Centre 54 Scarva Road, Banbridge, County Down BT32 3QD T: 028 4062 3491 E: info@fergusonsirishlinen.com W: www.fergusonsirishlinen.com
The Somme Heritage Centre 233 Bangor Road, Newtownards, County Down BT23 7PH T: 028 9182 3202 E: enquiry.shc@hotmail.co.uk W: www.irishsoldier.org
Ulster Folk and Transport Museum Cultra, Holywood, Co Down BT18 0EU T: 028 9042 8428 E: info@nmni.com W: www.nmni.com/uftm

County Fermanagh
Fermanagh County Museum Enniskillen Castle Castle Barracks, Enniskillen, County Fermanagh BT74 7HL T: 028 66 32 5000 E: castle@fermanagh.gov.uk W: www.enniskillencastle.co.uk
Roslea Heritage Centre Church St, Roslea, Enniskillen, County Fermanagh BT74 7DW T: (028) 67751750

County Londonderry
Foyle Valley Railway Museum Foyle Rd, Londonderry, County Londonderry BT48 6SQ T: (028) 71265234
Garvagh Museum 142 Main St, Garvagh, Coleraine, County Londonderry BT51 5AE T: (028) 295 58216 E: info@garvaghmuseum.com W: www.garvaghmuseum.com
Londonderry Harbour Museum Harbour Square, Londonderry, County Londonderry BT48 6AF T: 028 7137 7331 E: museums@derrycity.gov.uk W: www.derrycity.gov.uk

County Tyrone
The Ulster History Park Cullion, Lislap, County Tyrone BT79 7SU T: (028) 8164 8188 E: info@omagh.gov.uk W: www.omagh.gov.uk/historypark.htm
Ulster American Folk Park Centre for Migration Studies, Mellon Rd, Castletown, Omagh, County Tyrone BT78 5QY T: (028) 8225 6315 E: info@nmni.com W: www.nmni.com

Ireland
Dublin Civic Museum 58 South William Street, Dublin, 2 T: +353 679 4260
Garda Siochana Museum & Archives The Records Tower, Dublin, 2 T: +353 1 6719 597 E: j_herlihy@esatclear.ie W: www.esatclear.ie/~garda/museum.html
Irish Jewish Museum 3 - 4 Walworth Road, South Circular Road, Dublin, 8 T: +353 857 067 357 E: museum@jewishireland.org

Isle of Man
Regimental Museum of the Manx Regiment The MacClellan Hall, Tromode Road, Douglas, Isle of Man T: 01624 803146

Channel Islands
Alderney
The Alderney Society Museum Alderney GY9 3TG T: 01481 823222
Guernsey
18th Century Loopholed Tower PO Box 23, St Peter Port, Guernsey GY1 3AN
Clarence Battery Fort George, St Peter Port, Guernsey
Fort Grey Rocquaine Bay, St Saviours, Guernsey
German Direction Finding Tower PO Box 23, St Peter Port, Guernsey GY1 3AN
German Occupation Museum Les Houards, Forest, Guernsey GY8 0BG T: 01481 328205 W: www.aboutbritain.com/OccupationMuseum.htm
German Military Underground Hospital La Vassalerie Road, St Andrew's, Guernsey T: 01481 239100
German Naval Signals Headquarters St Jacques, Guernsey
La Valette Underground Military Museum St Peter Port, Guernsey T: 01481 722300
Royal Guernsey Militia and Royal Geurnsey Light Infantry Castle Comet, St Peter Port, Guernsey T: 01481 726518 W: www.museum.guernsey.net/castle.htm
Jersey
Elizabeth Castle - Jersey Militia St Aubin's Bay, St Helier, Jersey T: 01534 633300
German Underground Hospital Meadowbank, St Lawrence, Jersey T: 01534 863442
Island Fortress Occupation Museum 9 Esplanade, St Helier, Jersey T: 01534 633300
La Hougue Bie Grouville, Jersey T: 01534 633300
Maritime Museum and Occupation Tapestry Gallery New North Quay, St Helier, Jersey T: 01534 811043 E: marketing@jerseyheritagetrust.org W: www.jerseyheritagetrust.org
Mont Orgueil Castle Gorey, St Martin, Jersey T: 01534 633300
Noirmont Command Bunker Noirmont Point, St Brelade, Jersey T: 01534 482089
St Peter's Bunker Museum of Wartime German Equipment and Occupation Relics La Petite Rue De L'eglise, St Peter, Jersey JE3 7AF T: 01534 723136
The Channel Islands Military Museum The Five Mile Road, St Ouen, Jersey T: 01534 23136
Sark
German Occupation Museum Rue Lucas, Sark, Sark T: 01481 832564

Military Museums

100 Bomb Group Memorial Museum Common Road, Dickleburgh, Diss, IP21 4PH T: 01379 740708
101 (Northumbrian) Regt Royal Artillery (Volunteers) Museum Napier Armoury, Gateshead, NE8 4HX T: 0191 239 6130
4th Battalion East Yorkshire Regt Collection Kingston upon Hull City Museums, Wilberforce House, 23-25 High Street, Kingston upon Hull, HU1 T: 01482 613902
50 and 61 Sduadrons Museum The Lawn, Union Road, Lincoln,
A Soldier's Life 15th/19th The King's Royal Hussars
Northumberland Hussars and Light Dragoons Discovery Museum, Blandford Square, Newcastle-upon-Tyne, NE1 4JA T: 0191 232 6789 E: ralph.thompson@twmuseums.org.uk
Abington Museum and Museum of The Northamptonshire Regt Abington Park Museum, Abington, NN1 5LW T: 01604 635412 W: www.northampton.gov.uk/museums
Airbourne Forces Museum Browning Barracks, Aldershot, GU11 2BU T: 01252 349619
Army Medical Services Museum Keogh Barracks, Ash Vale, Aldershot, GU12 5RQ T: 01252 868612 E: armymedicalmuseum@btinternet.com W: www.ams-museum.org.uk
Army Medical Services Museum Keogh Barracks, Ash Vale, Aldershot, GU12 5RQ T: 01252 868612 E: museum@keogh72.freeserve.co.uk
Bankfield Museum & Gallery Boothtown Rd, Halifax, HX3 6HG T: 01422 354823 E: bankfield-museum@calderdale.gov.uk W: www.calderdale.gov.uk
Battle of Britain Memorial Flight R A F Coningsby, Coningsby, LN4 4SY
Battlefields Trust 33 High Green, Brooke, Norwich, NR15 1HR T: 01508 558145 E: BattlefieldTrust@aol.com W: www.battlefieldstrust.com

Bedford Museum Bedfordshire Yeomanry Castle Lane, Bedford, MK40 3XD T: 01234 353323 W: www.bedfordmuseum.org
Bedfordshire & Hertfordshire Regimental Museum Wardown Park, Luton, LU2 7HA T: 01582 546722 W: www.luton.gov.uk
Berkshire and Westminster Dragoons Museum Cavalry House, Duke of York's Headquarters, Kings Road, Chelsea, London, SW3 4SC T: 020 7414 5233
Blake Museum Blake Street, Bridgwater, TA6 3NB T: 01278 456127 E: museums@sedgemoor.gov.uk W: www.sedgemoor.gov.uk
Bomber County Aviation Museum Ex RAF Hemswell, Hemswell Cliff, Gainsborough, T: 01724 855410
Border Regt & Kings Own Royal Border Regt Museum Queen Mary's Tower, The Castle, Carlisle, CA3 8UR T: 01228 532774 E: borderregiment@aol.com W: www.armymuseums.org
Bournemouth Aviation Museum Hanger 600, Bournemouth International Airport, Christchurch, BH23 6SE T: 01202 580858 E: admin@aviation-museum.co.uk W: www.aviation-museum.co.uk
Brecknock Militia Howell Harris Museum, Coleg Trefeca, Brecon, LD3 0PP T: 01874 711423 E: post@trefeca.org.uk W: www.trefeca.org.uk
Brenzett Aeronautical Museum Ivychurch Road, Brenzett, Romney Marsh, TN29 0EE T: 01233 627911 W: www.aboutbritain.com/renzettAeronauticalMuseum
Britain at War Experience Winston Churchill, 64-66 Tooley Street, London Bridge, London, SE1 2TF T: 020 7403 3171 E: britainatwar@dial.pipex.com W: www.britainatwar.co.uk
Brixham Heritage Museum Bolton Cross, Brixham, TQ5 8LZ T: 01803 856267 E: mail@brixhamheritage.org.uk W: www.brixhamheritage.org.uk

Buckinghamshire Military Museum Trust Collection Old Gaol Museum, Market Hill, Buckingham, MK18 13X T: 01280 823020

Buffs Regimental Museum The Royal Museum & Art Gallery, 18 High Street, Canterbury, CT1 2RA T: 01227-452747 W: www.canterbury-museums.co.uk

Cheshire Military Museum The Castle, Chester, CH1 2DN T: 01244 327617

Cheshire Military Museum The Castle, Chester, CH1 2DN T: 01244 327617 W: www.chester.cc.uk/militarymuseum

Cholmondeley Collection of Model Soldiers Houghton Hall, Houghton, Kings Lynn, PE31 6UE T: 01485 528569 E: administrator@houghtonhall.com W: www.houghtonhall.com

Coldstream Guards Record Office Wellington Barracks, Birdcage Walk, London, SW1E 6HQ

Commonwealth War Graves Commission 2 Marlow Road, Maidenhead, SL6 7DX T: 01628-634221 W: www.cwgc.org

Cosford Royal Air Force Museum Cosford , Shifnal, TF11 8UP T: 01902 376200 E: cosford@rafmuseum.org W: www.rafmuseum.org

Cranwell Avation Heritage Centre Heath Farm, North Raunceby, Near Cranwell, Sleaford, NG34 8QR T: 01529 488490

D-Day Museum and Overlord Museum Clarence Esplanade, Southsea, PO5 3NT T: 023 9282 7261

De Havilland Heritage Centre inc The Mosquito Aircraft Museum PO Box 107, Salisbury Hall, London Colney, AL10 1EX T: 01727 822051 W: www.hertsmuseums.org

Dover Castle Dover, CT16 1HU T: 01304 211067

Duke of Cornwall's Light Infantry Museum The Keep, Bodmin, PL31 1EG T: 01208 72810 W: www.britrishlightinfantry.org.ca

Duke of Wellington's Regimental Museum Bankfield Museum, Akroyd Park, Boothtown Road, Halifax, HX3 6HG T: 01422 354823

Durham Light Infantry Museum Aykley Heads, Durham, DH1 5TU T: 0191-384-2214 E: dli@durham.gov.uk W: www.durham.gov.uk/dli

East Essex Aviation Society & Museum Martello Tower, Point Clear, Clacton on Sea, T: 01255 428020

East Lancashire Regt Towneley Hall, Burnley, BB11 3RQ T: 01282424213 E: towneleyhall@burnley.gov.uk W: www.towneleyhall.org.uk

Eden Camp Museum Malton, YO17 6RT T: 01653 697777 E: admin@edencamp.co.uk W: www.edencamp.co.uk

Essex Regiment Museum Oaklands Park, Moulsham St, Chelmsford CM2 9AQ T: 01245 605701 E: pompadour@chelmsford.gov.uk W: www.chelmsford.gov.uk/museums

Essex Secret Bunker Crown Building, Shrublands Road, Mistley, CO11 1HS T: 01206 392271 (24 hour information line)

Essex Volunteer Units Colchester Museums, 14 Ryegate Road, Colchester, CO1 1YG T: 01206 282935

Essex Yeomanry Collection Springfield Lyons TA Centre, Colchester Road, Chelmsford , CM2 5TA T: 01245 462298

Explosion! The Museum of Naval Firepower Priddy's Hard, Gosport, PO12 4LE T: 023 9258 6505 E: info@explosion.org.uk W: www.explosion.org.uk

Firepower - The Royal Artillery Museum Royal Arsenal (West), Warren Lane, Woolwich, London, London SE18 6ST T: 020 8312 7125 E: info@firepower.org.uk W: www.firepower.org.uk

Flambards Village and Cornwall Aircraft Park Flambards Village Theme Park, Culdrose Manor, Helston, TR13 0GA T: 01326 573404 E: info@flambards.co.uk W: www.flambards.co.uk

Fleet Air Arm Museum Records Research Centre RNAS Yeovilton, Nr Ilchester BA22 8HT T: 01935 840565 E: BarbaraG@fleetairarm.com SusanD@fleetairarm.com W: www.fleetairarm.com/en-GB/research.aspx

Fort Armherst Dock Road, Chatham , ME4 4UB T: 01634 847747 W: www.fortamhurst.org.uk

Fort Luton Museum Magpie Hall Road, Chatham, ME4 5XJ T: 01634 813969

Fusiliers Museum of Northumberland The Abbot's Tower, Alnwick Castle, Alnwick, Northumberland NE66 1NG T: 01665-602151 E: fusnorthld@aol.com W: www.northumberlandfusiliers.org.uk/

Fusiliers' London Volunteer Museum 213 Balham High Road, London, SW17 7BQ T: 020 8672 1168

Green Howards Regimental Museum Trinity Church Square, Richmond DL10 4QN T: 01748 826 561 E: museum@greenhowards.org.uk W: www.greenhowards.org.uk/

Grenadier Guards Record Office Wellington Barracks, Birdcage Walk, London, SW1E 6HQ E: rhqgrengds@yahoo.co.uk

Hertfordshire Regiment Museum 18 Bull Plain, Hertford, SG14 1DT T: 01992 582686 W: www.hertfordmuseum.org

Historic Ships and The Naval Dockyard HM Naval Base, Portsmouth, PO1 3LR T: 023 9286 1512 W: www.flagship.org.uk

Historic Warships at Birkenhead East Float Dock, Dock Road, Birkenhead, L41 1DJ T: 0151 6501573 W: www.warships.freeserve.co.uk

HMS Ganges Museum Victory House, Shotley Point Marina, Ipswich, IP9 1QJ T: 01473 684749

HMS Victory Victory Gate, HM Naval Base, Portsmouth, PO1 3LR T: (023) 9277 8600 E: info@hmswarrior.org W: www.hmswarrior.org

Honourable Artillery Company Armoury House, City Road, London, EC1Y 2BQ T: 020 7382 1537 W: www.hac.org.uk

HQ No 11 (Fighter) Group Battle of Britain Operations Room RAF Uxbridge, Uxbridge, UB10 0RZ T: 01895 815400

Imperial War Museum Lambeth Road, London, SE1 6HZ T: 020 7416 5342 E: collections@iwm.org.uk W: www.iwm.org.uk

Inns of Court and City Yeomanry Museum 10 Stone buildings, Lincoln's Inn, London, WC2A 3TG T: 020 7405 8112

Irish Guards Record Office Wellington Barracks, Birdcage Walk, London, SW1E 6HQ W: www.army.mod/ig~assoc

James Clavell Library Royal Arsenal (West), Warren Lane, Woolwich, London, SE18 6ST T: 020 8312 7125 W: www.firepower.org.uk

Kelvedon Hatch Secret Nuclear Bunker Kelvedon Hall Lane, Kelvedon Hatch, Brentwood, CM15 0LB T: 01277 364883 E: bunker@japar.demon.co.uk W: www.japar.demon.co.uk

Kent Battle of Britain Museum Aerodrome Road, Hawkinge, Folkestone, CT18 7AG T: 01303 893140

King's Own Royal Regimental Museum The City Museum, Market Square, Lancaster, Lancashire LA1 1HT T: 01524 64637 E: kingsownmuseum@iname.com W: www.kingsownmuseum.plus.com

King's Own Scottish Borderers Museum The Barracks, The Parade, Berwick upon Tweed TD15 1DG T: 01289 307426 W: www.kosb.co.uk/

King's Own Yorkshire Light Infantry Regimental Gallery Doncaster Museum and Art Gallery, Chequer Road, Doncaster DN1 2AE T: 01302 734293 E: museum@doncaster.gov.uk W: www.doncaster.gov.uk/museums

King's Regiment Collection Museum of Liverpool, Dock Traffic Office, Albert Dock, Liverpool, Merseyside L3 4AX T: 0151 478 4065 Closed - The new Museum of Liverpool is to open in 2011 E: karen.orourke@liverpoolmuseums.org.uk W: www.army.mod.uk/lancs

Kohima Museum Imphal Barracks, Fulford Road, York, Yorkshire YO10 4HD T: 01904 665806 E: thekohimamuseum@hotmail.com

Lashenden Air Warfare Museum Headcorn Aerodrome, Headcorn, Nr Ashford, TN27 9HX T: 01622 890226

Leeds Rifles Museum c/o 7 Wentworth Court, Raistrick, Brighouse, HD6 3XD

Leicestershire Yeomanry, Leicestershire Tigers Museum Loughborough War Memorial, Queen's Park, Loughborough, T: 01509 263370

London Irish Rifles Regimental Museum Duke of York's Headquarters, Kings Road, Chelsea, London, SW3 4SA

Midland Air Museum Coventry airport, Baginton, CV8 3AZ T: 024 7630 1033 W: www.discover.co.uk/~mam/

Ministry of Defence - Royal Naval Personnel Records Centre CS(RM)2 Navy Search, Bourne Avenue, Hayes, UB3 1RF

Montrose Air Station Heritage Centre Waldron Road, Montrose, Angus DD10 9BB T: 01674 678 222 E: rafmontrose@aol.com W: www.rafmontrose.org.uk

Museum of Army Chaplaincy Amport House,Andover, SP11 8BG T: 01264 773144 ex 4248 E: rachdcurator@tiscali.co.uk W: www.army.mod.uk/chaps/museum/index.htm

Museum of Army Flying Middle Wallop, Stockbridge, SO20 8DY T: 01980 674421 W: www.flying-museum.org.uk

Museum of Army Transport Flemingate, Beverley, HU17 0NG T: 01482 860445

Museum of Barnstaple & North Devon incorporating Royal Devon Yeomanry Museum Peter A Boyd, The Square, Barnstaple, EX32 8LN T: 01271 346 747

Museum of Defence Intelligence Chicksands, Shefford, SG17 5PR T: 01462 752340

Museum of Lancashire (Queen's Lancashire Regt Duke of Lancaster's Own Yeomanry Lancashire Hussars 14th/20th King's Hussars) Stanley Street, Preston, PR1 4YP T: 01772 534075

Museum of the Manchester Regt Ashton Town Hall, Market Place, Ashton-u-Lyne, OL6 6DL T: 0161 342 3078 W: www.tameside.gov.uk

Museum of the Queen's Lancashire Regt (East South and Loyal (North Lancashire) Regiments, Lancashire Regt (PWV) and The Queen's Lancashire Regt Fulwood Barracks, Preston, PR2 8AA T: 01772 260362 E: rhq.qlr@talk21.com

Museum of The Staffordshire Regt Whittington Barracks, Lichfield, WS14 9PY T: 0121 311 3240 E: museum@rhqstaffords.fsnet.co.uk

Museum of the Staffordshire Yeomanry The Ancient High House, Greengate Street, Stafford, ST16 2HS T: 01785 619130

National Army Museum Department of Archives, Photographs, Film & Sound Royal Hospital Road, London, SW3 4HT T: 020 7730 0717 E: apfs@nam.ac.uk W: www.nam.ac.uk

National Army Museum Royal Hospital Road, Chelsea, London, SW3 4HT T: 020 7730 0717 E: info@nam.ac.uk W: www.nam.ac.uk

National Maritime Museum Romney Road, Greenwich, London, London SE10 9NF T: 020 8858 4422 E: library@nmm.ac.uk manuscripts@nmm.ac.uk W: www.nmm.ac.uk

National Museum of the Royal Navy HM Naval Base (PP66), Portsmouth, PO1 3NH T: 023 9272 3795 E: library@nmrm.org.uk W: www.royalnavalmuseum.org

Newarke Houses Museum incorporating The Royal Leicestershire Regimental Museum The Newwarke, Leicester LE2 7BY T: 0116 225 4980 E: museums@leicester.gov.uk W: www.leicester.gov.uk/museums

Norfolk and Suffolk Aviation Museum - East Anglia's Aviation Heritage Centre Buckeroo Way, The Street, Flixton, Bungay, NR35 1NZ T: 01986 896644 E: nsam.flixton@virgin.net W: www.aviationmuseum.net

North East Aircraft Museum & Military Vehicles Museum Washington Road, Sunderland SR5 3HZ T: 0191 519 0662 E:info@neam.co.uk W:www.neam.co.uk

North East War Memorials Project Bilsdale, Ulgham, Morpeth, NE61 3AR T: 01670 790465 E: janet@newmp.org.uk W: www.newmp.org.uk

Oxfordshire and Buckinghamshire Light Infantry Regimental Museum Slade Park, Headington, Oxford OX3 7JL T: 01865 780128

Pembroke Yeomanry, Royal Pembroke Militia, Pembrokeshire Volunteers Museum Scolton Manor Museum, Spittal, Haverfordwest, Pembrokeshire SA62 5QL T: 01437 731328

Princess Louise's Kensington Regt Museum Duke of York's Headquarters, Kings Road, Chelsea, London, SW3 4RX

Princess of Wales's Royal Regt & Queen's Regt Museum Howe Barracks, Canterbury, CT1 1JY T: 01227-818056

Queen's Own Mercian Yeomanry Museum Bridgeman House, Cavan Drive Dawley, Telford, TF4 2BQ T: 01952 632930

Queen's Royal Surrey Regt Museum (Queen's Royal, East Surrey & Queen's Royal Surrey Regiments) Clandon Park, West Clandon, Guildford, GU4 7RQ T: 01483 223419 W: www.surrey-online.co.uk/queenssurreys www.queensroyalsurreys.org.uk

R.A.F. Regt Museum Home of The RAF Regiment, R A F Honington, Bury St Edmonds, IP31 1EE T: 01359 269561 ext 7824

R.E.M.E. Museum of Technology Isaac Newton Road, Arborfield, Reading, RG2 9NJ T: 0118 976 3375 W: www.rememuseum.org.uk

RAF Digby Ops Room Museum RAF Digby, Scopwick, Lincoln, LN4 3LH T: 01526 327503 W: www.airops.freeserve.co.uk

RAF Manston History Museum The Airfield, Manston Road, Ramsgate, CT11 5DF T: 01843 825224 W: www.rafmuseum.fsnet.co.uk

RAF Witchford Display of Memorabilia Grovemere Building, Lancaster Way Business Park, Ely, T: 01353 666666

Regimental Museum 13th/18th Royal Hussars & The Light Dragoons Cannon Hall, Cawthorne, Barnsley, S75 4AT T: 01226 790270

Regimental Museum of the 9th/12th Royal Lancers Derby City Museum and Art Gallery, The Strand, Derby, DE1 1BS T: 01332 716656 W: www.derby.gov.uk/museums

Regimental Museum of The Queen's Own Hussars (The 3rd King's Own Hussars and 7th Queen's Own Hussars) The Lord Leycester Hospital, High Street, Warwick, CV34 4EW T: 01926 492035 E: trooper@qohm.fsnet.co.uk W: www.qohmuseum.org.uk

Regimental Museum Royal Logistic Corps Princess Royal Barracks, Deepcut, Camberley, GU16 6RW T: 01252 833371 W: www.army-rlc.co.uk/museum

RGBW (Salisbury) Museum The Wardrobe, 58 The Close, Salisbury, SP1 2EX T: 01722 419419 W: www.thewardrobe.org.uk

RHQ Scots Guards Archives Wellington Barracks, Birdcage Walk, London, SW1E 6HQ E: sgarchives@dial.pipex.com

Royal Air Force Museum Grahame Park Way, Hendon, London, NW9 5LL T: (020) 8200 1763 W: www.rafmuseum.org.uk

Royal Berkshire Yeomanry Cavalry Museum T A Centre, Bolton Rd, Windsor SL4 3JG T: 01753 860600 W: www.army.mod.uk/signals/organisation/8748.aspx?rating

Royal Dragoon Guards Military Museum (4th/7th Royal Dragoon Guards & 5th Royal Inniskilling Dragoon Guards) 3A Tower Street, York YO1 9SB T: 01904 461010 E: hhq@rdgmuseum.org.uk W: www.rdgmuseum.org.uk/

Royal Engineers Library Brompton Barracks, Chatham, ME4 4UX T: 01634 822416

Royal Gunpowder Mills administrative Office, Beaulieu drive, Powdermill Lane, Waltham Abbey, EN9 1JY T: 01992 767022 W: www.royalgunpowder.co.uk

Royal Hampshire Regimental Museum Serle's House, Southgate Street, Winchester, SO23 9EG T: 01962 863658

Royal Leicestershire Regt Museum Gallery New Walk Museum, New Walk, Leicester, LE1 7FA T: 0116 2470403

Royal Leicestershire Regimental Gallery New Walk Museum, 53 New Walk, Leicester, LE1 7AE T: 0116 247 3220 W: www.leicestermuseums.co.uk

Royal Lincolnshire Regt Lincolnshire Yeomanry Museum Old Barracks, Burton Road, Lincoln, LN1 3LY T: 01522-528448

Royal Marines Museum Eastney, Southsea, PO4 9PX T: (023) 9281 9385 Exts 224 W: www.royalmarinesmuseum.co.uk

Royal Military Police Museum Roussillon Barracks, Chichester, PO19 6BL T: 01243 534225 E: museum@rhqrmp.freeserve.co.uk W: www.rhqrmp.freeserve.co.uk

Royal Military School of Music Museum Kneller Hall, Twickenham, TW2 7DU T: 020 8744 8652

Royal Naval Museum Buildings 1 - 7, College Road, HM Naval Base, Portsmouth, PO1 3LJ T: (023) 9283 9766 W: www.royalnavalmuseum.org

Royal Naval Patrol Association Museum Sparrows Nest, Lowestoft, NR32 1XG T: 01502 586250

Royal Navy Submarine Museum Haslar Jetty Road, Gosport, PO12 2AS T: (023) 92510354 E: admin@rnsubmus.co.uk W: www.rnsubsmus.co.uk

Royal Norfolk Regimental Museum Shirehall, Market Avenue, Norwich, NR1 3JQ T: 01603 493649 W: www..norfolk.gov.uk

Royal Wiltshire Yeomanry Museum A (RWY) Sqn Royal Yeomanry, Church Place, Swindon, SN1 5EH T: 01793 523865

Sandhurst Collection Royal Military Academy Sandhurst, Camberley, GU15 4PQ T: 01276 412489

Shropshire Regimental Museum (King's Shropshire Light Infantry, Shropshire Yeomanry) Shropshire Militia, Volunteers and TA The Castle, Shrewsbury, SY1 2AT T: 01743 358516 W: www.shropshireregimental.co.uk

Soldiers of Gloucestershire Museum Gloucester Docks, Commercial Road, Gloucester, GL1 2EH T: 01452 522682

Solway Aviation Museum Carlisle Airport, Carlisle, CA6 4NW T: 01228 573823

Solway Aviation Museum Aviation House, Carlisle Airport, Carlisle , CA6 4NW T: 01227 573823 W: www.solway-aviation-museum.org.uk

Somerset Military Museum (Somerset Light Infantry, Yeomanry Militia and Volunteers) County Museum The County Museum, Taunton Castle, Taunton, TA1 4AA T: 01823 333434 E: info@sommilmuseum.org.uk W: www.sommilmuseum.org.uk

South Lancashire Regt Prince of Wales Volunteers Museum Peninsula Barracks, Warrington,

Spitfire and Hurricane Memorial Building The Airfield, Manston Road, Ramsgate, CT11 5DF T: 01843 821940 W: www.spitfire-museum.com

Staff College Museum Old Staff College Building, Camberley, GU15 4NP T: 01276 412719

Suffolk Regt Museum The Keep, Gibraltar Barracks, Out Risbygate Street, Bury St Edmonds, IP33 3RN

Sussex Combined Services Museum (Royal Sussex Regt and Queen's Royal Irish Hussars) Redoubt Fortress, Royal Parade, Eastbourne, BN22 7AQ T: 01323 410300

Sussex Yeomanry Museum Newhaven Fort, Fort Road, Newhaven, BN9 9DS T: 01273 517622 E: info@newhavenfort.org.uk W: www.newhavenfort.org

Tangmere Military Aviation Museum Tangmere, Chichester, PO20 2ES T: 01243 775223 W: www.tangmere-museum.org.uk

Tank Museum Bovington, BH20 6JG T: 01929 405096 E: librarian@tankmuseum.co.uk W: www.tankmuseum.co.uk

The Association of Jewish Ex-Service Men and Women Military Museum AJEX House, East Bank, Stamford, London, N16 5RT T: 020 8800 2844 W: www.ajex.org.uk

The Buffs Regimental Museum The Royal Museum, 18 High Street, Canterbury, CT1 2JE T: 01227 452747

The Commandery Civil War Museum Sidbury, Worcester, WR1 2HU T: 01905 361821 E: thecommandery@cityofworcester.gov.uk W: www.worcestercitymuseums.org.uk

The Devonshire and Dorset Regt (Archives) RHQ Wyvern Barracks, Barrack Road, Exeter, EX2 6AR T: 01392 492436

The Fusiliers Museum (Lancashire) Wellington Barracks, Bolton Road, Bury, BL8 2PL T: 0161 764 2208

The Gurkha Museum Peninsula Barracks, Romsey Road, Winchester, Hampshire SO23 8TS T: 01962 842832 E: curator@thegurkhamuseum.co.uk W: www.thegurkhamuseum.co.uk

The Highlanders' Museum Archives Fort George, Ardersier, Inverness IV1 7TD T: 0131-310-8701 E: info@thehighlandersmuseum.com W: www.thehighlandersmuseum.com

The Household Cavalry Museum Combermere Barracks, Windsor, SL4 3DN T: 01753 755112

The Infantry and Small Arms School Corps Weapons Collection HQ SASC, HQ infantry, Warminster Training Centre, Warminster, BA12 0DJ T: 01985 222487

The Keep Military Museum The Keep, Bridport Road, Dorchester, Dorset DT1 1RN T: 01305 264066 E: info@keepmilitarymuseum.org W: www.keepmilitarymuseum.org

The King's Royal Hussars Museum (10th Royal Hussars PWO 11th Hussars PAO and The Royal Hussars PWO) Peninsula Barracks, Romsey Road, Winchester, SO23 8TS T: 01962 828540 E: beresford@krhmuseum.freeserve.co.uk W: www.hants.gov.uk/leisure/museum/royalhus/index.html

The Light Infantry Museum Peninsula Barracks, Romsey Road, Winchester, SO23 8TS T: 01962 868550

The Muckleburgh Collection Weybourne, Holt, NR25 7EG T: 01263 588210 W: www.muckleburgh.co.uk

The Museum of The Adjutant General's Corps RHQ Adjutant General's Corps, Worthy Down, Winchester, SO21 2RG T: 01962 887435

The Museum of Berkshire Aviation Trust Mohawk Way, off Bader Way, Woodley, Reading, Berkshire RG5 4UE T: 0118 944 8089 E: museumofberkshireaviation@fly.to W: http://fly.to/museumofberkshireaviation

The Museum of the Worcestershire Yeomanry Cavalry Worcester City Museum & Art Gallery, Foregate St, Worcester, WR1 1DT T: 01905 25371 E: tbridges@cityofworcester.gov.uk W: www.worcestercitymuseums.org.uk

The Nothe Fort Museum of Coastal Defence Barrack Road, Weymouth , DT4 5UF T: 01305 787243

The Polish Institute and Sikorski Museum 20 Princes Gate, London, SW7 1QA T: 020 7589 9249

The Potteries Museum & Art Gallery Bethesda Street, Hanley, Stoke-On-Trent, ST1 3DE T: 01782 232323 E: museums@stoke.gov.uk W: www.stoke.gov.uk/museums

The Queen's Own Royal West Kent Regt Museum Maidstone Museum and Art Gallery, St. Faith's Street, Maidstone, ME14 1LH T: 01622 602842 E: simonlace@maidstone.gov.uk

The Queen's Royal Lancers Regimental Museum (16th/5th and 17th/21st Lancers) Belvoir Castle, Grantham, NG32 1PD T: 0115 957 3295

The Regimental Museum RHQ The London Scottish Regiment, 95 Horseferry Road, Westminster, London, SW1P 2DX T: 020 7630 1639 E: archiveslsregt@aol.com W: www.londonscottishregt.org

The Royal Green Jackets Museum (Oxford and Bucks Light Infantry King's Royal Rifle Corps and The Rifle Brigade) Peninsula Barracks, Romsey Road, Winchester, SO23 8TS T: 01962 828549 E: museum@royalgreenjackets.co.uk W: www.royalgreenjackets.co.uk

The Royal Regt of Fusiliers H M Tower of London, London, EC3N 4AB T: (020) 7488 5610

The Royal Regt of Fusiliers Museum (Royal Warwickshire) St. John's House, Warwick , CV34 4NF T: 01926 491653

The Shuttleworth Collection Old Warden Aerodrome, Old Warden Park, Biggleswade, SG18 9EA T: 01767 627288 E: enquire@shuttleworth.org W: www.shuttleworth.org

The Worcestershire Regiment Museum Worcester City Museum & Art Gallery, Foregate Street, Worcester WR1 1DT T: 01905 25371 W: www.worcestercitymuseums.org.uk

Warwickshire Yeomanry Museum The Court House, Jury Street, Warwick, CV34 4EW T: 01926 492212 E: wtc.admin@btclick.com W: www.armymuseums.org.uk

Wellesborough Aviation Museum Control Tower Entrance, Wellesborough, Warwick, CV34 4EW

Wellington Aviation Museum Broadway Road, Moreton in the Marsh, GL56 0BG T: 01608 650323 W: www.wellingtonaviation.org

Welsh Guards Record Office Wellington Barracks, Birdcage Walk, London, SW1E 6HQ T: 020 7414 3291

WFR Museum (Sherwood Foresters Collection) of The Mercian Regiment The Castle, Nottingham NG1 6EL T: 0115 946 5415 E: rhqmercian.notts@btconnect.com W: www.wfrmuseum.org.uk www.army.mod.uk/mercian

Worcestershire Regt Archives (Worcestershire and Sherwood Forester's Regiment) RHQ WFR Norton Barracks, Worcester, WR5 2PA T: 01905 354359 E: rhg_wfr@lineone.net

York and Lancaster Regimental Museum Library and Arts Centre, Walker Place, Rotherham S65 1JH T: 01709 336633 E: yorkandlancsmuseum@rotherham.gov.uk W: www.rotherham.gov.uk

Yorkshire Air Museum Halifax Way, Elvington, York YO41 4AU T: 01904 608595 E: museum@yorkshireairmuseum.co.uk W: www.yorkshireairmuseum.co.uk

Wales

1st The Queen's Dragoon Guards Regimental Museum Cardiff Castle, Cardiff CF10 2RB T: (029) 2078 1271 E: curator@qdg.org.uk W: www.qdg.org.uk

Llandudno Royal Artillery Llandudno Museum, 17-19 Gloddaeth Street, Llandudno, Gwynedd LL30 2DD T: 01492 876517

Nelson Museum & Local History Centre Priory St, Monmouth, NP5 3XA T: 01600 710630 E: nelsonmuseum@monmouthshire.gov.uk

Pembroke Yeomanry, Royal Pembroke Militia, Pembrokeshire Volunteers Museum Scolton Manor Museum, Spittal, Haverfordwest, Pembrokeshire SA62 5QL T: 01437 731328

Powysland Museum The Canal Wharf, Welshpool, Powys SY21 7AQ T: 01938 554656 W: http://powysmuseums.powys.gov.uk

The Regimental Museum of The Royal Welsh (formerly South Wales Borderers) The Barracks, Brecon, Powys LD3 7EB T: 01874 613 906 F: 01874 613 275 E: martin.everett@rrw.org.uk W: www.rrw.org.uk
Information on South Wales Borderers, Welch Regiment, Monmouthshire Regiment - previously 24th, 41st and 69th Foot.

The Royal Monmouthshire Royal Engineers (Militia) Castle and Regimental Museum, The Castle, Monmouth NP25 3BS T: 01600-712935 E: curator@monmouthcastlemuseum.org.uk W: www.monmouthcastlemuseum.org.uk

The Royal Welch Fusiliers Regimental Museum The Queen's Tower, The Castle, Caernarfon, Gwynedd LL55 2AY T: 01286 673362 E: rwfusiliers@callnetuk.com W: www.rwfmuseum.org.uk

Scotland

Atholl Highlanders Blair Castle, Blair Atholl PH18 5TL T: 01796 481207 E: office@blair-castle.co.uk W: www.blair-castle.co.uk

Ayrshire Yeomanry Museum Rozelle House, Monument Road, Alloway by Ayr, Ayrshire KA7 4NQ T: 01292 445400 (Museum)

Culloden Visitor Centre Culloden Moor, Inverness, inverness-shire IV2 5EU T: 01463 790607 E: dsmyth@nts.org.uk W: www.nts.org.uk

Fife and Forfar Yeomanry Museum Yeomanry House, Castlebrook Road, Cupar, Fife KY15 4BL T: 01334 656155

HM Frigate Unicorn Victoria Dock, South Victoria Dock Road, Dundee, DD1 3BP T: 01382 200893 E: frigateunicorn@hotmail.com W: www.frigateunicorn.org

Montrose Air Station Museum Waldron Road, Montrose, Angus DD10 9BB T: 01674 673107 E: info@RAFmontrose.org.uk W: www.RAFmontrose.org.uk

Museum of The Royal Highland Fusilers (Royal Scots Fusilers and Highland Light Infantry) 518 Sauchiehall Street, Glasgow, G2 3LW T: 0141 332 0961 W: www.rhf.org.uk

Queen's Own Cameron Highlanders Fort George, Arderseir, Inverness, Inverness-shire IV1 2TD T: 01667 462777

Regimental Museum Argyll and Sutherland Highlanders Stirling Castle, Stirling, Stirlingshire FK8 1EH T: 01786 475165

Regimental Museum of The Highlanders (The Queen's Own Highlanders Collection) Fort George, Inverness-shire IV2 7TD T: 01463 224380 E: rhqthehighlanders@btopenworld.com

Royal Scots Regimental Museum The Castle, Edinburgh, EH1 2YT T: 0131-310-5014 E: rhqroyalscots@edinburghcastle.fsnet.co.uk W: www.theroyalscots.co.uk

Scottish Horse Regimental Archives - Dunkeld Cathedral Dunkeld, PH8 0AW T: 01350 727614

Stromness Museum 52 Alfred Street, Stromness T: 01856 850025

The Cameronians (Scottish Rifles) Museum & Low Parks Museum c/o Low Parks Museum, 129 Muir Street, Hamilton, Lanarkshire ML3 6BJ T: 01698 452163

West Lowland Fencibles Culzean Castle, Maybole KA19 8LE T: 01655 884455 E: culzean@nts.org.uk W: www.culzeancastle.net

Northern Ireland

Royal Inniskilling Fusiliers Regimental Museum The Castle, Enniskillen, Co Fermanagh BT74 7HL T: (028) 66323142

Royal Irish Fusilers Museum Sovereign's House, Mall East, Armagh, BT61 9DL T: (028) 3752 2911 W: www.rirfus-museum.freeserve.co.uk

Royal Ulster Rifles Regimental Museum RHQ Royal Irish Regiment, 5 Waring Street, Belfast, BT1 2EW T: (028) 90232086 E: rurmuseum@yahoo.co.uk W: www.rurmuseum.tripod.com

The Museum Of The Royal Irish Regt St. Patricks Barracks, Demesne Avenue, Ballymena, County Antrim BT43 7BH T: (028) 2566 1386 E: hqrirish@royalirishregiment.co.uk W: www.royalirishregiment.co.uk

The Somme Heritage Centre 233 Bangor Road, Newtownards, County Down BT23 7PH T: 028 9182 3202 E: sommeassociation@dnet.co.uk W: www.irishsoldier.org

Ulster Aviation Heritage Centre The Maze Regeneration Site, Halftown Road, Lisburn, BT27 5RF E: info@ulsteraviationsociety.org W: www.ulsteraviationsociety.org

Channel Islands

18th Century Loopholed Tower PO Box 23, St Peter Port, Guernsey GY1 3AN

Clarence Battery Fort George, St Peter Port, Guernsey

Elizabeth Castle - Jersey Militia St Aubin's Bay, St Helier, Jersey T: 01534 633300

Fort Grey Rocquaine Bay, St Saviours, Guernsey

German Direction Finding Tower PO Box 23, St Peter Port, Guernsey GY1 3AN

German Military Underground Hospital La Vassalerie Road, St Andrew's, Guernsey T: 01481 239100

German Naval Signals Headquarters St Jacques, Guernsey

German Occupation Museum Les Houards, Forest, Guernsey GY8 0BG T: 01481 328205 W: www.aboutbritain.com/OccupationMuseum.htm

German Occupation Museum Rue Lucas, Sark, Sark T: 01481 832564

German Underground Hospital Meadowbank, St Lawrence, Jersey T: 01534 863442

Island Fortress Occupation Museum 9 Esplanade, St Helier, Jersey T: 01534 633300

La Hougue Bie Grouville, Jersey T: 01534 633300

La Valette Underground Military Museum St Peter Port, Guernsey

T: 01481 722300

Maritime Museum and Occupation Tapestry Gallery New North Quay, St Helier, Jersey T: 01534 811043 E: marketing@jerseyheritagetrust.org W: www.jerseyheritagetrust.org

Noirmont Command Bunker Noirmont Point, St Brelade, Jersey T: 01534 482089

Royal Guernsey Militia and Royal Geurnsey Light Infantry Castle Comet, St Peter Port, Guernsey T: 01481 726518 W: www.museum.guernsey.net/castle.htm

St Peter's Bunker Museum of Wartime German Equipment and Occupation Relics La Petite Rue De L'eglise, St Peter, Jersey JE3 7AF T: 01534 723136

The Channel Islands Military Museum The Five Mile Road, St Ouen, Jersey T: 01534 23136

Belgium

In Flanders Fields Museum Lakenhallen, Grote Markt 34, Ieper, B-8900 T: 00-32-(0)-57-22-85-84 W: www.inflandersfields.be

Police Records & Museums

Devon & Cornwall Constabulary Museum Middlemoor, Exeter, Devon EX2 7HQ T: 01392 203025

Essex Police Museum Police Headquarters, PO Box 2, Springfield, Chelmsford, Essex CM2 6DA T: 01245 457 150 E: museum@essex.pnn.police.uk W: www.essex.police.uk/museum/

Friends of The Metropolitan Police Historical Collection PO Box 27970, London, SE7 7XY E: historicstore@met.police.uk W: www.met.police.uk/history/friends.htm

Garda Historical Society 8 Aisling Close, Ballincollig, County Cork T: +353 86 806 0385 E: J_herlihy@esatclear.ie W: www.esatclear.ie/~ric

Garda Siochana Museum & Archives The Records Tower, Dublin, 2 T: +353 1 6719 597 E: j_herlihy@esatclear.ie W: www.esatclear.ie/~garda/museum.html

Garda Siochana Museum & Archives The Records Tower, Dublin, 2 T: +353 1 6719 597 E: j_herlihy@esatclear.ie W: www.esatclear.ie/~garda/museum.html

Glasgow Police Heritage Society c/o The Glasgow Police Museum, 1/1 30 Bell Street, Merchant City, Glasgow, G1 1LG T: 0141 552 1818 E: curator@policemuseum.org.uk W: www.policemuseum.org.uk

Glasgow Police Museum 1/1 30 Bell Street, Merchant City, Glasgow, G1 1LG T: 0141 552 1818 E: curator@policemuseum.org.uk W: www.policemusaeum.org.uk

GMP Museum & Archives 57a Newton Street, Northern Quarter, Manchester, Greater Manchester M1 1ET T: 0161 856 3287/4500 E: police.museum@gmp.police.uk W: www.gmp.police.uk/museum

Kent Police Museum The Historic Dockyard, Chatham, Kent ME4 4TZ T: 01634 403260 E: info@kent-police-museum.co.uk W: www.kent-police-museum.co.uk

Metropolitan Police Archives Room 517, Wellington House, 67-73 Buckingham Gate, London, SW1E 6BE T: 020 7230 7186 W: www.met.police.uk/history/archives.htm

Metropolitan Police Historical Museum c/o T.P.H.Q. Fin & Res, 4th Floor, Victoria Embankment, London, SW1A 2JL T: (020) 8305-2824 E: webmaster@fomphc.org.uk W: www.fomphc.org.uk/

National Police Officers' Roll of Honour Roll of Honour Project, Lancashire Contabulary Headquarters, Hutton, Preston, Lancashire PR4 5SB

Police History Society 64 Nore Marsh Road, Wootton Bassett, Wiltshire SN4 8BH E: info@policehistorysociety.co.uk W: www.policehistorysociety.co.uk

Ripon Prison & Police Museum Ripon Museum Trust, St Marygate, Ripon, North Yorkshire HG4 1LX T: 01765-690799 E: info@riponmuseums.co.uk W: www.riponmuseums.co.uk/html/prison.htm

Royal Military Police Museum Roussillon Barracks, Chichester, Sussex PO19 6BL T: 01243 534225 E: museum@rhqrmp.freeserve.co.uk W: www.rhqrmp.freeserve.co.uk

Sheffield Police and Fire Museum 101-109 West Bar, Sheffield, South Yorkshire S3 8TP T: 0114 249 1999 W: www.hedgepig.freeserve.co.uk

South Wales Police Museum Police Headquarters, Cowbridge Road, Bridgend, Glamorgan CF31 3SU T: 01656 303207 E: GlamRO@cardiff.gov.uk W: www.southwalespolicemuseum.org.uk/

Surrey Police Museum Mount Browne, Sandy Lane, Guildford, Surrey GU3 1HG T: 01483 638744 E: 7454@surrey.police.uk W: www.surrey.police.uk/museum/default.asp www.surrey.police.uk/about/history.asp

Tetbury Police Museum The Old Courthouse, 63 Long Street, Tetbury, Gloucestershire GL8 8AA T: 01666 504670 E: tourism@tetbury.org W: www.visittetbury.co.uk/police-museum/

Thames Valley Police Museum Sulhamstead, Nr Reading, Berkshire RG7 4DX T: 0118 932 5748 E: ken.wells@thamesvalley.pnn.police.uk W: www.thamesvalley.police.uk

The North Eastern Police History Society 1 Darley Court, Plawsworth, Chester le Street, County Durham DH2 3LQ T: 0191 371 0276 E: janicestothard@aol.com W: www.communigate.co.uk/ne/nepolicehistory/

West Midlands Police Museum Sparkhill Police Station, Stratford Rd, Sparkhill, Birmingham, West Midlands B11 4EA T: 0121 626 7181

List of Current Police Forces

England and Wales - Avon and Somerset Constabulary, Bedfordshire Police, Cambridgeshire Constabulary, Cheshire Constabulary, City of London Police, Cleveland Constabulary, Cumbria Constabulary, Derbyshire Constabulary, Devon and Cornwall Constabulary, Dorset Police, Durham Constabulary, Dyfed-Powys Police, Essex Police, Gloucestershire Constabulary, Greater Manchester Police, Gwent Constabulary, Hampshire Constabulary, Hertfordshire Constabulary, Humberside Police, Kent County Constabulary, Lancashire Constabulary, Leicestershire Constabulary, Lincolnshire Police, Merseyside Police, Metropolitan Police, Norfolk Constabulary, North Wales Police - Heddlu Gogledd Cymru , North Yorkshire Police, Northamptonshire Police, Northumbria Police, Nottinghamshire Constabulary, South Wales Police - Heddlu de Cymru, South Yorkshire Police, Staffordshire Police, Suffolk Constabulary, Surrey Constabulary, Sussex Police, Thames Valley Police, Warwickshire Constabulary, West Mercia Police, West Midlands Police, West Yorkshire Police, Wiltshire Constabulary

Non Geographic Police Forces
British Transport Police, Ministry of Defence Police, UK Atomic Energy Constabulary, Port of Dover Police, The National Crime Squad

Scotland - Central Scotland Police, Dumfries and Galloway Constabulary, Fife Constabulary, Grampian Police, Lothian and Borders Police, Northern Constabulary, Strathclyde Police, Tayside Police

Ireland
Northern Ireland - Police Service of Northern Ireland (formerly Royal Ulster Constabulary)

Republic of Ireland - Garda Síochána

Channel Islands - Guernsey Police, States of Jersey Police

Isle of Man - Isle of Man Constabulary

Other Forces - Royal Military Police, Belfast Harbour Police, Mersey Tunnels Police, Port of Bristol Police, Port of Tilbury London Police, Royal Parks Constabulary, Port of Liverpool Police

Index to Advertisers

index

~~~~~~~~~

About the Editors & Publishers

Robert Blatchford LL.B (Hons)

is a law graduate of The University of Hull, England. He is a member of The Society of Genealogists as well as Cleveland, The City of York, Devon, Dyfed, Glamorgan, Somerset & Dorset & Gwent Family History Societies. He is a former Chairman of The City of York FHS and former Vice Chairman of the North East Group of Family History Societies. He has undertaken research in England, Wales, Scotland, Belgium and France as well as in Ireland, Australia and the United States. He has edited and published each issue of *The Family and Local History Handbook*. A Data CD has been produced with all previous issues of the Handbook in pdf format. He has also published *Herbert Chapman on Football* - a facsimile.

Elizabeth Blatchford

has been involved in genealogy and family history for over 20 years. She is a member of several family and local history societies. Elizabeth has been involved with this publication since its inception and has assisted with the editing of several editions. Since taking early retirement from Local Governement Elizabeth is fully involved in the editing of *The Family and Local History Handbook*. She has an NVQ consultancy business and is fully involved with her four grandchildren and her new kitten, Alfie!

Production Information

For the technically minded, all design, layout and preparation is done in house on Apple Macintosh computers, 27 inch and 20 inch Intel iMacs, a G4 Power Book, and an iPad. Software used includes using Quark Xpress 8, Adobe Photoshop CS4 and Adobe Acrobat 9 Pro. The *Handbook* is produced electronically.

The electronic files are sent to the printers and are printed directly to paper. The first time the files are seen in book form is when the *Handbook* is delivered from the printers.

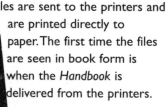

The Family & Local History Handbook 13

ISSN 1745-3887 ISBN 978 0 9552399 4 6

Published by

Robert Blatchford Publishing Ltd

33 Nursery Road, Nether Poppleton YORK, YO26 6NN U.K.

T: 01904 332638 E: sales@genealogical.co.uk W: www.genealogical.co.uk

The Genealogical Services Directory

Volume 1 Published March 1997 ISBN 0 9530297 0 0 ISSN 1368-9150
Volume 2 Published January 1998 ISBN 0 9530297 1 9 ISSN 1368-9150
Volume 3 Published January 1999 ISBN 0 9530297 2 7 ISSN 1368-9150
Volume 4 Published January 2000 ISBN 0 9530297 3 5 ISSN 1368-9150

The Family & Local History Handbook

Volume 5 Published January 2001 ISBN 0 9530297 4 3
Volume 6 Published February 2002 ISBN 0 9530297 5 1
Volume 7 Published February 2003 ISBN 0 9530297 6 X
Volume 8 Published March 2004 ISBN 0 9530297 7 8
Volume 9 Published March 2005 ISBN 0 9530297 8 6
Volume 10 Published September 2006 ISBN 978 0 9530297 9 2
Volume 11 Published May 2008 ISBN 978 0 9552399 1 5
Volumes 1 - 10 Omnibus CD Published March 2009 ISBN 978 0 9552399 2 2
Volume 12 Published November 2009 ISBN 978 0 9552399 3 9
Volume 13 Published May 2011 ISBN 978 0 9552399 4 6

Printed by Warwick Printing Caswell Road, Leamington Spa, Warwickshire CV31 1QD
T: 01926 883355 E: sales@warwickprinting.co.uk W: www.warwickprinting.co.uk

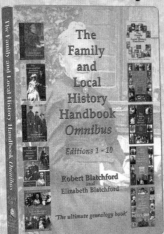

National Burial Index

This index wil enable you to look up your ancesters burials on your own PC without any subscription to pay. All the data is supplied on CD so you don't even need to be connected to the internet.

This third edition released February 2010 includes the 13 million burials from the second edition plus a further 5m to bring the total to over 18m records.

Price £29.95 + £1p&p

10% discount off the above price if you quote coupon code 'NBFLHH' at the checkout.

There are even more counties (see website) and parish registers covered for England and Wales from 1538 onwards. It is still not a complete index to all burials, but represents an enormous effort by Family History Societies and Groups to make available a large amount of information easily searchable in your own home. The National Burial Index, known as the NBI, is quality British data at an affordable price.

What will you find out if an ancestor burial is on the CD?

The information provided in the National Burial Index, taken from parish, non-conformist, Roman Catholic and cemetery registers , includes where available:

- County of burial
- Parish or cemetery where the event of burial was recorded
- Date of burial
- Forename(s) of the deceased
- Surname of the deceased
- Age
- The society or group that transcribed the record

See the full range and order online at:

www.my-history.co.uk

Tel: 01709 586758
4 Mexborough Business Centre, College Road,
Mexborough, South Yorkshire, S64 9JP